FASTI ECCLESIÆ SCOTICANÆ

FASTI ECCLESIÆ SCOTICANÆ

THE SUCCESSION OF MINISTERS
IN THE CHURCH OF SCOTLAND
FROM THE REFORMATION

VOLUME XI

MINISTERS OF THE CHURCH FROM
1 JANUARY 1976 TO 30 SEPTEMBER 1999

Edited for the Board of Practice and Procedure
of the Church of Scotland
by the Reverend

FINLAY ANGUS JOHN MACDONALD

MA, BD, PhD

Editorial Assistant
MONICA STEWART
MA, CPS

T&T CLARK
EDINBURGH

T&T CLARK LTD
59 GEORGE STREET
EDINBURGH EH2 2LQ
SCOTLAND

www.tandtclark.co.uk

First published 2000

ISBN 0 567 08750 6

British Library Cataloguing-in-Publication Data
A catalogue record for this book is available from the British Library

Typeset by Waverley Typesetters, Galashiels
Manufactured in Great Britain

CONTENTS

ABBREVIATIONS

addl	additional	lab	laboratory
admin	adminstrative	lic	licensed
agricult	agricultural	loc ten	locum tenens
app	appointed, appointment	m	married
assgnd, assgn	assigned, assignment	non-grad	non-graduating
Assoc	Associate	ord	ordained, ordination
asst	assistant	Orig Sec	Original Secession
asstshp	assistantship	OStJ	Order of St John
Aux	Auxiliary	OUP	Oxford University Press
b	born	presb	presbytery
CCC	Colonial and Continental	publ	publications
	Committee	RAChD	Royal Army Chaplains
cont	continued		Department
CStJ	Cross, Order of St John	RNCS	Royal Naval Chaplaincy
CUP	Cambridge University Press		Service
d	daughter	RE	Religious Education
dem	demitted	rep	representative
dept	department	res	resigned
Eccl	Ecclesiastical	ret	retired
educ	educated, education	s	son
esp	especially	SCHS	Scottish Church History
FES	*Fasti Ecclesiæ Scoticanæ*		Society
FMC	Foreign Mission Committee	term	terminable
	(now Board of World Mission)	tr	translation/translated (Publ)
FUF	*Fasti of the United Free*	trans	translated
	Church of Scotland,	univ	university
	Edinburgh, 1956	UFC	United Free Church
ind	inducted	URC	United Reformed Church
introd	introduced	VSO	Voluntary Service Overseas
KStJ	Knight of Justice, Order of St	w	wife
	John	WCC	World Council of Churches

PREFACE

It was in 1866 that Hew Scott completed the work which resulted in the first edition of *Fasti Ecclesiæ Scoticanæ*. The Latin means 'Register of Officials of the Church of Scotland' and Scott's purpose, in his own words, was 'to present a comprehensive account of the succession of ministers of the Church of Scotland since the period of the Reformation'. This volume, the eleventh in the series, takes the record forward from 1975 to the present. As in previous volumes the entries are arranged under presbyteries. However, it should be noted that synods were abolished in 1992.

While editorial responsibility has rested with me as Principal Clerk, the detailed work has been undertaken by Monica Stewart, Editorial Assistant. I gladly acknowledge my considerable indebtedness to her. Thanks are also due to Faith Brennan who designed the database and has provided invaluable IT support throughout the project, to Maurice Berrill who proof read the final text before publication and to T&T Clark Ltd., Publishers. The co-operation of Presbytery Clerks and ministers in supplying information, checking forms and returning them by due deadlines has been a vital aspect of the work and this also is gratefully recognised.

Finally, a particular word of thanks is due to the Very Rev Dr Andrew Herron, who, as a labour of love, maintained his own record of ministerial changes since the publication of Volume X. This meticulously detailed work, generously made available, gave a 'head start' to the publication of the current volume.

FINLAY A. J. MACDONALD
Editor

Edinburgh
2 February 2000

PRESBYTERY OF EDINBURGH

FULL-TIME PRESBYTERY CLERKS (FES X, 3)

1965 ROBERT MURRAY
(FES IX, 472; X, 3, 280), dem from Buckhaven St Michael's to take up app as Clerk to Presb of Edinburgh 1 Nov 1965; ret 4 Dec 1973; died 18 Sep 1983.

1973 ALEXANDER GORDON McGILLIVRAY
(FES IX, 137; X, 3, 81, 374), dem from Nairn High on app as Clerk to Presb of Edinburgh 4 Dec 1973; Depute Clerk of General Assembly 1971–93; Principal Clerk of General Assembly 1993–94; ret 13 Apr 1993; Editor of *Year Book* 1990–; d Jean m Gordon Hay; d Ann m Gordon McDougall; Publ: *An Introduction to Practice and Procedure in the Church of Scotland* (private, 1995); *The Office of Session Clerk* (Board of Parish Education, 1995); *The Church of Scotland* (St Andrew Press, 1996); *Nairn and the Disruption* (Polwarth Press, 1999).

1993 WILLIAM PETER GRAHAM
(FES X, 60), dem from Bonkyl and Preston with Chirnside with Edrom Allanton on app as Clerk to Presb of Edinburgh 12 Apr 1993; Publ: Chapter on Bonkyl, Preston and Chirnside in *Third Statistical Account of Scotland* Vol XXIII, County of Berwick (Scottish Academic Press, 1992).

ABERCORN (FES I, 189; VIII, 36; IX, 57; X, 34)

Linked 20 Dec 1974 with Dalmeny.

1948 WILLIAM MAIR
(FES IX, 57, 605; X, 34), trans from Fraserburgh St Andrew's to Abercorn North 22 Jul 1948; ret 30 Nov 1974; died 30 Dec 1981.

1974 ERIC WILLIAM SINCLAIR JEFFREY
(FES IX, 737; X, 36, 420), ind to Dalmeny 10 Apr 1969; became minister of linked charge with Abercorn 20 Dec 1974, see Dalmeny.

1980 IVOR GIBSON
(FES X, 275), res as teacher of Religious Education and ind to Abercorn with Dalmeny 4 Jul 1980; ret 31 Aug 1993; m 6 Aug 1960 Margaret Gillespie b 16 Jan 1938 d of William G. and Anne Jamieson Bishop Neilson; Children: Fiona Anne b 11 Nov 1963 m Ashby; Roger Hamilton b 19 Nov 1966.

1995 JAMES BROWN
(FES X, 104), trans from Glencaple with Lowther to Abercorn with Dalmeny 17 Jan 1995; Open University 1990–97 (BA, DHSW, DPsych).

ALBANY DEAF CHURCH OF EDINBURGH (FES X, 3)

Name changed from Albany Church for the Deaf to Albany Deaf Church of Edinburgh 3 May 1988.

1966 GEORGE SMITH
B 13 Feb 1926 at Hillside, s of William Henderson Gerard S. and Margaret Drummie; educ Montrose Academy 1938–42; Diploma (Deaf Welfare Exam Board) 1963; Diploma (Chaplains to Deaf People) 1970; Society for Deaf People (Aberdeen and North East) 1956–59; (North and East Lancs) 1959–62; (Edinburgh and East of Scotland) 1962; lic by Presb of Edinburgh; m 27 Jan 9145 Doreen Catherine Strachan d of James S. and Agnes Glendy Sutherland; Children: George Dorian b 13 Dec 1947 m Janet Grant; Morag Catherine b 8 Dec 1952 m James Lawrence; ord and ind to Albany Church for the Deaf 21 Jun 1966; died 21 Jun 1987; MBE 1987.

1988 MALCOLM McINTOSH REW
(FES X, 351), dem from Pitsligo 30 Jun 1980 and app Asst at Albany Deaf Church of Edinburgh; ind to same charge 17 Feb 1988; dem 1992.

1993 RICHARD DURNO
ord as Aux by Presb of Glasgow during assgn at John Ross Memorial Church for Deaf People, Glasgow 7 May 1989; assgnd to Albany Deaf Church of Edinburgh 1993; assgn terminated Jun 1998, entered full-time ministry.

1998 MARY KATHRYN WEIR
(FES X, 440), returned from Canada and introd as Community minister for ministry among Deaf People and as minister of Albany Deaf Church of Edinburgh 31 Mar 1998; res 30 Apr 1999; m (2) 28 Mar 1987 Malcolm Colin Cloete Graham s of Walter Gerald Cloete G. and Nellore Alice Lee Swan; Publ: *Intimate Conversations: Lenten Reflections on Psalms* (United Church of Canada, 1988).

BALERNO (FUF 1; FES IX, 1; X, 3)

1948 ROBERT SMITH
(FES IX, 1, 760; X, 3), res from app in Prague and ind to Balerno 21 Oct 1948; ret 24 Sep 1972; died 22 Jun 1989.

1973 DAVID DINNES OGSTON
(FES X, 3), ord by Presb of Edinburgh during assistantship at St Giles' 1 Mar 1970; ind to Balerno 6 Jun 1973; trans to Perth St John's 28 Apr 1980.

1980 HENRY ARTHUR SHEPHERD
(FES X, 329, 456), res as Asst Sec Dept of Education and ind to Balerno 18 Dec 1980; app to Christ Church, Bermuda 6 Feb 1993.

1993 MARTIN JAMES McKEAN
B 3 Oct 1957 at Edinburgh, s of James Black McGillivray M. and Estelle Margaret Mair; educ John Watson's, Edinburgh 1962–74; University of Edinburgh 1977–83 (BD, DipMin); Trainee Valuation Surveyor 1974–77; lic by Presb of Edinburgh 3 Jul 1983; asst Glasgow St John's Renfield 1983–84; m 23 Apr 1988 Audrey Margaret Beat b 16 Jun 1961 d of David B. and Elizabeth Mathieson; Children: Ross Martin b 12 May 1989; Rachel Elizabeth b 17 Nov 1990; ord and ind to Old Cumnock Old 13 Dec 1984; became minister of linked charge with Lugar 26 Feb 1989; trans to Balerno 30 Jun 1993.

1996 CHARLES WILLIAM HARCOURT BARRINGTON
B 6 Apr 1942 at London, s of John Harcourt B. and Margaretta Marion Whitfield-Hayes; educ Clifton College, Bristol 1955–60; University of Cambridge 1962–65 (MA); University of Edinburgh 1983–86 (BD); Jordanhill College, Glasgow 1990–91 (PGCE); Royal Navy 1960–68; Teaching 1968–74; Yacht Chartering 1975–83; loc ten Lochalsh 1987–88, 1988–89; lic by Presb of Edinburgh, 1986; m 6 Mar 1976 Veronica Anne Finlay b 14 May 1944 d of Ian Robertson F. and Mary Scott Pringle; Children: John b 22 May 1977; Louisa b 14 Jun 1979; Katharine b 18 Jul 1981; introd as Assoc at Balerno 15 Dec 1996; ord by Presb of Edinburgh 6 Feb 1997.

BARCLAY (FES X, 4, 6)

Formed 27 Apr 1980 by union of Barclay Bruntsfield and Chalmers Lauriston.

1966 ERIC CRAIG
(FES X, 6, 188), trans from Blantyre Livingstone Memorial to Chalmers Lauriston 28 Apr 1966; ret 20 Apr 1980; d Alison m John Noble; s Peter m Jeanette Marshall; d Rosemary m Kenneth Scott.

1980 DAVID GRAHAM LEITCH
(FES X, 321), trans from Inchbrayock Ferryden to Barclay 25 Oct 1980; Chaplain to Royal Hospital for Sick Children, Edinburgh; Addl children: Anna Catherine b 12 Jun 1976; d Sarah m Andrew Morrice.

BLACKHALL ST COLUMBA'S (FES I, 14; VIII, 5; IX, 4; X, 4)

1952 ROBERT JAMES WATSON MATHEWSON
(FES IX, 4, 169; X, 4), trans from Ayr Cathcart to St Columba's 4 Jun 1952; ret 31 Oct 1975; died 7 Oct 1989.

1976 ERNEST GEORGE SANGSTER
(FES X, 325, 442), trans from Aberdeen Beechgrove to St Columba's 5 May 1976; trans to Alva 1 Jul 1990.

1987 SARAH ELIZABETH CARMICHAEL NICOL
dem from Aberdeen St John's Church for Deaf People and introd as Assoc at Blackhall St Columba's 13 Sep 1987; introd as Assoc at Christ Church, Bermuda 1 Sep 1991.

1991 ALEXANDER BLACKIE DOUGLAS
B 12 Feb 1947 at Jedburgh, educ Jedburgh Grammar 1952–62; Scottish Bible College 1969–71; University of Aberdeen 1974–79 (BD); Lyle & Scott Knitwear, Hawick 1962–68; lic by Presb of Paisley, Apr 1979; m 14 Aug 1971 Cynthia Lorna Gilbertson b 30 Apr 1945 d of Marjorie Hutton Hart-Davies; Children: Craig Alexander b 21 Jan 1973; Grant Jonathan b 13 Aug 1974; ord and ind to Paisley St Columba Foxbar 22 Aug 1979; trans to Prestwick Kingcase 27 Mar 1985; trans to St Columba's 10 Apr 1991.

BRISTO MEMORIAL CRAIGMILLAR (FUF 3; FES IX, 5; X, 4)

1965 WILLIAM CROMIE NELSON
(FES IX, 744; X, 4, 424), res from service with FMC in N India 31 Jan 1965 and ind to Bristo Memorial Craigmillar 11 Feb 1965; trans to Southend 6 Jul 1978.

1978 ERIC WILLIAM SINCLAIR JEFFREY
(FES IX, 737; X, 36, 420), trans from Abercorn with Dalmeny to Bristo Memorial Craigmillar 16 Nov 1978; ret 1 Jul 1994; s Richard m Anna Louise Ukairo; d Janet m Christian Heinzinger.

1994 ANGUS LOW BAYNE
(FES X, 208, 239), dem from Crossford with Kirkfieldbank and emigrated to S Africa 30 Sep 1975; ind to Wynberg Presb Church, Presb of Cape Town 1 Oct 1975; app by Presb of Toronto, United Church of Canada 1 Jul 1989; app teacher, Totonto 1 Jul 1991; ind to Bristo Memorial Craigmillar 30 Nov 1994; University of S Africa 1985–86 (BTh), 1989–91 (MTh); University of Toronto 1990–91 (BEd); d Susan m Nicholas Cook.

BROUGHTON ST MARY'S (FES X, 4, 24)

Formed 26 Aug 1992 by union of Broughton McDonald and St Mary's (linkage with St Stephen's terminated 26 Aug 1992).

1957 NORMAN McGATHAN BOWMAN
(FES IX, 246, 359, 729; X, 24, 215), trans from Bonhill Old to St Mary's 3 Jul 1957; dem 15 Sep 1964 to take up app as Lecturer at Napier Technical College, Edinburgh; s Norman m Noreen Armstrong; s John m Sally Fearn; s Alistair m Yvonne Aikman; d Agnes m Dennis Shoat; Publ: *Seed Thoughts in Prose and Verse* (Rowan Mountain Press, USA, 1992); various articles.

1965 ALEXANDER ALLAN McARTHUR
(FES IX, 609, 783; X, 24, 171, 350), trans from Glasgow Pollokshields-Titwood to St Mary's 16 Jun 1965; died 30 Sep 1986.

1973 IAIN ALASDAIR ELDERS
(FES X, 4, 5, 35), trans from Cumbernauld Abronhill to Broughton Place 15 Feb 1973; became minister of united charge with McDonald Road 2 May 1974 and of united charge with St Mary's 26 Aug 1992.

1988 ROBERT JOHNSTON
(FES X, 300), trans from Dundee Camperdown to St Mary's with St Stephen's 10 Aug 1988; trans to Aberluthnott with Laurencekirk 18 Jun 1992.

CANONGATE (FES I, 23; VIII, 7; IX, 6; X, 5)

1937 RONALD WILLIAM VERNON SELBY WRIGHT
(FES IX, 8; X, 5), ord and ind to the Canongate 7 Jan 1937; Moderator of General Assembly 1972–73; ret 30 Sep 1977; died 24 Oct 1995.

1978 CHARLES ROBERTSON
(FES X, 379), trans from Kiltearn to the Canongate 16 Jun 1978.

CARRICK KNOWE (FES IX, 8; X, 5)

1971 WILLIAM WARD CLINKENBEARD
(FES X, 6), ord by Platte Presb and ind to Wood River, Nebraska (United Presb Church, USA) 10 Nov 1966; admitted by General Assembly 1971 and ind to Carrick Knowe 1 Jul 1971; d Helen m Carlile; Publ: *The Contemporary Lesson* (Bavelaw Press, 1990); co-author of *Full on the Eye* (Bavelaw Press, 1994); *Mind the Gap: Moving between Pulpit and Pew* (Bravelaw Press, 1998).

CLUNY (FES X, 6, 25, 24)

Formed 24 Jan 1974 by union of South Morningside and St Matthew's.

1942 ROBERT CAMPBELL MALSEED MATHERS
(FES IX, 40, 317; X, 24), ind to St Matthew's 22 Jan 1942; ret 24 Jan 1974; introd as Assoc at Edinburgh St Andrew's and St George's 31 Mar 1974; Chaplain (part-time) to Edinburgh City Hospital 1979–93; died 9 Jul 1999.

1973 GEORGE ALEXANDER MORRISON MUNRO
(FES X, 6, 25, 315), trans from Arbroath St Margaret's to Morningside South 17 Oct 1973; became minister of united charge with St Matthew's 24 Jan 1974.

COLINTON (FES I, 2; VIII, 1; IX, 9; X, 6)

1964 WILLIAM BRYCE JOHNSTON
(FES IX, 57; X, 6, 34, 134), trans from Greenock St George's to Colinton 3 Jun 1964; ret 30 Sep 1991; Moderator of General Assembly 1980–81; Chaplain to the Queen 1981–91; Extra Chaplain to the Queen from 1991; DD (Aberdeen) 1980; DLitt (Heriot-Watt) 1989; d Rosemary m C S McCulloch; Addl publ: Contributor to *Ethics and Defence* (SCM, 1976).

1992 GEORGE JAMES WHYTE
B 1 Apr 1955 at Elderslie, s of Thomas Wilson W. and Isabella Gowans Fairbairn; educ Paisley Grammar 1967–73; University of Glasgow 1973–76 (BSc), 1977–80 (BD); Police Constable 1976–77; lic by Presb of Paisley 25 Jun 1980; asst Paisley Sherwood 1980–81; m 21 Jun 1977 Moira Elizabeth Ewing b 11 Jul 1957 d of Cecil E. and Violet McLean; Children: Duncan George b 5 Dec 1982; Calum Ewing b 2 Jul 1984; Hannah Ruth b 10 Sep 1996; ord and ind to Kilchrenan and Dalavich with Muckairn 25 May 1981; trans to Glasgow Langside 25 Jun 1985; trans to Colinton 8 Apr 1992.

COLINTON MAINS (FES IX, 9; X, 6)

1976 JOHN STUART MILL
B 1 Oct 1945 at Stirling, s of John Stuart M. and Janet Reid Stewart; educ Hutchesons' Boys' Grammar, Glasgow 1957–63; University of Glasgow 1963–66 (MA), 1970–73 (BD); University of Strathclyde 1966–67 (MBA); Moray House College, Edinburgh 1980–81 (DipEd); Management Trainee in Aeronautics Industry 1967–69; lic by Presb of Glasgow 28 Jun 1973; asst Edinburgh St Giles' Cathedral 1973–75; m 17 Mar 1973 Elizabeth Pamela Muir b 10 May 1948 d of James Samuel Cameron M. and Betty Douglas Gratton; Children: Adrian Cameron Stuart b 11 Apr 1975; ord by Presb of Edinburgh during assistantship at St Giles' 7 Apr 1974; ind to Colinton Mains 25 Feb 1976; dem 1 Sep 1980 to enter teaching profession; app teacher of RE 22 Aug 1983; Chaplain (part-time) to Napier University 1984–90.

1980 JOHN HENDRY CRICHTON FENEMORE
B 16 Nov 1927 at Glasgow, s of Stephen Hendry F. and Elizabeth Black Crichton; educ Eastwood Secondary, Glasgow 1932–41; University of Glasgow 1976–79; Police Officer 1948–76; lic by Presb of Glasgow 29 Jun 1979; asst Glasgow St John's Renfield 1979–80; m 27 Mar 1953 Sarah Paterson Dawson b 2 Mar 1933 d of Archibald

Paterson D. and Ann Nairn Davren; Children: John b 3 Nov 1957; Sheila b 22 Mar 1959; Lynn b 5 Dec 1963; Alistair b 18 Jan 1966; ord and ind to Colinton Mains 18 Oct 1980; ret 30 Apr 1993.

1993 IAN ANDREW McQUARRIE
B 31 Mar 1947 at Glasgow, s of William M. and Elizabeth Brannigan Conway; educ Allan Glen's, Glasgow 1959–65; University of Glasgow 1988–92 (BD); Sales Admin 1970–88; lic by Presb of Glasgow 26 Jun 1992; asst Glasgow Sandyhills 1992–93; m 9 Jun 1972 Helen Thomson Watters b 30 Apr 1944 d of George Thomson W. and Margaret Scott Sharp; Children: Andrew Ian b 15 Apr 1976; Scott Thomson b 9 Aug 1978; Ross Conway b 4 Oct 1981; ord and ind to Colinton Mains 27 Oct 1993.

CORSTORPHINE CRAIGSBANK (FES IX, 10; X, 7)

1971 GEORGE DARLINGTON WILSON GRUBB
(FES X, 7), ind to Craigsbank 23 Dec 1971; University of Edinburgh 1971 (CPS), 1974–78 (BD); Open University 1974 (BA), 1983 (BPh); San Francisco Theological Seminary 1993 (DMin); Councillor, South Queensferry Ward 1999.

1986 ANN INGLIS
B 1 Mar 1950 at Ismailia, Egypt, d of Arthur Benson George McGuigan and Dorothy Wooton; educ James Gillespie's, Edinburgh 1962–68; University of Dundee 1968–72 (LLB); University of Edinburgh 1979–82 (BD); Advocate 1974–79; lic by Presb of Edinburgh 4 Jul 1982; asst Edinburgh Tron Kirk Moredun 1982–83; m 3 Jun 1975 John Fletcher Inglis b 16 Nov 1940 s of David Ballard I. and Caroline Lipson Minor; Children: Sarah Ann b 15 Dec 1975; David John b 4 Sep 1977; ord by Presb of Edinburgh and introd as Assoc at Craigsbank 9 Oct 1986.

CORSTORPHINE OLD (FES I, 5; VIII, 1; IX, 10; X, 7)

1976 JOHN (IAN) DARROCH BRADY
(FES X, 192), trans from Coatbridge Gartsherrie to Corstorphine Old 24 Mar 1976; s John m Maureen Elaine McCalley; s Derek died 20 Apr 1997.

CORSTORPHINE ST ANNE'S (FES I, 9; VIII, 4; IX, 10; X, 7)

1951 JAMES MACMILLAN
(FES IX, 10, 176 (2); X, 7), trans from Girvan St Andrew's to St Anne's 21 Sep 1951; ret 31 Dec 1975; died 27 Apr 1993.

1976 JAMES WILLIAM HILL
(FES X, 40), trans from Kirkliston to St Anne's 11 Jun 1976; Publ: Contributor to *Worship Now* (St Andrew Press, 1972).

CORSTORPHINE ST NINIAN'S (FUF 1; FES IX, 10; X, 7)

1966 COLIN ROSS MARTIN
(FES X, 7, 423), res from app with Colonial and Continental Committee at Buenos Aires St Andrew's and ind to St Ninian's 7 Sep 1966; ret 30 Sep 1994; died 21 Dec 1996.

1995 ALEXANDER THOMSON STEWART
B 11 Oct 1949 at Glasgow, s of John McKenzie S. and Mary McKenzie Campbell; educ High Possil Senior Secondary and Albert Senior Secondary, Glasgow; University of Glasgow 1969–74 (MA, BD); lic by Presb of Glasgow, Jun 1974; asst Glasgow St Margaret's Knightswood 1974–75; m 17 Jul 1971 Elizabeth Margaret Loggie b 4 Nov 1947 d of Thomas L. and Elizabeth Lyon; Children: Nicola Elizabeth b 5 Aug 1974; Angela Norma b 22 Sep 1977; ord and ind to Carluke Kirkton 29 May 1975; trans to Glasgow Cathcart Old 15 Nov 1980; trans to St Ninian's 31 May 1995.

CRAIGENTINNY ST CHRISTOPHER'S (FES IX, 11; X, 7)

Continued vacancy 1997–1999.

1959 DUNCAN SHAW
(FES IX, 40; FES X, 7, 24), trans from Edinburgh St Margaret's to Craigentinny St Christopher's 9 Sep 1959; ret 31 Jan 1997 in interests of re-adjustment; CStJ 1978; Romanian Patriarchal Cross 1978; Bundesverdienst Kreuz 1980; KStJ 1983; Order of St Sergius, Russian Orthodox Church 1987; Commander of Merit, Sovereign Military Order of Malta 1987; Romanian Patriarchal Cross for Hierarchs 1988; Dr hc (Edinburgh) 1990; Order of St Vladimir, Russian Orthodox Church 1997; Treasurer, Scottish Record Society 1964–97, President 1998–; Secretary, General Council, Univ of Edinburgh 1965–93, Secretary, General Council Trust 1982–90; Advisory Committee, Conference of European Churches 1970–86; Councillor, Society of Antiquaries of Scotland 1974–85; Trustee, National Museum of Antiquities, Scotland 1974–85; Editorial Director, Edina Press 1974–99, Managing Director 1999–; Lecturer in Theological German, Univ of Edinburgh 1975–81; Consultative Committee, Selly Oak Colleges, Birmingham 1976–87; Librarian, Priory of Scotland, OStJ 1978–86; Founder and Chairman of Council, Scottish Society for Reformation History 1980–; Visiting Lecturer, Orthodox Theological Academies of Sibiu and Bucharest, Universities of Munich, Heidelberg, Montreal, Mainz 1978–91; Member of Chapter General, London, OStJ 1984–93; Chairman, City of Edinburgh Justices Committee 1984–87; Chancellor, Priory of Scotland, OStJ 1986–92; Moderator of General Assembly 1987–88; Chairman, Instant Muscle Scotland Trust and IMS plc 1988–92; Director IMS plc, London 1988–96; Director, Centre for Theological Exploration, USA 1989–96; Trustee, Edinburgh Old Town Charitable

Trust 1989–; Liveryman, Worshipful Company of Scriveners, City of London 1990; Freeman, City of London 1990; Patron, HTVESK, Norway 1993–; Trustee, The Luigi and Laura Dallapiccola Foundation 1997–; w Ilse Peiter died 15 Feb 1989; m (2) 10 Aug 1991 Anna Libera d of Luigi Dallapiccola and Laura Coen Luggatto; d Hedda m Douglas John Greig; s Neil m Miriam Ribeiro de Barros; Publ: *John Knox and Mary, Queen of Scots* (1979); contributed foreword and supervised tr of G W Locher, *Zwingli's Thought: New Perspectives* (1981); contributor to and co-editor (with I B Cowan) of *The Renaissance and Reformation in Scotland: Essays in Honour of Gordon Donaldson* (1983); *A Voice in the Wilderness* (1995); *Valedictory Speech* (1997); contributor to *Die Zürcher Reformation: Ausstrahlungen und Rückwirkungen* (ed A Schindler, 1999).

1974   COLIN FINNIE MILLER
(FES IX, 420; X, 250), res as Dean of the Chapel and Professor, Hamilton College, Clinton New York 31 Jul 1970; introd as Assoc at Craigentinny St Christopher's 1 Jan 1974; ret 1984; died 2 Jan 1988.

1997   DOUGLAS MACPHERSON MAIN
dem from Errol with Kilspindie and Rait and introd as Interim minister at St Christopher's 13 Feb 1997; introd as Interim minister at Addiewell with Longridge and Breich with Stoneyburn 10 Nov 1998.

1999   LILLY CLARK EASTON
B 2 Oct 1953 at Johnstone, d of Ian Fraser and Helen McLaren Clark; educ Johnstone High 1966–70; University of Glasgow 1993–97 (BD); Laboratory Supervisor 1970–76; Print Room Operator (part-time) 1986–90; lic by Presb of Paisley, Aug 1997; asst Bishopton Erskine 1997–98; m 27 Dec 1971 Alexander Glen Easton b 21 Jan 1945 s of John Hunter E. and Margaret Glen; Children: Lynn b 17 Feb 1976 (adopted); Fraser b 21 Sep 1979; ord and ind to Craigentinny St Christopher's 26 Jan 1999.

CRAIGLOCKHART (FES I, 9; VIII, 4; IX, 11; X, 7)

1976   ALASTAIR HENDERSON SYMINGTON
(FES X, 448), res from RAF Chaplains' Branch and ind to Craiglockhart 22 Feb 1976; trans to Bearsden New Kilpatrick 21 Feb 1985.

1985   ANDREW FREELAND HEADDEN
B 7 Oct 1955 at Glasgow, s of George Frederick H. and Jean Keir; educ The High School of Glasgow and Douglas Academy 1971–77; University of Stirling 1974–77 (BA); University of Edinburgh 1977–80 (BD); lic by Presb of West Lothian 29 Jun 1980; asst Cadder 1980–81; m 13 Oct 1978 Sheena Elizabeth Hutchison d of Robert and Mary H; Children: Peter b 11 Dec 1981; Findlay b 11 Aug 1983; ord and ind to Motherwell North 10 Jun 1981; trans to Craiglockhart 11 Sep 1985; dem 2 Apr 1991 to take up app with Paxton Presb Church, Harrisburg, PA, USA.

1991   ANDREW RITCHIE
B 17 Apr 1952 at Dunfermline, s of David R. and Helen Reid Hall; educ Queen Anne High, Dunfermline 1964–68; University of Edinburgh 1978–83 (BD, DipMin); Banking 1968–76; lic by Presb of Dunfermline 3 Jul 1983; asst Dundee St Mary's 1983–84; m 8 Sep 1978 Sheila McKenzie Borrowman b 13 May 1957 d of Albert B. and Jane McKenzie Duff; Children: Neil Douglas b 19 Mar 1981; Matthew David b 9 Apr 1985; Ewan Stewart b 18 Apr 1987; Ayesha Helen Jane b 7 Sep 1992; ord and ind to Airdrie Clarkston 22 Jun 1984; trans to Craiglockhart 16 Oct 1991; Chaplain to Royal Hospital for Sick Children, Edinburgh.

CRAIGMILLAR PARK (FUF 6; FES IX, 11; X, 8)

1966   IAN MACTAGGART
(FES IX 315; X, 8, 16, 185, 455), ind to Mayfield South 20 Oct 1960; became minister of united charge with Craigmillar Park 3 Apr 1966; ret 30 Jun 1983.

1984   WILLIAM PATERSON
trans from Bridge of Weir St Machar's Ranfurly to Craigmillar Park 1 Mar 1984; trans to Bonkyl and Preston with Chirnside with Edrom Allanton 21 Oct 1993.

1994   SARAH ELIZABETH CARMICHAEL NICOL
B 14 Mar 1959 at Kitwe, Zambia, d of Allan Pollok Blue Hamilton and Margaret McCombie Mac-Callum; educ Ndola Dominican Convent, Zambia, St Bride's, Helensburgh and Inverness Royal Academy 1971–76; University of Aberdeen 1976–80 (BSc), 1980–83 (BD); lic by Presb of Inverness 30 Jun 1983; asst Edinburgh Albany Church for Deaf People 1983–84; m 23 Sep 1983 Stewart Nicol b 14 Jan 1952 s of Harold N. and Isabella Munro; Children: Deborah Joanne b 4 Sep 1997; ord and ind to Aberdeen St John's Church for Deaf People 20 Mar 1985; introd as Assoc at Edinburgh Blackhall St Columba's 13 Sep 1987; introd as Assoc at Christ Church, Bermuda 1 Sep 1991; ind to Craigmillar Park 20 Apr 1994.

CRAMOND (FES I, 10; VIII, 4; IX, 12; X, 8)

1957   CAMPBELL MACKENZIE MACLEAN
(FES IX, 391; X, 8, 233), trans from Campbeltown Longrow to Cramond 26 Apr 1957; ret 30 Apr 1992.

1993   GEORGE RUSSELL BARR
B 15 Oct 1953 at Kilmarnock, s of George B. and Isobel Leckie; educ Kilmarnock Academy 1965–71; University of Edinburgh 1972–75 (BA), 1975–78 (BD), 1993–94 (MTh); lic by Presb of Irvine and

Kilmarnock 29 Jun 1978; asst Jedburgh Old with Edgerston with Ancrum 1978–79; m 18 Jul 1978 Margaret Wyllie b 29 Nov 1954 d of Robert W. and Mary Hamilton; Children: Robert Wyllie b 15 Dec 1979; Lindsey Margaret b 3 Dec 1981; ord and ind to Garthamlock and Craigend East 10 Jul 1979; trans to Greenock St Luke's 4 May 1988; trans to Cramond 21 Apr 1993.

1997   IVOR MAXWELL HOMEWOOD
B 24 Jun 1944 at Rochester, s of Francis Stephen Peter H. and Diana Sydney Joan Purcell; educ Maidstone Grammar 1949–61; University of Strathclyde 1987–88 (MSc); University of Edinburgh 1992–95 (BD); British Army NCO 1961–65 and Officer 1966–92; lic by Presb of Edinburgh 2 Jul 1995; asst Edinburgh Murrayfield 1995–96; m (1) 16 Dec 1967 Valerie Ann Child b 24 May 1941 d of David Thomas C. and Joan Alderton; divorced 1977, m (2) 4 Oct 1980 Helen Elizabeth Erskine b 18 Jan 1950 d of Harold E. and Elizabeth Gothard McIntosh; Children: Rachel Helen b 22 Apr 1982; Richard Erskine b 13 Apr 1984; ord by Presb of Edinburgh and introd as Assoc at Cramond Kirk 9 Jan 1997; app Chaplain (part-time) to HMP Edinburgh 15 Mar 1999.

CURRIE (FES I, 14; VIII, 5; IX, 2; X, 3)

1965   GORDON McDONALD SIMPSON
(FES X, 3, 191), trans from Chapelhall to Currie 19 Jul 1965; dem 16 Nov 1981; ind to Leslie Trinity 20 Apr 1988.

1982   GORDON McLEAN
(FES X, 234, 357), trans from Killean and Kilchenzie to Currie 27 May 1982; dem 31 Mar 1992 and emigrated to USA.

1992   WILLIS ARTHUR JONES
(FES X, 272), dem from Dunfermline Erskine 31 May 1968 to return to USA; ind to Currie 10 Dec 1992.

1994   EWAN ROBERT KELLY
ord by Presb of Edinburgh and introd as Assoc at Currie 13 Jan 1994; introd as Chaplain to Glasgow Southern General Hospital Jun 1995.

1996   PETER WILLIAM NIMMO
ord by Presb of Edinburgh and introd as Assoc at Currie Kirk 24 Apr 1996; ind to Glasgow High Carntyne 17 Jun 1998.

DALMENY (FES I, 200; VIII, 40; IX, 59; X, 36)

Linked 20 Dec 1974 with Abercorn.

1947   WILLIAM COWIE FARQUHARSON
(FUF 362; FES IX, 59, 478, 524, 577; X, 36), trans from Fintray to Dalmeny 20 Feb 1947; ret 31 Jul 1968; died 20 Jun 1985.

1969   ERIC WILLIAM SINCLAIR JEFFREY
(FES IX, 737; X, 36, 420), res from service with FMC and ind to Dalmeny 10 Apr 1969; became minister of linked charge with Abercorn 20 Dec 1974; trans to Edinburgh Bristo Memorial Craigmillar 16 Nov 1978.

1980   IVOR GIBSON
(FES X, 275), ind to Abercorn with Dalmeny 4 Jul 1980, see Abercorn.

1995   JAMES BROWN
(FES X, 104), trans from Glencaple with Lowther to Abercorn with Dalmeny 17 Jan 1995.

DAVIDSON'S MAINS (FUF 2; FES IX, 12; X, 8)

1966   JAMES MONAGHAN
(FES IX, 467; X, 8, 280, 359), trans from Burntisland St Columba's to Davidson's Mains 17 May 1966 [not 1977 as in Vol X, 8]; ret 5 Jan 1988; died 25 Jun 1994.

1988   JEREMY RICHARD HUNTER MIDDLETON
B 19 Mar 1953 at Kilbarchan, s of Cecil M. and Jill Train Hunter; educ Charterhouse 1966–70; University of Edinburgh 1971–75 (LLB), 1976–79 (BD); lic by Presb of Edinburgh, Jul 1979; asst Largs St John's 1975–80; m 14 Jul 1977 Susan Margaret Hay b 5 Apr 1955 d of John H. and Margaret McArthur; Children: Jonathan Paul b 27 Mar 1979; Peter Jeremy b 20 May 1981; Andrew David b 26 Feb 1986; ord and ind to Cumbernauld Kildrum 19 Nov 1980; trans to Davidson's Mains 13 Jul 1988.

DEAN (FES I, 30; VII, 8; IX, 12; X, 8)

1953   HENRY JAMES YOUNG
(FES IX, 13; X, 8), ord and ind to Dean 22 Jul 1953; ret 28 Feb 1974.

1974   WILLIAM THOMS WEBSTER
(FES IX, 9, 470; X, 7, 8, 17), trans from Edinburgh Muirhouse to Dean 13 Nov 1974; ret 30 Sep 1986; d Margaret m Peter Branfield.

1987   JAMES GORDON GRANT
(FES X, 107, 335), trans from Troon Portland to Dean 18 Nov 1987; ret 30 Jun 1997; m (2) 24 Jul 1999 Pamela Bruce Robertson; d Catherine m Herve Parienti; s Ian m Irene Gilfillan; s David m Linda Parienti; Publ: Editor of *Walking with God* (St Andrew Press, 1996).

1998   MARK MANFIELD FOSTER
B 21 Jul 1969 at Glasgow, s of Peter Arundel F. and Audrey Elizabeth Manfield; educ Keil School, Dumbarton 1981–87; University of Glasgow 1987–92 (BSc); University of Edinburgh 1993–96 (BD); Volunteer, Scottish Churches World Exchange 1992–93; lic by Presb of Dumbarton 26 Jun 1996; asst Edinburgh St Michael's 1996–98; ord and ind to Edinburgh Dean 19 Mar 1998.

DRYLAW (FES IX, 13; X, 8)

1969 JOHN ERNEST McQUILKEN
(FES X, 8), ord and ind to Drylaw 10 Jun 1969; trans to Caddonfoot with Selkirk Heatherlie 19 Apr 1978.

1978 ISOBEL JEAN MOLLINS KELLY
app Asst Baird Research Fellow, Board of Education 1 Sep 1975; ind to Drylaw 25 Oct 1978; trans to Livingston Craigshill St Columba's 28 Feb 1985.

1985 IAN YOUNG GILMOUR
ord and ind to Drylaw 12 Sep 1985; trans to Edinburgh South Leith 27 Sep 1995.

1996 ADRIAN JAMES TAIT RENNIE
B 8 Apr 1963 at Aberdeen, s of John Diamond R. and Jessie Catherine Tait; educ Paisley Grammar 1975–80; University of Strathclyde 1980–83 (BA); University of Glasgow 1983–86 (BD); lic by Presb of Melrose and Peebles 29 Jun 1986; asst Glasgow King's Park 1986–88; m 15 Jun 1990 Jean Haddow Gibson b 30 Jul 1962 d of John G. and Jessie Sommerville; Children: Calum Christopher Gibson b 1 Jul 1994; ord by Presb of Glasgow during assistantship at King's Park 7 May 1987; ind to Glasgow Calton New with St Andrew's 12 May 1988; dem on app as Warden, MacLeod Centre, Iona Aug 1994; ind to Drylaw 15 Mar 1996.

DUDDINGSTON (FES I, 17; VIII, 6; IX, 13; X, 8)

1972 WILLIAM HEGGIE WILSON RAMSAY
(FES X, 8, 313), trans from Rattray to Duddingston 10 Feb 1972; ret 31 Jul 1989; died 31 Jul 1999; d Hannah m Smith; d Geertruida m Riddell.

1990 DAVID DONALDSON
(FES X, 29, 418), trans from Dundee Whitfield to Duddingston 31 Aug 1990; University of Dundee 1988 (DEd); Addl children: Andrew David b 12 Apr 1977; Catriona Ruth b 26 Apr 1984.

FAIRMILEHEAD (FES IX, 13; X, 9)

1974 MURRAY CHALMERS
(FES X, 9, 41), trans from Larbert West to Fairmilehead 16 Jan 1974; dem on app as Chaplain to Royal Edinburgh Hospital 1 Aug 1991.

1992 IAN DAVID MILLER
B 10 Mar 1937 at Milngavie, s of Thomas Henderson Adam M. and Agnes Margaret Robertson; educ Merchiston Castle, Edinburgh; University of Glasgow 1957–62 (MA); University of Edinburgh 1988–90; Marketing 1962–76; General Secretary 1976–88; lic by Presb of Edinburgh 1 Jul 1990; asst Edinburgh St Ninian's Corstorphine 1990–92; m 20 Feb 1976 Deborah Jane Halpin b 5 Jul 1944 d of Richard H. and Hilary Keighley-Bell; Children: Calum Alexander b 5 Feb 1978; ord by Presb of Edinburgh and introd as Assoc at Fairmilehead 25 Nov 1992; ret 9 Mar 1999.

1992 JOHN ROBERT MUNRO
B 23 Nov 1948 at Glasgow, s of Robert M. and Elizabeth Renfrew; educ Whitehill Secondary, Glasgow 1961–68; Royal Scottish Academy of Music and Drama 1969–72 (Dip Speech/Drama); University of Glasgow 1969–72 (Dip Dramatic Art); University of Edinburgh 1972–75 (BD); Shipping Clerk 1968–69; lic by Presb of Glasgow; asst Edinburgh Palmerston Place 1975–76; m 19 Sep 1973 Lillian Primrose b 2 Apr 1951 d of William P. and Lily Wright; Children: Emily Jane b 12 Feb 1980; ord and ind to Edinburgh St Bernard's Davidson 22 Oct 1976; introd as Assoc at Stockbridge St Bernard's 26 Nov 1980; ind to same charge 31 Jul 1983; trans to Fairmilehead 15 Jan 1992.

GILMERTON (FES I, 148; VIII, 27; IX, 14; X, 9)

1962 DONALD McLEAN SKINNER
(FES X, 9), ord and ind to Gilmerton 27 Sep 1962; Chaplain to Liberton Hospital, Edinburgh; app Justice of the Peace for County and City of Edinburgh 1975; Founder (1976) and Hon Director of 'Pioneer Tec' (Training for Industry); MBE 1985; Fellow of Institution of Engineers and Shipbuilders 1991.

1992 ANNE RIVERS LITHGOW
ord by Presb of Edinburgh and introd as Assoc at Gilmerton 24 Jun 1992; ind to Dunglass 18 Aug 1994.

GORGIE (FES X, 5, 26)

Formed 5 Aug 1979 by union of Cairns Memorial and Tynecastle.

1934 IAN AITKEN MACKENZIE
(FUF 366; FES IX, 6, 483; X, 5), trans from Methilhill to Cairns Memorial 24 Oct 1934; ret 5 Sep 1971; died 9 Sep 1988.

1972 PETER DAVID McDONALD
(FES X, 5), ord and ind to Cairns Memorial 18 May 1972; trans to Ratho 2 Mar 1979.

1975 ROBERT WILLIAM BRUCE
(FES IX, 249, 467; X, 17, 26, 147), dem from Newhaven-on-Forth 31 Mar 1974; introd on term app to Tynecastle 17 Feb 1975; ret 6 Mar 1979; died 21 Sep 1995.

1980 CHARLES MURRAY STEWART
(FES IX, 84; X, 26, 52), res as Director of Youth and Community Work, YMCA and ind to Gorgie 7 Feb 1980; introd to Lausanne 29 Apr 1985.

1986 DAVID JOHN BOYD ANDERSON
(FES X, 37), trans from Falkirk Bainsford to Gorgie 16 Jan 1986; dem on app as General Secretary of Evangelical Alliance Scotland 30 Sep 1994.

1995   PETER IAN BARBER
B 14 Oct 1956 at Edinburgh, s of Wilfred Ian David
B. and Dorothy Stark; educ Royal High School,
Edinburgh 1969–74; University of Edinburgh 1976–
80 (MA), 1980–83 (BD); Clerical Officer, Scottish
Office 1974–75; lic by Presb of Edinburgh, Jun
1983; asst Rutherglen Stonelaw 1983–84; m 11
Jul 1983 Norda Jane McRitchie b 3 Feb 1960 d of
Norman and Daveen M; Children: Jonathan b 10
Apr 1986; Christopher b 31 Dec 1987; ord and ind
to Glasgow St Margaret's Tollcross with Tollcross
Park 5 Sep 1984; became minister of united charge
29 Jun 1994; trans to Gorgie 22 Jan 1995.

GRANTON (FES VIII, 27; IX, 14; X, 9)
1969   WILLIAM COLVILLE THOMAS
(FES X, 9, 62), trans from Westruther with
Legerwood to Granton 19 Apr 1969; dem 13 Sep
1977 and app News Editor of Forfar Times 1 Oct
1977; Tutor (Continuing Education), University of
Edinburgh 1979–81; Asst Director and Head of
Resident Services, Richmond Fellowship 1981–84;
Specialist in Psychotherapy 1984–92; app Assoc
at St Luke's URC, Eastbourne 1992; app Chaplain
to Herdmanflat Psychiatric Hospital, Haddington 8
Feb 1999.

1978   NORMAN LIVINGSTONE FAULDS
(FES X, 330, 332), trans from Aberdeen St
George's-Tillydrone to Granton 28 Sep 1978; trans
to Aberlady with Gullane 13 Mar 1986.

1986   ELIZABETH MARGARET HENDERSON
ord by Presb of Ayr during assistantship at
Castlehill, Apr 1985; ind to Granton 19 Oct 1986;
trans to Edinburgh Richmond Craigmillar 7 May
1997.

1998   FRANCES LYNNE MACMURCHIE
B 2 Jan 1968 at Edinburgh, d of William Campbell
M. and Frances Anne Heweit Paton; educ Dalkeith
High 1980–86; University of Edinburgh 1986–91
(LLB, DipLP); University of St Andrews 1993–96
(BD); Trainee Solicitor 1991–93; lic by Presb of
Lothian 4 Jul 1996; asst Aberdeen Ferryhill 1996–
98; ord and ind to Granton 27 Jan 1998.

GREENBANK (FUF 10; FES IX, 15; X, 9)
1950   DONALD GEORGE MACKINTOSH
MACKAY
(FES IX, 15, 559, 739; X, 9), trans from Aberdeen
Carden Place to Greenbank 2 Jun 1950; ret 30 Jun
1982; died 26 Jul 1991.

1983   IAN GRAY SCOTT
(FES X, 262), trans from Aberdeen Holburn Central
to Greenbank 26 Jan 1983; m 3 Aug 1979
Alexandra Angus b 10 Oct 1949 d of John A. and
Elizabeth Ann Forbes; Children: Alison Isabel b 22
Feb 1983; Publ: Occasional sermons in the
Expository Times (T&T Clark).

GREENSIDE (FES I, 32; VIII, 8; IX, 15; X, 10, 11)

Formed 22 Jan 1978 by union of Greenside
(union 12 Jan 1975 of Abbey and Greenside) and
Hillside.

1941   JOHN BROADFOOT
(FES IX, 2, 282, 476; X, 3), trans from Glasgow
New Bridgegate to Abbey 25 Jun 1941; ret 31 Dec
1974; died 20 Jul 1978.

1968   JAMES WATSON
(FES X, 10 (2)), ord and ind to Greenside 21
Sep 1968; became minister of united charge
with Hopetoun 13 Jan 1974, of united charge
with Abbey 12 Jan 1975 and of united charge with
Hillside 22 Jan 1978; dem on app as Environmental
Health Officer for Stonehaven and Caithness 30
Jan 1981.

1968   ALEXANDER HUTTON PATERSON
(FES IX, 64, 745; X, 11, 39), trans from Grangemouth Dundas to Hillside 3 Oct 1968; ret 31 Mar
1977; died 24 Jul 1980.

1981   ANDREW FRASER ANDERSON
B 2 Sep 1944 at Aberdeen, s of Alfred Fraser A.
and Margaret Gray Spence; educ Harrow School,
Middlesex 1958–63; University of Oxford 1964–67
(MA); University of Edinburgh 1977–80 (BD); Sales
and Marketing, Dickinson Robinson Group 1967–
77; lic by Presb of Edinburgh 6 Jul 1980; asst
Edinburgh Greenside 1980–81; m 16 May 1970
Hazel Neary b 11 Sep 1944 d of Gerard James N.
and Dorothea Mary Cleary; Children: James b 8
Oct 1974; Mark b 2 Aug 1978; ord and ind to
Greenside 15 Oct 1981.

GREYFRIARS TOLBOOTH AND HIGHLAND
(FES I, 33, 37; VIII, 9; IX, 15; X,10, 26)

Formed 28 Feb 1979 by union of Greyfriars and
The Highland Church Tolbooth St John's.

1949   ROBERT STUART LOUDEN
(FES IX, 15, 174, 569; X, 10), trans from Dailly to
Greyfriars 14 Jul 1949; ret 30 Jun 1978; died 26
Mar 1991.

1967   EWEN ANGUS MACLEAN
(FES IX, 391, 404; X, 11, 20, 233), trans from
Edinburgh Restalrig to Highland Tolbooth St John's
28 Nov 1967; became minister of united charge
with Greyfriars 28 Feb 1979; ret 27 Jun 1982 but
continued as Gaelic Services minister; s Alastair
m Elspeth Hollis; d Katharine m George MacLeod
Halliday; Publ: *Eilthireachd nan Eilean* (Gairm
Gaelic Quarterly, 1994); *Eilean I* and *Saoghal
Mosach* (Gairm Gaelic Quarterly, 1995); *An Da
Eilthireachd* (Gairm Gaelic Quarterly, 1996); *A 'Dol
dhan t-Searmon ri La Geamhraidh o shean* (New
Writing Scotland, 1996); *Pasaids Neonach* (forthcoming).

1983 DAVID MACKAY BECKETT
(FES X, 119), trans from Largs Clark Memorial to Greyfriars Tolbooth and Highland 2 Feb 1983; s Paul m Eliza Tappe; Publ: *The Lord's Supper* (Handsel Press, 1984); *The Word in Season* (Canterbury Press, 1988); sermons on worship (Friends of Greyfriars, 1990).

HIGH KIRK (ST GILES') (FES I, 48; VIII, 10; IX, 16; X, 10)

1973 GILLEASBUIG IAIN MACMILLAN
(FES X, 10, 393), trans from Portree to St Giles' 3 May 1973; Chaplain to the Queen in Scotland since 1979; Extra Chaplain to the Queen in Scotland 1978–79; Dean of the Order of the Thistle since 1989; Hon Chaplain to Royal Scottish Academy; Alma College Michigan 1997; FRCS Edinburgh (Hon) 1998; Dr *hc* (Edinburgh) 1998; CVO 1999; Publ: *A Workable Belief* (St Andrew Press, 1993).

1992 JOHN PHILIP NEWELL
Joint-Warden of Iona Abbey, Iona Community 1988–92; app Asst at St Giles' 1 May 1992; app Warden of Spirituality, Anglican Diocese of Portsmouth 1 Sep 1995.

1995 DAVID KELMAN ROBERTSON
(FES X, 32), app Asst at St Giles' 1 Sep 1995; died 10 Sep 1998.

1997 IAIN KAY STIVEN
(FES X, 426), ret from Strachur and Strathlachlan 4 Jul 1997; app Asst at St Giles' 1 Oct 1997.

1997 KAREN KATRINA WATSON
B 4 Apr 1967 at Edinburgh, d of David Henry Campbell and Catherine Craik Dean; educ Portobello High 1979–85; University of Edinburgh 1990–94 (BD), 1994–95 (MTh); Senior Actuarial Clerk 1985–90; lic by Presb of Edinburgh 19 Nov 1995; asst Edinburgh St Giles' Cathedral 1996–97; m 5 Aug 1989 Craig McIntosh Watson b 30 Sep 1963; Children: Cameron Alexander b 23 Jan 1996; ord by Presb of Edinburgh and app Asst at St Giles' Cathedral 28 Dec 1997.

HOLY TRINITY (FES X, 11)

1962 ROBERT CUMMING WHITE
(FES X, 11, 211), trans from Law to Holy Trinity 7 Nov 1962; trans to Thornhill 12 Apr 1976.

1977 (ALEXANDER) ALASTAIR McKENZIE MORRICE
(FES X, 72), trans from Galashiels St John's to Holy Trinity 9 Jan 1977; trans to Rutherglen Stonelaw 23 Apr 1987.

1977 CHRISTOPHER DAVID PARK
ord by Presb of Edinburgh and introd as Assoc at Holy Trinity 23 Jun 1977; ind to Paisley St Ninian's Ferguslie 11 Nov 1981.

1982 KENNETH WILLIAM DONALD
ord by Presb of Edinburgh and introd as Assoc at Holy Trinity 23 Mar 1982; ind to Aberdeen Stockethill 20 Mar 1986.

1986 JOHN KYNOCH COLLARD
ord by Presb of Edinburgh and introd as Assoc at Holy Trinity 20 Aug 1986; ind to East Kilbride Claremont 3 Oct 1991.

1988 STANLEY ALEXANDER BROOK
B 25 Apr 1950 at Dundee, s of Stanley Alexander B. and Mary Ann Harris; educ Morgan Academy, Dundee 1955–68; University of Glasgow 1970–76 (BD, CPS); Journalism 1968; Social Work 1969–70; lic by Presb of Dundee 24 Jun 1976; asst Dyce 1976–77; m 1 Apr 1972 Lorna Watt Goodwin b 8 Jun 1950 d of Daniel G. and Taylor; Children: Eleanor Rose b 16 Oct 1973 m Matthew Buchanan; Victoria b 29 Dec 1975 m James Duce; Stanley b 16 Feb 1977; Douglas b 19 Jul 1979; ord and ind to Dundee Menzieshill 17 Aug 1977; trans to Holy Trinity 6 Jan 1988; Publ: Poem in *Life and Work* (1997); Paper in *Forward Together* (1997).

1992 MICHAEL SIDNEY DAWSON
B 20 Jul 1939 at London, s of Sidney Ronald D. and Levy/Leighton; educ Coopers Company School, London; East Grinstead Grammar and Sevenoaks School, Kent 1950–57; Brunel C.A.T (now Brunel University) 1958–62 (BTech); University of Edinburgh 1975–83 (BD); MIMECHE (Chartered Engineer); Aero Engine and Metrology 1958–64; Electricity Supply Industry 1964–75; lic by Presb of Dunfermline 29 Jun 1978; asst Rosyth 1978–79; m 25 Jul 1964 Penelope Ann Sharp b 12 Feb 1940 d of John Neville S. and Joan Hughes; Children: Angela b 24 Oct 1965 m Gerald Bishop; David b 21 Feb 1967 m Lesley Conlan; ord and ind to Kilmadock 15 Nov 1979; introd as Assoc at Holy Trinity 1 Jun 1992.

HOLYROOD ABBEY (FUF 11; FES IX, 17; X, 11)

1958 JAMES PHILIP
(FES IX, 614; X, 11, 353), trans from Gardenstown to Holyrood Abbey 15 Jan 1958; ret 31 Oct 1997; s William m Rebecca Carswell; d Jennifer m Nigel Barge; Addl publ: *The Power of God* (Gray, 1987); *Up Against It* (Christian Focus, 1991).

1994 ANDREW ALEXANDER DOWNIE
Assoc at Holyrood Abbey 1992–94; ord by Presb of Edinburgh 11 May 1994 and continued as Assoc at Holyrood Abbey; app Chaplain to Saughton Prison 19 May 1997; app Chaplain (full-time) to Kilmarnock Prison 22 Feb 1999.

1998 PHILIP ROBERTSON HAIR
B 24 Mar 1953 at Glasgow, s of Adam H. and Jean Nicholson; educ Clydebank High and Shawlands Academy 1965–71; University of Edinburgh 1973–79 (BD, CPS); Asst Warden, Glenshee Lodge

1971–73; lic by Presb of Glasgow, Jun 1979; asst Glasgow Chryston 1979–81; m 4 Aug 1979 Lynda Ann Cupples b 24 Apr 1957 d of Derek C. and Martha Stewart; Children: Rachel Elizabeth b 27 Mar 1983; Alastair Stewart b 1 May 1986; ord by Presb of Glasgow during assistantship at Chryston 5 Mar 1980; ind to Lochbroom and Ullapool 4 Jun 1982; trans to Holyrood Abbey 12 Jun 1998.

INVERLEITH (FUF 20; FES IX, 17; X, 11)

1975   DONALD HUGH DAVIDSON
(FES X, 11, 206), trans from Biggar St Mary's to Inverleith 10 Dec 1975.

JUNIPER GREEN (FES X, 12, 11)

Formed 10 Mar 1974 by union of Juniper Green St Andrew's and Juniper Green St Margaret's.

1962   ERIC ADDIS McCALL DAVIDSON
(FES IX, 423, 628; X, 12, 293, 359), trans from Cameron with Largoward to Juniper Green St Margaret's 24 Jan 1962; ret 3 Feb 1973; died 27 Oct 1987.

1968   GEORGE GORDON CAMERON
(FES X, 12 (2), 113, 417), trans from Kilmarnock St Ninian's Bellfield to St Andrew's Juniper Green 19 Nov 1968; became minister of united charge with St Margaret's 10 Mar 1974; ret 3 Mar 1997.

1998   BERNARD PETER LODGE
B 19 Feb 1939 at St Monans, s of Kenneth Kingsley L. and Minnie Gibbs; educ Kilsyth Academy 1950–55; University of Glasgow 1962–64; Scottish Congregational College 1964–67; University of London [external] 1967 (BD); Property Management and Surveying 1956–62; lic by Scottish Congregational Union 18 Jun 1967; asst Augine-Bristo Congregational Church 1964–67; m 29 Aug 1964 Margaret Benson Russell b 22 Jun 1940 d of Robert R. and Margaret Benson; Children: Susan Margaret b 5 Jun 1968 m Morris; Fiona Jane b 1 Mar 1970 m Destexhe; ord by Scottish Congregational Union and ind to Partick Congregational Church 18 Jun 1967; admitted by General Assembly and introd as Assoc at Bearsden New Kilpatrick 6 Jun 1975; ind to Kilmacolm Old 18 Apr 1980; introd as Interim minister at Juniper Green 5 Mar 1998.

KAIMES LOCKHART MEMORIAL (FES IX, 6; X, 5)

Name changed from Burdiehouse to Kaimes Lockhart Memorial 26 Mar 1989.

1963   JAMES ERIC McANDREW BAIKIE
(FES IX, 515; X, 5, 305), trans from Dundee St James' to Burdiehouse 4 Sep 1963; ret 8 May 1975; died 30 Mar 1987.

1975   GEORGE IRVINE HASTIE
(FES X, 5), ord by Presb of Ayr during assistantship at Troon Old 18 Feb 1971; ind to Burdiehouse 27 Nov 1975; dem 1 Feb 1987; ind to Cowdenbeath Cairns 11 May 1988.

1988   IAIN A MACDONALD
dem from Iona and Ross of Mull with Kilfinichen and Kilvickeon 31 Oct 1987; ind to Burdiehouse 17 Feb 1988; died 24 Apr 1990.

1989   MARIA ANNETTE GEERTRUDIS PLATE
dem from Cardenden St Fothad's and introd as Assoc at Kaimes Lockhart Memorial 14 Nov 1989; ind to same charge 28 Nov 1990; trans to South Ronaldsay and Burray 25 Aug 1994.

1991   DOUGLAS FREW STEVENSON
ord by Presb of Edinburgh and introd as Assoc at Kaimes Lockhart Memorial 2 Jul 1991; ind to Musselburgh St Andrew's High 9 Jun 1994.

1995   IAIN DOUGLAS PENMAN
B 1 Dec 1951 at Bedford, s of Larmont Douglas P. and Edith Margaret Scott; educ Solihull School, Warwickshire 1960–66, 1968–70; Edinburgh Academy 1966–68; University of Edinburgh 1970–74 (BD), 1974–75 (BD), 1975–76 (Dip Missionary Studies); lic by Presb of Edinburgh, Jul 1976; asst Bo' ness 1976–77; m 14 Aug 1978 Doreen Weir Robertson b 6 Sep 1950 d of John Brown R. and Dorothy Weir; Children: Ruth Dorothy b 20 Feb 1981; ord by Presb of Lothian and app Asst at Cockenzie and Port Seton Old 7 Oct 1977; ind to Coldstream 9 Oct 1980; became minister of linked charge with Eccles 26 Feb 1985; trans to Kaimes Lockhart Memorial 3 May 1995.

KIRK O' FIELD (FES X, 12, 24)

Formed 6 May 1984 by union of St Paul's Newington and Kirk o' Field.

1967   ALEXANDER KETCHEN CASSELLS
(FES X, 24, 342), trans from Leochel Cushnie and Lynturk to St Paul's Newington 19 Oct 1967; trans to Leuchars St Athernase with Guardbridge 20 Jan 1983.

1974   FARQUHAR MACDONALD McARTHUR
(FES X, 12), ord and ind to Kirk o' Field 1 May 1974; became minister of united charge with St Paul's Newington 6 May 1984; died 31 Jul 1995.

1996   IAN DOUGLAS MAXWELL
B 21 Sep 1952 at Bonneville, Haute Savoie, France, s of William M. and Ruth Christina Holloway; educ Rutherglen Academy and George Heriot's, Edinburgh 1964–70; University of Edinburgh 1970–73 (MA), 1973–76 (BD), 1995 (PhD); lic by Presb of Edinburgh, 1976; asst Glasgow Cathcart Old 1976–77; m 20 Aug 1976 Ellen de Boer b 3 Mar 1956 d of Wopke de B. and Aaltje Wielink; Children: Elspeth b 17 Jun 1982; Alison b 15 May 1986;

Rachel b 4 Feb 1991; ord by Presb of Edinburgh, Oct 1977 and app for service with Church of Pakistan at Sindh; app Chaplain to Sefula School, Zambia Jun 1979; introd as Assoc at Paisley St Ninian's Ferguslie 28 Oct 1982; res on app as Conference Manager, Carberry Tower Jun 1990; res and ind to Kirk o' Field Jul 1996.

KIRKLISTON (FES X, 40)

1969   JAMES WILLIAM HILL
(FES X, 40), ind to Kirkliston 24 Jun 1969; trans to Edinburgh Corstorphine St Anne's 11 Jun 1976.

1976   JOHN MURRIE
(FES IX, 783; X, 423), res as Warden and Minister of Church of Scotland Centre, Tiberias, Israel and ind to Kirkliston 27 Oct 1976; ret 12 Jan 1996; Chaplain to HM Prison Edinburgh 1979–96; s William m Karen Una Connaughton; Publ: Children's addresses in the *Expository Times* (T&T Clark 1976–96).

1996   GLENDA JANE KEATING
B 30 Sep 1950 at North Shields, d of Stanley Wilfred Hunt and Agnes May; educ Tynemouth High 1961–66; University of Dundee 1991–92 ('Access Course'); University of St Andrews 1992–95 (MTh); Queen Alexandra's Royal Army Nursing Corps 1967–71; Ninewells Hospital, Dundee 1975–92; lic by Presb of Dundee 28 Jun 1995; m 10 Apr 1971 Robert William Keating b 25 May 1948 s of Robert Francis K. and Lillian Dobbie; Children: Alister b 23 Jan 1972 m Tracy Stebbings; Stewart b 6 Mar 1975; ord and ind to Kirkliston 26 Jun 1996.

LEITH NORTH (FES X, 13, 14)

Formed 13 Jun 1982 by union of Leith St Ninian's Ferry Road and Leith North and Bonnington.

1962   DAVID HARKNESS LOGAN
(FES IX, 205; X, 14, 117), trans from Kilbirnie West to St Ninian's Ferry Road 13 Jun 1962; ret 13 Jun 1982; died 15 Nov 1985.

1965   DOUGLAS CLARKE
(FES IX, 149; X, 13 (2), 88, 109, 417), trans from Hurlford to Leith Bonnington 24 Nov 1965; became minister of united charge with Leith North 31 Jan 1968; ret 31 Dec 1979; died 2 May 1996.

1980   WILLIAM GEORGE NEILL
(FES X, 34, 179), trans from Glasgow Scotstoun East to Leith North and Bonnington 30 Oct 1980; became minister of united charge with St Ninian's Ferry Road 13 Jun 1982; trans to Ayr St Andrew's 26 Nov 1986.

1987   ALISTAIR GERALD CRICHTON McGREGOR
B 15 Oct 1937 at Sevenoaks, Kent, s of James Reid M. and Dorothy Janet Comrie; educ Charterhouse 1948–55; University of Oxford 1958–61 (BA); University of Edinburgh 1961–63 (LLB), 1983–86 (BD); Solicitor 1964–66; Advocate 1967–80; QC 1980–82; lic by Presb of Edinburgh 29 Jun 1986; asst Edinburgh Colinton 1986–87; m 7 Aug 1966 Margaret Dick Lees b 21 Jan 1939 d of David Jackson L. and Smith; Children: David James b 10 Feb 1969; Elizabeth Janet b 19 Dec 1970; Euan Reid b 12 Jan 1973; ord and ind to Leith North 5 Aug 1987.

LEITH SOUTH (FES X, 14)

1969   JOHN McKENZIE KELLET
(FES X, 14 (2), 303), trans from Dundee Menzieshill to Leith South 20 Mar 1969; ret 31 Oct 1994; s Malcolm m Carole Ann Gibson; d Lorna m William Edwin Martin; Publ: *The Iona Pilgrimage* (Wild Goose Publs, 1986); various articles for *Liturgical Review* and Church Service Society.

1973   JAMES SCOTT MARSHALL
(FES IX, 21, 252; X, 13, 14), dem from Leith Kirkgate in favour of union 24 Jun 1973; introd as Assoc at South Leith same date; ret 1979; d Morag m David Wood; s Donald m Isobel Neill; Publ: *Calendar of Irregular Marriages in South Leith 1697–1818* (Scottish Record Society, 1968); *Old Leith at Leisure* (Edina Press, 1976); *Old Leith at Work* (Edina Press, 1977); *Old Leith, the Caring Community* (Edina Press, 1979); *The Church in the Midst* (Edina Press, 1983); *The Life and Times of Leith* (John Donald, 1986); *North Leith Parish Church—First 500 Years* (St Andrew Press, 1993).

1995   IAN YOUNG GILMOUR
B 7 Sep 1956 at Glasgow, s of David G. and Mary Wallace Moyes; educ Clifton High and Coatbridge High 1968–74; University of Glasgow 1979–84 (BD, CMin); Royal Bank of Scotland 1974–76; Strathclyde Regional Council (Finance) 1976–78; Patrick & Co (Chartered Accountants) 1978–79; lic by Presb of Glasgow 25 Jun 1984; asst Glasgow Garthamlock and Craigend East 1984–85; m 19 Mar 1977 Donna Wallace b 30 May 1958 d of Donald W. and Elizabeth McGlynn; Children: Jennifer Elaine b 15 Dec 1978; Gillian Anne b 24 Aug 1980; ord and ind to Edinburgh Drylaw 12 Sep 1985; trans to South Leith 27 Sep 1995; Publ: Co-author of *Full on the Eye* (Bavelaw Press, 1994).

1996   JENNIFER BOOTH
B 19 Jan 1939 at Stafford, d of Geoffrey Moody and Doris Heeler; educ Esdaile and Lansdowne House, Edinburgh 1950–57; University of Edinburgh 1990–93 (LTh); Community Leader, YWCA 1979–85; Secretary for One Parent Families Scotland 1986–90; lic by Presb of Edinburgh 6 Jul 1993; asst Edinburgh St Andrew's and St George's 1993–95; m 31 Jul 1966 Gavin Arthur Booth b 6 Sep 1943 s of Alexander B. and Ethel Fairweather; Children: Andrew b 1 Jul 1969; Sarah b 9 May 1972 m Roger Wilkins; introd as Assoc (part-time) at

South Leith 6 Nov 1996; ord by Presb of Edinburgh 8 Dec 1996; Chaplain to Saughton Prison (part-time) 1995–98.

LEITH ST ANDREW'S (FES X, 13)

Formed 2 Sep 1973 by union of Claremont and St Andrew's Place.

1955 JOHN BROTHERSTONE HERRIOT
(FES IX, 529; X, 13, 312), trans from Lintrathen and Kingoldrum to Claremont 2 Jun 1955; ret 2 Sep 1973; died 12 Jan 1981.

1974 ROBERT RAE
(FES X, 13, 265), trans from Kilmadock to St Andrew's 3 Apr 1974; dem on app as Chaplain to Dundee Teaching Hospitals 1 Apr 1983.

1984 JOHN COOK
(FES X, 158), trans from Easterhouse St George's and St Peter's to St Andrew's 31 Jan 1984; Publ: *Spirit of Scotland* (BBC, 1979).

LEITH ST SERF'S (FES I, 115; VIII, 23; IX, 23; X, 14)

1946 FRANCIS GORDON FINDLAY
(FES IX, 23; X, 14), ord and ind to St Serf's 25 Jun 1946; ret 31 Oct 1975; died 16 May 1982.

1976 JOHN REX BEATTY
B 26 Oct 1920 at Taichow, China, s of John Colley B. and Claudia Isabelle; educ Trent College 1930–38; University of Aberdeen 1974–76; lic by Presb of Inverness 16 Jun 1976; m (2) 19 Jan 1952 Jill Gillette b 30 Jul 1916; Children: Diana Rosemary b 3 May 1948 m Anthony Knight; Dawn Jennifer b 12 Dec 1952; David Rex b 9 Dec 1954 m Ishbel Morrison; ord and ind to St Serf's 28 Sep 1976; died 7 May 1983.

1984 STANLEY WILLIAM PEAT
B 5 May 1929 at Edinburgh, s of George P. and Mary Goodall Henderson; educ George Heriot's, Edinburgh 1941–46; University of Edinburgh 1949–57 (BSc, PhD), 1973–76 (BD); Assistant (Physics), University of Edinburgh 1955–57; Lecturer, then Senior Lecturer (Physics), Heriot-Watt College/University 1957–73; lic by Presb of Edinburgh, Jul 1976; asst Edinburgh Corstorphine St Ninian's 1976–77; m 22 Jun 1956 Elizabeth Eleanor Smith b 12 Feb 1933 d of Charles and Isabella S; Children: Michael John b 17 Jun 1957; Karen Louise b 2 Feb 1959; ord and ind to Carluke St John's 11 May 1977; trans to St Serf's 11 Oct 1984; ret 30 Jun 1991.

1991 PETER HARRY DONALD
ord and ind to St Serf's 5 Sep 1991; trans to Inverness Crown 10 Dec 1998.

1999 SARA R EMBLETON
ind to St Serf's 28 Sep 1999.

LEITH ST THOMAS' JUNCTION ROAD (FES X, 14, 13)

Formed 11 May 1975 by union of St Thomas' and Junction Road.

1969 DONALD CAMPBELL STEWART
(FES X, 14 (2), 29, 425), res from app with Overseas Council at Buenos Aires, Argentina and ind to St Thomas' 28 Feb 1969; became minister of united charge with Junction Road 11 May 1975; ret 31 Oct 1990; died 1 Jan 1996.

1991 SHIRLEY BLAIR
ord by Presb of Edinburgh during assistantship at St Cuthbert's 1990; ind to St Thomas' Junction Road 4 Sep 1991.

LEITH WARDIE (FUF 17; FES IX, 24; X,14)

1961 THOMAS THOMSON
(FES IX, 402; X, 15, 240), trans from Oban Dunollie Road to Leith Wardie 25 Sep 1961; Chaplain (part-time) to Edinburgh Young Offenders Institution 1965–75; ret 31 Jul 1990.

1990 BRIAN CARLYLE HILSLEY
B 19 May 1955 at Springholm, s of Henry John H. and Margaret Jane Gass Watson; educ Castle Douglas High and Kirkcudbright Academy 1967–73; University of Aberdeen 1973–76 (LLB); University of Edinburgh 1986–89 (BD); Solicitor 1976–86; lic by Presb of Edinburgh 2 Jul 1989; asst Edinburgh Corstorphine St Ninian's 1989–90; m 11 Apr 1981 Dorothy Anne Forsyth b 9 May 1959 d of James Duncan F. and Margaret Burns Nicholson; Children: Michael Thomas b 5 Dec 1989; ord and ind to Wardie 27 Sep 1990.

LIBERTON (FES I, 170; VIII, 31; IX, 24; X, 15)

1942 CAMPBELL FERENBACH
(FES IX, 24, 292, 505; X, 15), trans from Glasgow Ruchill to Liberton 11 Mar 1942; ret 31 Dec 1970; died 12 Feb 1996.

1971 JOHN WILLIAM MORRISON CAMERON
(FES X, 15, 53, 170), trans from Glasgow Pollokshields Glencairn to Liberton 1 Jul 1971; ret 14 Jul 1996; s Richard m Elaine Essery; d Lois m Graham Carnie.

1996 JOHN NICOL YOUNG
B 5 Dec 1955 at Sialkot, Pakistan, s of William Galbraith Y. and Elizabeth Crawford Wiseman; educ George Heriot's, Edinburgh 1968–73; University of Edinburgh 1974–79 (MA), 1979–86 (PhD), 1992–95 (BD); Co-ordinator Multicultural Education Centre 1983–88; Research Worker, Board of World Mission 1988–92; lic by Presb of Edinburgh 2 Jul 1995; asst Edinburgh Craiglockhart 1995–96; m 9 Feb 1980 Lindsay Wormald b 5 Jul 1956 d of Eric and Georgina W; Children: Lucy b 21 Sep 1985; William b 3 Apr 1988; ord and ind to Liberton 14 Nov 1996.

LIBERTON NORTHFIELD (FUF 17; FES IX, 25; X, 15)

1949   GEORGE CARSE
(FES IX, 25, 529; X, 15), trans from Lethendy and Kinloch to Liberton Northfield 7 Sep 1949; dem 11 Oct 1959; died 21 Mar 1997.

1960   JOHN ANDERSON GRAY
(FES IX, 237; X, 15, 138, 186, 232, 445), ret from service with RAChD and ind to Liberton Northfield 19 Apr 1960; trans to Strone and Ardentinny 11 Aug 1965.

1966   ROBERT SMILLIE CHRISTIE
(FES X, 15, 113), ind Liberton Northfield 11 Apr 1966; trans to Kilmarnock West High 14 Jun 1973.

1974   LYON GEORGE BLAIR
(FES X, 15, 217), trans from Clydebank St James' to Liberton Northfield 17 Jan 1974; ret 23 Sep 1975.

1976   ANDREW A D GARDINER
ord and ind to Liberton Northfield 29 Apr 1976; dem 4 Sep 1986.

1987   WILLIAM HALLIDAY THOMSON
(FES X, 30, 327), trans from Glenrothes St Columba's to Liberton Northfield 17 Dec 1987; ret 30 Jun 1999.

LOCKHART MEMORIAL (FES VIII, 31; IX, 25; X, 15)

Congregation dissolved 31 Oct 1987.

1949   JAMES CLYNE MIDDLETON
(FES IX, 25; X, 15), ord by Presb of Edinburgh during assistantship at North Leith 7 May 1947; ind to Lockhart Memorial 27 Jul 1949; ret 31 Oct 1987; died 15 Apr 1993.

LONDON ROAD (FUF 17; FES IX, 26; X, 15)

1964   WILLIAM SCOTT REID
(FES IX, 746; X, 4, 15), trans from Edinburgh Bristo Memorial to London Road 20 Oct 1964; ret 30 Jun 1990; app Asst at Edinburgh Cluny 1 Apr 1991; RD 1975; s Christian m Dyer; d Beatrice m Hood; d Monica m Lloyd; Publ: *Religious Attitudes in Later Life* (Age Concern, 1976); *A Study of Religious Attitudes of the Elderly* (Age and Ageing, 1978); *Transitions in Middle and Later Life* (British Society of Gerontology, 1980); *Religious Attitudes in Later Life* (British Psychological Society, 1992).

1991   WILLIAM LISTER ARMITAGE
B 25 Mar 1941 at Glasgow, s of Henry Nicol A. and Flora McDonald; educ Albert Road Academy 1953–59; Jordanhill College, Glasgow 1966–67 (PGCE); University of Strathclyde 1967 (BSc); University of Edinburgh 1976 (BD); Flour Miller 1959–62; Teaching 1967–76; lic by Presb of West Lothian, Jul 1976; ord and ind to Bonnyrigg 28 Jul 1976; trans to London Road 28 Jan 1991.

MARCHMONT ST GILES' (FES X, 16)

Formed 11 Jun 1972 by union of Warrender, West St Giles' and Grange.

1961   JAMES CLARENCE FINLAYSON
(FES IX, 262, 287, 297, 374; X, 9, 176), trans from Glasgow St James' (Pollok) to the Grange 23 Feb 1961; ret 11 Jun 1972 in interests of union; loc ten South Morningside 1972–73, Fairmilehead 1973–74, St Nicholas' Sighthill 1975–76; Publ: *Launching Out. Christian Healing in Scotland* (private, 1994).

1966   JOHN MACDONALD ROSE
(FES IX, 19, 538, 651, 747; X, 12, 27, 402), trans from Kirkwall St Magnus to West St Giles' 14 Oct 1966; dem in interests of union 11 Jun 1972; died 3 Nov 1995.

1974   DONALD MURRAY STEPHEN
(FES X, 16, 103), trans from Kirkoswald to Marchmont St Giles' 31 Jan 1974; w Hilda died 8 Jul 1999; Addl children: David John b 11 Feb 1980; d Alison m Robin Alexander Leslie Munro.

1991   ELSPETH GILLIAN DOUGALL
B 2 Sep 1936 at Newport-on-Tay, d of Andrew Laird Swinton and Margaret McArtney Martin; educ Dundee High 1945–54; University of St Andrews 1954–57 (MA); University of Edinburgh 1957–58 (DSS), 1985–88 (BD); Personnel Officer 1988–89; lic by Presb of Edinburgh 5 Jul 1987; m 7 Jan 1960 Ian Cunningham Dougall b 27 Nov 1929 s of James Watson Cunningham D. and Annie McGibbon Eadie; Children: Bruce Swinton b 22 Jun 1961, died 15 Sep 1988; Neil James b 8 Feb 1963; Ninian Martin Eadie b 7 Sep 1965; ord in Kikuyu by Presb Church of East Africa 29 Jan 1989; ind to Marchmont St Giles' (joint ministry) 5 Dec 1991.

MAYFIELD SALISBURY (FES X, 16, 25)

Formed 7 Feb 1993 by union of Mayfield and Salisbury (new name adopted for Newington South and Hope Park 1 Jan 1959).

1930   ROBERT TAYLOR
(FUF 188; FES IX, 17, 29, 331; X, 18, 25), trans from Hamilton Saffronhall Associate Antiburgher to Hope Park 19 Nov 1930; became minister of united charge with Newington South 20 Oct 1940; ret 31 Mar 1967; died 23 Dec 1979.

1959   WILLIAM JAMES GILMOUR McDONALD
(FES IX, 466; X, 16, 276), trans from Limekilns to Mayfield 28 May 1959; DD (Edinburgh) 1987; Moderator of General Assembly 1989–90; ret 30 Nov 1992; s Roderick m Diane McNally.

1967   BRIAN CLIFFORD CASEBOW
(FES X, 25, 200), trans from Motherwell St Margaret's to Salisbury 18 Oct 1967; ret 31 Jan 1993; s Peter m Carolyn Lawrie; s Richard m Beverley Fenton.

1993 ALEXANDER WATT YOUNG
B 26 Jul 1959 at Stirling, s of Matthew Jenkins Y. and Jessie Mitchell; educ Bannockburn High and Stirling High 1971–76; Falkirk College of Technology 1976–80 (SLT); University of Glasgow 1980–86 (BD, DipMin); Princeton Theological Seminary, USA 1986–87 (ThM); Lab Technician 1976–80; lic by Presb of Stirling 8 Jul 1986; asst Falkirk Old and St Modan's 1987–88; m 28 Aug 1988 Pamela Margaret Walker b 3 Aug 1960 d of Earl W. and Gladys Venable; Children: Chloe Ann b 2 Oct 1991; Abigail Jane b 23 Nov 1994; ord and ind to Ardrossan Barony St John's 26 Jun 1988; trans to Mayfield Salisbury 1 Sep 1993.

1994 ALISON PATERSON McDONALD MATHESON
res from app at the Scottish Mission, Budapest 1 Mar 1994 and introd as Assoc at Mayfield Salisbury 1 Dec 1994; ind to Musselburgh Northesk 10 Oct 1998.

MORNINGSIDE BRAID (FES X, 16, 4)

Formed 12 May 1990 by union of Morningside and Braid.

1940 FRANK WOOD
(FES IX, 14, 27, 218; X, 16, 17), trans from Kilbarchan West to Morningside 30 May 1940; became minister of united charge with Morningside High 12 Jun 1960; ret 4 May 1969; died 6 Jan 1989.

1948 RODERICK SMITH
(FES IX, 5, 665, 688; X, 4), trans from Urray and Kilchrist to Braid 6 Oct 1948; ret 31 Dec 1976; died 13 Mar 1989.

1970 JOHN FRASER KIRK
(FES X, 17, 281, 319), trans from Forfar St James' to Morningside 5 Feb 1970; ret 12 May 1990; died 25 Oct 1999; Publ: 'Power to Hand' (Outline, 1986).

1977 ANGUS WILSON MORRISON
(FES X, 97, 334), trans from Cults West to Braid 30 Jun 1977; trans to Kildalton and Oa 20 Oct 1989.

1991 JOHN RENWICK WELLS
B 22 Dec 1961 at Edinburgh, s of George Huntly W. and Angusina McLean; educ Galashiels Academy 1973–79; University of St Andrews 1979–83 (BD); University of Durham 1984–85 (PGCE); University of Edinburgh 1986–88 (DipMin); Teaching (RE) 1984–86; lic by Presb of Melrose and Peebles 14 Sep 1988; asst Edinburgh Viewforth 1988–90; ord and ind to Morningside Braid 29 Jan 1991; app Chaplain (part-time) to Saughton Prison.

MORNINGSIDE UNITED (FES X, 18)

Formed 12 Jun 1980 by union of North Morningside and Morningside Congregational Church.

1975 JOHN STEWART MILLER
(FES IX, 115; X, 18, 65, 148, 357), trans from Cabrach and Mortlach to North Morningside with Morningside Congregational 20 Mar 1975; became minister of united charge 12 Jun 1980; ret 30 Sep 1997; Publ: Contributor to *Worship Now* (1972); sermons in *The Expository Times* (T&T Clark).

1998 JOHN R SMITH
minister of Congregational Union of Scotland, admitted to a seat in the Presb of Edinburgh in terms of Act X, 1998; ind to Morningside United 1998.

MUIRHOUSE ST ANDREW'S (FES X, 17)

Known as Muirhouse until 1995.

1975 HENRY STANLEY COWPER HOOD
(FES X, 17, 420), res from service with Overseas Council and ind to Muirhouse 25 Feb 1975; trans to Glasgow Anderston Kelvingrove 11 Jun 1980.

1980 FREDERICK DAVID FITZGERALD SHEWAN
(FES X, 50), trans from Musselburgh Northesk to St Andrew's 20 Nov 1980; d Rachel m Robin Cleland.

MURRAYFIELD (FES I, 86; VIII, 13; IX, 28; X, 17)

1964 GEORGE BROWN CAMERON SANGSTER

(FES IX, 435, 566; X, 17, 329), trans from Aberdeen Queen's Cross to Murrayfield 9 Sep 1964; introd as Assoc at Nairobi St Andrew's, Kenya 30 Apr 1980.

1980 CLARENCE WILLIAM MUSGRAVE
B 27 Mar 1939 at Belfast, s of Clarence Wilfred M. and Annie Kirkpatrick; educ Royal Belfast Academical Institution 1950–57; Trinity College, Dublin 1957–61 (BA); University of Edinburgh 1961–04 (BD); San Francisco Theological Seminary 1964–65 (ThM); lic by Presb of Edinburgh 22 Apr 1964; asst Edinburgh Blackhall St Columba's 1962–64; m 21 Jul 1964 Joan Evelyn McCammon b 10 Sep 1937 d of William John M. and Sarah McKee; Children: Peter Clarence William b 16 Aug 1966; Vivienne Anne Jane b 8 Mar 1968; Diane Evelyn Margaret b 20 Jun 1971 m Colin McDonell; ord by Presb of Edinburgh and app by Overseas Council for service with United Church of Zambia 27 Nov 1966; returned from Zambia and ind to Murrayfield 29 Oct 1980.

1997 WILLIAM ROBERT TAYLOR
introd as Assoc at Murrayfield 1 Sep 1997; ind to Cavers and Kirkton with Hawick St Mary's and Old 18 Sep 1998.

NEW RESTALRIG (FUF 25; FES IX, 34; X, 18)

1951   GAVIN BARR
(FES IX, 34, 209; X, 18), trans from Saltcoats
Landsborough to New Restalrig 2 May 1951; ret 5
Oct 1971; died 28 Dec 1993.

1972   IAN ANDERSON CLARK
(FES X, 18), ord and ind to New Restalrig 17 May
1972; dem 31 Oct 1978 on app as Principal of St
Colm's College, Edinburgh; app by Presb Church
in Canada, Jun 1983.

1979   IAIN CAMERON BARCLAY
ret from RAChD and ind to New Restalrig 31 May
1979; trans to Kilfinan with Kyles 8 Nov 1988.

1989   FERGUS ALEXANDER ROBERTSON
(FES X, 372 (2)), trans from Inverness Dalneigh
and Bona to New Restalrig 22 Jun 1989; trans to
Dalneigh and Bona 10 Aug 1999.

NEWHAVEN (FES X, 17)

1975   ALEXANDER REID AITKEN
(FES X, 17, 172), trans from Glasgow Rockvilla to
Newhaven 16 Jan 1975; ret 30 Sep 1997; Addl
children: John Robertson b 22 Mar 1976; Kenneth
Alexander b 17 Apr 1980.

1998   GRANT MACLAUGHLAN
B 6 Aug 1971 at Dundee, s of Catherine Hazel M.;
educ Menzieshill High, Dundee 1983–89; Dundee
Institute of Technology 1989–92 (BA); University
of St Andrews 1993–96 (BD); Café Manager 1992–
93; lic by Presb of Dundee 23 Jun 1996; asst
Dundee Mains 1996–97; m 23 Jul 1994 Gill; ord
and ind to Newhaven 29 Jan 1998.

NEWINGTON AND ST LEONARD'S (FES IX, 29;
X, 18)

Congregation dissolved 31 Jul 1976.

1957   MATTHEW SHIELDS
(FES IX, 51; X, 18, 29), trans from Broxburn St
John's to Newington and St Leonard's 29 Nov 1957;
ret 31 Jul 1976; died 25 Aug 1990.

NORTH MERCHISTON (FUF 9; FES IX, 30; X, 18)

Congregation dissolved 31 Oct 1986.

1966   KEITH SIMPSON PATON ROBINSON
(FES IX, 47; X, 18, 32, 46), trans from Walkerburn
to North Merchiston 6 Sep 1966; Chaplain (part-
time) to Royal Victoria Hospital, Edinburgh; ret 31
Oct 1986; s Norman m Suzanne Johnston.

OLD KIRK (FES I, 69, 77; VIII, 12; IX, 30; X, 18)

1975   THOMAS JOHN GORDON
(FES X, 18), ord by Presb of Glasgow during
assistantship at Easterhouse St George's and

St Peter's 3 Apr 1974; ind to Old Kirk 23 Jun
1975; trans to Edinburgh Viewforth 20 Nov
1982.

1983   IAN ANDREW MOIR
(FES X, 423), res as Asst Secretary, Overseas
Council and ind to the Old Kirk 25 Aug 1983; dem
on app by National Mission as Urban Priority Areas
Adviser 1 Nov 1991.

1992   THOMAS PRESTON
B 4 Sep 1948 at Edinburgh, s of Thomas P. and
Janet Harris Taylor; educ Galashiels Academy
1959–64; University of Edinburgh 1970–76 (BD,
CCEd); Inland Revenue 1964–65; Ministry of
Power 1965–68; DHSS 1968–70; lic by Presb of
Melrose and Peebles 7 Jul 1976; asst London
Crown Court 1976–78; ord and ind to Port Glasgow
Hamilton Bardrainney 31 May 1978; trans to
Bedrule with Denholm with Minto 17 May 1989;
trans to the Old Kirk 28 Jun 1992.

PALMERSTON PLACE (FES X, 15, 18)

Formed 2 May 1976 by union of Palmerston Place
and Lothian Road.

1968   JOHN WILLIAM CUMMING
(FES IX, 542; X, 18, 19, 298, 374), trans from Nairn
Old to Palmerston Place 14 Mar 1968; became
minister of united charge with Belford 5 Apr 1970
and with Lothian Road 2 May 1976; ret 31 Dec
1985; died 30 Dec 1987.

1986   JOHN PEARSON CHALMERS
trans from Renton Trinity to Palmerston Place 1
Oct 1986; app Depute Secretary, Board of Ministry
1 Oct 1995.

1990   IAN WILLIAM ALEXANDER
ord by Presb of Edinburgh and app Asst at
Palmerston Place 3 Jun 1990; app Education and
Communication Officer, Presb United Nations
Office, New York City 1 Sep 1992.

**1996   COLIN ANDREW MACALISTER
SINCLAIR**
B 16 Sep 1953 at Glasgow, s of Alexander S. and
Isobel McCulloch; educ Glasgow Academy 1960–
70; University of Stirling 1970–74 (BA); University
of Edinburgh 1977–80 (BD); Scripture Union Staff
Worker, Zambia 1974–77; lic by Presb of Glasgow,
Jun 1980; asst Edinburgh Palmerston Place 1980–
82; m 2 Jun 1981 Ruth Mary Murray b 13 Jun 1956
d of David M. and Moira Allerdyce; Children:
Joanna Ruth b 2 Sep 1983; Timothy David b 21
Oct 1986; Rachel Mary b 26 Jul 1990; Bethany Joy
b I May 1996; ord by Presb of Edinburgh 4 May
1981; ind to Newton-on-Ayr 28 Mar 1982; dem to
take up app as General Director, Scripture Union
Scotland 1 Aug 1988; ind to Palmerston Place 28
Aug 1996.

PILRIG ST PAUL'S (FES X, 14, 19)

Formed 24 Feb 1999 by union of Pilrig and Dalmeny Street and Leith St Paul's.

1969   GEORGE IRVING
(FES IX, 177, 478; X, 14, 40, 103), trans from Kirkliston to St Paul's 30 Jul 1969; dem 31 Jul 1977; introd as Assoc at Canonbie with Langholm Ewes and Westerkirk 15 Jan 1981.

1971   THOMAS McLURE LOGAN
(FES X, 19), ord by Presb of Falkirk during assistantship at Cumbernauld Kildrum 7 May 1970; ind to Pilrig and Dalmeny Street 25 Jun 1971; trans to Irvine St Andrew's 16 Mar 1978.

1978   COLIN RAYMOND WILLIAMSON
(FES X, 89), trans from Auchencairn with Rerrick to St Paul's 30 Jun 1978; trans to Aberdalgie and Dupplin with Forteviot 11 Oct 1984.

1978   ALEXANDER AYTON FAIRWEATHER
(FES X, 354), ind to Monquhitter with New Byth 31 Oct 1971; trans to Pilrig and Dalmeny Street 20 Dec 1978; trans to Kilmorack and Erchless 11 Jun 1987.

1985   JOHN MOFFAT TAIT
B 24 Feb 1946 at Kirkcaldy, s of Ernest T. and Janet Wallace Smith Pearson; educ Boroughmuir Secondary, Edinburgh 1958–64; Heriot-Watt University 1964–69; University of Edinburgh 1981–84 (BD); Research and Development Chemist 1969–73; Quality Assurance Engineer 1973–78; Quality Control Laboratory Supervisor 1978–81; lic by Presb of Falkirk 29 Jun 1984; asst Falkirk Old 1984–85; m 14 Apr 1973 Marlyn Ann Trotter b 8 Dec 1948 d of James Muir T. and Margaret James Morris Mancor; Children: Colin Andrew b 22 Nov 1980; Alan James b 20 Jun 1982; ord and ind to St Paul's 17 Jul 1985; became minister of united charge with Pilrig and Dalmeny Street 24 Feb 1999.

1988   WILLIAM IAIN CRAIGDALLIE DUNN
B 9 Sep 1933 at Edinburgh, s of John Craigdallie D. and Jemima Agnes Bell Goodall; educ George Watson's, Edinburgh 1938–52; Edinburgh College of Art 1954–58 (DA); Moray House College, Edinburgh 1964–65 (PGCE); University of Edinburgh 1980–82 (LTh); Thomas Nelson & Sons Ltd 1958–63; Draffens of Dundee 1961–62; Scotsman Publs Ltd 1963–64; Teaching 1965–80; lic by Presb of Edinburgh, Feb 1982; asst Edinburgh Cluny 1982–83; m 29 Sep 1962 Margaret Patricia Muirhead b 15 Sep 1938 d of William George M. and Mary Young Wilson; Children: Malcolm William b 11 Feb 1964; Gillian Craigdallie b 7 May 1965; Stuart Wilson b 19 Aug 1967; ord and ind to Cellardyke 17 May 1983; trans to Pilrig and Dalmeny Street 19 Jan 1988; ret 30 Sep 1998; Publ: *The Art and Craft of Screenprinting* (British Printing Society, 1975–76).

POLWARTH (FES X, 5, 11)

Formed 29 Nov 1981 by union of Candlish and John Ker Memorial.

1946   PHILIP CONACHER
(FES IX, 17, 576; X, 11), trans from Durris to John Ker Memorial 20 Feb 1946; dem on grounds of ill-health 31 Jul 1968; died 19 Apr 1995.

1959   ANDREW JAMES HEATLIE
(FES IX, 176; X, 5, 102), trans from Girvan South to Candlish 14 Jan 1959; ret 1 Dec 1981; died 19 May 1994.

1970   CLARENCE ALEXANDER GRANT
(FES X, 11, 94, 255), trans from Kirkinner and introd to John Ker Memorial (term) 2 Apr 1970; ret 31 Aug 1978; died 15 May 1999.

1980   DOUGLAS MILLAR MURRAY
res from term app at Callander St Bride's and ind to John Ker Memorial in deferred union with Candlish 29 May 1980; became minister of united charge 29 Nov 1981; app Lecturer in Eccl History, University of Glasgow 1 Oct 1989.

1990   WILLIAM BROWN
(FES X, 48), trans from Dalkeith St Nicholas' Buccleuch to Polwarth 9 Apr 1990; ret 31 Dec 1997; s Colin m Stacie North; d Fiona m Michael Axton.

1998   JOHN KENDALL SOMERVILLE McMAHON
B 5 Feb 1971 at Stirling, s of Anne Ferguson Bayne Kendall; educ Wallace High, Stirling 1982–89; University of Edinburgh 1989–93 (MA), 1994–96 (BD); Dartmouth College, NH, USA 1992; University of St Andrews 1993–94; lic by Presb of Stirling 27 Jun 1996; asst London Crown Court 1996–98; ord and ind to Polwarth 26 Feb 1998.

PORTOBELLO OLD (FES X, 19)

Name changed 1999 from Portobello Old and Windsor Place.

1969   ROBERT CAMBRIDGE SYMINGTON
(FES X, 19, 250), trans from Burrelton with Collace to Portobello Old 15 Jan 1969; became minister of united charge with Windsor Place 1 Oct 1973; trans to Killearn 26 Nov 1981.

1982   IAN GRAHAM WOTHERSPOON
(FES X, 23, 102, 289, 413), trans from Collessie and Ladybank to Old and Windsor Place 13 Jul 1982; trans to Gordon St Michael's with Greenlaw with Legerwood with Westruther 9 Apr 1991.

1991   NEIL BUCHANAN
B 27 Feb 1956 at Perth, s of Norman B. and Marion Lindsay McKenzie; educ Knightswood Secondary, Glasgow 1968–72; St Colm's College, Edinburgh 1979–81; University of Glasgow 1985–90 (BD);

Industry and Commerce 1972–79; Church Lay Agent 1982–85; lic by Presb of Glasgow 3 Jul 1990; asst Motherwell St Mary's 1990–91; m 5 May 1984 Marion Clements Allan b 5 May 1956 d of Samuel A. and Elizabeth Davie; Children: Kirsteen Elizabeth b 11 Dec 1985; Stewart Lindsay b 5 Sep 1989; Rebekah Morna Joy b 12 Nov 1993; ord and ind to Portobello Old and Windsor Place 1 Sep 1991.

PORTOBELLO ST JAMES' (FES I, 21; VIII, 6; IX, 32; X, 19)

1974 KENNETH MACLEAN BETHUNE
(FES X, 19), trans from Glasgow Jordanvale to Portobello St James' 14 Jun 1974; ret 31 Oct 1980; died 5 Mar 1983.

1981 MALCOLM McALLISTER MACDOUGALL
B 20 Mar 1952 at Greenock, s of Alexander M. and Elizabeth Penny McCowan McAllister; educ Greenock Academy and Kelvinside Academy, Glasgow 1964–70; University of Edinburgh 1978 (BD), 1980 (DipChEd); Moray House College, Edinburgh 1979 (Teaching Dip); Accountancy 1970–72; Banking 1972–74; lic by Presb of Greenock 21 Jan 1981; asst Edinburgh Greenbank 1980–81; m 18 Oct 1980 Janet Fiona MacVicar b 30 Jul 1956 d of Archibald M. and Jean MacDonald Hamilton; Children: Alastair Neil b 7 May 1983; Fiona Elizabeth b 29 Nov 1988; ord and ind to Portobello St James' 1 Oct 1981.

PORTOBELLO ST PHILIP'S JOPPA (FUF 24; FES IX, 33; X, 19)

1969 GLYN REES TAVERNER
(FES X, 19, 47, 111), trans from Kilmarnock Henderson to St Philip's Joppa 23 Jul 1969; trans to Mertoun with St Boswells 5 Oct 1983.

1984 PETER S CAMERON
ord and ind to St Philip's Joppa 30 Apr 1984; dem 30 Sep 1987 on app as Lecturer in New Testament, University of Edinburgh.

1988 JOHN WEIR COOK
(FES X, 111, 417), trans from Kilmarnock Henderson to St Philip's Joppa 10 Feb 1988; Publ: *The Word Among the Words* (1987); *What Makes a Heretic Tick?* (Sabbatical Thesis, 1995); sermon in *Preacher of the Year 1996*.

1998 ALISON MARY JACK
B 4 Mar 1967 at Bridge of Allan, d of Matthew Dudgeon J. and Jean Christine Jackson; educ High School of Stirling 1979–85; University of Edinburgh 1985–89 (MA), 1989–92 (BD), 1992–96 (PhD); lic by Presb of Stirling 29 Jun 1992; asst Edinburgh Portobello St Philip's Joppa 1996–97; m 25 Jul 1992 Paul Gerrard Davies b 8 Jul 1966 s of John Keri D. and Marjory Phillips Jones; Children: Iain

Matthew b 23 Jul 1998; ord by Presb of Edinburgh and introd as Assoc at St Philip's Joppa 22 Feb 1998; Publ: *Texts Reading Texts, Sacred and Secular* (Sheffield Academic Press, 1999).

PRIESTFIELD (FES X, 20)
Formed 6 Oct 1974 by union of Prestonfield and Rosehall.

1947 THOMAS ANGUS KERR
(FES IX, 33, 53; X, 20), trans from Harthill and Benhar to Prestonfield 25 Aug 1947; ret 31 Aug 1973; died 14 Nov 1976.

1963 ROBERT RAINY PHILIP
(FES IX, 224, 574; X, 21, 128), trans from Paisley St George's to Rosehall 15 Nov 1963; ret 30 Nov 1969; died 7 May 1993.

1971 HAMISH McINTYRE
(FES IX, 376, 449, 653; X, 21, 29, 371), dem from Inverness Dalneigh and introd on term app to Rosehall 15 Jul 1971; app term on union with Prestonfield 6 Oct 1974.

1975 ALISTAIR SKINNER
(FES X, 20, 301), trans from Dundee Douglas and Angus to Priestfield 9 Oct 1975; ret 31 Oct 1989; d Mairi m Christopher Burnett; Publ: Contributor to *Faithquest* (Collins, 1985–87).

1990 THOMAS NELSON JOHNSTON
(FES X, 402), trans from Buckie South and West to Priestfield 26 Apr 1990; m 30 Jul 1977 Jennifer Ann Baxter b 17 May 1947 d of Francis William B. and Marjory Pullan; Children: Alison Ruth b 5 Sep 1978; Miriam Ann b 1 Apr 1980; Andrew Scott b 11 Aug 1983; Ross William b 5 Jun 1985.

QUEENSFERRY (FES X, 42)

1971 JOHN GILBERT CARRIE
(FES X, 42), ord and ind to Queensferry 18 Nov 1971; s Gordon m Emma Wyllie; Publ: *The Iona Solar Energy Project* (Church of Scotland, 1978); *The Primary School Assembly: Theory and Practice* (Church of Scotland, 1991).

RATHO (FES I, 181; VIII, 34; IX, 46; X, 27)

1948 CYRIL JONES
(FES IX, 46, 467; X, 27 (2)), trans from Lochgelly St Andrew's to Ratho with Wilkieston 18 Feb 1948; became minister of united charge 23 Mar 1969; ret 31 Aug 1978; died 10 May 1996.

1979 PETER DAVID McDONALD
(FES X, 5), trans from Edinburgh Cairns Memorial to Ratho 2 Mar 1979; ret 30 Nov 1984; died 22 Oct 1996.

1985 MICHAEL RICHARD RENNIE SHEWAN
ord and ind to Ratho 26 Jun 1985; trans to
Auchterarder 1 Aug 1998.

1999 IAN JAMES WELLS
B 2 Nov 1956 at Edinburgh, educ Gracemount
Secondary, Edinburgh 1962–74; University of
Edinburgh 1993–97 (BD); Post Office Manager
1974–93; lic by Presb of Edinburgh 6 Jul 1997; asst
Edinburgh St Catherine's Argyle 1997–99; ord and
ind to Ratho 14 Apr 1999.

REID MEMORIAL (FUF 11; FES IX, 34; X, 20)
1954 IAN MACDONALD MACGREGOR
(FES IX, 34, 83; X, 20), trans from Rosewell to Reid
Memorial 6 Jan 1954; ret 15 Nov 1984; died 16
Sep 1985.

1985 BRIAN McFARLANE EMBLETON
B 5 Mar 1947 at St Andrews, s of James Austyn E.
and Isobel McFarlane Anderson; educ Broughton
Secondary, Edinburgh 1959–65; University of
Edinburgh 1970–74 (BD),1974–75 (CPS); Civil
Service 1966–70; lic by Presb of Edinburgh 9 Jul
1975; asst Glasgow St George's and St Peter's
Easterhouse 1975–77; m (1) 1 Apr 1977 Mary
Davidson McLean Haxton b 2 Aug 1949, died 14
Sep 1989 d of John Allan H. and Margaret Watson
Rule Beveridge; Children: Jennifer McFarlane b
17 Nov 1980; Alan Beveridge b 6 Sep 1983; m (2)
1 Jun 1991 Sara Roseanna Campbell b 28 Feb
1960 d of Leonard C. and Margaret Elizabeth
Reddick; Children: Victoria Helen b 6 Feb 1994;
ord by Presb of Glasgow during assistantship at
St George's and St Peter's 20 Apr 1976; ind to
Kilmarnock Shortlees 9 Mar 1977; trans to Reid
Memorial 21 Aug 1985.

RICHMOND CRAIGMILLAR (FES X, 20)
Linkage with Newcraighall terminated 4 Dec 1983
in favour of union.

1970 JOHN LAWLESS COWIE
(FES IX, 455; X, 20, 269, 278), dem from Rosyth
and introd on term app to Richmond Craigmillar
28 Oct 1970; became minister of linked charge with
Newcraighall 8 Apr 1973; dem 30 Jun 1977 on app
by Christian Fellowship of Healing, Edinburgh.

1970 DAVID DOUGLAS GALBRAITH
(FES X, 21), introd as Assoc at Richmond
Craigmillar 25 Oct 1970; Tutor (part-time) in
Practical Theology, University of Edinburgh 1971–
77; ind to Strathkinness 30 Jun 1977.

1978 MARY GORDON SPOWART
ord and ind to Richmond Craigmillar with
Newcraighall 2 Feb 1978; became minister of
united charge 4 Dec 1983; trans to Papa Westray
with Westray 3 Dec 1986.

1987 MARY OLIVER McKENZIE
B 2 Nov 1931 at Glasgow, d of John M. and
Christina Fulton; educ Kings Park Secondary,
Glasgow 1944–48; University of Glasgow 1970–
71 (CPS), 1973–76; Insurance Clerkess 1952–58;
Civil Service (Clerical) 1949–52; Deaconess and
Missionary 1958–76; lic by Presb of Glasgow 27
Jun 1976; ord by Presb of Glasgow and introd as
Assoc Community minister, Drumchapel 15 Oct
1976; introd as Community minister, Drumchapel
19 Jun 1980; ind to Richmond Craigmillar 12 Jun
1987; ret 9 Nov 1996.

1997 ELIZABETH MARGARET HENDERSON
B 5 Dec 1959 at Glasgow, d of William McLaren H.
and Hilda Benzie; educ Laurel Bank, Glasgow
1965–77; University of Aberdeen 1977–81 (MA);
University of Edinburgh 1981–84 (BD), 1996 (MTh);
lic by Presb of Edinburgh 1 Jul 1984; asst Ayr
Castlehill 1984–86; ord by Presb of Ayr during
assistantship at Castlehill, Apr 1985; ind to
Edinburgh Granton 19 Oct 1986; trans to Richmond
Craigmillar 7 May 1997.

SLATEFORD LONGSTONE (FES X, 25)
1970 ROBERT LAWSON MANSON
(FES X, 25, 423), res as Lecturer at St Colm's
College, Edinburgh and ind to Slateford Longstone
7 Jan 1970; dem 31 Jan 1986 and app Asst
Chaplain to Royal Edinburgh Hospital and
Gogarburn Hospital.

1986 WILLIAM ROBERT TAYLOR
ind to Slateford Longstone 9 Sep 1986; dem to take
up place as full-time student at University of
Edinburgh 10 Oct 1993.

1994 GORDON ROBERT PALMER
B 29 Jul 1957 at Glasgow, s of Robert P. and
Elizabeth McDonald McKay; educ Mackie
Academy, Stonehaven and Aberdeen Grammar
1962–75; University of Edinburgh 1975–79 (MA),
1981–84 (BD); Pittsburgh Theological Seminary,
USA 1985–86 (STM); Youth Work 1979–80; Hotel
Porter 1980–81; lic by Presb of Edinburgh, Jun
1984; asst Edinburgh South Leith 1984–85; m 10
Jul 1987 Karen Susan Taylor b 19 Oct 1960 d of
James T. and Helen Lochead; Children: Jennifer
Grace b 3 Aug 1992, died 3 Aug 1992; Ruth Joy b
7 Sep 1994; Sally Jane b 26 Feb 1997; ord and ind
to Glasgow Ruchazie 7 Oct 1986; trans to Slateford
Longstone 24 Feb 1994.

ST ANDREW'S AND ST GEORGE'S (FES X, 21)
1956 WILLIAM CECIL BIGWOOD
(FES IX, 511, 583, 628; X, 21, 23, 338), ord and
ind to St George's 20 Jul 1956; became minister of
linked charge with St Andrew's 6 Jun 1962 and of
united charge 7 Jun 1964; ret 30 Jun 1971; died
22 Nov 1995.

1972 WILLIAM ANDREW WYLIE
(FES IX, 251; X, 21, 148, 413, 456), res as General Secretary, Scottish Churches' Council and ind to St Andrew's and St George's 9 Feb 1972; dem on app as Industrial Chaplain for Inverclyde 20 Jun 1985.

1978 MARY IRENE LEVISON
B 8 Jan 1923 at Oxford, d of David Colville Lusk and Mary Theodora Colville; educ St Leonard's, St Andrews 1936–41; University of Oxford 1941–43 and 1946–47 (BA); University of Edinburgh 1950–53 (BD); Universities of Heidelberg and Basel 1953–54; Civil Service 1943–46; Deaconess, Musselburgh Inveresk 1954–58; Tutor, St Colm's College, Edinburgh 1958–61; Asst Chaplain to University of Edinburgh 1961–64; lic by Presb of Dalkeith 30 Jan 1957; m 9 Sep 1965 Frederick Levison b 3 Aug 1910, died 27 May 1999, s of Leon L. and Katie Barnes; ord by Presb of Edinburgh and app Asst at St Andrew's and St George's 30 Nov 1978; Chaplain to Retail Trade, Edinburgh from 1 Sep 1978; ret 31 Aug 1983; app Chaplain to the Queen in Scotland 11 May 1991; app Extra Chaplain to the Queen in Scotland 29 Jan 1993; DD (Edinburgh) 1994; Publ: *Royal Mail* (A Handbook for Bible Classes, Church of Scotland, 1962); *Wrestling with the Church* (Arthur James, 1992).

1983 RICHARD FRASER BAXTER
(FES IX, 728; X, 86, 416), dem from Kirkmahoe 30 Sep 1982; Asst at St Andrew's and St George's 1983–90; Interim Director, Church of Scotland Centre, Tiberias, Israel Apr-Dec 1990; Assoc (part-time) at South Leith 1991–95; app Chaplain to ministers and others within Presb of Edinburgh 1998; d Julie divorced from Simon Thomas Brooke, m Thomas Scott Carroll; d Alison m David Richard Findlay; s James m Deborah Anne Goldthorpe; Publ: Contributions to *Africa Praise* (Littleworth, 1969); cartoons in *People with a Purpose* (Committee of Forty, 1978); cartoons in *Against the Grain* and *Making the Most of It* (SRT), *Spotlight* (Woman's Guild), *The Scandal of Poverty* (Mowbray, 1983); illustrations in *North of the Zambezi* (Handsel, 1998).

1986 ANDREW RANKIN COWIE McLELLAN
(FES X, 132), trans from Stirling Viewfield to St Andrew's and St George's 30 Apr 1986; Moderator-Designate to General Assembly 2000–2001; Children: Andrew James and Ian Martin b 31 Jan 1979; Publ: *Preaching for These People* (Mowbray, 1997).

1990 KENNETH JOHN PATTISON
res as Chaplain to Glasgow Royal Infirmary and introd as Assoc at St Andrew's and St George's Aug 1990; ind to Kilmuir and Logie Easter 12 Jan 1996.

ST ANDREW'S CLERMISTON (FES X, 21)

1960 JOHN GRAHAM
(FES IX, 653; X, 21, 372), trans from Inverness Merkinch to St Andrew's Clermiston 3 Feb 1960; ret 31 Oct 1984; s David m Joan Helm; s Andrew m Elizabeth Richardson.

1985 ALISTER JOHN GOSS
(FES X, 271), res as Industrial Chaplain (URC) and ind to St Andrew's Clermiston 24 Jul 1985; dem on app as Industrial Chaplain for Inverclyde and West Coast 4 Oct 1987.

1988 PHILIP TAYLOR
B 29 Jul 1950 at Fyvie, University of Aberdeen 1978–82 (LTh, DPS); Nursing 1966–72; Civil Service 1973–78; lic by Presb of Aberdeen 28 Jun 1982; asst Aberdeen Mastrick 1982–83; m 30 Mar 1977 Brenda Schimangki b 2 Jun 1954; Children: Paul Philip b 28 Nov 1977; ord and ind to Kilmorack and Erchless 21 Jul 1983; dem 5 Apr 1986; ind to St Andrew's Clermiston 24 Mar 1988; dem 6 Aug 1988.

1989 ALISTAIR HUGH KEIL
B 21 Feb 1955 at Aberdeen, s of Hugh K. and Mary Ann Taylor Proctor; educ Elgin Academy 1960–72; University of Edinburgh 1976–82 (BD, DipMin); Friedrich-Schiller-Universität, Jena, Germany 1986–87; Bank Clerk 1972–75; lic by Presb of Moray 5 Dec 1982; asst Edinburgh Richmond Craigmillar 1982–83; Liberton Kirk 1983–86; m 7 Sep 1990 Karen Ann McVicar b 13 Apr 1960 d of William M. and Doreen Spiers; Children: Elaine Patricia b 4 Jul 1992; Alison Catriona b 18 Mar 1995; ord and ind to St Andrew's Clermiston 26 Jan 1989.

ST CATHERINE'S ARGYLE (FES X, 22)

1953 JOHN DONALD ROSS
(FES IX, 3, 413, 634; X, 3, 22), trans from Grantown South to Argyle Place 14 May 1953; became minister of united charge with St Catherine's in Grange 30 Jun 1968; ret 30 Nov 1974; died 9 Jul 1987.

1975 VICTOR WILLIAM NELSON LAIDLAW
(FES X, 22), ord and ind to St Catherine's Argyle 2 Jul 1975.

ST COLM'S (FES X, 22)

1966 IAN PATERSON RENTON
(FES X, 8, 22), trans from St Mark's, Greenwich (Presb Church of England) to Dalry-Haymarket 7 Jan 1966; became minister of united charge with St Bride's 7 Jun 1973; ret 1 Nov 1990; Officer OStJ; s Jamie m Linda Napier; d Ruth m David Dickerson; Publ: *A Study of Social Change: The History of Dalry-Haymarket* (private, 1968).

1991 STEWART McKEAN McPHERSON
B 22 Apr 1957 at Lanark, s of William Muir M. and Sheena McKean Campbell; educ Cumnock Academy 1968–73; University of Glasgow 1983–88 (BD, CMin); RNMD; Nursing 1976–79; lic by Presb of Ardrossan 8 Oct 1988; asst Glasgow St John's Renfield 1990–91; Children: Matthew Jack b 20 Aug 1988; Madeleine b 11 Nov 1991; ord and ind to St Colm's 21 Aug 1991.

ST CUTHBERT'S (FES I, 93; VIII, 15; IX, 37; X, 22)

1956 ROBERT LEONARD SMALL
(FES IX, 12, 50, 197; X, 8, 23), trans from Edinburgh Cramond to St Cuthbert's 14 Jun 1956; ret 30 Sep 1975; died 8 Apr 1994.

1976 THOMAS CUTHBERTSON CUTHELL
(FES X, 32), trans from Uphall North to St Cuthbert's 11 May 1976.

1997 PETER NEILSON
(FES X, 167), res as National Adviser in Mission and Evangelism and Director of Training, St Ninian's Centre, Crieff and introd as Assoc at St Cuthbert's 6 Aug 1997; Addl children: Susan Elinor b 19 Mar 1979; d Pauline m Paul Harry Beautyman; d Jane m Gareth John McKeith Saunders.

ST DAVID'S BROOMHOUSE (FES X, 23)

1951 JOHN STIRLING
(FUF 548; FES IX, 750; X, 23 (2), 426), res from app with FMC at Rajputana and introd to St David's Morrison Street 18 Mar 1951; ind as minister in full status 4 Mar 1955; became minister of united charge with Broomhouse Church Extension 17 Sep 1961; ret 30 Sep 1963; died 19 Apr 1979.

1958 WILLIAM WATSON JOHNSTON
(FUF 441; FES IX, 558, 599, 605; X, 4, 345), ret from Keithhall and Kinkell 5 Mar 1958; introd to Broomhouse (term) 1 Jun 1958; ret 31 Oct 1960; died 19 Feb 1976.

1964 RONALD NEWMAN SEWELL
(FES X, 23, 52, 97), trans from Wigtown to St David's Broomhouse 29 Jan 1964; trans to Penicuik South 19 Oct 1973.

1974 CHRISTOPHER PETER WHITE
(FES X, 23), ord and ind to St David's Broomhouse 4 Apr 1974; dem on app as Principal of Glasgow Bible Training Institute 1 Jul 1990.

1991 NEIL JAMES DOUGALL
B 8 Feb 1963 at Nairobi, Kenya, s of Ian Cunningham D. and Elspeth Gillian Swinton; educ George Heriot's, Edinburgh 1968–80; University of Aberdeen 1981–85 (BD); University of Glasgow 1987–89 (DipMin); Scripture Union Worker, Zimbabwe 1985–87; lic by Presb of Edinburgh 2 Jul 1989; asst Glasgow Temple Anniesland 1989–

90; m 31 Aug 1989 Helen Elizabeth Idle b 25 Feb 1965 d of Edward Thomas I. and Elizabeth Urwin; Children: Anna Elizabeth b 11 Jun 1992; Ruth Margaret b 15 Aug 1994; ord and ind to St David's 15 Jan 1991; app Chair of Scripture Union Scotland Sep 1999.

ST GEORGE'S WEST (FUF 28; FES IX, 39; X, 23)

1965 WILLIAM DAVID RANALD CATTANACH
(FES IX, 230; X, 23, 135, 325), trans from Aberdeen Beechgrove to St George's West 29 Apr 1965; app to Geneva 3 May 1984.

1985 ROBERT LINDSAY GLOVER
(FES X, 51), trans from Arbroath Knox's and St Vigean's to St George's West 30 Oct 1985; trans to Cockenzie and Port Seton Chalmers Memorial 6 Jun 1997.

1995 ELIZABETH MARSHALL CURRAN
ord by Presb of Edinburgh and introd as Assoc at St George's West 2 Feb 1995; ind to Aberlour 7 May 1998.

1998 PETER JAMES MACDONALD
B 22 Mar 1958 at Dumbarton, s of Donald M. and Jessie McIntyre; educ Vale of Leven Academy 1970–76; University of Glasgow 1979–83 (BD); University of Edinburgh 1983–85 (DipMin); Banking 1977–79; lic by Presb of Dumbarton 28 Jun 1985; asst Edinburgh The Old Kirk 1985–86; m 24 Jun 1983 Lesley Anne Orr b 14 Nov 1957 d of John Fleming O. and Janet Johnson; Children: Callum b 21 Aug 1989; Lorn b 10 Sep 1992; ord by Presb of Edinburgh and app National Young Adult Adviser 25 May 1986; ind to Kirkcaldy Torbain 1 Sep 1990; trans to St George's West 1 May 1998.

ST JOHN'S OXGANGS (FES X, 24)

Church Extension 1957. Transportation of Leith St John's.

1938 JOHN EDMUND HAMILTON
(FES VIII, 22; IX, 22; X, 13), trans from Edinburgh St Michael's to Leith St John's East 18 May 1938; dem 30 Sep 1953; died 15 Mar 1982.

1957 JOHN FLEMING ORR
(FES IX, 144; X, 24, 85), trans from Kirkconnel St Conal's to St John's 5 Sep 1957; ret 30 Nov 1987.

1988 JAMES RONALD DICK
(FES X, 118), trans from Corsock with Kirkpatrick Durham to St John's 17 Aug 1988; dem on app as Chaplain to Borders General Hospital 15 Sep 1997.

1997 YVONNE EMILY SUSAN ATKINS
B 4 Jul 1958 at Musselburgh, d of Alexander Sked and Mary Gwendoline Brawn; educ Preston Lodge High, 1970–74; University of Edinburgh 1991–95

(BD); Nursing 1976–90; Civil Service 1990–91; lic by Presb of Lothian 3 Aug 1995; asst Aberlady with Gullane 1995–97; m 10 Jul 1978 Denis Atkins b 14 Aug 1952 s of Danial A. and Mary Banks; Children: Lynsey Michelle b 13 Sep 1979; Nicola Louise b 17 Oct 1982; ord and ind to St John's 17 Jun 1997.

ST LUKE'S (FES I, 110; VIII, 31; IX, 40; X, 24)

Congregation dissolved 12 Dec 1982.

1955 THOMAS ANDERSON DOWNIE
(FES IX, 372, 461; X, 24, 222), trans from Milngavie St Paul's to St Luke's 7 Dec 1955; ret 28 Feb 1981; died 25 Aug 1988.

ST MARGARET'S (FES X, 15, 20)

Formed 5 Apr 1992 by union of Lochend and Restalrig.

1972 WILLIAM CARMICHAEL
(FES X, 20), ord and ind to Restalrig 3 Feb 1972; ret 31 Dec 1987; s Donald m Amaia Zulaika.

1975 JOHN JAMES STANLEY WHYTE
(FES IX, 794; X, 15, 30, 61, 225, 411, 449), res from term app at Broxburn West and ind to Lochend 19 Mar 1975; ret 30 Sep 1985; died 5 Mar 1994.

1986 JOHN WHITELAW DICKSON
B 21 Feb 1959 at Edinburgh, s of James Whitelaw D. and Euphemia McIntosh Amos; educ St Peter's, Musselburgh and Musselburgh Grammar 1963–76; University of Edinburgh 1979–85 (MA, BD); East Lothian District Council 1976–79; lic by Presb of Lothian 30 Jun 1985; asst Dundee St Mary's 1985–86; ord and ind to Lochend 30 Jul 1986; became minister of linked charge with Restalrig, then of united charge 5 Apr 1992; dem 30 Sep 1994.

1995 EWAN RITCHIE AITKEN
B 27 Apr 1962 at Paisley, s of Douglas A. and Fiona Ritchie; educ Woodmill High, Dunfermline 1974–80; University of Sussex 1981–85 (BA); University of Edinburgh 1987–90 (BD); Youth Work 1980–81; Vice-President, Students' Union 1982–83; Secretary, Student Christian Movement 1985–87; Interim Pastor, Buffalo, New York 1990–91; lic by Presb of Dunfermline, 1990; asst Edinburgh South Leith 1991–93; m 27 Jul 1991 Hilary Brown b 17 May 1967 d of Robin Graeme B. and Sybil Clarke; Children: Keir MacLeod b 29 May 1998; ord by Presb of Edinburgh during assistantship at South Leith 6 Jun 1992; ind to St Margaret's 22 Sep 1995; elected to City of Edinburgh Council (Restalrig Ward) 6 May 1999.

ST MARGARET'S (FES 1, 112; VIII, 22; IX, 40; X, 24)

Congregation dissolved 29 Jun 1969.

1963 ALEXANDER MACANDREW GILLESPIE
(FES IX, 73; X, 24, 44), dem from Lyne and Manor and introd to St Margaret's 27 Mar 1963; dem 29 Jun 1969; died 8 Sep 1984.

ST MARTIN'S (FES X, 24)

1968 COLIN GLYNN FREDERICK BROCKIE
(FES X, 24), ord by Presb of Aberdeen during assistantship at Mastrick 1 Oct 1967; ind to St Martin's 11 Jul 1968; trans to Kilmarnock Grange 15 Mar 1978.

1978 WENDY FAIRWAY DRAKE
ord and ind to St Martin's 26 Oct 1978; trans to Cockpen and Carrington with Lasswade with Rosewell 13 Feb 1992.

1992 DUGALD JAMES RADCLIFFE CAMERON
res as Assoc at Inverurie St Andrew's and ind to St Martin's 19 Aug 1992; trans to Glasgow St John's Renfield 4 Mar 1999.

1999 ELIZABETH JEANIE BURNS ROSS
B 2 Jan 1956 at Aberdeen, d of Meston Charles Christie and Elizabeth Downie; educ Bridge of Don, Aberdeen 1961–72; Aberdeen College of Commerce; University of Aberdeen (BD); Secretarial Work 1972–83; lic by Presb of Aberdeen 29 Jun 1993; asst Aberdeen Holburn West 1993–94; m 10 Jan 1976 divorced 1 Jun 1987; Children: Fiona Christie b 7 Feb 1978; Steven Malcolm b 23 Mar 1980; ord by Presb of Aberdeen and introd as Assoc at Holburn West 7 Mar 1996; ind to St Martin's 20 Oct 1999; Publ: *The Jubilee Community: A New Form of Being the Church* (Theology in Scotland, 1996).

ST MICHAEL'S (FES I, 114; VIII, 22; IX, 40; X, 24)

1948 ADRIAN GRAY WATT
(FES IX, 40, 317; X, 24), trans from Baillieston Old to St Michael's 6 Oct 1948; ret 30 Jun 1980; died 29 Mar 1990.

1980 MARGARET RAE FORRESTER
B 23 Nov 1937 at Edinburgh, d of William Rae McDonald and Mary Kate Macaskill; educ George Watson's, Edinburgh 1943–56; University of Edinburgh 1957–61 (MA), 1961–64 (BD); lic by Presb of Edinburgh 15 Apr 1964; asst Edinburgh St George's West 1978; m 9 Jun 1964 Duncan Baillie Forrester b 10 Nov 1933 s of William Roxburgh F. and Isobel Margaret Stewart McColl; Children: Donald McColl b 12 Sep 1966; Catriona Macaskill b 11 Apr 1968; ord and ind to Telscombe Cliffs URC, Sussex 23 Jan 1974; ind to St Michael's 4 Dec 1980; app Chaplain to Napier University 4 Dec 1980; Publ: Contributor to *Hymns for a Day* (St Andrew Press, 1982); contributor to *In Good Company* (Wild Goose Publs, 1999).

ST NICHOLAS' SIGHTHILL (FES IX, 41; X, 24)

1942 ROBERT COLLINS DICK
(FES IX, 41, 685; X, 24), trans from Wick West to
St Nicholas' Sighthill 11 Dec 1942; ret 31 Aug 1970;
died 16 Dec 1987.

1971 ANDREW IRELAND
(FES X, 24, 99), trans from Darlington New to St
Nicholas' Sighthill 17 Feb 1971; dem 15 Aug 1975
to enter teaching profession; Assoc (Hon) at
Dunfermline Abbey 1990–; Open University 1975–
78 (BA); Open University 1978–80 (DRD); s Alan
m Sheena Kinghorn.

1976 KENNETH JAMES MACKAY
(FES X, 303), trans from Dundee Maryfield Victoria
Street to St Nicholas' Sighthill 30 Jan 1976;
Chaplain to Princess Margaret Rose Hopsital,
Edinburgh; Addl children: Sarah Janet b 23 Aug
1977.

ST STEPHEN'S COMELY BANK (FUF 31; FES
IX, 42; X, 25)

1963 JOHN WILSON CRAIG
(FES IX, 362; X, 25, 216), trans from Clydebank
Radnor Park to St Stephen's Comely Bank 10 Dec
1963; ret 28 Feb 1990; s Ian m Margaret McCalley;
s Donald m Debra Silversides; s Duncan m
Jacqueline Staromlynska.

1990 IAN THOMAS McKEE
B 17 Mar 1953 at Bangor, Co Down, s of Thomas
Lancelot M. and Elizabeth Baxter; educ Grosvenor
High, Belfast 1964–71; Edge Hill College of Educa-
tion, Ormskirk, Lancs 1971–75 (BEd); Queen's
University, Belfast 1977–90 (BD); Teaching
(primary) 1975–77; lic by Presb of East Belfast
11 Jun 1980; asst West Kirk Presb Church,
Shankhill Road, Belfast 1979–83; m 18 Jul 1981
Annette Marie Gartland b 6 Nov 1953; Children:
David Ian b 3 Mar 1983; Jonathan Mark b 26 Feb
1985; Sarah Liesle b 3 Feb 1988; ord by Presb of
South Belfast during assistantship at West Kirk
Presb Church, Shankhill Road, Belfast 21 Jan
1981; ind to Bangor St Andrew's 31 Mar 1983; ind
to St Stephen's Comley Bank 5 Oct 1990; dem 30
Apr 1996.

1996 GRAHAM THOMSON DICKSON
B 18 Apr 1959 at Stranraer, s of John Irving D. and
Annie Agnes McMaster; educ George Heriot's,
Edinburgh; University of Aberdeen 1977–81 (MA),
1981–84 (BD); lic by Presb of Aberdeen 28 Jun
1984; asst Larbert Old 1984–85; m 25 Jun 1983
Alison Jane Hughes b 29 Jul 1959 d of Denis H.
and Jeanette Forsyth; Children: Lee b 14 Nov 1992;
ord and ind to New Luce with Old Luce 11 Jun 1985;
trans to St Stephen's Comely Bank 28 Nov
1996; Publ: Contributor to *God, Family and
Sexuality* (Handsel Press, 1997); *Sabbath and
Lord's Day* (Rutherford House, 1999).

STENHOUSE ST AIDAN'S (FES X, 21, 25)

Stenhouse Saughton and St Aidan's linked 1983,
then united 6 Jun 1993.

1964 ADAM SCOTT CURRIE
(FES IX, 603, 724, 788; X, 21, 413, 445), ret from
Royal Naval Chaplaincy Service and ind to St
Aidan's 22 Jan 1964; died 3 May 1982.

1967 WILLIAM MAXWELL
(FES X, 26, 161 (2)), dem from Glasgow Hall
Memorial and introd on term app to Stenhouse
Saughton 2 Mar 1967; ind to same charge 21 Jul
1970; ret 28 Nov 1983; died 30 May 1994.

1983 SYDNEY EDWIN PEEBLES
BEVERIDGE
(FES X, 287, 335), trans from Leven Scoonie to St
Aidan's with Stenhouse Saughton 15 Dec 1983;
trans to Brydekirk with Hoddam 9 Jun 1993.

1994 MARY BROWN MORRISON
B 10 Sep 1935 at Edinburgh, d of Alexander Osler
and Jane Forrest Brown; educ James Gillespie's,
Edinburgh 1940–53; University of Edinburgh 1953–
57 (MA); Moray House College, Edinburgh 1957–
58 (Sec Teacher's Cert, DipEd); University of
Edinburgh 1975–78 (BD); Teaching 1958–63; lic
by Presb of Lothian 3 Jul 1978; m 5 Oct 1963
Peter Keith Morrison b 3 Jan 1928 s of Donald
John M. and Patricia Sinclair Keith; Children:
Christine Jane b 25 Dec 1964 m Keith Bowden;
Catriona Mary b 29 Dec 1966 m Marc Prowe;
Alastair Peter b 8 Mar 1969; Flora Patricia b 25
May 1972 m David Johnston; ord and ind to
Dunfermline Townhill 26 Sep 1978; dem on app
as Adviser in Mission and Evangelism, Dept of
National Mission 1 Nov 1986; ind to Carmichael
Covington and Pettinain 19 Feb 1992; trans to
Stenhouse St Aidan's 12 Jan 1994.

STOCKBRIDGE (FES X, 25, 22)

Formed 18 Oct 1992 by union of St Bernard's
(union 26 Nov 1980 of St Bernard's and St
Bernard's Davidson) and St Stephen's (linkage with
St Mary's terminated 26 Aug 1992).

1949 ALEXANDER IAN DUNLOP
(FES IX, 41; X, 25), ind to St Stephen's 30 Sep
1949; ret 31 Jul 1986; s Alexander m Anne
Chamberlain; s John m Elizabeth Smith; Addl publ:
Kirks of Edinburgh (Scottish Record Society, 1988);
The Scottish Ministers' Widows' Fund (St Andrew
Press, 1992); various essays and lectures for
Scottish Church History Society.

1958 GEORGE ALEXANDER YOUNG
(FES IX, 70; X, 22, 43), trans from Winchburgh to
St Bernard's 14 Jun 1958; became minister of
united charge with St Bernard's Davidson 26 Nov
1980; ret 31 Jul 1983; died 3 Dec 1991.

1969　CHARLES PATERSON SMITH
(FES IX, 652, 670; X, 22, 371), trans from Inverness Crown to St Bernard's Davidson 3 Sep 1969; ret 30 Apr 1976; died 12 Jun 1999; d Heather m Thompson; s David m Channon; d Rosemary m Manson; s Charles m Hinch.

1976　JOHN ROBERT MUNRO
ord and ind to St Bernard's Davidson 22 Oct 1976; introd as Assoc at Stockbridge St Bernard's 26 Nov 1980; ind to same charge 31 Jul 1983; trans to Edinburgh Fairmilehead 15 Jan 1992.

1988　ROBERT JOHNSTON
(FES X, 300), trans from Dundee Camperdown to St Mary's with St Stephen's 10 Aug 1988; trans to Aberluthnott with Laurencekirk 18 Jun 1992.

1993　ANNE TAYLOR LOGAN
B 4 Oct 1954 at Falkirk, d of William Muir Mechie and Annie McGregor Taylor; educ West Calder High 1966–72; University of Edinburgh 1972–76 (MA), 1976–79 (BD), 1994–96 (MTh); lic by Presb of West Lothian 8 Jul 1979; asst Edinburgh Carrick Knowe 1979–81; m 26 Mar 1977 Michael Robert Logan b 8 Mar 1954 s of Charles Mitchell L. and Dorothea Grace Byres; Children: Jonathan William b 29 Apr 1983; Christopher Michael b 30 May 1985; ord by Presb of Edinburgh 15 Mar 1981; Asst (part-time) at Edinburgh Liberton 1981–82 and Edinburgh St Martin's 1983–85; Neighbourhood minister at Edinburgh St George's West 1986–93; ind to Stockbridge 20 Jun 1993; Chaplain (part-time) to Western General Hospital, Edinburgh.

STOCKBRIDGE (FUF 32; FES IX, 43; X, 26)

Congregation dissolved 23 Nov 1975.

1945　JOHN HOUSTON YULE
(FES IX, 43, 165, 507; X, 26), trans from Dundee Craigiebank to Stockbridge 10 Oct 1945; ret 23 Nov 1975; died 28 Jan 1986.

TRON KIRK MOREDUN (FES I, 134; VIII, 25; IX, 43; X, 26)

1968　RONALD McNISH MAXTON
(FES X, 26, 136), trans from Inverkip to the Tron Kirk Moredun 9 May 1968; introd as Assoc at Dollar with Glendevon with Muckhart 29 Mar 1989.

1989　STEPHEN MANNERS
B 30 Apr 1962 at Dumfries, s of Keith M. and Sylvia McMorran; educ Maxwelltown High and Dumfries Academy 1973–80; University of Glasgow 1980–83, 1985–88; Psychiatric Nursing 1983–85; lic by Presb of Glasgow 5 Jul 1988; asst Glasgow Temple Anniesland 1988–89; m 13 Jul 1985 Katharine McMillan b 8 Feb 1958 d of Norman M. and Heather Kelly; Children: Paula and Rachel b 6 Aug 1987; Joanna b 28 Feb 1990; Lucy b 7 Nov 1992; ord and ind to the Tron Kirk Moredun 21 Sep 1989.

VIEWFORTH (FES X, 27)

1974　IAN PERCY DOUGLAS
(FES X, 27), ord and ind to Viewforth 8 May 1974; trans to Aberdeen Craigiebuckler 3 Jun 1982.

1982　THOMAS JOHN GORDON
(FES X, 18), trans from Edinburgh Old Kirk to Viewforth 20 Nov 1982; dem to take up app as Chaplain and Adviser in Spiritual Care, Marie Curie Centre, Edinburgh 1 Oct 1994.

1995　ANTHONY PETER THORNTHWAITE
B 16 Feb 1951 at Evesham, Worcs, s of Eric James T. and Ethel Lydia Hood; educ Thurso High 1963–69; University of St Andrews 1991–94 (MTh); Squadron Leader (RAF) 1970–91; lic by Presb of St Andrews 7 Jul 1994; asst Leven St Andrew's 1994–95; m 22 Apr 1978 Sheila Robertson Wilkinson b 25 Mar 1954 d of William Roderick W. and Jean Robertson McLean; Children: Emma Louise b 25 Mar 1979; Lorna Jane b 12 Feb 1981; Holly Elizabeth b 12 Nov 1985; Victoria Anne b 25 Sep 1989; Samuel Peter b 12 Jul 1994; ord and ind to Viewforth 22 Nov 1995.

PRESBYTERY OF WEST LOTHIAN

ADDIEWELL (FES I, 1; VIII, 1; IX, 1; X, 28)

Linkage with West Kirk of Calder terminated 1 Feb 1985 in favour of linkage with Longridge and Breich with Stoneyburn.

1933 JAMES SIMPSON ROBSON
(FES IX, 1), ord and ind to Addiewell 4 Dec 1933; trans to Nottingham 21 Sep 1939; died 6 Oct 1988.

1969 THOMAS BORLAND SHEARER DUNDAS
(FES X, 28), ord and ind to Addiewell with West Kirk of Calder 1 Oct 1969; continued as minister of West Kirk of Calder following termination of linkage 1 Feb 1985; ret 30 Sep 1996.

1985 RONALD GALL
ord and ind to Addiewell with Longridge and Breich with Stoneyburn 6 Oct 1985; trans to Connel 12 Oct 1991.

1993 JAMES CRAIG HARRIS
ind to Addiewell with Longridge and Breich with Stoneyburn 6 Jan 1993; died 12 Feb 1997.

1998 DOUGLAS MACPHERSON MAIN
B 27 Feb 1944 at Perth, s of Robert M. and Elizabeth Anderson MacPherson; educ Perth Academy 1955–60; University of St Andrews 1981–85 (BD); Aircraft Engineer (RAF) 1961–81; lic by Presb of St Andrews, 1985; asst Leuchars St Athernase 1985–86; m 15 Feb 1964 Christine Jean Wilkins b 5 Feb 1946 d of Henry Francis Herbert W. and Muriel James; Children: Deborah b 26 Oct 1965 m Colin Adamson; Janine b 15 Sep 1966; David b 10 May 1968 m Julie Gillingham; Victoria b 7 Oct 1971; ord and ind to Errol with Kilspindie and Rait 23 Jul 1986; introd as Interim minister at Edinburgh Craigentinny St Christopher's 13 Feb 1997; introd as Interim minister at Addiewell with Longridge and Breich with Stoneyburn 10 Nov 1998.

ARMADALE (FES X, 28)

1953 EMMANUEL ROBERTSON
(FES IX, 49; X, 28), ord and ind to Armadale 30 Jul 1953; ret 31 Oct 1993; s Harry m Robina Elizabeth Elder; s Andrew m Dorothy Jane Evans.

1994 GEOFFREY HOWARD SMART
B 5 Dec 1944 at Portsmouth, s of Samuel S. and May Berry; educ Maidenhead Grammar 1956–61;

University of Glasgow 1990–93 (LTh); Retail 1964–72; Medical Sales 1972–90; lic by Presb of Stirling 30 Jun 1993; asst Tullibody St Serf's 1993–94; m 17 Sep 1966 Agnes Low b 15 Aug 1941 d of James L. and Annie Black; Children: Alison b 12 Mar 1974; ord and ind to Armadale 5 May 1994.

AVONBRIDGE (FUF 35; FES IX, 49; X, 28)

Linked 28 Dec 1970 with Torphichen.

1970 THOMAS CRICHTON
(FES X, 32), ord and ind to Torphichen 23 Jun 1965; became minister of linked charge with Avonbridge 28 Dec 1970; dem on app as Chaplain to St John's Hospital, Livingston 1 Oct 1989.

1990 MARJORY MACASKILL
ord and ind to Avonbridge with Torphichen 29 May 1990; dem 12 Jul 1998 on app as Chaplain to University of Strathclyde.

BATHGATE BOGHALL (FES X, 28)

1970 JOHN McLEAN
(FES X, 28, 422), res from service with Overseas Council in India and ind to Boghall 22 Jul 1970; s John m Ann Mackie; d Morna m Graham Hall; s Neil m Pamela Ruth Candea.

BATHGATE HIGH (FES I, 192; VIII, 36; IX, 50; X, 28)

1974 JOHN WILLIAM BIRD
(FES X, 26, 29), trans from Tynecastle to Bathgate High 12 Sep 1974; ret 30 Jan 1997.

1998 RONALD GEORGE GREIG
B 2 Apr 1952 at Edinburgh, s of Douglas George G. and Hazel Enid Margaret Hay; educ George Heriot's, Edinburgh 1964–70; University of Edinburgh 1979–83 (MA), 1983–86 (BD); Bank Officer 1970–74; Building Society Clerk 1974–79; lic by Presb of Falkirk 25 Jun 1986; asst Howe of Fife 1986–87; m 9 Aug 1986 Barbara-Ann Hall b 3 Apr 1960 d of Thomas H. and Margaret Russell; Children: Rosalind b 10 May 1987; David b 4 Apr 1990; Rachael b 5 Jan 1995; ord and ind to Redgorton with Stanley 22 Jul 1987; trans to Bathgate High 31 Mar 1998.

BATHGATE ST DAVID'S (FUF 35; FES IX, 50; X, 29)

1975 DAVID DONALDSON
(FES X, 29, 418), res from service with Overseas Council in Taiwan and ind to St David's 23 Oct 1975; trans to Dundee Whitfield 18 Aug 1982.

1984 ELLIOT GRAY STIRRAT WARDLAW
B 12 Oct 1956 at Edinburgh, s of Elliot Alexander W. and Elizabeth Johnston Stirrat; educ Edinburgh Academy 1961–74; University of Edinburgh 1974–78 (BA), 1978–79 (BD), 1981–82 (DipMin); lic by Presb of Aberdeen 27 Apr 1983; asst Aberdeen Northfield 1982–83; ord and ind to St David's 1 Mar 1984.

BATHGATE ST JOHN'S (FUF 35; FES IX, 50; X, 29)

1971 IAN WILLIAM McCREE
(FES X, 29), ord and ind to St John's 12 May 1971; trans to Glenrothes St Margaret's 24 Mar 1977.

1978 DUNCAN SHAW
B 10 Apr 1947 at High Blantyre, s of Robert Ferguson S. and Sarah McMillan Graham; educ St John's Grammar, Hamilton and Hamilton Academy 1959–66; University of Glasgow 1968–76 (BD, MTh); Accounts Clerk 1966–68; lic by Presb of Hamilton 31 May 1974; asst Glasgow Netherlee 1974–77; m 27 May 1987 Margaret Sutherland Wingate b 16 Apr 1944 d of John W. and Margaret McKenzie Goudie; Spouse's children from previous marriage: Ranald Alexander b 28 Feb 1971; John Allison Smith b 12 May 1972; Catriona Andrea b 9 Feb 1976; ord by Presb of Glasgow during assistantship at Netherlee 13 Jan 1975; ind to St John's 23 Feb 1978.

BLACKBURN (FUF 36; FES IX, 50; X, 29)

1953 ANDREW ANDERSON FYFE
(FES IX, 50; X, 29), ord by Presb of Edinburgh and app Asst at The Old Kirk 21 Oct 1951; ind to Blackburn 23 Jan 1953; dem 8 Aug 1957; died 25 Feb 1985.

1957 DONALD CAMPBELL STEWART
(FES X, 14 (2), 29, 425), ord and ind to Blackburn 18 Dec 1957; dem to take up app with Overseas Council in Argentina 22 Dec 1963.

1964 JOHN ARNOLD FLETCHER
(FES IX, 138; X, 29, 82, 419), res from app with Colonial and Continental Committee in Aden and ind to Blackburn 25 Jun 1964; ret 30 Apr 1997; d Bernice m Koppl; d Flaine m Smigliani.

1998 ROBERT ALEXANDER ANDERSON
B 3 Apr 1947 at Kilwinning, s of Alexander Mark Reid and Jessie A; educ Kilwinning High and Irvine Royal Academy 1952–65; University of Glasgow

1967–74 (MA, BD); University of Oxford 1975–78 (DPhil); Hospital Admin Trainee 1965–67; lic by Presb of Ardrossan 1 Oct 1973; asst Edinburgh Greenbank 1974–75; app by Board of World Mission as Tutor at St Paul's College, Limuru, Kenya 1980; ord by Presb of Kiambu, Presb Church of E Africa, Kenya 5 Aug 1984; ind to Overtown 15 Dec 1986; app Chaplain to University of Edinburgh 1 Apr 1989; res from app 31 Jul 1994; app Development Officer, Carberry Tower 1 Sep 1994; ind to Blackburn 29 Apr 1998; Publ: *Burns 1990* (Carlyle Society, 1990); *Intimations of Love Divine* (Leaping Salmon Trust, 1996); *Stop the World I Want to Think* (Leaping Salmon Trust, 1998).

BLACKRIDGE (FUF 36; FES IX, 51; X, 29)

Linked 10 Jul 1978 with Harthill St Andrew's.

1969 CLAUDE SAMUEL REDDICK
(FES IX, 455; X, 29, 269, 283, 341, 360), trans from Kirkcaldy Loughborough Road to Blackridge 18 Feb 1969; ret 31 Dec 1973; died 18 Dec 1982.

1974 HAMISH McINTYRE
(FES IX, 376, 449, 653; X, 21, 29, 371), res from term app at Rosehall and introd on term app to Blackridge 27 Nov 1974; ret 31 Mar 1978; died 29 Apr 1983.

1979 HARRY WARNER HARDIE
B 21 May 1940 at Galashiels, s of Thomas Cochrane H. and Elizabeth Warner; educ Galashiels Academy 1952–56; Bible Training Institute, Glasgow 1964–66 (DCRK); University of Edinburgh 1974–78 (BD); Butcher 1956–64; Missionary, Evangelical Union of S America 1968–73; lic by Presb of Edinburgh 2 Jul 1979; asst St Andrews St Leonard's with Cameron with Largoward 1978–79; m 27 Mar 1969 Sheena Legge b 15 Jul 1940 d of William L. and Kellas; Children: Fiona Ann b 2 Apr 1970 m John Gary Millar; Katrina Elizabeth b 27 May 1971 m Nigel McCullough; Sheena Felicity b 7 Oct 1977; ord and ind to Blackridge with Harthill St Andrew's 17 May 1979.

BROXBURN (FES X, 29)

1976 ANDREW MOYES
(FES X, 141, 165), trans from Glasgow Linthouse to Broxburn 18 Feb 1976; ret 30 Jun 1992.

1992 RICHARD TELFORD CORBETT
B 15 Apr 1952 at Perth, s of John Telford C. and Margaret MacGregor; educ Perth Academy 1964–70; University of Aberdeen 1970–74 (BSc), 1974–75 (MSc), 1975–78 (PhD), 1988–91 (BD); Research Scientist 1978–88; lic by Presb of Aberdeen 27 Jun 1991; asst Aberdeen Newhills 1991–92; m 12 Nov 1977 May Alexandria Todd b 12 Jun 1955 d of Alexander T. and Margaret

Williams; Children: Elizabeth Jane b 12 Mar 1982; Joanna Margaret b 4 Apr 1984; Sarah Anne b 11 Apr 1986; ord and ind to Broxburn 4 Nov 1992.

FAULDHOUSE ST ANDREW'S (FES X, 30)

Formed 10 Dec 1973 by union of Fauldhouse and Fauldhouse Crofthead. Linked same date with Longridge and Breich. Linkage terminated 1 Feb 1985.

1971 WILLIAM MENZIES KENNY
(FES X, 30, 219), dem from Dumbarton St Andrew's 31 Dec 1968; introd on term app to Fauldhouse Crofthead with Longridge and Breich 25 Aug 1971; ret 10 Dec 1973.

1974 WILLIAM NEILSON THOMSON HODGE
(FES X, 31, 358), trans from Drumblade to St Andrew's with Longridge and Breich 20 Jun 1974; trans to Longside 7 Sep 1978.

1979 CHARLES McCURDY
dem from Kirkcubbin (Presb Church in Ireland) and ind to St Andrew's with Longridge and Breich 15 Aug 1979; trans to Kirkmaiden 28 Jun 1984.

1985 SAMUEL HOSAIN
trans from Calderbank with Chapelhall to St Andrew's 2 Jul 1985; trans to Stewarton John Knox 24 Jun 1993.

1994 ALAN THOMSON McKEAN
trans from Kirkmichael, Straloch and Glenshee to St Andrew's 23 Mar 1994; trans to Barthol Chapel with Tarves 14 Oct 1999.

HARTHILL ST ANDREW'S (FES IX, 54; X, 31)

Linked 10 Jul 1978 with Blackridge.

1971 BERTRAM ANDREW LYON
(FES X, 31), ord and ind to St Andrew's 7 Oct 1971; trans to Fraserburgh West 9 Mar 1978.

1979 HARRY WARNER HARDIE
ord and ind to Blackridge with Harthill St Andrew's 17 May 1979, see Blackridge.

KIRK OF CALDER (FES X, 32)

Formed 25 Nov 1956 by union of Mid Calder Bridgend and Mid Calder St John's.

1949 DAVID WILLIAM ROSIE
(FES IX, 46, 162; X, 32 (2)), trans from Stranraer St Margaret's to St John's 19 Oct 1949; became minister of united charge with Bridgend 25 Nov 1956; ret 31 Jan 1981; died 20 Feb 1981.

1981 JOHN McLINTOCK POVEY
B 6 Mar 1956 at Glasgow, s of George Mackay P. and Helen Thomson Jack Abernethy; educ Paisley Grammar 1968–74; University of Glasgow 1974–

77 (MA), 1977–80 (BD); lic by Presb of Paisley 25 Jun 1980; asst Loanhead 1980–81; m 26 Jul 1980 Linda Rosalind Shiells b 30 May 1959 d of Robert Oliver S. and Audrey Margaret Mackay Forsyth; Children: Lesley Clare b 17 Nov 1983; Colin John b 1 Jul 1985; Stephen Robert George b 7 Jun 1988; ord and ind to Kirk of Calder 7 Jul 1981; Publ: *The Origins of the Parish of Mid Calder and its First Church* (1997); *Kirk of Calder: the Church and Education* (1997); *Kirk of Calder: Witchcraft in the Parish* (1997).

KIRKNEWTON AND EAST CALDER (FES X, 27)

1962 WILLIAM MUIR MECHIE
(FES IX, 65; X, 27, 40), trans from Haggs to Kirknewton and East Calder 11 Apr 1962; ret 31 Jan 1984; d Margaret m Rigg; d Jane m Gent; d Anne m Logan; d Christine m Fraser.

1984 ALLAN BROWN
ord and ind to Kirknewton and East Calder 12 Jun 1984; dem 16 Apr 1989.

1989 JOHN MACCOLL
ord and ind to Kirknewton and East Calder 27 Sep 1989; dem 31 Aug 1992.

1993 ANN MARSHALL BALLENTINE
B 27 Dec 1942 at Bellshill, d of William B. and Isabella Goodall Henderson; educ West Calder High 1955–61; University of Edinburgh 1961–65 (MA), 1974–76 (BD); Moray House College, Edinburgh 1965–66 (DREd); Teaching 1966–69, 1972–74; Travelling Secretary UCCF; Deaconess at Cumbernauld Condorrat 1976–81; lic by Presb of Falkirk 9 Jun 1981; ord and ind to Airth 30 Sep 1981; trans to Kirknewton and East Calder 6 Jul 1993.

LINLITHGOW ST MICHAEL'S (FES I, 214; VIII, 44; IX, 66; X, 41)

1959 DAVID STEEL
(FES IX, 365, 473, 750, 800; X, 41, 425), res from service with Overseas Council and ind to St Michael's 12 Jan 1959; Moderator of General Assembly 1974–5; ret 20 Nov 1976; LLD (Dundee) 1977; Lecturer, Columbia Seminary, Atlanta, USA 1977–85; Theologian Associate, Peachtree Church, Atlanta 1977–85; Publ: *Preaching Through the Year* (John Knox Press, 1980); *Preaching Through the Year* [2nd ed] (St Andrew Press, 1998); articles in religious journals 1943–96.

1977 JOHN LOVE PATERSON
(FES X, 424, 442), res as Chaplain to University of Stirling and ind to St Michael's 17 Mar 1977; Chaplain to the Queen in Scotland from 1996.

1991 RANALD STUART ROBERTSON GAULD
ord and introd as Assoc at St Michael's 25 Sep 1991; trans to Keith St Rufus and Botriphnie 5 Oct 1995.

LINLITHGOW ST NINIAN'S CRAIGMAILEN (FES IX, 67; X, 41)

1969 WILLIAM JOHNSTONE McMILLAN
(FES X, 41), ord and ind to St Ninian's Craig-mailen 31 Aug 1969; trans to New Erskine 23 Aug 1979.

1980 SAMUEL McCURDY HARRIS
(FES X, 88), trans from Urr to St Ninian's Craigmailen 27 Mar 1980; trans to Stranraer Old 9 Jan 1990.

1990 IAIN C MORRISON
ord and ind to St Ninian's Craigmailen 4 Sep 1990.

LIVINGSTON ECUMENICAL PARISH

Incorporating the Worship Centres at:

CARMONDEAN AND CRAIGSHILL (ST COLUMBA'S) (FES X, 31)

Craigshill St Columba's united 1 Jan 1998 with Ladywell St Paul's and Dedridge and incorporating Carmondean and Knightsridge.

1966 JAMES MAITLAND
(FES IX, 37, 479; X, 31, 186), trans from Airdrie West to Craigshill St Columba's 6 Jan 1966; ret 31 Jan 1983; died 20 Aug 1996.

1985 ISOBEL JEAN MOLLINS KELLY
trans from Edinburgh Drylaw to Craigshill St Columba's 28 Feb 1985; trans to Greenock St Margaret's 10 Nov 1998.

KNIGHTSRIDGE AND LADYWELL (ST PAUL'S) (FES X, 31)

Ladywell St Paul's united 1 Jan 1998 with Craigshill St Columba's and Dedridge and incorporating Carmondean and Knightsridge.

1974 JOHN McLEOD
(FES X, 31, 422), res from service with FMC in N India and ind to St Paul's 20 Nov 1974; trans to Resolis and Urquhart 27 Feb 1986.

1987 COLIN RUTHERFORD DOUGLAS
(FES X, 186), trans from Airdrie St Columba's to Livingston Ecumenical Parish, Dedridge 30 Jun 1987; internal move within parish to Knightsridge and Ladywell 6 Oct 1996.

DEDRIDGE (THE LANTHORN)

Church Extension 7 May 1974. United 1 Jan 1998 with Craigshill St Columba's and Ladywell St Paul's and incorporating Carmondean and Knightsridge.

1987 COLIN RUTHERFORD DOUGLAS
(FES X, 186), trans from Airdrie St Columba's to Livingston Ecumenical Parish, Dedridge 30 Jun 1987; internal move within parish to Knightsridge and Ladywell 6 Oct 1996.

LIVINGSTON OLD (FES X, 31)

Formerly called Livingston.

1969 ANTHONY RICHARD DALLISON
(FES X, 31), ord and ind to Livingston 30 Sep 1969; dem 27 Jul 1977.

1978 WILLIAM EWING SMITH
B 25 Apr 1928 at Uddingston, s of George S. and Annie Stirling Ewing; educ Uddingston Grammar 1933–45; Royal Technical College 1952 (BSc); University of Edinburgh 1956–59; Electrical Engineer, Metropolitan Vickers, Manchester 1952–56; lic by Presb of Edinburgh, May 1959; asst New College Missionary Society and Edinburgh Greenside 1959–60; Burnhead 1960–61; m 24 Aug 1961 Agnes Hill b 14 Apr 1936 d of Hugh H. and Alice French; Children: Martin Brownlee Ewing b 14 Jul 1962; Alaisdair Lindsay b 25 Aug 1964; David Alexander George b 29 Jun 1968; ord by Presb of Hamilton 7 Jan 1962; service with Overseas Council in Ajmer, Rajasthan, India 1962–72; app by Diocese of Delhi, Church of N India, to St James', Delhi Jan 1973; ind to Livingston Old 30 Mar 1978; ret 30 Sep 1994; Assoc of Royal Technical College (ARTC).

1995 GRAHAM WALTON SMITH
B 17 Sep 1946 at Edinburgh, s of William S. and Christina Bell Walton; educ Townhead Junior Secondary School and Lenzie Academy 1951–64; University of St Andrews 1964–67; University of London 1979–85 (BA [external]); University of Glasgow 1991–94 (BD); Bookselling 1971–75; Publishing 1975–85; Company Director 1985–91; lic by Presb of Glasgow 4 Jul 1994; asst Falkirk Old 1994–95; m 16 Jun 1979 Rosemary Sheila James b 17 Mar 1947 d of Dennis J. and Mary Ada Annie Boarer; ord and ind to Livingston Old 14 Sep 1995.

LONGRIDGE AND BREICH (FUF 39; FES IX, 54; X, 31)

Linked 1 Feb 1985 with Addiewell and Stoneyburn.

1971 WILLIAM MENZIES KENNY
(FES X, 30, 219), introd on term app to Fauldhouse Crofthead with Longridge and Breich 25 Aug 1971, see Fauldhouse.

1974 WILLIAM NEILSON THOMSON HODGE
(FES X, 31, 358), ind to Fauldhouse St Andrew's with Longridge and Breich 20 Jun 1974, see Fauldhouse.

1979   CHARLES McCURDY
ind to Fauldhouse St Andrew's with Longridge and
Breich 15 Aug 1979, see Fauldhouse.

1985   RONALD GALL
ord and ind to Addiewell with Longridge and Breich
with Stoneyburn 6 Oct 1985; trans to Connel 12
Oct 1991.

1993   JAMES CRAIG HARRIS
ind to Addiewell with Longridge and Breich with
Stoneyburn 6 Jan 1993; died 12 Feb 1997.

1998   DOUGLAS MACPHERSON MAIN
introd as Interim minister at Addiewell with
Longridge and Breich with Stoneyburn 10 Nov
1998, see Addiewell.

**PARDOVAN, KINGSCAVIL AND
WINCHBURGH** (FES X, 42, 43)

Formed 1 Jul 1997 by union of Pardovan and
Kingscavil and Winchburgh.

1958   RONALD NEIL GRANT MURRAY
(FES IX, 161; X, 43, 96, 151), trans from
Glasgow Barony North to Winchburgh 19 Dec
1958; became minister of linked charge with
Pardovan and Kingscavil 28 Feb 1965; ret 2 Nov
1986.

1987   ALAN M GRUBER
ord and ind to Pardovan and Kingscavil with
Winchburgh 25 Jun 1987; dem 31 Jul 1996 to enter
teaching profession.

1998   ALEXANDER SCOTT MARSHALL
B 25 Mar 1955 at Glasgow, s of Alexander
Campbell M. and Margaret Brown Toward Bell;
educ Bathgate Academy 1967–73; Napier
College, Edinburgh 1973–76 (DipComm); Moray
House College, Edinburgh 1976–77 (CSE);
University of Aberdeen 1979–83 (BD); Care
Asst, Board of Social Responsibility 1977–79; lic
by Presb of West Lothian 30 Jun 1983; asst
Aberdeen Garthdee 1983–84; m 4 Sep 1981
Suzanne Robertson b 10 Mar 1958 d of James
Forbes R. and Norma Craighead; Children: Laura
b 21 Jun 1987; ord by Presb of Edinburgh and
introd as Community minister at Drylaw,
Muirhouse and The Old Kirk 30 Aug 1984; ind to
Pardovan Kingscavil and Winchburgh 30 Jun
1998.

POLBETH HARWOOD (FES X, 32)

Formerly known as West Calder Harwood.

1959   DAVID KELMAN ROBERTSON
(FES X, 32), ind to Harwood 16 Dec 1959; ret 31
Oct 1992; app Asst at Edinburgh St Giles'
Cathedral 1 Sep 1995; died 10 Sep 1998; d Susan
m Prentice.

1994   WILLIAM McLAREN
B 19 Nov 1963 at Campbeltown, s of William M.
and Elizabeth Downie; educ Tarbert Secondary
and Oban High 1976–82; University of Dundee
1982–86 (MA); University of Edinburgh 1986–89
(BD); lic by Presb of South Argyll 30 Jun 1989;
asst Dundee St Mary's 1989–90; ord by Presb of
Greenock and introd as Assoc at the Old West
Kirk 22 Aug 1990; ind to Polbeth Harwood 27 Jan
1994.

STONEYBURN (FUF 1; FES IX, 46; X, 32)

Linked 1 Feb 1985 with Addiewell with Longridge
and Breich.

1958   JOHN THOMAS KIRKHOPE MITCHELL
(FES X, 32, 217), trans from Dalmuir Ross
Memorial to Stoneyburn 9 Oct 1958; ret 31 Oct
1981; died 25 Apr 1986.

1982   BRIAN SYDNEY SHERET
ord and ind to Stoneyburn 7 Dec 1982; dem 31
Jan 1985; ind to Blairbeth Rodger Memorial 1 Mar
1990.

1985   RONALD GALL
ord and ind to Addiewell with Longridge and Breich
with Stoneyburn 6 Oct 1985; trans to Connel 12
Oct 1991.

1993   JAMES CRAIG HARRIS
ind to Addiewell with Longridge and Breich with
Stoneyburn 6 Jan 1993; died 12 Feb 1997.

1998   DOUGLAS MACPHERSON MAIN
introd as Interim minister at Addiewell with
Longridge and Breich with Stoneyburn 10 Nov
1998, see Addiewell.

STRATHBROCK (FES X, 30, 32)

Formed 5 Aug 1976 by union of Ecclesmachan
and Uphall North.

1955   GEORGE WILLIAM BORTHWICK
EDMOND
(FES IX, 144, 571; X, 30, 332), trans from Torry to
Ecclesmachan 27 Jan 1955; dem 31 Dec 1975;
died 28 Jul 1991.

1966   THOMAS CUTHBERTSON CUTHELL
(FES X, 32), ord by Presb of Edinburgh during
assistantship at St Giles' 12 Oct 1965; ind to Uphall
North 16 Nov 1966; trans to Edinburgh St
Cuthbert's 11 May 1976.

1977   BRIAN CRAIG RUTHERFORD
ord and ind to Strathbrock 20 Jul 1977; dem on
app by Board of World Mission to Greyfriars St
Ann's, Trinidad, West Indies 8 Aug 1983.

1984   DAVID WILLIAM BLACK
(FES X, 244), res from service with United Church
of Jamaica and Grand Cayman and ind to
Strathbrock 9 Jan 1984.

TORPHICHEN (FES IX, 55; X, 32)

Linked 28 Dec 1970 with Avonbridge.

1965 THOMAS CRICHTON
(FES X, 32), ord and ind to Torphichen 23 Jun 1965; became minister of linked charge with Avonbridge 28 Dec 1970; dem on app as Chaplain to St John's Hospital, Livingston 1 Oct 1989.

1990 MARJORY MACASKILL
ord and ind to Avonbridge with Torphichen 29 May 1990, see Avonbridge.

UPHALL SOUTH (FUF 41; FES IX, 56; X, 32)

1961 ALAN BELL FORREST
(FES X, 32, 223), trans from Renton Millburn to Uphall South 21 Feb 1961; ret 16 May 1993; Clerk to Presb of Livingston and Bathgate 1970–76 and to Presb of West Lothian 1976–81; Clerk to Synod of Lothian 1976–92.

1994 WALTER MILLAR RITCHIE
(FES X, 312), trans from Appin with Lismore to Uphall South 15 Sep 1994; ret 30 Sep 1999.

WEST KIRK OF CALDER (FES X, 33)

Linkage with Addiewell terminated 1 Feb 1985.

1969 THOMAS BORLAND SHEARER DUNDAS
(FES X, 28), ord and ind to Addiewell with West Kirk of Calder 1 Oct 1969; continued as minister of West Kirk of Calder following termination of linkage 1 Feb 1985; ret 30 Sep 1996; m (2) 8 Jun 1996 Deirdre Adair b 4 Jul 1951 d of Albert A. and Matilda Elizabeth Middleton; d Morag m James Fraser.

1997 MARY DOUGAL DILBEY
B 30 May 1941 at Mallaig, d of Harry Claude D. and Elizabeth Dougal Smith; educ Inverness Royal Academy 1946–59; Moray House College, Edinburgh 1959–62 (DCE), 1970–71 (ACE); University of Edinburgh 1989–93 (BD); University of Tubingen 1991–92; Teacher at Lady Lovat's School, Morar 1962–66, George Watson's, Edinburgh 1966–89; lic by Presb of Edinburgh 4 Jul 1993; asst Edinburgh St Ninian's Corstorphine 1993–95; ord and ind to West Kirk of Calder 15 May 1997.

WHITBURN BRUCEFIELD (FUF 41; FES IX, 56; X, 33)

1935 WILLIAM BLACK McMARTIN
(FES IX, 56; X, 33), ord and ind to Brucefield 4 Sep 1935; ret 30 Apr 1977; died 15 Apr 1981.

1977 ROBERT BROUGH
(FES X, 58), trans from Tranent Wishart St Andrew's to Brucefield 17 Nov 1977; s Colin m Helen Carron-Brown; Publ: *Two Links in a Chain* (Wishart St Andrew's Church, 1977).

WHITBURN SOUTH (FES I, 235; VIII, 50; IX, 56; X, 33)

1956 WILLIAM HUME
(FES IX, 160; X, 33, 95), trans from Lochryan and Glenapp to Whitburn South 15 Feb 1956; ret 31 Dec 1983; died 25 Jan 1996.

1984 GAVIN W FORREST
ord and ind to Whitburn South 19 Jun 1984; dem 6 May 1987.

1988 GORDON ANGUS McCRACKEN
B 8 Jul 1956 at Glasgow, s of Cornelius Crawford M. and Agnes Scanlan Johnston; educ Woodside Senior Secondary, Glasgow 1968–73; University of Glasgow 1982–87 (BD, CMin); Building Services Engineer 1973–82; lic by Presb of Glasgow 2 Jul 1987; asst Glasgow Knightswood St Margaret's 1987–88; m 31 Jan 1992 ord and ind to Whitburn South 7 Jun 1988.

PRESBYTERY OF LOTHIAN

ABERLADY (FES X, 53)

Linked 1 Jan 1986 with Gullane.

1970   ROBERT CRANSTON LENNIE
(FES IX, 198, 228; X, 53, 132), trans from Gourock St John's to Aberlady 2 Sep 1970; ret 31 Dec 1985; died 8 Nov 1999.

1986   NORMAN LIVINGSTONE FAULDS
(FES X, 330, 332), trans from Edinburgh Granton to Aberlady with Gullane 13 Mar 1986.

ATHELSTANEFORD (FES X, 53)

Linked 9 Jun 1974 with Whitekirk and Tyninghame.

1944 ALEXANDER DOWNIE THOMSON
(FES IX, 86; X, 53), ord and ind to Athelstaneford 6 Dec 1944; ret 15 May 1974; died 8 Feb 1995.

1974   JOHN LIVINGSTON BLAIR
(FES X, 58, 355), dem from Banff Trinity and Alva and introd as Assoc at Dunbar with Whitekirk and Tyninghame 10 Mar 1971; became minister of linked charge of Athelstaneford with Whitekirk and Tyninghame 21 Jul 1974; ret 31 Aug 1976; died 27 Mar 1981.

1976   KENNETH DONALD FRASER WALKER
B 4 Sep 1942 at Tarbert, Argyll, s of John W. and Mary Hyslop; educ Girvan High, 1954–61; University of Edinburgh 1968–71 (MA), 1971–74 (BD); Banking 1961–67; lic by Presb of Edinburgh 10 Jul 1974; asst Bearsden South 1974–75; m 18 Jul 1974 Veronica McClay Fraser b 2 Aug 1948 d of Robert Maitland F. and Dorothy Greenop Stone; Children: Alison b 8 May 1976; Kenneth b 17 Oct 1978; Kirsten b 25 May 1981; Lesley b 11 Jan 1983; Graham b 9 Oct 1984; ord and ind to Athelstaneford with Whitekirk and Tyninghame 15 Dec 1976; Publ: *Three Orders for Holy Communion with Panel on Worship* (OUP, 1986); editor of centenary publication for Scottish Church Society, 1998.

BELHAVEN (FES I, 402; VIII, 105, IX, 86; X, 53)

Linked 24 Jul 1977 with Spott.

1948   JOHN STEIN McMARTIN
(FES IX, 86; X, 53), ind to Belhaven 28 Mar 1948; ret 30 Apr 1977; died 28 Jun 1997.

1978   LAURENCE HARVEY TWADDLE
B 17 Oct 1950 at Glasgow, s of Sarah Crawford Summerhill; educ Whitehill Secondary and Duncanrig Secondary 1962–68; University of St Andrews 1968–72 (MA); University of Edinburgh 1972–75 (BD), 1994 (MTh); lic by Presb of Edinburgh, 1976; asst Edinburgh St Cuthbert's 1976–78; m 29 Sep 1973 Alison Mary Stringer b 25 Jan 1950 d of Basil S. and Mary Civil; Children: Mary Ruth b 25 Jun 1982; Sarah Joanna b 15 Apr 1986; John Barnabus b 11 Apr 1987; ord by Presb of Edinburgh during assistantship at St Cuthbert's 1977; ind to Belhaven with Spott 27 Apr 1978; Publ: *Pray Today* (Holy Tryst, 1985); *Making Sense of English Words in Religion* (Chambers, 1992).

BOLTON AND SALTOUN (FES I, 356, 391; VIII, 87, 100; IX, 86; X, 53)

Linked 17 Oct 1979 with Humbie with Yester.

1959   GEORGE WILLIAM HUGH LOUDON
(FES IX, 104, 340, 444; X, 53, 203), trans from Uddingston Trinity to Bolton and Saltoun 23 Sep 1959; ret 30 Sep 1979; died 7 May 1990.

1979   ALLAN DAVIDSON SCOTT
ord and ind to Humbie with Yester 26 Oct 1977; became minister of linked charge with Bolton and Saltoun 17 Oct 1979, see Humbie.

1985   JOHN MILLER WILSON
(FES X, 318, 427), res from service with Board of World Mission in Ghana and ind to Bolton and Saltoun with Humbie with Yester 21 Feb 1985; trans to Altnaharra and Farr 14 Aug 1998.

1999   DONALD PIRIE
(FES X, 207), trans from Lenzie Old to Bolton and Saltoun with Humbie with Yester 12 Aug 1999.

BONNYRIGG (FUF 54; FES IX, 77; FES X, 47)

1970   JOHN CHALMERS NICOL
(FES X, 47, 424), res from app with Overseas Council in Argentina and ind to Bonnyrigg 23 Jun 1970; dem 30 Nov 1975 to take up app as Secretary of Edinburgh Local Health Council.

1976   WILLIAM LISTER ARMITAGE
ord and ind to Bonnyrigg 28 Jul 1976; trans to Edinburgh London Road 28 Jan 1991.

1991   JOHN MITCHELL
B 15 Nov 1953 at Lanark, s of Alexander M. and
Janet Benham; educ Calderhead High, Shotts
1959–68; Motherwell Technical College/
Coatbridge Technical College 1970–74; University
of Glasgow 1985–90 (LTh, CMin); Maintenance
Electrician 1974–85; lic by Presb of Hamilton 26
Jun 1990; m 3 Apr 1976 Elizabeth Crombie Laing
b 11 May 1952 d of Charles L. and Mary Cairns;
Children: Louise b 13 Jul 1978; Lisa b 3 Oct 1990;
ord and ind to Bonnyrigg 14 Aug 1991.

BORTHWICK (FES I, 301; VIII, 67; IX, 77; X,
47)

Linkage with Heriot terminated 22 Mar 1981 in
favour of linkage with Newtongrange.

1964   JOSEPH BLAIR GILLON
(FES IX, 19, 517, 556; X, 12, 47), res as Secretary
of Scottish Reformation Society and ind to
Borthwick with Heriot 23 Sep 1964; ret 31 Dec
1980.

1981   WILLIAM DOUGLAS HAMILTON
ind to Newtongrange 12 Aug 1976; became
minister of linked charge with Borthwick 22 Mar
1981; trans to Greenock St George's North 4 Dec
1986.

1987   JOHN LEWIS McPAKE
B 28 May 1961 at Bellshill, s of John Ramsay M.
and Florence Maria Gilfillan; educ Hunter High,
East Kilbride 1973–78; University of Strathclyde
1978–81 (BA); University of Glasgow 1982–85
(BD); University of Edinburgh 1990–94 part-time
(PhD); lic by Presb of Edinburgh 16 Nov 1986; asst
Queensferry 1985–87; m 8 Mar 1986 Ellen
McLaren Davidson b 9 Dec 1961 d of Thomas D.
and Margaret McLaren; Children: Jennifer
McLaren b 16 Dec 1987; Gillian Louise b 14 Jun
1989; Kirsteen Ellen b 29 Jul 1991; ord and ind
to Borthwick with Newtongrange 23 Jul 1987;
Publ: PhD thesis: 'H R Mackintosh, T F Torrance
and the reception of the theology of Karl Barth
in Scotland—with particular reference to the
concept of the self-revelation of God' (1994); *Hugh
Ross Mackintosh and the Direction of Scottish
Theology* in *Theology in Scotland* 3 (No 1)
(1996), pp. 41–54; *John McConnachie as the
original advocate of the theology of Karl Barth in
Scotland: The primacy of Revelation* in *Scottish
Bulletin of Evangelical Theology* 14 (No 2) (1996),
pp. 101–114.

**COCKENZIE AND PORT SETON CHALMERS
MEMORIAL** (FUF 61; FES IX, 87; FES X, 53)

1964   GEOFFREY HORNE UNDERWOOD
(FES X, 53), ord and ind to Cockenzie Chalmers
Memorial 3 Sep 1964; ret 30 Sep 1992; University
of Edinburgh 1982–85 (BD); s Brian m Dhana; d
Jayne m Martin Scott; s Mark m Pauline.

1993   IAN WISEMAN
B 27 Apr 1959 at Lerwick, s of John William W.
and Elizabeth Dow; educ Anderson High, Lerwick
1971–76; Aberdeen College of Commerce 1976–
80; University of Aberdeen 1989–92 (BTh); lic by
Presb of Aberdeen 25 Jun 1992; asst Aberdeen
Mastrick 1992–93; m 19 Nov 1982 Catherine
MacPhail Morrison b 22 Sep 1957 d of Donald
Roderick and Catherine Annie M; Children:
Deborah Joy b 30 Aug 1985; Nicola Ruth Elizabeth
b 19 Jan 1987; Naomi Margaret b 18 Dec 1992;
ord and ind to Cockenzie and Port Seton Chalmers
Memorial 26 Jun 1993; dem 5 Oct 1995 on app as
Asst Warden of Greyfriars Homeless Hostel,
Edinburgh; ret 1 Apr 1998.

1997   ROBERT LINDSAY GLOVER
(FES X, 51), trans from Edinburgh St George's
West to Cockenzie and Port Seton Chalmers
Memorial 6 Jun 1997; Addl children: Anne
Louise b 16 Jan 1978; Ruth Lindsay b 4 Sep
1981.

COCKENZIE AND PORT SETON OLD (FES I,
358; VIII, 88; IX, 88; X, 53)

1956   JOHN LAIDLAW SMELLIE
(FES IX, 130; X, 53, 76), trans from Annan Erskine
to Cockenzie Old 31 Aug 1956; dem 30 Sep 1976;
died 30 Sep 1994.

1980   SAMUEL JAMES KNOX
(FES X, 327), res as Lecturer at Trinity Theological
College, Nigeria and ind to Cockenzie and Port
Seton Old 28 Dec 1980; ret 30 Sep 1985; died 24
Jan 1998.

1986   JAMES SMILLIE ANNALL COWAN
ord and ind to Cockenzie and Port Seton Old 26
Feb 1986; trans to Greenock Ardgowan 19 Nov
1992.

1993   RONALD JOHN MAXWELL STITT
B 13 May 1948 at Glasgow, educ Shawlands
Academy, Glasgow 1952–63; University of
Glasgow 1972–77 (LTh); American Bible
College, Florida, 1979 (ThM), 1981 (BREd);
International Seminary, Florida 1984 (DMin); Open
University 1997 (BA); FSAScot 1995;
Accountancy; Law; Civil Service 1963–72; lic
by Presb of Glasgow, 1977; asst East Kilbride
Old 1977–78; Glasgow King's Park 1978–79; ord
and ind to Kilwinning Mansefield 16 May 1979;
trans to Cockenzie and Port Seton Old 30 Jun
1993.

COCKPEN AND CARRINGTON (FES X, 47)

Linkage of Carrington and Temple terminated 1
Jun 1975 to allow union of Cockpen and
Carrington. Linked 27 Nov 1977 with Lasswade.
Further linked 14 Jul 1991 with Rosewell.

1970 CRICHTON ROBERTSON
(FES IX, 89, 136, 374, 564; X, 47 (2), 223), trans from Rhu with Shandon to Carrington with Temple 28 Apr 1970; became minister of united charge with Cockpen 1 Jun 1975 and of linked charge with Lasswade 27 Nov 1977; ret 25 Jun 1978.

1978 MARION DAPHNE WALKER SMITH
ord and ind to Cockpen and Carrington with Lasswade 25 Oct 1978; trans to Gorbals 4 Oct 1979 (compassionate grounds).

1980 JAMES BROWN
(FES X, 104), trans from Maybole West to Cockpen and Carrington with Lasswade 13 Feb 1980; trans to Crawford with Lowther 14 Mar 1991.

1992 WENDY FAIRWAY DRAKE
B 12 Feb 1951 at Glasgow, d of Charles Colin Campbell Gillon and Audrey Fairway; educ Hillhead High, Glasgow 1963–68; University of St Andrews 1968–74 (BD); University of Aberdeen 1974–75; lic by Presb of Aberdeen 23 Apr 1975; asst Aberdeen Mastrick 1975–76; m 27 Jun 1972 Stephen John D. b 6 Nov 1949 s of Cyril Leslie James D. and Ruby Eunice Maunder; Children: Judith Lesley b 23 Jul 1980; John Charles b 20 Jul 1984; ord and ind to Edinburgh St Martin's 26 Oct 1978; trans to Cockpen and Carrington with Lasswade with Rosewell 13 Feb 1992.

CRANSTOUN, CRICHTON AND FORD (FES IX, 78; X, 48)

Linked 9 Jul 1980 with Fala and Soutra.

1958 JOHN BLACK LOGAN
(FES IX, 41, 304, 527; X, 48, 311), trans from Coupar Angus Abbey to Cranstoun, Crichton and Ford 15 May 1958; ret 31 Aug 1970; died 20 Jan 1987.

1971 GEORGE ALEXANDER TURNER
(FES X, 48), ord and ind to Cranstoun, Crichton and Ford 13 Jan 1971; dem 3 Oct 1976 to take up app with Presb Church in Canada, Ontario.

1977 EDWARD ANTHONY HOWARTH SAWERS
(FES X, 142, 180, 193), trans from East Kilbride Claremont to Cranstoun, Crichton and Ford 12 May 1977; became minister of linked charge with Fala and Soutra 9 Jul 1980; ret 1 May 1989; d Rosemary m Dominic Hugh Gray.

1989 PETER MITCHELL GARDNER
B 18 Jun 1961 at Glasgow, s of Joseph G. and Catherine Marshall Mitchell; educ Douglas Academy, Milngavie 1973–79; University of St Andrews (MA); University of Edinburgh (BD); Addiction Counsellor 1984–85; lic by Presb of Dumbarton 5 Jul 1987; asst Edinburgh St Cuthbert's 1987–89; m 21 Sep 1985 Heidi Clausen b 21 Jan 1962 d of Hans Kristian C. and Agnes

Hildersley; ord by Presb of Edinburgh during assistantship at St Cuthbert's 26 Jun 1988; ind to Cranstoun, Crichton and Ford with Fala and Soutra 20 Jul 1989.

DALKEITH ST JOHN'S AND KING'S PARK (FUF 55; FES IX, 78; X, 48)

1948 HUBERT LORRAINE BLACK
(FES IX, 78, 165; X, 48), trans from Newton Stewart St John's to St John's and King's Park 16 Dec 1948; ret 10 Jan 1958; died 5 Oct 1998.

1958 DUNCAN McKENZIE BRUCE
(FES IX, 565; X, 48, 268, 328), trans from Aberdeen Northfield to St John's and King's Park 30 Jun 1958; trans to Stirling North 16 Jan 1963.

1963 ANDREW BEVERIDGE DOIG
(FES IX, 732; X, 48, 418), res from service with FMC in Malawi and ind to St John's and King's Park 14 May 1963; dem 31 Aug 1972 on app as Secretary of Scottish National Bible Society.

1973 GEORGE ELRICK McCABE
(FES X, 48, 265), trans from Glendevon with Muckhart to St John's and King's Park 21 Feb 1973; ret 30 Sep 1987; died 6 May 1992.

1988 ALISTAIR KEITH RIDLAND
B 14 Sep 1955 at Leith, s of William Henry R. and Ada Louisa MacKenzie; educ Leith Academy 1967–73; University of Edinburgh 1974–78 (MA), 1978–81 (BD); lic by Presb of Edinburgh 5 Jul 1981; asst Glasgow Netherlee 1981–82; ord and ind to Ayr Annbank 15 Dec 1982; trans to St John's and King's Park 12 May 1988.

DALKEITH ST NICHOLAS' BUCCLEUCH (FES X, 48)

Formed 25 Nov 1979 by union of Dalkeith St Nicholas' and Buccleuch.

1950 MAGNUS JAMES GARSON MACINTOSH
(FES IX, 78, 251, 278; X, 48), trans from Stamperland to St Nicholas' 29 Jun 1950; died 11 Jan 1979.

1972 WILLIAM BROWN
(FES X, 48), ord and ind to Buccleuch 8 Dec 1972; became minister of united charge with St Nicholas' 25 Nov 1979; trans to Edinburgh Polwarth 9 Apr 1990.

1991 JAMES EDWARD ANDREWS
B 2 May 1945 at Downpatrick, N Ireland, s of James Derby A. and Harriet Norah Innes; educ Larne Grammar and Belfast Royal Academy; Magee University College, Londonderry 1965–68; Trinity College, Dublin 1968–70 (BA, MA); Manchester Polytechnic 1972–73 (DCG); University of Edinburgh 1981–84 (BD); Careers Officer 1970–81; lic by Presb of West Lothian 30

Jun 1984; asst Alloway 1984; Jedburgh Old with Ancrum with Edgerston 1985; m 19 Apr 1974 Margaret Elizabeth McWhirter b 8 Mar 1946 d of Samuel Robert M. and Evelyn May Coe; Children: Matthew Samuel b 18 Jun 1975; Robert Jonathan b 12 Feb 1979; ord and ind to Ardrishaig with South Knapdale 25 Oct 1985; trans to St Nicholas' Buccleuch 20 Jun 1991.

DIRLETON (FES I, 358; VIII, 88; IX, 88; X, 53)

Linked 1 Oct 1989 with North Berwick Abbey.

1968   IAN WEIR FRASER
(FES IX, 586; X, 53, 340), trans from Braemar to Dirleton 26 Sep 1968; ret 30 Sep 1989; died 29 Jan 1992.

1989   PATRICK HAMILTON CASHMAN
ord and ind to North Berwick Abbey 21 Jun 1985; became minister of linked charge with Dirleton 1 Oct 1989; ret 30 Apr 1998.

1998   DAVID JOHN GRAHAM
B 22 Nov 1955 at Hawick, s of Francis Inglis G. and Jane Elizabeth Dodds; educ Uddingston Grammar 1968–74; University of Aberdeen 1974–78 (BSc), 1978–81 (BD); University of Glasgow 1984–91 (PhD); lic by Presb of Aberdeen 15 Jun 1981; asst Motherwell South Dalziel 1981–82; Milngavie St Paul's 1982–83; m 21 Jun 1982 Mary Scollon MacIntyre Blevins b 10 Jan 1958 d of Robert B. and Jessica MacIntyre; Children: Lucilla Mary b 8 Sep 1988; ord by Presb of Dumbarton during assistantship at Milngavie St Paul's 15 Sep 1982; app to Glasgow Bible College Aug 1983; ind to Dirleton with North Berwick Abbey 10 Dec 1998; Tyndale New Testament Lecturer, Jul 2000; Publ: *The Dilemma of the Male Feminist Critic* in *Talking it Over: Perspectives on Women and Religion* (Trinity St Mungo Press, 1996); *Christ Imagery in Recent Film* in *Images of Christ* (Sheffield Academic Press, 1996); contributor to *Explorations in Theology and Film. Movies and Meaning* (Blackwell, 1997); *Comments on Commentaries: Matthew* (Biblical Studies Bulletin, 1997); *Pastoral Care in the New Testament* in *A History of Pastoral Care* (Cassell, 1999); *Matthew* in Two Horizons Commentary Series (Eerdmans, 2000); *Jewish and Early Christian Views of Illness, Healing and Medicine* (ISHM Symposium, forthcoming); *Matthew* in New Testament Readings Series (Routledge, forthcoming).

DUNBAR (FES X, 54)

Formed 20 Mar 1966 by union of Dunbar Abbey and Dunbar Old.

1949   THOMAS LOTHIAN
(FES IX, 88; X, 54), ord and ind to Dunbar Abbey 2 Mar 1949; ret 30 Apr 1955; died 11 Aug 1981.

1956   WALTER LEWIS LEWIS
(FES IX, 473, 757; X, 54, 280, 421), trans from Cardenden St Fothad's to Dunbar Abbey 21 Mar 1956; died 18 Mar 1966.

1966   WILLIAM RIDDELL CHALMERS
(FES X, 54, 177), trans from Glasgow St Nicholas' Cardonald to Dunbar 20 Oct 1966; ret 31 Oct 1992.

1993   ALEXANDER BUCHAN NOBLE
trans from Stirling St Mark's to Dunbar 16 Sep 1993; trans to Fyvie with Rothienorman 23 Sep 1999.

DUNGLASS (FES X, 53, 55, 56)

Formed 13 Feb 1994 by union of Cockburnspath, Innerwick and Oldhamstocks.

1965   DUNCAN McMILLAN TURNER
(FES IX, 555, 602, 652; X, 55, 323, 339), trans from Alford with Tullynessle and Forbes to Innerwick and Spott 29 Oct 1965; ret 30 Jun 1977.

1965   DAVID FAIRLEY SPENCE DICK
(FES IX, 1, 20; X, 12, 53), trans from Leith Bonnington to Cockburnspath with Oldhamstocks 29 Apr 1965; ret 31 Jul 1976; died 29 Jul 1991.

1977   BRUCE ROBERTSON
(FES IX, 662; X, 246, 379), res as Asst at Edinburgh St Giles' Cathedral and ind to Cockburnspath with Innerwick with Oldhamstocks 14 Dec 1977; dem 30 Sep 1982 and introd to the Scots Kirk, Paris.

1982   PARAIC REAMONN
ind to Cockburnspath with Innerwick with Oldhamstocks 15 Dec 1982; dem 31 Aug 1993 on app as Communications Secretary, World Alliance of Reformed Churches, Geneva.

1994   ANNE RIVERS LITHGOW
B 17 Dec 1948 at London, d of Oswald Horne and Jean Winifred Rivers; educ Fidelis Convent, London 1959–67; University of Edinburgh 1967–70 (MA), 1987–90 (BD); lic by Presb of Lothian 25 Apr 1991; asst Dalkeith St John's and King's Park 1990–92; m 28 Mar 1970 Robert Somerville Lithgow b 16 Jan 1943 s of William L. and Janet Liddle Clapham; Children: William David b 15 Apr 1971; Edward Francis b 12 Jan 1974; Rebecca Jean b 4 Sep 1978; ord by Presb of Edinburgh and introd as Assoc at Gilmerton 24 Jun 1992; ind to Dunglass 18 Aug 1994.

FALA AND SOUTRA (FES IX, 79; X, 48)

Linked 9 Jul 1980 with Cranstoun, Crichton and Ford.

1949   DANIEL BLADES
(FUF 314; FES IX, 79; X, 48), trans from Stirling South to Fala and Soutra 3 Jun 1949; ret 8 Jul 1980; died 19 Mar 1990.

1980   EDWARD ANTHONY HOWARTH
SAWERS
(FES X, 142, 180, 193), ind to Cranstoun, Crichton
and Ford 12 May 1977; became minister of linked
charge with Fala and Soutra 9 Jul 1980, see
Cranstoun.

1989   PETER MITCHELL GARDNER
ind to Cranstoun, Crichton and Ford with Fala and
Soutra 20 Jul 1989, see Cranstoun.

GARVALD AND MORHAM (FES X, 54)

Linked 13 Nov 1980 with Haddington West.

1966   ROBERT RICHARD CAMERON
CUNNINGHAM
(FES IX, 108, 254; X, 54, 66, 67), trans from
Jedburgh Trinity to Garvald and Morham 21 Sep
1966; ret 31 Oct 1978; died 10 Dec 1994.

1979   IAN WALKER
res from app with United Church of Zambia and
ind to Garvald and Morham 15 Aug 1979; became
minister of linked charge with Haddington West 13
Nov 1980; dem on app by Board of Education as
Tutor, St Colm's College 16 Sep 1984.

1985   ALASTAIR HUNTER GRAY
trans from Methil to Garvald and Morham with
Haddington West 21 Feb 1985; trans to Lochgilphead 5 Jul 1996.

1997   CAMERON MACKENZIE
B 4 Feb 1960 at Paisley, s of Alexander M. and
McKinnon; educ Castlehead High, Paisley 1965–
76; University of Glasgow 1991–95 (BD); Hair-
dresser 1979–87; Taxi Driver 1987–91; lic by
Presb of Paisley 29 Aug 1995; m 5 Aug 1993 Dilma
Ferreira b 5 Jun 1969 d of Francesco de Assis F.
and Carvalho; Children: Pedro Samuel Ferreira b
4 Sep 1997; Lucas Benjamin Ferreira b 14 Apr
1999; ord and ind to Garvald and Morham with
Haddington West 10 Jul 1997.

GLADSMUIR (FES I, 366; VIII, 90; IX, 89; X, 54)

Linked 11 May 1984 with Longniddry.

1955   ROBERT SYED SHAHJAHAN SHIRLAW
(FES IX, 54; X, 31, 54), trans from Livingston to
Gladsmuir 13 Apr 1955; ret 11 May 1984; died 4
Feb 1995.

1984   ANDREW GRAHAM BLACK
(FES X, 55), ind to Longniddry 25 Oct 1973;
became minister of linked charge with Gladsmuir
11 May 1984.

1992   FLORENCE ANNE UNDERWOOD
B 23 Sep 1930 at Stockport, d of Robert Redfern
and Annie Clegg; educ Greek Street High,
Stockport 1935–44; University of Edinburgh 1982–
86 (BD); Inland Revenue 1946–55; Dental Nurse

1955–56; lic by Presb of Lothian 5 Jun 1986;
asst Edinburgh Portobello St Philip's Joppa
1986–88; m 29 Nov 1952 Geoffrey Horne Underwood b 6 Nov 1928 s of Harry U. and Lily Horne;
Children: Brian b 19 Aug 1947 m Dhana; Jayne
Elizabeth b 25 Sep 1956 m Martin Scott; Mark
Geoffrey b 10 Mar 1962 m Pauline; Stephen
Raymond b 19 Feb 1967; ord by Presb of Lothian
and app Asst at Gladsmuir with Longniddry 22 Oct
1992.

GLENCORSE (FES I, 321; VIII, 73; IX, 79; X,
48)

Linked 10 Jul 1968 with Roslin.

1968   ROBERT KELLAS HALL
(FES X, 48), ord and ind to Glencorse with Roslin
11 Dec 1968; trans to Carnock 16 Oct 1980.

1981   JAMES ALLISON MANSON
ord and ind to Glencorse with Roslin 23 Apr 1981.

GOREBRIDGE (FES X, 48)

Formed 1 Oct 1975 by union of Temple, Gorebridge St Paul's and Gorebridge Stobhill.

1958   BERNARD ANDREW HEARFIELD
(FES IX, 175; X, 49, 101), trans from Dalmellington
Lamloch to Stobhill 26 Mar 1958; ret 31 Mar 1960;
died 2 Nov 1996.

1960   HENRY RAMSAY MANN FRASER
(FES IX, 710; X, 49, 192, 247, 388, 404), trans
from Thurso West to Stobhill 26 Oct 1960; trans
under mutual eligibility to Bolton St Andrew's 3 Jun
1970; trans to Logierait 1 Oct 1972.

1967   NIGEL ALEXANDER MALCOLM
MACKENZIE
(FES IX, 143, 272, 759; X, 49, 161, 331), trans
from Aberdeen St Mary's to St Paul's 10 May 1967;
ret 21 Nov 1974; died 4 May 1981.

1971   ANDREW DAVID KELTIE ARNOTT
(FES X, 48, 49), ord and ind to Stobhill 12 May
1971; became minister of united charge with
Temple and St Paul's 1 Oct 1975; trans to Glasgow
Netherlee 12 May 1977.

1977   ROBERT CLARK
(FES X, 301), trans from Dundee Fairmuir to
Gorebridge 29 Sep 1977; trans to North Bute 19
Jan 1982.

1982   STUART HEADLEY ROBERTSON
ord and ind to Gorebridge 27 May 1982; trans to
East Kilbride Mossneuk 21 Nov 1989.

1990   JUDITH ANNE HUGGETT
ord and ind to Gorebridge 16 Aug 1990; dem 15
Nov 1998 on app as Chaplain to Crosshouse
Hospital.

GULLANE (FES IX, 89; X, 54)

Linked 1 Jan 1986 with Aberlady.

1971 DAVID HUTCHISON WHITEFORD
(FES IX, 794; X, 54, 449), [corrections: BD (1946), not (1945) and s David Simpson Cuninghame, not Cunningham—both in Vol IX, 794]; ret from RAChD 12 Mar 1971 [not 31 Jan 1971, as in Vol X, 449] and ind to Gullane 17 Feb 1971; ret 31 Aug 1985; s David m Lucy Shankland; d Kathleen m David Anderson; d Emily m Alistair Bell.

1986 NORMAN LIVINGSTONE FAULDS
(FES X, 330, 332), trans from Edinburgh Granton to Aberlady with Gullane 13 Mar 1986.

HADDINGTON ST MARY'S (FES IX, 90; X, 54)

1970 JAMES FRAZER RIACH
(FES X, 54, 144), trans from East Kilbride Westwood to St Mary's 22 Oct 1970; dem 28 Feb 1979 and emigrated to USA.

1979 ALASDAIR WILLIAM MACDONELL
(FES X, 202, 333), trans from Barthol Chapel with Tarves to St Mary's 26 Sep 1979; ret 12 Oct 1992; d Ruth m Andrew Ruck; d Jennifer m Nicholas Denniston; d Hilary m Alastair Tulloch; s David m Jane Noble; d Lucy m John Wrinn.

1993 CLIFFORD ERYL HUGHES
B 16 Dec 1936 at Newport, Monmouthshire, s of Richard Arthur H. and Ellen Elizabeth Evans; educ Dulwich College, London 1949–56; University of Cambridge 1956–59 (MA); Moray House College, Edinburgh 1969 (CEd); University of Edinburgh 1988–91 (BD); Freelance singer; Headmaster (Beaconhurst School, Bridge of Allan and Loretto Junior School) 1975–86; lic by Presb of Lothian; asst Haddington St Mary's 1992; m 7 Aug 1965 Kathleen MacKenzie Craig b 5 Feb 1939 d of Arthur C. and Kathleen de Laval Willis; Children: Richard Mackenzie b 11 Jan 1967; Clare de Laval b 7 Jan 1969; ord and ind to St Mary's 28 Mar 1993; Publ: *A Singular Solace* (cassette of sacred songs).

HADDINGTON WEST (FUF 63; FES IX, 90; X, 55)

Linked 13 Nov 1980 with Garvald and Morham.

1955 JOSEPH SILLARS RITCHIE
(FES IX, 26, 49; X, 16, 55), trans from Edinburgh McDonald Road to Haddington West 19 May 1955; ret 31 Oct 1980; died 9 Nov 1996.

1980 IAN WALKER
ind to Garvald and Morham 15 Aug 1979; became minister of linked charge with Haddington West 13 Nov 1980, see Garvald and Morham.

1985 ALASTAIR HUNTER GRAY
trans from Methil to Garvald and Morham with Haddington West 21 Feb 1985; trans to Lochgilphead 5 Jul 1996.

1997 CAMERON MACKENZIE
ord and ind to Garvald and Morham with Haddington West 10 Jul 1997, see Garvald.

HOWGATE (FUF 56; FES IX, 80; X, 49)

Linked 10 Jan 1979 with Penicuik South.

1969 ALEXANDER ARNOT FLEMING
(FES IX, 63; X, 43 (2), 49), trans from Stenhouse and Carron to Howgate 9 Sep 1969; ret 31 Oct 1978; died 3 Jan 1990.

1979 RONALD NEWMAN SEWELL
(FES X, 23, 52, 97), ind to Penicuik South 19 Oct 1973; became minister of linked charge with Howgate 10 Jan 1979, see Penicuik South.

1985 FRANK RIBBONS
B 29 May 1952 at Dundee, s of James R. and Anne Milsch; educ Perth Academy 1964–70; University of Aberdeen 1970–74 (MA), 1974–75 (DEd), 1981–84 (BD); Teaching 1975–81; lic by Presb of Aberdeen, 1984; asst Aberdeen Kirk of St Nicholas 1984–85; m 1 Sep 1972 Catriona Munro b 9 Mar 1950 d of William M. and Mundina McLeod; Children: Sophie Ann b 1 Mar 1978; Rebecca Mairi b 9 Dec 1979; Nicholas William James b 13 Jun 1983; ord and ind to Howgate with Penicuik South 21 Aug 1985.

HUMBIE (FUF 63; FES I, 375, VIII, 95; IX, 90; X, 55)

Linked 18 May 1977 with Yester. Further linked 17 Oct 1979 with Bolton and Saltoun.

1969 WILLIAM HENRY ROGAN
(FES IX, 166, 220, 369; X, 55, 126), trans from Paisley Abbey to Humbie 20 Sep 1969; ret 31 Oct 1974; died 11 Jun 1987.

1977 ALLAN DAVIDSON SCOTT
ord and ind to Humbie with Yester 26 Oct 1977; became minister of linked charge with Bolton and Saltoun 17 Oct 1979; introd to Daviot with Rayne (term) 14 Jun 1984.

1985 JOHN MILLER WILSON
(FES X, 318, 427), ind to Bolton and Saltoun with Humbie with Yester 21 Feb 1985, see Bolton and Saltoun.

1999 DONALD PIRIE
(FES X, 207), trans from Lenzie Old to Bolton and Saltoun with Humbie with Yester 12 Aug 1999.

LASSWADE (FES X, 49)

Linked 27 Nov 1977 with Cockpen and Carrington.

1957　RONALD CHARLES KENNEDY
(FES IX, 55; X, 31, 49), trans from Longriggend and Meadowfield to Lasswade 23 Jan 1957; ret 30 Sep 1977; died 21 Mar 1978.

1978　MARION DAPHNE WALKER SMITH
ord and ind to Cockpen and Carrington with Lasswade 25 Oct 1978, see Cockpen.

1980　JAMES BROWN
(FES X, 104), trans from Maybole West to Cockpen and Carrington with Lasswade 13 Feb 1980; trans to Crawford with Lowther 14 Mar 1991.

1992　WENDY FAIRWAY DRAKE
ind to Cockpen and Carrington with Lasswade with Rosewell 13 Feb 1992, see Cockpen.

LOANHEAD (FES X, 49, 50)

Formed 8 Jan 1978 by union of Loanhead East and Loanhead West.

1969　NORMAN CHRISTOPHER MACRAE
(FES IX, 742; X, 49, 290, 422), trans from Cupar Bonnygate to Loanhead East 26 Feb 1969; became minister of linked charge with Loanhead West 8 Jan 1978; ret 21 Jan 1985; Chaplain (part-time) to Edinburgh Royal Infirmary 14 Oct 1985 to 30 Sep 1998.

1974　DONALD GILLIES
(FES X, 29, 50, 375, 398, 404), trans from Broxburn St Andrew's and introd to Loanhead West (term) 5 Dec 1974; ret 31 Dec 1976.

1985　ROBERT WILLIAM THOMPSON
trans form Glasgow Dennistoun Blackfriars to Loanhead 30 Oct 1985; died 6 Jan 1991.

1991　ANDREW FORTUNE SWAN
B 25 Mar 1954 at Edinburgh, s of Harold Thomas S. and Elisabeth Anne Ede; educ Fettes College, Edinburgh 1967–71; University of Edinburgh 1976–82 (BD, DipMin); Mechanic 1971–5; lic by Presb of Edinburgh, 1982; asst Edinburgh Mayfield 1981–82, Muirhouse 1983; m (1) Astrid Beckmann b 15 Jan 1958, died 10 May 1990, d of Elmar B. and Lotte Scholzel; Children: Eileadh Catriona b 16 Apr 1984; Anna Fortune b 13 Mar 1986; m (2) Loraine Elizabeth Haugh b 29 Oct 1958 d of Gordon H. and Isobel Bradley; ord and ind to Buittle and Kelton with Castle Douglas St Andrew's 22 Sep 1983; became minister of Buittle and Kelton follow-ing termination of linkage with Castle Douglas St Andrew's 27 Dec 1989; trans to Loanhead 24 Oct 1991; Publ: *Causewayend to Castle Douglas* (Penman, 1986); *Dumfries Station Hotel—A Centenary* and *G & SWR Signalling* (Glasgow and South Western Railway Association, 1997).

LONGNIDDRY (FES IX, 91; X, 55)

Linked 11 May 1984 with Gladsmuir.

1973　ANDREW GRAHAM BLACK
(FES X, 55), ind to Longniddry 25 Oct 1973; became minister of linked charge with Gladsmuir 11 May 1984; s Malcolm m Manuela Girnus.

1992　FLORENCE ANNE UNDERWOOD
app Asst at Gladsmuir with Longniddry 22 Oct 1992, see Gladsmuir.

MUSSELBURGH NORTHESK (FES I, 338; VIII, 80; IX, 82; X, 50)

1970　FREDERICK DAVID FITZGERALD SHEWAN
(FES X, 50), ord and ind to Northesk 23 Jul 1970; trans to Edinburgh Muirhouse 20 Nov 1980.

1981　RONALD HUNT BROWN
(FES X, 266), trans from Kincardine-in-Menteith with Norrieston to Northesk 21 Jul 1981; ret 18 Jan 1998; d Rona m Frazer McVinnie.

1998　ALISON PATERSON McDONALD MATHESON
B 28 Jan 1963 at Dundee, d of James Lawrence McDonald and Ellie Noble; educ Morgan Academy, Dundee 1975–81; University of St Andrews 1981–86 (MA); University of Edinburgh 1986–89 (BD); lic by Presb of Dundee 13 Aug 1989; asst Helensburgh The West Kirk 1989–90; Larbert West 1990–91; m 5 Feb 1994 Iain Gunn Matheson b 4 Mar 1956 s of Dugald Black M. and Mary McPherson; ord by Presb of Europe 16 Jun 1991; introd to Scottish Mission, Budapest 1 Mar 1991; introd as Assoc at Edinburgh Mayfield Salisbury 1 Dec 1994; ind to Northesk 10 Sep 1998.

MUSSELBURGH ST ANDREW'S HIGH (FES X, 50)

Formed 3 Nov 1985 by union of Musselburgh High and Musselburgh St Andrew's.

1947　ALEXANDER ERNEST LUMSDEN PATERSON
(FES IX, 51, 81; X, 50), trans from Blackridge to Musselburgh High 14 Sep 1947; ret 31 Oct 1985; died 21 Aug 1995.

1960　WILLIAM DONALD LAIRD
(FES X, 50), ord by Presb of Glasgow 29 Jun 1939; ind to St Andrew's 30 Nov 1960; ret 31 Oct 1985; died 11 Feb 1997.

1986　SHEILAGH MARGARET KESTING
trans from Overtown to St Andrew's High 25 Jun 1986; dem to take up app as Secretary for Ecumenical Relations 1 Oct 1993.

1994　DOUGLAS FREW STEVENSON
res as Assoc at Edinburgh Kaimes Lockhart Memorial and ind to St Andrew's High 9 Jun 1994; dem on app as Chaplain to Edinburgh Royal Infirmary 1 Feb 1999.

1999 VIOLET CATHERINE CLARK McKAY
B 7 Jul 1953 at Dunfermline, d of Robert John McLaren Oliver and Violet Hunter; educ Beath Senior High, Cowdenbeath 1965–70; University of Edinburgh 1982–86 (BD),1986–87 (CCE); Bank Clerkess/Teller 1970–74; Library Asst 1981–82; lic by Presb of Dunfermline 5 Jul 1987; asst Lochgelly Macainsh 1987–88; m 4 Aug 1973 Thomas McKay b 1 Dec 1950 s of John M. and Sarah Lynch; Children: Catherine Violet b 15 Dec 1974; Dawn Emily b 16 Jul 1977; ord and ind to Glenrothes St Ninian's 19 May 1988; trans to St Andrew's High 4 Oct 1999.

MUSSELBURGH ST CLEMENT'S AND ST NINIAN'S (FES X, 50)

Formed 1987 when St Clement's (Mission Station of Musselburgh St Michael's Inveresk) was integrated with St Ninian's.

1968 GEORGE WILSON CHARLTON
(FES IX, 397; X, 51, 269), trans from Tullibody St Serf's to St Ninian's 7 Jan 1968; trans to Fort Augustus with Glengarry 18 Sep 1987.

1988 ALEXANDER FERNIE BONAR
ord and ind to St Clement's and St Ninian's 24 Jul 1988; trans to Fowlis Wester with Madderty with Monzie 24 Apr 1996.

1997 MOIRA McDONALD
B 6 Jan 1969 at Elderslie, d of James McDonald and Ishbel Mearns Fernie; educ Renfrew High 1980–86; University of Dundee 1986–90 (MA); University of Edinburgh 1992–95 (BD); Chaplaincy Asst, University of London 1990–92; lic by Presb of Edinburgh 2 Jul 1995; asst Edinburgh Cramond 1995–97; m 9 Dec 1995 Ian Gates b 16 Sep 1957 s of Michael Lawrence G. and Jean Elizabeth Pearson; ord and ind to St Clement's and St Ninian's 15 May 1997.

MUSSELBURGH ST MICHAEL'S INVERESK (FES I, 324; VIII, 75; IX, 82; X, 50)

Formerly appeared as Musselburgh Inveresk.

1959 TOM SIDNEY SENIOR ADAMSON
(FES IX, 148, 227, 387; X, 50, 231), trans from Rothesay High Kirk to St Michael's Inveresk 4 Feb 1959; ret 31 Aug 1985; w Margaret died 16 Jan 1992.

1987 ALEXANDER EWING STRACHAN
(FES X, 265), trans from Caputh and Clunie to St Michael's Inveresk 15 Jan 1987; trans to Guernsey St Andrew's in the Grange 27 Mar 1998.

1999 ANDREW B DICK
trans from Tullibody St Serf's to St Michael's Inveresk 5 Aug 1999.

NEWBATTLE (FES I, 331; VII, 79; IX, 82; X, 51)

1976 WILLIAM JOHN MACDONALD
ord and ind to Newbattle 22 Jul 1976; trans to Gairloch and Dundonnell 10 Aug 1984.

1985 IAIN MACNEE
trans from Glasgow South Carntyne to Newbattle 20 Jun 1985; trans to Girvan South 18 May 1988.

1989 JARED WOODS HAY
B 22 Sep 1952 at Irvine, s of Robert Foster Geates H. and Annie Woods; educ Prestwick Academy and Ayr Academy 1965–70; London Bible College 1976–79 (BA); University of Aberdeen 1985 (MTh); University of Edinburgh 1984–86 (DipMin); Banking 1970–76; Travelling Secretary, Universities and Colleges Christian Fellowship 1979–83; lic by Presb of Edinburgh 29 Jun 1986; asst Edinburgh Cluny 1986–88; m 28 Nov 1987 Jane Ledgett McLeod b 31 Oct 1955 d of John Ledgett M. and Jean Hamilton McGhee; Children: Catriona Jane b 14 Oct 1992; Ian Robert b 24 May 1994; ord by Presb of Edinburgh during assistantship at Cluny 30 Aug 1987; ind to Newbattle 16 Mar 1989.

NEWTON (FES I, 336; VIII, 80; IX, 82; X, 51)

1971 ROBERT LINDSAY GLOVER
(FES X, 51), ord and ind to Newton 11 May 1971; trans to Arbroath St Vigean's and Auchmithie 11 Feb 1976.

1976 JAMES ROBERTSON
(FES X, 201 (2)), trans from Kirk o' Shotts to Newton 17 Jun 1976.

NEWTONGRANGE (FUF 58; FES IX, 83; X, 51)

Linked 22 Mar 1981 with Borthwick.

1957 JOHN ALEXANDER TURNBALL BEATTIE
(FES IX, 729, 756, 795; X, 51, 416), res from service with FMC at Calabar and ind to Newtongrange 18 Dec 1957; ret 30 Apr 1964; died 15 Sep 1987.

1964 ROBERT SIMSON MACNICOL
(FES IX, 741; X, 51, 422), res as Chaplain to Edinburgh Royal High School and ind to Newtongrange 16 Sep 1964; ret 15 Jun 1976; died 13 Apr 1986.

1976 WILLIAM DOUGLAS HAMILTON
ord by Presb of Glasgow during assistantship at Cathcart Old 21 Apr 1975; ind to Newtongrange 12 Aug 1976; became minister of linked charge with Borthwick 22 Mar 1981; trans to Greenock St George's North 4 Dec 1986.

1987 JOHN LEWIS McPAKE
ord and ind to Borthwick with Newtongrange 23 Jul 1987.

NORTH BERWICK ABBEY (FUF 64; FES IX, 91; X, 55)

Linked 1 Oct 1989 with Dirleton.

1965 ROBERT NICHOL BELL
(FES IX, 3, 94, 478; X, 3, 55), trans from Edinburgh Barclay to North Berwick Abbey 12 Aug 1965; ret 31 Oct 1974; died 25 Dec 1988.

1975 JAMES GRAHAME LEES
(FES IX, 312, 431; X, 16, 55, 183, 305), trans from Edinburgh Lothian Road to North Berwick Abbey 24 Sep 1975; ret 31 May 1984; died 26 Nov 1990.

1985 PATRICK HAMILTON CASHMAN
B 22 Feb 1933 at Co Cork, S Ireland, s of Thomas C. and Susan Elizabeth Good; educ Wilson's Hospital School 1946–51; Trinity College, Dublin 1951–55 (BSc); University of Edinburgh 1983–84; Materials Scientist; Technical Manager; Hi-tech Consultant 1955–83; lic by Presb of Melrose and Peebles 25 Jun 1984; asst Galashiels St Aidan's 1984–85; m 22 Sep 1962 Margaret Dorothy Abbott b 20 Jul 1934 d of Reginald Victor A. and Dorothy Bale; Children: Andrew Hamilton b 1 Aug 1963; John Philip b 16 Sep 1965; Stuart Reginald b 21 Jul 1972; ord and ind to North Berwick Abbey 21 Jun 1985; became minister of linked charge with Dirleton 1 Oct 1989; ret 30 Apr 1998.

1998 DAVID JOHN GRAHAM
ind to Dirleton with North Berwick Abbey 10 Dec 1998, see Dirleton.

NORTH BERWICK ST ANDREW BLACKADDER (FES X, 55, 56)

Formed 5 Mar 1989 by union of North Berwick St Andrew's and North Berwick Blackadder.

1952 WALTER McGILL FERRIER
(FES IX, 93, 316; X, 56), trans from Airdrie High to St Andrew's 23 Oct 1952; ret 31 Jul 1988; died 12 Oct 1991.

1960 DONALD JOHN BARKER McALISTER
(FES IX, 409; X, 56, 243), trans from Fort William MacIntosh Memorial to Blackadder 14 Apr 1960; ret 5 Mar 1989; s Bryan m Ann Robertson; d Deirdrie m William Gerrie; d Kathryn m Simon Loveless; Addl publ: *Blackadder Sermons* (Blackadder Church 1984).

1989 EDWARD CRAINIEY McKENNA
B 15 Aug 1959 at Chingola, Zambia, s of Thomas James M. and Isabella Fairliey Crainiey; educ Peebles High 1971–77; University of Edinburgh 1979–83 (BD); University of Aberdeen 1983–85 (DPS); Care Asst, Board of Social Responsibility 1978–79; lic by Presb of Edinburgh 30 Jun 1985; asst Glasgow Garthamlock 1985–86; Edinburgh South Queensferry 1989; m 2 Oct 1987 Heather Louise Robertson b 30 Jun 1958 d of John Lyall R. and June Powrie; Children: Jonathan Edward b 20 Aug 1988; Carolyn Wendy b 24 Aug 1990; Christian Lyall Robertson b 26 Dec 1993; ord and ind to St Andrew Blackadder 14 Nov 1989.

ORMISTON (FES IX, 93; X, 56)

Linkage with Prestonpans Grange terminated 29 Nov 1981 in favour of linkage with Pencaitland.

1975 ARTHUR THOMAS HILL
(FES X, 57, 209), ind to Prestonpans Grange 23 Apr 1970; became minister of linked charge with Ormiston 27 Jul 1975, see Prestongrange.

1981 LEON DAVID LEVISON
(FES IX, 79, 800; X, 56, 281), ind to Pencaitland 16 Apr 1970; became minister of linked charge with Ormiston 29 Nov 1981, see Pencaitland.

1982 COLIN VICTOR DONALDSON
B 27 Aug 1934 at Tayport, s of James Reginald D. and Winifred Logan; educ Merchiston Castle, Edinburgh 1948–53; University of St Andrews 1977–80; Marketing Director, James Donaldson & Sons Ltd 1956–77; lic by Presb of St Andrews 6 Jul 1980; asst Presb Church of Toms River, New Jersey 1980–81; m 4 Jul 1959 Marion Christina Duncan b 6 Nov 1934 d of James Brodie D. and Gertrude Malcolm; Children: Gillian Ruth b 27 Jun 1960 m David Couper; Colin Peter b 4 Jun 1962 m Clare Rawle; ord and ind to Ormiston with Pencaitland 28 Apr 1982; ret 31 Jul 1998; Exchange with Presb Church of New Zealand 1994–95.

1999 MARK MALCOLM
ord and ind to Ormiston with Pencaitland 27 Aug 1999.

PENCAITLAND (FES IX, 93; X, 56)

Linked 29 Nov 1981 with Ormiston.

1925 GEORGE GRANDISON MORGAN
(FES VIII, 99; IX, 93 (2); X, 56), ord and ind to Pencaitland Old 26 Feb 1925; became minister of united charge with West 27 Oct 1935; ret 15 Mar 1963; died 6 Nov 1983.

1964 JOHN MACFARLANE WILSON
(FES X, 56), ord and ind to Pencaitland 27 Feb 1964; dem 14 Oct 1969.

1970 LEON DAVID LEVISON
(FES IX, 79, 800; X, 56, 281), trans from Glenrothes St Columba's to Pencaitland 16 Apr 1970; became minister of linked charge with Ormiston 29 Nov 1981; ret 1 Jan 1982; s David m (1) Jill Henderson, died 1980, m (2) Rosemary Dean; d Elizabeth m Duncan MacDougal Galbraith; Addl publ: *Reflections* (Wild Goose Publs, 1997).

1982 COLIN VICTOR DONALDSON
ord and ind to Ormiston with Pencaitland 28 Apr 1982, see Ormiston.

1999 MARK MALCOLM
ord and ind to Ormiston with Pencaitland 27 Aug 1999.

PENICUIK NORTH (FUF 59; FES IX, 83; X, 51)

1974 JAMES GORDON MATHEW
(FES X, 51), ind to Penicuik North 12 Nov 1974; trans to Aberdeen Woodside 13 May 1982.

1982 JOHN WILKIE FRASER
(FES X, 120), trans from Stevenston Ardeer to Penicuik North 17 Nov 1982; Children: Joy b 26 Sep 1977; Jennifer b 6 Feb 1981; Jonathan b 23 Aug 1983.

PENICUIK SOUTH (FUF 59; FES IX, 84; X, 52)

Linked 10 Jan 1979 with Howgate.

1973 RONALD NEWMAN SEWELL
(FES X, 23, 52, 97), trans from Edinburgh St David's Broomhouse to Penicuik South 19 Oct 1973; became minister of linked charge with Howgate 10 Jan 1979; ret 30 Jun 1985; died 12 Sep 1989.

1985 FRANK RIBBONS
ord and ind to Howgate with Penicuik South 21 Aug 1985, see Howgate.

PENICUIK ST MUNGO'S (FES I, 343; VIII, 81; IX, 83; X, 51)

1960 ARCHIBALD JOHNSTON RODDAN RICHMOND
(FES IX, 535, 648; X, 51, 321), trans from Guthrie and Rescobie to St Mungo's 14 Sep 1960; ret 31 Oct 1984; died 12 Apr 1988.

1985 WILLIAM DRENNAN IRVING
B 31 Aug 1940 at Stoneyburn, s of Alexander Drennan I. and Elizabeth Keys Paterson; educ St Mary's, Bathgate 1945–55; University of Edinburgh 1981–84 (LTh); HM Forces 1958–81; lic by Presb of Edinburgh 1 Jul 1984; asst Edinburgh Fairmilehead 1984–85; m 18 Apr 1964 Esther Marjoribanks; Children: Fiona Ann b 13 Jul 1968 m Taylor; Paul b 7 Feb 1972; ord and ind to St Mungo's 15 May 1985.

PRESTONPANS PRESTONGRANGE (FES X, 57)

Linkage of Grange with Ormiston terminated 14 Nov 1981 to allow union of Grange and Preston.

1970 ARTHUR THOMAS HILL
(FES X, 57, 209), trans from Forth to Grange 23 Apr 1970; became minister of linked charge with Ormiston 27 Jul 1975; ret 5 Nov 1981; Clerk to Presb of Lothian 1983–92; w Margaret died 6 Sep 1980; m (2) 16 Dec 1989 Catherine Ritchie Craig b 9 Feb 1937.

1973 ROBERT COLIN MAXWELL MORTON
(FES X, 57, 125), trans from Linwood to Preston 8 Mar 1973; became minister of united charge with Grange 14 Nov 1981; introd to Jerusalem St Andrew's 14 Jul 1988.

1988 MOIRA HERKES
trans from Bedrule with Denholm with Minto to Prestongrange 8 Nov 1988; introd as Assoc at Dunblane Cathedral 24 Mar 1994.

1994 ROBERT RUSSELL SIMPSON
B 25 Dec 1952 at Edinburgh, s of Patrick William S. and Elizabeth Anne Wilson; educ Rugby 1966–71; University of Oxford 1971–74 (BA), 1974–75 (PGCE); University of Edinburgh 1990–93 (BD); Development Engineering 1975–90; lic by Presb of Edinburgh, 1993; asst Edinburgh St Catherine's Argyle 1993–94; m 4 Jul 1975 Lorraine Vivienne Southeim Turner b 9 May 1953 d of Humphrey James T. and Stephanie Eugenie Keller; Children: Russell James b 6 Apr 1978; Adrian Christopher b 16 Aug 1979; Andrew Douglas Peter b 13 Oct 1981; ord and ind to Prestongrange 27 Oct 1994.

ROSEWELL (FES I, 346; VIII, 82; IX, 84; X, 52)

Continued vacancy from 1987 until 1991. Linked 14 Jul 1991 with Cockpen and Carrington linked with Lasswade.

1966 JAMES HARVEY SINCLAIR
(FES X, 52), ord and ind to Rosewell 4 May 1966; introd as Assoc at Ashkirk with Caddonfoot with Selkirk 8 Sep 1987.

1992 WENDY FAIRWAY DRAKE
ind to Cockpen and Carrington with Lasswade with Rosewell 13 Feb 1992, see Cockpen.

ROSLIN (FES IX, 84; X, 52)

Linked 10 Jul 1968 with Glencorse.

1951 HUGH ERSKINE FRASER
(FES IX, 85, 426, 734; X, 52), trans from Perth Bridgend to Roslin 12 Dec 1951; ret 30 Jun 1968; died 29 Sep 1998.

1968 ROBERT KELLAS HALL
(FES X, 48), ord and ind to Glencorse with Roslin 11 Dec 1968; trans to Carnock 16 Oct 1980.

1981 JAMES ALLISON MANSON
ord and ind to Glencorse with Roslin 23 Apr 1981.

SPOTT (FES I, 417; VIII, 112; IX, 94; X, 57)

Union with Innerwick severed at General Assembly 1977. Linked 24 Jul 1977 with Belhaven.

1965 DUNCAN McMILLAN TURNER
(FES IX, 555, 602, 652; X, 55, 323, 339), trans from Alford with Tullynessle and Forbes to Innerwick and Spott 29 Oct 1965; ret 30 Jun 1977.

1978 LAURENCE HARVEY TWADDLE
ind to Belhaven with Spott 27 Apr 1978, see Belhaven.

TRANENT (FES X, 58)

Formed 27 Apr 1980 by union of Tranent Old and Tranent Wishart St Andrew's.

1953 ALEXANDER McDOUGALL MILLER
(FES IX, 95, 325; X, 58), res from app with FMC at Calabar, Nigeria and ind to Tranent Old 29 Oct 1953; became minister of united charge with Wishart St Andrew's 27 Apr 1980; ret 31 Dec 1985; died 16 Jul 1988.

1968 ROBERT BROUGH
(FES X, 58), ord and ind to Wishart St Andrew's 24 Jul 1968; trans to Whitburn Brucefield 17 Nov 1977.

1986 THOMAS MORRISON HOGG
B 18 Oct 1942 at Galashiels, s of Hugh Fraser H. and Jane Mary Telfer Borthwick Morrison; educ Galashiels Academy 1954–60; University of Edinburgh 1980–84 (BD); Quantity Surveyor 1960–80; lic by Presb of Melrose and Peebles 28 Jun 1984; m 16 Jul 1971 Kathleen Ross b 8 Aug 1943 d of William Fallon R. and Ann Cant Martin; Children: Sheena Anne b 17 Dec 1972; Lousie Jane b 26 Jun 1975; ord and ind to Tranent 2 Sep 1986.

TRAPRAIN (FES X, 56, 57, 58)

Formed 30 Sep 1999 by union of Prestonkirk, Stenton and Whittingehame.

1961 JOHN GRANT LEVACK
(FES IX, 234, 671; X, 56, 136), trans from Greenock West to Prestonkirk 5 Apr 1961; ret 30 Sep 1974; died 16 Oct 1999.

1963 WILLIAM ROY SANDERSON
(FES IX, 256, 467; X, 57, 151), trans from Glasgow The Barony to Stenton with Whittingehame 4 Apr 1963; ret 30 Nov 1973; Extra Chaplain to HM Queen in Scotland from 1977; s Arthur m Isobel Halliday; s Cecil m Elizabeth Cole; s Ronald m Pao Chem Liao; d Irene m Philip Morse.

1974 KENNETH GRANT HUGHES
(FES X, 31, 57, 137), trans from Livingston St Paul's to Stenton with Whittingehame 14 Aug 1974; became minister of linked charge with Prestonkirk 6 Oct 1974; trans to London Crown Court 16 Apr 1986.

1986 JAMES BARBOUR LAWSON
(FES X, 446), res as Officer-in-Charge, Simpson House, Edinburgh and ind to Prestonkirk with Stenton with Whittingehame 24 Sep 1986; trans to South Uist 25 Mar 1998.

WHITEKIRK AND TYNINGHAME (FES I, 422; VIII, 113; IX, 95; X, 58)

Linked 9 Jun 1974 with Athelstaneford.

1971 JOHN LIVINGSTON BLAIR
(FES X, 58, 355), introd as Assoc at Dunbar with Whitekirk and Tyninghame 10 Mar 1971; became minister of linked charge of Athelstaneford with Whitekirk and Tyninghame 21 Jul 1974, see Athelstaneford.

1976 KENNETH DONALD FRASER WALKER
ord and ind to Athelstaneford with Whitekirk and Tyninghame 15 Dec 1976.

YESTER (FES I, 398; VIII, 103; IX, 96; X, 58)

Linked 18 May 1977 with Humbie. Further linked 17 Oct 1979 with Bolton and Saltoun.

1960 GEORGE DOUGLAS MONRO
(FES IX, 9, 103; X, 6, 58), trans from Edinburgh Colinton Mains to Yester 24 Jun 1960; ret 31 Jul 1975; Hon Asst at Edinburgh Colinton 1980–90.

1977 ALLAN DAVIDSON SCOTT
ord and ind to Humbie with Yester 26 Oct 1977, see Humbie.

1985 JOHN MILLER WILSON
(FES X, 318, 427), ind to Bolton and Saltoun with Humbie with Yester 21 Feb 1985, see Bolton and Saltoun.

1999 DONALD PIRIE
(FES X, 207), trans from Lenzie Old to Bolton and Saltoun with Humbie with Yester 12 Aug 1999.

PRESBYTERY OF MELROSE AND PEEBLES

ASHKIRK (FES II, 168; VIII, 148; IX, 113; X, 71)

Linked 30 Jun 1961 with Lilliesleaf. Further linked 8 May 1977 with Bowden. Both linkages terminated 1 Sep 1983 in favour of linkage with Selkirk Lawson Memorial. Linked with Selkirk with Caddonfoot 8 Jun 1986 following union of Selkirk Lawson Memorial, Selkirk Heatherlie and Selkirk St Mary's West. Linkage with Caddonfoot terminated 2 Jul 1992.

1969 HENRY MONCRIEFF JAMIESON
(FES IX, 789; X, 71, 446), ret from RAF Chaplains' Branch and ind to Ashkirk with Lilliesleaf 8 Oct 1969; ret 31 May 1976.

1977 THOMAS WILSON DONALD
ord and ind to Ashkirk with Bowden with Lilliesleaf 28 Jul 1977, see Bowden.

1983 JOHN WATSON SLACK
(FES X, 408), ind to Selkirk Lawson Memorial 16 Aug 1978; became minister of linked charge with Ashkirk 1 Sep 1983, see Selkirk.

1986 IAN MORRISON STRACHAN
(FES X, 132, 190, 426), trans from Gourock St John's to Selkirk with Ashkirk with Caddonfoot 4 Dec 1986; ret 31 Aug 1994.

1987 JAMES HARVEY SINCLAIR
(FES X, 52), trans from Rosewell and introd as Assoc at Ashkirk with Caddonfoot with Selkirk 8 Sep 1987; ind to Auchencairn and Rerrick with Buittle and Kelton 18 Jun 1992.

1995 JAMES WILSON CAMPBELL
B 3 Mar 1955 at Falkirk, s of Graham C. and Williamina Wilson; educ Falkirk High 1967–72; Calendar Park College, Falkirk 1972–75 (DCE); University of St Andrews 1988–92 (BD); Teaching 1975–88; lic by Presb of Falkirk 25 Jun 1992; asst Erskine 1992–93; Bethesda Presb Church, Aberdeen, USA 1993–94; Bearsden New Kilpatrick 1994–95; ord and ind to Ashkirk with Selkirk 21 Jun 1995.

BOWDEN (FES II, 171; VIII, 148; IX, 121; X, 71)

Linked 8 May 1977 with Ashkirk with Lilliesleaf. Linkage with Ashkirk terminated 1 Sep 1983. Linkage with Lilliesleaf terminated 20 Oct 1994 in favour of linkage with Newtown.

1968 ALEXANDER SMITH HUTCHISON
(FES IX, 374, 423; X, 71, 251, 325, 328), trans from Aberdeen Melville and Carden Place to Bowden 31 Jul 1968; ret 3 Feb 1977; died 2 Oct 1994.

1977 THOMAS WILSON DONALD
B 31 Dec 1923 at Glasgow, s of Matthew D. and Eliza Wilson; educ Hillhead High, Glasgow 1928–39; Institute of Chartered Accountants of Scotland 1941–42, 1946–48 (CA); University of Glasgow 1974–77 (LTh); Royal Navy 1942–46; Chartered Accountant 1948–74; lic by Presb of Glasgow 30 Jun 1977; m 10 Sep 1949 Margaret Ethel Mitchell b 20 Nov 1924 d of James Millar Allan M. and Ethel Jane Pearson; Children: Katherine Rae b 12 Nov 1951 m Hutchison; Matthew James b 17 Jan 1954; Thomas Hugh b 18 Feb 1958; Rachel Margaret b 26 Nov 1959 m Potter; ord and ind to Ashkirk with Bowden with Lilliesleaf 28 Jul 1977; continued as minister of Bowden with Lilliesleaf after termination of linkage with Ashkirk 1 Sep 1983; ret 31 Aug 1987.

1988 JAMES WATSON
(FES X, 10 (2)), trans from Wick Old to Bowden with Lilliesleaf 6 Apr 1988; ret 30 Jun 1994; app Chaplain (part-time) to Dunoon General Hospital 1 Jun 1996.

1994 ALASDAIR (ALEXANDER) JAMES MORTON
(FES X, 83, 423), res as General Secretary, Dept of Education and ind to Maxton with Newtown 26 Sep 1991; became minister of Bowden with Newtown 20 Oct 1994; d Catriona Margaret m Anand Michel Ramkissoon; d Karen Elspeth m Manikumarian Krishnan; Publ: Contributor to *A Dictionary of Religious Education* (SCM, 1984); *Christian Teaching in Scottish Schools* (Education Committee, 1988).

BROUGHTON, GLENHOLM AND KILBUCHO
(FES I, 240; VIII, 52; IX, 71; X, 44)

Linked 27 Jun 1967 with Skirling. Further linked 26 Jan 1977 with Stobo and Drumelzier with Tweedsmuir.

1951 ALEXANDER VICTOR SMART
(FUF 187; IX, 71, 233, 329, 365; X, 44), trans from Greenock Trinity to Broughton, Glenholm and Kilbucho 6 Jun 1951; ret 27 Jun 1967; died 8 Nov 1984.

1967   THOMAS ROBERTS ROBERTSON
(FES IX, 295; X, 44, 111, 174), trans from
Kilmarnock Old High to Broughton, Glenholm and
Kilbucho with Skirling 29 Nov 1967; ret 1 Apr 1976;
w Hannah died 26 Jan 1988; Addl publ: *The Story
of the Kirk in Kirkcudbright* (*Church News*, 1983)*;
The Human Situation in War* (Dumfries and
Galloway Libraries, 1995); *Lesson from the Battle
of Kirkcudbright* (*Galloway News*, 1997); numerous
articles and pastoral letters.

1977   JAMES BOYD PRENTICE BULLOCH
(FES IX, 74, 95; X, 45), trans from Tranent Old to
Stobo and Drumelzier 1 Apr 1953; became minister
of linked charge with Tweedsmuir 10 Apr 1960 and
with Broughton, Glenholm and Kilbucho with
Skirling 26 Jan 1977; ret 22 Sep 1980; died 13
Apr 1981.

1980   JOHN DIAMOND RENNIE
(FES X, 130, 331), [correction: Martha Sharp
Diamond, not Dismond as in Vol X, 130]; trans from
Paisley Wallneuk to Broughton Glenholm and
Kilbucho with Skirling with Stobo and Drumelzier
with Tweedsmuir 26 Sep 1980; ret 30 Apr 1996; s
Adrian m Jean Gibson; d Fiona m Steven John
Horrell.

1996   RACHEL JEAN WAYLAND DOBIE
B 17 Aug 1942 at Forres, d of Archibald James
Stuart Miller and Chrissie Carruthers Fergusson;
educ Buckhaven High and Dumfries Academy
1954–60; Jordanhill College, Glasgow 1960–63
(DipPEd); University of Edinburgh 1993–95 (LTh);
Teaching 1963–80; lic by Presb of Dumfries and
Kirkcudbright 14 Sep 1990; asst Dalbeattie with Urr
1990–91; m 17 Jul 1964 Kirkpatrick Harold Dobie
b 21 Jul 1940 s of Kirkpatrick D. and Dulcie Frances
Mole; Children: Kirkpatrick Stuart b 22 Sep 1965;
Nicola Jane b 5 Jun 1967 m Douglas MacKenzie;
ord as Aux by Presb of Dumfries and Kirkcudbright
and assgnd to Dalbeattie with Urr 30 Aug 1991;
ind to Broughton Glenholm and Kilbucho with
Skirling with Stobo and Drumelzier with
Tweedsmuir (full-time ministry) 6 Sep 1996; Publ:
Time Together (St Andrew Press, 1981); Sunday
School material for Board of Parish Education (St
Andrew Press and Harper Collins, 1980s).

CADDONFOOT (FES II, 173; VIII, 149; IX, 121; X,
71)

Linkage with Ashkirk with Selkirk terminated 2 Jul
1992. Linked same date with Galashiels St Ninian's.

1949   DONALD MACCUISH
(FES IX, 121, 386, 404, 405, 656; X, 71), trans
from Port Bannatyne St Bruoc's to Caddonfoot 20
May 1949; ret 8 Jan 1978; died 6 Dec 1992.

1978   JOHN ERNEST McQUILKEN
(FES X, 8), trans from Edinburgh Drylaw to
Caddonfoot with Selkirk Heatherlie 19 Apr 1978;
trans to Glenaray and Inveraray 19 Jan 1983.

1983   THOMAS CRANSTONE BOGLE
ord and introd to Caddonfoot with Selkirk Heatherlie
(term) 29 Sep 1983; ind to Dumfries Lochside with
Terregles 22 Apr 1986.

1986   IAN MORRISON STRACHAN
(FES X, 132, 190, 426), trans from Gourock St
John's to Selkirk with Ashkirk with Caddonfoot 4
Dec 1986; ret 31 Aug 1994.

1987   JAMES HARVEY SINCLAIR
(FES X, 52), trans from Rosewell and introd as
Assoc at Ashkirk with Caddonfoot with Selkirk 8
Sep 1987; ind to Auchencairn and Rerrick with
Buittle and Kelton 18 Jun 1992.

1992   DAVID JOHN KELLAS
(FES X, 39, 226), ind to Galashiels St Ninian's
18 May 1983; became minister of linked charge
with Caddonfoot 2 Jul 1992, see St Ninian's.

1999   HILARY W SMITH
ord and ind to Caddonfoot with Galashiels St
Ninian's 23 Sep 1999.

CARLOPS (FUF 54; FES IX, 77; X, 44)

Linked 27 Mar 1985 with Kirkurd and Newlands.

1959   ALEXANDER CASEBY
(FES IX 575; X, 44, 334), trans from Drumoak to
Carlops 15 Apr 1959; ret 31 Mar 1965; died 14
May 1991.

1965   THOMAS MILLER PHILLIPS
(FES IX, 200, 231; X, 46, 133), ind to West Linton
St Andrew's 24 Jun 1964; became minister of
linked charge with Carlops 3 Nov 1965, see West
Linton.

1985   THOMAS WOTHERSPOON BURT
B 2 Apr 1948 at Glasgow, s of Peter Lawrence B.
and Mary Loudon Sanders; educ Hurst Grange and
Strathallan 1956–66; University of Edinburgh
1966–73 (BD, DipCEd, CEd, DipREd); Chaplain
to Oundle School 1975–76, 1979; Asst minister,
Bulawayo City Presb Church, Bulawayo 1976–78;
Scripture Union Staff Worker 1979–81; lic by Presb
of Glasgow 28 Jun 1973; asst Milngavie St Luke's
1973–75; m 20 Feb 1983 Rosemary Joy Callis b
18 Jul 1952 d of David Henry and Phyllis Margaret
C; Children: Peter James Grainger b 15 Apr 1983;
Sarah Joy b 13 Jan 1985; ord by Presb of
Mashonaland, Zimbabwe and ind to Hatfield Presb
Church, Harare 6 Aug 1982; ind to Carlops with
Kirkurd and Newlands with West Linton St
Andrew's 27 Mar 1985.

CHANNELKIRK (FES II, 146; VIII, 143; IX, 121;
X, 71)

Linked 1 Jul 1973 with Lauder Old.

1957 GEORGE KINNEAR WOOD
(FUF 109; FES IX, 149, 155, 221, 339, 535, 543; X, 71, 126), trans from Paisley George Street to Channelkirk 24 Oct 1957; ret 9 Oct 1966; died 29 Dec 1989.

1973 RICHARD FORBES JAMES
(FES IX, 239, 533; X, 73, 141), trans from Glasgow Blairbeth to Lauder Old 12 Oct 1961; became minister of linked charge with Channelkirk 1 Jul 1973; ret 30 Aug 1982; died 8 Aug 1991.

1982 DUNCAN JAMES McGREGOR
B 17 Jul 1935 at Edinburgh, s of Duncan Gerald M. and Elizabeth Alice Muir Reith; educ Edinburgh Academy 1942–53; University of Edinburgh 1977–80; Paper Making and Paper Trade 1955–69; Life Insurance 1969–77; lic by Presb of Edinburgh 6 Jul 1980; asst Edinburgh Tron Kirk Moredun 1980–81; m 2 Aug 1958 Constance Ann Aitchison b 13 Apr 1934 d of Robert A. and Jessie Swanson; Children: Andrew Duncan b 23 Jul 1959; Angus Robert b 17 Apr 1963 m Denholm; Roderick Innes b 6 Apr 1966 m Brandon; ord and ind to Channelkirk with Lauder Old 10 Sep 1982; ret 30 Sep 1996.

1997 JOHN MILLAR SHIELDS
(FES X, 345), ret from RAChD and ind to Channelkirk with Lauder Old 22 Aug 1997; d Jane m Cameron McKay.

EARLSTON (FES IX, 122; X, 71)

1946 JOHN HENRY DUNCAN
(FES IX, 122, 733; X, 71), trans from Lennoxtown to Earlston 25 Sep 1946; ret 30 Sep 1976.

1977 DAVID WISHART TORRANCE
(FES X, 31, 332), [correction: Bellshill Primary School 1929–30, not Academy as in Vol X, 332; omission from Vol X: 'Tell Scotland' (Home Mission Committee) Jan to Oct 1955]; trans from Aberdeen Summerhill to Earlston 30 Mar 1977; ret 30 Nov 1991; Asst at Dirleton with North Berwick Abbey 1992–1998; Addl publ: Editor of *The Witness of the Jews to God* (Handsel Press, 1982); *The Mission of Christians and Jews* (Handsel Press, 1986); co-author of *Anti-Semitism and Christian Responsibility* (Handsel Press, 1986); editor of *God, Family and Sexuality* (Handsel Press 1997); co-author of *A Passion for Christ* (Handsel Press, 1999).

1992 MICHAEL DAVID SCOULER
B 25 May 1961 at Glasgow, s of Campbell Buchanan S. and June Brown; educ Woodfarm Secondary and Earlston High, Glasgow 1973–78; University of Strathclyde 1978–82 (BSc); University of Edinburgh 1984–87 (BD); Banking 1982–83; lic by Presb of Glasgow 2 Jul 1987; asst Aberdeen Northfield 1987–88; m 20 Jul 1991 Katherine Patricia Ashmore b 27 Feb 1969 d of Donald Arthur A. and Patricia Eve Newell; Children: Jenny Louise b 17 Sep 1992; Heather Ann b 29 Jun 1994; ord by Presb of Aberdeen and app by RAChD 27 Jun 1988; ind to Earlston 19 Mar 1992; MBE 1989.

EDDLESTON (FES I, 270; VIII, 58; IX, 71; X, 44)

Linked 16 Aug 1977 with Peebles Old. Further linked with Lyne and Manor 2 Sep 1984. Arrangement with Lyne and Manor terminated 16 Jul 1992.

1971 JAMES SUTHERLAND DUNNETT
(FES IX, 107, 583; X, 13, 44, 338), trans from Edinburgh Leith St Andrew's Place to Eddleston 17 Nov 1971; ret 16 Aug 1977; died 18 May 1978.

1977 DAVID COCKBURN MACFARLANE
(FES X, 45, 53), trans from Aberlady to Peebles Old 29 Apr 1970; became minister of linked charge with Eddleston 16 Aug 1977 and of linked charge with Lyne and Manor 2 Sep 1984; ret 30 Apr 1997.

1984 ANDREW PAXTON LEES
introd as Assoc at Peebles Old with Eddleston with Lyne and Manor 5 Sep 1984, see Peebles Old.

1988 NANCY MEADE NORMAN
ord by Presb of Peebles and introd as Assoc at Eddleston with Lyne and Manor with Peebles Old 12 Jun 1988; loc ten Lyne and Manor Jan 1995; ind to same charge 29 May 1998.

1997 JAMES BISHOP MACLEAN
B 25 Mar 1960 at Stornoway, s of George Bishop M. and Catherine MacLeod; educ Nicolson Institute, Stornoway 1972–78; University of St Andrews 1978–85 (MTheol, DipPTheol); lic by Presb of Lewis 26 Jun 1985; asst Stornoway Martin's Memorial 1985–86; m 10 Oct 1986 Diana Helen Fairgrieve b 20 Sep 1966 d of George F. and Diana Fraser; ord and ind to Barra 5 Jun 1986; dem to take up app with RAChD 8 May 1990; ind to Eddleston with Peebles Old 14 Nov 1997.

ETTRICK (FES X, 71, 72)

Formed 15 May 1976 by union of Ettrick, Buccleuch and Kirkhope. Linked 16 May 1976 with Yarrow.

1976 GEORGE FULLERTON MONTEATH THOMSON
(FES X, 75, 83, 359), ind to Yarrow 7 Jul 1966; became minister of linked charge with Ettrick 16 May 1976, see Yarrow.

1986 BRUCE BAIRNSFATHER LAWRIE
(FES X, 125), res from app at Lucaya Presb Church of Scotland, Freeport, Bahamas and ind to Ettrick with Yarrow 15 Jan 1986.

GALASHIELS OLD AND ST PAUL'S (FES II, 176; VIII, 149; IX, 123; X, 72)

1951 ANGUS MACDONALD
(FES IX, 123, 329; X, 72), trans from Hamilton Avon Street to Old and St Paul's 4 Jul 1951; died 6 Mar 1978.

1978 JAMES BERNARD WALKER
(FES X, 304), res as Assoc at Dundee Mid Craigie with Wallacetown and ind to Old and St Paul's 15 Nov 1978; dem to take up app as Principal of Queen's College, Birmingham 7 Apr 1987.

1988 LESLIE McMILLAN STEELE
(FES X, 354), trans from Macduff Gardner to Old and St Paul's 19 Feb 1988; Addl children: Jane b 11 Jan 1977; Ruth b 11 Apr 1979.

GALASHIELS ST AIDAN'S (FES X, 72)

Formed 3 Jan 1975 by union of Ladhope and St Cuthbert's. Change of name from Galashiels Ladhope St Cuthbert's to Galashiels St Aidan's 3 Mar 1981.

1943 DAVID RAMAGE CURRIE
(FES IX, 124; X, 72), ind to Galashiels St Cuthbert's 24 Feb 1943; ret 20 Oct 1974; died 21 Jul 1988.

1971 ALEXANDER EDDINGTON ROGERSON
(FES IX, 82, 137; X, 44, 50, 72 (2), 291), trans from Eddleston to Galashiels Ladhope 10 Mar 1971; became minister of united charge with St Cuthbert's 3 Jan 1975; ret 30 Sep 1980; s John m Helen Nimmo.

1981 JACK MUNRO BROWN
B 27 Apr 1947 at Glasgow, s of Kenneth Munro B. and Iris Joy Arundale; educ Kelvinside Academy, Glasgow 1969–65; University of St Andrews 1965–69 (BSc); Moray House College, Edinburgh 1969–70 (DipREd); University of Edinburgh 1972–75 (BD); Teaching 1970–72; lic by Presb of Edinburgh 9 Jul 1995; asst Edinburgh Carrick Knowe 1975–76; m 15 Sep 1973 Eileen Margaret Omay b 8 Jan 1949 d of James Ritchie O. and Margaret May; Children: Philip Kenneth b 18 Sep 1976; Christopher James b 30 Jun 1978; Susan Margaret b 8 Jul 1983; ord and ind to Prestwick South 13 Jan 1977; trans to St Aidan's 18 Feb 1981.

GALASHIELS ST JOHN'S (FUF 88; FES IX, 124; X, 72)

1968 (ALEXANDER) ALASTAIR McKENZIE MORRICE
(FES X, 72), ord and ind to St John's 2 May 1968; trans to Edinburgh Holy Trinity 9 Jan 1977.

1977 RONALD WILLIAM BURNS
B 25 Dec 1940 at Glasgow, s of Matthew Duncan B. and Mildred Young; educ Bellahouston Secondary, Glasgow 1951–56; University of Glasgow 1971–76 (BD); Quantity Surveyor 1956–71; lic by Presb of Glasgow, Jun 1976; asst Glasgow Greenbank 1976–77; m 11 Dec 1965 Irene Mary

Fleming b 12 Dec 1943 d of James Prestley F. and Mary Jack; Children: Mary Louise b 17 Apr 1967; Duncan James b 23 Feb 1970; Peter b 24 Mar 1972; ord and ind to St John's 9 Jun 1977; dem charge and status 7 Mar 1982.

1982 STEPHEN FRANK CLIPSTON
B 31 Jul 1955 at Gillingham, Kent, s of Raymond Frank C. and Jessie Ogilvie Thomson McIntosh; educ Mackie Academy, Stonehaven 1967–73; University of Glasgow 1973–76 (MA), 1978–81 (BD); lic by Presb of Glasgow 30 Jun 1981; asst Glasgow St David's Knightswood 1981–82; m 24 Jul 1978 Elaine Margaret Jack b 7 Jun 1955 d of David Ronald J. and Eleanor Craig Lumsden Clark; Children: David Andrew b 19 May 1979; Joanne Ruth b 1 Aug 1980; Euan Philip and Alasdair Stephen b 5 Jan 1982; Morag Elizabeth and Jonathan Alexander b 17 Dec 1984; ord and ind to St John's 24 Sep 1982.

GALASHIELS ST NINIAN'S (FES X, 72)

Formed 10 Mar 1977 by union of Galashiels St Andrew's and Galashiels St Columba's. Linked 2 Jul 1992 with Caddonfoot.

1955 RONALD BARCLAY NEILL
(FES IX, 157, 487; X, 72, 290), trans from Cupar St John's to St Andrew's 13 Jul 1955; ret 30 Sep 1975; died 4 Aug 1979.

1969 JOHN ALFRED SHERRARD
(FES X, 72, 300, 313), trans from Dundee Camperdown to St Columba's 24 Sep 1969; became minister of united charge with St Andrew's 10 Mar 1977; trans to Glamis with Inverarity and Kinnettles 26 Oct 1982.

1983 DAVID JOHN KELLAS
(FES X, 39, 226), trans from Falkirk St James' to St Ninian's 18 May 1983; became minister of linked charge with Caddonfoot 2 Jul 1992; trans to Kilfinan with Kyles 27 Nov 1998; w Carol died 16 May 1994.

1999 HILARY W SMITH
ord and ind to Caddonfoot with Galashiels St Ninian's 23 Sep 1999.

INNERLEITHEN (FES X, 44)

Linked 2 Sep 1975 with Walkerburn. Further linked 11 Jul 1984 with Traquair.

1952 JAMES MACKINTOSH ALEXANDER
(FES IX, 72, 727; X, 44), res from service with FMC in Livingstonia, Malawi and ind to Innerleithen Old 24 Sep 1952; ret 7 Feb 1960; died 5 Jan 1985.

1960 DAVID DOIG
(FES IX, 338, 366, 481, 562; X, 44, 326), trans from Aberdeen Holburn Central to Innerleithen 14 Oct 1960; died 19 Jan 1969.

1969　WILLIAM KNOX BOWIE
(FES IX, 255; X, 44, 150), trans from Glasgow Tron St Mary's to Innerleithen 11 Sep 1969; became minister of linked charge with Walkerburn 2 Sep 1975; ret 30 Jun 1984; died 29 Nov 1995.

1985　JOHN WILSON
B 31 Aug 1944 at Glasgow, s of James Walker W. and Marion Kerr McDonald; educ Victoria Drive, Glasgow 1957–63; Stow College of Engineering, Glasgow 1963–70 (HNC); University of Glasgow 1978–83 (BD, CPS); Civil/Structural Engineering 1963–78; lic by Presb of Lanark 22 Jun 1983; asst Hamilton Old 1983–84; m 10 Jul 1970 Elizabeth Fyvie Smith b 7 Nov 1948 d of George Fyvie S. and Marion Brown Maclaren; Children: Susan Marion b 17 Mar 1973; Gail Elizabeth b 5 Aug 1975; ord and ind to Innerleithen with Traquair with Walkerburn 3 Jan 1985.

KIRKURD AND NEWLANDS (FES X, 44, 45)

Formed 18 Nov 1984 by union of Kirkurd and Newlands.

1935　FREDERICK SMITH
(FUF 303; FES IX, 71, 72, 440; X, 44), res from Blythbridge in interests of union 3 Feb 1935; ind to Kirkurd 14 May 1935; ret 31 Jul 1959; died 28 May 1979.

1957　JAMES ALEXANDER WILLIAMSON
(FES VIII, 721; IX, 794; X, 45, 449), res from RAChD and ind to Newlands 10 Apr 1957; became minister of linked charge with Kirkurd 29 Jul 1962; ret 30 Sep 1970; died 28 Sep 1989.

1971　RICHARD ANDERSON BAIGRIE
(FES IX, 728; X, 31, 44, 416), trans from Harthill St Andrew's to Kirkurd with Newlands 14 Apr 1971; ret 26 Mar 1985; Clerk to Presb of Bathgate 1957–64, to Presb of Livingston and Bathgate 1964–71, to Presb of Peebles 1971–75, to Presb of Melrose and Peebles 1975–85; Editor of Verbatim Reports of General Assembly from 1970; d Jean m Gordon Downie; d Sheilagh m Stewart Clark; s Richard m Jeanette Orr.

1985　THOMAS WOTHERSPOON BURT
ind to Carlops with Kirkurd and Newlands with West Linton St Andrew's 27 Mar 1985, see Carlops.

LAUDER OLD (FES II, 153; VIII, 144; IX, 125; X, 73)

Linked 1 Jul 1973 with Channelkirk.

1961　RICHARD FORBES JAMES
(FES IX, 239, 533; X, 73, 141), trans from Glasgow Blairbeth to Lauder Old 12 Oct 1961; became minister of linked charge with Channelkirk 1 Jul 1973; ret 30 Aug 1982; died 8 Aug 1991.

1982　DUNCAN JAMES McGREGOR
ord and ind to Channelkirk with Lauder Old 10 Sep 1982, see Channelkirk.

1997　JOHN MILLAR SHIELDS
(FES X, 345), ind to Channelkirk with Lauder Old 22 Aug 1997, see Channelkirk.

LYNE AND MANOR (FES IX, 73; X, 44)

Linked 2 Sep 1984 with Eddleston with Peebles Old. Linkage terminated 16 Jul 1992.

1964　HARRY ENTWISTLE TURNER
(FES X, 45), ord and ind to Lyne and Manor 27 Nov 1964; ret 31 May 1983; died 18 Sep 1987.

1984　DAVID COCKBURN MACFARLANE
(FES X, 45, 53), trans from Aberlady to Peebles Old 29 Apr 1970; became minister of linked charge with Eddleston 16 Aug 1977 and of linked charge with Lyne and Manor 2 Sep 1984; ret 30 Apr 1997.

1984　ANDREW PAXTON LEES
introd as Assoc at Peebles Old with Eddleston with Lyne and Manor 5 Sep 1984, see Peebles Old.

1988　NANCY MEADE NORMAN
B 24 Sep 1947 at Richmond, Virginia, USA, d of Guy Robert N. and Anne Thomas Eubank; educ Hermitage High, Richmond 1961–65; Westhampton College, University of Richmond 1965–69 (BA); Union Theological Seminary, Richmond 1971–75 (MDiv); University of Edinburgh 1975–76 (MTh); lic by Presb of Edinburgh 29 Jun 1986; asst Edinburgh St Giles' Cathedral 1977–82; locum Chaplain's Asst, Royal Infirmary, Edinburgh 1984–85; Edinburgh St Ninian's Corstorphine 1985–87; ord by Presb of Peebles and introd as Assoc at Eddleston with Lyne and Manor with Peebles Old 12 Jun 1988; loc ten Biggar Feb to Nov 1995; loc ten Lyne and Manor Jan 1995; app Tutor (part-time) at Westminster College, Oxford, Jul 1996; app Chaplain (part-time) to ministers in Presb of Edinburgh Mar 1998; ind to Lyne and Manor 29 May 1998.

MAXTON AND MERTOUN (FES X, 73)

Linkage terminated 20 Aug 1981 allowing Maxton to link with Newtown and Mertoun to link with St Boswells. Maxton and Mertoun united 18 Oct 1994 (linkage of Maxton with Newtown terminated same date). Linked 18 Oct 1994 with St Boswells.

1969　ROBERT McLEISH GREER
(FES X, 73), trans from Singapore and ind under mutual eligibility to Maxton with Mertoun 3 Jul 1969; ret 20 Aug 1981; died 16 Apr 1994.

1981　GEORGE ADAM BUCHANAN-SMITH
B 4 Mar 1929 at Currie, s of Alick Drummond B. and Mary Kathleen Smith; educ Edinburgh

Academy 1937–42; Trinity College, Glenalmond 1943–47; University of Edinburgh 1948–51 (MA), 1951–54 (BD); Union Theological Seminary, USA 1954–55 (MDiv); North West Quebec Parishes, United Church of Canada 1955–56; lic by Presb of Edinburgh 15 Apr 1954; m 4 Sep 1961 Isabel Angela Margaret Bowden b 28 May 1934 d of W E Bowden and F A M Backler; Children: Fiona McIntosh (stepdaughter) b 24 Jun 1960; Hannah Mary b 30 Jun 1962; George Adam Edward b 22 Jul 1964; Stuart Hunter b 7 May 1966; ord by Presb of Glasgow and app as Asst at The Cathedral 10 Jun 1956; Warden, St Francis-in-the-East Church House, Glasgow 1957–60; Chaplain to Fettes College, Edinburgh 1960–81; Housemaster, Fettes College 1967–79; ind to Mertoun with St Boswells 19 Aug 1981; died 24 Feb 1983.

1981 KENNETH THOMAS THOMSON
(FES X, 319, 402), introd on term app to Newtown 24 Feb 1977; became minister of linked charge with Maxton 20 Aug 1981, see Newtown.

1983 GLYN REES TAVERNER
(FES X, 19, 47, 111), trans from Edinburgh Portobello St Philip's Joppa to Mertoun with St Boswells 5 Oct 1983; became minister of united charge with Maxton 18 Oct 1994; ret 31 Oct 1995; s Michael m Tracy Gilpin.

1985 IAN GERARD GRAINGER
B 10 Apr 1925 at Newcastle-upon-Tyne, s of Valentine G. and Emma Harris; educ Heaton Secondary 1936–43; University of Durham 1946–50 (BSc); University of Edinburgh 1984–85; Member of the Institution of Civil Engineers; Engineering 1950–70; Administrator, Lundy Island 1970–77; Chief Engineer to Government of Kiribati, Tarawa, Central Pacific 1977–83; lic by Presb of Edinburgh 30 Jun 1985; m 28 Jun 1950 Georgina Jeffrey Polson b 3 Dec 1925 d of Thoms P. and Margaret Black MacCallum; Children: Ian Jonathan b 16 Jun 1956; Alison Joan b 19 Feb 1958; Thomas Polson b 3 Feb 1965; ord and introd on term app to Maxton with Newtown 23 Oct 1985; dem 30 Apr 1991.

1991 ALASDAIR (ALEXANDER) JAMES MORTON
(FES X, 83, 423), ind to Maxton with Newton 26 Sep 1991; became minister of Bowden with Newton 20 Oct 1994, see Bowden.

1996 BRUCE FERGUSON NEILL
(FES X, 274, 447), ret from Royal Naval Chaplaincy Service and ind to Maxton and Mertoun with St Boswells 26 Jan 1996; Addl children: Fergus Samuel b 13 Feb 1982.

MELROSE (FES X, 73)

Formed 6 Oct 1984 by union of Melrose High Cross and Melrose St Cuthbert's.

1950 THOMAS HENRY KEIR
(FES IX, 127, 426, 505, 562; X, 73), trans from Aberdeen Holburn West to St Cuthbert's 28 Sep 1950; ret 9 Apr 1972; died 12 Mar 1994.

1971 JOHN HERON MACDONALD
(FES IX, 650; X, 29, 73, 86, 370), trans from New Abbey to High Cross 13 May 1971; ret 31 May 1975; died 15 Jul 1995.

1972 ROBERT JOHN HENDERSON
(FES X, 73, 218, 366), trans from Elgin St Giles' to St Cuthbert's 18 Oct 1972; trans to Cairneyhill with Limekilns 23 Feb 1984.

1976 GEORGE IAN GRIFFITHS
(FES IX, 342, 359; X, 204), trans from Wishaw Chalmers to High Cross 23 Jan 1976; ret 6 Oct 1984; died 30 Oct 1985.

1984 ALISTAIR GEORGE BENNETT
B 4 May 1952 at Bridge of Allan, s of William Stirling B. and Hilda Gall Hardie; educ Inverurie Academy and Waid Academy, Anstruther 1964–70; University of St Andrews 1970–73 (BSc); University of Edinburgh 1973–76 (BD); lic by Presb of St Andrews 27 Jun 1976; asst Linlithgow St Michael's 1976–78; m 18 Sep 1974 Judith Helen Morris b 11 Mar 1953 d of James Reginald Spence M. and Marjorie Tyson; Children: Scott Alistair b 19 Apr 1976; Lyndsey Anne Stirling b 24 Jul 1979; Lauren Helen b 6 Sep 1982; ord and ind to Hamilton Trinity 12 Apr 1978; trans to Melrose 15 Nov 1984.

NEWTOWN (FUF 91; FES IX, 127; X, 74)

Linked 20 Aug 1981 with Maxton. Arrangement terminated 18 Oct 1994 in favour of linkage with Bowden.

1977 KENNETH THOMAS THOMSON
(FES X, 319, 402), dem from Sanday and introd on term app to Newtown 24 Feb 1977; became minister of linked charge with Maxton 20 Aug 1981; trans to Sanquhar St Bride's 15 Nov 1985.

1985 IAN GERARD GRAINGER
ord and introd on term app to Maxton with Newtown 23 Oct 1985, see Maxton and Mertoun.

1991 ALASDAIR (ALEXANDER) JAMES MORTON
(FES X, 83, 423), ind to Maxton with Newton 26 Sep 1991; became minister of Bowden with Newton 20 Oct 1994, see Bowden.

PEEBLES OLD (FES I, 285; VIII, 61; IX, 74; X, 45)

Linked 16 Aug 1977 with Eddleston. Further linked 2 Sep 1984 with Lyne and Manor. Arrangement terminated 16 Jul 1992.

1970   DAVID COCKBURN MACFARLANE
(FES X, 45, 53), trans from Aberlady to Peebles Old 29 Apr 1970; became minister of linked charge with Eddleston 16 Aug 1977 and of linked charge with Lyne and Manor 2 Sep 1984; ret 30 Apr 1997; s Alasdair m Fiona Margaret Johnston; s Iain m Jennifer Garvie; Addl publ: *The Church in Peebles* (Mainstream, 1990).

1984   ANDREW PAXTON LEES
ord by Presb of Melrose and Peebles and introd as Assoc at Peebles Old with Eddleston with Lyne and Manor 5 Sep 1984; ind to Gourock Ashton 19 Nov 1987.

1988   NANCY MEADE NORMAN
introd as Assoc at Eddleston with Lyne and Manor with Peebles Old 12 Jun 1988, see Eddleston.

1997   JAMES BISHOP MACLEAN
ret from RAChD and ind to Eddleston with Peebles Old 14 Nov 1997.

PEEBLES ST ANDREW'S LECKIE (FES X, 45)

Formed 5 May 1976 by union of Peebles St Andrew's and Peebles Leckie Memorial.

1967   ALBERT CRAIG
(FES IX, 731; X, 45, 417), ret from service with Overseas Council in India and ind to St Andrew's 6 Sep 1967; became minister of united charge with Leckie Memorial 5 May 1976; ret 31 Mar 1977; died 13 Jun 1985.

1977   DUNCAN MACGILLIVRAY
ord and ind to St Andrew's Leckie 20 May 1977; app to Rotterdam 31 May 1983.

1983   JAMES HENDERSON WALLACE
(FES X, 276), trans from Lochcraig to St Andrew's Leckie 14 Nov 1983; Addl children: Graham Mark b 16 Oct 1982; d Margaret Jane m Shaun Kinahan.

SELKIRK PARISH (FES X, 74)

Formed 8 Jun 1986 by union of Selkirk Heatherlie, Lawson Memorial and St Mary's West. Linked with Ashkirk with Caddonfoot same date. Linkage with Caddonfoot terminated 2 Jul 1992.

1963   WILLIAM FREDERICK LAING
(FES X, 74, 218), trans from Motherwell Dalziel High to St Mary's West 10 Oct 1963; ret 30 Jun 1986; d Alice m Timothy Paul Simons.

1966   EDWARD MACKAY
(FES IX, 105; X, 62, 74, 107, 187), trans from Drongan The Schaw Kirk to Heatherlie 15 Sep 1966; ret 31 Mar 1977; died 26 May 1993.

1972   KENNETH GEORGE ANDERSON
(FES X, 74, 415), res from app with Overseas Council at Scots Kirk, Bombay, India and ind to

Lawson Memorial 22 Jun 1972; dem 15 Jan 1978 on app by Union Church, Hong Kong.

1978   JOHN ERNEST McQUILKEN
(FES X, 8), ind to Caddonfoot with Heatherlie 19 Apr 1978, see Caddonfoot.

1978   JOHN WATSON SLACK
(FES X, 408), trans from Scunthorpe (Presb Church of England) to Lawson Memorial 16 Aug 1978; became minister of linked charge with Ashkirk 1 Sep 1983; ret 31 Jul 1985; s John m Ruth Lacey; d Helen m Derek Young; d Fiona m James Hewlett.

1983   THOMAS CRANSTONE BOGLE
ord and introd to Caddonfoot with Selkirk Heatherlie (term) 29 Sep 1983; ind to Dumfries Lochside with Terregles 22 Apr 1986.

1986   IAN MORRISON STRACHAN
(FES X, 132, 190, 426), trans from Gourock St John's to Selkirk with Ashkirk with Caddonfoot 4 Dec 1986; ret 31 Aug 1994.

1987   JAMES HARVEY SINCLAIR
(FES X, 52), trans from Rosewell and introd as Assoc at Ashkirk with Caddonfoot with Selkirk 8 Sep 1987; ind to Auchencairn and Rerrick with Buittle and Kelton 18 Jun 1992.

1995   JAMES WILSON CAMPBELL
ord and ind to Ashkirk with Selkirk 21 Jun 1995, see Ashkirk.

SKIRLING (FES I, 257; VIII, 55; IX, 353; X, 45)

Linked 27 Jun 1967 with Broughton, Glenholm and Kilbucho.

1951   GEORGE GORDON WATT
(FE IX, 136, 353; X, 45), trans from St Mungo to Skirling 8 Jun 1951; ret 16 Oct 1965; died 8 Jan 1978.

1967   THOMAS ROBERTS ROBERTSON
(FES IX, 295; X, 44, 111, 174), ind to Broughton, Glenholm and Kilbucho with Skirling 29 Nov 1967, see Broughton.

1977   JAMES BOYD PRENTICE BULLOCH
(FES IX, 74, 95; X, 45), trans from Tranent Old to Stobo and Drumelzier 1 Apr 1953; became minister of linked charge with Tweedsmuir 10 Apr 1960 and with Broughton, Glenholm and Kilbucho with Skirling 26 Jan 1977; ret 22 Sep 1980; died 13 Apr 1981.

1980   JOHN DIAMOND RENNIE
(FES X, 130, 331), ind to Broughton Glenholm and Kilbucho with Skirling with Stobo and Drumelzier with Tweedsmuir 26 Sep 1980, see Broughton.

1996   RACHEL JEAN WAYLAND DOBIE
ind to Broughton Glenholm and Kilbucho with Skirling with Stobo and Drumelzier with Tweedsmuir 6 Sep 1996, see Broughton.

ST BOSWELLS (FES IX, 127; X, 74)

Linked 19 Aug 1981 with Mertoun. Linkage continues following union of Maxton and Mertoun 18 Oct 1994.

1952   DAVID PRIESTLEY LEISHMAN
(FES IX, 127, 163, 181; X, 74), trans from Ochiltree to St Boswells 20 Mar 1952; ret 7 Apr 1973; died 16 Oct 1989.

1973   LILIAN MARGARET BRUCE
(FES X, 74), trans from Currie to St Boswells 23 Nov 1973; dem on app with Overseas Council for service in Tanzania 24 Jul 1980.

1981   GEORGE ADAM BUCHANAN-SMITH
ind to Mertoun with St Boswells 19 Aug 1981, see Maxton and Mertoun.

1983   GLYN REES TAVERNER
(FES X, 19, 47, 111), ind to Mertoun with St Boswells 5 Oct 1983; became minister of united charge with Maxton 18 Oct 1994, see Maxton and Mertoun.

1996   BRUCE FERGUSON NEILL
(FES X, 274, 447), ret from Royal Naval Chaplaincy Service and ind to Maxton and Mertoun with St Boswells 26 Jan 1996, see Maxton and Mertoun.

STOBO AND DRUMELZIER (FES IX, 74; X, 45)

Linked 26 Jan 1977 with Broughton, Glenholm and Kilbucho and with Skirling.

1953   JAMES BOYD PRENTICE BULLOCH
(FES IX, 74, 95; X, 45), trans from Tranent Old to Stobo and Drumelzier 1 Apr 1953; became minister of linked charge with Tweedsmuir 10 Apr 1960 and with Broughton, Glenholm and Kilbucho with Skirling 26 Jan 1977; ret 22 Sep 1980; died 13 Apr 1981.

1980   JOHN DIAMOND RENNIE
(FES X, 130, 331), ind to Broughton Glenholm and Kilbucho with Skirling with Stobo and Drumelzier with Tweedsmuir 26 Sep 1980, see Broughton.

1996   RACHEL JEAN WAYLAND DOBIE
ind to Broughton Glenholm and Kilbucho with Skirling with Stobo and Drumelzier with Tweedsmuir 6 Sep 1996, see Broughton.

STOW ST MARY OF WEDALE AND HERIOT (FES X, 49, 75)

Formed 27 May 1992 by union of Stow St Mary of Wedale and Heriot.

1957   JAMES ELPHINSTONE PIRIE
(FUF 333; FES IX, 267, 578, 724, 792; X, 49, 336), trans from Kinellar and Blackburn to Heriot 17 Apr 1957; ret 26 Apr 1962; died 1 Jan 1986.

1964   JOSEPH BLAIR GILLON
(FES IX, 19, 517, 556; X, 12, 47), res as Secretary of Scottish Reformation Society and ind to Borthwick with Heriot 23 Sep 1964; ret 31 Dec 1980.

1966   CHARLES ALEXANDER DUNCAN
(FES X, 75, 95), trans from Lochryan and Glenapp to Stow St Mary of Wedale 18 Mar 1966; became minister of linked charge with Heriot 4 Jun 1981; ret 31 Mar 1992; Clerk to Presb of Melrose 1972–75; Joint Clerk to Presb of Melrose and Peebles 1975–85; Clerk 1985–95; s Innes m Una Patricia Thorburn.

1992   STANLEY KENNON
B 26 Feb 1960 at Broxburn, s of William Stanley K. and Susan Frances Taylor; educ Hermitage Academy, Helensburgh 1972–78; Open University 1982–88 (BA); University of Edinburgh 1985–89 (BD), 1990 (CCEd); Retailing (Supervisory Management) 1978–85; lic by Presb of Dumbarton 1 Jul 1990; asst Edinburgh Viewforth 1990–92; m 13 Dec 1986 Aileen Margaret Stewart b 1 Apr 1959 d of Archibald Thomson S. and Annie Elliott; Children: Naomi Alexandra b 4 Jun 1993; Reuben Matthew b 29 Dec 1995; ord and ind to Stow St Mary of Wedale and Heriot 17 Aug 1992.

TRAQUAIR (FES I, 292; VIII, 65; IX, 75; X, 46)

Linked 11 Jul 1984 with Innerleithen with Walkerburn.

1962   HARRY JOHN DODD
(FUF 73; IX, 103, 128, 280; X, 46, 74), trans from Selkirk St Mary's to Traquair 8 Mar 1962; ret 31 Oct 1970; died 30 Sep 1981.

1971   JAMES SMITH CLARK
(FES IX, 59, 201; X, 36, 46), trans from Cumbernauld to Traquair 23 Mar 1971; ret 30 Sep 1978; died 4 Jan 1994.

1979   ARCHIBALD MACCALLUM CAMPBELL
(FES IX, 257, 444; X, 89, 151, 161, 278, 326), trans from Aberdeen Denburn to Traquair 21 Jun 1979; ret 30 Jun 1984; died 2 Jan 1988.

1985   JOHN WILSON
ord and ind to Innerleithen with Traquair with Walkerburn 3 Jan 1985, see Innerleithen.

TWEEDSMUIR (FES I, 295; VIII, 65; IX, 75; X, 46)

Linked 26 Jan 1977 with Broughton, Glenholm and Kilbucho.

1960   JAMES BOYD PRENTICE BULLOCH
(FES IX, 74, 95; X, 45), trans from Tranent Old to Stobo and Drumelzier 1 Apr 1953; became minister of linked charge with Tweedsmuir 10 Apr 1960 and with Broughton, Glenholm and Kilbucho with Skirling 26 Jan 1977; ret 22 Sep 1980; died 13 Apr 1981.

1980 JOHN DIAMOND RENNIE
(FES X, 130, 331), ind to Broughton Glenholm and Kilbucho with Skirling with Stobo and Drumelzier with Tweedsmuir 26 Sep 1980, see Broughton.

1996 RACHEL JEAN WAYLAND DOBIE
ind to Broughton Glenholm and Kilbucho with Skirling with Stobo and Drumelzier with Tweedsmuir 6 Sep 1996, see Broughton.

WALKERBURN (FES I, 298; VIII, 65; IX, 75; X, 46)

Linked 2 Sep 1975 with Innerleithen.

1967 ROBERT WADDELL
(FES IX, 752; X, 46, 359, 426), trans from Glass to Walkerburn 21 Apr 1967; ret 30 Apr 1974; died 20 May 1988.

1975 WILLIAM KNOX BOWIE
(FES IX, 255; X, 44, 150), trans from Glasgow Tron St Mary's to Innerleithen 11 Sep 1969; became minister of linked charge with Walkerburn 2 Sep 1975; ret 30 Jun 1984; died 29 Nov 1995.

1985 JOHN WILSON
ord and ind to Innerleithen with Traquair with Walkerburn 3 Jan 1985, see Innerleithen.

WEST LINTON ST ANDREW'S (FES I, 298; VIII, 66; IX, 75; X, 46)

Linked 27 Mar 1985 with Kirkurd and Newlands.

1964 THOMAS MILLER PHILLIPS
(FES IX, 200, 231; X, 46, 133), trans from Greenock Mid Kirk to St Andrew's 24 Jun 1964; became minister of linked charge with Carlops 3 Nov 1965; ret 31 Aug 1984; died 31 Jul 1996.

1985 THOMAS WOTHERSPOON BURT
ind to Carlops with Kirkurd and Newlands with West Linton St Andrew's 27 Mar 1985, see Carlops.

YARROW (FES II, 196; VIII, 154; IX, 129; X, 75)

Linked 16 May 1976 with Ettrick.

1966 GEORGE FULLERTON MONTEATH THOMSON
(FES X, 75, 83, 359), trans from Dumfries Lochside to Yarrow 7 Jul 1966; became minister of linked charge with Ettrick 16 May 1976; introd as Assoc at Dollar with Glendevon with Muckhart 12 Oct 1985.

1986 BRUCE BAIRNSFATHER LAWRIE
(FES X, 125), ind to Ettrick with Yarrow 15 Jan 1986, see Ettrick.

PRESBYTERY OF DUNS

AYTON (FES IX, 97; X, 59)

Linked 1 Jun 1969 with Burnmouth. Further linked 11 Sep 1984 with Grantshouse and Houndwood with Reston.

1969   JOHN TENNANT PEAT
(FES IX, 128; X, 59, 74, 222), trans from Milngavie St Paul's to Ayton with Burnmouth 11 Dec 1969; ret 15 Nov 1977; died 2 Apr 1988.

1978   DUNCAN WILLIAM McINTOSH ANDERSON
ord and ind to Ayton with Burnmouth 4 May 1978; trans to Glasgow New Cathcart 1 Sep 1982.

1983   DAVID JAMES HEBENTON
(FES X, 141, 201), res as Principal teacher at Barrhead High and ind to Ayton with Burnmouth 8 Sep 1983; became minister of linked charge with Grantshouse and Houndwood with Reston 11 Sep 1984; s David m Sandra Campbell; d Margaret m Euphemia Hepburn Wilson; d Fiona m Henry Allan Walker.

BERWICK ST ANDREW'S WALLACE GREEN AND LOWICK (FES X, 59, 409, 411)

Formed 1 May 1988 by union of Berwick-on-Tweed St Andrew's, Wallace Green and Lowick.

1962   GORDON JOHNSTON
(FES X, 409, 411), ord and introd to Berwick Tweedmouth with Lowick 19 Dec 1962; became minister of united charge with St Andrew's 10 Dec 1972; died 28 Sep 1982.

1975   WILLIAM GRAHAM MONTEITH
(FES X, 59), ord by Presb of Dumbarton during assistantship at Drumchapel St Andrew's 17 Mar 1974; ind to Wallace Green 30 Oct 1975; became minister of linked charge with Lowick; trans to Flotta and Fara with Hoy and Graemsay with Walls Old 15 May 1985.

1986   JAMES BLAIKIE
(FES X, 408), trans from Aberluthnott with Laurencekirk to St Andrew's with Wallace Green with Lowick 26 Sep 1986; became minister of united charge 1 May 1988; ret 5 Aug 1997; Addl children: Elizabeth Mary b 20 Jul 1970; s Norman m Elizabeth Duncan; d Heather m Timothy Beverage; s Iain deceased.

1999   ALISON ANN MEIKLE
B 30 Apr 1963 at Lanark, d of George Alexander Milne Haston and Joy Burns Brown; educ Larkhall Academy 1975–81; College of Nursing (S Eastern District), Glasgow 1981–84 (RGN); Lanarkshire College of Midwifery, Bellshill 1985–86 (RM); University of Glasgow 1993–97 (BD); Staff Nurse 1984–87; Staff Midwife 1987–93; lic by Presb of Hamilton 1 Sep 1997; m 31 Aug 1989 Hugh Meikle b 25 Jul 1946 s of Thomas Thomson M. and Barbara Orr; Children: Euan Thomas Haston b 20 Feb 1992; ord and ind to Berwick St Andrew's Wallace Green and Lowick 9 Feb 1999.

BONKYL AND PRESTON (FES II, 4; VIII, 115; IX, 98; X, 59)

Linked 15 Jul 1973 with Chirnside. Further linked 17 Sep 1978 with Edrom Allanton.

1973   WILLIAM PETER GRAHAM
(FES X, 60), ind to Chirnside 8 Aug 1968; became minister of linked charge with Bonkyl and Preston 15 Jul 1973, see Chirnside.

1993   WILLIAM PATERSON
B 5 Jun 1936 at Airdrie, s of Robert P. and Jean Thomson Lewis; educ Glasgow Academy 1945–53; University of Glasgow 1971–76 (BD); lic by Presb of Hamilton, 1976; asst Cadder 1976–77; m 25 Apr 1962 Evelyn Jean Davie Marshall b 8 Dec 1936, died 28 May 1996, d of Andrew Hamilton Scobie M. and Georgina Elisabeth Wilson; Children: Robert Douglas b 20 Feb 1964 m Jan Meldrum; Muriel Elisabeth Wilson b 24 Aug 1966 m Mark Kinghorn; ord and ind to Bridge of Weir St Machar's Ranfurly 31 Aug 1977; trans to Edinburgh Craigmillar Park 1 Mar 1984; trans to Bonkyl and Preston with Chirnside with Edrom Allanton 21 Oct 1993.

BURNMOUTH (FUF 68; FES IX, 98; X, 59)

Linked 1 Jun 1969 with Ayton. Further linked 11 Sep 1984 with Grantshouse and Houndswood with Reston.

1969   JOHN TENNANT PEAT
(FES IX, 128; X, 59, 74, 222), trans from Milngavie St Paul's to Ayton with Burnmouth 11 Dec 1969; ret 15 Nov 1977; died 2 Apr 1988.

1978 DUNCAN WILLIAM McINTOSH ANDERSON
ord and ind to Ayton with Burnmouth 4 May 1978, see Ayton.

1983 DAVID JAMES HEBENTON
(FES X, 141, 201), ind to Ayton with Burnmouth 8 Sep 1983; became minister of linked charge with Grantshouse and Houndwood with Reston 11 Sep 1984, see Ayton.

CHIRNSIDE (FES IX, 98; X, 59)

Linked 15 Jul 1973 with Bonkyl and Preston.

1968 WILLIAM PETER GRAHAM
(FES X, 60), ind to Chirnside 8 Aug 1968; became minister of linked charge with Bonkyl and Preston 15 Jul 1973 and of linked charge with Edrom Allanton 17 Sep 1978; dem on app as Clerk to Presb of Edinburgh 12 Apr 1993.

1993 WILLIAM PATERSON
ind to Bonkyl and Preston with Chirnside with Edrom Allanton 21 Oct 1993, see Bonkyl.

COLDINGHAM (FES IX, 99; X 60)

Linked 1 Jan 1965 with St Abb's. Further linked 1 Jul 1987 with Eyemouth.

1951 WILLIAM HOWARD PURDIE
(FES IX, 99, 141, 319; X, 60), trans from Dumfries South to Coldingham Priory 23 Jan 1951; became minister of linked charge with St Abb's 1 Jan 1965; ret 30 Apr 1972; died 15 Feb 1984.

1972 JAMES MORE MACLEOD FRANCIS
(FES X, 60), ord and ind to Coldingham with St Abb's 27 Sep 1972; dem 31 Aug 1975 on app as Lecturer in New Testament Studies and Ethics, Sunderland Polytechnic.

1976 JAMES ALEXANDER BRYDON MABEN
(FES X, 63), trans from Castleton with Saughtree to Coldingham with St Abb's 25 Feb 1976; ret 30 Apr 1987; died 25 Apr 1995; d Dorothy m Fred Macnicoll; s Robert m Kathleen Sturrock; d Barbara m Graham Clark; d Karen m Neil Craig.

1987 DANIEL G LINDSAY
ind to Eyemouth 19 Jun 1979; became minister of linked charge with Coldingham with St Abb's 1 Jul 1987.

COLDSTREAM (FES X, 63)

Linked 26 Feb 1985 with Eccles.

1973 HUGH FINDLAY KERR
(FES X, 63, 420), res from service with Overseas Council in Tiberias, Israel and ind to Coldstream 8 Nov 1973; introd to Lausanne 28 Apr 1980.

1980 IAIN DOUGLAS PENMAN
ord by Presb of Lothian 7 Oct 1977 and app Asst at Cockenzie and Port Seton Old; ind to Coldstream 9 Oct 1980; became minister of linked charge with Eccles 26 Feb 1985; trans to Edinburgh Kaimes Lockhart Memorial 3 May 1995.

1995 JAMES SCHOFIELD HARRISON CUTLER
B 10 Oct 1946 at Hamilton, s of John Frederick C. and Margaret Robertson Shaw; educ Dalziel High, Motherwell 1958–63; Member of the Institute of Structural Engineers 1971; University of Glasgow 1982–85 (BD); Structural Engineering 1963–82; lic by Presb of Lanark 30 Jun 1985; asst Lanark St Nicholas' 1985–86; m 26 Apr 1969 Agnes Carson McFadyen Ewing b 18 Jun 1947 d of Matthew E. and Marion Stewart; Children: Stewart John b 16 Feb 1972 m Liza Jane Cross; Jillian Marion b 21 Jan 1975; ord and ind to Kilmun with Strone and Ardentinny 22 Aug 1986; trans to Coldstream with Eccles 20 Oct 1995.

DUNS PARISH (FES X, 60)

Formed 4 Jul 1976 by union of Duns Old and Boston with Duns South.

1935 MALCOLM McCALLUM
(FES IX, 100; X, 60), ord and ind to Duns South 14 Jul 1935; ret 30 Jun 1976; died 30 Dec 1978.

1967 HUGH MACKAY
(FES X, 60, 173), trans from Glasgow St Bride's to Duns Old and Boston 2 Mar 1967; became minister of united charge with Duns South 4 Jul 1976; ret 31 Aug 1998; died 6 Jan 1999.

1999 ANDREW ALEXANDER MORRICE
B 14 Feb 1973 at Galashiels, s of Alastair M. and Mary Gossip; educ Currie High and Stonelaw High 1984–90; University of Dundee 1990–94 (MA); University of Edinburgh 1994–97 (BD); lic by Presb of Edinburgh, Jun 1997; asst Edinburgh Slateford Longstone 1997–99; m 27 Aug 1994 Sarah Leitch b 16 Jun 1972 d of Graham L. and Mary Cullington; Children: Peter b 23 Aug 1998; ord and ind to Duns 28 May 1999.

ECCLES (FES II, 12; VIII, 117; IX, 107; X, 64)

Linkage with Leitholm terminated 13 Jun 1976. Linked same date with Greenlaw. Arrangement terminated 27 Feb 1985. Linked same date with Coldstream.

1951 JAMES INGLIS CRAWFORD FINNIE
(FES IX, 107, 389; X, 64), trans from Strachur and Strathlachlan to Eccles 18 Sep 1951; became minister of linked charge with Leitholm 6 Dec 1959; ret 13 Jun 1976; died 28 Sep 1990.

1976 FREDERICK LEVISON
(FES IX, 36, 527; X, 22, 61), ind to Greenlaw 25
Sep 1968; became minister of linked charge with
Eccles 13 Jun 1976, see Greenlaw.

1978 JOHN (IAN) MANSON PATERSON
(FES IX, 745, 800; X, 295, 332), trans from St
Andrews Hope Park to Eccles with Greenlaw 15
Mar 1978; ret 11 Jan 1985; s Michael m Elspeth
Bell; d Ruth m Richard Russell.

1985 IAIN DOUGLAS PENMAN
ind to Coldstream 9 Oct 1980; became minister of
linked charge with Eccles 26 Feb 1985, see
Coldstream.

1995 JAMES SCHOFIELD HARRISON CUTLER
ind to Coldstream with Eccles 20 Oct 1995, see
Coldstream.

EDROM ALLANTON (FES X, 60)

Linked 17 Sep 1978 with Bonkyl and Preston with
Chirnside.

1948 JOHN MACDONALD
(FES IX, 100, 411; X, 60), trans from Ballachulish
to Edrom Allanton 10 Jun 1948; ret 31 Jul 1978;
died 24 Oct 1979.

1978 WILLIAM PETER GRAHAM
(FES X, 60), ind to Chirnside 8 Aug 1968; became
minister of linked charge with Edrom Allanton 17
Sep 1978, see Chirnside.

1993 WILLIAM PATERSON
ind to Bonkyl and Preston with Chirnside with
Edrom Allanton 21 Oct 1993, see Bonkyl.

EYEMOUTH (FES IX, 100; X, 60)

Linked 1 Jul 1987 with Coldingham with St Abb's.

1958 ALEXANDER LAMB
(FES IX, 410; X, 60, 244), trans from Kinlochleven
to Eyemouth 5 Dec 1958; died 7 Jan 1979.

1979 DANIEL G LINDSAY
ord by Presb of Paisley during assistantship at New
Erskine 1978; ind to Eyemouth 19 Jun 1979;
became minister of linked charge with Coldingham
with St Abb's 1 Jul 1987.

FOGO AND SWINTON (FES X, 60, 62)

Formed 13 Jun 1976 by union of Fogo and Swinton.
Linked same date with Leitholm. Further linked 31
Jan 1978 with Ladykirk with Whitsome.

1962 FRANCIS JOSEPH LAUGHLAN
McLAUGHLAN
(FUF 45; FES IX, 60, 361, 566, 625, 654; X, 62,
373), trans from Inverness Old High to Swinton 28
Feb 1962; ret 28 May 1967; died 19 Dec 1989.

1967 ROBERT MARTIN
(FES X, 60, 117), ord and ind to Fogo with
Swinton 22 Nov 1967; trans to Kilbirnie Barony 29
Oct 1975.

1976 ALAN CHARLES DAVID CARTWRIGHT
B 14 Jul 1947 at Glasgow, s of Joseph C. and
Catherine Allan Christie Honeyman; educ Hutche-
sons' Grammar, Glasgow 1959–65; University of
Strathclyde 1965–68 (BSc); University of Glasgow
1972–75 (BD); Statistician 1968–72; lic by Presb
of Lochaber 25 Jun 1975; asst Cameron with
Largoward with St Andrews St Leonard's 1975–
76; m 2 Sep 1970 Mary Elizabeth Lawson Bissett
b 31 Jan 1947 d of William Campbell B. and
Margaret Elizabeth Allan Lawson Matthew;
Children: Charles David b 1 Jun 1971; Margaret
Amelia Catherine b 28 Oct 1973 m Alan Richard
Denison; Rosemary Anne b 28 Sep 1977; ord
and ind to Fogo and Swinton with Leitholm 19
Aug 1976; became minister of linked charge
with Ladykirk with Whitsome 31 Jan 1978;
Clerk to Presb of Duns 1994–99; Publ: Articles
on Fogo, Ladykirk and Swinton in *Third
Statistical Account* (Scottish Academic Press); *A
History of the Churches in the Presbytery of Duns*
in *History of the Berwickshire Naturalists*, Vol 46
(1995).

FOULDEN AND MORDINGTON (FES II, 47, 56;
VIII, 126, 128; IX, 101; X, 60)

Linked 26 Nov 1978 with Hutton, Fishwick and
Paxton.

1968 JOHN COLVILLE LUSK
(FES IX, 55; X, 32, 60), dem from Uphall North 16
May 1966; ind to Foulden and Mordington 21 Feb
1968; ret 30 Jun 1978; died 9 Jun 1997.

1978 WILLIAM GAVIN DUNNETT
(FES X, 56, 61), trans from Ormiston to Hutton
and Fishwick and Paxton 11 Jul 1974; became
minister of linked charge with Foulden and
Mordington 26 Nov 1978; ret 1 Oct 1985.

1986 GERALDINE HENRIETTA HOPE
B 29 May 1942 at Epsom, Surrey, d of James Hilton
Webster and Ada Rosina McIntosh; educ Leith
Academy 1954–60; University of Edinburgh 1969–
73 (MA), 1974–78 (BD); lic by Presb of Edinburgh,
Jul 1978; asst Edinburgh Murrayfield; m 9 Apr 1978
Iain Gibson Hope b 29 Jun 1942 s of Alexander
Crosbie H. and Jane Trotter Gibson; Children:
Douglas Iain b 8 Jul 1979; ord and ind to Foulden
and Mordington with Hutton, Fishwick and Paxton
19 Aug 1986.

GORDON ST MICHAEL'S (FES II, 151; VIII, 144;
IX, 101; X, 60)

Linked 27 Feb 1985 with Greenlaw.

1971 ROBERT MAITLAND FRASER
(FES IX, 683, 734; X, 61, 280, 419), trans from Buckhaven St David's to Gordon St Michael's with Legerwood with Westruther 13 Jan 1971; ret 30 Sep 1979; died 11 Nov 1994.

1979 ALLAN MACINNES MACLEOD
(FES IX, 64, 791; X, 447), res from Gibraltar St Andrew's 1978 and ind to Gordon St Michael's with Legerwood with Westruther 13 Dec 1979; ret 11 Jan 1985.

1985 ROBERT DAVID HIGHAM
ord and ind to Gordon St Michael's with Greenlaw with Legerwood with Westruther 14 Jun 1985; dem 1 Sep 1990 on app as Lecturer, Northumbria Bible College.

1991 IAN GRAHAM WOTHERSPOON
(FES X, 23, 102, 289, 413), trans from Portobello Old and Windsor Place to Gordon St Michael's with Greenlaw with Legerwood with Westruther 9 Apr 1991; trans to Coatbridge St Andrew's 23 Jun 1994.

1995 THOMAS SINCLAIR NICHOLSON
B 2 Aug 1954 at Kirkwall, s of David Park N. and Margaret Morrison Sinclair; educ St Margaret's Hope Junior Secondary and Kirkwall Grammar 1966–73; University of Aberdeen 1973–77 (BD), 1977–78, 1979–80 (DPS); Lay Missionary, Presb Church in Canada 1978–79; lic by Presb of Orkney 3 Aug 1980; asst East Kilbride Old 1980–81; m 5 Aug 1978 Catherine Jane MacPhail b 4 Apr 1951 d of Franklin Lane M. and Helen Gordon Drope; Children: Elizabeth Donna b 24 Feb 1982; Jessica Laine b 13 Nov 1983; David Blair b 21 Nov 1985; ord by Presb of Orkney and app Missionary with Presb Church in Taiwan 9 Jun 1982; ind to Gordon St Michael's, Greenlaw, Legerwood and Westruther 1 May 1995; Publ: *Introduction to the Presbyterian Church in Taiwan* (Presb Church in Taiwan, 1987); English editor of *Self-determination: The Case for Taiwan* (Taiwan Church Press, 1988); editor of *Taiwan—Its International and Ecumenical Status and Role* (Presb Church in Taiwan, 1994).

GRANTSHOUSE AND HOUNDWOOD (FES X, 61)

Linked 11 Sep 1984 with Ayton with Burnmouth with Reston.

1968 SAMUEL McGEACHIE
(FES IX, 622; X, 34, 61 (2), 216, 333, 360), trans from Airth to Grantshouse with Houndwood 27 Nov 1968; became minister of Grantshouse and Houndwood with Reston 3 Jun 1973; trans to Lochgoilhead and Kilmorich 14 Sep 1978.

1979 HECTOR MACPHERSON
(FES X, 240, 241), trans from Tiree and Coll to Grantshouse and Houndwood with Reston 27 Mar 1979; ret 31 Aug 1984; died 2 Feb 1987.

1984 DAVID JAMES HEBENTON
(FES X, 141, 201), ind to Ayton with Burnmouth 8 Sep 1983; became minister of linked charge with Grantshouse and Houndwood with Reston 11 Sep 1984, see Ayton.

GREENLAW (FES IX, 102; X, 61)

Linked 13 Jun 1976 with Eccles. Arrangement terminated 27 Feb 1985 in favour of linkage with Gordon St Michael's.

1968 FREDERICK LEVISON
(FES IX, 36, 527; X, 22, 61), trans from Edinburgh St Bernard's Davidson to Greenlaw 25 Sep 1968; became minister of linked charge with Eccles 13 Jun 1976; ret 30 Sep 1977; died 27 May 1999; d Eleanor m Donald Pirie; d Elspeth m Malcolm Beaton; d Freda m Kevin Butler; Addl publ: *The Gospel at Infant Baptism* (St Andrew Press, 1980); *Christian and Jew. Leon Levison 1881–1936* (Pentland Press, 1989); *The Prospect of Heaven* (Wild Goose Publs, 1997).

1978 JOHN (IAN) MANSON PATERSON
(FES IX, 745, 800; X, 295, 332), ind to Eccles with Greenlaw 15 Mar 1978, see Eccles.

1985 ROBERT DAVID HIGHAM
ind to Gordon St Michael's with Greenlaw with Legerwood with Westruther 14 Jun 1985, see Gordon St Michael's.

1991 IAN GRAHAM WOTHERSPOON
ind to Gordon St Michael's with Greenlaw with Legerwood with Westruther 9 Apr 1991, see Gordon St Michael's.

1995 THOMAS SINCLAIR NICHOLSON
ind to Gordon St Michael's, Greenlaw, Legerwood and Westruther 1 May 1995, see Gordon St Michael's.

HUTTON AND FISHWICK AND PAXTON (FES X, 61)

Linked 26 Nov 1978 with Foulden and Mordington.

1974 WILLIAM GAVIN DUNNETT
(FES X, 56, 61), trans from Ormiston to Hutton and Fishwick and Paxton 11 Jul 1974; became minister of linked charge with Foulden and Mordington 26 Nov 1978; ret 1 Oct 1985.

1986 GERALDINE HENRIETTA HOPE
ord and ind to Foulden and Mordington with Hutton, Fishwick and Paxton 19 Aug 1986.

KIRK OF LAMMERMUIR (FES X, 59, 62)

Formed 10 Mar 1983 by union of Abbey St Bathan's and Cranshaws and Longformacus. Linked 5 Jul 1983 with Langton and Polwarth.

1948 CRICHTON EDWARD EDDY
(FES IX, 97; X, 59), res from app as Asst at
Paisley Abbey and ind to St Bathan's and
Cranshaws 22 Oct 1948; became minister of linked
charge with Longformacus 1 Apr 1973; died 5 Jun
1982.

1966 WALTER KIRKPATRICK GIBB
(FES IX, 138, 552; X, 62, 321), trans from Kinneff
to Longformacus 18 May 1966; ret 30 Sep 1972;
died 30 Mar 1982.

1983 ALEXANDER SLORACH
B 5 Aug 1937 at Glasgow, s of Lennox Gordon S.
and Jessie Gilmour; educ Leith Academy 1949–
54; University of Edinburgh 1967–70 (BD); CA
Apprenticeship and Qualification 1954–60;
Accountant with Board of World Mission in N
Rhodesia and Zambia 1961–66; lic by Presb of
Edinburgh 17 Jun 1970; m 27 Dec 1969 Ruth
Leonora Russell b 27 Apr 1942, died 29 Jun 1999,
d of William R. and Gladys Cargo; Children:
Sarah Dorothy b 4 Feb 1971; Amy Anna b 9 Aug
1974; ord in Kasama by Northern Presb of United
Church of Zambia 22 Aug 1971; Service with
Board of World Mission in Zambia 1970–82;
admitted by General Assembly 1983 and ind to
Kirk of Lammermuir with Langton and Polwarth 5
Jul 1983.

LADYKIRK (FES II, 53; VIII, 127; IX, 102; X, 61)
Linked 5 May 1955 with Whitsome. Further linked
31 Jan 1978 with Fogo and Swinton with Leitholm.

1958 ALEXANDER ARTHUR EWING
(FES IX, 174, 182, 301; X, 61, 101), trans from
Ayr Crosshill to Ladykirk with Whitsome 5 Dec
1958; ret 30 Nov 1970; died 7 Oct 1984.

1971 WELLESLEY GRAHAME BAILEY
(FES IX, 728; X, 24, 61, 416), res from service
with Overseas Council in Pakistan and ind to
Ladykirk with Whitsome 2 Jun 1971; ret 31 Jan
1978; Asst at London St Columba's Pont Street
1978–80; s Alan died 8 Mar 1992.

1978 ALAN CHARLES DAVID CARTWRIGHT
ord and ind to Fogo and Swinton with Leitholm 19
Aug 1976; became minister of linked charge with
Ladykirk with Whitsome 31 Jan 1978.

LANGTON AND POLWARTH (FES IX, 103; X, 61)
Linked 5 Jul 1983 with Kirk of Lammermuir.

1972 JAMES ANDREW HALL
(FES X, 58, 62, 188), trans from Blantyre
Livingstone Memorial to Langton and Polwarth
30 Aug 1972; ret 5 Jul 1983; died 11 Jan 1992.

1983 ALEXANDER SLORACH
ind to Kirk of Lammermuir with Langton and
Polwarth 5 Jul 1983, see Kirk of Lammermuir.

LEGERWOOD (FES II, 155; VIII, 144; IX, 125; X,
62)

Linked 27 Feb 1985 with Gordon St Michael's with
Greenlaw.

1953 DOUGLAS GORDON McLEAN
(FES VIII, 317; IX, 125, 382; X, 62), trans from
Innellan to Legerwood 12 May 1953; ret 24 Nov
1963; died 27 Jan 1985.

1964 WILLIAM COLVILLE THOMAS
(FES X, 9, 62), ord and ind to Legerwood with
Westruther 14 May 1964; trans to Edinburgh
Granton 9 Apr 1969.

1971 ROBERT MAITLAND FRASER
(FES IX, 683, 734; X, 61, 280, 419), trans from
Buckhaven St David's to Gordon St Michael's
with Legerwood with Westruther 13 Jan 1971; ret
30 Sep 1979; died 11 Nov 1994.

1979 ALLAN MACINNES MACLEOD
(FES IX, 64, 791; X, 447), ind to Gordon St
Michael's with Legerwood with Westruther 13 Dec
1979, see Gordon St Michael's.

1985 ROBERT DAVID HIGHAM
ind to Gordon St Michael's with Greenlaw with
Legerwood with Westruther 14 Jun 1985, see
Gordon St Michael's.

1991 IAN GRAHAM WOTHERSPOON
ind to Gordon St Michael's with Greenlaw with
Legerwood with Westruther 9 Apr 1991, see
Gordon St Michael's.

1995 THOMAS SINCLAIR NICHOLSON
ind to Gordon St Michael's, Greenlaw, Legerwood
and Westruther 1 May 1995, see Gordon St
Michael's.

LEITHOLM (FUF 79; FES IX, 110; X, 68)
Linkage with Eccles terminated 13 Jun 1976
in favour of linkage with Fogo and Swinton.
Further linked 31 Jan 1978 with Ladykirk with
Whitsome.

1959 JAMES INGLIS CRAWFORD FINNIE
(FES IX, 107, 389; X, 64), trans from Strachur and
Strathlachlan to Eccles 18 Sep 1951; became
minister of linked charge with Leitholm 6 Dec 1959;
ret 13 Jun 1976; died 28 Sep 1990.

1976 ALAN CHARLES DAVID CARTWRIGHT
ord and ind to Fogo and Swinton with Leitholm 19
Aug 1976; became minister of linked charge with
Ladykirk with Whitsome 31 Jan 1978.

RESTON (FUF 73; FES IX, 103; X, 62)
Linked 11 Sep 1984 with Ayton.

1973 SAMUEL McGEACHIE
(FES IX, 622; X, 34, 61 (2), 216, 333, 360), ind to Grantshouse with Houndwood 27 Nov 1968; became minister of Grantshouse and Houndwood with Reston 3 Jun 1973, see Grantshouse.

1979 HECTOR MACPHERSON
(FES X, 240, 241), trans from Tiree and Coll to Grantshouse and Houndwood with Reston 27 Mar 1979; ret 31 Aug 1984; died 2 Feb 1987.

1984 DAVID JAMES HEBENTON
(FES X, 141, 201), ind to Ayton with Burnmouth 8 Sep 1983; became minister of linked charge with Grantshouse and Houndwood with Reston 11 Sep 1984, see Ayton.

ST ABB'S (FUF 73; FES IX, 104; X, 62)

Linked 1 Jan 1965 with Coldingham. Further linked 1 Jul 1987 with Eyemouth.

1946 ROBERT DEWAR BURNETT
(FES IX, 104; X, 62), ord and ind to St Abbs 28 Aug 1946; ret 18 Apr 1963; died 3 May 1990.

1965 WILLIAM HOWARD PURDIE
(FES IX, 99, 141, 319; X, 60), trans from Dumfries South to Coldingham Priory 23 Jan 1951; became minister of linked charge with St Abb's 1 Jan 1965; ret 30 Apr 1972; died 15 Feb 1984.

1972 JAMES MORE MACLEOD FRANCIS
ord and ind to Coldingham with St Abb's 27 Sep 1972, see Coldingham.

1976 JAMES ALEXANDER BRYDON MABEN
(FES X, 63), ind to Coldingham with St Abb's 25 Feb 1976, see Coldingham.

1987 DANIEL G LINDSAY
ind to Eyemouth 19 Jun 1979; became minister of linked charge with Coldingham with St Abb's 1 Jul 1987.

WESTRUTHER (FUF 74; FES II, 165; VIII, 147; IX, 105; X, 62)

Linked 27 Feb 1985 with Gordon St Michael's with Greenlaw.

1964 WILLIAM COLVILLE THOMAS
(FES X, 9, 62), ord and ind to Legerwood with Westruther 14 May 1964; trans to Edinburgh Granton 9 Apr 1969.

1971 ROBERT MAITLAND FRASER
(FES IX, 683, 734; X, 61, 280, 419), trans from Buckhaven St David's to Gordon St Michael's with Legerwood with Westruther 13 Jan 1971; ret 30 Sep 1979; died 11 Nov 1994.

1979 ALLAN MACINNES MACLEOD
(FES IX, 64, 791; X, 447), ind to Gordon St Michael's with Legerwood with Westruther 13 Dec 1979, see Gordon St Michael's.

1985 ROBERT DAVID HIGHAM
ind to Gordon St Michael's with Greenlaw with Legerwood with Westruther 14 Jun 1985, see Gordon St Michael's.

1991 IAN GRAHAM WOTHERSPOON
ind to Gordon St Michael's with Greenlaw with Legerwood with Westruther 9 Apr 1991, see Gordon St Michael's.

1995 THOMAS SINCLAIR NICHOLSON
ind to Gordon St Michael's, Greenlaw, Legerwood and Westruther 1 May 1995, see Gordon St Michael's.

WHITSOME (FES II, 63; VIII, 128; IX, 105; X, 62)

Linked 5 May 1955 with Fogo with Swinton. Further linked 31 Jan 1978 with Fogo and Swinton with Leitholm.

1958 ALEXANDER ARTHUR EWING
(FES IX, 174, 182, 301; X, 61, 101), trans from Ayr Crosshill to Ladykirk with Whitsome 5 Dec 1958; ret 30 Nov 1970; died 7 Oct 1984.

1971 WELLESLEY GRAHAME BAILEY
(FES IX, 728; X, 24, 61, 416), ind to Ladykirk with Whitsome 2 Jun 1971, see Ladykirk.

1978 ALAN CHARLES DAVID CARTWRIGHT
ord and ind to Fogo and Swinton with Leitholm 19 Aug 1976; became minister of linked charge with Ladykirk with Whitsome 31 Jan 1978.

PRESBYTERY OF JEDBURGH

ANCRUM (FES IX, 106; X, 63)

Linkage with Minto terminated 3 Oct 1976. Linked same date with Jedburgh Old. Arrangement terminated 16 Apr 1991 to allow union of Jedburgh Old and Edgerston. Ancrum linked 21 Oct 1994 with Lilliesleaf. Further linked 19 Feb 1999 with Crailing and Eckford.

1950   PETER BRYCE GUNN
(FES IX, 106; X, 63), trans from Roxburgh to Ancrum 7 Apr 1950; became minister of linked charge with Minto 1 May 1968; ret 30 Sep 1976; died 6 Jul 1979.

1976   RONALD STANTON BLAKEY
(FES X, 67, 85, 187), trans from Bellshill West to Jedburgh Old 14 Dec 1972; became minister of linked charge with Ancrum 3 Oct 1976, see Jedburgh Old.

1981   WILLIAM HAISLEY MOORE
(FES X, 204), trans from Wishaw Old to Ancrum with Edgerston with Jedburgh Old 25 Nov 1981; dem 3 Sep 1990 on app as Scottish Secretary, Boys Brigade; ret 31 Mar 1996.

1991   WILLIAM FRANK CAMPBELL
B 9 Mar 1957 at Paisley, s of William Cross C. and Marjorie Margaret Sheelagh Nelson; educ Rutherglen Academy and Cathkin High, Cambuslang 1967–73; University of Strathclyde 1973–76 (BA); University of Glasgow 1985–88 (BD); Accountant, Caterpillar Tractor Co Ltd, Uddingston 1976–78; Secretary, Queen's Park FC, Glasgow 1979–81; Legal Asst, Messrs Maclay Murray and Spens, Glasgow 1981–83; Senior Admin Asst, Dumfries & Galloway Regional Council 1983–85; lic by Presb of Glasgow 5 Jul 1988; asst Ayr The Auld Kirk 1988–89; m 24 Jan 1991 Alexis Carnegie Graham b 23 Mar 1957 d of Edward G. and Barbara Lindsay Young Watson; Children from spouse's previous marriage: Lisa Christina b 14 Jan 1978; Laura Barbara b 9 Jun 1980; Alistair James b 8 Mar 1984; ord and ind to Irvine Relief Bourtreehill 6 Jun 1989; dem 30 Apr 1991; ind to Ancrum 15 Oct 1991; became minister of linked charge with Lilliesleaf 21 Oct 1994 and of linked charge with Crailing and Eckford 19 Feb 1999.

BEDRULE (FES II, 102; VIII, 135; IX, 113; X, 63)

Linked 1 Oct 1963 with Denholm. Further linked 7 Oct 1976 with Minto.

1945   THOMAS McGINN
(FES VIII, 160; IX, 84, 113, 146; X, 63), trans from Roslin to Bedrule 15 Jun 1945; ret 30 Sep 1963; died 7 Aug 1976.

1963   ROBERT WAUGH
(FES IX, 114; X, 63, 64), ind to Denholm 21 Jul 1954; became minister of linked charge with Bedrule 1 Oct 1963, see Denholm.

1975   JAMES FRASER FALCONER
(FES IX, 209; X, 63, 120, 328), trans from Aberdeen Mannofield to Bedrule with Denholm 19 Mar 1975; became minister of linked charge with Minto 7 Oct 1976; ret 31 Dec 1977; died 9 Nov 1989.

1978   JOHN THOMSON STUART
(FES X, 150, 448), ret from RAChD and ind to Bedrule with Denholm with Minto 30 Aug 1978; trans to Duffus, Spynie and Hopeman 23 Nov 1984.

1985   MOIRA HERKES
ord and ind to Bedrule with Denholm with Minto 10 Jun 1985; trans to Prestonpans Prestongrange 8 Nov 1988.

1989   THOMAS PRESTON
trans from Port Glasgow Hamilton Bardrainney to Bedrule with Denholm with Minto 17 May 1989; trans to Edinburgh Old Kirk 28 Jun 1992.

1992   WILLIAM MACGREGOR LONGMUIR
B 30 May 1936 at Swinton, s of James Boyd L. and Bethia Liddell MacGregor; educ Berwickshire High, Duns 1948–54; Open University 1978–79; University of Edinburgh 1980–83 (LTh); National Service (RAF) 1954–56; Home Civil Service 1954–80; lic by Presb of Edinburgh 3 Jul 1983; asst Edinburgh Cluny 1983–84; m 1 Sep 1984 Helen Uprichard b 6 May 1950 d of Joseph U. and Harriet McCleery; Children: Ruth MacGregor b 22 Jul 1985; Hannah Beth b 13 Jan 1987; ord and introd to Lanark Cairns 6 Sep 1984; ind 31 Aug 1989; trans to Bedrule with Denholm with Minto 27 Nov 1992.

CAVERS AND KIRKTON (FES X, 63, 67)

Formed 22 Aug 1976 by union of Cavers and Kirkton. Temporary linkage with Hawick St Mary's same date. Arrangement terminated 8 Mar 1988 in favour of linkage with Hobkirk and Southdean. This linkage was terminated 7 Jul 1996 in favour of previous linkage with Hawick St Mary's and Old.

1955 WILLIAM WELSH
(FES IX, 77, 149, 370; X, 63, 221), trans from Kilbowie to Cavers with Kirkton 5 Aug 1955; ret 31 Aug 1975; died 10 Jan 1976.

1976 DUNCAN CLARK
(FES X, 65, 270), trans from Ballingry to Hawick St Mary's 27 Jan 1971; became minister of linked charge with Cavers and Kirkton 22 Aug 1976; died 19 Oct 1984.

1985 ALEXANDER CLOWES McCARTNEY
(FES X, 275), ind to Hawick St Mary's with Cavers and Kirkton 11 Dec 1985, see St Mary's.

1988 ADAM McCALL BOWIE
B 13 Aug 1928 at Edinburgh, s of John B. and Helen Hay; educ Leith Academy 1940–42; University of Glasgow 1973–76 (LTh); Electrician 1942–57; RAF 1946–48; lic by Presb of Annandale 17 Jun 1976; m 7 Feb 1959 Ivy Lillian MacDonald b 1 Oct 1931 d of Elizabeth M; Children: Jean Elizabeth b 1 Nov 1959 m Stuart McCallum; Alison Mary b 1 Dec 1962; Angus John b 17 Jun 1972; ord and ind to King Edward 30 Jul 1976; became minister of linked charge with Gamrie 1 Jun 1978; trans to Dull and Weem with Fortingall and Glenlyon 23 Aug 1981; trans to Cavers and Kirkton with Hobkirk and Southdean 24 Aug 1988; ret 31 May 1996.

1996 DAVID WILLIAM GILMOUR BURT
ord and ind to Hawick St Mary's and Old 21 Jun 1989; became minister of linked charge with Cavers and Kirkton 7 Jul 1996; trans to Hamilton Hillhouse 22 Jan 1998.

1998 WILLIAM ROBERT TAYLOR
B 5 Aug 1958 at Airdrie, s of William T. and Elizabeth McMaster; educ High School of Glasgow 1967–75; University of Glasgow 1975–79 (MA); University of Edinburgh 1979–82 (BD), 1993–94 (MTh); lic by Presb of Hamilton 1 Jul 1982; asst East Kilbride Old 1982–83; m 7 Aug 1982 Alison Anne Wason b 19 Jul 1961 d of William W. and Annie Macrae Henderson; Children: Duncan Andrew William b 10 Sep 1986; Catriona Elspeth Joanne b 25 Nov 1988; divorced 17 Nov 1995; m (2) 6 Mar 1999 Lorna Margaret Mackenzie b 5 Nov 1954 d of David MacKay and Sheila Margaret Corcoran; ord by Presb of Perth and app Summer Mission Organiser and Youth Officer, St Ninian's, Crieff 29 Jun 1983; ind to Slateford Longstone 9 Sep 1986; dem to take up place as full-time student

at University of Edinburgh 10 Oct 1993; app Chaplain to Southfield Hospital, Edinburgh and Youth Work Organiser, Murrayfield, Edinburgh 1 Aug 1994 (part-time); app Chaplain (part-time) to Saughton Prison, Edinburgh 1 Nov 1994; introd as Assoc at Murrayfield 1 Sep 1997; ind to Cavers and Kirkton with Hawick St Mary's and Old 18 Sep 1998.

CRAILING AND ECKFORD (FES X, 64)

Formed 24 Jul 1977 by union of Crailing and Eckford. Linked same date with Oxnam with Roxburgh. Linkage terminated 19 Feb 1999. Linked same date with Ancrum with Lilliesleaf.

1931 ANDREW LOW McGREGOR MACKENZIE
(FES VIII, 177; IX, 107, 145; X, 64), trans from Lochrutton to Crailing 24 Sep 1931; ret 5 Jul 1960; died 22 Sep 1983.

1955 JAMES VICTOR LOGAN
(FES IX, 200, 516; X, 64, 306), trans from Dundee St Mark's to Eckford 16 Apr 1955; became minister of linked charge with Crailing 6 Jul 1960; ret 31 May 1977; died 25 Feb 1990.

1977 WILLIAM MOFFAT DREW THOMPSON
(FES IX, 111; X, 68), ord and ind to Oxnam 23 Jun 1950; became minister of linked charge with Roxburgh 4 Jul 1961and of linked charge with Crailing and Eckford 24 Jul 1977; dem 25 Dec 1997.

1999 WILLIAM FRANK CAMPBELL
ind to Ancrum 15 Oct 1991; became minister of linked charge with Crailing and Eckford 19 Feb 1999.

DENHOLM (FUF 81; FES IX, 114; X, 64)

Linked 1 Oct 1963 with Bedrule. Further linked 7 Oct 1976 with Minto.

1954 ROBERT WAUGH
(FES IX, 114; X, 63, 64), admitted by General Assembly 1954 and ind to Denholm 21 Jul 1954; became minister of linked charge with Bedrule 1 Oct 1963; ret 31 Jul 1974; died 19 Feb 1985.

1975 JAMES FRASER FALCONER
(FES IX, 209; X, 63, 120, 328), ind to Bedrule with Denholm 19 Mar 1975; became minister of linked charge with Minto 7 Oct 1976, see Bedrule.

1978 JOHN THOMSON STUART
(FES X, 150, 448), ind to Bedrule with Denholm with Minto 30 Aug 1978, see Bedrule.

1985 MOIRA HERKES
ord and ind to Bedrule with Denholm with Minto 10 Jun 1985; trans to Prestonpans Prestongrange 8 Nov 1988.

1989   THOMAS PRESTON
trans from Port Glasgow Hamilton Bardrainney to
Bedrule with Denholm with Minto 17 May 1989;
trans to Edinburgh Old Kirk 28 Jun 1992.

1992   WILLIAM MACGREGOR LONGMUIR
ind to Bedrule with Denholm with Minto 27 Nov
1992, see Bedrule.

HAWICK BURNFOOT (FES IX, 114; X, 64)

Linkage with Wilton terminated 21 Feb 1978.

1973   GEORGE WATSON
(FES IX, 547; X, 66, 317), trans from Brechin
Maisondieu to Hawick Wilton 6 Apr 1960; became
minister of linked charge with Hawick Burnfoot 15
Nov 1973 (until 21 Feb 1978) and of linked charge
with Teviothead 2 Apr 1989; ret 30 Nov 1991; died
15 Apr 1998.

1978   COLIN FORRESTER-PATON
(FES X, 66, 424), res from service with Overseas
Council in Ghana and introd as Assoc at Hawick
Wilton with Burnfoot 15 Nov 1973; ind to Hawick
Burnfoot 18 May 1978 following termination of
linkage; ret 21 Nov 1983; app Chaplain to HM the
Queen in Scotland 1981; app Extra Chaplain 5 Apr
1988; Publ: Editor of *Hugh Douglas: One Man's
Ministry* (St Andrew Press, 1993).

1984   JAMES MORTON COWIE
ind to Fordyce 5 Oct 1978; trans to Hawick Burnfoot
17 May 1984; introd as Community minister at
Edinburgh Craigmillar and app Chaplain to Thistle
Foundation 1 Sep 1996.

1997   CHARLES JOHN FINNIE
B 13 Mar 1961 at Perth, s of Charles John F. and
Maureen Murdoch Hillis Brown; educ Penilee
Secondary, Glasgow 1973–79; University of
Aberdeen 1984–89 (LTh, DPS); Sales Asst/
Storeman 1979–81; lic by Presb of Glasgow 3
Jul 1989; asst Newhills Aberdeen 1989–90; m 4
Aug 1984 Lynne Mary Gosland b 11 Aug 1963
d of Archibald Williams G. and Elizabeth
Watson Howard; Children: Mark Charles b 30
May 1989; Stephen David b 14 Apr 1991; Anna
Elizabeth May b 20 Apr 1994; ord and ind
to Caldercruix, Longriggend and Meadowfield
22 Jan 1991; ind to Hawick Burnfoot 30 May
1997.

HAWICK ST MARY'S AND OLD (FES X, 64, 65)

Formed 25 Jan 1989 by union of Hawick St Mary's
and Hawick Old. Linked 7 Jul 1996 with Cavers
and Kirkton.

1971   DUNCAN CLARK
(FES X, 65, 270), trans from Ballingry to Hawick
St Mary's 27 Jan 1971; became minister of linked
charge with Cavers and Kirkton 22 Aug 1976; died
19 Oct 1984.

1971   DAVID LIVINGSTON WRIGHT
(FES X, 53, 65, 319), trans from Forfar Lowson
Memorial to Hawick Old 14 Jan 1971; became
minister of linked charge with Teviothead 4 Jun
1972; trans to Stornoway St Columba 18 Feb 1986.

1985   ALEXANDER CLOWES McCARTNEY
(FES X, 275), trans from Kelty to St Mary's with
Cavers and Kirkton 11 Dec 1985; trans to Caputh
and Clunie 9 Nov 1987.

1989   DAVID WILLIAM GILMOUR BURT
ord and ind to Hawick St Mary's and Old 21 Jun
1989; became minister of linked charge with
Cavers and Kirkton 7 Jul 1996; trans to Hamilton
Hillhouse 22 Jan 1998.

1998   WILLIAM ROBERT TAYLOR
ind to Cavers and Kirkton with Hawick St Mary's
and Old 18 Sep 1998, see Cavers.

HAWICK TEVIOT AND ROBERTON (FES X, 65,
68)

Formed 30 Jun 1996 by union of Hawick Teviot
(formed 22 Mar 1988 by union of St George's
West and St Margaret's and Wilton South) and
Roberton.

1963   ROBERT LOCKHART
(FES IX, 6, 299, 533; X, 5, 65), trans from
Edinburgh Burdiehouse to St Margaret's and Wilton
South 23 Apr 1963; ret 31 Mar 1972; died 13 Jan
1980.

1967   THOMAS NEILSON HOOD
(FES X, 65), ord and ind to Hawick St George's
West 20 Apr 1967; died 24 Sep 1982.

1972   ROBERT McCONNELL
(FES X, 69, 407), trans from Tingwall to Roberton
with Teviothead 12 Jan 1966; became minister of
Roberton with Hawick St Margaret's and Wilton
South 2 Jan 1972; ret 31 Oct 1983.

1984   NEIL ROBERT COMBE
B 7 Aug 1949 at Stockport, Cheshire, s of Robert
Davidson C. and Betty Wylie; educ Nottingham
High 1960–67; University of Dundee 1967–71
(BSc); University of Sheffield 1972–73 (MSc);
University of Glasgow 1978–81 (BD); Information
Science Trainee 1971–72; Information Science
Research 1973–75; Library Systems Analyst 1975–
78; lic by Presb of Glasgow 11 Aug 1981; asst
Glasgow Chryston 1982–83; m 29 Jul 1978 Janet
Kirsteen Fraser b 21 May 1952 d of James
McLaren F. and Ruth Marsh; Children: Esther Joy
b 8 Jan 1981; Hannah Elizabeth b 28 Jan 1983;
Jonathan Paul b 10 Sep 1985; ord and ind to
Hawick St George's West with St Margaret's and
Wilton South with Roberton 28 Mar 1984; became
minister of united charge of Hawick Teviot 22 Mar
1988 and of united charge of Teviot and Roberton
30 Jun 1996.

HAWICK TRINITY (FES X, 65)

Formed 29 May 1959 by union of Hawick East Bank, Hawick St Andrew's and Hawick St John's.

1956 WILLIAM WOOD
(FES IX, 133, 291; X, 65, 78), dem from Half Morton 21 Apr 1956 and introd on term app to St John's; ret 29 May 1959; died 28 Oct 1977.

1959 DENNIS LEADBEATER
(FES IX, 361; X, 66, 216, 321), trans from Clydebank Hamilton Memorial to Trinity 2 Dec 1959; trans to The Glens 24 Nov 1971.

1972 EDWARD PETER LINDSAY THOMSON
(FES X, 66, 150), trans from Glasgow Balornock to Trinity 26 Apr 1972; s Edward William Stuart b 1 Feb 1967 m Andonella Arnone; s David Lindsay b 11 Oct 1969 m Anna Mary Winifred Sorensen; d Helen Margaret Rose b 30 Dec 1972 m Simon Peter Leach.

HAWICK WILTON (FES II, 142; VIII, 142; IX, 117; X, 66)

Linkage with Burnfoot terminated 21 Feb 1978. Linked 2 Apr 1989 with Teviothead.

1960 GEORGE WATSON
(FES IX, 547; X, 66, 317), trans from Brechin Maisondieu to Hawick Wilton 6 Apr 1960; became minister of linked charge with Hawick Burnfoot 15 Nov 1973 (until 21 Feb 1978) and of linked charge with Teviothead 2 Apr 1989; ret 30 Nov 1991; died 15 Apr 1998.

1992 BRIAN ROBERT HENDRIE
ord and ind to Hawick Wilton with Teviothead 24 Jan 1992; trans to Falkirk Bainsford 27 Aug 1997.

1998 JOHN SHEDDEN
(FES X, 88), ret from RAF Chaplains' Branch and ind to Hawick Wilton with Teviothead 29 May 1998; d Miranda m Edwards.

HOBKIRK AND SOUTHDEAN (FES X, 66, 69)

Formed 6 Mar 1988 by union of Hobkirk and Southdean and linked with Cavers and Kirkton. Linkage terminated 7 Jul 1996.

1954 STEPHEN GOODBRAND
(FES IX, 117; X, 66), res from service with Overseas Council in Ceylon and ind to Hobkirk 1 Apr 1954; became minister of linked charge with Southdean 1 Apr 1973; ret 31 Mar 1982; died 28 Jan 1997.

1983 JAMES CARSON STRACHAN
(FES IX, 421, 793; X, 93, 349, 448), trans from Mossgreen and Crossgates to Hobkirk with Southdean 11 May 1983; ret 31 Mar 1987; died 19 Mar 1989.

1988 ADAM McCALL BOWIE
trans from Dull and Weem with Fortingall and Glenlyon to Cavers and Kirkton with Hobkirk and Southdean 24 Aug 1988, see Cavers and Kirkton.

JEDBURGH OLD AND EDGERSTON (FES X, 64, 66)

Jedburgh Old temporarily linked with Ancrum 3 Oct 1976. Arrangement terminated 16 Apr 1991. Jedburgh Old and Edgerston united 24 Apr 1991.

1949 DAVID WHITEFORD
(FUF 184; FES IX, 22, 114, 326; X, 64), trans from Leith St Andrew's Place to Edgerston 23 Sep 1949; ret 31 Jul 1960; died 28 Apr 1976.

1960 JOHN ROBERTS
(FES IX, 120; X, 69), ind to Southdean 27 Apr 1951; became minister of linked charge with Edgerston 23 Oct 1960; died 31 Oct 1965.

1966 GEORGE BLAIR URQUHART
(FES IX, 333, 618; X, 64, 181, 355), trans from Springburn North to Edgerston with Southdean 2 Sep 1966; died 2 Sep 1972.

1972 RONALD STANTON BLAKEY
(FES X, 67, 85, 187), trans from Bellshill West to Jedburgh Old 14 Dec 1972; became minister of linked charge with Edgerston 18 Mar 1973; further linked with Ancrum 3 Oct 1976; dem on app as Asst Secretary, Dept of Education 1 Apr 1981.

1981 WILLIAM HAISLEY MOORE
ind to Ancrum with Edgerston with Jedburgh Old 25 Nov 1981, see Ancrum.

1992 BRUCE McNICOL
(FES X, 35), trans from Cumbernauld Condorrat to Jedburgh Old and Edgerston 1 May 1992; m 3 Jul 1989 Nancy Marian Helen Forrester b 7 Jul 1952 d of Alexander Scott Forrest F. and Nancy Margaret Anderson; Children: Alastair Alexander b 29 Aug 1990; Catherine Margaret b 27 Dec 1991.

JEDBURGH TRINITY (FES X, 67)

1967 JOHN ALLAN RIDDELL
(FES X, 67), ord and ind to Trinity 5 Oct 1967.

KELSO NORTH AND EDNAM (FES X, 67)

Formed 5 Oct 1980 by union of Kelso Trinity North and Kelso St John's Edenside and Ednam.

1938 JAMES FALLOON
(FES IX, 109 (2); X, 67), ord and ind to Kelso North 9 Mar 1938; became minister of united charge with Trinity 24 Nov 1940; died 28 Jun 1979.

1980   DONALD RUTHERFORD GADDES
(FES X, 67), ind to St John's Edenside and Ednam
14 Jan 1970; minister of linked charge with
Sprouston 1974–88; became minister of united
charge with Trinity North 5 Oct 1980; ret 3 Apr
1994; w Jean died 25 Nov 1996; Publ: *Henry
Francis Lyte* (Kelso North Church, 1993); *One of
Zion's Gates* (Kelso North Church, 1996).

1994   TOM McDONALD
B 22 Jan 1953 at Dunfermline, s of John M. and
Janet Renwick; educ Beath High 1966–71; Edin-
burgh College of Commerce 1971–74 (DipCom);
Moray House College, Edinburgh 1974–75
(PGCE); University of Edinburgh 1990–93 (BD);
Teaching 1975–90; lic by Presb of Dunfermline 4
Jul 1993; asst Melrose 1993–94; ord and ind to
Kelso North and Ednam 27 Jul 1994.

KELSO OLD AND SPROUSTON (FES X, 67,
69)
Formed 20 Dec 1988 by union of Kelso Old and
Sprouston.

1939   ALEXANDER HUNTER WRAY
(FES IX, 111, 118; X, 69), trans from Langholm
Erskine to Sprouston 11 Jan 1939; ret 20 Oct 1962;
died 14 Oct 1976.

1946   ROBERT HAMILTON
(FES IX, 109, 151; FES X, 67), trans from Anwoth
to Kelso Old 9 Jan 1946; ret 31 Oct 1979; s
Alexander m Rosemary Patricia Stocks; d Elizabeth
m Colin James Hunter.

1962   JOHN ANGUS MACGILP
(FES IX, 110, 610; X, 68), ind to Linton 6 Mar 1947;
became minister of linked charge with Makerstoun
12 May 1957 (linkage terminated 21 Oct 1962),
then of linked charge with Sprouston 21 Oct 1962;
ret 21 May 1974.

1974   DONALD RUTHERFORD GADDES
(FES X, 67), ind to Kelso St John's Edenside and
Ednam 14 Jan 1970; became minister of linked
charge with Sprouston 23 Jun 1974, see Kelso
North and Ednam.

1982   GEORGE DUDLEY ANDREW FOX
(FES X, 93), trans from Ballantrae and introd to
Kelso Old (term) 14 Mar 1982; ind to same charge
16 Dec 1984; ret 31 Dec 1988; Publ: *Pit-Polo-Pulpit*
(O Dickson, MPA, 1997).

1989   MARION ELIZABETH DODD
B 19 Apr 1941 at Stirling, d of Harry John D. and
Ida Alice Mary Ross; educ Selkirk High and
Esdaile, Edinburgh 1953–59; University of
Edinburgh 1959–62 (MA), 1984–87 (BD), 1989
(LRAM); Foreign Office (Russian Translation)
1962–64; Iron and Steel Institute (Editor) 1964–
67; BBC Singers 1967–84; lic by Presb of England,
Jul 1987; asst Edinburgh Colinton 1987–89; ord

by Presb of Edinburgh during assistantship at
Colinton, Aug 1988; ind to Kelso Old and Sprouston
25 Aug 1989.

LIDDESDALE (FES X, 63, 68, 69)
Formed 25 Jun 1993 by union of Castleton and
Saughtree (united 1 Aug 1976) and Newcastleton
Congregational Church.

1952   GEORGE HAROLD MAKIN
(FUF 514; FES IX, 119, 594, 624, 703; X, 69), trans
from Lynturk to Castleton with Saughtree 27 Jul
1952; ret 27 Jul 1960; died 13 Apr 1989.

1961   ARCHIBALD LAMONT
(FES IX, 396; X, 63, 234, 236, 253), trans from
Kilchoman to Castleton with Saughtree 9 Mar 1961;
trans to Perth Letham 17 Dec 1964.

1965   JAMES ALEXANDER BRYDON MABEN
(FES X, 63), ord and ind to Castleton with
Saughtree 15 Jul 1965; trans to Coldingham with
St Abb's 25 Feb 1976.

1979   REGINALD FRANKLIN CAMPBELL
ord and ind to Castleton and Saughtree with
Newcastleton Congregational Church 14 Jun 1979;
trans to Cumbernauld Kildrum 16 Feb 1989.

1989   ALAN DAVID REID
B 5 Feb 1963 at Victoria, Hong Kong, s of Ian
Alexander R. and Anne Grizel Cochrane; educ
Grove Academy, Broughty Ferry and Dunblane
High 1975–81; University of St Andrews 1981–
85 (MA); University of Edinburgh 1985–88
(BD); lic by Presb of Stirling 30 Jun 1988; asst
Howe of Fife 1988–89; m 7 Sep 1991 Christine
May Douglas b 24 Mar 1961 d of Alexander
King D. and May Kathleen Stroud; Children:
Alexander Mark b 7 Apr 1994; Douglas Ian b 21
Jul 1996; ord and ind to Castleton and Saughtree
with Newcastleton Congregational Church 8 Sep
1989; became minister of united charge 25 Jun
1993.

LILLIESLEAF (FUF 84; FES II, 182; VIII, 151; IX,
126; X, 73)
Linked 30 Jun 1961 with Ashkirk. Further linked 8
May 1977 with Bowden. Linkage with Ashkirk
terminated 1 Sep 1983. Linkage with Bowden
terminated 21 Oct 1994 in favour of linkage with
Ancrum. Further linked 19 Feb 1999 with Crailing
and Eckford.

1969   HENRY MONCRIEFF JAMIESON
(FES IX, 789; X, 71, 446), ret from RAF Chaplains'
Branch and ind to Ashkirk with Lilliesleaf 8 Oct
1969; ret 31 May 1976.

1977   THOMAS WILSON DONALD
ord and ind to Ashkirk with Bowden with Lilliesleaf
28 Jul 1977, see Bowden.

1988 JAMES WATSON
(FES X, 10 (2)), ind to Bowden with Lilliesleaf 6 Apr 1988, see Bowden.

1994 WILLIAM FRANK CAMPBELL
ind to Ancrum 8 Oct 1991; became minister of linked charge with Lilliesleaf 21 Oct 1994, see Ancrum.

LINTON (FES II, 75; VIII, 131; IX, 110; X, 68)

Linked 23 Jun 1974 with Morebattle and Hownam with Yetholm.

1947 JOHN ANGUS MACGILP
(FES IX, 110, 610; X, 68), trans from Pitsligo to Linton 6 Mar 1947; became minister of linked charge with Makerstoun 12 May 1957 (linkage terminated 21 Oct 1962), then of linked charge with Sprouston 21 Oct 1962; ret 21 May 1974; died 5 Apr 1985.

1974 JOSEPH BROWN
(FES X, 50, 68 (2), 70, 238, 444), ind to Hownam with Morebattle with Yetholm 20 Jul 1967; became minister of linked charge with Linton 23 Jun 1974, see Hownam.

1991 ROBIN DUNLOP McHAFFIE
B 12 Jul 1948 at Glasgow, s of William M. and Margaret Lauder McLellan; educ Bishopbriggs High and Lenzie Academy 1960–66; University of Glasgow 1973–78 (BD); Management Trainee 1967–71; Publicity Manager 1971–73; lic by Presb of Glasgow, Jun 1978; m 20 Jul 1968 Hazel Wallace Lyons b 21 Feb 1950 d of John L. and Jenny Wallace; Children: Sara Elizabeth b 12 Aug 1981; Emma Mary b 26 Mar 1985; Claire Jenny b 16 Mar 1988; ord by Presb of Glasgow during app at Trinity College Calton Mission, May 1979; ind to Glasgow Kinning Park 1 Jun 1981; trans to Linton with Morebattle and Hownam with Yetholm 25 Aug 1991.

MAKERSTOUN AND SMAILHOLM (FES X, 68)

United for second time 1 Jan 1986. Linked 8 Jul 1975 with Stichill, Hume and Nenthorn.

1957 JOHN ANGUS MACGILP
(FES IX, 110, 610; X, 68), ind to Linton 6 Mar 1947; became minister of linked charge with Makerstoun 12 May 1957 (linkage terminated 21 Oct 1962), then of linked charge with Sprouston 21 Oct 1962; ret 21 May 1974.

1966 DAVID SLOAN WALKER
(FES IX, 158, 222, 264; X, 68, 93, 261), trans from Alloa West to Makerstoun with Smailholm 5 Oct 1966; became minister of linked charge with Stichill, Hume and Nenthorn 8 Jul 1975; ret 31 Mar 1978.

1978 JOHN DONALD HENDERSON
(FES IX, 564; X, 88, 290, 328, 356), trans from Cupar Old and St Michael of Tarvit to Makerstoun with Smailholm with Stichill, Hume and Nenthorn 17 Nov 1978; trans to Cluny with Monymusk 18 Nov 1982.

1983 BRUCE JOHN LAIRD HAY
(FES X, 226, 445), ret from RAChD and ind to Makerstoun with Smailholm with Stichill, Hume and Nenthorn 1 Nov 1983; became minister of united charge of Makerstoun and Smailholm with Stichill, Hume and Nenthorn 1 Jan 1986; ret 31 Oct 1997; d Sophia died 1991; d Helen m Barker; d Caroline m Marsden; d Catriona m Cree; s John m Kist.

MINTO (FES II, 131; VIII, 140; IX, 119; X, 68)

Linkage with Ancrum terminated 3 Oct 1976. Linked 7 Oct 1976 with Bedrule.

1968 PETER BRYCE GUNN
(FES IX, 106; X, 63), trans from Roxburgh to Ancrum 7 Apr 1950; became minister of linked charge with Minto 1 May 1968; ret 30 Sep 1976; died 6 Jul 1979.

1976 JAMES FRASER FALCONER
(FES IX, 209; X, 63, 120, 328), ind to Bedrule with Denholm 19 Mar 1975; became minister of linked charge with Minto 7 Oct 1976, see Bedrule.

1978 JOHN THOMSON STUART
(FES X, 150, 448), ind to Bedrule with Denholm with Minto 30 Aug 1978, see Bedrule.

1985 MOIRA HERKES
ord and ind to Bedrule with Denholm with Minto 10 Jun 1985; trans to Prestonpans Prestongrange 8 Nov 1988.

1989 THOMAS PRESTON
trans from Port Glasgow Hamilton Bardrainney to Bedrule with Denholm with Minto 17 May 1989; trans to Edinburgh Old Kirk 28 Jun 1992.

1992 WILLIAM MACGREGOR LONGMUIR
ind to Bedrule with Denholm with Minto 27 Nov 1992, see Bedrule.

MOREBATTLE AND HOWNAM (FES X, 68)

Linked 23 Jun 1974 with Linton with Yetholm.

1956 OLIVER KENNETH WALLACE MACFADDEN
(FES VIII, 134; IX, 112; X, 70), ord and ind to Yetholm 20 Aug 1925; became minister of linked charge with Hownam 25 Nov 1956 and of linked charge with Morebattle 1 Aug 1963; ret 31 Aug 1966; died 24 Mar 1992.

1967   JOSEPH BROWN
(FES X, 50, 68 (2), 70, 238, 444), trans from Musselburgh St Ninian's to Hownam with Morebattle with Yetholm 20 Jul 1967; became minister of linked charge with Linton 23 Jun 1974; ret 1 Apr 1991; d Rosemary m Mark Riley; s Logan m Karen Sinclair.

1991   ROBIN DUNLOP McHAFFIE
ind to Linton with Morebattle and Hownam with Yetholm 25 Aug 1991, see Linton.

OXNAM (FES II, 134; VIII, 141; IX, 111; X, 68)

Linked 24 Jul 1977 with Crailing and Eckford with Roxburgh. Linkage terminated 3 Feb 1999. Continued vacancy declared.

1950   WILLIAM MOFFAT DREW THOMPSON
(FES IX, 111; X, 68), ord and ind to Oxnam 23 Jun 1950; became minister of linked charge with Roxburgh 4 Jul 1961 and of linked charge with Crailing and Eckford 24 Jul 1977; dem 25 Dec 1997; s David m Petronella Juliana Matyisin; s Edward m Rebecca Ann Hewitt; d Jane m (1) Antony Charles Vaughan Wynn (2) George Edward Ramsden; d Agnes m James Michael Joicey.

ROXBURGH (FES II, 86; VIII, 132; IX, 111; X, 69)

Linked 24 Jul 1977 with Crailing and Eckford with Oxnam. Linkage terminated 19 Feb 1999.

1961   WILLIAM MOFFAT DREW THOMPSON
(FES IX, 111; X, 68), ord and ind to Oxnam 23 Jun 1950; became minister of linked charge with Roxburgh 4 Jul 1961and of linked charge with Crailing and Eckford 24 Jul 1977; dem 25 Dec 1997.

STICHILL, HUME AND NENTHORN (FES IX, 112; X, 69)

Linking arrangement with Makerstoun with Smailholm re-established 8 Jul 1975. Continued following union of Makerstoun and Smailholm 1 Jan 1986.

1956   DONALD FRASER FINDLAY
(FES IX, 247, 417; X, 69, 247), trans from Moulin and Pitlochry West to Stichill Hume and Nenthorn 17 May 1956; became minister of linked charge with Makerstoun and Smailholm 7 May 1963 (arrangement terminated 20 Feb 1964); ret 30 Sep 1974; died 8 Aug 1976.

1966   DAVID SLOAN WALKER
(FES IX, 158, 222, 264; X, 68, 93, 261), trans from Alloa West to Makerstoun with Smailholm 5 Oct 1966; became minister of linked charge with Stichill, Hume and Nenthorn 8 Jul 1975; ret 31 Mar 1978.

1978   JOHN DONALD HENDERSON
(FES IX, 564; X, 88, 290, 328, 356), ind to Makerstoun with Smailholm with Stichill, Hume and Nenthorn 17 Nov 1978, see Makerstoun.

1983   BRUCE JOHN LAIRD HAY
(FES X, 226, 445), ind to Makerstoun with Smailholm with Stichill, Hume and Nenthorn 1 Nov 1983; became minister of united charge of Makerstoun and Smailholm with Stichill, Hume and Nenthorn 1 Jan 1986, see Makerstoun and Smailholm.

TEVIOTHEAD (FES II, 140; VIII, 141; IX, 120; X, 69)

Linkage with Hawick Old terminated 25 Jan 1989. Linked 2 Apr 1989 with Hawick Wilton.

1972   DAVID LIVINGSTON WRIGHT
(FES X, 53, 65, 319), trans from Forfar Lowson Memorial to Hawick Old 14 Jan 1971; became minister of linked charge with Teviothead 4 Jun 1972; trans to Stornoway St Columba 18 Feb 1986.

1989   GEORGE WATSON
(FES IX, 547; X, 66, 317), trans from Brechin Maisondieu to Hawick Wilton 6 Apr 1960; became minister of linked charge with Hawick Burnfoot 15 Nov 1973 (until 21 Feb 1978) and of linked charge with Teviothead 2 Apr 1989; ret 30 Nov 1991; died 15 Apr 1998.

1992   BRIAN ROBERT HENDRIE
ord and ind to Hawick Wilton with Teviothead 24 Jan 1992; trans to Falkirk Bainsford 27 Aug 1997.

1998   JOHN SHEDDEN
(FES X, 88), ind to Hawick Wilton with Teviothead 29 May 1998, see Hawick.

YETHOLM (FES IX, 112; X, 70)

Linked 23 Jun 1974 with Morebattle and Hownam with Linton.

1925   OLIVER KENNETH WALLACE MACFADDEN
(FES VIII, 134; IX, 112; X, 70), ord and ind to Yetholm 20 Aug 1925; became minister of linked charge with Hownam 25 Nov 1956 and of linked charge with Morebattle 1 Aug 1963; ret 31 Aug 1966; died 24 Mar 1992.

1967   JOSEPH BROWN
(FES X, 50, 68 (2), 70, 238, 444), ind to Hownam with Morebattle with Yetholm 20 Jul 1967; became minister of linked charge with Linton 23 Jun 1974, see Hownam.

1991   ROBIN DUNLOP McHAFFIE
ind to Linton with Morebattle and Hownam with Yetholm 25 Aug 1991, see Linton.

PRESBYTERY OF ANNANDALE AND ESKDALE

ANNAN OLD (FES II, 241; VIII, 165; IX, 130; X, 76)

1974 WILLIAM BROWN FERGUSON
(FES X, 76), ind to Annan Old 28 Aug 1974; trans to Glasgow Broomhill 18 Feb 1987.

1987 ANDREW FRATER
ord and ind to Annan Old 20 Aug 1987; trans to Milngavie Cairns 16 Mar 1994.

1995 STUART DOUGLAS ROGERSON
trans from Baillieston Mure Memorial to Annan Old 31 Aug 1995; trans to Strathaven West 25 Sep 1996.

1997 DUNCAN JAMES MACPHERSON
B 26 Apr 1967 at Hardgate, s of Alexander Calderwood and Christine Isobel M; educ Glasgow Academy 1972–84; University of Glasgow 1984–88 (BSc), 1989–92 (BD); lic by Presb of Dumbarton 28 Jun 1992; asst Milngavie Cairns 1992–93; m 3 Jul 1993 Jillian Margaret Robertson b 22 Jun 1971 d of Marjorie and John R; ord by Presb of Dumbarton during assistantship at Cairns 6 Oct 1993; introd as Assoc and Youth minister, Christ Church, Bermuda 10 Oct 1993; app Asst (part-time) at Canonbie with Langholm, Ewes and Westerkirk 22 Oct 1995; ind to Annan Old 22 Apr 1997.

ANNAN ST ANDREW'S GREENKNOWE ERSKINE (FES X, 76)

Formed 24 Feb 1974 by union of Annan St Andrew's Greenknowe and Annan Erskine.

1967 ROBERT CRAWFORD
(FES IX, 264; X, 76, 121, 156), trans from Whiting Bay to Annan Erskine 7 Jun 1967; ret 31 Jan 1973.

1969 ANDREW WHITTINGHAM RAE
(FES IX, 128; X, 9, 74, 76 (2)), trans from Edinburgh Fountainbridge to Annan St Andrew's Greenknowe 3 Sep 1969; became minister of united charge with Annan Erskine 24 Feb 1974; ret 31 Dec 1987; d Helen m Black.

1988 ALAN CHALMERS ROSS
B 16 May 1944 at Renfrew, s of Hubert Chalmers R. and Isabella Galloway; educ John Neilson Institute, Paisley 1949–62; Institute of Chartered Accountants of Scotland and University of Glasgow 1965 (CA); Accountancy, (Arthur Young & Co), Australia 1970–78; University of St Andrews 1978–81 (BD); lic by Presb of Paisley 1 Sep 1981; asst St Andrews St Leonard's with Cameron and Largoward 1981–82; Accountancy and Assoc ministry, Presb Church of East Africa, Nairobi 1983–87; ord and ind to St Andrew's Greenknowe Erskine 17 Feb 1988; ret 21 Sep 1997; Scottish Secretary of Feed the Minds 1998–; m 29 Aug 1970 Kay Vivienne Sarll b 24 Nov 1941 d of Arthur S. and Jean Matthews; Children: Morag Victoria b 1 Aug 1972; Callum Chalmers b 25 Oct 1974.

1998 GEORGE KERR LIND
B 3 Jan 1952 at Dumfries, s of George Kerr L. and Margaret Primrose Clark Thomson; educ Dumfries High 1965–68; Chartered Institute of Bankers in Scotland 1968–73 (MCIBS); University of Glasgow 1993–96 (BD); Banking 1968–93; lic by Presb of Falkirk 30 Jun 1996; asst Falkirk Camelon St John's 1996–98; m 26 Apr 1979 Rebecca Adamson Donaldson b 22 Aug 1946 d of John D. and Elizabeth Hannay; ord and ind to St Andrew's Greenknowe Erskine 30 Mar 1998.

APPLEGARTH AND SIBBALDBIE (FES II, 199; VIII, 155; IX, 131; X, 76)

Linked 30 Apr 1980 with Lochmaben.

1972 GEORGE FORGAN KYDD
(FES X, 76, 239), trans from Kilbrandon and Kilchattan to Applegarth and Sibbaldbie 6 Apr 1972; ret 30 Apr 1980; died 17 Dec 1991.

1980 JOHN JACKSON CARRUTHERS OWEN
(FES X, 187), trans from Baillieston St Andrew's to Lochmaben 10 Jan 1980; became minister of linked charge with Applegarth and Sibbaldbie 30 Apr 1980.

BRYDEKIRK (FES II, 242; VIII, 166; IX, 131; X, 76)

Linked 26 Mar 1972 with Hoddam.

1963 JOSEPH MAYCOCK
(FES IX, 153, 479; X, 77, 90), trans from Castle Douglas St Andrew's to Brydekirk 28 Aug 1963; ret 31 Dec 1969; died 12 Nov 1983.

1972 ANDREW GILLESPIE JENKINS
(FES X, 78, 79), ind to Hoddam 4 Apr 1968; became minister of linked charge with Brydekirk 26 Mar 1972, see Hoddam.

1978 NICHOLAS DOUGLAS CHETWYND ARCHER
(FES X, 415), res from service with Overseas Council in Livingstonia, Malawi and ind to Brydekirk with Hoddam 27 Apr 1978; dem 31 Aug 1982; ind to Dores and Boleskin 19 May 1983.

1983 GEORGE IRVING
(FES IX, 177, 478; X, 14, 40, 103), res as Assoc at Canonbie with Langholm Ewes and Westerkirk and introd to Brydekirk with Hoddam (term) 26 Oct 1983; ret 30 Nov 1986; died 4 May 1990.

1987 ALAN HUNTER STUART TAYLOR
(FES X, 80, 365, 401), trans from Holm to Brydekirk with Hoddam 14 Oct 1987; ret 31 Jul 1992; University of Edinburgh 1990–96 (MPhil); Publ: 'The Emergence of Second Century Christianity as a Distinctive Religion: Pagan Perception and Criticism' (Thesis, Univ of Edinburgh, 1996).

1993 SYDNEY EDWIN PEEBLES BEVERIDGE
(FES X, 287, 335), trans from Edinburgh St Aidan's with Stenhouse Saughton to Brydekirk with Hoddam 9 Jun 1993; s Andrew m Shirley Nicol Soutar; s Michael m Fiona Margaret Cowan.

CANONBIE (FUF 81; FES II, 228; VIII, 162; IX, 113; X, 77)

Linkage with Longtown terminated 9 Oct 1980 in favour of linkage with Langholm, Ewes and Westerkirk. This arrangement terminated 1 Dec 1998.

1930 ANDREW WELSH FARMS
(FES VI, 132; VIII, 613; IX, 113, 634; X, 77), trans from Glenlivet to Canonbie 21 Nov 1930; became minister of linked charge with Longtown 1 Jul 1955; ret 30 Jun 1969; died 3 Aug 1976.

1970 JOHN WILLIAM MOULE
(FES X, 77), ord and ind to Canonbie with Longtown 18 Mar 1970; ret 31 Aug 1979; died 29 Apr 1981.

1980 JOHN BALLANTYNE CAIRNS
(FES X, 42), ind to Ewes and Westerkirk with Langholm 16 Apr 1975; became minister of united charge 1 Aug 1980 and of linked charge with Canonbie 9 Oct 1980, see Langholm, Ewes and Westerkirk.

1981 GEORGE IRVING
(FES IX, 177, 478; X, 14, 40, 103), dem from Edinburgh Leith St Paul's 31 Jul 1977; introd as Assoc at Canonbie with Langholm Ewes and Westerkirk 15 Jan 1981; introd to Brydekirk with Hoddam (term) 26 Oct 1983.

1986 JAMES BROWNLEE WATSON
(FES X, 273), dem from Dunfermline Erskine on app as Co-ordinator of Voluntary Services, Bangour Village Hospital 27 May 1972; ind to Canonbie with Langholm, Ewes and Westerkirk 26 Feb 1986; dem 7 Jan 1990; m (2) 11 Nov 1977 Jess Brownlie b 28 Sep 1943 d of James Chambers and Betty Cutler; Children: Fiona Anne b 8 May 1979; Jennifer Louise b 10 Mar 1981.

1990 IAIN MACKENZIE
(FES X, 138, 152), trans from Port Glasgow St Martin's to Canonbie with Langholm, Ewes and Westerkirk 18 Sep 1990; trans to Tarbat 29 Jul 1998.

1999 LINDA J WILLIAMS
res as Assoc at Inverurie St Andrew's 29 Feb 1996; ind to Canonbie 28 May 1999.

CARLISLE CHAPEL STREET (FES VII, 464; VIII, 724; IX, 718; X, 77)

Linked 6 Oct 1980 with Longtown St Andrew's.

1973 WESLEY STEPHEN WILLIAM POOLE
(FES X, 77), trans under mutual eligibility from Presb Church in Ireland and ind to Carlisle 28 Mar 1973; ret 31 Jul 1976.

1977 EWEN SINCLAIR NICOLL
(FES X, 303), trans from Dundee Mains of Fintry to Carlisle 4 Feb 1977; became minister of linked charge with Longtown St Andrew's 6 Oct 1980; trans to Lochalsh and Stromeferry 3 Feb 1984.

1984 JOHN DEAN MASSON
B 13 Jul 1955 at Port Glasgow, s of Charles Blakely M. and Isabel Reid; educ Greenock Academy 1967–73; University of St Andrews 1973–77 (MA), University of Aberdeen 1977–80 (BD), 1980–83 (PhD); Open University 1993–95 (BSc); Queen's University, Belfast 1996–99 (DClinPsych); lic by Presb of Aberdeen, Jun 1980; asst Aberdeen North of St Andrew 1983–84; m (1) 17 Feb 1979 Isabel Duncan b 17 Apr 1957 d of Philip and Margaret D; Children: Alasdair b 9 Apr 1985; divorced, m (2) 23 Jun 1990 Margaret Willis b 25 Nov 1958 d of Joseph and Mary; ord and ind to Carlisle with Longtown St Andrew's 4 Jul 1984; dem 11 Jan 1987 to take up app with Inland Revenue; res Sep 1996 to take up app as Clinical Psychologist in field of learning disabilities.

1987 WILLIAM DAVID BROWN
B 21 Aug 1948 at Edinburgh, s of Eric B. and Elizabeth McLaren; educ Forrester High, Edinburgh 1960–64; Moray House College, Edinburgh 1976–78 (CQSW); University of Edinburgh 1983–86 (BD); Civil Service 1965–70; Social Work 1970–83; lic by Presb of Melrose and Peebles 29 Jun 1986; asst Upper Tweeddale 1986–87; m 21 Aug 1971 Shirley Armour b 7 Dec 1947 d of Joseph A.

and Violet Hiddleston; Children: Susan b 18 Nov 1973; David b 9 Jan 1976; ord and ind to Carlisle Chapel Street with Longtown St Andrew's 6 May 1987.

1992 SANDRA BLACK
introd as Assoc at Carlisle Chapel Street with Longtown St Andrew's and at Gretna Old, Gretna St Andrew's and Half Morton and Kirkpatrick Fleming 30 Apr 1992; app by Yorkhill NHS Trust, Glasgow, as Hospital Chaplain 8 Sep 1997.

DALTON (FES II, 201; VIII, 155; IX, 131; X, 77)

Linked 13 Nov 1957 with Hightae. Further linked 1 Jul 1976 with St Mungo.

1958 JOHN HALL PATTERSON
(FES IX, 501, 745; X, 77), [correction: Patterson, not Paterson as in Vol X, 77]; res from service with FMC in Bombay, India and ind to Dalton with Hightae 30 Jul 1958; ret 29 Feb 1976; died 28 Jan 1992.

1976 JAMES S GRIEVE
ord and ind to Dalton with Hightae with St Mungo 16 Nov 1976; died 5 Feb 1987.

1988 WILLIAM LOGAN KIRK
B 6 Jun 1931 at Gullane, s of Henry Bruce K. and Catherine Stewart Paterson Logan; educ Merchiston Castle, Edinburgh 1936–49; University of Edinburgh 1951–57 (MA, BD), 1965–66 (CAg); University of Aberdeen 1966–68 (MTh); Farm Work 1959–66, 1968–86; lic by Presb of Haddington and Dunbar 9 Apr 1957; asst Edinburgh St Giles' Cathedral 1957–59, Muirhouse 1986–87; ord and ind to Dalton with Hightae with St Mungo 15 Mar 1988.

DORNOCK (FES II, 244; VIII, 167; IX, 132; X, 77)

1926 CHARLES EDWARD STEWART
(FES VIII, 167; IX, 132; X, 77), ord and ind to Dornock 8 Apr 1926; ret 31 Dec 1966; died 28 Jun 1994.

1967 RONALD STANLEY SEAMAN
(FES X, 77), ord and ind to Dornock 4 May 1967; d Ilona m Michael Peter Swale; d Morven m Steven Walker.

ESKDALEMUIR (FES II, 232; VIII, 162; IX, 132; X, 77)

Linked 8 Aug 1962 with Hutton and Corrie. Further linked 31 Dec 1986 with Tundergarth.

1962 JOHN CAMPBELL LOUGH
(FES IX, 60, 355; X, 77, 79, 184, 212), ind to Hutton and Corrie 27 Jan 1960; became minister of linked charge with Eskdalemuir 8 Aug 1962; died 16 Apr 1979.

1980 ALEXANDER CAMERON GIBSON
(FES X, 109, 374), trans from Nairn Old to Eskdalemuir with Hutton and Corrie 9 Sep 1980; became minister of linked charge with Tundergarth 31 Dec 1986; ret 30 Jun 1990; s Ian m Maria Stewart; s David m Shirley Clark; s Alan m Jill Littlewood; Publ: *Vet in the Vestry* (Lochar and Penguin, 1987); *Poultry in the Pulpit* (Lochar, 1988); *Dog Collar Diary* (House of Lochar, 1995).

1991 JOHN GROOM MILLER
trans from Sandsting and Aithsting with Walls to Eskdalemuir with Hutton and Corrie with Tundergarth 13 Feb 1991; trans to Port Glasgow St Martin's 14 May 1998.

GRETNA OLD, ST ANDREW'S AND HALF MORTON AND KIRKPATRICK FLEMING (FES X, 77, 78, 79)

Formed 30 Sep 1981 by union of Gretna Old, St Andrew's, Half Morton and Kirkpatrick Fleming.

1936 WILLIAM PORTER FRASER
(FES IX, 133; X, 78), ord and ind to St Andrew's 29 Apr 1936; ret 3 Jan 1975; died 8 Jul 1981.

1968 JAMES CHARLES GREGORY
(FES X, 78), ord and ind to Kirkpatrick Fleming with Half Morton 11 Oct 1968; trans to Blantyre St Andrew's 2 Feb 1978.

1975 CHARLES BRYAN HASTON
(FES X, 78), ord and ind to Gretna Old with Gretna St Andrew's 6 Aug 1975; became minister of united charge with Half Morton and Kirkpatrick Fleming 30 Sep 1981; app Clerk (part-time) to Presb of Annandale and Eskdale 28 Jun 1983.

1980 WILLIAM BLACK
(FES X, 297), dem from Carnoustie Panbride 30 Sep 1978; introd to Half Morton and Kirkpatrick Fleming (term) 20 Feb 1980; ind to Kirkinner with Sorbie 19 Nov 1981.

1992 SANDRA BLACK
introd as Assoc at Carlisle Chapel Street with St Andrew's and at Gretna Old, Gretna St Andrew's and Half Morton and Kirkpatrick Fleming 30 Apr 1992, see Carlisle.

HIGHTAE (FUF 97; FES IX, 133; X, 78)

Linked 13 Nov 1957 with Dalton.

1958 JOHN HALL PATTERSON
(FES IX, 501, 745; X, 77), ind to Dalton with Hightae 30 Jul 1958, see Dalton.

1976 JAMES S GRIEVE
ord and ind to Dalton with Hightae with St Mungo 16 Nov 1976; died 5 Feb 1987.

1988 WILLIAM LOGAN KIRK
ord and ind to Dalton with Hightae with St Mungo
15 Mar 1988, see Dalton.

HODDAM (FES II, 248; VIII, 168; IX, 133; X, 78)

Linked 26 Mar 1972 with Brydekirk.

1968 ANDREW GILLESPIE JENKINS
(FES X, 78, 79), trans from Johnstone with Hope
Memorial to Hoddam 4 Apr 1968; became minister
of linked charge with Brydekirk 26 Mar 1972; trans
to Inch 17 Aug 1977.

1978 NICHOLAS DOUGLAS CHETWYND
ARCHER
(FES X, 415), ind to Brydekirk with Hoddam 27
Apr 1978, see Brydekirk.

1983 GEORGE IRVING
(FES IX, 177, 478; X, 14, 40, 103), introd to
Brydekirk with Hoddam (term) 26 Oct 1983, see
Brydekirk.

1987 ALAN HUNTER STUART TAYLOR
(FES X, 80, 365, 401), ind to Brydekirk with
Hoddam 14 Oct 1987, see Brydekirk.

1993 SYDNEY EDWIN PEEBLES
BEVERIDGE
(FES X, 287, 335), ind to Brydekirk with Hoddam
9 Jun 1993, see Brydekirk.

HUTTON AND CORRIE (FES II, 205; VIII, 156;
IX, 134; X, 79)

Linked 8 Aug 1962 with Eskdalemuir.

1960 JOHN CAMPBELL LOUGH
(FES IX, 60, 355; X, 77, 79, 184, 212), res from
term app at Glasgow Woodside 6 Sep 1959; ind to
Hutton and Corrie 27 Jan 1960; became minister
of linked charge with Eskdalemuir 8 Aug 1962; died
16 Apr 1979.

1980 ALEXANDER CAMERON GIBSON
(FES X, 109, 374), trans from Nairn Old to
Eskdalemuir with Hutton and Corrie 9 Sep 1980;
became minister of linked charge with Tundergarth
31 Dec 1986; ret 30 Jun 1990.

1991 JOHN GROOM MILLER
ind to Eskdalemuir with Hutton and Corrie with
Tundergarth 13 Feb 1991, see Eskdalemuir.

JOHNSTONE (FES X, 79)

Linked 18 Feb 1971 with Kirkpatrick Juxta.

1971 IAN GAIRDNER RAMSAY
(FES X, 79, 402), trans from Sanday to Johnstone
with Kirkpatrick Juxta 6 Oct 1971; died 16 Mar
1984.

1986 JOHN MASSON STEWART
(FES X, 74, 172, 178), trans from Glasgow Renfield
St Stephen's to Johnstone with Kirkpatrick Juxta
17 Jun 1986; d Christine m Fitzpatrick.

KIRKPATRICK JUXTA (FES II, 210; VIII, 157; IX,
134; X, 79)

Linked 18 Feb 1971 with Johnstone.

1971 IAN GAIRDNER RAMSAY
(FES X, 79, 402), trans from Sanday to Johnstone
with Kirkpatrick Juxta 6 Oct 1971; died 16 Mar
1984.

1986 JOHN MASSON STEWART
(FES X, 74, 172, 178), trans from Glasgow Renfield
St Stephen's to Johnstone with Kirkpatrick Juxta
17 Jun 1986.

KIRTLE-EAGLESFIELD (FES X, 79)

Linked 17 Apr 1972 with Middlebie with Waterbeck.

1960 HUGH EDWARD BAIKIE
(FES IX, 728; X, 79, 416), res from service with
Overseas Council at Rajasthan and ind to Kirtle-
Eaglesfield 17 Feb 1960; ret 30 Sep 1971; died 28
Oct 1981.

1972 CHARLES RAYMOND VINCENT
(FES IX, 433; X, 79, 97, 106, 257), trans from
Wigtown to Kirtle-Eaglesfield with Middlebie with
Waterbeck 2 Nov 1972; trans to Stonehouse St
Ninian's 7 May 1981.

1983 ERIC BURKINSHAW
(FES X, 277), trans from Coatbridge Gartsherrie
to Kirtle-Eaglesfield with Middlebie with Waterbeck
8 Nov 1983; ret 30 Apr 1986; died 26 Jan 1999.

1987 LESLIE WILLIAM THORNE
ord and ind to Kirtle-Eaglesfield with Middlebie
with Waterbeck 21 Jul 1987; trans to Coatbridge
Coats 29 Sep 1992.

1993 FREDA MARSHALL
ord and ind to Kirtle-Eaglesfield with Middlebie with
Waterbeck 26 May 1993; trans to Colonsay and
Oronsay with Kilbrandon and Kilchattan 15 Aug
1997.

1999 TREVOR CHARLES WILLIAMS
trans from Peterculter St Peter's to Kirtle-
Eaglesfield with Middlebie with Waterbeck 12
Jan 1999.

LANGHOLM, EWES AND WESTERKIRK (FES X,
64, 67, 69)

Formed 1 Aug 1980 by union of Langholm, Ewes
and Westerkirk. Linked 9 Oct 1980 with Canonbie.
Linkage terminated 1 Dec 1998.

1956 MATTHEW JAMES CAMERON DINWOODIE
(FES IX, 375, 455, 557; X, 67, 224), trans from Rosneath to Langholm Erskine 27 Jun 1956; ret 31 Mar 1970; died 8 Apr 1979.

1960 THOMAS CALVERT
(FES IX, 186, 413, 787; X, 67), dem from Blackburn St George's and ind under mutual eligibility to Langholm Old 9 Jun 1960; ret 31 Aug 1973; died 11 Oct 1983.

1975 JOHN BALLANTYNE CAIRNS
(FES X, 42), ord by Presb of Elgin during assistantship at Elgin St Giles' 20 Jan 1974; ind to Ewes and Westerkirk with Langholm 16 Apr 1975; became minister of united charge 1 Aug 1980 and of linked charge with Canonbie 9 Oct 1980; trans to Dumbarton Riverside 29 Aug 1985.

1981 GEORGE IRVING
(FES IX, 177, 478; X, 14, 40, 103), introd as Assoc at Canonbie with Langholm Ewes and Westerkirk 15 Jan 1981, see Canonbie.

1986 JAMES BROWNLEE WATSON
(FES X, 273), ind to Canonbie with Langholm, Ewes and Westerkirk 26 Feb 1986, see Canonbie.

1990 IAIN MACKENZIE
(FES X, 138, 152), trans from Port Glasgow St Martin's to Canonbie with Langholm, Ewes and Westerkirk 18 Sep 1990; trans to Tarbat 29 Jul 1998.

LOCHMABEN (FES X, 80)

Linked 30 Apr 1980 with Applegarth and Sibbaldbie.

1971 ROBERT McREADY FARQUHARSON
(FES X, 80, 275), trans from Kelty North to Lochmaben 22 Sep 1971; died 3 Mar 1979.

1980 JOHN JACKSON CARRUTHERS OWEN
(FES X, 187), trans from Baillieston St Andrew's to Lochmaben 10 Jan 1980; became minister of linked charge with Applegarth and Sibbaldbie 30 Apr 1980.

LOCKERBIE DRYFESDALE (FES X, 80)

Formed 31 Dec 1986 by union of Lockerbie Dryfesdale and Trinity and Lockerbie St Cuthbert's. Linkage of St Cuthbert's with Tundergarth terminated same date.

1939 JOHN FLETCHER
(FES IX, 136; X, 80), ord and ind to Lockerbie Trinity 1 Sep 1939; ret 29 Feb 1972; died 17 Mar 1990.

1958 HUGH DEWI GRIFFITH
(FES X, 80), res from RAChD and ind to St Cuthbert's 25 Sep 1958; became minister of linked

charge with Tundergarth 1 Feb 1963; ret 31 Dec 1986; died 11 Oct 1991.

1966 JAMES MITCHELL ANNAND
(FES X, 80 (2), 243), trans from Fort William Duncansburgh to Dryfesdale 14 Jun 1966; became minister of united charge with Trinity 22 Feb 1973 and of united charge with St Cuthbert's 31 Dec 1986; ret 3 Jul 1995.

1996 DAVID ALMOND
B 3 Dec 1946 at Edinburgh, s of Bernard A. and Dorothy Roseberry Tait; educ Broughton Senior Secondary, Edinburgh 1959–65; University of Edinburgh 1991–95 (BD); Employment Adviser; Recruitment Consultant 1966–91; lic by Presb of Dunfermline; asst Dalgety 1995–96; m 23 May 1986 Anne Christina Norris b 30 Aug 1938 d of Harold Gordon N. and Annie Melrose Young; ord and ind to Dryfesdale 10 Sep 1996.

LONGTOWN ST ANDREW'S (FES X, 66)

Linked 6 Oct 1980 with Carlisle Chapel Street.

1955 ANDREW WELSH FARMS
(FES VI, 132; VIII, 613; IX, 113, 634; X, 77), ind to Canonbie 21 Nov 1930; became minister of linked charge with Longtown 1 Jul 1955, see Canonbie.

1970 JOHN WILLIAM MOULE
(FES X, 77), ord and ind to Canonbie with Longtown 18 Mar 1970; ret 31 Aug 1979; died 29 Apr 1981.

1980 EWEN SINCLAIR NICOLL
(FES X, 303), ind to Carlisle 4 Feb 1977; became minister of linked charge with Longtown St Andrew's 6 Oct 1980, see Carlisle.

1984 JOHN DEAN MASSON
ord and ind to Carlisle with Longtown St Andrew's 4 Jul 1984, see Carlisle.

1987 WILLIAM DAVID BROWN
ord and ind to Carlisle Chapel Street with Longtown St Andrew's 6 May 1987, see Carlisle.

1992 SANDRA BLACK
introd as Assoc at Carlisle Chapel Street with St Andrew's and at Gretna Old, Gretna St Andrew's and Half Morton and Kirkpatrick Fleming 30 Apr 1992, see Carlisle.

MIDDLEBIE (FES II, 252; VIII, 169; IX, 136; X, 80)

Linked 23 Jul 1959 with Waterbeck. Further linked 17 Apr 1972 with Kirtle-Eaglesfield.

1949 HUGH ALEXANDER REID MACFARLANE
(FES IX, 59, 136; X, 81), trans from Carron to Middlebie with Eaglesfield 26 Jan 1949; became minister of linked charge with Waterbeck 23 Jul 1959; ret 18 Apr 1972; died 5 May 1987.

1972 CHARLES RAYMOND VINCENT
(FES IX, 433; X, 79, 97, 106, 257), ind to Kirtle-Eaglesfield with Middlebie with Waterbeck 2 Nov 1972, see Kirtle-Eaglesfield.

1983 ERIC BURKINSHAW
(FES X, 277), ind to Kirtle-Eaglesfield with Middlebie with Waterbeck 8 Nov 1983, see Kirtle-Eaglesfield.

1987 LESLIE WILLIAM THORNE
ord and ind to Kirtle-Eaglesfield with Middlebie 21 Jul 1987, see Kirtle-Eaglesfield.

1993 FREDA MARSHALL
ord and ind to Kirtle-Eaglesfield with Middlebie with Waterbeck 26 May 1993, see Kirtle-Eaglesfield.

1999 TREVOR CHARLES WILLIAMS
trans from Peterculter St Peter's to Kirtle-Eaglesfield with Middlebie with Waterbeck 12 Jan 1999.

MOFFAT (FES X, 81)

Formed 8 Aug 1960 by union of Moffat St Andrew's and Moffat Well Road. Linked 18 Feb 1971 with Wamphray.

1946 DONALD MACDONALD
(FES VII, 575; VIII, 256; IX, 136, 739; X, 81), res as Senior Staff Chaplain in India and ind to Moffat Well Road 15 Jul 1946; ret 31 Oct 1958; died 21 Nov 1986.

1961 GEORGE GORDON CAMPBELL
(FES IX, 11, 150, 474; X, 7, 81, 297), trans from Edinburgh Craiglockhart to Moffat 5 Apr 1961; became minister of linked charge with Wamphray 18 Feb 1971; trans to Abernyte 23 Jan 1974.

1975 GERALD CHRISTOPHER MOULE
(FES X, 81), ord by Presb of Aberdeen during assistantship at West of St Nicholas 3 Mar 1974; ind to Moffat with Wamphray 19 Mar 1975; dem 30 Sep 1999; Addl children: Emily Jane b 10 Jan 1980.

ST MUNGO (FES II, 220; VIII, 160; IX, 136; X, 81)

Linked 1 Jul 1976 with Dalton.

1967 ROBERT WILLIAM MATHESON
(FES IX, 502, 680, 742; X, 32, 56, 81), trans from Ormiston to St Mungo 24 Oct 1967; ret 31 Dec 1975; died 28 Jun 1988.

1976 JAMES S GRIEVE
ord and ind to Dalton with Hightae with St Mungo 16 Nov 1976; died 5 Feb 1987.

1988 WILLIAM LOGAN KIRK
ord and ind to Dalton with Hightae with St Mungo 15 Mar 1988, see Dalton.

TUNDERGARTH (FES II, 222; VIII, 161; IX, 137; X, 81)

Linkage with Lockerbie St Cuthbert's terminated 31 Dec 1986. Linked same date with Eskdalemuir.

1955 JOHN WILLIAM FAIRBAIRN
(FES X, 81), ord and ind to Tundergarth 16 Nov 1955; ret 31 Dec 1963; died 11 Oct 1984.

1963 HUGH DEWI GRIFFITH
(FES X, 80), ind to Lockerbie St Cuthbert's 25 Sep 1958; became minister of linked charge with Tundergarth 1 Feb 1963, see St Cuthbert's.

1986 ALEXANDER CAMERON GIBSON
(FES X, 109, 374), trans from Nairn Old to Eskdalemuir with Hutton and Corrie 9 Sep 1980; became minister of linked charge with Tundergarth 31 Dec 1986; ret 30 Jun 1990.

1991 JOHN GROOM MILLER
ind to Eskdalemuir with Hutton and Corrie with Tundergarth 13 Feb 1991, see Eskdalemuir.

WAMPHRAY (FES II, 224; VIII, 161; IX, 137; X, 81)

Linked 18 Feb 1971 with Moffat.

1975 GERALD CHRISTOPHER MOULE
(FES X, 81), ind to Moffat with Wamphray 19 Mar 1975, see Moffat.

WATERBECK (FUF 100; FES IX, 137; X, 81)

Linked 23 Jul 1959 with Middlebie. Further linked 17 Apr 1972 with Kirtle-Eaglesfield.

1959 HUGH ALEXANDER REID MACFARLANE
(FES IX, 59, 136; X, 81), ind to Middlebie with Eaglesfield 26 Jan 1949; became minister of linked charge with Waterbeck 23 Jul 1959, see Middlebie.

1972 CHARLES RAYMOND VINCENT
(FES IX, 433; X, 79, 97, 106, 257), ind to Kirtle-Eaglesfield with Middlebie with Waterbeck 2 Nov 1972, see Kirtle-Eaglesfield.

1983 ERIC BURKINSHAW
(FES X, 277), ind to Kirtle-Eaglesfield with Middlebie with Waterbeck 8 Nov 1983, see Kirtle-Eaglesfield.

1987 LESLIE WILLIAM THORNE
ord and ind to Kirtle-Eaglesfield with Middlebie with Waterbeck 21 Jul 1987, see Kirtle-Eaglesfield.

1993 FREDA MARSHALL
ord and ind to Kirtle-Eaglesfield with Middlebie with Waterbeck 26 May 1993, see Kirtle-Eaglesfield.

1999 TREVOR CHARLES WILLIAMS
trans from Peterculter St Peter's to Kirtle-Eaglesfield with Middlebie with Waterbeck 12 Jan 1999.

PRESBYTERY OF DUMFRIES AND KIRKCUDBRIGHT

ANWOTH AND GIRTHON (FES II, 385; VIII, 199; IX, 151; X, 89)

Linked 22 Mar 1990 with Borgue.

1971 JEOFFREYS JAMES ARTHUR CARMICHAEL
(FES IX, 348; X, 80, 89, 91, 209), trans from Lochmaben to Girthon 18 Mar 1971; became minister of united charge with Anwoth 25 Oct 1975; ret 15 Nov 1983; died 4 Aug 1994.

1984 CALLUM THOMSON O' DONNELL
ord and ind to Anwoth and Girthon 12 Jun 1984; trans to Troon Old 12 Nov 1989.

1990 AUSTIN URQUHART ERSKINE
B 29 Sep 1935 at Glasgow, s of George Maxwell E. and Elizabeth Rae McIntyre Paterson; educ North Kelvinside, Glasgow 1947–52; University of Glasgow 1982–85 (non-grad course); Structural Engineering 1952–82; lic by Presb of Glasgow 23 Jan 1986; asst Glasgow High Carntyne 1984–85, Partick East and Dowanhill 1985–86; m 4 Apr 1966 Sheila Margaret Campbell b 20 Nov 1931 d of Gordon C. and Jane Wilson; ord and ind to Banff St Mary's 13 Jun 1986; trans to Anwoth and Girthon with Borgue 25 Jul 1990.

AUCHENCAIRN AND RERRICK (FES X, 89, 92)

Continued vacancy from 1987 until 1991. Formed 10 Nov 1991 by union of Auchencairn and Rerrick. Linked same date with Buittle and Kelton.

1972 COLIN RAYMOND WILLIAMSON
(FES X, 89), ord and ind to Auchencairn with Rerrick 17 May 1972; trans to Leith St Paul's 30 Jun 1978.

1979 WILLIAM MUIR McPHERSON
(FES X, 107, 160), trans from Glasgow Gorbals to Auchencairn with Rerrick 16 Mar 1979; ret 31 Dec 1986; died 10 Feb 1991.

1992 JAMES HARVEY SINCLAIR
(FES X, 52), trans from Ashkirk with Caddonfoot with Selkirk to Auchencairn and Rerrick with Buittle and Kelton 18 Jun 1992; University of Edinburgh 1986–87 (DipMin).

BALMACLELLAN AND KELLS (FES X, 89, 91)

Formed 9 Dec 1992 by union of Balmaclellan and Kells. Linked with Dalry same date. Further linked with Carsphairn 24 Apr 1994. (Balmaclellan with Kells linked with Balmaghie 22 Oct 1978 until 9 Mar 1988).

1968 PETER DAVID THOMSON
(FES X, 89), ord and ind to Balmaclellan with Kells 14 Jun 1968; trans to Comrie and Strowan 27 Apr 1978.

1979 DAVID MURRAY McKAY
ord and ind to Balmaclellan with Balmaghie with Kells 31 Jul 1979; trans to Fyvie 13 Mar 1987.

1988 ROBERT HUGH DRUMMOND
(FES X, 77, 287, 381), trans from Pitsligo with Sandhaven to Balmaclellan with Kells 29 Sep 1988; ret 31 Oct 1991.

1993 WILLIAM CLEMENT ROBB
(FES X, 405), trans from Catrine with Sorn to Balmaclellan and Kells with Dalry 2 Jun 1993; dem 30 Aug 1993.

1994 DAVID SINCLAIR BARTHOLOMEW
B 2 Jul 1956 at Edinburgh, s of Robert Gordon B. and Jean Symington Thin; educ Edinburgh Academy 1962–74; University of St Andrews 1974–78 (BSc); University of Birmingham 1978–79 (MSc); University of Leicester 1980–84 (PhD); University of Aberdeen 1989–92 (BD); Geologist with Zimbabwe Geological Survey 1984–89; lic by Presb of Aberdeen 25 Jun 1992; asst Dyce 1993–94; m 15 Aug 1992 Heidi Louise Wilson b 8 Mar 1971 d of Stephen Scott and Florence Jean Elizabeth W; Children: Fiona Jean b 7 Nov 1994; James Riddell b 21 Aug 1996; Stuart Scott b 27 May 1999; ord and ind to Balmaclellan and Kells with Carsphairn with Dalry 12 Oct 1994;   Publ: Various geological publications.

BALMAGHIE (FES IX, 151; X, 89)

Linked with Balmaclellan 22 Oct 1978. Arrangement terminated 9 Mar 1988. Linked with Tarff and Twynholm same date.

1968 JAMES KNOX NAPIER
(FES IX, 533, 567; X, 89, 110, 329), trans from Irvine Relief to Balmaghie 6 Jun 1968; ret 31 May 1978.

1979   DAVID MURRAY McKAY
ord and ind to Balmaclellan with Balmaghie with Kells 31 Jul 1979; trans to Fyvie 13 Mar 1987.

1988   CHRISTOPHER WALLACE
B 27 Jan 1960 at Stirling, s of John W. and Jean Nicol; educ Lornshill Academy, Alloa 1972–76; University of Glasgow 1985 (BD), 1987 (DipMin); Distillers Co Ltd 1976–78; lic by Presb of Glasgow 1 Sep 1987; asst East Kilbride Claremont 1987–88; Jul 1981 Mary McGilp: Children: Jonathan b 1982; Andrew b 1986; Rebekah b 1990; ord and ind to Balmaghie with Tarff and Twynholm 12 Jul 1988; app Chaplain (part-time) to Dumfries Prison 1 Sep 1993.

BORGUE (FES IX, 152; X, 89)

Linked 22 May 1977 with Tongland with Twynholm. Linkage terminated 9 Mar 1988. Linked 22 Mar 1990 with Anworth and Girthon.

1964   JOHN McKIE HUNTER
(FES IX, 129, 163, 450; X, 89, 266), trans from Logie Kirk to Borgue 28 Oct 1964; ret 16 Jul 1970; died 4 Feb 1991.

1971   WILLIAM DOUGLAS HUTCHEON
(FE IX, 157, 425; X, 89, 340), trans from Corgaff and Strathdon to Borgue 16 Sep 1971; ret 31 Mar 1977; died 4 May 1977.

1977   BRUCE RITCHIE
ord and ind to Borgue with Tongland with Twynholm, Oct 1977; trans to Crieff St Andrew's and St Michael's 3 Jun 1987.

1990   AUSTIN URQUHART ERSKINE
ind to Anworth and Girthon with Borgue 25 Jul 1990, see Anworth.

BUITTLE AND KELTON (FES X, 90, 91)

Formed 20 Mar 1983 by union of Buittle and Kelton. Linked same date with Castle Douglas St Andrew's. Linkage terminated 24 Sep 1989. Linked 10 Nov 1991 with Auchencairn and Rerrick.

1959   RICHARD THOMAS HASSALL
(FES IX, 381; X, 90, 144, 228), trans from Glasgow Giffnock Orchard Park to Buittle 28 Jan 1959; ret 31 Aug 1965; died 16 Apr 1980.

1966   EDWARD RANKINE MARR
(FES IX, 217, 416; X, 90, 124), trans from Johnstone St Andrew's Trinity to Buittle 5 May 1966; ret 1 Apr 1977; Publ: 'The Story of Buittle Parish Church' (private, 1977).

1969   THOMAS WATERTON LUND
(FES IX, 58, 214, 306, 379, 451; X, 91, 267), trans from Sauchie to Kelton 1 May 1969; became minister of linked charge with Buittle 2 Oct 1977; ret 30 Jun 1982; died 2 May 1991.

1983   ANDREW FORTUNE SWAN
ord and ind to Buittle and Kelton with Castle Douglas St Andrew's 22 Sep 1983; became minister of Buittle and Kelton following termination of linkage with Castle Douglas St Andrew's 27 Dec 1989; trans to Loanhead 24 Oct 1991.

1992   JAMES HARVEY SINCLAIR
(FES X, 52), trans from Ashkirk with Caddonfoot with Selkirk to Auchencairn and Rerrick with Buittle and Kelton 18 Jun 1992.

CAERLAVEROCK (FUF 105; FES VIII, 170; IX, 138; X, 82)

Linked 2 Oct 1983 with Dumfries St Michael's and South. Arrangement terminated 1 Jul 1996. Continued vacancy declared.

1960   THOMAS DEWAR POLLOCK
(FES IX, 132; X, 82), trans under mutual eligibility from Presb Church of England and ind to Caerlaverock and Glencaple 28 Jan 1960; ret 31 Oct 1981; died 16 Sep 1987.

1983   JOHN PAGAN
ind to Dumfries St Michael's 7 Sep 1978; became minister of linked charge with Caerlaverock 2 Oct 1983; ret 31 Dec 1994; died 15 Feb 1998.

1983   ALBERT BROWN ELDER
(FES X, 84), ord and ind to South and Townhead 1 Dec 1960; became Collegiate minister of united charge with St Michael's linked with Caerlaverock 2 Oct 1983, see Dumfries St Michael's and South.

CARSPHAIRN (FES IX, 153; X, 90)

Linked 24 Feb 1972 with Dalry. Linkage terminated 9 Dec 1992. Linked 24 Apr 1994 with Balmaclellan and Kells with Dalry.

1961   JOHN ALEXANDER
(FES IX, 420, 507, 605, 704; X, 90, 301), trans from Dundee Downfield Strathmartine to Carsphairn 2 Nov 1961; ret 30 Jul 1970; died 2 Dec 1980.

1972   JOHN ROBERT MILLER
(FES X, 35, 90, 206), trans from Bonnybridge to Carsphairn with Dalry 24 Aug 1972; ret 9 Dec 1992; d Josephine m Sutcliffe; d Amanda m Craig; Publ: *The Kirk at Carsphairn 1640–1990* (McElroy, 1990).

1994   DAVID SINCLAIR BARTHOLOMEW
ord and ind to Balmaclellan and Kells with Carsphairn with Dalry 12 Oct 1994, see Balmaclellan.

CASTLE DOUGLAS PARISH (FES X, 90)

Formed 27 Dec 1989 by union of Castle Douglas St Andrew's and St Ringan's. Linkage (20 Mar 1983) of Castle Douglas St Andrew's with Buittle and Kelton terminated 27 Dec 1989 to allow for union. Linkage (6 Jan 1979) of Castle Douglas St Ringan's with Crossmichael and Parton terminated 27 Dec 1989.

1960 ROBERT HAMILL
(FES X, 90, 445), ret from RAChD and ind to Castle Douglas St Ringan's 25 Feb 1960; ret 27 Dec 1989.

1964 JAMES ANDREW BYERS
(FES IX, 168; X, 90, 98, 188), trans from Blantyre Stonefield to St Andrew's 19 Mar 1964; ret 20 Mar 1983; died 23 Dec 1985.

1983 ANDREW FORTUNE SWAN
ord and ind to Buittle and Kelton with Castle Douglas St Andrew's 22 Sep 1983; became minister of Buittle and Kelton following termination of linkage with Castle Douglas St Andrew's 27 Dec 1989; trans to Loanhead 24 Oct 1991.

1990 JOHN HAMILTON FRASER
(FES X, 128), dem from Fagley and Eccleshill, URC, Bradford and ind to Castle Douglas 3 Jul 1990.

CLOSEBURN (FES II, 309; VIII, 182; IX, 138; X, 82)

Linked 27 Apr 1980 with Durisdeer.

1960 DONALD JOHN MACGREGOR
(FES IX, 210; X, 82, 120), trans from Shiskine to Closeburn 9 Jun 1960; ret 31 Oct 1979; died 26 Sep 1996.

1980 JAMES WILLIAM SCOTT
(FES IX, 142; X, 84), ind to Durisdeer 24 Sep 1953; became minister of linked charge with Closeburn 27 Apr 1980.

COLVEND, SOUTHWICK AND KIRKBEAN (FES X, 82, 85)

Formed 11 Jun 1978 by union of Colvend and Southwick and Kirkbean.

1974 THOMAS SCOTT
(FES IX, 560, 706; X, 50, 85, 326, 425), trans from Loanhead West to Kirkbean 7 Mar 1974; died 16 Dec 1977.

1974 IAN WILLIAM ROBERTSON
(FES X, 82, 109, 157, 171), trans from Glasgow Crosshill Queen's Park to Colvend and Southwick 26 Sep 1974; became minister of united charge with Kirkbean 11 Jun 1978; ret 31 Dec 1995; s David died 22 Jul 1996; s Graham m Debby Welsh.

1996 DANNY KNIGHT
B 19 Jun 1943 at London, s of Leslie K. and Joan Hollidge; educ Solihull School 1955–61; College of Saints Mark and John, London 1962–65; University of St Andrews 1986–90; Bookselling and Publishing 1970–85; lic by Presb of Perth 1 Jul 1990; asst Scone Old 1990–91; m 3 Jul 1971 Helen Wightman b 13 Jan 1943 d of Donald Fraser W. and Jane Thomson Small Denholm; Children: Gary (adopted) b 22 Jul 1968; Gavin Fraser b 27 Apr 1972; ord and ind to Sandsting and Aithsting with Walls 4 Jul 1991; trans to Colvend, Southwick and Kirkbean 2 Jul 1996.

CORSOCK AND KIRKPATRICK DURHAM (FES X, 90, 91)

Formed 17 May 1989 by union of Corsock and Kirkpatrick Durham. Linked same date with Crossmichael and Parton.

1946 GEORGE BAIN BURNET
(FUF 255; FES IX, 154, 458; X, 90), ind to Corsock 17 Oct 1946; ret 28 Feb 1957; died 2 May 1979.

1958 JAMES LYLE MACLEOD
(FES IX, 396, 597, 709), trans from Queensferry to Balmaclellan with Corsock 31 Jul 1958; trans to Latheron 25 Oct 1962.

1959 GRAHAM MURRAY LITTLE
(FES IX, 10, 72, 474; X, 44, 91), trans from Eddleston to Kirkpatrick Durham 23 Jul 1959; became minister of linked charge with Corsock 7 Jul 1963; ret 26 Apr 1970; died 31 May 1976.

1970 ANDREW CAMPBELL MACKAY
(FES X, 90), directed moral rearmament work in Italy 1950–70; ind to Corsock with Kirkpatrick Durham 11 Nov 1970; died 14 Jun 1981.

1982 JAMES RONALD DICK
(FES X, 118), trans from Dundee Whitfield to Corsock with Kirkpatrick Durham 22 Nov 1982; trans to Edinburgh St John's Oxgangs 17 Aug 1988.

1990 ROBERT COLQUHOUN WOTHERSPOON
B 18 Aug 1934 at Rutherglen, s of James Wright W. and Agnes Colquhoun; educ Rutherglen Academy 1946–49; Langside College 1969–70; University of Glasgow 1970–75 (LTh); Factory Worker 1950–56; Assurance Agent 1956–63; Field Salesman, Scottish Gas 1963–69; lic by Presb of Glasgow 26 Jun 1975; asst Glasgow Sandyhills 1973–75; Chryston 1975–76; m 28 Jun 1964 Margaret Hendry b 13 Jan 1935 d of James Smith H. and Mary Cherry; Children: David b 27 Jan 1966 m Catherine Varty; Kirsten Mary b 7 May 1969; ord and ind to Strichen 24 Jun 1976; trans to Glasgow Castlemilk West 13 Mar 1980; trans to Corsock and Kirkpatrick Durham with Crossmichael and Parton 30 Jan 1990; ret 28 Feb 1998.

CROSSMICHAEL AND PARTON (FES X, 90, 91)

Formed 17 May 1989 by union of Crossmichael and Parton. Linked same date with Corsock and Kirkpatrick Durham.

1929   GEORGE DRUMMOND SUMMERS
(FES VIII 436; IX, 156; X, 91), trans from West
Wemyss to Parton 14 Nov 1929; ret 30 Nov 1961;
died 25 Dec 1980.

1962   DAVID CHAPLIN
(FES IX, 337; X, 38, 90, 167, 201, 417), res from
service with Overseas Council and ind to
Crossmichael with Parton 1 Mar 1962; trans to
Glasgow Netherton St Matthew's 21 Feb 1968.

1968   ALEXANDER WHITE RAMSAY KEITH
(FES IX, 14, 709; X, 9, 90, 176), trans from
Glasgow St James' (Pollok) to Crossmichael with
Parton 31 Oct 1968; dem charge and status 6 Feb
1974.

1975   ROBERT CHRISTOPHER IRVING
(FES X, 91, 136), trans from Inverkip to Crossmichael with Parton 2 May 1975; ret 31 Dec 1979;
died 20 May 1999.

1990   ROBERT COLQUHOUN WOTHERSPOON
trans from Glasgow Castlemilk West to Corsock
and Kirkpatrick Durham with Crossmichael and
Parton 30 Jan 1990; ret 28 Feb 1998.

CUMMERTREES (FES II, 243; VIII, 166; IX, 139;
X, 82)

Linked 31 Mar 1969 with Ruthwell and Mount
Kedar. Further linked 26 Oct 1980 with Mouswald.

1969   WILLIAM EDWARD WILLIAMSON
(FES IX, 200; X, 82, 114, 219), trans from
Dumbarton North to Cummertrees with Ruthwell
and Mount Kedar 2 Oct 1969; ret 26 Oct 1980;
died 30 Sep 1991.

1981   THOMAS CRAWFORD BALLENTINE
B 1 Jul 1937 at Ahoghill, Co Antrim, N Ireland, s of
Alexander B. and Hannah; educ Ballymena
Academy 1949–55; University of Leeds 1975–78
(MPhil); University of Edinburgh 1978–81 (BD);
Manager of Textile Mill 1959–69; Lecturer at
Scottish College of Textiles 1969–78; lic by Presb
of Melrose and Peebles 23 Jun 1981; m 1 Apr 1961
Marion Chalmers Sanderson b 1 May 1940 d of
Thomas Charters S. and Mary Fairley Jackson;
Children: Dorothy Margaret b 24 Feb 1962; David
Crawford b 20 Apr 1964; Thomas Alexander Derek
b 28 Oct 1967; Diane Elizabeth b 15 Apr 1971;
ord and ind to Cummertrees with Mouswald with
Ruthwell 20 Aug 1981; dem 11 Oct 1983 on app
by Presb Church in Ireland.

1984   ROBERT MORRISON NICOL
ord and ind to Cummertrees with Mouswald with
Ruthwell 16 Aug 1984; trans to Jersey St
Columba's 28 Feb 1991.

1991   JAMES WILLIAMSON
B 6 May 1944 at Edinburgh, s of James W. and
Agnes Storie; educ Musselburgh Grammar 1956–
60; University of Edinburgh 1972–75 (BA), 1988–

91 (BD); Moray House College, Edinburgh 1975–
76 (DCE); Accounancy 1960–71; Teaching 1976–
88; lic by Presb of Lothian 9 Sep 1984; m 15 Oct
1977 Morag Joan Moreland b 29 Jan 1954 d of
John M. and Sarah Marr (adoptive parents);
Children: Andrew Ian b 7 Mar 1980; Nicola
Christine b 10 Dec 1982; ord as Aux by Presb of
Lothian and assgnd to Haddington West with
Garvald and Morham 16 Feb 1986; ind to
Cummertrees with Mouswald with Ruthwell (full-
time ministry) 1 Aug 1991.

DALBEATTIE (FES X, 82, 83)

Formed 9 Dec 1988 by union of Dalbeattie
Craignair and Dalbeattie Park. Linkage of Dalbeattie Craignair with Urr continues after union.

1959   RODERICK PETTIGREW
(FES X, 83), ord and ind to Dalbeattie Park with
Kirkgunzeon 3 Dec 1959; ret 30 Apr 1987; died 7
Aug 1993.

1961   NEIL DOUGLAS CRAIG
(FES IX, 115, 346; X, 83, 207), trans from Carstairs
to Dalbeattie Craignair 19 Oct 1961; became
minister of linked charge with Urr 1 Jun 1980; ret
31 Aug 1987.

1988   NORMAN McKENZIE HUTCHESON
(FES X, 284), trans from Kirkcaldy St Andrew's to
Dalbeattie with Urr 11 Aug 1988; Children: Morna
Ann b 17 Apr 1977; Catriona Ann b 19 May 1979.

DALRY (FES IX, 154; X, 91)

Linkage with Carsphairn terminated 9 Dec 1992.
Linked same date with Balmaclellan and Kells.

1927   HAROLD GEORGE MULLO WEIR
(FES VIII, 204; IX, 154 (2); X, 91), [correction: FES
VIII, not VII as in Vol X, 91]; ord and ind to Dalry
28 Sep 1927; became minister of united charge
with St John's 18 Dec 1949; ret 24 Feb 1972; died
23 Mar 1985.

1972   JOHN ROBERT MILLER
(FES X, 35, 90, 206), ind to Carsphairn with Dalry
24 Aug 1972, see Carsphairn.

1993   WILLIAM CLEMENT ROBB
(FES X, 405), ind to Balmaclellan and Kells with
Dalry 2 Jun 1993, see Balmaclellan.

1994   DAVID SINCLAIR BARTHOLOMEW
ord and ind to Balmaclellan and Kells with Carsphairn with Dalry 12 Oct 1994, see Balmaclellan.

DUMFRIES GREYFRIARS (FES II, 269; VIII, 172;
IX, 140; X, 83)

1945   JOHN MELROSE
(FES IX, 140, 195, 289; X, 83), trans from Glasgow
Possilpark to Greyfriars 11 Oct 1945; ret 4 Jun
1972; died 2 Nov 1983.

1973 ALASDAIR (ALEXANDER) JAMES MORTON
(FES X, 83, 423), res from service with Overseas Council in Zambia and ind to Greyfriars 29 Mar 1973; dem 1 Oct 1977 on app as General Secretary, Dept of Education.

1978 ALAN HENRY WARD
ord and ind to Greyfriars 6 Apr 1978; trans to Cambuslang Old 13 Nov 1985.

1987 DAVID ROBERT BLACK
ord by Presb of Edinburgh during assistantship at South Leith 23 May 1986; ind to Greyfriars 19 Aug 1987; trans to Glasgow Pollokshields 17 Apr 1997.

1999 WALTER CAMPBELL CAMPBELL-JACK
B 14 Sep 1946 at Campbeltown, s of Archibald Ormiston J. and Agnes McTear Williamson Campbell; educ Dalkeith High 1959–62; Edinburgh College of Commerce 1969–71; Moray House College, Edinburgh 1971–74; University of Edinburgh 1974–78 (BD); University of Aberdeen 1987 (MTh); University of Edinburgh 1993 (PhD); lic by Presb of Edinburgh, Jul 1978; asst Nairn Old 1978–79; m 9 Sep 1967 Elizabeth Ruth Pugsley b 6 Sep 1946 d of Alfred John P. and Emily May Watts; Children: Fiona Elizabeth Claire b 17 Nov 1972; Diarmid Eoghan Thomas b 7 Apr 1975; Mairi Rebecca Rowena b 18 Oct 1978; Hamish Fergus Nathan b 20 Feb 1981; ord by Presb of Inverness during assistantship at Nairn Old 24 Apr 1979; ind to Knockbain 20 Mar 1980; Lecturer (part-time) at Highland Theological Institute and Evangelical Theological College of Wales; trans to Greyfriars 12 Mar 1999.

DUMFRIES LINCLUDEN (FES IX, 140; X, 83)

Linked 1 Feb 1962 with Holywood.

1961 JOHN CORDINER
(FES X, 83, 303), trans from Dundee Mains of Fintry to Lincluden 9 Mar 1961; became minister of linked charge with Holywood 1 Feb 1962; trans to Portpatrick 14 Jul 1981.

1982 MARY LAWSON HUTCHISON
B 8 Jul 1929 at Stirling, d of Joseph Keary and Catherine Anderson; educ Stirling High; University of Stirling; University of Edinburgh 1976–80 (BD); Secretary 1947–61, 1963–76; lic by Presb of Stirling 6 Jul 1980; asst Logie 1980–81; m 23 Nov 1951 John Hutchison b 20 Jan 1930, died 1989, s of William H. and Margaret Drummond; Children: William Kenneth b 28 Mar 1953; Catherine Mary b 31 Dec 1957 m Ian Hamilton; ord and ind to Lincluden with Holywood 20 Jan 1982; app Chaplain to Cresswell Maternity Hospital 1984 and to Dumfries and Galloway Royal Infirmary 1995; ret from Lincluden with Holywood 31 Jan 1995.

1995 JOHN SPENCER
(FES X, 52), ord and ind to Penicuik South 10 Oct 1962; dem 31 Dec 1967; Teaching 1968–91; introd as Assoc at Edinburgh Gorgie 19 Aug 1991; ind to Lincluden with Holywood 4 Apr 1995; m (2) 18 Oct 1980 Marion Rose Tait b 24 Dec 1937 d of Thomas T. and Rose Lundie.

DUMFRIES LOCHSIDE (FES X, 83)

Linked 27 Sep 1981 with Terregles. Linkage terminated 27 May 1997.

1976 DOUGLAS ALEXANDER OAG NICOL
ord by Presb of Auchterarder during assistantship at St Ninian's Centre, Crieff; ind to Lochside 28 Oct 1976; became minister of linked charge with Terregles 27 Sep 1981; trans to Kilmacolm St Columba 13 Jul 1982.

1983 JULIAN SINCLAIR TURNBULL
B 1 Apr 1955 at Glasgow, s of Ivor Sinclair T. and Vera Hilary Tullis Gillies; educ Hutchesons' Grammar, Glasgow 1966–72; University of Glasgow 1972–76 (BSc), 1976–79 (BD); University of Edinburgh 1985–86 (MSc); lic by Presb of Glasgow 29 Jun 1979; asst Hamilton Old and Auchingramont 1979–81; m 12 Mar 1983 Susan Patricia Dann b 11 Jul 1957 d of Frank Walter D. and Patricia Wethel Richardson; Children: Benjamin Spencer b 9 Dec 1991; ord by Presb of Hamilton during assistantship at Hamilton Old and Auchingramont 15 Jun 1980; ind to Lochside with Terregles 17 Feb 1983; dem to take up app as Departmental Computing Officer, University of Edinburgh 1 Oct 1986; res to take up app as Software Quality Assurance Engineer 14 Jul 1997.

1986 THOMAS CRANSTONE BOGLE
res from term app at Caddonfoot with Selkirk Heatherlie and ind to Lochside with Terregles 22 Apr 1986; trans to Fisherton with Maybole West 21 Aug 1996.

1997 THOMAS MITCHELL BRYSON
B 2 Mar 1959 at Glasgow, s of James Tait Crighton B. and Susannah Storrie Mitchell; educ Queen Anne High, Dunfermline and Beath Junior High, Cowdenbeath 1971–75; Lauder Technical College, Dunfermline; University of Edinburgh 1994 (BD); Craftsman Electrician 1976–90; lic by Presb of West Lothian 29 Aug 1995; asst Carluke Kirkton 1995–96; Wishaw St Mark's 1996–97; m 3 Sep 1983 Jane Milne Gunn b 7 Jan 1953 d of John G. and Isabella Brown Wood; Children: James Tait Crighton b 28 Feb 1985; ord and ind to Lochside 12 Aug 1997.

DUMFRIES MAXWELLTOWN WEST (FUF 107, FES IX, 140; X, 84)

1944 HENRY GLEN ALEXANDER SIMMONS
(FES IX, 140; X, 84), trans from Glasgow Parkhead East to Maxwelltown West 27 Apr 1944; died 25 Apr 1983.

1984   GORDON MATTHEW ALEXANDER SAVAGE
B 25 Aug 1951 at Old Kilpatrick, s of Thomas S. and Margaret Whytock Campbell; educ Glasgow Academy 1960–69; University of Edinburgh 1969–75 (MA, BD); lic by Presb of Dumbarton 29 Jun 1975; asst Dyce 1975–76; Dunblane Cathedral 1976–77; m 24 Oct 1981 Mairi Janet MacKenzie b 2 Apr 1956 d of Alastair George M. and Mary Jane MacKinnon; Children: David Gordon b 11 May 1989; Alasdair Thomas b 27 Jun 1991; ord and ind to Almondbank St Serf's with Logiealmond 31 Aug 1977; became minister of Almondbank Tibbermore with Logiealmond 5 Oct 1977; Junior Clerk to Perth Presb 1981–84; trans to Maxwelltown West 2 Feb 1984; app Clerk to Presb of Dumfries and Kirkcudbright 7 Oct 1987.

DUMFRIES ST GEORGE'S (FUF 103; FES IX, 141; X, 84)

1969   STUART FRANKLIN ASTLEY PRYCE
(FES X, 84, 120), trans from Saltcoats North to St George's 27 Aug 1969; ret 30 Apr 1997.

1997   DONALD CAMPBELL
ord and ind to St George's 27 Nov 1997.

DUMFRIES ST MARY'S (FES II, 270; VIII, 173; IX, 141; X, 84)

1957   IAN SWANSTON CRAN KNOX
(FES IX, 450; X, 84, 266), trans from Menstrie to St Mary's 25 Nov 1957; ret 30 Nov 1986; died 10 Apr 1995.

1987   GRAHAM DOUGLAS SUTHERLAND DEANS
B 15 Aug 1953 at Aberdeen, s of John Bell D. and Marjory Cumming Sutherland Douglas; educ Mackie Academy, Stonehaven 1965–71; University of Aberdeen 1971–77 (MA, BD); Westminster College, Oxford (and Scottish Churches Open College) 1995–98 (MTh [Oxon], 1999); lic by Presb of Aberdeen 29 Jun 1977; asst Edinburgh Corstorphine Craigsbank 1977–78; m 15 Aug 1981 Marina Punler b 14 Oct 1941 d of Alexander P. and Jane Henderson; ord and ind to Denbeath 24 Aug 1978; became minister of linked charge with Methilhill 3 Dec 1978; trans to St Mary's 8 Jul 1987; Publ: *A History of Denbeath Church* (Denbeath Church, 1980); *The Cup of Hate and the Cup of Love* (T&T Clark, 1983); *Stand Up for Jesus* (T&T Clark, 1987); *The Twelve Apostles* (T&T Clark, 1988); *Hymnody and Belonging: The Words of Hymnody* (Commercial Press, 1999); *Hymnody and Belonging: The Music of Hymnody* (Commercial Press, 1999); *Presbyterian Praise* (Pentland Press, 1999).

DUMFRIES ST MICHAEL'S AND SOUTH (FES X, 84)

Formed 2 Oct 1983 by union of Dumfries St Michael's and Dumfries South and Townhead. Linked same date with Caerlaverock. Linkage terminated 1 Jul 1996.

1960   ALBERT BROWN ELDER
(FES X, 84), ord and ind to South and Townhead 1 Dec 1960; became Collegiate minister of united charge with St Michael's linked with Caerlaverock 2 Oct 1983; became sole minister of charge following termination of linkage 1 Jul 1996; ret 30 Jun 1998.

1970   JOHN POWERS BATES
(FES X, 84, 302), trans from Dundee Lochee St Luke's to St Michael's 17 Apr 1970; dem 31 Jul 1977.

1978   JOHN PAGAN
ind to St Michael's 7 Sep 1978; became minister of united charge with South and Townhead and of linked charge with Caerlaverock 2 Oct 1983; ret 31 Dec 1994; died 15 Feb 1998.

1999   MAURICE SAMUEL BOND
B 25 Jun 1952 at Augher, Co Tyrone, s of Robert James B. and Mary Agnas Irwin; educ Limavady Secondary 1963–67; University of Nottingham 1974–77 (BA); University of Cambridge 1977–78 (DipEd); Queen's University, Belfast (part-time) 1978–80 (MTh); University of Dublin (part-time) 1990–95 (PhD); Apprentice Joiner 1967–72; Teaching 1979–80; lic by Presb of Templepatrick 15 Jun 1980; asst St John's Presb Church, Belfast 1981–83; m 19 Feb 1976 Tokuko Kawashima b 13 Mar 1951 d of Kuighi and Sueko K; Children: Sarah Nana Kazuko b 9 Aug 1977; Jonathan Syina Stephen Robert b 14 Oct 1981; ord and ind to St John's Presb Church, Belfast 18 Jan 1983; trans to First Ballynahinch Presb Church, Co Down 10 Mar 1985; ind to Dundee Downfield South 10 Apr 1991; trans to St Michael's and South 7 Jul 1999; Publ: *Reconciling Memories* (St Columba Press, 1988); *Presence* (*Theology in Scotland*, 1997).

DUMFRIES TROQUEER (FES X, 83, 84)

Maxwelltown Laurieknowe and Troqueer united 5 Aug 1976 as Dumfries Laurieknowe Troqueer. Laurieknowe dropped from name 3 Nov 1991.

1952   JOSEPH LEWIS MANGLES
(FES IX, 142, 227, 465; X, 84), trans from Kinross West to Troqueer 11 Dec 1952; ret 31 Dec 1975; died 18 Aug 1978.

1971   WILLIAM LOWRIE IRVINE
(FES IX, 328; X, 83, 110, 193), trans from Irvine St Paul's to Maxwelltown Laurieknowe 28 Oct 1971; ret 5 Aug 1976; died 7 Dec 1986.

1977 WILLIAM MONCUR McKENZIE
(FES X, 422), res from service with United Church of Zambia and ind to Laurieknowe Troqueer 10 Jun 1977; ret 30 Dec 1993; s John m Lorna Moffat; d Margaret m David Gurney; d Christine m John Wakefield; Publ: Secretary/Exegete: Bemba Bible, Zambia (United Bible Societies, 1983).

1994 WILLIAM WILSON KELLY
B 25 Nov 1949 at Glengarnock, s of David John K. and Margaret Wilson; educ Speir's School, Beith 1954–68; University of Glasgow 1968–72 (BSc), 1990–93 (BD); Scottish Agricultural College 1974–76; Scottish Milk Marketing Board 1976–90; lic by Presb of Ardrossan 7 Jul 1993; asst Dunfermline Gillespie 1993–94; m 18 Jun 1969 Joy Drummond b 1 Jan 1951 d of John D. and Jean Dickie; Children: Caroline b 25 Sep 1969; Mark b 7 Nov 1971; ord and ind to Troqueer 1 Jun 1994; app Chaplain (part-time) to Dumfries Prison.

DUNSCORE (FES IX, 142; X, 84)

Linked 8 Dec 1977 with Glencairn and Moniaive.

1966 JOHN WILLIAM GORDON MASTERTON
(FES IX, 115, 232; X, 84, 135), trans from Greenock St Paul's to Dunscore 6 Oct 1966; ret 1 Apr 1970; m (2) 27 Sep 1979 Margaret Gordon Middlemass b 29 Nov 1925 d of George M. and Margaret Grieve; s Gordon (from previous marriage) m Janette Stewart; d Kathleen (from previous marriage) m Park; Addl publ: *Speaking of Burns* (MacDonald, 1980); *Prayers For Use In Church II* (St Andrew Press, 1993).

1970 DUGALD CAMPBELL ALEXANDER
(FES IX, 181, 504, 683; X, 84, 288, 388), trans from Windygates and Balgonie to Dunscore 30 Nov 1970; ret 30 Jun 1977.

1978 ARCHIBALD IAIN CAMPBELL
(FES X, 40), dem from Grangemouth Kirk of the Holy Rood 30 Sep 1971 to enter teaching profession; ind to Dunscore with Glencairn and Moniaive 28 Jul 1978; dem 5 Oct 1984; loc ten Deerness with St Andrew's Oct 1984.

1985 ARTHUR DAVID COURTENAY GREER
(FES X, 163 (2), 419), res as Assoc at Dundee Whitfield and ind to Dunscore with Glencairn and Moniaive 4 Jun 1985; trans to Barra 29 Jul 1993.

1994 CHRISTINE MACKENZIE SIME
B 29 May 1955 at Edinburgh, d of John Mackintosh Mackenzie S. and Elizabeth Wood; educ James Gillespie's, Edinburgh 1967–73; University of Edinburgh 1973–77 (BSc), 1990–93 (BD); Medical Research Technician 1977–90; lic by Presb of Edinburgh 4 Jul 1993; ord and ind to Dunscore with Glencairn and Moniaive 30 Aug 1994.

DURISDEER (FUF 110; FES II, 312; VIII, 182; IX, 142; X, 84)

Linked 27 Apr 1980 with Closeburn.

1953 JAMES WILLIAM SCOTT
(FES IX, 142; X, 84), ord by Presb of Dunfermline during assistantship at Dunfermline Abbey 24 Feb 1952; ind to Durisdeer 24 Sep 1953; became minister of linked charge with Closeburn 27 Apr 1980.

GLENCAIRN AND MONIAIVE (FES X, 85)

Linked 8 Dec 1977 with Dunscore.

1962 JOHN RICHARD
(FES IX, 138, 543 (2); X, 85, 321, 331), trans from Aberdeen St Nicholas South Kincorth to Glencairn and Moniaive 26 Apr 1962; became minister of linked charge with Tynron 27 Nov 1966; ret 11 Dec 1977; died 19 Jul 1987.

1978 ARCHIBALD IAIN CAMPBELL
(FES X, 40), ind to Dunscore with Glencairn and Moniaive 28 Jul 1978, see Dunscore.

1985 ARTHUR DAVID COURTENAY GREER
(FES X, 163 (2), 419), ind to Dunscore with Glencairn and Moniaive 4 Jun 1985, see Dunscore.

1994 CHRISTINE MACKENZIE SIME
ord and ind to Dunscore with Glencairn and Moniaive 30 Aug 1994, see Dunscore.

HOLYWOOD (FES II, 274; VIII, 173; IX, 143; X, 85)

Linked 1 Feb 1962 with Dumfries Lincluden.

1962 JOHN CORDINER
(FES X, 83, 303), ind to Lincluden 9 Mar 1961; became minister of linked charge with Holywood 1 Feb 1962, see Lincluden.

1982 MARY LAWSON HUTCHISON
ord and ind to Dumfries Lincluden with Holywood 20 Jan 1982, see Lincluden.

1995 JOHN SPENCER
(FES X, 52), ind to Dumfries Lincluden with Holywood 4 Apr 1995, see Lincluden.

KIRKCONNEL (FES X, 85)

Formed 27 Feb 1983 by union of Kirkconnel St Conal's and Kirkconnel St Mark's.

1969 JOHN DAVID JONES
trans under mutual eligibility from Hebburn St Andrew's, Newcastle (Presb Church of England) to St Mark's 4 Jun 1969; ret 30 Nov 1972.

1975 ALEXANDER GRAINGER STODDART
(FES X, 85), ord and ind to St Conal's with St
Mark's 21 Aug 1975; trans to Peterculter St Peter's
9 Dec 1982.

1983 HAROLD GEORGE MUDALIAR
B 22 Feb 1937 at Calcutta, India, s of Arokiaswamy
Shankar M. and Isabella Louisa Nelson; educ
Stewart School, Cuttack, India 1940–54; Calcutta
Bible College, 1955–57; Union Biblical Seminary
(affiliated to Serampore University) 1968–70 (GTh),
1971–73 (BD); University of Aberdeen 1973–76;
University of Edinburgh 1981–82; Teacher and
Hostel Warden, Stewart School, Cuttack 1957–59;
Air India 1959–60; Director, Youth for Christ,
Calcutta 1960–66 and Madras 1966–68; Minister,
Ling Liang Chinese Churches, Calcutta 1970–71;
Asst minister, Union Church, Landour 1972; Hon
Asst minister, Emmanuel Methodist Church,
Madras 1973; Director, East/West Ministeries,
Edinburgh 1978–81; lic by Presb of Edinburgh 4
Jul 1982; asst Edinburgh Juniper Green 1982–83;
m 23 Oct 1967 Dinah Khurshid Tharasingh,
divorced 30 Oct 1980; Children: Paulus b 12 Sep
1968, died 12 Sep 1968; Tabitha Aloma Vanessa
b 7 May 1970; Samantha Abigail Sophia b 1 May
1973; ord and ind to Kirkconnel 18 Aug 1983; died
22 Jan 1992.

1992 ALAN MACGREGOR
ord and ind to Kirkconnel 2 Oct 1992; trans to Banff
with King Edward 27 Mar 1998.

1999 DAVID DEAS MELVILLE
B 12 Mar 1943 at Kirkcaldy, s of James M. and
Agnes Stewart Deas; educ Kirkcaldy High 1948–
60; Kirkcaldy Technical College 1960–68 (HNC);
University of London 1983–86 (BD); Research
Chemist 1960–73; Policeman 1973–78; Sales Rep
1978–83; lic by Presb of Falkirk 30 Jun 1988; asst
Falkirk St Andrew's 1988–89; m 23 Aug 1985 Irene
Williamson b 18 Jul 1958 d of John W. and Violet
McGuinness; Children: Andrew b 2 Sep 1990; ord
and ind to Dunnet with Olrig 1 Sep 1989; trans to
Kirkconnel 22 Jan 1999.

KIRKCUDBRIGHT PARISH (FES X, 91)

Formed 11 May 1983 by union of Kirkcudbright St
Cuthbert's and Kirkcudbright St Mary's.

1964 ADAM JACK
(FES IX, 274, 479, 513; X, 91, 304), trans from
Dundee Ryehill to St Cuthbert's 22 Oct 1964; ret
31 Jul 1974; died 30 May 1994.

1966 JAMES LAMB HEPBURN
(FES IX, 736; X, 91, 420), res from service with
Overseas Council in Malawi and ind to St Mary's
14 Apr 1966; introd to Ardoch (term) 11 May 1983.

1975 WILLIAM GRAINGER ALLAN
(FES X, 91, 174, 348), trans from Glasgow St
Enoch's-Hogganfield to St Cuthbert's 4 Mar 1975;
dem 31 May 1978.

1980 WILLIAM STEWART WILSON
B 8 Mar 1934 at Stromness, s of Stewart W. and
Jacobina Stout; educ Stromness Academy 1939–
57; Gray's School of Art, Aberdeen 1957–61 (DA);
Aberdeen Teacher Training College 1961–62;
University of Aberdeen 1977–79; Army 1962–64;
Teaching 1964–69, 1973–77; General Merchant
1969–73; lic by Presb of Aberdeen, 1979; asst
Aberdeen Mastrick 1979–80; m (1) Sheila Stevens
b 21 Aug 1938 d of Bertram S. and Maggie
Clouston; Children: Steven b 19 Mar 1966; Serena
b 7 Oct 1971; m (2) 30 Jun 1996 Patricia Florence
b 14 Nov 1930 d of John F. and Mary Ann Kidd;
Children from spouse's previous marriage: Murray
Chalmers b 6 Feb 1963; ord and ind to St
Cuthbert's 4 Jun 1980; became minister of united
charge with St Mary's 11 May 1983; ret 31 Aug
1997; Publ: Shipwrecks of Fair Isle.

1998 DOUGLAS ROBERT IRVING
B 24 May 1951 at Stranraer, s of Thomas Kerr I.
and Elizabeth Chatham McInroy; educ Stranraer
High 1963–69; University of Dundee 1969–72
(LLB); University of Edinburgh 1980–83 (BD);
Solicitor 1974–80; lic by Presb of Edinburgh 3 Jul
1983; asst Edinburgh Tron Kirk Moredun 1983–
84; m 8 Aug 1987 Hilary Frances Bell b 7 May
1962 d of Francis William Albert B. and Margaret
Isabella Rafferty; Children: Roan Thomas Bell b
29 Dec 1988; Jean Elizabeth Margaret b 1 Jul
1993; ord and ind to Kilbirnie Auld Kirk 8 Aug 1984;
trans to Kirkcudbright 16 Apr 1998.

KIRKGUNZEON (FES II, 279; VIII, 174; IX, 144;
X, 86)

Continued vacancy since 1987.

1959 RODERICK PETTIGREW
(FES X, 83), ord and ind to Dalbeattie Park with
Kirkgunzeon 3 Dec 1959; ret 30 Apr 1987; died 7
Aug 1993.

KIRKMAHOE (FUF 106; FES II, 281; VIII, 175; IX,
145; X, 86)

1975 RICHARD FRASER BAXTER
(FES IX, 728; X, 86, 416), [correction: res from
service with Overseas Council, not Overseas
House as in Vol X, 86]; res as Warden of Scottish
Churches' House, Dunblane and ind to Kirkmahoe
11 Sep 1975; dem 30 Sep 1982; Asst at Edinburgh
St Andrew's and St George's 1983–90.

1984 MARION DAPHNE WALKER SMITH
B at Kimberley, S Africa, d of Joseph Abbott S.
and Elisabeth Beveridge; University of Glasgow
1971–77 (BD, CPS); Private Secretary and
Personal Asst; lic by Presb of Glasgow 25 Jun
1976; ord and ind to Cockpen and Carrington with
Lasswade 25 Oct 1978; trans to Gorbals 4 Oct
1979 (compassionate grounds); trans to Kirkmahoe
6 Sep 1984; dem 31 Dec 1989.

1991 JOHN EDWARD GISBEY
(FES X, 128), res as Senior Lecturer at Queen's College, Glasgow and ind to Kirkmahoe 1 Nov 1991; dem 31 Jan 1996; ind to Thornhill 5 Jun 1997.

1996 DENNIS SINCLAIR ROSE
B 16 Dec 1945 at Glasgow, s of Robert John R. and Margaret Bain Reid; educ Yoker Secondary, Glasgow 1950–62; Glasgow Bible College 1989–90; University of Cambridge (DTh); University of Glasgow 1992–95; Business Management 1974–89; Sales Rep 1972–74; lic by Presb of Ardrossan 4 Jul 1995; asst West Kilbride St Andrew's 1994–96; m 1 Jun 1978 Marilyn Wilson b 14 Sep 1949 d of George W. and Howard; Children: David Sinclair b 8 May 1969 m Wendy; Stuart John b 7 Feb 1972; Allison Jane b 2 Mar 1977; ord and ind to Kirkmahoe 19 Dec 1996.

KIRKMICHAEL (FES X, 86)

Linked 13 Sep 1981 with Torthorwald.

1970 FRASER IAN MACDONALD
(FES IX, 29, 111, 673; X, 88), ind to Tinwald 9 Feb 1956; became minister of linked charge with Kirkmichael and Garvell 22 Oct 1970, see Tinwald.

1985 JAMES SMITH LEISHMAN
(FES X, 216, 377), trans from Patna Waterside to Kirkmichael with Tinwald with Torthorwald 16 Jan 1985; ret 31 Mar 1999; Addl children: Douglas Mark b 14 Jan 1977.

KIRKPATRICK-IRONGRAY (FES II, 287; VIII, 176; IX, 145; X, 86)

Linked 12 Sep 1982 with Lochrutton. Further linked 27 May 1997 with Terregles.

1957 WILLIAM BALLANTINE AITKEN
(FES X, 86), ind to Kirkpatrick-Irongray 24 Apr 1957; became minister of linked charge with Lochrutton 12 Sep 1982; ret 31 Dec 1986; died 30 Jan 1991.

1987 DAVID KEITH PATTERSON BENNETT
(FES X, 358), trans from Findochty with Portknockie to Kirkpatrick-Irongray with Lochrutton 30 Aug 1987; became minister of linked charge with Terregles 27 May 1997.

LOCHEND (FUF 106; FES IX, 145; X, 86)

Linked 25 May 1952 with New Abbey.

1971 WILLIAM HOLLAND
(FES X, 86, 357), res as Assoc at Mortlach with Cabrach and ind to Lochend with New Abbey 23 Dec 1971, see New Abbey.

LOCHRUTTON (FES II, 290; VIII, 177; IX, 145; X, 86)

Linkage with Terregles terminated 27 Sep 1981. Linked 12 Sep 1982 with Kirkpatrick-Irongray. Further linked 27 May 1997 with Terregles.

1975 WILLIAM SCRYMGOUR RHODES
(FES IX, 746; X, 86), res from service with Overseas Council at Serampore College, India and ind to Lochrutton with Terregles 10 Apr 1975; dem 31 Jul 1977 and re-app by Overseas Council to Serampore.

1982 WILLIAM BALLANTINE AITKEN
(FES X, 86), ind to Kirkpatrick-Irongray 24 Apr 1957; became minister of linked charge with Lochrutton 12 Sep 1982; ret 31 Dec 1986; died 30 Jan 1991.

1987 DAVID KEITH PATTERSON BENNETT
(FES X, 358), trans from Findochty with Portknockie to Kirkpatrick-Irongray with Lochrutton 30 Aug 1987; became minister of linked charge with Terregles 27 May 1997.

MOUSWALD (FES II, 318; VIII, 159; IX, 146; X, 87)

Linkage with Torthorwald terminated 26 Oct 1980. Linked with Cummertrees same date.

1965 JAMES COULTER
(FES X, 87), trans from Carrickfergus to Mouswald with Torthorwald 17 Jun 1965; ret 31 Mar 1970; died 11 Jan 1977.

1970 HAROLD MEREDITH
(FES X, 87, 172, 246), trans from Glasgow Ruchill to Mouswald with Torthorwald 27 Aug 1970; ret 30 Nov 1979; died 29 Sep 1989.

1981 THOMAS CRAWFORD BALLENTINE
ord and ind to Cummertrees with Mouswald with Ruthwell 20 Aug 1981, see Cummertrees.

1984 ROBERT MORRISON NICOL
ord and ind to Cummertrees with Mouswald with Ruthwell 16 Aug 1984; trans to Jersey St Columba's 28 Feb 1991.

1991 JAMES WILLIAMSON
ind to Cummertrees with Mouswald with Ruthwell 1 Aug 1991, see Cummertrees.

NEW ABBEY (FES II, 293; VIII, 177; IX, 147; X, 87)

Linked 25 May 1952 with Lochend.

1971 WILLIAM HOLLAND
(FES X, 86, 357), res as Assoc at Mortlach with Cabrach and ind to Lochend with New Abbey 23 Dec 1971; d Helen Ruth m Michael Wilson; d Dorothy Jane m Alex Meikle; d Mary Elizabeth m

Charles Merchant; s William Alexander m Audrey Duncan; Publ: *New Abbey Poors Fund: 1820–1835* (1990).

PENPONT KEIR AND TYNRON (FES X, 87, 88)

Formed 25 May 1980 by union of Penpont, Keir and Tynron.

1949   JOHN HUTCHISON ALEXANDER INGLIS (FES IX, 147, 202, 233; X, 87 (2)), trans from Greenock Union Street to Penpont 21 Apr 1949; became minister of united charge with Keir 2 Oct 1957; ret 20 Oct 1973; died 11 Feb 1993.

1974   JAMES GRANT (FES X, 83, 87, 401, 403), trans from Holm to Penpont and Keir 13 Jun 1974; became minister of united charge with Tynron 25 May 1980; ret 31 Jul 1987; s Christopher m Maureen Cook; d Marie m Eric Coltart.

1988   JAMES ROSS WILKIE (FES X, 113, 355), res as Director of Glenthorne Youth Treatment Centre, DHSS and ind to Penpont Keir and Tynron 1 Jun 1988; ret 1 Dec 1993; s David m Randall; d Elizabeth m Noon; s Andrew m Brooks.

1994   ROBERT BRUCE GEHRKE B 20 Apr 1956 at Redruth, Cornwall, s of Johannes Emil Wilhelm G. and Eleanor Wright Bruce; educ West Calder High and Craigshill High, Livingston 1968–74; Heriot-Watt University 1974–78 (BSc); University of Edinburgh 1990–93 (BD); Electrical Engineering 1978–90; lic by Presb of Edinburgh 4 Jul 1993; asst Edinburgh Barclay 1993–94; m 1 Sep 1979 Fiona Ramsay Steele b 22 Dec 1955 d of John Ramsay S. and Jean Sheena Nicolson; Children: John Mark b 27 Oct 1982; Ruth Jane b 16 Nov 1984; Jamie Sheena b 9 Oct 1987; ord and ind to Penpont Keir and Tynron 20 Jul 1994.

RUTHWELL (FES IX, 147; X, 87)

Linked 31 Mar 1969 with Cummertrees. Further linked 26 Oct 1980 with Mouswald. Mount Kedar dropped from name.

1969   WILLIAM EDWARD WILLIAMSON (FES IX, 200; X, 82, 114, 219), trans from Dumbarton North to Cummertrees with Ruthwell and Mount Kedar 2 Oct 1969; ret 26 Oct 1980; died 30 Sep 1991.

1981   THOMAS CRAWFORD BALLENTINE ord and ind to Cummertrees with Mouswald with Ruthwell 20 Aug 1981, see Cummertrees.

1984   ROBERT MORRISON NICOL ord and ind to Cummertrees with Mouswald with Ruthwell 16 Aug 1984; trans to Jersey St Columba's 28 Feb 1991.

1991   JAMES WILLIAMSON ind to Cummertrees with Mouswald with Ruthwell 1 Aug 1991, see Cummertrees.

SANQUHAR ST BRIDE'S (FES II, 324; VIII, 185; IX, 148; X, 87)

1949   JOHN DAVIDSON (FES IX, 47, 148; X, 87), trans from West Calder Harwood to St Bride's 5 Jul 1949; ret 31 Oct 1974; died 7 Mar 1983.

1976   GEORGE CRANSTON ord and ind to St Bride's 30 Sep 1976; Chaplain to Dumfries Young Offenders Institution 1977–83; trans to Rutherglen Wardlawhill 24 Nov 1983.

1985   KENNETH THOMAS THOMSON (FES X, 319, 402), trans from Maxton with Newtown to St Bride's 15 Nov 1985; died 5 May 1991; JP Ettrick and Lauderdale 1983–84; JP Nithsdale 1986; Addl children: Niall Anthony; s Stephen m Louise Pennington Fraser.

1991   DAVID GEORGE ADAMS ord and ind to St Bride's 12 Dec 1991; trans to Cowdenbeath Trinity 29 Apr 1999.

SANQUHAR ST NINIAN'S (FUF 108; FES IX, 148; X, 87)

Congregation dissolved 21 Mar 1976.

1960   DAVID STEWART ELDER (FES IX, 733; X, 88, 418), res as Secretary of Scottish Mission at Accra, Ghana and ind to St Ninian's 25 Nov 1960; ret 16 Sep 1974; died 1 Jul 1994.

TARFF AND TWYNHOLM (FES X, 92)

Tongland with Twynholm linked 22 May 1977 with Borgue. Arrangement terminated 9 Mar 1988. Tongland and Twynholm united same date as Tarff and Twynholm. Linked same date with Balmaghie.

1940   JOHN GOOD (FES IX, 156; X, 92), ord and ind to Twynholm 20 Mar 1940; became minister of linked charge with Tongland 1 Mar 1960; ret 22 May 1977; died 23 Mar 1996; w Janet died 4 Sep 1981.

1977   BRUCE RITCHIE ord and ind to Borgue with Tongland with Twynholm, Oct 1977; trans to Crieff St Andrew's and St Michael's 3 Jun 1987.

1988   CHRISTOPHER WALLACE ord and ind to Balmaghie with Tarff and Twynholm 12 Jul 1988, see Balmaghie.

TERREGLES (FES II, 296; VIII, 178; IX, 149; X, 88)

Linkage with Lochrutton terminated 27 Sep 1981 in favour of linkage with Dumfries Lochside. Linkage terminated 27 May 1997 in favour of linkage with Kirkpatrick-Irongray with Lochrutton.

1975 WILLIAM SCRYMGOUR RHODES
(FES IX, 746; X, 86), ind to Lochrutton with Terregles 10 Apr 1975, see Lochrutton.

1983 JULIAN SINCLAIR TURNBULL
ind to Lochside with Terregles 17 Feb 1983, see Lochside.

1986 THOMAS CRANSTONE BOGLE
ind to Lochside with Terregles 22 Apr 1986, see Lochside.

1997 DAVID KEITH PATTERSON BENNETT
(FES X, 358), trans from Findochty with Portknockie to Kirkpatrick-Irongray with Lochrutton 30 Aug 1987; became minister of linked charge with Terregles 27 May 1997.

THORNHILL (FES X, 88)

1976 ROBERT CUMMING WHITE
(FES X, 11, 211), trans from Edinburgh Holy Trinity to Thornhill 12 Apr 1976; ret 30 Jun 1996; died 15 Jun 1999; s William m Alison.

1997 JOHN EDWARD GISBEY
(FES X, 128), dem from Kirkmahoe 31 Jan 1996; ind to Thornhill 5 Jun 1997; University of Glasgow 1978–85 (DEd); Glasgow College of Food Technology 1982–84; Member of MHCIMA and GTC; d Louise McArthur m Ferrier; d Evelyn Isobel Rose m Farrell. .

TINWALD FES II, 297; VIII, 179; IX, 149; X, 88)

Linked 22 Oct 1970 with Kirkmichael and Garvell. Further linked 13 Sep 1981 with Torthorwald. Garvell dropped from name.

1956 FRASER IAN MACDONALD
(FES IX, 29, 111, 673; X, 88), trans from Roxburgh to Tinwald 9 Feb 1956; became minister of linked charge with Kirkmichael and Garvell 22 Oct 1970

and of linked charge with Torthorwald 13 Sep 1981; died 14 Oct 1983.

1985 JAMES SMITH LEISHMAN
(FES X, 216, 377), trans from Patna Waterside to Kirkmichael with Tinwald with Torthorwald 16 Jan 1985; ret 31 Mar 1999.

TORTHORWALD (FES II, 299; VIII, 180; IX, 149; X, 88)

Linked 13 Sep 1981 with Kirkmichael with Tinwald.

1965 JAMES COULTER
(FES X, 87), trans from Carrickfergus to Mouswald with Torthorwald 17 Jun 1965; ret 31 Mar 1970; died 11 Jan 1977.

1970 HAROLD MEREDITH
(FES X, 87, 172, 246), trans from Glasgow Ruchill to Mouswald with Torthorwald 27 Aug 1970; ret 30 Nov 1979; died 29 Sep 1989.

1981 FRASER IAN MACDONALD
ind to Tinwald 9 Feb 1956; became minister of linked charge with Torthorwald 13 Sep 1981, see Tinwald.

1985 JAMES SMITH LEISHMAN
(FES X, 216, 377), trans from Patna Waterside to Kirkmichael with Tinwald with Torthorwald 16 Jan 1985; ret 31 Mar 1999.

URR (FES II, 304; VIII, 180; IX, 150; X, 88)

Linked 1 Jun 1980 with Dalbeattie.

1974 SAMUEL McCURDY HARRIS
(FES X, 88), ord and ind to Urr 5 Jun 1974; trans to Linlithgow St Ninian's Craigmailen 27 Mar 1980.

1980 NEIL DOUGLAS CRAIG
(FES IX, 115, 346; X, 83, 207), trans from Carstairs to Dalbeattie Craignair 19 Oct 1961; became minister of linked charge with Urr 1 Jun 1980; ret 31 Aug 1987.

1988 NORMAN McKENZIE HUTCHESON
(FES X, 284), trans from Kirkcaldy St Andrew's to Dalbeattie with Urr 11 Aug 1988.

PRESBYTERY OF WIGTOWN AND STRANRAER

BARGRENNAN (FES II, 359; VIII, 193; IX, 163; X, 93)

Linkage with Monigaff terminated 12 Jan 1994 in favour of linking with Newton Stewart Penninghame St John's.

1962 RONALD MIDDLETON FARQUHAR (FES X, 95), ord and ind to Monigaff 10 Apr 1957; became minister of linked charge with Bargrennan 9 May 1962; died 11 Jul 1986.

1987 ALEXANDER MALCOLM RAMSAY ind to Bargrennan with Monigaff 15 Jul 1987; dem 31 Dec 1993 on app by Board of World Mission for service in Guatemala.

1994 NEIL GREGOR CAMPBELL ind to Penninghame St John's 5 Jul 1989; became minister of linked charge with Bargrennan 12 Jan 1994.

ERVIE KIRKCOLM (FES IX, 158; X, 93)

Linked 1 Jul 1985 with Leswalt.

1971 ALASTAIR WILLIAM MURDOCH SANDERSON (FES X, 93), ord and ind to Ervie and Kirkcolm 21 Sep 1971; trans to Glasgow Shawlands Cross 24 Nov 1976.

1977 IAN RING B 17 Jun 1933 at Glasgow, s of John R. and May Matheson; educ Hyndland Secondary, Glasgow 1945–48; Langside College, Glasgow 1971–72; University of Glasgow 1972–76 (BD); lic by Presb of Glasgow 25 Jun 1976; asst Glasgow Knightswood St Margaret's 1976–77; m 26 Mar 1959 Magdalene Jean Todd b 19 Feb 1929 d of John T. and Magdalene Ross; Children: Kenneth David b 28 Dec 1959; Judith Ann b 8 Oct 1962; Alison Jane b 24 Mar 1966; ord and ind to Ervie Kirkcolm 15 Jun 1977; dem 30 Jun 1981.

1982 ALEXANDER BROWN CAIRNS B 20 May 1932 at Methilhill, s of Robert C. and Elizabeth Penman; educ Kirkcaldy High 1943–48; University of Edinburgh 1952–55 (MA); Scottish Congregational College 1955–57; Hamilton College 1974–75 (Dip History and RE); Apprentice Architect 1948–52; m 22 Dec 1956 Dorothy Stuart Wilson b 17 Apr 1935 d of Thomas W. and Isabella

Falconer; Children: Dorothy Ann b 28 Sep 1958 m Ewen Miller; Robin Alexander b 14 Oct 1960; ord by Congregational Union of Scotland at Newburgh, Fife 15 Jul 1957; trans to Morison Memorial Congregational Church, Clydebank 5 Jan 1962; ind to Ervie Kirkcolm 20 Sep 1982; became minister of linked charge with Leswalt 1 Jul 1985; ret 20 May 1997.

1997 MICHAEL JOHN SHEPPARD B 7 Mar 1950 at London, s of John Charles Paul Jean S. and Maureen Isobel Hewitt; educ Plaistow Grammar, London 1961–66; University of Glasgow 1992–96 (BD); Quantity Surveyor and Estimator 1966–92; lic by Presb of Glasgow 1 Jul 1996; m 15 Nov 1975 Helen McEwan McKenzie b 3 Mar 1953 d of William Jack M. and Helen Graham Finlayson McEwan; Children: Jason b 18 May 1973; Catherine (Katie) Elizabeth b 20 Mar 1978 (both adopted); ord and ind to Ervie Kirkcolm with Leswalt 4 Dec 1997.

GLASSERTON AND ISLE OF WHITHORN (FES IX, 163; X, 94)

Linked 2 May 1990 with Whithorn St Ninian's Priory.

1955 WILLIAM CAMPBELL COWIE (FES X, 94), ord and ind to Glasserton and Isle of Whithorn 16 Jun 1955; ret 30 Apr 1990; died 18 Jan 1997.

1990 ALEXANDER IAIN CURRIE B 22 May 1959 at Glasgow, s of Alexander Edward C. and Margaret Walker Thomson Anderson; educ Cathkin High and Coatbridge High 1971–77; University of Glasgow 1984–89 (BD, CPS); Stockroom Manager 1977–79; Social Work (Church of Scotland) 1979–84; lic by Presb of Glasgow, Jun 1989; asst Kilsyth Burns and Old 1989–90; m 10 Sep 1983 Kirsty Walker Fleming b 31 Oct 1962 d of James Norman F. and Elizabeth Walker; Children: Alexander James b 4 Jan 1988; Gregor Iain b 20 Mar 1991; ord and ind to Glasserton and Isle of Whithorn with Whithorn St Ninian's Priory 2 Aug 1990.

INCH (FES X, 94, 95)

Inch linked 20 Oct 1982 with Stranraer St Andrew's. Linkage continues following union of Inch and Lochryan 1 Jul 1985.

1961 ARTHUR FORMSTON
(FES IX, 359, 377, 379; X, 94, 226), trans from North Knapdale Inverlussa and Bellanoch to Inch 15 Mar 1961; ret 31 Dec 1976; died 11 May 1996.

1966 WILLIAM McCALLUM
(FES IX, 393; X, 95, 234, 257), trans from Blackford to Lochryan and Glenapp 12 Oct 1966; ret 30 Nov 1984; died 10 Nov 1995.

1977 ANDREW GILLESPIE JENKINS
(FES X, 78, 79), trans from Hoddam with Brydekirk to Inch 17 Aug 1977; ret 20 Oct 1982 in interests of re-adjustment; died 22 May 1998; w Jean died 17 Nov 1977; m (2) 9 Mar 1979 Elizabeth Ann Dunn b 6 Jan 1942 d of George Eric D. and Elizabeth Anderson Laird; s Archibald m Catherine Mackie.

1983 THOMAS O' LEARY
ord and ind to Inch with Stranraer St Andrew's 11 May 1983; became minister of united charge with Lochryan 1 Jul 1985; dem to take up app with Board of World Mission in Colombo, Sri Lanka Jan 1988.

1988 JOHN HEPBURN BURNS
B 9 Sep 1959 at Dingwall, s of Thomas Sanderson Hepburn B. and Elizabeth Maud Kesting; educ Dingwall Academy 1964–77; University of St Andrews 1977–81 (BSc), 1981–84 (BD); lic by Presb of Ross 28 Sep 1984; asst Dundee St Mary's 1984–85; London St Columba's Pont Street 1985–88; by Presb of England during assistantship at St Columba's Pont Street, Oct 1985; ind to Inch with Stranraer St Andrew's 3 Mar 1988.

KIRKCOWAN (FES IX, 164; X, 94)

Linked 31 Mar 1982 with Wigtown.

1971 ROBERT LAWRENCE JOHNSTONE
(FES IX, 670; X, 94, 170, 383), trans from Glasgow Pollok to Kirkcowan 10 Mar 1971; ret 31 Dec 1976; died 26 May 1988.

1977 QUINTIN FINLAY
(FES X, 99), ord by Presb of Ayr and introd as Assoc at Castlehill 29 Jan 1975; introd on term app to Kirkcowan 29 Jun 1977; res from app 31 Oct 1981; ind to North Bute 16 Feb 1983.

1982 PHILIP LUDWIK MAJCHER
ord and ind to Kirkcowan with Wigtown 23 Jun 1982; dem on app by RAChD 7 Sep 1987.

1988 MARTIN THOMSON
B 24 Oct 1959 at Bellshill, s of Herbert Martin T. and Jean Patterson; educ Coatbridge High and Bannerman High 1971–77; University of St Andrews 1977–81 (BSc); University of Edinburgh and Moray House College 1981–82 (DEd, PGCE); University of Glasgow 1984–87 (BD); Teaching

1982–84; lic by Presb of Hamilton 26 Jun 1987; asst Glasgow Chryston 1987–88; m 18 Oct 1983 Lorna Sutherland Walker b 22 Jan 1960 d of Ranald Martin W. and Georgina McCombie Stewart; Children: Philip Martin b 16 Mar 1989; Jonathan Mark b 27 Feb 1991; Lewis David b 21 Feb 1995; ord and ind to Kirkcowan with Wigtown 18 May 1988.

KIRKINNER (FES IX, 364; VIII, 194; IX, 164; X, 94)

Linked 8 Jun 1981 with Sorbie.

1970 JAMES RANKIN
(FES IX, 267, 483 (2); X, 94, 287), trans from Thornton to Kirkinner 25 Sep 1970; ret 31 Aug 1978; died 4 Feb 1985.

1979 DAVID ROBERT BAILLIE
ord and ind to Kirkinner 24 Jan 1979; trans to Crawford with Lowther 22 Apr 1981.

1981 WILLIAM BLACK
(FES X, 297), res from term app at Half Morton and Kirkpatrick Fleming and ind to Kirkinner with Sorbie 19 Nov 1981; trans to Durness with Kinlochbervie 29 May 1986.

1986 JEFFREY MAURICE MEAD
B 12 Nov 1946 at Edinburgh, s of Maurice M. and Jean Hoy Wilson; educ Boroughmuir Senior Secondary, Edinburgh 1958–63; University of Edinburgh 1970–74 (MA), 1974–77 (BD); Banking 1963–69; lic by Presb of Edinburgh; asst Edinburgh St George's West 1977–79; Children: Paul b 25 May 1970 m Dorothy MacDonald; Robert b 8 Jun 1977; ord by Presb of Edinburgh during assistantship at St George's West; ind to Kirkinner with Sorbie 26 Sep 1986.

KIRKMABRECK (FES IX, 164; X, 94)

Linked 5 Jan 1996 with Monigaff.

1971 JOHN HARRISON PRESCOTT
(FES IX, 94, 159), trans from Glasgow Garthamlock to Kirkmabreck 12 May 1971; ret 6 Jan 1985; died 14 Oct 1994.

1985 DAVID WHITE McCREADIE
(FES X, 167, 359), trans from Callander St Kessog's to Kirkmabreck 18 Apr 1985; ret 31 Dec 1995; d Jacqueline m Spiers.

1994 HUGH DAVIDSON STEELE
B 3 Jul 1955 at Glasgow, s of Hugh Davidson S. and Ann Bryce MacLennan; educ Hermitage Academy, Helensburgh 1968–72 and Weymouth College, Dorset 1987–89; University of Aberdeen 1989–93 (LTh, DipMin); Royal Navy Air Craft Engineer 1972–87; Royal Sailors' Rest 1987–89; lic by Presb of Aberdeen; asst Aberdeen Mastrick 1993–94; m 30 Jul 1988 Deborah Jean Booth b 1

Jan 1958 d of John Leander and Harriet B; Children: Alistair James b 10 Jun 1989; Harriet Ann b 23 Nov 1990; Evelyn Mairi b 23 Oct 1992; ord and ind to Monigaff 17 Jun 1994; became minister of linked charge with Kirkmabreck 5 Jan 1996.

KIRKMAIDEN (FES IX, 159; X, 94)

Linked 10 Feb 1988 with Stoneykirk.

1943   JOHN INGLIS ANDREWS
(FES IX, 159; X, 94), ord and ind to Kirkmaiden 17 Mar 1943; ret 31 Jan 1983; w Jean died 1998.

1984   CHARLES McCURDY
B 14 Feb 1937 at Mountnorris, Co Armagh, N Ireland, s of Andrew M. and Florence Alexandra Flack; educ Newry Grammar 1949–55; Trinity College, Dublin 1955–59 (BA); Queen's University, Belfast 1973 (BD); lic by Presb of Letterkenny, Jun 1962; ord and ind to Carnmoney Presb Church 21 Nov 1962; trans to Hilltown/Clonduff Presb Churches, Iveagh 24 Feb 1966; trans to Kirkcubbin Presb Church 6 Dec 1973; ind to Fauldhouse St Andrew's with Longridge and Breich 15 Aug 1979; trans to Kirkmaiden 28 Jun 1984; dem 12 Jan 1987 to take up app with Presb Church in Ireland.

1988   DUNCAN MACGILLIVRAY
res from app at Rotterdam and ind to Kirkmaiden with Stoneykirk 16 May 1988; ret 30 Jun 1995; died 10 Jan 1997.

1995   IAN McILROY
ord and ind to Kirkmaiden with Stoneykirk 19 Jan 1995.

LESWALT (FES II, 342; VIII, 189; IX, 160; X, 95)

Linked 1 Jul 1985 with Ervie Kirkcolm.

1959   OLIVER MARSHALL OGILVY
(FES X, 95), ord and ind to Leswalt 30 Sep 1959; ret 28 Jun 1985; s Angus m Carol Dinnes; d Jane m Alan Webb.

1985   ALEXANDER BROWN CAIRNS
ind to Ervie Kirkcolm 20 Sep 1982; became minister of linked charge with Leswalt 1 Jul 1985; ret 20 May 1997.

1997   MICHAEL JOHN SHEPPARD
ord and ind to Ervie Kirkcolm with Leswalt 4 Dec 1997, see Ervie.

MOCHRUM (FES II, 369; VIII, 195; IX, 164; X, 95)

1971   WILLIAM JOHN MURRAY JESSON
(FES X, 95), ord and ind to Mochrum 23 Sep 1971; ret 30 Sep 1984; d Lesley m James Maxwell Carruthers.

1985   ANDREW R M PATTERSON
ord and ind to Mochrum 12 Jun 1985; dem 31 Aug 1988.

1989   JOHN HUBERT INNES WATT
(FES X, 213, 301, 439), Lecturer in Religious Education, Hamilton College of Education 1966–82; transferred to Jordanhill College of Education 1 Sep 1982; res 30 Jun 1985 and ind to Mochrum 9 Mar 1989; ret 30 Jun 1994.

1995   ROGER ALFRED FRANCIS DEAN
B 17 Sep 1939 at Whitton, Middlesex, s of Raylton Arthur Warren D. and Florence Mary Whitelock; educ Slough Grammar and Shawlands Academy, Glasgow 1951–55; University of Glasgow 1979–82 (LTh); Electronic Engineering 1956–61; Railway Telecommunications Engineer 1961–79; lic by Presb of Ayr 1 Jul 1982; asst Alloway 1982–83; m 5 Jun 1965 Elizabeth Smith Richardson b 29 Jul 1938 d of Charles Ferrier R. and Jessie Ewart Malcolm; Children: Alan Michael b 13 May 1966 m Hazel Booker; Pamela Joan b 17 Sep 1967 m David Gardner; Kevin Mark b 1 Jul 1971; ord and ind to Dennyloanhead with Haggs 29 Jun 1983; dem on app as Chaplain to Royal Caledonian Schools, Bushey, Herts 1 Sep 1990; ind to Mochrum 25 Jan 1995; Chaplain (part-time) to Penninghame Prison; Publ: *Galloway Gazette— Pulpit and Pen* (*Galloway Gazette*, 1997–98).

MONIGAFF (FES II, 371; VIII, 195, IX, 165; X, 95)

Linked 5 Jan 1996 with Kirkmabreck.

1957   RONALD MIDDLETON FARQUHAR
(FES X, 95), ord and ind to Monigaff 10 Apr 1957; became minister of linked charge with Bargrennan 9 May 1962; died 11 Jul 1986.

1987   ALEXANDER MALCOLM RAMSAY
ind to Bargrennan with Monigaff 15 Jul 1987, see Bargrennan.

1994   HUGH DAVIDSON STEELE
ord and ind to Monigaff 17 Jun 1994; became minister of linked charge with Kirkmabreck 5 Jan 1996, see Kirkmabreck.

NEW LUCE (FES II, 345; VIII, 190; IX, 160; X, 95)

Linked 10 Mar 1969 with Old Luce.

1969   WILLIAM GUTHRIE TRAN
(FES IX, 151, 533; X, 45, 96, 319), ind to Old Luce 29 Aug 1962; became minister of linked charge with New Luce 10 Mar 1969, see Old Luce.

1974   ALEXANDER JOHN ROBERTSON
(FES X, 95), ord and ind to New Luce with Old Luce 12 Jun 1974; trans to Baldernock 27 Feb 1985.

1985   GRAHAM THOMSON DICKSON
ord and ind to New Luce with Old Luce 11 Jun 1985; trans to Edinburgh St Stephen's Comely Bank 28 Nov 1996.

1997 THOMAS MILLAR McWHIRTER
B 3 Aug 1963 at Ballymena, Co Antrim, s of James Kilpatrick M. and Jean Bradshaw; educ Ballymena Academy 1975–82; University of Edinburgh 1982–86 (MA); University of Strathclyde 1986–87 (MSc); University of Aberdeen 1987–90 (BD); lic by Presb of Ballymena, Jun 1991; asst Dundonald, Presb Church of Ireland 1991–97; m 8 Aug 1995 Alison Catherine Wylie b 25 Sep 1965 d of James McCord W. and Isabella Morrow; Children: Charis Rebecca b 13 Sep 1996; Andrew John b 8 May 1998; ord by Presb of East Belfast during assistantship at Dundonald 31 Jan 1992; ind to New Luce with Old Luce 13 Jun 1997.

**NEWTON STEWART PENNINGHAME
ST JOHN'S** (FES X, 95, 96)

Linked 12 Jan 1994 with Bargrennan.

1971 WILLIAM SINCLAIR ARMSTRONG
(FES IX, 647; X, 96 (2), 113, 131, 368), trans from Kilmarnock St Marnock's to Penninghame 18 Aug 1971; became minister of united charge with Newton Stewart St John's 5 Oct 1971; dem 31 Oct 1988; died 2 Nov 1996.

1989 NEIL GREGOR CAMPBELL
B 5 May 1961 at Brighton, s of Gregor C. and Campbell; educ George Watson's, Edinburgh 1971–79; University of Edinburgh 1979–82 (BA), 1984–87 (BD); Hospital Porter 1982–84; lic by Presb of Edinburgh 5 Jul 1988; asst Edinburgh Palmerston Place 1987–89; m 22 Jun 1985 Elizabeth Sharp b 4 Jan 1959 d of Daniel S. and Watt; Children: Neil Donald b 18 May 1989; Peter Sharp b 21 Mar 1991; Lisa Ruth Catherine b 23 Feb 1993; ord by Presb of Edinburgh during assistantship at Palmerston Place 6 Aug 1988; ind to Penninghame St John's 5 Jul 1989; became minister of linked charge with Bargrennan 12 Jan 1994; Chaplain (part-time) to Penninghame Prison; Publ: *Penninghame St John's 1841–1991* (1991); contributor to *Prayers for Today's World* (Kingsway, 1993); *Penninghame: The Study of a Parish* (1998).

OLD LUCE (FES X, 96)

Linked 10 Mar 1969 with New Luce.

1962 WILLIAM GUTHRIE TRAN
(FES IX, 151, 533; X, 45, 96, 319), trans from Peebles Leckie Memorial to Old Luce 29 Aug 1962; became minister of linked charge with New Luce 10 Mar 1969; ret 8 Feb 1974; died 13 Apr 1980.

1974 ALEXANDER JOHN ROBERTSON
(FES X, 95), ord and ind to New Luce with Old Luce 12 Jun 1974; trans to Baldernock 27 Feb 1985.

1985 GRAHAM THOMSON DICKSON
ord and ind to New Luce with Old Luce 11 Jun 1985; trans to Edinburgh St Stephen's Comely Bank 28 Nov 1996.

1997 THOMAS MILLAR McWHIRTER
ind to New Luce with Old Luce 13 Jun 1997, see New Luce.

PORTPATRICK (FES IX, 161; X, 96)

Linked 9 Jun 1987 with Stranraer St Ninian's.

1968 SAMUEL MURDOCH McNAUGHT
(FES X, 96, 284), ord and ind to Portpatrick 1 May 1968; trans to Kirkcaldy St John's 29 Apr 1975.

1976 PAUL BASIL HILTON
(FES IX, 288; X, 40, 171, 230), trans from Lochgoilhead and Kilmorich to Portpatrick 18 Mar 1976; ret 20 Apr 1981; died 22 Sep 1984.

1981 JOHN CORDINER
(FES X, 83, 303), trans from Dumfries Lincluden with Holywood to Portpatrick 14 Jul 1981; ret 30 Sep 1986; d Ann m Forrest.

1987 THOMAS WILKINSON McGILL
(FES X, 97), ord and ind to St Ninian's 28 Jun 1972; became minister of linked charge with Portpatrick 9 Jun 1987; ret 14 Apr 1990.

1990 KEITH EDWARD OFFOR
B 3 Feb 1945 at Lanark, s of Charles Edward O. and Millicent Jane Figg; educ Airdrie Academy and Ayr Academy 1956–62; University of Edinburgh 1985–89; Building Society Manager 1968–85; lic by Presb of Dunfermline 2 Jul 1989; asst Lochgelly Macainsh 1989–90; m 22 Jul 1967 Mary Kay b 7 Nov 1944 d of John K. and Margaret Frew; Children: Graeme Edward b 30 Mar 1969 m Allison; Alastair John b 3 Aug 1971; Gillian Mary b 6 Dec 1974 m Peter Scott; ord and ind to Portpatrick with Stranraer St Ninian's 13 Jun 1990; dem charge and status Aug 1999.

SORBIE (FES IX, 166; X, 96)

Linked 8 Jun 1981 with Kirkinner.

1963 JOHN PRINGLE CROSGROVE
(FES IX, 385, 568; X, 96, 330), trans from Aberdeen St Clement's East to Sorbie 25 Mar 1963; ret 8 Jun 1981; died 27 May 1989.

1981 WILLIAM BLACK
(FES X, 297), ind to Kirkinner with Sorbie 19 Nov 1981, see Kirkinner.

1986 JEFFREY MAURICE MEAD
ind to Kirkinner with Sorbie 26 Sep 1986, see Kirkinner.

STONEYKIRK (FES X, 96)

Linked 10 Feb 1988 with Kirkmaiden.

1958 JAMES ALEXANDER CAMPBELL
(FES X, 93, 96), ord and ind to Ardwell-Sandhead 8 Jan 1958; became minister of united charge with Stoneykirk 28 Aug 1974; ret 30 Apr 1987.

1988   DUNCAN MACGILLIVRAY
res from app at Rotterdam and ind to Kirkmaiden with Stoneykirk 16 May 1988; ret 30 Jun 1995; died 10 Jan 1997.

1995   IAN McILROY
ord and ind to Kirkmaiden with Stoneykirk 19 Jan 1995.

STRANRAER HIGH KIRK (FES X, 96)

1957   ALEXANDER BURGESS
(FES IX, 194, 730; X, 96, 110), trans from Irvine Wilson Fullarton to Stranraer High Kirk 24 Apr 1957; ret 31 Aug 1985; died 7 May 1996.

1986   DAVID WILLIAM DUTTON
B 18 Sep 1947 at Jarrow, s of Arthur Leonard D. and Agnes Potter Murray; educ Jarrow Grammar 1959–66; University of Dundee 1967–70 (CSA); Westminster College, Cambridge 1970–73 (Exit Cert); Open University 1975–80 (BA); Civil Service 1966–67; m 11 Aug 1973 Sandra Rennie Pearce b 18 Apr 1951 d of Stanley Morton P. and Agnes McKechnie Rennie; Children: Alastair Peter b 5 Dec 1975; ord by Northumberland District Council of the URC and ind to Felton and Widdrington 14 Jul 1973; trans to Guisborough and Lingdale (URC) 30 Apr 1977; ind to Papa Westray with Westray 1 Feb 1980; trans to The High Kirk 12 Mar 1986.

STRANRAER OLD (FES II, 355; VIII, 192; IX, 161; X, 96)

1969   JAMES GUTHRIE THOMSON
(FES X, 96, 130), trans from Glasgow Penilee St Andrew to Stranraer Old 16 Oct 1969; dem 30 Sep 1983.

1985   GILBERT LITTLE THOMSON
trans from Wishaw Chalmers to Stranraer Old 5 May 1985; trans to Glenrothes Christ's Kirk on the Green 30 Jun 1989.

1990   SAMUEL McCURDY HARRIS
(FES X, 88), trans from Linlithgow St Ninian's Craigmailen to Stranraer Old 9 Jan 1990; Addl children: Ruth Isabella Clement b 24 Nov 1976; Rachel Grace Pollock b 29 Jun 1979; Publ: *Not a Silent God*, *My Father's House*, *How can we sing the Lord's song?* (*The Expository Times*, T&T Clark, 1982).

STRANRAER ST ANDREW'S (FUF 120; FES IX, 162; X, 96)

Linked 20 Oct 1982 with Inch.

1962   WILLIAM PAUL MONTEATH
(FES IX, 251, 340; X, 97, 149), trans from Thornliebank Spiersbridge to St Andrew's 17 Apr 1962; ret 7 Feb 1982; died 17 Oct 1983.

1983   THOMAS O' LEARY
ord and ind to Inch with St Andrew's 11 May 1983, see Inch.

1988   JOHN HEPBURN BURNS
ind to Inch with St Andrew's 3 Mar 1988, see Inch.

STRANRAER ST NINIAN'S (FUF 121; FES IX, 162; X, 97)

Linked 9 Jun 1987 with Portpatrick.

1972   THOMAS WILKINSON McGILL
(FES X, 97), ord and ind to St Ninian's 28 Jun 1972; became minister of linked charge with Portpatrick 9 Jun 1987; ret 14 Apr 1990.

1990   KEITH EDWARD OFFOR
ord and ind to Portpatrick with St Ninian's 13 Jun 1990, see Portpatrick.

WHITHORN ST NINIAN'S PRIORY (FES IX, 166; X, 97)

Linked 2 May 1990 with Glasserton and Isle of Whithorn.

1974   BASIL BARKHAM
(FES X, 97), trans from Berwick Wallace Green to St Ninian's Priory 6 Jun 1974; ret 31 Aug 1980; died 27 Apr 1982.

1980   WILLIAM McDOWALL MACMILLAN
ord and ind to St Ninian's Priory 26 Nov 1980; trans to Auchterhouse with Murroes and Tealing 25 Oct 1989.

1990   ALEXANDER IAIN CURRIE
ord and ind to Glasserton and Isle of Whithorn with Whithorn St Ninian's Priory 2 Aug 1990, see Glasserton.

WIGTOWN (FES IX, 167; X, 97)

Linked 31 Mar 1982 with Kirkcowan.

1973   JAMES GRANT SUTTIE STEWART THOMSON
(FES IX, 782; X, 97, 174, 439), trans from Glasgow St David's Knightswood to Wigtown 13 Jun 1973; ret 31 Oct 1981; Addl publ: Various contributions to biblical commentaries.

1982   PHILIP LUDWIK MAJCHER
ord and ind to Kirkcowan with Wigtown 23 Jun 1982; dem on app by RAChD 7 Sep 1987.

1988   MARTIN THOMSON
ord and ind to Kirkcowan with Wigtown 18 May 1988, see Kirkcowan.

PRESBYTERY OF AYR

ALLOWAY (FES III, 1; VIII, 211; IX, 168; X, 98)

1961 LUDOVIC WILLIAM GRANT GRAY
(FES IX, 455, 570; X, 98, 331), trans from Aberdeen St Nicholas' Union Grove to Alloway 17 May 1961; ret 31 Oct 1977; died 13 Nov 1978.

1978 JOSEPH WALTER McGINTY
(FES X, 34, 261), trans from Alloa North to Alloway 11 Apr 1978; ret 31 Jul 1998; University of Strathclyde 1991–95 (PhD); Publ: *Literary, Philosophical and Theological Influences on Robert Burns* (Univ of Strathclyde 1995); *John Goldie and Robert Burns* in *Studies in Scottish Literature* Vol XXIX ed by G Ross Roy (Univ of S Carolina, 1996); *Through a Glass Brightly—Alloway's Stained Glass* (Alloway, 1999).

1999 NEIL ANDREW McNAUGHT
B 16 Sep 1961 at Elderslie, s of Henry William Rigby M. and Ruth McLay; educ John Neilson Institute, Paisley 1973–79; University of Glasgow 1979–83 (BD), 1983–85 (MA); lic by Presb of Paisley 27 Jun 1985; asst Paisley Sherwood 1986–87; m 14 Feb 1987 Jill McMillan b 31 May 1964 d of James M. and Sarah Muir; Children: Andrew b 23 Jan 1989; Alan b 6 Aug 1990; Fraser b 20 Dec 1993; ord and ind to Gourock St John's 1 Oct 1987; trans to Alloway 24 Jun 1999.

ANNBANK (FES X, 98)

1969 CHARLES JOHN BIRNIE
(FES X, 98), ord and ind to Annbank 22 Oct 1969; trans to Aberdour with Tyrie 6 May 1982.

1982 ALISTAIR KEITH RIDLAND
ord and ind to Annbank 15 Dec 1982; trans to Dalkeith St John's and King's Park 12 May 1988.

1989 KENNETH LINDSAY JOHNSTON
(FES X, 141), trans from Glasgow Blairbeth Roger Memorial to Annbank 15 Feb 1989; Open University 1976–81 (BA).

ARNSHEEN BARRHILL (FES IX, 157; X, 93)

Linked 1 Aug 1982 with Colmonell.

1954 JAMES McCULLOCH NELSON
(FES IX, 157, 534; X, 93), trans from Glenprosen and Clova to Arnsheen Barrhill to 17 Feb 1954; ret 31 Jul 1982; died 25 Aug 1987.

1982 JAMES FARQUHAR LYALL
(FES IX, 789; X, 446), ind to Colmonell 28 Jan 1981; became minister of linked charge with Arnsheen Barrhill 1 Aug 1982, see Colmonell.

1990 JOHN OWAIN AB IFOR JONES
res as Assoc at Mearns and ind to Arnsheen Barrhill with Colmonell 4 Apr 1990; trans to Glasgow Langside 27 May 1998.

1999 JOHN STEWART LOCHRIE
(FES X, 101, 441), res as Chaplain to the Students' Assoc, University of Strathclyde 1987; ind to Arnsheen Barrhill with Colmonell 23 Mar 1999.

AUCHINLECK (FES X, 98)

Formed 4 Sep 1983 by union of Auchinleck Barony and Auchinleck Peden.

1941 CHARLES LIVINGSTONE JOHNSTON
(FES IX, 169; X, 98), ord and ind to Auchinleck Peden 26 Mar 1941; ret 30 Oct 1980; died 26 Apr 1996.

1967 DANIEL McCALLUM ROBERTSON
(FES X, 37, 98), trans from Falkirk Camelon Trinity to Auchinleck Barony 28 Sep 1967; became minister of linked charge with Auchinleck Peden 2 Nov 1980 and of united charge 4 Sep 1983; s Garry m Annette Elizabeth Wilson; d Iona m Allan MacDonald.

AYR AULD KIRK OF AYR (FES X, 98,99)

Formed 2 Aug 1981 by union of The Auld Kirk of Ayr and Darlington New.

1952 WILLIAM PRENTICE HOWAT
(FES IX, 172, 443; X, 98), trans from Bridge of Allan Chalmers to the Auld Kirk 30 Jan 1952; ret 31 May 1981; died 18 May 1994.

1971 ROBERT DOUGLAS HAIG YOUNG GLOVER
(FES X, 99), ord and ind to Darlington New 26 Aug 1971; trans to Luss 8 May 1980.

1982 THOMAS ALAN WHITEWAY GARRITY
(FES X, 348), trans from Fraserburgh South to the Auld Kirk 24 Feb 1982; dem 28 Feb 1999 on app by Board of World Mission to Bermuda; University of Edinburgh 1993–96 [part-time] (MTh).

1999   DAVID RANKIN GEMMELL
B 27 Feb 1963 at Girvan, s of Robert Clark G. and
Catherine Bruce Davidson; educ Carrick Academy
1974–79; University of Glasgow 1984–87 (MA),
1987–90 (BD); Clerical Asst 1979–83; lic by Presb
of Ayr 14 Jul 1990; asst Girvan North 1990–91; m
12 Sep 1982 Helen Margaret Pringle b 22 Oct 1963
d of James Bruce P. and Anne Malone; Children:
Kirstin Helen b 28 Jan 1983; Jonathan David b 22
Apr 1987; ord and ind to Fenwick 1 Aug 1991; trans
to the Auld Kirk 30 Sep 1999.

AYR CASTLEHILL (FES X, 99)

1967   MICHAEL MURE DICKIE
(FES X, 29, 99, 361), trans from Bathgate St
David's to Castlehill 14 Dec 1967; ret 1 Sep 1993;
s (Michael) Mure m Anna Hood; d Elspeth m Erick
Mauricia; d (Lenora) Jane m Fritz Lehmann.

1994   IAN ROBERT STIRLING
B 3 Jun 1963 at Dumfries, s of James S. and Alice
Mary Nichol; educ Queen Elizabeth High, Hexham
and Oban High; University of Edinburgh 1981–86
(BSc), 1986–89 (BD); lic by Presb of South Argyll
30 Jun 1989; asst Edinburgh St Andrew's and St
George's; m 9 Jul 1988 Amanda Jane Robinson b
14 Jan 1965 d of Peter R. and Susan Haslam;
Children: Nicola Amy b 16 Apr 1991; James
Alexander b 20 Feb 1993; Benjamin Andrew b 30
Jul 1996; ord and ind to Cowie with Plean 7 Jun
1990; trans to Castlehill 9 Jun 1994.

AYR NEWTON-ON-AYR (FES X, 99)

1945   WILLIAM HORNER WHALLEY
(FES IX, 150, 170; X, 99 (2)), trans from Urr to
Newton-on-Ayr Old 17 Oct 1945; became minister
of united charge with Newton-on-Ayr New 4 Jul
1962; died 10 Jul 1981.

1982   COLIN ANDREW MACALISTER SINCLAIR
ord by Presb of Edinburgh 4 May 1981; ind to
Newton-on-Ayr 28 Mar 1982; dem to take up app
as General Director, Scripture Union Scotland 1
Aug 1988.

1989   GEORGE STEWART BIRSE
B 13 Apr 1948 at Broughty Ferry, s of Francis
Arthur B. and Agnes Walker Coutts; educ Dun-
fermline High 1953–65; Institute of Chartered
Accountants of Scotland 1965–73 (CA); University
of Edinburgh 1976–79 (BD); Open University
1993–96 (BSc); Accountancy 1965–76; lic by
Presb of Edinburgh 31 May 1979; asst Cum-
bernauld Kildrum 1979–80; m 29 Jun 1976
Sandra Elisabeth Borthwick b 30 Apr 1956 d of
George Williamson B. and Margaret McLachlan;
Children: Elaine b 1 Sep 1978; Laura b 29 Apr
1981; Jennifer b 13 Apr 1985; ord and ind to
Barrhead Bourock 14 May 1980; trans to Newton-
on-Ayr 19 Jan 1989.

AYR ST ANDREW'S (FUF 125; FES IX, 170; X,
100)

1947   GEORGE HANSON BOYD
(FES IX, 170, 265; X, 100), trans from Glasgow
Dennistoun to St Andrew's 24 Sep 1947; ret 8 Mar
1978; died 21 Jan 1983.

1978   JAMES HOSIE
(FES X, 134, 163, 257), trans from Glasgow King's
Park to St Andrew's 30 Aug 1978; trans to Burra
Isle with Tingwall 26 Jul 1986.

1986   WILLIAM GEORGE NEILL
(FES X, 34, 179), trans from Edinburgh Leith North
to St Andrew's 26 Nov 1986; dem 30 Sep 1999 to
take up full-time study at Jordanhill College,
Glasgow (post-grad course in RE); Addl children:
Kenneth George b 10 Aug 1978; d Heather m Ian
Lyle.

AYR ST COLUMBA (FES X, 99, 100)

Formed 1 Jan 1981 by union of Cathcart, Sandgate
and Trinity.

1946   ROBERT DAVID McDOWELL JOHNSTON
(FES IX, 50, 171, 487; X, 100), trans from Bathgate
St John's to Sandgate 13 Mar 1946; ret 28 Jun
1973; died 4 Dec 1992.

1952   JAMES HYSLOP TELFER
(FES IX, 172, 518; X, 100), trans from Dundee
Wishart Memorial to Trinity 18 Sep 1952; ret 31
Dec 1979; died 5 Oct 1994.

1963   ANGUS MACDONALD NICOLSON
(FES IX, 191, 219, 304; X, 99, 179), trans from
Glasgow Scotstoun West to Cathcart 20 May 1963;
died 20 Aug 1976.

1974   ALASDAIR McINNES
(FES X, 86, 100), trans from Lochrutton with Terregles to Sandgate 19 Jun 1974; introd as Assoc to
united charge with Cathcart and Trinity 1 Jan 1981;
ret 13 Sep 1981; died 6 Sep 1988.

1977   LINDSAY H EWART
ord and introd to Ayr Cathcart (term) 23 Feb 1977;
ind to Lochgoilhead and Kilmorich 23 Oct 1981.

1981   WILLIAM JAMES CHRISTMAN
(FES X, 20, 165), trans from Glasgow Lansdowne
to St Columba 3 Jun 1981; dem 28 Feb 1991 on
app as Chaplain to HM Prison Shotts.

1991   FRASER ROBERT AITKEN
B 8 Jan 1953 at Paisley, s of Robert A. and
Margaret Swan Thomson; educ John Neilson Institution, Paisley 1964–70; University of Glasgow
1970–74 (MA), 1974–77 (BD); lic by Presb of
Paisley 28 Jun 1977; asst Paisley Abbey 1976–
77; Edinburgh Fairmilehead 1977–78; ord and ind
to Neilston 28 Jun 1978; trans to Girvan North 5
Jan 1984; trans to St Columba 21 Aug 1991.

1995 IAN McKELL STUART McINNES
ord by Presb of Ayr and introd as Assoc at St Columba 15 Mar 1995; ind to Glasgow Blawarthill 18 Jun 1997.

AYR ST JAMES' (FES III, 15; VIII, 313; IX, 170; X, 100)

1960 CHARLES EDWARD OFFOR
(FES IX, 316; X, 100, 185), trans from Airdrie Jackson to St James' 20 Jan 1960; ret 30 Jun 1982; died 27 Sep 1990.

1983 JAMES S CAMPBELL
trans from Kames and Kilbride with Kilfinan with Tighnabruaich to St James' 6 Jan 1983; ret 1992; died 6 Apr 1996.

1992 GILLIAN ELIZABETH WEIGHTON
B 5 Apr 1967 at Bellshill, d of John Millar Hunter and Mary Wasson Johnston Biggart; educ Earnock High, Hamilton 1979–85; University of St Andrews 1985–89 (BD); University of Glasgow 1989–90 (CMin); Union Theological Seminary, New York 1990–91 (STM); lic by Presb of Hamilton 2 Jul 1992; asst Dundee The High Kirk 1991–92; m 3 Aug 1992 Alister Grant Weighton b 29 Nov 1961 s of Gilbert W. and Betsy Mathieson Walker Grant; ord and ind to St James' 17 Sep 1992.

AYR ST LEONARD'S (FES III, 15; VIII, 213; IX, 171; X, 100)

1962 CAMPBELL MILNE SAUNDERS
(FES IX, 637; X, 100, 364), trans from Newtonmore to St Leonard's 14 Feb 1962; ret 17 May 1989.

1989 ROBERT LYNN
B 29 Mar 1946 at Glasgow, s of David L. and Catherine Lynch; educ Inverness High 1958–61; University of Aberdeen 1978–83 (BD), 1983–85 (MA); Retail 1961–64; Post Office 1964–67; British Airways 1967–78; lic by Presb of Inverness 5 Jul 1983; asst Bellshill West 1983–84; m 15 Feb 1985 Gillian Mary Porter b 4 Oct 1959 d of James Alexander McEwan P. and Margaret Primrose Keenan; Children: Hilary b 1 Feb 1987; David James b 6 May 1988; ord and ind to Fordyce 1 Nov 1984; trans to St Leonard's 8 Nov 1989.

AYR ST QUIVOX (FES X, 99, 106)

Formed 6 Sep 1981 by union of St Quivox and Ayr Lochside.

1941 WILLIAM LYLE BROWN WILSON
(FES IX, 184; X, 106), ord and ind to St Quivox 29 Oct 1941; ret 30 Apr 1978; died 29 Dec 1983.

1959 JOHN SHAND PHILLIPS
(FES IX, 368, 506, 646, 746; X, 99, 220), trans from Fintry to Lochside 25 Feb 1959; ret 30 Jun 1978.

1978 ROBERT FLEMING BROWN
(FES X, 159), trans from Garthamlock and Craig-end East to St Quivox 8 Nov 1978; became minister of united charge with Lochside 6 Sep 1981; trans to Aberdeen Queen's Cross 15 Nov 1984.

1985 GORDON MACRAE
ord and ind to St Quivox 12 Jun 1985; dem 17 Sep 1987; ind to Glasgow Tron St Mary's 11 Jan 1990.

1988 DAVID THOMAS NESS
(FES X, 102), trans from Dundonald to St Quivox 8 Jun 1988; Addl children: Fiona Hazel b 10 Dec 1976; m (2) 10 Mar 1995 Moira Anne McFarlane b 25 Dec 1944 d of Charles M. and Peebles.

1989 ANGUS RANKIN MATHIESON
ord by Presb of Edinburgh during assistantship at South Leith 10 Jul 1988; introd as Community minister at St Quivox 16 Aug 1989; dem to take up app as Education and Development Officer, Board of Ministry 1 Apr 1998.

AYR WALLACETOWN (FES III, 16; VIII, 213; IX, 172; X, 100)

1945 ARCHIBALD JOHN SCRUBY
(FES IX, 52, 172; 100), trans from Fauldhouse to Wallacetown 11 Apr 1945; ret 5 Mar 1968; died 1 Dec 1991.

1968 ANDREW MONTGOMERY McPHAIL
(FES X, 100), ord and ind to Wallacetown 18 Sep 1968; Open University 1975–78 (BA); d Gwen m Craig White.

BALLANTRAE (FES X, 93, 95)

Formed 1 Jul 1985 by union of Ballantrae and Glenapp.

1966 HARRY MILES LEITH
(FES IX, 590, 702; X, 54, 93, 368, 400), trans from Garvald and Morham to Ballantrae 24 Feb 1966; ret 30 Apr 1972; died 31 Jan 1984.

1972 GEORGE DUDLEY ANDREW FOX
(FES X, 93), ord and ind to Ballantrae 21 Sep 1972; introd to Kelso Old (term) 14 Mar 1982; ind to same charge 16 Dec 1984.

1983 THOMAS DRYSDALE LIND
(FES X, 379), trans from Kilmorack and Erchless to Ballantrae 12 Jan 1983; became minister of united charge with Glenapp 1 Jul 1985; dem 30 Jun 1986.

1987 ISOBEL JARVIE BRAIN
B 4 Jul 1930 at Glasgow, d of George Whitehall Taylor and Anne Russell; educ Hillhead High, Glasgow 1935–48; University of Glasgow 1948–51 (MA), Trinity College 1985–86; Jordanhill College, Glasgow 1951–52; Teaching 1952–69, 1972–85; lic by Presb of Glasgow 30 Jun 1986;

asst Jordanhill 1985–86; m 29 Jun 1962 Ernest John Brain b 12 Nov 1908; Children: Catriona Lorna b 12 Oct 1969; ord and ind to Ballantrae 24 Mar 1987; ret 30 Sep 1997.

1998 ROBERT PATTERSON BELL
(FES X, 190, 203), trans from Cambuslang St Andrew's to Ballantrae 20 Jan 1998; d Aileen m Alan Porte; s Andrew m Laura Gordon, divorced.

BARR (FES III, 17; VIII, 214; IX, 173; X, 100)

Linked 11 Jan 1976 with Dailly.

1957 SIMON CHARLES DAVID FERGUSSON
(FES X, 100), ord and ind to Barr St Andrew's 23 Oct 1957; ret 6 Feb 1975; died 6 Jan 1982.

1976 RICHARD SMITH
ord and ind to Barr with Dailly 10 Jun 1976; trans to Denny Old 17 Aug 1983.

1984 GEORGE GRAHAM HELON
B 10 Jan 1930 at Maxwelltown, s of James Frederick H. and Jessie Agnes Graham; educ Dumfries Academy 1940–44; Open University 1973–77 (BA); University of Glasgow 1977–80 (BD); Hairdressing 1944–48, 1950–77; Gordon Highlanders 1948–50; lic by Presb of Dumfries and Kirkcudbright 26 Jun 1980; asst Kirkmahoe 1980–81; m 10 Jan 1966 Flora Heather MacDougall d of Donald M. and Jean Findlayson; Children: Alison Anne b 11 Nov 1966 m Dunse; George Graham b 17 Jun 1970; ord and ind to Barr with Dailly 11 Jan 1984.

CATRINE (FES X, 100)

Linked 1 Sep 1978 with Sorn.

1955 JAMES DICKSON
(FES IX, 230; X, 100, 133), trans from Greenock Ladyburn to Catrine 14 Dec 1955; ret 31 Aug 1978; died 9 Apr 1979.

1979 ALEXANDER McEWAN WELSH
ord and ind to Catrine with Sorn 27 Feb 1979; trans to Glasgow Dennistoun Blackfriars 15 May 1986.

1986 WILLIAM CLEMENT ROBB
(FES X, 405), trans from Kilberry with Tarbert to Catrine with Sorn 19 Nov 1986; trans to Balmaclellan and Kells with Dalry 2 Jun 1993.

1994 GEORGE ANGUS CHALMERS
(FES X, 37, 61), trans from Banchory-Ternan West to Catrine with Sorn 15 Sep 1994; d Pamela m Grant Affleck; Publ: *I Saw the Man* [song] (Stainer & Bell, 1978).

COLMONELL (FES II, 333; VIII, 188; IX, 158; X, 93)

Linked 1 Aug 1982 with Arnsheen Barrhill.

1925 JAMES BROWN
(FES VIII, 188; IX, 158; X, 93), ord and ind to Colmonell 17 Sep 1925; ret 31 May 1962; died 18 Feb 1982.

1963 JAMES CARSON STRACHAN
(FES IX, 421, 793; X, 93, 349, 448), ret from RAChD and ind to Colmonell 14 Feb 1963; trans to Lonmay with Rathen West 22 Nov 1967.

1968 JAMES HAY HAMILTON
(FES IX, 274, 387; X, 93, 162), trans from Glasgow Hyndland to Colmonell 12 Jun 1968; ret 28 Feb 1978; died 3 Oct 1991.

1979 HENRY L KIRK
ind to Colmonell 26 Sep 1979; dem 20 Oct 1980.

1981 JAMES FARQUHAR LYALL
(FES IX, 789; X, 446), ret from RAChD and ind to Colmonell 28 Jan 1981; became minister of linked charge with Arnsheen Barrhill 1 Aug 1982; ret 15 Nov 1989; s Ian m Helen O' Donnel.

1990 JOHN OWAIN AB IFOR JONES
ind to Arnsheen Barrhill with Colmonell 4 Apr 1990, see Arnsheen.

1999 JOHN STEWART LOCHRIE
(FES X, 101, 441), ind to Arnsheen Barrhill with Colmonell 23 Mar 1999, see Arnsheen.

COYLTON (FES III, 20; IX, 173; X, 101)

Linked 8 Oct 1991 with Drongan The Schaw Kirk.

1932 ANDREW ELVIN HART
(FES V, 459; VIII, 517; IX, 173, 574; X, 101), trans from Cookney to Coylton 1 Sep 1932; ret 7 Apr 1962; died 20 Oct 1981.

1962 HERBERT KITCHENER NEIL
(FES IX, 327; X, 101, 192, 244, 267, 278), trans from Port of Menteith and Gartmore to Coylton 28 Oct 1962; trans to Kilmonivaig 28 May 1968.

1968 RICHARD HALDANE MARTIN McALPINE
(FES X, 101), ord and ind to Coylton 17 Oct 1968; trans to Lochgoilhead and Kilmorich 1 Nov 1990.

1992 PAUL ROBERT RUSSELL
B 26 Jul 1955 at Glasgow, s of Robert Andrew R. and Frances Margaret Watson; educ Ayr Academy 1967–73; University of Glasgow 1973–78 (MA), 1978–82 (BD); lic by Presb of Ayr 5 Jul 1983; asst Montrose Old 1982–83; m 10 Oct 1986 Shirley Anne Walker b 20 Mar 1961 d of James W. and Evelyn Speirs; Children: Kirsten Iona Megan b 5 Jun 1991; Caitlin Ilona Mhairi b 8 Oct 1993; Matthew Michael Stuart b 16 Aug 1995; ord and ind to Clydebank Radnor Park 17 Feb 1984; trans to Coylton with Drongan The Schaw Kirk 9 Jan 1992.

CRAIGIE (FES III, 22; VIII, 214; IX, 188; X, 101)

Linked 30 Apr 1959 with Symington.

1929   GEORGE ALEXANDER MACKEGGIE
(FES VI, 426; VIII, 645; IX, 188, 645), trans from Kinloss to Craigie 11 Nov 1929; ret 16 Apr 1958; died 15 Dec 1984.

1959   THOMAS RITCHIE
(FES IX, 110, 185; X, 106), ind to Symington 6 Aug 1946; became minister of linked charge with Craigie 30 Apr 1959; died 17 Nov 1968.

1969   ALEXANDER SMART SUTHERLAND
(FES IX, 389; X, 106, 232), dem from Bolton St Andrew's (Presb Church of England) and ind to Craigie with Symington 30 Sep 1969; ret 30 Nov 1987; s Alistair m Linda Northcote; s William m Gwendoline Anderson; s Kenneth m Sandra McDavid; s Ross m Carolyn Crombie; d Elizabeth m Robert Young.

1988   MARGARET WHYTE
B at Paisley, educ Paisley Grammar 1963–68; Open University 1974–80 (BA); University of Glasgow 1983–86 (BD); lic by Presb of Paisley 3 Jul 1986; m 1974 T D P Whyte; Children: Victoria b 1976; Sarah b 1979; ord and ind to Craigie with Symington 30 May 1988; Chaplain to West Lowland Battalion, Army Cadet Force.

CROSSHILL (FES IX, 173; X, 101)

Linked 30 Aug 1981 with Dalrymple.

1969   JAMES CRICHTON
(FES X, 101), ord and ind to Crosshill 16 Jul 1969; became minister of linked charge with Dalrymple 30 Aug 1981; Addl children: James; Publ: *The Story of the Crosshill Churches* (*Cumnock Chronicle*, 1976); *The Carrick Covenanters* (*Cumnock Chronicle*, 1978); *Mixed Company* (St Andrew Press, 1988).

DAILLY (FES IX, 174; X, 101)

Linked 11 Jan 1976 with Barr.

1976   RICHARD SMITH
ord and ind to Barr with Dailly 10 Jun 1976; trans to Denny Old 17 Aug 1983.

1984   GEORGE GRAHAM HELON
ord and ind to Barr with Dailly 11 Jan 1984, see Barr.

DALMELLINGTON (FES X, 101)

Formed 30 Oct 1983 by union of Dalmellington Kirk o' the Covenant and Dalmellington Lamloch Bellsbank.

1950   JOHN MORTON
(FES IX, 174, X, 101), ord and ind to Dalmellington Kirk o' the Covenant 24 Sep 1950; ret 16 Oct 1983.

1974   JAMES KERR
(FES IX, 73, 169, 365; X, 99, 101, 115, 420), res from app with Overseas Council at Nassau St Andrew's, Bahamas 31 May 1973; introd on term app to Dalmellington Lamloch Bellsbank 19 Dec 1974; ret 31 Dec 1979; died 27 Sep 1981.

1984   KEITH WILLIAM ROSS
ord and ind to Dalmellington 19 Sep 1984; trans to Glasgow Toryglen 20 Mar 1991.

1991   ALISON ELIZABETH SHAW DAVIDGE
ord by Presb of Ardrossan during assistantship at Largs Clark Memorial 30 Oct 1990; ind to Dalmellington 24 Oct 1991; trans to Paisley Martyrs' 1 Oct 1997.

1999   KENNETH BURGOYNE YORKE
B 13 Jun 1939 at Aberdeen, s of James Burgoyne Y. and Elizabeth McCallum; educ Prestwick High 1951–55; University of Glasgow 1977–81 (BD); University of Strathclyde 1992–93 (DEd); Motor Engineering 1956–77; lic by Presb of Ayr 28 Jun 1981; asst Alloway 1981–82; m (1) 13 Aug 1966 Ann Ironside Brown b 7 Jul 1941 d of James B. and Charlotte Caldwell; Children: Kenneth James b 31 Jan 1968; Callum Peter b 16 Aug 1969; m (2) 15 May 1991 Margaret McIntyre b 5 Apr 1948 d of Harold Raymond Beggs and Margaret Sands; Children: Eiley b 22 Sep 1990; ord and ind to Kirn 5 May 1982; trans to Ochiltree with Stair 25 Aug 1987; teacher of Religious and Moral Educ 1993–99; ind to Dalmellington 9 Mar 1999.

DALRYMPLE (FES IX, 175; X, 102)

Linked 30 Aug 1981 with Cosshill.

1972   GEORGE RORISON GILCHRIST
(FES IX, 213, 654; X, 102, 155, 372), trans from Glasgow Cathcart Old to Dalrymple 29 Nov 1972; ret 30 Aug 1980; s James m Heather Ann Cargey.

1981   JAMES CRICHTON
(FES X, 101), ord and ind to Crosshill 16 Jul 1969; became minister of linked charge with Dalrymple 30 Aug 1981.

DRONGAN THE SCHAW KIRK (FUF 132; FES IX, 185; X, 107)

Linked 8 Oct 1991 with Coylton.

1949   GEORGE LINDSAY HUNTER
(FES IX, 185; X, 107), ord and ind to The Schaw Kirk 29 Jun 1949; dem 29 Sep 1960 to enter teaching profession (RE); ret 27 Jun 1982; Children: Margaret b 5 Nov 1959; Publ: 'The Life and Work of Gaston Frommel' (PhD Thesis lodged with Edinburgh University).

1961   EDWARD MACKAY
(FES IX, 105; X, 62, 74, 107, 187), trans from Bargeddie to The Schaw Kirk 28 Jun 1961; trans to Selkirk Heatherlie 15 Sep 1966.

1967 WILLIAM MUIR McPHERSON
(FES X, 107, 160), ord and ind to The Schaw Kirk 23 Feb 1967; trans to Glasgow Gorbals 22 Nov 1973.

1974 GORDON DAVID JAMIESON
(FES X, 107), ord and ind to The Schaw Kirk 1 May 1974; trans to Elie with Kilconquhar and Colinsburgh 25 Jul 1979.

1980 JAMES SIDNEY ALLISON SMITH
(FES X, 224, 339, 404), trans from Alford with Tullynessle and Forbes with Keig to The Schaw Kirk 30 Apr 1980; ret 30 Sep 1991; d Susan m Vincent McCulloch (separated).

1992 PAUL ROBERT RUSSELL
ind to Coylton with The Schaw Kirk 9 Jan 1992, see Coylton.

DUNDONALD (FES IX, 175; X, 102)

1972 DAVID THOMAS NESS
(FES X, 102), ord and ind to Dundonald 17 May 1972; trans to Ayr St Quivox 8 Jun 1988.

1988 ROBERT MAYES
B 16 Jun 1951 at Lanark, s of John Shaw M. and Barbara Elizabeth Thomson; educ Lesmahagow Higher Grade School and Larkhall Academy 1963–69; University of St Andrews 1976–80 (BD); University of Glasgow 1980–81 (CMin); Local Government Officer 1969–76; lic by Presb of Lanark 30 Jun 1981; asst Troon St Meddan's 1981–82; m 17 Jun 1982 Catriona Girvan Gray McGreish b 19 Aug 1958 d of John Edward Lee M. and Elizabeth Girvan Black; Children: Elizabeth Ruth b 23 Jan 1985; Ruaridh b 11 Aug 1987; Margaret Catherine b 15 Dec 1989; ord and ind to Wishaw Old 12 May 1982; trans to Dundonald 13 Dec 1988.

FISHERTON (FES III, 37; VIII, 317; IX, 175; X, 102)
Linked 17 May 1978 with Maybole West.

1969 DAVID NAIRN McLEISH
(FES IX, 343, 432, 508, 681; X, 102, 256, 387), trans from Olrig to Fisherton 10 Apr 1969; ret 31 Dec 1977; m 21 Mar 1978 Mary Graham Coltart Anderson b 5 Mar 1916 d of Jonathan Ranken A. and Marian Goodall-Copestake; Publ: *Jesus Christ, Lover and Life-Giver* (private, 1991).

1980 DONALD WILSON PURVIS
B 21 May 1934 at Glasgow, s of John Aitken P. and Elizabeth Fergsuon; educ Albert Secondary, Glasgow 1946–49; University of Glasgow 1976–79 (DTh); lic by Presb of Lanark 3 Jun 1979; asst Motherwell Dalziel 1979–80; m 19 May 1962 Elizabeth Nicholson b 21 Jul 1939 d of Mr and Mrs George N; Children: Carol Ann b 13 Mar 1963; Sandra Lorraine b 28 Apr 1964; Claire Elizabeth b

17 Jan 1979; ord and ind to Fisherton with Maybole West 16 Jul 1980; ret 30 Sep 1985; died 12 May 1995.

1986 JOHN STUART
B 19 Mar 1957 at Glasgow, s of Andrew Alexander S. and Evelyn McLay; educ Colston Secondary, Glasgow 1969–75; University of Glasgow 1979–85 (BD, DipMin); lic by Presb of Glasgow 1 Jul 1985; asst Glasgow Shettleston Old 1985–86; m 4 Jul 1981 Evelyn Mary Smith d of William George S. and Barbera Carson Cowie; ord and ind to Fisherton with Maybole West 30 Apr 1986; dem 31 May 1995 and emigrated to USA.

1996 THOMAS CRANSTONE BOGLE
B 7 Jul 1939 at Hawick, s of David B. and Catherine Sloan; educ Hawick High 1944–58; University of St Andrews 1958–62; University of Edinburgh 1962–64, 1966–70 (BD, CPS); Moray House College, Edinburgh 1970–71 (HDREd); Youth Work 1963–64; Teaching 1971–83; lic by Presb of Shetland 30 Nov 1982; m 2 Aug 1976 Patricia Josephine McKenna b 4 Mar 1949 d of Henry Peter Mullen and Flora Hamilton; Children: Alan b 8 Apr 1968 m Lynn Elliot; Kirsteen Flora b 2 Apr 1971; Lindsey Catherine Sloan b 22 Jun 1977; Victoria Norma McKenna b 3 Dec 1980; ord and introd to Caddonfoot with Selkirk Heatherlie (term) 29 Sep 1983; ind to Dumfries Lochside with Terregles 22 Apr 1986; trans to Fisherton with Maybole West 21 Aug 1996.

GIRVAN NORTH (FES X, 102)
Formed 15 Feb 1973 by union of Girvan Old and Girvan St Andrew's.

1952 JAMES PETRIE EDGAR WIGHTMAN
(FES IX, 176, 192; X, 102), trans from Irvine Fullarton to St Andrew's 26 Mar 1952; ret 15 Feb 1973.

1973 EDWARD VANCE SIMPSON
(FES X, 102), ord by Presb of Elgin during assistantship at St Giles' 20 Feb 1972; ind to Girvan North 6 Jun 1973; trans to Giffnock South 29 Jun 1983.

1984 FRASER ROBERT AITKEN
trans from Neilston to Girvan North 5 Jan 1984; trans to Ayr St Columba 21 Aug 1991.

1992 JOSEPH ANTHONY KAVANAGH
ord and ind to Girvan North 25 Feb 1992; trans to Glasgow Mearns 8 May 1998.

1999 DOUGLAS GORDON McNAB
B 3 Jul 1955 at Glasgow, s of Gordon William M. and Alicia Read Bradley; educ Royal High, Edinburgh 1967–73; University of Edinburgh 1976 (BA), 1997 (BD); Teaching 1978–94; lic by Presb of West Lothian 26 Jun 1997; asst Kirk of Calder 1997–99; m 7 Jul 1984 Lorraine Miller b 30

Nov 1962 d of David Archibald M. and Frater; Children: Iain Douglas b 22 Sep 1986; Ross William b 27 Jun 1989; ord and ind to Girvan North 26 Jan 1999.

GIRVAN SOUTH (FES III, 43; VIII, 218; IX, 176; X, 102)

1967 ALASTAIR FERGUSON LAMONT
(FES X, 102, 421), res from service with Overseas Council in Chile and ind to Girvan South 1 Mar 1967; trans to Aberdeen Denburn 16 Jan 1980.

1980 ROBERT COOK
ord and ind to Girvan South 26 Jun 1980; dem 30 Sep 1987.

1988 IAIN MACNEE
trans from Newbattle to Girvan South 18 May 1988; trans to Canisbay with Keiss 17 Feb 1998.

1999 IAN KENNETH McLACHLAN
B 15 Aug 1953 at Edinburgh, s of Hugh Baird M. and Helen Urquhart Gilfillan; educ George Watson's, Edinburgh 1965–71; University of St Andrews 1971–77 (MA, BD); Dundee College of Education 1977–78 (PGCE); Teaching (RE) 1978–97, 1998–99; lic by Presb of Edinburgh, 1977; asst Dundee Barnhill St Margaret's 1997–98; ord and ind to Girvan South in deferred linkage with Barr and Dailly 19 Jan 1999.

KIRKMICHAEL (FES III, 44; VIII, 219; IX, 177; X, 103)

Linked 1 Apr 1971 with Straiton St Cuthbert's.

1971 WALTER DONALD McKECHNIE MOFFAT
(FES IX, 189, 571, 619; X,103, 151, 356), trans from Glasgow Bellahouston to Kirkmichael with Straiton St Cuthbert's 8 Jul 1971; ret 31 May 1985; died 13 Jan 1987.

1985 WILLIAM GERALD JONES
B 2 Nov 1956 at Irvine, s of William Wallace J. and Helen Cook; educ Dalry High and Garnock Academy, Kilbirnie 1969–74; University of Glasgow 1974–78 (MA), 1980–82 (BD); University of St Andrews 1978–80; Princeton Theological Seminary, New Jersey 1982–83 (ThM); lic by Presb of Ardrossan 30 Jun 1982; asst Glasgow Cathedral 1983–85; m 3 Apr 1991 Janet Blackstock b 16 Feb 1952 d of John B. and Janet Derby; ord by Presb of Glasgow during assistantship at Glasgow Cathedral 26 Jun 1984; ind to Kirkmichael with Straiton St Cuthbert's 23 Oct 1985; app Asst Chaplain and Officer, Order of St Lazarus of Jerusalem 1995; Church Service Society 1986–98; Societas Liturgica from 1989; Society for Liturgical Study from 1995; Publ: *Prayers for the Chapel Royal in Scotland* (private, 1989); contributor to *Worshipping Together* (St Andrew Press, 1991); contributor to *Common Order* (St Andrew Press, 1994).

KIRKOSWALD (FES IX, 177; X, 103)

1974 JAMES ALEXANDER GUTHRIE
(FES X, 103, 194), trans from Greengairs to Kirkoswald 17 Jul 1974; d Elspeth m Cunningham; Publ: *'A Corner of Carrick'* (*Carrick Gazette* 1979, 1981; Alex Gardner 1991).

LUGAR (FES III, 48; VIII, 220; IX, 177; X, 103)

Linkage with Old Cumnock St Ninian's terminated 26 Feb 1989. Linked same date with Old Cumnock Old.

1958 IAN MACDONALD TWEEDLIE
(FES X, 103), ind to Lugar 16 Oct 1958; became minister of linked charge with St Ninian's 20 Dec 1961; died 27 Jul 1988.

1989 MARTIN JAMES McKEAN
ord and ind to Old Cumnock Old 13 Dec 1984; became minister of linked charge with Lugar 26 Feb 1989; trans to Balerno 30 Jun 1993.

1994 JOHN WILLIAM PATERSON
B 7 Jun 1954 at Dumfries, s of William P. and Doris Craik Halliday; educ Dumfries Academy 1959–72; Stirling University 1972–76 (BSc, DipEd); Royal Military Academy, Sandhurst 1976–77; University of St Andrews 1990–93 (BD); British Army 1976–84; Principal of private school, Pakistan 1984–90; lic by Presb of Dumfries 4 Jul 1993; asst Largo Newburn with Largo St David's 1993–94; m 23 Jul 1983 Margery Grace Macaulay b 1 Jun 1956 d of Francis M. and Muriel Wilson; ord and ind to Lugar with Old Cumnock Old 15 Jun 1994.

MAUCHLINE (FES X, 103)

Formed 14 Jan 1976 by union of Mauchline Old and Mauchline North.

1948 JAMES CRUICKSHANK GLENNIE
(FES IX, 178, 194, 734; X, 103), trans from Kilmarnock Glencairn to Mauchline Old 12 May 1948; ret 31 Dec 1975; died 13 Jan 1980.

1953 ALLAN STEWART
(FES IX, 178; X, 103), ord and ind to Mauchline North 8 Apr 1953; dem 30 Sep 1975; died 24 Jul 1979.

1976 CHARLES SMITH MORRICE
(FES X, 200, 423), res from app with Board of World Mission in Argentina and ind to Mauchline 23 Jun 1976; dem to take up app with Board of World Mission in Kenya 1 Sep 1990; Publ: *A Brief History of Mauchline Parish Church* (1979).

1991 ALAN BARCLAY TELFER
B 14 Feb 1956 at Glasgow, s of Walter T. and Ismay McAslan Barclay; educ Eastwood Senior High, Glasgow 1967–73; Paisley College of Technology 1975–79 (BA, CQSW); University of Glasgow 1979–82 (BD); Office Junior in Stock

Exchange 1973–75; lic by Presb of Glasgow 28 Jun 1982; m 23 Jun 1983 Marjory May Crawford b 15 Jan 1957 d of Robert C. and Emma McAlister; Children: Andrew b 11 Jul 1984; Peter b 4 Aug 1987; Fiona b 23 Oct 1992; ord and ind to Falkirk St James' 30 Aug 1983; trans to Mauchline 14 Mar 1991.

MAYBOLE CARGILL-KINCRAIG (FES IX, 179; X, 103)

Congregation dissolved 3 May 1978.

1967   WALTER RENNIE
(FES X, 103, 244), trans from Kilmonivaig to Cargill-Kincraig 16 Oct 1967; ret 30 Apr 1978; died 20 Feb 1991.

MAYBOLE OLD (FES III, 50; VIII, 221; IX, 179; X, 103)

1943   GEORGE BROWN ANDERSON
(FES IX, 179, 329; X, 103), trans from Hamilton Auchingramont North to Maybole Old 1 Oct 1943; ret 30 Sep 1981; died 7 Jun 1988.

1982   ANDREW GORDON REID
ord and ind to Maybole Old 18 Jun 1982; trans to Dunfermline Gillespie Memorial 15 Dec 1988.

1989   COLIN CHARLES RENWICK
ord and ind to Maybole Old 12 Jul 1989; trans to Glasgow Jordanhill 28 Aug 1996.

1998   DAVID WHITEMAN
B 22 Feb 1960 at Blyth, Northumberland, s of Henry W. and Joy I' Anson; educ Manor Park, Newcastle-on-Tyne 1971–77; University of Edinburgh 1992–96; Buyer 1978–92; lic by Presb of Falkirk, 1996; m 14 Jul 1990 Susan Farmer b 5 Jun 1967 d of Douglas and Heather F; Children: Rachel Susan b 28 May 1996; Rebecca Joy b 19 Dec 1997; ord and ind to Maybole Old 10 Feb 1998.

MAYBOLE WEST (FES III, 54; VIII, 222; IX, 179; X, 103)

Linked 17 May 1978 with Fisherton.

1973   JAMES BROWN
(FES X, 104), ord and ind to Maybole West 16 May 1973; became minister of linked charge with Fisherton 17 May 1978; trans to Cockpen and Carrington with Lasswade 13 Feb 1980.

1980   DONALD WILSON PURVIS
ord and ind to Fisherton with Maybole West 16 Jul 1980, see Fisherton.

1986   JOHN STUART
ord and ind to Fisherton with Maybole West 30 Apr 1986, see Fisherton.

1996   THOMAS CRANSTONE BOGLE
ind to Fisherton with Maybole West 21 Aug 1996, see Fisherton.

MONKTON AND PRESTWICK NORTH (FES X, 104, 106)

Formed 31 May 1981 by union of Prestwick North and Monkton and Prestwick (St Cuthbert's).

1947   DONALD MURDOCH CASKIE
(FES IX, 179, 208, 325; X, 104), trans from Coatbridge Coats to Monkton and Prestwick 3 Sep 1947; ret 31 May 1981; died 26 Jul 1992.

1965   PHILIP WILFRID POWELL PETTY
(FES IX, 746; X, 106, 424), res as Deputy Warden of St Ninian's, Crieff and ind to Prestwick North 28 Apr 1965; Chaplain to Stratheden Hospital 1989; ret 30 Sep 1979; d Margaret m Kennedy.

1981   ARTHUR FRANCIS STODDART KENT
(FES X, 187, 420), trans from Bellshill West to Monkton and Prestwick North 9 Dec 1981; ret 30 Jun 1999; d Elaine m John Patience; d Valerie m George Latham.

MUIRKIRK (FES IX, 180; X, 104)

1970   ROY ARCHIBALD STEWART
(FES IX, 720, 764; X, 104, 183), trans from Glasgow Victoria Tollcross to Muirkirk 29 Apr 1970; ret 31 May 1972; died 14 Jul 1987.

1973   JAMES LESLIE GUTHRIE
(FES X, 104), ord and ind to Muirkirk 10 Jan 1973; dem 6 Nov 1987.

1987   WILLIAM HANNAH
B 25 Jul 1934 at Ayr, s of John Alexander H. and Margaret Gemmell Cairns; educ Ayr Grammar 1939–50; University of Glasgow 1982–86 (BD); Journalism 1950–62; Editor, Ayr Advertiser 1962–66; Asst Editor, ICI 1966–68; Public Relations Manager, Burroughs Corporation 1968–82; lic by Presb of Glasgow 30 Jun 1986; asst Cadder 1986–87; Marion Gillon Matheson b 12 May 1937 d of John Imrie Miller M. and Ruth Dickson; Children: John Alexander Matheson b 28 Jul 1959 m Fiona Harvie; William b 5 Sep 1962 m Morag Brown; Ruth Dickson b 15 Apr 1964 m Stuart Hay; James Cairns b 27 Apr 1967 m Karen Stewart; ord and ind to Muirkirk 16 Sep 1987.

NEW CUMNOCK (FES X, 104, 105)

Formed 28 Mar 1982 by union of New Cumnock Arthur Memorial and New Cumnock Old (union 10 May 1961 of New Cumnock Bank and New Cumnock Martyrs').

1936   ANDREW REID LOWRIE
(FES IX, 180, 459; X, 104), trans from Crossgates to New Cumnock Arthur Memorial 27 Feb 1936; pastoral tie severed 30 Jun 1963; died 24 Oct 1983.

1949 JOSEPH BUCHANAN
(FUF 309; FES IX, 114, 181, 223, 446; X, 104), trans from Edgerston to New Cumnock Bank 27 Mar 1949; ret 31 Oct 1959; died 19 Sep 1976.

1953 DAVID CLARK MACPHERSON
(FES IX, 181, 205, 356; X, 104, 105), trans from Alexandria North to New Cumnock Martyrs' 13 May 1953; became minister of linked charge with New Cumnock Bank 1 May 1960 and of united charge 10 May 1961; ret 31 Jul 1974; died 3 Nov 1987.

1964 JAMES WADDELL
(FES X, 104), ord and introd on term app to New Cumnock Arthur Memorial 30 Apr 1964; app terminated 31 Jul 1966.

1966 JAMES COLQUHOUN
(FES X, 104), ind to New Cumnock Arthur Memorial 14 Jun 1966; dem and returned to USA 30 Sep 1970.

1971 DUNCAN McDIARMID
(FES X, 85, 89, 104), trans from Kirkbean to New Cumnock Arthur Memorial 12 May 1971; ret 30 Sep 1976; died 4 Jun 1985.

1974 MORRIS COWPER COULL
(FES X, 105), ord and ind to New Cumnock Old 27 Nov 1974; became minister of united charge with New Cumnock Arthur Memorial 28 Mar 1982; trans to Glasgow Hillington Park 24 Feb 1983.

1983 ANDREW FLEMING McGURK
ord and ind to New Cumnock 27 Jun 1983; trans to Largs St John's 7 Jan 1993.

1993 GORDON KENNEDY
B 15 Sep 1963 in England, s of David K. and Grace Jewell; educ Crookston Castle Secondary 1975–80; University of Strathclyde 1980–85 (BSc); University of Glasgow 1989–92 (BD); Civil Engineering 1985–89; lic by Presb of Glasgow 26 Jun 1992; asst Bearsden North 1992–93; m 14 Mar 1987 Fiona Marshalsay b 20 Aug 1960 d of James Dowie M. and Isabella Armit Gow; Children: John Stephen b 27 Apr 1994; Andrew Philip b 18 Aug 1999; ord and ind to New Cumnock 16 Jun 1993.

OCHILTREE (FES IX, 181; X, 105)

Linked 6 Jan 1979 with Stair.

1967 JAMES CURRIE
(FES X, 72, 105), trans from Galashiels St John's to Ochiltree 19 Jul 1967; ret 31 Oct 1970; died 1 Oct 1986.

1971 JOHN HERON
(FES IX, 184; X, 95, 105, 106, 202), trans from Mochrum to Ochiltree 22 Apr 1971; ret 6 Jan 1979.

1979 RAYMOND DAVID MACKENZIE
ord and ind to Stair 9 May 1978; became minister of linked charge with Ochiltree 6 Jan 1979, see Stair.

1987 KENNETH BURGOYNE YORKE
trans from Kirn to Ochiltree with Stair 25 Aug 1987; app teacher of Religious and Moral Educ 16 Aug 1993.

1993 KEVIN MACKENZIE
trans from Wemyss to Ochiltree with Stair 30 Mar 1993; trans to East Kilbride Westwood 12 Dec 1996.

1997 CAROLYN MAI BAKER
B 1 Aug 1943 at Colchester, d of John Emrys Jones and Christina Nicol Stott; educ Colchester County High and Gairloch High; University of Aberdeen 1991–95 (BD); Social Work 1972–89; lic by Presb of Aberdeen 14 Nov 1995; m 31 Aug 1963 Colin Ernest Baker b 22 Feb 1941 s of Ernest and Violet B; Children: David Emrys b 26 Mar 1967 m Sheila; ord and ind to Ochiltree with Stair 16 Sep 1997.

OLD CUMNOCK CRICHTON WEST (FES IX, 181; X, 105)

Linked 7 May 1989 with Old Cumnock St Ninian's.

1950 JOHN HASTINGS MILLAR
(FES IX, 182, 272; X, 105), dem from Crichton West 30 Jun 1960 to enter teaching profession; ret 18 Apr 1986; w Veronica died; m (2) 7 Aug 1964 Elizabeth Stevenson Watson d of James W. and Susan Jane Livingston; died 30 Jun 1999.

1960 GEORGE STUART YOUNG
(FES X, 105, 310), ord and ind to Crichton West 20 Mar 1961; trans to Blairgowrie St Andrew's 20 Mar 1969.

1969 BRYAN LAUGHLIN TOMLINSON
(FES X, 105), ord and ind to Crichton West 29 Jun 1969; trans to Kirkcaldy Abbotshall 24 Apr 1980.

1981 EUPHEMIA CRAWFORD CAMPBELL
B 7 Mar 1922 at Glasgow, d of John Robertson and Euphemia Crawford; educ Battlefield Secondary, Glasgow 1933–36; University of Glasgow 1977–80 (BD); Clerkess 1936–41; Wartime Engineer 1941–45; lic by Presb of Glasgow, Jul 1980; m 19 May 1951 George Campbell b 22 Nov 1915 s of William C. and Elizabeth Smith; Children: Elspeth Margaret b 11 Jan 1962 m Fergus McCann; ord and ind to Crichton West 9 Jan 1981; became minister of linked charge with St Ninian's 7 May 1989; ret 29 Sep 1991.

1992 DUNCAN CAMPBELL EDDIE
ord and ind to Crichton West with St Ninian's 16 Jan 1992; trans to Aberdeen Holburn West 14 Oct 1999.

OLD CUMNOCK OLD (FES III, 24; IX, 182; X, 105)

Linked 26 Feb 1989 with Lugar.

1927   JOHN DOUGLAS McCLYMONT
(FES VIII, 215; FES IX, 182; X, 105), ord and ind to Old Cumnock Old 23 Nov 1927; ret Feb 1972; died 23 Sep 1982.

1972   JAMES BAILLIE FERGUSON
(FES X, 105), ord and ind to Old Cumnock Old 20 Jun 1972; trans to Lenzie Union 19 Jun 1984.

1984   MARTIN JAMES McKEAN
ord and ind to Old Cumnock Old 13 Dec 1984; became minister of linked charge with Lugar 26 Feb 1989; trans to Balerno 30 Jun 1993.

1994   JOHN WILLIAM PATERSON
ord and ind to Lugar with Old Cumnock Old 15 Jun 1994, see Lugar.

OLD CUMNOCK ST NINIAN'S (FES X, 105)

Linkage with Lugar terminated 26 Feb 1989. Linked 7 May 1989 with Old Cumnock Crichton West.

1961   IAN MACDONALD TWEEDLIE
(FES X, 103), ind to Lugar 16 Oct 1958; became minister of linked charge with St Ninian's 20 Dec 1961; died 27 Jul 1988.

1989   EUPHEMIA CRAWFORD CAMPBELL
ord and ind to Old Cumnock Crichton West 9 Jan 1981; became minister of linked charge with St Ninian's 7 May 1989; ret 29 Sep 1991.

1992   DUNCAN CAMPBELL EDDIE
ord and ind to Old Cumnock Crichton West with St Ninian's 16 Jan 1992, see Crichton West.

PATNA WATERSIDE (FES X, 105, 107)

Formed 29 Jun 1980 by union of Patna and Waterside and Lethanhill.

1945   DAVID GRAY JOHNSTON
(FES IX, 183; X, 105), ind to Patna 14 Mar 1945; ret 30 Apr 1971; died 30 May 1984.

1967   JOHN THOMAS GILBERT SCOLLAY
(FES X, 107, 135, 208), res from term app at Greenock South 28 Feb 1965; introd on term app to Waterside and Lethanhill 20 Apr 1967; ret 25 Jun 1972; died 2 Sep 1992.

1972   WILLIAM WELSH HALLIDAY BAIRD
(FES X, 105), ord and ind to Patna with Waterside and Lethanhill 26 Sep 1972; dem 18 Jan 1979.

1980   JAMES SMITH LEISHMAN
(FES X, 216, 377), trans from Alness to Patna Waterside 22 Oct 1980; trans to Kirkmichael with Tinwald with Torthorwald 16 Jan 1985.

1985   LINDSAY H EWART
trans from Lochgoilhead and Kilmorich to Patna Waterside 8 Jul 1985; died 21 Jan 1986.

1986   GAIR PORTER
ord and ind to Patna Waterside 6 Aug 1986; dem 6 Sep 1988.

1989   THOMAS ALEXANDER BERTRAM
(FES X, 358), res as teacher (RE) and ind to Patna Waterside 18 Apr 1989; app Secretary of National Church Assoc Oct 1994; ret 31 Dec 1995; Publ: Articles in National Church Assoc publs; editor of *Search the Scriptures* (private, 1998).

PRESTWICK KINGCASE (FES IX, 183; X, 106)

1968   JAMES LOGAN
(FES IX, 222; X, 106, 127), trans from Paisley Martyrs' Memorial to Kingcase 17 Jul 1968; died 18 Mar 1977.

1978   DUNCAN MUIR McLAREN
(FES X, 172), trans from Glasgow Ruchill to Kingcase 18 Sep 1978; trans to Glasgow Mosspark 18 Oct 1984.

1985   ALEXANDER BLACKIE DOUGLAS
trans from Paisley St Columba Foxbar to Kingcase 27 Mar 1985; trans to Edinburgh Blackhall St Columba 10 Apr 1991.

1991   IAN PURVES
B 12 Mar 1946 at Paisley, s of John P. and Joan Edwards Brodie; educ John Neilson Institute, Paisley 1951–61; University of Glasgow 1972–78 (LTh, CPS); lic by Presb of Paisley 29 Jun 1978; asst Paisley St Mark's Oldhall 1975–78; m 6 Jul 1974 Elizabeth Stirling Barr b 16 Mar 1946 d of John B. and Jessie Blue Raeburn; Children: Jocelyn Elizabeth b 7 Sep 1978; Gregor Ian b 2 May 1981; Russell John b 26 Mar 1986; ord and ind to Thornliebank 17 May 1979; trans to Johnstone St Paul's 17 May 1984; trans to Kingcase 25 Sep 1991; dem 19 Apr 1996.

1997   THOMAS DAVID WATSON
B 6 May 1961 at Lisburn, N Ireland, s of David Henry Alexander W. and Muriel Jean Sprunt; educ Wallace High, Lisburn and Kilsyth Academy 1972–79; University of Glasgow 1979–83 (BSc); University of Edinburgh 1984–87 (BD); lic by Presb of St Andrews 28 Jun 1987; asst Dundee Parish (St Mary's) 1987–88; m 30 Aug 1990 Julie Anne Stewart b 5 Jan 1963 d of Eric S. and Helen Atkinson; Children: Kirsty Helen b 17 Apr 1993; Mairi Jean b 1 May 1995; ord by Presb of Lorn and Mull and introd as Assoc at Kilmore and Oban 22 Sep 1988; ind to Kingcase 15 Jan 1997.

PRESTWICK SOUTH (FUF 132; IX, 183; X, 106)

1977 JACK MUNRO BROWN
ord and ind to Prestwick South 13 Jan 1977; trans to Galashiels St Aidan's 18 Feb 1981.

1981 THOMAS BARR GIRDWOOD
(FES IX, 333; X, 111, 179, 198), trans from Kirn to Prestwick South 28 Oct 1981; ret 31 Dec 1988; died 5 Feb 1997.

1989 KENNETH CHARLES ELLIOTT
B 18 Dec 1959 at Elderslie, s of William E. and Ann Taylor; educ Castlehead High, Paisley and Paisley Grammar 1971–77; University of Glasgow 1983–88 (BD, CMin); Civil Service 1977–83; lic by Presb of Paisley 31 Aug 1988; asst Paisley Martyrs' 1988–89; m 5 Jul 1985 Fiona Ann Smellie b 31 Jan 1962 d of Alexander S. and Jan Hunter; Children: Richard Alan b 30 Mar 1990; David Stuart b 24 Mar 1992; ord and ind to Prestwick South 1 Nov 1989.

PRESTWICK ST NICHOLAS' (FES III, 58; VIII, 223; IX, 183; X, 106)

1961 WILLIAM HUMPHREY HAMILTON
(FES IX, 124, 304; X, 106, 179), trans from Glasgow Shawlands Cross to St Nicholas' 11 Jan 1961; ret 1 Dec 1984; died 17 Feb 1998.

1985 GEORGE ROBERTSON FIDDES
B 31 Oct 1953 at Dundee, s of George Murray F. and Jeannie Shearer Cooper; educ Morgan Academy, Dundee 1964–69; University of Glasgow 1971–78 (BD); Apprentice Engineer 1969–71; lic by Presb of Dundee 12 Nov 1978; asst Armadale 1978–79; m 16 Jun 1978 Carol Anne Black b 16 Oct 1954 d of Francis Noel B. and Jean Walker Geddes Stoddart; ord and ind to Auchterless 2 Aug 1979; trans to St Nicholas' 19 Jun 1985.

SORN (FES III, 67; VIII, 224; IX, 184; X, 106)

Linked 1 Sep 1978 with Catrine.

1967 DAVID REID
(FES IX, 401, 506; X, 106, 300), trans from Dundee Clepington to Sorn 17 May 1967; died 10 Oct 1977.

1979 ALEXANDER McEWAN WELSH
ord and ind to Catrine with Sorn 27 Feb 1979; trans to Glasgow Dennistoun Blackfriars 15 May 1986.

1986 WILLIAM CLEMENT ROBB
(FES X, 405), ind to Catrine with Sorn 19 Nov 1986, see Catrine.

1994 GEORGE ANGUS CHALMERS
(FFS X, 37, 61), ind to Catrine with Sorn 15 Sep 1994, see Catrine.

STAIR (FES III, 69; VIII, 224; IX, 184; X, 106)

Linked 6 Jan 1979 with Ochiltree.

1957 ANDREW PRINGLE
(FES IX, 102; X, 61, 106), [correction: Ladykirk, not Ladybank as in Vol X, 106]; trans from Ladykirk with Whitsome to Stair 28 Aug 1957; ret 31 Aug 1976; died 27 Oct 1988.

1978 RAYMOND DAVID MACKENZIE
ord and ind to Stair 9 May 1978; became minister of linked charge with Ochiltree 6 Jan 1979; trans to Hamilton Burnbank with Hamilton North 13 Mar 1987.

1987 KENNETH BURGOYNE YORKE
ind to Ochiltree with Stair 25 Aug 1987, see Ochiltree.

1993 KEVIN MACKENZIE
trans from Wemyss to Ochiltree with Stair 30 Mar 1993; trans to East Kilbride Westwood 12 Dec 1996.

1997 CAROLYN MAI BAKER
ord and ind to Ochiltree with Stair 16 Sep 1997, see Ochiltree.

STRAITON ST CUTHBERT'S (FES III, 71; VIII, 225; IX, 184; X, 106)

Linked 1 Apr 1971 with Kirkmichael.

1928 JOHN FOSTER McCALLUM
(FES V, 284; VIII, 225; FES IX, 184; X, 106), trans from Dunnichen to St Cuthbert's 15 Aug 1928; ret 31 Mar 1971; died 16 Jun 1984.

1971 WALTER DONALD McKECHNIE MOFFAT
(FES IX, 189, 571, 619; X,103, 151, 356), trans from Glasgow Bellahouston to Kirkmichael with Straiton St Cuthbert's 8 Jul 1971; ret 31 May 1985; died 13 Jan 1987.

1985 WILLIAM GERALD JONES
ind to Kirkmichael with Straiton St Cuthbert's 23 Oct 1985, see Kirkmichael.

SYMINGTON (FES IX, 185; X, 106)

Linked 30 Apr 1959 with Craigie.

1969 ALEXANDER SMART SUTHERLAND
(FES IX, 389; X, 106, 232), ind to Craigie with Symington 30 Sep 1969, see Craigie.

1988 MARGARET WHYTE
ord and ind to Craigie with Symington 30 May 1988, see Craigie.

TARBOLTON (FES IX, 185; X, 106)

1967 IAN UIDHIST MACDONALD
(FES X, 106, 241), trans from Strathfillan to Tarbolton 27 Apr 1967; ret 30 Nov 1997; s Neil m Anne Flynn; s David m Susan Biggar.

1999 MARY CATHERINE SHAW
B 11 Jul 1950 at London, d of Bryan Edward
Plunkett and Margaret Joyce Gittins; educ Hornsey
High School for Girls, London and Cavendish
School, Hemel Hempstead 1961–68; University of
Glasgow 1992–95 (LTh); Cook and Housekeeper
1980–83; Admin 1988–91; lic by Presb of Dumfries
and Kirkcudbright 18 Jul 1995; asst Annan St
Andrew's Greenknowe Erskine 1995–96; m 31 Mar
1970 John Shaw b 27 Jan 1947 s of James
Frederick Anthony S. and Jean Winifred Robinson;
divorced 1999; Children: James Robert b 24 Jun
1972; William John b 24 Jul 1974; Rebecca Jane
b 13 Jul 1977 m Alan Paul McClean; ord by Presb
of Greenock and introd as Assoc at Old Gourock
and Ashton 10 Apr 1997; ind to Tarbolton in
deferred linkage with Annbank 12 Jan 1999.

TROON OLD (FES III, 77; VIII, 227; IX, 186; X,
107)

1973 JOHN GORDON WEBSTER
(FES X, 107, 427), res from app with Dr Graham's
Homes, Kalimpong, India and ind to Troon Old 5
Dec 1973; trans to Glasgow St John's Renfield 26
Apr 1989.

1989 CALLUM THOMSON O' DONNELL
trans from Anwoth and Girthon to Troon Old 12
Nov 1989; trans to Southend 4 Sep 1997.

1998 ALASTAIR HENDERSON SYMINGTON
(FES X, 448), trans from Bearsden New Kilpatrick
to Troon Old 12 May 1998; Chaplain to the Queen
in Scotland from 1996; Addl children: Fiona
Margaret b 22 May 1977; d Karen m Iain Stewart
Blair Russell; Publ: Co-author of *Readers Digest
Family Guide to the Bible* (*Readers Digest*, 1984);
For God's Sake, Ask! (St Andrew Press, 1993).

TROON PORTLAND (FUF 133; FES IX, 186; X,
107)

1965 JAMES GORDON GRANT
(FES X, 107, 335), trans from Dyce to Portland 29
Sep 1965; trans to Edinburgh Dean 18 Nov 1987.

1988 EDWARD JOSEPH THOMPSON
B 13 May 1956 at Carrickfergus, Co Antrim, s of
Joseph T. and Margaret Esdale; educ Carrick-
fergus Grammar 1971–75; University of Durham
1975–78 (BA); University of Edinburgh 1978–81
(BD); Visiting Chaplain, Merchiston School,
Edinburgh 1982–83; lic by Presb of West Lothian

30 Jun 1981; asst Edinburgh St George's West
1981–83; m 9 Sep 1978 Elizabeth Margaret
Patterson b 22 Sep 1956 d of William P. and
Audrey Lamb; Children: Simon James b 25 Aug
1983; Richard John b 21 Apr 1985; Andrew Gordon
b 30 Mar 1988; ord by Presb of Edinburgh during
assistantship at St George's West 6 Jun 1982; ind
to Golspie 21 Apr 1983; trans to Portland 1 Jun
1988; dem 31 Aug 1995 to take up app at Second
Presb Church, Kansas City, USA.

1996 ROBERT FRANKLIN BARDIN
B 6 Feb 1956 at Asheboro, N Carolina, USA, s of
William Earl B. and Joyce Batts; educ Sanderson
High, Raleigh, N Carolina 1970–74; North Carolina
State University 1974–78 (BA); Union Theological
Seminary, Richmond 1978–82 (DMin); lic by Presb
of Orange, Apr 1978; asst Salisbury Presb Church
1979–80, 1981–82; Tinkling Spring Presb Church
1980–81; m 11 Aug 1979 Karen Marie Chamblee
b 27 Apr 1957 d of Donald Vance C. and Barbara
Pickett; Children: Mary Elizabeth b 20 Jun 1984;
Hannah Marie b 28 Apr 1987; ord and ind to Stuarts
Draft, Virginia 8 Aug 1982; trans to Finley Memorial
Presb Church 8 Aug 1982; trans to St Andrew's
Covenant Presb Church Jul 1987; ind to Portland
27 Jun 1996; dem 3 Mar 1998.

1998 RONALD MITCHELL HALDANE BOYD
B 1 May 1967 at St Andrews, s of Ronald Haldane
B. and Nan Gilmour Mitchell; educ Bell Baxter
High School, Cupar 1979–85; University of St
Andrews 1985–90 (BD), 1990–91 (DipTh); lic by
Presb of St Andrews 3 Jul 1991; asst Bearsden
New Kilpatrick 1991–93; m 20 Feb 1999 Hazel
Williamson; ord and ind to Dumbarton West Kirk 5
May 1993; trans to Portland 29 Sep 1998.

TROON ST MEDDAN'S (FUF 133; FES IX, 186;
X, 107)

1948 HAROLD GLOVER REID
(FES IX, 186, 437; X, 107), trans from Madderty
to St Meddan's 18 May 1948; ret 2 Nov 1970; died
17 May 1989.

1971 DAVID GENTLES HAMILTON
(FES X, 107), ord and ind to St Meddan's 6 May
1971; trans to Bearsden South 25 Oct 1978.

1979 DAVID LITTLE HARPER
(FES X, 126), trans from New Erskine to St
Meddan's 23 Apr 1979; Addl children: Keith b 18
Sep 1976.

PRESBYTERY OF IRVINE AND KILMARNOCK

CROSSHOUSE (FES III, 84; VIII, 229; IX, 188; X, 108)

1973 ROBERT MILREE KENT
(FES X, 108), ord and ind to Crosshouse 26 Sep 1973; trans to Hamilton St John's 18 Apr 1981.

1981 IAN G GRANT
ord and ind to Crosshouse 23 Sep 1981; dem 31 Jan 1991.

1991 RONA MACDONALD YOUNG
B 4 May 1950 at Glasgow, d of Leslie McGilvray Greenlees and Jessie Dunlop MacDonald; educ Marr College, Troon 1962–68; Craigie College, Ayr 1968–71 (DEd); University of Glasgow 1986–90 (BD); Teaching (Primary) 1971–75; lic by Presb of Ayr 11 Jul 1990; asst Irvine Old 1990–91; m 2 Aug 1972 Thomas Cuthbert Young b 17 May 1948 s of Robert Cunningham Y. and Elizabeth Johnstone Cuthbert; Children: Fiona b 24 Aug 1975; Aileen b 24 Feb 1978; ord and ind to Crosshouse 11 Dec 1991.

DARVEL (FES X, 108)

Formed 3 Dec 1992 by union of Darvel Central and Darvel Irvine Bank and Easton Memorial.

1937 IAN McGREGOR WALLACE COLLINS
(FES IX, 188; X, 108), ord and ind to Darvel Central 29 Sep 1937; ret 30 Nov 1992; died 9 Nov 1998.

1972 ALEXANDER MATTHEWS McILROY
(FES X, 108), ord and ind to Irvine Bank and Easton Memorial 27 Sep 1972; ret 31 Mar 1987.

1988 ELIZABETH JOAN ELLIOT McINTYRE
ord and ind to Irvine Bank and Easton Memorial 18 Aug 1988; trans to Glasgow Langside 10 Sep 1992.

1993 ROBERT TRAVERS
B 5 Nov 1950 at Kilwinning, s of William T. and Margaret Millar Kilpatrick; educ Stevenston High and Irvine Royal Academy 1963–69; Open University 1979–89 (BA); University of Glasgow 1989–92 (BD); Hospital Lab Technician 1969–73; Health Physics 1974–89; lic by Presb of Ardrossan 9 Sep 1992; asst Stevenston Livingstone 1993–94; m 19 Aug 1974 Elizabeth Berry b 14 May 1953 d of William B. and Isabella Ferguson; Children: Kirsty Elizabeth b 3 Mar 1975; Robert William b 11 Feb 1977; Fiona Kilpatrick b 4 Jun 1980; ord and ind to Darvel 10 Jun 1993.

DREGHORN AND SPRINGSIDE (FES X, 108, 114)

Formed 18 Mar 1993 by union of Dreghorn and Pearston Old and Perceton and Dreghorn.

1970 WILLIAM STUART DUNN
(FES X, 108), ord and ind to Dreghorn and Pearston Old 3 Jun 1970; trans to Motherwell Crosshill 15 Sep 1982.

1977 STUART MACLEAN GOUDIE
(FES IX, 117; X, 66, 104), res as Lecturer in Religious Education and introd to Perceton and Dreghorn (term) 25 Aug 1977; ret 31 Oct 1988; d Margaret m Degnan; Anne m Aspden.

1983 GARY EDWARD HORSBURGH
B 16 Oct 1947 at Edinburgh, s of Thomas H. and Georgina Sinclair Hodgson; educ Forrester High, Edinburgh 1960–64; Free Church of Scotland College 1970–74; University of Stirling 1974–75; University of Edinburgh 1975–77 (BA); Civil Service 1964–70; lic by Presb of Edinburgh (Free Church of Scotland) 21 Jun 1977; m 27 Sep 1969 Janice McGeorge b 6 Jun 1948 d of Stephen Brennan M. and Jane Cunningham Jackson; Children: Simon Gary b 12 Nov 1973; Joanne Kathryn b 21 Mar 1986; ord by Edinburgh Free Church and ind to Kirkcaldy 10 Oct 1977; ind to Dreghorn and Pearston Old 6 Apr 1983; became minister of united charge with Perceton and Dreghorn 18 Mar 1993.

1989 IAN ROBERT BOYD
ord and ind to Perceton and Dreghorn 16 May 1989; dem 31 Aug 1992; ind to Netherlee 28 May 1997.

DUNLOP (FES X, 109)

1972 JAMES CURRIE
(FES IX, 373; X, 109, 176 (2), 223), trans from Glasgow St James' (Pollok) to Dunlop 6 Apr 1972; died 18 Apr 1987.

1988 JOHN ROBERT PAGE
ord and ind to Dunlop 9 Jun 1988; app by Board of World Mission to Costa del Sol with Gibraltar St Andrew's 3 Mar 1996.

1996   MAUREEN MARY DUNCAN
B 29 Dec 1944 at Edinburgh, d of John Hutson and Hannah Weatherhead Mason; educ Musselburgh Grammar 1960–63; University of Edinburgh 1991–95 (BD); lic by Presb of Edinburgh 2 Jul 1995; asst Edinburgh Wardie 1995–96; m 11 May 1968 Ronald George Duncan b 29 Jan 1942 s of Robert D. and Alison Wilson; Children: Hazel Susan b 8 May 1973; Kirsty Hannah b 4 May 1977; ord and ind to Dunlop 9 Oct 1996.

FENWICK (FES IX, 190; X, 109)

1969   DONALD STEWART
(FES IX, 379, 383; X, 109, 124, 229), trans from Glasgow Househillwood St Christopher's to Fenwick 23 Jan 1969; Chaplain to Torrance House Hospital, Kilmarnock; ret 20 Nov 1984; d Morven m James Murray McKenna; d Glenda m Ian Richard Mascall.

1985   GORDON FRASER HAY MACNAUGHTON
ord by Presb of Glasgow during assistantship at Newlands South 9 Jun 1982; ind to Fenwick 12 Jun 1985; dem on app as Chaplain to University of Dundee 1 Apr 1991.

1991   DAVID RANKIN GEMMELL
ord and ind to Fenwick 1 Aug 1991; trans to Ayr the Auld Kirk 30 Sep 1999.

GALSTON (FES X, 109)

Formed 27 May 1980 by union of Galston New and Galston Old.

1948   ROBERT CUMMINGS JAMIESON
(FES IX, 191, 488, X, 109), ord by Presb of Stranraer 1 Mar 1943 and ind to Edenshead 16 Dec 1943; trans to Galston Old 6 Oct 1948; ret 28 May 1980; d Ishbel m Michael Barron; s William m Joanne Croker.

1970   GORDON HARROW KEIR
(FES X, 109), ord and ind to Galston New 14 May 1970; died 9 Mar 1978.

1980   THOMAS JAMES LOUDON BLAIR
trans from Dundee Wallacetown to Galston 3 Dec 1980; Clerk of Presb of Irvine and Kilmarnock 1986–91; s Loudon Thomas m Rachel Nieto; d Shiona Patricia m Andrew Millar; Publ: Series of booklets publ by Education Dept 1980s.

1990   JOHN HENRY BINDON TAYLOR
(FES IX, 140; X, 83, 110), dem from Irvine St Andrew's to enter teaching profession 1 Dec 1969; ret as Head Teacher of Auchenharvie Academy 1 May 1989; introd as Assoc at Galston 1 Jan 1990; FEIS 1996; s Andrew m Shona Lauder; d Jane m Alan Cunningham.

HURLFORD (FES X, 109)

Formed 26 Oct 1995 by union of Hurlford Kirk and Hurlford Reid Memorial.

1967   DUNCAN ELLIOTT McCLEMENTS
(FES X, 109), ord and ind to Reid Memorial 19 Jan 1967; trans to Falkirk Grahamston United 1 Dec 1976.

1974   JAMES McNAUGHTON BRODIE
(FES X, 109, 416), res from service with Overseas Council in India and ind to Hurlford Kirk 22 Aug 1974; ret 30 Oct 1994; pastor of Kathmandu International Christian Congregation, Nepal 1995–97.

1977   ALAN GREIG
ord and ind to Reid Memorial 28 Jul 1977; dem on app by Board of World Mission and Unity for service in Zambia 21 Sep 1983.

1985   ELIZABETH WOOD HOUSTON
ord and ind to Reid Memorial 22 Jan 1985; trans to Alexandria 11 Jan 1995.

1996   JAMES DONALD McCULLOCH
B 11 Apr 1951 at Coatbridge, s of James Donald M. and Agnes Robertson Watt; educ Coatbridge High 1963–69; Glasgow College of Building and Printing 1968–76; University of Glasgow 1991–95 (BD); Newspaper and Commercial Compositor 1969–91; Graduate Member Institute of Printing 1982; Member of Institute of Printing London 1995; lic by Presb of Hamilton 30 Aug 1995; asst Bothwell 1995–96; m 29 Sep 1973 Ann Cameron Johnston b 4 Jan 1954 d of Robert J. and Susan Halbert Grant; Children: Fiona Ann b 2 Jul 1977; Lorna Ann b 13 May 1984; ord and ind to Hurlford 18 Sep 1996.

IRVINE FULLARTON (FES III, 38; VIII, 218; IX, 192; X, 109)

1953   PETER GEORGE THOMSON
(FES IX, 192, 472; X, 109), trans from St David's Buckhaven to Fullarton 21 Jan 1953; ret 31 Mar 1989; s Paul m Michele Perrone; s Mark m Jo Anne Ford; d Pamela m Robert Martin; Publ: *The Good Cause* (Cunningham District Council, 1989); *Crail Church Through the Centuries* (Crail Parish Church, 1999).

1989   NEIL URQUHART
B 29 Apr 1962 at Lagos, Nigeria, s of Alexander William U. and Brenda Young; educ Largs Academy 1973–79; University of Aberdeen 1981–85 (BD); University of Edinburgh 1986–88 (DipMin); Royal Bank of Scotland 1979–81; lic by Presb of Irvine and Kilmarnock; asst Chryston; m 21 May 1988 Dorothy Jean Chalmers b 6 Sep 1962 d of George C. and Jean Sutherland; Children: Alexander Lee b 2 Aug 1990; Amy Louise b 20 Feb 1992; Zoe Joy b 6 Apr 1995; ord and ind to Fullarton, Aug 1989.

IRVINE GIRDLE TOLL
Extension Charge 1978.

1978 JAMES ROY
(FES X, 118), dem from Kilwinning Mansefield on grounds of ill-health 31 Jan 1973; ind to Girdle Toll 25 Oct 1978; ret 31 Oct 1982; Open University 1985 (BA); Chaplain (part-time) to Ayrshire General Hospital from 1 Dec 1990; Editor of Presb Magazine, *The Fountain* from 1995.

1983 CHRISTINA MACFARLAN LANE
B 22 Jun 1932 at Dumbarton, d of Robert MacFarlan McDougall and Janet Lobban; educ Dumbarton Academy 1944–46; University of Glasgow 1978–82 (BD); Shop Asst 1946–47; Office Work 1947–78; lic by Presb of Dumbarton 27 Jun 1982; asst Clydebank Radnor 1982–83; ord and ind to Girdle Toll 11 Aug 1983; ret 30 Sep 1999.

IRVINE MURE (FUF 138; FES IX, 192; X, 109)

1969 ROBERT DUNCAN SAWERS
(FES IX, 748; X, 110, 305, 425), trans from Dundee St James' to Irvine Mure 26 Feb 1969; died 27 Feb 1976.

1976 HUGH MUIR ADAMSON
B 23 Oct 1947 at Dunfermline, s of William A. and Rebecca Welch; educ Dunfermline High 1959–65; University of Edinburgh 1969–73 (BD), 1975 (DPS); Civil Service (Agriculture and Fisheries) 1965–66; Ministry of Defence (Air) 1966–69; lic by Presb of Edinburgh 9 Jul 1975; asst Edinburgh Corstorphine Craigsbank 1975–76; m 28 Sep 1974 Anne Johnstone b 18 Mar 1943 d of William J. and Annie Ferguson Galt Pettigrew; Children: Graham William b 7 Feb 1976; Alistair Paul b 4 Oct 1977; Ruth Elizabeth b 27 Aug 1980; ord and ind to Irvine Mure 29 Sep 1976.

IRVINE OLD (FES III, 97; VIII, 232; IX, 193; X, 110)

1928 ALEXANDER MACARA
(FES VIII, 232; FES IX, 193; X, 110), ord and ind to Irvine Old 20 Sep 1928; ret 30 Sep 1978; died 21 Sep 1992.

1979 JAMES GREIG
(FES X, 191, 202, 419), trans from Chapelton with Strathaven Rankin to Irvine Old 27 Feb 1979; ret 30 Jun 1999; d Grace m Alan Kay (divorced); d Wilma m John Andrews; d Lorna m Joseph Brown (divorced).

IRVINE RELIEF BOURTREEHILL (FUF 138; FES IX, 193; X, 110)

Multi-purpose church completed and dedicated 3 Aug 1977. Relief congregation transported to this area from West Road, Irvine.

1976 ROBERT M LESLIE
ord and ind to Relief 18 Jun 1976; died 2 Aug 1981.

1982 ALISTAIR NEIL SHAW
ord and ind to Relief Bourtreehill 18 Mar 1982; trans to Kilmarnock Laigh 31 Oct 1988.

1989 WILLIAM FRANK CAMPBELL
ord and ind to Relief Bourtreehill 6 Jun 1989; dem 30 Apr 1991; ind to Ancrum 15 Oct 1991.

1992 WILLIAM GRAY
(FES X, 270), trans from Kirkintilloch St Columba's to Relief Bourtreehill 25 Mar 1992; dem 28 Feb 1994.

1995 ROBERT ANDREW HAMILTON
B 13 Jul 1967, s of Andrew H. and Hazel Agnes Stirling Brown; educ Auchenharvie Academy, Stevenston 1979–86; Glasgow College of Technology 1986–89 (BA); University of Edinburgh 1990–93 (BD); Volunteer in Tiberias 1990; Relief work, Board of Social Responsibility 1989–90; lic by Presb of Ardrossan 7 Jul 1993; asst Edinburgh St Philip's Joppa 1992–93; m 23 Aug 1991 Carol Jean Coubrough b 21 Aug 1965 d of William Smellie C. and Agnes McAlpine Waterston; Children: Daniel Robert b 29 Jan 1999; ord and ind to Relief Bourtreehill 12 Jan 1995.

IRVINE ST ANDREW'S (FES IX, 193; X, 110)

1970 JOHN WILLIAM FORSYTH HARRIS
(FES X, 110), ind to St Andrew's 5 Mar 1970; trans to Motherwell St Mary's 31 Aug 1977.

1978 THOMAS McLURE LOGAN
(FES X, 19), trans from Edinburgh Pilrig and Dalmeny Street to St Andrew's 16 Mar 1978; trans to Clydebank Abbotsford 30 Aug 1988.

1989 JOHN ANTHONY CAMPBELL
B 29 Oct 1932 at Bellshill, s of John C. and Margaret Christie; educ Rothesay Academy 1937–46; University of St Andrews 1985–87; Apprentice Printer 1946–55; National Service (RASC) 1955–57; Theatre Manager 1957–76; Hotelier 1976–78; Sub Post Master 1978–87; lic by Presb of Perth 2 Oct 1983; m 6 Oct 1959 Isabell Robertson b 25 Jul 1934 d of Charles R. and Euphemia Auld; Children: Nicola b 26 Mar 1963 m Derek Anderson; Fiona b 3 Jul 1966 m Graeme Ednie; Gregor b 10 Feb 1969 m Carolyn Miller; ord by Presb of Perth for Aux ministry 16 Sep 1984; assgns at Perth St John's, St Stephen's, St Leonard's-in-the-Fields, Craigie and Kinnoull 1984–89; ind to St Andrew's (full-time ministry) 28 Jun 1989; ret 26 Jun 1998.

1999 MORAG ANN DAWSON
B 1 Nov 1952 at Gorebridge, d of John Beattie and Isabella Kerr Lockhart; educ Greenhall High, Gorebridge 1965–70; University of Edinburgh 1992–96 (BD); Customer Services Asst 1997–98; Care Asst, Board of Social Responsibility 1996–

97; lic by Presb of Edinburgh 28 Jun 1998; asst Edinburgh St Andrew's Clermiston 1998–99; m 13 Jul 1974 Thomas Dawson b 21 Aug 1951 s of Thomas D. and Wotherspoon; divorced 1989; Children: Ewan Beattie and Barbara Wotherspoon b 11 Jun 1979; ord and ind to St Andrew's 29 Sep 1999.

KILMARNOCK GRANGE (FUF 139; IX, 194; X, 111)

1967   GEORGE LAURIE MARR
(FES X, 111, 293), trans from Anstruther St Adrian's to Grange 30 Aug 1967; dem 5 Oct 1977.

1978   COLIN GLYNN FREDERICK BROCKIE
(FES X, 24), trans from Edinburgh St Martin's to Grange 15 Mar 1978; Addl children: Martin Glynn b 19 Sep 1981.

KILMARNOCK HENDERSON (FUF 140; FES IX, 194; X, 111)

1970   JOHN WEIR COOK
(FES X, 111, 417), res from service with Overseas Council at St Andrew's Calcutta and ind to Henderson 8 Feb 1970; trans to Edinburgh Portobello St Philip's Joppa 10 Feb 1988.

1971   GORDON CALDERWOOD MACPHERSON
B 6 Apr 1938 at Glasgow, s of Alexander M. and Jean McCulloch Calderwood; educ Glasgow Academy 1943–55; University of Glasgow 1955–58 (MA), 1958–61 (BD); Duke University, N Carolina, USA 1961–62 (MTh); lic by Presb of Glasgow, Mar 1961; m (1) 11 Jul 1961 Elisabeth Lloyd MacLean b 3 Jul 1939 d of Neil M. and Rosalind Steeds; Children: Roderick Alexander b 21 May 1963; Elisabeth Louise b 6 May 1966 m Antony Stackhouse; Claire Suzanne b 5 Sep 1967 m Iain Miller; m (2) 21 Nov 1992 Gillian Maud Barrett b 27 Mar 1943; stepdaughter Alexandra Camplin b 22 Feb 1972; app Asst Chaplain to University of Glasgow 1 Oct 1962; ord by Presb of Glasgow 1963; introd as Assoc at Henderson 1 Sep 1971; res from app 1988.

1989   DAVID WILLIAM LACY
B 26 Apr 1952 at Inverness, s of Peter Lindsay L. and Agnes Smith Hislop; educ Aberdeen Grammar and Glasgow High 1963–69; University of Strathclyde 1969–72 (BA); University of Glasgow 1972–75 (BD); lic by Presb of Dumbarton 29 Jun 1975; asst Edinburgh St George's West 1975–76; m 21 Oct 1974 Joan Stewart Robertson b 27 Jul 1951 d of Alexander R. and Margaret MacMurray Adam; Children: Michael Peter b 26 May 1979; Claire Margaret b 29 Sep 1980; ord by Presb of Edinburgh during assistantship at St George's West 4 Apr 1976; ind to Glasgow Knightswood St Margaret's 28 Jun 1977; became minister of

united charge with Netherton St Matthew's 2 Jun 1982; trans to Henderson 12 Jan 1989; Publ: *Fifty Years of Worship* (Knightswood St Margaret's, 1982).

KILMARNOCK HOWARD ST ANDREW'S (FES X, 111, 112)

Formed 29 Aug 1984 by union of Kilmarnock St Andrew's North and Kilmarnock Howard.

1961   ROBERT ALLAN
(FES IX, 384; X, 112, 230), trans from Kirn St Andrew's to St Andrew's North 15 May 1961; ret 31 Oct 1982; died 26 Sep 1986.

1968   GIBSON KENNEDY BOATH
(FES IX, 382; X, 59, 111, 153, 228), trans from Chirnside to Kilmarnock Howard 15 May 1968; became minister of united charge with St Andrew's North 29 Aug 1984; ret 30 Apr 1989; Open University 1976–79 (BA); FSA(Scot).

1989   MALCOLM MACLEOD
B 13 Feb 1953 at Stornoway, s of Duncan M. and Jessie Barbara MacKillop; educ Sir E Scott Junior Secondary, Tarbert and Portree High 1965–71; University of Stirling 1971–75 (BA); University of Edinburgh 1975–78 (BD); lic by Presb of Uist 5 Jul 1978; asst Cadder 1978–79; m 2 Jul 1982 Ada Vanbeck Cousin b 14 Nov 1959 d of James C. and Janet Catherine Penman; Children; Beth Joy b 10 Dec 1984; Duncan James b 15 Feb 1987; ord by Presb of Aberdeen and introd as Assoc at St Machar's Cathedral 30 Sep 1979; ind to Arbroath Old 9 Jul 1984; trans to Howard St Andrew's 9 Aug 1989.

KILMARNOCK LAIGH (FES III, 104; VIII, 233; IX, 195; X, 111)

1967   MELVILLE FREDERICK SCHOFIELD
(FES X, 111, 126), trans from Paisley Canal Street to the Laigh Kirk 22 Nov 1967; dem to take up app as Chaplain to Edinburgh Northern Hospitals Group 1 Mar 1988.

1988   ALISTAIR NEIL SHAW
trans from Irvine Relief Bourtreehill to the Laigh Kirk 31 Oct 1988; trans to Glasgow Greenbank 27 Oct 1999.

KILMARNOCK OLD HIGH KIRK (FES III, 109; VIII, 233; IX, 195; X, 111)

1968   ALEXANDER MACDONALD
(FES X, 111), ind to the Old High Kirk 17 Apr 1968; trans to Paisley St Andrew's 15 Feb 1978.

1979   WILLIAM MILLER HALL
(FES X, 201), trans from Shotts Calderhead to the Old High Kirk 20 Jan 1979; Children: Martin David b 19 Aug 1975; Valerie Jane b 25 Sep 1979.

KILMARNOCK RICCARTON (FES III, 63; VIII, 224; IX, 196; X, 112)

1968 THOMAS WRIGHT JARVIE
(FES IX, 518; X, 112, 307), trans from Dundee Wishart Memorial to Riccarton 25 Sep 1968.

KILMARNOCK SHORTLEES (FES IX, 197; X, 113)

1960 JAMES PARKER SERVICE
(FES IX, 176; X, 102, 113), trans from Fisherton to Shortlees 20 Apr 1960; trans to Chapel of Garioch 11 Aug 1976.

1977 BRIAN McFARLANE EMBLETON
ord by Presb of Glasgow during assistantship at St George's and St Peter's Easterhouse 20 Apr 1976; ind to Shortlees 9 Mar 1977; trans to Edinburgh Reid Memorial 21 Aug 1985.

1986 JACK HOLT
ord by Presb of Glasgow during assistantship at Broom 18 Apr 1985; ind to Shortlees 16 Apr 1986; trans to Birse and Feughside 22 Sep 1994.

1996 ROLF HEINZ BILLES
B 30 Apr 1967 at Hermannstadt, Romania, s of Julius Heinz B. and Hannelore Mathilde Hempert; educ Isolde Kurz Gymnasium, Reutlingen, Germany 1980–86; University of Tübingen, Germany 1987–90, 1991–92; University of Edinburgh 1990–91; University of Glasgow 1992–94 (BD); lic by Presb of Glasgow 4 Jul 1994; asst Glasgow Renfield St Stephen's 1994–96; m 19 Jul 1991 Shirley Anne McMeeking b 14 Mar 1968 d of Thomas Alexander M. and Joyce Catherine Cochran; Children: Anna Jane b 28 Apr 1995; Rachel Joyce b 22 Mar 1997; ord and ind to Shortlees 24 Jan 1996.

KILMARNOCK ST ANDREW'S GLENCAIRN (FES X, 112)

1970 ROBERT ALEXANDER KYLE MARTIN
(FES X, 112, 270), trans from Beath with Cowdenbeath Guthrie Memorial to St Andrew's Glencairn 5 Nov 1970.

KILMARNOCK ST JOHN'S ONTHANK (FES X, 112)

1964 JAMES MACKAY MACDONALD
(FES X, 112), ord and ind to St John's Onthank 30 Oct 1964; ret 30 Jun 1987; University of Cambridge 1964 (Dip Rel Studies); University of London 1965 (BD [external]), 1989–93 (ThD [external]).

1987 ROBERT I JOHNSTONE
trans from Meldrum and Bourtrie to St John's Onthank 19 Oct 1987; dem 28 Feb 1989.

1989 WILLIAM T CULLEN
trans from Cowie with Plean to St John's Onthank 28 Nov 1989; dem 15 Sep 1996.

1997 SUSAN MARY ANDERSON
B 29 Mar 1949 at Kirton, Lincolnshire, d of Noel Robert Cranfield Chaplin and Margaret Greta Cumberworth; educ Boston High School for Girls 1954–68; Royal Manchester College of Music 1968–71 (GRSM, ARMCM); University of Glasgow 1991–94 (BD); Piano Teacher 1971–87; Clinical Liaison Officer, Epilepsy Assoc 1987–91; lic by Presb of Stirling 4 Nov 1994; asst Bridge of Allan Holy Trinity 1994–96; m 31 Jul 1971 David John Williamson Anderson b 28 Sep 1950 s of James Williamson A. and Helen Lugton Montgomery Graham; Children: Rachel Sarah b 22 Dec 1972 m John Murray; Kathryn Helen b 30 Jun 1975; ord and ind to St John's Onthank 24 Apr 1997.

KILMARNOCK ST KENTIGERN'S (FES X, 113)

1969 STEWART DUNCAN JEFFREY
(FES X, 113, 386), trans from Berriedale and Dunbeath Ross to St Kentigern's 27 Apr 1969; trans to Aberdeen St George's-Tilldyrone 22 Nov 1978.

1979 MALCOLM McNEILL WALKER HARE
(FES X, 39, 164), trans from Glasgow Langside Hill to St Kentigern's 26 Apr 1979; ret 30 Jun 1994.

1995 STUART GRANT BARCLAY
B 5 Jul 1965 at Glasgow, s of Stuart Hugh Taylor B. and Janie Margaret Grant; educ Armadale Academy 1977–83; University of Glasgow 1983–87 (LLB), 1987–88 (DipLP); University of Edinburgh 1991–94 (BD); Solicitor 1988–91; lic by Presb of Falkirk 9 Aug 1994; asst Bo' ness St Andrew's 1994–95; m 9 Dec 1989 Karen Jane Harper b 18 Jul 1966 d of Geoffrey Edmunds H. and Catherine McIntyre McEwan; Children: Kathryn Ruth b 25 May 1994; Andrew Stuart b 18 Apr 1996; Kirsten Jane b 10 May 1998; ord and ind to St Kentigern's 14 Jun 1995; Chaplain to Ayrshire Mission to Deaf People.

KILMARNOCK ST MARNOCK'S (FES III, 111; VII, 233; IX, 197; X, 113)

1976 THOMAS TAIT SCOTT
(FES X, 117), trans from Kildonan with Whiting Bay to St Marnock's 14 Jan 1976; ret 31 Mar 1989; d Lynn m Lee Bryan.

1989 JAMES McNAUGHTAN
B 8 Apr 1957 at Renfrew, s of James M. and Catherine Howie; educ Camphill High, Paisley 1962–75; University of Glasgow 1976–80 (BD), 1980–82 (DipMin); lic by Presb of Paisley 1 Jul 1982; asst Paisley Sherwood 1982–83; m 17 Jul 1982 Elspeth Thomson 3 Nov 1956 d of James T.

and Elizabeth Greig Young; Children: Andrew
James b 22 Apr 1984; Neil John b 28 Mar 1986;
Russell Greig b 8 Nov 1988; Ailsa Elizabeth b 9
Oct 1993; ord and ind to Dundee Douglas and
Angus 15 Sep 1983; trans to St Marnock's 22 Aug
1989.

KILMARNOCK ST NINIAN'S BELLFIELD (FES X, 113)

1969 STEWART GRAHAM MATTHEW
(FES X, 113), ord and ind to St Ninian's Bellfield
17 Apr 1969; dem 10 Aug 1979 on app as Adult
Adviser, Dept of Education.

1979 GARETH WILLIAM DAVIES
B 29 Sep 1945 at West Glamorgan, Wales, s of
Harold D. and Phyllis Mary Winnifred Bowen; educ
Stradey Secondary Modern and Gwen Draeth
Valley Grammar 1958–62; University of Edin-
burgh 1972–75 (BA), 1976–78 (BD); Technician
1964–71; lic by Presb of Edinburgh 2 Jul 1978;
asst Chryston 1978–79; m 3 Jul 1981 Linda Jean
Martin b 20 Jun 1950 d of John Hume M. and
Mary Hall; ord and ind to St Ninian's Bellfield 22
Dec 1979; dem 30 Sep 1994 to take up further
study.

1995 ALISON HELEN BURNSIDE
B 13 Jun 1964 at Johnstone, d of John Hannah
and Josephine Helen Gillan; educ Johnstone High
1976–82; University of Glasgow 1982–85 (MA),
1986–89 (BD); Youth Share Volunteer, Pakistan
1985–86; lic by Presb of Paisley 5 Sep 1989; asst
Alloa St Mungo's 1989–90; m 13 Jun 1990 William
Angus MacKay Burnside b 12 Nov 1965 s of
William B. and Nessie Hamilton Anderson Irving;
Children: Angus John b 29 Nov 1997; ord by Presb
of Hamilton and introd as Community minister at
Motherwell North and Motherwell St Andrew's 5
Dec 1990; ind to St Ninian's Bellfield 21 Sep 1995;
dem 30 Apr 1999.

KILMARNOCK WEST HIGH (FUF 140; FES IX, 197; X, 113)

1973 ROBERT SMILLIE CHRISTIE
(FES X, 15, 113), trans from Edinburgh Liberton
Northfield to West High 14 Jun 1973; d Susan m
Watson.

KILMAURS ST MAUR'S GLENCAIRN (FES X, 113)

1963 DONALD PATIENCE
(FES X, 114, 145, 448), trans from Kilsyth The
Burns to St Maur's Glencairn 12 Dec 1963; ret 30
Jun 1993; s Charles m Jacqueline Tyack.

1993 JOHN ALEXANDER URQUHART
B 23 Jan 1966 at Inverness, s of William Hector
U. and Ann Catherine MacKenzie; educ Inver-
ness Royal Academy; St Colm's College,

Edinburgh 1984–86; University of St Andrews
1988–92 (BD); Care Asst, Nursing Home 1987–
88; lic by Presb of Dundee 18 Jun 1992; asst
Dundee Meadowside St Paul's 1992–93; m
25 Mar 1987 Barbara Strachan b 17 Dec 1952 d
of Charles S. and Barbara Millar; Children: Eilidh
Barbara b 22 Mar 1988; John MacEwan b 12
Sep 1991; ord and ind to St Maur's Glencairn 29
Nov 1993.

NEWMILNS LOUDOUN (FES X, 114)

Formed 30 Sep 1980 by union of Newmilns
Loudoun East and Newmilns Loudoun Old.

1940 EDWARD THOMAS HEWITT
(FES IX, 199, 524; X, 114), trans from Airlie to
Loudoun Old 5 Sep 1940; ret 30 Sep 1980; died
10 Jan 1999.

1979 IAN HAMILTON
B 29 Mar 1950 at Lennoxtown, s of John McDowall
H. and Barbara Rooney McCann; educ Woodside
Senior Secondary, Glasgow 1962–68; University
of Strathclyde 1968–72 (BA); University of
Edinburgh 1972–75 (BD), 1976–79 (MPhil); lic by
Presb of Glasgow 25 Jun 1975; asst Aberdeen
Northfield 1975–76; m 3 Jul 1980 Joan Ross b 12
Jan 1952 d of Leslie and Marjorie R.; Children:
David Iain b 12 Sep 1981; Jonathan William b 12
Nov 1983; Rebecca Joan b 31 May 1986; Sarah
Kathryn b 29 Sep 1994; ord and ind to Newmilns
Loudoun East in deferred union with Loudoun Old
30 Aug 1979; became minister of united charge
30 Sep 1980; dem 16 Jul 1999 to become minister
of Evangelical Presb Church of England and
Wales, Cambridge; Publ: *Calvin's Doctrine of
Scripture* (Rutherford House, 1984); *Relevance of
Westminster Confession for Today* (Burning Bush,
1985); *Women Elders and the Kirk* (Christian
Focus, 1990); *Erosion of Calvinist Orthodoxy*
(Rutherford House, 1990); various articles in
*Scottish Dictionary of Church History and
Theology*.

STEWARTON JOHN KNOX (FUF 145; FES IX, 200; X, 114)

1971 GEORGE HOUSTOUN CAMPBELL
(FES X, 114, 417), res from service with Overseas
Council in Malawi and ind to John Knox 24 Jun
1971; died 30 Sep 1992; d Morag m Graham
Whitman; s Ian m Karen McManus; d Sheena m
Mukesh Amin; Addl publ: *Trigger-Happy* (John
Paul, The Preacher's Press, 1993); *The Kirk at the
Cape* (private, 1993).

1993 SAMUEL HOSAIN
B 15 Apr 1941 at Larache, Morocco, s of Larbi
H. and Fatoum Lamarti; educ Quranic School,
Larache Islamic College 1952–58; University
of Glasgow 1974–78 (BD), 1989–91 (MTh);

lic by Presb of Irvine and Kilmarnock 3 Jul 1979; asst Irvine Fullarton 1978–79; m 16 Jun 1979 Elizabeth Kirkwood d of Alexander K. and Annie Robertson; ord and ind to Calderbank with Chapelhall 26 Sep 1979; trans to Fauldhouse St Andrew's 2 Jul 1985; trans to John Knox 24 Jun 1993.

STEWARTON ST COLUMBA'S (FES X, 114)

1962 PHILIP MACKIE McCARDEL
(FES IX, 375; X, 114, 131, 224), trans from Renfrew North to St Columba's 14 Apr 1962; ret 17 Nov 1989; died 24 Feb 1993.

1989 ALEXANDER JOHN GEDDES
(FES X, 45, 129), trans from Aberdeen Langstane Kirk to St Columba's 18 May 1989; ret 31 Mar 1998.

1999 ELIZABETH ANN WADDELL
B 25 Jun 1949 at Motherwell, d of James Smith Taylor and Catherine Buchanan Livingston; educ Brandon High, Motherwell 1954–65; University of Glasgow 1993–97 (BD); Nursing (Sister/Nurse Manager) 1967–97; lic by Presb of Hamilton 1 Sep 1997; m 7 Aug 1971 John Scott Waddell b 30 Mar 1949 s of David Scott W. and Mary Greenshields Brownlee; divorced 25 Nov 1993; Children: Lee Ann b 14 Mar 1976; John Nicholas b 16 Sep 1979; ord and ind to St Columba's 25 Feb 1999.

PRESBYTERY OF ARDROSSAN

ARDROSSAN BARONY ST JOHN'S (FES X, 115)

Formed 24 Sep 1987 by union of Ardrossan Barony and Ardrossan St John's.

1960 JAMES EWING
(FES IX, 217, 277; X, 97, 115, 164), trans from Whithorn Priory to The Barony 7 Dec 1960; ret 31 Aug 1987; d Alison m Mann; d Helen m Cameron.

1972 DONALD MACKAY
(FES IX, 466; X, 64, 102, 115, 276, 411), trans from Hawick Burnfoot to St John's 19 Dec 1972; ret 31 Mar 1985; admitted to Fellow College of Preachers (RAF) 1978; Fellow Society of Antiquaries 1990; MBE 1995; d Dorothy m Fairbairn.

1988 ALEXANDER WATT YOUNG
ord and ind to Barony St John's 26 Jun 1988; trans to Edinburgh Mayfield Salisbury 1 Sep 1993.

1994 WILLIAM JACKSON
ord and ind to Barony St John's 19 May 1994; trans to Perth Craigie 9 Sep 1998.

1999 COLIN ALEXANDER SUTHERLAND
B 11 Nov 1941 at Helensburgh, s of Robert Alexander S. and Marjory Morton McWilliams; educ Hermitage Secondary, Helensburgh 1946–58; Clydebank College 1981–84 (DIIM); University of Glasgow 1990–93 (LTh); Engineering 1964–73; Purchasing 1973–90; lic by Presb of Dumbarton 4 Jul 1993; asst Dumbarton Riverside 1993–95; m 2 Oct 1971 Myra Shortreid Nellis b 19 Jan 1941 d of Andrew N. and Anne Feggans; Children: Andrea Marjory b 14 Apr 1975 m Grant Easton; ord and ind to Cowie with Plean 23 Mar 1995; trans to Barony St John's 3 Jun 1999.

ARDROSSAN PARK (FUF 148; FES IX, 201; X, 115)

1972 GEORGE BAYNE WILSON
(FES IX, 74, 284; X, 115, 168, 204), trans from Wishaw Craigneuk to Ardrossan Park 22 Mar 1972; died 16 Mar 1977.

1977 KENNETH JOHN PATTISON
res as Principal of Kapeni CCAP Theological College, Blantyre and ind to Ardrossan Park 27 Oct 1977; dem to take up app as Chaplain to Glasgow Royal Infirmary Jun 1984.

1985 ALEXANDER SELLARS DOWNIE
B 15 Apr 1932 at Hamilton, s of Alexander D. and Agnes Reddiex; educ Albert Senior Secondary, Glasgow 1944–46; University of Edinburgh 1957–59; University of Glasgow 1974–77; Salesman 1946–57; Sales Rep 1959–74; lic by Presb of Glasgow 30 Jun 1977; asst Glasgow Cathcart South 1977–78; m 8 Jul 1957 Robertina Milne b 18 Jul 1937 d of Robert M. and Mary Clarkson; Children: Alexander b 9 Oct 1958 m Tracy Morrow; Robert b 28 Nov 1960 m Lorna McCrorie; ord and ind to Fallin 1 Nov 1978; trans to Ardrossan Park 6 Jun 1985; ret 31 May 1997.

1998 WILLIAM ROGER JOHNSTON
B 1 May 1948 at Irvine, s of Hendry McLean Curdy J. and Letitia Coulter Ross; educ Belmont Academy and Ayr College; University of Glasgow 1992–96 (BD); Butcher 1964–91; lic by Presb of Ayr 21 Jul 1996; asst Ayr St Leonard's 1996–98; m 30 Mar 1968 Anne Murphy Bone b 18 May 1947 d of James B. and Agnes Johnston; Children: Shona b 28 Nov 1973 m Shaun Lidbury; Graeme b 9 Aug 1975; ord and ind to Ardrossan Park 28 Jan 1998.

BEITH HIGH (FES III, 84; VIII, 229; IX, 202; X, 115)

Linked 29 May 1996 with Beith Trinity.

1970 ALISTAIR JOHN DUNLOP
(FES X, 115, 322), trans from Kirriemuir St Ninian's to Beith High 8 Dec 1970; trans to Saddell and Carradale 22 Feb 1979.

1979 DAVID JOHN HISLOP HARBISON
(FES X, 195, 408), trans from Hamilton Hillhouse to Beith High 4 Oct 1979; became minister of linked charge with Trinity 29 May 1996; ret 12 Sep 1998; d Margaret m Andrew Evans; s Malcolm m Karen Bell; d Kathleen m Nicolas Digby.

1996 FIONA CALVIN ROSS
B 16 Apr 1970 at Irvine, d of Thomas James Strike R. and Jean Boyd Calvin; educ Auchenharvie Academy, Stevenston 1982–88; University of Glasgow 1988–94 (BD, DipMin); lic by Presb of Ardrossan 5 Jul 1994; asst Stevenston Livingstone 1994–95; ord by Presb of Ardrossan and introd as Assoc at Beith High with Trinity 25 Jun 1996.

1998   ANDREW ROXBURGH BLACK
B 13 Nov 1952 at Newmilns, s of Archibald B. and Hannah White; educ Hurlford Junior Secondary 1957–67; University of Glasgow 1981–85 (BD), 1985–86 (CMin); Care Asst 1972–73; Postman 1973–79; lic by Presb of Irvine and Kilmarnock 26 Jun 1986; asst Irvine Old 1981–82; Irvine Fullarton 1982–85; Dalry St Margaret's 1986–87; m 14 Jun 1974 Isabel Hunter b 10 Jul 1954 d of William John Stewart H. and Martha Hamilton Gillies Allan; Children: Vicky b 12 May 1977; Stephen Andrew b 31 Jul 1979; Claire Margaret b 24 Jan 1983; ord and ind to Glasgow Pollokshaws 6 May 1987; app Chaplain (part-time) to Low Moss Prison 1 Sep 1988; trans to Beith High with Trinity 14 Dec 1998.

BEITH TRINITY (FUF 164; FES IX, 202; X, 115)

Linked 29 May 1996 with Beith High.

1952   HUGH SHANKLAND McCULLOCH YOUNG
(FES IX, 149, 202; X, 115), trans from Tinwald to Beith Trinity 2 Apr 1952; ret 31 Mar 1980; died 7 Jul 1981.

1980   W DUNCAN CAPEWELL
ord and ind to Beith Trinity 25 Sep 1980; ret 31 Oct 1995; died 2 Mar 1996.

1996   DAVID JOHN HISLOP HARBISON
(FES X, 195, 408), ind to Beith High 4 Oct 1979; became minister of linked charge with Trinity 29 May 1996, see Beith High.

1996   FIONA CALVIN ROSS
ord and introd as Assoc at Beith High with Trinity 25 Jun 1996, see Beith High.

1998   ANDREW ROXBURGH BLACK
ind to Beith High with Trinity 14 Dec 1998, see Beith High.

BRODICK (FES IX, 202; X, 115)

Linked 13 Jan 1957 with Corrie.

1974   IAN MACLEOD
(FES X, 115, 126), trans from Paisley Canal Street to Brodick with Corrie 17 May 1974; Open University 1976–78 (BA); University of Glasgow 1987–89 (MTh), 1989–94 (PhD); divorced 1983; m (2) 1 Sep 1984 Agnes Helen McBirnie b 6 Dec 1942 d of William Lees and Agnes Johnstone; d Shona May MacLeod m Atkins; spouse's children from previous marriage: Elaine b 3 Nov 1966 m Campbell; Janice b 28 Nov 1969 m Walker; Publ: Co-author of *Talks for Children* (St Andrew Press, 1988); *Preaching on the Lord's Supper* (Mowbray, 1990; Hendricksons, 1994); editor of, and contributor to, *More Talks for Children* (St Andrew Press, 1992); editor of, and contributor to, *Even More Talks for Children* (St Andrew Press, 1997); various articles and sermons for journals.

CORRIE (FES IV, 47; VIII, 322; IX, 202; X, 116)

Linked 13 Jan 1957 with Brodick.

1974   IAN MACLEOD
(FES X, 115, 126), trans from Paisley Canal Street to Brodick with Corrie 17 May 1974, see Brodick.

CUMBRAE (FES X, 116)

Formed 7 Mar 1971 by union of Millport East and Millport West.

1957   JAMES MORTON
(FES IX, 39, 492, 653; X, 119, 292), trans from Newburgh St Katherine's to Millport West 25 Sep 1957; ret 28 Feb 1971; died 17 Jul 1995.

1965   EWEN CAMERON
(FES IX, 83, 102; X, 51, 119), trans from Penicuik North to Millport East 15 May 1965; ret 28 Feb 1971; died 2 Oct 1988.

1971   ANDREW McLAREN SMITH
(FES X, 116), ord and ind to Cumbrae 27 Nov 1971; ret 31 Aug 1997.

1998   MARJORY HUNTER MACKAY
B 15 Jun 1943 at Motherwell, d of Andrew Wilson and Agnes Marshall Hunter White; educ Hamilton Academy 1948–60; Jordanhill College, Glasgow 1960–63 (DipEd); University of Edinburgh 1989–94 (BD, CChEd); Teaching 1963–78; Company Director 1975–present; lic by Presb of Melrose and Peebles 19 Jul 1994; asst Melrose 1994–96; m 15 Jul 1965 Angus Campbell Mackay b 14 Jun 1941 s of Angus Campbell M. and Annie McNeill Livingston; Children: Alison Jill b 22 Jan 1969; Bronwen Ann b 13 Oct 1971; Emily Marjory b 29 Nov 1978; ord and ind to Cumbrae 1 May 1998.

DALRY ST MARGARET'S (FES III, 84; VIII, 229; IX, 203; X, 116)

1947   ROBERT KIRKLAND
(FES IX, 37, 115, 203; X, 116), trans from Edinburgh St Bride's to St Margaret's 26 Dec 1947; ret 30 Jun 1973; died 13 Sep 1985.

1973   ALEXANDER DOUGLAS LAMB
(FES X, 116, 407), trans from Unst to St Margaret's 15 Nov 1973; s Rognvald m Sheila Anderson; s John m Charlotte Lydia Gittins; s David m Sean Morgan-Davies.

DALRY TRINITY (FES X, 116)

1969   DAVID IAIN MONTGOMERY GRANT
(FES X, 116), ord and ind to Trinity 14 Nov 1969.

FAIRLIE (FES X, 116)

Formed 7 Jan 1968 by union of Fairlie St Margaret's and Fairlie St Paul's.

1946 THOMAS JAMES GORDON WEIR
(FES IX, 130, 204, 542; X, 116), dem from Carnoustie Newton Panbride 1944; ind to St Margaret's 20 Feb 1946; ret 7 Jan 1968; died 27 Jul 1987.

1968 DONALD MACLEOD
(FES IX, 661, 690, 694; X, 116, 393), trans from Portree to Fairlie 28 Aug 1968; ret 31 Dec 1979; died 22 Jan 1990.

1980 ROBERT JOHN THORBURN
B 26 Sep 1952 at Edinburgh, s of Robert King T. and Jean Scott McFarlane Reid; educ George Heriot's, Edinburgh 1957–70; University of Edinburgh 1970–75 (BD), 1975–77 (DPS); lic by Presb of Lothian 30 Jun 1977; asst Glasgow Cathedral 1977–80; m 2 Jul 1977 Gail Elizabeth Givan b 3 Oct 1953 d of Walker G. and Christine Cadigan; Children: John William b 17 Feb 1981; Kaye Walker b 15 Oct 1984; ord by Presb of Glasgow during assistantship at Glasgow Cathedral 30 Mar 1998; ind to Fairlie 24 Jun 1980.

FERGUSHILL (FES III, 96; VIII, 231; IX, 204; X, 116)

Linked 2 Mar 1958 with Kilwinning Erskine.

1975 RUDOLF DEHN
(FES X, 118), ord and ind to Kilwinning Erskine with Fergushill 9 Dec 1975; dem 30 Jun 1985; died 5 Apr 1991.

1987 THOMAS MALCOLM FULLARTON DUFF
B 30 Mar 1957 at Paisley, s of William Leslie Gordon D. and Helen Fullarton; educ Trinity College, Glenalmond 1970–75; University of Aberdeen 1975–79 (MA), 1981–84 (BD); Teaching (voluntary), Kenya 1979–81; lic by Presb of Aberdeen 28 Jun 1984; asst London Crown Court 1984–85; m 4 Nov 1989 Sandra Karen Rai b 15 Feb 1961 d of Andrew and Srikumari R; Children: Asaph William Sangeet b 13 Mar 1992; Abigail Kanchan Helen b 14 Mar 1994; ord by Presb of Aberdeen 26 Jun 1985 and app for service with Presb Church of E Africa in Dar-es-Salaam, Tanzania; ind to Fergushill with Kilwinning Erskine 9 Jan 1987.

KILBIRNIE AULD KIRK (FES X, 116, 117)

Formed 1 Jun 1978 by union of Glengarnock and Kilbirnie Barony.

1954 JOSEPH HUGHES HOUSTON
(FES IX, 204, 702; X, 116), trans from Evie to Glengarnock 8 Jul 1954; ret 1 Jun 1978; died 29 Jan 1986.

1975 ROBERT MARTIN
(FES X, 60, 117), trans from Swinton to Kilbirnie Barony 29 Oct 1975; dem 6 Dec 1977.

1978 FERGUS MACPHERSON
(FES IX, 741; X, 135, 422), res as Research Historian, Zambia and ind to the Auld Kirk Jun 1978; dem 19 Mar 1984 on app as World Mission Secretary to British Council of Churches, London.

1984 DOUGLAS ROBERT IRVING
ord and ind to the Auld Kirk 8 Aug 1984; trans to Kirkcudbright 16 Apr 1998.

1999 IAN WARRENDER BENZIE
B 15 Jan 1949 at Greenock, s of John B. and Hilda Ayling; educ Greenock Academy; University of Glasgow 1994 (BD); Banking 1967–94; lic by Presb of Dunoon 9 Jul 1997; m 19 Apr 1974 Elizabeth Young b 12 Sep 1951 d of James Y. and Alice Evans; Children: Jonathan b 4 Jul 1976; Jillian b 18 May 1980; ord and ind to the Auld Kirk 19 Mar 1999.

KILBIRNIE ST COLUMBA'S (FES X, 117)

1975 ALEXANDER THOMSON
(FES X, 117), ind to St Columba's 4 Jun 1975; trans to Ardler, Kettins and Meigle 18 Aug 1982.

1983 DAVID BROSTER
B 14 Mar 1944 at Liverpool, s of William B. and Olwen Evans; educ Liverpool Institute High 1955–61; University of Wales 1965–69 (DipTh, CPS); Open University 1977–83 (BA); Postal and Telegraph Officer 1961–65; lic by Presb Church of Wales 24 Sep 1969; m 10 Aug 1968 Margaret Ann Mercer b 13 Aug 1946 d of Arthur M. and Mabel Raffe; Children: Sian b 8 May 1971; Bethan b 10 Jun 1973; ord by Presb Church of Wales and ind to Tredegar Park Place 24 Sep 1969; trans to Liverpool Clubmoor (PCW) 1 Sep 1978; ind to St Columba's 1 Mar 1983.

KILMORY (FES X, 117)

Union with Kildonan dissolved 29 Feb 1968. Linked same date with Shiskine. This arrangement terminated 6 Nov 1977. Linked with Lamlash same date.

1954 JAMES BISSET
(FES IX, 206, 272, 413; X, 118), trans from Braes of Rannoch to Kilmory and Kildonan 22 Dec 1954; ret 29 Feb 1968; died 14 Dec 1984.

1969 RICHARD ALEXANDER FISHWICK
(FES X, 117, 202, 290), trans from Uddingston Burnhead to Kilmory with Shiskine 22 Jan 1969; ret 31 May 1977; died 2 Nov 1983.

1977 DOUGLAS GILBERT PROVAN FULTON
(FES X, 118), ord and ind to Lamlash 28 Aug 1958; became minister of linked charge with Kilmory 6 Nov 1977; ret 31 Oct 1992; died 23 May 1994.

1993 WILLIAM McDOWALL MACMILLAN
B 2 Feb 1933 at Glasgow, s of John M. and Jeannie Cross; educ Possil High, Glasgow 1936–47; University of Glasgow 1977–90 (LTh); Engineering 1947–69; Training Adviser 1969–77; lic by Presb of Paisley; m 8 Jun 1957 Georgina Jackson Wright b 6 Oct 1931 d of Duncan W. and Georgina Agnew; Children: Ian b 8 May 1959; Kenneth b 4 Aug 1962; Alison b 5 May 1964; Sheena b 15 Jan 1967; ord and ind to Whithorn St Ninian's Priory 26 Nov 1980; trans to Auchterhouse with Murroes and Tealing 25 Oct 1989; trans to Kilmory with Lamlash 18 Nov 1993; ret 2 Feb 1998.

1998 WILLIAM BROWN ROSS
B 27 Aug 1941 at Kirkcaldy, s of James R. and Catherine Louis Sime; educ Auchtermuchty Secondary 1946–56; University of St Andrews 1982–85 (LTh); University of Edinburgh 1985–86 (CPS); Apprentice Joiner 1956–61; Parachute Regiment 1961–65; Weapons Technician (RAF) 1971–82; lic by Presb of St Andrews 13 Dec 1987; m 4 Jun 1966 Maureen Roy Noble b 28 Jul 1938 d of James Sutherland N. and Dow; Children: James b 10 Oct 1967; Mark b 5 Mar 1968; ord and ind to Findochty with Portknockie 7 Oct 1988; trans to Alvie and Insh and app Warden of Badenoch Centre 13 Dec 1995; trans to Kilmory with Lamlash 30 Sep 1998.

KILWINNING ABBEY (FES III, 116; VIII, 234; IX, 206; X, 118)

1975 IAN JAMES McCLELLAND REID
(FES IX, 31; X, 18, 118, 455), Leader of Iona Community 1967–1974; ind to Kilwinning Abbey 19 May 1975; ret 3 Nov 1986; died 20 Feb 1997.

1987 WILLIAM BUCHAN
B 26 Sep 1936 at Peterhead, educ Peterhead Academy; University of Leeds; University of London; University of Strathclyde; Personnel Management 1966–85; lic by Presb of Stirling, Dec 1986; asst Alloa St Mungo's 1985–87; m 29 Mar 1958 Hazel Alice b 11 Nov 1935; Children: Lesley Alice b 20 Apr 1962 m Edwards; Ruth Anne b 6 Apr 1963; Iona Lyn b 11 Oct 1965 m McCullogh; William Bruce b 9 Oct 1967; ord and ind to Kilwinning Abbey 4 Mar 1987.

KILWINNING ERSKINE (FUF 151; FES IX, 206; X, 118)

Linked 2 Mar 1958 with Fergushill.

1975 RUDOLF DEHN
(FES X, 118), ord and ind to Kilwinning Erskine with Forgushill 9 Dec 1975; dem 30 Jun 1985; died 5 Apr 1991.

1987 THOMAS MALCOLM FULLARTON DUFF
ind to Fergushill with Kilwinning Erskine 9 Jan 1987, see Fergushill.

KILWINNING MANSEFIELD TRINITY (FES X, 118)

New Charge 1 Jan 1999. Congregation of Kilwinning Mansefield transported.

1973 JAMES RONALD DICK
(FES X, 118), ord and ind to Mansefield 19 Jun 1973; trans to Dundee Whitfield 29 Nov 1978.

1979 RONALD JOHN MAXWELL STITT
ord and ind to Mansefield 16 May 1979; trans to Cockenzie and Port Seton Old 30 Jun 1993.

1999 DOUGLAS STUART PATERSON
B 9 Apr 1944 at East Grinstead, Sussex, s of Alexander P. and Alice Kent; educ Shawlands Academy, Glasgow 1949–62; University of Glasgow 1962–66 (MA); Glasgow School of Art 1966–69 (DipTP); University of Edinburgh 1972–75 (BD); MRTPI 1972; Planning Offier, City of Glasgow Corporation 1966–68; Planning Officer, East Kilbride Development Corporation 1969–72; lic by Presb of Falkirk, Jun 1975; asst Cumbernauld St Mungo's 1975–77; ord by Presb of Falkirk during assistantship at St Mungo's 4 Mar 1976; introd as Assoc 5 May 1978; ind 14 May 1984; introd as Community minister, Kilwinning 26 Sep 1995; ind to Mansefield Trinity 21 Apr 1999.

LAMLASH (FES IX, 207; X, 118)

Linked 6 Nov 1977 with Kilmory.

1958 DOUGLAS GILBERT PROVAN FULTON
(FES X, 118), ord and ind to Lamlash 28 Aug 1958; became minister of linked charge with Kilmory 6 Nov 1977; ret 31 Oct 1992; died 23 May 1994.

1993 WILLIAM McDOWALL MACMILLAN
ind to Kilmory with Lamlash 18 Nov 1993, see Kilmory.

1998 WILLIAM BROWN ROSS
ind to Kilmory with Lamlash 30 Sep 1998, see Kilmory.

LARGS CLARK MEMORIAL (FUF 152; FES IX, 207; X, 118)

1966 DAVID MACKAY BECKETT
(FES X, 119), ord by Presb of Dundee during assistantship at St Mary's 10 Mar 1964; ind to Clark Memorial 8 May 1966; trans to Edinburgh Greyfriars Tolbooth and Highland 2 Feb 1983.

1983 GEORGE MELVYN WOOD
ord by Presb of England during assistantship at Crown Court 20 Jun 1982; ind to Clark Memorial 12 Jul 1983; trans to Cullen and Deskford 5 Dec 1997.

1998 STEPHEN JAMES SMITH
B 3 Nov 1961 at Dunfermline, s of John S. and Euphemia McKenzie Ogston; educ Beath High, Cowdenbeath 1973–79; Heriot-Watt University 1979–83 (BSc); University of Edinburgh 1988–91 (BD); Stocks/Shares Account Controller 1984–86; Pharmaceutical Rep 1986–88; lic by Presb of Dunfermline 30 Jun 1991; asst Ayr The Auld Kirk 1991–93; m 14 Jun 1986 Jacqueline Johnston b 29 Apr 1965 d of John J. and Martha Faulds; Children: Ewan Jonathan b 4 Apr 1990; Lewis James b 1 Feb 1993; ord and ind to Monifieth St Rule's 8 Mar 1993; trans to Clark Memorial 11 Dec 1998.

LARGS ST COLUMBA'S (FES III, 214; VIII, 250; IX, 207; X, 119)

1928 DAVID BROOK BAXTER
(FES VIII, 250; IX, 207; X, 119), trans from Dunlop to St Columba's 2 Oct 1928; ret 31 Oct 1965; died 22 Feb 1983.

1966 WALTER STANLEY CARR
(FES IX, 462; X, 119, 194, 273, 274), trans from Hamilton Avon Street with Brandon to St Columba's 25 Aug 1966; ret 30 Sep 1991; d Anne m Philip Collins.

1992 DAVID MURRAY McKAY
B 5 Jan 1952 at Edinburgh, s of John Alexander Murray M. and Eliza Brotherstone; educ Galashiels Academy 1964–70; University of Edinburgh 1970–77 (MA, BD); lic by Presb of Moray 10 Jul 1977; asst Edinburgh Greenbank 1977–79; m 14 Oct 1985 Agnes Jordan Allan Cameron Paton d of Robert Galt P. and Helen Allan; ord and ind to Balmaclellan with Balmaghie with Kells 31 Jul 1979; trans to Fyvie 13 Mar 1987; trans to St Columba's 2 Apr 1992.

LARGS ST JOHN'S (FUF 152; FES IX, 207; X, 119)

1952 WILLIAM MORTON MAUCHLINE
(FES IX, 172, 208, 215; X, 119), trans from Ayr Trinity to St John's 23 Apr 1952; ret 30 Nov 1971; died 31 Mar 1999.

1972 DAVID WILLOX MACLAGAN
(FES X, 119, 143), trans from East Kilbride Moncreiff to St John's 14 Feb 1972; ret 31 Dec 1991; d Amelia m Robertson; d Eileen m Cochrane.

1993 ANDREW FLEMING McGURK
B 28 Dec 1946 at Linlithgow, s of Peter Stevenson M. and Jean Stenhouse Fleming; educ Hermitage Secondary, Helensburgh 1958–64; Stow College, Glasgow 1964–68 (HNC); Paisley College of Technology 1968–69 (LRIC); University of Glasgow 1978–82 (BD); Laboratory Asst 1964–70; Laboratory Supervisor 1970–78; lic by Presb of Ardrossan, Jul 1982; asst Largs Clark Memorial

1982–83; m 4 Oct 1969 Sheila Anne Whyte b 23 Feb 1948 d of Archibald W. and Catherine Bell; Children: Fiona Helen b 24 Sep 1971; David Andrew b 17 Jun 1975; Neil Jonathan b 1 Dec 1977, died 5 Dec 1977; ord and ind to New Cumnock 27 Jun 1983; trans to St John's 7 Jan 1993.

LOCHRANZA AND PIRNMILL (FES IX, 393; X, 119)

Linked 6 Nov 1977 with Shiskine.

1965 JAMES LESLIE DOW
(FES IX, 229, 256, 732; X, 119, 132), trans from Greenock Cartsburn-Augine to Lochranza and Pirnmill 28 Oct 1965; died 26 May 1977.

1978 ROBERT McINTYRE WALKER
ord and ind to Lochranza and Pirnmill with Shiskine 22 Jun 1978; dem 31 Jul 1983 on app to Samuel Bill Theological College, Abak, Nigeria.

1984 ANDREW BARRIE
B 7 Aug 1957 at Hamilton, s of Andrew B. and Mary Strachan Downs; educ Uddingston Grammar; University of Strathclyde 1975–79 (BSc); University of Aberdeen 1979–82 (BD); lic by Presb of Hamilton; asst Largs St John's 1982–84; m 15 Jul 1982 Sheila Catherine Miller d of Stanley M. and Catherine Bell; Children: Andrew Alastair b 12 Jun 1987; Karen Danielle b 14 Apr 1990; ord and ind to Lochranza and Pirnmill with Shiskine 8 Feb 1984.

SALTCOATS NEW TRINITY (FES X, 119, 120)

Formed 4 Jul 1993 by union of Saltcoats Erskine and Saltcoats Landsborough Trinity.

1954 DAVID GORDON WEIR
(FES IX, 210, 610; X, 120 (2)), trans from Rosehearty to Saltcoats Trinity 11 Aug 1954; became minister of united charge with Landsborough 6 Oct 1968; ret 30 Apr 1992; s Robert m Mary McDonald.

1954 HUGH KIRKWOOD
(FES IX, 156, 208, 684; X, 119), trans from Rerrwick to Saltcoats Erskine 7 Jul 1954; ret 31 Oct 1981.

1982 BARRY WILLIAM DUNSMORE
ord and ind to Saltcoats Erskine 29 Sep 1982; trans to Stirling St Columba's 4 Feb 1988.

1988 MARGARET THOMSON
B 3 May 1930 at Glasgow, d of John W. and Mary Findlay McKay; educ Victoria Drive Secondary, Glasgow 1942–44; Dowanhill Secretarial College, 1944–45; University of Glasgow 1983–87 (BD); Secretary 1945–54,1971–82; lic by Presb of Glasgow 2 Jul 1987; asst Glasgow Mosspark 1987–88; m 13 Mar 1952 James Barbour Thomson

b 18 Oct 1928 s of Peter Loudon T. and Helen Barbour; Children: Alan James b 22 Jul 1954 m Maura Robertson; Dorothy Margaret b 1 Aug 1956 m David Gillespie; David John b 12 Jan 1958 m Rhona Ramsay; ord and ind to Saltcoats Erskine 28 Jun 1988; ret 30 Jun 1993.

1994 ALEXANDER DUNCAN McCALLUM
B 31 Mar 1940 at Largs, s of Duncan McColl M. and Jean Hunter; educ Largs Higher Grade School and Ardrossan Academy 1945–59; Scottish Hotel School 1960–63 (Dip); University of Glasgow 1983–86 (BD); Hotel Management and Lecturing 1960–83; lic by Presb of Ardrossan 2 Jul 1984; m 16 Dec 1963 Josephine Stokes b 29 Aug 1940 d of Thomas S. and McBride; Children: Alasdair b 1 Jun 1965; Scott b 17 Oct 1968 m Karen Muir; Heather b 20 Aug 1973; ord and ind to Kilberry with Tarbert 24 Jun 1987; trans to New Trinity 3 Feb 1994.

SALTCOATS NORTH (FES III, 81; VIII, 228; IX, 209; X, 120)

1970 JOHN HANNAH ROBERTSON
(FES X, 120, 195), trans from Hamilton Burnbank to Saltcoats North 22 Apr 1970; ret 30 Nov 1992; died 24 Oct 1997.

1993 CALUM DONALD MACDONALD
B 23 Mar 1960 at Glasgow, s of Donald M. and Kate Ann; educ North Kelvinside Comprehensive, Glasgow 1965–78; University of Glasgow 1987–92 (BD, CMin); Medical Laboratory 1978–87; lic by Presb of Glasgow 23 Jun 1992; asst Glasgow Broomhill 1992–93; m 23 Aug 1984 Wilma McNab b 8 Sep 1958 d of William M. and Margaret Given; Children: Mark Calum b 14 Aug 1987; Stephen James b 13 Jul 1990; ord and ind to Saltcoats North 10 Aug 1993.

SALTCOATS ST CUTHBERT'S SOUTH BEACH (FES X, 120)

1965 ERNEST GEORGE BALLS
(FES IX, 64, 336, 476; X, 120, 200), trans from Motherwell South Dalziel to St Cuthbert's South Beach 2 Jun 1965; ret 30 Jun 1980; died 20 Jul 1998.

1980 JOHN JOHNSTON
(FES X, 152), trans from Glasgow Blackfriars to St Cuthbert's South Beach 4 Dec 1980; dem on app as Chaplain to the Dumfries Hospitals 1 Nov 1987.

1988 BRIAN HENRY OXBURGH
B 12 Apr 1954 at Glasgow, s of Roy Francis O. and Mary Adeline Woodward; educ Rutherglen Academy and Cathkin High 1966–72; University of Strathclyde 1972–76 (BSc); University of Glasgow 1977–80 (BD); lic by Presb of Glasgow 23 Jun 1980; asst Glasgow Netherlee 1979–80; m

3 Sep 1977 Linda Bridges b 27 Nov 1951 d of Harry B. and Helen Shields; Children: Michelle b 13 Jun 1979; Laura b 20 Jan 1981; Angela b 11 Jan 1987; Stephen b 1 Feb 1988; ord and ind to Dunnichen Letham and Kirkden 9 Jul 1980; trans to St Cuthbert's South Beach 29 Jun 1988.

SHISKINE (FUF 288; FES IX, 210; X, 120)

Linked 6 Nov 1977 with Lochranza and Pirnmill.

1969 RICHARD ALEXANDER FISHWICK
(FES X, 117, 202, 290), trans from Uddingston Burnhead to Kilmory with Shiskine 22 Jan 1969; ret 31 May 1977; died 2 Nov 1983.

1978 ROBERT McINTYRE WALKER
ord and ind to Lochranza and Pirnmill with Shiskine 22 Jun 1978; dem 31 Jul 1983 on app to Samuel Bill Theological College, Abak, Nigeria.

1984 ANDREW BARRIE
ord and ind to Lochranza and Pirnmill with Shiskine 8 Feb 1984, see Lochranza.

STEVENSTON ARDEER (FUF 148; FES IX, 210; X, 120)

1974 JOHN WILKIE FRASER
(FES X, 120), ord and ind to Ardeer 28 Aug 1974; trans to Penicuik North 17 Nov 1982.

1983 FERGUS CAMERON BUCHANAN
ord by Presb of Glasgow during assistantship at Glasgow Cathedral 5 May 1982; ind to Ardeer 2 Jun 1983; trans to Milngavie St Paul's 19 Apr 1988.

1989 GEORGE GRAY FLETCHER
B 12 May 1961 at Glasgow, s of Christopher Kerr F. and Mary Arton Campbell; educ Bellahouston Academy, Glasgow 1973–79; University of Strathclyde 1979–83 (BSc); University of Glasgow 1984–87 (BD); Glasgow District Council 1983–84; lic by Presb of Glasgow; asst Giffnock Orchardhill 1987–89; m 10 Oct 1987 Maureen Ann Daly b 22 Aug 1962 d of John D. and Jessie Jack; Children: Graeme Jonathan b 19 Apr 1990; Alastair Duncan b 24 Sep 1993; ord and ind to Ardeer 16 Feb 1989.

STEVENSTON HIGH (FES III, 122; VIII, 235; IX, 210; X, 121)

1963 JOHN HERON
(FES IX, 247, 736; X, 121, 146), trans from Kirkintilloch St David's Memorial to Stevenston High 9 Oct 1963; ret 31 Jul 1975; died 14 Feb 1987.

1976 THOMAS MACINTYRE
ord by Glasgow and West (UFC) and ind to Shieldhall and Drumoyne (UFC) 31 Oct 1972; ind to Stevenston High 11 Mar 1976; trans to Paisley Wallneuk North 10 Aug 1988.

1989   ANN CHRISTINA McCOOL
B 7 Jan 1951 at Glasgow, d of Iain Cameron
McPhedran and May McNeil; educ Cranhill Com-
prehensive, Glasgow 1963–69; Assoc of London
College of Music and Drama 1968; Royal
Scottish Academy of Music and Drama 1970–73
(DSD, IPA); Jordanhill College, Glasgow 1973–74
(PGCE); University of Glasgow 1985–88 (BD);
Teaching 1974–76, 1983–85; lic by Presb of
Dumbarton 10 Jul 1988; m 31 Dec 1971 Robert
Ure McCool b 8 Dec 1943 s of Alexander M. and
Williamina Park; Children: Martin b 22 Jun 1976;
Gordon b 23 Dec 1980; ord and ind to Stevenston
High 16 May 1989.

STEVENSTON LIVINGSTONE (FUF 153; FES IX,
210; X, 121)

1960   IAIN McDOUGALL ROY
(FES X, 121), ord and ind to Livingstone 5 Jul 1960;
ret 17 Nov 1997; Publ: Contributor to *Preachers'
Handbook* and *Light for our Path* (IBRA 1988–99);
contributor to *Dictionary of Scottish Church History*
(Rutherford House, 1991); contributor to *More
Talks for Children* (St Andrew Press, 1992); con-
tributor to *Even More Talks for Children* (St Andrew
Press, 1997).

1999   JOHN MARSHALL MORTON LAFFERTY
B 11 Oct 1944 at Cleland, s of John Gilmour L. and
Mary Jane Orr Morton; educ Wishaw High 1949–
62; Glasgow College of Commerce and Distribution
1962–66 (ACII); University of Glasgow 1994–97
(BD); Financial Services 1962–79; Company
Chairman 1979–94; lic by Presb of Glasgow 3 Jul
1997; asst Bearsden New Kilpatrick 1997–98;
Glasgow Hyndland 1998–99; m 2 Mar 1968 Moira
Jean Rae b 25 Nov 1946 d of Allan R. and Jean
Neilson Revie; Children: Karen b 28 Jul 1972; John
Allan b 11 Dec 1973; Allan Gilmour Morton b 27
Jan 1981; ord and ind to Livingstone in deferred
linkage with Stevenston Ardeer 18 Feb 1999.

WEST KILBRIDE OVERTON (FUF 154; FES IX,
211; X, 121)

1956   WILLIAM BURNSIDE
(FES IX, 307; X, 121, 181), trans from Glasgow
Springburn North to Overton 21 Mar 1956; ret 31
Oct 1982; s John m Gillian Mary Samuel.

1983   NORMAN CRUICKSHANK
B 14 Aug 1937 at Glasgow, s of Alfred C. and
Jessie Mutch Henry; educ Knightswood Secon-
dary, Glasgow 1949–53; Engineering TEng (CEI)
AMI Prod E; Jordanhill College, Glasgow (FE
Teach Cert); Open University 1972–75 (BA);
University of Glasgow 1978–81 (BD); Mechanical
Engineering 1953–67; Lecturer in Mechanical
Engineering 1967–78; lic by Presb of Glasgow, Jun
1981; asst Strathblane 1978–80; Milngavie St
Luke's 1980–81; Springburn 1981–82; m 24 Jun
1961 Janet Gardner Johnston b 19 Jan 1938 d of
Charles J. and Jean McIlroy; Children: Ruth

Jennifer b 3 Jul 1963 m Alister Bull; Graeme
Norman b 24 Jul 1965 m Lillaine Brannan; ord and
ind to Overton 13 Apr 1983.

WEST KILBRIDE ST ANDREW'S (FES X, 121)

Formed 17 Mar 1974 by union of West Kilbride
Barony and West Kilbride St Bride's.

1968   JOHN WILLIAM GOUDIE
(FES IX, 291, 486; X, 121, 148, 171), trans from
Stamperland to West Kilbride Barony 10 Jan 1968;
ret 16 Mar 1974; died 18 Feb 1994.

1975   NORMAN MACDONALD PRITCHARD
(FES X, 121), trans from Edinburgh St George's
West to St Andrew's 20 Aug 1975; dem 30 Sep
1979 to take up app at Scots Kirk, Melbourne,
Australia.

1980   DUNCAN ROSS MITCHELL
B 5 May 1942 at Boddam, s of Duncan Sinclair
M. and Catherine Ross; educ Hyndland Senior
Secondary, Glasgow 1947–59; University of
Strathclyde 1965–69 (BA); University of Glasgow
1969–72 (BD); Life Assurance Valuation Clerk
1959–64; Hospital Clerk 1964–65; lic by Presb of
Glasgow and the West (UFC) 20 Jun 1972; m 16
Aug 1968 Sandra McDonald Fearns Brown b 26
Nov 1948 d of Edward B. and Sarah Fearns;
Children: Sarah Fiona b 18 May 1969; Fazer Ross
b 4 May 1972; Scott Edward Duncan b 26 Jan
1981; ord by UFC and ind to Craigmailen 21 Jun
1972; admitted by General Assembly 1980; ind to
St Andrew's 25 Mar 1980; Publ: Contibutor to *Even
More Talks for Children* (St Andrew Press, 1997);
weekly column in *Linlithgowshire Journal and
Gazette* 1974–80.

WHITING BAY AND KILDONAN (FES X, 171,
121)

Formed 13 Dec 1993 by union of Whiting Bay and
Kildonan.

1968   THOMAS TAIT SCOTT
(FES X, 117), ord and ind to Kildonan with Whiting
Bay 7 Aug 1968; trans to Kilmarnock St Marnock's
14 Jan 1976.

1976   ALEXANDER STRICKLAND
(FES X, 275), trans from Inverkeithing St John's
with North Queensferry to Kildonan with Whiting
Bay 20 Aug 1976; trans to Dairsie with Kemback
with Strathkinness 22 Oct 1981.

1982   ELIZABETH ROBERTSON LEISHMAN
WATSON
B 28 Mar 1956 at Whitburn, d of David W. and
Elizabeth Stewart; educ Whitburn Academy 1968–
74; University of Edinburgh 1974–77 (BA), 1977–
80 (BD); lic by Presb of West Lothian 29 Jun 1980;
asst Ayr Castlehill 1980–82; ord by Presb of Ayr
during assistantship at Castlehill 1 Apr 1981; ind
to Whiting Bay and Kildonan 31 Mar 1982.

PRESBYTERY OF LANARK

BIGGAR (FES X, 206)

Formed 26 Aug 1976 by union of Biggar Gillespie Moat Park and Biggar St Mary's.

1946 JOHN WARNOCK
(FES IX, 200, 295, 343; X, 206), trans from Glasgow Knightswood St David's to Gillespie Moat Park 6 Sep 1946; became minister of linked charge with Elsrickle 6 Sep 1961; ret 28 Feb 1975.

1977 ANGUS CAMERON MACKENZIE
(FES X, 200, 277), trans from Motherwell St Mary's to Biggar 9 Mar 1977; ret 30 Nov 1994; s Fergus m Margaret Linden; s Roderick m Johanna Bannon; s Martin m Catherine Dempster.

1995 GAVIN JOHN ELLIOTT
B 12 Jun 1950 at Perth, s of John Alexander E. and Stella McCombie; educ Perth Academy 1962–68; University of Aberdeen 1968–72 (MA), 1972–75 (BD); lic by Presb of Aberdeen 29 Jun 1975; asst Edinburgh South Leith 1975–77; m 31 Jul 1971 Rachel Ann Jones b 6 Nov 1950 d of John Hugh J. and Ida Fairhead; Children: Jonathan b 31 Oct 1975; Kirsten b 4 Apr 1978; Rosalind b 21 Feb 1981; Gareth b 7 May 1985; ord by Presb of Edinburgh during assistantship at South Leith 13 Jun 1976; ind to Glasgow Carntyne Old 5 May 1977; dem on app as Mission Partner with United Church of Zambia in Lusaka, Mar 1983; ind to South Uist 29 Aug 1989; trans to Biggar 29 Nov 1995.

BLACK MOUNT (FES X, 209)

Formed 14 Oct 1976 by union of Dunsyre, Dolphinton, Walston and Elsrickle.

1961 JAMES ANDERSON BALLANTYNE
(FES X, 209), ord and ind to Dunsyre, Dolphinton and Walston 5 Oct 1961; became minister of united charge with Elsrickle 14 Oct 1976; dem 30 Jun 1985; died 20 Sep 1990.

1986 IAN SMEATON SANDILANDS
B 26 Oct 1932 at Edinburgh, s of Thomas Smeaton S. and Ruth Sutherland Thompson; educ Broughton Secondary, Edinburgh 1944–50; University of Edinburgh 1983–85; National Service 1950–53; Advertising 1954–61; Telecommunications 1961–82; lic by Presb of Edinburgh 19 Feb 1986; asst

Edinburgh St Martin's 1985–86; m 16 Aug 1956 Elizabeth Johnston Stark b 30 Sep 1934 d of John S. and Jean Anderson: Children: Stewart Ian b 24 May 1957 m Gillian; Neil John b 1 May 1961; ord and ind to Black Mount 20 Aug 1986; ret 1 Aug 1999.

CAIRNGRYFFE (FES X, 207, 208, 212)

Formed 30 Mar 1995 by union of Carmichael, Covington, Thankerton and Pettinain. Linked with Symington same date.

1948 WILLIAM MARSHALL CUMMING
(FES IX, 189, 269, 353; X, 212), trans from Glasgow Gilmorehill to Pettinain 17 Sep 1948; became minister of linked charge with Carmichael 30 Mar 1952; ret 30 Sep 1972; died 15 Apr 1992.

1965 JOHN STEVEN THOMSON
(FES IX, 41, 350, 468; X, 24, 190, 208), trans from Cambuslang St Paul's to Covington and Thankerton St Michael's with Libberton and Quothquan 17 Jun 1965; ret 30 Nov 1972.

1973 JAMES ALEXANDER ROBERTSON MACKENZIE
(FES IX, 682, 740; X, 191, 207, 309, 387), trans from Coatbridge Blairhill to Carmichael with Pettinain with Covington and Thankerton 29 Aug 1973; trans to Largo St David's 25 Oct 1979.

1980 BRIAN RAMSAY
ord and ind to Carmichael with Covington and Thankerton with Pettinain 14 May 1980; trans to Aberlemno with Guthrie and Rescobie 15 Mar 1984.

1985 ANDREW ELLIOT LAMBIE
(FES X, 216, 406), res as Assoc at Ellon and ind to Carmichael with Covington and Thankerton with Pettinain 12 Jun 1985; ret 31 Dec 1991; s Hector m Sorrell Evans.

1992 MARY BROWN MORRISON
res as Adviser in Mission and Evangelism, Dept of National Mission and ind to Carmichael Covington and Pettinain 19 Feb 1992; trans to Edinburgh Stenhouse St Aidan's 12 Jan 1994.

1995 THOMAS JOHN BROWN
B 11 Nov 1941 at Falkirk, s of John B. and Jemima Jarvie Clark; educ Falkirk High 1953–59; University of Edinburgh 1968–71 (MA), 1990–93 (BD); Moray House College, Edinburgh 1971–72 (PGCE); Coal Merchant 1959–67; Teaching 1972–90; lic by Presb of Falkirk 29 Jun 1993; m 31 Oct 1964 Kathryn Inglis Bertram b 25 Apr 1944 d of John B. and Catherine Inglis; Children: David John William b 21 Jul 1966 m Loginie Govender; Alan Robert b 16 Jul 1969 m Deborah Eales; ord and ind to Cairngryffe with Symington 19 Sep 1995.

CARLUKE KIRKTON (FUF 197; FES IX, 344; X, 206)

1967 ERNEST ROSS DUNCAN SMART
(FES X, 167, 206), ord by Presb of Hamilton during assistantship at South Dalziel 19 Oct 1966; ind to Kirkton 28 Jun 1967; trans to Glasgow Merrylea 21 Nov 1974.

1975 ALEXANDER THOMSON STEWART
ord and ind to Kirkton 29 May 1975; trans to Glasgow Cathcart Old 15 Nov 1980.

1981 HUGH MAXWELL WALLACE
ord by Presb of Moray during assistantship at Elgin St Giles' 17 Feb 1980; ind to Kirkton 17 Jun 1981; trans to Glasgow Mount Florida 12 Feb 1987.

1987 IAIN DICKSON CUNNINGHAM
B 12 Apr 1954 at Port Glasgow, s of Thomas C. and Elizabeth Helen Croal Dickson; educ Hamilton Academy 1966–72; University of Glasgow 1972–75 (MA), 1975–78 (BD); lic by Presb of Hamilton 29 Jun 1978; asst Ayr Castlehill 1978–80; m 2 Jul 1977 Dawn Gibson b 8 Mar 1956 d of William G. and Heather Melvin; Children: Ross Iain b 19 Oct 1982; Linsay Dawn b 12 Apr 1984; Ailsa Ruth b 21 Feb 1986; Heather Amy Elizabeth b 10 Jan 1989; ord by Presb of Ayr during assistantship at Castlehill 9 May 1979; ind to Duntocher Trinity 12 Jun 1980; trans to Kirkton 29 Oct 1987; Publ: Hymn: *God the Father of Creation* (OUP, 1988); Hymn: *Spirit of Truth and Grace* (St Andrew Press, 1998).

CARLUKE ST ANDREW'S (FES III, 284; VIII, 265; IX, 344; X, 206)

1969 ROBIN DOBSON YATES
(FES X, 206), ord and ind to St Andrew's 26 Feb 1969; trans to Cambuslang Flemington Hallside 1 May 1980.

1980 JOHN MAXWELL BIRRELL
res as Warden, Stroove House and ind to St Andrew's 26 Nov 1980; trans to Forfar St Margaret's 22 Sep 1988.

1989 HELEN ELIZABETH JAMIESON
B 9 Aug 1959 at Irvine, d of Hugh Rodger Sloan and Margaret Muir Lithgow; educ Irvine Royal Academy 1971–77; Craigie College of Education 1977–80 (DipEd); University of Glasgow 1984–88 (BD); Teaching 1981–82; Clerical Officer (NHS) 1982–84; lic by Presb of Irvine and Kilmarnock 30 Jun 1988; asst Galston 1988–89; m 2 Jul 1990 Robert Hill Jamieson b 15 Apr 1953 s of David McRoberts J. and Margaret Hill; Children: Linda Margaret b 28 Dec 1994; Eilidh Sloan b 3 Aug 1998; ord and ind to St Andrew's 7 Jun 1989.

CARLUKE ST JOHN'S (FUF 198; FES IX, 344; X, 206)

1970 JAMES STANLEY FIRTH
(FES X, 206), ord and ind to St John's 19 Jun 1970; dem 31 Aug 1976.

1977 STANLEY WILLIAM PEAT
ord and ind to St John's 11 May 1977; trans to Edinburgh Leith St Serf's 11 Oct 1984.

1985 WILLIAM F STORRAR
ord by Presb of Glasgow and app Asst at Cadder 1984; ind to St John's 25 Jun 1985; dem 1 May 1991; University of Glasgow from 1996.

1991 MICHAEL WILLIAM FREW
B 16 May 1951 at Edinburgh, s of Alexander Daniel Ramsay F. and Margaret Isobel Mailer; educ Peebles High and Broughton Secondary, Edinburgh 1963–69; University of Edinburgh 1969–72 (BSc), 1973–76 (BD); Care Asst 1972–73; lic by Presb of Edinburgh, 1996; asst Ellon 1976–77; m 12 Sep 1975 Margaret Smith b 27 May 1949 d of Charles S. and Elizabeth Young; Children: Joanna b 6 Apr 1979; Douglas b 1 Nov 1980; Malcolm b 18 Dec 1981; David b 16 Oct 1984; ord and ind to Alloa West 30 Oct 1978; dem 15 Jan 1987 on app as Regional Organiser for Evangelism 1 Feb 1987; ind to St John's 3 Oct 1991.

CARNWATH (FES IX, 345; X, 207)

1939 HENRY NORMAN WILLOX
(FES IX, 275, 295, 345; X, 207), [correction: Willox, not Wilcox as in Vol X, 207]; trans from Glasgow Kelvinhaugh to Carnwath 17 Mar 1939; ret 31 Jul 1971; died 29 Jan 1998; w Adeline died 11 Mar 1983.

1971 WILLIAM JOHN MIDDLETON
(FES X, 89, 207), trans from Auchencairn with Rerrick to Carnwath 14 Dec 1971; dem 31 Jan 1978.

1978 BEVERLY GILBERT DOUGLAS DAVIDSON GAULD
(FES X, 445), ret from RAChD and ind to Carnwath 27 Jun 1978.

CARSTAIRS (FES IX, 345; X, 207)
Linked 21 May 1966 with Carstairs Junction.

1975 DONALD PIRIE
(FES X, 207), ord and ind to Carstairs with Carstairs Junction 30 Apr 1975; trans to Lenzie Old 2 Feb 1984.

1984 MELVILLE DOIG CROSTHWAITE
ord and ind to Carstairs with Carstairs Junction 29 Aug 1984; trans to Larbert East 16 Nov 1995.

1996 JOHN MELVYN COOGAN
B 24 Dec 1941 at Glasgow, s of John Charles C. and Nancy Deans; educ Allan Glen's, Glasgow 1947–57; Stow College of Engineering, Glasgow 1972, 1977; Glasgow Bible Training Institute 1986–88; University of Glasgow 1988–91 (LTh); Engineering and Building Maintenance; lic by Presb of Ardrossan 11 Sep 1991; asst Kilbirnie St Columba's 1991–92; ord and ind to Arisaig and The Small Isles 9 May 1992; dem 2 Feb 1994; ind to Carstairs with Carstairs Junction 14 Nov 1996.

CARSTAIRS JUNCTION (FES IX, 345; X, 207)

Linked 21 May 1966 with Carstairs.

1975 DONALD PIRIE
(FES X, 207), ord and ind to Carstairs with Carstairs Junction 30 Apr 1975; trans to Lenzie Old 2 Feb 1984.

1984 MELVILLE DOIG CROSTHWAITE
ord and ind to Carstairs with Carstairs Junction 29 Aug 1984; trans to Larbert East 16 Nov 1995.

1996 JOHN MELVYN COOGAN
ind to Carstairs with Carstairs Junction 14 Nov 1996, see Carstairs.

COALBURN (FUF 198; FES IX, 346; X, 207)

Linked 23 Jul 1998 with Lesmahagow Old.

1961 BRIAN FRANK CROSS
(FES X, 207), ord and ind to Coalburn 19 Jan 1961; ret 30 Jun 1998.

1998 SHEILA MARGARET MITCHELL
ord and ind to Lesmahagow Old 23 Nov 1995; became minister of linked charge with Coalburn 23 Jul 1998.

CROSSFORD (FUF 199; FES IX, 347; X, 208)

Linked 24 Aug 1973 with Kirkfieldbank.

1971 ANGUS LOW BAYNE
(FES X, 208, 239), ind to Crossford 21 Apr 1971; became minister of linked charge with Kirkfieldbank 24 Aug 1973; dem and emigrated to S Africa 30 Sep 1975.

1976 ROBERT JAMES McMAHON
(FES X, 422), res from service with Overseas Council in India 22 Aug 1975; employed by Overseas Council in Scotland until ind to Crossford with Kirkfieldbank 4 Mar 1976; ret 28 Jan 1997; s John m Sally Ann Bratt; Publ: *To God be the Glory* (Masihi Sahitya Sanstha, 1970).

1997 STEVEN REID
B 2 Apr 1958 at Glasgow, s of Hugh R. and Helen McIntyre McDonald; educ Allan Glen's, Glasgow 1970–75; University of Glasgow 1975–79 (BAcc), 1985–88 (BD); Accountancy 1979–85; lic by Presb of Glasgow 5 Jul 1988; asst Cambuslang Trinity St Paul's 1988–89; m 25 Mar 1989 Heather Craik b 26 Mar 1966 d of Iain and Fiona C; ord and ind to Dunfermline North 15 Jun 1989; trans to Crossford with Kirkfieldbank 3 Oct 1997.

CULTER (FES I, 245; VIII, 53; IX, 347; X, 208)

Linked 1 Dec 1972 with Libberton and Quothquan. Further linked with Symington 4 Jan 1978.

1962 RONALD SCOTT THOMSON
(FES IX, 505, 628; X, 208, 299), trans from Dundee Broughty Ferry St Stephen's to Culter 5 Sep 1962; ret 30 Sep 1971; died 14 Nov 1981.

1973 JAMES WILLIAM FULLER
(FES X, 208), ord and ind to Culter with Libberton and Quothquan 3 Jun 1973; introd to Rome St Andrew's 16 Jun 1976.

1977 PETER JOHN MACEWAN
(FES IX, 593, X, 255, 342, 413), trans from Perth St Stephen's to Culter with Libberton and Quothquan 11 Aug 1977; became minister of linked charge with Symington 4 Jan 1978; ret 13 Oct 1986; died 30 Apr 1990.

1987 SUSAN GAZARD COWELL
ord by Presb of Edinburgh during assistantship at Greenbank 25 May 1986; ind to Culter with Libberton and Quothquan with Symington 23 Apr 1987; introd to Budapest St Columba's 20 Jun 1994.

1997 STEPHEN ANTON PACITTI
(FES X, 170, 378), returned from Taiwan and ind to Culter with Libberton and Quothquan 27 Feb 1997; Addl children: Benjamin Antony b 24 Aug 1975; s Stephen Mark m Caroline Brotherhood.

DOUGLAS ST BRIDE'S (FES X, 209)

Linked 18 May 1977 with Douglas Water and Rigside.

1964 JOSEPH HARDIE
(FES IX, 193; X, 110, 196, 209), trans from Hamilton South and Quarter to St Bride's 24 Jun 1964; became minister of linked charge with Douglas Water and Rigside 18 May 1977; dem 30 Sep 1988; died 16 Sep 1997.

1979 KENNETH HAROLD FISHER
(FES X, 406), dem from Dunrossness 9 May 1979 and introd as Assoc at Douglas St Bride's with Douglas Water with Rigside; res 16 Apr 1980; ind to Eday with Stronsay Moncur Memorial 3 Jul 1990.

1989 FRANK ALEXANDER GOSLING
ord and ind to St Bride's with Douglas Water and Rigside 28 Jun 1989; dem and resigned status 4 Jan 1991.

1991 LAWRIE INGRAM LENNOX
B 30 Jul 1941 at Glasgow, s of William Brand and Frances Millicent L; educ Hutchesons' Boys' Grammar, Glasgow 1953–58; University of Glasgow 1959–64 (MA, DipEd), 1986–89 (BD); Jordanhill College, Glasgow 1963–64 (PGCE); Teaching 1964–86; lic by Presb of Ayr 4 Jul 1989; asst Crosshill with Dalrymple 1989–90; ord and ind to St Bride's with Douglas Water and Rigside 24 Jun 1991.

DOUGLAS WATER AND RIGSIDE (FES X, 209)

Linked 18 May 1977 with Douglas St Bride's.

1971 ADAM GIRVAN
(FES X, 209), ord and ind to Douglas Water and Rigside 15 May 1971; trans to Old Kilpatrick Bowling 25 Jun 1976.

1977 JOSEPH HARDIE
(FES IX, 193; X, 110, 196, 209), ind to Douglas St Bride's 24 Jun 1964; became minister of linked charge with Douglas Water and Rigside 18 May 1977, see St Bride's.

1979 KENNETH HAROLD FISHER
(FES X, 406), introd as Assoc at Douglas St Bride's with Douglas Water with Rigside 9 May 1979, see St Bride's.

1981 JAMES ALEXANDER RETTIE
ord by Presb of Lanark and introd as Assoc at Douglas Water and Rigside 20 Aug 1981; trans to Melness and Eriboll with Tongue 29 Nov 1984.

1985 AGNES ALEXANDER REID
ord by Presb of Lanark and introd as Assoc at Douglas Water and Rigside 30 Oct 1985; ind to Auchindoir and Kildrummy 18 Apr 1989.

1989 FRANK ALEXANDER GOSLING
ord and ind to Douglas St Bride's with Douglas Water and Rigside 28 Jun 1989, see St Bride's.

1991 LAWRIE INGRAM LENNOX
ord and ind to Douglas St Bride's with Douglas Water and Rigside 24 Jun 1991, see St Bride's.

FORTH ST PAUL'S (FES X, 209)

Formed 7 Nov 1975 by union of Forth and Haywood, Wilsontown and Braehead.

1969 LAURENCE SMITH McLAUCHLAN
(FES IX, 35, 49; X, 21, 210, 374), trans from Moy Dalarossie and Tomatin to Haywood, Wilsontown and Braehead 30 Oct 1969; ret on grounds of ill-health 31 Oct 1974.

1976 THOMAS P HEGGIE
ord and ind to St Paul's 29 Apr 1976; trans to Nairn Old 26 Mar 1981.

1981 DAVID DONALD SCOTT
ord and ind to St Paul's 22 Sep 1981; trans to Logie Kirk 1 Mar 1990.

1990 ALISON JAFFREY
ord and ind to St Paul's 27 Sep 1990; ret on grounds of ill-health 25 Oct 1995; introd to Auchaber United with Auchterless (part-time) 27 Sep 1999.

1996 JAMES BAIN
B 10 Oct 1964 at Cowdenbeath, s of James B. and Mary Milligan McFadyen; educ Beath High, Cowdenbeath 1978–82; University of Aberdeen 1982–86 (BD); University of Edinburgh 1986–88 (DipMin); Open University 1991 (Cert Hosp Mang); Management and Health Education (NHS) 1990–94; lic by Presb of Dunfermline 1 Jul 1988; asst Bearsden North 1994–96; ord and ind to St Paul's 27 Jun 1996.

GLENCAPLE (FES X, 208, 209)

Formed 12 May 1994 by union of Duneaton (union 1 Nov 1971 of Lamington and Wandel, Crawfordjohn and Abington, Wiston and Roberton) and Crawford. Linked same date with Lowther.

1934 EBENEZER GRANDISON COWIE SCOTT
(FES IX, 350; X, 210), ord and ind to Lamington and Wandel 21 May 1934; ret 1 Nov 1971; died 1 Jan 1977.

1951 ALEXANDER SPRING ARCHIBALD
(FUF 80; FES IX, 108, 110, 346, 616; X, 208), res from app at St James' Wanganni, New Zealand and ind to Crawford 29 Nov 1951; ret 30 Sep 1972; died 1 Jun 1992.

1952 MARTIN ANDREW SIMPSON
(FES IX, 355, 749; X, 212), res as Professor of History, Scottish Churches College, Calcutta and ind to Wiston and Roberton 30 Jun 1952; ret 1 Nov 1971; died 16 May 1985.

1972 ROBERT INCH JOHNSTONE
(FES IX, 611; X, 55, 209, 351), trans from Longniddry to Duneaton 4 Oct 1972; dem 5 Nov 1977 to enter teaching profession (RE); died 27 Jul 1984.

1973 JOHN NELSON
(FES IX, 744; X, 208, 424), res from app at St Andrew's, Calcutta, India and ind to Crawford and Elvanfoot with Leadhills and Wanlockhead 15 Nov 1973; ret 31 Dec 1980; d Mary m Gordon Millar; s David m Denise Shaw.

1978 MOSES DONALDSON
(FES X, 239), trans from Isle of Mull to Duneaton 18 Oct 1978; trans to Fort Augustus with Glengarry 15 Oct 1993.

1981 DAVID ROBERT BAILLIE
B 6 Jul 1925 at Musselburgh, s of Jasper Martin B. and Jean Livingstone; educ Musselburgh Grammar 1930–43; University of Edinburgh; Journalist Photography 1947–55; Scientific Photography (MOD) 1955–75; lic by Presb of Stirling 12 Jun 1977; asst Stirling St Ninian's 1977–78; m 10 Mar 1962 Irene Brenda Martin b 12 Mar 1933 d of Edwin M. and Elsie Hance; Children: Duncan Martin b 1 Apr 1963; Andrew Jasper b 10 Feb 1965; Mary Rachel b 12 Jun 1970; ord and ind to Kirkinner 24 Jan 1979; trans to Crawford with Lowther 22 Apr 1981; ret 6 Jul 1990.

1991 JAMES BROWN
(FES X, 104), trans from Cockpen and Carrington with Lasswade to Crawford with Lowther 14 Mar 1991; became minister of united charge with Duneaton 12 May 1994; trans to Abercorn with Dalmeny 17 Jan 1995.

1995 ANDREW MUNRO
B 1 Jan 1936 at Port Glasgow, s of Alexander M. and Janet Clark Lambert McCracken; educ North Manchester Grammar 1946–51; University of Aberdeen 1960–64 (MA); University of Glasgow 1964–67 (BD); Universities of Tubingen, Glasgow and Aberdeen 1967–71 (PhD); Trainee Accountant and RAF 1956–60; Teaching 1971–72; lic by Presb of Greenock, Mar 1967; m 27 Jul 1963 Sheila Murdoch Smith b 11 Nov 1940 d of Charles Henry Irvine S. and Janet Ramsey Ross; Children: Shelagh Janet b 26 Jun 1964 m James Clark; Iain Ross b 21 Jul 1967; ord by Presb of Strathbogie and Fordyce, Sep 1972 and app by Overseas Council for service in Ghana; res on app as Principal teacher, Elgin Academy 1976; Religious Education Adviser, Dumfries and Galloway Regional Council 1979–86; ind to Glencaple with Lowther 22 Aug 1995.

KIRKFIELDBANK (FES III, 305; VIII, 269; IX, 349; X, 210)

Linked 24 Aug 1973 with Crossford.

1961 JOHN BUCHANAN
(FES IX, 149, 312, 367; X, 210, 216 (2), 219), trans from Duntocher East to Kirkfieldbank 27 Jun 1961; ret 31 Jul 1973; died 18 Oct 1976.

1973 ANGUS LOW BAYNE
(FES X, 208, 239), ind to Crossford 21 Apr 1971; became minister of linked charge with Kirkfieldbank 24 Aug 1973; dem and emigrated to S Africa 30 Sep 1975.

1976 ROBERT JAMES McMAHON
(FES X, 422), ind to Crossford with Kirkfieldbank 4 Mar 1976, see Crossford.

1997 STEVEN REID
ind to Crossford with Kirkfieldbank 3 Oct 1997, see Crossford.

KIRKMUIRHILL (FUF 190; FES IX, 349; X, 210)

1974 DAVID ANDREW YOUNG
(FES X, 210), ord by Presb of Livingston and Bathgate during assistantship at Bathgate High 19 Sep 1972; ind to Kirkmuirhill 28 Mar 1974.

LANARK GREYFRIARS (FES X, 210)

Formed 28 May 1993 by union of Lanark Cairns and Lanark St Kentigern's.

1966 JAMES PATTERSON WILSON
(FES X, 65, 210), trans from Hawick St Mary's to St Kentigern's 16 Aug 1966; ret 31 Dec 1991; died 12 Feb 1993.

1973 DAVID ALEXANDER KENNEDY
(FES X, 165, 210, 231), trans from Glasgow Langside Old to Lanark Cairns 30 Jun 1973; ret 31 Oct 1983.

1984 WILLIAM MACGREGOR LONGMUIR
ord and introd to Cairns 6 Sep 1984; ind 31 Aug 1989; trans to Bedrule with Denholm with Minto 27 Nov 1992.

1993 DAVID ARTHUR COLLINS
B 15 Jun 1951 at Dumbarton, s of Arthur C. and Constance Kingsley MacDonald; educ Clydebank High 1963–69; University of Glasgow 1969–73 (BSc); Jordanhill College, Glasgow 1973–74 (PGCE); University of St Andrews 1989–92 (BD); Teaching 1974–79; Museum Education/Management 1979–89; lic by Presb of St Andrews 1 Jul 1992; asst Howe of Fife 1992–93; m 29 Jul 1977 Catherine Gray b 12 Nov 1954 d of Thomas Gilfillan G. and Ella Murray Cobb; Children: Alastair David b 5 May 1982; Malcolm John b 15 Apr 1984; ord and ind to Greyfriars (joint ministry) 8 Oct 1993.

1993 CATHERINE COLLINS
B 12 Nov 1954 at Hastings, d of Thomas Gilfillan Gray and Ella Murray Cobb; educ Kelso High 1965–72; University of St Andrews 1972–76 (MA), 1989–92 (BD); Moray House College, Edinburgh 1976–77 (PGCE); lic by Presb of St Andrews 1 Jul 1992; asst Glenrothes St Columba's 1992–93; m 29 Jul 1977 David Arthur Collins b 15 Jun 1951 s of Arthur C. and Constance Kingsley MacDonald; Children: Alastair David b 5 May 1982; Malcolm John b 15 Apr 1984; ord and ind to Greyfriars (joint ministry) 8 Oct 1993.

LANARK ST NICHOLAS' (FES X, 211)

1972 JOHN HEDLEY McINDOE
(FES X, 211, 304), trans from Dundee Park to St Nicholas' 6 Jan 1972; trans to London St Columba's with Newcastle St Andrew's 12 Feb 1988.

1988 JOHN MORRIA ARNOTT THOMSON
B 27 Feb 1949 at Buckhaven, s of Peter George
T. and Pamela Iris Marian Thorne; educ Irvine
Royal Academy 1961–67; University of Glasgow
1972–76 (BD); Columbia Theological Seminary,
Atlanta, USA 1976–77 (ThM); Civil Service 1968–
70; Local Government Officer 1970–72; lic by
Presb of Irvine and Kilmarnock 28 Sep 1977; asst
Troon St Meddan's 1976–77; m 21 Nov 1971
Marlene Jeffrey Logan b 5 Aug 1951 d of George
Jeffrey L. and Mary Hunter McGregor Cassels;
Children: Laura Marlene Jeffrey b 18 Dec 1978;
Stephen George Morria b 14 Dec 1981; ord and
ind to Houston and Killellan 11 May 1978; trans to
St Nicholas' 20 Sep 1988.

LAW (FES IX, 351; X, 211)

1968 WILLIAM ARCHIBALD FREW IZETT
(FES X, 211), ord and ind to Law 11 Sep 1968;
d Rhona m Michael Stewart Goss; s Ian m
Alison Henderson; d Christine m Scott Simon
Waugh.

LESMAHAGOW ABBEYGREEN (FUF 201; FES
IX, 352; X, 211)

1954 ROBERT BERNARD WILLIAM WALKER
(FES IX 352, 752; X, 211), ind to Abbeygreen 6
Apr 1954; ret 31 Oct 1981; s Donald m Judith
Veitch Anderson.

1982 DAVID SMYTH CARMICHAEL
ord and ind to Abbeygreen 2 Sep 1982.

LESMAHAGOW OLD (FES III, 313; VIII, 271; IX,
352; X, 211)

Linked 23 Jul 1998 with Coalburn.

1969 WILLIAM NIVEN
(FES X, 196, 211), trans from Hamilton Laighstonehall to Lesmahagow Old 8 Jan 1969; ret 31
Aug 1994; d Linda m Caldwell; d Kirsten m Jensen;
d Judith m Pow.

1995 SHEILA MARGARET MITCHELL
B 24 Jul 1970 at Edinburgh, d of Hamish Gordon
M. and Anne Brisbane Kennedy; educ Longcroft
Secondary, Beverley, N Humberside and Arran
High, Lamlash 1982–88; University of Edinburgh
1988–93 (BD, MTh); lic by Presb of Ardrossan 13
Jul 1994; asst Edinburgh St Giles' Cathedral 1994–
95; ord and ind to Lesmahagow Old 23 Nov 1995;
became minister of linked charge with Coalburn
23 Jul 1998.

LIBBERTON AND QUOTHQUAN (FES VIII, 55;
IX, 352; X, 212)

Linked 1 Dec 1972 with Culter. Further linked 4
Jan 1978 with Symington.

1973 JAMES WILLIAM FULLER
(FES X, 208), ord and ind to Culter with Libberton
and Quothquan 3 Jun 1973; introd to Rome St
Andrew's 16 Jun 1976.

1977 PETER JOHN MACEWAN
(FES IX, 593, X, 255, 342, 413), ind to Culter with
Libberton and Quothquan 11 Aug 1977; became
minister of linked charge with Symington 4 Jan
1978, see Culter.

1987 SUSAN GAZARD COWELL
ind to Culter with Libberton and Quothquan with
Symington 23 Apr 1987, see Culter.

1997 STEPHEN ANTON PACITTI
(FES X, 170, 378), ind to Culter with Libberton and
Quothquan 27 Feb 1997, see Culter.

LOWTHER (FES IX, 355; X, 212)

Formerly known as Leadhills and Wanlockhead.
Linkage with Crawford terminated 12 May 1994.
Linked same date with Glencaple.

1981 DAVID ROBERT BAILLIE
ind to Crawford with Lowther 22 Apr 1981, see
Glencaple.

1991 JAMES BROWN
(FES X, 104), trans from Cockpen and Carrington
with Lasswade to Crawford with Lowther 14 Mar
1991; became minister of united charge with
Duneaton 12 May 1994; trans to Abercorn with
Dalmeny 17 Jan 1995.

1995 ANDREW MUNRO
ind to Glencaple with Lowther 22 Aug 1995, see
Glencaple.

SYMINGTON (FES IX, 354; X, 212)

Linked 4 Jan 1978 with Culter with Libberton and
Quothquan. Linkage terminated 30 Mar 1995.
Linked same date with Cairngryffe.

1964 ALEXANDER MAXWELL DUFF
(FES IX, 340; X, 130, 203, 212), trans from Penilee
St Andrew's to Symington 28 May 1964; ret 31
Dec 1977; died 14 Mar 1988.

1978 PETER JOHN MACEWAN
(FES IX, 593, X, 255, 342, 413), ind to Culter with
Libberton and Quothquan 11 Aug 1977; became
minister of linked charge with Symington 4 Jan
1978, see Culter.

1987 SUSAN GAZARD COWELL
ind to Culter with Libberton and Quothquan with
Symington 23 Apr 1987, see Culter.

1995 THOMAS JOHN BROWN
ord and ind to Cairngryffe with Symington 19 Sep
1995, see Cairngryffe.

PRESBYTERY OF PAISLEY

FULL-TIME PRESBYTERY CLERK (FES X, 122)

1972 WILLIAM WARBURTON MITCHELL BELL (FES IX, 464, 538; X, 122, 314), dem from Barrhead Arthurlie on app as Clerk to Presb of Paisley (full-time) and Chaplain to Royal Alexandra Infirmary, Paisley 30 Oct 1972; app Clerk to Synod of Clydesdale 8 Oct 1981; ret 31 Dec 1983; died 20 Feb 1999.

BARRHEAD ARTHURLIE (FUF 163; FES IX, 212; X, 122)

1973 JOHN CAMPBELL
(FES X, 122), ord and ind to Barrhead Arthurlie 16 May 1973; trans to Glasgow Sherbrooke St Gilbert's 12 Jun 1980.

1980 QUINTIN ALEXANDER BLANE
ord by Presb of Edinburgh during assistantship at St Giles' 3 Jun 1979; ind to Barrhead Arthurlie 28 Oct 1980; trans to Bellshill West 25 Oct 1994.

1995 TERENCE CAMPAIGNE MORAN
B 24 Jun 1960 at Glasgow, s of Joseph M. and Margaret Donnachie Scott Smith; educ Waverley Secondary, Drumchapel 1972–78; University of Glasgow 1989–93 (BD, CMin); Police Officer 1979–85; lic by Presb of Glasgow, Jul 1993; asst The Auld Kirk of Ayr 1993–94; Glasgow Sandyford 1994–95; m 29 May 1984 divorced 1988; m (2) 17 Sep 1993, divorced 1998; Children: Ellie Brown b 21 Mar 1995; ord and ind to Barrhead Arthurlie 31 Aug 1995; dem 3 Apr 1998.

1998 JAMES SMILLIE ANNALL COWAN
B 13 Jan 1959 at Irvine, s of James C. and Moira Annall; educ James Hamilton Academy, Kilmarnock 1971–76; University of Edinburgh 1977–81 (BD), 1981–83 (DipMin); Warehouse Storeman 1976–77; Car Valet 1984–86; lic by Presb of Irvine and Kilmarnock, Nov 1983; asst Edinburgh Richmond Craigmillar 1983–84; m 28 Jun 1980 Nadia Toni b 10 Mar 1958 d of Ferruccio T. and Helen Mackie; Children: Laura b 17 Mar 1985; Amy b 29 Dec 1986; ord and ind to Cockenzie and Port Seton Old 26 Feb 1986; trans to Greenock Ardgowan 19 Nov 1992; trans to Barrhead Arthurlie 10 Dec 1998.

BARRHEAD BOUROCK (FES III, 131; VIII, 237; IX, 212; X, 122)

1969 FRANK JAMES GARDNER
(FES X, 122), ind to Barrhead Bourock 1 Oct 1969; trans to Gourock Old 28 Oct 1979.

1980 GEORGE STEWART BIRSE
ord and ind to Barrhead Bourock 14 May 1980; trans to Newton-on-Ayr 19 Jan 1989.

1989 ADAM JOHNSTON JARRON HOOD
ord and ind to Barrhead Bourock 29 Jun 1989; dem to take up place at University of Oxford 1 Oct 1994; app Deputy Director, Research Centre, Queen's College, Birmingham 1 Sep 1999.

1995 MAUREEN LEITCH
B 23 Mar 1946 at Bonnybridge, d of Robert Campbell Ferguson and Agnes Gillies Dyet; educ Denny High 1958–64; Dunfermline College of Physical Education 1964–67 (DipPEd); University of Stirling 1982–85 (BA); University of Edinburgh 1991–94 (BD); Teaching 1967–85; Development Education Officer 1988–91; lic by Presb of Falkirk 3 Aug 1994; m 6 Aug 1974 Angus Forbes Leitch b 16 Feb 1944 s of James Forbes L. and Christina Williamson Robertson; Children: Alexander James b 12 Oct 1980; Lynsey Ann b 1 Sep 1983; ord and ind to Barrhead Bourock 15 Aug 1995.

BARRHEAD SOUTH AND LEVERN (FES X, 122, 125)

Formed 29 May 1985 by union of Barrhead South and Levern and Nitshill (area of South Nitshill detached and adjoined to parish of Glasgow Priesthill).

1940 ROBERT SMITH
(FES IX, 218, 499; X, 125), trans from Pittenweem St Fillan's to Levern and Nitshill 28 Sep 1940; ret 19 Nov 1973; died 12 Sep 1997.

1972 JOHN McLAREN SPIERS
(FES X, 122), ord and ind to Barrhead South 7 Jun 1972; trans to Giffnock Orchardhill 5 Mar 1977.

1974 BRUCE BAIRNSFATHER LAWRIE
(FES X, 125), ord and ind to Levern and Nitshill 21 Aug 1974; dem 29 Sep 1981 on app by Board of World Mission for service with Lucaya Presb Church, Freeport, Bahamas.

1977   ROBERT MACARTHUR HETHERINGTON
(FES X, 315, 420), res from term app at Arbroath
Inverbrothock and ind to Barrhead South 24 Aug
1977; became minister of united charge with
Levern and Nitshill 29 May 1985.

BISHOPTON (FES X, 122)

Name changed 1999 from Bishopton Erskine
(union 1 Apr 1971 of Bishopton Old Erskine and
Bishopton Rossland).

1960   IAN FORBES McCULLOCH
(FES IX, 62, 229; X, 38, 123), [correction:
Bishopton Rossland, not Erskine as in Vol X, 38];
trans from Falkirk Grahamston to Bishopton
Rossland 11 Feb 1960; ret 31 Mar 1971; died 12
May 1976.

1970   DOUGLAS NIVEN ALEXANDER
(FES X, 122, 123), res as Warden of Iona Com-
munity House, Glasgow and ind to Bishopton Old
Erskine 26 Aug 1970; became minister of united
charge with Bishopton Rossland 1 Apr 1971; ret 8
Apr 1999; d Susan m David Cooper.

BRIDGE OF WEIR FREELAND (FUF 164; FES
IX, 213; X, 123)

Linkage with Houston and Killellan terminated 30
Oct 1977.

1953   HENRY CUMMING
(FES IX, 213, 434, 533; X, 123), trans from Forfar
Lowson Memorial to Freeland 8 Oct 1953; ret 6
Jun 1972; died 12 Jun 1997.

1972   GEORGE KEITH McEWAN MORTIMER
(FES IX, 262, 444; X, 124, 154), ind to Houston
and Killellan 28 Sep 1960; became minister of
linked charge with Freeland 6 Sep 1972, see
Houston.

1978   ANDREW GORDON NIMMO WILSON
ord by Presb of Dundee during assistantship at St
Mary's 31 Mar 1977; ind to Freeland 10 May 1978;
trans to Aberdeen Rubislaw 10 Dec 1987.

1988   KENNETH NELSON GRAY
B 27 Jan 1961 at Dunfermline, s of George Currie
G. and Anne Tennent Robertson; educ Cathkin
High, Glasgow 1972–78; University of Strath-
clyde 1978–82 (BA); University of Glasgow 1984–
87 (BD); Accountancy 1982–84; lic by Presb of
Glasgow 2 Jul 1987; asst Paisley Sherwood 1987–
88; m 15 Aug 1987 Alison Jane Wilson d of James
W. and Elizabeth Macdonald; ord and ind to
Freeland 28 Jun 1988.

BRIDGE OF WEIR ST MACHAR'S RANFURLY
(FES III, 131; VIII, 237; IX, 214; X, 123)

Formed 28 Aug 1968 by union of Bridge of Weir
Ranfurly and Bridge of Weir St Machar's.

1952   LLANDELS BONAR BISHOP
(FES IX, 66, 199, 214, 721; X, 123), trans from
Linlithgow Craigmailen to St Machar's 30 Sep
1952; ret 15 Oct 1960; died 25 Sep 1981.

1962   DONALD ANGUS MACLEOD
(FES X, 123, 155, 189, 236), trans from Glasgow
Castlemilk West to St Machar's with Ranfurly 19
Sep 1962; dem 30 Jun 1967 to take up teaching
post in Canada.

1969   ALASTAIR FLEMING McCORMICK
(FES X, 123, 230), trans from Kirn St Andrew's to
St Machar's Ranfurly 1 May 1969; trans to Perth
St Andrew's 19 Jan 1977.

1977   WILLIAM PATERSON
ord and ind to St Machar's Ranfurly 31 Aug 1977;
trans to Edinburgh Craigmillar Park 1 Mar 1984.

1984   THOMAS CAMPBELL PITKEATHLY
ord and ind to St Machar's Ranfurly 25 Sep 1984;
introd to Brussels St Andrew's 25 Oct 1991.

1992   SUZANNE DUNLEAVY
B 9 Jan 1951 at Edinburgh, d of Charles D. and
Marjorie Deward Murphy; educ Bathgate Academy
1963–69; Callander Park College of Education,
Falkirk 1969–72 (DipPEd); University of Edinburgh
1985–89 (BD); Teaching (primary) 1972–85; lic by
Presb of West Lothian 4 Jul 1989; asst London St
Columba's Pont Street 1990–92; ord by Presb of
England during assistantship at St Columba's Pont
Street 30 Sep 1990; ind to St Machar's Ranfurly 8
May 1992.

CALDWELL (FES III, 132; VIII, 237; IX, 214; X,
123)

1971   EDWIN LOWE
(FES IX, 320; X, 120, 123, 189, 245), trans from
Aberfeldy to Caldwell 17 Feb 1971; ret 30
Sepember 1988; d Christine died 7 Jan 1991; s
Kenneth m Margaret MacMillan.

1989   JOHN PATTISON CUBIE
(FES X, 127, 190), trans from Cambuslang Trinity
St Paul's to Caldwell 1 Mar 1989; ret 30 Jun 1999;
s John m Vanessa Lancefield; s Andrew m Joan
Crockett; Publ: Sermons and children's talks in
Expository Times (T&T Clark).

1999   JOHN CAMPBELL
(FES X, 122), res as Adviser in Mission and
Evangelism, Dept of National Mission and ind to
Caldwell 29 Sep 1999; University of Glasgow
1984–87 (MA); Open University 1993–96 (BSc); d
Jane died 8 Jul 1996.

ELDERSLIE KIRK (FES X, 123)

Formed 2 Nov 1977 by union of Elderslie East and
Elderslie West.

1943 DAVID RAMSAY
(FES IX, 214, 381; X, 123), trans from Colintraive to Elderslie West 20 Feb 1943; ret 31 Aug 1970; died 15 Sep 1981.

1954 ALEXANDER RALSTON
(FES IX, 214, 608, 707; X, 123), trans from New Deer North to Elderslie East 7 Apr 1954; ret 2 Nov 1977; died 3 Jan 1991.

1971 DONALD KEITH
(FES IX, 123), ord and ind to Elderslie Kirk 5 May 1971; dem on app by Royal Naval Chaplaincy Service 14 Apr 1977.

1978 WILLIAM CURRIE HEWITT
ord by Presb of Ayr during assistantship at Castlehill 17 Feb 1977; ind to Elderslie Kirk 7 Jun 1978; trans to Greenock St Luke's 3 Mar 1994.

1994 DAVID NEIL McLACHLAN
B 25 Feb 1956 at Kirn, s of Duncan M. and Agnes McCreadie Fenwick; educ John Neilson Institute, Paisley 1968–74; University of Glasgow 1979–84 (BD, CMin); Strathclyde Police Fingerprint Dept 1974–76; Town Planning 1977–79; lic by Presb of Paisley 27 Nov 1984; asst Paisley Martyrs 1984–85; m 22 Aug 1981 Yvonne Gailey b 13 Mar 1957 d of Robert G. and May Riddell; Children: David Jamie b 22 Jan 1986; Robert Fenwick b 28 Sep 1987; separated; ord and ind to Glasgow Gorbals 5 Jun 1985; trans to Elderslie Kirk 29 Sep 1994; Publ: *The Times Best Sermons of 1996* (Cassell, 1996).

HOUSTON AND KILLELLAN (FES III, 141; VIII, 239; IX, 215; X, 124)

Linkage with Bridge of Weir Freeland terminated 30 Oct 1977.

1960 GEORGE KEITH McEWAN MORTIMER
(FES IX, 262, 444; X, 124, 154), trans from Glasgow Carntyne Old to Houston and Killellan 28 Sep 1960; became minister of linked charge with Bridge of Weir Freeland 6 Sep 1972; ret 30 Sep 1977; died 17 Dec 1980.

1978 JOHN MORRIA ARNOTT THOMSON
ord and ind to Houston and Killellan 11 May 1978; trans to Lanark St Nicholas' 20 Sep 1988.

1989 GEORGINA MARTHA BAXENDALE
B 18 Aug 1950 at Motherwell, d of George Robertson Naismith and Catherine McFarlane Wood; educ Brandon High and Dalziel High, Motherwell 1962–68; University of Glasgow 1976–80 (BD); Teaching and Translating 1972–76; lic by Presb of Hamilton, Jun 1980; m 10 Apr 1984 Ronald Hugh Baxendale b 20 Apr 1952; divorced 1996; Children: Laura Jane b 13 Jun 1985; James George Edward b 24 May 1988; ord and ind to Coatbridge Blairhill Dundyvan 14 May 1981; dem 30 Sep 1986 on app as Assoc Chaplain to University of Glasgow; ind to Houston and Killellan 28 Jun 1989.

HOWWOOD (FES III, 143; VIII, 239; IX, 215; X, 124)

1947 JOHN CAMPBELL
(FES IX, 215, 391; X, 124), trans from Campbeltown Lorne Street to Howwood 16 Dec 1947; died 26 Jun 1977.

1978 JOHN McARTHUR
(FES X, 126), trans from Neilston to Howwood 2 Feb 1978; ret 31 Jul 1985; died 20 Aug 1993.

1985 PHYLLIS MARY WILSON
ord and ind to Howwood 7 Nov 1985; trans to Motherwell South Dalziel 24 Nov 1994.

1995 BENJAMIN JOHN ANTHONY ABELEDO
B 14 Aug 1958 at Barcelona, Spain, s of Indalecio A. and Remedios Llorys; educ Parish of Arenal Secondary School, Mallorca 1962–72; Nazarene Theological College (affiliated to Univ of Manchester) 1984–90 (BTh, DipTh, PTh); Paratroop Regiment 1976–79; Nursing 1981–83; lic by Church of the Nazarene 1 Jun 1988; asst Glasgow Penilee St Andrew's 1994–95; m 28 Jun 1980 Marie Connolly b 5 Jul 1956 d of Daniel Duffy C. and Mary Rowan Donnelly; Children: Cassia b 22 Jan 1982; Stephen b 15 Aug 1984; Nadine b 31 Dec 1989; ord by Church of the Nazarene (Swanick) 9 May 1991; ind to Howwood 27 Jun 1995; Officer in RAChD from 12 May 1998.

INCHINNAN (FES IX, 216; X, 124)

1970 JAMES ALAN COATS MATHERS
(FES IX, 427; X, 124, 253, 323), trans from Montrose St George's and Trinity to Inchinnan 30 Jan 1970; ret 30 Sepember 1989; s Neal m Debra Horvath; s John m Patricia Susan George; s Alan m Morna Anderson.

1990 LESLIE GAVIN DONAGHY
ord and ind to Inchinnan 30 May 1990; dem 31 Aug 1994 to enter teaching profession (RE); ind to Dumbarton St Andrew's 2 Jul 1998.

1995 MARILYN MACLAINE
B 18 Oct 1943 at Edinburgh, d of Reginald Farnell and Marion Gill Stewart; educ Boroughmuir Secondary, Edinburgh 1958–60; University of Edinburgh 1988–91 (LTh); Security Officer 1969–86; lic by Presb of Edinburgh 7 Jul 1991; asst Edinburgh St Nicholas' Sighthill 1991–92; m 22 Sep 1962 Donald John MacLaine b 31 Jul 1941 s of John Findlayson M. and Lily MacLennan; Children: Kevin Bruce b 20 Oct 1965; Martin James b 8 Jun 1968; ord and ind to Inchinnan 27 Apr 1995.

JOHNSTONE HIGH (FES III, 146; VIII, 239; IX, 216; X, 124)

1952 ARTHUR FAWCETT
(FES IX, 216; X, 124), ord and ind to Johnstone High 25 Nov 1952; died 14 Dec 1976.

1976 JAMES SKIMINS
ord and ind to Johnstone High 30 Sep 1976; dem 12 Oct 1982.

1983 ALBERT EDWARD SMITH
ord and ind to Johnstone High 2 Jun 1983; trans to Dunkeld 14 Nov 1990.

1991 RANDOLPH SCOTT
B 26 May 1946 at Airdrie, s of James S. and Janet Brown Mitchell Gray; educ Clifton High, Coatbridge 1958–61; University of Glasgow 1984–90 (BD, MA); Accountancy 1961–84; lic by Presb of Hamilton 26 Jun 1990; m 9 Dec 1972 Louise Main b 3 Nov 1948 d of Thomas M. and Lily Hazlie; Children: Greig b 14 Apr 1975; Jill b 28 Aug 1978; ord and ind to Johnstone High 20 Jun 1991.

JOHNSTONE ST ANDREW'S TRINITY (FES IX, 217; X, 124)
1974 JAMES CHALMERS MACCOLL
(FES X, 124, 240), trans from Oban Christ's Church Dunollie to St Andrew's Trinity 17 Apr 1974; m 6 Apr 1957 Margaret Palmer Gwynne b 5 Jul 1935 d of David Brynmor Lloyd-G. and Margaret Palmer Swan Dunlop; Children: Elizabeth b 17 Jan 1959 m Ian Dickman; John b 27 Jul 1960 m Deborah White; David b 18 Apr 1963 m Gillian Brown; Andrew b 12 Aug 1969.

JOHNSTONE ST PAUL'S (FES X, 124)
1975 CHARLES REILLY JONES
B 28 Sep 1942 at Edinburgh, s of Charles Reilly J. and Jessie Livingstone; educ Niddrie Marischal Secondary (now Castle Brae) 1955–58; University of Edinburgh 1970–74 (BD); lic by Presb of Edinburgh 6 Oct 1974; asst Edinburgh Carrick Knowe 1974–75; m 5 Feb 1966 Elizabeth Anne King b 26 Feb 1943; Children: Jennifer b 22 Mar 1967; Martin b 3 Apr 1969; Beverley b 16 Jul 1973; ord and ind to St Paul's 29 Apr 1975; dem 11 Oct 1983.

1984 IAN PURVES
trans from Thornliebank to St Paul's 17 May 1984; trans to Prestwick Kingcase 25 Sep 1991.

1992 JAMES ANDREW SPENCE BOAG
B 24 Oct 1955 at Greenock, s of James B. and Isabella Smyth; educ Port Glasgow High 1960–71; University of Edinburgh 1986–90 (BD); University of Glasgow 1990–91 (CMin); Shipbuilding 1971–84; lic by Presb of Greenock 1 Sep 1991; asst Greenock St Luke's 1991–92; m 14 Feb 1975 Christine Elizabeth McFeeley b 7 Nov 1952 d of William M. and Ann Cook; Children: Richard b 6 Mar 1978; Jonathan b 2 Mar 1983; ord and ind to St Paul's 13 May 1992.

KILBARCHAN EAST (FUF 166; FES IX, 217; X, 125)
1975 CHARLES BLAIR GILLON
(FES X, 125), ord and ind to Kilbarchan East 30 Jul 1975; trans to Glasgow Ibrox 31 Jan 1980.

1980 STANLEY WILLIAM PALMER
B 20 Nov 1932 at Birmingham, s of Charles Henry P. and May Florance Rodgers; educ Kings Norton Grammar, Birmingham 1943–48; University of Glasgow 1976–80 (BD); Sales Manager, Cadbury Schweppes 1953–76; lic by Presb of Dumbarton 17 Jun 1980; asst Milngavie Cairns 1976–78; Faifley 1978–80; m 27 Mar 1958 Margaret Anne Frier b 30 Dec 1934 d of John Douglas F. and Margaret Greig; Children: Joy Margaret b 1 Oct 1959 m Purkiss; Alan Charles b 21 Dec 1962; Ruth May b 5 May 1964 m Caldwell; Mary Elizabeth b 17 Jun 1966 m Borland; ord and ind to Kilbarchan East 10 Sep 1980; ret 30 Jun 1991.

1994 ALISTER WILLIAM BULL
B 11 May 1964 at Glasgow, s of Geoffrey Taylor B. and Agnes Johnstone Templeton; educ Balfron High and Douglas Academy, Milngavie 1976–81; Glasgow College of Building and Printing 1981–84 (Higher Dip Print); University of London (external) 1986–90 (BD); University of Glasgow 1990–92 (DipMin); Printing Administrator 1984–86; lic by Presb of Ardrossan 9 Sep 1992; asst Aberdeen Newhills 1992–93; m 17 Aug 1985 Ruth Jennifer Cruickshank b 3 Jul 1963 d of Norman C. and Johnson; Children: Carron Ruth b 9 May 1988; Marc Alister b 20 Jun 1990; Jordan Matthew b 14 Jun 1993; ord and ind to Kilbarchan East 11 Jan 1994.

KILBARCHAN WEST (FES III, 148; VIII, 240; IX, 218; X, 125)
1955 ANDREW KERR
(FES IX, 540; X, 125, 315), trans from Arbroath to Kilbarchan West 16 Mar 1955; ret 1 Dec 1991.

1994 ARTHUR SHERRATT
B 10 Feb 1944 at Paisley, s of Arthur S. and Mary Jane Thomson Nixon; educ Camphill Secondary, Paisley 1956–60; University of Glasgow 1989–93 (BD); Mechanical Engineering 1960–76; Sales Rep 1976–82; Taxi Driver 1982–89; lic by Presb of Paisley 26 Aug 1993; asst Elderslie Kirk 1993–94; m 6 Mar 1965 Susan Docherty b 1 Mar 1946 d of John D. and Elizabeth Johnston; Children: Karen Elizabeth b 28 Oct 1966 m Stewart Rafferty; Kim Jane b 12 Jun 1969; ord and ind to Kilbarchan West 5 May 1994.

LINWOOD (FES III, 152; VIII, 241; IX, 218; X, 125)
1973 JOHN WHITEFORD DRUMMOND
(FES X, 125), ind to Linwood 27 Sep 1973; trans to Rutherglen West 24 Jun 1986.

1987 THOMAS EDWARD MARSHALL
B 16 Apr 1954 at Lennoxtown, s of Alec M. and Martha Cameron Heggarty; educ Woodside Secondary, Glasgow 1966–71; Glasgow College of Technology 1973–75 (HNC); University of Glasgow 1981–86 (BD, CMin); School Laboratory Technician 1973–74; Medical Physics Technician 1974–81; lic by Presb of Glasgow 30 Jun 1986; asst Govan Old 1986–87; m 18 Aug 1973 Florence Mills b 18 Jan 1955 d of George Harold M. and Elizabeth Reilly; Children: Nicola b 10 Feb 1977; David Edward b 8 Sep 1979; Adam b 16 Nov 1984; ord and ind to Linwood 5 May 1987.

LOCHWINNOCH (FES IX, 219; X, 125)

1962 RODERICK McLEOD
(FES IX, 202; X, 116, 125), trans from Dalry Courthill to Lochwinnoch 14 Feb 1962; ret 31 Jul 1990.

1992 THOMAS O' LEARY
B 29 Dec 1945 at Aberdeen, s of Thomas O. and Annie Kynoch Watkins; educ Rutherglen Academy 1957–63; University of Glasgow 1977–82 (BD, CMin); Gas Engineering 1963–77; lic by Presb of Irvine and Kilmarnock 23 Jun 1982; asst Troon St Meddan's 1982–83; m 4 Feb 1970 Carolyn Sword Aitken; Children: Susan Douglas b 9 Jan 1971 m Jamie Bower; Ross Watkins b 16 Jan 1973; ord and ind to Inch with Stranraer St Andrew's 11 May 1983; became minister of united charge with Lochryan 1 Jul 1985; dem to take up app with Board of World Mission in Colombo, Sri Lanka Jan 1988; ind to Lochwinnoch 2 Sep 1992; ret 30 Jun 1998.

1999 ROBIN NORMAN ALLISON
B 15 Sep 1967 at Bishopbriggs, s of James Norman A. and Caroline Elizabeth Gibson; educ Peebles High 1980–85; University of Edinburgh 1986–92 (BD, DipMin); Hotel Porter 1985–86; lic by Presb of Melrose and Peebles 14 Jul 1992; asst Edinburgh Palmerston Place 1992–94; m 25 Apr 1992 Julia MacRae b 22 Jul 1969 d of Gordon Duncan M. and Elizabeth Helen Stuart; Children: Emily Victoria b 23 Mar 1995; Rebecca Elizabeth b 4 Jan 1997; Lucy Catherine b 13 Oct 1998; ord and ind to Kelty 16 Feb 1994; trans to Lochwinnoch 14 Apr 1999.

NEILSTON (FES X, 126)

1968 JOHN McARTHUR
(FES X, 126), admitted to Church of Scotland and ind to Neilston 3 Jul 1968; trans to Howwood 2 Feb 1978.

1978 FRASER ROBERT AITKEN
ord and ind to Neilston 28 Jun 1978; trans to Girvan North 5 Jan 1984.

1984 ALEXANDER MACDONALD
(FES X, 111), trans from Paisley St Andrew's to Neilston 26 Jun 1984; Publ: *Man of Principle* (1994), *A Straight Furrow* (1996), *The Word of Life* (1998)—all publ by Alexander Fleming Appreciation Society.

NEW ERSKINE (FES X, 126)

1972 DAVID LITTLE HARPER
(FES X, 126), ord and ind to New Erskine 25 Jun 1972; trans to Troon St Meddan's 23 Apr 1979.

1979 WILLIAM JOHNSTONE McMILLAN
(FES X, 41), trans from Linlithgow St Ninian's Craigmailen to New Erskine 23 Aug 1979; trans to Sandsting and Aithsting with Walls and Sandness 8 Mar 1997.

1998 IAN WILSON BELL
B 20 Aug 1944 at Auchinleck, s of Harold B. and Margaret Tanner; educ Cumnock Academy 1955–58; Stow College, Glasgow 1958–63 (CuG); Kilmarnock Academy 1964–65 (FTC); University of Glasgow 1987–89 (LTh); Electronics Engineering 1962–87; lic by Presb of Ayr 4 Jul 1989; asst Ayr Auld Kirk 1989–90; m 26 Mar 1965 May Armstrong b 22 Jul 1944 d of Robert A. and Margaret Kirk; Children: Alison b 16 Apr 1966 m Dickie; Colin b 19 Feb 1969; Gillian b 10 May 1973; ord and ind to Greenock St Margaret's 30 May 1990; trans to New Erskine 11 Feb 1998.

PAISLEY ABBEY (FES III, 160; VIII, 242; IX, 220; X, 126)

1970 JAMES DARLING ROSS
(FES IX, 155; X, 91, 126, 287), trans from Scoonie (Leven) to Paisley Abbey 10 Jun 1970; died 7 Jun 1977.

1978 JOHNSTON REID McKAY
(FES X, 151), trans from Glasgow Bellahouston-Steven to Paisley Abbey 30 May 1978; dem on app as Senior Producer, BBC Religious Broadcasting 1 Jul 1987.

1988 ALAN DAVID BIRSS
B 5 Jun 1953 at Ellon, s of David B. and Gladys May Slessor; educ Glenwood Junior High, Glenrothes and Glenrothes High 1965–71; University of St Andrews 1971–75 (MA); University of Edinburgh 1975–78 (BD); lic by Presb of Kirkcaldy 4 Jul 1978; asst Dundee St Mary's 1978–81; m 30 Jul 1981 Carol Margaret Pearson b 6 Apr 1957 d of Ronald Matthew P. and Eileen Florance Jack; ord by Presb of Dundee during assistantship at St Mary's 18 Apr 1979; ind to Inverkeithing St Peter's 10 Sep 1982; trans to Paisley Abbey 2 Mar 1988.

PAISLEY ABBEY CLOSE (FUF 168; FES IX, 220; X, 126)

Congregation dissolved 30 Apr 1965.

1940 JOHN WILLIAM BURNSIDE
(FUF 39; FES IX, 54, 220, 507; X, 126), trans from Dundee Strathmartine to Abbey Close 9 Jul 1940; ret 30 Apr 1965; died 9 Oct 1987.

PAISLEY CASTLEHEAD (FES X, 126)
Formed 25 Jun 1975 by union of Paisley Canal Street and Paisley Middle.

1947 JAMES FISHER HENDERSON BURNS
(FES IX, 222, 244; X, 126, 128), trans from East Kilbride West to Paisley Middle 10 Dec 1947; became minister of linked charge with Mossvale 23 Sep 1964 and of united charge with Canal Street 25 Jun 1975; died 5 Apr 1976.

1976 JOHN YOUNG
admitted by General Assembly 1976 and ind to Castlehead 28 Sep 1976; trans to Airdrie Broomknoll 6 Jun 1989.

1990 GORDON KIRKWOOD
res as Assoc at Skene and ind to Castlehead 27 Mar 1990; trans to Glasgow Anderston Kelvingrove 29 Oct 1997.

1998 ESTHER JOHNSTON NINIAN
B 29 Oct 1952 at Glasgow, d of Robert McNicol N. and Mary Dryden Brown; educ Hutchesons' Grammar, Glasgow 1963–70; University of Aberdeen 1970–73 (MA); University of Strathclyde 1974–75 (Dip Librarianship); University of Glasgow 1989–92 (BD); Local Government 1975–89; lic by Presb of Paisley 20 Aug 1992; asst Glasgow Cathcart Old 1992–93; ord and ind to Hamilton Gilmour and Whitehill 17 Jun 1993; trans to Castlehead 15 Sep 1998.

PAISLEY GLENBURN (FES X, 127)

1970 MALCOLM WRIGHT
(FES X, 127), ord and ind to Glenburn 23 Jun 1970; trans to Craigrownie with Rosneath St Modan's 16 Nov 1984.

1985 FRANCIS DEANE DIXON
B 19 Jan 1958 at Port Glasgow, s of Henry D. and Eva May; educ Port Glasgow High 1970–74; Manchester College 1978–81 (BTh); University of Glasgow 1981–84 (BD); lic by Presb of Greenock 27 Jun 1984; asst Paisley Sherwood 1984–85; m 16 Jun 1979 Linda McPherson Bell b 16 Jun 1957 d of Joseph More and Grace B; Children: Mark Stewart b 30 Jun 1983; Christopher Joseph b 6 Mar 1987; ord and ind to Glenburn 27 May 1985; dem 31 May 1993.

1994 GEORGE CONNOR MACKAY
B 30 Apr 1960 at Glasgow, s of Robert Laurie M. and Kathleen Connor; educ Govan High 1972–76; University of Glasgow 1984–89 (BD, CMin); Jordanhill College, Glasgow 1990–91 (CertEd); University of Glasgow 1996–98 (DPC); Sales Asst

and Dept Supervisor 1976–83; Teaching 1991–94; lic by Presb of Glasgow 3 Jul 1989; asst Glasgow Langside 1987–89; Paisley Sherwood 1989–90; divorced; Children: Craig Robert b 15 Aug 1987; ord and ind to Glenburn 23 Mar 1994.

PAISLEY LAIGH (FES X, 128)
Formed 19 Sepember 1985 by union of St Andrew's and St George's.

1959 JOHN CRUICKSHANKS SCOTT
(FES IX, 116, 684; X, 65, 128), trans from Hawick St Mary's to St Andrew's 6 Jun 1959; died 24 Jul 1977.

1978 ALEXANDER MACDONALD
(FES X, 111), trans from Kilmarnock Old High to St Andrew's 15 Feb 1978; trans to Neilston 26 Jun 1984.

1985 THOMAS MILLAR CANT
(FES X, 129, 392), trans from Plockton and Kyle to St George's 14 Jun 1972; became minister of united charge with St Andrew's 19 Sep 1985; s James m Avril Jackson; d Coleen m Alistair Hope.

PAISLEY LYLESLAND (FUF 168; FES, 221; X, 127)

1971 LAWSON RICHARD BROWN
(FES X, 127, 169, 416), res from app with Overseas Council in Freeport, Grand Bahama and ind to Lylesland 2 Nov 1971; trans to St Leonard's with Cameron with Largoward 6 Feb 1980.

1980 THOMAS MATHIESON McWILLIAM
(FES X, 143, 305), trans from East Kilbride Greenhills to Lylesland 27 Aug 1980; trans to Contin, Apr 1997.

1998 ANDREW WATT BRADLEY
(FES X, 185), trans from Auchterarder to Lylesland 13 Jan 1998; Addl children: Nicholas Andrew b 25 Sep 1978.

PAISLEY MARTYRS' (FES X, 127)
Formed 19 Sep 1979 by union of Martyrs' and Martyrs' Memorial.

1969 GEORGE PRENTICE
(FES X, 127, 193), trans from Coatbridge Townhead to Martyrs' Memorial 15 Jan 1969; became minister of united charge with Martyrs' 19 Sep 1979; ret 31 Jul 1997; Geneva Theological College, USA 1976 (BTh); Open University 1982 (BA); d Eileen m Stewart Cummings; s Gordon m Janet Dunsmuir; Publ: *Church and Congregation* (Gleniffer Press, 1978).

1969 DAVID CAMPBELL McLEOD
(FES X, 127), ord and ind to Martyrs' 9 Jul 1969; trans to Dundee Fairmuir 8 Jun 1978.

1997 ALISON ELIZABETH SHAW DAVIDGE
B 16 Aug 1964 at Greenock, d of Alexander
Ferguson and Elizabeth McMinn; educ Largs
Academy 1976–82; University of Edinburgh 1982–
86 (MA), 1986–89 (BD), 1990–91 (Research
Student); lic by Presb of Ardrossan, Sep 1989;
asst Falkirk Old and St Modan's 1989–90; m 24
Jul 1989 Peter Louis Vere Davidge b 7 Oct 1966 s
of Cecil Vere D. and Phillipa Felicia Goldwyre
Lester; ord by Presb of Ardrossan during
assistantship at Largs Clark Memorial 30 Oct
1990; ind to Dalmellington 24 Oct 1991; trans to
Martyrs' 1 Oct 1997.

PAISLEY OAKSHAW TRINITY (FES X, 127, 128,
129)

Formed 16 Mar 1994 by union of Orr Square and
Oakshaw Trinity (union 29 Aug 1991 of High, St
John's and School Wynd Congregational Church).

1948 ROBERT MORRISON
(FES IX, 198, 223; X, 128), trans from Kilmaurs
Glencairn to Orr Square 10 Jun 1948; ret 2 Jan
1994; died 6 Jul 1998.

1966 ALEXANDER JOHN GEDDES
(FES X, 45, 129), trans from Peebles St Andrew's
to Paisley St John's 17 Nov 1966; trans to
Aberdeen Langstane Kirk 6 Dec 1979.

1967 JOHN ROBERTSON
(FES X, 40, 127), trans from Haggs to Paisley High
29 Nov 1967; dem 15 Nov 1982 to take up app at
Glasgow Westercraigs Rehabilitation Hostel
(Family Support Unit); died 3 Oct 1988.

1980 IAN SAMUEL CURRIE
(FES X, 191), trans from Coatbridge Blairhill
Dundyvan to St John's 22 Oct 1980; became
minister of united charge with Paisley High and
School Wynd Congregational Church 29 Aug 1991
and of united charge with Orr Square 16 Mar 1994;
Addl children: John Stuart b 8 Aug 1977.

1983 CHRISTOPHER LEON LEVISON
(FES X, 201), res as Assoc Chaplain to University
of Aberdeen and ind to Paisley High 30 Aug 1983;
became minister of united charge with St John's
and School Wynd Congregational Church 29 Aug
1991; dem 4 Oct 1998 on app as Chaplain to
Victoria Infirmary, Glasgow.

PAISLEY SANDYFORD (THREAD STREET)
(FES X, 130)

1947 ROBERT LARMOUR SIM
(FES IX, 217, 226; X, 130), trans from Kilbarchan
East to Thread Street 10 Jun 1947; became
minister of Sandyford (Thread Street) following
transportation of congregation 14 May 1969; ret
31 Oct 1979; died 9 Jul 1989.

1980 DAVID KAY
B 18 Oct 1943 at Bridge of Allan, s of Joseph K.
and Doreen Sutherland Hadgraft; educ Clydebank
High 1948–59; University of Strathclyde 1967–71
(BA); University of Glasgow 1971–74 (BD), 1980
(MTh); Sales Rep 1959–66; lic by Presb of
Glasgow and the West (UFC) 11 Jun 1974; m 21
Jun 1974 Margaret McArthur b 17 Apr 1945 d of
William Hunter M. and Agnes Hepburn Mac-
Pherson; Children: Elaine b 27 Nov 1976; Alistair
b 8 Dec 1984; ord and ind to Broxburn St Nicholas'
(UFC) 30 Jul 1974; ind to Sandyford 28 May
1980; Publ: *A Maundy Thursday Meditation* (CCBI,
1991).

PAISLEY SHERWOOD GREENLAW (FES X, 127,
130)

Formed 22 Jan 1997 by union of Sherwood and
Greenlaw.

1950 WILLIAM ROBERTSON
(FES IX, 194, 221, 359; X, 127), trans from Bonhill
Old to Paisley Greenlaw 8 Nov 1950; ret 7 Nov
1975; died 26 Apr 1993.

1965 DUNCAN McLACHLAN
(FES X, 130, 230, 274), trans from Dunfermline
St Margaret's to Paisley Sherwood 23 Jun
1965; ret 2 Aug 1992; s David m Yvonne Lilian
Gailey.

1976 JOHN PATON RENTON
ord and ind to Paisley Greenlaw 24 Jun 1976; trans
to Kemnay 18 Oct 1990.

1991 HELEN PERCY
ord and ind to Paisley Greenlaw 12 Dec 1991;
introd as Assoc at Airlie Kingoldrum and
Ruthven with Glenisla with Kilry with Lintrathen 9
Jun 1994.

1993 ALEXANDER (ALASDAIR) FRANCIS
CAMERON
B 15 Sep 1942 at Inverness, s of Alastair C. and
Mary Ann Grant; educ Beauly Junior Secondary
and Inverness Royal Academy 1947–60; Univer-
sity of Glasgow 1963–64 (CA); University of
Aberdeen 1981–85 (BD); Accountancy 1965–81;
lic by Presb of Aberdeen 26 Jun 1985; asst
Aberdeen Northfield 1985–86; m 28 Jul 1969
Patricia Margaret Wheeler b 30 May 1947 d of
Lewis Ross W. and Denise Purdy; Children: Ewan
Alexander b 26 May 1972; Bruce David b 28 Feb
1974; ord and ind to Perth Kinnoull 20 Aug 1986;
trans to Paisley Sherwood 23 Mar 1993; became
minister of united charge with Paisley Greenlaw
22 Jan 1997.

1998 MAY BELL
ord by Presb of Paisley and app Asst at Sherwood
Greenlaw 18 Jun 1998.

PAISLEY ST COLUMBA FOXBAR (FES X, 128)

1939 ALEXANDER CARMICHAEL MACGILLIVRAY
(FES IX, 224, 400; X, 128 (2)), trans from Kilbrandon and Kilchattan to St Columba 12 Dec 1939; became minister of transported Church Extension Charge of St Columba Foxbar 17 Dec 1958; ret 8 Oct 1972; died 31 Aug 1977.

1973 JOHN HAMILTON FRASER
(FES X, 128), ord and ind to St Columba Foxbar 9 May 1973; trans to Rutherglen Wardlawhill 2 Feb 1979.

1979 ALEXANDER BLACKIE DOUGLAS
ord and ind to St Columba Foxbar 22 Aug 1979; trans to Prestwick Kingcase 27 Mar 1985.

1985 ANTHONY JOHN ROBERT FOWLER
B 14 Aug 1953 at Birmingham, s of Alan Geoffrey F. and Eunice Barker; educ Moseley Grammar, Birmingham 1964–71; University of Southampton 1971–74 (BSc); University of Edinburgh 1978–81 (BD); Accountancy 1974–78; lic by Presb of Edinburgh 5 Jul 1981; asst Largs St John's 1981–82; m 16 Sep 1978 Linda Mitchell b 26 Nov 1955 d of John Jackson M. and Elizabeth Kilpatrick McCririck; Children: David Alan b 5 May 1980; Joanna Elizabeth Margaret b 6 Apr 1983; ord and ind to Durness with Kinlochbervie 14 Jul 1982; trans to St Columba Foxbar 28 Nov 1985.

PAISLEY ST JAMES' (FUF 172; FES IX, 224; X, 129)

1955 SAMUEL SCARLETT DALY
(FES IX, 292, 623; X, 129, 172), trans from Glasgow Ruchill to St James' 16 Feb 1955; ret 30 Jun 1984; died 13 Aug 1994.

1986 THOMAS ROBERT CAMPBELL
B 24 Jul 1959 at Glasgow, s of George C. and Jeanie Skinner; educ Renfrew High 1964–75; University of Glasgow 1979–85 (MA, BD); Pharmaceutical Chemistry Technician 1975–79; lic by Presb of Paisley, Jun 1985; asst Paisley Sherwood 1985–86; m 10 Oct 1981 Elaine Ailsa Craig b 8 Jul 1959 d of David C. and Gardner; Children: Rebecca Jean b 15 Feb 1989; Hannah Victoria b 12 Jul 1991; ord and ind to St James' 29 May 1986; dem 9 May 1993 on app as Admin Manager, Health Board.

1994 ELEANOR JANE McMAHON
B 2 Dec 1962 at Baillieston, d of Patrick M. and Anne Elizabeth McNicholl; educ Earnock High, Hamilton 1974–79; University of Glasgow and Jordanhill College, Glasgow 1979–83 (BEd); University of Aberdeen 1989–92 (BD); Teaching 1983–89; lic by Presb of Hamilton 24 Jun 1992; asst London St Columba's, Pont Street 1992–94; ord and ind to St James' 26 Aug 1994.

PAISLEY ST LUKE'S (FES X, 129)

1974 GEORGE MILLAR GRAHAM
(FES X, 129, 284, 357), trans from Kirkcaldy St John's to St Luke's 29 Aug 1974; dem 8 Mar 1983.

1984 HARRY BELL MEALYEA
ord and ind to St Luke's 12 Mar 1984; trans to Bargeddie 23 Jun 1993.

1994 DANIEL RITCHIE MARSHALL GILLON
B 7 Jan 1952 at Irvine, s of Hugh G. and Mary Ritchie Marshall; educ Ayr Academy 1963–69; University of Edinburgh 1987–92 (BD, DipMin); Sheriff Clerk's Branch, Scottish Courts Service 1972–87; lic by Presb of West Lothian 30 Sep 1992; asst Kirk of Calder 1992–94; m 17 Mar 1972 Janet Mary Barbour b 8 Jun 1953 d of Thomas Galt B. and Yvonne Mary May Furnell; Children: Amy Louise b 28 Apr 1974; Benjamin Thomas b 6 Apr 1978; ord and ind to St Luke's 24 Feb 1994.

PAISLEY ST MARK'S OLDHALL (FES IX, 225; X, 129)

1974 ALEXANDER McDONALD
(FES X, 29, 129), trans from Bathgate St David's to St Mark's Oldhall 5 Jun 1974; dem 11 Oct 1988 on app as General Secretary, Board of Ministry; Open University 1978 (BA).

1989 ALISTAIR HOGARTH MORRISON
B 12 Sep 1943 at Glasgow, s of James M. and Janetta Harvey Hogarth; educ Jordanhill College School, Glasgow 1948–62; Jordanhill College, Glasgow 1964–66 (DYCS); University of Aberdeen 1981–84 (BTh); City of Glasgow and Strathclyde Police Force 1962–64, 1968–81; lic by Presb of Gordon 26 Jun 1984; asst Inverurie St Andrew's 1984–85; m 24 Dec 1971 Grace Clark b 3 Nov 1940, died 29 Dec 1995; Children: Fiona b 27 Jan 1973; Stuart b 22 Jan 1975; ord and ind to Elgin High 31 May 1985; trans to St Mark's 27 Sep 1989.

PAISLEY ST MATTHEW'S (FES X, 129)

Formed 30 Apr 1969 by union of St George's East and Wellmeadow. Congregation dissolved 14 Jun 1988.

1932 ALEXANDER GEORGE FORTUNE
(FUF 376; FES IX, 224, 523; X, 129), trans from Tayport Queen Street to St George's East 26 Jan 1932; ret 31 Aug 1968; died 21 Dec 1985.

1969 JAMES ROBERT MOFFETT
(FES X, 129, 130), trans from Kilwinning UOS Church to Paisley UOS Church 6 May 1947; (acceded Assembly 1956 and named Paisley Wellmeadow); became minister of united charge with St George's East 30 Apr 1969; ret 26 Feb 1979; s Robert m Elaine McCormick; d Kathleen m Ross Campbell; s James m Vivienne Bell.

1979 JAMES CARRUTHERS GORRIE GREIG
(FES X, 82), Lecturer (RE) at Jordanhill College, Glasgow 1963–79; ind to St Matthew's 25 Jun 1979; dem on app as Translator, WCC, Geneva 14 May 1986.

PAISLEY ST NINIAN'S FERGUSLIE (FES IX, 225; X, 130)

1974 ALASTAIR OSBORNE
(FES X, 130), introd on term app to St Ninian's Ferguslie Park 16 May 1974; res 30 Sep 1980; introd as Community minister at Ayr St Quivox 1 Sep 1981.

1976 JAMES SNEDDON BLACK
B 14 Dec 1947 at Edinburgh, s of George B. and Janet Walker; educ Dalkeith High 1960–66; University of Edinburgh 1969–73 (BD), 1973–75 (DPS); Customs and Excise Officer 1966–69; lic by Presb of Dalkeith 6 Jul 1975; asst Paisley St Ninian's Ferguslie 1975–76; m 30 Jul 1970 Christine Fraser b 18 Feb 1949 d of William Hugh F. and Gwendoline Thomas; Children: Fraser b 2 Apr 1972 m Michelle Duke; Robert b 29 Jun 1974; ord by Presb of Paisley and introd as Assoc at St Ninian's Ferguslie 29 Apr 1976; dem 1 Mar 1978 and app Personnel Manager, Scottish Newcastle Brewers 6 Mar 1978; app Personnel Manager of United Distillers 3 Sep 1991.

1978 WILLIAM PETER FINLAY
(FES X, 391, 419), res as Assoc at Lochcarron and Shieldaig with Torridon and Kinlochewe and introd as Assoc to St Ninian's Ferguslie (term) 1 Apr 1978; dem 30 Sep 1980; Union Church of Tripoli Jan 1982.

1981 CHRISTOPHER DAVID PARK
res from app at Edinburgh Holy Trinity and ind to St Ninian's Ferguslie 11 Nov 1981; trans to Glasgow Colston Milton 24 Nov 1994.

1982 IAN DOUGLAS MAXWELL
res as Chaplain to Sefula School, Zambia and introd as Assoc at St Ninian's Ferguslie 28 Oct 1982; app Conference Manager, Carberry Tower Jun 1990.

1995 ARCHIE SPEIRS
B 25 Jun 1954 at Paisley, s of John Balyntine S. and Dorothy Niven; educ Camphill High, Paisley 1967–72; University of Glasgow 1990–93 (BD); Computer Engineering 1978–88; lic by Presb of Paisley 14 Aug 1993; m 4 Mar 1978 Katrina Bell Haldane b 8 Mar 1956 d of Thomas H. and Catherine Bell; Children: Christopher John b 29 Sep 1980; Richard Thomas b 4 Mar 1982; ord and ind to St Ninian's Ferguslie 29 Jun 1995.

PAISLEY WALLNEUK NORTH (FES X, 127, 130)

Formed 19 Jan 1983 by union of Merksworth and Wallneuk.

1969 JOHN DIAMOND RENNIE
(FES X, 130, 331), trans from Aberdeen St Nicholas South of Kincorth to Wallneuk 7 May 1969; trans to Broughton Glenholm and Kilbucho with Skirling with Stobo and Drumelzier with Tweedsmuir 26 Sep 1980.

1976 IAIN ALEXANDER WHYTE
(FES X, 427), res as Lecturer at Falkirk College of Technology and ind to Merksworth 1 Jan 1976; dem to take up app as Chaplain to University of St Andrews 1 Oct 1981.

1981 WILLIAM GRANT RAMSAY
admitted by General Assembly and ind to Wallneuk 24 Jun 1981; became minister of united charge with Merksworth 19 Jan 1983; trans to Glasgow Springburn 7 Jan 1988.

1988 THOMAS MACINTYRE
B 13 Jan 1946 at Inverness, s of Thomas Stirling M. and Janet Elizabeth Stevenson; educ Dumfries Academy 1951–68; University of Edinburgh 1968–70 (MA), 1970–72 (BD); lic by Presb of Lothian and Borders (UFC) 13 Jun 1972; m 30 Jun 1972 Marian Elizabeth Jane Porter b 14 Oct 1946 d of James P. and Laura Williamson; Children: Lewis b 12 Feb 1976; Vaila b 13 Aug 1980; Struan b 25 Mar 1983; ord by Glasgow and West (UFC) and ind to Shieldhall and Drumoyne (UFC) 31 Oct 1972; ind to Stevenston High 11 Mar 1976; trans to Wallneuk North 10 Aug 1988.

RENFREW MOORPARK (FES X, 131)

(Formerly Renfrew Rutherford Memorial). Congregation dissolved 6 Oct 1992.

1954 JAMES AITKEN RULE
(FES IX, 227; X, 131), ord by Presb of Glasgow during assistantship at Cathcart Old 29 Jun 1952; ind to Rutherford Memorial 17 Feb 1954; ret 30 Jun 1991; Addl children: Ewan Macdonald b 29 Dec 1968.

RENFREW NORTH (FUF 174; IX, 227; X, 131)

1973 ARTHUR PARR BARRIE
(FES X, 131), ord and ind to Renfrew North 6 Jun 1973; trans to Hamilton Cadzow 13 Jan 1979.

1979 ELIZABETH LORNA HOOD
B 21 Apr 1953 at Irvine, d of James Mitchell and Elizabeth McPike Watson Sharpe; educ Kilmarnock Academy 1965–71; University of Glasgow 1971–74 (MA), 1974–77 (BD); lic by Presb of Irvine and Kilmarnock 29 Jun 1977; asst Edinburgh St Ninian's Corstorphine 1977–79; m 7 Jul 1979 Peter Finlay Hood b 23 Feb 1955 s of Peter Alexander H. and Margaret Spiers Hill; Children: Laura Elizabeth b 8 Jun 1984; Michael Peter b 20 Sep 1988; ord by Presb of Edinburgh during assistantship at St Ninian's 16 Apr 1978; ind to Renfrew North 26 Jun 1979.

RENFREW OLD (FES III, 184; VIII, 245; IX, 227; X, 131)

1963   PETER MACNEE HOUSTON
(FES IX, 341; X, 131, 203), trans from Wishaw Craigneuk Belhaven to Renfrew Old 6 Jun 1963; ret 30 Jun 1997; d Margaret m Borland.

1980   MARGARET FORSYTH CURRIE
ord by Presb of Paisley and app Asst at Renfrew Old 9 Jul 1980; introd as Community minister at Greenock Cartsdyke 23 Mar 1982.

1998   ALEXANDER C WARK
trans from Methil to Renfrew Old 23 Sep 1998.

RENFREW TRINITY (FUF 174; FES IX, 227; X, 131)

1967   GILBERT DRUMMOND
(FES X, 131, 323), trans from Montrose St Luke's and St John's to Trinity 18 Jan 1967; ret 28 Feb 1988; died 15 Sepember 1998; d Christine m Damsie; d Arlene m Huzzard.

1988   ANDREW THOMSON
B 12 Mar 1946 at Kilwinning, s of William T. and Annie McNeish; educ Kilwinning High 1951–62; Open University 1978–81 (BA); British Rail 1962–68; ICI 1968–73; m 5 Apr 1969 Eleanor Morrison; Children: Andrew b 17 Feb 1981; Jennifer b 24 May 1978; m (2) 17 May 1995 Elizabeth Kean b 1 May 1950 d of Thomas Alston and Diana Smith; ord by Congregational Union of Scotland and ind to Stewarton Congregational Church 25 Jun 1976; trans to Coatbridge Congregational Church 1 May 1979; admitted by General Assembly 1982 and ind to Campbeltown Lowland 1 Jul 1982; trans to Trinity 19 Oct 1988; ret 30 Sep 1991.

1992   STUART CHARLES STEELL
B 12 Dec 1960 at Glasgow, s of Samuel S. and Margaret; educ Knightswood Secondary, Glasgow 1972–77; University of Glasgow 1986–91 (BD, CMin); Plumber 1977–81; General Maintenance Engineer 1981–86; lic by Presb of Falkirk 27 Jun 1991; m 16 Apr 1983 Carol Whyte b 29 May 1959 d of Stanley W. and Janette Gillespie; Children: Craig Duncan b 20 Oct 1986; Gillian Elizabeth b 25 Jan 1990; ord and ind to Trinity 23 Sep 1992.

PRESBYTERY OF GREENOCK

GOUROCK ST JOHN'S (FUF 156; FES IX, 228; X, 132)

1970 IAN MORRISON STRACHAN
(FES X, 132, 190, 426), trans from Cambuslang St Paul's to St John's 13 Dec 1970; trans to Selkirk with Ashkirk with Caddonfoot 4 Dec 1986.

1987 NEIL ANDREW McNAUGHT
ord and ind to St John's 1 Oct 1987; trans to Alloway 24 Jun 1999.

GREENOCK ARDGOWAN (FES X, 134, 135)

Formed 19 Feb 1992 by union of Greenock St Andrew's and Greenock The Union.

1959 ANDREW STARK TAYLOR
(FES X, 135), ord and ind to The Union 28 Oct 1959; ret 16 Feb 1992; d Moira m Alan Urquhart.

1965 ALEXANDER STEVENSON
(FES IX, 209; X, 119, 134 (2), 158), dem from Glasgow Eastbank and introd on term app to St Andrew's 24 Mar 1965; ind 7 May 1967 on union with Trinity; ret 30 Jun 1976.

1977 IAN WALTER BLACK
ord by Presb of Glasgow during assistantship at The Cathedral 3 Jun 1976; ind to St Andrew's 13 Apr 1977; trans to Grangemouth Zetland 15 Aug 1991.

1992 JAMES SMILLIE ANNALL COWAN
trans from Cockenzie and Port Seton Old to Ardgowan 19 Nov 1992; trans to Barrhead Arthurlie 10 Dec 1998.

GREENOCK CARTSDYKE (FES X, 132)

Formed 30 Apr 1981 by union of Greenock Cartsburn Augine and Greenock Crawfordsburn.

1946 SYDNEY HOBSON ROBB
(FES IX, 229; X, 132), ind to Crawfordsburn 20 Feb 1946; ret 20 Sep 1981; died 14 Apr 1999.

1971 ANDREW RANKIN COWIE McLELLAN
(FES X, 132), ind to Cartsburn Augine 29 Sep 1971; trans to Stirling Viewfield 27 Aug 1980.

1981 PETER WEBSTER
B 1 Oct 1949 at Edinburgh, s of Alexander Allan W. and Elizabeth Frances Doctor; educ Gourock High and Greenock High 1961–68; University of Glasgow 1971–74 (BD); University of Edinburgh 1974–76 (DPS); Trainee Systems Analyst 1969–71; lic by Presb of Greenock 24 Jun 1976; asst Alloa St Mungo's 1976–77; m 15 Oct 1971 Patricia Margaret Shipp b 13 Aug 1951 d of Reginald Verah S. and Maud Wishart Bradley: Children: Jennie Valerie b 7 Mar 1977; Alison Margaret b 13 Oct 1978; Timothy Christopher b 29 Oct 1979; ord by Presb of Aberdeen and introd on term app to Woodside North 22 Jun 1977; ind to Cartsdyke 15 Sep 1981.

GREENOCK FINNART ST PAUL'S (FES X, 133, 135)

Formed 15 Mar 1978 by union of Greenock St Paul's and Greenock Finnart.

1937 DONALD HUGH STEWART
(FUF 363; FES IX, 109, 229, 479; X, 133), trans from Kelso St John's Edenside to Finnart 5 May 1937; ret 30 Sep 1967; died 22 Jul 1989.

1968 DAVID REID EASTON
(FES IX, 23, 33; X, 14, 135), trans from Edinburgh Leith St Paul's to St Paul's 18 Dec 1968; ret 30 Sep 1977; died 24 Sep 1997.

1969 JOHNSTON REID McKAY
(FES IX, 308; X, 133, 181), trans from Glasgow Stevenson Memorial to Finnart 26 Jan 1969; became minister of united charge with St Paul's 15 Mar 1978; ret 31 Dec 1978; died 25 Jul 1990.

1979 DAVID MILL
B 17 Jan 1949 at Dundee, s of William M. and Arnot Whitton Miller; educ Morgan Academy, Dundee 1961–67; University of St Andrews 1967–71 (MA), 1971–73 (post-grad research); University of Edinburgh 1974–77 (BD); Warden of holiday home for physically disabled children 1973–74; lic by Presb of Dundee 26 Jun 1977; asst Hamilton Old and Auchingramont 1977–79; m (1) 25 Sep 1971 Ingrid Juliane Wilson b 19 Apr 1951 d of Richard Andrew W. and Lia Wilhelmine Berta Schluter; Children: Ruth Whitton b 26 Oct 1973; Christina Juliane b 26 Mar 1975; Jonathan Richard

b 19 Sep 1977; divorced 11 Mar 1987; m (2) 8 Apr 1989 Evlyn Helen Williams b 19 Jan 1945 d of Lennard Percival W. and Helen Meikle Barr Hawke; ord by Presb of Hamilton during assistantship at Hamilton Old and Auchingramont 16 Apr 1978; ind to Finnart St Paul's 30 May 1979.

GREENOCK OLD WEST KIRK (FES X, 134)

Formed 10 Jan 1979 by union of Greenock North and Greenock St Columba Gaelic.

1959   DONALD MORRISON
(FES IX, 393, 507; X, 134, 301), trans from Dundee Downfield South to St Columba Gaelic 16 Dec 1959; became minister of united charge with North 10 Jan 1979; ret 11 Jul 1980; died 19 Jul 1981.

1970   ROBERT URQUHART
(FES IX, 504, 550; X, 134, 268, 299), trans from Stirling St Mark's to Greenock North 16 Apr 1970; ret 31 Jul 1978; died 15 Nov 1982.

1980   JOHN BANKS
ind to the Old West Kirk 19 Oct 1980; dem 31 Dec 1988 on app as Chaplain to Ailsa Hospital, Ayr.

1988   JAMES THOMSON FIELDS
ord by Presb of Greenock and introd as Assoc at the Old West Kirk 28 Jun 1988; app Manager of Counselling Services, Yorkhill NHS Trust, Glasgow 1 Dec 1995.

1990   WILLIAM McLAREN
ord by Presb of Greenock and introd as Assoc at the Old West Kirk 22 Aug 1990; ind to Polbeth Harwood 27 Jan 1994.

1997   COLIN IAN WILLIAM JOHNSON
B 27 Jun 1956 at Wallsend, England, s of John J. and Margaret Scott MacDowall Hussey; educ Royal Grammar, Newcastle 1967–74; University of St Andrews 1975–79 (MA); University of Glasgow 1992–95 (BD); Banking 1979–92; lic by Presb of Dumbarton 5 Jul 1995; m 26 Jun 1982 Elspeth MacGregor McPhee b 5 Nov 1957 d of Duncan Cameron M. and Elizabeth Anderson MacGregor; Children: Moira Beth Margaret b 6 May 1985; Kirsty Ann Catriona b 13 Mar 1988; ord and ind to the Old West Kirk 12 Jun 1997.

GREENOCK ST GEORGE'S NORTH (FES X, 133, 134)

Formed 18 Aug 1983 by union of Greenock St George's and Greenock Martyrs' and North.

1970   JAMES STEWART PYPER
(FES IX, 442; X, 134, 161, 262), trans from Glasgow Hillington Park to St George's 14 May 1970; became minister of united charge with Martyrs' and North 18 Aug 1983; ret 31 Mar 1986.

1975   JOSEPH BALDWIN PERRY
(FES X, 133, 157, 302), trans from Glasgow Dennistoun to Martyrs' and North 23 Mar 1975; dem 31 Jan 1983; introd on term app to Farnell with Chaplaincy at Stracathro Hospital 18 Oct 1984.

1986   WILLIAM DOUGLAS HAMILTON
B 6 Jul 1944 at Dumfries, s of William H. and Esther McLellan Sands Telfer; educ Stranraer High 1948–63; University of Glasgow 1969–74 (BD); Medical Laboratory Technology 1963–68; lic by Presb of Glasgow 27 Jun 1974; asst Glasgow Cathcart Old 1974–76; m 23 Mar 1974 Agnes Laurie Stevenson b 14 Mar 1955 d of Hugh Hamill S. and Catherine McVicar Watson; Children: Alasdair Scott b 14 Jun 1977; Kenneth Douglas b 2 Feb 1981; ord by Presb of Glasgow during assistantship at Cathcart Old 21 Apr 1975; ind to Newtongrange 12 Aug 1976; became minister of linked charge with Borthwick 22 Mar 1981; trans to St George's North 4 Dec 1986.

GREENOCK ST LUKE'S (FES X, 134, 135)

Formed 30 Sep 1987 by union of Greenock St Mark's Greenbank and Greenock The Old Kirk.

1963   ALEXANDER CHESTNUT
(FES X, 135), trans from Loughbrickland and Scarva (Presb Church in Ireland) to St Mark's Greenbank 14 Mar 1963; Chaplain (part-time) to Greenock Prison 1971–81, 1986–93; ret 30 Sep 1987; MBE 1992; d Catherine m David William Service; d Rachel m Hamish Elder Potts; d Alexandra m Wylie.

1967   JAMES MARSHALL BUTTERY SCOULAR
(FES IX, 79, X, 49, 134, 221), trans from Jamestown to The Old Kirk 19 Sep 1967; trans to Kippen 13 Jun 1986.

1988   GEORGE RUSSELL BARR
trans from Garthamlock and Craigend East to St Luke's 4 May 1988; trans to Edinburgh Cramond 21 Apr 1993.

1994   WILLIAM CURRIE HEWITT
B 6 Apr 1951 at Kilmarnock, s of Robert Bunten H. and Mary Hamilton Mair Roberts; educ Kilmarnock Academy 1962–68; University of Glasgow 1970–76 (BD, DipPS); lic by Presb of Irvine and Kilmarnock 14 Jul 1976; asst Ayr Castlehill 1976–78; m 16 Jun 1976 Moira Elizabeth MacLeod b 6 Oct 1949 d of Ronald Alexander M. and Catherine Paterson; Children: Rhona Catherine b 28 Sep 1977; Martin William b 1 Oct 1980; Neil Robert b 20 Feb 1989; ord by Presb of Ayr during assistantship at Castlehill 17 Feb 1977; ind to Elderslie Kirk 7 Jun 1978; trans to St Luke's 3 Mar 1994.

1995 ELIZABETH ANNE CRUMLISH
ord by Presb of Greenock and introd as Assoc at Greenock St Luke's 30 Aug 1995; app by Inverclyde Royal NHS Trust as Hospital Chaplain 1 Oct 1996.

GREENOCK ST MARGARET'S (FES IX, 232; X, 135)

1950 ANDREW SWAN
(FES IX, 232, 588 (2); X, 135), trans from Logie-Coldstone to St Margaret's 30 Jan 1950; ret 8 Oct 1983.

1984 COLIN MACEWEN ANDERSON
(FES X, 18, 452), res as Industrial Chaplain on lower reaches of the Clyde and ind to St Margaret's 12 Apr 1984; dem on app as Chaplain to University of Glasgow 2 Oct 1989.

1990 IAN WILSON BELL
ord and ind to St Margaret's 30 May 1990; trans to New Erskine 11 Feb 1998.

1998 ISOBEL JEAN MOLLINS KELLY
B 14 Jan 1945 at Glasgow, d of Hugh and Elizabeth K; educ Hutchesons' Grammar, Glasgow 1956–62; University of Glasgow 1962–66 (MA); Jordanhill College, Glasgow 1966–67 (Cert Sec Educ); University of Glasgow 1970 (DipEd); University of Edinburgh 1970–73 (BD); Teaching 1967–70; lic by Presb of Glasgow, Jun 1973; asst Edinburgh Pilrig Dalmeny Street 1973–75; ord by Presb of Edinburgh during assistantship at Pilrig Dalmeny Street 22 Sep 1974; app Asst Baird Research Fellow, Board of Education 1 Sep 1975; ind to Edinburgh Drylaw 25 Oct 1978; trans to Livingston Craigshill St Columba's 28 Feb 1985; trans to St Margaret's 10 Nov 1998.

GREENOCK ST NINIAN'S (FES X, 135)

1975 JAMES HENRY ROBERTSON
(FES X, 135), ord and ind to St Ninian's 16 Apr 1975; trans to Thornliebank 20 Feb 1985.

1985 ALLAN GLEN McINTYRE
B 10 Feb 1952 at Irvine, s of Neil M. and Matilda Scott Irving; educ Marr College, Troon 1963–69; University of Glasgow 1977–82 (BD), 1984 (CMin); Scottish Aviation (Prestwick) 1969–70; Technician (Glasgow Museums) 1970–74; lic by Presb of Ayr 10 Mar 1985; ord and ind to St Ninian's 28 Nov 1985.

GREENOCK THE MOUNT KIRK (FES X, 134, 135)

Formed 24 Nov 1982 by union of Greenock Mount Pleasant and Greenock South Park.

1937 JOHN McCALLUM YOUNG
(FES IX, 231; X, 134), ord and ind to Mount Pleasant 2 Sep 1937; became minister of linked charge with Wellpark 13 Oct 1957 (congregation dissolved 31 May 1979) and of united charge with South Park 24 Nov 1982; ret 17 Oct 1983; died 27 Jan 1987.

1965 JAMES HAMILTON SIMPSON
(FES X, 135), ind to South Park 29 Sep 1965; became Collegiate minister of united charge with Mount Pleasant 24 Nov 1982; Addl children: David Alexander b 28 Mar 1976; s James m Suzanne Maree Brannigan.

GREENOCK WELLPARK (FUF 160; FES IX, 233; X, 136)

Congregation dissolved 31 May 1979.

1957 JOHN McCALLUM YOUNG
(FES IX, 231; X, 134), ord and ind to Mount Pleasant 2 Sep 1937; minister of linked charge with Wellpark 13 Oct 1957 until dissolution of congregation 31 May 1979.

GREENOCK WELLPARK MID KIRK (FES X, 133, 136)

Formed 6 Mar 1996 by union of Greenock Wellpark West and Greenock Mid Kirk.

1939 JAMES THOMSON RUNCIMAN
(FES IX, 234; X, 136), ind to Wellpark West 22 Jun 1939; ret 31 Oct 1973; died 1 Feb 1994.

1965 ALEXANDER PORTEOUS
(FES X, 133), ord and ind to Mid Kirk 6 Jan 1965; ret 2 May 1987; d Sandra m Stephen Thornton; s Colin m Wendy Lamont.

1974 SIDNEY HALL COLEMAN
(FES X, 136), res from app at Southminster, Oklahoma City and ind to Wellpark West 25 Apr 1974; trans to Glasgow Merrylea 25 Feb 1982.

1983 WILLIAM SHACKLETON
(FES X, 175), trans from Glasgow St Francis-in-the-East to Wellpark West 12 May 1983; dem 3 Mar 1996; President, Bridgeton Business Club 1981 and 1982, Secretary and Treasurer 1999; Chief Steward, Regional League of Men's Fellowships; Leader, Church House Youth Club; s Scott m Gillian Fiona Smillie; d Joy m Andrew David Bailey; Publ: Articles for *Life and Work* and *Glasgow Herald*; prize-winning short story in *Scots Magazine* 1990.

1988 RONALD GEORGE LAWSON
(FES X, 114), trans from Dumbarton St Andrew's to Mid Kirk 12 Oct 1988; became minister of united charge with Wellpark West 6 Mar 1996; ret 31 Aug 1999; m 17 Apr 1976 Beryl Read b 2 May

1939 d of Donald R. and Alice Roberts; Children: David Read b 29 Aug 1978; Angela Georgene (adopted) b 29 May 1980; George (adopted) b 5 Jun 1981.

INVERKIP (FES IX, 234; X, 136)

1976　WILLIAM BONOMY
(FES IX, 729; X, 253, 337, 416), trans from Perth St Andrew's to Inverkip 25 Feb 1976; ret 30 Jun 1987; d Sheila m Robert Rennie; w Margaret died 17 Oct 1996.

1987　MICHAEL JOHN ERSKINE
res as Assoc at Ellon and ind to Inverkip 25 Nov 1987; trans to Craignish with Kilninver and Kilmelford 24 Feb 1992.

1992　MANSON COUTTS MERCHANT
B 23 Aug 1958 at Torphins, s of Henry Reid M. and Constance Robertson Mortimer; educ Bankhead Academy, Aberdeen 1970–75; University of Aberdeen 1986–91 (BD, CPS); Clydesdale Bank 1975–85; Abbey Life Assurance 1985; Nursing Asst, Royal Cornhill Hospital 1985–86; lic by Presb of Aberdeen 27 Jun 1991; asst Aberdeen Northfield 1991–92; m 25 Jun 1983 Sheena Frances Duncan b 22 Jan 1964 d of George Alexander D. and Polly Thomson Fowlie; Children: Laura Amy b 28 Nov 1986; Jennifer Frances b 14 May 1989; Jonathan Ian b 1 Oct 1994; ord and ind to Inverkip 4 Jun 1992; dem 31 Aug 1997 and emigrated to USA.

1998　JANET ELIZABETH GILLIES
B 17 Apr 1949 at Huddersfield, d of William Beaumont and Barbara May Kilburn; educ Huddersfield High 1960–66; University of Edinburgh 1991–95 (BD); Nursing and Midwifery 1967–91 (RGN, Huddersfield 1970; SCM, Edinburgh 1972); lic by Presb of Dunfermline 3 Jul 1995; asst Lochgelly St Andrew's 1995–97; m 1 Jun 1974 David Johnston Gillies b 28 Apr 1949 s of George Watson G. and Celia Anne McCormack; Children: Anna Jane b 21 Oct 1976; Matthew David b 8 Dec 1980; ord and ind to Inverkip 5 May 1998.

KILMACOLM OLD (FES III, 211; VIII, 249; IX, 235; X, 136)

1969　JOHN BARR
(FES X, 136, 170, 182), dem from St Andrew's, Frognal Lane, Hampstead (Presb Church of England) and ind to Kilmacolm Old 29 May 1969; ret 30 Sep 1979; s Peter m Carolyn Mary Seel.

1980　BERNARD PETER LODGE
res from app as Assoc at Bearsden New Kilpatrick and ind to Kilmacolm Old 18 Apr 1980; introd as Interim minister at Edinburgh Juniper Green 5 Mar 1998.

1998　GORDON DUNLOP IRVING
B 23 Jul 1953 at Kilmarnock, s of Donald Crawford I. and Mary Ross Dunlop; educ Belmont High, Ayr and Carrick Academy, Maybole 1965–71; University of Glasgow 1989–93 (BD); Banking 1971–72; Housing 1972–73; Newcastle Art College 1973–74; Silk Screen Printer 1974–78; Prestwick Circuits 1978–89; lic by Presb of Ayr 4 Jul 1993; asst Ayr St Columba 1994; m 31 Jul 1980 Jane Hunter Crawford b 17 Mar 1956 d of James C. and Joyce Walker; Children: Ross Martin b 8 Jan 1993; Crawford Kieran b 14 Apr 1995; ord and ind to Dundee Stobswell 20 Sep 1994; trans to Kilmacolm Old 26 Nov 1998.

KILMACOLM ST COLUMBA (FES X, 137)

1968　FREDERICK JOHN MARSHALL
(FES X, 137, 218), trans from Drumchapel Old to Kilmacolm St Columba 17 Apr 1968; introd to Christ Church, Bermuda 31 Dec 1981.

1982　DOUGLAS ALEXANDER OAG NICOL
trans from Dumfries Lochside with Terregles to St Columba 13 Jul 1982; dem to take up app as General Secretary, Board of National Mission 1 Sep 1991.

1992　ROBERT DOUGLAS CRANSTON
B 4 Apr 1960 at Bellshill, s of George C. and Mora Bingham; educ High School of Glasgow and Dumfries Academy 1971–77; University of Glasgow; lic by Presb of Glasgow, 1985; m 1 Jul 1983 Christine Martha Barbour b 14 Jun 1953 d of Tom B. and Jean Watson; Children: Stephen Robert; Ruth Christine; ord and ind to Denny Westpark 1 Sep 1986; trans to St Columba 3 Sep 1992; Publ: Sermons (*Christian Digest*, 1997–98).

LANGBANK (FES IX, 235; X, 137)

1953　QUINTIN GOLDER
(FES IX, 236, 305, 511; X, 137), trans from Glasgow Shearer Memorial to Langbank 3 Jun 1953; ret 30 Jun 1976; died 28 Jul 1984.

1977　WALTER VERNON STONE
(FES IX, 750; X, 426), res as Scottish Secretary, United Society for Christian Literature and ind to Langbank 30 Mar 1977; ret 31 Aug 1985; s Michael m Josephine.

1986　EUSTACE ANNESLEY
B 6 Apr 1931 at Co Tyrone, N Ireland, s of William A. and Margaret Paterson; educ Foyle College, Londonderry 1943–48; Queen's University, Belfast 1948–52 (BSc); Open University 1978 (BA); lic by Presb of Belfast 20 Jun 1955; asst Whitehouse Church, Belfast; m 11 Sep 1957 Sarah Hazel Clarke, died 6 Mar 1987, d of Thomas Alexander and Frances Louise C: Children: Thomas William Paterson b 27 Dec 1958 m Jennifer Lowry; Jennifer

Lois b 12 Jun 1960 m David Cuthbertson; Carolyn Margaret b 8 Nov 1960 m Edward Thompson; ord and ind to Cranshaw Presb Church 7 Jul 1957; Chaplain to HM Forces 1963–86; ind to Langbank 12 Mar 1986; died 23 May 1997.

1998 ANNA SCOTT RODWELL
B 10 Nov 1967 at Kelso, d of Thomas William Brown and Anne Scott Mitchell; educ Kelso High and Berwickshire High 1979–85; University of Aberdeen 1985–90 (BD); University of Glasgow 1991–93 (DipMin); lic by Presb of Duns 4 Jul 1993; asst Paisley Sherwood Greenlaw 1996–97; m 17 Sep 1993 Terry Moran b 24 Jun 1961 s of Joseph M. and Margaret Smith; Children: Ellie b 21 Mar 1995; m (2) 20 Jun 1998 Damon Rodwell b 21 Sep 1967 s of Robert Richard R. and Hilary Harbord; Children: Hamish b 8 Jul 1999; ord and ind to Langbank 25 Mar 1998.

OLD GOUROCK AND ASHTON (FES X, 132)

Formed 17 May 1989 by union of Gourock Old and Gourock Ashton.

1938 JOHN BIRNIE ALLAN
(FES IX, 221, 228), trans from Paisley George Street to Gourock Old 30 Nov 1938; dem 25 Jun 1946; died 10 Aug 1987.

1947 WILLIAM EASDON CASKIE
(FES IX, 33, 228; X, 132, 246), ind to Gourock Old 25 Feb 1947; trans to Dull and Weem 23 Sep 1966.

1966 JOHN HENRY WHYTE
(FES X, 132), trans from Molesworth Presb Church, Cookstown, N Ireland to Gourock Ashton 25 Jun 1966; Clerk to Presb of Greenock 1969–86; ret 31 Oct 1986; s David m Frances Anne Finch.

1967 JAMES ALEXANDER KEITH ANGUS
(FES X, 78, 132), trans from Hoddam to Gourock Old 18 May 1967; trans to Braemar with Crathie 2 Apr 1979.

1979 FRANK JAMES GARDNER
(FES X, 122), trans from Barrhead Bourock to Gourock Old 28 Oct 1979; became minister of united charge with Ashton 17 May 1989; Addl children: Grant b 15 Jan 1976; d Lynne m John Barr; s Mark m Michelle McNaught.

1987 ANDREW PAXTON LEES
res as Assoc at Peebles Old with Eddleston with Lyne and Manor and ind to Gourock Ashton 19 Nov 1987; trans to Glasgow Knightswood St Margaret's 15 Jun 1989.

1993 JAMES HENDERSON LOUDON MELROSE
(FES X, 41, 437), res as Principal Lecturer in Religious Studies, Hamilton/Jordanhill Colleges of Education and introd as Assoc at Old Gourock and Ashton 28 Jun 1993; ret 31 Oct 1996; s Hamish m Linda; s Andrew m Dianne; s Calum m Irene; Publ: Various teacher training publs (Hamilton/Jordanhill Colleges, 1970–90).

1997 MARY CATHERINE SHAW
ord by Presb of Greenock and introd as Assoc at Old Gourock and Ashton 10 Apr 1997; ind to Tarbolton in deferred linkage with Annbank 12 Jan 1999.

PORT GLASGOW HAMILTON BARDRAINNEY (FES X, 137)

1967 DAVID JOHN COURTNEY EASTON
(FES X, 137), ord by Presb of Garioch 14 Nov 1965 and app Asst at Inverurie St Andrew's; ind to Hamilton Bardrainney 25 Jan 1967; trans to Burnside 6 Jun 1977.

1978 THOMAS PRESTON
ord and ind to Hamilton Bardrainney 31 May 1978; trans to Bedrule with Denholm with Minto 17 May 1989.

1990 DAVID JOHN McADAM
B 29 Sep 1963 at Dumfries, s of Robert M. and Agnes Green Harkness; educ Marr College, Troon 1975–80; University of Edinburgh 1980–84 (BSc), 1985–88 (BD); lic by Presb of Edinburgh 3 Jul 1988; asst Edinburgh Old Kirk 1988–89; m 12 Aug 1988 Margaret Elizabeth Ramsey b 15 Jun 1962 d of Matthew Drummond R. and Elizabeth Wilson McKay; Children: Rachel Zoe Ramsey b 15 Apr 1992; Stephen Matthew Ramsey b 23 May 1994; ord and ind to Hamilton Bardrainney 25 Apr 1990.

PORT GLASGOW NEWARK (FES III, 217; VIII, 250; IX, 236; X, 137)

Congregation dissolved 18 Oct 1987.

1973 WILLIAM LARMOUR HASLETT
(FES X, 137), ind to Newark 17 Jan 1973; dem 31 May 1986.

PORT GLASGOW ST ANDREW'S (FES X, 138)

Formed 27 Jan 1983 by union of St Andrew's and West.

1960 DAVID COUSER GORDON
(FES IX, 148; X, 87, 138), trans from Sanquhar St Ninian's to Port Glasgow West 5 May 1960; trans to Gigha and Cara 20 Apr 1982.

1973 ERNEST MARTIN SCOTT
(FES X, 138, 178), trans from Glasgow St Thomas' Gallowgate to St Andrew's 14 Mar 1973; became minister of united charge with Port Glasgow West 27 Jan 1983; ret 31 May 1992; University of Aberdeen 1995 (MA); s Ian m Rosemary Ballantyne.

1993 ANDREW THOMAS MACLEAN
B 1 Feb 1950 at Abadan, Iran, s of Thomas M. and Alice Wood Irvine; educ Bearsden Academy 1962–66; University of Stirling 1972–76 (BA); University of Edinburgh 1976–79 (BD); Insurance 1966–70; Production 1970–72; lic by Presb of Dumbarton, 1979; asst Loanhead 1979–80; m 28 Jul 1979 Alison Douglas Blair b 31 May 1958 d of Peter Douglas B. and Mary Blair Lawrie; Children: Alice Jane b 17 Sep 1981; Peter Martin b 5 Jun 1983; ord and ind to Aberdeen Stockethill 8 May 1980; app Chaplain to Students' Assoc, University of Strathclyde 1 Sep 1985; ind to St Andrew's 30 Mar 1993; Salzburg Seminar (Fellow) 1987.

PORT GLASGOW ST MARTIN'S (FES IX, 237; X, 138)

1966 FRANCIS CAMPBELL TOLLICK
(FES X, 138, 292, 426), trans from Cupar Springfield to St Martin's 29 Sep 1966; dem 20 Jun 1972 to enter teaching profession; Principal teacher of RE, Buckhaven High 1975–90; Quality Practitioner from 1990.

1973 IAIN MACKENZIE
(FES X, 138, 152), trans from Glasgow Blochairn to St Martin's 7 Mar 1973; trans to Canonbie with Langholm, Ewes and Westerkirk 18 Sep 1990.

1991 LYNN WYLIE JOLLY
B 6 Apr 1963 at Glasgow, d of James J. and Jean Helen Wylie; educ Clydebank High 1975–81; University of Glasgow 1982–88 (BD, MTh); lic by Presb of Glasgow 8 Jul 1988; asst Dundee Roseangle Ryehill 1989–91; ord and ind to St Martin's 31 May 1991; dem 13 Jul 1997.

1998 JOHN GROOM MILLER
B 29 Mar 1940 at Kilmarnock, educ Kilmarnock Academy 1951–55; Stow College of Engineering, Glasgow 1957–61 (CGLI); University of Glasgow 1968–72 (BEd); Central School of Religion 1986–88 (LTh), 1991–96 (BD), 1999 (MTh); Welding and Fabrication, Lab Technician 1956–66; lic by Presb of Irvine and Kilmarnock, Jun 1982; asst Kilmarnock Riccarton 1982–83; ord by Presb of Irvine and Kilmarnock and app by RAF Chaplains' Branch 17 Jun 1983; ind to Sandsting and Aithsting with Walls 5 Nov 1988; trans to Eskdalemuir with Hutton and Corrie with Tundergarth 13 Feb 1991; trans to St Martin's 14 May 1998.

SKELMORLIE AND WEMYSS BAY (FES X, 138)
Formed 22 Oct 1972 by union of Skelmorlie and Wemyss Bay North and Skelmorlie and Wemyss Bay South.

1961 DONALD CURRIE CASKIE
(FES IX, 133, 722; X, 139, 413), trans from Paris to Skelmorlie and Wemyss Bay North 11 Jan 1961; ret 28 Sep 1968; died 22 Dec 1983.

1970 WILLIAM RUSSELL KENNEDY
(FES IX, 268; X, 112 (2), 139 (2), 159), trans from Kilmarnock St Andrew's Glencairn to Skelmorlie and Wemyss Bay North 26 Feb 1970; became minister of united charge with Skelmorlie and Wemyss Bay South 22 Oct 1972; ret 30 Sep 1978; died 1 Jul 1988.

1979 WILLIAM ROBERT ARMSTRONG
B 17 Jul 1942 at New Galloway, s of Robert Montgomery A. and Jessie Jane Hunter Dick; educ Kirkcudbright Academy 1958–61; University of Edinburgh 1973–78 (BD); Mechanical Engineering 1961–73; lic by Presb of Dunfermline 29 Jun 1978; asst West Kilbride St Andrew's 1978–79; m 11 Oct 1969 Laura Arnott Carswell d of Andrew C. and Margaret Annie Smith; Children: Helen Margaret b 3 Mar 1974; David William b 30 Apr 1976; Joanne Ruth b 21 Jul 1978; ord and ind to Skelmorlie and Wemyss Bay 16 May 1979.

PRESBYTERY OF GLASGOW

1959 ANDREW HERRON
(FES IX, 215, 218; X, 124, 140), dem from Houston and Killellan to take up app as Clerk to Presb of Glasgow 31 Oct 1959; ret 30 Oct 1981; Editor of Church of Scotland *Year Book* 1960–92; Baird Lecturer 1985; LLD (Strathclyde); DD (Glasgow); Publ: Guides to—*Congregational Affairs* 1978; *The Presbytery* 1983; *The Ministry* 1987; *Ministerial Income* 1987 (St Andrew Press); *The Laws and Practice of the Kirk* (Chapter House, 1995).

1970 HAMISH ALASTAIR STEWART BRYDONE
(FES IX, 618, 714; X, 140, 406), dem from North-mavine on app as Asst Clerk (full-time) to Presb of Glasgow 1 Sep 1970; died 30 Oct 1979.

1980 ALEXANDER CUNNINGHAM
(FES X, 203, 217), dem from Uddingston Chalmers and app Clerk to Presb of Glasgow 5 Jun 1980; d Anne m James Culley Stewart.

ANDERSTON KELVINGROVE (FES X, 149, 163)

Formed 19 Apr 1979 by union of Anderston (union 18 Dec 1968 of Anderston Old, Anderston and St Peter's and St Mark's-Lancefield) and Kelvingrove.

1928 HERBERT ALEXANDER DARG ALEXANDER
(FUF 208; FES IX, 253; X, 149), trans from Harthill to Anderston Old 13 Dec 1928; ret 18 Dec 1968; died 2 Jan 1981.

1957 ARCHIBALD RUSSELL
(FES IX, 17; X, 11, 149, 177, 218), trans from Edinburgh Holyrood Abbey to St Mark's-Lancefield 20 Jun 1957; became minister of united charge with Anderston Old and Anderston and St Peter's 18 Dec 1968; introd as Community minister at Drumchapel 31 Jan 1973.

1964 ARTHUR DAVID COURTENAY GREER
(FES X, 163 (2), 419), ind to Kelvingrove 8 Jan 1964; dem on app to Dept of Education 1 Sep 1978.

1974 ALEXANDER DAVID MOORE GRAHAM
(FES X, 149), ind to Anderston 24 Jan 1974; became minister of united charge with Kelvingrove 19 Apr 1979; dem 31 Jan 1980 on app as Warden of Iona Abbey.

1979 ROBERT CAMPBELL ROBERTSON
(FES X, 455), res as Warden of Community House, Glasgow (Iona Community) and introd as Assoc at Anderston Kelvingrove 19 Apr 1979; became Community minister; died 13 Sep 1989.

1980 HENRY STANLEY COWPER HOOD
(FES X, 17, 420), trans from Edinburgh Muirhouse to Anderston Kelvingrove 11 Jun 1980; trans to London Crown Court 7 Nov 1991.

1992 PETER McENHILL
ord and ind to Anderston Kelvingrove 23 Jun 1992; dem 30 Sep 1996 to take up app as Lecturer at Westminster College, University of Cambridge.

1997 GORDON KIRKWOOD
B 15 Dec 1962 at Edinburgh, s of Henry Bowman Timmins K. and Margaret Parson; educ Bellshill Academy 1974–79; University of Strathclyde 1979–83 (BSc); University of Glasgow 1983–86 (BD); lic by Presb of Hamilton 26 Jun 1986; asst Glasgow Greenbank 1986–88; ord by Presb of Glasgow during assistantship at Greenbank 3 Dec 1987; introd as Assoc at Skene 12 Apr 1988; ind to Paisley Castlehead 27 Mar 1990; trans to Anderston Kelvingrove 29 Oct 1997.

BAILLIESTON MURE MEMORIAL (FUF 176; FES IX, 317; X, 186)

1942 ROBERT LAW KINNIS
(FES IX, 317, 470; X, 186), trans from Tulliallan to Mure Memorial 12 Sep 1942; ret 4 Feb 1972.

1972 JOHN ANDERSON GRAY
(FES IX, 237; X, 15, 138, 186, 232, 445), trans from Strone and Ardentinny to Mure Memorial 9 Nov 1972; ret 27 Apr 1986; s Andrew m Anne Elizabeth Aitkenhead.

1986 STUART DOUGLAS ROGERSON
trans from Kilmchoman with Portnahaven to Mure Memorial 8 Oct 1986; trans to Annan Old 31 Aug 1995.

1996 ALLAN SCOTT VINT
B 8 Aug 1964 at Longridge, s of George Scott V. and Catherine Butler; educ Whitburn Academy 1976–82; University of Aberdeen 1982–85 (BSc), 1985–88 (BD); lic by Presb of Aberdeen, 1988; asst Aberdeen Northfield 1988–89; m 31 Aug 1983

Hazel Miller Archer b 15 Jan 1965 d of Alexander A. and Janet Dewar; Children: Rachel Louise b 5 Apr 1986; ord and ind to Motherwell St Andrew's 19 Jun 1989; trans to Mure Memorial 29 May 1996.

BAILLIESTON ST ANDREW'S (FES X, 187)

1956   ALEXANDER CAMERON WALKER
(FES IX, 44; X, 26, 186), trans from Edinburgh Tynecastle to Baillieston Old 19 Jan 1956; ret 30 Nov 1966; died 7 Apr 1991.

1967   JOHN JACKSON CARRUTHERS OWEN
(FES X, 187), ord and ind to St Andrew's 28 Jun 1967; trans to Lochmaben 10 Jan 1980.

1980   THOMAS CALDWELL HOUSTON
(FES X, 420), res from app at Jerusalem St Andrew's and ind to St Andrew's 30 Apr 1980.

BALSHAGRAY VICTORIA PARK (FES X, 150, 183)

Formed 24 Jan 1991 by union of Balshagray and Victoria Park.

1964   WILLIAM THOMSON ALLAN
(FES IX, 477; X, 183, 283), trans from Kirkcaldy Abbotsford Hayfield to Victoria Park 25 Feb 1964; died 23 Aug 1977.

1975   ROBERT STEWART FRIZZELL
(FES X, 150, 169), res from term app at Glasgow Partick Anderson and ind to Balshagray 2 Apr 1975; trans to Wick Old 29 Dec 1988.

1978   ALLAN FREDERICK WEBSTER
ord and ind to Victoria Park 28 Jun 1978; trans to Dunnichen, Letham and Kirkden 11 Jan 1990.

1989   DAVID LAMONT COURT
B 13 Jun 1962 at Salisbury, s of William C. and Heather Ann Turner; educ Lesmahagow High and Larkhall Academy 1974–80; University of Strathclyde 1980–84 (BSc); University of Glasgow 1985–88 (BD); Insurance Salesman 1984–85; lic by Presb of Lanark 29 Jun 1988; asst Falkirk Old and St Modan's 1988–89; m 30 Mar 1989 Alison Lindsay Cook b 27 Aug 1965 d of David Lindsay C. and Irene Winning Morton; Children: Samuel William b 19 Jul 1993; Jonathan David b 30 Mar 1996; Ruth Lindsay b 28 Jun 1999; ord and ind to Balshagray 21 Jun 1989; became minister of united charge with Victoria Park 24 Jan 1991.

BANTON (FES III, 371; VIII, 285; IX, 239; X, 140)

Linked 15 Jun 1975 with Twechar.

1969   MICHAEL McCULLOCH BOGLE
(FES IX, 729; X, 72, 140, 416), trans from Ettrick and Buccleuch with Kirkhope to Banton 7 Aug 1969; ret 4 Jun 1975; w Frieda died Mar 1964; m (2) 3 Dec 1966 Catherine Hood Slimmon b 25 Apr

1905, died 2 Sep 1990, d of James Alexander S. and Elizabeth Ursula Maclean.

1975   WILLIAM ALEXANDER TINDALL
(FES X, 140), admitted by General Assembly 1975 and ind to Banton with Twechar 4 Nov 1975; died 22 Jul 1977.

1978   MICHAEL ROBERT PHILIP
ord and ind to Banton with Twechar 16 Mar 1978; trans to Blairgowrie St Mary's South 13 Jan 1988.

1989   JEAN RAMAGE MITCHELL BLACKLEY
B 21 Jan 1931 at Bishopbriggs, d of Alexander Millar Stirling and Margaret Murdoch Ewing Thomson; educ The Park School, Glasgow 1936–49; Jordanhill College, Glasgow 1949–53 (DEd); University of Glasgow 1978–83 (BD); Teaching (primary) 1953–57, 1969–78; lic by Presb of Glasgow 8 Nov 1983; m 28 Sep 1957 Robert Blackley b 22 Apr 1916, died 28 Jan 1967 s of James B. and Jessie Johnston; ord and ind to Banton with Twechar 9 Mar 1989.

BARLANARK GREYFRIARS (FES X, 150)

1976   JAMES WYLIE MACDONALD
ord and ind to Greyfriars 2 Jun 1976; trans to Lerwick and Bressay 6 Jul 1981.

1982   THOMAS LEONARD POLLOCK
ord and ind to Greyfriars 13 May 1982; trans to Airdrie Clarkston 2 Jun 1992.

1992   JAMES STEELE ALLISON CUNNINGHAM
B 24 Mar 1935 at Calderbank, s of Alexander C. and Jean Brownlie Steele Allison; educ Airdrie Academy 1946–52; University of Glasgow 1952–56 (MA), 1956–59 (BD); University of Oxford 1959–62 (BLitt); Princeton University, USA 1963–65 (PhD); Instructor in New Testament, Princeton Theological Seminary 1962–65; Asst Professor of Classics, McMaster University, Ontario, Canada 1965–68; Edward North Professor of Classics, Hamilton College, Clinton, New York 1968–89; lic by Presb of Hamilton 17 Apr 1959; m (1) 25 Jan 1965 Mary Frances Johnson b 8 Oct 1940 d of Frank Harris J. and Mary Frances McGhee; Children: Alexander Harris b 25 Jun 1966 m Theresa Lynn Kennedy; Mary Frances Allison b 2 Oct 1970; m (2) 8 Aug 1988 Elma Isabel Fulton b 8 Jun 1941 d of James F. and Isabella Macdonald; ord and ind to Greyfriars 26 Nov 1992.

BARONY RAMSHORN (FES X, 151, 177)

Formed 16 Sep 1982 by union of The Barony and St Paul's (Outer High) and St David's (Ramshorn). Congregation dissolved 7 Oct 1985.

1957   MATTHEW LIDDELL
(FES IX, 149, 333; X, 177, 198), trans from Larkhall Trinity to St Paul's (Outer High) and St David's

(Ramshorn) 2 Oct 1957; ret 16 Sep 1982; d Eleanor m Bruce Christer; s John m Laura Jefferies; s David m Moira Clark.

1971 JAMES WILSON ANDERSON
(FES IX, 359, 412, 536; X, 151, 245), res from BBC (Religious Broadcasting) and ind to The Barony 5 May 1971; ret 31 Oct 1978; died 8 May 1983.

1979 COLIN IAN MACLEAN
(FES X, 385, 398, 422), res from app at Trinidad Greyfriars St Ann's and ind to The Barony 24 Oct 1979; became minister of united charge with St Paul's (Outer High) and St David's (Ramshorn) 16 Sep 1982; introd to Rome St Andrew's 30 Sep 1983.

BATTLEFIELD EAST (FES X, 151, 164)

Formed 7 Jun 1979 by union of Langside Hill and Battlefield East.

1924 ARCHIBALD CHISHOLM
(FUF 231; FES IX, 277), dem from Glasgow Langside Hill 1939; died 18 May 1977.

1940 GEORGE SCOTT
(FES VI, 175; VIII, 244; IX, 277, 282, 562; X, 164), trans from Aberdeen Holburn Central to Langside Hill 27 Sep 1940; ret 30 Sep 1962; died 10 Nov 1964.

1963 MALCOLM McNEILL WALKER HARE
(FES X, 39, 164), trans from Grangemouth Charing Cross to Langside Hill 4 Sep 1963; trans to Kilmarnock St Kentigern's 26 Apr 1979.

1968 ERIC GORDON MILTON
(FES X, 151, 351), trans from Pitsligo to Battlefield East 23 Apr 1968; trans to Jersey St Columba's 27 Jul 1976.

1977 ALAN CAMERON RAEBURN
(FES X, 387), trans from Lybster and Bruan to Battlefield East 16 Mar 1977; became minister of united charge with Langside Hill 7 Jun 1979; Addl children: David b 12 Jun 1979.

BELHAVEN WESTBOURNE (FES X, 151)

Congregation dissolved 14 Oct 1990.

1946 JOHN STUART CAMERON
(FES VI, 29; VIII, 307; IX, 307, 312; X, 183), trans from Belfast Malone Presb Church to Westbourne 2 May 1946; became minister of united charge with Belhaven 23 Oct 1960; ret 31 Dec 1960; died 8 Sep 1976.

1961 DAVID JOHNSTONE
(FES IX, 166; X, 97, 151, 326), trans from Aberdeen East and Belmont to Belhaven Westbourne 6 Sep 1961; ret 4 Oct 1987.

BISHOPBRIGGS KENMURE (FUF 203; FES IX, 239; X, 140)

1968 PHILIP HOWARD JONES
(FES X, 140), ord and ind to Kenmure 16 Jun 1968; ret 30 Jun 1987; s Martyn m Sheila McCallum; d Alice m Aaron Longwe.

1987 DONALD STUART CRAWFORD
ord and ind to Kenmure 1 Oct 1987; suspended 1991.

1992 IAIN ARCHIBALD LAING
(FES X, 177), trans from Kingarth and Kilchattan Bay with Rothesay The High Kirk to Kenmure 29 Jun 1992; Addl children: Alastair Iain b 30 Mar 1978; Andrew Stephen b 24 Dec 1984.

BISHOPBRIGGS SPRINGFIELD (FES X, 141)

1954 JAMES CRAN
(FES IX, 51, 97, 156, 261; X, 141, 154), trans from Broxburn St Nicholas' to Cambridge Street 15 Feb 1954; became minister of united charge with Bishopbriggs Springfield 5 Sep 1968; died 25 Jun 1977.

1978 WILLIAM EWART
(FES X, 274), trans from Dunfermline Townhill to Springfield Cambridge 26 Jan 1978; Addl children: Christopher John William b 17 Sep 1977.

BLAIRBETH RODGER MEMORIAL (FES IX, 239; X, 141)

Formerly known as Blairbeth.

1969 KENNETH LINDSAY JOHNSTON
(FES X, 141), ord and ind to Blairbeth 25 Sep 1969; trans to Annbank 15 Feb 1989.

1990 BRIAN SYDNEY SHERET
B 9 Jun 1944 at Aberdeen, s of Sydney Glashan S. and Ruth Park; educ Robert Gordon's College, Aberdeen 1956–62; University of Aberdeen 1962–66 (MA), 1966–69 (BD); University of Oxford 1969–72 (DPhil); locums in Aberdeen 1973–82; lic by Presb of Aberdeen 24 Apr 1969; asst Edinburgh Corstorphine Old 1972–73; ord and ind to Stoneyburn 7 Dec 1982; dem 31 Jan 1985; ind to Rodger Memorial 1 Mar 1990.

BLAWARTHILL (FES IX, 358; X, 214)

1950 JAMES McKAY
(FES IX, 359; X, 214), res as Asst at Hamilton Old and ind to Blawarthill 17 Jan 1950; ret 1 Jun 1986; died 17 Mar 1993.

1987 NEIL WYLIE GALBRAITH
ord and ind to Blawarthill 13 May 1987; trans to Glasgow Cathcart Old 1 May 1996.

1997 IAN McKELL STUART McINNES
B 23 Feb 1960 at Irvine, s of David M. and Mary Thow Pitcaithly; educ Ravenspark Academy, Irvine 1972–77; Glasgow Bible Training Institute 1987 (DTh); King's College, London 1987–90 (BD); University of Glasgow 1991–93 (DipMin); ARCO Storeman 1977–78; Hospital Storeman 1978–79; Relief Manager/Bar Tender 1979–82; Asst Chaplain, Independent Churches' Chaplaincy, London 1990–91; lic by Presb of Irvine and Kilmarnock 30 Jun 1993; asst Kilmarnock Grange 1993–95; m 30 Jun 1991 Elizabeth Anne Gibson b 6 May 1951 d of Thomas G. and Annie Murray; ord by Presb of Ayr and introd as Assoc at St Columba 15 Mar 1995; ind to Blawarthill 18 Jun 1997; app Chaplain (part-time) to Barlinnie Prison.

BRIDGETON ST FRANCIS IN THE EAST (FES X, 152, 175)

Formed 26 Jun 1986 by union of Bridgeton and St Francis-in-the-East.

1960 WILLIAM SHACKLETON
(FES X, 175), ord and ind to St Francis-in-the-East 19 Sep 1960; trans to Greenock Wellpark West 12 May 1983.

1960 JOHN TURNER LANG
(FES IX, 278; X, 152, 153, 165), trans from Glasgow Laurieston Renwick to Bridgeton and Newhall 7 Jun 1960; became minister of united charge with London Road St Clement's 15 Jan 1967; trans to Glasgow St James' (Pollok) 30 Jan 1986.

1984 HOWARD ROBERT HUDSON
B 14 Sep 1955 at Darlington, s of Thomas Howard H. and Eleanor Pringle; educ High School of Glasgow 1964–73; University of Glasgow 1973–77 (MA), 1977–81 (BD); lic by Presb of Glasgow 30 Jun 1981; asst Glasgow King's Park 1979–80, Calton New with St Andrew's 1981–84; m 17 Apr 1982 Sandra Elizabeth Jack b 16 Oct 1956 d of Alexander Donald Gordon J. and Betty Kilgour; Children: Alan Robert b 29 Dec 1983; Mark Alexander b 28 Aug 1986; ord by Presb of Glasgow during assistantship at Calton New with St Andrew's 4 Mar 1982; ind to St Francis-in-the-East 22 Feb 1984; became minister of united charge with Bridgeton 26 Jun 1986.

BROOM (FES IX, 239; X, 141)

1958 WELSH NEILSON PETERKIN
(FES IX, 141; X, 84, 141), trans from Dumfries St George's to Broom 20 Mar 1958; ret 1 Aug 1986.

1987 JAMES WHYTE
B 26 Apr 1946 at Glasgow, s of James W. and Margaret Burgh Stobo; educ Penilee High, Glasgow 1951–63; Jordanhill College, Glasgow 1966–69 (DCE); University of Glasgow 1977–81

(BD); Community Education Officer 1969–77; Planning Engineer 1963–67; lic by Presb of Paisley 4 Jul 1981; asst Barrhead Arthurlie 1977–78; Pailsey St Mark's Oldhall 1978–81; m 24 Jan 1970 Norma Isabella West b 13 Feb 1945 d of Arthur William W. and Isabella Black Shaw; Children: Kenneth James Arthur b 15 Aug 1974; Janet Margaret Isabel b 28 May 1976; Lorna Margaret b 12 Sep 1980; ord and ind to Coupar Angus Abbey 27 Aug 1981; trans to Broom 5 Feb 1987.

BROOMHILL (FUF 236; FES IX, 260; X, 153)

1938 DANIEL McKENZIE BUCHANAN
(FUF 338; FES IX, 260; X, 153), trans from London Golders Green to Broomhill 11 Oct 1938; ret 6 Oct 1962; died 3 Mar 1985.

1963 JAMES AITCHISON
(FES IX, 42, 374; X, 25, 153), trans from Edinburgh St Stephen's Comley Bank to Broomhill 15 May 1963; ret 30 Sep 1986; died 13 Feb 1994.

1987 WILLIAM BROWN FERGUSON
(FES X, 76), trans from Annan Old to Broomhill 18 Feb 1987.

BURNSIDE (FES IX, 240; X, 141)

1954 JAMES ADAM LINDSAY
(FES IX, 232, 240, 487; X, 141), trans from Greenock St George's to Burnside 9 Sep 1954; ret 31 Dec 1976; s Malcolm m Lesley Wyllie; d Alison m Hugh McKirdy; d Elizabeth m Keith Burrell.

1977 DAVID JOHN COURTNEY EASTON
(FES X, 137), trans from Port Glasgow Hamilton Bardrainney to Burnside 6 Jun 1977; Addl children: Susan b 28 Aug 1978; s Simon m Sharon Clark.

BUSBY (FES X, 141)

Busby East and Busby West linked 5 Oct 1975, united 5 Apr 1990.

1939 ALASTAIR DOVE MACCALMAN
(FES IX, 241, 252; X, 141), trans from Torrance to Busby West 5 Oct 1939; ret 31 May 1974; died 29 Jul 1998.

1975 LAURENCE ARTHUR BROWN WHITLEY
(FES X, 141), ord and ind to Busby East with Busby West 11 Dec 1975; trans to Montrose Old 24 Sep 1985.

1986 ARCHIBALD IAIN CAMPBELL
(FES X, 40), ind to Busby East with West 12 Jun 1986; became minister of united charge 5 Apr 1990; ret 30 Jun 1997; divorced 1984, m (2) 26 Mar 1985 Gillian Sarah Fry b 11 Sep 1941 d of Gerald and Esme Day; d Ruth m Gavin Howie; d Susan m Andrew Williams.

1998 JEREMY CHRISTOPHER EVE
B 18 Nov 1956 at Ipswich, s of Robin Charles Roger E. and Agnes Craig Kelly; educ Crewkerne Grammar and Plymouth College 1967–74; University of Dundee 1974–78 (BSc); University of Glasgow 1991–94 (BD); Jordanhill College, Glasgow 1985–86; Computer Programming 1981–84; Youth Work 1984–91; lic by Presb of Glasgow 4 Jul 1994; asst Glasgow Netherlee 1995–98; m 31 Mar 1989 Michelle Hampton b 6 Aug 1965 d of James H. and Fox; Children: Stephen James b 11 Dec 1989; Lucy b 19 Feb 1991; Alice b 9 Jul 1996; Becky b 5 Feb 1999; ord by Presb of Glasgow during assistantship at Netherlee 7 Sep 1995; ind to Busby 20 Jan 1998.

CADDER (FES III, 372; IX, 241; X, 141)

1974 WILLIAM JACK BEAUMONT
(FES X, 51, 141, 416), trans from Penicuik North to Cadder 12 Jun 1974; ret 30 Sep 1993; died 26 Sep 1998.

1994 HENRY DANE SHERRARD
(FES X, 413), trans from Buckhaven to Cadder 9 Mar 1994; trans to Arrochar with Luss 14 Dec 1998.

1999 GRAHAM SOMERVILLE FINCH
B 22 Oct 1950 at Falkirk, s of John Somerville F. and Jean Graham Evans; educ Falkirk High 1962–68; University of St Andrews 1968–72 (MA); University of Aberdeen 1972–75 (BD); lic by Presb of Aberdeen; asst Edinburgh St Giles' 1975–77; m 13 Aug 1974 Louise Jane Richardson b 3 Mar 1952 d of Robert Paterson R. and Louise Margaret Neill; Children: John Sutherland b 28 Jul 1978; Kathryn Louise b 26 Aug 1982; ord and ind to Sanday 20 Jul 1977; became minister of linked charge with North Ronaldsay 9 Oct 1978; trans to Stonehaven Fetteresso 21 Apr 1983; trans to Cadder 22 Sep 1999.

CALTON PARKHEAD (FES X, 153, 157, 169)

Formed 6 Oct 1977 by union of Calton Old, Dalmarnock Old and Parkhead.

1945 DANIEL MACLURE WILSON
(FES IX, 265, 709; X, 157), dem from Stromness Victoria Street 26 Oct 1942; ind to Dalmarnock Old 20 Mar 1945; ret 31 Dec 1963; died 28 Nov 1976.

1965 CHARLES GORDON STRACHAN
(FES X, 157), ind to Dalmarnock Old 20 Jan 1965; dem 30 Sep 1970.

1969 ALEXANDER FRANCIS GRIMSTONE
(FES IX, 251; X, 148, 153, 262, 339, 406), trans from Fetlar to Calton Old 3 Nov 1969; became minister of united charge with Dalmarnock Old and Parkhead 6 Oct 1977; ret 30 Sep 1986; Assoc at Glasgow Cathedral from 1 Oct 1986; s Alastair m Joyce Johnston.

1971 PETER WILLIAM MILLAR
(FES X, 157), ord and ind to Dalmarnock Old 10 Jan 1971; dem 31 Aug 1976 and app by Overseas Council for service in S India 4 Jan 1977.

1987 SAMUEL GERARD VICTOR CRAWFORD
B 17 Feb 1929 at Dublin, s of George C. and Mary Alice Rourke; educ Stevenson College, Edinburgh 1976–77; University of Edinburgh 1977–80; Printer 1944–64; Missionary (Church of Scotland) 1965–76; lic by Presb of Edinburgh, 1980; m 3 Apr 1954 Iris Francis Anderson b 9 Apr 1932 d of Charles A. and Maud Davey; Children: Olive Susan b 19 Nov 1955 m Pohlman; Shirley Anne b 12 Aug 1958 m Francis; Deirdrie Jean b 10 Jun 1965 m Upman; Colum Barry b 6 Jun 1971; ord and ind to Acharacle with Ardnamurchan 19 Aug 1980; trans to Calton Parkhead 28 Jan 1987; ret 31 Oct 1991.

1992 RONALD ANDERSON
B 14 Nov 1947 at Motherwell, s of William A. and Maria Anson Main; educ New Stevenston Secondary 1952–62; University of St Andrews 1983–88 (BD), 1989–90 (DipTh); Spray Painter 1978–81; lic by Presb of Kirkcaldy 16 Sep 1990; asst Markinch 1990–91; Kirkcaldy St Brycedale 1991–92; m 1 Aug 1972 Mary Scott Anderson b 29 Aug 1949 d of Gavin Young A. and Clara Close; Children: Drew b 23 Sep 1969 m Tracy Martin; Ron b 16 Apr 1971; ord and ind to Calton Parkhead 30 Apr 1992.

CAMBUSLANG FLEMINGTON HALLSIDE (FES X, 189)

1937 ANDREW ROBERTSON SILLERS
(FES IX, 321, 353; X, 189 (2)), trans from Rigside to Flemington 2 Mar 1937; became minister of united charge with Hallside and Newton 5 Jun 1974; ret 31 Oct 1979; died 26 Feb 1982.

1980 ROBIN DOBSON YATES
(FES X, 206), trans from Carluke St Andrew's to Flemington Hallside 1 May 1980; ret 31 Jan 1984.

1984 ROBERT DAVID CURRIE
B 5 Jun 1948 at Barrhead, s of Henry C. and Christina Cross Auld; educ John Neilson Institution, Paisley; University of Glasgow 1966–70 (BSc), 1980–83 (BD); Teaching (Geography) 1971–80; lic by Presb of Paisley 23 Jun 1983; asst Renfrew Old 1983–84; m 12 May 1984 Marion Pauline Ross b 18 Dec 1951 d of Gordon R. and Audrey Birchell; Children: Rosemary Ann b 25 Sep 1988; Fiona Ruth b 30 Aug 1990; ord and ind to Flemington Hallside 29 Nov 1984.

CAMBUSLANG OLD (FES III, 234; VIII, 254; IX, 322; X, 189)

1936 JOHN KENNEDY
(FES IX, 322, 373; X, 189), trans from Old Kilpatrick to Cambuslang Old 11 Mar 1936; ret 30 Sep 1966; died 23 Jul 1983.

1967 IAN MURRAY POLLOCK DAVIDSON
(FES X, 111, 189, 258), trans from Kilmarnock Grange to Cambuslang Old 17 May 1967; trans to Stirling Allan Park South with Church of the Holy Rude 25 Apr 1985.

1985 ALAN HENRY WARD
B 2 Jun 1948 at Glasgow, s of James Henry W. and Irene Jessie McCall; educ Hillhead High, Glasgow 1960–66; University of Glasgow 1966–70 (MA); Jordanhill College, Glasgow 1970–71 (PGCE); University of Edinburgh 1973–76 (BD); Teaching 1971–73; lic by Presb of West Lothian 11 Jun 1976; asst St Andrews St Leonard's with Cameron and Largoward 1976–78; m 29 Jun 1973 Alison Lindsay Stead b 22 May 1951 d of Donald Maurice S. and Joan Aitkenhead; Children: Michael James b 6 Mar 1979; Simon Donald b 11 Sep 1980; ord and ind to Dumfries Greyfriars 6 Apr 1978; trans to Cambuslang Old 13 Nov 1985; Publ: *The Effectiveness of TLS* (St Colm's College, 1993).

CAMBUSLANG ST ANDREW'S (FES X, 190)

Name changed from Cambuslang Rosebank and West to St Andrew's 1966.

1956 ROBERT BLACK KINCAID
(FES IX, 148, 230, 261; X, 133, 190), trans from Greenock Martyrs' and North to Cambuslang Rosebank and West 4 Apr 1956; ret 30 Apr 1974; died 27 Jul 1980.

1974 ROBERT PATTERSON BELL
(FES X, 190, 203), trans from Craigneuk-Belhaven to St Andrew's 30 Oct 1974; trans to Ballantrae 20 Jan 1998.

1998 JOHN STEVENSON
B 14 Oct 1942 at Motherwell, s of Peter S. and Helen Duffy; educ Motherwell Central School 1947–58; University of Glasgow (LTh); Company Director 1980–92; lic by Presb of Hamilton 30 Aug 1995; asst Cambuslang St Andrew's 1995–98; m 20 Oct 1965 Isobel Paterson Brown b 5 Apr 1944 d of John B. and Grace Morris; Children: Jonathan Mark b 6 Feb 1970 m Ursula; Janie Kristian b 17 Jul 1973; ord and ind to St Andrew's 23 Apr 1998.

CAMBUSLANG TRINITY ST PAUL'S (FES X, 190)

Formed 5 May 1987 by union of Cambuslang Trinity and Cambuslang St Paul's.

1968 JOHN PATTISON CUBIE
(FES X, 127, 190), trans from Paisley Martyrs' to Trinity 11 Dec 1968; became minister of united charge with St Paul's 5 May 1987; trans to Caldwell 1 Mar 1989.

1971 ANDREW RUSSELL HAMILTON
(FES IX, 189, 266; X, 157 (2), 190), trans form Glasgow Crosshill Victoria to St Paul's 3 Nov 1971; ret 5 May 1987; died 9 Jun 1993.

1989 DAVID STEWART
B 19 Oct 1949 at Glasgow, s of John S. and Eveline Masterton; educ Hyndland Secondary, Glasgow 1961–67; University of Aberdeen 1967–71 (MA), 1971–72 (DipEd), 1972–75 (BD), 1978 (MTh); St John's College, Nottingham 1990–93 (DPC); lic by Presb of Glasgow 26 Jun 1975; asst New Erskine 1975–76; m 6 Aug 1976 Margaret Elizabeth Hamlet b 27 Oct 1948 d of Ronald H. and Ruth Pocock; ord and ind to Kirkintilloch Park 4 Aug 1977; became minister of linked charge with Torrance 19 Mar 1983; trans to Trinity St Paul's 30 Aug 1989; Publ: '*Aberdeen Doctors' and the Covenanters* (Journal of Scottish Church History Society, Vol 22, part 1, 1984); *Church Computing* (*Life and Work*, 1995).

CAMPHILL-QUEEN'S PARK (FES IX, 261; X, 154)

Congregation dissolved 31 Dec 1991.

1947 WILLIAM FINDLAY GRIEVE
(FES IX, 200, 261, 652; X, 154), trans from Inverness Crown to Camphill-Queen's Park 8 May 1947; ret 31 Dec 1971; died 27 Mar 1993.

1972 JAMES ARCHIBALD MARSHALL
(FES X, 154, 219), trans form Duntocher to Camphill-Queen's Park 14 Sep 1972; ret 30 Apr 1987; died 22 Nov 1998.

CAMPSIE (FES X, 142)

Formed 31 May 1978 by union of Campsie High and Campsie Trinity.

1949 ALEXANDER ABERCROMBY MORRISON
(FES IX, 91, 241; X, 142), trans from Innerwick to Campsie High 19 Jan 1949; became minister of united charge with Trinity 31 May 1978; ret 31 Aug 1979; died 14 Jun 1997.

1972 EUPHEMIA HELEN CLOUSTON IRVINE
(FES X, 142), ord and ind to Campsie Trinity with Milton of Campsie 1 Jun 1972; continued as minister of Milton of Campsie following termination of linkage with Trinity 31 May 1978; ret 28 Aug 1988.

1980 JOHN MACKENZIE ROBERTSON
Asst at Glasgow St George's Tron 1975–80; ind to Campsie 19 Mar 1980; dem 10 Mar 1992.

1993 DAVID JOHN TORRANCE
B 25 Oct 1962 at Edinburgh, s of David Wishart T. and Mary Elizabeth Barton; educ Aberdeen Grammar and Earlston High 1974–80; University of Aberdeen 1980–84 (BD); University of Edinburgh

1986–88 (DipMin); Financial and Insurance Advisor 1984–6; lic by Presb of Melrose and Peebles, Nov 1988; asst Edinburgh St Michael's 1988–89; Ayr Castlehill 1989–90, 1991; Mearns 1992–93; m (1) 19 Sep 1983 Rebecca Jane Knowles b 6 Mar 1962; divorced Sep 1990; m (2) 12 Jul 1996 Ann Rylance b 7 May 1961; ord and ind to Campsie 18 Mar 1993.

CARDONALD (FES III, 132; VIII, 237; IX, 261; X, 154)

1971 JOHN STEVENSON
(FES X, 154, 268), trans from Leven St John's to Cardonald 21 Apr 1971; trans to Kirriemuir Old 16 Feb 1983.

1983 ERIC McLACHLAN
B 2 Apr 1943 at Glasgow, s of Alexander Pinkerton M. and Elizabeth Cairns; educ Eastpark, Glasgow 1955–58; University of Glasgow 1970–75 (BD, CPS); Export Shipping Clerk 1955–69; lic by Presb of Glasgow, Jun 1976; asst Glasgow Trinity Possil and Henry Drummond 1970–74; Glasgow St Margaret's Knightswood 1974–75; m 29 Mar 1969 Janis Barron b 8 Feb 1947 d of David Bradshaw Wright B. and Livingstone; ord and ind to Connel 23 Jan 1978; trans to Cardonald 27 Oct 1983.

CARMUNNOCK (FES III, 378; VIII, 286; IX, 242; X, 142)

1972 JAMES REID
(FES IX, 376; X, 20, 142, 224), res from service with Presb Church of W Australia in Perth and ind to Carmunnock 23 Mar 1972; returned to Australia to take up app with Presb Church in Manly, New South Wales 15 Mar 1977.

1977 HENRY HUTCHISON
(FES IX, 208, 265; X, 157), London College of Music 1951 (LLCM); University of Glasgow 1955 (PhD); University of Toronto 1962 (BEd); University of Glasgow 1973–75 (MLitt); res as Lecturer in Education, University of Glasgow and ind to Carmunnock 20 Nov 1977; ret 31 Jan 1993; Publ: *The Church and Spiritual Healing* (Rider, 1955); *A Faith to Live By* (W A Wilde, USA, 1959); *Kirk Life in Old Carmunnock* (Kirk Session, 1978); *God Believes in You* (Eyre & Spottiswoode, 1980); *Well I'm Blessed!* (Eyre & Spottiswoode, 1981); *Healing Through Worship* (Eyre & Spottiswoode, 1981); *A Faith that Conquers* (St Andrew Press, 1982).

1993 ROBERT JAMES MASSON ANDERSON
B 21 Feb 1947 at Arbroath, s of Robert Masson A. and Fileen Margaret Minter; educ Portland Secondary 1958–62; University of Glasgow 1989–92 (BD); Civil Service 1965–89; lic by Presb of Glasgow 26 Jun 1992; asst Glasgow Shettleston Old 1992–93; ord and ind to Carmunnock 26 May 1993; app Chaplain (part-time) to Barlinnie Prison.

CARMYLE (FUF 205; FES IX, 242; X, 142)

Linked 22 Feb 1978 with Kenmuir Mount Vernon.

1956 DAVID HAMILTON McMAHON
(FES IX, 245, 762; X, 142), res from app with Jewish Mission Committee at Alexandria St Andrew's, Egypt and ind to Carmyle 23 Feb 1956; ret 21 Sep 1977; died 17 Mar 1986.

1978 HERBERT MARSHALL GIBSON
(FES X, 197, 229), ind to Kenmuir Mount Vernon 24 Apr 1974; became minister of linked charge with Carmyle 22 Feb 1978; trans to Glasgow St Thomas' Gallowgate 29 Apr 1982.

1982 JAMES McBRIDE DAVIES
ord and ind to Carmyle with Kenmuir Mount Vernon 25 Nov 1982; trans to Aberdeen St Stephen's 22 Feb 1989.

1989 WILLIAM BRUCE McDOWALL
ord and ind to Carmyle with Kenmuir Mount Vernon 25 Aug 1989; trans to Uddingston Park 4 Mar 1999.

1999 MURDO MACLEAN
B 17 Jun 1965 at Glasgow, s of Murdo M. and Janet Nicol Morrison; educ Lochend Secondary 1977–81; University of Glasgow 1991–95 (BD), 1995–96 (CMin); Zoo Keeper, Zoological Society of Glasgow and West of Scotland 1981–91; lic by Presb of Glasgow 1 Jul 1996; asst Glasgow Burnside 1996–97; m 22 Jul 1995 Alison Macdonald b 16 Sep 1964 d of Kenneth M. and Jean Cation; ord by Presb of Glasgow and introd as Assoc at St George's Tron 2 Jul 1997; ind to Carmyle with Kenmuir Mount Vernon 4 Nov 1999.

CARNTYNE OLD (FUF 252; FES IX, 262; X, 154)

Linked 4 May 1983 with Eastbank.

1961 ROBERT McILWRAITH CULLEN
(FES X, 154, 254, 313), trans from Newtyle to Carntyne Old 10 May 1961; ret 29 Feb 1976; died 14 Jan 1978.

1977 GAVIN JOHN ELLIOTT
ord by Presb of Edinburgh during assistantship at South Leith 13 Jun 1976; ind to Carntyne Old 5 May 1977; dem on app as Mission Partner with United Church of Zambia, Lusaka, Mar 1983.

1983 RONALD ALEXANDER STEPHEN CRAIG
B 25 Dec 1951 at Aberdeen, s of Ronald Anderson C. and Marjorie Simmonds Bain; educ Aberdeen Grammar 1957–70; University of Glasgow 1970–73 (BAcc), 1979–82 (BD); University of Strathclyde 1973–74 (PDPM); Industrial Relations Officer 1974–79; lic by Presb of Glasgow 28 Jun 1982; asst Glasgow Cardonald 1982–83; m 23 Sep 1978 Grace Russell Allison b 7 Apr 1954 d of James A. and Marion Taylor MacMillan; Children: Andrew James b 2 May 1981; John Ronald b 2 Nov 1983; ord and ind to Carntyne Old with Eastbank 23 Aug 1983.

CARNWADRIC (FES IX, 262, 276; X, 154)

1953 DOUGLAS DUGALD McPHAIL
(FES IX, 277; X, 154, 163), ord and ind to Kingston-Union 15 Nov 1950; became minister of transported charge of Carnwadric 20 Sep 1953; ret 30 Nov 1982; died 2 Aug 1993.

1983 GRAEME KERR BELL
B 17 Sep 1952 at Paisley, s of James B. and May Hamilton Aitken Dickson; educ Camphill Secondary, Paisley 1965–70; University of Strathclyde 1970–74 (BA); University of Edinburgh 1974–75 (CMS); University of Aberdeen 1979–82 (BD); General Treasurer, CCAP, Blantyre Synod, Malawi 1975–78; Care Asst, Church of Scotland 1979; lic by Presb of Paisley 1 Jul 1982; asst Glasgow Garthamlock and Craigend East 1982–83; m 5 Aug 1983 Sandra Louise Neeson b 9 Sep 1950 d of William and Agnes N; Children: Gordon Neeson and Kenneth Dickson b 14 Aug 1985; ord and ind to Carnwadric 24 Jun 1983.

CASTLEMILK EAST (FES X, 154)

1971 JOHN DUNLOP MILLER
(FES X, 154), ord and ind to Castlemilk East 17 Jan 1971; Addl children: James Ian b 16 May 1976.

CASTLEMILK WEST (FES X, 155)

1963 JAMES MILLAR
(FES IX, 198; X, 113, 155), trans from Kilmaurs Glencairn with Kilmaurs St Maur's to Castlemilk West 24 Apr 1963; trans to Glasgow Shawlands Old 29 Aug 1979.

1980 ROBERT COLQUHOUN WOTHERSPOON
trans from Strichen to Castlemilk West 13 Mar 1980; trans to Corsock and Kirkpatrick Durham with Crossmichael and Parton 30 Jan 1990.

1990 JAMES NIVEN RUDDOCK McNEIL
ord and ind to Castlemilk West 28 Jul 1990; trans to Alva 30 Oct 1997.

1998 CHARLES MILLAR CAMERON
B 31 May 1951 at Glasgow, s of Charles C. and Elizabeth Ann Jones; educ Woodside Secondary, Glasgow 1963–70; University of Stirling 1971–74 (BA); University of Glasgow 1974–77 (BD), 1984 (PhD); Western Theological Seminary, USA 1978–79; lic by Presb of Glasgow 30 Jun 1977; asst Paisley Sherwood 1977–78; m 18 Oct 1980 Sharon Elizabeth Tweed b 30 Jul 1955 d of Thomas T; Children: Daniel Thomas b 9 Jul 1986; ord and ind to Dunfermline St Ninian's 26 Feb 1980; dem 8 Feb 1996 on app by Presb Church in Ireland; ind to Castlemilk West 7 Sep 1998.

CATHCART OLD (FES III, 381; VIII, 286; IX, 262; X, 155)

1973 CHARLES COLIN CAMPBELL GILLON
(FES IX, 152; X, 90, 155, 167, 172), trans from Glasgow Renfield to Cathcart Old 14 Jun 1973; dem 30 Apr 1980 to take up app at First Presb Church, Georgetown, Washington DC.

1980 ALEXANDER THOMSON STEWART
trans from Carluke Kirkton to Cathcart Old 15 Nov 1980; trans to Edinburgh Corstorphine St Ninian's 31 May 1995.

1996 NEIL WYLIE GALBRAITH
B 3 Feb 1953 at Greenock, s of Neil W. and McAleese; educ Greenock High 1958–70; James Watt College; University of Glasgow 1981–86 (BD, CMin); Commercial Artist 1970–81; lic by Presb of Greenock; asst Port Glasgow St Andrew's 1986–87; m 11 Jan 1974 Mags Caskie b 12 Jan 1954 d of Harry C. and Craig; Children: Ryan b 12 Apr 1976; Ross b 6 Apr 1978; ord and ind to Glasgow Blawarthill 13 May 1987; trans to Cathcart Old 1 May 1996; Publ: *People Just Like Me* (BAA, 1986).

CATHCART SOUTH (FUF 214; IX, 262; X, 155)

1930 JOHN LANDELS KENT
(FUF 266; FES IX, 251, 262; X, 155), trans from Thornliebank Spiersbridge to Cathcart South 19 Sep 1930; ret 15 Sep 1971; died 5 Aug 1980.

1972 HUGH RUTHERFORD WYLLIE
(FES X, 155, 192), trans from Coatbridge Dunbeth to Cathcart South 12 Jan 1972; trans to Hamilton Old 21 Oct 1981.

1982 GEORGE FAIRLIE
(FES X, 306, 385), trans from Dundee St Peter's to Cathcart South 1 Apr 1982; trans to Crail with Kingsbarns 3 Nov 1989.

1990 ANDREW McGILL SMILLIE
B 14 Dec 1944 at Dumbarton, s of Andrew S. and Janet Cameron; educ Dumbarton Academy 1949–59; University of Glasgow 1986–89 (LTh); Motor Mechanic 1959–65; Management Services Officer 1965–86; lic by Presb of Dumbarton 9 Jul 1989; m 31 Aug 1968 Joyce Elizabeth Evans b 28 Nov 1946 d of William E. and Elizabeth Nimmo; Children: Craig b 1 Sep 1970 m Kathryn Whale; Karen b 12 Jul 1973 m Graham Hogg; ord and ind to Cathcart South 20 Jun 1990.

CATHEDRAL (ST MUNGO'S OR HIGH) (FES III, 451; VIII, 304; IX, 262; X, 155)

1953 DAVID ALEXANDER ROSS McGREGOR
(FES IX, 38), Asst at Glasgow Cathedral 1953–55, then Hon Asst; died 10 May 1999.

1967 WILLIAM JAMES MORRIS
(FES IX, 472; X, 155, 279, 350), trans from Peterhead Old to Glasgow Cathedral 25 Oct 1967; Dean of the Chapel Royal in Scotland 1991–96; Publ: *A Walk Around Glasgow Cathedral* (Society of Friends of Glasgow Cathedral).

CHRYSTON (FES IX, 243; X, 142)

1936 GEORGE WHITFIELD MACARTHUR
(FES IX, 242, 243, 266; X, 142), trans from Glasgow East Park to Chryston East 14 Apr 1936; became minister of united charge with West 5 Mar 1950; ret 31 Dec 1970; died 23 Feb 1985.

1971 WILLIAM GORDON HAGGARTY
(FES X, 142), ord and ind to Chryston 8 Sep 1971; trans to Aberdeen North of St Andrew 30 Sep 1976.

1977 MARTIN ANGUS WILLIAM ALLEN
B 5 Aug 1942 at St Andrews, s of Charles Headley A. and Janet Carmichael Dunn; educ Dundee High 1954–60; University of St Andrews 1960–64 (MA); University of Edinburgh 1971–74 (BD); Covenant Seminary, St Louis, Missouri, USA 1975–76 (ThM); Education and Training, Scottish Gas 1964–71; lic by Presb of Edinburgh 29 Jun 1974; asst Edinburgh Wester Hailes 1974–75; m 24 Jun 1968 Wilma Ann Roger Legge b 16 Dec 1944 d of William Roger L. and Isabella Dey McDonald Kellas; Children: Peter William Martin b 13 Mar 1973 m Sheona Gray; David Stephen b 27 Jun 1975; ord and ind to Chryston 17 Feb 1977.

1998 JOHN DUNCAN URQUHART
B 11 Apr 1966 at Stornoway, s of John U. and Christina Nellie MacLennan; educ Leverhulme Memorial School and Sir E Scott School, Harris and Nicolson Institute, Stornoway 1978–84; Glasgow School of Art 1984–88; University of Aberdeen 1993–96; Reporter and Presenter, BBC Scotland 1988–93; lic by Presb of Uist, Jun 1996; asst Chryston 1996–98; m 6 Mar 1998 Muriel Ann MacKinnon b 5 Nov 1972 d of Ian Alpen M. and Annie MacRae MacIver; Children: Mairead Anna b 9 Apr 1999; ord by Presb of Glasgow and introd as Assoc at Chryston 2 Apr 1998.

COLSTON MILTON (FES IX, 263; X, 156)

1950 JOHN McKENZIE STEWART
(FES IX, 263; X, 156), ord and ind to Colston Milton 18 May 1950; ret 30 Sep 1980; died 12 Aug 1989.

1981 JOHN PROCTOR
ord and ind to Colston Milton 6 May 1981; dem 31 Aug 1986 to take up app with URC.

1986 DAVID JAMES TAYLOR
trans from Stracathro with Brechin Maison Dieu to Colston Milton 10 Dec 1986; trans to Iona with Kilfinichen and Kilvickeon and Ross of Mull 9 Oct 1993.

1994 CHRISTOPHER DAVID PARK
B 8 Jun 1949 at Bridge of Weir, s of Robert P. and Eva Carter; educ Watford Grammar 1961–67; University of Edinburgh 1967–71 (BSc), 1973–76 (BD); Agricultural Engineering Research 1971–73; lic by Presb of Edinburgh 4 Jul 1976; asst Aberdeen St Machar's Cathedral 1976–77; m 24 Jul 1971 Moira Lindsay b 8 Jul 1950 d of Benjamin L. and Jean Rintoul; Children: Fiona b 19 Oct 1974; Douglas b 3 Jul 1976; Catriona b 9 Jan 1978; Steven b 9 Apr 1981; David b 8 Oct 1986; ord by Presb of Edinburgh and introd as Assoc at Holy Trinity 23 Jun 1977; ind to Paisley St Ninian's Ferguslie 11 Nov 1981; trans to Colston Milton 24 Nov 1994.

COLSTON WELLPARK (FES III, 406; VIII, 292; IX, 263; X, 156)

1974 ALFRED BOWIE
(FES X, 156), ord and ind to Colston Wellpark 20 Jun 1974; trans to Alford with Keig with Tullynessle and Forbes 30 Sep 1987.

1988 DAVID MITCHELL
ord and ind to Colston Wellpark 23 Jun 1988; dem 1 Aug 1998 on app as Chaplain to Marie Curie Hospice, Huntershill.

1999 CHRISTINE MARGARET GOLDIE
B 9 Mar 1959 at Glasgow, d of Albert Davidson G. and Christina Kennedy Cuthbert; educ Jordanhill School, Glasgow 1964–77; University of Glasgow 1977–80 (LLB), 1980–83 (BD), 1993–97 (MTh); lic by Presb of Glasgow 23 Jun 1983; asst West Kilbride St Andrew's 1983–84; ord and ind to Clydebank St Cuthbert's 8 May 1984; dem on app as Chaplain to Glasgow Polytechnic 17 Feb 1992; ind to Colston Wellpark 8 Apr 1999.

CRANHILL (FES IX, 264; X, 156)

1969 ROBERT JOHN REID
(FES X, 156, 306), trans under mutual eligibility from Presb Church in Ireland and ind to Cranhill 24 Apr 1969; dem 12 Apr 1984 and introd on term app to Mossgreen and Crossgates.

1985 IAIN MACLEOD GREENSHIELDS
ord and ind to Cranhill 1 May 1985; trans to Larkhall St Machan's 2 May 1993.

1994 JAMES AIRD TREVORROW
(FES X, 409), res from app at Danesholme and Kingswood Ecumenical Experiment, Corby and ind to Cranhill 11 Apr 1994; divorced 24 Jan 1970; m (2) 1 May 1976 Isabel Agnes Davie b 4 Mar 1939 d of George and Isabel D.

CROFTFOOT (FUF 221; FES IX, 264; X, 156)

1973 HUGH SAWERS
(FES X, 52, 156), trans from Penicuik South to Croftfoot 16 May 1973; dem 30 Jun 1979; ind to Motherwell St Andrew's 28 Oct 1981.

1979 JAMES MULHOLLAND MARTIN
(FES X, 30), trans from Caldercruix, Longriggend and Meadowfield to Croftfoot 8 Nov 1979; dem 14 Jul 1985.

1986 JOHN MINTO LLOYD
B 23 Jul 1942 at Glasgow, s of John Minto L. and Helen Jack Millar; educ High School of Glasgow 1947–59; University of Glasgow 1978–83 (BD, CMin); Banking 1959–78; lic by Presb of Glasgow 27 Jun 1983; asst Glasgow Cathcart 1983–84; m (1) 15 Sep 1969 Dorothy May Thomson b 11 Mar 1945, died 12 Nov 1984 d of James T. and Williamina McCulloch; Children: Michelle Helen and Sharon Catherine b 15 Oct 1972; Elizabeth Claire b 8 Dec 1978; Christopher John b 26 Mar 1981; m (2) 5 Sep 1986 Anne Taylor b 10 Feb 1962 d of Robert Stuart and Elizabeth Hendry; Children: David Andrew b 14 Jul 1987; Laura Anne b 22 May 1990; Jonathan Mark b 10 Mar 1993; ord and ind to Bundaberg, Queensland (Uniting Church in Australia) 27 Jul 1984; ind to Croftfoot 8 May 1986.

CROSSHILL QUEEN'S PARK (FES X, 157)

1974 WILLIAM MARSH
(FES X, 157), ord by Presb of Glasgow during assistantship at Netherlee 6 Dec 1972; ind to Queen's Park 27 Dec 1974; died 18 Mar 1997.

DENNISTOUN BLACKFRIARS (FES X, 152, 158)

Formed 6 May 1982 by union of Dennistoun, Dennistoun South and Blackfriars.

1965 JOHN JOHNSTON
(FES X, 152), ind to Blackfriars 12 May 1965; trans to Saltcoats St Cuthbert's South Beach 4 Dec 1980.

1982 ROBERT WILLIAM THOMPSON
trans under mutual eligibility from UFC and ind to Blackfriars 2 Dec 1982; trans to Loanhead 30 Oct 1985.

1986 ALEXANDER McEWAN WELSH
trans from Catrine with Sorn to Blackfriars 15 May 1986; dem 31 Aug 1994 to enter teaching profession.

DENNISTOUN CENTRAL (FES X, 157)

Formed 24 Jan 1975 by union of Trinity-Duke Street, Bluevale and Whitevale and Rutherford.

1958 WILLIAM JAMES HUTTON
(FES IX, 181, 757; X, 105, 182), dem from Glasgow Trinity-Duke Street 31 Jan 1966; Asst at Glasgow Shettleston Old 1966–69; entered teaching profession Jan 1970; died 3 Dec 1994.

1966 IAIN LACHLAN GILLIES
(FES X, 105, 152, 237), trans from Ochiltree to Bluevale and Whitevale 19 Oct 1966; ret 24 Jan 1975; died 18 Nov 1998; d Joyce m Kenneth Wilkie.

1975 WILLIAM HAMILTON
(FES IX, 242; X, 93, 142, 157, 182), trans from Ervie and Kirkcolm to Trinity-Duke Street 30 Mar 1967; became Collegiate minister of united charge with Rutherford, Bluevale and Whitevale 24 Jan 1975; ret 28 Feb 1977; died 28 Feb 1994.

1975 THOMAS LESLIE BARR
(FES X, 157, 173), ord and ind to Rutherford 29 May 1969; became minister of united charge with Bluevale and Whitevale and Trinity-Duke Street 24 Jan 1975; trans to Kinross 28 Aug 1979.

1980 JOHN CAIRNS BECK
(FES X, 387), trans from Halkirk with Westerdale and Halsary to Dennistoun Central 10 Jul 1980; trans to Alves and Burghead with Kinloss and Findhorn 28 Jun 1995.

1996 ADAMINA YOUNGER
B 23 May 1939 at Glasgow, d of James Lennox and Margaret Brown; educ High Possil Senior Secondary, Glasgow 1944–57; Jordanhill College, Glasgow 1957–61 (PGCE); University of Glasgow 1974–78 (BD); Teaching (Infants) 1961–68; Lecturing (Educ) 1968–74; lic by Presb of Greenock 28 Jun 1977; asst Gourock St John's 1977–78; m 15 Jul 1964 George Younger b 30 Dec 1940 s of James Y. and Catherine Allison; Children: Gillian Ann May b 8 Dec 1967; Stephen Kelly b 22 Nov 1968; Jaqueline Ann Girvan b 13 Mar 1972; ord and ind to Clydebank Radnor Park 13 Sep 1978; dem on app as Young Adult Adviser, Board of Education 15 Mar 1983; Owner of Roslea Café, Glasgow 10 Jun 1986; ind to Glasgow Garthamlock and Craigend East 2 Nov 1988; trans to Dennistoun Central 28 Jan 1996.

DRUMCHAPEL DRUMRY ST MARY'S (FES X, 218)

1967 ROBERT ERSKINE GILBERT
(FES X, 218, 333), trans from Aberdeen Torry to Drumry St Mary's 1 Feb 1967; died 26 Jun 1991.

1992 HILDA CHRISTINE SMITH
B 15 Nov 1960 at Glasgow, d of Andrew Mackie S. and Catherine; educ Stanley Green High, Paisley 1972–78; University of Glasgow 1978–84 (MA), 1984–88 (BD); Care Asst, Drug Rehabilitation 1989–90; lic by United Free Church of Scotland 21 Jun 1988; asst Rothesay Trinity 1990–92; ord and ind to St Mary's 27 Aug 1992.

DRUMCHAPEL ST ANDREW'S (FES X, 218)

Formed 31 Aug 1995 by union of Drumchapel St Andrew's and Drumchapel Old.

1969 KINNINBURGH JOHN TURNBULL
(FES IX, 286; X, 150, 169, 218), trans from Glasgow Barlanark Greyfriars to Drumchapel Old 15 Jan 1969; trans to Bridge of Allan Holy Trinity 14 Dec 1976.

1975 EDWARD MACBEAN HALDANE LEWIS
(FES X, 170, 218), trans from Glasgow Plantation with Pollok Street to St Andrew's 16 Feb 1975; ret 31 Dec 1993.

1977 DAVID ALLAN KEDDIE
(FES X, 163, 230), ind to Drumchapel Old 20 Apr 1977; dem 23 May 1983 to enter teaching profession; app teacher of RE, Clydebank High 30 Apr 1983; app School Chaplain and Principal teacher (RE), Kelvinside Academy 26 Aug 1984.

1984 JOHN STEWART PURVES
B 8 Jan 1958 at Edinburgh, s of D Stewart P. and Marjory Gilruth; educ Stewart's Melville, Edinburgh 1963–75; University of Edinburgh 1976–79 (LLB), 1979–82 (BD); lic by Presb of Edinburgh 4 Jul 1982; asst Glasgow King's Park 1982–84; ord by Presb of Glasgow during assistantship at King's Park 5 May 1983; ind to Drumchapel Old 7 Jun 1984; became minister of united charge with St Andrew's 31 Aug 1995; Publ: *King David* (Ladybird, 1983).

1996 ELIZABETH MILLS GREGSON
B 10 Jul 1933 at Glasgow, d of William Laurie Wyper and Martha Anderson Mills; educ Bellahouston Academy, Glasgow 1938–45; Jordanhill College, Glasgow 1969–72 (Teaching Diploma); Open University 1972–76 (BA); University of Glasgow 1992 (BD); Teaching (primary) 1973–86; lic by Presb of Glasgow, Jul 1988; m 12 Mar 1955 John George Gregson b 15 Sep 1931, died Apr 1990, s of Leslie Victor G. and Margaret Sheddon McLay; Children: Leslie Douglas b 7 Dec 1956; Christine Laurie b 25 Dec 1959 m James Gow Copeland; Kenneth William b 24 Apr 1963 m Susanne Kondes; ord by Presb of Glasgow and app Asst (part-time) at St Andrew's 29 Aug 1996.

1996 KAY GILCHRIST
ord by Presb of Glasgow and introd as Assoc at St Andrew's 15 Feb 1996; dem 24 Jan 1999 on app as Chaplain to Rachel House Children's Hospice, Kinross.

DRUMCHAPEL ST MARK'S (FES X, 218)

1970 ROBERT HOWAT DUNCAN
(FES X, 132, 218, 418), trans from Greenock Cartsburn-Augine to St Mark's 20 Oct 1970; dem 31 Mar 1982.

1983 ROBERT ALASDAIR CALVERT
ord and ind to St Mark's 11 Aug 1983; introd to Rotterdam 1 Aug 1995.

1996 ELIZABETH SMITH
ord and ind to St Mark's 20 Jun 1996.

EAGLESHAM OLD AND CARSWELL (FES X, 142)

1960 ALEXANDER MURDOCH BENNETT
(FES IX, 394; X, 142, 234), trans from Saddell and Carradale to Eaglesham Old and Carswell 12 May 1960; died 30 Jan 1988.

1988 WILLIAM DOUGLAS LINDSAY
B 22 Apr 1939 at Glasgow, s of William Thomson L. and Ellen Baird Millar; educ High School of Glasgow 1952–57; University of Glasgow 1972–77 (BD, CPS); Shipping and Forwarding Agents 1957–72; lic by Presb of Glasgow 30 Jun 1977; asst Glasgow Yoker Old 1973–74, Hyndland 1974–75, Broomhill 1975–77, Dennistoun Central 1977–78; m 4 May 1963 Marjory Edmund Webster b 22 Feb 1939 d of John Sutherland W. and Margaret Robson George; Children: Fiona Margaret b 14 Mar 1964; Kenneth Richard b 1 May 1967 m Marion Blair Donald Cameron; ord and ind to Glasgow Partick South 1 Jun 1978; trans to Eaglesham Old and Carswell 20 Sep 1988.

EASTBANK (FUF 252; FES IX, 266; X, 158)

Linked 4 May 1983 with Carntyne Old.

1972 THOMAS ALASTAIR McLACHLAN
(FES X, 158), ord and ind to Eastbank 15 Jun 1972; trans to Kilsyth Burns and Old 5 Jan 1983.

1983 RONALD ALEXANDER STEPHEN CRAIG
ord and ind to Carntyne Old with Eastbank 23 Aug 1983, see Carntyne Old.

EASTERHOUSE ST GEORGE'S AND ST PETER'S (FES X, 158)

1968 JOHN COOK
(FES X, 158), ord by Presb of Dundee during assistantship at Menzieshill 29 Mar 1967; ind to St George's and St Peter's 27 Aug 1968; trans to Leith St Andrew's 31 Jan 1984.

1984 MALCOLM CUTHBERTSON
B 3 Apr 1956 at Glasgow, s of John Gardner C. and Jean Watson; educ Grangemouth High 1968–74; University of Stirling 1974–77 (BA); University of Aberdeen 1980–83 (BD); University of Edinburgh 1996–; lic by Presb of Falkirk 14 Jun 1983; asst London Crown Court 1983–84; m (1) 13 Apr 1985 Deborah Diane Beaubrun b 8 Mar 1958; Children: David b 12 Apr 1989; m (2) 14 Dec 1992 Catherine Fennel b 22 Jun 1952; ord and ind to St George's and St Peter's 30 Jun 1984; app non-executive Director of Glasgow Dental Hospital and School Trust 1 Apr 1994.

EASTWOOD (FES III, 133; VIII, 183; IX, 267; X, 158)

1960 IAN BRUCE DOYLE
(FES IX, 335; X, 159, 200), trans from Motherwell St Mary's to Eastwood 27 Sep 1960; dem on app as Depute-Secretary, Dept of National Mission 1 Mar 1977.

1977 ARCHIBALD ROBERTSON
(FES X, 171), app Chaplain (part-time) to Royal Hospital for Sick Children, Glasgow 1 Feb 1972;

trans from Glasgow Queen's Park West to East-wood 27 Oct 1977; ret 1 Apr 1999; s John m Catriona Adam.

FERNHILL AND CATHKIN (FES X, 147)

1972   IAN RIDDOCK FISHER
(FES X, 104, 147), trans from Maybole West to Fernhill and Cathkin 19 Oct 1972; dem 7 Aug 1989 on app as Secretary, Board of Stewardship and Finance.

1990   DOUGLAS WOODBURN WALLACE
B 23 Sep 1955 at Greenock, s of Henry Brownlee W. and Margaret Elizabeth Douglas; educ Greenock Academy; University of Edinburgh 1973–80 (MA, BD); lic by Presb of Greenock 29 Jun 1980; asst Glasgow Calton New with St Andrew's 1980–82; m 30 May 1981 Janet Rosalind Lee b 1 Aug 1957 d of Norman L. and Sybil Thorndyke; Children: Ian Gordon b 14 Nov 1982; Andrew David b 20 Aug 1984; ord by Presb of Glasgow during assistantship at Calton New 7 May 1981; ind to Kilmodan and Colintraive 26 May 1982; trans to Fernhill and Cathkin 29 Mar 1990.

GAIRBRAID (FUF 220; FES IX, 268; X, 159)

1971   IAN CAMPBELL MACKENZIE
(FES X, 159), ord by Presb of Glasgow 9 Jul 1970 and ind to Gairbraid 9 Dec 1971; m 28 Apr 1973 Mary Johnstone Thomson b 28 Apr 1941 d of James Hastings T. and Mary Dickson Johnstone; Children: Ruth Anne b 11 Nov 1977; Elspeth Mary b 22 Jun 1979.

GARDNER STREET (FUF 238; FES IX, 269; X, 159)

1924   KENNETH GILLIES
(FUF 238; FES IX, 269; X, 159), ord and ind to Gardner Street 29 May 1924; died 26 Jul 1976.

1977   DAVID MACINNES
(FES X, 397), trans from Kinloch to Gardner Street 8 Apr 1977; trans to Kilmuir and Paible 3 May 1993.

1994   RODERICK MORRISON
(FES X, 396), trans from Stornoway High to Gardner Street 7 Oct 1994; Children: Roderick William b 18 Feb 1980; Muriel Dawn b 28 Sep 1981.

GARTCOSH (FES VIII, 293; IX, 244; X, 144)

Linked 23 Apr 1985 with Glenboig.

1973   JOHN McKENDRY
(FES X, 144, 181, 188, 379), trans from Glasgow Summerfield to Gartcosh 15 Nov 1973; ret 31 Jan 1983; died 25 Aug 1996.

1985   ALEXANDER MAYER FRASER
B 30 Mar 1954 at Nkana, Zambia, s of John Gilles F. and Jessie MacKenzie Mayer; educ Hillhead High, Glasgow 1966–72; University of St Andrews 1972–77 (BD); University of Glasgow 1981–83 (DipMin); Army Officer 1977–81; lic by Presb of Glasgow 27 Mar 1983; asst Milngavie St Paul's 1983–84; m 12 Sep 1981 Susan Marjorie Mac-Gregor b 21 Oct 1957 d of Carrick John M. and May Souter; Children: Morven May b 4 Jan 1988; Ewan John b 16 Oct 1990; Murdo Alexander b 9 Oct 1994; ord and ind to Gartcosh with Glenboig 3 Oct 1985.

GARTHAMLOCK AND CRAIGEND EAST (FES X, 159)

1971   ROBERT FLEMING BROWN
(FES X, 159), ord and ind to Garthamlock and Craigend East 7 Dec 1971; trans to Ayr St Quivox 8 Nov 1978.

1979   GEORGE RUSSELL BARR
ord and ind to Garthamlock and Craigend East 10 Jul 1979; trans to Greenock St Luke's 4 May 1988.

1988   ADAMINA YOUNGER
ind to Garthamlock and Craigend East 2 Nov 1988; trans to Glasgow Dennistoun Central 28 Jan 1996.

1996   VALERIE JUNE DUFF
B 7 Mar 1953 at Dundee, d of William MacLeod D. and Joan Barclay Jamieson; educ Carnoustie High 1965–70; Columbia Seminary 1987–93 (DMin); St Colm's College, Edinburgh 1977–79; Financial Admin 1970–77; Church of Scotland Deaconess 1980–93; ord in Greater Atlanta 23 Jul 1993; ind to Garthamlock and Craigend East 7 Nov 1996.

GIFFNOCK ORCHARDHILL (FUF 207; FES IX, 245; X, 144)

1936   HAMISH CURRIE MACKENZIE
(FUF 306; FES IX, 245, 443; X, 144), trans from Bridge of Allan Chalmers to Orchardhill 4 Jun 1936; ret 30 Jun 1976; died 13 Sep 1980.

1977   JOHN McLAREN SPIERS
(FES X, 122), trans from Barrhead South to Orchardhill 5 Mar 1977; University of Glasgow 1995 (MTh); Children: Jillian Watson McLaren b 17 Jul 1981; Jennifer Diane Young b 25 Feb 1983.

GIFFNOCK SOUTH (FES III, 138; VIII, 239; IX, 245; X, 144)

1949   WILFRID JAMES TOWART
(FES IX, 245; X, 144), res from app with RAChD and ind to Giffnock South 13 Jan 1949; trans to Glasgow Priesthill 3 Nov 1982.

1983   EDWARD VANCE SIMPSON
(FES X, 102), trans from Girvan North to Giffnock
South 29 Jun 1983; app Chaplain (part-time) to
Barlinnie Prison; Addl children: David Vance b 24
Sep 1976; Colin William b 24 Jan 1979; Mhairi
Scott and Emma Hawthorn b 7 Jul 1982.

GIFFNOCK THE PARK (FES X, 144)

1974   MICHAEL GIBSON
(FES X, 144), ord and ind to The Park 25 Oct 1974.

GLENBOIG (FUF 185; FES IX, 328; X, 194)

Linked 23 Apr 1985 with Gartcosh.

1960   CRAWFORD STEVENSON KING
(FES X, 194), ord by Presb of Edinburgh 19 Feb
1958; ind to Glenboig 2 Mar 1960; ret 31 Oct 1984.

1985   ALEXANDER MAYER FRASER
ord and ind to Gartcosh with Glenboig 3 Oct 1985,
see Gartcosh.

GORBALS (FES X, 160)

Formed 31 Jan 1973 by union of Gorbals-John
Knox, Laurieston-Renwick, Abbotsford-Chalmers
and St Ninian's-Wynd.

1949   JAMES DOUGLAS WALLACE
(FES IX, 253, 614; X, 149), trans from Gardens-
town to Abbotsford-Chalmers 14 Sep 1949; ret 30
Nov 1966; died 5 Jul 1984.

1950   JOHN MACKIE BISSET
(FES IX 301, 604; X, 177), res from RAChD and
ind to St Ninian's-Wynd 9 Sep 1950; became
minister of linked charge with Abbotsford-Chalmers
5 Jan 1967; ret 31 Jan 1973; died 16 Mar 1998.

1973   WILLIAM MUIR McPHERSON
(FES X, 107, 160), trans from Ayr The Schaw Kirk
to Gorbals 22 Nov 1973; trans to Auchencairn with
Rerrick 16 Mar 1979.

1979   MARION DAPHNE WALKER SMITH
trans from Cockpen and Carrington with Lasswade
to Gorbals 4 Oct 1979 (compassionate grounds);
trans to Kirkmahoe 6 Sep 1984.

1985   DAVID NEIL McLACHLAN
ord and ind to the Gorbals 5 Jun 1985; trans to
Elderslie Kirk 29 Sep 1994.

1996   WILLIAM G McKAIG
introd as Assoc at Gorbals 31 Oct 1996.

1996   IAN FRANCIS GALLOWAY
B 4 May 1952 at Johnston, s of William G. and
Margaret McKay; educ Hutchesons' Grammar,
Glasgow and George Heriot's, Edinburgh 1961–
70; Heriot-Watt University 1970–73 (BA); University
of Glasgow 1973–76 (BD); lic by Presb of

Edinburgh 4 Jul 1976; asst Edinburgh Old Kirk
1976–78; m (1) 28 Sep 1973 Kathryn Orr b 6 Aug
1952 d of John Fleming O. and Janet Johnston;
Children: David John b 31 Mar 1979; Duncan
Callum b 18 Aug 1981; Helen Catriona b 16 Nov
1983; divorced, m (2) 9 Mar 1996 Julie Ann Gibson
b 5 Oct 1965; Children: Rebecca Amy b 10 May
1998; ord by Presb of Edinburgh during assistantship at the Old Kirk 12 Jun 1977; app National
Youth Adviser, Dept of Education Aug 1978; app
Joint-Warden, Iona Abbey 1 Mar 1983; ind to
Glasgow Lansdowne 8 Dec 1988; dem 31 May
1991; ind to Gorbals 9 May 1996.

GOVAN OLD (FES III, 409; VIII, 293; IX, 270; X,
160)

Formed 7 Oct 1993 by union of Govan Old and
Elder Park Macgregor Memorial.

1960   DAVID CAMPBELL ORR
(FES IX, 473; X, 160, 280), trans from Burntisland
St Columba's to Govan Old 23 Jun 1960; ret 15
Oct 1980; died 27 Feb 1993.

1970   JOHN GILLIES FRASER
(FES IX, 734; X, 159, 166, 419), res from service
with Board of World Mission in Zambia and ind to
Macgregor Memorial 19 May 1960; became
minister of united charge with Elder Park 22 Apr
1970; ret 30 Sep 1986; died 5 Aug 1998; d
Catherine m Peter Nicolson; s Alexander m Susan
McGregor.

1981   WILLIAM JOHN HARVEY
(FES X, 165, 454), trans from Stirling St Mark's to
Govan Old 3 Sep 1981; dem 30 Jun 1988 to take
up app as Leader of Iona Community.

1989   THOMAS ALEXANDER DAVIDSON
KELLY
B 10 Mar 1949 at Edinburgh, s of Frederick Nevill
D. and Mary Lyon Campbell MacLeod; educ
Edinburgh Academy 1956–67; University of
Edinburgh 1967–71 (MA), 1971–74 (BD); lic by
Presb of Edinburgh 10 Jul 1974; asst Dundee St
Mary's 1974–76; m 16 Feb 1980 Kim McArthur b
27 Oct 1949 d of Neil Munro M. and Anne Lavery
Walker; Children: Neil Alexander b 29 Nov 1980;
Campbell Eoin Thomas b 18 Sep 1984; Anne
Frances Ruth b 5 Nov 1986, died 21 Mar 1987;
ord by Presb of Dundee during assistantship at St
Mary's 10 Apr 1975; ind to Kilberry with Tarbert 5
Jul 1976; app by RAChD 5 Jul 1982; ind to Govan
Old 22 Jun 1989; Publ: *The Prebend of Govan:
1150–1560* (Friends of Govan Old, 1994); *What
happened to the Sancta Sanctis?* (Record of
Church Service Society No. 27, 1994); *The Govan
collection in the context of local history* and *The
Partick hogback hunt* in *Govan and its Early
Medieval Sculpture*, ed Anna Ritchie (Alan Sutton,
1994); *'Common Order' (1994): Pioneering spirit
or reflective mode?* in *To Glorify God*, eds Bryan
D Spinks and Iain R Torrance (T&T Clark, 1999).

1989 ALBERT STUART DICKSON
(FES X, 29, 51, 173), res as Assoc at Glasgow Calton New with St Andrew's and introd to Elder Park Macgregor Memorial (term) 22 Jun 1989; introd as Assoc following union with Govan Old 7 Oct 1993; ret 31 Aug 1995; d Fiona m Michael Ford (died 1984).

1996 MICHAEL STANLEY EDWARDS
B 13 Feb 1944 at Glasgow, s of Stanley Frederick E. and Sarah Violet Deans Sibbald; educ Hillhead High and Allan Glen's, Glasgow 1949–60; University of Glasgow 1976–81 (BD); Electronic Engineering and Company Directorships 1961–75; lic by Presb of Glasgow, 1981; asst Glasgow St Margaret's Knightswood 1981–82; m 2 May 1964 Irene Jean Wilson b 26 Apr 1943 d of Percy Alfred and Violet W; Children: Suzanne Fiona b 21 Apr 1966 m Lindsay; James Michael Wilson b 15 Sep 1969 m Kay; ord by Presb of Glasgow and app by RAF Chaplains' Branch 26 Apr 1982; introd as Govan Community minister and Assoc at Govan Old 7 Feb 1996.

GOVANHILL TRINITY (FES X, 154, 160)

Formed 17 May 1989 by union of Govanhill and Candlish-Polmadie (union 12 May 1968 of Candlish Memorial and Polmadie).

1931 ARCHIBALD GLEN
(FUF 69; FES IX, 98, 261; X, 154), trans from Chirnside North to Candlish Memorial 15 Sep 1931; ret 30 Sep 1967; died 4 Jul 1978.

1961 RICHARD PORTER
(FES IX, 52; X, 30, 160), trans from Caldercruix to Govanhill 11 May 1961; ret 30 Jun 1988; d Margaret m Richardson; Publ: '100 Years of Witness and Service' (Govanhill Church, 1980).

1968 ALEXANDER GEORGE ALLAN
(FES X, 154, 263), trans from Cowie to Candlish-Polmadie 6 Sep 1968; ret 17 May 1989; s Stuart died 1988.

1990 TOMAS MICHAL BISEK
B 30 Nov 1939 at Prague, Czech Republic, s of Frantisek B. and Lydie Jurenova; educ Czech Technical Institute, Prague 1957–62; Theological Faculty, Prague 1965–69; Union Theological Seminary, New York 1969–70 (STM); Pastor of the Evangelical Church of the Czech Brethren 1970–82; m 1 Jul 1966 Daniela b 15 Sep 1947; Children: Lucie b 14 Sep 1969; Lukas b 28 Mar 1971; Ester b 17 Dec 1972; Benjamin b 13 Aug 1974; introd as Assoc at Cumbernauld Condorrat 21 Jul 1985; ind to Govanhill Trinity 22 Feb 1990; dem 30 Sep 1996 to return to the Czec Republic; Publ: Articles for *Life and Work* (1988).

1997 SIGRID MARTEN
B 18 Apr 1963 at Boeel, Germany, d of Werner Wilhelm Marten and Helga Esmark; educ Klaus-Harms-Schule, Kappeln, Germany 1973–83; Kirchliche Hochschule Bethel 1983–85; University of Hamburg 1985–91; University of Edinburgh 1994–95 (CPS); lic by Presb of Edinburgh 19 Nov 1995; asst Edinburgh North Leith 1996–97; m 4 Jun 1994; ord and ind to Govanhill Trinity 6 Nov 1997.

GREENBANK (FES III, 138; VIII, 239; IX, 245; X, 144)

1971 ANGUS TAYLOR STEWART
(FES X, 42, 145, 178), trans from Glasgow St Stephen's to Greenbank 30 Mar 1971; ret 10 Aug 1999; Publ: 'Keywords of Faith' (St Andrew Press).

1992 RODERICK GORDON HAMILTON
ord by Presb of Glasgow and introd as Assoc at Greenbank; ind to Clydebank Abbotsford 19 Jun 1996.

1997 FIONA MARGARET ELIZABETH GARDNER
B 15 Jan 1966 at Glasgow, d of Edward Birrill Harrison and Mary Gray; educ Douglas Academy, Milngavie 1977–83; University of Glasgow 1983–87 (MA), 1987–93 (MLitt), 1992–95 (BD); Care Asst, Board of Social Responsibility 1990–92; lic by Presb of Glasgow 12 Feb 1997; asst Glasgow Greenbank; m 25 Jun 1994 Colin Scarle Gardner b 9 Sep 1956 s of Thomas G. and Audrey Rita Scarle; Children: Andrew James b 7 Aug 1999; ord by Presb of Glasgow and app Asst at Greenbank 12 Feb 1997.

1999 ALISTAIR NEIL SHAW
B 6 Jul 1953 at Kilbarchan, s of Alexander Currie S. and Agnes Lyall Mitchell; educ Paisley Grammar 1965–71; University of Glasgow 1971–76 (MA), 1976–79 (BD); lic by Presb of Paisley 28 Jun 1979; asst Edinburgh Liberton 1980–81; m 11 Jul 1983 Brenda Bruce b 20 Feb 1959 d of Robert B. and Aileen Cruickshank McKenna; Children: Alison Elizabeth b 30 Oct 1986; Lindsay Susan b 26 Sep 1989; ord and ind to Irvine Relief Bourtreehill 18 Mar 1982; trans to Kilmarnock the Laigh Kirk 31 Oct 1988; trans to Greenbank 27 Oct 1999.

GREYFRIARS AND ALEXANDRA PARADE (FES IX, 272; X, 161)

Congregation dissolved 30 Sep 1966.

1929 JOHN WARNOCK
(FUF 207; FES IX, 253, 272; X, 161), trans from Crail to Alexandra Parade 12 Sep 1929; became minister of united charge with Garngad 30 Jan 1946 and of united charge with Greyfriars 3 Jun 1951; ret 30 Sep 1966; died 1 May 1981.

HIGH CARNTYNE (FES IX, 272; X, 161)

1954 JAMES MARTIN
(FES IX, 199, 272; X, 161), trans from Newmilns West to High Carntyne 20 Jan 1954; ret 31 Dec 1987; DD (Glasgow) 1983; d Heather m David Cole; d Lesley m Douglas Sommerville; Addl publ: *A Plain Man in the Holy Land* (St Andrew Press, 1978); *People in the Jesus Story* (St Andrew Press, 1980); pop-up books for children (Collins,1978–80); *Listening to the Bible* (St Andrew Press, 1983); *William Barclay: A Personal Memoir* (St Andrew Press, 1984); *My Friend Bobby* (Arthur James, 1989); *Suffering Man, Loving God* (Harper Collins, 1990); *It's You, Minister* (Chapter House, 1990); *It's My Belief* (St Andrew Press, 1991); *Travels in the Holy Land* (Lochar, 1991); *God Collared* (Chapter House, 1992); *William Barclay in a Nutshell* (Handsel Press, 1992); *You Can't be Serious* (Pentland Press, 1995); *More about Bobby* (Chapter House, 1997); *A Parish Minister's Hats* (Chapter House, 1997); *Grit for the Road of Life* (Chapter House, 1998); *Seen from my Manse Window* (Chapter House, 1999); *More Grit for Life's Road* (Chapter House, 1999).

1988 JOHN DAVIDSON HEGARTY
ord and ind to High Carntyne 24 Aug 1988; trans to Cupar St John's 20 Nov 1997.

1998 PETER WILLIAM NIMMO
B 19 Jan 1966 at Dumbarton, s of William N. and Mary Elizabeth Allan; educ Vale of Leven Academy, Alexandria 1977–83; Glasgow College of Technology 1983–85 (SHND Business Studies); University of Glasgow 1987–91 (BD); Princeton Theological Seminary, New Jersey 1991–92 (ThM); Joiner 1985–87; Hospital Porter 1992–94; lic by Presb of Dumbarton 28 Jun 1992; asst Edinburgh St John's Oxgangs 1995–96; m 31 Jul 1993 Katharina Giere b 9 May 1968 d of Walter Gustav Wolfgang G. and Elke Johanna Engelmann; Children: Daniel b 4 Dec 1997; ord by Presb of Edinburgh and introd as Assoc at Currie Kirk 24 Apr 1996; ind to High Carntyne 17 Jun 1998; Publ: *Power without Glory—25 Years on* (*Trinity College Bulletin*, 1992); *Sin, Evil and Job. Monotheism as a Psychological and Pastoral Problem* (*Pastoral Psychology*, USA, Vol 42, No 6, 1994).

HILLINGTON PARK (FUF 214; FES IX, 273; X, 161)

1971 KENNETH MACKENZIE ANDERSON
(FES IX, 728; X, 161), res from service with Overseas Council in N India and Pakistan and ind to Hillington Park 15 Apr 1971; dem 31 Jul 1982.

1983 MORRIS COWPER COULL
(FES X, 105), trans from New Cumnock to Hillington Park 24 Feb 1983; trans to Stirling Allan Park South with Church of the Holy Rude 29 Feb 1996.

1997 IAIN MORRISON
B 29 Oct 1958 at Harris, s of Christina Morrison; educ Sir E Scott School, Tarbert and Nicolson Institute, Stornoway 1970–75; Glasgow College of Building and Printing 1975–77 (OND); University of Glasgow 1985–90 (BD, CPS); Local Authority Technician 1977–83; Insurance Agent 1983–85; lic by Presb of Lewis 4 Jul 1990; asst Bearsden North 1990–91; m 2 Aug 1989 Sheena Morrison b 14 Jan 1957 d of P K Morrison and Williamina MacLeod; Children: Christopher b 31 Jul 1984; Patricia b 7 Mar 1987; ord and ind to Campbeltown Lorne and Lowland 16 May 1991; trans to Hillington Park 14 Jan 1997.

HOUSEHILLWOOD ST CHRISTOPHER'S (FES IX, 214; X, 124)

1975 WILLIAM HOWARD ELLIS
(FES IX, 213; X, 99, 123, 124, 151, 418, 445), trans from Glasgow Barlanark Greyfriars to Househillwood St Christopher's 28 Nov 1975; ret 31 Oct 1980; died 20 Aug 1991.

1981 WILLIAM CLEMENT ROBB
(FES X, 405), dem from Delting 31 Oct 1976; ind to Househillwood St Christopher's 25 Mar 1981; trans to Kilberry with Tarbert 21 Jan 1983.

1983 ALAN KENNETH SORENSEN
B 16 Apr 1957 at Dalmuir, s of Scott Stevenson S. and Mary Norton; educ Hutchesons' Boys' Grammar, Glasgow 1969–74; University of Glasgow 1974–80 (BD, DipMin); University of Edinburgh [part-time] 1991–93 (MTh); Retail Management 1980–82; lic by Presb of Glasgow 26 Jun 1980; asst Glasgow Cathcart South 1982–83; ord and ind to Househillwood St Christopher's 28 Jun 1983.

HUTCHESONTOWN (FES X, 173)

Name changed from Rutherglen Road 1987. Congregation dissolved 30 Sep 1995.

1973 DENIS IAN SUTHERLAND
(FES X, 173), res as minister to travelling people and ind to Rutherglen Road 16 Aug 1973; ret 30 Apr 1995.

HYNDLAND (FES III, 417; VIII, 295; IX, 273; X, 162)

1968 JOHN ANDERSON MACNAUGHTON
(FES IX, 293; X, 162, 173, 203), trans from Uddingston Park to Hyndland 12 Dec 1968; ret 31 Oct 1989; d Margaret m Phillip Burton; s Duncan m Catriona Joss.

1990 JOHN CAIRNS CHRISTIE
B 9 Jul 1947 at Glasgow, s of John Cairns C. and Agnes Ritchie; educ Hermitage Academy, Helensburgh 1959–66; University of Strathclyde

1968–71 (BSc); Paisley College 1975–77 (CBiol, MIBiol); University of Glasgow 1986–89 (BD); Analytical Chemist 1966–68; Teaching 1972–86; lic by Presb of Glasgow 2 Jul 1989; asst Glasgow Mosspark 1989–90; m (1) 16 Sep 1972 Elizabeth McDonald McIntosh b 28 May 1945, died 21 May 1993 d of John M. and Isabella Brisland; Children: Elizabeth Margaret b 4 Apr 1976; m (2) 3 Jan 1995 Annette Cooke Carnegie Evans b 28 May 1944 d of William Hamill and Margaret Carnegie; ord and ind to Hyndland 7 Jun 1990.

IBROX (FUF 228; FES IX, 274; X, 162, 151)

Formed 1 Oct 1978 by union of Bellahouston-Steven and Ibrox.

1964 ROBERT THOMSON BONE
(FES X, 162), ind to Ibrox 3 Dec 1964; dem 1 Sep 1979 on app by Overseas Council for service at Livingstonia, Malawi.

1971 JOHNSTON REID McKAY
(FES X, 151), ind to Bellahouston-Steven 25 Nov 1971; trans to Paisley Abbey 30 May 1978.

1980 CHARLES BLAIR GILLON
(FES X, 125), ord and ind to Kilbarchan East 30 Jul 1975; trans to Ibrox 31 Jan 1980; app Chaplain (part-time) to Barlinnie Prison; w Patience died 21 Nov 1980; m (2) 30 Jun 1983 Linda Smith b 12 Jul 1956 d of Robert S. and Marlene Robertson; Children: Robert Blair b 27 Mar 1985; Blair Hector b 11 Dec 1987; Lucy Charlotte Doris b 13 Mar 1991.

JOHN ROSS MEMORIAL (for Deaf People)

Became Church of Scotland congregation 31 Aug 1983. New building in Gorbals dedicated 28 Sep 1989. Linked 29 Apr 1993 with Rutherglen West. Arrangement terminated 25 Jun 1998.

1982 HUGH BAIRD HANEY
Chaplain to Deaf People, Paisley 1975–82; ind to John Ross Memorial 1982; ret 28 Feb 1991.

1993 JOHN WHITEFORD DRUMMOND
(FES X, 125), trans from Linwood to Rutherglen West 24 Jun 1986; minister of linked charge with John Ross Memorial from 29 Apr 1993 until 25 Jun 1998.

1993 JANETTE BLACK
introd as Assoc at Rutherglen West with John Ross Memorial 29 Apr 1993, see Rutherglen West.

1998 RICHARD DURNO
B 4 Mar 1951 at Aberdeen, s of Kenneth Campbell D. and Margaret Mackie; educ Hilton Secondary, Aberdeen 1963–66; Bible Training Institute, Glasgow 1981–83 (Readers Cert); Church of Scotland Aux Ministry Course 1983–85; Poly-technic of North London (now Univ of N London) 1986–88 (DSW, CQSW); Social Work 1978–98; lic by Presb of Glasgow 26 Jan 1986; m 19 Jun 1982 Linda Elizabeth Adam b 7 Mar 1957 d of William Cairns A. and Evelyn Helen Thiems; Children: Justine Linda b 9 Nov 1988; Meghan Richarda b 4 Nov 1988; ord by Presb of Glasgow during assgn at John Ross Memorial Church for Deaf People 7 May 1989; assgnd to Albany Deaf Church of Edinburgh 1993; assgn terminated Jun 1998, entered full-time ministry; introd as Community minister at John Ross Memorial Church for Deaf People, Glasgow 25 Jun 1998; also app Chaplain to Schools for the Deaf.

JORDANHILL (FUF 229; FES IX, 275; X, 162)

1960 JAMES McMICHAEL ORR
(FES X, 162, 257, 424), trans from Auchterarder St Andrew's and West to Jordanhill 20 May 1960; trans to Aberfoyle 1 Dec 1976.

1977 FINLAY ANGUS JOHN MACDONALD
(FES X, 266), trans from Menstrie to Jordanhill 2 Jun 1977; dem on app as Assoc Principal Clerk to General Assembly 1 May 1996.

1996 COLIN CHARLES RENWICK
B 15 Dec 1962 at Perth, s of Donald R. and Vera Winifred Skett; educ Breadalbane Academy, Aberfeldy 1967–80; University of Glasgow 1980–84 (BMus); University of Aberdeen 1985–88 (BD); lic by Presb of Dunkeld and Meigle 30 Jun 1988; asst Rothesay Trinity 1988–89; m 17 Sep 1994 Eilidh Catriona Halliday b 2 Feb 1962 d of Kenneth Charles Robertson H. and Helen Sim Campbell; ord and ind to Maybole Old 12 Jul 1989; trans to Jordanhill 28 Aug 1996.

KELVIN STEVENSON MEMORIAL (FES X, 162, 181)

Formed 18 Jan 1979 by union of Kelvin (union 30 Jan 1975 of Kelvinside East Park and Wilton) and Stevenson Memorial.

1942 CHARLES DOUGLAS HAMILTON
(FES IX, 314, 544; X, 184), trans from Panbride to Wilton 18 Dec 1942; ret 30 Jan 1975; died 1 Jan 1988.

1956 WILLIAM McAREAVEY
(FES X, 158, 162, 163), ind to East Park 29 Nov 1956; became minister of united charge with Kelvinside Old 18 Oct 1967, of united charge with Wilton 30 Jan 1975 and of united charge with Stevenson Memorial 18 Jan 1979.

KELVINSIDE HILLHEAD (FES X, 152, 163)

Formed 18 May 1978 by union of Kelvinside-Botanic Gardens and Belmont and Hillhead.

1938 ALAN BOYD ROBSON
(FES IX, 275; X, 163), trans from Presb Church of England and ind to Kelvinside-Botanic Gardens 15 Dec 1938; became Collegiate minister of united charge with Belmont and Hillhead 18 May 1978; ret 31 Dec 1978; died 13 Nov 1986.

1959 GEORGE McKENZIE DENNY GRIEVE
(FES IX, 109, 369; X, 152, 221), trans from Helensburgh St Bride's to Belmont and Hillhead 9 Sep 1959; became minister of united charge with Kelvinside-Botanic Gardens 18 May 1978; died 26 Apr 1987.

1987 VALERIE GRACE COWAN WATSON
B 11 May 1949 at Greenock, d of Archibald McAffer W. and Sheila Cowan Stewart; educ Woodside Secondary, Glasgow and Coatbridge High 1961–66; University of Glasgow 1966–70 (MA), 1982–85 (BD); Union Theological Seminary, New York 1986–87 (STM); Teaching 1970–71; Local Government Careers Service 1971–82; lic by Presb of Paisley 27 Jun 1985; asst Glasgow Knightswood St Margaret's 1985–86; ord and ind to Kelvinside Hillhead 22 Oct 1987; dem 30 Sep 1999 to take up full-time study.

KENMUIR MOUNT VERNON (FES III, 265; VIII, 261; IX, 322; X, 197)

Linked 22 Feb 1978 with Carmyle.

1947 WILLIAM MARTIN
(FES IX, 332, 742; X, 197), res as Missionary Professor of English, Wilson College, Bombay and ind to Kenmuir Mount Vernon 27 Nov 1947; ret 30 Sep 1973; died 4 Nov 1994.

1974 HERBERT MARSHALL GIBSON
(FES X, 197, 229), ind to Kenmuir Mount Vernon 24 Apr 1974; became minister of linked charge with Carmyle 22 Feb 1978; trans to Glasgow St Thomas' Gallowgate 29 Apr 1982.

1982 JAMES McBRIDE DAVIES
ord and ind to Carmyle with Kenmuir Mount Vernon 25 Nov 1982; trans to Aberdeen St Stephen's 22 Feb 1989.

1989 WILLIAM BRUCE McDOWALL
ord and ind to Carmyle with Kenmuir Mount Vernon 25 Aug 1989; trans to Uddingston Park 4 Mar 1999.

1999 MURDO MACLEAN
ind to Carmyle with Kenmuir Mount Vernon 4 Nov 1999, see Carmyle.

KENT ROAD ST VINCENT'S (FES IX, 276; X, 163)

Congregation dissolved 31 Jul 1977.

1972 ALEXANDER THOMAS HAIN TAYLOR
(FES IX, 751; X, 57, 163, 426), res from United Theological College, Kingston, Jamaica and ind to St Vincent's 12 Apr 1972; dem 31 Jul 1977; introd to Dunoon St Cuthbert's (term) 1 Jun 1978.

KILSYTH ANDERSON (FUF 50; FES IX, 245; X, 145)

1968 JAMES ROSS
(FES X, 145), ord and ind to Anderson 22 Apr 1968; ret 31 Oct 1998; d Christine m Frank; s David m Alison.

1999 CHARLES MACDONALD MACKINNON
B 10 Feb 1954 at Kuala Lumpur, Malaya, s of Lachlan and Mary Flora M.; educ Oban High 1966–72; Central College of Commerce, Glasgow 1972–73; University of Glasgow 1983–88 (BD, CMin); Banking 1973–83; lic by Presb of Glasgow 5 Jul 1988; asst Glasgow St James' Pollock 1988–89; m 29 Jun 1985 Catherine Calder Brims b 19 Oct 1953 d of George Douglas B. and Barbara Irving Swanson Calder; Children: Mairi Brims b 14 Jan 1987; Andrew Charles b 14 Mar 1989; ord and ind to Urray and Kilchrist 10 Aug 1989; trans to Anderson 25 Aug 1999.

KILSYTH BURNS AND OLD (FES X, 145)

Formed 23 Feb 1975 by union of Kilsyth Burns and Kilsyth Old.

1966 WILLIAM FRASER WILLS
(FES IX, 296, 357, 371, 555; X, 145, 180, 222), trans from Glasgow Springburn Hill to Kilsyth Burns 28 Sep 1966; ret 30 Sep 1974.

1975 DAVID HENRY ALEXANDER WATSON
(FES X, 145), trans under mutual eligibility from Harmony Hill, Lambeg (Presb Church in Ireland) and ind to Burns and Old 25 Jun 1975; introd to Anstruther (term) 29 Jun 1982.

1983 THOMAS ALASTAIR McLACHLAN
(FES X, 158), trans from Glasgow Eastbank to Burns and Old 5 Jan 1983; Children: Donald Alasdair b 30 Apr 1975; Kenneth Edward b 17 Aug 1977.

KING'S PARK (FES IX, 276; X, 163)

1968 JAMES HOSIE
(FES X, 134, 163, 257), trans from Greenock St George's to King's Park 26 Sep 1968; trans to Ayr St Andrew's 30 Aug 1978.

1979 GEORGE STEWART SMITH
(FES X, 223), trans from Renton Trinity to King's Park 22 Mar 1979.

KINNING PARK (FES X, 164)

Formed 19 Nov 1978 by union of Cessnock, Kinning Park and St Andrew's Plantation.

1948 ROBERT HAMILTON PORTER
(FES IX, 102, 285, 458), trans from Greenlaw Fairbairn Memorial to Paisley Road 17 Nov 1948 (united 8 Jun 1958 with White Memorial as Cessnock); dem 30 Nov 1951; died 9 Apr 1989.

1969 ADRIAN HAY STEPHEN
(FES IX, 294, 606; X, 164, 355), dem from Boharm and introd on term app to Kinning Park 27 Nov 1969; ret 31 Jul 1978; died 29 Jan 1996.

1975 JOHN MACLEAN
(FES IX, 131; X, 10, 11, 76, 173, 204), res from Wishaw Craigneuk (term) and introd to St Andrew's Plantation 9 Oct 1975 (term); ret 20 Apr 1977.

1981 ROBIN DUNLOP McHAFFIE
res from Glasgow Trinity College Calton Mission and ind to Kinning Park 1 Jun 1981; trans to Linton with Morebattle and Hownam with Yetholm 25 Aug 1991.

1991 STEWART JACKSON LAMONT
(FES X, 456), ind to Kinning Park 2 Dec 1991; dem 31 May 1999 on app as Executive Secretary, Church and Society Commission, Conference of European Churches, Brussels.

KIRKINTILLOCH HILLHEAD (FES IX, 246; X, 145)

1956 THOMAS BOYD MILLER
(FES IX, 360, 712, 715, 716; X, 145, 215), trans from Bowling to Hillhead 9 Oct 1956; ret 5 Apr 1977; died 1 Jan 1989.

1977 GEORGE ANDERSON ROSS FORBES
(FES X, 156), trans from Glasgow Cowlairs-Somerville to Hillhead 27 Sep 1977; Addl children: Alice Helen b 5 Feb 1979.

KIRKINTILLOCH ST COLUMBA'S (FES X, 146)

1976 WILLIAM GRAY
(FES X, 270), trans from Ballingry to St Columba's 24 Aug 1976; trans to Irvine Relief Bourtreehill 25 Mar 1992.

1992 DAVID McMASTER WHITE
B 28 Feb 1950 at Glasgow, s of James W. and Margaret Purvis; educ Victoria Drive Secondary, Glasgow 1961–66; University of Strathclyde 1971–75 (BA); Baptist Theological College of Scotland 1975–78 (Dip); University of London 1975–78 (BD); Insurance Underwriter 1966–71; asst Bishopbriggs Springfield 1991–92; m 3 Jul 1987 Anne Wallace Fyte b 22 Aug 1960 d of John F. and Anne Porteous; Children: Emma Elizabeth b 20 May 1989; David Fyfe b 17 Mar 1991; Bethany Margaret b 12 Oct 1994; ord by Baptist Union of Scotland and ind to Falkirk Baptist Church 16 Jan 1988; admitted by General Assembly 1991; ind to St Columba's 1 Oct 1992.

KIRKINTILLOCH ST DAVID'S MEMORIAL PARK (FES X, 145, 146)

Formed 16 May 1991 by union of Kirkintilloch St David's Memorial and Kirkintilloch Park (linked with Torrance 19 Mar 1983 until 13 May 1990).

1938 ALEXANDER KING MACKAY
(FES IX, 246; X, 145), ord and ind to Park 24 Jun 1938; ret 30 Sep 1976; died 11 Mar 1997.

1964 ARTHUR WILLIAM ALEXANDER MAIN
(FES X, 146, 301), trans from Dundee Douglas and Angus to St David's Memorial 3 Jun 1964; dem 30 Sep 1970 to enter teaching profession; s John m Selamawit Germai; d Pamela m Ammar Zwain; d Kathryn m Stuart Alexander Clark.

1971 WILLIAM JOHN MACLEOD
(FES X, 146, 241), trans from Tiree to St David's Memorial 16 Jun 1971; ret 1 Sep 1988; d Christeen m Lavery; s Neil m Gardner.

1977 DAVID STEWART
ord and ind to Park 4 Aug 1977; became minister of linked charge with Torrance 19 Mar 1983; trans to Cambuslang Trinity St Paul's 30 Aug 1989.

1989 JOHN HAY PATERSON
B 13 Jun 1935 at Glasgow, s of James Gibson P. and Jean Watt Hay; educ Hutchesons' Grammar 1940–52; University of Glasgow 1972–76 (BD); Fireplaces and Heating Business 1952–72; lic by Presb of Glasgow 25 Jun 1976; asst East Kilbride Claremont 1976–77; m 3 Nov 1956 Ishbel Marian Mitchell b 22 Jul 1934 d of David M. and Margaret Robb; Children: Jacqueline Anne b 5 Feb 1958; Jennifer Jane b 22 Jun 1960 m Robert Anderson; Christine Gillian b 6 Jun 1962; ord and ind to Airdrie Flowerhill 2 Jun 1977; trans to St David's Memorial 23 Feb 1989; became minister of united charge with Park 16 May 1991.

KIRKINTILLOCH ST MARY'S (FES III, 481; VIII, 309; IX, 247; X, 146)

1947 FRANK HAUGHTON
(FES IX, 247, 478; X, 146), trans from Kirkcaldy Gallatown to St Mary's 9 Sep 1947; s Frank m Marilyn; s Gillies m Moreen.

KNIGHTSWOOD ST MARGARET'S (FES VIII, 279; IX, 371; X, 222)

Formed 2 Jun 1982 by union of Knightswood St Margaret's and Netherton St Matthew's.

1965 THOMAS DOUGLAS ALLSOP
(FES X, 222, 322 (2)), trans from Kirriemuir St Andrew's to Knightswood St Margaret's 2 Sep 1965; trans to Aberdeen Beechgrove 13 Jan 1977.

1973 EVERETT JOHN PATON
(FES X, 119, 167, 371), trans from Erchless to Netherton St Matthew's 20 Dec 1973; ret 31 Jul 1980; died 23 May 1990.

1977 DAVID WILLIAM LACY
ord by Presb of Edinburgh during assistantship at St George's West 4 Apr 1976; ind to Knightswood

St Margaret's 28 Jun 1977; became minister of united charge with Netherton St Matthew's 2 Jun 1982; trans to Kilmarnock Henderson 12 Jan 1989.

1989   ANDREW PAXTON LEES
B 26 Nov 1951 at Glasgow, s of James Grahame L. and Helen Elizabeth Paxton; educ Dundee High and Daniel Stewart's College, Edinburgh 1964–68; University of Edinburgh 1978–83 (BD); Motor Retail: Service Supervisor 1968–77; Parts Manager 1977–78; lic by Presb of Edinburgh 3 Jul 1983; asst Peebles Old with Eddleston with Lyne and Manor 1983–84; m 26 Apr 1975 Carole Mattocks b 25 Dec 1953 d of William M. and Muriel Mitchell; Children: Kirstine b 7 May 1982; Calum b 30 Dec 1983; ord by Presb of Melrose and Peebles and introd as Assoc at Peebles Old with Eddleston with Lyne and Manor 5 Sep 1984; ind to Gourock Ashton 19 Nov 1987; trans to St Margaret's 15 Jun 1989.

LANGSIDE (FES X, 151, 164)

Formed 27 Mar 1975 by union of Langside Old and Battlefield Erskine (union 24 Nov 1971 of Battlefield West and Erskine Rose). Name changed 10 May 1983 from Langside and Battlefield Erskine to Langside.

1937   STANLEY CRAIG MUNRO
(FES IX, 72, 257; X, 151), trans from Innerleithen Craigside to Battlefield West 14 May 1937; became minister of united charge with Erskine Rose 24 Nov 1971; ret 31 Oct 1973; died 3 May 1983.

1974   JOHN DURHAM ROSS
(FES X, 151, 164), admitted by General Assembly 1974 and ind to Battlefield Erskine 6 Jun 1974; became minister of united charge with Langside Old 27 Mar 1975; dem on app as Industrial Chaplain for Dundee 31 Jan 1985.

1985   GEORGE JAMES WHYTE
trans from Kilchrenan and Dalavich with Muckairn to Langside 25 Jun 1985; trans to Edinburgh Colinton 8 Apr 1992.

1992   ELIZABETH JOAN ELLIOT McINTYRE
trans from Darvel Irvine Bank and Easton Memorial to Langside 10 Sep 1992; died 8 Aug 1997.

1998   JOHN OWAIN AB IFOR JONES
B 16 May 1957 at St Asaph, Wales, s of John Ifor J. and Lily Eirwen; educ Syr Hugh Owen, Caernarfon 1970–75; University of St Andrews 1979 (MA); University of London 1995 (BD); Fellow of Society of Antiquaries of Scotland 1993; m 27 May 1988 Carolyn Mary Healy b 4 Feb 1954 d of John Patrick H. and Mary Aloysius Luby; ord by Union of Welsh Independents 1 Oct 1981; admitted by General Assembly 1987; introd as Assoc at Mearns 1988; ind to Arnsheen Barrhill with Colmonell 4 Apr 1990; trans to Langside 27 May 1998.

LANSDOWNE (FES X, 165)

1976   WILLIAM JAMES CHRISTMAN
(FES X, 20, 165), trans from Glasgow Lochwood to Lansdowne 26 Nov 1976; trans to Ayr St Columba 3 Jun 1981.

1981   JOHN LEANDER MILLAR
ord and ind to Lansdowne 24 Oct 1981; trans to Duncansburgh with Kilmonivaig 24 Sep 1987.

1988   IAN FRANCIS GALLOWAY
Joint-Warden, Iona Abbey 1983–88; ind to Lansdowne 8 Dec 1988; dem 31 May 1991; ind to Gorbals 9 May 1996.

1992   ROY JAMES MURRAY HENDERSON
B 21 Mar 1963 at Paisley, s of Norman Murray H. and Elizabeth Marion Harvey; educ Garnock Academy 1973–79; University of Glasgow 1981–84 (BD), 1984–86 (DipMin); lic by Presb of Ardrossan 2 Jul 1986; asst Edinburgh Old Kirk 1986–87; m 1 Jul 1987 Jane Catherine Elizabeth Wilson b 3 Aug 1964 d of Thomas W. and Jean Allan; Children: Jennifer Mhairi b 10 Jul 1990; James Allan b 22 Jun 1994; ord and ind to Alexandria St Andrew's 28 Oct 1987; trans to Lansdowne 24 Jun 1992.

LENZIE OLD (FES III, 486; VIII, 310; IX, 248; X, 146)

1949   JOHN CRAWFORD
(FES IX, 248, 653; X, 146), trans from Inverness Merkinch St Mark's to Lenzie Old 7 Sep 1949; ret 30 Sep 1970; died 7 Dec 1985.

1971   ALEXANDER FISHER FLEMING
(FES X, 146, 280), trans from Buckhaven St Michael's to Lenzie Old 16 Apr 1971; trans to Strathblane 26 Jan 1983.

1984   DONALD PIRIE
(FES X, 207), trans from Carstairs with Carstairs Junction to Lenzie Old 2 Feb 1984; trans to Bolton and Saltoun with Humbie with Yester 12 Aug 1999.

LENZIE UNION (FUF 263; FES IX, 248; X, 146)

1923   EDWIN BAIN MACLURE
(FUF 263; FES IX, 248; X, 146), trans from Dumbarton Bridgend to Lenzie Union 1 Jun 1923; ret 30 Sep 1961; died 25 Apr 1982.

1962   DAVID WILSON ORROCK
(FES IX, 318; X, 146, 159, 187), trans from Finnieston to Lenzie Union 27 Mar 1962; ret 30 Sep 1983; died 24 Jan 1999.

1984   JAMES BAILLIE FERGUSON
(FES X, 105), trans from Old Cumnock Old to Lenzie Union 19 Jun 1984; Addl children: Angus b 30 Aug 1978; s Gregor m Kathryn Tyson.

LINTHOUSE ST KENNETH'S (FES X, 165, 176)

Formed 2 May 1976 by union of Linthouse and St Kenneth's.

1949 THOMAS LEE LOW
(FES IX, 298, 352; X, 176), ind to St Kenneth's 12 Jan 1949; ret 2 May 1976; died 5 Apr 1978.

1976 GRAHAM KEITH BLOUNT
ord and ind to Linthouse St Kenneth's 28 Sep 1976; trans to Bridge of Allan Chalmers and also app Chaplain (part-time) to University of Stirling 12 Oct 1983.

1984 ANNE JESSIE McINROY HARPER
res as Education Field Officer, Dept of Education and ind to Linthouse St Kenneth's 6 Jun 1984; dem on app as Chaplain to Glasgow Royal Infirmary 1 Dec 1990.

1991 JAMES MACFARLANE
B 15 Sep 1946 at Bellshill, s of James M. and Mary Muirhead; educ Wishaw High; University of St Andrews 1972–76 (MTh), 1976–80 (PhD); Teaching 1980–89; lic by Presb of St Andrews 1 Jul 1990; asst St Andrews St Leonard's 1990–91; m (1) 20 Mar 1976 Eve Milne b 23 May 1939 d of James M. and Helen Scott; m (2) 27 Jul 1998 Jean Thomson b 23 Oct 1936 d of George T. and Agnes Irving; Children from previous marriage: Janet Moss b 31 Aug 1963; Matthew Moss b 17 May 1967; ord and ind to Linthouse St Kenneth's 13 Nov 1991.

LOCHWOOD (FES X, 165)

1970 WILLIAM JAMES CHRISTMAN
(FES X, 20, 165), trans from Edinburgh Richmond Craigmillar to Lochwood 23 Mar 1970; trans to Glasgow Lansdowne 26 Nov 1976.

1977 IAIN McCORMICK GORING
ord by Presb of Dumbarton during assistantship at Milngavie St Luke's 1 Feb 1976; ind to Lochwood 3 Jun 1977; trans to Callander 6 Jun 1985.

1986 HUGH FINDLAY WATT
ord and ind to Lochwood 13 Jan 1986; trans to Urquhart and Glenmoriston 11 Jan 1996.

1996 KEITH McLEOD STEVEN
res as Assoc at Glasgow Renfield St Stephen's and ind to Lochwood 9 Sep 1996; dem 8 Apr 1997.

1997 STUART MATTHEW DUFF
B 10 Apr 1954 at Edinburgh, s of Matthew D. and Florence Winifred Turland; educ Bo'ness Academy 1966–69; Bible Training Institute 1974–77 (Dip); Glasgow Bible College 1992–94 (BA); University of Edinburgh 1994–96; Plumber 1969–74; Church Asst 1977–79; Missionary (Philippines) 1979–92; lic by Presb of Falkirk 30 Jul 1996; asst Grangemouth Zetland 1996–97; m 2 Jul 1977 Irene Violet Aitken b 8 Feb 1948 d of Robert A. and Anne

Kingston; Children: Jonathan Andrew b 9 Nov 1980; Stephen Matthew b 5 Aug 1984; ord and ind to Lochwood 17 Dec 1997.

MARTYRS', THE (FES X, 166)

1962 GEORGE MEARNS STEVENSON
(FES IX, 635, 765; X, 166, 224), trans from Rosneath St Modan's to The Martyrs' 3 Sep 1962; ret 30 Sep 1984; died 1 Apr 1996.

1985 ELAINE HEATHER MACRAE
ord and ind to The Martyrs' 26 Sep 1985; dem 31 Jan 1994.

1995 EWEN MACLEAN
B 20 Mar 1964 at Harris, s of Donald Allan M. and Dolina Campbell; educ Sir E Scott School, Harris and Nicolson Institute, Stornoway 1969–82; University of Paisley 1985–88 (BA); University of Glasgow 1988–91 (BD); lic by Presb of Lewis 28 Jun 1991; asst Glasgow Chryston 1991–93; m 30 Mar 1995 Audrey Wilson b 9 Jun 1973 d of John W. and Linda McNeill; ord and ind to The Martyrs' 1 Feb 1995.

MARYHILL (FES X, 166)

Maryhill High linked 24 Sep 1986 with Maryhill Old. Congregations united 5 May 1998.

1949 DAVID THOMSON HISLOP
(FES IX, 130, 281; X, 166), trans from Annan Erskine to Maryhill High 27 Apr 1949; ret 1 May 1983; died 9 Sep 1999.

1960 WILLIAM CADZOW McCORMICK
(FES IX, 223, 377; X, 128, 166), trans from Paisley Oakshaw West to Maryhill Old 2 Mar 1960; ret 30 Sep 1983; d Janice m Urquhart; d Christine m Gray; Publ: *Selected Poems* (private, 1989).

1987 ANTHONY JOHN DOUGLAS CRAIG
B 28 Aug 1942 at Glasgow, s of John Sommerville C. and Agnes Marbank Marshall; educ Gordonstoun 1956–60; University of Aberdeen 1981–86 (BD); Full-time voluntary work with The Oxford Group/Moral Re-armament 1960–81; lic by Presb of Gordon 6 Jul 1986; asst Aberdeen Northfield 1986–87; m 12 Jan 1974 Anne Mary Wood b 17 May 1949 d of Alexander Lawson W. and Mary Walford Wilson; Children: Edith Dron b 4 Sep 1979; Jenny-Anne Lawson b 1 Jul 1983; John Marshall b 3 Nov 1985; Iona Stewart b 9 Mar 1990; ord and ind to Maryhill High with Maryhill Old 3 Sep 1987; became minister of united charge 5 May 1998.

1988 MARGARET HENDRY JOHNSTON
B 21 May 1958 at Glasgow, d of Thomas J. and Margaret White Hendry; educ Knightswood Secondary, Glasgow 1970–75; Jordanhill College, Glasgow 1975–78 (DPEd); University of Edinburgh 1981–85 (BD); lic by Presb of Glasgow 1 Jul 1985;

asst Glasgow Govan Old 1985–86; ord by Presb of Glasgow and introd as Assoc at Maryhill High with Maryhill Old 24 Mar 1988.

MAXWELL MEARNS CASTLE (FES X, 146)

1969 WILLIAM ARBUCKLE
(FES IX, 327, 364; X, 146, 202, 217), trans from Strathaven Avendale Old to Maxwell Mearns Castle 30 Oct 1969; dem 30 Sep 1981.

1982 ALEXANDER McKINNON ROGER
ord and introd on term app to Mearns Castle 30 Sep 1982; res 2 Nov 1992 on app as National Chaplain to Scottish Prison Service.

1993 DAVID CRAIG CAMERON
B 4 Dec 1956 at Paisley, s of Evan C. and Irene Alison Craig; educ Penilee Secondary, Glasgow 1969–74; Glasgow College of Building and Printing (part-time) 1974–80 (HNC, IQS); University of Glasgow 1987–92 (BD); Quantity Surveying 1974–87; lic by Presb of Glasgow 26 Jun 1992; asst Glasgow Carnwadric 1992; m 12 Oct 1979 Lesley Marjory Allan b 27 Feb 1955 d of James Kennedy A. and Christina Smith Blackwood; Children: Lyndsay Gillian b 11 Aug 1982; Matthew David b 22 Aug 1984; Mark Allan b 20 May 1987; ord and ind to Maxwell Mearns Castle 24 Jun 1993.

MEARNS (FES III, 154; VIII, 242; IX, 248; X, 146)

1960 DAVID ANDERSON BLACK
(FES IX, 486; X, 146, 168, 289), trans from Glasgow Partick Old to Mearns 15 May 1960; trans to Cleish 25 Oct 1978.

1979 RODERICK DUNCAN McKENZIE CAMPBELL
B 1 Aug 1943 at Glasgow, s of Thomas Gemmell C. and Frances Alexandrina Campbell MacKenzie; educ Daniel Stewart's, Edinburgh and Arbroath High 1949–61; Jordanhill College, Glasgow 1963–66 (Diploma Tech Subjects); University of Edinburgh 1970–74 (BD); Teaching 1966–70; lic by Presb of Angus 10 Jul 1974; asst Drumchapel Old 1974–75; m 10 Sep 1977 Susan Norman b 22 Sep 1949 d of Thomas Arthur N. and Sheila Mabel Gill; Children: Catriona Frances Gill b 8 Nov 1979; Sheona Margaret b 22 Mar 1982; ord by Presb of Angus and app by Board of World Mission for service at St Andrew's, Nairobi, Kenya 1 Jun 1975; ind to Mearns 1 Jun 1979; dem 30 Sep 1997; loc ten Glasgow Ruchazie 1997–99, loc ten Glasgow Eastwood 1999; app Chairman, Victoria NHS Trust 1 Jan 1997; Chaplain TA 1980–99; TD 1992 and Bar 1998; Publ: *Kirk and Party* (private, 1988); *Challenge to Change—Theology in Scotland* (Univ of St Andrews, 1997).

1988 JOHN OWAIN AB IFOR JONES
admitted by General Assembly 1987; introd as Assoc at Mearns 1988; ind to Arnsheen Barrhill with Colmonell 4 Apr 1990.

1998 JOSEPH ANTHONY KAVANAGH
B 27 Jan 1957 at Glasgow, s of James John K. and Mary Gronan; educ St Mirin's Academy, Paisley 1968–73; University of St Andrews 1986–91 (BD, DipPTh); Accounts 1979–81; Car Factory Worker 1977–79; lic by Presb of St Andrews 3 Jul 1991; m 30 Jun 1980 Mary Pamela McMillan b 18 Aug 1954 d of John M. and Catherine Hayes; Children: Jason Robert b 17 Dec 1972; Deborah Anne b 26 Apr 1979; Judith Mary b 1 Feb 1985; Benjamin James b 6 Mar 1987; ord and ind to Girvan North 25 Feb 1992; trans to Mearns 28 May 1998.

MERRYLEA (FES III, 425; VIII, 298; IX, 281; X, 167)

1950 IRONSIDE SIMPSON
(FES IX, 64, 281, 504; X, 167), trans from Broughty Ferry East to Merrylea 15 Mar 1950; ret 31 May 1974; died 23 Sep 1983.

1974 ERNEST ROSS DUNCAN SMART
(FES X, 167, 206), trans from Carluke Kirkton to Merrylea 21 Nov 1974; dem 31 Aug 1981 and emigrated to USA.

1982 SIDNEY HALL COLEMAN
(FES X, 136), trans from Greenock Wellpark West to Merrylea 25 Feb 1982; s Malcolm m Susan Heywood.

MILTON OF CAMPSIE (see X, 142)

Former Mission Church of Campsie High. Raised to full status 26 May 1964 and linked with Campsie Trinity 21 Jun 1964. Linkage terminated 31 May 1978.

1972 EUPHEMIA HELEN CLOUSTON IRVINE
(FES X, 142), ord and ind to Campsie Trinity with Milton of Campsie 1 Jun 1972; continued as minister of Milton of Campsie following termination of linkage with Trinity 31 May 1978; ret 28 Aug 1988.

1988 DIANE ELIZABETH STEWART
B 7 Dec 1946 at Glasgow, d of William Thomson S. and Elizabeth Struthers Jarvie; educ Albert Senior Secondary, Glasgow 1959–63; University of Glasgow 1982–87 (BD, CMin); Shorthand Typist 1963–64; Civil Service 1964–82; lic by Presb of Glasgow 2 Jul 1987; asst Bishopbriggs Springfield Cambridge 1987–88; ord and ind to Milton of Campsie 9 Nov 1988.

MOSSPARK (FES VIII, 244; IX, 282; X, 167)

1975 DAVID MACKIE
(FES X, 167, 360, 422), trans from Keith St Rufus to Mosspark 6 Nov 1975; trans to Strachur and Strathlachlan 11 Feb 1981.

1981 DONALD KEITH
(FES IX, 123), res from app with Royal Naval Chaplaincy Service 14 Apr 1981 and ind to Mosspark 7 Jun 1981; dem 14 May 1984 and re-app by RNCS.

1984 DUNCAN MUIR McLAREN
(FES X, 172), trans from Prestwick Kingcase to Mosspark 18 Oct 1984; Geneva College 1984 (PhD); m 2 Jul 1978 Irene MacDonald Bruce b 10 Jul 1947 d of Thomas Laidlaw B. and Catherine MacDonald; Children: Kirsten Irene b 18 Dec 1979; Morag Rhona b 16 Mar 1981; Fraser Muir b 31 Oct 1984; Publ: *A Holy Land Tour Booklet* (private, 1993).

MOUNT FLORIDA (FUF 233; FES IX, 282; X, 167)

1975 PETER NEILSON
(FES X, 167), ord and ind to Mount Florida 10 Jan 1975; dem on app as National Organiser for Evangelism 1 Jun 1986.

1987 HUGH MAXWELL WALLACE
B 30 Apr 1953 at Glasgow, s of Maxwell Dewar W. and Annie Muriel Williams; educ Glasgow Academy 1958–71; University of Glasgow 1973–77 (BD), 1977–79 (MA); Quantity Surveying 1971–73; lic by Presb of Glasgow 5 Jul 1979; asst Elgin St Giles' 1979–81; m 18 Aug 1979 Elizabeth Rae Tran b 22 Aug 1957 d of Andrew Smith T. and Elizabeth Reid; Children: David Tran b 5 Dec 1984; Hugh Alasdair b 4 Sep 1986; Andrew Maxwell b 11 Feb 1990; ord by Presb of Moray during assistantship at Elgin St Giles' 17 Feb 1980; ind to Carluke Kirkton 17 Jun 1981; trans to Mount Florida 12 Feb 1987.

NETHERLEE (FUF 233; FES IX, 248; X, 147)

1947 STANLEY DAVID MAIR
(FES IX, 248; X, 147), res from RAChD and ind to Netherlee 18 Apr 1947; died 1 Aug 1976.

1977 ANDREW DAVID KELTIE ARNOTT
(FES X, 48, 49), trans from Gorebridge to Netherlee 12 May 1977; trans to St Andrews Hope Park 5 Dec 1996.

1997 IAN ROBERT BOYD
B 29 Nov 1961 at Ayr, s of Andrew Graham B. and Margaret Kirkland; educ Prestwick Academy 1973–78; University of Glasgow 1981–88 (MA, BD); University of Edinburgh 1991–; lic by Presb of Ayr 13 Jul 1988; asst Glasgow Knightswood St Margaret's 1988–89; m 13 Jul 1985 Carolyn Templeton; Children: Hannah Margaret b 19 Jun 1989; Michael Robert b 20 Feb 1991; ord and ind to Perceton and Dreghorn 16 May 1989; dem 31 Aug 1992; ind to Netherlee 28 May 1997; Publ: *What are the Clergy For?* (SPCK, 1995).

1998 JENNIFER MACRAE
B 10 Apr 1954 at Glasgow, d of Gordon Milne and Margaret Kirkpatrick Smith; educ Hillhead High,

Glasgow 1966–72; Unversity of Glasgow 1972–75 (MA), 1994–97 (BD); Teaching 1976–81; Computer Training 1984–93; lic by Presb of Glasgow 3 Jul 1997; asst Glasgow Wellington 1997–98; m 28 Dec 1977 James Stewart Macrae b 9 Sep 1948 s of James M. and Helen MacLean Stewart; Children: Laura Susan b 9 Sep 1981; Elaine Jennifer b 11 Jul 1985; ord by Presb of Glasgow and app Asst at Netherlee 1 Dec 1998.

NEW CATHCART (FUF 234; FES IX, 283; X, 168)

1923 JOHN ADAMSON FINLAY
(FUF 234; FES IX, 283; X, 168), ord and ind to New Cathcart 8 Nov 1923; ret 23 Nov 1958; died 23 Mar 1978.

1959 SAMUEL McCRORIE AITKENHEAD
(FES IX, 139; X, 83, 168), trans from Dalbeattie Park to New Cathcart 22 Jun 1959; ret 31 Oct 1981; died 11 Jun 1995.

1982 DUNCAN WILLIAM McINTOSH ANDERSON
trans from Ayton with Burnmouth to New Cathcart 1 Sep 1982; suspended 1987.

1988 JOHN MURNING
ord and ind to New Cathcart 31 Aug 1988; dem 13 Jun 1999 on app by RAChD.

NEW GOVAN (FES X, 174, 176, 177)

Formed 14 Apr 1982 by union of Govan Trinity (union 16 Sep 1976 of St Columba Summertown and St Kiarian's Dean Park) and St Mary's Fairfield.

1937 THOMAS MOFFAT MURCHISON
(FES IX, 294, 687; X, 174 (2)), trans from Glenelg to St Columba Copland Road 18 Nov 1937; became minister of united charge with Summer-town 20 Jan 1966; ret 5 Aug 1972; died 9 Jan 1984.

1940 DAVID WEBSTER McMURTRIE
(FES IX, 308, 511; X, 181), trans from Mid Craigie to Summertown 26 Jan 1940; ret 31 Jan 1965; d Kathleen m Holmes; d Elizabeth m Starritt.

1946 ROBERT JAMES FENTON
(FES IX, 161, 298; X, 176), trans from Stoneykirk to St Kiarian's Dean Park 22 Jan 1946; ret 16 Sep 1976.

1947 KENNETH STEWART
(FES IX, 268, 379; X, 159), res as Port Chaplain, Port of Glasgow and ind to Fairfield 17 Apr 1947; ret 1 May 1975; died 25 Sep 1987.

1954 ROBERT EASTON
(FES IX, 299, 323, 606; X, 177 (2)), trans from Glasgow Cambuslang West to St Mary's Govan 12 Dec 1954; became minister of united charge with Fairfield 1 May 1975 and of united charge with Govan Trinity 14 Apr 1982; ret 31 Oct 1988; died 23 Nov 1992.

1974 DAVID McCLURE MITCHELL
(FES X, 174, 192, 267), trans from Plean to St Columba Summertown 1 May 1974; became minister of united charge with St Kiaran's Dean Park 16 Sep 1976; ret 30 Sep 1981; died 14 Dec 1985.

1989 JOHN PATRICK WRIGHT
B 17 Jan 1940 at Ambala, Punjab, India, s of David Patrick W; educ Loretto School, Musselburgh; University of Glasgow 1970–75 (BD); Captain in Regular Army 1958–64; Training Officer, Rolls Royce 1964–70; lic by Presb of Glasgow 25 Jun 1975; m 26 Mar 1966 Nancy Mary; Children: David b 1967; Neil b 1969; Bruce b 1973; ord and ind to Kildalton and Oa 27 Nov 1977; introd to Fort William Duncansburgh (term) 14 Apr 1983; res from app 31 Jul 1986; ind to New Govan 20 Jun 1989.

NEWLANDS SOUTH (FUF 234; FES IX, 283; X, 168)

1968 ALWYN JAMES CECIL MACFARLANE
(FES IX, 661; X, 19, 23, 168, 378), trans from Edinburgh Portobello Old to Newlands South 4 Sep 1968; dem 12 Jan 1985; introd as Assoc at Scots Church, Melbourne, Australia 10 Oct 1984; ret 10 Feb 1988; Chaplain to the Queen in Scotland from 1977.

1985 IAIN FERGUSON PATON
trans from Banchory-Ternan West to Newlands South 6 Oct 1985; introd to Jerusalem St Andrew's 1 Mar 1997.

1997 JOHN DEAS WHITEFORD
B 17 May 1951 at Rhynie, s of Robert Stockbridge W. and Joan Caroline Deas; educ Barrhead High, John Neilson Institute, Paisley and Aberdeen Grammar 1963–69; University of Aberdeen 1969–72 (MA); University of Glasgow 1973–75 (CQSW, DSW), 1985–88 (BD); Social Work 1975–85; lic by Presb of Dunkeld and Meigle 27 Jun 1988; asst Perth St Leonard's-in-the-Fields and Trinity 1988–89; m 16 Jun 1978 Rose-Marie Edholm b 11 May 1950 d of Gunnar E. and Iris Ejebro; Children: Anneli Astrid Karolina b 19 Jul 1980; Sonia Joan Elizabeth b 17 Jan 1983; Camilla Rosalind b 25 Jun 1986; David Alexander b 9 Mar 1990; ord and ind to Stonehaven Dunnottar 22 Jun 1989; trans to Newlands South 27 Nov 1997.

NEWTON MEARNS (FUF 264; FES IX, 249; X, 147)

1931 WILLIAM MURRAY MACKAY
(FES IX, 249; X, 147), ord and ind to Newton Mearns 11 Sep 1931; ret 31 Oct 1976; died 4 Oct 1994.

1977 GRAHAM REGINALD GEORGE CARTLIDGE
B 8 Dec 1950 at Edinburgh, s of Reginald James C. and Dorothy Margaret Hurford; educ George Heriot's, Edinburgh 1955–68; University of St Andrews 1968–72 (MA); University of Edinburgh 1972–75 (BD); Union Theological Seminary, New York 1975–76 (STM); Jordanhill College, Glasgow 1993–94 (PGCE); lic by Presb of Edinburgh 9 Jul 1975; asst Paisley Abbey 1976–77; m 3 Jul 1981 Elaine Allison Bunting b 19 May 1953 d of Stanley B. and Audrey O' Donnell; Children: Christopher William James b 18 Jun 1982; Timothy Robert Graham b 3 Oct 1984; Peter David b 21 Feb 1990; ord and ind to Newton Mearns 26 Jun 1977; dem 24 Aug 1993 to enter teaching profession; app Teacher of RE, Kilmarnock Academy 15 Aug 1994; app Asst Principal teacher (RE, MEd), Woodfarm High, Thornliebank 1 Feb 1997; app Principal teacher (RE, MEd), Penilee Secondary, Glasgow 16 Aug 1999.

1994 ANGUS KERR
B 8 Nov 1957 at Glasgow, s of Angus K. and Jean Cochrane Brownlee; educ Uddingston Grammar 1970–76; University of Aberdeen 1976–80 (BD); University of Glasgow 1980–81 (CMin); Princeton Theological Seminary, USA 1981–82 (ThM); lic by Presb of Glasgow 28 Jun 1982; asst Ayr Castlehill 1982–84; m 28 Apr 1984 Catherine Hughes Kerr b 6 Sep 1952 d of Robert Kennedy K. and Gladys White Hughes; Children: Cameron Angus b 15 Aug 1985; Laura Kathryn b 1 May 1987; ord by Presb of Ayr during assistantship at Castlehill 20 Apr 1983; app by RAChD 1 Jun 1984; ind to Kirkcaldy Viewforth 1 May 1987; trans to Newton Mearns 5 Jan 1994.

NORTH KELVINSIDE (FUF 234; FES IX, 284; X, 168)

1971 WILLIAM GRAHAM ALSTON
(FES X, 168, 387), trans from Lybster and Bruan to North Kelvinside 17 Mar 1971; d Fiona m Richard Swainston; d Morag m Fergus McNeill; s Angus m Emma Jane Arnold; Publ: *Disciples not Decisions* (BTI, 1974); *Planning Schedule* (Commercial Services, 1979).

PARTICK SOUTH (FES X, 168, 169)

Formed 3 Oct 1977 by union of Partick Anderson and Newton Place.

1966 DONALD NORMAN MACDONALD
(FES X, 168), ind to Newton Place 17 Nov 1966; dem 12 Apr 1977 to take up app with BBC.

1972 ROBERT STEWART FRIZZELL
(FES X, 150, 169), ord and introd on term app to Partick Anderson 26 Jun 1972; res from app and ind to Balshagray 2 Apr 1975.

1978 WILLIAM DOUGLAS LINDSAY
ord and ind to Partick South 1 Jun 1978; trans to Eaglesham Old and Carswell 20 Sep 1988.

1989 KENNETH DAVID STOTT
ord and ind to Partick South 28 Jun 1989; trans to Dundee Chalmers Ardler 15 Jan 1997.

1997 ALAN LINKLATER DUNNETT
B 24 Jul 1950 at Edinburgh, s of William D. and Enid Ethel Daphne Stuart; educ Edinburgh Academy 1961–68; University of Edinburgh 1968–71 (LLB), 1988–91 (BD); Solicitor 1971–88; lic by Presb of Edinburgh 4 Jul 1991; asst Edinburgh Juniper Green 1991–93; m 1 Aug 1975 Linda Weir McColl b 22 Jan 1953 d of Andrew Weir M. and Margaret Stewart; Children: Ruth Joanna Stewart b 5 Apr 1977; John Mark Linklater b 23 Sep 1980; Joel Daniel b 30 Oct 1984; ord by Presb of Glasgow 16 Mar 1994; introd as Chaplain to University of Strathclyde 1 Oct 1993; ind to Partick South 11 Dec 1997.

PARTICK TRINITY (FES X, 158, 168, 169)

Formed 9 May 1990 by union of Partick East and Dowanhill (union 4 Sep 1984 of Partick East and Dowanhill) and Old Partick.

1964 GORDON JOSEPH ANGUS MANSON
(FES X, 169, 266), trans from Menstrie to Partick East 1 Oct 1964; became minister of united charge with Dowanhill 4 Sep 1984; ret 1 Nov 1989; died 12 Dec 1994.

1966 JOHN JOLLY
(FES IX, 563, 570; X, 152 (2), 169, 331), [correction: ord 15 Oct 1950, not Nov as in Vol IX, 570]; trans from Glasgow Bluevale and Whitevale to Old Partick 29 Mar 1966; ret 10 Jul 1990; d Ann m Paul Smyth; s Andrew m Christine Hobbins.

1969 ROBERT CURRIE
(FES X, 158, 215), trans from Boquhanran to Dowanhill 27 Feb 1969; dem and introd as Community minister at Partick 25 Jun 1984.

1990 JOHN DILLON
trans from Clydebank Faifley to Partick Trinity 25 Oct 1990; dem 31 Aug 1993.

1994 STUART JAMES SMITH
B 27 Jun 1966 at Glasgow, s of Blair S. and Eunice Stuart Wink; educ Hutchesons' Grammar, Glasgow 1978–83; University of Glasgow 1983–87 (BEng), 1990–93 (BD); Civil Engineering 1987–90; lic by Presb of Glasgow 1 Jul 1993; asst Glasgow Temple Anniesland 1993–94; m 23 Jul 1993 Elspeth Anne McTaggart b 18 Aug 1964 d of Neil M. and Anne Nisbet; Children: Cameron Boston b 2 Jul 1995; Catriona Helen b 9 Aug 1999; ord and ind to Trinity 24 Aug 1994.

PENILEE ST ANDREW'S (FES IX, 226; X, 130)

1970 DAVID IAN ISDALE
(FES IX, 200; X, 114, 131), trans from Stewarton John Knox to Penilee St Andrew 25 Nov 1970; introd to Inverchaolain and Toward (term) 27 Apr 1977.

1977 JOHN COLIN CASKIE
ord and ind to Penilee St Andrew 1 Jul 1977; trans to Carnoustie 21 Oct 1983.

1984 ESTHER MARY MARGARETHA JAMIESON
B 31 Mar 1954 at Bern, Switzerland, d of James Waterson Leitch and Hedwig Barbara Elisabeth Aeschlimann; educ Madchen Gymnasium, Basel, Switzerland 1965–73; University of Basel 1973–75; Royal Scottish Academy of Music and Drama 1975–78 (DDA); University of Glasgow 1979–82 (BD); Acting 1978–79; lic by Presb of Glasgow 28 Jun 1982; asst Glasgow Broom 1979–80, Crosshill Queen's Park 1980–81, Belhaven Westbourne 1981–82, St John's Renfield 1982–83; m 7 Oct 1999 Ian McIntyre Jamieson; ord and ind to Penilee St Andrew 30 Mar 1984.

POLLOK (FUF 239; FES IX, 287; X, 170)

Congregation dissolved 30 Jun 1976.

1972 JOHN GARDNER OLIVER
(FES X, 170, 188, 411), dem from Blantyre Livingstone Memorial on health grounds 13 Jun 1967; introd on term app to Pollok 27 Jun 1972; ind to Eddrachillis 18 May 1977.

POLLOKSHAWS (FES X, 170)

Formed 1 Jun 1965 by union of Auldfield and Shawholm.

1963 WALTER THOMAS CURRIE
(FES X, 150, 170), ord and ind to Auldfield 27 Aug 1963; became minister of united charge with Shawholm 1 Jun 1965; ret 10 Oct 1976; died 12 Jan 1996.

1977 RONALD JOHNSTONE
ord and ind to Pollokshaws 10 May 1977; trans to Thurso West 10 May 1984.

1984 JACQUELINE RUTH UNSWORTH
ord and ind to Pollokshaws 28 Nov 1984; dem 31 Oct 1987.

1987 ANDREW ROXBURGH BLACK
ord and ind to Pollokshaws 6 May 1987; trans to Beith High with Trinity 14 Dec 1998.

POLLOKSHIELDS (FES X, 170, 171)

Formed 1 Jan 1977 by union of Pollokshields Glencairn, Pollokshields Kenmure and Pollokshields-Titwood.

1965 HENRY THOMSON
(FES X, 170, 230), trans from Lochgoilhead and Kilmorich to Pollokshields Kenmure 30 Sep 1965; became minister of united charge with Pollokshields Glencairn and Pollokshields-Titwood 1 Jan 1977; ret 31 Dec 1990; died 9 Feb 1994.

1966 ARTHUR HOWAT GRAY
(FES IX, 296, 565; X, 129, 171, 328), trans from Paisley St John's to Pollokshields-Titwood 21 Apr 1966; ret 28 Feb 1975; died 26 Jun 1981.

1972 STEPHEN ANTON PACITTI
(FES X, 170, 378), trans from Dundonnell to Pollokshields Glencairn 16 Jan 1972; dem on app by Board of World Mission for service with Presb Church in Taiwan 28 Sep 1977.

1977 REBECCA McCRAE LEASK
ord by Presb of Glasgow and introd as Assoc at Pollokshields 18 May 1977; introd to Callander St Bride's 15 Mar 1981 (term).

1991 PHILLIP EARNSHAW
B 27 Dec 1938 at Holmfirth, Yorkshire, s of Chris E. and Eleanor Mary Dakin; educ Penistone Grammar 1949–53; Open University 1977–79 (BA); University of Stirling 1979–82 (BSc); University of Glasgow 1982–85 (BD); Mechanical Engineering 1953–79; lic by Presb of Glasgow, Jun 1985; asst Lenzie Union 1982–83; Bearsden Killermont 1983–85; Bishopbriggs Springfield Cambridge 1985–86; m 5 May 1973 Anne Robertson Patterson McAndrew 15 Jul 1941 d of William M. and Jean Patterson; Children: Christopher William b 3 Nov 1973; William McAndrew b 20 Feb 1975; Jane Eleanor b 23 Apr 1977; ord and ind to Stromness 5 Jun 1986; trans to Pollokshields 5 Jun 1991; ret 31 Dec 1996.

1997 DAVID ROBERT BLACK
B 7 Jun 1960 at Forres, s of Robert Charles B. and Josephine Main Stewart; educ Lossiemouth High 1972–78; University of Edinburgh 1978–82 (MA), 1982–85 (BD); lic by Presb of Moray 5 Jul 1985; asst Edinburgh South Leith 1985–87; m 14 Jun 1986 Sandra Anderson b 31 Jul 1959 d of James and Margaret A; Children: Lucy Claire b 30 Apr 1995; ord by Presb of Edinburgh during assistantship at South Leith 23 May 1986; ind to Dumfries Greyfriars 19 Aug 1987; trans to Pollokshields 17 Apr 1997.

POSSILPARK (FES X, 171)

Formed 9 Apr 1975 by union of Possilpark and Rockvilla.

1951 JAMES MURRAY HUTCHESON
(FES IX, 289, 482; X, 171 (2)), trans from Leven St John's to Possilpark 16 May 1951; became minister of united charge with Rockvilla 9 Apr 1975; Chaplain (part-time) to Barlinnie Prison 1959–69;

Chaplain (part-time) to Gartloch Hospital 1969–78; ret 31 Oct 1987; s Norman m Elizabeth Gilchrist Anderson; d Linore m Ernest Newall.

1988 MARTIN RICHARD FORREST
B 11 May 1956 at Greenock, s of Alan Leslie F. and Mary Paterson Lyons; educ Gourock High and Greenock Academy 1968–74; University of Strathclyde 1974–78 (BA); University of Aberdeen 1981–84 (BD); University of Cape Town 1986–88 (MA); Teaching (voluntary) in Kenya, Church Missionary Society 1978–80; lic by Presb of Greenock 23 Jun 1984; asst Edinburgh West Pilton 1984–85; m 11 Jan 1991 Janice Ann Henderson b 29 Mar 1964 d of Charles H. and Mary Stuart; Children: Rachel Ann b 2 Oct 1992; ord and ind to Possilpark 4 Feb 1988; Publ: *Learning from the Struggle in Bonhoeffer's Christological Ethic* (*Journal of Theology for S Africa*, 1987).

PRIESTHILL AND NITSHILL (FES IX, 226; X, 171)

Following union 29 May 1985 of Barrhead South and Levern and Nitshill (Presb of Paisley), the area of South Nitshill was detached from parish of Levern and Nitshill and adjoined to parish of Priesthill.

1966 WILLIAM MACKAY
(FES X, 171), [correction: b 9 Jun 1906, not 1907 as in Vol X, 171]; admitted by General Assembly 1964; ind to Priesthill 3 Mar 1966; ret 31 Oct 1974; died 22 Jan 1982.

1976 JOHN BAIN BURNETT
(FES X, 405, 416), returned from service with Board of World Mission in Buenos Aires and ind to Priesthill 1 Oct 1976; introd as Assoc at Dollar with Glendevon with Muckhart 26 Sep 1979.

1982 WILFRID JAMES TOWART
(FES IX, 245; X, 144), trans from Giffnock South to Priesthill 3 Nov 1982; ret 2 Mar 1987; died 8 Jan 1995.

1986 JOHN FORBES
ord by Presb of Glasgow and introd as Assoc at Priesthill 3 Jun 1986; dem 1988; died 11 Dec 1995.

1987 DEREK HARRY NIMMO POPE
ord and ind to Priesthill and Nitshill 6 Jun 1987; trans to Motherwell North 6 Jun 1995.

1988 DOUGLAS MARK NICOL
B 5 Jun 1955 at Glasgow, s of John Mathie N. and Elizabeth Watson McKechnie; educ King's Park Secondary, Glasgow 1967–72; University of Glasgow 1973–74 (CA), 1983–86 (BD); Apprentice Chartered Accountant 1972–77; Chartered Accountant 1977–79; Postman (part-time) 1979–80, (full time) 1980–83; lic by Presb of Glasgow 30 Jun 1986; asst Glasgow Newlands South 1986–88; m 27 Oct 1989 Aileen Susan Watson b 29 Jun 1961 d of John W. and Irene Margaret Jean

Hannah Walker; ord by Presb of Glasgow during assistantship at Newlands South 14 May 1987; introd as Assoc at Priesthill and Nitshill 18 May 1988; ind to same charge 31 Jan 1996.

1998 MORRIS MACKENZIE DUTCH
B 27 Jul 1951 at Paisley, s of Oliver Kay D. and Ada Morrison; educ West Secondary, Paisley 1956–66; University of Glasgow 1987–91 (BD); Mechanical Engineering 1992–98; lic by Presb of Glasgow 27 Jun 1991; asst Glasgow Priesthill and Nitshill 1998; m 21 Jul 1973 Margaret Abernethy Milne b 20 Oct 1951 d of Alexander M. and Isabelle Paterson; Children: David Alexander b 10 Oct 1978; Anna Margaret b 25 Mar 1983; ord by Presb of Glasgow and introd as Assoc at Priesthill and Nitshill 3 Jun 1998; dem 31 Dec 1998.

RENFIELD ST STEPHEN'S (FES X, 172)

1972 JOHN MASSON STEWART
(FES X, 74, 172, 178), trans from Selkirk Lawson Memorial to St Stephen's 13 Jan 1972; became minister of united charge with Renfield 18 Apr 1974; trans to Johnstone with Kirkpatrick Juxta 17 Jun 1986.

1976 ANGUS TURNER
ord by Presb of Glasgow and introd as Assoc at Renfield St Stephen's 22 Jun 1976; res 31 Jul 1990 and app Industrial Chaplain for Glasgow Sep 1990.

1987 DAVID WARD LUNAN
(FES X, 153, 368), trans from St Andrew's-Lhanbryd to Renfield St Stephen's 18 Sep 1987; Children: Andrew David; Gordon Ward; Iain Mellis; Malcolm Young.

1991 KEITH McLEOD STEVEN
dem from East Kilbride Claremont and introd as Assoc at Renfield St Stephen's 11 Apr 1991; ind to Glasgow Lochwood 9 Sep 1996.

ROBROYSTON
New Charge 1997.

1999 KEITH DAVID McKILLOP
B 25 Jun 1969 at Glasgow, s of Peter Docherty M. and Agnes Nelson Ewart; educ Kirkintilloch High 1981–86; University of Glasgow 1986–92 (MB, ChB), 1994–97 (BD); Doctor (Medicine) 1992–94, 1995–97 (part-time), 1997–98 (full-time); lic by Presb of Glasgow, Jul 1997; asst Glasgow St Paul's Provanmill 1998–99; m 1 Sep 1990 Catriona Helen Mitchell b 3 Oct 1962 d of Alex M. and Ann Austin; Children: Lauren Ann b 17 May 1993; David Ewart b 16 Jan 1995; ord and ind to Robroyston 30 Jun 1999.

RUCHAZIE (FES IX, 292; X, 172)

1954 ROBERT DAVIDSON
(FES IX, 288, 292; X, 172), trans from Glasgow Pollok Street to Ruchazie 6 May 1954; ret 30 Jun 1980; died 21 May 1996.

1981 DAVID WILLIAM DENNISTON
ord and ind to Ruchazie 1 May 1981; trans to Kennoway 19 Jun 1986.

1986 GORDON ROBERT PALMER
ord and ind to Ruchazie 7 Oct 1986; trans to Edinburgh Slateford Longstone 24 Feb 1994.

1995 JAMES STENHOUSE DICK
B 20 May 1939 at Kirkcaldy, s of Peter Herd D. and Margaret Ingram Saunders Stenhouse; educ Kirkcaldy High 1945–51; University of St Andrews 1957–62 (MA); Moray House College, Edinburgh 1962–63; University of Aberdeen 1985–87 (BTh); Teaching 1963–85; lic by Presb of Aberdeen, 1986; asst Aberdeen St Columba's Bridge of Don 1987–88; ord and ind to Echt with Midmar 17 May 1988; trans to Ruchazie 1995; ret 30 Sep 1997.

1999 WILLIAM FORSYTH HUNTER
B 2 Feb 1960 at Dunfermline, s of David Scott H. and Georgina Kelly; educ Queen Anne High, Dunfermline 1972–78; University of Edinburgh 1978–82 (MA); University of Aberdeen 1982–85 (BD); lic by Presb of Edinburgh 20 Jun 1985; asst Buckhaven 1985–86; ord by Presb of Perth and app Summer Mission Organiser/Youth Officer at St Ninian's, Crieff 20 Jun 1986; ind to Aberdeen Middlefield 7 Aug 1991; trans to Ruchazie 2 Mar 1999; Publ: Contributor to *Ace* Teen Magazine (FYT/Church of Scotland, 1986).

RUCHILL (FUF 245; FES IX, 292; X, 172)
Formed 24 Mar 1976 by union of Ruchill and St Cuthbert's Queen's Cross.

1955 WILLIAM McROBERTS
(FES IX, 363; X, 172, 217), trans from Clydebank West to Ruchill 20 Sep 1955; dem to enter teaching profession 15 Jan 1967; died 5 May 1998.

1967 HAROLD MEREDITH
(FES X, 87, 172, 246), trans from Tenandry to Ruchill 12 Oct 1967; trans to Mouswald with Torthorwald 27 Aug 1970.

1971 DUNCAN MUIR McLAREN
(FES X, 172), ord and ind to Ruchill 28 May 1971; trans to Prestwick Kingcase 18 Sep 1978.

1976 WILLIAM ALEXANDER McFARLANE
(FES IX, 77, 468; X, 47, 174, 330), trans from Aberdeen St Clement's West to St Cuthbert's Queen's Cross 21 Feb 1962; dem 24 Mar 1976; app Asst at Glasgow Maryhill Old 1976; ret 15 Nov 1978; died 29 Mar 1995.

1978 STEWART LANG
ord and ind to Ruchill 24 Aug 1978; dem 14 Jan 1992.

1992 JOHN CLYNE MATTHEWS
B 29 May 1944 at Glasgow, s of Neil McBride M. and Isabella Clark Clyne; educ Kennedy Street Secondary, Glasgow 1949–59; University of Glasgow 1980–86 (BD, MA), 1988–92 (MTh); American General Electric Inc (Managing Director) until 1980; lic by Presb of Dumbarton 30 Jun 1986; asst Bearsden Killermont 1980–82; Glasgow Temple Anniesland 1982–83, Govan Old 1983–84, Hyndland 1984–85, St Francis-in-the-East 1985–86; m 26 Oct 1966 Mabel Low b 5 Apr 1941 d of Cecil L. and Edna Simpson; Children: Linsey b 23 Dec 1967; Kenneth b 22 Aug 1970; Stuart b 7 Mar 1974; ord and ind to Ruchill 3 Sep 1992.

RUTHERGLEN OLD (FES X, 147)

Formed 15 Jan 1981 by union of Rutherglen East and Rutherglen Old (formed 25 Jul 1976 by union of Rutherglen Old and Summerfield).

1960 KENNETH McMILLAN BLAIR
(FES X, 172), ord and ind to Rockcliffe 20 Sep 1960 (united 8 Oct 1970 with Hall Memorial Fairbairn as Summerfield); ret 8 Oct 1970; died 25 Jun 1982.

1967 ROBERT GORDON MACROBERT
(FES IX, 306; X, 147, 180, 217), trans from Dumbarton Craigrownie to Old and Greenhill 17 May 1967; became minister of united charge with Summerfield 25 Jul 1976 and of united charge with Rutherglen East 15 Jan 1981; died 2 May 1984.

1972 BRIAN STUART COOPER DONALD
(FES X, 147, 418), res from service with Overseas Council in Pakistan and ind to Rutherglen East 17 Apr 1972; trans to Monquhitter with New Byth 28 Sep 1979.

1985 ALEXANDER THOMSON
(FES X, 117), trans from Ardler, Kettins and Meigle to Rutherglen Old 6 May 1985; University of Edinburgh [part-time] (MPhil); University of Aberdeen [part-time] 1985 (PhD); Addl children: Derek b 6 Jun 1977; Publ: *Tradition and Authority in Science and Theology* (Scottish Academic Press, 1987).

RUTHERGLEN STONELAW (FUF 265; FES IX, 250; X, 148)

1957 THOMAS MORTON
(FES IX, 117, 300; X, 148, 177), trans from St Nicholas' Cardonald to Stonelaw 18 Jun 1957; ret 31 Oct 1986.

1987 (ALEXANDER) ALASTAIR McKENZIE MORRICE
(FES X, 72), trans from Edinburgh Holy Trinity to Stonelaw 23 Apr 1987; Addl children: Christiana b 28 Oct 1978 (adopted); s Peter m Sharon Pilling; s Andrew m Sarah Leitch.

RUTHERGLEN WARDLAWHILL (FES III, 492; VIII, 311; IX, 250; X, 148)

1962 ALASTAIR MACDONALD GIBSON
(FES IX, 57, 576; X, 148, 335), trans from Ellon to Wardlawhill 26 Apr 1962; ret 1978; died 29 Mar 1982.

1979 JOHN HAMILTON FRASER
(FES X, 128), trans from Paisley St Columba Foxbar to Wardlawhill 2 Feb 1979; dem on app to St Columba's and New Lendal, URC, York 12 Mar 1983.

1983 GEORGE CRANSTON
B 20 Mar 1936 at New Stevenson, Motherwell, s of Robert C. and Margaret Swann Watson; educ Dalziel High, Motherwell 1941–52; University of Aberdeen 1964–66 (lay missionary course); University of Glasgow 1972–76 (BD); Draughtsman 1952–64; Lay missionary (Church of Scotland) 1966–72; lic by Presb of Glasgow, 1976; asst Glasgow Cathcart South 1975–76; m 8 Jun 1959 Mary (Mora) Bingham b 26 Sep 1935 d of William B. and Mary McAlister; Children: Douglas b 4 Apr 1960 m Christine; Graham b 14 Jul 1964 m Tereesa; ord and ind to Sanquhar St Bride's 30 Sep 1976; trans to Wardlawhill 24 Nov 1983; app Chaplain (part-time) to Low Moss Prison.

RUTHERGLEN WEST (FES X, 148)

Linked 29 Apr 1993 with John Ross Memorial for Deaf People. Arrangement terminated 25 Jun 1998.

1944 ALLAN BOWIE
(FES IX, 250; X, 148 (2)), ord and ind to Rutherglen West 23 Feb 1944; ret 2 Nov 1985; died 17 Mar 1998.

1986 JOHN WHITEFORD DRUMMOND
(FES X, 125), trans from Linwood to Rutherglen West 24 Jun 1986; minister of linked charge with John Ross Memorial from 29 Apr 1993 until 25 Jun 1998; Addl children: Ruth Morrison b 7 Jan 1977; Robert William Whiteford b 6 Jun 1982; Grace Stewart b 18 Dec 1984.

1993 JANETTE BLACK
ord by Presb of Glasgow and introd as Assoc at Rutherglen West with John Ross Memorial 29 Apr 1993; res from app 1997.

SANDYFORD HENDERSON MEMORIAL (FES IX, 303; X, 178)

1956 GEORGE MACKENZIE PHILIP
(FES X, 179), ind to Sandyford Henderson Memorial 19 Oct 1956; ret 31 Oct 1996; s John m Rosalyn Weekes; d Ruth m David McLeish; Publ: *Daily Bible Reading Notes* (Congregational Record, 1959–96 monthly); *Kingdom Against Kingdom* (Congregation, 1985); *Lord from the Depths* (Gray, 1986); *Apostles' Creed* (Christian Focus, 1990); *Freedom Through Obedience* (Christian Focus, 1992).

1997 CHRISTOPHER PETER WHITE
(FES X, 23), res from app as Assoc at Glasgow St George's Tron and ind to Sandyford Henderson Memorial 12 Jun 1997; m 8 Jan 1977 Elizabeth Mary Marshall Gilbertson b 6 Jul 1945 d of Michael Henry Marshall G. and Jean Irving Scott Moncrieff; Children: David Alexander b 31 May 1978; Robert John b 10 Oct 1979; Elizabeth Anna b 5 Sep 1981; Naomi Sarah b 9 Jul 1985; Publ: *Introduction to the Christian Faith* (Rutherford House, 1990); *The Effective Pastor* (Christian Focus, 1998).

SANDYHILLS (FUF 253; FES IX, 250; X, 148)

1968 ROBERT CARMONT
(FES X, 148, 279, 329), trans from Aberdeen Northfield to Sandyhills 29 Apr 1968; ret 28 Feb 1994; d Sheila m Andrew Lindsay.

1994 JOHN PAYNE FAWCETT MARTINDALE
B 26 Apr 1956 at Glasgow, s of Richard M. and Jeanie Boyd Payne; educ North Kelvinside, Glasgow 1968–74; Glasgow College of Building and Printing 1974–78 (BSc); Heriot-Watt University 1984–86 (MSc); University of Glasgow 1990–93 (BD); Fellow of Royal Institution of Chartered Surveyors (FRICS); Member of British Institute of Management (MBIM); Quantity Surveying 1978–90; lic by Presb of Glasgow 1 Jul 1993; asst Glasgow Strathbungo Queen's Park 1993–94; m 8 Jul 1978 Jaan French b 23 Nov 1952 d of Robert Muir F. and Catherine McInnes Anderson; Children: Aaron John b 29 Jan 1982; Joy Elizabeth b 13 Dec 1983; ord and ind to Sandyhills 17 Aug 1994.

SCOTSTOUN AND WHITEINCH (FES X, 160, 162, 179)

Formed 3 Sep 1992 by union of Scotstoun (union 7 Dec 1988 of Scotstoun East and Scotstoun West) and Whiteinch (union 30 Apr 1981 of Jordanvale and Gordon Park).

1963 GEORGE HUNTER
(FES IX, 482; X, 137, 179, 286), trans from Port Glasgow Newark to Scotstoun West 28 Nov 1963; ret 31 Oct 1987; s Douglas m Margo Cowan; s Crawford m Bridget Grealis; s George m Margaret Rowley; d Rosemary m Christopher Jacketts.

1972 GAVIN JOHN McFADYEN
(FES X, 116, 160, 202), trans from Uddingston Burnhead to Gordon Park 28 Sep 1972; became minister of united charge with Jordanvale 30 Apr 1981; ret 3 Sep 1992.

1975 WILLIAM GEORGE NEILL
(FES X, 34, 179), trans from Blackbraes and Shieldhill to Scotstoun East 3 Apr 1975; trans to Edinburgh North Leith and Bonnington 30 Oct 1980.

1981 ALEXANDER ROBERTSON
admitted by General Assembly 1980 and ind to Scotstoun East 27 Aug 1981; trans to Aberluthnott with Laurencekirk 6 Nov 1987.

1989 JAMES GORDON MATHEW
(FES X, 51), trans from Aberdeen Woodside to Scotstoun 29 Jun 1989; became minister of united charge with Whiteinch 3 Sep 1992; trans to Clackmannan 1 Jul 1999.

1993 ALAN McWILLIAM
B 20 Jun 1968 at Dundee, s of Thomas Mathieson M. and Patricia Godfrey; educ Stanley Green High, Paisley 1980–86; University of Glasgow 1989–92 (BD); lic by Presb of Glasgow 24 Jun 1992; asst Edinburgh Holy Trinity 1992–93; m 28 Aug 1988 Diane Christine Drysdale b 16 Jan 1968 d of Anthony D. and Christine Searil; Children: David Stuart b 26 Nov 1996; Steven John b 2 Feb 1999; ord by Presb of Glasgow and introd as Assoc at Scotstoun and Whiteinch 24 Nov 1993.

SHAWLANDS (FES X, 179)

Formed 3 Sep 1998 by union of Shawlands Cross and Shawlands Old.

1958 JAMES CALDWELL
(FES IX, 213, 536; X, 179 (2), 322), trans from Kirriemuir St Ninian's to Shawlands Old 14 May 1958; became minister of united charge with Langside Avenue 27 Jan 1963; trans to Abernethy and Dron 14 Jun 1978.

1961 THOMAS BARR GIRDWOOD
(FES IX, 333; X, 111, 179, 198), trans from Kilmarnock Grange to Shawlands Cross 21 Jun 1961; trans to Kirn 31 Mar 1976.

1976 ALASTAIR WILLIAM MURDOCH SANDERSON
(FES X, 93), trans from Ervie and Kirkcolm to Shawlands Cross 24 Nov 1976; became minister of united charge with Shawlands Old 3 Sep 1998; Addl children: Ewan Thomson b 27 Jan 1977; d Carol m Cakiroglu; s Peter m Plompen.

1979 JAMES MILLAR
(FES IX, 198; X, 113, 155), trans from Glasgow Castlemilk West to Shawlands Old 29 Aug 1979; ret 10 Dec 1989; d Joyce m Maxwell; s Ian m

Evans; m (2) Kathleen Rosemary Annie Grant b 23 Aug 1945 d of Henry McQueen G. and Mabel Kathleen Jenner.

1990 ALASTAIR DAVID McLAY
B 10 Jan 1963 at Glasgow, s of James M. and Margaret Adams Brady; educ King's Park Secondary, Glasgow 1968–81; University of Strathclyde 1981–85 (BSc); University of Glasgow 1985–88 (BD); lic by Presb of Glasgow 5 Jul 1988; asst Glasgow Newlands South 1988–90; m 16 Jul 1988 Gail Margaret McAulay b 27 Sep 1966 d of Peter George M. and Florence Tugela Adams; Children: Mhairi Iona b 22 Oct 1993; Catriona Ruth b 2 Oct 1995; ord by Presb of Glasgow during assistantship at Newlands South 11 May 1989; ind to Shawlands Old 29 Aug 1990; introd as Assoc at Shawlands 3 Sep 1998.

SHERBROOKE ST GILBERT'S (FES IX, 305; X, 180)

1952 DAVID NOEL FISHER
(FES IX, 305, 340, 343; X, 180), trans from Uddingston Chalmers to Sherbrooke St Gilbert's 27 Mar 1952; ret 31 Dec 1979; w Margaret died 22 Sep 1988; s Alexander m Fiona Brown; d Marion m Andrew Ian Gordon Nelson; d Sheena m Iain Graham.

1980 JOHN CAMPBELL
(FES X, 122), trans from Barrhead Arthurlie to Sherbrooke St Gilbert's 12 Jun 1980; dem to take up app as Adviser in Mission and Evangelism, Dept of National Mission 1 Jan 1987.

1987 DONALD MACLEOD
B 4 Jan 1943 at Glasgow, s of Calum and Sylvia M; educ Hyndland, Glasgow 1955–60; Royal Scottish Academy of Music 1965–68 (DRSAM); Jordanhill College, Glasgow 1970–71; University of Glasgow 1983–86 (BD); Banking 1960–65; Teaching 1969–70; Professional Musician 1971–83; lic by Presb of Glasgow 30 Jun 1986; asst Bishopbriggs Springfield Cambridge 1986–87; m 10 Jul 1969 Elspeth Williamson b 7 Sep 1941 d of Jack W. and Lorna Johnston; Children: Colin b 2 Jun 1971 m Helen Tyson; Fiona b 21 Jun 1974; Fraser b 5 Nov 1977; ord and ind to Sherbrooke St Gilbert's 27 May 1987; Publ: Co-editor of *With a Loud Noise Skilfully* (Panel on Worship, 1995).

SHETTLESTON OLD (FES III, 489; VIII, 311; IX, 305; X, 180)

1973 ROBERT MILNE TUTON
(FES X, 156, 180, 243), trans from Glasgow Colston Wellpark to Shettleston Old 29 Aug 1973; ret 31 Jan 1995.

1995 ALISON JOAN ROSS
ord and ind to Shettleston Old 4 Oct 1995; trans to Kilchoman with Portnahaven 1 Apr 1998.

1999 DAVID KIRK SPEED
(FES X, 237), trans from Aberfoyle with Port of Menteith to Shettleston Old 3 Aug 1999.

SOUTH CARNTYNE (FES IX, 306; X, 180)

1976 IAIN MACNEE
ord by Presb of Greenock during assistantship at Port Glasgow Hamilton Bardrainney 30 May 1975; ind to South Carntyne 27 May 1976; trans to Newbattle 20 Jun 1985.

1986 ALEXANDER HANLEY GREEN
ord and ind to South Carntyne 5 Feb 1986; trans to Strathblane 2 Nov 1995.

1996 GARY NEIL WILSON
B 15 Jan 1961 at Glasgow, s of George W. and Isabel Neil; educ Colston Secondary 1973–77; St Colm's College, Edinburgh 1989–91 (Cert in Diaconal Min); University of Edinburgh 1991–95 (BD); Template Maker 1977–84; Hussmann Craig Nicol 1984–89; lic by Presb of Edinburgh 2 Jul 1995; asst Portree 1995–96; m 28 Mar 1992 Helen Ackford b 19 Nov 1961 d of Brian A. and Myrtle Wright; Children: Andrew Jonathan b 6 May 1995; Sarah Elizabeth b 4 Jan 1997; Rachel Helen b 12 Mar 1999; ord and ind to South Carntyne 28 Nov 1996.

SOUTH SHAWLANDS (FUF 254; FES IX, 307; X, 180)

1968 THOMAS GRACIE MACFARLANE
(FES X, 39, 180, 421), trans from Falkirk St James' to South Shawlands 12 Sep 1968; ret 10 Dec 1992; s Kenneth m Deborah Hope Davidson.

1993 LILY FLEMING HAWTHORN McKINNON
B 6 Oct 1948 at Paisley, d of Neil Hawthorn and Lily McDonald Fleming; educ Dalry High 1953–67; University of Aberdeen 1967–70 (MA); University of Glasgow 1986–87, 1989–91 (BD); Teaching 1970–71, 1981–84; Employment Training Officer 1988–89; lic by Presb of Glasgow 27 Jun 1991; asst Glasgow Wellington 1991–92, St John's Renfield 1992–93; m 16 Sep 1972 Graeme Iain McKinnon b 24 Sep 1950 s of Donald Iain M. and Dora Ann White; Children: Laura Victoria b 7 Aug 1973; Nelson Paul b 29 Dec 1974; Daniel Lewis b 4 Apr 1976; Emma Louise b 7 Nov 1978; ord and ind to South Shawlands 6 May 1993; dem 31 Jan 1999; Chaplain to Prince and Princess of Wales Hospice 1995–99.

SPRINGBURN (FES X, 156, 162, 180, 181, 183)

Formed 11 May 1978 by union of Cowlairs-Somerville, Johnstone, Sighthill, Springburn North Hill and Wellfield.

1951 JOHN HENRY PRENDERGAST
(FES IX, 21, 76, 306; X, 180), trans from Edinburgh Leith Junction Road to Sighthill 18 Oct 1951; ret 13 Jun 1978; died 4 Mar 1983.

1961 FRANK MYERS
(FES X, 183), ord and ind to Wellfield 30 Aug 1961; became minister of united charge with Cowlairs-Somerville, Johnstone, Sighthill and Springburn North Hill 11 May 1978; ret 31 Oct 1987; Pastoral Assoc at Glasgow St George's Tron 1988–98; Open University 1994 (BA); d Judith m Thomas McGibbon; Publ: *History of Springburn Churches* (lodged Springburn Museum).

1967 WILLIAM INGLIS MILLER
(FES IX, 560, 569, 588, 604, 648; X, 162, 166, 342), trans from Glasgow London Road St Clement's to Johnstone 1 Nov 1967; ret 28 Feb 1974; died 20 Jul 1976.

1967 CHARLES CAMERON
(FES IX, 574; X, 181, 334, 338), trans from Stonehaven South to Springburn North Hill 15 Jun 1967; dem 15 Jul 1978.

1971 GEORGE ANDERSON ROSS FORBES
ord and ind to Cowlairs-Somerville 30 Sep 1971; trans to Kirkintilloch Hillhead 27 Sep 1977.

1978 SHEILA BLOUNT
ord by Presb of Glasgow and introd as Assoc at Springburn 27 Sep 1978; res from app 30 Sep 1981; ind to Falkirk Old and St Modan's (joint ministry) 22 Jun 1990.

1988 WILLIAM GRANT RAMSAY
B 31 May 1935 at Dundee, s of William Craig R. and Isabella Cooney; educ Logie Secondary, Dundee 1947–50; University of Aberdeen 1962–64; United Free Church College, Edinburgh 1964–67; Commercial Artist 1950–53, 1953–62; National Service 1953–55; lic by Presb of Dundee (United Free Church) 3 Jun 1967; m 9 Jul 1966 Lydia Shepherd Angus b 22 Oct 1942 d of Arthur Fisher A. and Annie Barron; Children: William Arthur b 17 Jan 1968 m Ona Fraser; Gordon Leonard b 13 Oct 1969; Paul Richard b 16 Oct 1972; Elizabeth Lydia b 28 Jul 1974; ord and ind to Dysart with Buckhaven (UFC) 7 Jul 1967; trans to Glasgow Millerston (UFC) 22 Nov 1971; admitted by General Assembly and ind to Paisley Wallneuk 24 Jun 1981; became minister of united charge with Merksworth 19 Jan 1983; trans to Springburn 7 Jan 1988; ret 31 Jan 1999.

ST ANDREW'S EAST (FUF 246; FES IX, 293; X, 173)

1971 DAVID HOGG
(FES X, 173, 348), trans from Boddam to St Andrew's East 25 Mar 1971; ret 31 Mar 1991; died 21 May 1992.

1991 JANETTE GILLESPIE REID
B 6 Aug 1949 at Bellshill, d of Hugh Reid and Janet Hamilton Gillespie McCallum; educ Clifton High, Coatbridge 1954–64; University of Glasgow 1984–89 (BD, CMin); Comptometer Operator 1964–67; Bank Clerkess 1967–84; lic by Presb of Glasgow 3 Jul 1989; asst Glasgow Dennistoun Central 1988–89, Barlanark Greyfriars 1989–91; ord and ind to St Andrew's East 22 Oct 1991.

ST BRIDE'S (FES III, 436; VIII, 300; IX, 293; X, 173)

Congregation dissolved 30 Jun 1975.

1969 CHARLES GEORGE INGLIS
(FES IX, 789; X, 174, 446), ret from RAChD and introd to St Bride's 21 Oct 1969; app terminated on dissolution of congregation 30 Jun 1975; ret 30 Jun 1975.

ST COLUMBA (FES III, 436; VIII, 300; IX, 293; X, 174)

1955 ANGUS FERGUSON MACKINNON
(FES IX, 399, 687, 692; X, 174, 394), trans from Strath to St Columba 13 Sep 1955; ret 31 Dec 1980; died 9 May 1982.

1981 DONALD NORMAN MACDONALD
(FES X, 168), res from BBC and ind to St Columba 4 Nov 1981; dem 31 Dec 1987; died 16 Jul 1993.

1989 JOHN MURDO MACLEOD MACARTHUR
(FES X, 384, 397), dem from Strath and Sleat 2 Dec 1984; ind to St Columba 4 Apr 1989; ret 31 Dec 1996; Addl children: Anna Macleod b 30 Jan 1979.

ST DAVID'S KNIGHTSWOOD (FES IX, 295; X, 174)

1973 ALEXANDER MACLEAN GUNN
(FES X, 174, 389), trans from Wick St Andrew's-Thrumster to St David's Knightswood 6 Dec 1973; trans to Aberfeldy with Amulree and Strathbraan 1 Mar 1986.

1986 HOWARD GEORGE TAYLOR
trans from Innellan with Inverchaolain and Toward to St David's Knightswood 25 Sep 1986; dem 22 Sep 1998 to take up app as Chaplain and Lecturer, Heriot-Watt University.

1999 WILLIAM GRAHAM MURRAY THAIN
B 13 Oct 1958 at Elgin, s of James T. and Williamina Keiro; educ Forres Academy 1970–76; University of Strathclyde 1976–80 (LLB); University of Aberdeen 1984–87 (BD); Solicitor 1980–84; lic by Presb of Inverness 26 Jun 1987; asst Falkirk St Andrew's 1987–88; m 13 Sep 1984 Mary Barbara

Marwick b 4 Mar 1958 d of David Thomas M. and Elizabeth Blanche Blinkhorn Mackintosh; Children: David Thomas b 8 Nov 1985; Matthew James b 20 May 1990; ord and ind to Polmont Old 20 Jun 1988; trans to St David's Knightswood 25 May 1999.

ST ENOCH'S HOGGANFIELD (FES III, 441; VIII, 301; IX, 295; X, 174)

1975 DONALD MACLENNAN THOMSON
(FES X, 174), ord and ind to St Enoch's Hogganfield 29 Oct 1975; dem 9 Dec 1981; ind to Aberdeen Nigg 8 May 1986.

1982 ALEXANDER TAIT
B 7 Dec 1926, s of Joseph T. and Margaret Strong; University of Glasgow 1962–64; United Free Church College, Edinburgh 1964–67; Gardener 1945–54; Lay Missionary 1954–62; lic by Presb of Alloa and Dunfermline (UFC) 8 Apr 1967; m 29 Mar 1951 Janet Graham Campbell b 26 May 1927 d of James Darrie C. and Jenny Burns; Children: Jennifer Elizabeth b 23 Aug 1957; Alastair Graham b 5 May 1961; ord and ind to Sauchie Fishcross (UFC) 7 Jul 1967; ind to St Enoch's Hogganfield 19 Sep 1982; ret 31 Oct 1995.

1996 ANDREW JOHN PHILIP
B 18 Nov 1964 at Falkirk, s of James P. and Janet Ramsay Moodie June Trapp; educ Firrhill High, Edinburgh 1976–82; Napier College, Edinburgh 1982–87 (BSc); University of Edinburgh 1991–94 (BD); Retailing 1987–88; Production Engineering 1988–91; lic by Presb of Falkirk 9 Aug 1994; asst Aberdeen Newhills 1994–96; m 25 Nov 1995 Elizabeth-Ann Clark Osborne b 7 Jan 1974 d of Joseph O. and Janet Galloway Dowie; ord and ind to St Enoch's Hogganfield 14 Mar 1996.

ST GEORGE'S-IN-THE-FIELDS (FES III, 444; VIII, 302; IX, 296; X, 175)

Congregation dissolved 30 Jun 1980.

1959 JOHN WATSON BARKER
(FES IX, 197, 786; X, 175, 188, 444), res from term app at Blantyre Burleigh Memorial and ind to St George's-in-the-Fields 9 Mar 1959; ret 31 Dec 1979; died 14 Oct 1983.

ST GEORGE'S TRON (FES IX, 296; X, 175)

1965 GEORGE BAILLIE DUNCAN
(FES X, 107, 175), trans from Troon Portland to St George's Tron 4 Mar 1965; ret 14 Mar 1977; died 4 Apr 1997.

1977 ERIC JOHN ALEXANDER
(FES X, 114), trans from Newmilns Loudoun East to St George's Tron 25 Aug 1977; ret 30 Nov 1997; Addl publ: *Plainly Teaching the Word* (Toronto Press, 1982).

1982 ERIC JOHN WRIGHT
res as Lecturer in New Testament, All Nations Christian College, Ware, Herts and introd as Assoc at St George's Tron 1 Oct 1982; dem 1983.

1984 DAVID WILLIAM ELLIS
introd as Assoc at St George's Tron 3 Oct 1984; res 31 Aug 1989 to take up app as National Director of Overseas Missionary Fellowship.

1990 RICHARD GEORGE BUCKLEY
ord by Presb of Glasgow and introd as Assoc at St George's Tron 1 Jul 1990; ind to Glasgow Trinity Possil and Henry Drummond 9 Aug 1995.

1997 MURDO MACLEAN
ord by Presb of Glasgow and introd as Assoc at St George's Tron 2 Jul 1997; ind to Carmyle with Kenmuir Mount Vernon 4 Nov 1999.

1998 SINCLAIR BUCHANAN FERGUSON
(FES X, 407), res as Professor of Systematic Theology, Westminster Theological Seminary, Philadelphia, USA and ind to St George's Tron 1 Jul 1998; Addl children: John Charles Allan b 26 Feb 1980; Ruth Kathleen Elizabeth b 20 May 1981; s David m Katharine Anne Shaw; Publ: *Add to Your Faith* (Pickering & Inglis, 1980, Zondervan, 1982); *The Christian Life* (Hodder & Stoughton, 1981, Intervarsity Press, 1982); *Man Overboard!* (Pickering & Inglis, 1981, Tyndale House, 1982); *Grow in Grace* (Marshall, Morgan & Scott, 1982, NavPress, 1983); *Discovering God's Will* (Banner of Truth, Carlisle PA, 1982); *Handle with Care* (Hodder & Stoughton, 1982); *A Heart for God* (NavPress, 1985, Banner of Truth, 1987); *Kingdom Life in a Modern World* (NavPress, 1986, Banner of Truth, 1988); *Children of the Living God* (NavPress, 1987, Banner of Truth, 1989); *John Owen on the Christian Life* (Banner of Truth, Carlisle PA, 1987); *Undaunted Spirit* (Rutherford House, 1988); *Daniel* (Word, 1988); *Understanding the Gospel* (Kingsway, 1989); *Healthy Christian Growth* (Banner of Truth, Carlisle PA, 1991); *Read any Good Books?* (Banner of Truth, Carlisle PA, 1992); *Deserted by God?* (Baker Book House, 1993, Banner of Truth, 1996); *The Pundit's Folly* (Banner of Truth, Carlisle PA, 1995); *If I Should Die Before I Wake* (Baker Book House, Intervarsity Press, 1995); *The Holy Spirit* (Intervarsity Press, 1996, IVP, 1997); *Let's Study Philippians* (Banner of Truth, Carlisle PA, 1997); *The Big Book of Questions and Answers* (Christian Focus, 1997); editor of *New Dictionary of Theology* (Intervarsity Press, Leicester and Illinois, 1988).

ST JAMES' (POLLOK) (FES IX, 297; X, 175)

1970 ROBERT WILLIAM WILKIE IRVINE
(FES X, 83, 176), dem from Maxwelltown Laurieknowe and introd as Assoc at St James' (Pollok) 9 Apr 1970; ind to Glasgow Tron St Mary's 25 Mar 1976.

1973 WILLIAM THOMSON REVEL
(FES IX, 268, 607, 716, 717; X, 155, 159, 176),
trans from Glasgow Cessnock to St James' (Pollok)
1 Feb 1973; ret 31 Oct 1981; died 27 Jan 1990.

1982 IAN GEORGE GOUGH
(FES X, 316), trans from Arbuthnott with Kinneff
to St James' 17 Feb 1982; introd as Assoc at
Bearsden New Kilpatrick 17 Sep 1985.

1986 JOHN TURNER LANG
(FES IX, 278; X, 152, 153, 165), trans from
Glasgow Bridgeton to St James' (Pollok) 30 Jan
1986; ret 31 Jan 1991; died 10 Apr 1994.

1991 HELEN DONALDSON HAMILTON
B 21 Jun 1938 at Glasgow, d of Alexander H. and
Mary Greer; educ Albert Secondary, Glasgow
1950–53; University of Glasgow 1985–89; Nursing
1955–81 (RGN, RSCN, SCM, QN, HV); Civil
Service Government Adviser 1982–85; lic by Presb
of Ayr, Aug 1989; ord and ind to St James' (Pollok)
26 Jun 1991.

ST JOHN'S RENFIELD (FUF 248; FES IX, 297;
X, 176)

1966 JAMES ALEXANDER SIMPSON
(FES X, 38, 176), trans from Falkirk Grahamston
to St John's Renfield 20 Apr 1966; trans to Dornoch
Cathedral 21 Apr 1976.

1976 COLIN GEORGE McINTOSH
ord and ind to St John's Renfield 26 Aug 1976;
trans to Dunblane Cathedral 18 Aug 1988.

1989 JOHN GORDON WEBSTER
(FES X, 107, 427), trans from Troon Old to St
John's Renfield 26 Apr 1989; ret 1 Jul 1998.

1999 DUGALD JAMES RADCLIFFE CAMERON
B 16 Oct 1961 at Glasgow, s of Dugald C. and
Catherine Margaret Cormack; educ Victoria Drive,
Glasgow 1974–79; Glasgow Technical College
1982 (SNCH); University of Edinburgh 1984–89
(BD, DipMin), 1995–96 (MTh); Accountancy
Trainee 1980–84; lic by Presb of Dumbarton 15
Oct 1989; asst Edinburgh South Leith 1989–90; m
4 Nov 1989 Pauline Jean Radcliffe b 28 May 1967
d of Jim R. and Patricia Maunder; ord by Presb of
Gordon and introd as Assoc at Inverurie St
Andrew's 23 Aug 1990; ind to Edinburgh St Martin's
19 Aug 1992; trans to St John's Renfield 4 Mar
1999; Publ: *Celtic Christianity: Scotch Mist?*
(Scottish Episcopal Review, 1996); pastoral care
case study (SPCK, 1999).

ST LUKE'S AND ST ANDREW'S (FES X, 153,
173)

Formed 22 Jun 1993 by union of Calton New (union
of St Luke's and Macmillan-Calton, St John's
Chalmers and Greenhead Barrowfield) and St
Andrew's (linked from 1 Feb 1976).

1932 JOHN MACKENZIE
(FES IX, 259; X, 153, 160), ord and ind to Bridgeton
West and Barrowfield 22 Dec 1932; became
minister of united charge with Greenhead 25 Mar
1962; ret 28 Feb 1971; died 23 Oct 1993.

1955 WILLIAM DUNCAN CROMBIE
(FES IX, 142, 787; X, 153 (3), 166, 444), ret from
RAChD and ind to Macmillan-Calton 17 Feb 1955;
became minister of united charge with St Luke's 1
Dec 1961 and of united charge with St John's
Chalmers 1 Oct 1963; became minister of united
charge with Greenhead Barrowfield 2 Mar 1971 and
of linked charge with St Andrew's 1 Feb 1976; ret
31 Dec 1987; d Mary m Burrow; d Elizabeth m
Ward.

1964 JOHN HUNTER KENNEDY
(FES X, 173), ord and ind to St Andrew's 16 Nov
1964; dem 16 Nov 1968 to return to medical
profession.

1968 MALCOLM LEITH FISHER
(FES X, 153), ord by Presb of Glasgow during
assistantship at Govan Old 18 Jan 1967; introd as
Asst and Youth Leader at Calton New 16 Sep 1968;
ind to Falkirk Old 19 Jun 1979.

1970 ALEXANDER STEWART BORROWMAN
(FES IX, 149, 198, 385, 471; X, 153, 173, 230
(2)), trans from Glasgow Burnbank to St Andrew's
13 Apr 1970; ret 1 Feb 1976; died 14 Feb 1978.

1975 GRAHAM McLEAN FORSHAW
(FES X, 153), ord by Presb of Glasgow during
assistantship at Govan Old 16 Dec 1973; app
Club Organiser and Asst at Calton New 1 Nov 1975;
res Dec 1977 to take up employment outwith
Church.

1985 ALBERT STUART DICKSON
(FES X, 29, 51, 173), app Leader of Calton Youth
Club and Asst minister Calton New with St
Andrew's 1 Jan 1984; introd as Assoc 27 Mar 1985;
introd to Elder Park Macgregor Memorial (term)
22 Jun 1989.

1988 ADRIAN JAMES TAIT RENNIE
ord by Presb of Glasgow during assistantship at
King's Park 12 May 1988; ind to Calton New with
St Andrew's 12 May 1988; dem on app as Warden,
MacLeod Centre, Iona Aug 1994.

1995 IAN COLIN FRASER
B 4 Apr 1943 at Edinburgh, s of Colin F. and Alice
Galloway; educ Kirkcaldy High; Moray House
College, Edinburgh (DipYC); Open University (BA);
University of Glasgow (BD); Insurance 1959–65;
Community Work 1967–79; lic by Presb of
Greenock; m 8 Jul 1967 Linda Isobel Main b 6 Mar
1945 d of William and Isobel M; Children: Shona;
Sharon; Gordon; Alistair; ord by Presb of Greenock
and introd as Community minister at Cartsdyke,

Jul 1982; ind to St Luke's and St Andrew's 22 Feb 1995; Publ: *Community Ministry* (1986); *Community Ministry* (1989).

ST MARGARET'S POLMADIE (FES III, 450; VIII, 303; IX, 298; X, 176)

Congregation dissolved 31 May 1984.

1950 ROBERT MURRAY McGREGOR
(FES IX, 299; X, 176), ord and ind to St Margaret's Polmadie 2 Feb 1950; ret 31 Dec 1983; died 2 Mar 1994.

ST MARGARET'S TOLLCROSS PARK (FES X, 176, 181)

Formed 29 Jun 1994 by union of St Margaret's Tollcross and Tollcross Park (linked from 30 Jun 1983).

1958 ANDREW JOHN AITKEN
(FES IX, 144; X, 85, 181), trans from Kirkconnel St Mark's to Tollcross Park 15 Dec 1958; became minister of linked charge with Tollcross Central 3 Apr 1979; ret 30 Oct 1981; w Agnes died 11 May 1987; University of Greenwich 1995–97 (PhD).

1971 IAIN ARCHIBALD LAING
(FES X, 177), ord and ind to St Margaret's Tollcross 4 Nov 1971; trans to Kingarth and Kilchattan Bay with Rothesay The High Kirk 4 May 1983.

1984 PETER IAN BARBER
ord and ind to St Margaret's Tollcross with Tollcross Park 5 Sep 1984; became minister of united charge 29 Jun 1994; trans to Edinburgh Gorgie 22 Jan 1995.

1995 GEORGE McMILLAN MURRAY
B 27 Jul 1946 at Glasgow, s of James Wemyss M. and Jenny Neil Brown; educ Bernard Street, Glasgow and Duncanrig, East Kilbride 1951–61; Glasgow School of Art 1964–66 (Cert Graphic Design); University of Edinburgh 1990–93 (LTh); Window Dresser and Graphic Designer 1964–90; lic by Presb of Dunfermline 4 Jul 1993; asst Dunfermline Abbey 1993–94; m 19 May 1971 Gillian Mann b 28 Mar 1952 d of George M. and Martha Craig; Children: Jeremy George b 5 Mar 1973; Julie Sarah b 15 Sep 1976; David James b 24 Dec 1985; ord and ind to St Margaret's Tollcross Park 25 Oct 1995.

ST MICHAEL'S, CARNTYNE (FES III, 405; VIII, 292; IX, 300; X, 177)

Congregation dissolved 30 May 1965.

1956 HENRY ALBERT KENNEDY
(FES IX, 619; X, 177, 356), trans from Buckie West to St Michael's, Carntyne 5 Sep 1956; dem 31 Oct 1962 to enter teaching profession (RE); died 24 May 1983.

ST NICHOLAS' CARDONALD (FES IX, 300; X, 177)

1967 ALEXANDER CRAIB BARR
(FES IX, 114; X, 64, 177, 286), trans from Methil to St Nicholas' Cardonald 21 Jun 1967; ret 31 Jul 1992; d Eleanor m James Dinnett.

1992 RODERICK IAN TURNBULL MACDONALD
B 7 Jul 1960 at Glasgow, s of Robert Turnbull M. and Delia O'Donnell McSherry; educ Penilee Secondary, Glasgow, Stewarton High and Kilmarnock Academy 1972–78; University of Glasgow 1986–90 (BD), 1990–91 (CMin); Civil Service 1979–83; Community Work 1985–86; lic by Presb of Glasgow 27 Jun 1991; asst Dumbarton Riverside 1991–92; m 6 Jun 1992 Ann Stephanie McDougall b 11 Jun 1966 d of Robert M. and Winifred Stephanie Morrison; ord and ind to St Nicholas' 3 Dec 1992.

ST PAUL'S PROVANMILL (FES IX, 310; X, 177)

1973 ALASTAIR RAMSAY MOODIE
(FES X, 177), trans from Govan Old to St Paul's Provanmill 5 Sep 1973; dem 31 Oct 1984 on app as Chaplain to Crosshouse and Kirklandside Hospital 28 Nov 1984.

1985 ROBERT RUSSELL McLARTY
B 27 Jan 1956 at Ayr, s of Robert McTurk M. and Morag Campbell Thompson; educ Royal High School, Edinburgh 1967–72; University of Ediburgh 1972–7 (MA), 1977–78 (DArch); University of Glasgow 1981–84 (BD); Architecture 1975–76, 1978–81; lic by Presb of Glasgow 25 Jun 1984; asst Glasgow St John's Renfield 1984–85; m 20 Jul 1978 Susan Campbell Ritchie b 5 Jan 1954 d of Peter Roy R. and Catherine Johnina Cruickshanks Campbell; Children: Margaret and Iain b 3 Apr 1987; ord and ind to St Paul's Provanmill 30 May 1985; app Chaplain (part-time) to Barlinnie Prison 1 Apr 1998.

ST ROLLOX (FUF 250; FES IX, 302; X, 178)

1946 ROBERT GOURLAY BLACK
(FES IX, 302, 338; X, 178), trans from Stonehouse Hamilton Memorial to St Rollox 14 May 1946; ret 30 Sep 1966; died 5 Feb 1985.

1967 EDWARD GWYNFAI JONES
(FES X, 178), ind to St Rollox 20 Aug 1967; app Chaplain (part-time) to Stobhill Hospital, Glasgow 10 Sep 1968; Addl children: Helen Margretta b 2 Aug 1977; d Elspeth m Glen Cross.

ST THOMAS' GALLOWGATE (FES IX, 303; X, 178)

1974 ERIK McLEISH CRAMB
(FES X, 178), ord by Presb of Edinburgh during assistantship at the Old Kirk 15 Apr 1973; ind to St

Thomas' Gallowgate 30 Jan 1974; dem 19 Apr 1981 on app by Overseas Council for service in Kingston, Jamaica.

1982　HERBERT MARSHALL GIBSON
(FES X, 197, 229), trans from Carmyle with Kenmuir Mount Vernon to St Thomas' Gallowgate 29 Apr 1982; ret 9 Nov 1996; Open University 1986–95 (BA, BSc); d Justine m Timothy David Colmer.

1997　IRENE ANNE BRISTOW
B 30 Mar 1941 at Glasgow, d of Vivian Peter Sinclair and Isabella Carswell Milby; educ Strathbungo Senior Secondary 1953–56; University of Edinburgh 1984–88 (BD); Cost Accountancy 1960–74; lic by Presb of Falkirk 24 Aug 1988; asst Larbert West 1988–89; m 4 Dec 1971 John Bristow b 9 Aug 1930 s of James B. and Nellie Ward; Children: Kirsteen Anne b 14 Oct 1974; Martin John b 14 Aug 1978; ord and ind to Dumbarton St Andrew's 28 Jun 1989; trans to St Thomas' Gallowgate (75%) and app by Board of National Mission under new forms of ministry (25%) 7 Aug 1997.

STAMPERLAND (FES IX, 250; X, 148)

1968　ARCHIBALD FREELAND CHISHOLM
(FES X, 148, 417), res from service with FMC in S Africa and ind to Stamperland 16 May 1968; trans to Leven St Andrew's 28 Oct 1976.

1977　DAVID KIRK SPEED
(FES X, 237), trans from Kildalton and Oa to Stamperland 27 Jun 1977; trans to Aberfoyle with Port of Menteith 20 Nov 1986.

1987　ALASTAIR JACK CHERRY
B 13 Mar 1944 at Glasgow, s of William Jack C. and Elizabeth McGilchrist Davidson; educ Bellahouston Academy, Glasgow 1956–62; University of Glasgow 1976–80 (BD); Open University 1992–95 (BA); Joint Stock Banking 1963–76; lic by Presb of Glasgow 30 Jun 1981; asst Paisley Sherwood 1981–82; m 6 Aug 1969 Fiona Mairi Murchison b 21 Aug 1947 d of Thomas Moffat M. and Mary Black Morton Philip; Children: Graeme Thomas b 13 Mar 1972; Iain William b 1 May 1974; ord and ind to Leven Scoonie Kirk 10 Jun 1982; trans to Stamperland 1 Jul 1987.

STEPPS (FES X, 148)

Formed 6 Jan 1983 by union of Stepps St Andrew's and Stepps Whitehill.

1961　ROBERT ANDERSON PHILP
(FES IX, 746; X, 424), res from service with FMC in Kenya 28 Feb 1961 and ind to St Andrew's 27 Sep 1961; ret 1 Apr 1981; d Mary m Donald Michael Titterington; d Ethel m Alan McIntosh; d Dorothy m Duncan Robertson.

1972　FREDERICK COMERY MUIR
(FES X, 148, 368), trans from Lossiemouth St James' to Whitehill 24 Oct 1972; became minister of united charge with St Andrew's 6 Jan 1983; ret 30 Nov 1997; Assoc of Royal School of Church Music 1991; m 6 Jul 1976 Christine Elizabeth Dickie b 20 Jun 1943 d of Thomas Cullen Dickie and Jeanie King Gemmell; Children: Margaret Jean b 15 Jul 1977; Thomas William b 20 Jan 1981.

1998　KENNETH SMYTH BAIRD
B 3 Mar 1944 at Bangor, Co Down, N Ireland, s of John B. and May Bryce; educ Bangor Secondary Intermediate and Bangor Technical 1955–59; Queen's University, Belfast 1976–80 (MSc), 1982–87 (PhD); University of Edinburgh 1993–96 (BD); CEng 1973; MIMarE 1973; Mechanical and Marine Engineering 1959–66; Further Education 1966–93; lic by Presb of Edinburgh 7 Jul 1996; asst Edinburgh Barclay 1996–97, Wardie 1997–98; m 19 Dec 1967 Margaret Olive Shannon b 25 Jun 1947 d of Robert S. and Margaret Pyper; Children: Kevin Smyth Owen b 4 Oct 1968; Cara Margaret May b 18 Dec 1969 m Steven Williams; Susan Annette b 19 Feb 1971 m Jeremiah Barakat; Jonathan O' Connor b 20 May 1977; Bronya Ilona Siobhan b 24 Aug 1978 m Michael Hunt; ord and ind to Stepps 26 Mar 1998.

STRATHBUNGO QUEEN'S PARK (FES X, 171, 181)

Formed 3 May 1979 by union of Strathbungo and Queen's Park West.

1958　CECIL HUGH ROBERTSON MARTIN
(FES X, 181), ord and ind to Strathbungo 10 Apr 1958; dem 30 Sep 1978 to take up teaching app in Iceland.

1970　ARCHIBALD ROBERTSON
(FES X, 171), ord and ind to Queen's Park West 1 Oct 1970; trans to Glasgow Eastwood 27 Oct 1977.

1979　NORMA DRUMMOND STEWART
B 20 May 1936 at Glasgow, d of Norman Rutherford S. and Margaret Ellen Andrew Drummond; educ Hyndland Secondary, Glasgow 1948–54; University of Glasgow 1954–57 (MA); 1957–62 (MEd); Glasgow Bible Training Institute 1962–64 (DipBS); University of London [External] 1962–64 (DipTh); University of Glasgow 1974–77 (BD); Teaching 1958–62; Missionary 1965–74; lic by Presb of Glasgow 30 Jun 1977; asst Glasgow Greenbank 1977–79; ord by Presb of Glasgow during assistantship at Greenbank 8 Dec 1977; ind to Strathbungo Queen's Park 3 May 1979; ret 31 Jan 2000.

TEMPLE ANNIESLAND (FES X, 150, 181)

Formed 27 Jun 1984 by union of Temple and Anniesland Cross.

1946 HENRY CHRISTIE THOMSON
(FES IX, 254, 529; X, 150), trans from Lethendy and Kinloch to Anniesland Cross 3 Oct 1946; ret 4 Oct 1971; died 29 Oct 1999; Publ: 'Does God?' (Drummond Press, 1973).

1968 IAIN MILLER MACDOUGALL
(FES IX, 307; X, 181 (2)), trans from Glasgow Steven Memorial to Temple 24 Oct 1968; died 7 Dec 1982.

1972 ROBERT WILLIAM MOFFATT JOHNSTON
(FES X, 150, 216), trans from Clydebank Hamilton Memorial to Anniesland Cross 22 Mar 1972; became minister of united charge with Temple 27 Jun 1984; ret 31 Aug 1999; d Alison m Philip Brien; s Iain m Elaine Diver.

THORNLIEBANK (FES X, 149)

Formed 8 Sep 1977 by union of Thornliebank Spiersbridge and Thornliebank Woodlands.

1963 JOHN ALICK MACDONALD
(FES IX, 300, 311, 397, 401; X, 149, 183), trans from Glasgow Victoria Park to Spiersbridge 30 May 1963; became minister of united charge with Woodlands 8 Sep 1977; ret 8 Sep 1978; died 19 May 1995.

1979 IAN PURVES
ord and ind to Thornliebank 17 May 1979; trans to Johnstone St Paul's 17 May 1984.

1985 JAMES HENRY ROBERTSON
(FES X, 135), trans from Greenock St Ninian's to Thornliebank 20 Feb 1985; Chaplain (part-time) to Barlinnie Prison 1992–94; trans to Culloden The Barn 19 Aug 1994.

1995 ROBERT MUNGALL SILVER
B 16 Aug 1962 at Glasgow, s of John S. and Mary Minto Hilley; educ Ravenspark Academy, Irvine 1974–79; Glasgow College of Technology 1979–84 (BA); Jordanhill College, Glasgow 1985–86 (PGCE); University of Glasgow 1991–94 (BD); Teaching 1986–91; lic by Presb of Glasgow 4 Jul 1994; asst Glasgow Newlands South 1994–95; m 17 Jun 1995 Sharon Wallace b 19 Jul 1970 d of Charles W. and Jean Whitehill; Children: Joshua b 2 Jul 1997; Jordan b 10 Dec 1998; ord and ind to Thornliebank 2 Aug 1995.

TOLLCROSS CENTRAL (FUF 256; FES IX, 309; X, 181)

Linked with Tollcross Park 3 Apr 1979 until 30 Jun 1983. Congregation dissolved 21 Jun 1987.

1919 JAMES NEIL ALEXANDER
(FUF 256; FES IX, 309), dem from Glasgow Tollcross Central Nov 1954; died 10 Jan 1976.

1955 OSCAR BUSSEY
(FES IX, 276; X, 163, 181), trans from Glasgow Kent Road St Vincent to Tollcross Central 2 Jun 1955; ret 31 Jan 1977; died 25 Oct 1994.

1979 ANDREW JOHN AITKEN
(FES IX, 144; X, 85, 181), trans from Kirkconnel St Mark's to Tollcross Park 15 Dec 1958; became minister of linked charge with Tollcross Central 3 Apr 1979; ret 30 Oct 1981.

TORRANCE (FUF 267; FES IX, 252; X, 149)

Linked with Kirkintilloch Park 19 Mar 1983 until 13 May 1990.

1955 MURDO MACLEOD
(FES VII, 451; IX, 791; X, 149, 447), res from RAChD and ind to Torrance 2 Jun 1955; died 6 Sep 1980.

1983 DAVID STEWART
ord and ind to Park 4 Aug 1977; became minister of linked charge with Torrance 19 Mar 1983; trans to Cambuslang Trinity St Paul's 30 Aug 1989.

1991 NIGEL BARGE
B 24 Jul 1955 at Rhu, s of Ronald Mansfield B. and Elizabeth Anne Lamberton; educ Trinity College, Glenalmond 1968–73; University of St Andrews 1974–78 (BSc); Moray House College, Edinburgh (CEd); Teaching 1979–85; lic by Presb of Edinburgh, 1988; asst Inchbrayock with Montrose Melville South 1988–90; m 8 Feb 1992 Jennifer Philip b 2 Jan 1970 d of James P. and Mary Moffat; Children: Ruth Mary b 18 Jan 1995; Rachel Anne b 1 Sep 1996; Samuel Ronald b 17 Jan 1998; ord and ind to Torrance 21 Mar 1991.

TORYGLEN (FES IX, 309; X, 181)

1952 ANDREW JOHN ORR GORDON
(FES IX, 283, 309; X, 181), trans from Glasgow Newhall to Toryglen 24 Sep 1952; ret 31 Mar 1983; died 30 Jul 1998.

1984 STUART DOUGALL MACQUARRIE
ord and ind to Toryglen 14 Jun 1984; dem 28 Aug 1990 on app by Carers National Assoc.

1991 KEITH WILLIAM ROSS
B 4 Apr 1958 at Glasgow, s of William R. and Agnes Lawson; educ Hyndland Senior Secondary, Glasgow 1963–76; University of Dundee 1976–80 (MA); University of St Andrews 1980–83 (BD); lic by Presb of Dundee 26 Jun 1983; asst Buckhaven 1983–84; m (1) 17 Jun 1984 Katherine Layzer b 10 Oct 1963 d of Robert L. and Anne Harwood; Children: Faith Garrison b 9 Jan 1986; divorced 5 Apr 1987; m (2) 12 Apr 1996 Feri Salvesen b 3 May 1961 d of Robin S. and Sari Clark; Children: Ishbel Robin b 6 Nov 1997; Evelyn Deborah b 8 Mar 1999; ord and ind to Dalmellington 19 Sep 1984; trans to Toryglen 20 Mar 1991.

TOWNHEAD BLOCHAIRN (FES X, 182)

1958 FREDERICK WILBERT DUNDAS HOUSTON
(FES IX, 717; X, 182 (2)), trans from Mid Yell to Townhead 23 Jan 1958; became minister of united charge with Blochairn 13 Sep 1973; died 31 Mar 1987.

1988 WILLIAM PETER FINLAY
(FES X, 391, 419), ind to Townhead Blochairn 20 Oct 1988; m 31 Mar 1989 Marjorie Nicolson b 26 Apr 1950 d of Donald N. and Edna Holland; Children: Hamish Ian b 4 Aug 1994.

TRINITY POSSIL AND HENRY DRUMMOND (FES X, 182)

1966 ALEXANDER LEISHMAN WALKER
(FES X, 161, 182, 226, 244), trans from Kilmartin to Henry Drummond 8 Sep 1966; became minister of united charge with Trinity Possil 8 Jun 1967; ret 30 Jun 1988.

1988 ANDREW THOMSON BLAKE McGOWAN
trans from Aberdeen Causewayend to Trinity Possil and Henry Drummond 15 Sep 1988; dem to take up app as Director of Highland Theological Institute 1 Aug 1994.

1995 RICHARD GEORGE BUCKLEY
B 25 May 1957 at London, s of John Redmond B. and Joan Wynanda Olthoff; educ Falmouth Grammar and Falmouth Comprehensive 1968–75; Trinity College, Bristol 1975–78 (BD); University of Aberdeen 1978–79 (MTh); Notre Dame College of Education 1979–80 (PGCE); Teaching 1980–87; lic by Presb of Glasgow 3 Jul 1989; asst Glasgow Pollokshields 1989–90; m 11 Apr 1980 Margaret MacInnes Robertson b 12 Mar 1949 d of Donald MacInnes R. and Marion MacDonald; Children: Charis Robertson b 28 Feb 1981; Aaron Robertson b 1 Jul 1982; Esther Robertson b 5 Jul 1986; Rachel Robertson b 23 Mar 1990; ord by Presb of Glasgow and introd as Assoc at St George's Tron 1 Jul 1990; ind to Trinity Possil and Henry Drummond 9 Aug 1995.

TRON ST MARY'S (FES IX, 311; X, 182)

1976 ROBERT WILLIAM WILKIE IRVINE
(FES X, 83, 176), res as Assoc at Glasgow St James' (Pollok) and ind to Tron St Mary's 25 Mar 1976; trans to Kincardine-in-Menteith with Norrieston 18 Nov 1988.

1990 GORDON MACRAE
dem from Ayr St Quivox 17 Sep 1987; ind to Tron St Mary's 11 Jan 1990; trans to Kippen with Norrieston 22 Jan 1998.

1999 WILLIAM THOMAS SMYTH WILSON
B 15 Aug 1965 at Ballymoney, N Ireland, s of Thomas Smyth W. and Catherine Crothers; educ Coleraine Academical Institution 1977–85; Sunderland Polytechnic 1985–88 (BSc); University of Edinburgh 1994–97 (BD); Pharmacy 1988–94; lic by Presb of Edinburgh 6 Jul 1997; asst Inverness Kinmylies 1997–99; m 17 Oct 1997 Mairi Macdonald b 17 Feb 1966 d of William John M. and Jessie Ann MacLeod; ord and ind to Tron St Mary's 20 Jan 1999.

TWECHAR (FES III, 485; VIII, 319; IX, 252; X, 149)
Linked 15 Jun 1975 with Banton.

1975 WILLIAM ALEXANDER TINDALL
(FES X, 140), admitted by General Assembly 1975 and ind to Banton with Twechar 4 Nov 1975; died 22 Jul 1977.

1978 MICHAEL ROBERT PHILIP
ord and ind to Banton with Twechar 16 Mar 1978; trans to Blairgowrie St Mary's South 13 Jan 1988.

1989 JEAN RAMAGE MITCHELL BLACKLEY
ord and ind to Banton with Twechar 9 Mar 1989, see Banton.

VICTORIA TOLLCROSS (FUF 256; FES IX, 311; X, 183)

1971 RICHARD COLEY
(FES X, 183), ord and ind to Victoria Tollcross 12 May 1971.

WALLACEWELL (FES X, 150, 151)
Formed 22 Sep 1998 by union of Balornock North and Barmulloch (linked from 13 May 1983).

1954 JOHN RANKINE SMITH
(FES IX, 206, 256; X, 151), trans from Kilwinning Erskine to Barmulloch 17 Jun 1954; ret 30 Sep 1982; s David m Linda Watt; s James m Pamela Taylor; d Ailisa m Robin Thomson; s John m Kim Wylie.

1972 ELIZABETH WYLIE SUTHERLAND
(FES X, 150), ord and ind to Balornock North 7 Sep 1972; became minister of linked charge with Barmulloch 13 May 1983; ret 31 Oct 1996.

1999 JOHN BLACK MACGREGOR
B 4 Jul 1961 at Tarbert, Lochfyne, s of Duncan Campbell M. and Elizabeth Margaret Johnson Hall; educ Keil School, Dumbarton; Tarbert Secondary and Oban High 1973–78; University of Glasgow 1993–97 (BD); Footballer 1978–80; Self-employed 1980–95; lic by Presb of South Argyll 8 Jul 1997; asst Bishopbriggs Springfield Cambridge 1997–99; m 5 Oct 1985 Susan Anne McSporran b 20 Mar 1967 d of Alexander M. and Janette Kirkcaldy; Children: Lindsay b 20 Nov 1986; Kirsty b 25 Jul 1989; ord and ind to Wallacewell 25 Feb 1999.

WELLINGTON (FES X, 183)

1973 MAXWELL DAVIDSON CRAIG
(FES X, 38, 183 (2)), trans from Falkirk Graham-ston to Wellington 17 Jan 1973; trans to Aberdeen St Columba's Bridge of Don 21 Jan 1989.

1974 JOHN ALEXANDER GRIMSON
(FES IX, 735; X, 78, 184, 419), trans from Half Morton with Kirkpatrick Fleming to Woodlands 4 Oct 1966; introd as Assoc at Wellington following union of Woodlands and Wellington 30 May 1974; ret 31 Oct 1986; s John m Cheryl Batty; d Neiliann m John Dent-Jones.

1990 MALCOLM LEITH FISHER
(FES X, 153), trans from Falkirk Old and St Modan's to Wellington 1 Feb 1990; Addl children: Alasdair James b 17 Mar 1978; Duncan Uist b 22 Dec 1980; Shona Elspeth b 8 Jan 1983.

WILLIAMWOOD (FES IX, 252; X, 149)

1949 COLIN CAMPBELL
(FES IX, 206, 216, 252; X, 149), trans from Johnstone East to Williamwood 17 Nov 1949; ret 30 Sep 1989; w Margaret died 25 Jul 1995.

1990 GEORGE HUTTON BETHUNE STEEL
B 5 Nov 1957 at Paisley, s of James Herbert Bethune S. and Elizabeth Margaret McAllister; educ John Neilson Institute, Paisley 1969–75; University of Glasgow 1975–81 (BD, MA); lic by Presb of Paisley 1 Jul 1981; asst Glasgow Cardonald 1981–82; m 6 Jul 1976 Lesley Killoch Peters b 11 Dec 1952 d of John Killoch P. and Margaret Paterson Turnbull; Children: James Hutton b 30 Jul 1982; John George b 15 Jul 1984; Joy Catherine b 25 Apr 1988; ord and ind to Alva 23 Jun 1982; trans to Williamwood 21 Feb 1990.

YOKER OLD (FES III, 370; VIII, 284; IX, 375; X, 224)

Linked 27 May 1981 with Yoker St Matthew's.

1958 JOHN HARRIS HAMILTON
(FES IX, 309; X, 181, 224), trans from Glasgow Tollcross Park to Yoker Old 9 Apr 1958; ret 31 May 1980; died 17 May 1997.

1981 WILLIAM ANDERSON BRYDEN
B 12 Feb 1940 at Glasgow, s of Joseph George B. and Marion Murray Anderson; educ Rothesay Academy and Hillhead High, Glasgow 1952–57; University of Edinburgh 1972–77 (BD); University of Strathclyde 1984–85 (MBA); Life Assurance 1957–62; Computer Systems Design 1962–72; lic by Presb of Lothian, Jun 1976; asst Edinburgh Tron Kirk Moredun 1976–77; m 21 Sep 1968 Tessa Lucy Powell b 24 Jun 1943 d of Ronald Matthew Arthur P. and Ethel Maud Jackson; Children: Fiona Marion b 24 May 1970; Sheena Catherine b 15 Feb 1973; ord and ind to Corgarff and Strathdon with Glenbuchat-Towie 21 Sep 1977; trans to Yoker Old with St Matthew's 1 Jun 1981; ret 31 Mar 1984.

1984 ERIK McLEISH CRAMB
(FES X, 178), res from app with Overseas Council in Kingston, Jamaica and ind to Yoker Old with St Matthew's 29 Aug 1984; dem on app as Industrial Chaplain for Tayside and National Co-ordinator 21 Jun 1989.

1992 NEIL ALEXANDER SIMPSON
B 24 Aug 1952 at Bromley, s of William Ernest S. and Elizabeth Cormack; educ St Olave's Grammar, London and Archbishop Holgate's Grammar, York 1963–69; University of Durham 1970–73 (BA); University of London 1983–86 (BD); University of Edinburgh 1986–89 (PhD); Computer Management 1978–82; lic by Presb of East Lothian; asst North Berwick St Andrew's Blackadder 1992; m 23 May 1997 Isobel McKenzie b 28 May 1952; Children: William; Alexander; Samuel; Jonathan; ord and ind to Yoker Old with St Matthew's 29 Oct 1992.

YOKER ST MATTHEW'S (FES IX, 376; X, 224)

Vacant from 1971 until 1981. Linked 27 May 1981 with Yoker Old.

1981 WILLIAM ANDERSON BRYDEN
ind to Yoker Old with St Matthew's 1 Jun 1981, see Yoker Old.

1984 ERIK McLEISH CRAMB
(FES X, 178), ind to Yoker Old with St Matthew's 29 Aug 1984, see Yoker Old.

1992 NEIL ALEXANDER SIMPSON
ord and ind to Yoker Old with St Matthew's 29 Oct 1992, see Yoker Old.

PRESBYTERY OF HAMILTON

AIRDRIE BROOMKNOLL (FES X, 185, 189)

Linked 26 Aug 1998 with Calderbank.

1961 DUNCAN CAMERON McPHEE
(FES X, 102, 185), trans from Dalrymple to Broom-
knoll 20 Dec 1961; dem 1 Feb 1978 on app as
Secretary-Depute, Home Board; Clerk to Presb of
Hamilton 1972–78; ret 26 Oct 1993; d Elspeth m
Colin Ian William Johnson; s Iain m Susan
Harrison; d Ailsa m Robin Edward Hill; d Mairi m
James Leggatt.

1979 WILLIAM ABERNETHY
ord and ind to Broomknoll 25 Jan 1979; trans to
Glenrothes St Margaret's 18 Feb 1988.

1989 JOHN YOUNG
B 12 Feb 1934 at Glasgow, s of Matthew Swan
and Mary Jane Jardine Mathie; educ John Street
Secondary 1946–49; Scottish Congregational
College 1970–73; University of Glasgow 1982
(DipMin), 1986 (MTh); Pollokshields Congrega-
tional Church 1968–76; m 30 Dec 1961 Muriel Mary
Rennie b 1 Apr 1937 d of David and Janet R;
Children: Juliet Janet b 11 Jan 1965; Abigail
Jane b 14 Mar 1967; Emma Rennie b 9 Dec
1968; ord and ind to Dennistoun Wardlaw Con-
gregational Church 7 Jul 1963; admitted by General
Assembly 1976 and ind to Paisley Castlehead 28
Sep 1976; trans to Broomknoll 6 Jun 1989; became
minister of united charge with Calderbank 26 Aug
1998; ret 13 Jun 1999; Publ: *A Word in Your Ear*
(Heatherbank Press, 1986).

AIRDRIE CLARKSTON (FES III, 252; VIII, 255;
IX, 315; X, 185)

1975 ANDREW WATT BRADLEY
(FES X, 185), ord and ind to Clarkston 3 Jul 1975;
trans to Auchterarder 13 Oct 1983.

1984 ANDREW RITCHIE
ord and ind to Clarkston 22 Jun 1984; trans to
Edinburgh Craiglockhart 16 Oct 1991.

1992 THOMAS LEONARD POLLOCK
B 6 Oct 1954 at Glasgow, s of William Loudfoot P.
and Georgina McEwan Cummings Leonard; educ
Hyndland Senior Secondary, Glasgow 1967–73;
Glasgow College of Technology 1973–78 (DBS,
BA); University of Glasgow 1978–81 (BD);
University of Edinburgh 1994–96 (MTh); lic by

Presb of Glasgow 30 Jun 1981; asst Glasgow St
John's Renfield 1981–82; m 16 Jul 1982 Elaine
Elizabeth Gray b 27 Apr 1961 d of James G. and
Elizabeth Scott; Children: Mairi Gray b 14 Aug
1988; Neil Fraser b 14 Jan 1991; ord and ind to
Glasgow Barlanark Greyfriars 13 May 1982; trans
to Clarkston 2 Jun 1992.

AIRDRIE FLOWERHILL (FES III, 251; VIII, 258;
IX, 315; X, 185)

1956 JOHN BRUNTON CAMERON
(FES IX, 555, 730; X, 185, 417), res from service
with FMC in Calabar and ind to Flowerhill 12 Sep
1956; ret 31 Oct 1976; died 23 Jun 1978.

1977 JOHN HAY PATERSON
ord and ind to Flowerhill 2 Jun 1977; app Chaplain
(part-time) to Wester Moffat Hospital 1 Oct 1978
and to Monklands District General Hospital 1 Nov
1981; trans to Kirkintilloch St David's Memorial 23
Feb 1989.

1989 DAVID McNAIR CLARK
ord and ind to Flowerhill 31 Aug 1989; dem 7 Oct
1996 on app as General Director of Scripture Union
Scotland.

1997 ANDREW GARDNER
B 5 May 1966 at Glasgow, s of James Henry G.
and Hughina Somerville Crum; educ McLaren High,
Callander 1979–83; University of Glasgow 1984–
88 (BSc); University of Dundee 1989–92 (PhD);
University of St Andrews 1992–95 (BD); Research
Scientist, Scottish Crop Research Institute 1989–
92; loc ten at Douglas and Angus, Dundee 1997;
lic by Presb of Dundee 28 Jun 1995; asst Dundee
High Kirk 1995–97; m 3 Jul 1992 Julia Sandra Band
d of John David B. and Moira Joy Chalmers;
Children: Bethany Joanne b 27 Mar 1997; Karalyn
Rebecca b 14 Sep 1998; ord and ind to Flowerhill
12 Jun 1997.

AIRDRIE HIGH (FUF 175; FES IX, 316; X, 185)

1963 GEORGE McCABE
(FES X, 185), ord and ind to Airdrie High 2 Oct
1963; ret 28 Apr 1996.

1998 WILLIAM RICHARD HOUSTON
B 24 May 1957 at Johnstone, s of John H. and
Jessie McGill; educ Paisley Grammar 1969–75;

University of Glasgow 1975–79 (BSc); University of St Andrews 1993–96 (BD); Burroughs Machines 1980–82; Rodime Europe 1982–87; GEC Marconi 1987–93; lic by Presb of Kirkcaldy 30 Jun 1996; asst Leven St Andrew's 1993–94; Kirkcaldy Torbain 1994–95; Methil 1995–96; Kirkcaldy Linktown with Auchtertool 1996–98; m 3 Feb 1990 Helen Struthers b 1 May 1963 d of Matthew and Annette S; ord and ind to Airdrie High 12 Mar 1998.

AIRDRIE JACKSON (FUF 176; FES IX, 316; X, 185)

1960   WILLIAM WYLIE
(FES X, 186), ord and ind to Jackson 29 Jun 1960; dem 21 Sep 1997; died 15 Nov 1998.

1998   SHARON ELIZABETH FAIRBAIRN COLVIN
B 12 Jan 1943 at Bellshill, d of David Colville Osborne and Mary Elizabeth Nelson; educ Rutherglen Academy 1955–61; University of Glasgow 1980–84 (BD); lic by Presb of Hamilton 27 Jun 1984; asst Glasgow Greenbank 1984–85; m 25 Sep 1970 Richard Alexander Colvin b 1 May 1940 s of Denis Richard C. and Sarah Teresa Josephine Lynch; Children: Catherine Elizabeth b 25 Nov 1971; Sharon Eleanor b 4 Apr 1974; Richard Andrew b 19 Dec 1976; David Patrick b 19 Dec 1976; ord and ind to Ballingry 28 Jun 1985; trans to Jackson 17 Jun 1998.

AIRDRIE NEW MONKLAND (FES III, 271; VIII, 262; IX, 316; X, 186)

Linked 26 Jan 1977 with Greengairs.

1946   JAMES McCONNELL
(FES IX, 256, 316; X, 186), trans from Glasgow Barony North to New Monkland 5 Sep 1946; ret 31 Dec 1975; died 12 Jul 1983.

1977   ALAN ANDREW FORD
B 8 Jun 1948 at Glasgow, s of James F. and Elizabeth Reside Smith; educ High School of Glasgow 1960–65; Glasgow College of Commerce 1965–70 (AIB); University of Glasgow 1971–76 (BD); Bank of Scotland 1965–70; lic by Presb of Glasgow 25 Jun 1976; asst Dundee Mains of Fintry 1976–77; m 21 Sep 1972 Mary Douglas b 5 Oct 1948 d of Peter D. and Christina MacAulay; Children: Barbara Mary b 24 Mar 1977; Aileen Kirsty b 25 Jul 1978; ord and ind to New Monkland with Greengairs 13 Jul 1977.

AIRDRIE NEW WELLWYND (FES X, 186)

Formed 17 Sep 1995 by union of Airdrie Wellwynd and Airdrie West.

1957   THOMAS NICHOLSON
(FES IX, 67, 546; X, 186, 316), trans from Bervie to Wellwynd 17 Mar 1957; ret 30 Sep 1979; died 30 Oct 1980.

1975   GEORGE MITCHELL
(FES X, 186), trans under mutual eligibility from London Blackheath (Presb Church of England) to Airdrie West 17 Dec 1975; dem 31 May 1984; died 17 Apr 1989.

1980   ADAM JAMES LEARMONTH
(FES X, 199), trans from Motherwell North to Wellwynd 19 Nov 1980; ret 30 Sep 1993; s William m Ann Dunn.

1985   PETER MITCHELL GORDON
(FES X, 300, 316), trans from Brechin Cathedral to Airdrie West 5 Sep 1985; ret 17 Sep 1995; Publ: Contributor to *The Book of the Society of Friends of Brechin Cathedral*; contributor to *Airdrie West Parish Church: Its Life and Times 1834–1995* (1995); co-author of *Peter and Jane: Their Forebears, Relatives and Family* (1998).

1995   ROBERT FRASER PENNY
B 1 Nov 1959 at Perth, s of Andrew Fraser P. and Christina McGregor Robertson; educ Perth Academy 1964–77; University of Edinburgh 1977–80 (BA), 1980–83 (BD); lic by Presb of Perth 3 Jul 1983; asst Perth Letham St Mark's 1983–84; m 8 Jul 1982 Susan Claire Archibald b 28 Jan 1959 d of John Stevenson A. and Jane Elma Glendinning; Children: Andrew John b 9 Jan 1986; Katie Jane b 10 May 1988; ord and ind to Harray with Sandwick 13 Jun 1984; trans to New Wellwynd 31 May 1995.

AIRDRIE ST COLUMBA'S (FES X, 186)

1973   COLIN RUTHERFORD DOUGLAS
(FES X, 186), ind to St Columba's 26 Apr 1973; trans to Livingston Ecumenical Parish, Dedridge 30 Jun 1987.

1987   MARGARET FORSYTH CURRIE
B 14 Oct 1953 at Renfrew, d of Alexander Robertson C. and Ellen Edmiston Thompson Macfee; educ Paisley Grammar 1966–72; University of Aberdeen 1972–76 (BEd); University of Glasgow 1976–79 (BD); lic by Presb of Paisley 28 Jun 1979; asst Paisley St Mark's Oldhall 1979–80; ord by Presb of Paisley and app Asst at Renfrew Old 9 Jul 1980; introd as Community minister at Greenock Cartsdyke 23 Mar 1982; ind to St Columba's 17 Dec 1987.

BARGEDDIE (FES III, 226; VIII, 251; IX, 318; X, 187)

1962   JOHN ANGUS MACKENZIE
(FES IX, 587; X, 187, 341), trans from Finzean with Strachan to Bargeddie 31 Jan 1962; ret 31 Dec 1969 on grounds of ill-health; died 24 Oct 1991.

1970   ARCHIBALD FERGUSON DOIG
(FES X, 187, 216), trans from Clydebank Linnvale to Bargeddie 8 Jul 1970; dem 7 Oct 1975; died 16 May 1999.

1976 ALISTAIR MALCOLM
ord and ind to Bargeddie 16 Oct 1976; trans to
Inverness West 7 Nov 1992.

1993 HARRY BELL MEALYEA
B 14 Jan 1948 at Clydebank, s of Harry M. and
Melissa Resa Hume; educ Clydebank High 1960–
66; University of Strathclyde 1966–72 (BArch);
University of Glasgow 1979–81 (BD); Architecture
1972–74; Presb Church of Iran 1977–79; Presb
Church of Pakistan 1981–82; lic by Presb of
Glasgow, 1982; asst Glasgow Croftfoot 1982–84;
m 7 Jul 1975 Mary Thompson Mackie Scrimgeour
b 28 Mar 1952 d of Richard S. and Mary Mackie;
Children: Mark b 11 Jun 1982; William b 13 Mar
1984; Emily b 6 Aug 1985; Sarah Louise b 30 Dec
1990; ord and ind to Paisley St Luke's 12 Mar 1984;
trans to Bargeddie 23 Jun 1993.

BELLSHILL MACDONALD MEMORIAL (FUF
177; FES IX, 318; X, 187)

1942 ALBERT THOMSON
(FES IX, 110, 318; X, 187), trans from Morebattle
St Aidan's to MacDonald Memorial 21 Oct 1942;
ret 30 Sep 1972; died 19 Mar 1981.

1973 WILLIAM McCALLUM GLENCROSS
(FES X, 187, 408), trans from Whalsay and
Skerries to Macdonald Memorial 29 Jun 1973; ret
31 Jul 1999; d Claire m Liam Davey; d Denise m
Stephen Simpson.

BELLSHILL ORBISTON (FES IX, 318; X, 187)

Linked 15 Oct 1980 with Bellshill St Andrew's.

1974 ROBERT JAMES McKAY
(FES IX, 281; X, 167, 187, 273), trans from
Dunfermline St Andrew's to Orbiston 11 Jan 1974;
ret 15 Oct 1980; died 31 Dec 1980.

1981 CHARLES HUGH MOAR GREIG
ord by UFC and ind to Edinburgh Blackhall 24 Jul
1976; ind to Orbiston with St Andrew's 6 May 1981;
trans to Kinghorn 26 Oct 1988.

1989 HARRY MARTIN JOHN JOHNSTONE
B 12 May 1963 at Orpington, Kent, s of Robert J.
and Helen Scott Rae; educ Linlithgow Academy
1975–80; University of Edinburgh 1981–84 (MA);
University of Aberdeen 1984–87 (BD), 1988–89
(MTh); lic by Presb of West Lothian, Sep 1987;
asst Glasgow Castlemilk East 1987–88; m 24 Mar
1990 Susan Harvie b 14 Jun 1965 d of Robin H.
and Elizabeth Lumsden; Children: Robert Martin b
9 Jun 1993; David John b 27 Jul 1995; ord and ind
to Orbiston with St Andrew's 19 Sep 1989.

BELLSHILL ST ANDREW'S (FUF 177; FES IX,
318; X, 187)

Linked 15 Oct 1980 with Bellshill Orbiston.

1946 ALLAN RODGER MACPHERSON
(FES IX, 319, 478; X, 187), trans from Kirkcaldy
Invertiel North to St Andrew's 27 Jun 1946; ret 31
Dec 1969; died 30 Oct 1980.

1970 JAMES FORSYTH
(FES X, 187, 378), ord and ind to St Andrew's 24
Jun 1970; trans to Fortrose and Rosemarkie 30
May 1975.

1976 C BRIAN ROSS
ord and ind to St Andrew's 13 May 1976; dem 10
Sep 1979.

1981 CHARLES HUGH MOAR GREIG
ind to Bellshill Orbiston with St Andrew's 6 May
1981, see Orbiston.

1989 HARRY MARTIN JOHN JOHNSTONE
ord and ind to Orbiston with St Andrew's 19 Sep
1989, see Orbiston.

BELLSHILL WEST (FES III, 226; VIII, 252; IX, 319;
X, 187)

1973 ARTHUR FRANCIS STODDART KENT
(FES X, 187, 420), res from service with Overseas
Council in Jamaica and ind to Bellshill West 18
Oct 1973; trans to Monkton and Prestwick North 9
Dec 1981.

1982 JAMES WILSON McLEOD
admitted by General Assembly 1978; ind to
Bellshill West 15 May 1982; introd to Geneva 11
Jan 1994.

1994 QUINTIN ALEXANDER BLANE
B 30 Apr 1952 at Ayr, s of Quintin B. and Jean
Kerr Cannell; educ Ayr Academy 1964–70;
University of Glasgow 1970–74 (BSc), 1974–77
(BD); lic by Presb of Ayr 6 Jul 1977; asst Edinburgh
St Giles' 1977–80; ord by Presb of Edinburgh
during assistantship at St Giles' 3 Jun 1979; ind to
Barrhead Arthurlie 28 Oct 1980; trans to Bellshill
West 25 Oct 1994.

BLANTYRE LIVINGSTONE MEMORIAL (FUF
179; FES IX, 319; X, 188)

Continued vacancy from 1998.

1974 JAMES EDWARD HUNTER
(FES X, 188), ord and ind to Livingstone Memorial
18 Dec 1974; ret 10 Mar 1997; d Grace m Lindsay;
d Marion m Harkness; d Janet m Ritchie.

BLANTYRE OLD (FES III, 227; VIII, 252; IX, 320;
X, 188)

1971 JOHN NEISH NOTMAN
(FES X, 188, 224), trans from Yoker St Matthew's
to Blanytre Old 6 Oct 1971; died 5 Mar 1976.

1976 JOHN RICHARD SILCOX
ord and ind to Blantyre Old 16 Sep 1976; dem on app as Chaplain and Head of Dept of Religious, Moral and Philisophical Studies, Queen Victoria School, Dunblane 1 Sep 1984.

1985 PETER OWEN PRICE
ord by Methodist Conference and ind to Brays Road Church, Liverpool 1957; Chaplain, Royal Navy 1960–80; Principal Chaplain, Royal Navy 1981–84; admitted by General Assembly 1984 and ind to Blantyre Old 19 Mar 1985; ret 30 Sep 1996.

1997 ROSEMARY ANN SMITH
B 22 Mar 1944 at Hayling Island, Hampshire, d of William Henderson Kay and Hilda Rosemary Saggers; educ King's Road High, Rosyth 1955–60; University of Edinburgh 1992–96 (BD); GEC Marconi (Secretarial) 1978–92; loc ten Dunfermline St Andrew's Erskine 1997; lic by Presb of Dunfermline 23 Jun 1996; asst Dunfermline Gillespie Memorial 1996–97; m 13 Apr 1963, divorced; Children: Brian b 15 Apr 1964 m Christine; Neil b 15 Mar 1968; Jason b 5 May 1971; ord and ind to Blantyre Old 23 Oct 1997.

BLANTYRE ST ANDREW'S (FES X, 187, 188)

Formed 23 Jun 1976 by union of Blantyre Anderson and Blantyre Stonefield and Burleigh.

1975 ALEXANDER BUCHAN
(FES X, 188), ord and ind to Anderson with Stonefield Burleigh 25 Jun 1975; became minister of united charge 23 Jun 1976; trans to Whalsay and Skerries 19 Mar 1977; m 1 May 1976 Isabel Coulter Black b 16 Mar 1949 d of David and Catherine Coulter B; Children: David b 17 Jun 1977; Catherine b 28 Aug 1979.

1978 JAMES CHARLES GREGORY
(FES X, 78), trans from Kirkpatrick Fleming with Half Morton to St Andrew's 2 Feb 1978; ret 9 Oct 1992.

1993 IAN MEREDITH
B 14 Oct 1953 at Paisley, s of John Richard M. and Elizabeth MacFarlane; educ Stanley Green Secondary, Paisley 1965–69; Reid Kerr College, Paisley 1968–71; Cardonald Further Education College, Glasgow 1972–73; London Bible College 1973–77; Spurgeons College, London 1982–85 (BA); University of London 1987–89 (MTh); University of Edinburgh 1994–96 (MTh); Psychiatric Nursing 1971–74; m 2 Jan 1997 Marilyn Dawn Short b 25 Jun 1950 d of Benjamin S. and Margaret Thompson; ord by URC and ind to St Martin's Watford 4 May 1985; ind to St Andrew's 24 Aug 1993.

BOTHWELL (FES X, 189)

Formed 25 Aug 1976 by union of Bothwell St Bride's and Bothwell Kirkfield and Wooddean.

1945 THOMAS KIRKWOOD CAMPBELL
(FES IX, 298, 321; X, 189), trans from Glasgow St Kiaran's Dean Park to St Bride's 27 Jun 1945; ret 31 Oct 1975; died 31 Dec 1993.

1958 JOHN LOUGH
(FES IX, 303, 663; X, 178, 189), trans from Glasgow St Thomas' Gallowgate to Kirkfield and Wooddean 13 Mar 1958; ret 31 Dec 1973; died 12 Jul 1982.

1977 ROBERT JAMES STEWART
(FES X, 204, 258), trans from Comrie and Strowan to Bothwell 6 Jul 1977; trans to Orwell with Portmoak 15 Feb 1989.

1989 JAMES McALPINE GIBSON
B 31 Mar 1948 at Edinburgh, s of William G. and Agnes Taylor McAlpine; educ Daniel Stewart's, Edinburgh 1953–67; Edinburgh College of Speech and Drama 1972–75 (LRAM); University of Glasgow 1972–77 (LTh); General Building Contracting and Haulage Contracting 1967–72; lic by Presb of Glasgow 30 Jun 1977; asst Paisley Abbey 1977–78; m 15 Jul 1978 Doreen Margaret McCracken b 23 Jul 1952 d of James M. and Catherine Margaret Craig Adams; Children: Niall Adams b 1 Feb 1981; Valerie Jane b 7 Jan 1983; ord and ind to Grangemouth Old 11 Jul 1978; trans to Bothwell 3 Nov 1989.

CALDERBANK (FUF 180; FES III, 233; VIII, 254; IX, 321; X, 189)

Vacant 1974 until 1979. Linked 22 Feb 1979 with Chapelhall. Arrangement terminated 26 Aug 1998 to allow for linkage with Airdrie Broomknoll.

1979 SAMUEL HOSAIN
ord and ind to Calderbank with Chapelhall 26 Sep 1979; trans to Fauldhouse St Andrew's 2 Jul 1985.

1986 JAMES ROBERT NELSON
ord and ind to Chapelhall with Calderbank 3 Apr 1986, see Chapelhall.

CALDERCRUIX, LONGRIGGEND AND MEADOWFIELD (FES X, 30)

Formed 26 Jun 1973 by union of Caldercruix, Longriggend and Meadowfield.

1962 ANGUS MACLEOD
(FES IX, 407, 687, 695; X, 30, 241), trans from Tobermory to Caldercruix with Longriggend with Meadowfield 12 Apr 1962; ret 31 Aug 1972; died 11 Sep 1986.

1974 JAMES MULHOLLAND MARTIN
(FES X, 30), ord and ind to Caldercruix, Longriggend and Meadowfield 16 May 1974; trans to Glasgow Croftfoot 8 Nov 1979.

1980 ROBERT CARL NELSON
ord and ind to Caldercruix, Longriggend and
Meadowfield 28 May 1980; Chaplain to Longriggend Remand Institution 1984–90; trans to
Inverness Dalneigh and Bona 31 May 1990.

1991 CHARLES JOHN FINNIE
ord and ind to Caldercruix, Longriggend and
Meadowfield 22 Jan 1991; trans to Hawick Burnfoot
30 May 1997.

1998 IAN McINTYRE WATSON
B 18 Jun 1964 at Glasgow, s of John Irvine W.
and Eleanor Margaret Herald; educ Braidfield High,
Clydebank; University of Strathclyde 1982–86
(LLB), 1987 (DipLP); University of St Andrews
1992–95 (BD); Solicitor 1987–92; lic by Presb of
Perth 4 Aug 1995; asst Bethesda Presb Church,
North Carolina 1995–96; Dunfermline St Leonard's
1996–98; m 15 Jun 1991 Kim Crichton b 22 Apr
1969 d of James C. and Susan McMillan; ord and
ind to Caldercruix Longriggend and Meadowfield
18 Feb 1998.

CARFIN (FES IX, 323; X, 190)

Continued vacancy from 1967 until 1988. Linked 1
Apr 1988 with Newarthill.

1988 GEORGE STRACHAN NOBLE
(FES X, 200), ord and ind to Newarthill 30 Jun
1972; became minister of linked charge with Carfin
1 Apr 1988.

CHAPELHALL (FUF 181; FES IX, 323; X, 191)

Linked 22 Feb 1979 with Calderbank. Arrangement
terminated 26 Aug 1998.

1970 PETER MARTIN DAWES
(FES X, 191), trans under mutual eligibility from
Carcroft St Andrew's (Presb Church of England)
to Chapelhall 18 Nov 1970; trans to Trinity (URC),
Camden Town, London 28 Jul 1977.

1979 SAMUEL HOSAIN
ord and ind to Calderbank with Chapelhall 26
Sep 1979; trans to Fauldhouse St Andrew's 2 Jul
1985.

1986 JAMES ROBERT NELSON
B 27 Feb 1945 at Bellshill, s of Robert N. and
Elizabeth Shearer McColm; educ Uddingston
Grammar 1957–60; University of St Andrews
1979–84 (BD, DPTh); Joinery and Glazing 1960–
66, 1968–69; Secretary 1966–68; lic by Presb of
St Andrews 15 Jul 1984; asst St Andrews Hope
Park 1984–85; m 8 Oct 1983 Georgina Roden b
19 Oct 1957 d of William R. and Marion Henderson;
divorced 1 Dec 1997; ord and ind to Chapelhall
with Calderbank 3 Apr 1986; became minister of
Chapelhall following termination of linkage 26 Aug
1998.

CHAPELTON (FES IX, 324; X, 191)

Linked 15 Jun 1960 with Strathaven Rankin.

1968 JAMES GREIG
(FES X, 191, 202, 419), res from service with
Overseas Council in Kenya and ind to Chapelton
with Strathaven Rankin 5 Dec 1968; trans to Irvine
Old 27 Feb 1979.

1979 ALISTAIR LINDSAY JESSAMINE
ord and ind to Chapelton with Strathaven Rankin
28 Aug 1979; trans to Dunfermline Abbey 19 Mar
1991.

1991 SHAW JAMES PATERSON
B 13 Sep 1964 at Bellshill, s of James P. and Anne
Kerr Andrews Reid; educ Bellshill Academy and
Langside College 1976–82; University of Glasgow
1982–87 (BSc), 1987–90 (BD); lic by Presb of
Hamilton 26 Jun 1990; asst Hamilton Old 1990–
91; m 4 Sep 1987 Christine Russell b 3 Oct 1963
d of James Dougall R. and Marion Andrew Welsh
Miller; Children: Euan Shaw b 19 Mar 1993; Ross
James b 22 Dec 1995; Kirstie Mhariane b 10 Jul
1997; ord and ind to Chapelton with Strathaven
Rankin 29 Aug 1991; app Chaplain (part-time) to
Dungavel Prison.

CLELAND (FUF 182; FES III, 243; VIII, 255; IX,
324; X, 191)

1970 JAMES HAY WILSON
(FES X, 191), ord and ind to Cleland 18 May 1970;
app Clerk to Presb of Hamilton 5 Feb 1985; ret 31
May 1996 from Cleland; d Margaret Ann m John
Thomson Robb (deceased); d Janice m William
Andrew Baird.

1997 JOHN ANDREW JACKSON
B 2 Mar 1948 at Woburn, Mass, USA, s of Andrew
J. and Edyth Vera Hanover; educ Airdrie Academy
1961–67; Glasgow College of Technology 1980–
81 (DMS); University of Glasgow 1988–93 (BD);
Engineering 1972–79; Project Manager 1979–80;
Company Director 1980–92; lic by Presb of
Hamilton 29 Jun 1993; asst Hamilton St John's
1993–94; m (1) 17 Feb 1973 Elizabeth Margaret
McWilliam b 26 Jun 1949, died 15 Jun 1988 d of
Stuart Wilson M. and Margaret Elizabeth
McKendrick; Children: Roderick Andrew Stuart b
13 Dec 1976; Victoria Jane b 15 Sep 1979; m (2)
28 Jun 1993 Caroline Clark b 19 Mar 1957 d of
Robert Baird Hunter C. and Irene Alexia Brown;
ord and ind to Cleland 24 Nov 1997.

COATBRIDGE BLAIRHILL DUNDYVAN (FES X,
191)

Formed 11 Sep 1974 by union of Blairhill and
Dundyvan.

1947 GRIFFITH JOSEPH OWENS
(FES IX, 325; X, 192), admitted by General Assembly 1946; ord and ind to Dundyvan 24 Mar 1947; ret 11 Sep 1974; died 22 Aug 1984.

1975 IAN SAMUEL CURRIE
(FES X, 191), ord and ind to Blairhill Dundyvan 8 May 1975; trans to Paisley St John's 22 Oct 1980.

1981 GEORGINA MARTHA BAXENDALE
ord and ind to Blairhill Dundyvan 14 May 1981; dem 30 Sep 1986 on app as Assoc Chaplain to University of Glasgow.

1987 IAIN ALEXANDER WHYTE
(FES X, 427), res as Chaplain to University of St Andrews 1 Oct 1981 and ind to Blairhill Dundyvan 15 Jun 1987; app National Secretary, Christian Aid Scotland 1 Oct 1990.

1991 JOHN McLACHLAN BLACK
(FES X, 318, 444), res from RAF Chaplains' Branch and ind to Blairhill Dundyvan 21 Mar 1991; d Jane m Fox; d Ruth m Stretch.

COATBRIDGE CALDER (FES X, 192, 193)

Formed 7 Sep 1978 by union of Coatbridge Garturk and Coatbridge Whifflet.

1949 JOHN COWAN
(FES IX, 222, 326; X, 192), trans from Paisley Mossvale to Garturk 4 May 1949; ret 16 May 1977; died 18 May 1980.

1972 WILLIAM OMAND WINTHROP
(FES IX, 374; X, 193, 223), dem from Renton Old in interests of union 25 Jun 1969; introd on term app to Whifflet 29 Nov 1972; res 1978; died 27 Oct 1979.

1979 WILLIAM G McKAIG
ind to Calder 27 Apr 1979; dem 30 Jun 1983; ind to Peterculter St Peter's 26 Jun 1991.

1983 KEITH SAUNDERS
ord and ind to Calder 21 Dec 1983; dem 19 Sep 1999 to take up app as Chaplain to Glasgow Western Infirmary.

COATBRIDGE CLIFTON (FES X, 192)

Formed 21 Mar 1993 by union of Coatbridge Coats and Coatbridge Coatdyke.

1948 THOMAS JARDINE JOHNSTONE
(FES IX, 325; X, 192), ord and ind to Coats 29 Apr 1948; ret 31 Oct 1990; died 18 Aug 1998; Publ: Sermon *A City Set on an Hill* (Monklands Library, 1985).

1974 HENRY RAMSAY MANN FRASER
(FES IX, 710; X, 49, 192, 247, 388, 404), trans from Logierait to Coatdyke 14 Nov 1974; trans to Aberdeen John Knox Gerrard Street 6 Jul 1978.

1979 IAN WILLIAM MACBAIN
(FES X, 371), dem from Daviot and Dunlichity with Moy, Dalarossie and Tomatin 30 Sep 1976; ind to Coatdyke 29 Feb 1979; ret 31 Mar 1993; s Allan m Margaret Alexander; d June m David Grindley.

1992 LESLIE WILLIAM THORNE
B 11 Nov 1936 at Ruislip Manor, Middlesex, s of Philip T. and Agnes Gray Gifford; educ Hillhead High, Glasgow 1948–52; University of Glasgow 1983–86 (LTh); Open University 1994 (BA); Engineering 1952–83; lic by Presb of Paisley 28 Jun 1986; asst St Andrews St Leonard's with Cameron 1986–87; m 8 Apr 1974 Moira Walker b 11 Mar 1948, died 12 Feb 1998 d of Gavin W. and Mary Hill Jack Miller; ord and ind to Kirtle-Eaglesfield with Middlebie with Waterbeck 21 Jul 1987; trans to Coats 29 Sep 1992; became minister of united charge with Coatdyke 21 Mar 1993.

COATBRIDGE MIDDLE (FUF 184; FES IX, 326; X, 192)

1974 JOHN CAMPBELL
(FES X, 193), ord and ind to Coatbridge Middle 19 Dec 1974; ret 31 Aug 1985; died 11 Aug 1998.

1986 ANDREW MALTMAN McCANCE
B 27 Mar 1925 at Glasgow, s of Andrew Sillars M. and Jane McKinlay; educ Glasgow High 1935–43; Royal Technical College, Glasgow [now University of Strathclyde] 1944–45, 1948–50 (BSc); University of Glasgow 1983–84; Plant and Production Engineering, Albion Motors 1944–79; British Leyland 1979–80; Burdur Traktor Co., Turkey 1980–82; lic by Presb of Glasgow 25 Jun 1984; asst Bearsden South 1984–85; m (1) 23 Sep 1952 Jessie Olivia Mackay b 14 Dec 1933 d of William Murray M. and Isobel Thomson; Children: Valerie Ann b 30 May 1954 m Brolly; Andrew Murray b 4 Apr 1956 m Roff; Douglas Ian b 2 Jun 1967; divorced 22 Oct 1981; m (2) 8 Apr 1985 Corinne Dunn Coull b 28 Jul 1938 d of Robert Kidd C. and Jane Wilson Stewart; ord and ind to Coatbridge Middle 12 Mar 1986; ret 27 Mar 1995.

1996 JAMES GRIER
B 9 Jul 1940 at Glasgow, s of James G. and Ellen Rachael Wood; educ Albert Secondary, Glasgow 1952–55; University of Glasgow 1985–89 (BD); Printing 1955–74; Sales Rep 1974–85; lic by Presb of Glasgow 3 Jul 1989; asst Bishopbriggs Springfield Cambridge 1989–90; Glasgow High Carntyne 1990–91; m 20 Jun 1964 Moira MacGowan Campbell b 9 Nov 1941 d of Samuel Peter C. and Helen Carmichael MacGowan; Children: Lynn Alison b 28 Jun 1966; Gillian Karen b 26 Jun 1968 m Graham Hunter; ord by Presb of Lochcarron and Skye and introd as Assoc at Strath and Sleat 26 Apr 1991; ind to Coatbridge Middle 16 May 1996; Chaplain (part-time) to Monklands General Hospital, Airdrie.

COATBRIDGE OLD MONKLAND (FES III, 273; VIII, 262; IX, 327; X, 193)

1969 JAMES GIBSON MUNTON
(FES X, 193), ord and ind to Old Monkland 25 Jun 1969; Open University 1980 (BA); w Helen died 3 Jul 1982; m (2) 16 Apr 1984 Jaqueline McOwat b 23 Nov 1952 d of John M. and Margaret Edith McIntosh; s David m Linda Brown; d Jennifer m John Muir.

COATBRIDGE ST ANDREW'S (FES X, 192)

Formed 28 Feb 1993 by union of Coatbridge Dunbeth, Coatbridge Gartsherrie (continued vacancy from 1983–93) and Coatbridge Maxwell.

1967 JOHN (IAN) DARROCH BRADY
(FES X, 192), ord and ind to Gartsherrie 6 Sep 1967; trans to Edinburgh Corstorphine Old 24 Mar 1976.

1976 JAMES THOMSON McNAY
(FES X, 156, 198, 325), trans from Aberdeen Bon-Accord St Paul's to Maxwell 24 Mar 1976; died 19 Jul 1991.

1977 ERIC BURKINSHAW
(FES X, 277), trans from Mossgreen and Cross-gates to Gartsherrie 22 Sep 1977; trans to Kirtle-Eaglesfield with Middlebie with Waterbeck 8 Nov 1983.

1977 JAMES FREDERICK DUNN
(FES X, 144, 218, 219), trans from Dumbarton Riverside to Dunbeth 22 Sep 1977; ret 28 Feb 1993; d Marion m Kenneth McCracken; s James m Lloret McKenna.

1994 IAN GRAHAM WOTHERSPOON
(FES X, 23, 102, 289, 413), trans from Gordon St Michael's with Greenlaw with Legerwood with Westruther to St Andrew's 23 Jun 1994; Open University 1983–87 (BA); Clerk to Presb of Duns 1993–94; Addl children: Stewart Ian b 10 Jul 1976; d Shona m Mark Thomas.

COATBRIDGE TOWNHEAD (FES IX, 327; X, 193)

1969 WILLIAM MAYNE GILMOUR
(FES X, 193), ord and ind to Townhead 24 Sep 1969; trans to Bridge of Allan Chalmers with Lecropt 14 Nov 1979.

1980 CHARLES ARCHIBALD LEGGAT
ord and ind to Townhead 27 Aug 1980; trans to Dundee Craigiebank 7 Dec 1989.

1990 DEREK WALTER HUGHES
ord and ind to Townhead 18 Jun 1990; trans to Motherwell Dalziel St Andrew's 20 Sep 1996.

1997 DAVID PAXTON HOOD
B 9 Dec 1963 at Glasgow, s of David Paxton H. and Jean Stevenson Ross; educ Williamwood High and Eastwood High, Glasgow 1975–80; Glasgow

College of Technology 1980–84 (DipIOB[Scot]); University of Glasgow 1986–90 (BD), 1993–94 (CMin); Clydesdale Bank 1980–86; Dept of National Mission 1990–93; lic by Presb of Glasgow 4 Jul 1994; asst Glasgow Rutherglen Stonelaw 1994–96; m 20 Sep 1991 Janet Ruth Forbes b 18 Dec 1967 d of Iain F. and Ruth Macartney; Children: Jennifer Ruth b 16 Mar 1993; David Paxton b 25 Nov 1995; ord and ind to Townhead 29 May 1997.

DALSERF (FES III, 245; VIII, 256; IX, 328; X, 193)

1974 KEITH MACLEOD McROBB
(FES IX, 196, 440; X, 112, 150, 194), trans from Glasgow Balshagray to Dalserf 3 May 1974; ret 1 Dec 1981; died 28 Jul 1992.

1982 DAVID CAMERON McPHERSON
B 2 Jan 1948 at Glasgow, s of David Jeffrey M. and Margaret Busby; educ Queen's Park Secondary, Glasgow 1960–65; University of Strathclyde 1971–75 (BSc); University of Glasgow 1976–80 (BD); Trainee Telephone Engineer 1965–66; Corrosion Engineer 1975–76; lic by Presb of Glasgow, 1980; asst Burntisland and Auchtertool 1980–81; m 14 Jul 1983 Sharon Clarissa Jones b 19 Mar 1953 d of Frederick J. and Clarissa Price; Children: David Jones b 14 Dec 1997; ord and ind to Dalserf 2 Jun 1982.

EAST KILBRIDE CLAREMONT (FES X, 142)

1968 EDWARD ANTHONY HOWARTH SAWERS
(FES X, 142, 180, 193), trans from Glasgow South Shawlands to Claremont 24 Apr 1968; trans to Cranstoun, Crichton and Ford 12 May 1977.

1978 KEITH McLEOD STEVEN
ord and ind to Claremont 5 Jul 1978; introd as Assoc at Glasgow Renfield St Stephen's 11 Apr 1991.

1991 JOHN KYNOCH COLLARD
B 15 Mar 1957 at Oxford, s of Martin Kynoch C. and Frances Jean Archer; educ Bradfield College, Berkshire 1970–75; University of Cambridge 1976–79 (MA); University of Edinburgh 1982–85 (BD); Scottish and Newcastle Breweries 1979–82; lic by Presb of Edinburgh 30 Jun 1985; asst Edinburgh Murrayfield 1985–86; m 16 Aug 1980 Anne Morrison b 16 Aug 1958 d of Archie M. and Joan Wallace; Children: Graeme Kynoch b 5 Jan 1988; Robert Wallace b 5 Jan 1992; ord by Presb of Edinburgh and introd as Assoc at Holy Trinity 20 Aug 1986; trans to Claremont 3 Oct 1991.

EAST KILBRIDE GREENHILLS (FES X, 143)

1972 THOMAS MATHIESON McWILLIAM
(FES X, 143, 305), trans from Dundee St David's North to Greenhills 17 May 1972; trans to Paisley Lylesland 27 Aug 1980.

1981 ALEXANDER McKENZIE MILLAR
ord by Presb of Edinburgh during assistantship at South Leith 15 Jun 1980; ind to Greenhills 13 May 1981; trans to St Martin's with Scone New 19 Aug 1987.

1988 JOHN BREWSTER
B 19 Aug 1955 at Buckhaven, s of Robert B. and Margaret Thomson; educ Buckhaven High 1967–73; University of St Andrews 1973–77 (MA); University of Dundee 1977–78 (DipEd); Dundee College of Education 1977–78 (PGCE); University of Edinburgh 1982–85 (BD); Teaching 1978–82; lic by Presb of Kirkcaldy 2 Jul 1985; asst Aberdeen Kirk of St Nicholas 1985–88; ord and ind to Greenhills 21 Apr 1988.

1990 MATILDA WILSON
ord by Presb of Hamilton and introd as Assoc at Greenhills 1 Oct 1990; ind to Dysart 26 Aug 1998.

EAST KILBRIDE MONCREIFF (FUF 206; FES IX, 243; X, 143)

1972 ALEXANDER McLACHLAN
(FES X, 131, 143), trans from Renfrew North to Moncreiff 20 Sep 1972; dem 16 Sep 1983.

1983 ALASTAIR SWANSON LUSK
(FES X, 143), ord by Presb of Hamilton and introd as Assoc at Moncreiff 14 Feb 1974; ind to same charge 9 Nov 1983; Addl children: Cara b 16 Jun 1976; Graeme b 9 Mar 1979.

1984 JAMES BELL FALCONER
ord by Presb of Glasgow during assistantship at Broom Church 31 Mar 1982; introd as Assoc at Moncreiff 4 Apr 1984; app Chaplain to Kingseat and House of Daviot Hospitals 30 Oct 1989.

1989 IAN ANDREW MANSON
ord by Presb of Hamilton and introd as Assoc at Moncreiff 8 Jun 1989; ind to Clydebank St Cuthbert's 20 Oct 1992.

1993 NORMA PEEBLES ROBERTSON
ord and introd as Assoc at Moncreiff 8 Jun 1993; ind to Kincardine O'Neil with Lumphanan 11 Jun 1998.

EAST KILBRIDE MOSSNEUK

Church Extension 1991.

1989 STUART HEADLEY ROBERTSON
B 15 Dec 1935 at Newcastle-on-Tyne, s of Percy John R. and Florence May Miskelly; educ Heaton Technical School, Newcastle 1947–51; Rutherford College of Technology, Newcastle 1951–57 (ONC, HNC); University of Glasgow 1975–78 (MEng), 1978–81 (BD); Instrument Engineering 1951–65; General Management, Mine Safety Appliances 1965–78; lic by Presb of Glasgow 30 Jun 1981; asst Glasgow Anniesland Cross 1980–81;

Bearsden North 1981–82; m 24 Mar 1962 Roberta Burns b 12 Jul 1940 d of Robert Dempster B. and Martha Tilley Tate; Children: Gillian b 6 Apr 1964; Graeme Stuart b 17 May 1966; David Robert Kenneth b 15 May 1971; ord and ind to Gorebridge 27 May 1982; trans to Mossneuk 21 Nov 1989; died 4 Jun 1998.

EAST KILBRIDE OLD (FES III, 265; VIII, 261; IX, 244; X, 143)

1932 THOMAS KENNEDY JOHNSTONE
(FES VIII, 200; IX, 151, 244; X, 143), trans from Balmaclellan to East Kilbride Old 26 Oct 1932; ret 31 Aug 1960; died 10 Jan 1981.

1961 WALTER MILNE REID
(FES IX, 88, 435, 661, 664; X, 143, 259), trans from Crieff South to East Kilbride Old 17 May 1961; died 29 May 1974.

1975 JAMES GILFILLAN
(FES X, 143, 213), trans from Alexandria North to East Kilbride Old 16 Apr 1975; ret 31 Jan 1997; d Agnes m Alan Bowles; s James m Hazel Aitken; Editor of *Young Scotland* (1968–72); editor of *Yes* (1978–82); editor of *Ministers' Forum* (1993–99).

1998 DOUGLAS WILLIAM CLARK
B 13 Aug 1946 at Glasgow, s of William C. and Helen Scott; educ Dalmuir Secondary 1951–61; University of Glasgow 1988–91 (LTh); Clyde Port Authority 1961–84; lic by Presb of Glasgow, Jun 1992; m 4 Oct 1969 Janette Campbell b 19 Oct 1943 d of Kenneth C. and Ethel Orr; Children: Stuart William and Stephen Kenneth b 1 Dec 1971; ord and ind to Bellhelvie 25 May 1993; trans to East Kilbride Old 16 Feb 1998.

EAST KILBRIDE SOUTH (FES X, 143)

1958 PATRICK JOHN ROGERS HAMILTON
(FES IX, 244; X, 143 (2)), dem from East Kilbride West on app as first minister of Church Extension Charge of East Kilbride South 26 Mar 1958; ret 31 Aug 1979; s Paul m Reeta Chakrabarti; s Mark m Susan Duckworth.

1980 JOHN CLARKSON SHARP
B 30 Dec 1945 at Motherwell, s of Robert Eglinton S. and Isabella Agnes Burgess Morison; educ Dalziel High, Motherwell 1957–64; Coatbridge Technical College 1964–68 (HNC); University of Strathclyde 1968–70 (BSc); University of Glasgow 1972–78 (BD, PhD); Draughtsman 1964–68; Mechanical Engineering 1968–72; lic by Presb of Hamilton 2 Jul 1975; asst Motherwell Dalziel 1978–79; m 17 Oct 1970 Allison Black Morrison b 6 Dec 1938 d of William M. and Allison Jane Taylor; Children: Andrew Robert b 28 Sep 1971; Allison Ruth b 13 Sep 1973; John William b 20 May 1977; ord and ind to East Kilbride South 20 Feb 1980; Publ: *Life is for Everyone* (St Andrew Press, 1988); *Jesus is for Everyone* (St Andrew Press, 1992).

EAST KILBRIDE WEST (FUF 206; FES IX, 244; X, 143)

1975 MACKNIGHT CRAWFURD COWPER
(FES IX, 126; X, 73, 144, 444), res from RAChD and ind to East Kilbride West 10 Dec 1975; ret 20 Jul 1983; d Judith m William Wehmeyer.

1983 DAVID EDWARD PAXTON CURRIE
B 27 Jun 1950 at Glasgow, s of Duncan C. and Jessie Isabella Bryce Paxton; educ Duncanrig Secondary and Hunter High, East Kilbride 1962–67; University of Strathclyde 1970–74 (BSc); University of Glasgow 1979–82 (BD); Apprentice Metallurgist 1967–70; Production Engineer and Development Engineer 1974–79; lic by Presb of Hamilton 1 Jul 1982; asst Rutherglen Stonelaw 1982–83; m 22 Mar 1975 Gwen Ward b 15 Aug 1955 d of Timothy Ineson W. and Ethel Osborne; Children: David Ian b 27 Nov 1977; Jennifer Elizabeth b 10 Sep 1979; Merle Jane b 12 Aug 1982; John Graham 21 Apr 1986; ord and ind to East Kilbride West 14 Sep 1983.

EAST KILBRIDE WESTWOOD (FES X, 144)

1971 IAN DUNCAN PETRIE
(FES X, 144), ord by Presb of Aberdeen 3 May 1970 and ind to Westwood 29 Apr 1971; trans to Dundee St Andrew's 15 Jan 1986.

1986 JAMES GRAHAM BLACK
B 10 Feb 1952 at Motherwell, s of James B. and Elizabeth Emily McCallum Graham; educ Dalziel High, Motherwell 1964–70; University of Glasgow 1970–71, 1972–77 (BD, DPS); lic by Presb of Hamilton 29 Jun 1977; asst West Kilbride St Andrew's 1977–78; m 11 Jul 1979 Isobel Ann Hamilton d of Ian H. and Isobel Fortune; Children: Isobel b 8 Dec 1982; ord and ind to Hamilton North 30 Aug 1978; became minister of linked charge with Burnbank 13 Jan 1982; trans to Westwood 28 Aug 1986; died 16 Jan 1996.

1996 KEVIN MACKENZIE
B 30 Aug 1962 at Aberdeen, s of Roy M. and Henrietta Mary Strachan Craig; educ Gordon Schools, Huntly 1974–79; University of Aberdeen 1982–88 (BD, DPS); lic by Presb of Aberdeen 27 Jun 1988; asst Edinburgh Murrayfield 1988–89; m 16 Aug 1985 Linda Anne Wylie b 19 May 1962 d of Alexander W. and Anne Gillespie; Children: Hollie b 7 Oct 1986; Katie b 18 Apr 1989; Christopher b 29 Dec 1990; ord and ind to Wemyss 16 May 1989; trans to Ochiltree with Stair 30 Mar 1993; trans to Westwood 12 Dec 1996.

GLASFORD (FES III, 243; VIII, 258; IX, 328; X, 194)

Linked 31 Jan 1973 with Strathaven East.

1973 HECTOR JAMES STEEL
(FES IX, 339, 610; X, 202), ind to Strathaven East 28 Apr 1949; became minister of linked charge with Glasford 31 Jan 1973, see Strathaven.

1980 WILLIAM THOMPSON STEWART
B 12 Apr 1953 at Giffnock, s of John S. and Mary Murray Stewart Thompson; educ Woodfarm High, Giffnock and Shawlands Academy, Glasgow 1965–71; University of Glasgow 1971–78 (BD, DPS); lic by Presb of Falkirk 29 Jun 1978; asst Rutherglen Stonelaw 1978–79; m 29 Jun 1981 Sheila Ann Alison b 2 May 1957 d of Graham A. and Norma MacArthur Perry; Children: Euan John b 17 Jun 1985; Gillian Norma b 28 Nov 1988; ord and ind to Glasford with Strathaven East 6 Feb 1980; Publ: *Glasford: The Kirk and the Kingdom* (Mainsprint, 1988).

GREENGAIRS (FES IX, 329; X, 194)

Vacant from 1974 until 1977. Linked 26 Jan 1977 with Airdrie New Monkland.

1977 ALAN ANDREW FORD
ord and ind to New Monkland with Greengairs 13 Jul 1977, see New Monkland.

HAMILTON BURNBANK (FES III, 232; VIII, 254; IX, 330; X, 195)

Linked 13 Jan 1982 with Hamilton North.

1971 JOHN FREDERICK HART
(FES IX, 285, 516; X, 169, 184, 195, 280), trans from Glasgow Whitehill to Burnbank 20 Oct 1971; ret 31 Mar 1975; died 9 Apr 1983.

1978 RONALD MICHAEL LEEMAN CHILTON
(FES X, 390), trans from Applecross to Burnbank 2 Mar 1978; trans to Corgarff and Strathdon with Glenbuchat-Towie 15 Dec 1981.

1982 JAMES GRAHAM BLACK
ord and ind to Hamilton North 30 Aug 1978; became minister of linked charge with Burnbank 13 Jan 1982; trans to East Kilbride Westwood 28 Aug 1986.

1987 RAYMOND DAVID MACKENZIE
B 6 Dec 1947 at Glasgow, s of David Murdoch M. and Margaret Queen; educ Knightswood Secondary, Glasgow 1952–64; College of Commerce 1964–68 (SNC Business); Bible Training Institute 1970–72 (DTh); University of Glasgow 1972–77 (BD); City Line Shipping Co Ltd 1964–67; Albion Motors Ltd 1967–79; lic by Presb of Glasgow 30 Jun 1977; asst Bearsden Killermont 1973–75; Glasgow Scotstoun West 1975–76; Milngavie St Paul's 1976–77; Bathgate High 1977–78; m 25 Aug 1973 Susan Mary Hallett b 23 Apr 1946 d of Norman Frank H. and Doris Ethel Luck; Children: Gregor Raymond b 14 Apr 1976; Ross Norman b 14 Apr 1976; Morven Ann b 17 Dec

1981; ord and ind to Stair 9 May 1978; became minister of linked charge with Ochiltree 6 Jan 1979; trans to Burnbank with Hamilton North 13 Mar 1987.

HAMILTON CADZOW (FES III, 233; VIII, 254; IX, 330; X, 195)

1952 ANDREW McNEIL DOUGLAS
(FES IX, 100, 294, 330; X, 195), trans from Duns to Cadzow 25 Sep 1952; ret 31 Mar 1978; m (2) 25 Nov 1986 Eliza Barr Anderson b 30 Jun 1914 d of Hugh A. and Eliza Barr Harper; Publ: *Church and School in Scotland* (St Andrew Press, 1985).

1979 ARTHUR PARR BARRIE
(FES X, 131), ord and ind to Renfrew North 6 Jun 1973; trans to Cadzow 13 Jan 1979; Children: Kristeen Marion b 17 Feb 1977.

HAMILTON GILMOUR AND WHITEHILL (FES X, 195)

1972 ROBERT BROWN
(FES X, 195), admitted by General Assembly and ind to Gilmour and Whitehill 22 Mar 1972; trans to Kilbrandon and Kilchattan 25 Oct 1991.

1993 ESTHER JOHNSTON NINIAN
ord and ind to Gilmour and Whitehill 17 Jun 1993; trans to Paisley Castlehead 15 Sep 1998.

HAMILTON HILLHOUSE (FES X, 195)

1967 DAVID JOHN HISLOP HARBISON
(FES X, 195, 408), trans from Whalsay and Skerries to Hillhouse 20 Sep 1967; trans to Beith High 4 Oct 1979.

1980 JAMES GAULT MACKENZIE
ord and ind to Hillhouse 29 Feb 1980; trans to Jersey St Columba's 7 Mar 1997.

1998 DAVID WILLIAM GILMOUR BURT
B 30 Jul 1964 at Paisley, s of James Simpson B. and Margaret Anne Gilmour; educ Castlehead High, Paisley 1976–81; University of Glasgow 1981–87 (BD, DipMin); lic by Presb of Paisley 6 Oct 1987; asst Paisley St George's 1983–85; Paisley St John's 1985–87; m 29 Sep 1989 Shona Ann Miller b 24 Aug 1968 d of Robert Dinwoodie M. and Margaret McCrumb Mathie; ord and ind Hawick St Mary's and Old 21 Jun 1989; became minister of linked charge with Cavers and Kirkton 7 Jul 1996; trans to Hillhouse 22 Jan 1998.

HAMILTON NORTH (FES IX, 330; X, 196)

Linked 13 Jan 1982 with Hamilton Burnbank.

1964 HECTOR GRANT MACMILLAN
(FES X, 196), ord and ind to Hamilton North 19 Jun 1964; trans to Alyth 29 Dec 1976.

1978 JAMES GRAHAM BLACK
ord and ind to Hamilton North 30 Aug 1978; became minister of linked charge with Burnbank 13 Jan 1982; trans to East Kilbride Westwood 28 Aug 1986.

1987 RAYMOND DAVID MACKENZIE
ind to Hamilton Burnbank with North 13 Mar 1987, see Burnbank.

HAMILTON OLD (FES X, 196)

Auchingramont dropped from name 1980.

1973 DOUGLAS HOGARTH HAY MACNAUGHTON
(FES X, 41, 141, 196), trans from Cadder to Old and Auchingramont 29 Nov 1973; trans to Bearsden South 28 Aug 1981.

1981 HUGH RUTHERFORD WYLLIE
(FES X, 155, 192), trans from Glasgow Cathcart South to Hamilton Old 21 Oct 1981; Moderator of General Assembly 1992–93; Hon Freeman of Hamilton District Council 1992; DD (Aberdeen) 1993; Vice-Chairman Lanarkshire Healthcare NHS Trust 1996; Fellow of Chartered Institute of Bankers in Scotland 1997; Trustee, Lanarkshire Primary Care NHS Trust 1999; Chaplain to Royal British Legion Scotland (Hamilton); Chaplain to Burma Star Assoc (Lanarkshire); Chaplain to Strathclyde Police; d Hazel m Alastair Ewen Scott; d Helen m Hugh James Edward Henderson.

HAMILTON SOUTH (FUF 189; FES IX, 332; X, 196)

Linked 30 Sep 1956 with Quarter.

1975 BENJAMIN JOHNSTONE
(FES X, 196), ord by Presb of Inverness during assistantship at Nairn Old 1 May 1973; ind to Hamilton South with Quarter 9 Jul 1975; trans to Mallaig and The Small Isles 22 Sep 1989.

1990 WILLIAM ANGUS McKAY BURNSIDE
B 12 Nov 1965 at Glasgow, s of William B. and Nessie Johnstone; educ Cranhill Secondary, Glasgow 1977–83; Glasgow College of Technology 1983–86 (BA); University of Glasgow 1986–89 (BD); University of Strathclyde 1993–94 (PGCE); lic by Presb of Glasgow 10 Jul 1989; asst Aberdeen Northfield 1989–90; m 13 Jun 1990 Alison Hannah b 13 Jun 1964 d of John H. and Josephine Gillan; Children: Angus John b 29 Nov 1997; ord and ind to Hamilton South with Quarter 4 May 1990; dem 14 Aug 1994 to enter teaching profession (RE).

1994 FRASER KING TURNER
B 14 May 1942 at Glasgow, s of Peter T. and Mary King; educ Hyndland Senior Secondary 1953–56; Langside College, Glasgow 1987–88; University of Glasgow 1988–91 (LTh); lic by Presb of Hamilton 2 Jul 1991; asst Glasgow Burnside 1991–93, High

Carntyne 1992–93; m 11 Aug 1964 Margaret Tracey b 14 Sep 1939; Children: Jacqueline Mary; Tracy Louise; Kristine Margaret; ord and ind to Hamilton South with Quarter 21 Jan 1994; app Chaplain (part-time) to Dungavel Prison.

HAMILTON ST ANDREW'S (FES X, 196)

Formed 22 Feb 1967 by union of Hamilton Avon and Hamilton Brandon.

1927   JAMES ROBERTSON BUCHANAN
(FES IX, 329; X, 194), trans from Culross to Brandon 29 Jun 1927; ret 22 May 1954; died 20 Sep 1981.

1955   CLEMENT EDWIN PAULL
(FES IX, 640; X, 194, 356, 365), trans from Burghead to Brandon 7 Sep 1955; trans to Buckie West 17 Jan 1962.

1964   WALTER STANLEY CARR
(FES IX, 462; X, 119, 194, 273, 274), trans from Dunfermline St John's to Avon Street with Brandon 6 May 1964; trans to Largs St Columba's 25 Aug 1966.

1967   WILLIAM GEORGE BEATTIE
(FES IX, 195; X, 111, 182, 196), trans from Glasgow Trinity Possil to St Andrew's 2 Mar 1967; ret 31 Aug 1986; s Stephen m Catherine Gollan; d Esther m Robert Watson; s Richard m June Affleck; s Philip m Morag Fraser.

1987   NORMAN BARCLAY McKEE
ord and ind to St Andrew's 4 Jun 1987; trans to Uddingston Old 26 Oct 1994.

1995   NORMA MOORE
B 19 May 1952 at Dundee, d of James M. and Thomasina Henschlewood McKenzie; educ Harris Academy, Dundee 1964–70; University of Aberdeen 1970–75 (MA); South Bank Polytechnic, London 1975–76; University of Edinburgh 1990–93 (BD); Secretary and PA 1976–90; lic by Presb of England 27 Jun 1993; asst Glasgow Netherlee 1993–95; ord and ind to St Andrew's 18 Aug 1995.

HAMILTON ST JOHN'S (FUF 188; FES IX, 331; X, 196)

1967   JOHN EBENEZER BROWN
(FES IX, 299, 382, 480; X, 196, 284), trans from Kirkcaldy St Brycedale to St John's 20 Jun 1967; ret 15 Sep 1980; died 7 Dec 1998; DD (St Andrews) 1979; s Andrew m Clare Rencastle; Publ: *A Time to Serve* (Mainstream, 1994); sermons in *The Expository Times* (T&T Clark).

1981   ROBERT MILREE KENT
(FES X, 108), trans from Crosshouse to St John's 18 Apr 1981; m 6 Jul 1992 Lesley Janet Simpson b 28 Jan 1958 d of Ronald S. and Jean McGill; Children: Donald John Simpson b 28 Aug 1995; Andrew Ronald and Mark Robert b 6 May 1997.

HAMILTON TRINITY (FES X, 197)

1969   JAMES HARRISON HUDSON
(FES X, 197), ind to Laighstonehall (name changed to Trinity 1970) 26 Jun 1969; trans to Dundee McCheyne Memorial 23 Mar 1977.

1978   ALISTAIR GEORGE BENNETT
ord and ind to Trinity 12 Apr 1978; trans to Melrose 15 Nov 1984.

1985   IAIN GUNN MATHESON
ord and ind to Trinity 28 May 1985; dem 28 Feb 1991 on app by Board of World Mission to Prague.

1991   KAREN ELIZABETH HARBISON
B 25 Jan 1964 at Glasgow, d of James Parker Bell and Margo Jolly; educ Clydebank High 1975–81; University of Glasgow 1981–84 (MA), 1987–90 (BD); Youth Work 1984–87; lic by Presb of Dumbarton 1 Jul 1990; asst Dundee The High Kirk 1990–91; m 11 Aug 1990 Malcolm Ian Harbison b 4 Mar 1962 s of David H. and Winnifred Wright; Children: Duncan b 14 Aug 1993; Eilidh b 4 Apr 1998; ord and ind to Trinity 17 Sep 1991.

HAMILTON WEST (FUF 189; FES IX, 332; X, 197)

1974   JAMES STANLEY COOK
(FES X, 197), ord and ind to Hamilton West 21 Aug 1974; University of Strathclyde 1982, 1983–84 (Counselling Skills); University of Glasgow 1995–97 (Dip in Palliative Care); s Stephen m Ita Martina Lennon; s Iain m Mary McNally; d Lesley m Adrian Michael Jones.

HOLYTOWN (FES III, 264; VIII, 261; IX, 332; X, 197)

1973   NORMAN JOHN LINKENS
(FES X, 104, 138, 197), dem from Port Glasgow Old in interests of union 31 Oct 1971; ind to Holytown 14 Feb 1973; dem 31 Aug 1978.

1979   JAMES SOMMERVILLE SALMOND
B 13 Jan 1951 at Bangour, s of John Brown S. and Joan Lambie Copland; educ West Calder High and Whitburn Academy 1963–68; University of Leeds 1971–74 (BA); University of Edinburgh 1974–77 (BD, MTh); Central School of Religion 1983–86 (ThD); Bus Conductor/Driver 1968–78 (part-time while studying); lic by Presb of West Lothian 13 Nov 1977; asst Armadale 1977–78; m 10 Sep 1969 Catherine Florence Wildy b 31 Jan 1951 d of Henry Alfred W. and Margaret Mitchel; Children: Helen Copland b 12 Apr 1970 m Lindsay; Angela Margaret b 5 Feb 1975; Lorna Jane b 28 Jun 1978; Claire Frances b 22 Mar 1981; Calum James b 12 Sep 1986; loc ten Holytown 1978–79; ord and ind to Holytown 15 Oct 1979; Chaplain (part-time) to Monklands General Hospital, Airdrie; Publ: *Moody Blues* (Excalibur Press, 1992); *His Watchmen Are Blind* (National Church Assoc, 1993); *Any Dream Will Do* (Milne, 1997).

KIRK O' SHOTTS (FES X, 201)

Formed 19 Feb 1975 by union of Kirk o' Shotts and Shottsburn.

1930 JOHN DICKSON
(FES X, 202), trans from Arbroath (Orig Sec) to Shottsburn (Orig Sec) 12 Nov 1930; ret 19 Feb 1975; died 1 Oct 1979.

1950 JOHN WILLIAM McBRIDE
(FES IX, 338), ord and ind to Kirk o' Shotts 16 Aug 1950; dem Jan 1954 to emigrate to Canada; died 7 Dec 1996.

1954 DONALD MALCOLM MACLEOD
(FES IX, 338, 367; X, 201, 350), trans from Duntocher to Kirk o' Shotts 30 Jun 1954; trans to New Deer St Kane's 2 Apr 1959.

1960 ANDREW MEEK
(FES IX, 141, 330, 619; X, 84, 201), trans from Dumfries South and Townhead to Kirk o' Shotts 20 Apr 1960; died 24 Jul 1969.

1970 JAMES ROBERTSON
(FES X, 201 (2)), ord and ind to Kirk o' Shotts 1 Jul 1970; became minister of united charge with Shottsburn 19 Feb 1975; trans to Newton 17 Jun 1976.

1977 SHONA MORRIS
ord and ind to Kirk o' Shotts 23 Jun 1977; dem 31 Oct 1978.

1979 SHEILA MARGARET SPENCE
B 10 Feb 1940 at Bonnyrigg, d of Alexander Fraser White and Euphemia McGill Lothian; educ James Gillespie's High School for Girls, Edinburgh 1952–58; University of Edinburgh 1958–61 (MA), 1961–64 (BD); lic by Presb of Edinburgh 3 Jul 1977; asst Glasgow St James' (Pollok) 1964–65; Largs St John's 1965–68; m 4 Sep 1968 Archibald John S. b 9 Apr 1935 s of James S. and Annie Smith Kenmir; Children: Alan James b 8 Apr 1972; Mark Fraser b 21 Nov 1975; ord and ind to Kirk o' Shotts, Salsburgh 24 Oct 1979.

LARKHALL CHALMERS (FES X, 198)

Strutherhill dropped from name 1992.

1962 JAMES WHITTON
(FES X, 198, 386), trans from Berriedale and Dunbeath Ross to Chalmers 3 Oct 1962; died 15 Dec 1989.

1990 JAMES GRANGER HASTIE
B 10 Oct 1946 at Cambuslang, s of Archibald Hamilton H. and Edith Elizabeth Armstrong Granger; educ Allan Glen's, Glasgow 1958–63; Institute of Chartered Accountants of Scotland 1963–69 and University of Glasgow 1965–66 (CA); 1985–88 (BD); Apprentice Chartered Accountant 1963–69; General Manager/Partner Family Bakery

1969–82; Group Financial Controller 1983–84; lic by Presb of Hamilton 27 Jun 1988; asst Uddingston Viewpark 1988–90; m 19 Feb 1971 Rosalind Margaret Bell b 8 Sep 1947 d of James H. B. and Margaret Glidden; Children: Anita Joan b 9 Nov 1972; Andrew James b 24 Jan 1976; ord and ind to Chalmers 22 Sep 1990.

LARKHALL ST MACHAN'S (FES III, 270; VIII, 262; IX, 333; X, 198)

1968 GORDON WALKER BLAKE
(FES X, 86, 198), trans from Lochrutton with Terregles to St Machan's 17 Jan 1968; died 12 Feb 1982.

1982 ALEXANDER C WARK
ord and ind to St Machan's 16 Sep 1982; dem 30 Jun 1992 on app to Rotterdam.

1993 IAIN MACLEOD GREENSHIELDS
B 8 Mar 1954 at Glasgow, s of John Anthony Archibald G. and Catherine MacLeod; educ Victoria Drive, Glasgow 1965–70; ACMA 1976; University of Glasgow 1978–82 (BD); 1982–83 (CMin), 1986–88 (MTh); University of Cambridge 1985 (DRS); Weir Group Accounts 1970–77; lic by Presb of Glasgow 1 Jun 1984; asst Glasgow Broomhill 1983–84; m 22 Aug 1981 Linda Anne McGill b 1 Mar 1961 d of Ian Alistair M. and Anne MacLeod; Children: Alistair John b 19 May 1990; Ross MacLeod b 13 Aug 1991; Caitlin Anne b 2 Feb 1994; ord and ind to Cranhill 1 May 1985; trans to St Machan's 2 May 1993; Chaplain (part-time) to Longriggend Prison (now Shotts Prison); Chaplain to Hairmyres Hospital (part-time); Publ: *From the Heart* (Moorley's, 1987); *Treasure in Unsure Places* (Moorley's, 1997); *Prayer* (Moorley's, 1997); *In Control of the World* (Moorley's, 1997).

LARKHALL TRINITY (FUF 190; FES IX, 333; X, 198)

1958 ANGUS DONALD MACDONALD
(FES IX, 568, 657; X, 198, 330), trans from Aberdeen St George's in the West to Trinity 19 Mar 1958; ret 31 Dec 1985; died 5 Apr 1986.

1986 COLIN DAVID JOHNSTON
ord and ind to Trinity 21 Aug 1986; dem on app by Board of World Mission as Mission Partner with United Church of Zambia in Sefula, Maamba, Choma and Lusaka Central, Sep 1993.

1995 LINDSAY SCHLÜTER
B 13 Feb 1964 at Munich, Germany, d of Hans S. and Jean Maxwell Cameron; educ Lessing Gymnasium, Frankfurt 1974–83; University of Frankfurt 1983–85; University of Edinburgh 1985–86; University of Heidelberg 1986–90 (Theologisches Examen); University of Glasgow 1991–92 (CMin); Foreign Language Asst 1990–91; Tourist Guide 1991–92; lic by Presb of Moray 20 Sep 1992; asst

Glasgow Newlands South with Bridgeton St Francis-in-the-East 1993–94; loc ten Glasgow Ruchazie 1994–95; ord and ind to Trinity 19 Jan 1995; Accredited Counsellor of the Church of Scotland.

MOTHERWELL CLASON MEMORIAL (FUF 191; FES IX, 334; X, 198)

Congregation dissolved 13 Jun 1993.

1961 JOHN HANDLEY
(FES IX, 458; X, 198, 271), trans from Cowdenbeath Guthrie Memorial to Clason Memorial; ret 13 Jun 1993; s Ronald m Jane.

MOTHERWELL CROSSHILL (FES X, 199)

Formed 30 Jun 1971 by union of Motherwell Brandon and Motherwell Cairns.

1957 WILLIAM ALEXANDER SIMPSON
(FES IX, 680, 710; X, 198, 404), trans from Walls Old to Motherwell Cairns 1 May 1957; ret 30 Jun 1971; died 9 Aug 1986.

1972 DAVID JAMES FERGUSON
(FES X, 199, 407), trans from Tingwall to Crosshill 19 Jan 1972; trans to Bellie with Speymouth 26 Mar 1982.

1982 WILLIAM STUART DUNN
(FES X, 108), trans from Dreghorn and Pearston Old to Crosshill 15 Sep 1982; Addl children: Catriona Elizabeth b 22 Apr 1976; Kirsteen Iona b 18 Mar 1978; s Alasdair m Stephanie Helena Davison.

MOTHERWELL DALZIEL ST ANDREW'S (FES X, 199, 200)

Formed 1 Sep 1996 by union of Dalziel and St Andrew's.

1956 JAMES CONNOR MITCHELL
(FES IX, 64, 450; X, 199, 266), trans from Kippen to Dalziel North 8 Feb 1956; ret 31 Jul 1969; died 22 Nov 1991.

1968 WILLIAM CRAIK BRUCE
(FES X, 199 (2), 277), trans from Lochgelly St Andrew's to Dalziel High 13 Mar 1968; became minister of united charge with Dalziel North 2 Sep 1970; ret 31 Aug 1995; s David m Susan Cloney; s Thomas m Angela Hamil; s Andrew m Gillian Lyal.

1973 ALASTAIR JACK McTAVISH
(FES IX, 466, 511; X, 200, 303, 422), res from service with Overseas Council in Jamaica and ind to St Andrew's 21 Mar 1973; ret 30 Sep 1981; died 26 Oct 1995.

1981 HUGH SAWERS
(FES X, 52, 156), dem from Glasgow Croftfoot 30 Jun 1979; ind to St Andrew's 28 Oct 1981; dem 31 Jul 1988; Open University 1979–80 (BA); s Douglas m Karen Buttar; d Gillian m Peter Gray.

1989 ALLAN SCOTT VINT
ord and ind to St Andrew's 19 Jun 1989; trans to Baillieston Mure Memorial 29 May 1996.

1996 DEREK WALTER HUGHES
B 27 Apr 1960 at Motherwell, s of Angus H. and Ann Isabel Sutherland Ferguson Forrester; educ Garrion Academy, Wishaw 1972–78; University of Stirling 1978–81 (BSc, DipEd); University of Edinburgh 1986–89 (BD); Teaching (Berwickshire High School, Duns) 1982–86; lic by Presb of West Lothian 4 Jul 1989; asst Strathbrock 1989–90; m 3 Apr 1982 Elizabeth Haddow Hill McGhie b 20 Jan 1956 d of George Macreaddie M. and Mary Hill; Children: Diahann b 9 Jun 1983; Claire Elizabeth b 25 Jun 1985; David Christopher b 7 Nov 1989; ord and ind to Coatbridge Townhead 18 Jun 1990; trans to Dalziel St Andrew's 20 Sep 1996.

1998 COLIN MACBEATH BROUGH
B 7 Jun 1968 at Glasgow, s of Robin B. and Harriet Macbeath Hamilton; educ High School of Glasgow 1979–86; University of Edinburgh 1986–90 (BSc), 1993–96 (BD); Software Engineering 1990–93; lic by Presb of Edinburgh 7 Jul 1996; asst Edinburgh Davidson's Mains 1996–98; m 22 Jul 1995 Helen Mary Carron-Brown b 30 Jan 1972 d of John Andrew C. and Sue Mellor; Children: Peter Euan b 8 Jul 1997; Andrew Finlay b 23 Feb 1999; ord by Presb of Hamilton and introd as Assoc at Dalziel St Andrew's 11 May 1998.

MOTHERWELL MANSE ROAD (FUF 192; FES IX, 335; X, 199)

1974 THOMAS RALPH TAYLOR
(FES X, 199), ord and ind to Manse Road 4 Oct 1974; trans to Shotts Calderhead 10 Oct 1979.

1980 DAVID COWAN
(FES X, 408), dem from Clydebank St Andrew's 14 Jan 1979; introd to Manse Road (term) 23 Apr 1980; ind to Corby St Ninian's 1 Mar 1984.

1985 THOMAS JAMES GRANT SEATH
B 6 Jun 1926 at Greenock, s of John Berry S. and Helen Cameron; educ Greenock High 1939–45; Paisley Technical College 1945–51 (HNC, GCE); University of Glasgow 1975–79 (BD); Electronic Engineering; Reinforced Plastics Engineering; Management Development 1945–75; lic by Presb of Glasgow 29 Jun 1979; asst Glasgow St David's Knightswood 1979–80; m 17 Aug 1957 Isobel Drummond Strachan b 5 Dec 1925 d of Alexander Duncan S. and Isabella Drummond; Children: Andrea Muriel b 9 Jun 1951; Grant b 29 Jul 1959;

Lorna b 29 Jul 1959; ord and ind to Kincardine O'Neil with Lumphanan 25 Sep 1980; trans to Manse Road 20 Dec 1985; ret 30 Jun 1992; Chaplain (part-time) to Shotts Prison 1989–.

1993 RICHARD JOHN GILMOUR DARROCH
ord and ind to Manse Road 21 Sep 1993; trans to Upper Donside 29 Jun 1999.

MOTHERWELL NORTH (FES X, 199)

1966 ADAM JAMES LEARMONTH
(FES X, 199), ord and ind to Motherwell North 18 May 1966; trans to Airdrie Wellwynd 19 Nov 1980.

1981 ANDREW FREELAND HEADDEN
ord and ind to Motherwell North 10 Jun 1981; trans to Edinburgh Craiglockhart 11 Sep 1985.

1986 ALISON PAUL
ord and ind to Motherwell North 28 May 1986; trans to Rhu and Shandon 13 Dec 1994.

1995 DEREK HARRY NIMMO POPE
B 7 Apr 1953 at Strathaven, s of Harry Nimmo P. and Anne Beattie; educ Dalziel High, Motherwell 1966–71; Jordanhill College, Glasgow 1972–75 (DYCW); University of Glasgow 1982–86 (BD); Youth and Community Work 1975–82; lic by Presb of Paisley, 1986; asst Glasgow Castlemilk East 1986–87; m 22 Jan 1976 Helen Crawford b 18 Aug 1953 d of Wesley C. and Lilian Wright; Children: Anna b 7 Jan 1978; David b 1 Jun 1980; Katherine b 31 Mar 1984; Mark b 8 Feb 1989; ord and ind to Glasgow Priesthill and Nitshill 6 Jun 1987; trans to Motherwell North 6 Jun 1995; Chaplain (part-time) to Shotts Prison.

MOTHERWELL SOUTH DALZIEL (FES III, 250; VIII, 257; IX, 335; X, 200)

1966 IAN MACKENZIE FORBES
(FES IX, 243; X, 142, 184, 200), trans from Glasgow Woodlands to South Dalziel 2 Feb 1966; trans to Kemnay 12 Jan 1977.

1977 JAMES BROWN ALLAN
B 24 Apr 1936 at Coatbridge, s of James Brown A. and Sarah Bell Harkness; educ Gartsherrie Academy and Coatbridge Secondary; University of Aberdeen 1961–63; Scottish Congregational College 1963–65; Open University 1974–76 (BA); Social Work 1953–60 (National Service 1954–56); lic by Congregational Union; m 30 Jun 1965 Ann Russell b 29 Aug 1938 d of William R. and Rosina Ross; Children: Ross Graham b 8 Nov 1969; Kirstin Ann b 26 Jan 1973 m Stephen Whitefield; ord by Congregational Union and ind to Galashiels Congregational Church 18 Jun 1965; Secretary, Multilateral Church Conversation 1971–77; Barrhead Congregational Church 1970–77; admitted by General Assembly and ind to Motherwell South Dalziel 21 Sep 1977; ret Aug 1994 on grounds of ill-health.

1994 PHYLLIS MARY WILSON
B 18 Feb 1941 at Forres, d of James Falconer and Helen Fraser; educ Forres Academy 1953–59; Scottish College of Commerce 1959–63 (DipCom); Jordanhill College, Glasgow 1963–64 (DipRE); University of Glasgow 1982–84 (CMin); Teaching (Business Studies and RE) 1963–72; lic by Presb of Glasgow 6 Jun 1984; asst Rutherglen Stonelaw 1984–85; m 25 Sep 1971 Thomas Henry Wilson b 25 Sep 1943 s of Thomas W. and Catherine Nugent; Children: Julie b 16 Sep 1972; Gareth b 30 Nov 1976; Jennifer b 21 Aug 1979; ord and ind to Howwood 7 Nov 1985; trans to South Dalziel 24 Nov 1994.

MOTHERWELL ST MARGARET'S (FES X, 200)

1971 EDWARD WEIR
(FES X, 108, 200, 427), trans from Darvel Irvine Bank and Easton Memorial to St Margaret's 15 Dec 1971; died 2 Aug 1983.

1984 ANDREW McGILL CAMPBELL
B 1 Mar 1940 at Loth, Sutherland, s of Andrew McGill C. and Helen Munro McLaren; educ Lasswade Secondary 1951–52; Kirkwall Grammar 1953–55; Langside College, Glasgow; University of Glasgow 1979–83 (BD, CMin); Retail Sales Manager 1965–77; lic by Presb of Hamilton 23 Jun 1983; m 4 Jun 1959 Dora Margaret Proctor Bogle d of James Proctor B. and Margaret Johnstone Hetherington; Children: Yvonne b 11 Mar 1961; Andrew b 27 Feb 1965; James b 11 Dec 1970; ord and ind to St Margaret's 2 May 1984; Chaplain (part-time) to Shotts Prison.

MOTHERWELL ST MARY'S (FES III, 250; VII, 257; IX, 335; X, 200)

1961 ANGUS CAMERON MACKENZIE
(FES X, 200, 277), trans from Lumphinnans to St Mary's 19 Apr 1961; trans to Biggar 9 Mar 1977.

1977 JOHN WILLIAM FORSYTH HARRIS
(FES X, 110), trans from Irvine St Andrew's to St Mary's 31 Aug 1977; trans to Bearsden South 25 Feb 1987.

1987 DAVID WALLACE DOYLE
B 12 Apr 1948 at Glasgow, s of Ian Bruce D. and Anne Watt Wallace; educ Glasgow High 1960–66; University of Glasgow 1966–70 (MA), 1970–73 (BD); University of Cambridge 1974–77; lic by Presb of Glasgow 28 Jun 1973; asst East Kilbride Old 1973–74; m 6 Aug 1973 Alison Wightman Britton b 3 Mar 1948 d of James B. and Ellen Rankin; Children: Jennifer Ann b 6 Apr 1977; Graeme James b 23 Jan 1979; ord and ind to Tulliallan and Kincardine 26 Oct 1977; trans to St Mary's 16 Sep 1987.

NEW STEVENSTON WRANGHOLM KIRK (FUF 189; FES IX, 337; X, 201)

1965 DOUGLAS FRANK NOEL CRAWFORD
(FES IX, 731; X, 201, 417), res from service with Overseas Council in Livingstonia, Malawi and ind to Wrangholm Kirk 24 Feb 1965; trans to Braes of Rannoch with Foss and Rannoch 22 Sep 1978.

1979 BARBARA DIANE QUIGLEY
B 19 Nov 1953 at Dewsbury, Yorkshire, d of George Q. and Marjory Idle; educ Cockburn High, Leeds 1965–72; University of St Andrews 1972–77 (MTheol, DPS); Duke University, USA 1977–78 (ThM); University of Birmingham 1994–95 (PGCE); lic by Presb of St Andrews, Sep 1978; asst Dumbarton Riverside 1978–79; m 19 Nov 1988 David Michael Firth b 3 Oct 1951 s of Jack F. and Elaine Limbert; Children: Eilidh Elisabeth b 3 Feb 1990; ord and ind to Wrangholm Kirk 19 Dec 1979; dem 14 Jul 1991; app General Secretary, YWCA Scotland 1 Aug 1991; app Chaplain to New Cross Hospital, Wolverhampton 1 Aug 1992; res to take up teaching app, Wolverhampton 1 Sep 1995; app teacher at Carnoustie High 1 Sep 1997; app teacher at High School of Dundee 1 Sep 1998; Hon Asst minister at Dundee Fairmuir Sep 1998–Sep 1999; Publ: *It's not what you say* (Church of Scotland, 1984).

1992 PAUL AMED
B 3 Jun 1949 at Birmingham, s of Fazal A. and Phyliss Hazeldene; University of Aberdeen 1986–91 (LTh, DPS); Bricklayer 1964–66; Driver, Royal Corps Transport 1966–69; Fish Plant Operator 1971–74; Tar Plant Operator 1974–77; Plate Welder 1977–82; lic by Presb of Lewis 28 Jun 1991; m 4 Aug 1970 Catherine Ann MacDonald b 2 Mar 1952 d of Donald John M. and Jessie Annabella Mackay; Children: Dawn Morrison b 2 Mar 1972; Pauline Jane b 26 May 1973; ord and ind to Wrangholm Kirk 9 Jun 1992.

NEWARTHILL (FUF 192; FES IX, 336; X, 200)

Linked 1 Apr 1988 with Carfin.

1972 GEORGE STRACHAN NOBLE
(FES X, 200), ord and ind to Newarthill 30 Jun 1972; became minister of linked charge with Carfin 1 Apr 1988.

NEWMAINS BONKLE (FUF 196; FES IX, 336; X, 200)

Linked 7 Feb 1980 with Newmains Coltness Memorial.

1960 GEORGE DICKSON McMILLAN
(FES IX, 164, 357, 363; X, 54, 200, 214), trans from Garvald and Morham to Bonkle 23 Nov 1960; ret 30 Sep 1970; died 30 Aug 1978.

1971 ROBERT CAMPBELL
(FES IX, 53, 366; X, 128, 200, 218), dem from Paisley North 31 Aug 1967; ind to Bonkle 1 Dec 1971; ret 31 Dec 1978; died 7 Dec 1981.

1980 WILLIAM HUNTER FRAME
(FES X, 326), trans from Aberdeen Garthdee to Bonkle with Coltness Memorial 16 Jul 1980; ret 31 Aug 1988; died 28 Mar 1992.

1989 GRAHAM LAIRD DUFFIN
B 21 Oct 1959 at Dunfermline, s of Joseph D. and Patricia Anne Wilson; educ Kirkcaldy High 1971–77; University of Edinburgh 1977–81 (BSc), 1985–88 (BD); Moray House College, Edinburgh 1981–82 (DipEd); Youth Work 1982–83; Teaching 1983–85; lic by Presb of Edinburgh 3 Jul 1988; asst Edinburgh St David's Broomhouse 1988–89; m 30 Mar 1985 Agnes Jane Gray b 16 Aug 1964 d of William G. and Jessie Cairns; Children: Alan Steven b 5 Oct 1987; Laura Anne b 28 Apr 1990; Amy Jane b 12 Feb 1998; ord and ind to Bonkle with Coltness Memorial 11 May 1989.

NEWMAINS COLTNESS MEMORIAL (FES III, 244; VIII, 256; IX, 336; X, 200)

Linked 7 Feb 1980 with Newmains Bonkle.

1973 CHRISTOPHER LEON LEVISON
(FES X, 201), ind to Coltness Memorial 27 Jun 1973; dem on app as Assoc Chaplain to University of Aberdeen 20 Aug 1978.

1980 WILLIAM HUNTER FRAME
(FES X, 326), trans from Aberdeen Garthdee to Bonkle with Coltness Memorial 16 Jul 1980; ret 31 Aug 1988; died 28 Mar 1992.

1989 GRAHAM LAIRD DUFFIN
ord and ind to Bonkle with Coltness Memorial 11 May 1989, see Bonkle.

OVERTOWN (FES III, 275; VIII, 262; IX, 337; X, 201)

1940 JAMES LYON KERR
(FES IX, 337; X, 201), ord and ind to Overtown 29 May 1940; ret 28 Feb 1979; died 9 Sep 1989.

1980 SHEILAGH MARGARET KESTING
ord by Presb of Hamilton and introd to Overtown 12 Jan 1980; ind to same charge 25 Nov 1982; trans to Musselburgh St Andrew's High 25 Jun 1986.

1986 ROBERT ALEXANDER ANDERSON
res from service with Overseas Council in Kiambu, Kenya and ind to Overtown 15 Dec 1986; dem on app as Chaplain to University of Edinburgh 1 Apr 1989.

1990 JANET MARY HENDERSON
B 27 Jun 1954 at Glasgow, d of William Tait H. and Joan Nancy Sinclair; educ Duncanrig

Secondary, East Kilbride 1966–72; University of Edinburgh 1972–76 (MA), 1983–86 (BD), 1990 (PhD); Moray House College, Edinburgh 1976–77 (DEd); Teaching (History and RE) 1977–79; lic by Presb of Edinburgh 29 Jun 1986; asst Edinburgh Craigmillar Park 1986–87; Milngavie Cairns 1988–89; ord and ind to Overtown 28 Feb 1990.

QUARTER (FES III, 276; VIII, 262; IX, 337; X, 201)

Linked 30 Sep 1956 with Hamilton South.

1975 BENJAMIN JOHNSTONE
(FES X, 196), ind to Hamilton South with Quarter 9 Jul 1975, see Hamilton South.

1990 WILLIAM ANGUS McKAY BURNSIDE
ord and ind to Hamilton South with Quarter 4 May 1990, see Hamilton South.

1994 FRASER KING TURNER
ord and ind to Hamilton South with Quarter 21 Jan 1994, see Hamilton South.

SHOTTS CALDERHEAD ERSKINE (FES X, 201)

Formed 17 Oct 1989 by union of Shotts Calderhead and Shotts Erskine.

1958 ROGER MANSEL HOLLINS
(FES X, 201), ind to Calderhead 17 Dec 1958; dem 2 Oct 1962 to enter teaching profession (RE); app Principal Lecturer in Religious Education, Craigie College, Ayr 1965; ret 31 Dec 1988; s Graham m Catherine Taylor; d Caroline m David Carson, divorced; s Ian m Elaine Laughlin.

1963 GEORGE IRVINE FRANCIS
(FES IX, 56, 572, 610; X, 201, 351), dem from Calderhead 31 Mar 1972 to enter teaching profession; died 11 Nov 1984.

1964 JAMES WILSON SIM
(FES IX, 325; X, 192, 201), res as Warden of Community House (Iona Community), Glasgow and ind to Erskine 17 Sep 1964; ret 6 Sep 1989; died 29 Jan 1995.

1972 WILLIAM MILLER HALL
(FES X, 201), ord and ind to Calderhead 27 Sep 1972; trans to Kilmarnock The Old High Kirk 20 Jan 1979.

1979 THOMAS RALPH TAYLOR
(FES X, 199), trans from Motherwell Manse Road to Calderhead 10 Oct 1979; trans to Clackmannan 27 Sep 1984.

1985 WILLIAM DAVID BEATTIE
B 31 Aug 1956 at Motherwell, s of John Blyth B. and Margaret Smith; educ Wishaw High 1968–74; University of Aberdeen 1976–82 (BD, DPS); Banking 1974–76; lic by Presb of Aberdeen 28 Jun 1982; asst Skene 1982–83; m 8 Oct 1993 Sharon

Eadie b 22 Oct 1971 d of John E. and Elizabeth Donaldson; ord and ind to Calderhead 12 Feb 1985; became minister of united charge with Erskine 17 Oct 1989; Chaplain (part-time) to Shotts Prison; died 8 Nov 1999.

STONEHOUSE ST NINIAN'S (FES III, 279; VIII, 263; IX, 338; X, 202)

1957 ALEXANDER GEMMELL
(FES IX, 657; X, 202, 374), trans from Nairn High to St Ninian's 9 Oct 1957; Clerk to Presb of Hamilton 1980–84; ret 31 Oct 1980; died 15 Oct 1984.

1981 CHARLES RAYMOND VINCENT
(FES IX, 433; X, 79, 97, 106, 257), trans from Kirtle-Eaglesfield with Middlebie with Waterbeck to St Ninian's 7 May 1981; ret 30 Jun 1992.

1992 THOMAS NELSON
B 31 Jul 1953 at Glasgow, s of James N. and Mary Kellman; educ Garthamlock Secondary, Glasgow 1965–71; University of Strathclyde 1971–75 (BSc); University of Glasgow 1988–91 (BD); Columbia Theological Seminary, USA 1990–91; Civil Engineering 1975–88; lic by Presb of Ardrossan 11 Sep 1991; asst Dalry Trinity 1991–92; m 16 Sep 1977 Catherine Burns Findlay b 20 Jan 1955 d of James Graham F. and Catherine Miller Thomson; Children: Carolyn Miller b 17 Jul 1982; Mairi Elizabeth b 14 Mar 1985; James Findlay b 4 May 1988; ord and ind to St Ninian's 27 Oct 1992; Chaplain (part-time) to Longriggend Prison.

STRATHAVEN AVENDALE OLD AND DRUMCLOG (FES III, 222; VIII, 251; IX, 339; X, 202)

Drumclog added to name 1984.

1970 JAMES PRINGLE FRASER
(FES IX, 208; X, 119, 174, 185, 202), trans from Glasgow St Enoch's Hogganfield to Avendale Old and Drumclog 3 Jan 1970; ret 30 Sep 1988; d Alyson m Ian Harkness; s Euan m Gillian Page.

1988 ROBERT FORBES WALKER
B 2 Aug 1960 at Motherwell, s of Robert Forbes W. and Henrietta Black Harrison Galway; educ Dalziel High, Motherwell 1972–78; University of Glasgow 1978–82 (BSc), 1983–86 (BD); Princeton Theological Seminary, USA 1987–88 (ThM); Teaching 1982–83; lic by Presb of Hamilton 26 Jun 1986; asst Bearsden New Kilpatrick 1986–87; ord by Presb of Dumbarton during assistantship at New Kilpatrick 3 May 1987; ind to Avendale Old and Drumclog 30 Nov 1988.

STRATHAVEN EAST (FUF 193; FES IX, 339; X, 202)

Linked 31 Jan 1973 with Glasford.

1949 HECTOR JAMES STEEL
(FES IX, 339, 610; X, 202), trans from Roseharty to Strathaven East 28 Apr 1949; became minister of linked charge with Glasford 31 Jan 1973; ret 31 Aug 1979; died 26 Sep 1983.

1980 WILLIAM THOMPSON STEWART
ord and ind to Glasford with Strathaven East 6 Feb 1980, see Glasford.

STRATHAVEN RANKIN (FUF 193; FES IX, 339; X, 202)

Linked 15 Jun 1960 with Chapelton.

1968 JAMES GREIG
(FES X, 191, 202, 419), res from service with Overseas Council in Kenya and ind to Chapelton with Strathaven Rankin 5 Dec 1968; trans to Irvine Old 27 Feb 1979.

1979 ALISTAIR LINDSAY JESSAMINE
ord and ind to Chapelton with Strathaven Rankin 28 Aug 1979; trans to Dunfermline Abbey 19 Mar 1991.

1991 SHAW JAMES PATERSON
ord and ind to Chapelton with Strathaven Rankin 29 Aug 1991, see Chapelton.

STRATHAVEN WEST (FUF 194; FES IX, 339; X, 202)

Admitted upon Petition 26 May 1995.

1996 STUART DOUGLAS ROGERSON
B 27 Dec 1951 at Glasgow, s of William Brydon R. and Barbara Clayton; educ Rutherglen Academy 1963–69; University of Strathclyde 1969–72 (BSc); Jordanhill College, Glasgow 1972–73 (Post-grad Teaching Dip); University of Glasgow 1976–79 (BD); Teaching 1973–76; lic by Presb of Hamilton 28 Jun 1979; asst East Kilbride Old 1979–80; m 15 Aug 1973 Jennifer Munn b 10 Mar 1952 d of Walter M. and Janet Campbell; Children: Lesley Elizabeth b 3 Aug 1977; Anna Louise b 4 Jan 1980; Sarah Helen b 20 Oct 1982; ord and ind to Kilchoman with Portnahaven 4 Jun 1980; trans to Baillieston Mure Memorial 8 Oct 1986; trans to Annan Old 31 Aug 1995; trans to Strathaven West 25 Sep 1996.

UDDINGSTON BURNHEAD (FES X, 202)

1973 JAMES MARTIN GRADY
(FES X, 30, 202), trans from Fauldhouse Old to Burnhead 26 Sep 1973; ret 30 Sep 1992; died 28 Dec 1993; w June died 24 Sep 1986; m (2) 14 Jan 1989 Jeanette Williams Wallace b 9 Aug 1935 d of Archibald Knox and Margaret Crawford Paisley.

1993 ROBERT MACKENZIE
B 14 Jun 1964 at Glasgow, s of Alastair M. and Grace Smith; educ Glasgow Academy 1976–82;

University of Aberdeen 1982–86 (LLB); University of Edinburgh 1986–89 (BD); Seoul Presb Theological Seminary, Korea 1989–90; Assoc Minister, Shindang Central Presb Church, Seoul, Korea 1989–90; Staff Assoc, World Mission and Unity 1992; lic by Presb of Aberdeen; asst Queensferry 1990–91; ord and ind to Burnhead 12 Apr 1993.

UDDINGSTON OLD (FES X, 203)

Formed 25 Jun 1982 by union of Chalmers and Trinity. Name changed from Uddingston Chalmers Trinity to Uddingston Old 1984.

1969 ALEXANDER CUNNINGHAM
(FES X, 203, 217), trans from Clydebank Union to Chalmers 18 Jun 1969; app Asst Clerk to Presb of Hamilton 1 Oct 1972; app Clerk 1978; dem from Chalmers and app Clerk to Presb of Glasgow 5 Jun 1980.

1970 PHILIP ROSS MACKINTOSH MALLOCH
ord and ind to Trinity 23 Sep 1970; trans to Inchbrayock with Montrose Melville South 17 Sep 1981.

1983 ROBERT JOHN McDOUGALL ANDREW
(FES X, 243, 315, 364), trans from Kilmallie to Uddingston Old 27 Jan 1983; ret 1 Feb 1994; m (2) 8 Aug 1980 Anne Jones-Davies (nee Wylie); d Margaret Jean m Stephen Harding; d Kathleen Mary m David Greive; s Robert Gervase m Elizabeth Kennedy.

1994 NORMAN BARCLAY McKEE
B 27 Feb 1943 at Paisley, s of Norman M. and Marion Fraser Barclay; educ Paisley Grammar 1955–59; University of Glasgow 1982–86 (BD); Rolls Royce Ltd 1959–65; Administrator (NHS) 1965–82; lic by Presb of Lanark 29 Jun 1986; asst Lanark St Nicholas' 1986–87; m 9 Jun 1971 Anne Marion Morrison Tennant b 5 Jan 1951 d of Robert T. and Agnes McDonald; Children: Fraser Robert b 8 May 1974; Jamie McDonald b 19 Nov 1977; ord and ind to Hamilton St Andrew's 4 Jun 1987; trans to Uddingston Old 26 Oct 1994.

UDDINGSTON PARK (FUF 194; FES IX, 340; X, 203)

1974 JOHN WELSH MALCOLM
(FES IX, 18, 337; X, 12, 203, 413), res from app at Scots Church, Lausanne and ind to Park 13 Dec 1974; ret 30 Sep 1981.

1987 EARLSLEY MABIN WHITE
B 21 Feb 1928 at Fleetwood, Lancs, s of Matthew W. and Sarah Wright Beattie; Salvation Army College, London 1946–47; Salvation Army 1947–52; Western Theological College, Bristol 1953–57; University of Bristol 1954–57 (BA); lic by Gloucester County Union (Congregational Church)

10 Jun 1954; m 22 Jun 1953 Sylvia Ruth Hoskin b 30 Jul 1929 d of Edgar and Lilian H; Children: Paul b 22 Jan 1956 m Alison; Rosalyn b 6 Sep 1958 m Ian; Alastair b 12 Oct 1960; ord by Congregational Church in England and Wales and ind to Russell Town, Bristol 26 Jun 1957; Royal Navy Chaplain 1960–67; Teaching (English) 1968; Orchard Road Presb Church, Singapore 1969–77; Trinity Church, Ramsey, Isle of Man 1979–87; admitted by General Assembly 1987; ind to Park 30 Oct 1987; ret 21 Feb 1998.

1999 WILLIAM BRUCE McDOWALL
B 14 Sep 1960 at Glasgow, s of William John M. and Agnes Bruce McIntosh; educ Stonelaw High, Rutherglen 1972–78; University of Strathclyde 1978–82 (BA), 1982–83 (Dip Personnel Management); University of Glasgow 1985–88 (BD); Admin Asst, Glasgow Chamber of Commerce 1983–85; lic by Presb of Glasgow 27 Jun 1988; asst Glasgow Greenbank 1988–89; m 1 Sep 1984 Elizabeth Ann Cox b 21 Sep 1960 d of Charles Johnston C. and Margaret Fleming; Children: Colin John b 1 Nov 1989; Gregor Bruce b 15 Jul 1993; ord and ind to Glasgow Carmyle with Kenmuir Mount Vernon 25 Aug 1989; trans to Park 4 Mar 1999.

UDDINGSTON VIEWPARK (FES IX, 340; X, 203)

1967 GEORGE KIDD BARR
(FES X, 203), ord and ind to Viewpark 29 Nov 1967; ret 27 Jun 1993; University of Edinburgh 1991–94 (PhD); Publ: Technical papers on literary scalometry in *Irish Biblical Studies* (1995–98); *Literary and Linguistic Computing* (1997); *Expert Evidence* (1998).

1994 SCOTT STEIN McKENNA
B 3 Feb 1966 at Dunfermline, s of John M. and Jane Docherty Stein; educ Kirkton High, Dundee 1978–84; Dundee College of Technology 1984–87 (BA); University of St Andrews 1989–92 (BD); Accountancy 1987–89; lic by Presb of Dundee 18 Jun 1992; asst Glasgow Wellington 1992–94; m 18 Jul 1997 Shelagh Morag Laird b 2 Jun 1966 d of Brian L. and Morag Adams; ord and ind to Viewpark 27 Jan 1994; Chaplain (part-time) to Monklands General Hospital, Airdrie.

WISHAW CAMBUSNETHAN NORTH (FUF 186; FES IX, 341; X, 204)

1964 ALEXANDER GALLAN
(FES X, 204, 219), trans from Duntocher Trinity to Cambusnethan North 17 Jun 1964; ret 31 Dec 1988; d Jean m Michael Ward; s John m Jane Prentice; s David m Kitty Toua.

1989 MHORAG MACDONALD
B 6 Apr 1953 at Lagos, Nigeria, d of Douglas Hamilton M. and Margaret McCallum; educ Dumbarton Academy 1965–71; University of Glasgow 1971 76 (MA), 1985–88 (BD); Jordanhill

College, Glasgow 1977–78 (PGCE); Teaching 1978–83; Principal teacher 1983–85; lic by Presb of Dumbarton 10 Jul 1988; asst Bishopton Erskine 1988–89; ord and ind to Cambusnethan North 4 Sep 1989.

WISHAW CAMBUSNETHAN OLD AND MORNINGSIDE (FES X, 204)

Morningside was formerly a Mission Station.

1969 JOHN SHARP McBRIDE
(FES IX, 109, 337; X, 67, 204), trans form Kelso St John's Edenside and Ednam to Cambusnethan Old 29 Jan 1969; ret 31 Mar 1979; died 5 Apr 1990.

1980 DOUGLAS RAMSAY MURRAY
ind to Duke Street Congregational Church, Leith Sep 1969; admitted by General Assembly and ind to Cambusnethan Old 14 Feb 1980; introd to Lausanne 4 Feb 1994.

1995 IAIN CAMPBELL MURDOCH
B 16 Oct 1950 at Glasgow, s of John Duncan M. and Zoe Mann Hannay; educ Haileybury College, Hertford 1964–68; University of Oxford 1968–71(MA); University of Edinburgh 1971–73 (LLB), 1989–92 (BD); Moray House College, Edinburgh 1976–77 (DipEd); Law 1973–74; Teaching 1975–89; loc ten Edinburgh Kaimes Lockhart Memorial and Chaplain (temp) to City Hospital, Edinburgh 1994–95; lic by Presb of Edinburgh 5 Jul 1992; asst Edinburgh Duddingston Kirk 1992–94; m 4 Aug 1979 Elizabeth Jane Gibson b 29 Aug 1951 d of John G. and Jane Watt; Children: Rebecca Jane b 15 Feb 1982; David Peter Iain b 6 Jan 1986; ord and ind to Cambusnethan Old and Morningside 22 Feb 1995.

WISHAW CHALMERS (FUF 195; FES IX, 341; X, 204)

1976 GILBERT LITTLE THOMSON
admitted by General Assembly and ind to Chalmers 12 May 1976; trans to Stranraer Old 5 May 1985.

1985 CATHERINE WEIR OWEN
ord by Presb of Dumbarton during assistantship at Helensburgh West 6 May 1984; ind to Chalmers 25 Aug 1985; dem 1987; app Chaplain to Stirling Royal (part-time) Jun 1994.

1988 IAN OSBORNE COLTART
B 15 Apr 1943 at Glasgow, s of David Hope C. and Agnes Smith Biggart; educ Morrison's Academy, Crieff 1954–61; St Colm's College, Edinburgh (Missionary Training) 1966–67; University of Glasgow 1984–87 (BD); Trainee Chartered Accountant 1961–66; Missionary with Church of Scotland in India 1967–84; lic by Presb of Dumbarton 5 Jul 1987; asst Dumbarton Riverside 1987–88; m 7 Apr 1967 Florence Margaret Hart b 30 Mar 1937 d of Thomas H. and Stella Todd;

Children: Andrew b 20 May 1968 m Caroline Smith; Rosemary Anne b 11 Aug 1970; Alistair David Thomas b 24 Jun 1972 m Alison Weir; ord and ind to Chalmers 31 May 1988; Chaplain (part-time) to Longriggend Prison.

WISHAW CRAIGNEUK AND BELHAVEN (FES X, 204)

1976 IAIN PAUL
B 15 Jun 1939 at Glasgow, s of John P. and Margaret Middleton; educ Govan High, Glasgow; University of Strathclyde 1961 (BSc); University of Bristol 1967–69 (PhD); University of Sheffield (Post Doc Research); University of Edinburgh (BD, PhD); Member of Centre of Theological Inquiry, USA from 1979; Lecturer in Chemistry, University of London 1969–71; lic by Presb of Larbert, 1970; asst Kirkconnel 1974–75; m 20 Dec 1972 Elizabeth Russell d of Russell and Kidd; Children: Findlay b 2 Jun 1975; Liza b 2 Mar 1978; ord and ind to Craigneuk and Belhaven 28 Jan 1976; ret 31 Mar 1991; Publ: Three books on science and theology (1982–87); co-editor of *Science and Religion* (ESSAT Conference, 1990); numerous scientific publs.

1991 SCOTT RABY
B 24 Mar 1956 at Dundee, s of Stanley Henry R. and Annie Don Hamilton; educ Queen Anne High, Dunfermline 1968–74; University of Edinburgh 1981–85 (LTh); University of Glasgow 1985–87 (CMin); Grocery Retail Management 1975–80; lic by Presb of Dunfermline 1 Jul 1990; asst Arbroath Ladyloan St Columba's 1988–90; Inchbrayock with Montrose Melville South 1990–91; m 5 May 1990 Cherie Donaldson b 28 Apr 1963 d of Charles D. and Sheenagh Hendrickx; Children: Rebekah b 14 Sep 1994; Stephen b 2 Dec 1998; ord and ind to Craigneuk and Belhaven 19 Sep 1991.

WISHAW OLD (FES III, 282; VIII, 264; IX, 342; X, 204)

1970 WILLIAM HAISLEY MOORE
(FES X, 204), res from RAChD (Presb Church of Ireland) and ind to Wishaw Old 16 Dec 1970; trans to Ancrum with Edgerston with Jedburgh Old 25 Nov 1981.

1982 ROBERT MAYES
ord and ind to Wishaw Old 12 May 1982; trans to Dundonald 13 Dec 1988.

1989 JAMES DAVIDSON
B 7 Oct 1942 at Ayr, s of James D. and Margaret Love Farrel Cassells; educ Dalmellington Junior Secondary 1954–57 and Greenwood Academy, Irvine 1983–84; University of Glasgow 1984–88 (BD); Trainee Mining Engineer 1957–61; Army 1961–83; lic by Presb of Irvine and Kilmarnock 30 Jun 1988; asst Irvine Old 1988–89; m 19 Dec 1964 Elizabeth Brown Bruce d of John Orton Geddes B. and Elizabeth McAndrew Henderson; Children: Andrew John b 12 May 1967; Stuart James b 27 Aug 1974; ord and ind to Wishaw Old 22 Jun 1989.

WISHAW ST MARK'S (FES X, 204)

1967 HENRY JAMES WYLIE FINDLAY

(FES X, 204), ind to St Mark's 22 Nov 1967; Addl children: Simon James b 8 Oct 1974; Ruth Elizabeth Margaret b 11 Apr 1978.

WISHAW THORNLIE (FUF 195; FES IX, 342; X, 204)

1969 WILLIAM DIXON BROWN
(FES X, 25, 205), trans from Edinburgh Slateford Longstone to Thornlie 16 Apr 1969; ret 31 Jul 1989.

1990 EVELYN PHILLIPS HOPE
B 11 Jun 1934 at Glasgow, d of James Dickson H. and Elizabeth Phillips Neil; educ Shawlands Academy, Glasgow 1946–52; School of Radiography, Glasgow 1955; Robert Gordon's Institute of Technology, Aberdeen 1973 (CQSW); University of Glasgow 1983 (DAEd); Open University 1985 (BA); University of Glasgow 1986–89 (BD); Radiographer; Social Work; lic by Presb of Glasgow 3 Jul 1989; asst Glasgow King's Park 1989–90; ord and ind to Thornlie 26 Sep 1990; dem 8 Mar 1998.

1999 KLAUS OTTO FRITZ BUWERT
B 6 Apr 1956 at Dumfries, s of Hans B. and Irmgard Müller; educ Dumfries Academy; University of Edinburgh 1974–78 (LLB), 1980–83 (BD); lic by Presb of Dumfries and Kirkcudbright 10 Jul 1983; asst Troon St Meddan's 1983–84; m 8 Aug 1986 Maureen Macaulay b 12 Jul 1951 d of Peter M. and Eleanor Boyd MacFarlane; Children: Andrew b 26 Jun 1987; Jonathan b 29 Jun 1990; Stephen b 19 Feb 1992; ord and ind to Kinlochleven with Nether Lochaber 30 May 1984; trans to Thornlie 25 Aug 1999.

PRESBYTERY OF DUMBARTON

ALEXANDRIA (FES X, 213)

Formed 16 Feb 1994 by union of North and St Andrew's (union 27 Nov 1975 of Alexandria Old and Bonhill North).

1953 WILLIAM JAMES EDWIN MACFARLANE
(FES IX, 359; X, 213, 214), ord and ind to Bonhill North 28 Jan 1953; became minister of united charge with Alexandria Old 27 Nov 1975; ret 1 Feb 1987; d Margaret m David Cairnduff Ferrie.

1975 DOUGLAS WILLIAM BELL
(FES X, 213), ord and ind to Alexandria North 22 Oct 1975; ret 31 Oct 1993.

1987 ROY JAMES MURRAY HENDERSON
ord and ind to St Andrew's 28 Oct 1987; trans to Glasgow Lansdowne 24 Jun 1992.

1995 ELIZABETH WOOD HOUSTON
B 31 Jul 1953 at Dumbarton, d of Peter MacNee H. and Agnes Reston Beveridge; educ St Columba's, Kilmacolm 1964–71; University of Glasgow 1971–74 (MA), 1978 (DipEd), 1980–83 (BD); Teaching (English) 1975–80; lic by Presb of Paisley 23 Jun 1983; asst Paisley Sherwood 1983–84; ord and ind to Hurlford Reid Memorial 22 Jan 1985; trans to Alexandria 11 Jan 1995.

ARROCHAR (FES IX, 357; X, 213)

Linked 1 Sep 1986 with Luss.

1964 ROBERT KENNEDY WILLIAMSON
(FES IX, 419, 586, 754; X, 62, 181, 213, 336, 340), trans from Kingswells to Arrochar 30 Sep 1964; ret 31 Dec 1972; died 16 Aug 1986.

1973 ALBERT FLEMING BOLTON
(FES IX, 318, 594, 704; X, 187, 213), trans from Bellshill Orbiston to Arrochar 17 May 1973; ret 16 Jan 1983; died 7 Oct 1997.

1984 LESLIE CARNEW
ord and ind to Arrochar 22 Sep 1984; dem 31 Dec 1985.

1986 EWEN SINCLAIR NICOLL
(FES X, 303), trans from Lochalsh and Stromeferry to Arrochar with Luss 2 Oct 1986; ret 28 Feb 1998.

1998 HENRY DANE SHERRARD
(FES X, 413), trans from Cadder to Arrochar with Luss 14 Dec 1998; Princeton Theological Seminary, USA 1996—present (Doctor of Ministry).

BALDERNOCK (FES III, 327; VIII, 273; IX, 357; X, 214)

1967 THOMAS CHAPMAN ROBERTSON
(FES IX, 382, 460, 660; X, 214, 228), trans from Dunoon St John's to Baldernock 10 May 1967; ret 30 Nov 1970; died 3 Nov 1986.

1971 SAMUEL DEVLIN
(FES IX, 165, 591; X, 95, 147, 214), trans from Rutherglen East to Baldernock 8 Jul 1971; ret 30 Jun 1984; died 12 Apr 1989.

1985 ALEXANDER JOHN ROBERTSON
(FES X, 95), trans from New Luce with Old Luce to Baldernock 27 Feb 1985; ret 30 Jun 1993.

1994 HAROLD ANDREW MACLEAN STEVEN
(FES X, 355), trans from Banff Trinity and Alvah with King Edward to Baldernock 20 Apr 1994.

BEARSDEN KILLERMONT (FES IX, 371; X, 222)

1950 ROBERT JACK
(FES IX, 371; X, 222), ord and ind to Bearsden Killermont 15 Feb 1950; ret 31 May 1996; s James m Fiona Margaret McDonald.

1998 GORDON FRASER HAY MACNAUGHTON
B 27 Mar 1958 at Glasgow, s of Douglas Hogarth Hay M. and Sheila Beatrice Kellie; educ Glasgow Academy 1963–75; University of Glasgow 1975–78 (MA); University of Edinburgh 1978–81 (BD); Institute of Counselling 1999 (Dip in Clinical and Pastoral Counselling); lic by Presb of Hamilton 28 Jun 1981; asst Glasgow Newlands South 1981–85; m 27 Aug 1985 Isabel Carole Marks b 28 Dec 1960 d of Frederick Charles M. and Agnes Miller Bruce; Children: Lindsay Sheila b 18 Jun 1990; Isla Glen b 28 Jan 1993; ord by Presb of Glasgow during assistantship at Newlands South 9 Jun 1982; ind to Fenwick 12 Jun 1985; dem on app as Chaplain to University of Dundee 1 Apr 1991; ind to Killermont 26 Feb 1998; Publ: *Uniworship—A University Worship Book* (University of Dundee, 1991).

BEARSDEN NEW KILPATRICK (FES III, 355; VIII, 280; IX, 373; X, 223)

1973 DAVID SAGE MILLEN HAMILTON
(FES X, 23, 223, 290, 331), trans from Aberdeen West of St Nicholas to New Kilpatrick 24 Jan 1973; dem on app as Lecturer in Practical Theology, University of Glasgow 1 Aug 1984.

1975 BERNARD PETER LODGE
admitted by General Assembly and introd as Assoc at New Kilpatrick 6 Jun 1975; ind to Kilmacolm Old 18 Apr 1980.

1980 RALPH COLLEY PHILIP SMITH
(FES X, 283), res as Producer, Religious Television, BBC Scotland and indrod as Assoc at New Kilpatrick 12 Oct 1980; dem on app as Producer A-V Unit, Dept of Communication 1 Aug 1984.

1985 ALASTAIR HENDERSON SYMINGTON
(FES X, 448), trans from Edinburgh Craiglockhart to New Kilpatrick 21 Feb 1985; trans to Troon Old 12 May 1998.

1985 IAN GEORGE GOUGH
(FES X, 316), trans from Glasgow St James' (Pollok) and introd as Assoc at New Kilpatrick 17 Sep 1985; ind to Arbroath Knox's with St Vigean's 12 Sep 1990.

1999 DAVID DONALD SCOTT
B 4 Nov 1954 at Stirling, s of David S. and Hazel Lamont; educ Keil School, Dumbarton 1966–72; University of St Andrews 1972–76 (BSc); University of Edinburgh 1977–80 (BD); Church of Scotland Missionary (Teaching), Ghana 1976–77; lic by Presb of South Argyll 27 Jun 1980; asst Glasgow Barlanark Greyfriars 1980–81; m 12 Sep 1980 Mary-Catherine Cruise b 27 Jan 1954 d of Aaron Victor C. and Sara Bell Ingle; Children: David Peter b 12 Dec 1981; Anna Catherine b 12 Jul 1983; Colin John b 26 May 1985; Sarah Frances b 24 Jul 1987; ord and ind to Forth St Paul's 22 Sep 1981; trans to Logie Kirk 1 Mar 1990; trans to New Kilpatrick 28 Apr 1999.

BEARSDEN NORTH (FUF 203; FES IX, 358; X, 214)

1933 WILLIAM GEORGE DUNCAN MACLENNAN
(FUF 463; FES IX, 358, 640; X, 214), trans from Burghead to Bearsden North 4 Oct 1933; ret 31 Oct 1966; died 19 Feb 1981.

1967 DAVID PEACOCK MUNRO
(FES IX, 545; X, 99, 214, 314), trans from Ayr Castlehill to Bearsden North 30 Aug 1967; ret 30 Oct 1996; Clerk to Presb of Dumbarton from 9 Sep 1986; d Morag m Jean-Luc Landi.

1997 KEITH THOMAS BLACKWOOD
B 29 May 1969 at Motherwell, s of James Alasdair B. and Elizabeth Lennox Simpson; educ Dalziel

High, Motherwell 1981–86; University of Glasgow 1986–88 (BDS), 1988–91 (BD), 1993–95 (DipMin); Care Asst, Board of Social Responsibility 1993–95; lic by Presb of Hamilton 30 Aug 1995; asst Alloway 1995–97; m 16 Aug 1996 Katrina Mary Lee b 21 May 1974 d of Graham L. and Janette Ross; ord and ind to Bearsden North 15 May 1997.

BEARSDEN SOUTH (FUF 203; FES IX, 358; X, 214)

1967 WILLIAM BOYD ROBERTSON MACMILLAN
(FES X, 34, 214, 352), trans from Fyvie to Bearsden South 25 Apr 1967; trans to Dundee Parish Church (St Mary's) 8 Mar 1978.

1978 DAVID GENTLES HAMILTON
(FES X, 107), trans from Troon St Meddan's to Bearsden South 25 Oct 1978; dem on app as Curriculum Officer, Board of Parish Education 1 Nov 1980.

1981 DOUGLAS HOGARTH HAY MACNAUGHTON
(FES X, 41, 141, 196), trans from Hamilton Old to Bearsden South 28 Aug 1981; died 2 Jun 1986.

1987 JOHN WILLIAM FORSYTH HARRIS
(FES X, 110), trans from Motherwell St Mary's to Bearsden South 25 Feb 1987; d Fiona m Graeme Norman Stirling.

BEARSDEN WESTERTON FAIRLIE MEMORIAL (FES X, 224)

Linked with Dalmuir Overtoun 9 Sep 1984 until 13 Dec 1990.

1957 FREDERICK ALBERT SMITH
(FES IX, 356; X, 213, 224), trans from Alexandria Bridge Street to Westerton Fairlie Memorial 27 Jun 1957; ret 31 Mar 1979; died 26 May 1983.

1979 IAIN JAMES McINTOSH TELFER
ord by Presb of Moray during assistantship at Elgin St Giles' 17 Feb 1978; ind to Westerton Fairlie Memorial 20 Jun 1979; became minister of linked charge with Dalmuir Overtoun 9 Sep 1984; trans to Inverurie St Andrew's 3 Jul 1989.

1984 JAMES FORREST GATHERER
ord by Presb of Dumbarton and introd as Assoc at Westerton Fairlie Memorial with Dalmuir Overtoun 14 Sep 1984; ind to Dalmuir Barclay 13 Dec 1990.

1990 ERIC VALLANCE HUDSON
(FES X, 346), res as Religious Programmes Officer for Scottish Television and ind to Westerton Fairlie Memorial 11 Jan 1990; d Gillian m Gavin Coull; s Peter m Roisin O' Hagan.

BONHILL (FES X, 215)

Formed 20 Nov 1974 by union of Bonhill Old and Bonhill South.

1966 RALPH WYNNE FAIRWAY
(FES IX, 132, 244, 280, 511; X, 144, 215, 358), res from app as Asst at Largs St Columba's and ind to Bonhill South 28 Sep 1966; ret 31 Mar 1973; died 9 Mar 1987.

1975 IAN HUNTER MILLER
(FES X, 215), ord and ind to Bonhill 6 Aug 1975; Open University 1976–79 (BA).

CARDROSS (FES IX, 361; X, 215)

1951 ARCHIBALD ALEXANDER ORROCK
(FES IX, 361, 792; X, 215), ret from Royal Naval Chaplaincy Service and ind to Cardross 2 Feb 1951; dem 31 Oct 1964; Teaching (RE) 1964–82; Assoc at Dunblane Cathedral 1984–88; ret 8 Nov 1988.

1965 ANDREW JOHN SCOBIE
(FES X, 215), ord by Presb of Dumbarton during assistantship at Bearsden New Kilpatrick 28 Apr 1963; ind to Cardross 27 May 1965; Children: Rosemary Elizabeth b 16 May 1967 m Roknic; James Andrew Collier b 6 Nov 1968; Addl publ: Co-author of *New Ways to Worship* (St Andrew Press, 1980); contributor to *Songs of God's People* (OUP, 1988); contributor to *Worshipping Together* (St Andrew Press, 1991); contributor to *Common Order* (St Andrew Press, 1994).

CLYDEBANK ABBOTSFORD (FES X, 215)

Formed 25 Jun 1974 by union of Clydebank St James' and Clydebank West.

1956 STEWART PURVES WEBSTER BORTHWICK
(FES IX, 246; X, 145, 215, 217), trans from Kirkintilloch Hillhead to Clydebank West 18 Mar 1956; became minister of united charge with St James' 25 Jun 1974; ret 30 Sep 1987; died 6 Sep 1990.

1988 THOMAS McLURE LOGAN
(FES X, 19), trans from Irvine St Andrew's to Abbotsford 30 Aug 1988; ret 31 Oct 1995.

1996 RODERICK GORDON HAMILTON
B 4 Jan 1966 at Greenock, s of Gordon George H. and Maureen Stirling Millar; educ Gourock High and Greenock Academy 1976–83; University of Glasgow 1983–86 (MA), 1986–89 (BD); lic by Presb of Greenock, Oct 1989; asst Troon St Meddan's 1989–92; m 21 Jun 1991 Shirley Murray Mills b 15 Jun 1966 d of Samuel Scott and Annie M; ord by Presb of Glasgow and introd as Assoc at Greenbank 21 Apr 1992; ind to Abbotsford 19 Jun 1996.

CLYDEBANK FAIFLEY (FES X, 216)

1973 THOMAS GIRVAN WATSON
(FES X, 216), ord and ind to Faifley 17 Nov 1973; ret 31 Jul 1984; died 29 May 1987.

1985 JOHN DILLON
ord and ind to Faifley 28 May 1985; trans to Glasgow Partick Trinity 25 Oct 1990.

1991 GREGOR McINTYRE
B 19 Nov 1965 at Glasgow, s of Robert M. and Dorothy-Anne Johnston; educ Woodfarm High 1977–83; Universtiy of Glasgow 1983–87 (BSc), 1987–91 (BD); lic by Presb of Glasgow 3 Jul 1990; m 17 Jun 1989 Kathryn Stoddart b 23 Mar 1966 d of Robert S. and Chapman; Children: Alison Kirsty b 18 Jan 1998; ord and ind to Faifley 16 May 1991.

CLYDEBANK KILBOWIE ST ANDREW'S (FES X, 215, 217, 221)

Formed 9 May 1990 by union of Kilbowie and Clydebank St Andrew's (union 14 Jan 1976 of Boquhanran and Clydebank Union).

1956 ALEXANDER HAMILTON LAWSON
(FES IX, 94; X, 57, 221), trans from Prestonpans Grange to Kilbowie 9 Jan 1956; ret 31 Oct 1988; s Iain m Cecilia Macnamara; d Muriel m William Barlow; Publ: *Churches at the Crossroads* (Conference of European Churches, 1983); *Towards a Lasting Peace* (Conference of Bussum, Holland, 1985).

1972 ROBERT MENZIES FERGUSON ROSS
(FES IX, 287, 483; X, 169, 175, 210, 217), trans from Glasgow St George's Road to Clydebank Union 27 May 1972; became minister of linked charge with Boquhanran 29 Oct 1974; dem 31 Dec 1975; died 7 Jan 1989.

1976 DAVID COWAN
(FES X, 408), trans from Whalsay and Skerries to St Andrew's 31 May 1976; dem 14 Jan 1979; introd to Motherwell Manse Road (term) 23 Apr 1980.

1979 JOSEPH STEWART
ord and ind to St Andrew's 13 Jun 1979; trans to Dunoon St John's with Sandbank 5 Apr 1989.

1991 RODERICK JAMES GRAHAME
B 25 Jun 1964 at Dundee, s of Albert Scott G. and Margaret Burns Kinloch; educ Monifieth High 1976–82; University of Dundee 1982–83; University of St Andrews 1983–87 (BD); University of Aberdeen 1988–89 (CPS); lic by Presb of Dundee 13 Aug 1989; asst Bellshill West 1989–91; ord and ind to Kilbowie St Andrew's 13 Mar 1991.

CLYDEBANK RADNOR PARK (FUF 273; FES IX, 362; X, 216)

1971 THOMAS CRAWFORD RICHARDSON
(FES X, 216), ord and ind to Radnor Park 24 Nov 1971; trans to Cults West 1 Feb 1978.

1978 ADAMINA YOUNGER
ord and ind to Radnor Park 13 Sep 1978; dem on app as Young Adult Adviser, Board of Education 15 Mar 1983.

1984 PAUL ROBERT RUSSELL
ord and ind to Radnor Park 17 Feb 1984; trans to Coylton with Drongan The Schaw Kirk 9 Jan 1992.

1992 MARGARET JANE BOAG YULE
B 11 Aug 1954 at Paisley, d of Hugh McCutcheon Boag and Margaret Surgeoner Hunter; educ John Neilson Institute, Paisley 1966–71; Glasgow and West of Scotland College of Domestic Science 1971–74 (DDSc); Jordanhill College, Glasgow 1974–75 (PGCE); University of Glasgow 1987–91 (BD); Teaching 1975–87; lic by Presb of Paisley 20 Aug 1991; m 31 Jul 1976 Iain Webster Yule b 27 Feb 1954 s of John Hagan Y. and Margaret Jane Marshall Webster; Children: Brian Iain b 9 Jan 1981; Graham Boag b 15 Jul 1983; ord and ind to Radnor Park 18 Nov 1992.

CLYDEBANK ST CUTHBERT'S (FES X, 216)

Formed 27 Oct 1983 by union of Clydebank Hamilton Memorial and Clydebank Linnvale.

1975 STANLEY HILL
(FES X, 216, 351), trans from Pitsligo to Hamilton Memorial with Linnvale 16 Feb 1975; dem 30 Sep 1981; ind to Muiravonside 29 Nov 1984.

1984 CHRISTINE MARGARET GOLDIE
ord and ind to St Cuthbert's 8 May 1984; dem on app as Chaplain to Glasgow Polytechnic 17 Feb 1992.

1992 IAN ANDREW MANSON
B 29 Nov 1961 at Glasgow, s of Ian M. and Mae Scott; educ King's Park Secondary, Glasgow 1966–79; Glasgow School of Art 1979–83 (BA); University of Edinburgh 1985–88 (BD); lic by Presb of Edinburgh; m 23 Sep 1986 ord by Presb of Hamilton and introd as Assoc at East Kilbride Moncreiff 8 Jun 1989; ind to St Cuthbert's 20 Oct 1992.

CRAIGROWNIE (FES IX, 363; X, 217)

Linked 25 Apr 1984 with Rosneath St Modan's.

1967 CHARLES KEITH OMOND SPENCE
(FES IX, 272; X, 138, 161, 217), trans from Port Glasgow Old to Craigrownie 29 Nov 1967; Chaplain (TA) 1950–71; app Senior Chaplain (Scotland) 25 Oct 1962; subsequently Senior Chaplain to 52 (Lowland) Division; ret 30 Jun 1983.

1984 MALCOLM WRIGHT
(FES X, 127), trans from Paisley Glenburn to Craigrownie with Rosneath St Modan's 16 Nov 1984; Publ: Sermons in the *Expository Times* (T&T Clark): *Playing the Game with God* (1979); *All-encompassing Witness* (1987); *A Reckless Kind of Love* (1989); *The Joy of Reality* (1991); *The Household of God* (1997).

DALMUIR BARCLAY (FES X, 217, 223)

Formed 13 Dec 1990 by union of Dalmuir Overtoun (union 11 Jan 1976 of Dalmuir Old and Dalmuir Ross Memorial, linked with Bearsden Westerton 9 Sep 1984 until 13 Dec 1990) and Old Kilpatrick Barclay.

1944 COLIN CAMPBELL
(FES IX, 373, 377; X, 223), trans from Cumlodden and Lochfyneside to Old Kilpatrick Barclay 11 Jul 1944; died 13 Jul 1988.

1969 JOHN ALGIE BEATTIE
(FES IX, 706; X, 169, 187, 217, 402, 410), trans from Glasgow Plantation to Dalmuir Old 26 Mar 1969; became minister of united charge with Dalmuir Ross Memorial 11 Jan 1976; ret 30 Apr 1984.

1984 IAIN JAMES McINTOSH TELFER
ind to Westerton Fairlie Memorial 20 Jun 1979; became minister of linked charge with Dalmuir Overtoun 9 Sep 1984; trans to Inverurie St Andrew's 3 Jul 1989.

1990 JAMES FORREST GATHERER
B 27 Sep 1955 at Edinburgh, s of William Alexander G. and Jemima Mackay Forrest; educ Jordanhill School, Glasgow and George Heriot's, Edinburgh; Napier College, Edinburgh (Civil Engineering); University of Aberdeen 1979–83 (BD); Civil Engineering 1976–79; lic by Presb of Edinburgh; m 10 Oct 1987 Catherine Ebdon b 4 Apr 1961 d of Denis E. and Jean Carlo; Children: Peter James b Jun 1990; Adam John b May 1992; Lindsey Andrew b May 1997; ord by Presb of Dumbarton and introd as Assoc at Bearsden Westerton Fairlie Memorial with Dalmuir Overtoun 14 Sep 1984; ind to Barclay 13 Dec 1990.

DUMBARTON RIVERSIDE (FES X, 219)

Formed 18 Nov 1984 by union of Dumbarton Riverside (union 26 Jun 1972 of Dumbarton High, North and Old) and Dumbarton Knoxland.

1945 IAN ARTHUR GIRDWOOD EASTON
(FES IX, 366; X, 219), ord and ind to Dumbarton North 27 Jun 1945; dem 5 Mar 1957 on app as Head of Communications, Caterpillar Tractor Co; app Group Management Development Manager, Colvilles Ltd 1960; app Personnel Manager, University of Strathclyde Business School 1965; ret 30 Sep 1981.

1957 WILLIAM EDWARD WILLIAMSON
(FES IX, 200; X, 82, 114, 219), trans from Stewarton Cairns to Dumbarton North 16 Oct 1957; trans to Cummertrees with Ruthwell and Mount Kedar 2 Oct 1969.

1971 JAMES ARTHUR MACEWAN
(FES IX, 197; X, 113, 168 (2), 219, 402), trans from Westray with Papa Westray to Knoxland 24 Feb 1971; ret 30 Jun 1979; died 17 Jan 1996.

1972 JAMES FREDERICK DUNN
(FES X, 144, 218, 219), trans from Gartcosh to Dumbarton High 12 May 1965; became minister of united charge with Dumbarton North and Dumbarton Old 26 Jun 1972; trans to Coatbridge Dunbeth 22 Sep 1977.

1974 HENRY FINLAYSON CALDER NIVEN
(FES X, 219, 303), trans from Dundee Mains of Fintry to Riverside and ind as Collegiate minister 16 Jan 1974; died 6 Jul 1977.

1978 JAMES FERGUS MILLER
(FES X, 350), trans from Peterhead Old to Riverside 30 May 1978; trans to Dunblane Cathedral 12 Dec 1984.

1980 GEOFFREY LEE
(FES X, 347), trans from Aberdour with Tyrie to Knoxland 27 Feb 1980; ret 31 Oct 1984; died 27 Mar 1994.

1985 JOHN BALLANTYNE CAIRNS
(FES X, 42), trans from Canonbie with Langholm, Ewes and Westerkirk to Riverside 29 Aug 1985; Moderator of General Assembly 1999–2000; Publ: *Keeping Fit for Ministry* (St Andrew Press, 1989).

DUMBARTON ST ANDREW'S (FES X, 219)

1976 RONALD GEORGE LAWSON
(FES X, 114), trans from Perceton and Dreghorn to St Andrew's 27 May 1976; trans to Greenock Mid Kirk 12 Oct 1988.

1989 IRENE ANNE BRISTOW
ord and ind to St Andrew's 28 Jun 1989; trans to Glasgow St Thomas' Gallowgate (75%) and app by Board of National Mission under new forms of ministry (25%) 7 Aug 1997.

1998 LESLIE GAVIN DONAGHY
B 15 Apr 1962 at Helensburgh, s of William Albert Hillard D. and Mildred Adams; educ Clydebank High 1973–79; Stow College 1980–82 (ONC); University of Glasgow 1983–89 (BD, DipMin); University of Strathclyde (PGCE); MLSO Western Infirmary Glasgow 1980–83; lic by Presb of Dumbarton 9 Jul 1989; asst Bearsden South 1989–90; m 6 Jul 1985 Caroline Rae b 7 Oct 1964 d of David R. and Agnes MacIntyre; Children: Andrew James b 10 Oct 1992; Calum Michael b 14 Sep 1995; ord and ind to Inchinnan 30 May 1990; dem 31 Aug 1994 to enter teaching profession (RE); ind to St Andrew's 2 Jul 1998.

DUMBARTON THE WEST KIRK (FES X, 217, 218)

Formed 22 Apr 1984 by union of Dumbarton Bridgend and Dalreoch.

1960 JAMES MERCIER THOMSON
(FES IX, 199; X, 114, 218), trans from Newmilns Loudoun East to Bridgend 7 Sep 1960; became minister of united charge with Dalreoch 22 Apr 1984; introd as Assoc at Elgin St Giles' 31 Jul 1992.

1993 RONALD MITCHELL HALDANE BOYD
ord and ind to the West Kirk 5 May 1993; trans to Troon Portland 29 Sep 1998.

DUNTOCHER (FES X, 219, 220)

1973 EDWARD JOSEPH GEORGE HEWITT
(FES X, 219), ord and ind to Duntocher Trinity 16 May 1973; ret 31 Jan 1980; died 25 Jul 1988.

1980 IAIN DICKSON CUNNINGHAM
ord by Presb of Ayr during assistantship at Castlehill 9 May 1979; ind to Duntocher Trinity 12 Jun 1980; trans to Carluke Kirkton 29 Oct 1987.

1988 ROBIN JAMES McALPINE
ord and ind to Duntocher 9 Jun 1988; dem 11 Aug 1997 on app by Board of National Mission as East of Scotland Adviser in Mission and Evangelism 18 Sep 1997.

DUNTOCHER WEST (FUF 272; FES IX, 367; X, 220)

Congregation seceded to UF Church 11 Jan 1976.

1955 JOHN SIMPSON MUTCH
(FES V, 454; VIII, 463, 516; IX, 522, 592; X, 220, 341), trans from Glenbuchat to Duntocher West 23 Feb 1955; ret 30 Jun 1960; died 14 Jul 1977.

GARELOCHHEAD (FES IX, 368; X, 220)

1964 JAMES BALLANTINE MURRAY
(FES IX, 167, 495; X, 97, 220, 285), trans from Leslie Trinity to Garelochhead 13 May 1964; ret 30 Apr 1970; died 22 Jun 1981.

1970 HAROLD JAMES GARDINER TROUP
(FES IX, 482; X, 220, 275, 286), trans from Inverkeithing St James' and North to Garelochhead 6 Nov 1970; ret 30 Nov 1980.

1982 EWEN JOHN GILCHRIST
ord and ind to Garelochhead 9 Sep 1982; trans to Perth St Matthew's 1 May 1988.

1989 ALASTAIR STUART DUNCAN
B 20 Oct 1961 at Edinburgh, s of Malcolm
McGregor D. and Winifred Petrie Greenhorn; educ
George Watson's, Edinburgh; University of Edinburgh 1979–83 (MA), 1984–87 (BD); lic by Presb
of Edinburgh 5 Jul 1987; asst Edinburgh The Old
Kirk 1987–88; Aberdeen St George's Tillydrone
1988–89; m 29 Jun 1985 Ruth Catherine Jeffrey b
6 Mar 1963 d of Stewart Duncan J. and Margaret
Scott Bakie; Children: Stuart Malcolm b 22 Oct
1987; Elisabeth Grace b 1 Feb 1989; Helen Laura
b 7 Oct 1991; ord and ind to Garelochhead 31 May
1989.

HELENSBURGH PARK (FUF 272; FES IX, 369;
X, 221)

1947 GEORGE REID LOGAN
(FES IX, 141, 369, 446; X, 221), trans from Dumfries St George's to Helensburgh Park 8 Oct 1947;
ret 31 Jan 1977; died 26 Apr 1988.

1977 JAMES HASTIE BROWN
B 4 Apr 1939 at Glasgow, s of Thomas B. and
Agnes Burgess Hastie; educ Victoria Drive,
Glasgow 1951–55; University of Glasgow 1971–
76 (BD); Brewer's Stocktaker/Accountant 1955–
68; Brewer's Sales Rep 1968–71; lic by Presb of
Glasgow 25 Jun 1976; asst Glasgow Cardonald
1976–77; m 7 Jul 1962 Moyra Ferguson Walker b
29 Sep 1938 d of Robert W. and Mary McLean
Kean; Children: Kirstie Ferguson b 25 May 1968;
Elspeth McIntyre b 20 Aug 1970; Andrew McLean
b 7 Dec 1973; ord and ind to Helensburgh Park 22
Jun 1977.

HELENSBURGH ST COLUMBA (FUF 273; FES
IX, 370; X, 221)

1969 ANDREW SCOTLAND MITCHELL
(FES X, 109, 221), trans from Galston New to St
Columba 23 Oct 1969; dem 30 Apr 1982; Clerk
(part-time) to Presb of Dumbarton 1973–82;
Principal Officer for Scotland, British Sailors'
Society 1982–83; Principal Teacher (RE), Strath-
clyde Region 1983–89; Interim minister and part-
time teacher 1989–92; Open University 1986 (BA),
1988 (Adv DipEd [open]), 1990 (BA); ind to
Kilmaronock Gartocharn 22 Oct 1992.

1982 FREDERICK MINTY BOOTH
(FES X, 268), res as Youth and Development
Worker with United Church of Jamaica and Grand
Cayman and ind to St Columba 6 Nov 1982; d
Kirsteen m Mark Capon.

HELENSBURGH THE WEST KIRK (FES X, 220,
221)

Formed 9 Sep 1981 by union of Helensburgh
Old and St Andrew's and Helensburgh St Bride's.

1973 DAVID TINDAL REID
(FES X, 23, 37, 154, 220), trans from Edinburgh
St Cuthbert's to Old and St Andrew's 5 Sep 1973;
became minister of united charge with St Bride's
9 Sep 1981; trans to Cleish with Fossoway St Serf's
and Devonside 4 Dec 1985.

1974 ROBERT ALAN KNOX
(FES X, 120, 221, 446), trans from Stevenston
Ardeer to St Bride's 6 Feb 1974; dem 17 Feb 1980
on app by RAChD.

1986 DAVID WILLIAM CLARK
B 10 Feb 1949 at Kilmarnock, s of Frank C. and
Georgina Chalmers; educ Arbroath High 1961–67;
University of St Andrews 1967–71 (MA), 1971–74
(BD); lic by Presb of Dundee 27 Jun 1974; asst
Aberdeen St Machar's 1974–76; m 18 Sep 1982
Kathryn Anne Milne b 20 Sep 1949 d of Maurice
M. and Dorothy Smith; Children: Lyndsay Anne
b 5 Dec 1983; Lucy Kathryn b 13 Apr 1985;
Michael David b 15 Jul 1986; Ruth Elizabeth b
18 Dec 1991; ord by Presb of Aberdeen during
assistantship at St Machar's Cathedral, Mar 1975;
introd to Bridge of Allan Chalmers (term) 30 Sep
1976; ind to Cupar Old and St Michael of Tarvit 3
May 1979; trans to West Kirk of Helensburgh 1
Sep 1986.

JAMESTOWN (FES III, 348; VIII, 278; IX, 370; X,
221)

1968 ROBERT PATERSON
(FES IX, 192, 228, 276; X, 163, 221), trans from
Glasgow King's Park to Jamestown 7 Mar 1968;
ret 31 Mar 1979; died 20 Mar 1985.

1979 DONALD ARCHIBALD MACQUARRIE
ord and ind to Jamestown 28 Aug 1979; trans to
Fort William Duncansburgh with Kilmonivaig 22
Aug 1990.

1991 KENNETH GEORGE RUSSELL
B 21 Mar 1955 at Kirkcaldy, s of George R. and
Isobel Reilly; educ Buckhaven High and Dun-
fermline High 1960–73; University of Edinburgh
1980–85 (BD, CCE); Computing 1974–78; Youth
Work 1978–80; lic by Presb of Kirkcaldy 1 Jul 1995;
asst Markinch 1995–96; m 29 Apr 1978 Hilary Joan
Duncan b 6 Apr 1955 d of Peter D. and Dorothy
Williamson; Children: Ashley Hilary b 3 Apr 1981;
Neil Kenneth Peter b 27 Feb 1985; ord and ind to
Lochgelly St Andrew's 15 May 1986; introd as
Assoc at Buckhaven 7 Dec 1988; ind to Jamestown
20 Feb 1991.

KILMARONOCK GARTOCHARN (FES IX, 371;
X, 222)

1956 WALTER WILLIAM LYALL
(FES IX, 335; X, 200, 222), trans from Motherwell
St Andrew's to Kilmaronock Gartocharn 19 Dec
1956; ret 31 Mar 1992; died 28 May 1994.

1992 ANDREW SCOTLAND MITCHELL
(FES X, 109, 221), res as teacher (RE) and ind to
Kilmaronock Gartocharn 22 Oct 1992; m (2) 9 Oct
1980 Annie Strachan McKinnon b 31 May 1942 d
of Edward Gordon Howard M. and Isabella Wyper
Houston; stepdaughter Morag Houston Clinch.

LUSS (FES IX, 372; X, 222)

Linked 1 Sep 1986 with Arrochar.

1966 MARTIN BRYDON SHIELDS
(FES IX, 10, 534, 645; X, 7, 222), trans from
Edinburgh Corstorphine St Ninian's to Luss 31 Mar
1966; ret 30 Nov 1973; died 15 Nov 1989.

1974 JOHN WILSON WADDELL
(FES IX, 79, 315; X, 167, 185, 222), trans from
Glasgow Mount Florida to Luss 8 May 1974; died
4 Apr 1979.

1980 ROBERT DOUGLAS HAIG YOUNG
GLOVER
(FES X, 99), trans from Ayr Darlington New to Luss
8 May 1980; ret 31 Aug 1986; died 26 Aug 1998.

1986 EWEN SINCLAIR NICOLL
(FES X, 303), trans from Lochalsh and Stromeferry
to Arrochar with Luss 2 Oct 1986; ret 28 Feb 1998.

1998 HENRY DANE SHERRARD
(FES X, 413), ind to Arrochar with Luss 14 Dec
1998, see Arrochar.

MILNGAVIE CAIRNS (FUF 264; FES IX, 372; X,
222)

1964 JAMES ROY HERKLESS PATERSON
(FES X, 222, 252), trans from Perth Craigie to
Cairns 23 Sep 1964; ret 30 Sep 1993; died 30 Dec
1998; s Roger m Lesley Brown; Addl publ: *A Faith
for the Year 2000* (St Andrew Press, 1990).

1994 ANDREW FRATER
B 24 May 1961 at Glasgow, s of John Birch and
Elizabeth F; educ Williamwood High and Eastwood
High, Glasgow 1973–79; Glasgow College of
Technology 1979–83 (BA); University of Edinburgh
1983–86 (BD); lic by Presb of Glasgow 30 Jun
1986; asst Glasgow Pollokshields 1986–87; m 30
Dec 1987 Diana Christine Russell b 13 Aug 1965
d of John and Marion R; Children: Laura Elizabeth
b 10 Sep 1991; ord and ind to Annan Old 20 Aug
1987; trans to Cairns 16 Mar 1994.

MILNGAVIE ST LUKE'S (FUF 264; FES IX, 372;
X, 222)

1971 DOUGLAS MARTIN COPP
(FES X, 167, 222), trans from New Bridgegate to
St Luke's 19 Feb 1971; died 31 Dec 1995.

1997 RAMSAY BAXTER SHIELDS
trans from Fordyce to St Luke's 9 Apr 1997.

MILNGAVIE ST PAUL'S (FES III, 361; VIII, 282;
IX, 372; X, 222)

1970 JOHN MUNN KIRK PATERSON
(FES X, 29, 222), trans from Bathgate St John's to
St Paul's 24 Jun 1970; Moderator of General
Assembly 1984–85; ret 8 Oct 1987; DD (Aberdeen)
1986.

1988 FERGUS CAMERON BUCHANAN
B 26 Sep 1954 at Glasgow, s of Archiblad B. and
Elizabeth Cairns Green; educ Crookston Castle
Secondary 1967–73; University of Glasgow 1973–
78 (MA), 1978–81 (BD); lic by Presb of Glasgow
13 Jun 1981; asst Glasgow Cathedral 1981–83; m
3 Sep 1978 Gabrielle Alexina Bradley b 27 Nov
1956 d of James B. and Philomena Stew; Children:
Mark Cameron b 25 Aug 1983; Stephen John b 24
Aug 1985; Paul Gabriel b 22 Dec 1989; ord by
Presb of Glasgow during assistantship at Glasgow
Cathedral 5 May 1982; ind to Stevenston Ardeer 2
Jun 1983; trans to St Paul's 19 Apr 1988.

OLD KILPATRICK BOWLING (FES X, 223)

Formed 30 Nov 1975 by union of Old Kilpatrick
and Bowling.

1936 ARCHIBALD DUNCAN EUNSON
(FES IX, 259, 373; X, 223), trans from Glasgow
Bluevale to Old Kilpatrick 30 Sep 1936; ret 30 Nov
1975; died 11 Jan 1987.

1967 DANIEL BROCK DOYLE
(FES IX, 241, 366; X, 141, 215, 234), trans from
Saddell and Carradale to Bowling 12 Apr 1967;
ret 31 Jul 1974; died 15 Jun 1991.

1976 ADAM GIRVAN
(FES X, 209), trans from Douglas Water and
Rigside to Old Kilpatrick Bowling 25 Jun 1976; ret
31 Dec 1983; died 2 Dec 1991.

1984 ALASTAIR JAMES MACKICHAN
B 11 Apr 1951 at Rochdale, s of Ian Duncan M.
and Honor Elizabeth Mary Stearn; educ Hulme
Grammar, Oldham and Lawrence Sheriff Gram-
mar, Rugby 1962–69; University of Oxford 1969–
72 (MA); University of Edinburgh 1980–83 (BD);
Agriculture 1972–78; Social Work 1978–80; lic by
Presb of Edinburgh 3 Jul 1983; asst Edinburgh St
Giles' Cathedral 1983–84; m 27 Sep 1980 Jane
Margaret Lindsay b 13 Nov 1950 d of James
Kenneth L. and Wisteria Ethel Jolly; Children:
Calum Ian b 19 Jul 1983; Jamie Dugald b 9 Apr
1985; ord and ind to Old Kilpatrick Bowling 10 Dec
1984.

RENTON TRINITY (FES X, 223)

1970 GEORGE STEWART SMITH
(FES X, 223), ord by Presb of Greenock during
assistantship at St Ninian's 21 Apr 1966; ind to
Trinity 4 Jun 1970; trans to Glasgow King's Park
22 Mar 1979.

1979   JOHN PEARSON CHALMERS
ord and ind to Trinity 14 Jun 1979; trans to Edinburgh Palmerston Place 1 Oct 1986.

1987   AGNES ADAM MOORE
ord and ind to Trinity 23 Jun 1987; trans to Sauchie and Coalsnaughton 6 Jan 1995.

1995   CAMERON HUNTER LANGLANDS
ord and ind to Trinity 28 Jun 1995; dem 20 Sep 1999 on app as Health Care and Co-ordinating Chaplain, Greater Glasgow Primary Care NHS Trust.

RHU AND SHANDON (FES X, 224)

1971   ALEXANDER DOUGLAS STIRLING
(FES X, 42, 224), trans from Queensferry to Rhu and Shandon 6 Jun 1971; ret 30 Mar 1994; s David m Bianca Bailey; s Douglas m Gail Smith.

1994   ALISON PAUL
B 18 Nov 1946 at Glasgow, d of Clifford Stuart P. and Isobel Campbell Burns; educ Dumbarton Academy 1952–65; University of Glasgow 1965–70 (MA), 1982–85 (BD); University of Manchester 1976–77 (DTEO); Teaching (English), Germany 1970–76, 1977–82; lic by Presb of Dumbarton 28 Jun 1985; asst Helensburgh West Kirk 1985–86; ord and ind to Motherwell North 28 May 1986; trans to Rhu and Shandon 13 Dec 1994.

ROSNEATH ST MODAN'S (FES X, 224)

Linked 25 Apr 1984 with Craigrownie.

1963   MERRICKS ARNOTT
(FES IX, 145, 307, 560; X, 180, 224), trans from Glasgow South Shawlands to Rosneath 24 Apr 1963; ret 30 Jun 1972; died 19 Apr 1995.

1972   WILLIAM MEIKLEJOHN
(FES IX, 470, 606; X, 224, 278), trans from Tulliallan to Rosneath St Modan's 1 Nov 1972; ret 31 Oct 1978; died 6 Apr 1997.

1979   THOMAS FORREST SMITH
(FES X, 147, 274, 285), dem from Dunfermline St Ninian's and introd to Rosneath St Modan's (term) 1 Aug 1979; introd on term app to Arbuthnott with Kinneff 14 Apr 1982.

1984   MALCOLM WRIGHT
(FES X, 127), trans from Paisley Glenburn to Craigrownie with Rosneath St Modan's 16 Nov 1984.

PRESBYTERY OF SOUTH ARGYLL

ARDRISHAIG (FES IX, 377; X, 225)

Linked 10 Dec 1964 with South Knapdale.

1965 JOHN GARRIOCK ROSS
(FES IX, 122, 357; X, 47, 71, 225, 234), trans from Gigha and Cara to Ardrishaig with Knapdale South 4 Aug 1965; ret 31 Mar 1969; died 29 Sep 1983.

1969 HENRY CRAWFORD DONALDSON
(FES IX, 168, 237, 264, 799; X, 98, 225, 453), res as Home Organisation Secretary, Overseas Council and ind to Ardrishaig with South Knapdale 22 Oct 1969; ret 28 Feb 1978; died 11 Jun 1985.

1978 WILLIAM DOUGLAS WATT
ord and ind to Ardrishaig with South Knapdale 29 Nov 1978; trans to Aboyne with Dinnet 21 Jun 1985.

1985 JAMES EDWARD ANDREWS
ord and ind to Ardrishaig with South Knapdale 25 Oct 1985; trans to Dalkeith St Nicholas' Buccleuch 20 Jun 1991.

1992 JAMES HOSIE
(FES X, 134, 163, 257), trans from Burra Isle with Tingwall to Ardrishaig with South Knapdale 27 Mar 1992; ret 14 Jun 1998.

1998 DAVID CARRUTHERS
B 4 Jan 1960 at Dumfries, s of James and Ethel C; educ Lockerbie Academy 1972–77; University of Aberdeen 1994–97 (BD); Clydesdale Bank 1977–80; UK Atomic Energy Authority 1980–94; Graduate of Royal Society of Chemistry; lic by Presb of Caithness 6 Jul 1997; asst Drumoak with Durris and Peterculter Kelman Memorial 1997–98; m 7 Mar 1987 Alison Ruth Fair Stewart b 1 May 1960 d of Leslie and Jean S; Children: Philip b 9 Feb 1989; Naomi b 25 Sep 1990; Rachel b 27 Jul 1994; Beth b 10 May 1996; ord and ind to Ardrishaig with South Knapdale 11 Dec 1998.

CAMPBELTOWN HIGHLAND (FES IV, 48; VIII, 322; IX, 391; X, 233)

1964 CHARLES MALCOLM HENDERSON
(FES IX, 689; X, 225, 233, 393), trans from Glassary to Campbeltown Highland 8 Jul 1964; ret 30 Sep 1989.

1991 DONALD R LAWRIE
ord and ind to Campbeltown Highland 26 Jan 1991; pastoral tie severed 31 Mar 1996.

1997 MICHAEL JAMES LIND
B 15 Feb 1954 at Glasgow, s of James Young L. and Jean Dalrymple McNiven; educ Loretto School, Musselburgh 1962–72; University of Dundee 1972–76 (LLB); University of Edinburgh 1977–78 (non-grad law student), 1980–83 (BD); Scottish Widows 1976–77; Law Apprentice 1979–80; lic by Presb of Edinburgh 3 Jul 1983; asst Edinburgh Gorgie 1983–84; m 7 Aug 1980 Anne Welsh Malcolm b 20 Sep 1955 d of Hugh Welsh M. and Isabel Hill; Children: William James Young b 22 Jan 1984; Alexander Hugh Cunningham b 16 Feb 1986; Robert Donald McNiven b 29 Oct 1988; ord and ind to Duirinish 12 Oct 1984; trans to Campbeltown Highland 26 Sep 1997.

CAMPBELTOWN LORNE AND LOWLAND (FES X, 233)

Formed 5 Sep 1990 by union of Campbeltown Lorne Street and Campbeltown Lowland.

1945 JOHN RICHARDSON HAMILTON CORMACK
(FES IX, 392; X, 233 (2)), ind to Campbeltown Lowland Charge 24 Oct 1945; became minister of united charge with Longrow 5 May 1971; ret 31 May 1981; w Agnes died 4 Feb 1982; Publ: Co-author of *Highland Railway Locomotives* (Railway Correspondence and Travel Society, 1989, 1990).

1961 JAMES WILLIAM HOOD
(FES IX, 68; X, 42, 233), trans from Polmont Shieldhill to Lorne Street 3 May 1961; died 11 Nov 1987.

1982 ANDREW THOMSON
admitted by General Assembly 1982 and ind to Lowland 1 Jul 1982; trans to Renfrew Trinity 19 Oct 1988.

1991 IAIN MORRISON
ord and ind to Lorne and Lowland 16 May 1991; trans to Glasgow Hillington Park 14 Jan 1997.

1997 JOHN OSWALD
B 10 Oct 1947 at Glasgow, s of John O. and Agnes Clelland; educ Kelvinside Academy, Glasgow 1953–65; University of Edinburgh 1966–70 (BSc),

1970–73 (PhD), 1992–95 (BD); Agriculture Supply Industry (Management) 1973–92; lic by Presb of Melrose and Peebles 4 Jul 1995; asst Eddleston with Peebles Old 1995–97; m 28 Apr 1972 Barbara Roberta Wright b 12 Jul 1948 d of Joseph W. and Anne Burns; Children: John b 6 Feb 1975; ord and ind to Lorne and Lowland 3 Jun 1997.

CRAIGNISH (FES IV, 2; VIII, 312; IX, 377; X, 225)

Linkage with Kilmartin terminated 1 Nov 1974. Linked same date with Kilninver and Kilmelford.

1945 NEIL MACKAY
(FES IX, 377, 411; X, 225), trans from the Small Isles to Craignish 31 Oct 1945; ret 31 Aug 1967; died 8 Jul 1980.

1968 JOHN TURNER
(FES IX, 196, 505, 570, 606; X, 112, 225), trans from Kilmarnock Riccarton to Craignish with Kilmartin 10 Apr 1968; ret 31 Jul 1974; died 17 Jul 1978.

1975 ROBERT CRAIG MILLER CARMICHAEL
(FES IX, 393; X, 115, 119, 225, 311), trans from Eassie and Nevay with Newtyle to Craignish with Kilninver and Kilmelford 3 Apr 1975; ret 30 Jun 1991; d Shona Stewart b 10 Dec 1957; s Colin Roderick b 24 Dec 1963; d Fiona Mary b 20 Aug 1950 m Meins; d Kirsteen Miller b 7 Jun 1959 m Menzies;.

1992 MICHAEL JOHN ERSKINE
B 5 Apr 1956 at Bridge of Allan, s of John Francis Hervey Erskine and Pansy Constance Thorne; educ Belhaven School and Eton College 1964–75; University of Edinburgh 1976–80 (MA), 1981–84 (BD); lic by Presb of Stirling, 1985; asst Glasgow Govan Old 1984–85; m 5 Sep 1987 Jill Westwood d of Campbell W. and Helen Logan; Children: Laura Anne b 15 Apr 1990; Ewan Stewart b 14 Jun 1992; ord by Presb of Gordon and introd as Assoc at Ellon, 1985; ind to Inverkip 25 Nov 1987; trans to Craignish with Kilninver and Kilmelford 24 Feb 1992.

CUMLODDEN, LOCHFYNESIDE AND LOCHGAIR (FES X, 225)

Lochgair preaching station transferred from Glassary to Cumlodden and Lochfyneside 1983.

1960 JOHN ALEXANDER STABLES
(FES IX, 524; X, 225, 310), trans from Airlie to Cumlodden and Lochfyneside 5 Feb 1960; ret 4 May 1966; died 2 Apr 1985.

1966 ALEXANDER FRASER
(FES IX, 268, 380, 656, 681; X, 225, 373), trans from Inverness Kirkhill to Cumlodden and Lochfyneside 21 Sep 1966; ret 24 Feb 1978; died 11 Jul 1995.

1979 JAMES SHIRLAW PATERSON
(FES IX, 283, 365; X, 38, 218, 294), trans from Falkirk Old to Cumlodden and Lochfyneside 13 Feb 1979; ret 30 Sep 1984; died 24 Sep 1987.

1985 RODERICK MACLEOD
(FES X, 395), trans from Bernera to Cumlodden, Lochfyneside and Lochgair 20 Sep 1985; Depute Clerk to Presb of South Argyll from 1995; President, Scottish Gaelic Texts Society from 1996; University of Edinburgh 1977 (PhD); Open University 1994 (PhD); Addl publ: Editor of Gaelic Supplement to *Life and Work* from 1980; various articles (Gaelic and English) on Highland church history; *Gaidheal aig Harvard* (1986).

GIGHA AND CARA (FES IV, 54; VIII, 323; IX, 392; X, 233)

Continued vacancy declared 1998.

1973 JAMES ROBERTSON
(FES IX, 356; X, 130, 213, 234), dem from Paisley St Ninian's Ferguslie 31 Dec 1972; ind to Gigha and Cara 25 Apr 1973; ret 30 Apr 1981; died 25 Jun 1982.

1982 DAVID COUSER GORDON
(FES IX, 148; X, 87, 138), trans from Port Glasgow West to Gigha and Cara 20 Apr 1982; ret 31 Jul 1988 on medical grounds; d Sheila m Headley; s Andrew m Parker.

1990 HERBERT HERMANN FRIEDRICH GUNNEBERG
res as Assoc at Glenorchy and Innishael with Strathfillan and ind to Gigha and Cara 28 Mar 1990; ret 12 Jun 1998.

GLASSARY AND KILMARTIN AND FORD (FES X, 225, 226)

Formed 31 Mar 1982 by union of Glassary and Kilmartin. Name changed to include Ford 1 Jan 1997.

1965 WILLIAM COURTLAND BANNATYNE SMITH
(FES IX, 2, 711, 713; X, 3, 225), trans from Currie to Glassary 16 Jan 1965; ret 31 Oct 1974; died 8 Jun 1992.

1975 ARTHUR LAW
(FES X, 42, 225, 243), trans from Redding and Westquarter to Glassary and Kilmartin 6 Jun 1975; trans to Kincardine-in-Menteith with Norrieston 9 Dec 1981.

1982 NORMAN ROSS WHYTE
ord and ind to Glassary and Kilmartin 25 Aug 1982; trans to Burra Isle with Tingwall 3 Jun 1995.

1996 THOMAS JOSEPH REEVES MACKINNON
ord and ind to Glassary and Kilmartin 7 Jun 1996; trans to Carinish 11 Sep 1998.

1999 ALISON JOAN ROSS
B 19 Feb 1958, d of Ian Gerard Grainger and Georgina Jeffrey Polson; educ University of Edinburgh 1980 (BD); Moray House College, Edinburgh 1982 (CEd); University of Glasgow 1993 (CMin); Teacher (RE), Wallace Hall and Sanquhar Academies 1982–83; Teacher (RE and Comparative Government), Wells Cathedral School 1983–86; asst Nairn Old 1993; m 5 Aug 1996 Robert McWilliam Ross b 4 Jul 1963 s of Thomas Thomson R. and Christina McWilliam: Children: Anna Margaret b 21 Jun 1987; Gilliane Veronica b 27 Nov 1997; Alistair Joe b 26 Nov 1998; ord and ind to Glasgow Shettleston Old 4 Oct 1995; trans to Kilchoman with Portnahaven 1 Apr 1998; trans to Glassary and Kilmartin and Ford 25 Jun 1999.

GLENARAY AND INVERARAY (FES IX, 378; X, 226)

1973 ALEXANDER GEORGE SOMERVILLE
(FES IX, 749; X, 226, 425), res as Staffing Secretary of Overseas Council and ind to Glenaray and Inveraray 20 Jul 1973; Clerk to Synod of Argyll 1981–92; ret 30 Sep 1982; died 24 Oct 1999.

1983 JOHN ERNEST McQUILKEN
(FES X, 8), trans from Caddonfoot with Selkirk Heatherlie to Glenaray and Inveraray 19 Jan 1983; ret 30 Sep 1992; d Joyce m O' Dowd.

1993 WILLIAM BRIAN WILKINSON
(FES X, 240, 271), trans from Kirkwall East to Glenaray and Inveraray 23 Mar 1993.

JURA (FUF 291; FES IV, 69; VIII, 328; IX, 395; X, 236)

Continued vacancy from 1988 until 1992.

1975 PETER YOUNGSON
(FES X, 165, 236, 281), trans from Glenrothes St Columba's to Jura 31 Jul 1975; trans to Kirriemuir St Andrew's 14 Jan 1988.

1992 MAIRI CATRIONA BYERS
B 15 Nov 1932 at South Uist, d of Malcolm Laing and Mary Catherine McRury; educ Portree High and Dingwall Academy 1946–51; Inverness 1953–56 (RGN-RNI); Edinburgh 1956–57 (SCM SMMP); Aberdeen College of Education 1975–78; University of Aberdeen 1988–91 (BTh, CPS); Missionary Service (Ghana) 1960–71; Teaching 1978–86; lic by Presb of Buchan 26 Jun 1991; asst Auchterless with Rothienorman 1991–92; m 3 Apr 1959 Alan James Byers b 7 Apr 1926 s of George Laing B. and Eileen Gladys Baker; Children: Calum George b 15 Nov 1960 m Sally Duthie; David Laing b 21 Feb 1963 m Rachel Halstead; Mary Catherine b 30 Jan 1966 m Norman Craik; Andrew John b 19 Jul 1968 m Linda Cheesewright; ord and ind to Jura 28 Aug 1992; ret 31 Aug 1998.

1999 DWIN CAPSTICK
B 23 Dec 1941 at Sedbergh, Cumbria, s of Anthony C. and Marjorie Harper; educ Queen Elizabeth Grammar, Kirkby Lonsdale 1951–57; Hartley Victoria Methodist Theological College, Manchester 1964–67; Selly Oak Colleges, Birmingham 1967–68; Farming 1957–64; m 18 Jun 1966 Ruth Huddleston b 5 Sep 1940 d of Henry Winder H. and Elsie Park; Children: Anna b 31 Aug 1967; Naomi b 2 Aug 1969 m Paul Richardson; Peter Ndoma b 16 May 1973; ord by Methodist Conference, Manchester, 1970; Methodist Church of Sierra Leone, W Africa 1968–74; apps with Methodist Church in Blackpool (1974), Wensleydale (1977), South Craven (1983); Warden of Marrick Priory Outdoor Educ Centre, Richmond 1989; Deputy Warden of Wydale Hall, Scarborough 1995; ind to Jura 8 Jul 1999.

KILARROW (FES IV, 71; VIII, 328; IX, 395; X, 236)

Linked 14 Mar 1973 with Kilmeny.

1961 JOHN MUIR WATSON
(FES IX, 677; X, 236, 385, 388), trans from Watten to Kilarrow 1 Mar 1961; ret 30 Mar 1968; died 24 Dec 1983.

1969 JOHN STEWART
(FES X, 236), ord and ind to Kilarrow 27 Aug 1969; dem 14 Oct 1970.

1976 IAIN ROSS MUNRO
(FES X, 110, 257), trans from Irvine Relief to Kilarrow with Kilmeny 15 Jan 1976; trans to Barra 24 Mar 1982.

1982 JAMES AIRD TREVORROW
(FES X, 409), trans from Corby St Andrew's to Kilarrow with Kilmeny 7 Nov 1982; app to Danesholme and Kingswood Ecumenical Experiment, Corby 13 Nov 1987; Publ: *The Celtic Foundation* (1985), *The Norse Invasion* (1987), *The Parish Emerges* (1988), *The Days of the Lordship* (1991), *Turbulent Times* (1996)—all publ by Kilarrow Kirk Session.

1990 FRANCIS SYMINGTON GIBSON
(FES X, 147, 237, 454), res as Director of Board of Social Responsibility and ind to Kilarrow with Kilmeny 8 Feb 1990; DD (Academy of Ecumenical Indian Theology, Madras) 1991; ret 30 Sep 1995; Publ: Articles on alcohol and drug addiction (International Christian Federation for Alcohol and Drug Addiction, 1974–89).

1996 ANNE McIVOR
B 1 Sep 1946 at Campbeltown, d of Angus M. and Mary McCallum; educ Campbeltown Grammar 1958–65; Robert Gordon's Institute of Technology, Aberdeen 1965–68 (DND); University of Edinburgh 1990–94 (BD); Dietitian 1969–73; Langley House Trust (for ex-offenders) 1974–78; Senior Dietitian

1979–90; lic by Presb of Perth, 1994; asst Motherwell St Mary's 1994–96; ord and ind to Kilarrow with Kilmeny 31 May 1996.

KILBERRY (FES IV, 57; VIII, 324; IX, 392; X, 226)

Linked 29 Apr 1965 with Tarbert.

1965 WILLIAM EADIE
(FES IX, 316, 545; X, 185, 227), ind to Tarbert 26 Sep 1962; became minister of linked charge with Kilberry 29 Apr 1965, see Tarbert.

1976 THOMAS ALEXANDER DAVIDSON KELLY
ord by Presb of Dundee during assistantship at St Mary's 10 Apr 1975; ind to Kilberry with Tarbert 5 Jul 1976; app by RAChD 5 Jul 1982.

1983 WILLIAM CLEMENT ROBB
(FES X, 405), trans from Glasgow Househillwood St Christopher's to Kilberry with Tarbert 21 Jan 1983; trans to Catrine with Sorn 19 Nov 1986.

1987 ALEXANDER DUNCAN McCALLUM
ord and ind to Kilberry with Tarbert 24 Jun 1987; trans to Salcoats New Trinity 3 Feb 1994.

1995 JANE CHRISTIAN TAYLOR
B 7 Jul 1964 at Beckenham, Kent, d of Robert White T. and Annie Fraser; educ Langley Park School for Girls, Beckenham 1975–83; University of Edinburgh 1983–89 (BD, DipMin); St Paul's United Theological College, Limuru, Kenya 1988–89 (as part of DipMin course); lic by Presb of England 2 Jul 1989; asst Glasgow Cathcart Old 1989–90; Edinburgh St Giles' 1990–92; ord by Presb of Edinburgh during assistantship at St Giles' Cathedral 21 Oct 1990; ind to Kilberry with Tarbert 18 Jan 1995.

KILCALMONELL (FES X, 234)

Linked 29 Apr 1965 with Skipness.

1965 ALEXANDER ANDREW LAWSON
(FUF 546; FES IX, 102; X, 61, 234, 421), res from service with Overseas Council at Karachi and ind to Kilcalmonell with Skipness 23 Sep 1965; ret 31 Oct 1970; died 9 Aug 1988.

1971 ARCHIBALD LAMONT
(FES IX, 396; X, 63, 234, 236, 253), trans from Perth Letham to Kilcalmonell with Skipness 7 Sep 1971; dem 30 Sep 1992.

1993 CHARLES RICHARD WOOD
B 1 Nov 1940 at Burnley, s of Charles W. and Helen Mary Louise Davies; educ Queen Elizabeth Grammar, Blackburn; HMS Conway MN Officer Cadet School 1956–58; MN Officer 1958–62;

Teacher, Falklands Islands Gov Service 1964–68; National College for Youth Leaders, Leicester 1968–69 (DYW); Youth Tutor, Oxfordshire Education Authority 1970–73; University of Oxford 1972–73 (Cert Counselling); Project Director, 'Project Gambia', Oxfam 1974–77; Senior Regional Officer, Spastics Society 1977–81; Field Director, Voluntary Service Overseas, Tanzania 1981–82; General Manager, Eday Community Enterprises 1982–84; University of Aberdeen 1989–92 (LTh); lic by Presb of Buchan 2 Jul 1992; asst New Deer St Kane's 1992–93; m 10 Aug 1976 Arnrid Katherine Moore b 20 Aug 1947 d of T W M. and Mary Beumont Hudson; Children: Samuel Charles b 20 Dec 1977; Kirsty Mary b 21 Feb 1980; Suzanna Helen b 12 Dec 1982; ord and ind to Kilcalmonell with Skipness 21 Sep 1993; Fellow of Royal Geographical Society 1972; Publ: *Project Gambia* (Oxfam, 1977); *Wild Islands* (with Royal Geographical Society, 1980).

KILCHOMAN (FUF 290; FES IV, 72; VIII, 329; IX, 396; X, 236)

Linked 1 Apr 1958 with Portnahaven.

1976 WILLIAM ALEXANDER DUNDAS
(FES X, 243, 245, 279, 298), trans from Buckhaven to Kilchoman with Portnahaven 9 Jul 1976; died 25 Sep 1979.

1980 STUART DOUGLAS ROGERSON
ord and ind to Kilchoman with Portnahaven 4 Jun 1980; trans to Baillieston Mure Memorial 8 Oct 1986.

1987 ROBERT BELL DONALDSON
B 20 Nov 1928 at Tayport, s of David Alexander D. and Christina Miller; educ Dundee High 1941–46; University of St Andrews 1949–53; Rhodes University, S Africa 1962–68 (BSocSc); National Service 1946–49; lic by Presb of Dundee 9 Jun 1953; asst Salisbury Presb Church, S Rhodesia 1953–56; m (1) 26 Sep 1956 Margaret Everlie Perrow b 14 Jul 1936 d of Percival P. and Margaret Murray; Children: Andrew Robert b 28 Feb 1958; Philip David b 19 Feb 1959; Moyra Helen Christine b 14 Jan 1960 m Shaw; m (2) 4 Dec 1990 Kathleen Maureen Black b 17 May 1935 d of Harold Frederick Davidson and Kathleen Elinor McGeoch; Spouse's children from previous marriage: Douglas Lauchlan b 29 May 1962; Kathleen b 10 Dec 1964; Elizabeth b 22 May 1971; ord by Presb of Rhodesia during assistantship at Salisbury Presb Church 19 Aug 1953; ind to Kokstad, Presb Church of S Africa 16 Jan 1957; trans to Grahamstown Trinity (PCSA) 1 Mar 1962; ind to Kilchoman with Portnahaven 21 Oct 1987; ret 31 Mar 1997.

1998 ALISON JOAN ROSS
trans from Glasgow Shettleston Old to Kilchoman with Portnahaven 1 Apr 1998; trans to Glassary and Kilmartin and Ford 25 Jun 1999.

KILDALTON AND OA (FES X, 237)

Linkage with Kilmeny terminated 14 Mar 1973. Name changed from Kildalton same date.

1969 DAVID KIRK SPEED
(FES X, 237), ord and ind to Kildalton with Kilmeny 3 Jul 1969; became minister of Kildalton and Oa 14 Mar 1973; trans to Stamperland 27 Jun 1977.

1977 JOHN PATRICK WRIGHT
ord and ind to Kildalton and Oa 27 Nov 1977; introd to Fort William Duncansburgh (term) 14 Apr 1983.

1983 JEAN ELIZABETH STEWART
B 7 Sep 1921 at London, d of Joseph Moffett and Kate Hunter Panton; educ St Leonard's, St Andrews 1934–39; University of Aberdeen 1982–83; Secretary 1962–69, 1978–82; House Mistress and Teacher, Sherborne School for Girls 1969–78; lic by Presb of England 17 Jul 1983; m 22 Feb 1941 Ian Benson Stewart b 19 Sep 1919 (deceased) s of George Benson S. and Eleanor Rathbone; Children: Isla Mary b 27 Aug 1945 m John Stephen Taylor, m dissolved; ord and ind to Kildalton and Oa 7 Oct 1983; ret 28 Feb 1989; Chaplain to Islay Hospital 1989–92.

1989 ANGUS WILSON MORRISON
(FES X, 97, 334), trans from Edinburgh Braid to Kildalton and Oa 20 Oct 1989; ret 15 Feb 1999; Publ: Various reviews in *Scottish Journal of Theology.*

1999 NORMAN MACLEOD
B 25 Jun 1944 at Bayhead, N Uist, s of Donald M. and Margaret Flora Gillies; educ Portree High 1956–63; University of Aberdeen 1992–96 (BTh); Civil Service 1970–90; lic by Presb of Aberdeen 26 Jun 1997; asst Aberdeen Holburn Central 1997–99; m 30 Nov 1977 Sylvia Margaret James b 26 Sep 1947 d of William Henry J. and Kathleen Mary Collard; Children: Catriona Margaret b 20 Jul 1983; Eilidh Marie b 7 Sep 1985; ord and ind to Kildalton and Oa 5 Aug 1999.

KILLEAN AND KILCHENZIE (FES IV, 59; VIII, 324; IX, 392; X, 234)

1974 GORDON McLEAN
(FES X, 234, 357), res as Assoc at Cabrach and Mortlach and ind to Killean and Kilchenzie 24 Dec 1974; trans to Currie 27 May 1982.

1983 RICHARD MATHIES FINDLAY
(FES X, 40, 117 (2), 296), trans from St Monans to Killean and Kilchenzie 26 Jan 1983; died 27 Oct 1983.

1984 JOHN HARRIS PATON
B 10 May 1958 at Glasgow, s of William Hyslop P. and Joyce Harris; educ Glasgow Academy 1968–75; University of Glasgow 1975–79 (BSc); University of Edinburgh 1979–82 (BD); lic by Presb

of Edinburgh 4 Jul 1982; asst Edinburgh Fairmilehead 1982–84; m 27 Jun 1981 Marion Morrison b 27 Nov 1959 d of Ian M. and Jean Mitchell; ord by Presb of Edinburgh during assistantship at Fairmilehead 25 Sep 1983; ind to Killean and Kilchenzie 6 Jul 1984.

KILMENY (FES IV, 77; VIII, 329; IX, 396; X, 237)

Linkage with Kildalton terminated 14 Mar 1973. Linked same date with Kilarrow.

1969 DAVID KIRK SPEED
(FES X, 237), ord and ind to Kildalton with Kilmeny 3 Jul 1969; became minister of Kildalton and Oa 14 Mar 1973; trans to Stamperland 27 Jun 1977.

1976 IAIN ROSS MUNRO
(FES X, 110, 257), trans from Irvine Relief to Kilarrow with Kilmeny 15 Jan 1976; trans to Barra 24 Mar 1982.

1982 JAMES AIRD TREVORROW
(FES X, 409), trans from Corby St Andrew's to Kilarrow with Kilmeny 7 Nov 1982, see Kilarrow.

1990 FRANCIS SYMINGTON GIBSON
(FES X, 147, 237, 454), ind to Kilarrow with Kilmeny 8 Feb 1990, see Kilarrow.

1996 ANNE McIVOR
ord and ind to Kilarrow with Kilmeny 31 May 1996, see Kilarrow.

KILNINVER AND KILMELFORD (FUF 293; FES IV, 96; VIII, 334; IX, 401; X, 226)

Linked 1 Nov 1974 with Craignish.

1975 ROBERT CRAIG MILLER CARMICHAEL
(FES IX, 393; X, 115, 119, 225, 311), trans from Eassie and Nevay with Newtyle to Craignish with Kilninver and Kilmelford 3 Apr 1975; ret 30 Jun 1991.

1992 MICHAEL JOHN ERSKINE
trans from Inverkip to Craignish with Kilninver and Kilmelford 24 Feb 1992, see Craignish.

LOCHGILPHEAD (FES IV, 19; VIII, 315; IX, 379; X, 226)

1962 JOHN ROBERTSON CALLEN
(FES X, 226), ord and ind to Lochgilphead 8 May 1962; ret 30 Sep 1996; died 18 Aug 1998; s Fergus m Suzi Appleford; s Kenneth m Mairi Elizabeth MacCallum.

1996 ALASTAIR HUNTER GRAY
B 7 Apr 1953 at Glasgow, s of Hunter G. and Molly Deuchars; educ Coatbridge High 1965–71; University of St Andrews 1971–74 (MA), 1974–77 (BD); lic by Presb of St Andrews 1 Jun 1977; asst Jedburgh Old with Ancrum with Edgerston 1977–

78; m 4 Jan 1978 Anne Moira Buck b 21 Nov 1951 d of William B. and Jean Farley; Children: Colin Hunter b 5 Sep 1979; Kirsty Jane b 19 Jun 1981; Lorna Anne b 4 May 1983; ord and ind to Methil 18 Jun 1978; trans to Garvald and Morham with Haddington West 21 Feb 1985; trans to Lochgilphead 5 Jul 1996; Publ: *Pray Today 1984–85* (Church of Scotland, 1984); *Local Church Evangelism* (St Andrew Press, 1985); *Roots Going Deep* (Haddington West Church, 1996).

NORTH KNAPDALE (FES X, 226, 227)

Formed 2 Jun 1982 by union of Inverlussa and Bellanoch and Tayvallich.

1958   ALBERT JOHANNES GOODHEIR
(FES IX, 406; X, 227, 241), trans from Tiree and Hilypol to North Knapdale Tayvallich 9 Jan 1958; ret 31 Aug 1970; died 27 Dec 1995.

1971   DAVID MONTGOMERY
(FES X, 227), trans from Hamilton Old to North Knapdale Inverlussa and Bellanoch with Tayvallich 5 Mar 1971; became minister of united charge 2 Jun 1982; ret 30 Apr 1996.

1997   ROBERT JAMES MALLOCH
B 16 Sep 1958 at East Kilbride, s of Matthew M. and Margaret McIntyre McCraw; educ Claremont High, East Kilbride 1969–74; University of Glasgow 1981–85 (BD); Lab Technician 1974–81; lic by Presb of Hamilton 26 Jun 1986; m 27 Jul 1991 Margaret Hilary MacKenzie b 8 Oct 1958 d of Gordon M. and Beryl Honney; Children: Jennifer Hilary b 13 May 1993; Matthew Gordon Robert b 19 Jun 1995; ord by Presb of Hamilton and app by RAChD 1 Apr 1987; ind to Duror with Glencoe St Munda's 1 May 1991; trans to North Knapdale 1 Mar 1997.

PORTNAHAVEN (FUF 291; FES IV, 79; VIII, 329; IX, 397; X, 237)

Linked 1 Apr 1958 with Kilchoman.

1976   WILLIAM ALEXANDER DUNDAS
(FES X, 243, 245, 279, 298), trans from Buckhaven to Kilchoman with Portnahaven 9 Jul 1976; died 25 Sep 1979.

1980   STUART DOUGLAS ROGERSON
ord and ind to Kilchoman with Portnahaven 4 Jun 1980; trans to Baillieston Mure Memorial 8 Oct 1986.

1987   ROBERT BELL DONALDSON
ind to Kilchoman with Portnahaven 21 Oct 1987, see Kilchoman.

1998   ALISON JOAN ROSS
trans from Glasgow Shettleston Old to Kilchoman with Portnahaven 1 Apr 1998, see Kilchoman.

SADDELL AND CARRADALE (FES IX, 393; X, 234)

1967   JOHN EWEN MACINNES
(FES X, 234, 393), trans from Duirinish to Saddell and Carradale 22 Sep 1967; dem 30 Sep 1978; ind to Snizort 21 Dec 1979.

1979   ALISTAIR JOHN DUNLOP
(FES X, 115, 322), trans from Beith High to Saddell and Carradale 22 Feb 1979; s Andrew m Elizabeth Anne McMillan; s Alistair m Sharon Grimley; Publ: *A Grace for Carradale Golf Club* (Mainstream, 1990); *Antares* (*Oban Times*, 1990).

SKIPNESS (FES IV, 66; VIII, 326; IX, 394; X, 234)

Linked 29 Apr 1965 with Kilcalmonell.

1965   ALEXANDER ANDREW LAWSON
(FUF 546; FES IX, 102; X, 61, 234, 421), res from service with Overseas Council at Karachi and ind to Kilcalmonell with Skipness 23 Sep 1965; ret 31 Oct 1970; died 9 Aug 1988.

1971   ARCHIBALD LAMONT
(FES IX, 396; X, 63, 234, 236, 253), trans from Perth Letham to Kilcalmonell with Skipness 7 Sep 1971; dem 30 Sep 1992.

1993   CHARLES RICHARD WOOD
ord and ind to Kilcalmonell with Skipness 21 Sep 1993, see Kilcalmonell.

SOUTH KNAPDALE (FES IV, 18; VIII, 315; IX, 379; X, 226)

Linked 10 Dec 1964 with Ardrishaig.

1931   JOHN MACDONALD GILLIES
(FES VIII, 315; IX, 379, 380; X, 226), trans from Tarbert West to Knapdale South 4 Nov 1931; ret 10 Dec 1964; died 25 Jan 1982.

1965   JOHN GARRIOCK ROSS
(FES IX, 122, 357; X, 47, 71, 225, 234), trans from Gigha and Cara to Ardrishaig with Knapdale South 4 Aug 1965; ret 31 Mar 1969; died 29 Sep 1983.

1969   HENRY CRAWFORD DONALDSON
(FES IX, 168, 237, 264, 799; X, 98, 225, 453), res as Home Organisation Secretary, Overseas Council and ind to Ardrishaig with South Knapdale 22 Oct 1969; ret 28 Feb 1978; died 11 Jun 1985.

1978   WILLIAM DOUGLAS WATT
ord and ind to Ardrishaig with South Knapdale 29 Nov 1978; trans to Aboyne with Dinnet 21 Jun 1985.

1985   JAMES EDWARD ANDREWS
ord and ind to Ardrishaig with South Knapdale 25 Oct 1985; trans to Dalkeith St Nicholas' Buccleuch 20 Jun 1991.

1992 JAMES HOSIE
(FES X, 134, 163, 257), trans from Burra Isle with Tingwall to Ardrishaig with South Knapdale 27 Mar 1992; ret 14 Jun 1998.

1998 DAVID CARRUTHERS
ord and ind to Ardrishaig with South Knapdale 11 Dec 1998, see Ardrishaig.

SOUTHEND (FES IX, 394; X, 234)

1958 JAMES MARKS
(FES IX, 236; X, 137, 235), trans from Port Glasgow Hamilton to Southend 11 Jun 1958; ret 30 Apr 1971; died 4 Feb 1976.

1972 JOHN RUSSELL
(FES X, 235, 414), res from app at Scots Church, Rotterdam and ind to Southend 9 Feb 1972; trans to Tillicoultry 2 Feb 1978.

1978 WILLIAM CROMIE NELSON
(FES IX, 744; X, 4, 424), trans from Edinburgh Bristo Memorial Craigmillar to Southend 6 Jul 1978; ret 30 Apr 1987; died 18 Apr 1989.

1987 RODERICK HOUSTON McNIDDER
ord and ind to Southend 5 Jun 1987; dem to take up app as Hospital Chaplain (full-time), South Ayrshire NHS Trust 1 Apr 1997.

1997 CALLUM THOMSON O' DONNELL
B 18 Aug 1958 at Biggar, s of Thomas Thomson O. and Helen McKendrick Peacock; educ High School of Glasgow and Biggar High 1970–76; University of Glasgow 1976–83 (MA, BD); lic by Presb of Lanark, Jun 1983; asst Bearsden South 1983–84; m 7 Aug 1981 Anne Watt Murray d of Peter M. and Agnes Watt; Children: Ewan Thomas b 20 Dec 1984; Andrew James b 22 Sep 1986; ord and ind to Anwoth and Girthon 12 Jun 1984; trans to Troon Old 12 Nov 1989; trans to Southend 4 Sep 1997.

TARBERT (FES IX, 380; X, 227)

Linked 29 Apr 1965 with Kilberry.

1962 WILLIAM EADIE
(FES IX, 316, 545; X, 185, 227), trans from Airdrie High to Tarbert 26 Sep 1962; became minister of linked charge with Kilberry 29 Apr 1965; ret 31 Dec 1975; died 14 Jun 1995.

1976 THOMAS ALEXANDER DAVIDSON KELLY
ind to Kilberry with Tarbert 5 Jul 1976, see Kilberry.

1983 WILLIAM CLEMENT ROBB
(FES X, 405), ind to Kilberry with Tarbert 21 Jan 1983, see Kilberry.

1987 ALEXANDER DUNCAN McCALLUM
ord and ind to Kilberry with Tarbert 24 Jun 1987; trans to Salcoats New Trinity 3 Feb 1994.

1995 JANE CHRISTIAN TAYLOR
ind to Kilberry with Tarbert 18 Jan 1995, see Kilberry.

PRESBYTERY OF DUNOON

ASCOG (FUF 279; FES IX, 381; X, 228)

Linked 6 Jan 1957 with Rothesay Craigmore St Brendan's.

1957   ROBERT MORTON FULTON
(FES IX, 293, 386; X, 231), trans from Glasgow St Bride's to Rothesay Craigmore St Brendan's 17 Mar 1949; became minister of linked charge with Ascog 6 Jan 1957; ret 30 Sep 1985; died 7 Jun 1994.

1986   DUNCAN A BALLANTYNE
ord and ind to Ascog with Rothesay Craigmore St Brendan's 11 Jun 1986; dem 31 Mar 1999 to take up app with Presb Church of Wales.

DUNOON OLD AND ST CUTHBERT'S (FES X, 228)

Formed 24 Feb 1982 by union of Dunoon High Kirk and Dunoon St Cuthbert's.

1956   ALLAN MACLEOD
(FES IX, 643 (2); X, 228, 367), trans from Elgin South to the High Kirk 29 Feb 1956; ret 30 Sep 1981; died 25 Mar 1996.

1962   REDVERS BULLER ANDERSON
(FUF 38; FES IX, 20, 67, 124; X, 72, 228), trans from Galashiels St Mark's to St Cuthbert's 24 Jan 1962; ret 15 Feb 1966; died 8 Oct 1978.

1967   ALFRED JAMES ARMOUR
(FES IX, 133, 204, 460, 568, 612, 620; X, 228, 341, 357), trans from Deskford to St Cuthbert's 14 Jun 1967; trans to Strachan with Finzean 21 Oct 1970.

1971   WILLIAM PEEBLES
(FES IX, 161; X, 16, 89, 228, 337), trans from Skene to St Cuthbert's 15 Sep 1971; ret 30 Jun 1976; died 1 May 1983.

1978   ALEXANDER THOMAS HAIN TAYLOR
(FES IX, 751; X, 57, 163, 426), dem from Glasgow Kent Road St Vincent's 31 Jul 1977; introd to St Cuthbert's (term) 1 Jun 1978; ret 30 Sep 1981.

1982   RONALD ARTHUR ANDREW GALE
B 14 Dec 1932 at Glasgow, s of James Arthur G. and Helen Smeal Lang; educ Glasgow High School and Hutchesons' Grammar 1937–51; RAF College,

Cranwell 1951–54; University of Glasgow 1978–81 (LTh); Sales Management 1955–57; RAF 1957–78; lic by Presb of Glasgow 30 Jun 1981; asst Milngavie St Paul's 1981–82; m 18 Oct 1958 Catherine McLachlan Bowsie b 14 Sep 1931 d of James B. and Catherine Livingston; Children: Douglas b 17 Aug 1959 m Susan; Catherine b 19 May 1962 m Jeremy Summers; ord and ind to Dunoon Old and St Cuthbert's 6 Oct 1982; ret 31 Oct 1995.

1996   ISABEL PATRICIA LANG
B 11 Oct 1938 at Glasgow, d of John L. and Margaret McFarlane; educ Hillhead High, Glasgow 1950–56; University of Glasgow 1956–59 (BSc), 1992–94 (2 years of BD course); Teaching 1960–92; lic by Presb of Glasgow 4 Jul 1994; asst Jordanhill 1994–96; ord and ind to Dunoon Old and St Cuthbert's 23 Oct 1996.

DUNOON ST JOHN'S (FUF 277; FES IX, 382; X, 228)

Linked 1 Apr 1986 with Sandbank.

1945   ALEXANDER SALMOND RENTON
(FES IX, 319, 343, 382, 746), trans from Bellshill St Andrew's to St John's 12 Dec 1945; dem 23 Apr 1953 and emigrated to Montreal, Canada; died 26 Apr 1995.

1952   THOMAS CHAPMAN ROBERTSON
(FES IX, 382, 460, 660; X, 214, 228), ind to St John's 19 Nov 1952; trans to Baldernock 10 May 1967.

1968   JOHN GRAHAM
(FES IX, 498; X, 162, 228, 294, 297), trans from Carnoustie Panbride to St John's 28 Mar 1968; became minister of linked charge with Sandbank 1 Apr 1986; ret 31 Oct 1987; died 17 Jul 1998.

1989   JOSEPH STEWART
B 2 May 1941 at Harthill, s of John S. and Margaret Gillespie; educ Harthill Junior Secondary 1946–56; Fishmonger 1961–71; Bathgate Technical College 1971–73; University of Glasgow 1973–78; lic by Presb of West Lothian 20 Aug 1978; asst Polbeth Harwood 1978–79; m 5 Mar 1966 Margaret Earl b 16 Feb 1946 d of Andrew E. and Elizabeth Stevenson; Children: John b 12 Jun 1967; ord and ind to Clydebank St Andrew's 13 Jun 1979; trans to St John's with Sandbank 5 Apr 1989.

INNELLAN (FES X, 228)

Linked 13 May 1981 with Inverchaolain and Toward.

1968 ROBERT FREDERICK RUSSELL LOGAN
(FES IX, 225, 428, 568; X, 228 (2), 254), trans from Perth St Leonard's to Innellan Matheson with West 16 Jan 1968; became minister of united charge 9 Aug 1972; ret 31 Oct 1980; died 15 Feb 1984.

1981 HOWARD GEORGE TAYLOR
ord by Church of Central Africa Presb and ind to Zomba, Malawi 13 May 1971; ind to Innellan with Inverchaolain and Toward 27 Oct 1981; trans to Glasgow St David's Knightswood 25 Sep 1986.

1987 HUGH CONKEY
B 11 Jul 1957 at Paisley, s of Hugh C. and Margaret Blair; educ Allan Glen's, Glasgow 1969–75; University of Glasgow 1975–79 (BSc); University of Edinburgh 1982–85 (BD); Systems Programming 1979–82; lic by Presb of Edinburgh 30 Jun 1985; asst Inchbrayock with Montrose Melville South 1985–86; m 19 Jun 1982 Ailsa Anne Eaton b 17 Apr 1961 d of James Baird E. and Irene Russell: Children: Ruth b 23 Dec 1986; Rachel Alison b 28 Aug 1989; ord and ind to Innellan with Inverchaolain and Toward 22 Apr 1987.

INVERCHAOLAIN AND TOWARD (FES IV, 27; VIII, 317; IX, 383; X, 229)

Linked 13 May 1981 with Innellan.

1958 DOUGLAS FERGUSON MILLER SOMMERVILLE
(FES IX, 68, 132; X, 77, 229), trans from Gretna Old to Inverchaolain and Toward 26 Nov 1958; ret 31 May 1976; died 2 Jan 1996.

1977 DAVID IAN ISDALE
(FES IX, 200; X, 114, 131), dem from Glasgow Penilee St Andrew and introd to Inverchaolain and Toward (term) 27 Apr 1977; ret 7 Apr 1981; died 16 Oct 1982.

1981 HOWARD GEORGE TAYLOR
ind to Innellan with Inverchaolain and Toward 27 Oct 1981, see Innellan.

1987 HUGH CONKEY
ord and ind to Innellan with Inverchaolain and Toward 22 Apr 1987, see Innellan.

KILFINAN (FES X, 229)

Linked 27 Jan 1957 with Tighnabruaich. Further linked 28 Mar 1979 with Kames and Kilbride. Linkage with Tighnabruaich and with Kames and Kilbride terminated 4 Jul 1983. Linked with Kyles same date.

1973 ELLIS OWEN SHAW
(FES IX 748; X, 229, 425), res from service with Overseas Council in S India 30 Apr 1972 and ind to Kilfinan with Tighnabruaich 20 Sep 1973; ret 31 Oct 1978; died 1 Apr 1983.

1979 JAMES S CAMPBELL
ord and ind to Kames and Kilbride with Kilfinan with Tighnabruaich 26 Sep 1979; trans to Ayr St James' 6 Jan 1983.

1984 PETER BROWN
(FES IX, 786; X, 229, 270, 444), res from Royal Naval Chaplaincy Service 20 May 1981 and app Asst at Banchory-Ternan East with Durris; ind to Kilfinan with Kyles 8 Apr 1984; dem 30 Apr 1987; ind to Holm 30 Apr 1989.

1988 IAIN CAMERON BARCLAY
trans from Edinburgh New Restalrig to Kilfinan with Kyles 8 Nov 1988; dem to take up place as full-time student at Universtiy of Aberdeen 1996, also app Pastoral Asst at Beechgrove.

1998 DAVID JOHN KELLAS
(FES X, 39, 226), trans from Galashiels St Ninian's with Caddonfoot to Kilfinan with Kyles 27 Nov 1998.

KILMODAN AND COLINTRAIVE (FES X, 229)

1955 JOHN ALLAN SIM
(FES IX, 99, 478 (2); X, 229, 283), trans from Kirkcaldy Invertiel to Kilmodan and Colintraive 12 Jan 1955; ret 30 Nov 1966; died 25 Apr 1985.

1967 JAMES McGREGOR COUPER
(FES IX, 731; X, 229, 255, 417), trans from Redgorton to Kilmodan and Colintraive 1 Aug 1967; ret 30 Sep 1976.

1977 DAVID ARTHUR HARRIES
ind to Kilmodan and Colintraive 16 Mar 1977; dem 30 Jun 1981 on app as Principal Chaplain to British Sailors' Society.

1982 DOUGLAS WOODBURN WALLACE
ord by Presb of Glasgow during assistantship at Calton New 7 May 1981; ind to Kilmodan and Colintraive 26 May 1982; trans to Glasgow Fernhill and Cathkin 29 Mar 1990.

1991 DAVID PATRICK LOW'CUMMING
(FES X, 102, 354 (2), 366), res as Secretary Depute, Dept of Ministry and Mission and ind to Kilmodan and Colintraive 31 Oct 1991; ret 31 Oct 1997.

1998 ROBERT MAIR DONALD
(FES X, 303), res as Assoc at Abernyte with Inchture and Kinnaird with Longforgan and ind to Kilmodan and Colintraive 6 May 1998.

KILMUN ST MUNN'S (FES IV, 33; VIII, 318; IX, 384; X, 229)

Linkage with Sandbank terminated 1 Apr 1986. Linked with Strone and Ardentinny same date.

1929 ALEXANDER GILLON
(FES VIII, 319; IX, 384; X, 229), trans from Inverallochy to Kilmun St Munn's 16 Aug 1929; ret 28 Feb 1966; died 17 Feb 1977.

1968 GORDON WILLIAM GARNETT MAKINS
(FES IX, 415; X, 229, 246, 273), [correction: Gordon, not George as in Vol X, 229, 246, 273]; trans from Dunfermline North to Kilmun St Munn's with Sandbank 21 Aug 1968; ret 1 Apr 1986; died 18 Jul 1992.

1986 JAMES SCHOFIELD HARRISON CUTLER
ord and ind to Kilmun with Strone and Ardentinny 22 Aug 1986; trans to Coldstream with Eccles 20 Oct 1995.

1997 EVELYN MEIKLE YOUNG
B 14 Mar 1943 at Glasgow, d of Ronald Whiteford Reid and Agnes Hunter Baird; educ Laurel Bank, Glasgow 1953–60; University of Glasgow 1960–65 (BSc), 1980–83 (BD); University of Oxford 1965–66 (DipEd); Teaching 1966–67; University Tutor 1968–73; Teaching (Community Educ) 1976–80; lic by Presb of Paisley, Jun 1983; asst Bishopton Erskine 1983–84; m 28 Mar 1967 Alistair Young b 1 Nov 1944 s of Robert Y. and Jean Simon MacFarlane; Children: Hazel Nesta b 26 Mar 1969; Valerie Jean b 20 Jul 1972 m Ott; Richard Stephen b 28 Mar 1975; ord and ind to Larbert West 16 Aug 1984; dem on app as Asst/Deputy Secretary, Dept of Education 1 Feb 1991; ind to Kilmun with Strone and Ardentinny 1 Apr 1997.

KINGARTH AND KILCHATTAN BAY (FES IX, 384; X, 229)

Linked 23 Aug 1973 with Rothesay The High Kirk.

1973 ALEXANDER McALPINE KNOX
(FES X, 231 (2), 421), ind to Rothesay The High Kirk 19 Dec 1967; became minister of united charge with St John's 2 May 1973 and of linked charge with Kingarth and Kilchattan Bay 23 Aug 1973, see Rothesay.

1983 IAIN ARCHIBALD LAING
(FES X, 177), trans from Glasgow St Margaret's Tollcross to Kingarth and Kilchattan Bay with Rothesay The High Kirk 4 May 1983; trans to Bishopbriggs Kenmure 29 Jun 1992.

1993 GARY JOHN McINTYRE
ord and ind to Kingarth and Kilchattan Bay with Rothesay The High Kirk 12 May 1993; trans to Stirling St Ninians Old 19 Nov 1998.

KIRN (FES X, 230)

1971 DAVID ALLAN KEDDIE
(FES X, 163, 230), trans from Glasgow Kent Road St Vincent's to Kirn 18 Feb 1971; dem to take up app at Grace Presb Church, Calgary, Alberta 2 Oct 1975; Jordanhill College, Glasgow 1976–77 (PGCE).

1976 THOMAS BARR GIRDWOOD
(FES IX, 333; X, 111, 179, 198), trans from Glasgow Shawlands Cross to Kirn 31 Mar 1976; trans to Prestwick South 28 Oct 1981.

1982 KENNETH BURGOYNE YORKE
ord and ind to Kirn 5 May 1982; trans to Ochiltree with Stair 25 Aug 1987.

1988 MAY McGILL ALLISON
ord and ind to Kirn 31 May 1988.

KYLES (FES X, 229, 232)

Formed 4 Jul 1983 by union of Kames, Kilbride and Tighnabruaich. Linked same date with Kilfinan.

1973 ELLIS OWEN SHAW
(FES IX 748; X, 229, 425), ind to Kilfinan with Tighnabruaich 20 Sep 1973, see Kilfinan.

1975 JAMES JOHNSTON
(FES IX, 282, 391; X, 167, 229), trans from Glasgow Mosspark to Kames and Kilbride 12 Mar 1975; ret 31 Oct 1978; died 4 Jul 1979.

1979 JAMES S CAMPBELL
ord and ind to Kames and Kilbride with Kilfinan with Tighnabruaich 26 Sep 1979; trans to Ayr St James' 6 Jan 1983.

1984 PETER BROWN
(FES IX, 786; X, 229, 270, 444), ind to Kilfinan with Kyles 8 Apr 1984, see Kilfinan.

1988 IAIN CAMERON BARCLAY
ind to Kilfinan with Kyles 8 Nov 1988, see Kilfinan.

1998 DAVID JOHN KELLAS
(FES X, 39, 226), ind to Kilfinan with Kyles 27 Nov 1998, see Kilfinan.

LOCHGOILHEAD AND KILMORICH (FES IX, 385; X, 230)

1972 PAUL BASIL HILTON
(FES IX, 288; X, 40, 171, 230), trans from Grangemouth Kerse to Lochgoilhead and Kilmorich 30 Aug 1972; trans to Portpatrick 18 Mar 1976.

1978 SAMUEL McGEACHIE
(FES IX, 622; X, 34, 61 (2), 216, 333, 360), trans from Grantshouse and Houndwood with Reston to Lochgoilhead and Kilmorich 14 Sep 1978; ret 31 Mar 1981; died 25 Apr 1991.

1981 LINDSAY H EWART
res from term app at Ayr Cathcart and ind to Lochgoilhead and Kilmorich 23 Oct 1981; trans to Patna Waterside 8 Jul 1985.

1986 JAMES SCOTT MARSHALL
B 1 Jul 1930 at Edinburgh, s of James Scott M. and Florence May Jane Soutar; educ Rutherglen Academy and Glasgow High 1942–47; Faculty of Actuaries 1947–61 (FFA); University of Bristol 1964–68 (BA); University of Edinburgh 1967–69, 1970–71 (BD); Reformed Episcopal Seminary, USA 1969–70 (MDiv); Hamilton College of Education 1974–75 (DRE); Actuarial Clerk 1947–58; Actuary 1959–64; lic by Presb of Edinburgh, Jun 1971; asst Glenrothes St Ninian's 1971–72; East Kilbride Claremont 1973–74; ord and ind to Lochgoilhead and Kilmorich 3 Oct 1986; ret 10 Sep 1989.

1990 RICHARD HALDANE MARTIN McALPINE
(FES X, 101), ord and ind to Coylton 17 Oct 1968; trans to Lochgoilhead and Kilmorich 1 Nov 1990; ret 31 Oct 1999; d Anne m John Runciman Stead.

NORTH BUTE (FES X, 230)

New name for North Bute St Colmac's, St Bruoc's and St Ninian's. Continued vacancy from 1998.

1973 THOMAS CLIFFORD KELLY
(FES X, 230), admitted by General Assembly 1972; ord and ind to North Bute St Colmac's, St Bruoc's and St Ninian's 25 Jul 1973; trans to Cargill-Burrelton with Collace 9 Jul 1981.

1982 ROBERT CLARK
(FES X, 301), trans from Gorebridge to North Bute 19 Jan 1982; died 16 May 1982.

1983 QUINTIN FINLAY
(FES X, 99), res from term app at Kirkcowan 31 Oct 1981; ind to North Bute 16 Feb 1983; ret 31 Dec 1996.

ROTHESAY CRAIGMORE ST BRENDAN'S (FES IV, 22; VIII, 316; IX, 386; X, 231)

Linked 6 Jan 1957 with Ascog.

1949 ROBERT MORTON FULTON
(FES IX, 293, 386; X, 231), trans from Glasgow St Bride's to Craigmore St Brendan's 17 Mar 1949; became minister of linked charge with Ascog 6 Jan 1957; ret 30 Sep 1985; died 7 Jun 1994.

1986 DUNCAN A BALLANTYNE
ord and ind to Ascog with Craigmore St Brendan's 11 Jun 1986, see Ascog.

ROTHESAY THE HIGH KIRK (FES X, 231)

Formed 2 May 1973 by union of Rothesay St John's and Rothesay The High Kirk. Linked 23 Aug 1973 with Kingarth and Kilchattan Bay.

1957 JAMES DIXON DOUGLAS
(FES X, 231), ord and ind to Rothesay St John's 20 Feb 1957; dem 3 Sep 1957.

1958 JOHN RANKIN BELL
(FES IX, 341, 349; X, 210, 231), trans from Kirkmuirhill to Rothesay St John's 12 Mar 1958; ret 30 Apr 1973; died 2 Jan 1991.

1967 ALEXANDER McALPINE KNOX
(FES X, 231 (2), 421), res from app with FMc in W India and ind to The High Kirk 19 Dec 1967; became minister of united charge with St John's 2 May 1973 and of linked charge with Kingarth and Kilchattan Bay 23 Aug 1973; trans to Eassie and Nevay with Newtyle 14 Sep 1982.

1983 IAIN ARCHIBALD LAING
(FES X, 177), trans from Glasgow St Margaret's Tollcross to Kingarth and Kilchattan Bay with Rothesay The High Kirk 4 May 1983; trans to Bishopbriggs Kenmure 29 Jun 1992.

1993 GARY JOHN McINTYRE
ord and ind to Kingarth and Kilchattan Bay with Rothesay The High Kirk 12 May 1993; trans to Stirling St Ninians Old 19 Nov 1998.

ROTHESAY TRINITY (FES X, 231, 232)

Formed by union of Rothesay Trinity and Rothesay West 28 Aug 1979.

1967 JOHN RITCHIE MAY
(FES IX, 194, 631; X, 203, 232, 361), trans from Uddingston Viewpark to Rothesay West 7 Jun 1967; ret 31 Aug 1978; died 26 Jul 1994.

1970 ROBERT RONALD SAMUEL
(FES X, 231, 425), res from service with Overseas Council in S Africa and ind to Trinity 24 Jun 1970; d Lorna died 28 Jan 1985; s Leslie m Suzanne Felicity Hill.

SANDBANK (FES IX, 388; X, 232)

Linked 1 Apr 1986 with Dunoon St John's.

1968 GORDON WILLIAM GARNETT MAKINS
(FES IX, 415; X, 229, 246, 273), trans from Dunfermline North to Kilmun St Munn's with Sandbank 21 Aug 1968; ret 1 Apr 1986; died 18 Jul 1992.

1989 JOSEPH STEWART
ind to Dunoon St John's with Sandbank 5 Apr 1989, see Dunoon St John's.

STRACHUR AND STRATHLACHLAN (FES IX, 389; X, 232)

1965 FRANCIS SINCLAIR BANKS
(FES IX, 196, 208, 514; X, 232, 305), trans from Dundee St David's North to Strachur and Strathlachlan 27 Oct 1965; died 30 Jan 1978.

1978   WILLIAM REID FINDLAY
(FES IX, 194, 618; X, 111), trans from Banff Trinity
to Kilmarnock Henderson 10 Nov 1948; ret 3 Jun
1958; ind to Strachur and Strathlachlan 17 Jul
1978; dem 17 Jun 1980.

1981   DAVID MACKIE
(FES X, 167, 360, 422), trans from Glasgow Mosspark to Strachur and Strathlachlan 11 Feb 1981;
ret 31 Jan 1988; died 1 Nov 1994.

1988   IAIN KAY STIVEN
(FES X, 426), University of Edinburgh 1976–80
(MEd); loc ten Wick Old 1984–86; ind to Strachur
and Strathlachlan 16 Aug 1988; ret 4 Jul 1997;
app Asst at Edinburgh St Giles' Cathedral 1 Oct
1997; m (2) 13 Jun 1987 Susan Ralston Bucher b
17 Jan 1947 d of Robert B. and Jean Ralston;
Children: Hannah Isobel b 17 Oct 1988; Publ:
*Religious Education in Scotland: Blessing or
Betrayal?* (Edina Press, 1982).

1998   ROBERT KENNETH MACKENZIE
B 13 Feb 1950 at Madras, India, s of Robert
Paterson M. and Jessie Kirkwood Ree; educ
George Watson's, Edinburgh 1962–68; University
of Edinburgh 1968–72 (MA), 1972–75 (BD), 1976–
80 and 1982–84 (PhD); lic by Presb of Dunfermline
9 Jul 1975; asst Hamilton Old and Auchingramont
1975–77; m 12 Jul 1975 Susannah Russell
Copeland Clinton b 6 Jul 1952 d of Hugh C. and
Elizabeth Gibson Copeland; Children: Brannah
Elizabeth and Ellen Mairi b 11 Sep 1980; Catriona
Lucy b 6 Sep 1985; ord by Presb of Hamilton during
assistantship at Old and Auchingramont 9 May
1976; ind to Creich with Rosehall 30 Apr 1980;
trans to Brechin Cathedral 20 Mar 1986; became
minister of united charge with Brechin Maison Dieu
with Stracathro 4 Sep 1990; trans to Strachur and
Strachlachlan 17 Jun 1998; Publ: Contributor to
Third Statistical Account of Scotland (Scottish

Academic Press, 1988); contributor to *The Book
of the Society of Friends of Brechin Cathedral*
(Society of Friends of Brechin Cathedral, 1989,
1991, 1994, 1997).

STRONE AND ARDENTINNY (FES IX, 389; X,
232)

Linked 1 Apr 1986 with Kilmun St Munn's.

1973   DAVID DAVIDSON MITCHELL
(FES IX, 229; X, 133, 232, 302), trans from Dundee
Lochee West to Strone and Ardentinny 16 May
1973; ret 3 Nov 1981; died 9 Nov 1990.

1982   JOHN CRINDLE HOLLAND
B 6 May 1922 at Grangemouth, s of John H. and
Margaret Cameron; educ Grangemouth High
1927–36; University of Aberdeen 1964–66 (Lay
Missionary Training); Missionary, Perth Letham
1966–71 and Cumbernauld Kildrum 1971–74;
University of Glasgow 1974–76; Marine Engineer-
ing Apprentice 1936–40; Royal Navy 1940–47;
Chemical Engineering ICI and BP 1947–64; lic by
Presb of Falkirk 2 Jun 1976; m 20 May 1943 Olive
Rosina Postans b 30 Sep 1923 d of Henry P. and
Emily Stagg; Children: Margaret b 28 Mar 1945 m
McGregor; Leslie b 29 May 1948 m Harrower; ord
and ind to Haggs 18 Jun 1976; became minister of
linked charge with Dennyloanhead 25 Jul 1978;
trans to Strone and Ardentinny 4 Aug 1982; ret 31
May 1985.

1986   JAMES SCHOFIELD HARRISON CUTLER
ord and ind to Kilmun with Strone and Ardentinny
22 Aug 1986; trans to Coldstream with Eccles 20
Oct 1995.

1997   EVELYN MEIKLE YOUNG
ind to Kilmun with Strone and Ardentinny 1 Apr
1997, see Kilmun.

PRESBYTERY OF LORN AND MULL

APPIN (FES IX, 398; X, 238)

Linked 16 Dec 1980 with Lismore.

1948 KENNETH MALCOLM MACMILLAN
(FES IX, 398, 405, 689; X, 238), trans from Kilfinichen and Kilvickeon to Appin 16 Dec 1948; ret 16 Dec 1980; died 16 May 1994.

1981 WALTER MILLAR RITCHIE
(FES X, 312), trans from Kirkmichael Straloch and Glenshee to Appin with Lismore 29 Oct 1981; trans to Uphall South 15 Sep 1994.

1995 DOUGLAS ROBERT ROBERTSON
B 19 Jul 1964 at Dumfries, s of Charles Orr R. and Helen Jane Hughes; educ Boclair Academy 1976–81; University of Strathclyde 1981–85 (BSc); University of Aberdeen 1987–90 (BD); Production Engineering 1985–87; lic by Presb of Aberdeen 27 Jun 1990; asst Aberdeen St George's Tillydrone 1990–91; m 3 Oct 1986 Alison Macdonald b 19 Dec 1964 d of Ian M. and Karen McCuaig; Children: Eilidh b 4 Sep 1989; Mairi b 3 Nov 1992; Duncan b 12 Aug 1999; ord by Presb of Aberdeen during assistantship at St George's Tillydrone 27 Jun 1991; Assoc at Scots' Church, Melbourne (Presb Church of Australia) 1991–94; ind to Appin with Lismore 1 Jun 1995.

ARDCHATTAN (FES IX, 398; X, 238)

1956 NORMAN MACDONALD
(FES IX, 695 (2); X, 238, 396), trans from Manish-Scarista to Ardchattan 16 Nov 1956; ret 31 Jan 1984; died 30 Apr 1995.

1984 JEFFREY ALEXANDER McCORMICK
B 14 Jul 1959 at Glasgow, s of Alexander M. and Annie Blair Craig; educ Douglas Academy, Milngavie 1971–77; University of Glasgow 1977–83 (BD, DipMin); lic by Presb of Dumbarton 4 Dec 1983; asst Bearsden North 1983–84; m 17 Sep 1982 Fiona Susan Ann Thomson b 9 Sep 1960 d of Samuel James T. and Christina MacGregor MacTaggart; Children: Jeffrey Kenneth b 23 Jan 1985; Jamie Stuart b 3 Feb 1986; Donald Malcolm b 21 Sep 1987; ord and ind to Ardchattan 12 Sep 1984.

COLL (FUF 300; FES IV, 108; VIII, 338; IX, 404; X, 238)

Union with Tiree severed 29 Aug 1986 in favour of linkage. Linkage terminated 30 Apr 1994. Continued vacancy declared.

1973 HECTOR MACPHERSON
(FES X, 240, 241), trans from Lismore to Tiree and Coll 22 Oct 1973; trans to Grantshouse and Houndwood with Reston 27 Mar 1979.

1979 JAMES ALEXANDER MUNRO
ord and ind to Tiree and Coll 12 Jul 1979; trans to South Uist 15 Sep 1983.

1984 GEORGE MITCHELL DONALDSON
ord and ind to Tiree and Coll 15 Jun 1984; became minister of linked charge 29 Aug 1986; trans to Golspie 4 Mar 1989.

1990 NEIL MACKINNON
ord and ind to Coll with Tiree 30 May 1990; became minister of Tiree following termination of linkage 30 Apr 1994; trans to Longside 23 Nov 1995.

COLONSAY AND ORONSAY (FES IV, 69; VIII, 328; IX, 395; X, 236)

Continued vacancy from 1988 until 1997. Linked 1 Apr 1997 with Kilbrandon and Kilchattan.

1973 RONALD LINDSAY CRAWFORD
(FES X, 162, 236, 417), res from service with Overseas Council in Tanzania and ind to Colonsay and Oronsay 20 Aug 1973; ret 31 Oct 1988; died 10 Feb 1999.

1997 FREDA MARSHALL
B 21 Mar 1944 at Rutherglen, d of Frederick Henry Conway and Helen McCorkindale Thomson; educ Haberdashers' Aske's, Hatcham, London; University of St Andrews 1989–92 (BD); Fellow of Chartered Insurance Institute 1982 (FCII); Insurance Clerk 1962–67; Insurance Broker 1979–89; lic by Presb of Irvine and Kilmarnock 20 Jun 1992; asst Galston 1992–93; m 20 Aug 1965 Robert Inglis Marshall b 8 Nov 1943 s of John Boyd M. and Joan Crosbie Inglis; Children: Stephen John b 1 Aug 1968 m Nina Blakesley; Anthony Neil b 18 Jul 1971 m Lisa Nichol; Robert b 27 Mar 1975;

Christopher James b 16 Sep 1976; ord and ind to Kirtle-Eaglesfield with Middlebie with Waterbeck 26 May 1993; trans to Colonsay and Oronsay with Kilbrandon and Kilchattan 15 Aug 1997.

CONNEL (FES IV, 83; VIII, 332; IX, 399; X, 238)

1934 DUNCAN ARCHIBALD MACCALLUM (FES IX, 399; X, 238), ord and ind to Connel 1 Nov 1934; ret 31 Dec 1976; died 26 Dec 1989.

1978 ERIC McLACHLAN
ord and ind to Connel 23 Jan 1978; trans to Glasgow Cardonald 27 Oct 1983.

1984 WILLIAM ALEXANDER BINNIE RITCHIE
B 13 May 1932 at Bathgate, s of William Smith R. and Agnes Gray; educ Bathgate Academy 1943–49; University of St Andrews 1973–76 (MTh); lic by Presb of St Andrews 20 Jun 1976; asst Kennoway 1976–77; m 4 Jun 1955 Margaret Drummond Barton b 10 Jul 1931 d of Alexander Baird B. and Maggie Blair; Children: Eleanor Margaret b 13 May 1957; William Blair b 5 Sep 1959; ord and ind to Ballingry 19 May 1977; trans to Connel 16 May 1984; died 3 Feb 1991.

1991 RONALD GALL
B 27 Jun 1959 at Torphins, s of James Ross G. and Agnes Ogg; educ James Hamilton Academy, Kilmarnock 1971–77; University of Strathclyde 1977–81 (BSc); University of Aberdeen 1981–84 (BD); lic by Presb of Irvine and Kilmarnock 3 Jul 1984; asst Chryston 1984–85; m 17 Oct 1992 Lucy Rosalind Taylor b 7 Dec 1960 d of Peter Anthony T. and Valerie Burgess; Children: Cameron James b 18 Jul 1994; Thomas Peter b 15 Aug 1996; ord and ind to Addiewell with Longridge and Breich with Stoneyburn 6 Oct 1985; trans to Connel 12 Oct 1991.

GLENORCHY AND INNISHAEL (FES IX, 399; X, 238)

Linked 17 Nov 1980 with Strathfillan.

1971 THOMAS JACK McVEAN
(FES IX, 141, 382; X, 95, 133, 229, 238), trans from Newton Stewart St John's to Glenorchy and Innishael 5 Oct 1971; ret 20 Oct 1979; died 17 Mar 1986.

1981 HERBERT HERMANN FRIEDRICH GUNNEBERG
admitted by General Assembly 1981 and introd as Assoc at Glenorchy and Innishael with Strathfillan 1 Oct 1981; ind to Gigha and Cara 28 Mar 1990.

1981 WILLIAM TERVIT HOGG
B 9 Jan 1953 at Edinburgh, s of William H. and Frances Mary MacIntosh; educ Penicuik High 1964–70; University of St Andrews 1970–75 (MA), 1975–78 (BD); lic by Presb of St Andrews 25 Jun 1978; asst Dundee St Andrew's 1978–79; St

Andrews St Leonard's with Cameron and Largoward 1979–81; ord by Presb of St Andrews during assistantship at St Leonard's with Cameron and Largoward 2 Dec 1979; ind to Glenorchy and Innishael with Strathfillan 24 Sep 1981.

IONA AND ROSS OF MULL (FUF 300; FES IV, 110; VIII, 338; IX, 404; X, 238)

Linked 4 Jun 1985 with Kilfinichen and Kilvickeon.

1958 DAVID SIME STIVEN
(FES VIII, 526; IX, 82, 561; X, 50, 238), trans from Musselburgh Inveresk to Iona and Ross of Mull 15 Jul 1958; ret 31 May 1966; died 26 Dec 1986.

1969 HARRY GALBRAITH MILLER
(FES IX, 159, 379; X, 94, 124, 238), trans from Inchinnan to Iona and Ross of Mull 18 Jun 1969; ret 30 Apr 1985.

1986 IAIN A MACDONALD
ord and ind to Iona and Ross of Mull with Kilfinichen and Kilvickeon 4 Mar 1986; dem 31 Oct 1987; ind to Edinburgh Burdiehouse 17 Feb 1988.

1989 DONALD KERR PRENTICE
ord and ind to Iona and Ross of Mull with Kilfinichen and Kilvickeon 20 Jul 1989; dem on app by RAChD 1 May 1992.

1993 DAVID JAMES TAYLOR
B 26 Mar 1951 at Kirkcaldy, s of James T. and Jane Pae Rollo; educ Kirkcaldy High 1963–69; University of Edinburgh 1969–73 (MA), 1978–85 (BD); Teaching 1974–78; lic by Presb of Kirkcaldy 29 Jun 1981; asst Edinburgh Tron Kirk Moredun 1981–82; m 7 Apr 1984 Mary Watt Beveridge b 29 Jun 1957 d of William Mitchell B. and Edna Helen; Children: Neil William James b 8 Feb 1997; ord and ind to Stracathro with Brechin Maison Dieu 13 Jul 1982; trans to Glasgow Colston Milton 10 Dec 1986; trans to Iona with Kilfinichen and Kilvickeon and Ross of Mull 9 Oct 1993.

ISLE OF MULL, KILNINIAN AND KILMORE (FUF 300; FES IV, 114; VIII, 339; IX, 405; X, 239)

Linked 3 Apr 1979 with Tobermory with Salen and Ulva with Torosay and Kinlochspelvie with Kilfinichen and Kilvickeon. Linkage with Kilfinichen and Kilvickeon terminated 4 Jun 1985.

1969 ANGUS LOW BAYNE
(FES X, 208, 239), ord by Presb of Lorn and Mull and introd as Assoc at Kilninian and Kilmore with Tobermory 23 Jul 1969; ind to Crossford 21 Apr 1971.

1972 GORDON HOLROYD
(FES X, 239, 385, 407, 454), res as Asst Secretary of Social Service Committee and ind to Kilninian and Kilmore with Tobermory 7 Apr 1972; became minister of linked charge with Salen and Ulva and Torosay and Kinlochspelvie 12 Jul 1972; trans to Dingwall St Clement's 11 Dec 1979.

1972 MOSES DONALDSON
(FES X, 239), ord by Presb of Lorn and Mull and
introd as Assoc at Kilninian and Kilmore with
Tobermory with Salen and Ulva with Torosay and
Kinlochspelvie 7 Nov 1972; ind to Duneaton 18
Oct 1978.

1972 GEORGE MABON BAIN
(FES X, 240), ord by Presb of Lorn and Mull and
introd as Assoc at Kilninian and Kilmore with
Tobermory with Salen and Ulva with Torosay and
Kinlochspelvie 4 Jun 1972; trans to Gamrie with
King Edward 30 Mar 1982.

1978 MARGARET GILCHRIST McLEAN
ord by Presb of Lorn and Mull and introd as Assoc
to Isle of Mull parishes 3 Oct 1978; introd as
Community minister, Annandale and Eskdale 23
Aug 1984.

1980 ALAN THOMAS TAYLOR
ord and ind to Isle of Mull parishes 29 May 1980.

1981 RICHARD ARTHUR THOMAS GOODMAN
B 10 Nov 1921 at London, s of Henry Arthur G.
and Margaret Murphy; educ St Bernard's, Stepney,
London 1926–36; Kingsway Institute, London
1937–39 (CGRP); University of Glasgow 1962–
65 (DipCEd), 1974–76; RAF 1940–46; Post Office
Engineering Dept 1950–66; Lay Missionary,
Church of Scotland 1966–74; lic by Presb of Falkirk
2 Jul 1876; m 7 Sep 1946 Isabella Milne Stewart b
28 Sep 1922 d of Robert S. and Elizabeth Morrow;
Children: Robert Andrew b 4 May 1949 m Irene
Barrie; Thomas Stewart b 2 Aug 1951, died 1993,
m Janette Easton; ord and ind to Muiravonside 30
Jul 1976; introd as Assoc to Isle of Mull parishes
11 Oct 1981; ret 31 Aug 1986.

1987 WILLIAM POLLOCK
B 24 Mar 1949 at Glasgow, s of Robert Thomson
P. and Margaret Wilson; educ Hutchesons' Gram-
mar, Glasgow 1954–67; University of Glasgow
1967–71 (MA), 1971–74 (BD); University of
Cambridge 1974–77 (PhD); Joint-leader, Psychi-
atric Day Centre 1980–83; Psychological
Research, Church of England 1984–87; lic by
Presb of Dunoon, Sep 1977; asst Paisley Lylesland
1977–78; ord by Presb of Lorn and Mull and introd
as Assoc to Isle of Mull parishes 1 Sep 1987; Publ:
*A Theoretical Consideration of Selection for
Training for Ministry* (*Journal of Psychology and
Theology*, 1986).

KILBRANDON AND KILCHATTAN (FES IX, 400;
X, 238)

Linked 1 Apr 1997 with Colonsay and Oronsay.

1972 IAN CAMERON
(FES IX, 465; X, 85, 239, 275, 387), trans from
Reay to Kilbrandon and Kilchattan 30 Nov 1972;
ret 30 Jun 1981; s Kenneth m Helen McDonald
Simpson; s Alastair m Margaret Elizabeth Mann.

1982 MALCOLM ALEXANDER RITCHIE
(FES X, 224, 299), trans from Strathblane to
Kilbrandon and Kilchattan 8 Jun 1982; ret 8 Jun
1990; s John m Agnes Falcoz-Vigne; Publ: Reprint
of *Character and Claims of Freemasonry* by
Charles G Finney (Tentmaker Publ, 1996); tr into
French of *Pilgrim's Progress* Part 1 (forthcoming).

1991 ROBERT BROWN
(FES X, 195), trans from Hamilton Gilmour and
Whitehill to Kilbrandon and Kilchattan 25 Oct
1991; ret 31 Mar 1997; d Fiona m Iain Harris; d
Evelyn m Lee Ashley Messeder; s David m Helen
McLoughlin.

1997 FREDA MARSHALL
ind to Colonsay and Oronsay with Kilbrandon and
Kilchattan 15 Aug 1997, see Colonsay.

KILCHRENAN AND DALAVICH (FES IX, 400; X,
239)

Linked 17 Nov 1980 with Muckairn.

1973 JOHN MACGREGOR MACKECHNIE
(FES IX, 331, 614; X, 196 (2), 239), trans from
Hamilton Old and Auchingramont to Kilchrenan and
Dalavich 16 Mar 1973; ret 31 Dec 1978.

1981 GEORGE JAMES WHYTE
ord and ind to Kilchrenan and Dalavich with
Muckairn 25 May 1981; trans to Glasgow Langside
25 Jun 1985.

1986 JAMES FORSYTH
(FES X, 187, 378), res from term app at Contin-
Strathconon and ind to Kilchrenan and Dalavich
with Muckairn 6 Jan 1986; dem 31 Oct 1988; ind
to Fearn Abbey and Nigg Chapelhill 6 Aug 1994.

1989 WILLIAM JAMES LETHEM GALBRAITH
(FES X, 289), trans from Auchtermuchty to
Kilchrenan and Dalavich with Muckairn 8 Sep 1989;
ret 30 Jun 1996; s David m Margaret McDonald; s
Christopher m Lynn Smart; s Stephen m Angela
Byrne.

1996 MARGARET ROBB McRAE MILLAR
B 16 Jun 1942 at Dundee, d of Alexander M. and
Margaret Cobb; educ Camphill Secondary, Paisley
1947–60; Jordanhill College, Glasgow 1961–64
(DipChE); St Colm's College, Edinburgh 1966–67;
University of S Africa 1992–96 (BTh); Teaching
1964–66; Missionary (Church of Scotland) 1967–
96; ord by United Church of Zambia 1 May 1977;
Deaconess Tutor, United Church of Zambia 1975–
90; Moderator, then Bishop, N Western Presb,
Zambia 1991–95; ind to Kilchrenan and Dalavich
with Muckairn 1 Nov 1996.

KILFINICHEN AND KILVICKEON (FES X, 239)

Linkage with Isle of Mull parishes terminated 4 Jun
1985. Linked same date with Iona and Ross of
Mull.

1972 JAMES ARTHUR BREMNER
(FES X, 59, 239), trans from Bonkyl and Preston with Reston to Kilfinichen and Kilvickeon 8 Aug 1972; ret 31 Oct 1978; died 8 Nov 1978.

1979 GORDON HOLROYD
(FES X, 239, 385, 407, 454), ind to Kilninian and Kilmore with Tobermory 7 Apr 1972; became minister of linked charge with Salen and Ulva and Torosay and Kinlochspelvie 12 Jul 1972 and of further linkage with Kilfinichen and Kilvickeon 3 Apr 1979, see Kilninian and Kilmore.

1980 ALAN THOMAS TAYLOR
ord and ind to Isle of Mull parishes 29 May 1980.

1986 IAIN A MACDONALD
ord and ind to Iona and Ross of Mull with Kilfinichen and Kilvickeon 4 Mar 1986, see Iona.

1989 DONALD KERR PRENTICE
ord and ind to Iona and Ross of Mull with Kilfinichen and Kilvickeon 20 Jul 1989, see Iona.

1993 DAVID JAMES TAYLOR
ind to Iona with Kilfinichen and Kilvickeon and Ross of Mull 9 Oct 1993, see Iona.

KILMORE AND OBAN (FES X, 239, 240)

Formed 31 Dec 1983 by union of Kilmore and Kilbride Oban Old, Oban Christ's Church Dunollie and Oban St Columba's Argyll Square.

1967 JOHN MACLEOD
(FES X, 24, 239, 447), trans from Edinburgh St Paul's Newington to Kilmore and Kilbride Oban Old 5 Apr 1967; ret 31 Dec 1983; died 7 Dec 1995.

1968 GEORGE KERR HIGGINS
(FES X, 158, 240), trans from Easterhouse St George's and St Peter's to St Columba's Argyll Square 16 Jan 1968; dem 31 Dec 1977; s Daniel m Connolly; s Simon m Pigeon.

1974 WILLIAM BRIAN WILKINSON
(FES X, 240, 271), trans from Carnock to Christ's Church Dunollie 28 Nov 1974; became joint minister of united charge with Kilmore and Kilbride Oban Old and St Columba's Argyll Square 31 Dec 1983; trans to Kirkwall East 11 Nov 1987.

1979 ANDREW BLAIR CAMPBELL
B 25 Jun 1953 at Edinburgh, s of William Andrew C. and Jean Blair McGill; educ North Berwick High 1965–71; University of Edinburgh 1972–76 (BD), 1976–78 (DPS), 1995 (MTh); lic by Presb of Lothian, Jun 1978; asst Linlithgow St Michael's 1978–79; m 4 Sep 1976 Fiona McRobbie d of John M. and Victoria Brand; ord and ind to St Columba's Argyll Square 15 Nov 1979; became joint minister of united charge with Christ's Church Dunollie and Kilmore and Kilbride Oban Old 31 Dec 1983.

1988 THOMAS DAVID WATSON
ord by Presb of Lorn and Mull and introd as Assoc at Kilmore and Oban 22 Sep 1988; ind to Prestwick Kingcase 15 Jan 1997.

LISMORE (FES IV, 98; VIII, 335; IX, 401; X, 240)

Linked 16 Dec 1980 with Appin.

1974 JAMES MACKAY
(FES X, 194, 240), res from app with Presb Church in Canada and ind to Lismore 22 Aug 1974; ret 31 Jul 1978.

1981 WALTER MILLAR RITCHIE
(FES X, 312), trans from Kirkmichael Straloch and Glenshee to Appin with Lismore 29 Oct 1981; trans to Uphall South 15 Sep 1994.

1995 DOUGLAS ROBERT ROBERTSON
ind to Appin with Lismore 1 Jun 1995, see Appin.

MUCKAIRN (FES IV, 100; VIII, 335; IX, 401; X, 240)

Linked 17 Nov 1980 with Kilchrenan and Dalavich.

1968 DAVID OWER GALBRAITH
(FES IX, 201, 503; X, 240, 299), trans from Dundee Barnhill St Margaret's to Muckairn 25 Sep 1968; ret 30 Nov 1980.

1981 GEORGE JAMES WHYTE
ord and ind to Kilchrenan and Dalavich with Muckairn 25 May 1981, see Kilchrenan.

1986 JAMES FORSYTH
(FES X, 187, 378), ind to Kilchrenan and Dalavich with Muckairn 6 Jan 1986, see Kilchrenan and Dalavich.

1989 WILLIAM JAMES LETHEM GALBRAITH
(FES X, 289), trans from Auchtermuchty to Kilchrenan and Dalavich with Muckairn 8 Sep 1989; ret 30 Jun 1996.

1996 MARGARET ROBB McRAE MILLAR
ind to Kilchrenan and Dalavich with Muckairn 1 Nov 1996, see Kilchrenan.

SALEN AND ULVA (FUF 302; FES IV, 118, 124; VIII, 340, 342; IX, 406; X, 241)

Linked 3 Apr 1979 with Kilninian and Kilmore with Tobermory with Torosay and Kinlochspelvie with Kilfinichen and Kilvickeon. Linkage with Kilfinichen and Kilvickeon terminated 4 Jun 1985.

1966 JAMES MACRURIE
(FES IX, 742; X, 164, 241, 405, 422), trans from Delting to Salen and Ulva with Torosay and Kinlochspelvie 21 Oct 1966; ret 31 Dec 1971; died 11 Sep 1979.

1972 MOSES DONALDSON
(FES X, 239), introd as Assoc at Kilninian and Kilmore with Tobermory with Salen and Ulva with Torosay and Kinlochspelvie 7 Nov 1972, see Kilninian and Kilmore.

1972 GEORGE MABON BAIN
(FES X, 240), introd as Assoc at Kilninian and Kilmore with Tobermory with Salen and Ulva with Torosay and Kinlochspelvie 4 Jun 1972, see Isle of Mull.

1972 GORDON HOLROYD
(FES X, 239, 385, 407, 454), ind to Kilninian and Kilmore with Tobermory 7 Apr 1972; became minister of linked charge with Salen and Ulva and Torosay and Kinlochspelvie 12 Jul 1972, see Kilninian and Kilmore.

1981 RICHARD ARTHUR THOMAS GOODMAN
introd as Assoc to Isle of Mull parishes 11 Oct 1981, see Isle of Mull.

1987 WILLIAM POLLOCK
ord by Presb of Lorn and Mull and introd as Assoc to Isle of Mull parishes 1 Sep 1987, see Isle of Mull.

STRATHFILLAN (FES IX, 403; X, 241)

Linked 17 Nov 1980 with Glenorchy and Innishael.

1968 ALEXANDER IAN INGRAM
(FES X, 241), ind to Strathfillan 19 Dec 1968; ret 30 Apr 1974; died 16 Jan 1996.

1974 ROBERT MAULE-BROWN
(FES IX, 142, 182; X, 56 (2), 189, 241, 342, 400, 423), trans from Calderbank to Strathfillan 22 Nov 1974; trans to Strathy and Halladale 6 Jun 1978.

1981 WILLIAM TERVIT HOGG
ind to Glenorchy and Innishael with Strathfillan 24 Sep 1981, see Glenorchy.

1981 HERBERT HERMANN FRIEDRICH GUNNEBERG
introd as Assoc at Glenorchy and Innishael with Strathfillan 1 Oct 1981, see Glenorchy.

TIREE (FES X, 241)

Union with Coll severed 29 Aug 1986 in favour of linkage. Linkage terminated 30 Apr 1994.

1973 HECTOR MACPHERSON
(FES X, 240, 241), trans from Lismore to Tiree and Coll 22 Oct 1973; trans to Grantshouse and Houndwood with Reston 27 Mar 1979.

1979 JAMES ALEXANDER MUNRO
ord and ind to Tiree and Coll 12 Jul 1979; trans to South Uist 15 Sep 1983.

1984 GEORGE MITCHELL DONALDSON
ord and ind to Tiree and Coll 15 Jun 1984; became minister of linked charge 29 Aug 1986; trans to Golspie 4 Mar 1989.

1990 NEIL MACKINNON
ord and ind to Coll with Tiree 30 May 1990; became minister of Tiree following termination of linkage 30 Apr 1994; trans to Longside 23 Nov 1995.

1996 ROBERT DAVID HIGHAM
B 13 Mar 1937 at Bolton, Lancashire, s of Reginald H. and Dorothy Hough; educ Bolton School 1948–54; National Leathersellers College, London 1957–60 (Dip Leather Tech); University of Aberdeen 1980–84 (BD); Tannery Management 1960–69; Trade Journal Editor 1969–80; lic by Presb of Aberdeen 28 Jun 1984; asst Aberdeen North of St Andrew 1984–85; m 19 Dec 1964 Diana Mai Cochrane b 12 Aug 1942 d of David Jeffrey C. and Millicent Cowell; Children: Ruth b 6 Aug 1965 m Nicholas Butcher; Vivienne b 24 Jun 1968; Shirley b 15 Mar 1971 m Leslie McColm; ord and ind to Gordon St Michael's with Greenlaw with Legerwood with Westruther 14 Jun 1985; dem 1 Sep 1990 on app as Lecturer, Northumbria Bible College; ind to Tiree 19 Apr 1996.

TOBERMORY (FES IX, 406; X, 241)

Linked 3 Apr 1979 with Kilninian and Kilmore with Torosay and Kinlochspelvie with Salen and Ulva with Kilfinichen and Kilvickeon. Linkage with Kilfinichen and Kilvickeon terminated 4 Jun 1985.

1963 JONATHAN DARBY BROWN
(FUF 353; FES IX, 32 (2), 466, 562; X, 19, 241), trans from Edinburgh Portobello Old and Regent Street to Tobermory 14 Feb 1963; ret 8 May 1968; died 1 Nov 1988.

1969 ANGUS LOW BAYNE
(FES X, 208, 239), ord by Presb of Lorn and Mull and introd as Assoc at Kilninian and Kilmore with Tobermory 23 Jul 1969; ind to Crossford 21 Apr 1971.

1972 GORDON HOLROYD
(FES X, 239, 385, 407, 454), ind to Kilninian and Kilmore with Tobermory 7 Apr 1972, see Kilninian and Kilmore.

1972 GEORGE MABON BAIN
(FES X, 240), introd as Assoc at Kilninian and Kilmore with Tobermory with Salen and Ulva with Torosay and Kinlochspelvie 4 Jun 1972, see Isle of Mull.

1972 MOSES DONALDSON
(FES X, 239), introd as Assoc at Kilninian and Kilmore with Tobermory with Salen and Ulva with Torosay and Kinlochspelvie 7 Nov 1972, see Kilninian and Kilmore.

1978 HUGH CHARLES ORMISTON
(FES X, 306), dem from Dundee Whitfield and introd as Assoc at Tobermory 31 Jul 1978; app Industrial Chaplain in the Forth Valley 1 Nov 1980.

1981 RICHARD ARTHUR THOMAS GOODMAN
introd as Assoc to Isle of Mull parishes 11 Oct 1981, see Isle of Mull.

1987 WILLIAM POLLOCK
ord by Presb of Lorn and Mull and introd as Assoc to Isle of Mull parishes 1 Sep 1987, see Isle of Mull.

TOROSAY AND KINLOCHSPELVIE (FES IX, 407; X, 241)

Linked 3 Apr 1979 with Kilninian and Kilmore with Salen and Ulva with Kilfinichen and Kilvickeon. Linkage with Kilfinichen and Kilvickeon terminated 4 Jun 1985.

1966 JAMES MACRURIE
(FES IX, 742; X, 164, 241, 405, 422), trans from Delting to Salen and Ulva with Torosay and Kinlochspelvie 21 Oct 1966; ret 31 Dec 1971; died 11 Sep 1979.

1972 GEORGE MABON BAIN
(FES X, 240), introd as Assoc at Kilninian and Kilmore with Tobermory with Salen and Ulva with Torosay and Kinlochspelvie 4 Jun 1972, see Isle of Mull.

1972 GORDON HOLROYD
(FES X, 239, 385, 407, 454), ind to Kilninian and Kilmore with Tobermory 7 Apr 1972; became minister of linked charge with Salen and Ulva and Torosay and Kinlochspelvie 12 Jul 1972, see Kilninian and Kilmore.

1972 MOSES DONALDSON
(FES X, 239), introd as Assoc at Kilninian and Kilmore with Tobermory with Salen and Ulva with Torosay and Kinlochspelvie 7 Nov 1972, see Kilninian and Kilmore.

1981 RICHARD ARTHUR THOMAS GOODMAN
introd as Assoc to Isle of Mull parishes 11 Oct 1981, see Isle of Mull.

1987 WILLIAM POLLOCK
ord by Presb of Lorn and Mull and introd as Assoc to Isle of Mull parishes 1 Sep 1987, see Isle of Mull.

PRESBYTERY OF FALKIRK

AIRTH (FES X, 34)

1969 GEORGE GILLON
(FES IX, 541, 594; X, 34, 297), trans from Barry to Airth 16 Apr 1969; ret 30 Oct 1980; s Alexander m Meredith Wattison.

1981 ANN MARSHALL BALLENTINE
ord and ind to Airth 30 Sep 1981; trans to Kirknewton and East Calder 6 Jul 1993.

1994 JOHN HENRY FAIRFUL
B 26 Apr 1960 at Glasgow, s of William Marshall F. and Mary Cadden Stirling; educ High School of Glasgow 1972–78; University of St Andrews 1988–92 (BD); Accountancy 1978–79; Salvation Army Officer 1981–88; lic by Presb of Glasgow; asst Brightons 1993–94; ord and ind to Airth 8 Jun 1994; Chaplain (part-time) to Polmont Young Offenders Institution.

BLACKBRAES AND SHIELDHILL (FES X, 34)

1976 JOHN MARSHALL PATTERSON
B 17 Nov 1919 at Edinburgh, s of Henry Arnott Dewar P. and Mary Ewing; educ James Clark Secondary, Edinburgh 1931–34; University of Edinburgh 1974–76; Mechanical Engineering 1934–74; lic by Presb of Edinburgh 30 May 1976; m 1 May 1943 Margaret Roger McQueen b 26 Apr 1920 d of James Alexander M. and Beatrice Dorothea Rainy Dickie; ord and ind to Blackbraes and Shieldhill 28 Jun 1976; app Asst at Corstorphine Old 1 May 1988; ret 31 Dec 1987.

1988 JAMES ANDREW McMULLIN
(FES X, 338), trans from Aberdeen Stoneywood to Blackbraes and Shieldhill 15 Jun 1988; ret 31 Oct 1996; d Hilary m Morrison.

1997 JAMES HENRY DUNN CRAIG DRYSDALE
B 6 Jan 1941 at Glasgow, s of John William Mail Craig D. and Jeanie Mitchell Brown; educ Bellahouston Academy, Glasgow 1953–55; Stow College, Glasgow 1956–64 (FTC); University of Glasgow 1983–86 (LTh); Teaching 1963–65; Plater/Marker 1966–67; Fabrication and Welding Instructor 1967–73; Training Officer 1974–83; lic by Presb of Glasgow 30 Jun 1986; asst Glasgow St Nicholas' Cardonald 1983–85, Penilee St Andrew's 1985–86, Cathcart Old 1986–87; m 14

Sep 1962 Isabella Milne Nelson b 6 Oct 1940 d of William N. and Isabella Glen; Children: Stuart b 23 Dec 1964 m Linzi Copeland; Lesley b 14 May 1967 m Jim Adam Christie; ord and ind to Coupar Angus Abbey 9 Jul 1987; trans to Blackbraes and Shieldhill 20 Nov 1997; also Chaplain (part-time) to Polmont Young Offenders Institution.

BO'NESS OLD (FES I, 195; VIII, 37; IX, 57; X, 34)

1971 WILLIAM SUTHERLAND
(FES X, 34, 62), trans from Langton and Polwarth to Bo' ness Old 2 Dec 1971; ret 17 Apr 1992.

1994 WILLIAM McPHERSON
B 23 Oct 1958 at Clydebank, s of William M. and Margaret McLaren; educ Clydebank High 1970–76; Jordanhill College, Glasgow 1980 (DipEd); University of Edinburgh 1992 (BD); Project Leader, Save the Children Fund 1981–89; lic by Presb of Edinburgh 5 Jul 1992; asst Edinburgh Barclay 1992–93; ord and ind to Bo' ness Old 26 Jan 1994.

BO'NESS ST ANDREW'S (FUF 43; FES IX, 57; X, 34)

1976 JAMES HAMILTON
(FES X, 445), ret from RAChD and ind to St Andrew's 26 May 1976; dem 8 Mar 1981.

1981 ALBERT ORR BOGLE
B 3 Feb 1949 at Glasgow, s of James Proctor B. and Margaret Johnstone Heatherington; educ Woodside Secondary, Glasgow 1962–67; University of Glasgow 1975–80 (BD); University of Edinburgh 1996–98 (MTh); Banking 1967–75; lic by Presb of Glasgow, Jun 1980; asst Glasgow Cardonald 1980–81; m 31 Aug 1977 Martha Baird Craig Goldie d of David G. and Barbara Craig; Children: Sarah Jane b 1981; Stephen James b 1983; ord and ind to St Andrew's 16 Sep 1981; app National Evangelist (part-time) Jan 1998; Publ: *James Barr* (Scottish Church History Society Records, Vol 21, 1982); *The Lamplighter* (Well Oiled Music, 1987); *Pray Today* (Panel on Worship, 1987); *Run Scared No More* (Well Oiled Music, 1990); *Shekinah* (Well Oiled Music, 1994); *Brave* (Well Oiled Music, 1995); *Cardboard House* (Well Oiled Music, 1998).

BONNYBRIDGE ST HELEN'S (FES X, 35, 40)

Formed 31 Jul 1991 by union of Bonnybridge and High Bonnybridge St Helen's (linkage of Denny-loanhead and High Bonnybridge St Helen's terminated 7 Jul 1978).

1973   JOHN JACKSON
(FES X, 35, 63 (2)), trans from Coldstream to Bonnybridge 28 Feb 1973; ret 1 Apr 1990.

1978   JOHN WATSON
(FES X, 37, 342), trans from Leochel-Cushnie and Lynturk to Dennyloanhead with High Bonnybridge St Helen's 19 Sep 1972; became minister of High Bonnybridge St Helen's (term) following termination of linkage 7 Jul 1978; ret 31 May 1991.

1992   DONALD GEORGE BRUCE McCORKINDALE
B 27 Dec 1963 at Glasgow, s of Donald Gordon M. and Catherine Wilma Anne Bruce; educ Kelvinside Academy, Glasgow 1968–81; University of St Andrews 1983–91 (BD, DipMin); lic by Presb of Dumbarton 7 Jul 1991; asst Glasgow Netherlee 1991–92; m 7 Jun 1997 Lesley Rona Page b 2 Feb 1973 d of Ronald Andrew P. and Wilma Arnott Downs Roberts; ord and ind to Bonnybridge St Helen's 28 May 1992.

BOTHKENNAR AND CARRONSHORE (FES IV, 299; VIII, 388; IX, 58; X, 35)

1944   WILLIAM BUCHANAN MACLAREN
(FES IX, 58; X, 35), [correction: b at Ardbeg, Bute, not Ascog as in Vol IX, 58]; ord and ind to Bothkennar and Carronshore 5 Jul 1944; ret 1 Nov 1983; s Ian m Carole Begg; s Andrew m Sheena Waddell; s William m Janice Bellingham; Addl publ: *Annals of a Country Parish* (Falkirk Libraries).

1984   WILLIAM DICKIE WHITELAW
B 29 Apr 1929 at Irvine, s of William Dickie W. and Mary Wadell Chalmers; educ Irvine Royal Academy 1940–45; Glasgow School of Accountancy 1952–56 (ACCA); University of Glasgow 1981–84; Accountancy 1950–81; lic by Presb of Irvine and Kilmarnock 3 Jul 1984; m 1 Oct 1952 Mary Marshall Bowman b 25 Jun 1928 d of William Arthur B. and Marion Gray Thaw; Children: David Richard b 12 Feb 1955 m Susan McGown Greer; Alan William b 10 Jun 1960 m Shona Mary Geddes; Douglas Arthur b 11 Oct 1966; ord and ind to Bothkennar and Carronshore 25 Sep 1984; ret 31 Oct 1997.

1998   PATRICIA ANNE CARRUTH
B 16 Aug 1947 at Glasgow, d of David Brown and Anne Pagan; educ John Neilson Institution, Paisley 1959–65; University of Glasgow 1992–96 (BD); Clerkess 1965–72; School Secretary 1986–92; lic by Presb of Paisley 22 Aug 1996; m 5 Jul 1969 Gordon William Carruth b 24 Sep 1943 s of

Matthew C. and Jessie McMillan; Children: Kirsty Lynne b 4 Sep 1973; Lindsey Anne b 26 Jun 1978; ord and ind to Bothkennar and Carronshore 28 May 1998.

BRIGHTONS (FUF 52; FES IX, 68; X, 42)

Name changed from Polmont South 1977.

1967   CHARLES RATTRAY HERIOT
(FES X, 42, 140), trans from Bishopbriggs Kenmure to Polmont South 2 Nov 1967; ret 30 Jun 1996; s Crawford m Karen McColl; d Heather m David Allison.

1996   SCOTT ROSS McLAREN KIRKLAND
B 3 Dec 1963 at Glasgow, s of Andrew K. and Thelma Gallagher; educ Hyndland Secondary, Glasgow 1976–82; Derbyshire College of Higher Education 1982–86 (ACMA); University of Aberdeen 1990–95 (BD); Westminster Theological Seminary, USA 1992–94 (MAR); Accountancy 1982–90; lic by Presb of Glasgow 3 Jul 1995; asst Aberdeen Mannofield 1995–96; m 28 May 1994 Anita Tong b 4 Jan 1964 d of Zung T. and Ning Lai; Children: Priscilla b 7 Aug 1996; Sarah b 2 Feb 1998; ord and ind to Brightons 4 Sep 1996.

CARRIDEN (FES I, 198; VIII, 39; IX, 58; X, 35)

1965   NORMAN STANLEY SWAN
(FES X, 35), ord and ind to Carriden 6 Oct 1965; ret 30 Sep 1978; died 16 Sep 1983.

1978   IAIN MACLAREN ROBERTSON
(FES X, 86, 257), res 13 Sep 1978 from Aberuthven with Gask (term) and ind to Carriden 13 Dec 1978; ret 31 Dec 1992 on grounds of ill-health.

1993   ROBERT GORDON REID
B 16 Dec 1945 at Kirkcaldy, s of James Kinnell R. and Magdalene Swan Kerr; educ Buckhaven High 1957–64; Heriot-Watt University 1964–71 (BSc); University of St Andrews 1988–91 (BD); Electronics Engineer 1971–73; Project Engineer 1973–83; Asst Chief Electronics Engineer, Timex 1983–88; lic by Presb of Dundee 18 Jun 1992; asst Dundee Barnhill St Margaret's 1991–93; m 18 Dec 1975 Sheila Ann Jack b 9 Nov 1944 d of Alexander McPhail J. and Ann Conn Rice McKee; Children: Alasdair James b 23 Feb 1978; Fiona Ann b 3 Dec 1979; ord and ind to Carriden 14 Apr 1993.

CUMBERNAULD ABRONHILL (FES X, 35)

1973   DOUGLAS WILLIAM PHENIX
(FES X, 35, 275), trans from Kelty Oldfield to Abronhill 28 Sep 1973; dem 7 Jan 1980.

1980   FRASER METHVEN COMPTON STEWART
ord and ind to Abronhill 12 Jun 1980; trans to Ardler, Kettins and Meigle 12 Mar 1986.

1986 NEIL WILSON BARCLAY
B 7 Oct 1943 at West Kilbride, s of Thomas Ian B. and Janet Cook Wilson; educ Hutchesons' Grammar, Glasgow 1955–62; University of Glasgow 1962–65 (BSc), 1982–85 (BD); Jordanhill College, Glasgow 1965–66 (PGCE); University of New England, NSW, Australia 1970–72 (BEd); Teaching (Scotland and Australia) 1966–82; lic by Presb of Glasgow 1 Jul 1985; asst Glasgow Greenbank 1985–86; m 26 Dec 1973 Jennifer May Roulet b 15 May 1948 d of Eric Marcel R. and Violet Hopkins; Children: Keith b 25 Jun 1976; Lynne b 21 Sep 1982; ord and ind to Abronhill 13 Aug 1986.

CUMBERNAULD CONDORRAT (FES III, 384; VIII, 287; IX, 59; X, 35)

1963 JAMES KENNEDY ORD
(FES X, 35), ord and ind to Condorrat 9 Jan 1963; dem 31 Dec 1968 to enter teaching profession.

1969 BRUCE McNICOL
(FES X, 35), ind to Condorrat 13 Oct 1969; trans to Jedburgh Old and Edgerston 1 May 1992.

1985 TOMAS MICHAL BISEK
introd as Assoc at Condorrat 21 Jul 1985; ind to Glasgow Govanhill Trinity 22 Feb 1990.

1990 GEORGINA NELSON
ord and introd as Assoc at Condorrat 22 Aug 1990; app Chaplain to St John's Hospital, Livingston 1 Oct 1995.

1993 JOHN ALEXANDER McDONALD
B 20 Jan 1944 at Glasgow, s of Alexander M. and Mary Gray McFarlane; educ Albert Senior Secondary (now Springburn), Glasgow 1956–61; University of Glasgow 1968–71 (MA), 1974–77 (BD); Jordanhill College, Glasgow 1971–72 (DipEd); Ministry of Pensions and National Insurance 1961–65; Scottish Co-operative 1966–68; lic by Presb of Glasgow 30 Jun 1977; asst Edinburgh Tron Kirk Moredun 1977–78; m 29 Sep 1977 Agnes Forrest Cowan Hannah b 30 Apr 1947 d of William H. and Mary Lees Hamilton Cowan; ord and ind to Aberuthven with Dunning 28 Sep 1978; trans to Condorrat 18 Feb 1993; ret 30 Mar 1997.

1997 HUGH TAYLOR BROWN
B 15 Apr 1957 at Kilwinning, s of Hugh B. and Elizabeth Gray McMurtrie Anderson Lamb; educ Ravenspark Academy, Irvine 1969–72; University of Glasgow 1991–95 (BD), 1995–96 (CMin); Decorator 1972–91; lic by Presb of Irvine and Kilmarnock 27 Jun 1996; m (1) 27 Jan 1978 Catherine Mason b 7 Mar 1957 d of William M. and Agnes Forsyth; m (2) 27 Jun 1997 Fiona Cunningham Wotherspoon b 1 Dec 1966 d of Alexander W. and Lesley Winning; Children: Hannah Lucie Taylor b 10 Nov 1998; ord and ind to Condorrat 9 Oct 1997.

CUMBERNAULD KILDRUM (FES X, 35)

1970 ALAN MURRAY McPHERSON
(FES X, 36, 354), trans from Monquhitter to Kildrum 20 Nov 1970; dem 31 Jul 1980.

1980 JEREMY RICHARD HUNTER MIDDLETON
ord and ind to Kildrum 19 Nov 1980; trans to Edinburgh Davidson's Mains 13 Jul 1988.

1989 REGINALD FRANKLIN CAMPBELL
B 15 Feb 1951 at Edinburgh, s of Edward Crichton C. and Phyllis Gwendoline Franklin; educ Boroughmuir Secondary, Edinburgh 1963–69; Heriot-Watt University 1969–70; University of Edinburgh 1971–77 and Moray House College, Edinburgh 1975–76 (BD, DChEd); Catering 1970–71; lic by Presb of Edinburgh 3 Jul 1977; asst Largs St John's 1977–79; m 16 Jul 1977 Rosemary Anne Walker b 3 Jul 1954 d of George Adamson and Kathleen Margaret W; Children: Neil Alexander b 2 Jan 1987; ord and ind to Castleton and Saughtree with Newcastleton Congregational Church 14 Jun 1979; trans to Kildrum 16 Feb 1989; dem 31 Jul 1993.

1994 JAMES PATERSON NOBLE COCHRANE
B 4 May 1947 at Aberdeen, s of James Paterson Noble C. and Catherine McKenzie McKay; educ Hilton Academy, Aberdeen 1952–63; University of Edinburgh 1990–93 (LTh); Textile Buyer 1973–90; lic by Presb of Dunfermline 4 Jul 1993; asst South Queensferry 1993–94; m 19 Aug 1967 Patricia Christie b 17 Aug 1947 d of George C. and Isabella Lee; Children: Alison b 13 Sep 1968 m Colin Campbell; Michael James b 2 Apr 1970 m Philippa Lloyd; Graeme George b 30 Dec 1973 m Estelle Welsh; ord and ind to Kildrum 11 May 1994.

CUMBERNAULD OLD (FES IX, 59; X, 36)

1971 GEORGE HARKES
(FES X, 36, 161, 181, 361, 445), trans from Summerfield to Cumbernauld Old 19 Nov 1971; dem 31 Mar 1988; Chaplain to Newton Stewart Hospital 1991–98; ret 12 Apr 1998; Children: Andrew George b 24 Nov 1981; Peter Ewen b 29 Jun 1983.

1988 GRAHAM ALEXANDER DUNCAN
res as Tutor at Federal Theological Seminary of S Africa and ind to Cumbernauld Old 31 Aug 1988; dem 5 May 1998 to take up app with Board of World Mission as Lecturer, University of Fort Hare, S Africa.

1999 CATRIONA OGILVIE
B 15 Dec 1952 at Kampala, Uganda, E Africa, d of Philip Gordon Coutts and Alison May Heady; educ Dollar Academy 1963–70; University of St Andrews 1970–74 (MA); University of Glasgow 1994–97 (BD); Social Work 1974–78; Childminding 1987–94; lic by Presb of Lanark 28 Aug 1997; asst Motherwell St Mary's 1997–99; m 7 Aug 1976 Iain

Ogilvie b 21 Jun 1952 s of Ian Maurice O. and Frances Gillespie Gray; Children: Alexander Iain (Sandy) b 7 Jul 1979; Callum Philip b 16 Jun 1981; Euan David b 12 Nov 1984; ord and ind to Cumbernauld Old 16 Feb 1999.

CUMBERNAULD ST MUNGO'S (FES X, 36)

1972 KENNETH CHARLES LAWSON
(FES X, 36, 130), trans from Paisley South to St Mungo's 25 Feb 1972; dem 9 Mar 1984 on app as Adviser in Adult Education, Board of Parish Education.

1978 DOUGLAS STUART PATERSON
ord by Presb of Falkirk during assistantship at St Mungo's 4 Mar 1976; introd as Assoc 5 May 1978; ind to same charge 14 May 1984; introd as Community minister, Kilwinning 26 Sep 1995.

1984 DAVID ALEXANDER SYME FERGUSSON
ord by Presb of Falkirk and introd as Assoc at St Mungo's 19 Nov 1984; app Lecturer in Systematic Theology, University of Edinburgh 1 Oct 1986.

1986 ANGUS MACLEAN WELLS
B 22 Dec 1961 at Edinburgh, s of George Huntley and Angusina MacLean; educ Galashiels Academy 1973–79; University of Dundee 1979–80; University of St Andrews 1980–84 (BD); University of Edinburgh 1984–85 (DipMin); lic by Presb of Melrose and Peebles 30 Oct 1985; asst Perth St Leonard's-in-the-Fields and Trinity 1985–86; ord and introd as Assoc at St Mungo's 20 Nov 1986; dem 9 Nov 1993.

1996 WILLIAM SIMPSON WHITSON
(FES X, 192, 267, 329), dem from Coatbridge Dunbeth 7 Jan 1975; Jordanhill College, Glasgow 1975–76; Teaching (RE) 1976–95; ind to St Mungo's 17 Apr 1996; ret 30 Jun 1999; introd as Assoc at Perth St Matthew's 1 Sep 1999; marriage to Isobel Jean Lyle McNaught ended in divorce Sep 1978; m (2) 5 Sep 1980 Barbara Mills Buchan McLaren b 9 Mar 1937 d of James M. and Isabella Buchan; Children: Christopher James McLaren b 5 Oct 1975; Publ: Contributor to *Worship Now* (St Andrew Press, 1972); contributor to *Prayers for Contemporary Worship* (St Andrew Press, 1977).

DENNY OLD (FES IV, 303; VIII, 389; IX, 60; X, 36)

1943 ROBERT GEORGE LAWRIE
(FES IX, 60; X, 36), trans to Denny Old 15 Dec 1943; ret 31 Oct 1976; died 30 Nov 1992.

1977 ROBIN ALASDAIR ROSS
ord and ind to Denny Old 20 Apr 1977; dem 10 Oct 1982 and app to Tiberias, Israel 2 Feb 1983.

1983 RICHARD SMITH
B 25 Feb 1938 at Falkirk Redding, s of James S. and Amelia Carbis Cummings; educ Falkirk Technical High (now Graeme High) 1942–53; Heriot-Watt University 1958–60 (AICS); University of Glasgow 1970–75 (BD); Chartered Shipbroker 1953–70; lic by Presb of Falkirk 3 Jul 1975; asst Bo' ness Old 1975–76; m 21 Apr 1963 Georgina Wotherspoon Swinton b 13 Jun 1939 d of John S. and Ina Wotherspoon; Children: Hazel Carbis Swinton b 1 Dec 1965 m Kevin Gilmour; Lorna Dunlop McGregor b 9 Oct 1978; ord and ind to Barr with Dailly 10 Jun 1976; trans to Denny Old 17 Aug 1983; Sub-Chaplain to Order of St John Central Branch from 1990.

DENNY WESTPARK (FES X, 37)

1968 GEORGE ANGUS CHALMERS
(FES X, 37, 61), trans from Greenlaw to Westpark 5 Apr 1968; trans to Banchory-Ternan West 10 Mar 1986; University of Stirling 1980–84 (MLitt).

1986 ROBERT DOUGLAS CRANSTON
ord and ind to Denny Westpark 1 Sep 1986; trans to Kilmacolm St Columba 3 Sep 1992.

1993 MARK EDWARD JOHNSTONE
B 28 May 1968 at Glasgow, s of Charles J. and Jessie Black; educ Kingsridge Secondary, Drumchapel 1973–86; University of Glasgow 1986–89 (MA), 1989–92 (BD); lic by Presb of Glasgow 26 Jun 1992; asst Bishopbriggs Springfield Cambridge 1992–93; m 29 Sep 1990 Audrey Cameron b 1 Mar 1966 d of Angus C. and Heather Wills; Children: Ross b 21 Mar 1992; Gayle b 14 Nov 1993; Samuel b 7 Aug 1995; ord and ind to Westpark 10 May 1993; dem 31 May 1999 to take up app with United Church of Canada.

DENNYLOANHEAD (FUF 46; FES IX, 60; X, 37)

Linkage with High Bonnybridge St Helen's terminated 7 Jul 1978. Linked 25 Jul 1978 with Haggs. Arrangement terminated 28 Jun 1991. Congregation dissolved 1 Sep 1991.

1972 JOHN WATSON
(FES X, 37, 342), trans from Leochel-Cushnie and Lynturk to Dennyloanhead with High Bonnybridge St Helen's 19 Sep 1972; became minister of High Bonnybridge St Helen's (term) following termination of linkage 7 Jul 1978; ret 31 May 1991.

1978 JOHN CRINDLE HOLLAND
ord and ind to Haggs 18 Jun 1976; became minister of linked charge with Dennyloanhead 25 Jul 1978; trans to Strone and Ardentinny 4 Aug 1982.

1983 ROGER ALFRED FRANCIS DEAN
ord and ind to Dennyloanhead with Haggs 29 Jun 1983; dem on app as Chaplain to Royal Caledonian Schools, Bushey, Herts 1 Sep 1990.

DUNIPACE (FES X, 36)

Formed 8 Jan 1989 by union of Dunipace North and Dunipace Old.

1971 HENRY MUNROE
(FES X, 36), ord and ind to Dunipace North with Old 25 Aug 1971; ret 4 Sep 1988.

1989 JEAN WARDLAW GALLACHER
B 9 Jun 1962 at Helensburgh, d of Edward G. and Jeanie Gillespie Wardlaw; educ Vale of Leven Academy 1974–79; Clydebank College 1979–82; University of Glasgow 1982–86 (BD), 1987–88 (CMin); Columbia Theological Seminary, USA 1986–87 (CTh); lic by Presb of Dumbarton 10 Jul 1988; asst West Kirk of Helensburgh 1988–89; ord and ind to Dunipace 29 Jun 1989.

FALKIRK BAINSFORD (FUF 46; FES IX, 61; X, 37)

1974 DAVID JOHN BOYD ANDERSON
(FES X, 37), ord and ind to Bainsford 20 Nov 1974; trans to Edinburgh Gorgie 16 Jan 1986.

1986 FRANCIS DEREK GUNN
B 4 Jun 1950 at Edinburgh, s of Francis G. and Barbara Morrison; educ Portobello Secondary, Edinburgh 1962–68; University of St Andrews 1981–85 (BD); lic by Presb of St Andrews 30 Jun 1985; asst Edinburgh Corstorphine Craigsbank 1985–86; m 7 Oct 1978 Audrey Patricia Herd d of David Stewart H. and Mary Kirker; Children: David Alasdair b 3 Apr 1980; Caroline Elizabeth b 19 Apr 1982; Susan Jennifer b 28 Nov 1984; ord and ind to Bainsford 28 May 1986; dem 9 Feb 1997.

1997 BRIAN ROBERT HENDRIE
B 21 Sep 1962 at Ayr, s of Robert Woods H. and Sarah Wilson Merry; educ Ayr Academy 1975–81; University of Glasgow 1985–89 (BD), 1989–90 (CMin); Travel Agent 1981–85; lic by Presb of Ayr 11 Jul 1990; asst Prestwick Kingcase 1990–91; Falkirk St Andrew's West 1991–92; m 30 Jul 1989 Yvonne Hibbert Jamieson b 7 Apr 1966 d of George Barron J. and Sarah Brown; Children: Chloe Christine b 2 Jul 1997; ord and ind to Hawick Wilton with Teviothead 24 Jan 1992; trans to Bainsford 27 Aug 1997.

FALKIRK CAMELON IRVING (FUF 47; FES IX, 62; X, 38)

1962 JOHN McCALLUM
(FES X, 38), ord and ind to Irving 28 Nov 1962; ret 31 Jul 1998; d Fiona m Fellowes.

1999 SARAH (SALLY) FOSTER-FULTON
B 25 Apr 1964 at Beaufort, S Carolina, USA, d of William Harrell Foster and Gambrell Glenn; educ Seneca High School 1970–82; Presb College 1987 (BA); University of Glasgow 1991 (BD); Director of Christian Education 1988–90; lic by Presb of Falkirk; asst Dunipace; m 19 May 1990 Robert Stuart McColl Fulton b 31 Aug 1960 s of Robert F. and Young; Children: Jessie Alexandra b 6 Jul 1991; Sarah Grace b 22 Mar 1994; ord and ind to Camelon Irving (rev tenure) 10 Mar 1999.

FALKIRK CAMELON ST JOHN'S (FES I, 197; VIII, 38; IX, 61; X, 37)

Granted full status 2 Feb 1992.

1957 JAMES ROBSON
(FES IX 101; X, 37, 60), trans from Gordon St Michael's to Camelon St John's 7 Aug 1957; ret 30 Nov 1987; d Susan m Jackson.

1988 JAMES KENNEDY WALLACE
B 28 Oct 1959 at Lanarkshire, s of Alexander W. and Margaret Stevenson Kennedy; educ Hamilton Grammar 1972–78; University of Aberdeen 1980–83 (MA); University of St Andrews 1983–86 (BD); Union Theological Seminary, New York 1987–88 (STM); lic by Presb of Hamilton 26 Jun 1986; asst Bearsden North 1986–87; First Presb Church, Baldwin, New York 1987–88; m 18 Jun 1993 Catherine Machin d of John M. and Catherine Page; Children: Megan Elizabeth Bell b 16 Mar 1989; Ruth Catherine b 24 Dec 1995; ord and introd to Camelon St John's (term) 22 Jun 1988; ind 2 Feb 1992.

FALKIRK CAMELON TRINITY (FUF 48; FES IX, 61; X, 37)

Congregation dissolved 13 May 1973.

1956 JAMES WAUGH
(FES IX, 69, 181, 425, 529, 753; X, 37), introd on term app to Camelon Trinity 6 Jan 1956; ind to same charge 23 Oct 1957; dem 12 May 1959 to enter teaching profession; died 12 Mar 1998; w Margaret died 4 Jun 1982.

1960 DANIEL McCALLUM ROBERTSON
(FES X, 37, 98), ord and ind to Camelon Trinity 6 Sep 1960; trans to Auchinleck Barony 28 Sep 1967.

FALKIRK ERSKINE (FUF 47; FES IX, 61; X, 37)

1973 DAVID CHAPLIN
(FES IX, 337; X, 38, 90, 167, 201, 417), [correction: Netherton St Matthew's, not St Margaret's as in Vol X, 38]; trans from Glasgow Netherton St Matthew's to Erskine 24 Apr 1973; ret 31 Oct 1982; died 23 Aug 1991.

1983 GRAEME WATSON MACKINNON MUCKART
ord and ind to Erskine 12 Jul 1983; loc ten Carriden 1 Sep 1990; app to St Andrew's, Colombo, Sri Lanka 22 Jun 1992.

1990   BLAIR ROBERTSON
ord and ind to Erskine 23 Oct 1990; dem 20 Jul 1998 to take up app as Chaplain to Glasgow Southern General Hospital.

1999   GLEN DONALD MACAULAY
B 9 Jan 1952 at Musselburgh, s of Malcolm M. and Susan Johnstone; educ Preston Lodge High, Prestonpans 1964–70; University of Edinburgh 1994–97 (BD); Civil Service 1972–94; lic by Presb of Lothian 3 Jul 1997; asst Edinburgh Leith St Andrew's 1997–99; m 14 Apr 1971 Janet Dalgleish McDougall b 14 Apr 1953 d of Benjamin M. and Betsy Brown; Children: Jennifer Elizabeth b 31 Jul 1971; Callum Donald b 8 Apr 1974 m Lynsey Fraser; ord and ind to Erskine 17 Mar 1999.

FALKIRK GRAHAMSTON UNITED (FES X, 38)

1973   WILLIAM GORDON McDONALD
(FES X, 38 (2), 276), trans from Limekilns to Grahamston with Graham's Road 27 Jun 1973; became minister of united charge 15 Oct 1975; ret 31 Oct 1975; Children: Mary b 25 Jul 1971; Fiona b 21 Jun 1973 m Morrison.

1976   DUNCAN ELLIOTT McCLEMENTS
(FES X, 109), trans from Hurlford Reid Memorial to Grahamston United 1 Dec 1976; University of Edinburgh [part-time] 1982–85 (MTh); University of Manchester [part-time] 1987–90 (CRS); s David m Louise Jayne Elizabeth Marshall.

FALKIRK LAURIESTON (FES IX, 62; X, 38)

Linked 31 Dec 1979 with Redding and Westquarter.

1958   GAVIN SHANKS BROWN
(FES IX, 480, 640, 721; X, 38, 365), trans from Bellie to Laurieston 10 Dec 1958; ret 31 Dec 1979; died 3 Jul 1995.

1980   RONALD JOHN McDOWALL
B 2 Jun 1937 at Ayr, s of John M. and Mary Cherry; educ Ayr Grammar and Ayr Academy 1949–56; Paisley Technical College 1956–61 (ONC, HNC, CChem); University of Glasgow 1976–80 (BD); Scottish Agricultural Industries 1956–57; Research Chemist, ICI 1957–76; lic by Presb of Ayr 25 Jun 1980; m 19 May 1962 Helen Paterson Vance b 14 Sep 1936 d of John V. and Sarah Paterson Crosbie; Children: Kenneth John b 30 May 1965 m Janine Harkness; Fiona Sarah b 28 May 1966 m George Burgess; ord and ind to Laurieston with Redding and Westquarter 19 Sep 1980.

FALKIRK OLD AND ST MODAN'S (FES X, 38, 39)

Formed 22 Oct 1986 by union of Falkirk Old and Falkirk St Modan's.

1932   NEIL CAMPBELL
(FUF 121; FES IX, 63, 166; X, 39), trans from Whithorn St Ninian's to St Modan's 14 Dec 1932; ret 6 Sep 1972; died 23 May 1982.

1966   JAMES SHIRLAW PATERSON
(FES IX, 283, 365; X, 38, 218, 294), trans from Largo and Newburn to Falkirk Old 15 Jun 1966; trans to Cumlodden and Lochfyneside 13 Feb 1979.

1973   GRAHAM WATSON FOSTER
(FES X, 39), ord and ind to St Modan's 20 Jun 1973; trans to Invergordon 11 Aug 1978.

1979   RONALD WENDELL SMITH
B 23 Jan 1946 at New Glasgow, Nova Scotia, Canada, s of George Wendell Mortimer S. and Audrey Muriel Noddin; educ Sydney Mines High, Nova Scotia 1952–64; Acadia University 1965–68 (BA); University of New Brunswick 1968–69 (BEd); L'Université de Moncton 1969–70; University of Glasgow 1974–77 (BD); Teaching 1969–71; Lay Ministry 1971–74; lic by Presb of Glasgow 30 Jun 1977; asst Glasgow Ibrox 1975–76, Balshagray 1976–77; ord and ind to St Modan's 18 Jan 1979; introd as Assoc following union with Old 22 Oct 1986.

1979   MALCOLM LEITH FISHER
(FES X, 153), res as Asst and Youth Leader at Glasgow Calton New and ind to Falkirk Old 19 Jun 1979; became minister of united charge with St Modan's 22 Oct 1986; trans to Glasgow Wellington 1 Feb 1990.

1990   SHEILA BLOUNT
B 14 Oct 1953, d of Charles Colin Campbell Gillon and Audrey Fairway; educ Hillhead High, Glasgow 1965–71; University of St Andrews 1971–75 (BD); University of Strathclyde 1975–77 (BA); lic by Presb of Glasgow 30 Jun 1977; asst Glasgow Cardonald 1977–78; m 12 Sep 1974 Graham Keith Blount b 7 Apr 1951 s of George Keith B. and Caroline Victoria Brown: Children: Laura Carol b 13 Nov 1981; Lindsay May b 24 May 1983; ord by Presb of Glasgow and introd as Assoc at Springburn 27 Sep 1978; res from app 30 Sep 1981; ind to Old and St Modan's (joint ministry) 22 Jun 1990; ind as sole minister 19 Nov 1998; Chaplain (part-time) to HM Institution Corton Vale 1985–93; Chaplain (part-time) to Polmont Young Offenders Institution.

1990   GRAHAM KEITH BLOUNT
trans from Bridge of Allan Chalmers to Old and St Modan's (joint ministry) 22 Jun 1990; dem 20 Sep 1998 on app as Scottish Churches' Parliamentary Officer.

FALKIRK ST ANDREW'S WEST (FES X, 39)

Formed 3 Oct 1990 by union of Falkirk St Andrew's and Falkirk West.

1927 WILLIAM MORTON GRANT
(FUF 49; FES IX, 63; X, 39), trans from Auchtergaven to Falkirk West 14 Apr 1927; ret 30 Nov 1967; died 16 Aug 1987.

1968 MARTIN ROBERTSON BETSWORTH COUTTS REID
(FES X, 39, 385), trans from Strathy and Halladale to Falkirk West 14 May 1968; dem in interests of union 10 Oct 1990; ret 7 Oct 1993; University of London (external) 1999 (BD).

1972 ROBERT McGHEE
(FES X, 39, 51, 389, 389), trans from Newbattle to St Andrew's 15 May 1972; became minister of united charge with West 3 Oct 1990; died 18 Mar 1996.

1997 ALASTAIR MACKENZIE HORNE
B 31 Aug 1958 at Bellshill, s of James H. and Margaret Whitton Ferguson; educ Cathkin High, Glasgow 1970–76; University of Strathclyde 1976–80 (BSc); University of Glasgow 1985–88 (BD); lic by Presb of Lanark 30 Jun 1988; asst Hamilton St John's; m 28 Dec 1981 Elizabeth Anne Donaldson; Children: Douglas b 27 May 1987; Alison b 24 Dec 1991; ord and ind to Invergowrie 17 Oct 1989; trans to St Andrew's West 13 Feb 1997.

FALKIRK ST JAMES' (FUF 48; FES IX, 63; X, 39)

1972 DAVID JOHN KELLAS
(FES X, 39, 226), trans from Glenaray and Inveraray to St James' 29 Nov 1972; trans to Galashiels St Ninian's 18 May 1983.

1983 ALAN BARCLAY TELFER
ord and ind to St James' 30 Aug 1983; trans to Mauchline 14 Mar 1991.

1992 ERIC GEORGE McKIMMON
B 1 Apr 1951 at Co Tyrone, N Ireland, s of Thomas M. and Margaret Lucas; educ Castlederg Secondary and Strabane Grammar 1962–69; Queens University, Belfast 1974–78 (BA), 1984–87 [part-time] (MTh); University of Edinburgh 1979–81 (BD); Banking 1970–73; Inland Revenue 1973–74; lic by Presb of Strabane 26 Jun 1981; asst Monkstown Abbey Church 1980–81; Comber First Presb Church 1981–83; m 10 Jul 1982 Kathleen Helen Walker b 14 Mar 1960 d of James W. and Nancy Sloss; Children: Morag b 3 Jul 1984; Angus b 17 Feb 1986; Calum b 16 Jun 1988; ord by Presb of Down during assistantship at Comber First Presb Church 3 Jan 1983; ind to Tullyallen and Mountnorris 16 Apr 1984; trans to Claremont and Burt, Republic of Ireland 26 Mar 1988; ind to St James' 10 Jan 1992.

GRANGEMOUTH CHARING CROSS AND WEST (FES X, 39, 40)
Congregations linked 7 Oct 1976 and united 5 Apr 1978.

1960 MALCOLM NANFRED CORNER
(FES VIII, 626; FES IX, 641; X, 40, 366), trans from Drainie St Gerardine's to Grangemouth West 22 Apr 1960; ret 30 Nov 1969; died 24 Sep 1990.

1964 ALEXANDER ROBERTSON
(FES X, 39, 400), trans from Evie to Charing Cross 23 Sep 1964; became minister of linked charge with West 7 Oct 1976 and of united charge 5 Apr 1978; ret 30 Nov 1981; died 22 Feb 1987.

1971 THOMAS HAROLD BUXTON WELLER
(FES X, 40, 190), dem from Carfin 30 Jun 1967 and ind to Grangemouth West 15 Jun 1971; ret 30 Sep 1976; died 7 May 1989.

1982 DANIEL LAMB MATHERS
B 15 Dec 1935 at Peterhead, s of Daniel Parker M. and Ann Campbell Wilson; educ John Street Senior Secondary, Glasgow 1947–50; University of Glasgow 1973–78 (BD); Paint Industry 1950–58; National Service (RAF) 1958–60; Industrial Chemist 1962–73; lic by Presb of Falkirk 29 Jun 1978; asst Cumbernauld Kildrum 1978–79; m 27 Sep 1963 Alexena Smith b 12 Apr 1939 d of Alexander Smith and Margaret Aitken; Children: Iain Lamont b 10 Jul 1964 m Susan Charlotte Reid; Murray Neil b 25 Oct 1965; Bruce Douglas b 13 Apr 1970 m Shirley-Anne Crawford; ord and ind to Charing Cross and West 11 Oct 1982; Chaplain (part-time) to Polmont Young Offenders Institution.

GRANGEMOUTH DUNDAS (FUF 49; FES IX, 63; X, 39)

1969 DOUGLAS BLACK BLAIR
(FES X, 39), ord and ind to Grangemouth Dundas 11 Sep 1969; s Kenneth m Sara Manning.

GRANGEMOUTH KERSE (FES I, 210; VIII, 43; IX, 64; X, 40)

1973 EAN MACGREGOR SIMPSON
(FES X, 40, 229), trans from Kilbride and Tighnabruaich to Kerse 20 Feb 1973; dem 20 Apr 1992 on grounds of ill-health; died 21 Dec 1998.

1992 ANDREW CRAIG DONALD
B 4 Feb 1968 at Edinburgh, s of Brian Stuart Cooper D. and Cecilia Mary Craig; educ Stonelaw High, Rutherglen and Turriff Academy 1979–85; University of Aberdeen 1985–91 (BD, DPS); lic by Presb of Buchan 26 Jun 1991; asst Aberdeen Mannofield 1990–91; Bearsden North 1991–92; ord and ind to Kerse 23 Oct 1992; Chaplain to Falkirk and District Battalion, Boys' Brigade 1995–96, 1996–97; Regional Chaplain to Girls' Brigade for Central Region 1999–2000.

GRANGEMOUTH KIRK OF THE HOLY ROOD
(FES X, 40)

1972   GORDON FERGUSON
(FES X, 40), ord and ind to Kirk of the Holy Rood 3 May 1972; ret 31 May 1996; d Margaret m Tom Barker.

1996   JOANNE GIBSON FINLAY
B 3 Jan 1963 at Broxburn, d of Alexander Walker Robertson and Margaret Savage Stewart; educ Whitburn Academy 1968–81; Dundee College of Education 1981–84 (Dip Mus Ed); University of Edinburgh 1990–94 (BD); Teaching 1984–90; lic by Presb of West Lothian 7 Jul 1994; asst Brightons 1994–96; m 3 Jul 1985 Donald Brown Finlay b 27 Apr 1950 s of Daniel Martin F. and Isabella Thomson; ord and ind to Kirk of the Holy Rood 16 Aug 1996.

GRANGEMOUTH ZETLAND (FES X, 39, 40)

Formed 14 Mar 1991 by union of Grangemouth Grange and Grangemouth Old.

1954   WILLIAM RYRIE LYALL
(FES IX, 64; X, 39), ord and ind to Grange 2 Dec 1954; ret 30 Dec 1987; died 14 May 1991.

1964   DAVID SPOWART
(FE IX, 53, 749; X, 40, 253, 425), trans from Perth Letham to Grangemouth Old 2 Jun 1964; ret 28 Feb 1978; died 18 Feb 1994.

1978   JAMES McALPINE GIBSON
ord and ind to Grangemouth Old 11 Jul 1978; trans to Bothwell 3 Nov 1989.

1988   ELAINE WRIGHT McKINNON
ord and ind to Grangemouth Grange 18 Nov 1988; loc ten Edinburgh Slateford Longstone 1991; app by Board of World Mission as Chaplain to Alliance Girls' High School, Kenya 11 Jan 1992.

1991   IAN WALTER BLACK
B 20 Mar 1951 at Glasgow, s of John Henry Wilson B. and Isabella Gardiner Towers; educ Allan Glen's, Glasgow 1963–69; University of Edinburgh 1969–72 (MA), 1972–75 (BD); lic by Presb of Glasgow 3 Dec 1975; asst Glasgow Cathedral 1975–77; m 9 Aug 1975 Agnes Cowan b 18 Feb 1953 d of Hugh C. and Elizabeth Crosbie; Children: Richard John Cowan b 5 Jul 1979; Stephen Hugh b 23 Mar 1982; ord by Presb of Glasgow during assistantship at The Cathedral 3 Jun 1976; ind to Greenock St Andrew's 13 Apr 1977; trans to Zetland 15 Aug 1991.

HAGGS (FES IV, 309; VIII, 390; IX, 65; X, 40)

Linked 25 Jul 1978 with Dennyloanhead. Arrangement terminated 28 Jun 1991.

1976   JOHN CRINDLE HOLLAND
ord and ind to Haggs 18 Jun 1976; became minister of linked charge with Dennyloanhead 25 Jul 1978; trans to Strone and Ardentinny 4 Aug 1982.

1983   ROGER ALFRED FRANCIS DEAN
ord and ind to Dennyloanhead with Haggs 29 Jun 1983, see Dennyloanhead.

1991   ROBERT STUART McCOLL FULTON
ord and ind to Haggs 28 Jun 1991; dem 14 Jun 1998 on app as Special Adviser on Chaplaincy to HM Prison Services.

1998   HELEN FERGUS CHRISTIE
B 17 Mar 1950 at Edinburgh, d of Duncan Ferguson Morrison and Betsy Birrell Simpson; educ Lindsay High, Bathgate 1962–67; University of St Andrews 1992–96 (BD); Civil Service 1968–80; Caretaker 1986–92; lic by Presb of Dundee 18 Jun 1997; m 2 Aug 1975 Andrew Christie b 16 Jul 1947 s of David C. and Mary Tulloch; Children: Stewart Fraser b 14 Apr 1980; ord and ind to Haggs 9 Dec 1998.

LARBERT EAST (FUF 50; FES IX, 66; X, 41)

1964   ERIC JOHN MURRAY
(FES X, 41, 423), res from service with FMC in Kenya and ind to Larbert East 26 Feb 1964; ret 30 Jun 1995; d Fiona m Jardine; s Eric m Samantha Whittet.

1995   MELVILLE DOIG CROSTHWAITE
B 14 Aug 1956 at Sheffield, s of David Doig C. and Margaret McKelvie; educ Peterlee Grammar Tech-nical School 1967–74; University of Edinburgh 1974–79 (BD), 1982–83 (DipMin); Moray House College, Edinburgh 1979–80 (DEd); Teaching 1980–82; lic by Presb of West Lothian 30 Jun 1983; asst Armadale 1983–84; m 10 Jul 1982 Irene Margaret Brownie b 21 Mar 1957 d of Robert Allan B. and Irene Hare Niven; Children: Andrew Robert b 20 Apr 1984; Hannah Margaret b 4 May 1986; Peter David b 2 May 1988; Sarah Anne b 7 Apr 1991; ord and ind to Carstairs with Carstairs Junction 29 Aug 1984; trans to Larbert East 16 Nov 1995.

LARBERT OLD (FES X, 41)

1975   DAVID CHARLES SEARLE
(FES X, 41, 336), trans from Aberdeen Newhills to Larbert Old 8 Sep 1975; dem 15 May 1985 and ind to Hamilton Road Presb Church, Bangor, N Ireland 30 May 1985.

1985   CLIFFORD ALFRED JOHN RENNIE
(FES X, 383), trans from Altnaharra and Farr to Larbert Old 23 Aug 1985; Addl children: Athole James b 24 Aug 1978; Craig Andrew b 10 Jan 1980; Publ: *Goal Behind the Curtain* (Christian Focus, 1990); *Offside in Ecquatina* (Christian

Focus, 1991); *True Gold* (Christian Focus, 1992); contributor to *Daily Bread* and *Encounter with God* (Scripture Union, 1993–98).

LARBERT WEST (FUF 51; FES IX, 66; X, 41)

1974 ALAN HUTCHISON MACKAY
(FES X, 41), ord and ind to Larbert West 30 May 1974; trans to Broughty Ferry East 8 Mar 1984.

1984 EVELYN MEIKLE YOUNG
ord and ind to Larbert West 16 Aug 1984; dem on app as Asst/Deputy Secretary, Dept of Education 1 Feb 1991.

1991 ROBERT SCOTT TAYLOR ALLAN
ord and ind to Larbert West 21 Jun 1991; dem on app as Education and Development Officer, Board of Ministry 31 Jan 1999.

1999 GAVIN ROSS BOSWELL
B 11 Aug 1965 at Harare, Zimbabwe, s of Douglas Ernest B. and Rosemary Leeds; educ Pinetown Boys' High School, Pinetown, Natal, S Africa 1980–82; Rhodes University, Grahamstown, S Africa 1987–91 (BTh); National Military Service, S African Navy 1985–86; lic by Presb of Kingwilliamstown (PCSA) 1 Feb 1991; asst Cambridge Church, East London (PCSA) 1991–92; m 27 Apr 1996 Caroline Mary MacNaughtan b 29 Nov 1961 d of Charles M. and Jean Parsons; Children: Marion Rose b 1 Jun 1997; ord by Presb of Transvaal East and ind to St Andrew's, Brakpan, S Africa 4 Feb 1993; ind to Trinity PCSA, Greencroft, Harare, Zimbabwe 16 Jun 1995; ind to Larbert West 26 Aug 1999.

MUIRAVONSIDE (FES I, 221; VIII, 46; IX, 67; X, 42)

1976 RICHARD ARTHUR THOMAS GOODMAN
ord and ind to Muiravonside 30 Jul 1976; introd as Assoc to Isle of Mull parishes 11 Oct 1981.

1982 PETER E WRIGHT
dem from Evie with Rendall with Firth 1 Dec 1980; ind to Muiravonside 27 Apr 1982; dem 1 Jul 1984.

1984 STANLEY HILL
(FES X, 216, 351), dem from Clydebank Hamilton Memorial with Linnvale 30 Sep 1981; ind to Muiravonside 29 Nov 1984; ret 31 Dec 1998.

1999 JOAN ROSS
B 26 Jan 1956 at Renfrew, d of Richard R. and Lily Jackson Scott; educ Grove Academy, Broughty Ferry 1968–74; University of St Andrews 1974–78 (BSc), 1978–81 (PhD); University of Glasgow 1993–96 (BD); Post-Doctoral Research 1981–84; Polytechnic/University Admin 1985–93; lic by Presb of Paisley 22 Aug 1996; asst Kilmacolm Old 1996–98; ord and ind to Muiravonside 16 Jun 1999.

POLMONT OLD (FES I, 224; VIII, 47; IX, 68; X, 42)

Name changed from Polmont North 1977.

1954 HUGH TALMAN
(FES IX, 68; X, 42), trans from Kilwinning Mansefield to Polmont North 1 Apr 1954; ret 31 Dec 1987.

1988 WILLIAM GRAHAM MURRAY THAIN
ord and ind to Polmont Old 20 Jun 1988; trans to Glasgow St David's Knightswood 25 May 1999.

REDDING AND WESTQUARTER (FES IX, 68; X, 42)

Linked 31 Dec 1979 with Falkirk Laurieston.

1976 J ALLAN PAISLEY
ord and ind to Redding and Westquarter 25 Jun 1976; dem 31 Dec 1978.

1980 RONALD JOHN McDOWALL
ord and ind to Falkirk Laurieston with Redding and Westquarter 19 Sep 1980, see Laurieston.

SLAMANNAN (FES IX, 69; X, 42)

1938 WILLIAM IAIN GIRDWOOD WILSON
(FES IX, 69), ord and ind to Slamannan Balquatston 21 Dec 1938; dem 1941; app Assoc Professor of Bible, Davidson College, N Carolina, USA; died 22 Oct 1995.

1944 HOPE MONCRIEFF
(FUF 442; FES IX, 69), introd to Slamannan Balquatston 2 Feb 1944; res 13 Mar 1945.

1946 ALEXANDER DUNCAN CAMERON
(FES IX, 69, 506), trans from Dundee Chalmers to Slamannan (union of Slamannan Balquatston and Slamannan St Lawrence) 15 May 1946; died 8 Jun 1968.

1968 THOMAS GRAHAM FLEMING
(FES X, 42, 120, 194), trans from Stevenston Ardeer to Slamannan 6 Jan 1968; dem 31 Jan 1982.

1982 SAMUEL BRYCE OVENS
B 15 May 1938 at Blackburn, s of Thomas O. and Mary McBryde Bryce; educ Lindsay High, Bathgate 1948–53; University of Glasgow 1977–81 (BD); Electrician 1954–76; lic by Presb of Stirling 19 Jul 1981; asst Falkirk Old 1981–82; m 5 May 1957 Sheila Mary Robinson b 10 Nov 1933 d of Edgar R. and Wanda White; Children: Lesley Karon b 21 Nov 1958; Elizabeth Wanda b 30 Jun 1962 m Graeme Ramage; Isabella Eileen b 30 Jun 1962 m Vincent Green; ord and ind to Slamannan 11 Aug 1982; ret 31 Mar 1992.

1992　RAYMOND THOMSON
B 22 Feb 1952 at Paisley, s of Robert Wilson T. and Agnes Holmes Renton; educ Paisley Grammar 1964–70; University of Glasgow 1984–90 (BD, DipMin); Lab Technician 1971–75, 1977–82; lic by Presb of Paisley 15 Jan 1992; asst Paisley Martyrs 1990–91; Elderslie Kirk 1991–92; ord and ind to Slamannan 3 Jun 1992.

STENHOUSE AND CARRON (FES X, 34)

1969　ROBERT KEITH HARDIE
(FES X, 43), ord by Presb of Aberdeen during assistantship at St Machar's Cathedral 23 Jun 1968; ind to Stenhouse and Carron 3 Dec 1969; Addl children: David Keith Charles b 18 Dec 1981.

PRESBYTERY OF STIRLING

ABERFOYLE (FES IV, 334; VIII, 395; IX, 440; X, 261)

Linked 17 Mar 1983 with Port of Menteith.

1967   JOHN HERBERT BOYD MACPHAIL
(FES IX, 372, 660; X, 222, 261), dem from Milngavie Cairns 31 Dec 1963; ind to Aberfoyle 12 Jul 1967; ret 30 Apr 1976; died 19 Jul 1996.

1976   JAMES McMICHAEL ORR
(FES X, 162, 257, 424), trans from Jordanhill to Aberfoyle 1 Dec 1976; became minister of linked charge with Port of Menteith 17 Mar 1983; ret 31 Aug 1986.

1986   DAVID KIRK SPEED
(FES X, 237), trans from Stamperland to Aberfoyle with Port of Menteith 20 Nov 1986; trans to Glasgow Shettleston Old 3 Aug 1999.

ALLOA NORTH (FES X, 261)

Formed 1 Mar 1970 by union of Alloa Chalmers and Alloa St Andrew's.

1952   FREDERICK TIDD
(FES IX, 134, 440; X, 261), trans from Kirkpatrick-Juxta to Chalmers 9 Dec 1952; ret in interests of union 28 Feb 1970; died 10 Jan 1980.

1970   JOSEPH WALTER McGINTY
(FES X, 34, 261), trans from Blackbraes and Shieldhill to Alloa North 8 Sep 1970; trans to Alloway 11 Apr 1978.

1978   IAN WILLIAM FINLAY HAMILTON
ord and ind to Alloa North 3 Oct 1978; trans to Nairn Old 3 Oct 1986.

1988   DAVID STEWART FIFE COUPER
B 24 Sep 1956 at Pietermaritzburg, S Africa, s of David George C. and Jill Munro Lerwick; educ Fettes College, Edinburgh 1970–74; University of St Andrews 1975–79 (MA); University of Cambridge 1979–80 (PGCE); University of Aberdeen 1984–87 (BD); Teaching 1980–84; lic by Presb of Gordon 28 Jun 1987; asst South Queensferry 1987–88; m 29 Jul 1983 Gillian Ruth Donaldson b 27 Jun 1960 d of Colin Victor D. and Marion Christina Duncan; Children: Jennifer Ruth Lona b 30 Jul 1985; James David Scott b 6 Oct 1987; Timothy Peter Ross b 4 Sep 1989; ord and ind to Alloa North 18 May 1988.

ALLOA ST MUNGO'S (FES IV, 291; VIII, 386; IX, 440; X, 261)

1947   PETER PHILIP BRODIE
(FES IX, 247, 440; X, 261), trans from Kirkintilloch St Mary's to St Mungo's 28 Jan 1947; Moderator of General Assembly 1978–79; ret 31 Dec 1986; died 16 Oct 1990.

1987   KEITH FERRIER HALL
trans from Blairgowrie St Mary's South to St Mungo's 11 May 1987; trans to Dundee (St Mary's) 13 Jul 1994.

1996   ALAN FREW MUNRO DOWNIE
B 17 Nov 1946 at Uddingston, s of William D. and Margaret Herbertson McEwan Frew; educ Hamilton Academy and Langside College, Glasgow 1958–69; University of Glasgow 1969–73 (MA), 1973–76 (BD); Trainee Insurance Underwriter 1964–68; lic by Presb of Hamilton 28 Jun 1976; asst Largs St Columba's 1976–77; m 28 Jul 1973 Margaret Elizabeth Moore b 5 Aug 1948 d of William M. and Mary Milroy; Children: Jacqueline Irene Mary b 2 Jul 1976; Colin William Moore b 28 Jan 1980; Andrew Alan Frew b 23 Dec 1981; Laura Margaret Wilson b 1 Oct 1985; ord and ind to Dun with Hillside 19 Oct 1977; trans to St Mungo's 15 Feb 1997; Chaplain (part-time) to HMP Glenochil.

ALLOA WEST (FUF 304; FES IX, 441; X, 261)

1925   ALEXANDER CHISHOLM
(FUF 304; FES IX, 144; X, 261), dem from Alloa West 30 Sep 1954 to take up app as Lecturer in Church Music; ret 1959; died 19 Sep 1980.

1955   DAVID SLOAN WALKER
(FES IX, 158, 222, 264; X, 68, 93, 261), trans Ervie and Kirkcolm to Alloa West 26 Apr 1955; trans to Makerstoun with Smailholm 5 Oct 1966.

1967   GRAHAM NORRIE
(FES X, 261), ord and ind to Alloa West 28 Mar 1967; trans to Forfar East and Old 7 Jun 1978.

1978   MICHAEL WILLIAM FREW
ord and ind to Alloa West 30 Oct 1978; dem 15 Jan 1987 on app as Regional Organiser for Evangelism 1 Feb 1987.

1988 ALAN McKENZIE
B 18 Nov 1948 at Edinburgh, s of John M. and Margaret Haimes; educ Lochaber High, Fort William; University of Aberdeen 1966–70 (BSc); University of Sheffield 1970–73 (research student); Jordanhill College, Glasgow 1973 (PGCE); St Colm's College, Edinburgh 1976–77 (CSCC); University of Glasgow 1984–87 (BD); Teaching 1974–76; Overseas Missionary, Church of Scotland 1977–84; lic by Presb of Hamilton 26 Jun 1987; asst Glasgow Pollokshields 1987–88; m 18 Mar 1978 Margaret Hannah Sim b 27 Jan 1954 d of James Noble S. and Hannah Cormack; Children: Christine b 15 Oct 1980; Graeme b 26 Jul 1983; Stephen b 23 Oct 1989; ord and ind to Alloa West 13 Jul 1988; Publ: *Ben Nevis and Glen Nevis*, Map and Notes (Nevisport/Sheffield University, 1972).

ALVA (FES X, 261, 262)

Formed 3 Jun 1981 by union of Alva Eadie and Alva St Serf's.

1968 ALBERT GARDINER
(FES IX, 66; X, 41, 206, 262, 319), trans from Carluke St Andrew's to Alva Eadie with St Serf's 12 Jun 1968; died 6 Dec 1981.

1982 GEORGE HUTTON BETHUNE STEEL
ord and ind to Alva 23 Jun 1982; trans to Williamwood 21 Feb 1990.

1990 ERNEST GEORGE SANGSTER
(FES X, 325, 442), trans from Edinburgh Blackhall St Columba's to Alva 1 Jul 1990; ret 19 Jun 1997.

1997 JAMES NIVEN RUDDOCK McNEIL
B 20 Feb 1962 at Glasgow, s of James M. and Pearl Crump; educ Crookston Castle, Glasgow 1974–80; University of Strathclyde 1980–84 (BSc); University of Aberdeen 1985–88 (BD); Night Watchman 1984–85; lic by Presb of Aberdeen 27 Jun 1988; asst Glasgow King's Park 1988–89; m 4 Sep 1992 Roseanna Blue b 5 Mar 1953 d of John B. and Margaret King; Children: Iona b 5 Jul 1993; Cairy b 28 Dec 1994; James b 1 Sep 1997; ord and ind to Castlemilk West 28 Jul 1990; trans to Alva 30 Oct 1997.

BALFRON (FES X, 214)

Formed 11 Jul 1967 by union of Balfron North and Balfron South. Linked 21 Apr 1994 with Fintry.

1927 THOMAS HUTCHISON BURNS-BEGG
(FES VIII, 274; IX, 357; X, 214), ord and ind to Balfron North 1 Apr 1927; ret 11 Jul 1967; died 14 Nov 1977.

1967 JOHN JAMIESON
(FES X, 214), ord and ind to Balfron 19 Nov 1967; ret 1 Oct 1993; s Robert m Audrey Allan; s Thomas m Fiona Dando; s David m Linda Kilpatrick.

1994 JOHN TURNBULL
B 27 Apr 1941 at Edinburgh, s of John T. and Jean Herdman McNeil Currie; educ Trinity Academy, Edinburgh 1946–56; University of Edinburgh 1989–92 (LTh); Police Officer 1960–89; lic by Presb of Lothian 2 Jul 1992; asst Penicuik North 1992–93; m 7 Sep 1962 Moira Gertrude Jack b 20 Aug 1941 d of Russell J. and Gertrude Campbell; Children: Ruth Margaret b 21 Jun 1965; John Russell Andrew b 13 Aug 1968; ord and ind to Balfron with Fintry 3 Oct 1994.

BALQUHIDDER (FES IV, 337; VIII, 396; IX, 441; X, 262)

Linked 29 Aug 1996 with Killin and Ardeonaig.

1973 DONALD ROBERTSON FRASER
(FES IX, 83, 505 (2); X, 262, 299, 367), trans from Forres St Laurence to Balquhidder 16 Aug 1973; trans to Huntly Cairnie Glass 19 Sep 1980.

1982 JAMES WILLIAM BENSON
(FES X, 364), trans from Rothiemurchus and Aviemore to Balquhidder 25 Aug 1982; ret 30 Apr 1996; m (2) 26 Mar 1988 Maureen Scott d of Robert S. and Margaret Girvan; d Julia m William Morrow; d Rachel m Charles Cusworth; d Grace m Robin Smith.

1997 JOHN LINCOLN
B 22 Feb 1946 at Peterborough, s of Alan Edward L. and Betty Longland; educ South Shields Grammar 1957–63; Sunderland Polytechnic 1965–69 (HND); Enfield College of Technology 1971–72 (CEI); Open University 1983 (MPhil); University of Edinburgh 1982–85 (BD); Electronic Engineering 1966–70; Lecturer (Acoustics and Electronics) 1972–80; Self-employed 1980–82; lic by Presb of Lothian 20 Jun 1985; asst Edinburgh Colinton 1985–86; m 22 Nov 1980 Julie Marion Walker b 22 Jul 1953 d of Thomas Alexander W. and Anne Elizabeth Macmillan; Children: Thomas b 29 Aug 1985; Rachel b 21 Sep 1989; ord and ind to Altnaharra and Farr 3 Jun 1986; trans to Balquhidder with Killin and Ardeonaig 19 Jun 1997; Publ: Papers in the *Journal of the Institute of Musical Instrument Technology* and in *Proceedings of the Institute of Acoustics*.

BANNOCKBURN ALLAN (FES IV, 297; VIII, 387; IX, 442; X, 262)

1966 ROBERT ALEXANDER JONES
(FES X, 262), ord and ind to Bannockburn Allan 29 Jun 1966; trans to Marnoch 9 May 1985.

1986 ROBERT S FYALL
ord and ind to Bannockburn Allan 30 Jul 1986; dem 31 Dec 1989 to take up app as Tutor, St John's College, Durham.

1990 JAMES LANDELS
B 13 Jun 1948 at Glasgow, s of James L. and Sarah Craig; educ Possilpark Secondary, Glasgow 1953–63; University of Glasgow 1984–89 (BD, CMin); Numerical Control and Part Programmer 1963–84; lic by Presb of Glasgow 3 Jul 1989; asst Cambuslang 1989–90; m 2 Sep 1972 Mary Higgins b 18 Jul 1951 d of Ronald H. and Rita Anderson; Children: James b 13 Sep 1973; Colin b 6 Mar 1979; ord and ind to Bannockburn Allan 2 Oct 1990.

BANNOCKBURN LADYWELL (FUF 305; FES IX, 442; X, 262)

1961 THOMAS KINLOCH
(FES IX, 594 (2); X, 262, 342), trans from Leochel Cushnie and Lynturk to Ladywell 22 Mar 1961; ret 31 Dec 1978; died 28 Feb 1993.

1979 CHARLES DOUGLAS McMILLAN
ord and ind to Ladywell 31 May 1979; trans to Elgin High 2 Nov 1991.

1992 IAN J M McDONALD
trans from Deerness with St Andrews to Ladywell 30 Sep 1992; dem 31 Jul 1996 on app as Chaplain to Kirkcaldy Acute Hospitals.

1997 ELIZABETH MARY DUNCAN ROBERTSON
B 9 Jan 1964 at Paisley, d of James Duncan R. and Mary Mulligan; educ Victoria Drive Secondary, Glasgow 1976–81; University of Glasgow 1989–94 (BD, CMin); Nursing (Paediatric and General) 1981–88; lic by Presb of Glasgow 6 Sep 1995; ord and ind to Ladywell 21 Aug 1997.

BRIDGE OF ALLAN CHALMERS (FUF 306; FES IX, 443; X, 262)

Linked 9 May 1979 with Lecropt. Linkage terminated 3 Apr 1983.

1952 WILLIAM CALDWELL MACDONALD
(FUF 23; FES IX, 31, 443; X, 262), trans from Edinburgh Palmerston Place to Chalmers 24 Sep 1952; ret 26 Oct 1975; died 15 Sep 1987.

1976 DAVID WILLIAM CLARK
ord by Presb of Aberdeen during assistantship at St Machar's Cathedral, Mar 1975; introd to Chalmers (term) 30 Sep 1976; ind to Cupar Old and St Michael of Tarvit 3 May 1979.

1979 WILLIAM MAYNE GILMOUR
(FES X, 193), trans from Coatbridge Townhead to Chalmers with Lecropt 14 Nov 1979; became minister of Lecropt following termination of linkage with Chalmers 3 Apr 1983.

1983 GRAHAM KEITH BLOUNT
trans from Glasgow Linthouse St Kenneth's to Chalmers and also app Chaplain (part-time) to University of Stirling 12 Oct 1983; trans to Falkirk Old and St Modan's (joint ministry) 22 Jun 1990.

1990 ALAN ANDERSON STUART REID
(FES X, 206, 220), res as Chaplain to University of Aberdeen and ind to Chalmers 9 Jan 1990; ret 16 Aug 1995; Addl children: James Stuart b 1 Mar 1981; Publ: Co-author of *Key Words of Faith* (St Andrew Press, 1992).

1996 ALEXANDER GARDNER HORSBURGH
B 18 Jun 1968 at Edinburgh, s of John Millar Stuart H. and Johann Catriona Gardner; educ Edinburgh Academy 1973–86; University of Aberdeen 1986–90 (MA), 1990–93 (BD); lic by Presb of Edinburgh 4 Jul 1993; asst Kirkwall St Magnus Cathedral 1993–96; ord by Presb of Orkney during assistantship at St Magnus Cathedral 16 Mar 1995; ind to Chalmers 24 Oct 1996; Chaplain (part-time) to University of Stirling.

BRIDGE OF ALLAN HOLY TRINITY (FES IX, 443; X, 262)

1966 IAN GRAY SCOTT
(FES X, 262), ind to Holy Trinity 2 Jun 1966; trans to Aberdeen Holburn Central 11 Mar 1976.

1976 KINNINBURGH JOHN TURNBULL
(FES IX, 286; X, 150, 169, 218), trans from Glasgow Drumchapel Old to Holy Trinity 14 Dec 1976; ret 15 Nov 1984; died 6 Mar 1994.

1985 JOHN CHALMERS NICOL
(FES X, 47, 424), app Principal Admin Asst of Argyll and Clyde Health Board 11 Dec 1978; Member of Institute of Health Services Management 1977–79; ind to Holy Trinity 1 Aug 1985.

BUCHANAN (FES III, 333; VIII, 274; IX, 360; X, 215)

Linked 1 Jul 1959 with Drymen.

1960 IAN ALISTER GRAY
(FES IX, 59, 417; X, 215, 253), trans from Perth St Andrew's to Buchanan with Drymen 27 Jan 1960; ret 6 Jun 1981; s Donald m Sandra; s Alastair m Lindsey.

1981 WILLIAM JOHN ROBERTSON HAY
(FES X, 115, 285), trans from Leslie Trinity to Buchanan with Drymen 25 Aug 1981; ret 31 Dec 1995; Addl children: Alexander John b 19 Jun 1977.

1997 ALEXANDER JAMES MACPHERSON
B 27 Jan 1955 at Glasgow, s of Alex M. and Joan Martin; educ Douglas Academy, Milngavie 1967–71; University of Glasgow 1981–85 (BD); Royal Navy 1969–73; Bank of Scotland 1975–80; lic by Presb of Glasgow, Jul 1985; asst Milngavie St Paul's 1985–87; m 14 Jul 1984 Ruth Marwick b 1 Jun 1956 d of John and Elizabeth M; ord by Presb of Dumbarton during assistantship at Milngavie St Paul's 4 Jun 1986; ind to Cullen and Deskford 1 May 1987; trans to Buchanan with Drymen 16 Jan 1997.

BUCHLYVIE (FES IX, 444; X, 262)

Linked 17 Mar 1983 with Gartmore.

1962   JOHN MILLIGAN LAING
(FES IX, 84, 596; X, 52, 262), trans from Penicuik South to Buchlyvie 28 Mar 1962; became minister of linked charge with Gartmore 17 Mar 1983; ret 7 Jan 1986; d Catherine m Robertson; Publ: *Bannockburn Allan Church 150 Years 1939–89* (1989).

1986   MOIRA GRACE MACCORMICK
B 25 Aug 1938 at Glasgow, d of Robert Callander Smith and Helen Greenhorn; educ Hyndland Secondary, Glasgow 1943–55; University of Glasgow 1982–85 (LTh); Open University 1988–92 (BA); Agriculture 1955–62; Farm Secretary 1970–82; lic by Presb of Irvine and Kilmarnock 27 Jun 1985; asst Kilmarnock Laigh 1984–85; Galston 1985–86; m 11 Jul 1962 Duncan Neil MacCormick b 24 Jan 1939 s of John McGregor M. and Mary Ann McColl; Children: Mairi b 9 Jan 1964 m William Duff; Iain b 21 Sep 1965 m Caroline Wolff; ord and ind to Buchlyvie with Gartmore 3 Jun 1986.

CALLANDER (FES X, 263)

Formed 1 Apr 1985 by union of Callander St Kessog's and Callander St Bride's.

1951   MALCOLM ALEXANDER MACCORQUODALE
(FES IX, 401, 410, 444; X, 263), trans from Kinlochleven to St Kessog's 25 Apr 1951; died 23 Jun 1981.

1965   WILLIAM HAY WATSON
(FES IX, 752; X, 263, 427), ind to St Bride's 12 May 1965; dem to take up app with Presb Church, Salisbury, Rhodesia 31 Oct 1970.

1971   JAMES BROWN DONALD
(FES IX, 10, 169; X, 7, 263), dem from Edinburgh Corstorphine Craigsbank and introd on term app to St Bride's 22 Jun 1971; ret 31 Oct 1975; died 22 Dec 1983.

1976   DOUGLAS MILLAR MURRAY
ord and introd to St Bride's (term) 4 Aug 1976; ind to Edinburgh John Ker Memorial in deferred union with Candlish 29 May 1980.

1981   REBECCA McCRAE LEASK
B 23 Apr 1920 at Ardrossan, d of John Beggs and Isabella Sinclair Laidley; educ Ardrossan Academy 1925–39; West of Scotland Commercial College 1939–40 (Dip Foreign Corresp); Glasgow School of Speech Therapy 1951–54 (LCST); University of Reading 1965–66 (DTST); University of Edinburgh 1974–76; Private Secretary 1940–51; Speech Therapist, Ayrshire Schools 1954–57; Regional Speech Therapist, Glasgow Hospitals and West

of Scotland 1957–69; Lecturer in Speech Therapy, Jordanhill College, Glasgow 1965–69; Deputy Director, Dublin College of Speech Therapy 1969–74; lic by Presb of Edinburgh 4 Jul 1976; asst Paisley Lylesland 1976–77; m 17 Sep 1986 Leo Leask (formerly Tocher) b 3 Jul 1908 s of Robert Tocher and Jane McAllister Leask; ord by Presb of Glasgow and introd as Assoc at Pollokshields 18 May 1977; introd to St Bride's on term app 15 Mar 1981; ret 23 Apr 1985.

1982   DAVID WHITE McCREADIE
(FES X, 167, 359), trans from Huntly to St Kessog's 27 May 1982; trans to Kirkmabreck 18 Apr 1985.

1985   IAIN McCORMICK GORING
B 22 Jul 1950 at Edinburgh, s of John McCormick G. and Agnes Cuthbertson McLean; educ Dunfermline High 1962–68; University of Edinburgh 1968–71 (BSc),1972–75 (BD); Civil Service 1971–72; lic by Presb of Dunfermline 3 Jul 1975; asst Milngavie St Luke's 1975–77; m 29 Mar 1976 Janet Chisholm Page b 21 Jul 1951 d of James Chisholm P. and Florence Gertrude Beacall; Children: Steven McLean b 28 Sep 1978; Sally Chisholm b 28 Feb 1982; Colin McCormick b 23 Oct 1983; ord by Presb of Dumbarton during assistantship at Milngavie St Luke's 1 Feb 1976; ind to Glasgow Lochwood 3 Jun 1977; trans to Callander 6 Jun 1985.

CAMBUSBARRON THE BRUCE MEMORIAL (FUF 308; FES IX, 445; X, 263)

'The Bruce Memorial' added to name 13 May 1976.

1945   ALEXANDER ROBERTSON SPARKE
(FES IX, 445; X, 263), admitted by General Assembly as Licentiate 1945; ord and ind to Cambusbarron 26 Dec 1945; ret 31 Aug 1973; died 26 Mar 1977.

1974   WILLIAM CRAIG
(FES X, 263), ord and ind to Cambusbarron 5 Jun 1974; ret 15 Nov 1997; Open University 1976–78 (BA); s William m Sandra Margaret Banks; s John m Fiona Jane Smith.

1998   BRIAN GORDON WEBSTER
B 10 Nov 1946 at Edinburgh, s of Alexander Allan W. and Elizabeth Francis Doctor; educ Greenock High 1951–65; Paisley College of Technology 1966–72 (BSc); University of Glasgow 1993–96 (BD); MIERE 1976 Chartered Engineer; MIEE 1988; Electronic Engineer and Computer Consultant 1970–93; lic by Presb of Greenock 1 Sep 1996; asst Greenock St Luke's 1996–98; m 25 May 1973 Fiona Livingstone Black b 26 Jun 1951 d of Allan Douglas B. and Sine Livingstone Climie; Children: Allan Martin b 12 Sep 1974; Simon Gordon b 26 Sep 1977; Jonathan David b 13 Feb 1980; ord and ind to The Bruce Memorial 21 Aug 1998.

CLACKMANNAN (FES IX, 445; X, 263)

1933 THOMAS CROUTHER GORDON
(FUF 270; IX 362, 445; X, 263), trans from Clyde-
bank Union to Clackmannan 22 Feb 1933; ret 30
Jun 1966; died 23 Dec 1987.

1967 GEORGE ALEXANDER McCUTCHEON
(FES IX, 168; X, 98, 263), trans from Auchinleck
to Clackmannan 14 Mar 1967; ret 31 Mar 1984;
Clerk to Presb of Stirling 1985–94.

1984 THOMAS RALPH TAYLOR
(FES X, 199), trans from Shotts Calderhead to
Clackmannan 27 Sep 1984; dem 31 Aug 1990 and
app Chaplain (part-time) to Glenochil Young
Offenders Institution.

1991 ERIC DOUGLAS AITKEN
(FES X, 415), res from app with Buckhaven Parish
Church Agency and ind to Clackmannan 3 Oct
1991; ret 15 Nov 1998; s Ewan Ritchie m Hilary
Brown; s Stewart Gregor m Katherine Quinn; s
Ronald Douglas m Vivien Rollo; Publ: *Words for a
Living* (St Andrew Press, 1983).

1999 JAMES GORDON MATHEW
(FES X, 51), trans from Scotstoun and Whiteinch
to Clackmannan 1 Jul 1999; Addl children: Ian
Gordon Alexander b 26 Jun 1978.

COWIE (FUF 309; FES IX, 446; X, 263)

Linked 3 Nov 1974 with Plean.

1975 DAVID ANDERSON
(FES X, 264), ord and ind to Cowie with Plean 26
Feb 1975; trans to Aberlour 2 Aug 1983.

1984 WILLIAM T CULLEN
ord and ind to Cowie with Plean 23 Feb 1984; trans
to Kilmarnock St John's Onthank 28 Nov 1989.

1990 IAN ROBERT STIRLING
ord and ind to Cowie with Plean 7 Jun 1990; trans
to Ayr Castlehill 9 Jun 1994.

1995 COLIN ALEXANDER SUTHERLAND
ord and ind to Cowie with Plean 23 Mar 1995; trans
to Ardrossan Barony St John's 3 Jun 1999.

DOLLAR (FES X, 264)

Formed 13 Jun 1979 by union of Dollar St
Columba's and Dollar West. Linked same date with
Glendevon with Muckhart.

1948 ANDREW HUGHES
(FES IX, 108, 446; X, 264), trans from Jedburgh
Boston Blackfriars to St Columba's 16 Dec 1948;
ret 28 Feb 1979; died 14 Sep 1989.

1958 JOHN MACDOUGALL MACKINNON
(FES IX, 313; X, 184, 264), trans from Glasgow
White Memorial to Dollar West 13 Mar 1958; ret
31 Dcc 1973.

1975 ARTHUR RAYMOND CHARLES GASTON
(FES X, 264, 267), trans from Sauchie to Dollar
West with Glendevon with Muckhart 21 Jan 1975;
became minister of united charge with Dollar St
Columba's 13 Jun 1979; dem 21 Sep 1989 and
introd to Geneva.

1979 JOHN BAIN BURNETT
(FES X, 405, 416), dem from Glasgow Priesthill
and introd as Assoc at Dollar with Muckhart with
Glendevon 26 Sep 1979; ret 9 Oct 1985; s Peter
m Jennifer Barras; d Gillian m Charles Boland; d
Sally m Alexander Scott; s John m Anne Milen-
kovic; d Susan m Kenneth Hunter.

1985 GEORGE FULLERTON MONTEATH
THOMSON
(FES X, 75, 83, 359), dem from Ettrick with Yarrow
and introd as Assoc at Dollar with Glendevon with
Muckhart 12 Oct 1985; ret 31 Oct 1988.

1989 RONALD McNISH MAXTON
(FES X, 26, 136), dem from Edinburgh Tron Kirk
Moredun and introd as Assoc at Dollar with Glen-
devon with Muckhart 29 Mar 1989; ret 1 Oct 1994.

1990 JOHN PETER SANDISON PURVES
B 6 Aug 1948 at Edinburgh, s of John P. and Annie
Winifred Sandison; educ Bathgate Academy 1960–
66; University of Edinburgh 1966–70 (BSc);
University of Aberdeen 1974–77 (BD); Teaching
(VSO) 1970–72; Adventure Playground Leader
1972–74; lic by Presb of West Lothian 30 Jun 1977;
asst Rutherglen Stonelaw 1977–78; m 1 Aug 1978
Patricia Kennedy b 28 Feb 1954 d of Charles K.
and Jean Anderson; Children: James Kennedy b
9 Jan 1981; Ellen Anne b 25 Sep 1984; ord by
Presb of Aberdeen 26 Oct 1978 and app Asst
Chaplain to University of Aberdeen; app by Board
of World Mission as Missionary with United Church
of Jamaica and Grand Cayman 1 Mar 1983; ind to
Dollar with Glendevon with Muckhart 27 Feb 1990.

1995 MARGARET McARTHUR
B 24 Jan 1963 at Tillicoultry, d of Alexander Shaw
McAllister and Margaret Wright Lindop; educ Alva
Academy 1975–80; University of Edinburgh 1987–
93 (BD, DipMin); Trustee Savings Bank 1980–83;
Insurance 1984–87; lic by Presb of Stirling 1 Dec
1993; asst Stirling North 1993–95; m 8 May 1982
Neil Morrison McArthur b 8 Jun 1952 s of John M.
and Margaret Morrison; Children: John Alexander
Neil b 4 Oct 1983; David Lindop Morrison b 18
May 1985; ord by Presb of Striling and introd as
Assoc at Dollar with Glendevon with Muckhart 29
Jun 1995.

DRYMEN (FES IX, 365; X, 218)

Linked 1 Jul 1959 with Buchanan.

1960 IAN ALISTER GRAY
(FES IX, 59, 417; X, 215, 253), trans from Perth St
Andrew's to Buchanan with Drymen 27 Jan 1960;
ret 6 Jun 1981.

1981 WILLIAM JOHN ROBERTSON HAY
(FES X, 115, 285), ind to Buchanan with Drymen 25 Aug 1981, see Buchanan.

1997 ALEXANDER JAMES MACPHERSON
ind to Buchanan with Drymen 16 Jan 1997, see Buchanan.

DUNBLANE CATHEDRAL (FES IV, 342; VIII, 397; IX, 447; X, 264)

1966 JOHN RODGER GRAY
(FES IX, 302; X, 178 (2), 264), trans from Glasgow St Stephen's Blythswood to Dunblane Cathedral 18 Aug 1966; Moderator of General Assembly 1977–78; ret 31 May 1984; died 9 Aug 1984.

1985 JAMES FERGUS MILLER
(FES X, 350), trans from Dumbarton Riverside to Dunblane Cathedral 12 Dec 1984; dem 31 Jul 1987.

1988 COLIN GEORGE McINTOSH
B 5 Apr 1951 at Glasgow, s of George Marr and Mary Hill; educ Govan High 1963–69; University of Glasgow 1969–72 (MA), 1972–75 (BD); lic by Presb of Glasgow 26 Jun 1975; asst Edinburgh St Ninian's Corstorphine 1975–76; m 11 Jul 1975 Linda Mary Henderson b 26 Apr 1953 d of Robert H. and Catherine Emma Bell Patrick; Children: Carolyn Anne b 6 Jan 1978; Jennifer Ruth b 26 Sep 1979; ord and ind to Glasgow St John's Renfield 26 Aug 1976; trans to Dunblane Cathedral 18 Aug 1988.

1994 MOIRA HERKES
dem from Prestonpans Prestongrange and introd as Assoc at Dunblane Cathedral 24 Mar 1994; ind to Dunfermline St Andrew's Erskine 22 Mar 1998.

DUNBLANE ST BLANE'S (FES IX, 447; X, 264)

1952 ALEXANDER ROBERTS
(FES IX, 160, 287, 447; X, 264), trans from Glasgow Cornwall Street to St Blane's 1 Oct 1952; ret 31 Dec 1973; died 6 Feb 1993.

1975 WILLIAM SUNTER
(FES X, 150, 264), trans from Glasgow Tron Balornock to St Blane's 28 Aug 1975; introd to Kingswells (term) 17 Feb 1983.

1980 JOHN CLARK
(FES IX, 474; X, 218, 281, 282 (2)), trans from Kennoway to St Blane's 18 Sep 1980; ret 30 Jun 1988; died 26 Nov 1997.

1988 GEORGE GEMMELL CRINGLES
B 26 Feb 1952 at Wishaw, s of George Gemmell C. and Alexandrina Cleland Russell; educ Carluke High and Wishaw High 1964–70; University of Glasgow 1975–80 (BD, CMin); Shop Asst 1970–

72; Printers Auxiliary 1972–75; lic by Presb of Hamilton 26 Jun 1980; asst Glasgow St John's Renfield 1980–81; m 16 Apr 1981 Janet Hunter Mathie b 3 Jan 1953 d of John M. and Robina Wemyss Young; Children: Ewen James b 25 Aug 1982; Douglas Ross b 4 Jul 1987; ord and ind to Alness 29 May 1981; trans to St Blane's 1 Nov 1988; Publ: Postscript to *Third Statistical Account of Scotland*, Vol 13: Parish of Alness (Scottish Academic Press, 1987).

FALLIN (FES IX, 448; X, 264)

1967 JAMES POTTER REID DRYSDALE
(FES X, 265), ord and ind to Fallin 1 Jun 1967; trans to Brechin Southesk 1 Jun 1978.

1978 ALEXANDER SELLARS DOWNIE
ord and ind to Fallin 1 Nov 1978; trans to Ardrossan Park 6 Jun 1985.

1986 ELEANOR DONALDSON MUIR
B 20 Jan 1957 at Dundee, d of Allan Ramsey Muir and Grace Margaret Thomson; educ Carnoustie High 1969–73; St Colm's College, Edinburgh 1978–80 (Diaconal Training); University of St Andrews 1980–85 (MTh, DPTh); Secretarial Asst 1976–78; lic by Presb of Dundee, Jun 1985; asst Falkirk Old 1985–86; ord and ind to Fallin 5 Jun 1986; app Chaplain (part-time) to Polmaise Colliery Jun 1986; app Chaplain (part-time) to Cornton Vale Prison Oct 1990.

FINTRY (FES III, 345; VIII, 277; IX, 367; X, 220)

Linked 21 Apr 1994 with Balfron.

1968 JAMES CALLAN WILSON
(FES X, 220, 406), trans from Shetland Nesting to Fintry 18 Jan 1968; ret 30 Jun 1972; died 26 Jul 1986.

1972 DAVID JOHNSTON
(FES IX, 488; X, 220, 291, 371), trans from Croy and Dalcross with Cawdor to Fintry 6 Dec 1972; ret 30 Jun 1982; died 5 Jan 1985.

1982 HAMISH NORMAN MACKENZIE McINTOSH
(FES IX, 247, 342; X, 105, 118, 447), ret from RAF Chaplains' Branch and ind to Fintry 25 Nov 1982; ret 31 Dec 1987.

1988 ARTHUR JAMES DOHERTY
ord by Church of the Nazarene, 1957; Social Worker and locum minister (Church of Scotland) 1969–86; admitted by General Assembly 1988 and ind to Fintry 24 Oct 1988; ret 31 Oct 1993.

1994 JOHN TURNBULL
ord and ind to Balfron with Fintry 3 Oct 1994, see Balfron.

GARGUNNOCK (FES IV, 307; VII, 390; IX, 448; X, 265)

Linked 27 Sepember 1994 with Kincardine-in-Menteith.

1934   WILLIAM TURNER
(FES IX, 448; X, 265), ord and ind to Gargunnock 6 Apr 1934; minister of linked charge with Kincardine-in-Menteith from 22 Jun 1958 until 1 Nov 1964; ret 8 Aug 1970.

1971   ROBERT LINDSAY MUIRHEAD
(FES IX, 328; X, 159, 194, 265), trans from Glasgow Gairbraid to Gargunnock 6 Jan 1971; ret 22 Jun 1981; died 3 Feb 1994.

1982   CATHERINE ANNE HEPBURN
ord and ind to Gargunnock 23 Mar 1982; became minister of linked charge with Kincardine-in-Menteith 27 Sep 1994.

GARTMORE (FES IX, 448; X, 265)

Union with Port of Menteith converted to temporary linkage May 1976. Linked 17 Mar 1983 with Buchlyvie.

1969   DAVID STEWART
(FES IX, 793; X, 267, 448), ind to Port of Menteith and Gartmore 4 Dec 1969; became minister of linked charge, May 1976, see Port of Menteith.

1983   JOHN MILLIGAN LAING
(FES IX, 84, 596; X, 52, 262), ind to Buchlyvie 28 Mar 1962; became minister of linked charge with Gartmore 17 Mar 1983, see Buchlyvie.

1986   MOIRA GRACE MACCORMICK
ord and ind to Buchlyvie with Gartmore 3 Jun 1986, see Buchlyvie.

GLENDEVON (FES IV, 275; VIII, 381; IX, 437; X, 265)

Linked 1 Aug 1955 with Muckhart. Further linked with Dollar West 14 Jul 1974 and with Dollar 13 Jun 1979.

1975   ARTHUR RAYMOND CHARLES GASTON
(FES X, 264, 267), trans from Sauchie to Dollar West with Glendevon with Muckhart 21 Jan 1975; became minister of united charge with Dollar St Columba's 13 Jun 1979; dem 21 Sep 1989 and introd to Geneva.

1979   JOHN BAIN BURNETT
(FES X, 405, 416), introd as Assoc at Dollar with Glendevon with Muckhart 26 Sep 1979, see Dollar.

1985   GEORGE FULLERTON MONTEATH THOMSON
(FES X, 75, 83, 359), dem from Ettrick with Yarrow and introd as Assoc at Dollar with Glendevon with Muckhart 12 Oct 1985; ret 31 Oct 1988.

1989   RONALD McNISH MAXTON
(FES X, 26, 136), introd as Assoc at Dollar with Glendevon with Muckhart 29 Mar 1989, see Dollar.

1990   JOHN PETER SANDISON PURVES
ind to Dollar with Glendevon with Muckhart 27 Feb 1990, see Dollar.

1995   MARGARET McARTHUR
introd as Assoc at Dollar with Glendevon with Muckhart 29 Jun 1995, see Dollar.

KILLEARN (FES IX, 371; X, 221)

1962   JOHN BARCLAY SKELLY
(FES IX, 227, 318; X, 131, 221), trans from Renfrew Old to Killearn 5 Sep 1962; ret 30 Jun 1971; died 11 Jun 1982.

1972   STUART WILSON McWILLIAM
(FES IX, 225, 558; X, 183, 221, 325), trans from Glasgow Wellington to Killearn 27 Jan 1972; ret 30 Apr 1981; d Elizabeth died 15 Jun 1988; w Margaret died 7 Oct 1991; Publ: Articles in *Journal for Preachers* (Decator, USA, 1984, 1986).

1981   ROBERT CAMBRIDGE SYMINGTON
(FES X, 19, 250), trans from Edinburgh Portobello Old and Windsor Place to Killearn 26 Nov 1981; introd as Community minister, Lorn and Mull 5 May 1992.

1993   PHILIP ROSS MACKINTOSH MALLOCH
trans from Inchbrayock with Montrose Melville South to Killearn 2 Dec 1993; Addl children: Christopher b 10 Feb 1976; d Ruth m David Chalmers; s Stephen m Valerie Carter; Publ: *The Future of the Family* (St Andrew Press, 1992); *Marriage Plus* (Board of Social Responsibility, 1993).

KILLIN AND ARDEONAIG (FES IX, 416; X, 245, 247)

Linked 29 Aug 1996 with Balquhidder.

1955   JOHN RODGERS COLQUHOUN
(FES IX, 200, 510; X, 247, 302), trans from Dundee Lochee West to Killin 18 May 1955; became minister of linked charge with Ardeonaig 29 Jul 1957 and of united charge 30 Mar 1967; ret 31 Oct 1976; died 11 Jun 1983.

1977   JOHN McRAE
ord and ind to Killin and Ardeonaig 6 May 1977; dem 11 Nov 1982.

1983   DAVID JOHN HENDERSON McNAUGHTON
B 3 Mar 1941 at Comrie, s of David Baird M. and Christina Margaret McDonald Ross; educ Hillhead High, Glasgow; Institute of Chartered Accountants of Scotland 1959–64; University of Glasgow 1971–75 (BD); Chartered Accountant

1964–71; lic by Presb of Glasgow 19 Aug 1975; asst Greenbank 1975–76; m 6 Mar 1971 Dorothy Aerts b 19 Aug 1938 d of Adriaan Gregoor Lodovicus A. and Barbara Bain; Children: Karen Ann b 6 Aug 1963 m Copping; Claire Madeleine b 2 Feb 1972 m Sinclair; Andrew Peter b 4 Jul 1977; David George b 16 Nov 1978; ord and ind to Dundee Douglas and Angus 1 Jun 1976; trans to Killin and Ardeonaig 1 Jun 1983; dem 1 Jun 1996 to write; Publ: *McNaughton's Step by Step Guide to the Taxation of Ministers of Religion 1997–98* (private, 1998); denominational variants of *McNaughton's Step by Step Guide to the Taxation of Priests, Pastors or Ministers of Religion 1998–99* (private, 1999).

1997　JOHN LINCOLN
ind to Balquhidder with Killin and Ardeonaig 19 Jun 1997, see Balquhidder.

KILMADOCK (FES X, 265)

Vacant from 1992.

1974　ALEXANDER EWING STRACHAN
(FES X, 265), ord and ind to Kilmadock 26 Jun 1974; dem on app by Overseas Council to Trinidad Greyfriars and St Ann's 22 Jul 1979.

1979　MICHAEL SIDNEY DAWSON
ord and ind to Kilmadock 15 Nov 1979; introd as Assoc at Edinburgh Holy Trinity 1 Jun 1992.

KINCARDINE-IN-MENTEITH (FES IV, 348; VIII, 399; IX, 449; X, 265)

Linkage with Norrieston terminated 4 Apr 1994. Linked 27 Sepember 1994 with Gargunnock.

1974　RONALD HUNT BROWN
(FES X, 266), ord and ind to Kincardine-in-Menteith with Norrieston 3 Jul 1974; trans to Musselburgh Northesk 21 Jul 1981.

1981　ARTHUR LAW
(FES X, 42, 225, 243), trans from Glassary and Kilmartin to Kincardine-in-Menteith with Norrieston 9 Dec 1981; ret 30 Jun 1988.

1988　ROBERT WILLIAM WILKIE IRVINE
(FES X, 83, 176), trans from Glasgow Tron St Mary's to Kincardine-in-Menteith with Norrieston 18 Nov 1988; Chaplain (part-time) to HM Prison and Young Offenders Institution Glenochil; ret 31 Jul 1993; d Irene m Simon Jones.

1994　CATHERINE ANNE HEPBURN
ord and ind to Gargunnock 23 Mar 1982; became minister of linked charge with Kincardine-in-Menteith 27 Sep 1994.

KIPPEN (FES IX, 449; X, 266)

Linked 6 Mar 1997 with Norrieston.

1956　ROBERT WILLIAM ALEXANDER BEGG
(FES IX, 373, 591, 669, 716; X, 266, 339), trans from Alford to Kippen 12 Sep 1956; ret 31 Aug 1974; died 4 Nov 1991.

1975　DONALD MACAULAY MACDONALD
(FES IX, 372, 657; X, 11, 266, 374), trans from Edinburgh Inverleith to Kippen 9 Apr 1975; ret 31 Oct 1985; d Lorna m Pratt; d Margaret m Colquhoun; d Elspeth m Smith.

1986　JAMES MARSHALL BUTTERY SCOULAR
(FES IX, 79, X, 49, 134, 221), trans from Greenock The Old Kirk to Kippen 13 Jun 1986; ret 31 May 1996; d Fiona m Kenneth Storrier; s Allan m Nanette.

1998　GORDON MACRAE
trans from Glasgow Tron St Mary's to Kippen with Norrieston 22 Jan 1998.

LECROPT (FES IV, 353; VIII, 400; IX, 450; X, 266)

Linked 9 May 1979 with Bridge of Allan Chalmers. Linkage terminated 3 Apr 1983.

1967　WILLIAM STEWART
(FES IX, 750; X, 266, 426), res as Principal of Serampore College, Bengal and ind to Lecropt 2 May 1967; ret 30 Jun 1978; died 17 Mar 1989.

1979　WILLIAM MAYNE GILMOUR
(FES X, 193), trans from Coatbridge Townhead to Bridge of Allan Chalmers with Lecropt 14 Nov 1979; became minister of Lecropt following termination of linkage with Chalmers 3 Apr 1983; Children: Andrew Kenneth b 15 Apr 1974; Ruth Ann b 17 Dec 1975.

LOGIE (FES IV, 354; VIII, 400; IX, 450; X, 266)

1965　DAVID MACINTYRE BELL ARMOUR SMITH
(FES IX, 44; X, 27, 168, 266), trans from Glasgow Old Partick to Logie 29 Apr 1965; DUniv (Stirling) 1983; Moderator of General Assembly 1985–86; ret 31 Jul 1989; died 22 Nov 1997; s David m Nina Susanne Weber; s Donald m Alison Denny.

1990　DAVID DONALD SCOTT
trans from Forth St Paul's to Logie Kirk 1 Mar 1990; trans to Bearsden New Kilpatrick 28 Apr 1999.

MENSTRIE (FES IV, 357; VIII, 401; IX, 450; X, 266)

1971　FINLAY ANGUS JOHN MACDONALD
(FES X, 266), ord and ind to Menstrie 2 Jun 1971; trans to Glasgow Jordanhill 2 Jun 1977.

1977　GEORGE TAYLOR SHERRY
B 26 Apr 1938 at Holytown, s of Michael S. and Marie Taylor; educ Bellshill Academy 1943–56; University of Glasgow 1971–76 (LTh); Chemistry

1956–66; Technical Rep 1966–71; lic by Presb of Hamilton, Jun 1976; asst Bellshill West 1976–77; m 3 Sep 1964 Ellen Phillips b 2 Dec 1942 d of John P. and Annie Hooks; Children: Yvonne b 31 Dec 1964 m Gary Shiels; Gordon b 8 May 1966; Graeme b 30 Dec 1967; George Phillips b 25 Nov 1971; ord and ind to Menstrie 12 Oct 1977; app Chaplain (part-time) to Glenochil Young Offenders Institution.

MUCKHART (FES V, 67; VIII, 419; IX, 468; X, 266)

Linked 1 Aug 1955 with Glendevon. Further linked 14 Jul 1974 with Dollar West and with Dollar 13 Jun 1979.

1975 ARTHUR RAYMOND CHARLES GASTON
(FES X, 264, 267), trans from Sauchie to Dollar West with Glendevon with Muckhart 21 Jan 1975; became minister of united charge with Dollar St Columba's 13 Jun 1979; dem 21 Sep 1989 and introd to Geneva.

1979 JOHN BAIN BURNETT
(FES X, 405, 416), introd as Assoc at Dollar with Glendevon with Muckhart 26 Sep 1979, see Dollar.

1985 GEORGE FULLERTON MONTEATH THOMSON
(FES X, 75, 83, 359), dem from Ettrick with Yarrow and introd as Assoc at Dollar with Glendevon with Muckhart 12 Oct 1985; ret 31 Oct 1988.

1989 RONALD McNISH MAXTON
(FES X, 26, 136), introd as Assoc at Dollar with Glendevon with Muckhart 29 Mar 1989, see Dollar.

1990 JOHN PETER SANDISON PURVES
ind to Dollar with Glendevon with Muckhart 27 Feb 1990, see Dollar.

1995 MARGARET McARTHUR
introd as Assoc at Dollar with Glendevon with Muckhart 29 Jun 1995, see Dollar.

NORRIESTON (FUF 312; FES IV, 358; VIII, 401; IX, 451; X, 266)

Linkage with Kincardine-in-Menteith terminated 4 Apr 1994. Linked 6 Mar 1997 with Kippen.

1974 RONALD HUNT BROWN
(FES X, 266), ord and ind to Kincardine-in-Menteith with Norrieston 3 Jul 1974; trans to Musselburgh Northesk 21 Jul 1981.

1981 ARTHUR LAW
(FES X, 42, 225, 243), trans from Glassary and Kilmartin to Kincardine-in-Menteith with Norrieston 9 Dec 1981; ret 30 Jun 1988.

1988 ROBERT WILLIAM WILKIE IRVINE
(FES X, 83, 176), ind to Kincardine-in-Menteith with Norrieston 18 Nov 1988, see Kincardine-in-Menteith.

1998 GORDON MACRAE
trans from Glasgow Tron St Mary's to Kippen with Norrieston 22 Jan 1998.

PLEAN (FES IV, 312; VIII, 391; IX, 451; X, 267)

Linked 3 Nov 1974 with Cowie.

1975 DAVID ANDERSON
(FES X, 264), ord and ind to Cowie with Plean 26 Feb 1975; trans to Aberlour 2 Aug 1983.

1984 WILLIAM T CULLEN
ord and ind to Cowie with Plean 23 Feb 1984; trans to Kilmarnock St John's Onthank 28 Nov 1989.

1990 IAN ROBERT STIRLING
ord and ind to Cowie with Plean 7 Jun 1990; trans to Ayr Castlehill 9 Jun 1994.

1995 COLIN ALEXANDER SUTHERLAND
ord and ind to Cowie with Plean 23 Mar 1995; trans to Ardrossan Barony St John's 3 Jun 1999.

PORT OF MENTEITH (FES X, 267)

Union with Gartmore severed May 1976. Temporary linkage with Gartmore from same date. Linked with Aberfoyle 17 Mar 1983.

1969 DAVID STEWART
(FES IX, 793; X, 267, 448), res as Chaplain, Ministry of Defence and ind to Port of Menteith and Gartmore 4 Dec 1969; became minister of linked charge, May 1976; ret 4 Dec 1982; died 6 May 1986.

1983 JAMES McMICHAEL ORR
(FES X, 162, 257, 424), ind to Aberfoyle 1 Dec 1976; became minister of linked charge with Port of Menteith 17 Mar 1983, see Aberfoyle.

1986 DAVID KIRK SPEED
(FES X, 237), trans from Stamperland to Aberfoyle with Port of Menteith 20 Nov 1986; trans to Glasgow Shettleston Old 3 Aug 1999.

SAUCHIE AND COALSNAUGHTON (FES X, 263, 267)

Formed 14 Jul 1994 by union of Coalsnaughton and Sauchie.

1959 JOHN BARCLAY
(FES IX, 149, 316; X, 186, 263), trans form Airdrie South Bridge Street to Coalsnaughton with Tillycoultry West 16 Jul 1959; ret 31 Dec 1969; died 18 Dec 1976.

1970 GEORGE HUNTER FOX
(FES X, 204, 263, 319, 387), trans from Wishaw Old to Coalsnaughton with Tillicoultry West 29 Jul 1970; became minister of Coalsnaughton following termination of linkage 6 Jun 1976; ret 30 Jun 1977; died 27 Mar 1992.

1975 NORMAN SWINBURNE
(FES X, 267, 333), trans from Aberdeen Torry to Sauchie 1 Jul 1975; ret 31 Oct 1993; d Melanie m Stephen Ibbitson; d Sally m Rafael White.

1977 JAMES McLAREN RITCHIE
(FES IX, 747; X, 16, 339, 424), res from service with Overseas Council in Yemen Arab Republic and ind to Coalsnaughton 28 Sep 1977; ret 27 Sepember 1985; Clerk to Presb of Lothian 1991–94; s Ian m Alyson Dow; d Kirsten m Mark Underwood; s Michael m Theresa Deehan; Publ: Tr and annotation of the *History of the Mazru'i Dynasty of Mombasa* (British Academy and OUP, 1995).

1986 MALCOLM HERBERT MACRAE
B 27 Sep 1945 at Lima, Peru, s of Malcolm Roderick M. and Annabella MacLeod; educ Inverness High and Arbroath High 1959–63; Free Church of Scotland College, Edinburgh 1965–68; University of Aberdeen 1969–71 (MA); University of St Andrews 1987–95 (PhD); lic by Presb of Perth (Free Church) 15 Jun 1971; ord by Free Presb of Glasgow and ind to Coatbridge West 5 Nov 1971; admitted by General Assembly 1984; assistant-ships at Dunblane Cathedral and Mull 1984–86; ind to Coalsnaughton 28 May 1986; dem 31 Jul 1994; Chaplain (part-time) to County Hospital, Alloa 1986–94; Pastoral Asst at Stirling Allan Park South with Church of the Holy Rude 1994–96; Chaplain (part-time) to Sauchie Hospital and to Glenochil Young Offenders Institution from 1994; Publ: *Intuitionism* (PhD Thesis, 1995).

1995 AGNES ADAM MOORE
B 8 May 1952 at Stirling, d of David Moore and Ellen Thomson Scott; educ Stirling High 1964–68; University of Glasgow 1982–86 (BD); Clerical Officer 1968–82; lic by Presb of Stirling, Jun 1986; asst Glasgow St John's Renfield 1986–87; ord and ind to Renton Trinity 23 Jun 1987; trans to Sauchie and Coalsnaughton 6 Jan 1995.

STIRLING ALLAN PARK SOUTH (FUF 312; FES IX, 452; X, 267)

Linked 1 Jul 1984 with Stirling Church of the Holy Rude.

1950 IAIN DUNCAN MACCALLUM
(FES IX, 293, 454; X, 268, 269), trans from Glasgow St Clement's to Stirling South 31 Jan 1950; became minister of united charge with Stirling Allan Park 3 May 1970; ret 30 Jun 1984.

1985 IAN MURRAY POLLOCK DAVIDSON
(FES X, 111, 189, 258), trans from Cambuslang Old to Allan Park South with Church of the Holy Rude 25 Apr 1985; ret 31 Jul 1994; MBE (1993); s David m Lyn Haycock; Publ: *At the Sign of the Fish* (Cambuslang Old, 1975); *A Guide to the Church of the Holy Rude* (Church of the Holy Rude, 1990).

1996 MORRIS COWPER COULL
(FES X, 105), trans from Glasgow Hillington Park to Allan Park South with Church of the Holy Rude 29 Feb 1996; Children: Charles Stewart b 4 Mar 1976; Katherine Cowper b 3 May 1977.

STIRLING CHURCH OF THE HOLY RUDE (FES IX, 452; X, 268)

Linked 1 Jul 1984 with Stirling Allan Park South.

1955 CHARLES BENJAMIN EDIE
(FES IX, 18, 72; X, 12, 268), trans from Juniper Green St Margaret's to Church of the Holy Rude 13 Apr 1955; ret 30 Jun 1984.

1985 IAN MURRAY POLLOCK DAVIDSON
(FES X, 111, 189, 258), trans from Cambuslang Old to Allan Park South with Church of the Holy Rude 25 Apr 1985; ret 31 Jul 1994.

1996 MORRIS COWPER COULL
(FES X, 105), ind to Allan Park South with Church of the Holy Rude 29 Feb 1996, see Allan Park South.

STIRLING ERSKINE-MARYKIRK (FES IX, 452; X, 268)

Congregation dissolved 20 May 1969.

1948 ROBERT FERGUSON
(FES IX, 452, 580, 713; X, 268), trans from Newhills to Erskine-Marykirk 4 Nov 1948; ret 31 Dec 1968; died 28 Mar 1985.

STIRLING NORTH (FES IX, 328; VIII, 394; IX, 452; X, 268)

1963 DUNCAN McKENZIE BRUCE
(FES IX, 565; X, 48, 268, 328), trans from Dalkeith St John's and King's Park to Stirling North 16 Jan 1963; trans to Muthill 26 Oct 1977.

1978 PAUL MARTIN NEWMAN SEWELL
(FES X, 288), trans from Windygates and Balgonie to Stirling North 15 Mar 1978; Addl children: Steven b 29 May 1979.

STIRLING ST ANDREW'S (FUF 315; FES IX, 453; X, 268)

Congregation dissolved 18 Jun 1967.

1953 NORMAN BROOK
(FES IX, 420, 453, 556, 701; X, 268), trans from Montrose St Luke's and introd on term app to St Andrew's 9 Jun 1953; res from app 31 Mar 1965; died 30 Sep 1992.

STIRLING ST COLUMBA'S (FUF 313; FES IX, 453; X, 268)

1970 WILLIAM GRANT ANDERSON
(FES IX, 140, 334; X, 65, 199, 268), trans from Hawick Old to St Columba's 1 Oct 1970; ret 31 Oct 1985; died 18 May 1994.

1988 BARRY WILLIAM DUNSMORE
B 27 Jan 1954 at Glasgow, s of William D. and Mildred Laing; educ Hillhead High, Glasgow 1966–72; University of Glasgow 1974–80 (MA, BD); Hospital Admin 1972–74; lic by Presb of Glasgow 26 Jun 1980; asst Bearsden South 1981–82; m 12 Jul 1978 Hilda Burns b 22 Feb 1956 d of Thomas B. and Jessie Smith; Children: Jennifer Mimi b 9 May 1984; Philip Barry b 27 Nov 1986; ord and ind to Saltcoats Erskine 29 Sep 1982; trans to St Columba's 4 Feb 1988.

STIRLING ST MARK'S (FES IX, 453; X, 268)

1970 FREDERICK MINTY BOOTH
(FES X, 268), ord and ind to St Mark's 27 Aug 1970; dem on app by Board of World Mission for service with United Church of Jamaica and Grand Cayman in Brownsville, 14 Aug 1976.

1976 WILLIAM JOHN HARVEY
(FES X, 165, 454), Warden of Iona Abbey 1971–76; ind to St Mark's 21 Dec 1976; trans to Govan Old 3 Sep 1981.

1982 ALEXANDER BUCHAN NOBLE
ord and ind to St Mark's 6 Jan 1982; trans to Dunbar 16 Sep 1993.

1995 RODNEY PRENTICE TAYLOR ROBB
B 30 Oct 1948 at Dewsbury, Yorkshire, s of Douglas McKecknie R. and Caroline Torrance Prentice; educ Eastwood Secondary, Giffnock and George Watson's, Edinburgh 1959–64; University of Edinburgh 1988–92 (BD); Banking 1971–88; lic by Presb of Paisley 25 Feb 1993; m 7 Jun 1979 Christine Isabell Dunbar b 23 Feb 1956 d of Robert D. and Christina Sorley; Children: Gavin David b 25 Oct 1980; Mark Taylor b 1 Oct 1983; ord and ind to St Mark's 2 Mar 1995.

STIRLING ST NINIANS OLD (FES IV, 313; VIII, 391; IX, 453; X, 268)

1940 DAVID DICK
(FES VIII, 487; IX, 149, 454, 506; X, 268), trans from Torthorwald to St Ninians Old 12 Jun 1940; ret 30 Sep 1968; died 17 Apr 1984.

1969 JAMES STIRLING
(FES X, 261, 269), trans from Alloa St Andrew's to St Ninians Old 4 Jun 1969; ret 28 Feb 1998; s (James) Gregor m Yvonne Bowman; d Rhona m Anthony Bellis; s Fraser m Anne Coyne.

1998 GARY JOHN McINTYRE
B 15 Jun 1967 at Glasgow, s of John McPherson M. and Maria McIvor McSporran; educ Campbeltown Grammar 1979–85; University of Aberdeen 1986–90 (BD); University of Glasgow 1990–92 (DipMin); lic by Presb of South Argyll 26 Jun 1992; asst Upper Tweeddale 1992–93; ord and ind to Kingarth and Kilchattan Bay with Rothesay The High Kirk 12 May 1993; trans to St Ninians Old 19 Nov 1998.

STIRLING VIEWFIELD (FUF 314; FES IX, 454; X, 269)

1937 GEORGE THOMAS JAMIESON
(FES IX, 454; X, 269), ord by Presb of Edinburgh during assistantship at St Stephen's; ind to Viewfield 7 Sep 1937; ret 31 Oct 1969.

1970 JOHN SCOTT
(FES X, 269, 270), trans from Paisley Abbey to Viewfield 7 May 1970; trans to Aberdour St Fillan's 3 Dec 1975.

1976 ALASTAIR GILBERT HUNTER
ord and ind to Viewfield 27 May 1976; dem 31 Dec 1979 on app as Lecturer in Hebrew and Old Testament, University of Glasgow.

1980 ANDREW RANKIN COWIE McLELLAN
(FES X, 132), trans from Greenock Cartsburn Augine to Viewfield 27 Aug 1980; trans to Edinburgh St Andrew's and St George's 30 Apr 1986.

1987 IAIN AULAY MACLEOD MACRITCHIE
ord and ind to Viewfield 24 Jun 1987; introd as Pastoral Asst, Aberdeen Beechgrove and app Teaching Asst, Christ's College, University of Aberdeen 1 Oct 1992.

1995 IAN TAYLOR
B 4 Jul 1964 at Hamilton, s of William Joseph Bryce T. and Elizabeth Pye Henderson; educ Hamilton Grammar 1976–81; Assoc of the Chartered Institute of Bankers in Scotland 1987; University of Glasgow 1988–92 (BD); Princeton Theological Seminary, New Jersey 1992–93 (ThM); International Credit Analyst (Bank of Scotland) 1981–88; lic by Presb of Hamilton 31 Aug 1993; asst Wishaw St Mark's 1993–95; m 5 Jul 1990 Catherine Jane Kerr b 3 Dec 1965 d of David McVey K. and Andrewina Adams Scott; Children: Joshua David b 8 Jan 1995; ord and ind to Viewfield 26 Oct 1995.

STRATHBLANE (FES IX, 375; X, 224)

1969 MALCOLM ALEXANDER RITCHIE
(FES X, 224, 299), trans from Dundee Broughty Ferry St James' to Strathblane 13 Oct 1969; trans to Kilbrandon and Kilchattan 8 Jun 1982.

1983 ALEXANDER FISHER FLEMING
(FES X, 146, 280), trans from Lenzie Old to Strathblane 26 Jan 1983; ret 30 Jan 1995; s Iain m Juliette Howey; Publ: *The Stained Glass in Strathblane Parish Church* (Lomondside Press, 1994).

1995 ALEXANDER HANLEY GREEN
B 29 Sep 1944 at Glasgow, s of John G. and Adeline Dawson Hanley; educ Knightswood Secondary, Glasgow 1956–59; University of Glasgow 1976–80 (MA), 1980–83 (BD); Legal Profession 1960–76; lic by Presb of Dumbarton 13 Jan 1985; asst Milngavie Cairns 1984–86; m 3 Aug 1979 Jean Plant b 22 Aug 1952 d of Alex P. and Marion Reid; Children: David b 30 Aug 1981; Jennifer b 20 Aug 1983; Kirsty b 16 Dec 1986; ord and ind to Glasgow South Carntyne 5 Feb 1986; trans to Strathblane 2 Nov 1995.

TILLICOULTRY (FES X, 269)

Formed 6 Jun 1976 by union of Tillicoultry St Serf's and Tillicoultry West.

1956 PATRICK DOUGLAS GORDON CAMPBELL
(FES IX, 434; X, 258, 269), trans from Comrie Old to St Serf's 2 Oct 1956; became minister of united charge with West 6 Jun 1976; dem 9 Oct 1977 on app to Geneva.

1978 JOHN RUSSELL
(FES X, 235, 414), trans from Southend to Tillicoultry 2 Feb 1978; s Andrew m Justine Sarah Overton.

TULLIBODY ST SERF'S (FUF 316; FES IX, 455; X, 269)

1968 CHARLES CHIRNSIDE
(FES IX, 730; X, 269, 417), res from service with Overseas Council in Pakistan and ind to St Serf's 6 Jun 1968; ret 15 Jun 1986; s David m Susan Bain; d Fiona m Peter Johnson; d Ruth m Adrian Clarke.

1986 ANDREW B DICK
ord and ind to St Serf's 15 Oct 1986; trans to Musselburgh St Michael's Inveresk 5 Aug 1999.

PRESBYTERY OF DUNFERMLINE

ABERDOUR ST FILLAN'S (FES X, 270)

1965 DAVID WEDDERBURN RUTHERFORD
(FES IX, 356, 456, 747; X, 270 (2)), ind to Aberdour and Dalgety 22 Feb 1949; continued as minister of Aberdour St Fillan's after severence of union 30 Jun 1965; ret 30 May 1975; died 17 Sep 1999; d Jan m Isles.

1975 JOHN SCOTT
(FES X, 269, 270), trans from Stirling Viewfield to St Fillan's 3 Dec 1975; ret 30 Jun 1996; s John m Francesca Higgins; s Murray m Julie Smith; d Aileen m Paul Johnson.

1997 PETER BUCHANAN PARK
B 28 May 1949 at Glasgow, s of Eric P. and Mary Cox; educ Bellahouston Academy, Glasgow 1961–67; University of Glasgow 1992–95 (BD); Banking 1968–91; lic by Presb of Dumbarton 5 Jul 1995; m 16 Jun 1973 Mari Rae b 1 May 1952 d of Lewis R. and Elizabeth Anderson; Children: Graham Scott b 2 Apr 1976; Barry Andrew b 9 Nov 1978; ord and ind to St Fillan's 9 Jan 1997.

BALLINGRY (FES V, 57; VIII, 417; IX, 456; X, 270)

1971 WILLIAM GRAY
(FES X, 270), ord and ind to Ballingry 11 Aug 1971; trans to Kirkintilloch St Columba's 24 Aug 1976.

1977 WILLIAM ALEXANDER BINNIE RITCHIE
ord and ind to Ballingry 19 May 1977; trans to Connel 16 May 1984.

1985 SHARON ELIZABETH FAIRBAIRN COLVIN
ord and ind to Ballingry 28 Jun 1985; trans to Airdrie Jackson 17 Jun 1998.

BEATH AND COWDENBEATH NORTH (FES X, 270, 271)

Formed 9 Dec 1998 by union of Beath (linked 6 Feb 1962 with Cowdenbeath Guthrie Memorial) and Cowdenbeath North (union 1 Jun 1972 of Guthrie Memorial and Lumphinnans).

1929 GEORGE PORTEOUS McWILLIAM
(FES VI, 143; VIII, 406; IX, 456; X, 270), trans from Towie to Beath 16 Oct 1929; ret 1 May 1961; died 29 Sep 1984.

1969 PETER CRIGHTON RAE
(FES X, 270, 277), ord by Presb of Elgin during assistantship at Elgin St Giles' 25 Feb 1968; ind to Lumphinnans 27 Aug 1969; became minister of united charge of Cowdenbeath North with Beath 1 Jun 1972; became minister of united charge 9 Dec 1998; d Elizabeth m Timothy Lynn.

CAIRNEYHILL (FUF 345; FES IX, 457; X, 271)

Linkage with Torryburn and Newmills terminated 1 Sep 1983. Linked same date with Limekilns.

1946 WILLIAM LOUDON CUNNINGHAM
(FES IX, 323, 457, 580; X, 271), trans from Chapelhall to Cairneyhill 18 Dec 1946; ret 31 May 1968; died 20 Nov 1994.

1968 DAVID YULE ARCHIBALD
(FES X, 93, 278), trans from Bargrennan to Torryburn and Newmills 23 Aug 1961; became minister of linked charge with Cairneyhill 1 Jun 1968; ret 1 Aug 1983.

1984 ROBERT JOHN HENDERSON
(FES X, 73, 218, 366), trans from Melrose St Cuthbert's to Cairneyhill with Limekilns 23 Feb 1984; ret 30 Jun 1990; died 25 Apr 1999; w Margaret died 25 Jun 1982; m (2) 21 Jun 1983 Charlotte McKenzie Clunie b 23 Mar 1926 d of William Fingzies C. and Charlotte McKenzie; s Michael m Agnes Gillies; s John m Fionna Milne; d Rachel m John Taylor.

1990 NORMAN MILLER GRANT
B 22 Apr 1957 at Perth, s of Norman G. and Helen Miller; educ Galashiels Academy 1969–75; University of Edinburgh 1975–76, 1984–89 (BD, DipMin); Quality Controller 1976–84; lic by Presb of Edinburgh 1 Oct 1989; asst Edinburgh Barclay 1989–90; m 22 Aug 1980 Karen Penelope Constance Duncan b 15 Nov 1956 d of Andrew D. and Constance Godfrey; Children: Sarah Louise b 23 Feb 1984; Eleanor Kathryn b 28 Aug 1986; James Peter b 10 Jun 1990; ord and ind to Cairneyhill with Limekilns 26 Oct 1990.

CARNOCK AND OAKLEY (FES V, 7; VIII, 407; IX, 457; X, 271)

Name changed from Carnock 1994.

1975 ALISTER JOHN GOSS
(FES X, 271), ord and ind to Carnock 15 May 1975; dem on app as Industrial Chaplain (URC) in Hertfordshire and Bedfordshire 1 Jan 1980; ind to Edinburgh St Andrew's Clermiston 24 Jul 1985.

1980 ROBERT KELLAS HALL
(FES X, 48), trans from Glencorse with Roslin to Carnock 16 Oct 1980; ret 31 Jul 1988.

1989 ELIZABETH SHEDDON SMITH KENNY
B 6 Nov 1944 at Dunfermline, d of John K. and Euphemia Sheddon Glancy; educ Queen Anne School, Dunfermline 1956–60; University of Edinburgh 1983–87 (BD); Nursing and Midwifery 1963–73, 1976–83; Missionary in Peru 1973–76; lic by Presb of Dunfermline 5 Jul 1987; asst Dunfermline St Margaret's 1987–89; ord and ind to Carnock 17 Feb 1989.

COWDENBEATH TRINITY (FES X, 271, 277)

Formed 18 Nov 1998 by union of Cowdenbeath West with Mossgreen and Crossgates (linked 24 Apr 1986) and Cowdenbeath Cairns. Name changed 1999 from South to Trinity.

1962 JOHN ANGUS MACLEOD
(FES X, 38, 271), trans from Falkirk Irving Camelon to Cairns 27 Jun 1962; trans to Keith St Rufus 14 May 1976.

1968 ALEXANDER JAMES SHAW
(FES X, 271), ord and ind to Cowdenbeath West 1 May 1968; trans to Ardclach with Auldearn and Dalmore 20 Dec 1984.

1970 ERIC BURKINSHAW
(FES X, 277), ord and ind to Mossgreen and Crossgates 13 Jul 1970; trans to Coatbridge Gartsherrie 22 Sep 1977.

1976 SVEN (SVEINBJÖRN) SESSELIUS BJARNASON
ind to Cairns 24 Nov 1976; dem 31 Aug 1987; ind to Kirkmichael and Tomintoul 26 May 1992.

1978 JAMES CARSON STRACHAN
(FES IX, 421, 793; X, 93, 349, 448), trans from Lonmay with Rathen West to Mossgreen and Crossgates 25 Oct 1978; trans to Hobkirk with Southdean 11 May 1983.

1984 ROBERT JOHN REID
(FES X, 156, 306), dem from Glasgow Cranhill 12 Apr 1984 and introd on term app to Mossgreen and Crossgates; res from app 1985; died 5 Dec 1992.

1986 EVAN JOHN ROSS
B 6 Oct 1933 at Glasgow, s of Evan John R. and Jane Mowat; educ Shawlands Academy, Glasgow 1938–49; University of Glasgow 1959–60; University of Edinburgh 1981–84 (LTh); Commerce and Industry 1949–59; National Service (RAF) 1952–54; Social Work 1959–81; lic by Presb of Falkirk 27 Jun 1984; asst Bo'ness Old 1984–85; m 4 Sep 1959 Helena Rose Hamilton b 16 Jan 1931 d of Arthur William H. and Helen Ward; Children: Fiona Jane b 2 Feb 1961 m McGleave; Alison Helen b 14 Jun 1963; Kirsten Joy b 5 Feb 1967; ord and ind to Cowdenbeath West with Mossgreen Crossgates 24 Apr 1986; ret 6 Oct 1998.

1988 GEORGE IRVINE HASTIE
(FES X, 5), dem from Edinburgh Burdiehouse 1 Feb 1987; ind to Cairns 11 May 1988; trans to Mearns Coastal Parish 12 Feb 1998.

1999 DAVID GEORGE ADAMS
B 14 May 1946 at Kirkcaldy, s of David A. and Ada Watters; educ King Edward VI Grammar, Stafford 1951–62; University of St Andrews 1986–90 (BD); Insurance 1970–77; Self-employed 1977–89; lic by Presb of Kirkcaldy 17 Mar 1991; asst Methil 1989–90; Auchterderran with Kinglassie 1990–91; m 14 Oct 1967 Rosemary Worthington b 19 Jul 1947 d of Kenneth W. and Evelyn Hollinshead; Children: Denise b 17 Dec 1970; Christopher b 5 Feb 1975; Gillian b 11 Jul 1991; ord and ind to Sanquhar St Bride's 12 Dec 1991; trans to Trinity 29 Apr 1999.

CULROSS AND TORRYBURN (FES X, 272, 278)

Formed 1 Sep 1983 by union of Culross Abbey and Torryburn and Newmills.

1954 ARCHIBALD BARCLAY ANDERSON WILSON
(FES IX, 470, 712; X, 278), trans from Durham Waddington Street to Torryburn and Newmills 4 Mar 1954; dem 27 Aug 1960; died 10 Jan 1997.

1960 ANDREW QUEEN MORTON
(FES IX, 605; X, 272, 348), trans from Fraserburgh St Andrew's to Culross 29 Oct 1960; became minister of united charge with Torryburn and Newmills 1 Sep 1983; ret 31 Jan 1987; d Julian Thomas; Addl publ: *Literary Detection* (Bowker, 1978); co-author of *The Genesis of John* (1980); *The Making of Mark* (1996); *The Gathering of the Gospels* (1997).

1961 DAVID YULE ARCHIBALD
(FES X, 93, 278), trans from Bargrennan to Torryburn and Newmills 23 Aug 1961; became minister of linked charge with Cairneyhill 1 Jun 1968; ret 1 Aug 1983; w Isobel died 13 Oct 1997; d Margaret m Eric Brown.

1987 ALISON ESTHER PHYLLIS NORMAN
ord by Presb of Hamilton during assistantship at Hamilton Old 1 Mar 1987; ind to Culross and Torryburn 10 Sep 1987; dem 1 Oct 1992 on app by Royal Naval Chaplaincy Service.

1993 DAVID WILLIAMSON WHYTE
ord and ind to Culross and Torryburn 12 Feb 1993; trans to Boat of Garten and Kincardine with Duthil 5 Mar 1999.

DALGETY (FES V, 21; VIII, 408; IX, 459; X, 272)

1971 PETER KENNETH ELSTON
(FES X, 272), admitted by General Assembly 1969; Asst Edinburgh Tron Kirk Moredun 1969–70; ind to Dalgety 6 Jan 1971; ret 1 Nov 1999.

DUNFERMLINE ABBEY (FES IX, 460; X, 272)

1969 STEWART MACCOLL MACPHERSON
(FES IX, 104; X, 62, 171, 210, 272), trans from Glasgow Queen's Park West to Dunfermline Abbey 10 Sep 1969; ret 5 Nov 1990.

1991 ALISTAIR LINDSAY JESSAMINE
B 17 Jun 1949 at Hill of Beath, Fife, s of John J. and Helen Allan; educ Beath High, Cowdenbeath 1961–66; University of Edinburgh 1971–78 (MA, BD); Civil Service 1967–71; lic by Presb of Dunfermline 29 Jun 1978; asst Glasgow Newlands South 1978–79; m 3 Oct 1994 Eleanor Moore d of Andrew M. and Jeannie McRae; ord and ind to Chapelton with Strathaven Rankin 28 Aug 1979; trans to Dunfermline Abbey 19 Mar 1991.

DUNFERMLINE GILLESPIE MEMORIAL (FUF 348; FES IX, 460; X, 273)

1962 JOHN McCORMICK GORING
(FES X, 206, 273), trans from Carluke St John's to Gillespie Memorial 31 May 1962; ret 31 Aug 1988; s Iain m Janet Page; d Elspeth m Gordon Strachan; s Hugh m Julie Millar; d Alison m Anthony Cook.

1988 ANDREW GORDON REID
B 17 Jun 1943 at Glasgow, s of Andrew R. and Isabel Anderson; educ Eastbank Academy, Glasgow 1955–61; University of Glasgow 1961–64 (BSc); University of Edinburgh 1973–76 (BD); Teaching 1965–73 (Mathematics), 1976–82 (RE); lic by Presb of Bathgate, Jun 1970; m 29 Mar 1969 Evelyn Phair b 1 Aug 1947 d of Robert P. and Evelyn Munro; Children: Greg b 7 Jan 1970; Fiona Eilean b 20 Feb 1972; Catherine Isobel Evelyn b 8 Oct 1979; ord and ind to Maybole Old 18 Jun 1982; trans to Gillespie Memorial 15 Dec 1988.

DUNFERMLINE NORTH (FES VIII, 410; IX, 460; X, 273)

1968 GORDON FRASER CAMPBELL JENKINS
(FES X, 273), ord and ind to Dunfermline North 5 Dec 1968; dem to take up app as Deputy General Secretary, Board of Education 5 Sep 1988.

1989 STEVEN REID
ord and ind to Dunfermline North 15 Jun 1989; trans to Crossford with Kirkfieldbank 3 Oct 1997.

1998 GORDON FRASER CAMPBELL JENKINS
(FES X, 273), res as Asst Secretary, Board of Ministry 31 May 1997; loc ten Lochgelly Macainsh 1 Nov 1997; ind to Dunfermline North 25 Jun 1998; University of Edinburgh 1988 (PhD); d Marion m Lawson; Publ: *Goldfrum Church* (private, 1985); PhD Thesis: 'Establishment and Dissent in the Dunfermline Area 1733–1883' (Univ of Edinburgh, 1988); articles in *Dictionary of Scottish Church History and Theology* (T&T Clark, 1993).

DUNFERMLINE ST ANDREW'S ERSKINE (FES X, 273)

1974 JAMES LAIRD
(FES X, 273, 292), trans from Strathmiglo to St Andrew's Erskine 23 Jan 1974; died 30 Nov 1996.

1998 MOIRA HERKES
res as Assoc at Dunblane Cathedral and ind to St Andrew's Erskine 22 Mar 1998; trans to Brechin Gardner Memorial 20 Oct 1999.

DUNFERMLINE ST LEONARD'S (FES V, 41; VIII, 410; IX, 462; X, 273)

1957 ROBERT PATERSON MACKENZIE
(FES IX, 121, 740; X, 71, 273), trans from Channelkirk to St Leonard's 10 Apr 1957; Junior Clerk to Presb of Dunfermline and Kinross 1959–61; Clerk 1961–71; ret 31 May 1980; w Jessie died 27 May 1994.

1981 ALEXANDER BELL MITCHELL
B 28 Jun 1949 at Baillieston, s of David M. and Elizabeth Taylor; educ Uddingston Grammar 1960–65; Jordanhill College, Glasgow 1971–73 (DipTEd); University of Edinburgh 1975–79 (BD); Mechanical Engineering 1965–71; Teaching 1973–75; lic by Presb of Hamilton 28 Jun 1979; asst Dunblane Cathedral 1979–81; m 20 Mar 1976 Elizabeth Wallace Brodie b 14 Sep 1954 d of Thomas B. and Catherine Wallace; Children: Hazel b 27 Feb 1977; David b 12 Feb 1980; Kirsty b 31 Dec 1984; ord and ind to St Leonard's 18 Feb 1981.

DUNFERMLINE ST MARGARET'S (FUF 349; FES IX, 462; X, 274)

1948 ERIC MARR DUNCAN
(FES IX, 134, 463, 722; X, 274), res from World Student Christian Federation, Geneva and ind to St Margaret's 27 Oct 1948; dem 5 Feb 1960 to enter teaching profession (RE); died 23 Mar 1997.

1960 DUNCAN McLACHLAN
(FES X, 130, 230, 274), trans from Kirn St Margaret's to St Margaret's 21 Jun 1960; trans to Paisley Sherwood 23 Jun 1965.

1966 COLIN CAMPBELL REITH MACPHERSON
(FES X, 274, 345), trans from Inverurie West to St Margaret's 3 Feb 1966; ret 31 May 1996.

1996   FIONA MINA RICHARD
B 25 Feb 1962 at Abingdon, d of Harold William Nicolson and Martha Georgina Mitchell Roberts; educ Denny High 1974–79; Queen Margaret College, Edinburgh 1979–82 (BA); University of Stirling 1986–88 (CQSW); University of Glasgow 1992–95 (BD); VSO, Sri Lanka 1982–85; Social Work 1988–92; lic by Presb of Falkirk 27 Jun 1995; m 27 Jul 1995 Robert Richard b 11 Oct 1971 s of James R. and Martha McLean; ord and ind to St Margaret's 26 Sep 1996.

DUNFERMLINE ST NINIAN'S (FUF 349; FES IX, 461; X, 274)

1957   DOUGLAS BECK
(FES IX, 461, 611, 712, 714, 717; X, 273, 274), trans from Tyrie to St Andrew's South 15 Apr 1953; became minister of St Ninian's following transportation of congregation 15 May 1957; ret 31 Dec 1970; died 26 Apr 1993.

1971   THOMAS FORREST SMITH
(FES X, 147, 274, 285), trans from Leslie Trinity to St Ninian's 20 Aug 1971; introd to Rosneath St Modan's (term) 1 Aug 1979.

1980   CHARLES MILLAR CAMERON
ord and ind to St Ninian's 26 Feb 1980; dem 8 Feb 1996 on app by Presb Church in Ireland; ind to Glasgow Castlemilk West 7 Sep 1998.

1996   ELIZABETH ANNE FISK
B 10 Nov 1950 at Lennoxtown, Glasgow, d of Ronald Thomas Barnes and Mary Ann Duncan Johnstone; Glasgow South College of Nursing 1982–84 (SEN), 1986–88 (SRN); Adult Education Centre 1988–90 (SCE); University of Glasgow 1991–95 (BD); Greater Glasgow Health Board 1978–91; lic by Presb of Glasgow 3 Jul 1995; m 2 Feb 1970 Dennis Ernest Fisk s of Stanley Walter F. and Mary Simpson; Children: Carol Joan b 18 Aug 1970; Dennis Ernest b 27 Oct 1971 m Karen Elliot; Angela Elizabeth b 28 Aug 1973; ord and ind to St Ninian's 22 Aug 1996.

DUNFERMLINE ST PAUL'S (FES X, 274)

1964   FRANCIS TAYLOR SMITH
(FES, X 274, 365), trans from Aberlour to St Paul's 26 Oct 1964.

DUNFERMLINE TOWNHILL (FUF 255; FES V, 36; VIII, 410; IX, 463; X, 274)

1972   WILLIAM EWART
(FES X, 274), ind to Townhill 20 Jun 1972; trans to Bishopbriggs Springfield Cambridge 26 Jan 1978.

1978   MARY BROWN MORRISON
ord and ind to Townhill 26 Sep 1978; dem on app as Adviser in Mission and Evangelism, Dept of National Mission 1 Nov 1986.

1987   WILLIAM EDWARDS FARQUHAR
B 28 May 1941 at Lossiemouth, s of William F. and Alexanderina Gault Smith; educ Elgin Academy 1956–58; Open University 1978–83 (BA); University of Aberdeen 1983–86 (BD); Civil Service 1958–67; Royal Air Force 1967–83; lic by Presb of Moray 29 Jun 1986; asst Spynie, Duffus and Hopeman 1986–87; m 28 May 1966 Jean Margaret Stewart b 11 Sep 1943 d of Robert Mowatt S. and Flora Donaldson; Children: Deborah Jo b 29 Mar 1969 m Alastair Wallace Grierson; William Stuart b 17 Sep 1970; ord and ind to Townhill 12 Jun 1987; app Clerk to Presb of Dunfermline 19 Mar 1991.

INVERKEITHING ST JOHN'S (FUF 350; FES IX, 464; X, 275)

Linked 31 Jul 1958 with North Queensferry.

1971   ALEXANDER STRICKLAND
(FES X, 275), ord and ind to St John's with North Queensferry 5 May 1971; trans to Kildonan with Whiting Bay 20 Aug 1976.

1977   WILLIAM GORDON GLEN BAIRD
B 7 Jan 1928 at Glasgow, s of William B. and Sarah Park Kirkwood; educ William Hulme's Grammar, Manchester 1938–43; University of Glasgow 1949–52 [part-time] (DPA); Glasgow and West of Scotland Commercial College 1954–57 [part-time] (ACII); University of Edinburgh 1972–74; Clerk, LMS Railway Co 1943–44; Inland Revenue 1944–46; Royal Navy/Writer 1946–48; Ministry of Pensions and National Insurance 1948–66; Senior Exec Officer, HM Treasury 1967–68; Training Officer for Scotland, DHSS 1969–72; lic by Presb of Edinburgh 10 Jul 1974; asst Edinburgh St Ninian's Corstorphine 1974–75; m 3 Jun 1954 Morag Thorburn Crichton b 21 Jan 1928 d of Thomas Moir C. and Jane Helen Thorburn Burns; Children: Moira Carolyn b 7 May 1957 m Michael Eric Paton; Ronald William b 16 Jul 1959 m Gillian Isobel Gilmour Smith; ord and ind to St John's with North Queensferry 25 Aug 1977; ret 31 Mar 1993.

1995   SHEILA MUNRO
B 23 May 1963 at Stranraer, d of Charles M. and Mary Hughes; educ Stranraer Academy 1975–81; St Colm's College, Edinburgh 1986–88 (Diaconal Studies); University of Glasgow 1990–94 (BD); Sales Asst 1981; Secretarial/Clerical 1982–86; Deaconess 1988–90; lic by Presb of Wigtown and Stranraer, Jul 1994; asst Forres St Leonard's with Rafford with Dallas 1994–95; ord and ind to St John's with North Queensferry 6 Jul 1995.

INVERKEITHING ST PETER'S (FES V, 42; VIII, 411; IX, 464; X, 275)

1938   JOHN JOHNSTON
(FES IX, 464, 569; X, 275), trans from Aberdeen St Mary's to St Peter's 26 Jan 1938; ret 31 Dec 1981; died 6 Aug 1993.

1982   ALAN DAVID BIRSS
ord by Presb of Dundee during assistantship at St
Mary's 18 Apr 1979; ind to St Peter's 10 Sep 1982;
trans to Paisley Abbey 2 Mar 1988.

1988   GEORGE GRAY NICOL
B 15 Jul 1948 at Glasgow, s of George N. and
Mary Mill Smith; educ Allan Glen's, Glasgow 1960–
66; University of Glasgow 1972–77 (BD); University
of Oxford 1977–81 (DPhil); Insurance 1966–72;
Baptist Minister 1982–88; loc ten Kilchrenan and
Dalavich with Muckairn 1988; m 1 Sep 1979 Elaine
Shipton b 13 Feb 1949 d of Jack and Stella S;
Children: Callum George b 6 Dec 1981; Lyle David
b 5 Apr 1986; ord by Baptist Union and ind to King's
Sutton Baptist Church, Oxfordshire 22 May 1982;
admitted by General Assembly 1988 and ind to
St Peter's 22 Sep 1988; Publ: Articles, studies
and sermons in *Expository Times*, *Journal of
Theological Studies*, *Studia Theologica*, *Vetus
Testamentum*.

KELTY (FES X, 275)

1974   ALEXANDER CLOWES McCARTNEY
(FES X, 275), ord by Presb of Ayr during
assistantship at Castlehill 5 Dec 1973; ind to Kelty
12 Sep 1974; trans to Hawick St Mary's with Cavers
and Kirkton 11 Dec 1985; American Bible College
1975–76 (BTh).

1986   ALISTAIR JOHN DRUMMOND
B 3 Jun 1959 at Edinburgh, s of Robert Hugh and
May D; educ Glenrothes High 1973–77; University
of Edinburgh 1977–84 (BSc, BD); Princeton
Theological Seminary, New Jersey 1984–85 (ThM);
lic by Presb of Edinburgh 1 Jul 194; asst St
Andrews St Leonard's with Cameron 1985–86; m
12 Jul 1986 Su Yon Pak b 5 Nov 1960 d of Dong
Kyu P. and Yang Sook; ord and ind to Kelty 21
Aug 1986; dem 31 Aug 1993 and emigrated to
USA.

1994   ROBIN NORMAN ALLISON
ord and ind to Kelty 16 Feb 1994; trans to Lochwinnoch 14 Apr 1999.

LIMEKILNS (FUF 352; FES IX, 466; X, 276)

Linked 1 Sep 1983 with Cairneyhill.

1973   WILLIAM MILLAR WEIR
(FES IX, 81; X, 49, 133, 204, 276), trans from
Greenock Martyrs' and North to Limekilns 15 Feb
1973; ret 31 Aug 1983; died 13 Jan 1995.

1984   ROBERT JOHN HENDERSON
(FES X, 73, 218, 366), ind to Cairneyhill with
Limekilns 23 Feb 1984, see Cairneyhill.

1990   NORMAN MILLER GRANT
ord and ind to Cairneyhill with Limekilns 26 Oct
1990, see Cairneyhill.

LOCHCRAIG (FUF 350; FES IX, 466; X, 276)

1973   JAMES HENDERSON WALLACE
(FES X, 276), ord by Presb of Paisley 21 Feb 1973;
ind to Lochcraig 14 Nov 1973; trans to Peebles St
Andrew's Leckie 14 Nov 1983.

1984   JAMES FORD TODD
B 18 Feb 1953 at Larkhall, s of James Hunter T.
and Marion Ford; educ Larkhall Academy 1965–
70; University of Aberdeen 1973–79 (BD, CPS);
lic by Presb of Aberdeen 5 Dec 1979; asst Miln-
gavie St Paul's 1979–80; loc ten Glasgow Colston
Milton 1981; loc ten Kirkwall East 1982–83; m 3
Dec 1983 Christine Rae b 9 Jul 1956; Children:
Amy Caroline b 10 Oct 1984; ord and ind to
Lochcraig 16 May 1984; dem 30 Nov 1999.

LOCHGELLY CHURCHMOUNT (FUF 352, FES
IX, 466; X, 276)

Congregation dissolved 31 May 1980.

1962   FINLAY JOHN STEWART
(FES X, 276), admitted by General Assembly 1961;
ind to Churchmount 27 Feb 1962; ret 31 Dec 1979;
Publ: *Henry Drummond* (Macdonald Press, 1985);
also audio-visual of same title (Drummond Trust,
1983–84).

LOCHGELLY MACAINSH (FUF 353; FES IX, 466;
X, 276)

1962   NORMAN ROY MACASKILL
(FES X, 277), ord and ind to Lochgelly Macainsh
25 Apr 1962; Clerk to Presb of Dunfermline 1972–
91; trans to Kingussie 9 Apr 1991.

1992   JOHN WILLIAM KNOX
B 22 May 1937 at Renfrew, s of John K. and
Barbara Carlisle Mack; educ Galashiels Academy
1949–52; Moray House College, Edinburgh 1965–
67 (CQSW); University of St Andrews 1989–92
(MTh); Motor Engineering 1953–54; Social Work
1954–89; National Service 1955–57; lic by Presb
of Dundee 18 Jun 1992; m 10 Oct 1959 Ann
Sharpe b 22 Aug 1937 d of Percy S. and Mary
Louise Kirk; Children: Andrew Ian b 31 May 1960
m Fiona Blair; Gillian Ann b 6 May 1961 m David
Morrison; Heather Alexandra b 18 Oct 1964 m Alan
Fleming; ord and ind to Lochgelly Macainsh 15 Jul
1992; ret 31 Oct 1997.

1999   MARYANN RHODA RENNIE
B 20 Feb 1969 at Edinburgh, d of John William
Robertson and Alice Rosina Rudland; educ Bishop
Wand Church of England School, Sunbury and
Boroughmuir High, Edinburgh 1980–87; University
of Edinburgh 1990–94 (BD), 1994–95 (MTh),
1995–96 (CPS); Bank Officer 1987–90; lic by Presb
of Edinburgh 7 Jul 1996; asst Dalkeith St John's
and King's Park 1996–98; m 20 Aug 1994 Keith
James Rennie b 12 Mar 1968 s of James
Robertson R. and Frances Mary Traynor; ord and
ind to Lochgelly Macainsh 18 Mar 1998.

LOCHGELLY ST ANDREW'S (FES V, 111; VIII, 432; IX, 467; X, 277)

1968 JOHN MILTON TENNANT
(FES X, 277), ord and ind to St Andrew's 4 Jul 1968; died 7 Jun 1985.

1986 KENNETH GEORGE RUSSELL
ord and ind to St Andrew's 15 May 1986; introd as Assoc at Buckhaven 7 Dec 1988.

1990 ROBERT FARRELL DUNCAN
B 14 Sep 1936 at Dundee, s of Alexander Mackeral D. and Grace Farrell; educ Grove Academy, Broughty Ferry; Dundee College of Commerce; University of St Andrews 1974–77 (MTh); Dundee Teacher Training College 1977–78 (PGCE); Teaching 1978–88; Principal teacher (RE); lic by Presb of Dundee 29 Sep 1985; asst Dundee Strathmartine 1984–85, Albany Butterburn with St David's North 1988–89; m 17 Oct 1959 Isabel Margaret Douglas Paterson b 13 Sep 1938 d of William P. and Agnes Philip; Children: Heather Evon b 8 Oct 1960 m Leslie Hood; Derek William b 4 Jun 1963 m Kirsty Warburton; ord as Aux by Presb of Dundee and assgnd to Dundee St James' 28 Sep 1986; ind to St Andrew's (full-time ministry) 18 Jan 1990.

NORTH QUEENSFERRY (FUF 354; FES IX, 468; X, 277)

Linked 31 Jul 1958 with Inverkeithing St John's.

1971 ALEXANDER STRICKLAND
(FES X, 275), ord and ind to Inverkeithing St John's with North Queensferry 5 May 1971; trans to Kildonan with Whiting Bay 20 Aug 1976.

1977 WILLIAM GORDON GLEN BAIRD
ind to Inverkeithing St John's with North Queensferry 25 Aug 1977, see Inverkeithing.

1995 SHEILA MUNRO
ord and ind to Inverkeithing St John's with North Queensferry 6 Jul 1995, see Inverkeithing St John's.

ROSYTH (FES IX, 469; X, 278)

1971 STANLEY SCOULAR
(FES X, 199, 278), trans from Motherwell Manse Road to Rosyth 10 Feb 1971; ret 16 Oct 1999; s Iain m Debra Saunders; d Janet m David Hamilton Russell.

SALINE AND BLAIRINGONE (FES X, 270, 278)

Formed 1 Jan 1993 by union of Saline and Blairingone.

1953 ALEXANDER GEORGE DOWNIE
(FES IX, 470; X, 278), ord and ind to Saline 26 Feb 1953; became minister of linked charge with Blairingone 23 Feb 1958; died 15 Oct 1992.

1993 RICHARD HAMMOND
B 18 Feb 1952 at Redditch, Worcs, s of Richard Edmund H. and Enid Mary Smith; educ Redditch County High 1963–70; University of Strathclyde 1970–75 (BA); Jordanhill College, Glasgow 1975 (PGCE); University of Edinburgh 1989–92 (BD); Teaching 1976–80; Mission work with 'Navigators', Germany and Edinburgh 1980–89; lic by Presb of Edinburgh 5 Jul 1992; asst Edinburgh Davidson's Mains 1992–93; m 2 Jul 1977 Elizabeth Claire Mary Sieger b 30 Sep 1952 d of Albert Edward S. and Dorothy Marie Shannon; Children: Natalie Elizabeth b 31 May 1979; Peter Richard b 16 Oct 1982; ord and ind to Saline and Blairingone 28 May 1993.

TULLIALLAN AND KINCARDINE (FES X, 278)

Formed 24 Apr 1974 by union of Kincardine and Tulliallan.

1962 JONATHAN McCULLOUGH FLETCHER
(FES IX, 709 (2); X, 114, 276, 404), res from term app at Newmilns West and ind to Kincardine 28 Aug 1962; ret 31 Mar 1974; died 20 Dec 1989.

1974 FREDERICK CHARLES LEES
(FES X, 278), ord and ind to Tulliallan and Kincardine 10 Sep 1974; dem 8 Apr 1976.

1976 ALEXANDER McCOLL POOLE
B 22 Jul 1937 at Bellshill, s of Thomas Peat P. and Barbara McColl; educ Bellshill Academy 1949–52; University of Glasgow 1971–76 (BD); lic by Presb of Hamilton, Jul 1976; asst Stonehouse St Ninian's 1975–76; m 16 Mar 1956 Ann McEwan b 25 Jan 1938 d of John M. and Janet McConnell; Children: Alexander John Graeme b 28 Aug 1957; Heather Ann Elizabeth b 20 Dec 1964; ord and ind to Tulliallan and Kincardine 21 Oct 1976; died 17 May 1977.

1977 DAVID WALLACE DOYLE
ord and ind to Tulliallan and Kincardine 26 Oct 1977; trans to Motherwell St Mary's 16 Sep 1987.

1988 JAMES GILLON REDPATH
B 9 Mar 1956 at Kirkcaldy, s of Andrew Simon R. and Annie Smith Turnbull; educ Beath Senior High 1968–74; University of St Andrews 1982–87 (BD, DipPT); Librarian 1975–81; lic by Presb of St Andrews 25 Oct 1987; asst Forfar East and Old 1987–88; m 24 Sep 1983 Anne Morgan b 20 Mar 1963 d of David Duncan M. and Euphemia Dewar; ord and ind to Tulliallan and Kincardine 17 May 1988.

PRESBYTERY OF KIRKCALDY

AUCHTERDERRAN (FES V, 76; VIII, 422; IX, 471; X, 279)

Linked 2 Sep 1979 with Kinglassie. Further linked 18 Sep 1991 with Cardenden St Fothad's.

1959 KENNETH GOWAN OGILVIE
(FES IX, 611; X, 279, 351), trans from Strichen to Auchterderran 29 Apr 1959; dem 31 Dec 1968 to take up app as teacher of Religious Education, Edinburgh; ret 1978.

1970 ALASTAIR STEWART YOUNGER
(FES X, 279), ord by Presb of Stirling and Dunblane during assistantship at Alloa St Mungo's 8 Jun 1969; ind to Auchterderran 15 Jul 1970; trans to Inverness St Columba High 28 Apr 1976.

1977 JAMES EWEN ROSS CAMPBELL
(FES X, 417), res from service with FMC and ind to Auchterderran 28 Apr 1977; became minister of linked charge with Kinglassie 2 Sep 1979 and with Cardenden St Fothad's 18 Sep 1991.

AUCHTERTOOL (FES V, 78; VIII, 422; IX, 471; X, 279)

Linkage with Burntisland terminated 28 Feb 1987. Linked 31 Mar 1987 with Kirkcaldy Invertiel. Linkage continues following union of Invertiel and Bethelfield 8 Jan 1991.

1969 JOSEPH SMITH EASTON
(FES IX, 30, 467; X, 18, 280), ind to Burntisland St Andrew's 16 Feb 1966; became minister of linked charge with Auchtertool 18 May 1969, see Burntisland.

1977 DONALD MACFARLANE MACKENZIE
(FES IX, 684; X, 187, 280, 378, 388), ind to Burntisland St Columba's 24 Jan 1967; became minister of united charge with St Andrew's linked with Auchtertool 13 Mar 1977, see Burntisland.

1987 JOHN ALEXANDER COWIE
ord and ind to Invertiel 23 Jun 1983; became minister of linked charge with Auchtertool 31 Mar 1987; dem 31 Dec 1989 and introd to the English Reformed Church, Amsterdam 1990.

1991 GEORGE STRACHAN COWIE
ord and ind to Auchtertool with Kirkcaldy Linktown 21 Aug 1991; trans to Aberdeen Holburn Central 27 May 1999.

BUCKHAVEN (FES X, 279)

1973 WILLIAM ALEXANDER DUNDAS
(FES X, 243, 245, 279, 298), trans from Dundee Balgay St Thomas' to Buckhaven 15 Mar 1973; trans to Kilchoman with Portnahaven 9 Jul 1976.

1976 HENRY DANE SHERRARD
(FES X, 413), res from app in Genoa and ind to Buckhaven 21 Dec 1976; trans to Cadder 9 Mar 1994.

1988 KENNETH GEORGE RUSSELL
dem from Lochgelly St Andrew's and introd as Assoc at Buckhaven 7 Dec 1988; ind to Jamestown 20 Feb 1991.

1995 BRYCE CALDER
B 26 Dec 1966 at Bo'ness, s of Robert C. and Janette Black; educ Bo'ness Academy 1978–84; University of Edinburgh 1987–90 (MA), 1990–93 (BD); Metropolitan Police Force 1985–87; lic by Presb of Falkirk 28 Jun 1993; asst Troon St Meddan's 1993–94; m 1 Oct 1988 Helen Maureen Miller b 24 Sep 1967 d of Alistair M. and Maureen Scott; Children: Alexandrea b 8 Sep 1991; Andrew b 29 Nov 1995; ord and ind to Buckhaven 17 Jan 1995.

BURNTISLAND (FES X, 280)

Formed 13 Mar 1977 by union of Burntisland St Columba's and St Andrew's. Linked same date with Auchtertool. Linkage terminated 28 Feb 1987.

1966 JOSEPH SMITH EASTON
(FES IX, 30, 467; X, 18, 280), trans from Edinburgh North Merchiston to St Andrew's 16 Feb 1966; became minister of linked charge with Auchtertool 18 May 1969; died 20 Aug 1976.

1967 DONALD MACFARLANE MACKENZIE
(FES IX, 684; X, 187, 280, 378, 388), trans from Bellshill West to St Columba's 24 Jan 1967; became minister of united charge with St Andrew's linked with Auchtertool 13 Mar 1977; ret 30 Sep 1986.

1987   JOHN CHARLES DUNCAN
B 12 Mar 1956 at Dundee, s of John Charles D. and Anne Christine Norris; educ Logie Secondary, Dundee 1968–71; Dundee College of Commerce 1971–73 (SNC); University of Aberdeen 1981–85 (BD); Irish School of Ecumenics and Trinity College, Dublin 1985–86 (MPhil); Shipping Clerk 1973–81; lic by Presb of Dundee 7 Dec 1986; asst Glasgow Knightswood St Margaret's 1986–87; ord and ind to Burntisland 1 Oct 1987.

CARDENDEN ST FOTHAD'S (FES X, 280)

Linked 18 Sep 1991 with Auchterderran with Kinglassie.

1972   COLIN JOHN GROOM
(FES X, 280), admitted by General Assembly 1972 and ind to St Fothad's 8 Aug 1972; dem 28 Aug 1982.

1983   MARIA ANNETTE GEERTRUDIS PLATE
ord and ind to St Fothad's 5 Jul 1983; introd as Assoc at Edinburgh Kaimes Lockhart Memorial 14 Nov 1989.

1991   JAMES EWEN ROSS CAMPBELL
(FES X, 417), ind to Auchterderran 28 Apr 1977; became minister of linked charge with Kinglassie 2 Sep 1979 and with St Fothad's 18 Sep 1991.

DENBEATH (FUF 358; FES IX, 473; X, 280)

Linked 3 Dec 1978 with Methilhill.

1971   THOMAS WATT WILSON
(FES X, 49, 210, 230, 281), trans from Lochgoilhead and Kilmorich to Denbeath 15 Apr 1971; ret 3 Aug 1977; died 23 Mar 1999.

1978   GRAHAM DOUGLAS SUTHERLAND DEANS
ord and ind to Denbeath 24 Aug 1978; became minister of linked charge with Methilhill 3 Dec 1978; Depute Clerk and Treasurer, Presb of Kirkcaldy 1981–87; trans to Dumfries St Mary's 8 Jul 1987.

1988   ELISABETH FAITH CRANFIELD
B 8 Jun 1962 at Durham, d of Charles Ernest Burland C. and Ruth Elizabeth Gertrude Bole; educ Durham High 1973–80; University of St Andrews 1980–84 (MA); University of Aberdeen 1984–87 (BD); lic by Presb of Aberdeen 30 Jun 1987; asst Glasgow St John's Renfield 1987–88; ord and ind to Denbeath with Methilhill 30 Jun 1988.

DYSART (FES X, 281)

Formed 19 Nov 1972 by union of Dysart Barony and Dysart St Serf's.

1966   THOMAS CAMERON GEDDES
(FES X, 199, 281 (2)), trans from Motherwell North to Barony 18 Jan 1966; became minister of united charge with St Serf's 19 Nov 1972; died 23 Sep 1991.

1992   DAVID JOHN SMITH
ord and ind to Dysart 23 Mar 1992; trans to Leslie Trinity 23 Sep 1997.

1998   MATILDA WILSON
B 5 Oct 1946 at Edinburgh, d of Robert W. and Matilda Knight; St Colm's College, Edinburgh 1979–81 (DCS); University of Glasgow 1986–89 (LTh), 1994–96 (MTh); Self-employed 1958–79; lic by Presb of Edinburgh 2 Jul 1989; asst Edinburgh Colinton 1989–90; ord by Presb of Hamilton and introd as Assoc at East Kilbride Greenhills 1 Oct 1990; ind to Dysart 26 Aug 1998.

GLENROTHES CHRIST'S KIRK (FES X, 285)

Formerly known as Leslie Christ's Kirk on the Green. New name adopted 1991.

1969   IAN DOUGLAS GRANT SUTHERLAND
(FES IX, 289, 655; X, 285, 325, 373), trans from Inverness West to Christ's Kirk on the Green 22 Jan 1969; trans to Aberdeen Causewayend 25 Sep 1975.

1977   JOHN THOMAS HERBERTSON TAYLOR
(FES IX, 506, 595; X, 213, 230, 300, 321), dem from Glenesk and introd to Christ's Kirk on the Green (term) 15 May 1977; ret 13 May 1983; m (2) 20 Apr 1990 Elizabeth Coventry Mitchell b 13 Nov 1926 d of David More M. and Jean Beath Reid.

1983   PETER ALAN DUNCAN BERRILL
ord and ind to Christ's Kirk on the Green 27 Oct 1983; dem 30 Apr 1987 to enter teaching profession; ind to Aberluthnott with Laurencekirk 3 Jun 1999.

1989   GILBERT LITTLE THOMSON
B 20 Jun 1935 at Airdrie, s of Gilbert Little T. and Margaret Towers; educ Airdrie Academy; University of Aberdeen 1960–62; Scottish Congregational College 1962–65 (CMin); Newcastle Institute of Teacher Training Colleges 1968–70 (DEd); Open University 1971–74 (BA); Engineering 1950–60; National Service (RE) 1956–58; m 9 Aug 1965 Kathleen Margaret Dawson Booth b 3 Dec 1943 d of John B. and Annie Smart; Children: Karen b 9 Mar 1970 m Prescott; Mhairi b 16 Apr 1971 m Richard Ramsey; Kirsty b 17 Nov 1972; ord by Scottish Congregational Union and ind to Eyemouth 25 Jun 1965; admitted by General Assembly and ind to Wishaw Chalmers 12 May 1976; trans to Stranraer Old 5 May 1985; trans to Christ's Kirk on the Green 30 Jun 1989; ret 31 Dec 1996.

1997 JAMES McMILLAN
B 8 Apr 1957 at Bellshill, s of George Bath M. and Elizabeth Watt; educ Coatbridge High 1970–76; University of Glasgow 1991–95 (BD); Dept of Employment (Accounts) 1977–78; British Rail (Accounts) 1978–91; lic by Presb of Glasgow 6 Jul 1985; ord and ind to Christ's Kirk 16 Dec 1997.

GLENROTHES ST COLUMBA'S (FES X, 281)

1976 WILLIAM HALLIDAY THOMSON
(FES X, 30, 327), trans from Aberdeen John Knox Gerrard Street to St Columba's 29 Jan 1976; trans to Edinburgh Liberton Northfield 17 Dec 1987.

1988 ALISTAIR G McLEOD
ord and ind to St Columba's 28 Sep 1988.

GLENROTHES ST MARGARET'S (FES IX, 475; X, 281)

1964 WALLACE ALLEN SHAW
(FES X, 281), admitted by General Assembly 1963 and ind to St Margaret's 31 Jan 1964; dem 24 Aug 1976.

1977 IAN WILLIAM McCREE
(FES X, 29), trans from Bathgate St John's to St Margaret's 24 Mar 1977; trans to Clyne 3 Jul 1987.

1988 WILLIAM ABERNETHY
trans from Airdrie Broomknoll to St Margaret's 18 Feb 1988; dem 16 Oct 1993.

1994 JOHN PETER McLEAN
B 7 Jul 1948 at Bangor, Co Down, s of Peter M. and Jean Ferguson McMillan; educ Bangor Grammar 1959–67; Queen's University, Belfast 1967–70 (BSc); Moray House College, Edinburgh 1971–72 (Grad Cert Sec Educ); University of Ulster 1984–87 (BPhil); University of Edinburgh 1989–92 (BD); Accountancy 1970–71; Teaching 1972–89; lic by Presb of Dunfermline 12 Jul 1992; asst Dunfermline Gillespie Memorial 1992–93; m 5 Aug 1974 Elizabeth Agnes Watson Hilsley d of Henry H. and Jean Watson; Children: Janis Elizabeth b 4 Oct 1980; Alan John b 23 Jul 1982; ord and ind to St Margaret's 13 Jun 1994.

GLENROTHES ST NINIAN'S (FES X, 282)

1965 NORMAN MACLEOD
(FES X, 28, 282), trans from Armadale East to St Ninian's 29 Oct 1965; trans to Orwell with Portmoak 31 May 1978.

1978 MURDOCH MACKENZIE
res from service with Overseas Council in Madras, S India and ind to St Ninian's 24 Oct 1978; dem 31 Aug 1982.

1982 JAMES GLADSTONE MACDONALD PURVES
B 15 Mar 1955 at Edinburgh, s of James Gladstone P. and Mona Kathleen Macdonald; educ George Heriot's, Edinburgh 1965–73; University of Edinburgh 1973–80 (LLB, BD); lic by Presb of Edinburgh, Jul 1980; asst Skene 1980–81; m 28 Aug 1979 Jennifer Ross Kay d of Norman Ross and Kathleen K; Children: Sharon Kay b 22 May 1981; ord by Presb of Gordon and app Asst at Skene 8 Mar 1981; ind to St Ninian's 28 Jan 1982; dem 31 May 1987.

1988 VIOLET CATHERINE CLARK McKAY
ord and ind to St Ninian's 19 May 1988; trans to Musselburgh St Andrew's High 4 Oct 1999.

INNERLEVEN EAST (FES IX, 475; X, 282)

1975 JAMES LINDSAY TEMPLETON
(FES X, 282), ord and ind to Innerleven East 15 May 1975; Children: Kathryn Louise b 30 Aug 1982.

KENNOWAY, WINDYGATES AND BALGONIE ST KENNETH'S (FES X, 282, 288)

Formed 19 Mar 1997 by union of Kennoway and Windygates and Balgonie.

1960 JOHN CLARK
(FES IX, 474; X, 218, 281, 282 (2)), trans from Glasgow Drumchapel Drumry St Mary's to Kennoway Old 12 Dec 1960; became minister of united charge with Arnot 13 Apr 1975; trans to Dunblane St Blane's 18 Sep 1980.

1971 PAUL MARTIN NEWMAN SEWELL
(FES X, 288), ind to Windygates and Balgonie 2 Sep 1971; trans to Stirling North 15 Mar 1978.

1978 HEATHER CLAIRE OLSEN
ord and ind to Windygates and Balgonie 16 Aug 1978; dem 30 Sep 1996; ind to Creich with Rosehall 11 Jun 1999.

1981 ALEXANDER BUCHAN
(FES X, 188), ind to Kennoway on returning from Australia Mar 1981; dem 30 Jun 1985; ind to North Ronaldsay with Sanday 28 Nov 1989.

1986 DAVID WILLIAM DENNISTON
trans from Glasgow Ruchazie to Kennoway 19 Jun 1986; trans to Perth North 9 Oct 1996.

1997 RICHARD BAXTER
B 20 Jun 1961 at Bangor, N Ireland, s of Thomas George B. and Gertrude Elizabeth Fleming; educ Bangor Grammar 1972–79; University of Edinburgh 1979–83 (MA), 1993–96 (BD); University of Oxford 1983–86; Tax Inspector 1986–91, Tax Consultant 1991–93; lic by Presb of Kirkcaldy 30 Jun 1996; asst Kirkcaldy Pathhead 1996–97; m 30 Jun 1984 Sheryl Jane Hume b 14 Apr 1962 d of Francis John

H. and Jane Bellshaw Fraser; Children: Patrick Thomas b 15 Jun 1991; Amy Jane b 10 Apr 1993; ord and ind to Kennoway, Windygates and Balgonie 28 Oct 1997.

KINGHORN (FES X, 282)

Formed 8 Jan 1961 by union of Kinghorn Rosslands and Kinghorn St Leonard's.

1951 JOHN ANDREW NISBET
(FES IX, 103, 476; X, 282 (2)), trans from Longformacus to St Leonard's 28 Aug 1951; became minister of united charge with Rosslands 8 Jan 1961; ret 18 Sep 1977; died 1 Jun 1995.

1978 EVERARD WILLIAM KANT
(FES IX, 364; X, 28, 55 (2), 85, 217, 441), res as Chaplain to International Students, University of Glasgow and ind to Kinghorn 13 Apr 1978; ret 30 Apr 1988; University of Edinburgh 1994–95 (MTh); d Pauline m David Ogle.

1988 CHARLES HUGH MOAR GREIG
trans from Bellshill Orbiston with St Andrew's to Kinghorn 26 Oct 1988; trans to Dunrossness and St Ninian's inc Fair Isle with Sandwick Cunningsburgh and Quarff 18 Jan 1997.

1997 JAMES REID
B 27 Jul 1960 at Bellshill, s of Archibald Strang R. and Annie Easton Love McQueen; educ Larkhall Academy 1972–76; University of Edinburgh 1981–85 (BD); Scottish Congregational College 1981–85 (Cert); Auctioneer's Asst 1976–81; asst Edinburgh Morningside United 1984–85; m 2 May 1994 Marion Elizabeth Hunter b 5 Aug 1962 d of John H. and Eileen Elizabeth Logan; Children: Andrew John b 31 Jan 1997; ord by Congregational Union of Scotland and ind to Middleton Park, Bridge of Don 10 Aug 1985; trans to Avoch Congregational Church 24 Aug 1990; ind to Kinghorn 2 Sep 1997.

KINGLASSIE (FES V, 96; VIII, 426; IX, 476; X, 282)

Linked 2 Sep 1979 with Auchterderran.

1960 WILLIAM FINLAYSON YOUNG
(FES IX, 485, 607; X, 282, 349), trans from Maud to Kinglassie 4 May 1960; ret 26 Aug 1979; Publ: Editor of *A Poesy of Flowers* (1997).

1979 JAMES EWEN ROSS CAMPBELL
(FES X, 417), ind to Auchterderran 28 Apr 1977; became minister of linked charge with Kinglassie 2 Sep 1979.

KIRKCALDY ABBOTSHALL (FES X, 283)

Formed 2 Feb 1964 by union of Kirkcaldy Abbotshall and Kirkcaldy Raith.

1949 MAGNUS WILLIAM COOPER
(FES IX, 131, 477; X, 283 (2)), trans from Applegarth and Sibbaldbie to Abbotshall 9 Nov 1949; became minister of united charge with Raith 2 Feb 1964; ret 21 Jul 1979; s George m Nicola Smith.

1980 BRYAN LAUGHLIN TOMLINSON
(FES X, 105), trans from Old Cumnock Crichton West to Abbotshall 24 Apr 1980.

KIRKCALDY LINKTOWN (FES X, 283)

Formed 8 Jan 1991 by union of Kirkcaldy Bethelfield and Kirkcaldy Invertiel. Linked same date with Auchtertool.

1955 THOMAS McMILLAN FLEMING
(FES IX, 205; X, 117, 283), trans from Kilbirnie East to Invertiel 30 Aug 1955; ret 16 Oct 1982; died 17 Jun 1984.

1958 ROBERT CAMPBELL
(FES IX, 173; X, 100, 283, 369), trans from Speymouth and Garmouth to Bethelfield 24 Sep 1958; ret 25 Mar 1985; died 14 Feb 1997.

1983 JOHN ALEXANDER COWIE
ord and ind to Invertiel 23 Jun 1983; became minister of linked charge with Auchtertool 31 Mar 1987; dem 31 Dec 1989 and introd to the English Reformed Church, Amsterdam 1990.

1985 WILLIAM M ASHCROFT
ord and ind to Bethelfield 6 Aug 1985; dem 12 Aug 1990.

1991 GEORGE STRACHAN COWIE
ord and ind to Auchtertool with Kirkcaldy Linktown 21 Aug 1991; trans to Aberdeen Holburn Central 27 May 1999.

KIRKCALDY OLD (FES V, 102; VIII, 430; IX, 479; X, 283)

1960 JOHN GEDDES SIM
(FES IX, 296; X, 175, 284), trans from Glasgow St Francis-in-the-East to Kirkcaldy Old 24 Mar 1960; ret 30 Jun 1987; w Jean died 14 Aug 1993; s John m Margaret Ann Bell; s Peter m Gillian Mary Lennam; d Margaret m Peter Ibison; Addl publ: Founding editor of *Ministers' Forum* (Church of Scotland, 1978–93); *Memoir on a Marriage* (Finlay Press, 1999).

1988 JOHN ALEXANDER FERGUSON
ord and ind to Kirkcaldy Old 16 Jun 1988; trans to Peterculter 2 Sep 1999.

KIRKCALDY PATHHEAD (FES X, 284)

1956 (KARL) BERNHARD CITRON
(FES IX, 32; X, 284 (2)), res as Professor of Biblical Theology, Austin Presb Theological Seminary, USA 1 Jun 1955 and ind to Pathhead West 8 Feb

1956; became minister of united charge with Pathhead East 30 Apr 1958; ret 1 Oct 1975; died 19 Feb 1978.

1976   THOMAS DOUGLAS McROBERTS
B 18 Sep 1949 at Glasgow, s of Thomas M. and Elizabeth Crossan Douglas; educ Hutchesons' Grammar, Glasgow 1958–67; University of Glasgow 1967–74 (BD, CPS); lic by Presb of Glasgow 27 Jun 1974; asst East Kilbride Greenhills 1974–75; m 30 Jun 1972 Elspeth Jean Manson b 1 Jan 1952 d of Gordon Joseph Angus M. and Jean Baillie; Children: Kenneth Douglas b 1 Jan 1975; Alistair Thomas b 1 Jan 1975, died 30 Mar 1976; ord by Presb of Glasgow during assistantship at Greenhills 12 Jun 1975; ind to Pathhead 8 Jun 1976; dem 30 Sep 1978.

1979   ARCHIBALD MILLER MILLOY
ord and ind to Pathhead 16 May 1979; dem on app as Regional Adviser in Mission and Evangelism, Dept of National Mission 1 Aug 1992.

1993   JOHN DAVIDSON THOMSON
B 26 Jan 1940 at Airdrie, s of William T. and Janet Davidson; educ Airdrie Academy 1952–57; Coatbridge Technical College 1957–63 (LIM); University of Glasgow 1980–84 (BD); Production Metallurgist 1957–80; lic by Presb of Hamilton 27 Jun 1984; asst Bellshill West 1984–85; m 27 Dec 1962 Mary Webster Lees b 9 Feb 1941 d of William Ritchie L. and Helen Shillinglaw; Children: Aileen Davidson b 19 May 1967 m Barclay; Alison Ritchie b 29 Apr 1970 m Pert; ord and ind to Methil 19 Sep 1985; trans to Pathhead 16 Mar 1993.

KIRKCALDY ST ANDREW'S (FES X, 284)

1973   NORMAN McKENZIE HUTCHESON
(FES X, 284), ord and ind to St Andrew's 11 Jul 1973; trans to Dalbeattie with Urr 11 Aug 1988.

1989   DAVID JAMES HEPBURN LAING
trans from Dundee Craigiebank to St Andrew's 16 May 1989; trans to Cellardyke with Kilrenny 28 Jan 1999.

KIRKCALDY ST BRYCEDALE (FUF 363; FES IX, 480; X, 284)

1968   DAVID STUART PHILIP
(FES IX, 463; X, 86, 274, 284), trans from Kirkmahoe to St Brycedale 14 Dec 1968; dem 22 Oct 1978 and app by Board of World Mission to Costa del Sol with Gibraltar St Andrew's.

1979   JOHN KENNETH FROUDE
B 8 Dec 1950 at Glasgow, s of John Hosie F. and Dorothy Hall; educ Hillhead High, Glasgow 1962–69; University of Aberdeen 1972–76 (BD), 1976–78 (MA); lic by Presb of Aberdeen, Jun 1978; asst Aberdeen Northfield 1978–79; m 19 Sep 1973 Agnes-Ann Newton; ord and ind to St Brycedale 28 Aug 1979.

KIRKCALDY ST JOHN'S (FES V, 108; VIII, 431; IX, 480; X, 284)

1975   SAMUEL MURDOCH McNAUGHT
(FES X, 96, 284), trans from Portpatrick to St John's 29 Apr 1975; Children: Gordon Martin b 2 Sep 1972; Carol Lesley b 21 Jun 1975.

KIRKCALDY TEMPLEHALL (FES IX, 480; X, 285)

1971   BROCK AINSLIE WHITE
(FES X, 285), ord and ind to Templehall 28 Jan 1971; m 1 Nov 1980 Dreena Margaret Miller b 29 Dec 1950 d of Hugh Whiteford M. and Margaret Reid Spittal Mitchell; Children: Caroline Margrett b 13 Mar 1982; Neil Miller b 18 Feb 1984.

KIRKCALDY TORBAIN (FES X, 285)

1964   DENIS WARNOCK
(FES IX, 752; X, 285), res from service with Overseas Council in Kenya and S Africa and ind to Torbain 30 Apr 1964; ret 28 Feb 1990.

1990   PETER JAMES MACDONALD
res as National Young Adult Adviser and ind to Torbain 1 Sep 1990; trans to Edinburgh St George's West 1 May 1998.

1999   IAN JAMES ELSTON
B 18 Dec 1967 at Newcastle-on-Tyne, s of Peter Kenneth E. and Jessie Holmes; educ Inverkeithing High 1979–85; Napier College 1985–87 (HND); University of Edinburgh 1992–97 (BD, MTh); Clerk 1987–92; lic by Presb of Dunfermline 21 Sep 1997; asst Callander 1997–99; m 30 Aug 1997 Patricia Bertram b 5 Aug 1969 d of Robert William B. and Bridget Fallon; ord and ind to Torbain 27 Apr 1999.

KIRKCALDY VIEWFORTH (FES X, 283, 284)

Formed 23 Oct 1977 by union of Kirkcaldy Gallatown and Kirkcaldy Sinclairtown. Linked 1 Mar 1995 with Thornton.

1967   JAMES ROSS FULTON
(FES IX, 155, 468; X, 91, 283), trans from Balmaclellan with Kells to Gallatown 13 Jun 1967; ret 22 Oct 1977; died 9 Nov 1983.

1970   MATTHEW NOEL PATTERSON
(FES X, 77, 156, 253, 284), trans from Perth Moncrieffe to Sinclairtown 30 Apr 1970; became minister of united charge with Gallatown 23 Oct 1977; trans to Daviot and Dunlichity with Moy, Dalarossie and Tomatin 17 Oct 1979.

1980   GEORGE DAVIDSON WILKIE
(FES IX, 237; X, 138, 456), res as Industrial Adviser to Home Board and ind to Viewforth 2 May 1980; ret 31 Oct 1986; Addl publ: *Christian Thinking about Industrial Life* (St Andrew Press, 1980); *Role of*

Christians in Trade Unions (St Andrew Press, 1980); *Capital—A Moral Instrument* (St Andrew Press, 1992); founder and first editor of *Finance and Ethics Quarterly* (1993).

1987 ANGUS KERR
ret from RAChD and ind to Viewforth 1 May 1987; trans to Glasgow Newton Mearns 5 Jan 1994.

1995 DANIEL CONNOLLY
admitted by General Assembly and ind to Viewforth with Thornton 10 Jan 1995; dem 14 Feb 1999 on app by RAChD.

LESLIE TRINITY (FES X, 285)

1972 WILLIAM JOHN ROBERTSON HAY
(FES X, 115, 285), trans from Ardrossan St John's to Trinity 26 Apr 1972; trans to Buchanan with Drymen 25 Aug 1981.

1982 ALISTAIR THOMAS ELLIS WYNNE
B 23 Jun 1952 at Enniskillen, N Ireland, s of Thomas Laurence W. and Margaret Ruth Ellis; educ Montclair Junior High and Eastern Christian High, New Jersey 1963–69; College of William and Mary, Williamsburg, Virginia 1969–73 (BA); University of Edinburgh 1973–76 (BD); lic by Presb of Dumbarton 17 Jun 1980; asst Bearsden South 1979–80; m 27 Dec 1980 Judith Mary Wilson b 4 Feb 1947 d of Paul and Mary W; Community Church, Nicosia, Cyprus 1981; ord and ind to Trinity 25 Feb 1982; dem 31 May 1987.

1988 GORDON McDONALD SIMPSON
(FES X, 3, 191), ind to Trinity 20 Apr 1988; ret 30 Sep 1996; m 20 Oct 1984 Moira b 11 Jun 1953; Children: Keith; Claire.

1997 DAVID JOHN SMITH
B 10 Apr 1958 at Fontainbleau, France, s of David Melville Martin S. and Jean Mackie Swinton; educ Madras College, St Andrews 1970–76; University of Edinburgh 1985–89 (BD), 1989–90 (DipMin); Furniture Remover 1979–84; lic by Presb of St Andrews 23 Sep 1990; asst Edinburgh Cluny 1990–91; m 30 Jun 1989 Dale Fleming b 12 Sep 1961 d of Robert John F. and Wilhelmina Helen Dale; Children: Hazel Jennifer b 12 Jul 1994; Joy Heather and Andrew Timothy b 5 Sep 1997; ord and ind to Dysart 23 Mar 1992; trans to Trinity 23 Sep 1997.

LEVEN SCOONIE KIRK (FES V, 116; VIII, 434; IX, 483; X, 287)

1971 SYDNEY EDWIN PEEBLES BEVERIDGE
(FES X, 287, 335), trans from Echt with Midmar to Scoonie (Leven) 11 Feb 1971; trans to Edinburgh St Aidan's with Stenhouse Saughton 15 Dec 1983.

1982 ALASTAIR JACK CHERRY
ord and ind to Scoonie Kirk 10 Jun 1982; trans to Glasgow Stamperland 1 Jul 1987.

1987 EDGAR JOHN OGSTON
B 22 May 1950 at Dumfries, s of Bruce Kerr Newsome O. and Annie Gillespie Bell; educ Dumfries Academy 1955–68; University of Edinburgh 1968–72 (BSc), 1972–75 (BD); lic by Presb of Dumfries 17 Jul 1975; asst Elgin St Giles' 1975–77; m 26 Jul 1975 Jean McTaggart b 1 Dec 1948 d of Dugald William M. and Janet Christian Martin; Children: Stephen b 6 Sep 1976; Eileen b 17 Jun 1978; Heather b 21 Nov 1980; ord by Presb of Moray during assistantship at Elgin St Giles' 15 Feb 1976; ind to Kinlochleven 8 Jun 1977; became minister of linked charge with Nether Lochaber 13 Aug 1981; app by Board of World Mission for service with United Church of Jamaica and Grand Cayman 25 Jan 1984; ind to Scoonie Kirk 21 Dec 1987.

LEVEN ST ANDREW'S (FES X, 286)

Formed 6 Apr 1975 by union of Leven Forman and Leven St John's.

1954 WALTER MACFARLANE CALDERWOOD
(FES IX 116, 481; X, 286), trans from Hawick St Mary's to Leven Forman 17 Feb 1954; ret 30 Sep 1974; d Margaret m Brian Cavanagh.

1971 JOHN BARCLAY BURNS
(FES X, 286 (2)), ord and ind to St John's 26 Aug 1971; became minister of united charge with Forman 6 Apr 1975; dem 5 May 1976.

1976 ARCHIBALD FREELAND CHISHOLM
(FES X, 148, 417), trans from Stamperland to St Andrew's 28 Oct 1976; trans to Braes of Rannoch with Foss and Rannoch 17 Dec 1984.

1985 ALEXANDER RICHARD FORSYTH
B 30 Jan 1949 at Kirkcaldy, s of Alexander Richard F. and Harkes; educ Viewforth School, Kirkcaldy 1961–64; Overdale Theological College 1968–72 (CRK, DTh); Open University 1976–80 (BA); Geneva Theological College 1982–84 (MTh); Motor Engineering 1964–68; asst Balsall Heath Church of Christ 1972–73; m 20 Aug 1971 Jean Thomson Steedman b 25 May 1950 d of Robert Williamson S. and Agnes Thomson Anderson; Children: Julie Anne b 25 Oct 1973; Alexander Richard b 24 Jun 1975; ord during assistantship at Balsall Heath Church of Christ 24 Jul 1973; ind to St George's URC, Ashington; trans to St John's URC, Newcastle-on-Tyne; ind to St Andrew's 30 May 1985; Chaplain (TA) since 1983; Publ: *Help for Prayerless Christianity* (T&T Clark, 1975); *The Capacity to Care* (St George's House, Windsor, 1984); *Aquainted with Grief* (Geneva Theological College, 1984).

MARKINCH (FES X, 286)

Formed 27 Apr 1969 by union of Markinch St Drostan's and Markinch St Mark's.

1956 HUGH LYONS
(FES IX, 134, 475, 595; X, 282, 286), trans from Kennoway Arnot to St Mark's 5 Dec 1956; ret 27 Apr 1969; died 17 Apr 1978.

1972 IAN DINNING GORDON
(FES X, 286), ord and ind to Markinch 17 Oct 1972; d Judith m Hamish Mair; d Claire m Forsyth Black; d Laura m Kevin Rooney.

METHIL (FES V, 114; VIII, 433; IX, 482; X, 286)

1968 JAMES DUNCAN
(FES X, 287, 311), dem from Methil 21 Aug 1972 to enter teaching profession; app Principal teacher of Religious Education, Bell Baxter School, Cupar; died 23 Dec 1998.

1973 GEORGE FERGUSON McDONALD
(FES IX, 608; X, 101, 287, 350), trans from Dalmellington Lamloch with Bellsbank to Methil 1 Feb 1973; ret 31 Oct 1977; died 30 Nov 1996.

1978 ALASTAIR HUNTER GRAY
ord and ind to Methil 18 Jun 1978; trans to Garvald and Morham with Haddington West 21 Feb 1985.

1985 JOHN DAVIDSON THOMSON
ord and ind to Methil 19 Sep 1985; trans to Kirkcaldy Pathhead 16 Mar 1993.

1994 ALEXANDER C WARK
res from app at Rotterdam and ind to Methil 13 Feb 1994; trans to Renfrew Old 23 Sep 1998.

METHILHILL (FUF 366; FES IX, 482; X, 287)

Linked 3 Dec 1978 with Denbeath.

1946 ROBERT MOLLISON ESPLIN
(FES IX, 483; X, 287), ord and ind to Methilhill 24 Jan 1946; ret 30 Nov 1978; died 30 Apr 1986.

1978 GRAHAM DOUGLAS SUTHERLAND DEANS
ord and ind to Denbeath 24 Aug 1978; became minister of linked charge with Methilhill 3 Dec 1978; Depute Clerk and Treasurer, Presb of Kirkcaldy 1981–87; trans to Dumfries St Mary's 8 Jul 1987.

1988 ELISABETH FAITH CRANFIELD
ord and ind to Denbeath with Methilhill 30 Jun 1988, see Denbeath.

THORNTON (FES IX, 483; X, 287)

Linked 1 Mar 1995 with Kirkcaldy Viewforth.

1971 ROBERT HUGH DRUMMOND
(FES X, 77, 287, 381), trans from Kilmuir-Easter to Thornton 2 Jul 1971; trans to Pitsligo 13 Aug 1981.

1981 DAVID WEST GATT
B 17 Jan 1928 at Fraserburgh, s of David West G. and Winifred Mary Anderson; educ Fraserburgh Academy 1933–44; Scottish Congregational College 1969–73; University of Edinburgh 1970–73; Cost Accountant 1949–54; Accountant with British Rail 1954–61; Lecturer and Civil Defence Officer 1961–69; m 22 Dec 1956 Jeannie Slessor Watt b 13 May 1933 d of George W. and Louise Tait; Children: Alison Jane b 4 Apr 1961 m White; Iain Vincent b 28 Nov 1963; ord by Congregational Church and ind to Motherwell, Aug 1973; admitted by General Assembly and ind to Thornton 26 Nov 1981; ret 28 Feb 1995.

1995 DANIEL CONNOLLY
ind to Viewforth with Thornton 10 Jan 1995, see Viewforth.

WEMYSS (FES X, 288)

Formed 7 Mar 1976 by union of Wemyss St Adrian's and St George's and Wemyss St Mary's-by-the-Sea.

1950 JOHN WELSH
(FES IX, 164, 298, 484, 502; X, 288), trans from Auchterhouse to St Mary's-by-the-Sea 11 Apr 1950; ret 31 Jul 1975; died 27 May 1982.

1961 GEORGE VEITCH HENDRIE
(FES X, 281, 288), ord and ind to East Wemyss St George's 11 Oct 1961; became minister of united charge with West Wemyss St Aidrian's 12 Aug 1973 and of united charge with St Mary's-by-the-Sea 7 Mar 1976; died 8 Aug 1988.

1989 KEVIN MACKENZIE
ord and ind to Wemyss 16 May 1989; trans to Ochiltree with Stair 30 Mar 1993.

1993 JOAN EDITH ARBUTHNOTT
B 10 Jun 1946 at Inverurie, d of Robert Williamson Minto and Phoebe Rosemary Gareh; educ Inverurie Academy 1958–64; University of Aberdeen 1964–68 (MA); University of Edinburgh 1989–92 (BD); Parish Asst, South Queensferry 1988–89; lic by Presb of Edinburgh 5 Jul 1992; asst Edinburgh St Michael's 1992–93; m 10 Sep 1965 Gordon William Arbuthnott b 14 Mar 1942 d of Roy Gordon A. and Maggie Lobban; Children: David John b 28 Dec 1968; Peter Gordon b 3 Oct 1971; ord and ind to Wemyss 20 Dec 1993; dem 2 Dec 1997.

1999 KENNETH WILLIAM DONALD
B 26 Apr 1955 at Glasgow, s of Matthew and Marion D; educ High Possil and Possilpark, Glasgow 1967–73; Paisley College of Technology 1973–77 (BA); University of Edinburgh 1977–80 (BD); lic by Presb of Glasgow, Jun 1980; asst East Kilbride Westwood 1980–81; Edinburgh Holyrood Abbey 1981–82; m 25 Feb 1984 Moira Morris b 14

Feb 1963 d of David and Rita M; Children: Karen Laura b 21 May 1985; Mark Kenneth b 18 Mar 1987; Ashleigh Claire b 3 Feb 1990; Lisa Joy b 12 Nov 1992; Rachel Nicole b 29 Apr 1995; ord by Presb of Edinburgh and introd as Assoc at Holy Trinity 23 Mar 1982; ind to Aberdeen Stockethill 20 Mar 1986; dem 28 Feb 1995; ind to Wemyss 4 Mar 1999.

PRESBYTERY OF ST ANDREWS

ABDIE AND DUNBOG (FES X, 289)

Formed 12 Dec 1965 by union of Abdie and Dunbog. Linked 10 Apr 1983 with Newburgh.

1960   IVERACH NOEL McDONALD
(FES IX, 608, 790; X, 260, 289, 446), res from term app at Gask and introd on term app to Abdie 11 May 1960; ret 12 Dec 1965; died 27 Jul 1979.

1966   THOMAS JOHNSTON TITTERINGTON
(FES IX, 637; X, 137, 289, 364), trans from Port Glasgow Clune Park to Abdie and Dunbog 12 May 1966; ret 31 Mar 1983; died 29 Jan 1993.

1983   IAN TAYLOR
B 12 Oct 1932 at Dundee, s of Ian Goodsir Oliphant T. and Jemima Rattray Kydd; educ Dundee High 1939–51; University of St Andrews 1951–54 (BSc), 1956–57 (BEd); University of Sheffield 1974–75 (MA); University of Edinburgh 1979–81 (LTh); Teaching 1957–62; Lecturing (Maths) 1962–64; Senior Lecturer (Educ) 1964–79; lic by Presb of Edinburgh, Jun 1983; asst Edinburgh St Giles' Cathedral 1981–83; m 22 Jun 1956 Marjorie Ann Ogilvy Coupar b 23 Jun 1935 d of Benjamin Batchelor C. and Annie McCourtie; Children: Michael John b 20 Nov 1959 m Carol Pride; Richard Jeremy b 27 Apr 1961 m (1) Janet Hopley, divorced, m (2) Christina Metikaridis; Nichola Suzanne b 27 Nov 1965; ord and ind to Abdie and Dunbog with Newburgh 10 Aug 1983; ret 12 October 1997; Lecturing (Adult Educ) for Universities of St Andrews, Edinburgh, Cambridge, Hull, Leeds; Publ: *How to Produce Concert Versions of Gilbert and Sullivan* (Hale, 1972); *Maths for Mums and Dads* (Elliot, 1973); *The Gilbert and Sullivan Quiz Book* (William Luscombe, 1974); *The Opera Lover's Quiz Book* (William Luscombe, 1975); *Music and the Victorian Elementary School* (History of Education Society, 1976); video—John Knox (Church of Scotland, 1986).

1998   ROBERT JAMES VICTOR LOGAN
(FES X, 51, 371), trans from Inverness Crown to Abdie and Dunbog with Newburgh 19 Mar 1998; Publ: *The Lion, the Pit and the Snowy Day* (private, 1982).

ANSTRUTHER (FES X, 293)

Formed 1 Jan 1973 by union of Chalmers Memorial and St Adrian's.

1968   JAMES NAPIER HUTCHISON
(FES IX, 80; X, 14, 49, 59, 293), trans from Bonkyl and Preston with Reston to St Adrian's 18 Apr 1968; ret 31 Dec 1972; died 5 Sep 1996.

1973   CHARLES WILMAR MILLER
(FES IX, 149; X, 88, 147, 293, 334), trans from Cruden to Anstruther 1 Jun 1973; trans to Fowlis and Liff 24 Sep 1980.

1982   DAVID HENRY ALEXANDER WATSON
(FES X, 145), trans from Kilsyth Burns and Old and introd to Anstruther (term) 29 Jun 1982; ind 28 Jun 1987; ret 30 Sep 1993; s David m Julie Stewart; s Hugh m Sheena MacKenzie; d Jane m Allan Green; d Ruth m Michael Harrison.

1994   IAN ANDREW CATHCART
B 5 Apr 1964 at Glasgow, s of John Ian C. and Catherine Cubie Pollock; educ Hillpark Secondary, Glasgow 1975–81; Glasgow College of Building and Printing 1981–85; University of Glasgow 1989–92 (BD); Quantity Surveyor 1985–89; lic by Presb of Glasgow, Jun 1992; asst Glasgow King's Park 1992–94; m 6 Jul 1991 Jacqueline Olive Wardrope b 17 May 1963 d of William Richard W. and Olive Emma Sweet Johnston; Children: Ross John b 2 Jan 1994; Joshua Ian b 31 Mar 1997; Rebekah Jacqueline b 16 Feb 1999; ord and ind to Anstruther 28 Apr 1994.

AUCHTERMUCHTY (FES IX, 485; X, 289)

1973   WILLIAM JAMES LETHEM GALBRAITH
(FES X, 289), ord and ind to Auchtermuchty 27 Sep 1973; trans to Kilchrenan and Dalavich with Muckairn 8 Sep 1989.

1990   ANN GRANGER FRASER
B 4 Mar 1947 at Glasgow, d of Alexander Hunter Mackie and Margaret Murray; educ Govan High 1958–64; University of Glasgow 1983–88 (BD, CMin); Insurance Clerkess 1964–65; Airtraffic Control Asst 1965–68; lic by Presb of Paisley 31 Aug 1988; m 29 Sep 1967 Gilbert John Alexander Fraser b 9 Dec 1940 s of Alexander F. and Annie Gilbert; Children: Gary b 3 Jan 1969 m Lynne Campbell; Glen b 7 Jul 1970 m Vivienne Nairn; Gael b 5 Sep 1977; ord and ind to Auchtermuchty 16 Aug 1990.

BALMERINO (FES IX, 486; X, 289)

Vacant from 1978 until 1984. Linked 22 Jan 1984 with Wormit.

1938 ROBERT PEEBLES CONSTABLE
(FES IX, 39, 486; X, 289), trans from Edinburgh St James' to Balmerino 31 Mar 1938; died 11 Nov 1978.

1984 ANDREW LOCKHART STEVENSON
B 12 Dec 1926 at Beith, s of Andrew S. and Jessie Barclay; educ Spier's School, Beith 1938–44; Jordanhill College, Glasgow 1944–46 (DipPE); University of Glasgow 1945–46, 1948–50 (Dip Public Admin); University of London 1950–53 (LLB); University of Aberdeen 1975–78 (MLitt); National Service (RAF) 1946–48; Teaching (PE) 1948–66; Lecturing (PE) 1966–81; lic by Presb of Aberdeen 31 May 1984; m 10 Aug 1955 Jane Wilson Begg b 21 Apr 1927 d of Alexander Kidd B. and Catherine Purdon Shankland; Children: Catherine b 10 May 1957 m McKenna; Sheila b 13 Oct 1959 m Strachan; Andrew John b 4 Jul 1963; ord and ind to Balmerino with Wormit 25 Jul 1984; ret 31 Aug 1993.

1993 GRAEME WILLIAM BEEBEE
B 30 May 1965 at Ayr, s of John Benjamin B. and Maureen Elizabeth McMurtrie; educ Belmont Academy, Ayr 1977–83; Ayr College 1984 (NCBS); Falkirk College 1985–87 (SNDCS); University of St Andrews 1987–92 (BD); lic by Presb of Ayr 28 Jun 1992; asst Troon St Meddan's 1992–93; m 12 Aug 1995 Ailsa Blair b 26 Jun 1970 d of George Chisholm B. and Margaret MacDonald; ord and ind to Balmerino with Wormit 28 Oct 1993.

BOARHILLS AND DUNINO (FES X, 293, 294)

Boarhills with Dunino linked 23 Jun 1993 with St Andrews Martyrs'. Linkage continues following union of Boarhills and Dunino 1 May 1994.

1956 NORMAN ARTHUR LOGAN
(FUF 128; FES IX, 174, 259; X, 152, 294), trans from Glasgow Bluevale to Dunino 23 Nov 1956; ret 31 Aug 1965; died 21 Jun 1985.

1966 PETER CARSTAIRS DOUGLAS
(FES X, 293), ord and ind to Boarhills with Dunino 26 Feb 1966; ret 23 Jun 1993; divorced 1989, m (2) 18 Jul 1993 Patricia Anne Jackson.

1993 DAVID IAN SINCLAIR
ord and ind to Martyrs' 1 Nov 1990; became minister of linked charge with Boarhills with Dunino 23 Jun 1993 and of linked charge with Boarhills and Dunino 1 May 1994; dem 21 Mar 1999 on app as Secretary of Committee on Church and Nation.

CAMERON (FES V, 186; VIII, 454; IX, 495; X, 293)

Linked 1949 with Largoward. Further linked 17 Apr 1975 with St Andrews St Leonard's. Linkage with Largoward terminated 11 October 1983.

1962 DONALD GILLIES CUBIE
(FES X, 190, 277, 293), trans from Mossgreen and Crossgates to Cameron with Largoward 27 Sep 1962; ret 30 Jun 1973; died 13 Jul 1978.

1975 ANDREW BARCLAY McLELLAN
(FES IX, 198, 207, 644; X, 113, 296), ind to St Andrews St Leonard's 14 Jan 1960; became minister of linked charge with Cameron with Largoward 17 Apr 1975, see St Leonard's.

1980 LAWSON RICHARD BROWN
(FES X, 127, 169, 416), trans from Paisley Lylesland to St Leonard's with Cameron with Largoward 6 Feb 1980; became minister of St Leonard's with Cameron 11 Oct 1983; ret 31 Aug 1997.

1998 ALAN DOUGLAS McDONALD
B 6 Mar 1951 at Glasgow, s of Douglas Gordon M. and Robina Lindsay Bishop Craig; educ Glasgow Academy 1962–69; University of Strathclyde 1969–72 (LLB); University of Edinburgh 1975–78 (BD), 1994–96 (MTh); Apprentice Solicitor 1972–74; Solicitor 1974–75; lic by Presb of Edinburgh 2 Jul 1978; asst Edinburgh Greenside 1978–79; m 26 Jul 1975 Judith Margaret Allen b 23 May 1950 d of Arthur Charles A. and Kathleen Joy Hulatt; Children: Neil David b 16 Jan 1979; Alison Ruth b 22 Jul 1981; ord by Presb of Edinburgh and introd as Community minister at Drylaw, Muirhouse and the Old Kirk 25 Oct 1979; ind to Aberdeen Holburn Central 28 Jul 1983; trans to Cameron with St Leonard's 27 Aug 1998.

CARNBEE (FUF 374; FES V, 187; VIII, 455; IX, 495; X, 294)

Linked 28 Dec 1971 with Pittenweem.

1929 JOHN ANDREW INGLIS
(FES VIII, 82, 584; IX, 495, 608; X, 294), trans from Peterhead East to Carnbee 22 Nov 1929; ret 2 Jun 1960; died 21 Jun 1984.

1961 ARTHUR CROSS SCOBIE
(FES IX, 251, 484, 542; X, 148, 294), trans from Glasgow Stepps St Andrew's to Carnbee 16 Mar 1961; ret 31 May 1971; died 28 Jul 1972.

1971 CHARLES GEORGE THROWER
(FES X, 295, 426), ind to Pittenweem 27 Nov 1970; became minister of linked charge with Carnbee 28 Dec 1971, see Pittenweem.

CELLARDYKE (FES V, 191; VIII, 455; IX, 495; X, 294)

Linked 6 Sep 1988 with Kilrenny.

1952 JOHN MATHEWS
(FES IX, 495; X, 294), [correction: Mathews, not Matthews as in Vol X, 294]; trans from Carlisle Fisher Street to Cellardyke 9 Jan 1952; ret 30 Sep 1982; died 13 Sep 1991.

1983 WILLIAM IAIN CRAIGDALLIE DUNN
ord and ind to Cellardyke 17 May 1983; trans to Edinburgh Pilrig and Dalmeny Street 19 Jan 1988.

1989 FYFE BLAIR
ord and ind to Cellardyke with Kilrenny 26 Jun 1989; trans to Aberdeen Cove 1 Jan 1998.

1999 DAVID JAMES HEPBURN LAING
B 14 Apr 1949 at Portobello, s of James Allan L. and Norah McPhail Ritchie; educ Royal High School, Edinburgh and Elgin Academy 1954–68; University of St Andrews 1968–75 (BD, DPS); lic by Presb of Moray 27 Jun 1975; asst Aberdeen West of St Nicholas 1975–77; m 17 Aug 1974 Edith Mary Thomson Ramsay b 6 Aug 1952 d of Archibald Alfred Luke R. and Greta Amelia Laurie; Children: Ian David Ramsay b 2 Jun 1977; Andrew James Stewart b 10 Dec 1979; ord by Presb of Aberdeen during assistantship at West of St Nicholas 15 Mar 1976; introd to Lossiemouth St Gerardine's High (term) 15 Jun 1977 and ind to same charge Jun 1980; trans to Dundee Craigiebank 9 Nov 1982; trans to Kirkcaldy St Andrew's 16 May 1989; trans to Cellardyke with Kilrenny 28 Jan 1999.

CERES AND SPRINGFIELD (FES X, 289, 292)

Linkage of Springfield and Monimail terminated 6 Feb 1983. Ceres and Springfield linked 19 Jun 1983, then united 26 Feb 1989.

1967 GEORGE RENDLE LEATHEM
(FES IX, 37, 492, 560; X, 292, 326), trans from Aberdeen Ferryhill to Springfield 17 May 1967; ret 31 Mar 1975; died 7 Oct 1992.

1968 WALTER LEARMONTH
(FES X, 289), ord and ind to Ceres 21 Aug 1968; became minister of linked charge with Springfield 19 Jun 1983 and of united charge 26 Feb 1989; ret 16 Sep 1997.

1975 GEORGE IVORY LITHGOW McCASKILL
(FES IX, 648; X, 176, 252, 292, 369), ind to Monimail 13 Dec 1973; became minister of linked charge with Springfield 31 Mar 1975, see Monimail.

1998 MATTHEW ZACHARY ROSS
B 15 Nov 1967 at Dundee, s of Euan MacDonald R. and Jean Mary Palmer; educ Westminster School, London 1982–86; University of Edinburgh 1986–90 (LLB), 1993–96 (BD); House of Commons Research Asst 1990–91; Political Research 1991–93; lic by Presb of Edinburgh 7 Jul 1996; asst Edinburgh Duddingston 1996–98; ord and ind to Ceres and Springfield 4 Feb 1998.

CRAIL (FES IX, 495; X, 294)

Linked 26 Sep 1976 with Kingsbarns.

1915 WILLIAM MURRAY MILNE
(FES V, 195; VIII, 456; IX, 496; X, 294), trans from Macduff to Crail 17 Nov 1915; ret 31 May 1956; died 16 Dec 1982.

1956 WILLIAM JOHN MACINTYRE
(FES IX, 400; X, 238, 294), trans from Kilbrandon and Kilchattan to Crail 5 Dec 1956; became minister of linked charge with Kingsbarns 26 Sep 1976; ret 30 Sep 1989; DD (St Andrews) 1981; d Christine m David Livingstone Farquhar; s John m Kathryn Lucile Knight.

1989 GEORGE FAIRLIE
(FES X, 306, 385), trans from Glasgow Cathcart South to Crail with Kingsbarns 3 Nov 1989; d Catriona m Sandy Mack; s Alasdair m Mairi McLeod.

CREICH, FLISK AND KILMANY (FES X, 290)

Linked 6 Feb 1983 with Monimail.

1972 PETER McPHAIL
(FES IX, 66, 608; X, 41, 57, 290), trans from Prestonpans Preston to Creich, Flisk and Kilmany 11 May 1972; Clerk to the Synod of Fife; ret 31 Jan 1982; d Sheila m William Telfer; d Morag m Frank Williamson; d Fiona m Graham Ure.

1983 CLIFFORD STRONG
B 16 Nov 1930 at Aintree, nr Liverpool, s of Frederick S. and Florence May Moorcroft; educ Anfield School, Liverpool 1936–46; University of Glasgow 1979–82 (LTh); Shipping Superintendent 1953–79; lic by Presb of Dumbarton 27 Jun 1982; asst Bearsden South 1982–83; m 12 Aug 1954 Alice Rosemary Grant b 15 Oct 1927 d of Alexander G. and Jathi; Children: Colin Alexander b 4 Jul 1958 m Laura Miller; Alistair James b 22 Nov 1961; ord by Presb of Dumbarton during assistantship at Bearsden South 1983; ind to Creich, Flisk and Kilmany with Monimail 20 Sep 1983; ret 16 Nov 1995.

1996 MITCHELL COLLINS
B 20 Apr 1945 at St Andrews, s of George Wilkinson C. and Janet Gourlay Deas; educ Buckhaven High 1957–61; University of St Andrews 1989–93 (BD); University of Edinburgh 1994–95 (CPS); Clerical work 1961–76; Office Management 1976–82; lic by Presb of Kirkcaldy 18 Sep 1994; m 15 Jul 1967 Alexandra Guidi b 17 Oct 1945 d of James G. and Isabella Martin; Children: Susan b 8 Sep 1968 m Scott Fraser; Lynne b 22 Dec 1970; Michelle b 21 Feb 1974 m Colin McLean; ord and ind to Creich, Flisk and Kilmany with Monimail 13 Jun 1996.

CUPAR OLD AND ST MICHAEL OF TARVIT
(FES V, 141; VIII, 441; IX, 487; X, 290)

1972 JOHN DONALD HENDERSON
(FES IX, 564; X, 88, 290, 328, 356), trans from Thornhill to Cupar Old and St Michael of Tarvit 22 Jun 1972; trans to Makerstoun with Smailholm with Stichill, Hume and Nenthorn 17 Nov 1978.

1979 DAVID WILLIAM CLARK
res from term app at Bridge of Allan Chalmers and ind to Cupar Old and St Michael of Tarvit 3 May 1979; trans to the West Kirk of Helensburgh 1 Sep 1986.

1987 DEREK BROWNING
B 24 May 1962 at Edinburgh, s of John B. and Mary Winton Shanks; educ North Berwick High 1974–80; University of Oxford 1980–83 (MA); University of St Andrews 1983–86 (BD); Princeton Theological Seminary, USA 1994–97 (DipMin); lic by Presb of Lothian 4 Jul 1986; asst Troon St Meddan's 1986–87; ord and ind to Cupar Old and St Michael of Tarvit 4 Aug 1987.

CUPAR ST JOHN'S (FUF 370; FES IX, 487; X, 290)

1956 JAMES KIRK PORTEOUS
(FES IX, 424; X, 252, 290), trans from Logiealmond to St John's 16 Feb 1956; ret 9 Mar 1997.

1997 JOHN DAVIDSON HEGARTY
B 20 Nov 1941 at Edinburgh, s of Albert H. and Isabella Renwick Craig; educ Leith Academy 1953–58; University of Glasgow 1966–68; British Society of Commerce (external) 1974–76 (ABSC); University of Edinburgh 1985–88 (LTh); Accountancy 1958–66; Home Missionary (Church of Scotland) 1968–69; Management Accountancy 1970–78; Lay Missionary 1978–85; lic by Presb of Lothian 29 Jun 1988; m 27 Aug 1966 Linda May Thornton b 28 Aug 1945 d of James Burns Newlands T. and Mary May Greig Anderson; Children: Susan Jane b 21 Sep 1967 m Stephen Park; Shona Davidson b 31 May 1969 m Keith Mackay; John David b 22 Jul 1974; ord and ind to Glasgow High Carntyne 24 Aug 1988; trans to St John's 20 Nov 1997.

DAIRSIE (FUF 370; FES V, 148; VIII, 443; IX, 488; X, 290)

Linked 17 May 1970 with Kemback. Further linked 31 Jul 1980 with Strathkinness.

1970 FRANCIS WILLIAM RAE
(FES IX, 194, 262, 375; X, 154, 291), trans from Glasgow Cardonald to Dairsie with Kemback 3 Sep 1970; ret 31 Oct 1976; died 4 Jun 1994.

1977 JAMES ERIC STEWART LOW
(FES X, 12, 34, 250, 403, 421), dem from South Ronaldsay and Burray and introd to Dairsie with Kemback (term) 2 Oct 1977; ind to Carnoustie Panbride 10 May 1979.

1980 JAMES ARNOT HAMILTON
(FES X, 4, 354), trans from Edinburgh Barclay Bruntsfield to Dairsie with Kemback 21 Feb 1980; became minister of linked charge with Strathkinness 31 Jul 1980; died 5 Apr 1981.

1981 ALEXANDER STRICKLAND
(FES X, 275), trans from Kildonan with Whiting Bay to Dairsie with Kemback with Strathkinness 22 Oct 1981.

EDENSHEAD AND STRATHMIGLO (FES X, 291, 292)

Formed 1 May 1981 by union of Edenshead and Strathmiglo.

1965 HERBERT LLOYD MONRO CAMERON
(FES X, 291), ord and ind to Edenshead 4 Nov 1965; ret 26 Oct 1980; died 8 May 1989.

1974 WILLIAM CAMERON WALLACE
(FES IX, 240, 342; X, 204, 292, 452), res as Industrial Chaplain and ind to Strathmiglo 9 Oct 1974; became minister of united charge with Edenshead 1 May 1981; ret 30 Sep 1983; died 24 Apr 1987.

1984 THOMAS GRAY McCALLUM ROBERTSON
(FES X, 389), trans from Wick Old to Edenshead and Strathmiglo 24 May 1984; s Duncan m Jennifer Anne Connell.

ELIE (FES IX, 496; X, 294)

Linked 24 Apr 1977 with Kilconquhar and Colinsburgh.

1950 KENNETH DAVID MACKENZIE DOW
(FES IX, 163, 496, 765; X, 294), trans from Glasserton to Elie 28 Jun 1950; became minister of linked charge with Kilconquhar and Colinsburgh 24 Apr 1977; ret 30 Apr 1979; died 20 Feb 1986.

1979 GORDON DAVID JAMIESON
(FES X, 107), trans from Drongan The Schaw Kirk to Elie with Kilconquhar and Colinsburgh 25 Jul 1979; trans to Dundee Barnhill St Margaret's 12 Jun 1986.

1986 PETER MEAGER
(FES X, 447), ret from RAChD and ind to Elie with Kilconquhar and Colinsburgh 17 Dec 1986; dem 31 Jul 1998; app Clerk to Presb of St Andrews 1 Jul 1999; app Chaplain (part-time) to Murray Royal Hospital, Perth 1 Aug 1999; Open University 1995–96 (CMgmt); s Colin m Lorna Stevenson; d Elizabeth m Gordon Walsh.

1998 IAIN FERGUSON PATON
B 28 Jan 1941 at Edinburgh, s of Alexander P. and Jill Goold Ferguson; educ George Watson's, Edinburgh 1946–57; University of Edinburgh 1975–

79 (BD); Banking 1957–67; Company Secretary 1967–75; lic by Presb of Edinburgh, Jul 1979; asst Edinburgh St Ninian's Corstorphine 1979–80; m 20 Mar 1970 Marjorie Vickers MacDonald b 15 Oct 1943 d of David Alexander M. and Frances Dobson Fleming; Children: Douglas Alexander b 6 Aug 1972; Karen Marjorie b 19 Mar 1974 m Roger Yearsley; ord and ind to Banchory-Ternan West 29 May 1980; trans to Glasgow Newlands South 6 Oct 1985; introd to Jerusalem St Andrew's 1 Mar 1997; ind to Elie with Kilconquhar and Colinsburgh 7 Dec 1998.

FALKLAND (FES IX, 488; X, 291)

Linked 1 Jan 1981 with Freuchie.

1954   PETER RENNIE GRAHAM WALLACE
(FES IX, 72, 489; X, 291), trans from Innerleithen Craigside to Falkland 8 Apr 1954; became minister of linked charge with Freuchie 1 Jan 1981; ret 31 May 1984; died 31 Jul 1985.

1984   IAIN ALASTAIR MACKAY WRIGHT
ord by Presb of England during assistantship at St Columba's 17 Apr 1983; ind to Falkland with Freuchie 22 Nov 1984; dem 6 May 1989 on app as Director for Care, Scotland.

1990   JOHN WILLIAM JARVIE
B 15 Apr 1958 at Irvine, s of John J. and Margaret Ramsay; educ Rutherglen Academy, Stonelaw High and Cathkin High 1969–74; Glasgow College of Technology 1974–76 (SHND); University of Glasgow 1984–89 (BD, CMin); University of Edinburgh 1994–96 [part-time] (MTh); Accountancy 1976–84; lic by Presb of Glasgow 3 Jul 1989; asst Glasgow Langside 1985–86, Strathbungo Queen's Park 1986–87, St James' Pollok 1987–88; Strathaven East with Glasford 1988–89; Hamilton St John's 1989–90; m 1 Aug 1981 Karena Susan Langdon b 10 Jun 1960 d of Albert John L. and Georgina Kelly; Children: Iain James b 26 Jan 1988; Calum David b 20 Sep 1989; Duncan Peter b 11 May 1993; ord and ind to Falkland with Freuchie 4 Jul 1990.

FREUCHIE (FES V, 157; VIII, 447; IX, 489; X, 291)

Linked 1 Jan 1981 with Falkland.

1970   THOMAS KILGOUR POTTS
(FES IX, 204, 484, 559; X, 249, 291), trans from Abernethy with Dron to Freuchie 27 Jan 1970; died 26 Apr 1980.

1981   PETER RENNIE GRAHAM WALLACE
(FES IX, 72, 489; X, 291), ind to Falkland 8 Apr 1954; became minister of linked charge with Freuchie 1 Jan 1981, see Falkland.

1984   IAIN ALASTAIR MACKAY WRIGHT
ind to Falkland with Freuchie 22 Nov 1984, see Falkland.

1990   JOHN WILLIAM JARVIE
ord and ind to Falkland with Freuchie 4 Jul 1990, see Falkland.

HOWE OF FIFE (FES X, 289, 290, 291)

Formed 23 Jan 1983 by union of Collessie, Ladybank, Cults and Kettle.

1947   ALEXANDER PHILP
(FES IX, 231, 491; X, 289, 291), trans from Greenock North to Ladybank 28 Oct 1947; became minister of united charge with Collessie 7 Jan 1968; ret 30 Apr 1975; died 17 Jun 1980.

1964   ANGUS MACASKILL
(FES IX, 26, 543; X, 15, 290), trans from Edinburgh London Road to Cults with Kettle 23 Apr 1964; ret 30 Jun 1969; died 2 Sep 1983.

1970   GEORGE ALEXANDER MACLEAN HENDERSON
(FES IX, 376; X, 224, 290, 378, 419), dem from Fodderty and Strathpeffer 30 Jun 1962; ind to Cults with Kettle 15 Jan 1970; ret 16 Jan 1983; died 18 Jul 1989.

1975   IAN GRAHAM WOTHERSPOON
(FES X, 23, 102, 289, 413), res as Assoc at Edinburgh St Cuthbert's and ind to Collessie and Ladybank 16 Oct 1975; trans to Edinburgh Portobello Old and Windsor Place 13 Jul 1982.

1983   IAIN MACDONALD FORBES
(FES X, 395, 419, 453), trans from Benbecula to Howe of Fife 17 Feb 1983; dem on app by Board of World Mission to the Evangelical Church of Christ in Mozambique 31 Oct 1993.

1991   MARION JOYCE PATON
B 17 Jun 1951 at St Helen's, Merseyside, d of Ian Keith P. and Gwendolyn Ruth Mitchell; educ Huyton College and Morpeth Grammar for Girls 1962–70; University College, Cardiff 1970–73 (BMus); King Alfred's College, Winchester 1973–74 (PGCE); University of St Andrews 1987–90 (BD); Teaching 1974–77; Director of Music, Wentworth Milton Mount, Bournemouth 1977–87; lic by Presb of St Andrews 1 Jul 1990; ord by Presb of St Andrews and introd as Assoc to Howe of Fife 5 Dec 1991; ind to same charge 8 Sep 1994.

1996   MARION COWIE
B 31 Aug 1963 at Malta, d of John Andrew Edmiston and Marjory Ellen Aitken; educ Woodmill High, Dunfermline and Glenwood High, Glenrothes 1975–81; University of Glasgow 1982–86 (MA), 1986–89 (BD); lic by Presb of Dumbarton 9 Jul 1989; asst Glasgow Netherlee 1989–91; m 28 Jul 1989 George Strachan Cowie b 18 Nov 1963 s of Gordon Strachan C. and Angela Mary Whelband; Children: Graeme Strachan b 27 May 1991; Kirsty-Anne b 11 Apr 1994; ord by Presb of Glasgow during assistantship at Netherlee 11 May 1990; introd as Assoc at Howe of Fife 7 Nov 1996.

KEMBACK (FES V, 205; VIII, 458; IX, 497; X, 291)

Linked 17 May 1970 with Dairsie. Further linked 31 Jul 1980 with Strathkinness.

1970 FRANCIS WILLIAM RAE
(FES IX, 194, 262, 375; X, 154, 291), trans from Glasgow Cardonald to Dairsie with Kemback 3 Sep 1970; ret 31 Oct 1976; died 4 Jun 1994.

1977 JAMES ERIC STEWART LOW
introd to Dairsie with Kemback (term) 2 Oct 1977, see Dairsie.

1980 JAMES ARNOT HAMILTON
(FES X, 4, 354), ind to Dairsie with Kemback 21 Feb 1980, see Dairsie.

KILCONQUHAR AND COLINSBURGH (FES IX, 497; X, 294)

Linked 24 Apr 1977 with Elie.

1965 JAMES EADIE LYON
(FES IX, 1, 517; X, 294, 306), trans from Dundee Victoria Street to Kilconquhar and Colinsburgh 12 May 1965; ret 31 Jul 1976; died 1 Jan 1995.

1977 KENNETH DAVID MACKENZIE DOW
(FES IX, 163, 496, 765; X, 294), trans from Glasserton to Elie 28 Jun 1950; became minister of linked charge with Kilconquhar and Colinsburgh 24 Apr 1977; ret 30 Apr 1979; died 20 Feb 1986.

1979 GORDON DAVID JAMIESON
(FES X, 107), trans from Drongan The Schaw Kirk to Elie with Kilconquhar and Colinsburgh 25 Jul 1979; trans to Dundee Barnhill St Margaret's 12 Jun 1986.

1986 PETER MEAGER
(FES X, 447), ind to Elie with Kilconquhar and Colinsburgh 17 Dec 1986, see Elie.

1998 IAIN FERGUSON PATON
ind to Elie with Kilconquhar and Colinsburgh 7 Dec 1998, see Elie.

KILRENNY (FES V, 211; VIII, 459; IX, 497; X, 294)

Linked 6 Sep 1988 with Cellardyke.

1948 HAMISH STEWART DUNCAN MACNAB
(FES IX, 497; X, 294), ord and ind to Kilrenny 9 Jun 1948; ret 31 October 1987; s Iain m Jean Ritchie; d Amanda m Mark Schnee; d Judith m Peter Jones; s Gavin m Mary Stevenson; s Hamish m Sheila Hamilton.

1989 FYFE BLAIR
ind to Cellardyke with Kilrenny 26 Jun 1989, see Cellardyke.

1999 DAVID JAMES HEPBURN LAING
ind to Cellardyke with Kilrenny 28 Jan 1999, see Cellardyke.

KINGSBARNS (FES V, 215; VIII, 460; IX, 497; X, 294)

Linked 26 Sep 1976 with Crail.

1926 DOUGLAS GEORGE BISSET
(FES VIII, 460; IX, 497; X, 294), ord and ind to Kingsbarns 4 Jun 1926; ret 12 Oct 1974; died 18 Nov 1991.

1976 WILLIAM JOHN MACINTYRE
(FES IX, 400; X, 238, 294), ind to Crail 5 Dec 1956; became minister of linked charge with Kingsbarns 26 Sep 1976, see Crail.

1989 GEORGE FAIRLIE
(FES X, 306, 385), trans from Glasgow Cathcart South to Crail with Kingsbarns 3 Nov 1989.

LARGO AND NEWBURN (FES X, 294)

Linked 3 Jun 1987 with Largo St David's.

1967 DOUGLAS LISTER
(FES IX, 542; X, 294, 298, 345), trans from Inverurie St Andrew's to Largo and Newburn 25 Jan 1967; ret 31 October 1986; Addl publ: *The Day I Met Sandra* (1998).

1988 ROSEMARY FREW
B 2 Oct 1961 at Glasgow, d of Robert Ramsay Bone and Mary Donald; educ Williamwood Junior High, Eastwood Senior High and Linlithgow Academy 1973–79; University of Edinburgh 1979–82 (MA), 1983–86 (BD); lic by Presb of West Lothian 29 Jun 1986; asst Markinch 1986–87; m 8 Sep 1984 David James Allardyce Frew b 10 Mar 1955 s of James F. and Alice Campbell Montgomery; Children: Peter James b 29 Sep 1995; Rebecca Mhairi b 23 Jun 1998; ord and ind to Largo and Newburn with Largo St David's 4 May 1988.

LARGO ST DAVID'S (FUF 364; FES IX, 498; X, 294)

Linked 3 Jun 1987 with Largo and Newburn.

1972 THOMAS JAMES DYER
(FES IX, 58, 87, 542; X, 35, 295, 336), trans from Foveran to St David's 27 Jan 1972; ret 31 Mar 1979; died 10 Jan 1994.

1979 JAMES ALEXANDER ROBERTSON MACKENZIE
(FES IX, 682, 740; X, 191, 207, 309, 387), trans from Carmichael with Pettinain with Covington and Thankerton to St David's 25 Oct 1979; ret 31 Mar 1987.

1988 ROSEMARY FREW
ord and ind to Largo and Newburn with St David's 4 May 1988, see Largo and Newburn.

LARGOWARD (FES V, 220; VIII, 461; IX, 498; X, 295)

Linkage with Cameron with St Andrews St Leonard's terminated 11 October 1983. Linked same date with St Monans.

1962   DONALD GILLIES CUBIE
(FES X, 190, 277, 293), trans from Mossgreen and Crossgates to Cameron with Largoward 27 Sep 1962; ret 30 Jun 1973; died 13 Jul 1978.

1975   ANDREW BARCLAY McLELLAN
(FES IX, 198, 207, 644; X, 113, 296), ind to St Andrews St Leonard's 14 Jan 1960; became minister of linked charge with Cameron with Largoward 17 Apr 1975, see St Leonard's.

1980   LAWSON RICHARD BROWN
(FES X, 127, 169, 416), trans from Paisley Lyleskand to St Leonard's with Cameron with Largoward 6 Feb 1980; became minister of St Leonard's with Cameron 11 Oct 1983; ret 31 Aug 1997.

1983   DAVID REID
(FES X, 339, 448), ret from RAChD and ind to Largoward with St Monans 22 Nov 1983; ret 31 Aug 1992.

1993   GILBERT COOPER NISBET
B 28 May 1949 at Edinburgh, s of John Downie N. and Isabella Cooper Wight; educ George Heriot's, Edinburgh 1954–67; Institute of Chartered Accountants of Scotland 1967–72 (CA); University of St Andrews 1989–92 (BD); Accountancy 1967–89; lic by Presb of Angus 21 Jun 1992; asst Anstruther 1992–93; m 20 Dec 1975 Melinda Elizabeth Robinson b 20 Jul 1953 d of Leslie Gordon R. and Patricia Jackson; Children: John David b 12 Mar 1977; Robin James b 26 Sep 1978; Martin Gilbert b 27 Feb 1982; ord and ind to Largoward with St Monans 5 May 1993.

LEUCHARS ST ATHERNASE AND GUARDBRIDGE (FES IX, 498; X, 295)

Formed 10 Jan 1991 by union of Leuchars St Athernase and Guardbridge.

1958   WILLIAM ADAM
(FES IX, 254, 600; X, 150, 295), trans from Glasgow Auldfield to St Athernase with Guardbridge 25 Mar 1958; ret 31 Aug 1982; died 6 May 1997.

1983   ALEXANDER KETCHEN CASSELLS
(FES X, 24, 342), trans from Edinburgh St Paul's Newington to St Athernase with Guardbridge 20 Jan 1983; became minister of united charge 10 Jan 1991; ret 31 Jul 1997.

1998   ARTHUR RAYMOND CHARLES GASTON
(FES X, 264, 267), res as Staffing Secretary, Board of World Mission and ind to Leuchars St Athernase and Guardbridge 29 Oct 1998; s James m Jean Guthrie; d Gillian m Kok Seng Chan.

LOGIE (FES V, 163; VIII, 449; IX, 491; X, 291)

Congregation dissolved 29 Oct 1972.

1947   DONALD SINCLAIR
(FES IX, 323, 491, 625, 714; X, 291), trans from Cabrach to Logie 6 Nov 1947; ret 31 Mar 1972; died 14 Oct 1985.

MONIMAIL (FES IX, 491; X, 292)

Linkage with Springfield terminated 6 Feb 1983. Linked same date with Creich, Flisk and Kilmany.

1944   WILLIAM McCRAW
(FUF 372; FES IX, 486, 491; X, 292), ord and ind to Monimail (UFC) 27 Jul 1928; became minister of united charge of Monimail and Bow of Fife 1 Jan 1944; ret 31 May 1963; died 31 Dec 1990.

1963   JAMES GEORGE STEWART BLYTH
(FES X, 292, 341), ord and ind to Monimail 25 Sep 1963; trans to Glenmuick (Ballater) 6 Jun 1973.

1973   GEORGE IVORY LITHGOW McCASKILL
(FES IX, 648; X, 176, 252, 292, 369), res as teacher (RE) and ind to Monimail 13 Dec 1973; became minister of linked charge with Springfield 31 Mar 1975; returned to teaching (RE) 18 Aug 1980; ret 22 Apr 1990; Addl children: George Alexander b 4 Oct 1961; d Lindsey m Brown.

1983   CLIFFORD STRONG
ind to Creich, Flisk and Kilmany with Monimail 20 Sep 1983, see Creich.

1996   MITCHELL COLLINS
ord and ind to Creich, Flisk and Kilmany with Monimail 13 Jun 1996, see Creich.

NEWBURGH (FES X, 292)

Linked 10 Apr 1983 with Abdie and Dunbog.

1958   ALEXANDER GILCHRIST MORRISON MACKENZIE
(FES IX, 536; X, 292, 322), trans from Kirriemuir South to Newburgh 19 Jun 1958; ret 31 Aug 1982; died 18 Dec 1984.

1983   IAN TAYLOR
ord and ind to Abdie and Dunbog with Newburgh 10 Aug 1983, see Abdie.

1998   ROBERT JAMES VICTOR LOGAN
(FES X, 51, 371), trans from Inverness Crown to Abdie and Dunbog with Newburgh 19 Mar 1998.

NEWPORT-ON-TAY (FES X, 294, 308)

Formed 29 Jun 1980 by union of Newport St Fillan's, Newport St Thomas' and Forgan.

1951 ROBERT ALLAN HOWIESON
(FES IX, 45, 522, 736; X, 308), trans from Edinburgh West Coates to Newport St Thomas's 26 Apr 1951; ret 31 Jul 1977.

1954 ALBERT PENMAN BOGIE
(FES IX, 496, 682; X, 294), trans from Reay to Forgan 12 Aug 1954; ret 28 Aug 1979.

1958 ALEXANDER LAIDLAW McFARLANE MACLEAN
(FES IX, 147; X, 87, 308), trans from Ruthwell and Mount Kedar to St Fillan's 9 Oct 1958; became minister of united charge with Newport St Thomas's and Forgan 29 Jun 1980; ret 30 Apr 1985; died 13 Oct 1986.

1985 WALTER GRAHAM BLACK
ord by Presb of Dumbarton during assistantship at New Kilpatrick 11 Sep 1983; ind to Newport-on-Tay 6 Oct 1985; introd as Assoc at Aberdeen St Columba's Bridge of Don 6 Dec 1993.

1994 WILLIAM KENNETH PRYDE
B 16 Oct 1947 at Kirkcaldy, s of David Marne P. and Margaret Henderson Blair Thomson; educ Kirkcaldy Secondary and Kirkcaldy High 1959–65; Duncan of Jordanstone College, Dundee 1966–71 (DA); University of Edinburgh 1990–93 (BD); Architect 1971–90; Member of the Royal Institute of British Architects 1974 (RIBA), Assoc of the Royal Incorporation of Architects in Scotland 1974 (ARIAS); lic by Presb of Stirling 30 Jun 1993; m 23 Aug 1974 Elizabeth Grace Coutts b 18 Jan 1948 d of Daniel C. and Jessie Campbell Finnie; Children: Fraser Ross b 31 Dec 1980; Alison Morven b 21 Sep 1982; ord and ind to Newport-on-Tay 30 Jun 1994.

PITTENWEEM (FES IX, 499; X, 295)

Linked 28 Dec 1971 with Carnbee.

1942 JOHN SHARP DINWOODIE
(FUF 38; FES IX, 53, 149, 499; X, 295), trans from Thornhill Virginhall to Pittenweem 14 Jan 1942; ret 31 May 1970; died 9 Jun 1980.

1970 CHARLES GEORGE THROWER
(FES X, 295, 426), res from app with Overseas Council in Jamaica and ind to Pittenweem 27 Nov 1970; became minister of linked charge with Carnbee 28 Dec 1971; University of St Andrews 1975–77 (DPSS); d Tamara m Mark Turner; Publ: History and Visitors' Guide to Pittenweem Kirk and Priory (Pittenweem Church, 1981, 1989); Pictish Trail: Guide to East Neuk Churches (East Neuk Kirk Session, 1997).

ST ANDREWS HOLY TRINITY (FES V, 229; VIII, 464; IX, 499; X, 295)

First and Second charges united 10 May 1978.

1949 CHARLES ARMOUR
(FES IX, 499; X, 295), ind to St Andrew's Holy Trinity (Second Charge) 19 Jun 1949; became sole minister 10 May 1978; d Jacqueline m (2) Neil Goulding.

1968 CHARLES YOUNG McGLASHAN
(FES IX, 739, 790; X, 101, 295, 447), trans from Dailly to Holy Trinity (First Charge) 29 Sep 1968; ret 18 Jun 1977; died 3 Mar 1990.

ST ANDREWS HOPE PARK (FUF 377; FES IX, 500; X, 295)

1966 JOHN (IAN) MANSON PATERSON
(FES IX, 745, 800; X, 295, 332), trans from Aberdeen St Ninian's to Hope Park 23 Aug 1966; trans to Eccles with Greenlaw 15 Mar 1978.

1978 WILLIAM HENNEY
(FES X, 124, 313, 454), res as Asst Secretary, Dept of Education and ind to Hope Park 14 Dec 1978; ret 1 Jun 1996; DD (St Andrews) 1993; m (2) 2 Apr 1976 Margaret MacGradie b 23 Dec 1945 d of Norman M. and Mary MacKenzie; Children: Alison Margaret b 26 May 1977; Marion Christina b 19 Jun 1979; Gillian Mary b 15 Nov 1980; Laura Robertson b 28 Dec 1983.

1996 ANDREW DAVID KELTIE ARNOTT
(FES X, 48, 49), trans from Glasgow Netherlee to Hope Park 5 Dec 1996; Addl children: Kenneth David b 16 Oct 1978.

ST ANDREWS MARTYRS' (FUF 378; FES IX, 500; X, 295)

Linked 23 Jun 1993 with Boarhills and Dunino.

1958 JOHN WALLACE PATTERSON
(FES IX, 183; X, 106, 295), trans from Prestwick North to Martyrs' 25 Sep 1958; ret 31 October 1989; app Clerk to Presb of St Andrews 1 May 1974; app Clerk to Presb of St Andrews 1 Jan 1976 (following union of Presbs of Cupar and St Andrews); ret as Clerk 30 Jun 1999.

1990 DAVID IAN SINCLAIR
ord and ind to Martyrs' 1 Nov 1990; became minister of linked charge with Boarhills with Dunino 23 Jun 1993 and of linked charge with Boarhills and Dunino 1 May 1994; dem 21 Mar 1999 on app as Secretary of Committee on Church and Nation.

ST ANDREWS ST LEONARD'S (FES V, 242; VIII, 470; IX, 500; X, 296)

Linked 17 Apr 1975 with Cameron with Largoward. Linkage with Largoward terminated 11 October 1983.

1960 ANDREW BARCLAY McLELLAN
(FES IX, 198, 207, 644; X, 113, 296), trans from Kilmarnock West High to St Leonard's 14 Jan 1960; became minister of linked charge with Cameron with Largoward 17 Apr 1975; ret 3 May 1979; died 3 Dec 1980.

1980 LAWSON RICHARD BROWN
(FES X, 127, 169, 416), trans from Paisley Lyleland to St Leonard's with Cameron with Largoward 6 Feb 1980; became minister of St Leonard's with Cameron 11 Oct 1983; ret 31 Aug 1997.

1998 ALAN DOUGLAS McDONALD
ind to Cameron with St Leonard's 27 Aug 1998, see Cameron.

ST MONANS (FES IX, 501; X, 296)

Linked 11 October 1983 with Largoward.

1944 JOHN STEWART ROUGH
(FUF 365; FES IX, 501; X, 296), trans from Dumbarton North to St Monans 18 Oct 1944; ret 31 Dec 1971; died 2 Jul 1990.

1972 GORDON WILLIAM CRAIG
(FES X, 296, 444), ord and ind to St Monans 26 Jul 1972; dem 9 Sep 1974 on app by Royal Naval Chaplaincy Service.

1975 RICHARD MATHIES FINDLAY
(FES X, 40, 117 (2), 296), trans from Haggs to St Monans 9 Apr 1975; trans to Killean and Kilchenzie 26 Jan 1983.

1983 DAVID REID
(FES X, 339, 448), ret from RAChD and ind to Largoward with St Monans 22 Nov 1983; ret 31 Aug 1992.

1993 GILBERT COOPER NISBET
ord and ind to Largoward with St Monans 5 May 1993, see Largoward.

STRATHKINNESS (FUF 378; FES V, 244; VIII, 471; IX, 501; X, 296)

Linked 31 Jul 1980 with Dairsie with Kemback.

1961 JOHN ALEXANDER HALL
(FES IX, 79, 129, 135; X, 74, 296), trans from Selkirk West to Strathkinness 27 Sep 1961; ret 30 Jun 1968; died 7 Jul 1999.

1968 GEORGE ALESTAIR ALISON BENNETT
(FES IX, 314, 336; X, 136, 184, 296), trans from Kilmacolm Old to Strathkinness 5 Dec 1968; ret 31 Jul 1976; d Katherine m Stewart Hislop.

1977 DAVID DOUGLAS GALBRAITH
(FES X, 21), res as Assoc at Edinburgh Richmond Craigmillar and ind to Strathkinness 30 Jun 1977; dem on app as Lecturer (temp) in Practical Theology, University of St Andrews 1 Aug 1980.

1980 JAMES ARNOT HAMILTON
(FES X, 4, 354), ind to Dairsie with Kemback 21 Feb 1980; became minister of linked charge with Strathkinness 31 Jul 1980, see Dairsie.

TAYPORT (FES X, 308)

Formed 7 Dec 1978 by union of Tayport Queen Street and Tayport Erskine Ferryport-on-Craig.

1963 GEORGE STRATHEARN AYRE
(FES IX, 446; X, 263, 284, 309), trans from Kirkcaldy Raith to Tayport Queen Street 20 Jun 1963; introd to Dundee St James' (term) 10 May 1978.

1965 GEORGE LEVACK EDINGTON
(FES IX, 330; X, 195, 309, 372), trans from Inverness Hilton to Tayport Erskine Ferryport-on-Craig 12 May 1965; became minister of united charge with Queen Street 7 Dec 1978; ret 1 Jan 1990.

1990 COLIN JOHN DEMPSTER
B 18 Jan 1952 at Lanark, s of William Brown D. and Mary Renton; educ Biggar High 1964–68; Borders College, 1971–74 (RMN); Lanarkshire College 1976–78 (RGN); University of Glasgow 1984–89 (BD); Psychiatric Nursing and Social Work 1971–84; lic by Presb of Lanark, Jun 1989; asst Carluke St John's 1989–90; m 7 Dec 1974 Patricia Ann Kay b 19 Mar 1954 d of Frank K. and Nora McKinlay; Children: Jamie Scott b 22 May 1980; Craig William b 10 Jun 1991; ord and ind to Tayport 23 Aug 1990.

WORMIT (FES IX, 523; X, 309)

Linked 22 Jan 1984 with Balmerino.

1957 IAN HAMILTON McKENZIE ROBERTSON
(FES IX, 550; X, 309, 318), trans from Ferryden to Wormit 1 Nov 1957; ret 31 Oct 1983; died 20 Nov 1998.

1984 ANDREW LOCKHART STEVENSON
ord and ind to Balmerino with Wormit 25 Jul 1984, see Balmerino.

1993 GRAEME WILLIAM BEEBEE
ord and ind to Balmerino with Wormit 28 Oct 1993, see Balmerino.

PRESBYTERY OF DUNKELD AND MEIGLE

ABERFELDY (FES IX, 412; X, 245)

Linked 1 Nov 1973 with Amulree and Strathbraan. Further linked 17 Aug 1989 with Dull and Weem.

1971   HENRY MONTGOMERIE GIBSON
(FES X, 142, 245), trans from Glasgow Carmunnock to Aberfeldy 7 Oct 1971; became minister of linked charge with Amulree and Strathbraan 1 Nov 1973; trans to Dundee The High Kirk 31 Jan 1979.

1979   DAVID GEORGE STRACHAN
B 14 Jun 1952 at Edinburgh, s of Stanley George S. and Iris Winifred Luke; educ Merchiston Castle, Edinburgh 1965–70; University of Aberdeen 1970–77 (BD, DPS); lic by Presb of Angus 5 Jul 1977; asst Aberdeen North of St Andrew 1977–79; m (1) 15 Aug 1974 Helen Mary McBain b 1 Jan 1953 d of William M. and Mary Douglas; Children: Peter David b 9 Jul1979; Michael Douglas b 21 Feb 1981; m (2) 10 Sept 1988 Gwyneth Ann Hardy b 31 Mar 1960 d of Roy H. and Cynthia Battson; Children: Emma Gwen b 4 Nov 1991; ord by Presb of Aberdeen during assistantship at North of St Andrew 17 Mar 1978; ind to Aberfeldy with Amulree and Strathbraan 20 Jun 1979; dem on app as Community Channel Co-ordinator, Aberdeen Cable TV 20 Jul 1985; app Managing Director, Tern Television Production Ltd 28 Feb 1988; app Chairman of same 1 Jul 1992.

1986   ALEXANDER MACLEAN GUNN
(FES X, 174, 389), trans from Glasgow St David's Knightswood to Aberfeldy with Amulree and Strathbraan 1 Mar 1986; became minister of linked charge with Dull and Weem 17 Aug 1989; m 19 Jan 1979 Ruth Tennent Sinclair Rankine b 28 Oct 1947 d of William R. and Mary Wright; Children: Anne b 19 Nov 1979; Ian David b 9 Sept 1982.

ALYTH (FES X, 310)

Formed 10 Oct 1976 by union of Alyth Barony and Alyth High.

1933   JACOB SIBBALD CLARK
(FES IX, 525; X, 310), ord and ind to Alyth High 5 Apr 1933; ret 30 Sep 1976; died 13 Feb 1982.

1954   DAVID FYFE ANDERSON
(FES IX, 524; X, 310), ord and ind to Alyth Barony 6 Jan 1954; ret 29 Feb 1976; died 1 Jul 1986.

1976   HECTOR GRANT MACMILLAN
(FES X, 196), trans from Hamilton North to Alyth 29 Dec 1976; dem 1 Mar 1985 and introd as Assoc at Dundee Whitfield.

1985   GORDON OLIVER
res as Community minister, Hamilton Trinity and ind to Alyth 24 Oct 1985; introd to Lisbon St Andrew's 18 Jan 1998.

1998   NEIL NORMAN GARDNER
B 22 Aug 1965 at Edinburgh, s of Norman Steel G. and Isobel Telfer Selkirk; educ Dunbar Grammar 1977–83; University of St Andrews 1983–87 (MA); University of Edinburgh 1987–90 (BD); lic by Presb of Lothian 1 Jul 1990; asst Bearsden New Kilpatrick 1990–91; ord by Presb of Dumbarton and app by RAChD 29 May 1991; ind to Alyth 23 Sept 1998.

AMULREE AND STRATHBRAAN (FES IX, 412; X, 245)

Linked 1 Nov 1973 with Aberfeldy. Further linked 17 Aug 1989 with Dull and Weem.

1961   RODERICK McSWAN BOYD
(FES IX, 9, 139, 599, 668, 670; X, 82, 245), trans from Dalbeattie Craignair to Amulree and Strathbraan 4 May 1961; ret 30 Jun 1971; died 31 Aug 1976.

1973   HENRY MONTGOMERIE GIBSON
(FES X, 142, 245), trans from Glasgow Carmunnock to Aberfeldy 7 Oct 1971; became minister of linked charge with Amulree and Strathbraan 1 Nov 1973; trans to Dundee The High Kirk 31 Jan 1979.

1979   DAVID GEORGE STRACHAN
ind to Aberfeldy with Amulree and Strathbraan 20 Jun 1979, see Aberfeldy.

1986   ALEXANDER MACLEAN GUNN
(FES X, 174, 389), trans from Glasgow St David's Knightswood to Aberfeldy with Amulree and Strathbraan 1 Mar 1986; became minister of linked charge with Dull and Weem 17 Aug 1989.

ARDLER, KETTINS AND MEIGLE (FES X, 310, 312)

Formed 1 Dec 1981 by union of Ardler, Kettins and Meigle.

1949 JOHN FORBES LOVE
(FES IX, 529; X, 312), ord and ind to Meigle 24 Feb 1949; ret 1 Dec 1981; died 12 Aug 1986.

1959 RONALD MILLER BOYD SCOTT
(FUF 339; FES IX, 434, 514; X, 305, 312), trans from Dundee St Enoch's to Kettins 14 Apr 1959; became minister of linked charge with Ardler 30 Jun 1960; ret 10 Jun 1979; died 7 Apr 1985.

1982 ALEXANDER THOMSON
(FES X, 117), trans from Kilbirnie St Columba's to Ardler, Kettins and Meigle 18 Aug 1982; trans to Rutherglen Old 6 May 1985.

1986 FRASER METHVEN COMPTON STEWART
trans from Cumbernauld Abronhill to Ardler, Kettins and Meigle 12 Mar 1986; trans to Inverness Kinmylies 3 Nov 1992.

1993 ALBERT BROWN REID
(FES X, 210, 253), trans from Dundee Trinity to Ardler, Kettins and Meigle 15 Apr 1993; d Alison m Barry Robert Davidson.

BENDOCHY (FES V, 242; VIII, 472; IX, 525; X, 310)

Linked 28 Jan 1976 with Kinclaven. Linkage terminated 31 Dec 1988. Linked 1 Jan 1989 with Blairgowrie St Mary's South.

1951 DOUGLAS MACPHAIL BUCHANAN THORNTON
(FES IX, 525; X, 310), ord and ind to Bendochy 22 Aug 1951; ret 30 Apr 1965; died 17 Mar 1990.

1966 JAMES FERGUSON MACDONALD
(FES IX, 165, 790; X, 241, 310, 446), trans from Salen and Ulva with Torosay and Kinlochspelvie to Bendochy 20 Jan 1966; became minister of linked charge with Kinclaven 28 Jan 1976; ret 31 Jan 1984.

1984 ROLAND JOHN PORTCHMOUTH
B 4 Sep 1923 at London, s of Charles Frederick Howard P. and May Idena Monck; educ Kilburn Grammar, London 1935–40; Harrow School of Art 1946–49 (NDD); Hornsey School of Art 1949–50 (ATD); University of Edinburgh 1978–80; Teaching (Art), Lecturer in Art Education and Senior Lecturer in Art 1951–68; lic by Presb of Melrose and Peebles 29 May 1980; asst Peebles Old 1979–80; m 17 Jun 1972 Susan Mary Glass b 23 Jun 1940 d of Percy G. and Lily; Children: Lucy Clare b 17 Nov 1974; ord and ind to Grantully, Logierait and Strathtay 8 Dec 1980; trans to Bendochy with Kinclaven 18 Nov 1984; ret 31 Dec 1988; Publ: *Creative Crafts for Today* (Studio Vista, Vlklng, 1969); *Secondary School Art* (Studio Vista, Van Nostrand Reinhold, 1971); *All Kinds of Papercraft* (Studio Vista, Viking, 1972); *How to make things*

from the beach (Studio Vista, 1973); *Working in Collage* (Studio Vista, Viking 1973); *The Creatures of the Carp* (Canongate, 1977, Scottish Children's Press, 1998).

1989 MICHAEL ROBERT PHILIP
trans from Banton with Twechar to Blairgowrie St Mary's South 13 Jan 1988; became minister of linked charge with Bendochy 1 Jan 1989.

BLAIR ATHOLL AND STRUAN (FES IX, 413; X, 245)

1947 DONALD CAMERON
(FES IX, 396, 413; X, 245), trans from Kildalton to Blair Atholl and Struan 8 Oct 1947; ret 1979; died 28 Sep 1990.

1980 JAMES DUNCAN
B 28 Jan 1926 at Glasgow, s of Andrew D. and Mary Kirkwood Gribbon; educ Eastbank Academy, Glasgow 1931–43; University of Glasgow 1977–80; University of London (external) 1982 (BTh); Regular Army 1943–47 (seconded to Australian Army 1945–47); Harrisons and Crosfield, British Borneo 1947–48; Sales Management 1949–76; lic by Presb of Glasgow 10 Jun 1980; m (1) 3 Apr 1952 Jean Marshall Shiells b 2 Jun 1928, died 31 May 1975, d of David S. and Margaret Caldwell Johnston; Children: Andrew Kenneth b 14 Sept 1953 m Helen Armour Taylor; David James b 16 Oct 1958 m Cherri Anne Rippon; m (2) 22 Oct 1980 Christine Margaret Fisher b 3 Apr 1931 d of James Fisher and Christina Muir Crowe; ord and ind to Blair Atholl and Struan 17 Jul 1980; ret 29 Jan 1995.

1996 NEIL GOW
B 25 Dec 1945 at Redhill, Surrey, s of Alexander Hennessy Lumsden G. and Charlotte Pratt; educ Waverley Secondary and Knightswood Secondary, Glasgow 1958–64; University of Strathclyde 1964–68 (BSc); Jordanhill College, Glasgow 1970–71 (PGCE); University of Glasgow 1970–74 (MEd), 1991–94 (BD); Teaching (VSO) 1968–70; Teaching 1971–91; lic by Presb of Glasgow 4 Jul 1994; m 3 Jul 1973 Elizabeth Minter b 29 Nov 1947 d of Robert Egerton M. and Elizabeth McKinlay; Children: Ruth b 29 Jul 1976; Jill b 12 Dec 1979; ord and ind to Blair Atholl and Struan 21 Mar 1996.

BLAIRGOWRIE ST ANDREW'S (FUF 322; FES IX, 525; X, 310)

1951 ROBERT MELBOURNE HOWIESON
(FUF 360; FES IX, 196, 274, 475, 525; X, 310), trans from Kilmarnock St Andrew's North to St Andrew's 28 Jun 1951; ret 21 Jan 1968; died 30 Nov 1992.

1969 GEORGE STUART YOUNG
(FES X, 105, 310), trans from Old Cumnock Crichton West to St Andrew's 20 Mar 1969; ret 18 Nov 1996; s James m Louise; s George m Alison Giles; d Helen m Gordon.

1997 ROBERT SLOAN
B 19 Dec 1949 at Glasgow, s of Robert Miller S.
and Ann Jane O'Malley; educ Dennistoun Secondary, Glasgow 1961–64; University of Glasgow
1992–96 (BD); Stores Clerk 1965–73; Internal
Sales Clerk 1973–77; Production Planner 1977–
90; Stock Controller 1990–92; lic by Presb of
Glasgow 1 Jul 1996; asst Glasgow Newlands South
1996–97; m 10 Jun 1972 Lynda Anne Boag b 24
Feb 1952 d of John B. and Margaret Blanch Hill;
Children: Francis b 29 Oct 1974, died Oct 1974
and Paul b 29 Oct 1974, died Oct 1974; Angela
Lynda b 15 Dec 1975; Graham Robert b 27 Sept
1978; ord and ind to St Andrew's 14 May 1997;
app Hospital Chaplain (part-time) 1 Jan 1998.

BLAIRGOWRIE ST MARY'S SOUTH (FES X, 310)

Linked 1 Jan 1989 with Bendochy.

1929 JAMES LEITHEAD
(FES IX, 525; X, 310), ord and ind to St Mary's 13
Nov 1929; ret 30 Sep 1967; died 2 Mar 1985.

1969 NORMAN JOHN MACPHERSON
(FES IX, 657; X, 55, 310, 374), trans from Humbie
to St Mary's South 13 Mar 1969; dem on grounds
of ill-health 31 Aug 1980 and took up app as Admin
Officer with 'An Comunn Gaidhealach'; ret 31 Dec
1986; Children: Fiona Mary b 21 Apr 1956 m Arthur
Watt; Donald Neil b 21 Nov 1957 m Marion
Hayworth; Duncan John b 5 May 1959; Kenneth
Angus b 5 Nov 1963.

1981 KEITH FERRIER HALL
ord and ind to St Mary's South 7 May 1981; trans
to Alloa St Mungo's 11 May 1987.

1988 MICHAEL ROBERT PHILIP
B 15 Jul 1949 at Larbert, s of Alexander Robert P.
and Margaret Jean Brown; educ Grove Academy,
Broughty Ferry 1961–67; University of Dundee
1967–69; University of Edinburgh 1971–75 (BD),
1975–76 (CChEd); Bank Clerk 1969–71; lic by
Presb of Dundee, Jun 1976; asst Jedburgh Old
with Edgerston and Ancrum 1976–77; m 7 Aug
1976 Janice Hegarty b 16 Mar 1953 d of Henry H.
and Margaret Adamson; Children: Henry Robert b
7 Aug 1983; ord and ind to Banton with Twechar
16 Mar 1978; trans to St Mary's South 13 Jan 1988;
became minister of linked charge with Bendochy
1 Jan 1989.

BLAIRGOWRIE THE HILL (FES V, 255; VIII, 472;
IX, 526; X, 310)

Congregation dissolved 30 Jun 1976.

1949 ALEXANDER FOUBISTER TAYLOR
YOUNG
(FES IX, 155, 526; X, 310), trans from Rerrick to
The Hill 23 Jun 1949; ret 30 Jun 1976; died 14
Aug 1989.

BRAES OF RANNOCH (FES IV, 175; VIII, 354;
IX, 413; X, 245)

Linked 12 Oct 1955 with Kinloch Rannoch. Linkage
continues following union of Kinloch Rannoch and
Foss and Tummel 9 Oct 1977.

1959 THOMAS STRACHAN ALLAN LEIGHTON
(FES IX, 712; X, 245, 405), trans from Cunningsburgh to Braes of Rannoch with Kinloch Rannoch
2 Apr 1959; ret 31 Mar 1970; died 12 Jan 1983.

1973 WILLIAM MURDOCH MACLEAN
CAMPBELL
(FES X, 243, 245), res as Assoc at Kilmallie with
Glengarry and ind to Braes of Rannoch with Kinloch
Rannoch 3 May 1973; became minister of linked
charge with Foss and Rannoch 9 Oct 1977; trans
to Lundie and Muirhead of Liff 14 Apr 1978.

1978 DOUGLAS FRANK NOEL CRAWFORD
(FES IX, 731; X, 201, 417), trans from New
Stevenston Wrangholm to Braes of Rannoch with
Foss and Rannoch 22 Sept 1978; ret 30 Apr 1984;
died 4 Nov 1993.

1984 ARCHIBALD FREELAND CHISHOLM
(FES X, 148, 417), trans from Leven St Andrew's
to Braes of Rannoch with Foss and Rannoch 17
Dec 1984; Clerk to Presb of Dunkeld and Meigle
1992–96; ret 30 Nov 1997; d Barbara m Birrell; d
Nancy m Birse; d Sheila m Robertson.

1998 DAVID GENTLES HAMILTON
(FES X, 107), res from Board of Parish Education
and ind to Braes of Rannoch with Foss and
Rannoch 31 Mar 1998; Addl publ: *Sunday School
at a Glance* (PEP, 1983); *Discovering the Way*
(PEP, 1983); *Children: The Challenge to the
Church* (PEP, 1987); co-author of *Craftwork with
Children* (PEP, 1990); *Too Young to Matter?* (PEP,
1991); *How to Prepare Your Child for the Church*
(PEP, 1991); *How to Prepare Your Church for
Children* (PEP, 1991); *The Vows of Baptism* (PEP,
1992); *How to Prepare Your Child for the Lord's
Supper* (PEP, 1993); *So You're Thinking about
Opening the Table to Children* (PEP, 1993);
Teaching the Christian Faith (PEP, 1993); *Projects
with Children* (PEP, 1993); *The Insight Handbook*
and other volumes in *Insight* series (HarperCollins,
1995–97); editor of *Church and Home* series (St
Andrew Press, 1978–80); *Children of the Way* (St
Andrew Press, 1980–84); *The Faithquest* (William
Collins, 1984–88); other essays, articles and
resource material.

CAPUTH AND CLUNIE (FES X, 250, 311)

Formed 20 Oct 1983 by union of Clunie, Lethendy,
Kinloch, Caputh and Murthly. Linked 1 Jan 1989
with Kinclaven.

1949 FREDERICK FRASER ROUTLEDGE BELL
(FES IX, 129, 421; X, 250), trans from Selkirk West
to Caputh 19 Oct 1949; became minister of linked
charge with Murthly 15 Nov 1950; ret 30 Sep 1983;

Publ: *Diary of a Quiet Life*; *A Fisherman's Life*; *Caputh Parish—A History*; *Nature Notes and Short Stories*.

1957 JOHN FLEMING
(FES VIII, 248; IX, 155, 230, 246, 349, 353, 449; X, 145, 311), trans from Kilsyth Burns to Clunie 29 Mar 1957; ret 18 Feb 1962; died 3 Dec 1982.

1962 JAMES DUNCAN
(FES X, 287, 311), ord and ind to Clunie, Lethendy and Kinloch 6 Aug 1962; trans to Methil 29 Feb 1968.

1968 DAVID WILLIAM ROSS
(FES IX, 168, 467, 510; X, 303, 311), trans from Dundee Mains to Clunie, Lethendy and Kinloch 22 Aug 1968; died 27 Dec 1974.

1975 FREDERICK HASLEHURST FULTON
(FES IX, 360; X, 215, 311, 384), trans from Dornoch Cathedral to Clunie, Lethendy and Kinloch 8 Oct 1975; ret 4 Apr 1983.

1984 ALEXANDER EWING STRACHAN
(FES X, 265), res from service with Overseas Council at Trinidad Greyfriars and St Ann's and ind to Caputh and Clunie 29 Mar 1984; trans to Musselburgh St Michael's Inveresk 15 Jan 1987.

1987 ALEXANDER CLOWES McCARTNEY
(FES X, 275), trans from Hawick St Mary's with Cavers and Kirkton to Caputh and Clunie 9 Nov 1987; became minister of linked charge with Kinclaven 1 Jan 1989; ret 10 Nov 1995; s James m Elizabeth Carolyn Gallagher; d Elizabeth m Robin Gibson Chisholm.

1996 LINDA JEAN BROADLEY
B 15 Apr 1948 at Broxburn, d of John Craig Milne and Andrewina MacKenzie MacGregor; educ Lansdowne House, Edinburgh 1953–65; Dunfermline College 1965–68 (DipEd); University of Glasgow 1991–94 (LTh); Teaching 1968–69; lic by Presb of Lanark 11 Oct 1994; asst Moffat St Andrew's 1994–96; m 1 Aug 1968 Andrew Lewis B. b 18 Dec 1945 s of John Cameron B. and Elizabeth Patience; Children: Andrew John McKenzie b 8 May 1969 m Lucy Johnson; Jennifer Catherine b 14 Aug 1970; Karen Elizabeth b 11 Jun 1972 m George Renouf; Alistair Cameron b 17 Sept 1975; ord and ind to Caputh and Clunie with Kinclaven 18 Dec 1996.

COUPAR ANGUS ABBEY (FES IX, 527; X, 311)

1958 WILLIAM COCHRANE
(FES IX, 485, 598; X, 311, 345), trans from Inverurie West to Coupar Angus Abbey 10 Dec 1958; died 25 Oct 1980.

1981 JAMES WHYTE
ord and ind to Coupar Angus Abbey 27 Aug 1981; trans to Broom 5 Feb 1987.

1987 JAMES HENRY DUNN CRAIG DRYSDALE
ord and ind to Coupar Angus Abbey 9 Jul 1987; trans to Blackbraes and Shieldhill 20 Nov 1997.

1997 BRUCE DEMPSEY
B 16 May 1961 at Glasgow, s of John D. and Jane Ruddick; educ Queen Victoria School, Dunblane 1972–77; University of Glasgow 1992–96 (BD); Marine Sales Engineer 1978–89; Outdoor Activities Instructor 1989–92; lic by Presb of Dunkeld and Meigle 30 Jun 1996; m 8 Sep 1990 Kathryn Douglas b 31 Jul 1957 d of Mungo D. and Lena Hume; ord and ind to Coupar Angus Abbey 29 May 1997.

DULL AND WEEM (FES X, 246)

Linked 1 Feb 1981 with Fortingall and Glenlyon. Linkage terminated 17 Aug 1989 in favour of linkage with Aberfeldy with Amulree and Strathbraan.

1971 GEORGE MARSHALL DALE
(FES IX, 147, 459, 719; X, 188, 246, 266), trans from Blantyre Old to Dull and Weem 1 Apr 1971; ret 31 Dec 1979; died 24 Jan 1984.

1981 ADAM McCALL BOWIE
trans from Gamrie with King Edward to Dull and Weem with Fortingall and Glenlyon 23 Aug 1981; trans to Cavers and Kirkton with Hobkirk and Southdean 24 Aug 1988.

1989 ALEXANDER MACLEAN GUNN
(FES X, 174, 389), trans from Glasgow St David's Knightswood to Aberfeldy with Amulree and Strathbraan 1 Mar 1986; became minister of linked charge with Dull and Weem 17 Aug 1989.

DUNKELD (FES X, 246)

1924 THOMAS ROGER GILLIES
(FES VIII, 350; IX, 417; X, 247), ord and ind to Little Dunkeld 23 Oct 1924; ret 31 Oct 1974; died 24 Jun 1982.

1974 THOMAS DICK
(FES IX, 193; X, 110, 179, 246 (2)), trans from Glasgow Scotstoun East to Dunkeld and Dowally 1 Aug 1974; became minister of united charge with Little Dunkeld 1 Nov 1974; ret 31 Mar 1990.

1990 ALBERT EDWARD SMITH
trans from Johnstone High to Dunkeld 14 Nov 1990; trans to Methlick 19 Oct 1999.

FORTINGALL AND GLENLYON (FES X, 246)

Formed 20 Nov 1980 by union of Fortingall and Glenlyon. Linked 1 Feb 1981 with Dull and Weem. Linkage terminated 17 Aug 1989 in favour of linkage with Kenmore with Lawers (united 1 Oct 1990).

1946 DAVID TOWERS TAYLOR
(FES IX, 415; X, 246), ord and ind to Glenlyon 30 Oct 1946; became minister of linked charge with Fortingall 14 Jan 1954; ret 30 Apr 1958; died 19 Mar 1981.

1959 ROBERT BURNSIDE
(FES IX, 118, 477; X, 246, 283), trans from Kirk-caldy Dunnikier to Fortingall with Glenlyon 26 Feb 1959; died 8 Aug 1965.

1966 WILLIAM PATON HENDERSON
(FES IX 5, 89, 229, 653; X, 54, 246, 258, 435), res as Lecturer in RE, Aberdeen College of Education and ind to Fortingall with Glenlyon 27 Jan 1966; ret 27 Aug 1971; died 21 Jun 1986.

1972 DUNCAN PRIMROSE MACPHEE
(FES IX, 337; X, 225, 246, 283 (2)), trans from Kirkcaldy Dunnikier to Fortingall with Glenlyon 2 Mar 1972; introd on term app at Braemar 22 Apr 1976.

1976 ARTHUR WILLIAM BRUCE
(FES IX, 62, 563; X, 84, 239, 320), trans from Garvock St Cyrus to Fortingall with Glenlyon 26 Nov 1976; became minister of united charge 20 Nov 1980; ret 31 Jan 1981.

1981 ADAM McCALL BOWIE
ind to Dull and Weem with Fortingall and Glenlyon 23 Aug 1981, see Dull and Weem.

1989 KENNETH MACVICAR
(FES IX, 416; X, 247), ord and ind to Kenmore 10 Jul 1950; became minister of linked charge with Lawers 9 May 1957 and of linked charge with Fortingall and Glenlyon 17 Aug 1989; ret 30 Sep 1990; s Angus m Kay Boyle; s Cameron m Marylin McDougall; d Jean m David Ainsley; Publ: *The Wings of the Morning* (John Donald, 1997).

1990 JOHN THOMAS MANN
ord and ind to Fortingall and Glenlyon with Kenmore and Lawers 5 Dec 1990; trans to Durness and Kinlochbervie 23 Nov 1998.

1999 ANNE JANETTE BRENNAN
B 31 Jan 1955 at Glasgow, d of Edward McGartland and Janet Dawson Mackenzie Wright; educ Lenzie Academy 1967–73; University of Strathclyde 1973–77 (BSc); University of Glasgow 1993–96 (BD), 1996–99 (MTh); Pharmacist Manager 1978–81; Locum Pharmacist 1981–97; lic by Presb of Stirling 29 May 1997; asst Bears-den South 1997–99; m 1 Oct 1977 Brian Patrick Brennan b 24 Oct 1955 s of Patrick B. and Helen Howat Hamilton; Children: Sharon Patricia b 27 Apr 1981; Kathleen Mary b 26 May 1983; Kirsten Anne b 26 May 1983; ord and ind to Fortingall and Glenlyon with Kenmore and Lawers 30 Jun 1999.

FOSS AND RANNOCH (FES X, 246)

Formed 9 Oct 1977 by union of Foss and Tummel and Kinloch Rannoch. Linkage with Braes of Rannoch continues.

1959 THOMAS STRACHAN ALLAN LEIGHTON
(FES IX, 712; X, 245, 405), ind to Braes of Rannoch with Kinloch Rannoch 2 Apr 1959, see Braes of Rannoch.

1968 HAMISH (JAMES) NORMAN WALKER
(FES X, 246, 426), res from service with Overseas Council in India and ind to Foss and Tummell with Tenandry 29 Aug 1968; dem 4 Dec 1976 to take up app as General Secretary, Fellowship of Reconciliation.

1973 WILLIAM MURDOCH MACLEAN CAMPBELL
(FES X, 243, 245), res as Assoc at Kilmallie with Glengarry and ind to Braes of Rannoch with Kinloch Rannoch 3 May 1973; became minister of linked charge with Foss and Rannoch 9 Oct 1977; trans to Lundie and Muirhead of Liff 14 Apr 1978.

1978 DOUGLAS FRANK NOEL CRAWFORD
(FES IX, 731; X, 201, 417), trans from New Steven-ston Wrangholm to Braes of Rannoch with Foss and Rannoch 22 Sept 1978; ret 30 Apr 1984; died 4 Nov 1993.

1984 ARCHIBALD FREELAND CHISHOLM
(FES X, 148, 417), ind to Braes of Rannoch with Foss and Rannoch 17 Dec 1984, see Braes of Rannoch.

1998 DAVID GENTLES HAMILTON
(FES X, 107), ind to Braes of Rannoch with Foss and Rannoch 31 Mar 1998, see Braes of Rannoch.

GRANTULLY, LOGIERAIT AND STRATHTAY (FES X, 247)

Formed 1 Apr 1975 by union of Grantully, Logierait and Strathtay.

1967 ALASTAIR SCOTT CALDER
(FES IX, 235; X, 137 (2), 247), trans from Kilma-colm St Columba to Grantully and Strathtay 17 May 1967; ret 30 Nov 1974; died 13 Mar 1994.

1975 JOHN HARKESS OSTLER
(FES X, 247), ord and ind to Grantully, Logierait and Strathtay 30 Oct 1975; dem 31 Aug 1980 on app by RAF Chaplains' Branch.

1980 ROLAND JOHN PORTCHMOUTH
ord and ind to Grantully, Logierait and Strathtay 8 Dec 1980; trans to Bendochy with Kinclaven 18 Nov 1984.

1984 IRENE BRYDEN FRASER MILLER
B 31 Mar 1939 at Beechwood, Kettleholm, d of William John and Mary Miller Fraser; educ Perth Academy 1950–56; University of St Andrews 1956–

60 (MA), 1980–83 (BD); Moray House College, Edinburgh 1960–61; Teaching 1961–65; lic by Presb of Perth, 1983; asst Comrie 1983–84; m 14 Oct 1965 John William Miller b 16 May 1929 s of John McKinnie M. and Violet Munn; Children: Colin Gemmell Bryden b 9 Sept 1966; Catriona Helen b 29 Dec 1968; Shian Mary b 3 Jul 1971; ord and ind to Grantully, Logierait and Strathtay 29 Aug 1984; ret 31 Aug 1999.

KENMORE AND LAWERS (FES X, 247)

Kenmore with Lawers linked 17 Aug 1989 with Fortingall and Glenlyon. Kenmore and Lawers united 1 Oct 1990.

1950   KENNETH MACVICAR
(FES IX, 416; X, 247), ord and ind to Kenmore 10 Jul 1950; became minister of linked charge with Lawers 9 May 1957 and of linked charge with Fortingall and Glenlyon 17 Aug 1989; ret 30 Sep 1990.

1990   JOHN THOMAS MANN
ord and ind to Fortingall and Glenlyon with Kenmore and Lawers 5 Dec 1990, see Fortingall.

1999   ANNE JANETTE BRENNAN
ord and ind to Fortingall and Glenlyon with Kenmore and Lawers 30 Jun 1999, see Fortingall.

KINCLAVEN (FES IX, 424; X, 252)

Linked 28 Jan 1976 with Bendochy. Arrangement terminated 31 Dec 1988. Linked 1 Jan 1989 with Caputh and Clunie.

1966   JAMES FERGUSON MACDONALD
(FES IX, 165, 790; X, 241, 310, 446), trans from Salen and Ulva with Torosay and Kinlochspelvie to Bendochy 20 Jan 1966; became minister of linked charge with Kinclaven 28 Jan 1976; ret 31 Jan 1984.

1984   ROLAND JOHN PORTCHMOUTH
ind to Bendochy with Kinclaven 18 Nov 1984, see Bendochy.

1989   ALEXANDER CLOWES McCARTNEY
(FES X, 275), ind to Caputh and Clunie 9 Nov 1987; became minister of linked charge with Kinclaven 1 Jan 1989, see Caputh and Clunie.

1996   LINDA JEAN BROADLEY
ord and ind to Caputh and Clunie with Kinclaven 18 Dec 1996, see Caputh.

KIRKMICHAEL, STRALOCH AND GLENSHEE (FES X, 311, 312)

Formed 10 Dec 1978 by union of Kirkmichael, Straloch and Glenshee. Continued vacancy from 1994 until 1998. Linked 30 Apr 1998 with Rattray.

1961   DAVID ALEXANDER TOSH
(FES IX, 125; X, 73, 312), trans from Lauder Old to Kirkmichael and Straloch 14 Apr 1961; ret 26 Aug 1972; died 21 Jul 1993.

1973   DAVID MASTERTON DOIG
(FES X, 312, 403), res as Assoc at South Ronaldsay and Burray and ind to Glenshee and Glenericht 19 Oct 1973; dem 5 Mar 1978; introd as Assoc at Dundee Mid Craigie 19 Feb 1979.

1973   WALTER MILLAR RITCHIE
(FES X, 312), ord and ind to Kirkmichael and Straloch 16 May 1973; became minister of united charge with Glenshee 10 Dec 1978; trans to Appin and Lismore 29 Oct 1981.

1982   ALAN THOMSON McKEAN
ord and ind to Kirkmichael, Straloch and Glenshee 3 Sept 1982; trans to Fauldhouse St Andrew's 23 Mar 1994.

1998   HUGH CHARLES ORMISTON
(FES X, 306), res as Industrial Chaplain in the Forth Valley and ind to Kirkmichael Straloch and Glenshee with Rattray 30 Apr 1998; University of Glasgow 1984 (MPhil), 1989 (PhD); s Ewan m Gillian Keating.

PITLOCHRY (FES X, 247, 248)

Formed 1 Jan 1992 by union of Moulin, Pitlochry West and Pitlochry East.

1958   FRANK MARTIN
(FES X, 248), ord and ind to Pitlochry East 26 Nov 1958; ret 31 Dec 1990; s David m Jane; s Evan m Susan.

1973   WILLIAM GAULT SHANNON
(FES X, 167, 247, 455), res as Warden of St Ninian's, Crieff and ind to Moulin and Pitlochry West 30 Nov 1973; became minister of united charge with Pitlochry East 1 Jan 1992; ret 31 Jan 1998; s David m Cathie Galbraith.

1998   ALEXANDER MALCOLM RAMSAY
B 4 Mar 1957 at Livingstone, N Rhodesia (now Zambia), s of Norman James Gemmill R. and Rachael Mary Berkeley Cox; educ Merchiston Castle, Edinburgh and Lawrenceville School, New Jersey 1970–75; University of Cambridge 1975–78 (BA); University of Edinburgh 1978–80 (LLB), 1983–85 (DipMin); Solicitor 1982–83; lic by Presb of Edinburgh 30 Jun 1985; asst Edinburgh Fairmilehead 1985–87; m 4 Apr 1981 Catherine (Cati) Angela Balfour-Paul b 22 Mar 1959 d of Hugh Glencairn B. and Margaret Clare Ogilvy; Children: Megan Clare b 7 Mar 1986; Angus James b 18 Jun 1988; ord by Presb of Edinburgh during assistantship at Fairmilehead 25 May 1986; ind to Bargrennan with Monigaff 15 Jul 1987; dem 31 Dec 1993 on app by Board

of World Mission for service in Guatemala; Selly Oak Colleges, Birmingham Jan-Mar 1994, departed for Guatemala 15 Apr 1994; ind to Pitlochry 2 Jul 1998.

RATTRAY (FES IX, 530; X, 313)

Linked 30 Apr 1998 with Kirkmichael, Straloch and Glenshee.

1972 THOMAS WILLIAM TAIT

(FES X, 313), ord and ind to Rattray 18 Jul 1972; ret 19 Jul 1997; Children: Mahri b 17 Dec 1967 (adopted); Steven b 17 Aug 1969 (adopted); Alison Caroline b 19 Mar 1971.

1998 HUGH CHARLES ORMISTON

(FES X, 306), ind to Kirkmichael Straloch and Glenshee with Rattray 30 Apr 1998, see Kirkmichael.

TENANDRY (FES IV, 173; VIII, 353; IX, 418; see X, 246)

Linkage with Foss and Tummel terminated 8 Oct 1977. Continued vacancy declared.

1935 DUNCAN MACNAB SINCLAIR

(FES VIII, 343; IX, 55, 411, 418), trans from Longriggend and Meadowfield to Tenandry 6 Jun 1935; dem 31 Jan 1954; died 30 Mar 1977.

1954 GORDON WILLIAM GARNETT MAKINS

(FES IX, 415; X, 229, 246, 273), ord and ind to Foss and Tummel with Tenandry 7 Jul 1954; trans to Dunfermline North 15 Oct 1958.

1959 HAROLD MEREDITH

(FES X, 87, 172, 246), ord and ind to Foss and Tummel with Tenandry 27 Aug 1959; trans to Glasgow Ruchill 12 Oct 1967.

1968 HAMISH (JAMES) NORMAN WALKER

(FES X, 246, 426), ind to Foss and Tummell with Tenandry 29 Aug 1968, see Foss and Rannoch.

PRESBYTERY OF PERTH

ABERDALGIE AND DUPPLIN (FES IV, 193; VIII, 360; IX, 419; X, 249)

Linked 15 Apr 1982 with Forteviot.

1960 JOHN ANNAND FRASER
(FES VIII, 95; IX, 90, 331 (2); X, 196, 249), trans from Hamilton Old and Auchingramont (First Charge) to Aberdalgie and Dupplin 30 Nov 1960; ret 31 Oct 1970; died 3 Oct 1985.

1971 WILLIAM UIST MACDONALD
(FES IX, 300, 517; X, 249, 306), trans from Wallacetown to Aberdalgie and Dupplin 16 Jun 1971; became minister of linked charge with Forteviot 15 Apr 1982; ret 30 Apr 1984; s Alasdair m Catherine Susan Roberts; d Patricia m David Howes.

1984 COLIN RAYMOND WILLIAMSON
(FES X, 89), trans from Leith St Paul's to Aberdalgie and Dupplin with Forteviot 11 Oct 1984; Chaplain (part-time) to Perth Prison; m 6 Jul 1978 Arlene Elizabeth Geddes b 5 Aug 1957 d of John G. and Elizabeth Maxwell; Children: Rachel Clare b 11 Aug 1979; Hannah Emily b 31 Dec 1981; Colin Edward b 3 Apr 1983.

ABERNETHY AND DRON (FES X, 249)

Linked 26 Jun 1979 with Arngask.

1970 LESLIE GRAHAM WATT
(FES X, 47, 249, 427), res from app with Overseas Council in Chile 1 Dec 1969 and ind to Abernethy and Dron 26 Aug 1970; ret 25 Jun 1977; died 24 Jun 1991.

1978 JAMES CALDWELL
(FES IX, 213, 536; X, 179 (2), 322), trans from Glasgow Shawlands Old to Abernethy and Dron 14 Jun 1978; became minister of linked charge with Arngask 26 Jun 1979; ret 30 Jun 1984; died 29 Jan 1995.

1984 HUGH SCOULLER
B 15 Mar 1946 at Edinburgh, s of Hugh and Helen S; educ University of Edinburgh 1968–71 (BSc), 1980–83 (BD); lic by Presb of Lothian 3 Jul 1983; asst Bonnyrigg 1983–84; m 14 Aug 1965 Patricia Anne Downie b 5 Jan 1946 d of David Gray and Marie Irene D; Children: Hugh b 2 Dec 1967; Alan b 2 Nov 1976; Rhona b 5 Nov 1978; ord and ind to Abernethy and Dron with Arngask 10 Jan 1984; dem 31 Dec 1986.

1988 KENNETH GEORGE ANDERSON
(FES X, 74, 415), res from app with Union Church, Hong Kong and ind to Abernethy and Dron with Arngask 14 Jan 1988.

ABERUTHVEN (FUF 339; FES IX, 433; X, 257)

Linkage with Gask terminated 27 Sep 1978 in favour of linkage with Dunning.

1975 IAIN MACLAREN ROBERTSON
(FES X, 86, 257), dem from Kirkmahoe and introd to Aberuthven with Gask (term) 9 Apr 1975; res from app 27 Sep 1978 and ind to Carriden 13 Dec 1978.

1978 JOHN ALEXANDER McDONALD
ord and ind to Aberuthven with Dunning 28 Sep 1978; trans to Cumbernauld Condorrat 18 Feb 1993.

1993 ALAN JOHN ROY
(FES X, 304, 425), trans from Dundee Stobswell to Aberuthven with Dunning 24 Nov 1993; dem 30 Sep 1999; s Keith m Lois; s Colin m Jane; d Heather m Bryan Knight.

ALMONDBANK TIBBERMORE (FES X, 249, 252, 256)

Formed 5 Oct 1977 by union of Almondbank St Serf's and Tibbermore. Linkage with Logiealmond continued until 18 Jan 1995.

1957 WILLIAM STIVENS MORRIS
(FES IX, 466; X, 249, 276), trans from Lochcraig to St Serf's 20 Feb 1957; became minister of linked charge with Logiealmond 10 Apr 1968; ret 31 Jul 1976; died 28 Apr 1990.

1959 ROBERT ALEXANDER ORCHISON WYLIE
(FES IX, 273, 630; X, 162, 256), trans from Glasgow Hutchesontown and Caledonia Road to Tibbermore 17 Dec 1959; ret 31 Jul 1971; died 22 Jun 1981.

1972 ALEXANDER McRAE HOUSTON
(FES IX, 102, 250; X, 148, 256, 267, 420), res from app at Trinidad Greyfriars, Port of Spain and ind to Tibbermore 3 May 1972; ret 5 Oct 1977.

1977 GORDON MATTHEW ALEXANDER SAVAGE
ord and ind to Almondbank St Serf's with Logiealmond 31 Aug 1977; became minister of Almondbank Tibbermore with Logiealmond 5 Oct 1977; trans to Dumfries Maxwelltown West 2 Feb 1984.

1984 IAN MARR
B 26 Dec 1958 at Kirkwall, s of John Robert Bain and Isabella M; educ Kirkwall Grammar 1971–77; University of Aberdeen 1977–83 (MA, BD); lic by Presb of Aberdeen 1 Jul 1984; asst Dyce 1983–84; m 15 Jul 1984 Judith Anne Philip b 7 Sep 1961 d of John George Walker and Frances P; ord and ind to Almondbank Tibbermore with Logiealmond 5 Dec 1984; became minister of Almondbank Tibbermore following termination of linkage 18 Jan 1995; dem 30 Apr 1996.

1997 JAMES ALEXANDER SIMPSON
dem from Dornoch Cathedral and introd as Interim minister at Almondbank Tibbermore 7 May 1997; introd as Interim minister at Brechin Cathedral 15 Sep 1998.

1998 DONALD CAMPBELL
B 7 Apr 1951 at Dumbarton, s of Donald C. and Dorothy Dean; educ Dumbarton Academy 1956–67; University of Glasgow 1994–97 (BD); Telecommunications Technician 1967–94; lic by Presb of Dumbarton 6 Jul 1997; m 3 Mar 1973 Elizabeth Anne Johnston b 3 Mar 1951 d of William J. and Catherine Colquhon McKenna McKay; Children: Kirsty Jane b 27 Mar 1974; Gillian Iona b 30 Nov 1977; ord and ind to Almondbank Tibbermore 25 Nov 1998.

ARDOCH (FES IV, 257; VIII, 376; IX, 433; X, 257)
Linked 25 Apr 1984 with Blackford.

1969 DUGALD McKINNON
(FES IX, 638; X, 42, 227, 257, 364), [correction: Tarbert Argyll, not Tarbert Harris as in Vol X, 42]; trans from Redding and Westquarter to Ardoch 2 Jun 1969; ret 16 Jun 1982; died 13 Oct 1993.

1983 JAMES LAMB HEPBURN
(FES IX, 736; X, 91, 420), dem from Kirkcudbright St Mary's and introd to Ardoch (term) 11 May 1983; became minister of Ardoch with Blackford 25 Apr 1984; ret 30 Sep 1991; s Kenneth m Hong Yoke Lim.

1991 HAZEL WILSON
B 17 Apr 1950 at Banff, d of George Mackie and Margaret Helen Stewart; educ Banff Academy 1962–68; University of Aberdeen 1973 (MA), 1974 (DipEd), 1990 (BD); Aberdeen College of Education 1974 (PGCE); Robert Gordon's Institute of Technology 1979 (DMS); Buyer of Electrical and Instrumentation Equipment for Oil Platforms 1981–

86; Lecturer in Marketing 1986; lic by Presb of Aberdeen; asst Aberdeen St Machar's Cathedral 1990–91; ord and ind to Ardoch with Blackford 29 Nov 1991.

ARNGASK (FES IX, 420; X, 249)
Linked 26 Jun 1979 with Abernethy and Dron.

1970 ALASTAIR GILBERT STEVEN RAE
(FES IX, 5, 515; X, 54, 249, 306), trans from Gullane to Arngask 25 Aug 1970; ret 30 Sep 1978; died 2 Jan 1979.

1979 JAMES CALDWELL
(FES IX, 213, 536; X, 179 (2), 322), ind to Abernethy and Dron 14 Jun 1978; became minister of linked charge with Arngask 26 Jun 1979, see Abernethy.

1984 HUGH SCOULLER
ord and ind to Abernethy and Dron with Arngask 10 Jan 1984, see Abernethy.

1988 KENNETH GEORGE ANDERSON
(FES X, 74, 415), ind to Abernethy and Dron with Arngask 14 Jan 1988, see Abernethy.

AUCHTERARDER PARISH (FES X, 257)
Formed 6 Jul 1983 by union of Auchterarder Barony and Auchterarder St Andrew's and West.

1966 DONALD WILLIAM MACKENZIE
(FES IX, 378, 693; X, 226, 257), trans from Glenaray and Inveraray to Auchterarder Barony 12 Jan 1966; ret 6 Jul 1983; Publ: Co-author of *Tiree Bards and their Bardachd* (Society of West Highland and Island Historical Research, 1978); *The Worthy Translator: How the Scottish Gaels got the Scriptures in their own Tongue* (Society of Friends of Killin and Ardeonaig Parish Church, 1992); *Sin mar a bha. That's how it was. Recollections of an Ulva Boyhood* (Birlinn, 2000); Parish of Glenaray and Inveraray, Argyll for *Third Statistical Account* (Scottish Academic Press).

1971 HAMISH McINTOSH
(FES IX, 783; X, 5, 179, 257), trans from Edinburgh Broughton Place to Auchterarder St Andrew's and West 16 Dec 1971; ret 6 Jul 1983; s James Christopher b 28 Nov 1958 m Ailsa Elizabeth Stewart McLellan; d Elizabeth Anne b 19 Feb 1961 m William Edward Landles; s John Rowan b 26 Mar 1964 m Alison Severn; Addl publ: *Contracts of Employment and Influence of Class in First 30 Years of Livingstonia Mission* (*SCHS Record*, 1987); *Robert Laws as Preacher* 1985–87 and *Effect of 1914–18 War on Livingstonia Mission 1988–89* (*Bulletin of Scottish Institute of Missionary Studies*); *Robert Laws, Servant of Africa* (Handsel Press, 1993).

1983 ANDREW WATT BRADLEY
(FES X, 185), trans from Airdrie Clarkston to Auchterarder 13 Oct 1983; trans to Paisley Lylesland 13 Jan 1998.

1998 MICHAEL RICHARD RENNIE SHEWAN
B 23 Mar 1956 at Fyvie, s of Albert S. and Mary Jeannie Fitzgerald; educ Insch Secondary 1968–71; Clinterty Agricult College 1971–75 (NCA); Aberdeen College of Commerce 1978–79; University of Aberdeen 1979–85 (BD, CPS); Farming 1973–79; lic by Presb of Gordon, Oct 1984; asst Aberdeen Northfield 1984–85; m 16 Jun 1984 Judith Ann Alexander b 27 Jun 1957 d of William A. and Edna Barclay; Children: Hannah Mary b 26 Mar 1986; Rebecca Margaret b 16 Aug 1987; Gordon Alexander b 26 Dec 1990; ord and ind to Ratho 26 Jun 1985; trans to Auchterarder 1 Aug 1998.

AUCHTERGAVEN AND MONEYDIE (FES X, 250, 252)

Formed 7 Jan 1979 by union of Auchtergaven and Moneydie.

1934 JOHN CHISHOLM
(FUF 247; FES IX, 297, 425; X, 252), trans from Glasgow St George's Road to Moneydie 28 Mar 1934; ret 31 Oct 1978; died 22 Jan 1985.

1973 JAMES DONALD SMITH
(FES X, 250, 251, 334), trans from Cults East to Auchtergaven 5 Dec 1973; became minister of united charge with Moneydie 7 Jan 1979; ret 28 Nov 1981; died 15 Dec 1995.

1982 ROBERT McCRUM
ord and ind to Auchtergaven and Moneydie 5 May 1982; dem on app by Royal Naval Chaplaincy Service 20 Oct 1986.

1987 WILLIAM McGREGOR
B 7 Nov 1936 at Motherwell, s of Hamilton Gemmell M. and Annie Brown Pollock; educ Dalziel High, Motherwell 1948–51; Coatbridge Technical College 1952–58, 1962–63 (HNC Mech Eng); University of Glasgow 1983–86 (LTh); National Service RAF 1958–60; Mechanical Engineering 1961–64, 1965–83; lic by Presb of Stirling 26 Jun 1986; asst Dunblane Cathedral 1986–87; m 31 Aug 1963 Alison Christison Stewart Taylor b 29 Apr 1941 d of Percy Herbert T. and Alison Christison Stewart Thomson; Children: Angus Hamilton b 6 Jan 1968 m Rachel Dellow; Scott Laurie b 23 Apr 1972; ord and ind to Auchtergaven and Moneydie 6 May 1987.

BLACKFORD (FES IX, 434; X, 257)

Linked 25 Apr 1984 with Ardoch.

1967 JAMES BENJAMIN RENNIE
(FES X, 244, 258), trans from Kinlochleven to Blackford 29 Mar 1967; trans to Leochel Cushnie and Lynturk with Tough 1 Dec 1983.

1984 JAMES LAMB HEPBURN
(FES IX, 736; X, 91, 420), introd to Ardoch (term) 11 May 1983; became minister of Ardoch with Blackford 25 Apr 1984, see Ardoch.

1991 HAZEL WILSON
ord and ind to Ardoch with Blackford 29 Nov 1991, see Ardoch.

CARGILL-BURRELTON (FES X, 250)

Formed 20 Nov 1980 by union of Cargill and Burrelton with Collace.

1933 JOHN ADAMSON HONEY
(FES VIII, 189; IX, 159 (2), 421; X, 250), trans from Kirkmaiden to Cargill 9 Feb 1933; became minister of linked charge with St Martin's 1 Oct 1959; died 11 Nov 1979.

1965 ROBERT CAMBRIDGE SYMINGTON
(FES X, 19, 250), returned from Hong Kong Union Church and ind to Burrelton with Collace 10 Nov 1965; trans to Edinburgh Portobello Old 15 Jan 1969.

1969 JAMES LINDSAY KINNEAR WOOD
(FES X, 250), ord by Presb of Aberdeen during assistantship at West Church of St Nicholas 21 May 1967; ind to Burrelton with Collace 25 Jun 1969; became minister of united charge with Cargill 20 Nov 1980; trans to Ruthrieston West 16 Jan 1981.

1981 THOMAS CLIFFORD KELLY
(FES X, 230), trans from North Bute to Cargill-Burrelton with Collace 9 Jul 1981; trans to Ferintosh 3 May 1988.

1988 RICHARD ERNEST FRAZER
ord by Presb of Edinburgh during assistantship at St Giles' 14 Dec 1986; ind to Cargill-Burrelton with Collace 27 Nov 1988; trans to Aberdeen St Machar's Cathedral 14 Oct 1993.

1994 ROBERT JOHN WATT
B 26 Feb 1947 at Glasgow, s of Robert W. and Agnes Greig Kelly; educ Whitehill Secondary, Glasgow 1959–66; University of St Andrews 1988–92 (BD); Business Admin 1966–88; lic by Presb of Stirling 29 Jun 1992; asst Stirling Allan Park South with Holy Rude 1992–93; m 25 Jan 1974 Barbara Westwater b 23 Jun 1948 d of Peter Blair W. and Margery Whitehead; Children: Alasdair Greig b 21 Feb 1975 m Faye Louise Owens; Fiona Margery b 19 Jun 1978; ord and ind to Cargill-Burrelton with Collace 11 May 1994.

CLEISH (FES V, 60; VIII, 417; IX, 457; X, 271)

Linked 6 Apr 1980 with Fossoway St Serf's and Devonside.

1968   HUGH JAMES NICOL PURVES
(FES IX, 724, 792; X, 271, 414, 448), res from app at Scots Kirk, Paris and ind to Cleish 1 Mar 1968; ret 31 Oct 1977; died 9 Jan 1984.

1978   DAVID ANDERSON BLACK
(FES IX, 486; X, 146, 168, 289), trans from Mearns to Cleish 25 Oct 1978; became minister of linked charge with Fossoway St Serf's and Devonside 6 Apr 1980; dem 30 Apr 1985; died 5 Jan 1986.

1985   DAVID TINDAL REID
(FES X, 23, 37, 154, 220), trans from Helensburgh The West Kirk to Cleish with Fossoway St Serf's and Devonside 4 Dec 1985; ret 30 Sep 1993; d Judith m Mark Jardine; d Lorna m John Howell; s Peter m Ritva Lohilata.

1994   ANGUS DAVID MACLEOD
B 20 Jul 1946 at Glasgow, s of George M. and Margaret Cunningham Devine; educ Dornoch Academy 1951–64; University of St Andrews 1964–68 (MA); University of Edinburgh 1989–92 (BD); Ship Building and Steel Industry 1968–74; International Banking 1975–89; lic by Presb of Edinburgh 4 Jul 1992; asst Edinburgh St Giles' Cathedral 1992–94; m 23 Aug 1969 Jennifer Jean Scott b 12 Dec 1946 d of James S. and Jean Balfour Robertson; Children: Roderick b 11 May 1971; Douglas b 27 Jul 1974; ord by Presb of Edinburgh during assistantship at St Giles' 13 Jun 1993; ind to Cleish with Fossoway St Serf's and Devonside 4 May 1994.

COLLACE (FES IV, 199; VIII, 361; IX, 421; X, 250)

Linked 1 May 1965 with Burrelton. Linkage continues following union of Burrelton and Cargill 20 Nov 1980.

1947   ROBERT ROBERTSON
(FES IX, 421; X, 250), admitted by General Assembly 1947 and ind to Collace 17 Sep 1947; ret 1 May 1965; died 26 Nov 1992.

1965   ROBERT CAMBRIDGE SYMINGTON
(FES X, 19, 250), returned from Hong Kong Union Church and ind to Burrelton with Collace 10 Nov 1965; trans to Edinburgh Portobello Old 15 Jan 1969.

1969   JAMES LINDSAY KINNEAR WOOD
(FES X, 250), ind to Burrelton with Collace 25 Jun 1969; became minister of united charge with Cargill 20 Nov 1980, see Cargill-Burrelton.

1981   THOMAS CLIFFORD KELLY
(FES X, 230), trans from North Bute to Cargill-Burrelton with Collace 9 Jul 1981; trans to Ferintosh 3 May 1988.

1988   RICHARD ERNEST FRAZER
ind to Cargill-Burrelton with Collace 27 Nov 1988, see Cargill-Burrelton.

1994   ROBERT JOHN WATT
ord and ind to Cargill-Burrelton with Collace 11 May 1994, see Cargill-Burrelton.

COMRIE AND STROWAN (FES X, 258)

Linked 1 May 1979 with Dundurn.

1962   JOHN McGHIE
(FES IX, 62, 561; X, 258 (2), 326), trans from Aberdeen Greyfriars to Comrie Old and St Kessog's 21 Mar 1962; became minister of united charge with Monzievaird and Strowan 2 Sep 1964; ret 28 Feb 1967 on grounds of ill-health; died 16 May 1993.

1967   ROBERT JAMES STEWART
(FES X, 204, 258), trans from Wishaw St Mark's to Comrie and Strowan 5 Jul 1967; trans to Bothwell 6 Jul 1977.

1978   PETER DAVID THOMSON
(FES X, 89), trans from Balmaclellan with Kells to Comrie and Strowan 27 Apr 1978; became minister of linked charge with Dundurn 1 May 1979.

CRIEFF (FES X, 258, 259)

Formed 24 Jun 1997 by union of Crieff St Andrew's and St Michael's (united 3 May 1989) and Crieff South and Monzievaird.

1964   EDWARD STANLEY PEARSON HEAVENOR
(FES IX, 195, 756; X, 55, 258, 419), trans from North Berwick Abbey to St Michael's 25 Nov 1964; ret 1 Sep 1986; died 19 Sep 1992.

1964   ARCHIBALD HERBERT MINTO
(FES IX, 203, 271, 290; X, 171, 258), trans from Glasgow Queen's Park High to St Andrew's 16 Sep 1964; ret 30 Apr 1983; died 1 Mar 1997.

1966   HENRY ALEXANDER GARDNER TAIT
(FES X, 259), ord and ind to Crieff South and Monzievaird 19 Jan 1966; ret 24 Jun 1997.

1984   JAMES NEIL STEWART ALEXANDER
(FES IX, 322; X, 434), res from app at Rome St Andrew's 1983 and introd to Crieff St Andrew's (term) 12 Apr 1984; ret 3 Jun 1987; died 9 Dec 1996.

1987   BRUCE RITCHIE
B 3 Sep 1952 at Edinburgh, s of Thomas R. and Matilda Gray; educ Jedburgh Grammar and Hawick High; Heriot-Watt University 1970–73 (BSc); University of Edinburgh 1973–76 (BD); lic by Presb of Jedburgh 4 Jul 1976; asst Edinburgh Cluny 1976–77; m 10 Jul 1976 Gace Marion Macalpine Dow b 7 Jul 1949 d of Thomas Cramp D. and Marion Kenny Lawson; Children: Elizabeth Marion Janet b 28 Nov 1978; Alison Grace b 5 Aug 1980; ord and ind to Borgue with Tongland with Twynholm, Oct 1977; trans to Crieff St

Andrew's and St Michael's 3 Jun 1987; became minister of united charge with Crieff South and Monzievaird 24 Jun 1997; Publ: *The Logic of the Trinity* (*Scottish Bulletin of Evangelical Theology*, 1986).

DUNBARNEY (FES IX, 422; X, 251)

Linked 4 Apr 1982 with Forgandenny.

1960   WILLIAM JAMES ROSS
(FES IX, 58, 214; X, 35, 251), trans from Bonnybridge to Dunbarney 31 Aug 1960; ret 15 Oct 1981; died 15 May 1994.

1982   FERGUSON C McLACHLAN
ord and ind to Dunbarney with Forgandenny 14 Jul 1982; dem 31 Aug 1988.

1989   WILLIAM DUNCAN STENHOUSE
B 17 Dec 1940 at Gatehouse-of-Fleet, s of William Angus Campbell S. and Winifred Girgan; educ Kirkcudbright Academy 1952–58; University of Edinburgh 1958–61 (MA), 1985–88 (BD); Moray House College, Edinburgh 1961–62; Teaching 1962–85; lic by Presb of Dumfries and Kirkcudbright 10 Jul 1988; asst Cummertrees with Mouswald with Ruthwell 1988–89; m 18 Jul 1964 Esther Hannay b 14 May 1941 d of James H. and Florence Corkill; Children: Angus James b 28 Nov 1967 m Rosemary Stark; ord and ind to Dunbarney with Forgandenny 21 Jun 1989.

DUNDURN (FES IV, 288; VIII, 379; IX, 436; X, 259)

Linked 1 May 1979 with Comrie and Strowan.

1958   WILLIAM PATERSON
(FUF 45; FES IX, 59, 365, 522; X, 259, 308), trans from Newport St Fillan's to Dundurn 17 Feb 1958; ret 31 Jan 1967; died 2 Oct 1989.

1967   ANDERSON NICOL
(FES IX, 5, 422, 570; X, 259, 331), trans from Aberdeen West of St Nicholas to Dundurn 17 Jun 1967; died 1 Aug 1972.

1973   JOHN HUGH GUNN ROSS
(FES IX, 236; X, 9, 137, 259), trans from Edinburgh Fairmilehead to Dundurn 29 Mar 1973; ret 30 Apr 1979; s John m Frances Hunter Gordon; s Robin m Ann Aikman Smith; d Brigid m Donald William MacLeod.

1978   PETER DAVID THOMSON
(FES X, 89), trans from Balmaclellan with Kells to Comrie and Strowan 27 Apr 1978; became minister of linked charge with Dundurn 1 May 1979.

DUNNING (FES X, 259)

Linked 28 Sep 1978 with Aberuthven.

1972   HUGH BAIN
(FES X, 201, 259), trans from Newmains Coltness Memorial to Dunning 23 Nov 1972; dem 19 Feb 1978.

1978   JOHN ALEXANDER McDONALD
ind to Aberuthven with Dunning 28 Sep 1978, see Aberuthven.

1993   ALAN JOHN ROY
(FES X, 304, 425), ind to Aberuthven with Dunning 24 Nov 1993, see Aberuthven.

ERROL (FES IX, 422; X, 251)

Linked 28 May 1980 with Kilspindie and Rait with Kinfauns.

1966   DAVID ALEXANDER SUTHERLAND
(FES IX, 164, 221; X, 127, 192, 251), trans from Coatbridge Gartsherrie to Errol 16 Nov 1966; ret 31 Aug 1978; died 20 Sep 1981.

1979   PETER DOUGLAS WILSON
ord and ind to Errol 9 May 1979; became minister of linked charge with Kilspindie and Rait 28 May 1980; trans to Aberdeen St Columba's Bridge of Don 6 Feb 1986.

1986   DOUGLAS MACPHERSON MAIN
ord and ind to Errol with Kilspindie and Rait 23 Jul 1986; introd as Interim minister at Edinburgh Craigentinny St Christopher's 13 Feb 1997.

1997   JOHN MOFFAT PICKERING
B 23 Nov 1946 at London, s of Thomas Edward P. and Mabel Jessie Moffat Rigley; educ St Alban's, Hertfordshire 1958–65; University of Durham 1965–68 (BSc); University of Edinburgh 1968–69 (DipEd); Moray House College, Edinburgh; University of Edinburgh 1991–94 (BD); Teaching 1969–91; lic by Presb of Stirling 7 Jul 1994; asst Stirling St Columba's 1994–95; m 1 Apr 1978 Margaret Emslie Finnie b 11 Feb 1960 d of William F. and Katherine Ewan; Children: Thomas Emslie b 18 Jan 1979; Gillian Moffat b 14 Jan 1982; ord and ind to Errol with Kilspindie and Rait 1 Oct 1997.

FORGANDENNY (FUF 331; FES IV, 209; VIII, 363; IX, 423; X, 251)

Linkage with Forteviot terminated 14 Apr 1982. Linked same date with Dunbarney.

1974   GEORGE STEWART SHARP
(FES X, 251, 388), trans from Thurso West to Forgandenny with Forteviot 17 Apr 1974; died 6 Oct 1981.

1982   FERGUSON C McLACHLAN
ord and ind to Dunbarney with Forgandenny 14 Jul 1982; dem 31 Aug 1988.

1989 WILLIAM DUNCAN STENHOUSE
ord and ind to Dunbarney with Forgandenny 21 Jun 1989, see Dunbarney.

FORTEVIOT (FES X, 251)

Linkage with Forgandenny terminated 14 Apr 1982. Linked 15 Apr 1982 with Aberdalgie and Dupplin.

1938 ANDREW REID
(FES VII, 705; VIII, 151, IX, 123, 423, 762; X, 251 (2)), res from app at Alexandria St Andrew's, Egypt 1937 and ind to Forteviot 28 Jun 1938; became minister of united charge with Pathstruie 8 Jan 1957; ret 31 Dec 1959; died 29 Dec 1979.

1961 ANGUS MACASKILL
(FES IX, 408, 547, 658; X, 251, 317), trans from Brechin St Ninian's to Forgandenny with Forteviot 13 Sep 1961; died 7 Oct 1973.

1974 GEORGE STEWART SHARP
(FES X, 251, 388), trans from Thurso West to Forgandenny with Forteviot 17 Apr 1974; died 6 Oct 1981.

1982 WILLIAM UIST MACDONALD
(FES IX, 300, 517; X, 249, 306), ind to Aberdalgie and Dupplin 16 Jun 1971; became minister of linked charge with Forteviot 15 Apr 1982, see Aberdalgie.

1984 COLIN RAYMOND WILLIAMSON
(FES X, 89), ind to Aberdalgie and Dupplin with Forteviot 11 Oct 1984, see Aberdalgie.

FOSSOWAY ST SERF'S AND DEVONSIDE (FES X, 274)

Linked 6 Apr 1980 with Cleish.

1941 DUNCAN LIVINGSTONE McCONKEY
(FES IX, 464; X, 274 (2)), ord and ind to St Serf's 16 Jul 1941; became minister of united charge with Devonside 26 Jan 1964; ret 6 Apr 1980; died 2 Oct 1993.

1980 DAVID ANDERSON BLACK
ind to Cleish 25 Oct 1978; became minister of linked charge with Fossoway St Serf's and Devonside 6 Apr 1980, see Cleish.

1985 DAVID TINDAL REID
(FES X, 23, 37, 154, 220), ind to Cleish with Fossoway St Serf's and Devonside 4 Dec 1985, see Cleish.

1994 ANGUS DAVID MACLEOD
ind to Cleish with Fossoway St Serf's and Devonside 4 May 1994, see Cleish.

FOWLIS WESTER (FES IV, 272; VIII, 380; IX, 436; X, 259)

Linked 3 May 1961 with Monzie. Further linked 13 Jun 1984 with Madderty.

1969 FREDERICK PEARSON COPLAND SIMMONS
(FUF 246; FES IX, 292; X, 260), trans under mutual eligibility from Bournemouth (Presb Church of England) and ind to Fowlis Wester with Monzie 1 Oct 1969; ret 7 Jul 1974; died 22 Oct 1978.

1975 JOHN MACKAY COOKE
(FES IX, 282; X, 41, 167, 260, 268), trans from Larbert Old to Fowlis Wester with Monzie 28 Feb 1975; ret 31 Dec 1982; m (2) 1 Oct 1986 Elinor Muriel Logan (nee Halliday) b 9 May 1924 d of James Halliday and Nancy Scott; d Valery Elizabeth m Malcolm Prothero; s David m Ruth Salter.

1984 JOSEPH LOGAN LECKIE
(FES IX, 193; X, 35, 110, 302, 421), trans from Dundee Lochee St Luke's to Fowlis Wester with Madderty with Monzie 17 Jun 1984; ret 31 Dec 1995; s Gordon m Wendy; s Ross m Sophie; s Joseph m Blanche; s David m Henrietta; d Elizabeth m Peter; Addl publ: *God's Green Gifts* (Handsel, 1992); *Proceedings of the World Renewable Energy Congress* (Pergamum, 1992, 1994, 1996, 1998); *Christian Ecology* (1998); *Green Christians* (1998); *Prophecy Today* (1999); articles for *Coracle* (Iona Community).

1996 ALEXANDER FERNIE BONAR
B 19 Feb 1942 at Glasgow, s of William B. and Jane Charles Fernie; educ Lindsay High, Bathgate 1954–60; Coatbridge Technical College 1961–69 (HNC), 1970–72 (LRIC); University of Edinburgh 1985–88 (LTh); Works Chemist/Asst Works Manager 1960–70; Works Chemical Engineer 1970–73; Sales and Installation Engineer 1973–85; lic by Presb of West Lothian 19 Sep 1984; m 4 Sep 1965 Janet Catherine Lambie b 2 Sep 1943 d of Thomas L. and Mary Crombie Tripney; Children: Barbara Anne b 25 Apr 1978; ord and ind to Musselburgh St Clement's and St Ninian's 24 Jul 1988; trans to Fowlis Wester with Madderty with Monzie 24 Apr 1996; Chaplain (part-time) to Friarton Prison, Perth.

GASK (FES IV, 273; VIII, 380; IX, 437; X, 260)

Linkage with Aberuthen terminated 27 Sep 1978 in favour of linkage with Methven. Linkage continues following union of Methven and Logiealmond 18 Jan 1995.

1975 IAIN MACLAREN ROBERTSON
(FES X, 86, 257), dem from Kirkmahoe and introd to Aberuthven with Gask (term) 9 Apr 1975; res from app 27 Sep 1978 and ind to Carriden 13 Dec 1978.

1978 RICHARD CECIL ALLAN FOWLER
B 22 Oct 1937 at Nanyuki, Kenya, s of Wilfred Cecil F. and Margaret Worsley Harrison; educ Thomson's Falls, Kenton and Duke of York (now Lenana School), Nairobi, Kenya 1945–56; Plymouth and

Devonport Tech College 1958–61 (BSc); University of Exeter 1961–62 (CEd); University of Edinburgh 1965–67 (MSc); University of St Andrews 1974–77 (BD); Teaching 1963–65, 1967–73, 1974; Warden of Forestry Commission Visitor Centre 1973; lic by Presb of Kirkcaldy, 1977; m (1) 18 Oct 1965 Joan Pauline Gibson d of Neil G. and Clarice Broadbent; Children: Ruth Sharon b 29 Jul1966 m Walker; Pauline Joy b 16 Nov 1967 m (1) Gray, m (2) Stevenson; Josephine Mary b 1 Jan 1971 m Hamilton; m (2) Grace Christina Smith b 7 Aug 1925; ord and ind to Gask with Methven 27 Sep 1978; dem 10 Sep 1985 to re-enter teaching profession; ret 24 Aug 1997; Publ: *Methven Parish Church 1783–1983* (Danscot Print, Perth 1983).

1986   BRIAN BAIN
B 12 Sep 1942 at Aberdeenshire, s of Charles B. and Ivy Cameron; educ Cairney Junior Secondary School 1947–57 and Langside College, Glasgow 1972–73; University of Glasgow 1973–74, 1978–79 (LTh); previous employment: Farming; lic by Presb of Glasgow, 1979; asst Glasgow Govan 1976–77, St James' (Pollok) 1977–78; Paisley Sherwood 1979–80; m 30 Jun 1972 Coreen Margaret Mary Stephen b 23 Mar 1946 d of Adrian Hay S. and Margaret Smith; Children: David; Susan; ord and ind to Strichen 3 Jul 1980; trans to Gask with Methven 9 Apr 1986; became minister of united charge with Logiealmond 18 Jan 1995.

KILSPINDIE AND RAIT (FES IV, 213; VIII, 365; IX, 423; X, 251)

Linked 1 Sep 1955 with Kinfauns. Further linked 28 May 1980 with Errol.

1948   EDWARD BEAL
(FUF 373; FES IX, 323, 423, 493, 507; X, 251), trans from Airdrie Chapelhall to Kilspindie and Rait 2 Jun 1948; became minister of linked charge with Kinfauns 1 Sep 1955; ret 30 Sep 1965; died 15 Sep 1985.

1966   JOHN MACNEILL URQUHART
(FES IX, 91, 337; X, 200, 252), trans from Newmains Coltness Memorial to Kilspindie and Rait with Kinfauns 15 May 1966; ret 25 May 1980; d Sheila died 1 Dec 1991.

1980   PETER DOUGLAS WILSON
ord and ind to Errol 9 May 1979; became minister of linked charge with Kilspindie and Rait 28 May 1980, see Errol.

1986   DOUGLAS MACPHERSON MAIN
ord and ind to Errol with Kilspindie and Rait 23 Jul 1986, see Errol.

1997   JOHN MOFFAT PICKERING
ord and ind to Errol with Kilspindie and Rait 1 Oct 1997, see Errol.

KINROSS (FES X, 276)

Formed 11 Jan 1979 by union of Kinross East and Kinross West.

1962   DUNCAN MURDOCH MACKENZIE
(FES IX, 659, 690, 698; X, 276, 377), trans from Avoch North to Kinross West 8 Mar 1962; ret 11 Jan 1979; died 21 Aug 1994.

1965   ARCHIBALD EDMUNDS MILLAR
(FES X, 276), ord and ind to Kinross East 18 Feb 1965; trans to Perth St Stephen's 3 May 1978.

1979   THOMAS LESLIE BARR
(FES X, 157, 173), trans from Glasgow Dennistoun Central to Kinross 28 Aug 1979; ret on grounds of ill-health 31 Oct 1997; Addl children: Deborah Joy b 16 Nov 1984.

1998   JOHN PRINGLE LORIMER MUNRO
B 11 May 1947 at Edinburgh, s of Alan McKenzie M. and Anna Pringle Davidson; educ Edinburgh Academy 1952–65; University of Cambridge 1966–69 (MA); University of Edinburgh 1969–72 (BD), 1974–77 (PhD); lic by Presb of Edinburgh 21 Jun 1972; asst Cumbernauld St Mungo's 1972–74; m 28 Mar 1970 Patricia Ann Lawson b 5 Oct 1945 d of William L. and Edna Severn; Children: Ian William b 9 Sep 1974; Helen Patricia b 26 Mar 1977; ord by Presb of Stirling, Oct 1977 and app Chaplain to University of Stirling; app by Overseas Council as Lecturer at St Paul's United Theological College, Limuru, Kenya Sep 1982; ind to Arbroath Knox's with St Vigean's 11 May 1986; dem on app as Asst Secretary, Board of World Mission 1 Feb 1990; ind to Kinross 8 Jul 1998.

MADDERTY (FES IX, 437; X, 260)

Linkage with Trinity Gask and Kinkell terminated 13 Jun 1984 in favour of linkage with Fowlis Wester with Monzie.

1970   IAN ROBERT NEWTON MILLER
(FES IX, 198, X, 260), ind to Madderty with Trinity Gask and Kinkell 27 May 1970; ret 10 Apr 1977; died 28 Jan 1993.

1978   HARRY GREENWOOD
(FES X, 30, 349 (2)), trans from Longside to Madderty with Trinity Gask and Kinkell 19 Apr 1978; ret 13 Jun 1984; died 16 Dec 1997.

1984   JOSEPH LOGAN LECKIE
(FES IX, 193; X, 35, 110, 302, 421), ind to Fowlis Wester with Madderty with Monzie 17 Jun 1984, see Fowlis Wester.

1996   ALEXANDER FERNIE BONAR
ind to Fowlis Wester with Madderty with Monzie 24 Apr 1996, see Fowlis Wester.

METHVEN AND LOGIEALMOND (FES X, 252)

Methven linked 27 Sep 1978 with Gask. Linked charge united 18 Jan 1995 with Logiealmond.

1959　SAMUEL KENNEDY
(FES IX, 279 (2); X, 166, 252), trans from London Road St Clement's to Methven 17 Sep 1959; ret 30 Jun 1977; died 12 Apr 1994.

1968　WILLIAM STIVENS MORRIS
(FES IX, 466; X, 249, 276), ind to Almondbank St Serf's 20 Feb 1957; became minister of linked charge with Logiealmond 10 Apr 1968, see Almondbank Tibbermore.

1977　GORDON MATTHEW ALEXANDER SAVAGE
ord and ind to Almondbank St Serf's with Logiealmond 31 Aug 1977; became minister of Almondbank Tibbermore with Logiealmond 5 Oct 1977; trans to Dumfries Maxwelltown West 2 Feb 1984.

1978　RICHARD CECIL ALLAN FOWLER
ord and ind to Gask with Methven 27 Sep 1978; dem 10 Sep 1985 to re-enter teaching profession.

1984　IAN MARR
ord and ind to Almondbank Tibbermore with Logiealmond 5 Dec 1984; became minister of Almondbank Tibbermore following termination of linkage 18 Jan 1995.

1986　BRIAN BAIN
trans from Strichen to Gask with Methven 9 Apr 1986; became minister of united charge with Logiealmond 18 Jan 1995.

MONZIE (FES IX, 438; X, 260)

Linked 3 May 1961 with Fowlis Wester. Further linked 13 Jun 1984 with Madderty.

1969　FREDERICK PEARSON COPLAND SIMMONS
(FUF 246; FES IX, 292; X, 260), ind to Fowlis Wester with Monzie 1 Oct 1969, see Fowlis Wester.

1975　JOHN MACKAY COOKE
(FES IX, 282; X, 41, 167, 260, 268), trans from Larbert Old to Fowlis Wester with Monzie 28 Feb 1975; ret 31 Dec 1982.

1984　JOSEPH LOGAN LECKIE
(FES IX, 193; X, 35, 110, 302, 421), ind to Fowlis Wester with Madderty with Monzie 17 Jun 1984, see Fowlis Wester.

1996　ALEXANDER FERNIE BONAR
ind to Fowlis Wester with Madderty with Monzie 24 Apr 1996, see Fowlis Wester.

MUTHILL (FES IX, 438; X, 260)

Linked 13 Jun 1984 with Trinity Gask and Kinkell.

1952　IAIN CAMPBELL
(FES IX, 438, 730; X, 260), res from service with FMC at Ichang, China 1951 and ind to Muthill 23 Sep 1952; ret 31 Dec 1976; died 17 Apr 1977.

1977　DUNCAN McKENZIE BRUCE
(FES IX, 565; X, 48, 268, 328), trans from Stirling North to Muthill 26 Oct 1977; ret 31 May 1984; died 11 Sep 1997; s Neil m Barbara Humphries; d Blythe m Geoffrey Wood.

1984　STANLEY GEORGE STRACHAN
B 24 Sep 1925 at Alvah, s of George S. and Hilda Mary Jeanne Reid; educ Turriff Secondary 1931–43; University of Aberdeen 1946–50 (MA), 1982–83; University of Oxford 1950–51 (DipAgEc); University of Dundee 1968–69 (DipEd); Civil Service 1951–55; Potato Merchant 1955–72; Training Adviser 1972–82; lic by Presb of Angus; m (1) 25 Aug 1950 Iris Winifred Luke b 2 Sep 1929 d of Edwin Scott L. and Emma Edward; Children: David George b 14 Jun 1952 m Gwyneth Hardy; Sheila Gail b 25 Dec 1954; Susan Hilary b 25 Oct 1956 m Cameron Rose; Lesley Ann b 12 Jun 1959 m Charles Bilinda; m (2) 12 Apr 1996 Jennifer Jane Kertland b 1 Oct 1946 d of Robert John K. and Marjory Lorraine Fisher; ord and ind to Muthill with Trinity Gask and Kinkell 24 Sep 1984; dem 31 Dec 1993; ret 31 Dec 1995.

1994　ELINOR JANET GORDON
B 21 Jun 1950 at Perth, d of Peter G. and Isabella Waldie Thomson; educ Bell Baxter High, Cupar 1962–67; Moray House College, Edinburgh 1967–70 (DipEd); University of Edinburgh 1984–88 (BD); Teaching 1970–72; RAF 1972–78; Church of Scotland Diaconate 1981–84; lic by Presb of Edinburgh 3 Jul 1988; ord and ind to Delting with Nesting and Lunnasting 13 Aug 1988; trans to Muthill with Trinity Gask and Kinkell 11 Apr 1994.

ORWELL (FES X, 277)

Linked 31 May 1978 with Portmoak.

1956　THOMAS SHEARER
(FES IX, 215, 501; X, 124, 277), trans from Glasgow Househillwood St Christopher's to Orwell 30 Aug 1956; ret 30 Jun 1977; died 16 Feb 1994.

1978　NORMAN MACLEOD
(FES X, 28, 282), [correction: Glenrothes St Ninian's, not St Columba's as in Vol X, 28]; trans from Glenrothes St Ninian's to Orwell with Portmoak 31 May 1978; ret 30 Sep 1988.

1989　ROBERT JAMES STEWART
(FES X, 204, 258), trans from Bothwell to Orwell with Portmoak 15 Feb 1989; ret 30 Jun 1995; s Michael m Rachael Kelsey.

1995 UNA B STEWART
ord and ind to Orwell with Portmoak 4 Oct 1995.

PERTH CRAIGEND MONCREIFFE (FES X, 251)

Linkage with Rhynd continues following union of Craigend and Perth Moncreiffe 3 Apr 1974.

1953 HECTOR HOUSTON
(FES IX, 430; X, 251 (2)), ind to Craigend with Rhynd 29 Jul1953; became minister of united charge with Perth Moncreiffe 3 Apr 1974; ret 2 Jul 1990; died 27 May 1991.

1991 RIADA MARION MACMILLAN
B 30 Nov 1933 at Glasgow, d of Ian MacPherson and Elsa Cowan; educ Albert Senior Secondary, Glasgow 1945–49; University of Glasgow 1986–90 (BD); Photographic Retoucher 1949–56; Sales Asst 1976–86; lic by Presb of Glasgow 3 Jul 1990; asst Kirkintilloch St Columba's 1990–91; m 13 Jul 1956 Frank MacMillan b 27 Nov 1934 s of John M. and Joanna Gibb; Children: Cheryl b 14 Nov 1957 m Notman; Elsa b 29 Dec 1960; Andrew b 2 Jul 1969 m Maureen Carr; Mhairi b 8 Feb 1972; ord and ind to Craigend Moncreiffe with Rhynd 17 Jun 1991; ret 30 Nov 1998.

1999 ISOBEL RITCHIE BIRRELL
B 26 Sep 1950 at Glasgow, nee Wilson, educ East Bank Academy, Glasgow 1962–66; St Colm's College, Edinburgh 1970–72 (DCS); University of St Andrews 1972–74 (CPSS), 1991–94 (BD); Clerkess 1966–68; Clerkess/Bookkeeper 1968–70; lic by Presb of Angus 4 Jul 1994; m 23 Mar 1978 John Maxwell Birrell b 14 Apr 1946 s of John Frederick B. and Hilary Mary Granger; Children: Gillian Ruth b 8 Aug 1979; Claire Elizabeth b 24 Jun 1981; Nicola Rachel b 14 Mar 1985; ord by Presb of Angus and app Chaplain to Forfar Infirmary 4 Jul 1994; app Chaplain to Stracathro Hospital 1 Oct 1995 and to Sunnyside Royal 1 Feb 1996; app Chaplain to Murray Royal, Perth 1 Apr 1998; ind to Craigend Moncreiffe with Rhynd (part-time) with Chaplaincy, HM Prison, Perth 24 Mar 1999.

PERTH CRAIGIE (FES IV, 240; IX, 426; X, 252)

1965 MALCOLM NICHOLSON HENRY
(FES IX, 135; X, 80, 253, 420), res from service with CCC in Kenya and ind to Craigie 5 May 1965; ret 31 Aug 1987; d Alison m Stewart; d Jean m Hammond.

1988 JOHN RANKIN
(FES X, 337), trans from Stonehaven Dunnottar to Craigie 30 Nov 1988; died 30 Sep 1997.

1998 WILLIAM JACKSON
B 16 Dec 1955 at Glasgow, s of George J. and Henrietta Wilson; educ Craigbank Secondary 1968–72; University of Glasgow 1988–93 (BD, CMin); Local Government 1977–88; lic by Presb

of Paisley 17 Aug 1993; asst Glasgow Penilee St Andrew's 1993–94; m 17 Aug 1984 Linda Simpson b 16 Oct 1957 d of Robert S. and Stenhouse; Children: Paul b 21 Feb 1977; Martin b 30 Dec 1982; Steven b 30 Dec 1982; ord and ind to Ardrossan Barony St John's 19 May 1994; trans to Craigie 9 Sep 1998.

PERTH KINNOULL (FES II, 218; VIII, 366; IX, 426; X, 253)

1970 ROBERT RUSSELL BROWN
(FES IX, 350, 486, 716; X, 210, 211, 253), trans from Lanark St Nicholas' to Kinnoull 17 Sep 1970; ret 15 Jan 1986; w Isobel died 14 Aug 1996.

1986 ALEXANDER (ALASDAIR) FRANCIS CAMERON
ord and ind to Kinnoull 20 Aug 1986; trans to Paisley Sherwood 23 Mar 1993.

1993 JOHN FERGUS FERGUSON
B 9 May 1960 at Calderbraes, s of John Fergus F. and Mary Jane Baillie Gray; educ Fortrose Academy 1972–78; University of Aberdeen 1978–82 (MA), 1983–86 (BD); lic by Presb of Ross 22 Jul 1986; asst Dundee Ogilvie and Stobswell 1986–87; m 5 Jul 1985 Moira Alexandra Ross b 1 Jul 1958 d of William R. and Mina Margaret Morrison; Children: Julie Elizabeth b 10 Mar 1987; Katie Margaret b 25 Aug 1989; ord and ind to Birse and Feughside 3 Sep 1987; trans to Kinnoull 1 Dec 1993.

PERTH LETHAM ST MARK'S (FES X, 253, 254)

Formed 22 Jun 1977 by union of Perth Letham and Perth St Mark's.

1945 HAMISH SHARP
(FES IX, 370, 429, 430; X, 254), trans from Redgorton to St Mark's 5 Dec 1945; ret 22 Jun 1977; died 31 Jan 1979.

1972 ALBERT BROWN REID
(FES X, 210, 253), trans from Lanark Cairns to Letham 26 Jan 1972; became minister of united charge with St Mark's 22 Jun 1977; trans to Dundee Trinity 19 Nov 1981.

1982 GRAHAM RICHARD HOUSTON
trans from Kildonan and Loth Helmsdale to Letham St Mark's 6 May 1982; dem 30 Jun 1990 to take up app as Chaplain to Heriot-Watt University.

1990 ROBERT PATTERSON BOYLE
ord and ind to Letham St Mark's 28 Nov 1990; trans to Buckie North 9 Aug 1996.

1997 JAMES CULLY STEWART
B 22 Mar 1968 at Coatbridge, s of William Munn S. and Elizabeth Hazel Montgomery; educ Airdrie Academy 1981–85; University of Glasgow 1989–95 (BD, DipMin); Butcher 1985–88; lic by Presb of

Hamilton 20 Sep 1995; asst Airdrie Flowerhill 1995–97; m 12 Jul 1993 Anne Eleanor Cunningham b 22 Dec 1965 d of Alexander and Eleanor C; Children: Hannah Joy b 10 Jul1995; Adam James b 16 Aug 1997; Ruth Grace b 10 Aug 1999; ord and ind to Letham St Mark's 19 Mar 1997.

PERTH NORTH (FES X, 253, 254)

Formed 1 Sep 1985 by union of Perth North and Perth St Leonard's.

1950 JOHN ALEXANDER KITCHIN
(FES IX, 364; 427; X, 253), trans from Drumchapel to Perth North 29 Nov 1950; ret 31 Mar 1977; died 30 Oct 1994.

1968 ROBERTSON TAYLOR
(FES X, 254), admitted by General Assembly 1968 and ind to St Leonard's 21 Aug 1968; ret 31 Aug 1985; died 1 Jun 1996.

1974 ROBERT STITT HILL
(FES X, 311), introd as Assoc at Perth North 1 Jan 1974; ret 29 Jan 1978; Open University 1980–89 (BA); Publ: *The Sword Unsheathed* (Tell, 1992).

1978 ROBERT PATERSON SLOAN
(FES X, 381), trans from Invergordon to Perth North 1 Feb 1978; became minister of united charge with St Leonard's 1 Sep 1985; trans to Braemar with Crathie 18 Apr 1996.

1995 KENNETH IAN MACKENZIE
B 7 Apr 1959 at Glasgow, s of Ian Kenneth M. and Margaret Vera Mathieson; educ Millburn Secondary, Inverness and Inverness Royal Academy 1971–76; Royal Agricultural College 1978–79; University of Aberdeen 1983–88 (BD, CPS); Agriculture and Timber 1977–79; Farming (Manager/Partner) 1979–83; lic by Presb of Aberdeen, Jul 1988; asst Aberdeen Dyce 1988–91; m 18 Jun 1987 Jayne Louise Lovett b 23 Jan 1961 d of Ian L. and Margaret Murchison; Children: Mairi Louise b 27 Sep 1989; Catriona Murchison b 1 Jun 1991; Ruaridh Iain Lovat b 20 May 1993; Kirsty Margaret b 30 Nov 1995; ord by Presb of Aberdeen during assistantship at Dyce 16 Mar 1990; introd as Assoc Pastor at First Presb Church, Burlingame, USA 14 Aug 1991; res 31 Jul 1994 and introd as Assoc at Perth North 1 Jan 1995; res from app 24 Aug 1999.

1996 DAVID WILLIAM DENNISTON
B 23 Apr 1956 at Glasgow, s of William D. and Emily McLintock Bennett; educ Hutchesons' Grammar, Glasgow 1968–74; University of Glasgow 1974–80 (BD, DipMin); lic by Presb of Glasgow 26 Jun 1980; asst Glasgow Garthamlock and Craigend East 1980–81; m 25 Mar 1977 Jane MacFarlane Ross b 17 Feb 1957 d of Robert Templeton Cunningham R. and Jane MacFarlane; Children: Iain Robert Ross b 21 Jun 1979; David Graeme Ross b 8 Dec 1981; Ruth Jane b 18 Sep 1987; ord and ind to Glasgow Ruchazie 1 May

1981; trans to Kennoway 19 Jun 1986; trans to Perth North 9 Oct 1996.

PERTH ST ANDREW'S AND ST STEPHEN'S (FES X, 253, 255)

Formed 6 Jan 1991 by union of Perth St Andrew's and Perth St Stephen's.

1961 WILLIAM BONOMY
(FES IX, 729; X, 253, 337, 416), trans from Peterculter Kelman Memorial to St Andrew's 14 Jun 1961; trans to Inverkip 25 Feb 1976.

1977 ALASTAIR FLEMING McCORMICK
(FES X, 123, 230), trans from Bridge of Weir St Machar's Ranfurly to St Andrew's 19 Jan 1977; dem 15 Feb 1989 and app by Board of World Mission to Nassau, Bahamas.

1978 ARCHIBALD EDMUNDS MILLAR
(FES X, 276), trans from Kinross East to St Stephen's 3 May 1978; ret 6 Jan 1991; d Elizabeth m Key; s Andrew m McGuire.

1991 ALFRED GORDON DRUMMOND
B 11 May 1961 at Dunfermline, s of Alexander D. and Flora Fox; educ Dunfermline High; Glasgow Bible College 1982–85; University of Glasgow 1985–90; Fitter Apprenticeship, Rosyth Dockyard 1977–82; lic by Presb of Falkirk, Jun 1990; asst Chryston 1990–91; m 13 Aug 1983 Caroline Watson b 20 Feb 1961 d of David W. and Margaret Shepherd; Children: Jonathan David b 11 May 1988; Philip Peter b 4 Aug 1990; ord and ind to St Andrew's and St Stephen's 29 May 1991.

PERTH ST JOHN THE BAPTIST (FES IV, 226; VIII, 368; IX, 428; X, 253)

1973 ALLAN YOUNG
(FES X, 253), trans from Troon Old to St John's 2 May 1973; died 16 Apr 1979.

1980 DAVID DINNES OGSTON
(FES X, 3), trans from Balerno to St John's 28 Apr 1980; Children: Catherine Ann Hunter b 5 Jul 1973; Ruth Lindsay MacLeod b 7 Feb 1975; Publ: *Prayers* (Daghesh Forte, 1972); contributor to *Worship Now* (St Andrew Press, 1972); *Hemmert Bress* (Daghesh Lene, 1975); contributor to *The Living Doric* (Charles Murray Memorial Trust, 1985); *White Stone Country* (Ramsay Head Press, 1986); *Dry Stone Days* (Ramsay Head Press, 1988); contributor to *The New Makars* (Mercat Press, 1991); contributor to *Mak it New* (Mercat Press, 1995); contributor to *The Keekin-Gless* (Perth and Kinross Libraries, 1999).

PERTH ST LEONARD'S-IN-THE-FIELDS AND TRINITY (FES X, 254, 255)

Formed 22 Jun 1982 by union of Perth St Leonard's-in-the-Fields and Perth Trinity.

1947 THOMAS FOTHERINGHAM GIBB
(FES IX, 259, 429; X, 255), ret from RAF Chaplains' Branch and ind to Trinity 12 Feb 1947; ret 22 Jun 1982; died 24 Aug 1990.

1970 GORDON GRANT STEWART
(FES X, 47, 254), trans from Bonnyrigg to St Leonard's-in-the-Fields 29 Jan 1970; became minister of united charge with Perth Trinity 22 Jun 1982.

PERTH ST MATTHEW'S (FES X, 254)

Formed 1 May 1965 by union of Perth Bridgend, Perth Middle, Perth West and Perth Wilson.

1926 WILLIAM DRUMMOND HUNTER
(FUF 334; FES IX, 427; X, 253), trans from Alva Eadie to Middle 12 May 1926; ret 2 Sep 1963; died 12 Jul 1979.

1965 GEORGE HAMILTON HEARN McBRIDE
(FES IX, 246, 530; X, 132, 254, 312), trans from Gourock Ashton to St Matthew's 10 Dec 1965; ret 30 Sep 1987.

1988 EWEN JOHN GILCHRIST
B 2 Sep 1952 at Helensburgh, s of James G. and Mary Elizabeth McKernan; educ Bearsden Academy 1964–70; University of Edinburgh 1976–81 (BD, DipMin), 1993–95 (DTh); Journalism 1971–76; lic by Presb of Edinburgh 25 Oct 1981; asst Eddleston with Peebles Old 1981–82; m 16 Sep 1978 Susan Marion Jane Warren b 30 Dec 1953 d of Sydney W. and Jean McIntosh; Children: Jane Shona b 6 May 1981; Tabitha Anne b 13 Nov 1984; ord and ind to Garelochhead 9 Sep 1982; trans to St Matthew's 1 May 1988; Publ: Youth page of *Life & Work* 1984–86; monthly column for *Life & Work* 1986–88; *Getting Married in Church* (Lion, 1990).

PERTH ST PAUL'S (FES IV, 239; VIII, 370; IX, 429; X, 255)

Congregation dissolved 14 Jun 1988.

1954 NIGEL ROSS MACLEAN
(FES IX, 256, 429, 467; X, 255), trans from Glasgow Barony North to St Paul's 21 Jul 1954; ret 14 Aug 1986; s Iain m Joyce Frame; s Ronald m Christine Low.

PORTMOAK (FES V, 73; VIII, 420; IX, 469; X, 278)

Linked 31 May 1978 with Orwell.

1974 HERBERT KITCHENER NEIL
(FES IX, 327; X, 101, 192, 244, 267, 278), trans from Kilmonivaig to Portmoak 27 Feb 1974; ret 31 May 1978; died 3 Oct 1999.

1978 NORMAN MACLEOD
(FES X, 28, 282), ind to Orwell with Portmoak 31 May 1978, see Orwell.

1989 ROBERT JAMES STEWART
(FES X, 204, 258), ind to Orwell with Portmoak 15 Feb 1989, see Orwell.

1995 UNA B STEWART
ord and ind to Orwell with Portmoak 4 Oct 1995.

REDGORTON (FES IV, 241; VIII, 370; IX, 430; X, 255)

Linked 28 Jan 1981 with Stanley.

1968 MURRAY DONALDSON
(FES IX, 82, 713; X, 255, 329, 406), trans from Aberdeen Rosemount to Redgorton 1 May 1968; ret 1979; died 23 May 1989.

1981 ALASDAIR GIFFEN GRAHAM
ord and ind to Redgorton with Stanley 3 Jun 1981; trans to Arbroath St Margaret's 26 Nov 1986.

1987 RONALD GEORGE GREIG
ord and ind to Redgorton with Stanley 22 Jul 1987; trans to Bathgate High 31 Mar 1998.

1998 DEREK GRAFTON LAWSON
B 2 Feb 1949 at Dundee, s of Fettes Grafton L. and Lily Norrie Latto; educ Dundee High 1961–66; University of Dundee 1966–69 (LLB); University of St Andrews 1994–97 (BD); Law Apprentice 1969–71; Solicitor 1971–94; lic by Presb of St Andrews 2 Jul 1997; asst Elie with Kilconquhar and Colinsburgh 1997–98; St Andrews Hope Park 1998; m 19 Jun 1971 Moira Adamson Fraser Leighton b 17 Sep 1951 d of Norman George L. and Margaret Martin Brown Miller; Children: Paula Ann Fraser b 3 Sep 1973; Iain Grafton b 22 Sep 1975; ord and ind to Redgorton with Stanley 4 Nov 1998.

RHYND (FES IV, 243; VIII, 370; IX, 430; X, 255)

Linked 1 Feb 1953 with Craigend. Linkage continues following union of Craigend and Perth Moncreiffe 3 Apr 1974.

1922 JAMES LAMONT FYFE SCOTT
(FES IV, 245; IX, 430), trans from Creich to Rhynd 11 May 1922; dem 31 Aug 1952; died 20 Sep 1983.

1953 HECTOR HOUSTON
(FES IX, 430; X, 251 (2)), ind to Craigend with Rhynd 29 Jul 1953; became minister of united charge with Perth Moncreiffe 3 Apr 1974; ret 2 Jul 1990; died 27 May 1991.

1991 RIADA MARION MACMILLAN
ord and ind to Craigend Moncreiffe with Rhynd 17 Jun 1991, see Craigend Moncreiffe.

1999 ISOBEL RITCHIE BIRRELL
ind to Craigend Moncreiffe with Rhynd (part-time) with Chaplaincy, HM Prison, Perth 24 Mar 1999, see Craigend Moncreiffe.

SCONE NEW (FES IX, 431; X, 255)

Linked 19 Nov 1980 with St Martin's.

1962   JAMES SHIRRA
(FES IX, 363; X, 217, 255), trans from Clydebank Union to Scone New 27 Jun 1962; became minister of linked charge with St Martin's 19 Nov 1980; ret 28 Feb 1987.

1987   ALEXANDER McKENZIE MILLAR
trans from East Kilbride Greenhills to St Martin's with Scone New 19 Aug 1987.

SCONE OLD (FES IV, 250; VIII, 373; IX, 431; X, 256)

1949   RONALD ROBERTSON
(FES IX, 431, 688; X, 256), trans from Lochcarron to Scone Old 3 Jun 1949; ret 30 Nov 1982; died 22 Jul 1994.

1983   JOHN BRUCE THOMSON
(FES X, 388), trans from Thurso West to Scone Old 22 Jun 1983; Chaplain (part-time) to Perth Prison.

ST MADOES AND KINFAUNS (FES X, 252, 255)

Congregations linked 20 Oct 1982, then united 18 Jun 1989.

1966   JOHN MACNEILL URQUHART
(FES IX, 91, 337; X, 200, 252), ind to Kilspindie and Rait with Kinfauns 15 May 1966, see Kilspindie.

1968   CHARLES WILLIAM FRASER
(FES IX, 166, 498; X, 211, 255, 294), trans from Lesmahagow Old to St Madoes 23 Apr 1968; ret 23 Apr 1982; died 23 Sep 1983.

1983   MICHAEL JOHN WARD
ord and ind to Kinfauns with St Madoes 7 Dec 1983; became minister of united charge 18 Jun 1989; dem 22 Mar 1999 on app as Community minister, Presb of Orkney.

ST MARTIN'S (FES IV, 248; VIII, 372; IX, 431; X, 255)

Linkage with Cargill terminated 19 Nov 1980. Linked same date with Scone New.

1959   JOHN ADAMSON HONEY
(FES VIII, 189; IX, 159 (2), 421; X, 250), trans from Kirkmaiden to Cargill 9 Feb 1933; became minister of linked charge with St Martin's 1 Oct 1959; died 11 Nov 1979.

1980   JAMES SHIRRA
(FES IX, 363; X, 217, 255), trans from Clydebank Union to Scone New 27 Jun 1962; became minister

of linked charge with St Martin's 19 Nov 1980; ret 28 Feb 1987.

1987   ALEXANDER McKENZIE MILLAR
B 4 Jun 1953 at Glasgow, s of James M. and Sarah Noble Arthurs; educ Govan High 1965–71; University of Glasgow 1971–73, 1977–79 (MA); University of Edinburgh 1974–77 (BD); Open University Business School 1996 (MBA); lic by Presb of Paisley 28 Jun 1979; asst Edinburgh South Leith 1979–81; m 17 Jul 1980 Jennifer Margaret Davie b 4 Sep 1956 d of James Selkirk D. and Jane Lang McAlpine; Children: Rhona Jane Sarah b 24 Feb 1991; ord by Presb of Edinburgh during assistantship at South Leith 15 Jun 1980; ind to East Kilbride Greenhills 13 May 1981; trans to St Martin's with Scone New 19 Aug 1987; app Clerk (part-time) to Presb of Perth 16 Mar 1999.

STANLEY (FES X, 256)

Linked 28 Jan 1981 with Redgorton.

1959   IAIN DUNNET REID
(FES IX, 357; X, 213, 256), trans from Arrochar to Stanley 28 Oct 1959; ret 5 Jan 1981; died 20 Oct 1983; Addl children: Elspeth Mary b 3 May 1960.

1981   ALASDAIR GIFFEN GRAHAM
ord and ind to Redgorton with Stanley 3 Jun 1981; trans to Arbroath St Margaret's 26 Nov 1986.

1987   RONALD GEORGE GREIG
ord and ind to Redgorton with Stanley 22 Jul 1987; trans to Bathgate High 31 Mar 1998.

1998   DEREK GRAFTON LAWSON
ord and ind to Redgorton with Stanley 4 Nov 1998, see Redgorton.

TRINITY GASK AND KINKELL (FES IV, 286; VIII, 385; IX, 439; X, 260)

Linkage with Madderty terminated 13 Jun 1984 in favour of linkage with Muthill.

1970   IAN ROBERT NEWTON MILLER
(FES IX, 198, X, 260), ind to Madderty with Trinity Gask and Kinkell 27 May 1970; ret 10 Apr 1977; died 28 Jan 1993.

1978   HARRY GREENWOOD
(FES X, 30, 349 (2)), ind to Madderty with Trinity Gask and Kinkell 19 Apr 1978, see Madderty.

1984   STANLEY GEORGE STRACHAN
ord and ind to Muthill with Trinity Gask and Kinkell 24 Sep 1984, see Muthill.

1994   ELINOR JANET GORDON
ind to Muthill with Trinity Gask and Kinkell 11 Apr 1994, see Muthill.

PRESBYTERY OF DUNDEE

ABERNYTE (FES IX, 502; X, 297)

Linked 28 Feb 1983 with Inchture and Kinnaird and Longforgan.

1974 GEORGE GORDON CAMPBELL
(FES IX, 11, 150, 474; X, 7, 81, 297), trans from Moffat St Andrew's with Wamphray to Abernyte 23 Jan 1974; ret 28 Feb 1979; died 1 Oct 1980.

1983 ROBERT DALY
(FES IX, 320, 518; X, 307), trans from Blantyre Stonefield to Inchture and Kinnaird 24 Feb 1954; became minister of linked charge with Longforgan 4 Apr 1963 and with Abernyte 28 Feb 1983; died 15 Nov 1988.

1989 JAMES ALEXANDER PENRICE JACK
B 10 Dec 1960 at Bellshill, s of William Callan J. and Jean Alexander Penrice; educ Dalziel High, Motherwell 1971–76; University of Strathclyde 1977–81 (BSc), 1982–83 (BArch); University of Glasgow 1985–88 (BD); Architect 1983–85; lic by Presb of Hamilton 1 Jul 1988; asst Dundee St Mary's 1988–89; ord and ind to Abernyte with Inchture and Kinnaird with Longforgan 19 Sep 1989; Publ: *Summer in a Highland Parish* (St Andrew Press, 1986); *And You Visited Me* (Christian Focus, 1993).

ALBANY-BUTTERBURN (FES X, 298)

Linked 1 Jun 1986 with St David's North.

1962 GILBERT MOLLISON MOWAT
(FES IX, 321; X, 298 (2), 304), trans from Calderbank to Dundee Rosebank-Chapelshade 25 Feb 1958 (renamed Albany 1960); became minister of united charge with Butterburn 26 Sep 1962; ret 31 May 1986; d Margaret m Duthie.

1986 GIDEON GEORGE SCOTT
(FES X, 27, 305), trans from Edinburgh Wester Coates to St David's North 10 Apr 1973; became minister of linked charge with Albany-Butterburn 1 Jun 1986; m (2) 6 Apr 1991 Jean Logan Russell Carlile b 19 Sep 1953 d of Gavin Morrison Hamilton C. and Mary Thomson Davidson Logan; s Christopher m Eileen Tait; Addl publ: *Creativity and Conformity* (*Contact*, 1981).

AUCHTERHOUSE (FES V, 309; VIII, 485; IX, 502; X, 297)

Linked 27 Feb 1983 with Murroes and Tealing.

1968 JAMES HAMILTON
(FES X, 49, 297), trans from Loanhead East to Auchterhouse 28 Aug 1968; ret 31 Mar 1982.

1983 HELEN GIBSON JOHNSTONE
ord and ind to Auchterhouse with Murroes and Tealing 28 Sep 1983; dem 16 Feb 1989 to take up app with Board of World Mission in Zambia.

1989 WILLIAM McDOWALL MACMILLAN
trans from Whithorn St Ninian's Priory to Auchterhouse with Murroes and Tealing 25 Oct 1989; trans to Kilmory with Lamlash 18 Nov 1993.

1995 SYDNEY SAMUEL GRAHAM
ord by Presb of Greenock for Aux ministry 29 Oct 1987; University of Glasgow 1995 (MPhil), 1996 (BD); Asst at Paisley Abbey 1993–94; ind to Auchterhouse with Murroes and Tealing (full-time ministry) 23 Aug 1995.

BALGAY (FES X, 298)

Formed 10 Jul 1973 by union of Balgay St Thomas' and Martyrs'.

1946 JOHN ANDERSON MACDONALD
(FES IX, 511, 529; X, 298, 303), trans from Lintrathen and Kingoldrum to Martyrs' 23 Apr 1946; became minister of united charge with Balgay St Thomas' 10 Jul 1973; ret 31 Dec 1985; died 16 Oct 1989.

1987 GEORGE KLEMENS ROBSON
B 3 Feb 1946 at Aberdeen, s of Herbert R. and Jessie Christian Thomson; educ Peterculter Junior Secondary 1958–61; University of Aberdeen 1977–82 (LTh, DPS); Accountancy and Clerical 1961–77; lic by Presb of Aberdeen 28 Jun 1982; m 7 Oct 1967 Lynn Vater b 9 Apr 1947 d of Cyril V. and Iris Morgan; Children: Gillian b 26 Mar 1971 m Gary Silcock; ord and ind to Echt with Midmar 12 May 1983; trans to Balgay 23 Sep 1987.

BARNHILL ST MARGARET'S (FES V, 369; VIII, 495; IX, 503; X, 299)

1969 GEORGE WATT
(FES IX, 753; X, 8, 295, 299, 427), trans from Edinburgh Drylaw to Barnhill St Margaret's 6 Mar 1969; died 30 Sep 1985.

1986 GORDON DAVID JAMIESON
(FES X, 107), trans from Elie with Kilconquhar and Colinsburgh to Barnhill St Margaret's 12 Jun 1986; d Elspeth m Murray MacKenzie.

BONNETHILL (FUF 381; FES IX, 503; X, 299)

Congregation dissolved 31 Dec 1978.

1960 JAMES DENIS KEILLER
(FES IX, 61; X, 37, 299), [correction: Keiller, not Keillor as in FES X, 37, 299]; trans from Denny-loanhead to Bonnethill 23 Mar 1960; ret 31 Dec 1978; died 8 Jul 1990.

BROUGHTY FERRY EAST (FUF 379; FES IX, 504; X, 299)

1963 JAMES ARCHIBALD REID
(FES IX, 218, 313, 533; X, 299, 319), trans from Forfar Lowson Memorial to Broughty Ferry East 5 Jun 1963; ret 30 Apr 1983; died 22 Jul 1987.

1984 ALAN HUTCHISON MACKAY
(FES X, 41), [correction: s of Agnes Geekie Hutchison, not Agnes Geekie as in Vol X, 41]; trans from Larbert West to Broughty Ferry East 8 Mar 1984; m 16 Jul 1999 Janet Margaret Morton d of Robert Colin Morton and Carol Diane Pallo.

BROUGHTY FERRY ST AIDAN'S (FES V, 311; VIII, 485; IX, 504; X, 299)

1941 ANDREW MILNE MITCHELL GILES
(FES VIII, 540; IX, 504, 580 (2); X, 299), trans from Newmachar to St Aidan's 27 Aug 1941; ret 31 Dec 1967; died 12 Sep 1981.

1968 KEITH CAMPBELL
(FES X, 299, 366), trans from Edinkillie to St Aidan's 6 Jun 1968; died 13 Mar 1994.

1995 CAROLINE JACKSON
B 19 Mar 1957 at Kilmarnock, d of Robert Braid Hunter Clark and Irene Alexina Brown; educ Grange Academy, Kilmarnock 1969–75; University of St Andrews 1975–78 (MA); University of Glasgow 1991–94 (BD); Secretarial Work 1980–91; lic by Presb of Hamilton 29 Aug 1994; asst East Kilbride Westwood 1994–95; ord and ind to St Aidan's 6 Sep 1995.

BROUGHTY FERRY ST JAMES' (FES V, 312; VIII, 485; IX, 504; X, 299)

1970 THOMAS PARKER ROBERTSON
(FES X, 299, 378), trans from Dingwall St Clement's to St James' 10 Jun 1970; s Thomas m Marianne MacKay; Publ: *St James Parish Church, Broughty Ferry* (Trendell Simpson, 1990).

BROUGHTY FERRY ST LUKE'S AND QUEEN STREET (FES IX, 505; X, 299)

1959 SAMUEL GILLIES MACNAB
(FES IX, 266, 309; X, 108, 158, 299), trans from Darvel Irvine Bank and Easton Memorial to St Luke's and Queen Street 17 Dec 1959; ret 30 Sep 1994.

1996 PAULINE STEENBERGEN
B 2 Mar 1969 at Glasgow, d of Henry Dick Cummings S. and Margarete Montgomery; educ Hazelhead Academy, Aberdeen 1981–86; University of Aberdeen 1987–91 (MA); University of Edinburgh 1991–94 (BD); lic by Presb of Aberdeen 30 Jun 1994; asst South Queensferry 1994–96; m David George Pitkeathly b 26 Mar 1965 s of Denis Aitken P. and Isabel Gilmour Crerar; ord and ind to St Luke's and Queen Street 27 Mar 1996; dem 31 May 1999; Publ: *Christian Values* (ed MacDonald, T&T Clark, 1994).

BROUGHTY FERRY ST STEPHEN'S AND WEST (FES X, 300)

1974 JOHN URQUHART CAMERON
(FES X, 300), ord and ind to St Stephen's and West 25 Sep 1974; Marketing Executive, Pergamon Press 1976–81; Sports Journalist and Travel Writer with *Good Holiday Magazine*, *Good Ski Guide* 1981-present; University of Southern California 1982 (ThD); Publ: Articles on sport, travel and tourist industry (Hill Publs, 1981-present).

CAMPERDOWN (FES X, 300)

1973 ROBERT JOHNSTON
(FES X, 300), ord and ind to Camperdown 21 Nov 1973; trans to Edinburgh St Mary's with St Stephen's 10 Aug 1988.

1989 SHEILA CRAIK
B 11 Jul 1946 at Dundee, d of David Keith Barron and Christina Downes Stuart Cox; educ Logie Secondary, Dundee 1951–61; Dundee College; University of St Andrews 1982–87 (BD, DPTh); Secretary 1961–67, 1969–74; lic by Presb of Dundee 18 Sep 1988; asst Dundee St Peter's McCheyne 1988–89; m (1) 2 Apr 1966; Children: Alexander Rory Beaton b 26 Jun 1967 m Porani Husing; m (2) 29 Sep 1972 David Neil Sandeman Craik b 3 Jun 1941; Children: Richard David Barron b 10 Jul 1974; Roderick Jonathan McNab b 10 Aug 1976; ord and ind to Camperdown 2 May 1989.

CHALMERS ARDLER (FES X, 300)

1969 JAMES ERNEST POWRIE
(FES X, 300), ord and ind to Chalmers Ardler 10 Jun 1969; ret 31 Oct 1995.

1997   KENNETH DAVID STOTT
B 14 Dec 1962 at Montrose, s of David James S. and Rena Summers; educ Tynecastle High, Edinburgh 1967–81; University of Edinburgh 1981–85 (MA), 1985–88 (BD); lic by Presb of Edinburgh 3 Jul 1988; asst Brightons 1988–89; m 28 Jun 1986 Anne Maria Herron b 17 Jan 1964 d of James H. and Jessie Bradford; Children: Amy Elizabeth b 1 Nov 1989; Rachel Joy b 17 May 1991; Katie Grace b 25 Mar 1994; ord and ind to Glasgow Partick South 28 Jun 1989; trans to Chalmers Ardler 15 Jan 1997.

CLEPINGTON (FES V, 325; VIII, 497; IX, 506; X, 300)

1970   JOHN EDWARD HAWDON
(FES X, 300), ind to Clepington 14 Oct 1970; ret 31 Oct 1995; University of Edinburgh 1993–94 (MTh); s Andrew m Laura Traynor.

1997   ARTHUR ARMOUR CHRISTIE
B 28 Nov 1952 at St Andrews, s of Arthur Porteous C. and Jane Noble Cookson Armour; educ Kirkland High, Methil 1963–66; Fife College (MHCIMA); University of Edinburgh 1991–95 (BD); Catering Executive 1973–86; Personnel Manager 1986–89; lic by Presb of Dunfermline 3 Jul 1995; asst Auld Kirk of Ayr 1995–97; Grace Elizabeth Mara b 13 Mar 1954 d of John and Jean M; Children: Liam David b 11 Nov 1975 m Fiona; Cara Jane b 16 Dec 1976; ord and ind to Clepington 19 Feb 1997.

CRAIGIEBANK (FES IX, 506; X, 301)

Linked 11 Mar 1998 with Douglas and Angus.

1967   JAMES BEWS
(FES IX, 574, 684; X, 301, 389), trans from Wick Central to Craigiebank 14 Jun 1967; ret 31 Aug 1981; s James m Christine Moore, divorced; m (2) Heather McAlpine.

1982   DAVID JAMES HEPBURN LAING
trans from Lossiemouth St Gerardine's High to Craigiebank 9 Nov 1982; trans to Kirkcaldy St Andrew's 16 May 1989.

1989   CHARLES ARCHIBALD LEGGAT
trans from Coatbridge Townhead to Craigiebank 7 Dec 1989; ret 31 Dec 1995; died 11 Mar 1997.

1998   MICHAEL VICTOR ALEXANDER MAIR
(FES X, 219), trans from Aberdeen Holburn West to Craigiebank with Douglas and Angus 21 Oct 1998; Children: Eleanor Jane b 1 Sep 1971.

1999   EDITH F McMILLAN
dem from Dunrossness with Sandwick, Cunningsburgh and Quarff 4 Apr 1990; introd as Assoc at Craigiebank with Douglas and Angus 4 Aug 1999.

DOUGLAS AND ANGUS (FES X, 301)

Linked 11 Mar 1998 with Craigiebank.

1976   DAVID JOHN HENDERSON McNAUGHTON
ord and ind to Douglas and Angus 1 Jun 1976; trans to Killin and Ardeonaig 1 Jun 1983.

1983   JAMES McNAUGHTAN
ord and ind to Douglas and Angus 15 Sep 1983; trans to Kilmarnock St Marnock's 22 Aug 1989.

1990   JOHN RAE NOTMAN
ord and ind to Douglas and Angus 13 Jun 1990; trans to Portlethen 6 Mar 1997.

1998   MICHAEL VICTOR ALEXANDER MAIR
(FES X, 219), ind to Craigiebank with Douglas and Angus 21 Oct 1998, see Craigiebank.

1999   EDITH F McMILLAN
introd as Assoc at Craigiebank with Douglas and Angus 4 Aug 1999, see Craigiebank.

DOWNFIELD SOUTH (FUF 383; FES IX, 507; X, 301)

1960   CHARLES NICOLL
(FES IX, 501; X, 296, 301), trans from Strathkinness to Downfield South 23 Jun 1960; ret 31 Jul 1985; died 23 May 1991.

1986   ANDREW J WILSON
res as Assoc at Elgin St Giles' and ind to Downfield South 28 May 1986; dem 9 Sep 1991.

1991   MAURICE SAMUEL BOND
dem from First Ballynahinch Presb Church, Co Down and ind to Downfield South 10 Apr 1991; trans to Dumfries St Michael's and South 7 Jul 1999.

DUNDEE (ST MARY'S) (FES V, 313; VIII, 486; IX, 508; X, 301)

1951   HUGH OSBORNE DOUGLAS
(FES IX, 21, 482, 508; X, 301), trans from Edinburgh North Leith to St Mary's 19 Sep 1951; ret 31 Jul 1977; died 4 Jan 1986.

1978   WILLIAM BOYD ROBERTSON MACMILLAN
(FES X, 34, 214, 352), trans from Bearsden South to Dundee Parish Church (St Mary's) 8 Mar 1978; ret 31 Oct 1993; Chaplain to City of Dundee District Council 1978–93; Freeman of Dundee 1991; Chaplain in Ordinary to the Queen 1988–97; Extra Chaplain to the Queen in Scotland 1997-; Moderator of General Assembly 1991–92; LLD (Dundee) 1990; DD (Aberdeen) 1991; Prelate, Order of St John of Jerusalem (Scotland) 1993–96; Trustee Scottish National War Memorial 1994- .

1994   KEITH FERRIER HALL
B 20 Oct 1955 at Arbroath, s of Pearson Herald H. and Mary Watson Carrie; educ Arbroath High 1960–73; University of St Andrews 1973–79 (BD); lic by Presb of Angus 31 Aug 1979; asst Dundee (St Mary's) 1979–80; m 2 Sep 1978 Amilia Elaine Donaldson b 23 Nov 1959 d of Albert Carneigie D. and Helen Lee Coutts; Children: Keith Ramsay b 31 Jul 1987; Chloe Amilia and Russell Donaldson b 7 Dec 1988; ord and ind to Blairgowrie St Mary's South 7 May 1981; trans to Alloa St Mungo's 11 May 1987; trans to Dundee (St Mary's) 13 Jul 1994.

DUNDEE WEST (FES X, 302, 304, 306)
Formed 22 Sep 1999 by union of Roseangle Ryehill (union 3 Sep 1980 of Roseangle and Ryehill) and St Peter's McCheyne (union 24 Aug 1982 of St Peter's and McCheyne).

1940   DAVID GOOD GRAY
(FES IX, 463, 517; X, 306), trans from Dunfermline Townhill to St Peter's 23 Nov 1940; ret 30 Apr 1972; died 22 Apr 1990.

1952   DUNCAN GUNN DARROCH
(FES IX, 510, 662; X, 302), trans from Kilmorack to McCheyne 12 May 1952; ret 30 Jun 1976; died 13 May 1978.

1961   JAMES ALEXANDER BREMNER
(FES IX, 41; X, 24, 304, 306), trans from Edinburgh St Paul's Newington to St Mark's 5 Jan 1961; became minister of united charge with St John's (Roseangle) 12 Sep 1968; ret 30 Sep 1979; died 23 Sep 1989.

1965   JAMES MURDOCH ROGERS
(FES X, 304), ord and ind to Second Saintfield, Presb Church in Ireland, 24 Mar 1955; ind to Ryehill 18 Aug 1965; became minister of united charge with Roseangle 3 Sep 1980; app to Gibraltar St Andrew's with Costa del Sol 29 Sep 1993.

1973   GEORGE FAIRLIE
(FES X, 306, 385), ord by Presb of Sutherland and introd as Assoc at Lairg with Rogart 6 Apr 1971; ind to St Peter's 12 Apr 1973; trans to Glasgow Cathcart South 1 Apr 1982.

1977   JAMES HARRISON HUDSON
(FES X, 197), trans from Hamilton Trinity to McCheyne Memorial 23 Mar 1977; became minister of united charge with St Peter's 24 Aug 1982; dem 22 Sep 1999; Addl children: Jacquelyn Ellison Mhairi b 21 Oct 1977; d Carolyn m McLean; d Rosalyn m McIver; d Gwendolyn m Hannah; Addl publ: *Let the Fire Burn* (Handsel Press, 1978); *The Impact of Robert Murray McCheyne* (*Life & Work*, 1987).

1995   JOYCE LYNN
ord and ind to Roseangle Ryehill 1 Mar 1995; trans to Shapinsay 25 Nov 1998.

FAIRMUIR (FES V, 333; VIII, 488; IX, 508; X, 301)

1972   ROBERT CLARK
(FES X, 301), ord and ind to Fairmuir 14 Jun 1972; trans to Gorebridge 29 Sep 1977.

1978   DAVID CAMPBELL McLEOD
(FES X, 127), trans from Paisley Martyrs' to Fairmuir 8 Jun 1978; d Esther m Cobain.

FOWLIS AND LIFF (FES IX, 518; X, 307)
Linked 17 May 1995 with Lundie and Muirhead of Liff.

1954   WILLIAM OSLER NICOLL
(FES IX, 196, 485, 518, 538; X, 307), trans from Kilmarnock Riccarton to Fowlis and Liff 27 Jan 1954; ret 30 Sep 1979; died 14 Sep 1982.

1980   CHARLES WILMAR MILLER
(FES IX, 149; X, 88, 147, 293, 334), trans from Anstruther to Fowlis and Liff 24 Sep 1980; ret 27 Feb 1994; Chaplain (part-time) to Royal Dundee Liff Hospital 1981–; Religious Broadcasting Organiser for Radio Liff FM; s David m Jeannette Jamie; s John m Fiona Muirhead; s Andrew m Lynne Esplin; Publ: Cartoon in biography of Professor William Barclay (Paternoster Press, 1984); articles and cartoons in *Expository Times* (T&T Clark) and *Life & Work*.

1995   MARTYN ROBIN HADEN THOMAS
ord and ind to Lundie and Muirhead of Liff 22 Jun 1987; became minister of linked charge with Fowlis and Liff 17 May 1995.

HIGH KIRK (FUF 383; FES IX, 508; X, 301)

1942   ROY ROSS HOGG
(FES IX, 12, 509, 736; X, 301), trans from Edinburgh Davidson to The High Kirk 4 Dec 1942; ret 31 Jan 1978; died 9 Oct 1978.

1979   HENRY MONTGOMERIE GIBSON
(FES X, 142, 245), trans from Aberfeldy with Amulree to The High Kirk 31 Jan 1979; dem 30 Jun 1999; University of St Andrews 1984–88 (PhD).

INCHTURE AND KINNAIRD (FES IX, 518; X, 307)
Linked 4 Apr 1963 with Longforgan. Further linked 28 Feb 1983 with Abernyte.

1954   ROBERT DALY
(FES IX, 320, 518; X, 307), trans from Blantyre Stonefield to Inchture and Kinnaird 24 Feb 1954; became minister of linked charge with Longforgan 4 Apr 1963 and with Abernyte 28 Feb 1983; died 15 Nov 1988.

1989   JAMES ALEXANDER PENRICE JACK
ord and ind to Abernyte with Inchture and Kinnaird with Longforgan 19 Sep 1989, see Abernyte.

INVERGOWRIE (FES IX, 519; X, 307)

1961 IAIN ROBESON CRAIG
(FES IX, 191; X, 109, 171, 307), trans from Glasgow Pollokshields West to Invergowrie 14 Dec 1961; ret 31 Dec 1988.

1989 ALASTAIR MACKENZIE HORNE
ord and ind to Invergowrie 17 Oct 1989; trans to Falkirk St Andrew's West 13 Feb 1997.

1997 ROBERT JOHN RAMSAY
B 28 Oct 1951 at Alyth, s of George R. and Elizabeth Helen Great; educ Blairgowrie High 1963–69; University of Edinburgh 1969–73 (LLB); University of St Andrews 1982–85 (BD); Solicitor's Apprenticeship 1973–75; Lecturer in Law, University of Dundee 1975–79; Head of Legal Studies, Govt Admin College, Papua New Guinea 1979–82; lic by Presb of Dunkeld and Meigle 26 Jun 1985; asst Kirriemuir Old 1985–86; m 7 Sep 1974 Sheila Margaret Ball b 6 Mar 1955 d of Robert Alexander B. and Margaret Millar; Children: Susan Margaret b 13 Nov 1976; Catriona Jane b 29 Sep 1978; ord and ind to Glenisla with Kilry with Lintrathen 14 May 1986; became minister of linked charge with Airlie Kingoldrum and Ruthven 19 Jun 1994; trans to Invergowrie 3 Dec 1997.

LOCHEE OLD AND ST LUKE'S (FES X, 302)

Formed 30 Sep 1985 by union of Lochee Old (formerly called Lochee East-St Ninian's) and Lochee St Luke's.

1949 JOHN MACDONALD
(FES IX, 509; X, 302 (2)), ord and ind to Lochee St Ninian's 17 Nov 1949; became minister of united charge with Lochee East 23 Sep 1959; ret 30 Sep 1985.

1970 JOSEPH LOGAN LECKIE
(FES IX, 193; X, 35, 110, 302, 421), returned from service with Presb Church in USA and ind to Lochee St Luke's 31 Dec 1970; trans to Fowlis Wester with Madderty with Monzie 17 Jun 1984.

1985 ROY MACKENZIE
B 18 Jul 1931 at Aberdeen, s of William M. and Isabella Ferrier; educ Torry Intermediate 1942–45; Aberdeen College of Commerce 1978–79; University of Aberdeen 1979–82 (LTh); National Service 1949–51; Company Secretary; Manager, House Furnishing Co; General Manager; lic by Presb of Gordon, Jul 1982; m 7 Dec 1957 Henrietta Mary Strachan Craig b 27 Feb 1937 d of Thomas C. and Henrietta Strachan; Children: Karen m Keith Andrews; Kevin m Linda Wyllie; ord and ind to Alves and Burghead 22 Oct 1982; trans to Lochee Old and St Luke's 2 Oct 1985; died 24 Apr 1994.

1995 ELISABETH GILLIAN BRAID SPENCE
B 23 Jan 1957 at Dunfermline, d of James S. and Hilda Beckett; educ Queen Anne High, Dunfermline 1969–74; Dundee College of Education 1978–81

(DipEd); University of Edinburgh 1989–93 (BD); Child Therapist 1981–89; lic by Presb of Ross 6 Jul 1993; asst Edinburgh Oxgangs 1993–94; ord and ind to Lochee Old and St Luke's 16 Aug 1995; Publ: Contributor to *Christian Values* (T&T Clark, 1995).

LOCHEE WEST (FUF 384; FES IX, 510; X, 302)

1973 JAMES ALEXANDER ROY
(FES X, 302, 377), trans from Stonehaven Dunnottar to Lochee West 11 Dec 1973.

LOGIE AND ST JOHN'S CROSS (FES X, 302, 306)

Formed 31 Aug 1982 by union of Logie and St John's Cross.

1928 HENRY MATTHEW BARTLETT
(FES VIII, 489; IX, 510; X, 302), ord and ind to Logie 6 Jul 1928; ret 31 Jul 1969; died 28 Dec 1980.

1964 GEORGE RAMSAY RATTRAY MACKENZIE
(FES IX, 64, 198, 274; X, 162, 306), trans from Ibrox to St John's Cross 16 Mar 1964; became minister of united charge with Logie 31 Aug 1982; ret 31 Mar 1987.

1970 FRANK DEY
(FES X, 302, 341), trans from Finzean with Strachan and Birse to Logie 13 May 1970; ret 31 Aug 1982; died 22 Mar 1984.

1988 DAVID DOMINIC SMART
ord and ind to Logie and St John's Cross 15 Jul 1988; trans to Aberdeen Gilcomston South 18 Jun 1998.

1999 DAVID SINCLAIR SCOTT
B 13 Jun 1958 at Edinburgh, s of Ivan St Clair S. and Elizabeth Sinclair Robertson; educ George Watson's, Edinburgh 1970–76; University of Aberdeen 1976–80 (MA), 1983–86 (BD); Youthshare Volunteer, Kenya (Church of Scotland) 1980–81; Programme Secretary, YMCA 1981–83; lic by Presb of Aberdeen 30 Jun 1986; asst Falkirk Old and St Modan's 1986–87; m 16 Jul 1982 Susan Joyce Harman b 11 Mar 1959 d of Gerald Albert H. and Joyce Jenny Benzie; Children: Julie Elizabeth b 15 Jan 1985; Katie Louise b 11 Aug 1987; Paul Christopher b 7 Nov 1988; ord and ind to Invergordon 26 Jun 1987; trans to Logie and St John's Cross 20 Aug 1999.

LONGFORGAN (FES V, 351; VIII, 492; IX, 519; X, 307)

Linked 4 Apr 1963 with Longforgan. Further linked 28 Feb 1983 with Abernyte.

1963 ROBERT DALY
(FES IX, 320, 518; X, 307), trans from Blantyre Stonefield to Inchture and Kinnaird 24 Feb 1954; became minister of linked charge with Longforgan 4 Apr 1963 and with Abernyte 28 Feb 1983; died 15 Nov 1988.

1989 JAMES ALEXANDER PENRICE JACK
ord and ind to Abernyte with Inchture and Kinnaird with Longforgan 19 Sep 1989, see Abernyte.

LUNDIE AND MUIRHEAD OF LIFF (FES IX, 519; X, 307)

Linked 17 May 1995 with Fowlis and Liff.

1950 MATTHEW JOHN ROBERT LESTER
(FES IX, 519, 521; X, 307), ord and ind to Muirhead of Liff 20 Sep 1950; became minister of united charge with Lundie 7 Jun 1953; died 20 May 1977.

1978 WILLIAM MURDOCH MACLEAN CAMPBELL
(FES X, 243, 245), trans from Braes of Rannoch with Foss and Rannoch to Lundie and Muirhead of Liff 14 Apr 1978; dem on app as Chaplain to Royal Cornhill and Woodlands Hospitals, Aberdeen 18 Aug 1986.

1987 MARTYN ROBIN HADEN THOMAS
B 14 Apr 1934 at Stourbridge, Worcestershire, s of Percy Fred T. and Emily Kathleen Haden; educ Oldbury Grammar 1945–52; Advanced College of Technology, Birmingham (now Aston University) 1952–57 (CEng, MIStructE); University of Edinburgh 1984–86; Structural Steelwork Designer 1952–60; National Service (Royal Engineers) 1957–59; Senior Structural Engineer 1961–70; Missionary Engineer (Nepal) 1970–84; lic by Presb of Edinburgh 29 Jun 1986; asst Edinburgh Braid 1986–87; m 31 Jul 1971 Shirley Ann Snell b 2 Sep 1936 d of Sidney James S. and Millicent Winifred Riddle; Children: Mary Elizabeth b 2 Jul 1972, died 3 Jul 1972; Cherry Ruth b 18 Sep 1973; Peter Martyn Robert b 10 Jan 1975; ord and ind to Lundie and Muirhead of Liff 22 Jun 1987; became minister of linked charge with Fowlis and Liff 17 May 1995.

MAINS (FES V, 357; VIII, 493; IX, 510; X, 303)

1969 JOHN CLARK SCROGGIE
(FES IX, 703; X, 291, 303, 401), trans from Flisk and Kilmany to Mains 12 Mar 1969; ret 28 Feb 1985; m (2) 15 Jan 1996 Letitia Blance Cameron Steen b 27 Oct 1934 d of James Cameron S. and Catherine McIntosh Sanderson; d Catherine m David Robertson; d Helen m Harry Keith.

1985 KENNETH ROBERT THOM
ord and ind to Mains 25 Sep 1985; dem 18 Nov 1990 on app by RAF Chaplains' Branch.

1991 MICHAEL STEWART GOSS
B 31 Oct 1962 at Hawick, s of David William G. and Elaine Stewart; educ St Joseph's College, Dumfries and Dumfries Academy 1974–80; University of Aberdeen 1980–85 (BD), 1988–90 (DPS); Hotel Porter/Head Porter 1986–88; lic by Presb of Aberdeen 27 Jun 1990; asst Aberdeen Newhills 1990–91; m 30 Aug 1986 Rhona Young Izett b 27 Feb 1964 d of William Archibald Frew I. and Margaret Perrie Letham; Children: Andrew William b 13 Nov 1994; Aileen Stewart b 27 Oct 1998; ord and ind to Mains 21 Aug 1991.

MAINS OF FINTRY (FES IX, 511; X, 303)

1974 EWEN SINCLAIR NICOLL
(FES X, 303), ind to Mains of Fintry 28 Aug 1974; trans to Carlisle 4 Feb 1977.

1977 PETER MAURICE HUMPHRIS
B 3 Jun 1947 at Cambridge, s of Maurice H. and Audrey Allmark; educ Bedford School 1960–65; University of Aberdeen 1965–69 (BSc); Glasgow Bible Training Institute 1971–72; University of Glasgow 1972–75 (BD); Electrical Engineering 1969–71; lic by Presb of Glasgow 26 Jun 1975; asst Nairn Old 1975–77; m 29 Jul 1970 Kathleen Morrison b 27 Apr 1948 d of Alexander M. and Maimie Chisholm; Children: David b 16 Jul 1974 m Kirsten Beaumont; Douglas b 14 Jun 1976; Karen b 29 May 1978; Sarah b 14 Sep 1982; ord by Presb of Inverness during assistantship at Nairn Old 3 Mar 1976; ind to Mains of Fintry 10 Aug 1977; Publ: *Who's for Baptism?* (Handsel Press, 1978).

MEADOWSIDE ST PAUL'S (FES X, 303, 306)

Formed 4 Dec 1981 by union of Meadowside (formerly Albert Square and St George's) and St Paul's.

1952 BASIL GATHORNE HARDY
(FES IX, 516, 609; X, 306), trans from Peterhead East to St Paul's 25 Mar 1952; became minister of united charge with Meadowside 4 Dec 1981; ret 25 May 1984; m (2) 31 Jul 1982 Grace Allan Auchterlonie b 22 May 1928 d of William Watt A. and Sarah Allan Fotheringham; s Brian (from previous marriage) m Hilary Elizabeth Russell; d Avril (from previous marriage) m Alexander Peter Kopyto.

1956 JOHN BROWN COUPAR
(FES IX, 317; X, 186, 298, 303), trans from Airdrie Wellwynd to Albert Square and St George's 19 Sep 1956; ret 30 Sep 1980; died 22 Jan 1987.

1984 MAUDEEN I MACDOUGALL
d of John and Georgina M; educ Falkirk High 1964–70; University of Edinburgh 1971–77 (BA, BD); lic by Presb of Falkirk 30 Jun 1977; ord by Presb of West Lothian and ind to Livingston New Town as Community minister 4 Oct 1978; ind to Meadowside St Paul's 25 Sep 1984.

MENZIESHILL (FES X, 303)

1969 ROBERT MAIR DONALD
(FES X, 303), ord and ind to Menzieshill 9 Jul 1969; dem 30 Mar 1977 to take up app as Company Director of Laburn Building Services Ltd; Assoc at Abernyte with Inchture and Kinnaird with Longforgan 1994–98; Open University 1973–76 (BA); Addl children: Colin Graeme b 18 Feb 1976.

1977 STANLEY ALEXANDER BROOK
ord and ind to Menzieshill 17 Aug 1977; trans to Edinburgh Holy Trinity 6 Jan 1988.

1989 JACK MITCHELL
ord as Aux by Presb of Dundee and assgnd to Menzieshill 7 Jun 1987; ind to same charge 30 Mar 1989; ret 31 Mar 1996.

1996 HARRY JAMES BROWN
B 29 Apr 1944 at Carrickfergus, Co Antrim, s of Harry James B. and Martha Harbinson McReynolds; educ Ballyclare High 1955–61; Marine Radio College; University of St Andrews 1987–90 (LTh); Marine Radio Officer 1962–67; Company Salesman/Sales Manager 1969–87; lic by Presb of Dunfermline 1 Jul 1990; asst Dunfermline St Margaret's 1990–91; m 15 Jul 1967 Frances Elizabeth Ann Murphy b 18 Jun 1946 d of Samuel and Frances M; Children: Jonathan Ian Harry b 25 Aug 1970 m Lisa Anne Adair; David Samuel b 7 Jan 1974 m Renee Conlee; ord and ind to Benholm and Johnshaven with Garvock St Cyrus 11 Jul 1991; trans to Menzieshill 18 Dec 1996.

MID CRAIGIE (FES IX, 511; X, 303)

Temporarily linked with Wallacetown 1975–80.

1955 WILLIAM BULLMAN
(FES X, 303), ord and ind to Mid Craigie 20 Sep 1955; ret 1 Nov 1973; died 24 Apr 1977.

1975 JAMES BERNARD WALKER
(FES X, 304), ord by Presb of Dundee and introd as Assoc at Mid Craigie with Wallacetown 18 Jun 1975; ind to Galashiels Old and St Paul's 15 Nov 1978.

1979 DAVID MASTERTON DOIG
(FES X, 312, 403), dem from Glenshee and Glenericht 5 Mar 1978; introd as Assoc at Mid Craigie 19 Feb 1979; ind to same charge 29 Sep 1982; ret 30 Apr 1986; Addl children: Gillian Mhairi b 23 Mar 1979; d Deirdre m Woods; d Pauline m Macgregor; d Helen m Middleton; d Lilian m Hay.

1987 DOUGLAS J PAGE
ord and introd on term app to Mid Craigie 29 Apr 1987; res 31 May 1991.

1992 COLIN ALEXANDER STRONG
B 4 Jul 1958 at Dumbarton, s of Clifford S. and Alice Rosemary Grant; educ Keil School, Dumbarton 1970–75; University of Stirling 1975–78 (BSc); University of Aberdeen 1985–88 (BD); Applications Programmer 1979–84; Analyst/Programmer 1984–85; lic by Presb of Inverness 24 Jun 1988; asst Dundee Ogilvie and Stobswell 1988–89; m 29 Jul 1989 Laura Mary Rose Miller d of Robert M. and Mary Cowie; Children: Anna Mairi b 30 Mar 1997; Zoe Alice b 27 Jun 1999; ord and ind to Rousay 16 Jun 1989; trans to Mid Craigie 15 Jan 1992.

MONIFIETH PANMURE (FUF 391; FES IX, 520; X, 307)

1949 HARRY VALENTINE GIBBONS
(FES IX, 68, 520, 762; X, 307), service with RAChD 1940–46; ind to Panmure 26 Oct 1949; ret 26 Oct 1965; died 1 Aug 1991.

1967 ALEXANDER MACKENZIE JACK
(FES X, 307), trans under mutual eligibility from Goodmayes St Andrew's (Presb Church of England) to Panmure 8 Nov 1967; ret 31 Mar 1973.

1974 DAVID BLAIR JAMIESON
(FES X, 308), ord and ind to Panmure 15 Jan 1974; m (2) 22 Feb 1985 Valerie Nancy Maidment b 28 Feb 1954 d of Ronald Clifford John M. and Alice Blacklaws.

MONIFIETH SOUTH (FUF 392; FES IX, 521; X, 308)

1959 DONALD WILLIAM FRASER
(FES X, 308), ord by Presb of Dunfermline during assistantship at Dunfermline Abbey 13 Jul 1958; ind to Monifieth South 9 Jul 1959.

MONIFIETH ST RULE'S (FES V, 361; VIII, 494; IX, 520; X, 308)

1970 THOMAS MILROY
(FES X, 28, 308), trans from Bathgate Boghall to St Rule's 29 Apr 1970; ret 30 Sep 1992.

1993 STEPHEN JAMES SMITH
ord and ind to St Rule's 8 Mar 1993; trans to Largs Clark Memorial 11 Dec 1998.

1999 ROBERT WILLIAM MASSIE
B 21 Aug 1942 at Aberdeen, s of Jane Massie; educ Frederick Street School, Aberdeen 1954–57; University of Aberdeen 1985–88 (LTh); Brake Mechanic 1957–66; Lab Technician 1966–85; lic by Presb of Aberdeen 27 Jun 1988; asst Aberdeen Garthdee 1988–89; m 31 Aug 1963 Phyllis Fleming b 16 May 1943 d of James F. and Marjory Lawrance; Children: Stuart b 15 Sep 1964 m Margaret

Livingstone; Alison b 15 Mar 1969 m David Stewart; ord and ind to New Pitsligo 25 Aug 1989; became minister of linked charge with Aberdour 20 Jul 1995; trans to St Rule's 20 Oct 1999.

MONIKIE AND NEWBIGGING (FES X, 307, 308)

Linkage of Monifieth North and Newbigging with Monikie terminated 6 Jun 1984 in favour of union. Name changed 1985 to Monikie and Newbigging.

1961 WILLIAM DOUGLAS CHISHOLM
(FES IX, 302, 580, 731; X, 90, 178, 308), trans from Crossmichael to Monikie 17 May 1961; became minister of linked charge with Monifieth North and Newbigging 6 Sep 1967; ret 13 Sep 1983; d Elaine m Graham Myles; d Isabel m Keith Rouse; Publ: Monikie in *Third Statistical Account*, County of Angus a) *Precious Stones—Newbigging Church* b) *The Hillock—Monifieth North Church* (1979); *The Monikie Story—a Parish Social History* (Findlay, 1982).

1985 GORDON ROSS MACKENZIE
B 8 Jan 1948 at Nairn, s of Alexander M. and Freda Gordon Johnston; educ Nairn Academy 1960–65; University of Aberdeen 1965–69 (BScAgr); University of Glasgow 1972–75 (BD); Union Theological Seminary, Virginia 1975–76; Agricultural Adviser 1969–72; lic by Presb of Inverness 9 Jul 1975; m 4 Aug 1978 Sheila Macrae Davis b 15 Feb 1958 d of Henry Dunsmore D. and Jean Denny Gilchrist; Children: Sarah Jean b 18 Jun 1983; John Alexander b 7 Jan 1986; ord and ind to Kirkmichael and Tomintoul 26 Oct 1977; trans to Monikie and Newbigging 14 Feb 1985.

MURROES AND TEALING (FES X, 308, 309)

Formed 14 Dec 1982 by union of Murroes and Tealing. Linked 27 Feb 1983 with Auchterhouse.

1958 WILLIAM CHARLES SMITH
(FES IX, 592, 663; X, 309, 340), dem from Corgarff 14 Jan 1958 and introd on term app to Tealing; ret 1 Dec 1960; died 12 Jun 1980.

1962 JAMES KIDD
(FES X, 121, 309), trans from Whiting Bay to Tealing 24 Apr 1962; became minister of linked charge with Murroes 10 Dec 1963; ret 31 Mar 1983; died 29 Jun 1992.

1983 HELEN GIBSON JOHNSTONE
ord and ind to Auchterhouse with Murroes and Tealing 28 Sep 1983, see Auchterhouse.

1989 WILLIAM McDOWALL MACMILLAN
ind to Auchterhouse with Murroes and Tealing 25 Oct 1989, see Auchterhouse.

1995 SYDNEY SAMUEL GRAHAM
ind to Auchterhouse with Murroes and Tealing 23 Aug 1995, see Auchterhouse.

ST ANDREW'S (FES V, 363; VIII, 489; IX, 513; X, 305)

1950 THOMAS ROBERTSON STRATHERN CAMPBELL
(FES IX, 190, 513, 561; X, 305), trans from Aberdeen St Colm's to St Andrew's 13 Sep 1950; died 11 Feb 1985.

1986 IAN DUNCAN PETRIE
(FES X, 144), trans from East Kilbride Westwood to St Andrew's 15 Jan 1986; Chaplain (part-time) to Nine Incorporated and Three United Trades, Dundee; Addl children: Ewan Cownie b 30 Apr 1978.

ST COLUMBA'S (FES X, 305)

Congregation dissolved 24 Nov 1991.

1956 JOHN MACKAY NIMMO
(FES IX, 210, 267; X, 159, 301, 305), trans from Glasgow Elder Park to St Columba's 6 Jun 1956; died 6 Oct 1996.

ST DAVID'S NORTH (FUF 388; FES IX, 514; X, 305)

Linked 1 Jun 1986 with Albany-Butterburn.

1973 GIDEON GEORGE SCOTT
(FES X, 27, 305), ind to St David's North 10 Apr 1973; became minister of linked charge with Albany-Butterburn 1 Jun 1986, see Albany-Butterburn.

ST JAMES' (FUF 382; FES IX, 514; X, 305)

Congregation dissolved 1988.

1969 ANDREW DENIS WILLIAMS
(FES X, 305, 388), res as Asst at Grangemouth Kerse and ind to St James' 24 Sep 1969; dem 23 Jan 1977.

1978 GEORGE STRATHEARN AYRE
(FES IX, 446; X, 263, 284, 309), trans from Tayport Queen Street and introd to St James' (term) 10 May 1978; ret 11 May 1983; died 27 Jun 1989.

STOBSWELL (FES X, 304, 306)

Formed 29 Jun 1976 by union of Park and Maryfield Victoria Street. Stobswell united 9 Jan 1985 with Ogilvie as Ogilvie Stobswell. Renamed Stobswell 1991.

1952 JAMES EKRON LITTLE
(FES IX, 512, 610; X, 304), trans from Pitsligo to Ogilvie 7 Oct 1952; ret 31 Dec 1984; died 11 Feb 1993.

1971 KENNETH JAMES MACKAY
(FES X, 303), ord and introd on term app to Maryfield Victoria Street 24 Jun 1971; trans to Edinburgh St Nicholas' Sighthill 30 Jan 1976.

1972 ALAN JOHN ROY
(FES X, 304, 425), res from service with Overseas Council and ind to Dundee Park 16 Jun 1972; became minister of united charge with Maryfield Victoria Street 29 Jun 1976 and of united charge with Ogilvie 9 Jan 1985; trans to Aberuthven with Dunning 24 Nov 1993.

1994 GORDON DUNLOP IRVING
ord and ind to Stobswell 20 Sep 1994; trans to Kilmacolm Old 26 Nov 1998.

1999 JANE LOUISE BARRON
B 7 Oct 1962 at Shrewsbury, d of Frederick Reginald Houlston and Margaret Louise Bartlett; educ Alice Ottley School, Worcester 1966–81; University of Stirling 1981–85 (BA, DipED); University of Aberdeen 1993–96 (BD); Teaching (English) 1985–90; Radio Journalist and Producer 1990–93; lic by Presb of Kincardine and Deeside, May 1998; asst Aberdeen Queen's Cross 1998–99; m 25 Jul 1985 Ian George Barron b 6 Jul 1963 s of George B. and Evelyn Allan; ord and ind to Stobswell 1 Sep 1999.

STRATHMARTINE (FES IX, 507; X, 301)

Formerly Downfield Strathmartine.

1962 ROBERT GOVAN CLARKSON
(FES IX, 606; X, 301, 349), trans from Fraserburgh West to Strathmartine 28 Jun 1962; ret 7 Aug 1989; s Graeme m Moira Helen Dalgleish; s Fraser m Jeanine; s Robin m Isabel.

1990 STEWART McMILLAN
dem from Whalsay and Skerries 15 Jan 1988; ind to Strathmartine 5 Apr 1990.

THE STEEPLE (FES X, 306)

Formed 12 Oct 1978 by union of Dundee Old St Paul's and St David's and Wishart Memorial and Dundee The Steeple.

1959 ROBERT ARTHUR
(FES IX, 115, 292; X, 173, 304), trans from Rutherford to Old St Paul's and St David's 10 Feb 1959; ret 30 Sep 1975; died 27 Apr 1990.

1963 WALTER STRANG MONEY
(FES IX, 66, 116; X, 65, 119, 306), trans from Saltcoats Landsborough to The Steeple 11 Jun 1963; ret 12 Oct 1978; died 28 Jun 1989.

1976 JOHN STEIN
(FES X, 425), ind to Old St Paul's and St David's and Wishart Memorial 16 Mar 1976; became minister of united charge with The Steeple 12 Oct 1978; dem on app as Joint-Warden of Carberry Tower 1 May 1986.

1986 GRAHAM WATSON FOSTER
(FES X, 39), trans from Invergordon to The Steeple 18 Nov 1986; Chaplain (part-time) to Abertay University, Dundee; died 22 Jun 1999; Addl children: Mark Robert b 25 Jun 1978; Publ: *Pray Today 1990–91* (Prayer and Devotion Committee, 1990).

TRINITY (FES X, 299, 306)

Formed 29 Apr 1981 by union of Baxter Park, Wallacetown and St Matthew's.

1953 JAMES STEWART
(FES IX, 516; X, 306), ord and ind to St Matthew's 18 Aug 1953; ret 31 Mar 1980; died 27 May 1982.

1955 GILBERT CECIL McCUTCHEON
(FES IX, 625; X, 299, 357), trans from Drumblade to Baxter Park 5 Jun 1955; ret 30 Jun 1973; died 19 Jan 1994.

1971 THOMAS JAMES LOUDON BLAIR
(FES X, 142, 306), trans from Campsie Trinity with Milton of Campsie to Wallacetown 8 Dec 1971 (temporarily linked with Mid Craigie 1975–80); trans to Galston 3 Dec 1980.

1975 DONALD BAXTER JOHNSTONE
(FES X, 299, 405), trans from Burra Isles, Shetland to Baxter Park 21 Feb 1975; dem 31 Dec 1978; Addl children: John b 19 May 1976.

1981 ALBERT BROWN REID
(FES X, 210, 253), trans from Perth Letham St Mark's to Trinity 19 Nov 1981; trans to Ardler, Kettins and Meigle 15 Apr 1993.

1993 JAMES LYNCH WILSON
B 23 Mar 1957 at Airdrie, s of Alfred W. and Elizabeth Lynch; educ Airdrie Academy 1969–71, 1974–75; Graeme High, Falkirk 1971–73; Cumbernauld High 1973–74; University of Aberdeen 1980–85 (BD, CPS); lic by Presb of Hamilton 27 Jun 1985; m 10 Jul 1982 Esther Teresa Hird b 4 Dec 1959 d of Gordon H. and Isobel Kelman; Children: Naomi Elizabeth b 16 Jul 1983; Nathan Edward b 24 Sep 1985; Joel Gordon b 30 Sep 1987; Adin Alfred b 9 Apr 1989; ord and ind to Strichen 24 Sep 1986; trans to Trinity 20 Oct 1993.

WHITFIELD (FES X, 306)

1969 HUGH CHARLES ORMISTON
(FES X, 306), ord and ind to Whitfield 4 May 1969; introd as Assoc at Tobermory 31 Jul 1978.

1978 JAMES RONALD DICK
(FES X, 118), trans from Kilwinning Mansefield to Whitfield 29 Nov 1978; trans to Corsock with Kirkpatrick Durham 22 Nov 1982.

1981   ARTHUR DAVID COURTENAY GREER
(FES X, 163 (2), 419), res from Dept of Education
and introd as Assoc at Whitfield 1 Oct 1981; ind
to Dunscore with Glencairn and Moniaive 4 Jun
1985.

1982   DAVID DONALDSON
(FES X, 29, 418), trans from Bathgate St David's
to Whitfield 18 Aug 1982; trans to Edinburgh
Duddingston 31 Aug 1990.

1985   HECTOR GRANT MACMILLAN
(FES X, 196), [correction: MacMillan, not McMillan
as in FES X, 196]; dem from Alyth and introd
as Assoc at Whitfield 1 Mar 1985; ret 28 Feb
1990.

1991   GEORGE GAMMACK
B 17 Sep 1945 at Aberdeen, s of Ernest and
Elizabeth G; educ Aberdeen Grammar 1958–64;
University of Aberdeen 1964–68 (MA); University
of Exeter 1968–70; University of St Andrews 1981–
84 (BD); lic by Presb of St Andrews, Jul 1984; asst
Ceres with Springfield 1984–85; m 20 Jul 1973
Ann b 9 Mar 1946; Children: Emma b 11 Jul 1975;
Stephen b 10 Jan 1978; ord and introd as Assoc
at Aberdeen Mastrick 26 Sep 1985; ind to Whitfield
29 May 1991; ret 12 Sep 1999.

PRESBYTERY OF ANGUS

ABERLEMNO (FES V, 276; VIII, 479; IX, 532; X, 314)

Vacant from 1977 until 1983. Linked 17 Jun 1983 with Guthrie and Rescobie.

1959 ARTHUR COLIN RUSSELL
(FES X, 314), ord and ind to Aberlemno with Oathlaw 19 Nov 1959; continued as minister of Aberlemno following termination of linkage with Oathlaw 1 Jan 1962; ret 31 Dec 1976; d Margaret m Taylor; d Bridget m Corr; Addl publ: *Gold Coast to Ghana* (Pentland Press, 1996).

1984 BRIAN RAMSAY
B 24 Sep 1955 at Forfar, s of Joseph Patrick R. and Norma Easton Tasker; educ Websters Seminary, Kirriemuir; University of St Andrews 1973–79 (BD, DPS); lic by Presb of Angus 9 Sep 1979; asst Jedburgh Old with Ancrum with Edgerston 1979–80; m 28 Aug 1976 Christine Ann Jack b 25 Oct 1956; Children: Amy Lisa b 11 May 1979; Felicity Sarah b 16 Feb 1982; ord and ind to Carmichael with Covington and Thankerton with Pettinain 14 May 1980; trans to Aberlemno with Guthrie and Rescobie 15 Mar 1984; Publ: *By Hill and Loch* (Premier Printers, 1991).

AIRLIE KINGOLDRUM AND RUTHVEN (FES X, 310, 312, 313)

Formed 19 Jun 1994 by union of Airlie, Ruthven and Kingoldrum. Linked same date with Glenisla with Kilry with Lintrathen.

1955 GEORGE SCOTT MILL
(FES VII, 701; VIII, 740; IX, 89, 639, 743; X, 313, 365), trans from Alves to Ruthven 1 Jul 1955; ret 1 Aug 1965; died 7 Sep 1987.

1960 GORDON McINTOSH RAMSAY
(FES X, 310), ord and ind to Airlie 15 Nov 1960; became minister of linked charge with Ruthven 28 Nov 1965 and with Kingoldrum 5 Jan 1980; died 16 May 1993.

1994 ROBERT JOHN RAMSAY
ord and ind to Glenisla with Kilry with Lintrathen 14 May 1986; became minister of linked charge with Airlie Kingoldrum and Ruthven 19 Jun 1994; trans to Invergowrie 3 Dec 1997.

1994 HELEN PERCY
B 2 May 1965 at Epping, University of St Andrews 1983–87 (MTh), 1989–90 (DipPTh, FSIM); lic by Presb of St Andrews 1 Jul 1990; asst Edinburgh Mayfield 1990–91, Kaimes Lockhart Memorial 1991; ord and ind to Paisley Greenlaw 12 Dec 1991; introd as Assoc at Airlie Kingoldrum and Ruthven with Glenisla with Kilry with Lintrathen and app Chaplain to Noranside Prison 9 Jun 1994; dem 3 Dec 1997.

1999 LESLIE McEWEN BARRETT
B 24 May 1950 at Prestbury, Cheshire, s of Frank Jones B. and Janet B.; educ Didsbury Technical High 1961–67; University of St Andrews 1987–90 (BD); Chartered Surveyor (FRICS); lic by Presb of Perth 1 Jul 1990; m 18 Dec 1971 Ruth Templeton; Children: Anthony Leslie b 30 Sep 1973; William McEwen b 2 Nov 1974; Gillian Ruth b 14 Jun 1978; ord and ind to Barthol Chapel with Tarves 27 Jun 1991; introd as Interim minister at Airlie Ruthven and Kingoldrum with Glenisla with Kilry with Lintrathen 1 Mar 1999.

ARBIRLOT (FUF 394; FES V, 420; VIII, 508; IX, 538; X, 314)

Linked 8 Jan 1961 with Colliston. Further linked 28 Dec 1983 with Carmyllie.

1961 JAMES JOHNSTON TURNBULL
(FES IX, 45, 205; X, 27, 314), trans from Kirknewton and East Calder to Arbirlot with Colliston 19 Aug 1961; ret 31 May 1981.

1982 DAVID SHEPHERD ALLAN GRIEVE
(FES X, 271, 350), res as Adviser in Religious Education, Lanarkshire and Strathclyde Region and ind to Arbirlot with Colliston 17 Aug 1982; became minister of linked charge with Carmyllie 28 Dec 1983; ret 28 Feb 1991; s John m Susan Jackson; s Michael m Lynn Gordon; d Alison m Barry Applin.

1991 KENNETH BROWN
B 13 Aug 1962 at Greenock, s of Alexander B. and Agnes Johnstone; educ Cowdenknowes and Greenock Academy 1967–79; University of Aberdeen 1985–89 (BD), 1989–90 (CPS); University of St Andrews 1994–96 (MLitt); University of Keele 1997-present (PhD); Clerical Asst 1979–82; lic by Presb of Aberdeen 27 Jun 1990; asst Skene

Westhill 1990–91; m 5 Sep 1984 Catherine Blum b 22 Oct 1959 d of Rene B. and Anne-Marie Cessens; Children: Christopher b 11 Sep 1986; Dominic b 1 Sep 1989; Jeremy b 17 Mar 1991; ord and ind to Arbirlot with Carmyllie with Colliston 15 May 1991.

ARBROATH INVERBROTHOCK (FES V, 427; VIII, 509; IX, 539; X, 314)

Congregation dissolved 24 Oct 1977.

1971 ROBERT MACARTHUR HETHERINGTON (FES X, 315, 420), res from service with Overseas Council in S India and introd on term app to Inverbrothock 27 Oct 1971; ind to Barrhead South 24 Aug 1977.

ARBROATH KNOX'S (FUF 395; FES IX, 539; X, 315)

Linked 30 May 1982 with Arbroath St Vigean's.

1950 JOHN REID
(FES IX, 247, 539; X, 315), trans from Kirkintilloch South to Knox's 14 Jun 1950; ret 20 Nov 1981; died 4 May 1982.

1982 ROBERT LINDSAY GLOVER
(FES X, 51), trans from Newton to Arbroath St Vigean's and Auchmithie 11 Feb 1976; became minister of linked charge with Knox's 30 May 1982; trans to Edinburgh St George's West 30 Oct 1985.

1986 JOHN PRINGLE LORIMER MUNRO
res from service with Overseas Council in Kenya and ind to Knox's with St Vigean's 11 May 1986; dem on app as Asst Secretary, Board of World Mission 1 Feb 1990.

1990 IAN GEORGE GOUGH
(FES X, 316), res as Assoc at Bearsden New Kilpatrick and ind to Knox's with St Vigean's 12 Sep 1990; University of Aberdeen 1988 (MTh).

ARBROATH OLD AND ABBEY (FES X, 314, 315)

Formed 17 Jun 1990 by union of Arbroath Old and Arbroath Abbey.

1958 THOMAS GEMMELL CAMPBELL
(FES IX, 22, 586; X, 13, 315), trans from Edinburgh Leith St Andrew's to Arbroath Old 8 Jan 1958; ret 31 Dec 1983; died 22 Sep 1995.

1977 WALTER GORDON BEATTIE
(FES X, 96, 349), trans from Fraserburgh West to Arbroath Abbey 17 May 1977; became minister of united charge with Arbroath Old 17 Jun 1990; ret 31 Oct 1995; d Fiona m Christopher Durden.

1984 MALCOLM MACLEOD
res as Assoc at St Machar's Cathedral and ind to Arbroath Old 9 Jul 1984; trans to Kilmarnock Howard St Andrew's 9 Aug 1989.

1996 VALERIE LOUISE ALLEN
B 23 Aug 1961 at Belfast, d of James Eric A. and Brenda Kathleen Hunter; educ Richmond Lodge Grammar, Belfast 1966–80; University of Edinburgh 1980–83 (BMus); University of Ulster 1984–85 (MTD); Princeton Theological Seminary, New Jersey 1987–90 (MDiv); Teaching (Music) 1983–84; Voluntary Work 1985–87; ord by Presb of Maumee Valley, Ohio (Presb Church USA) 4 Nov 1990; ind to University Presb Church, Baton Rouge, Louisiana, USA 2 Dec 1990; ind to Old and Abbey 22 Aug 1996.

ARBROATH ST ANDREW'S (FES X, 315)

1959 IAN INGRAM SCOTT MACLEOD
(FES IX, 370; X, 221, 315), trans from Jamestown to St Andrew's 15 Dec 1959; ret 31 Oct 1991; Chaplain (part-time) to Little Cairnie Hospital, Arbroath 1986–97; d Anne m Stephen Abbott; d Alice m Richard Soutar; Publ: Articles for *Life & Work* 1960–70.

1992 WILLIAM MARTIN FAIR
B 25 Mar 1964 at Johnstone, s of William F. and Georgina Whitelaw; educ Woodfarm High 1969–81; University of Strathclyde 1981–85 (BA); University of Glasgow 1986–89 (BD); Youth and Community Work 1985–86; lic by Presb of Glasgow 3 Jul 1989; asst Bearsden Killermont 1987–89; Christ Church, Bermuda 1989–91; m 4 Jul 1987 Elaine Marion Wiley b 23 Mar 1964 d of Malcolm W. and Maureen Baird; Children: Callum b 19 Jun 1996; Andrew b 3 Nov 1998; ord and ind to St Andrew's 28 Jan 1992.

ARBROATH ST VIGEAN'S (FES X, 324)

Linked 30 May 1982 with Arbroath Knox's.

1959 HENRY RUSSELL FERRIE
(FES IX, 173, 479; X, 283, 324), trans from Kirkcaldy Old to St Vigean's and Auchmithie 1 Jul 1959; ret 30 Sep 1975; died 19 Feb 1993.

1976 ROBERT LINDSAY GLOVER
(FES X, 51), trans from Newton to St Vigean's and Auchmithie 11 Feb 1976; became minister of linked charge with Arbroath Knox's 30 May 1982; trans to Edinburgh St George's West 30 Oct 1985.

1986 JOHN PRINGLE LORIMER MUNRO
ind to Knox's with St Vigean's 11 May 1986, see Knox's.

1990 IAN GEORGE GOUGH
(FES X, 316), ind to Knox's with St Vigean's 12 Sep 1990, see Knox's.

ARBROATH WEST KIRK (FES X, 315)

Formed 28 Jun 1990 by union of Arbroath Ladyloan St Columba's and Arbroath St Margaret's.

1923 WILLIAM EWART GLADSTONE MILLAR
(FES V, 429; VIII, 509; IX, 540; X, 315), trans from Glasgow Laurieston to St Margaret's 18 Dec 1923; ret 10 Sep 1960; died 12 Oct 1982.

1957 KENNETH MACMILLAN
(FES IX, 53, 600; X, 314, 315 (2), 346), trans from Meldrum and Bourtie to Erskine with Princes Street 26 Nov 1957; became minister of united charge 1 Nov 1959 and joint minister of united charge with Ladyloan 27 Jun 1973; ret 16 Mar 1978; died 25 Aug 1993.

1961 ROBERT JOHN McDOUGALL ANDREW
(FES X, 243, 315, 364), trans from Rothiemurchus to St Margaret's 15 Jun 1961; trans to Kilmallie 23 Nov 1967.

1961 GAVIN DUNIPACE BROWNLIE
(FES X, 42, 315 (2)), trans from Redding and Westquarter to Ladyloan 3 Mar 1961; became minister of united charge with St Columba's 27 Jun 1973; ret 26 Jun 1990; d Joan m Shanks.

1968 GEORGE ALEXANDER MORRISON MUNRO
(FES X, 6, 25, 315), ord and ind to St Margaret's 20 Jun 1968; trans to Edinburgh South Morningside 17 Oct 1973.

1974 GEORGE BRYAN ROLLO
(FES X, 316), ord and ind to Arbroath St Margaret's 14 Aug 1974; trans to Elgin St Giles' 7 May 1986.

1986 ALASDAIR GIFFEN GRAHAM
B 20 Apr 1954 at Lanark, s of George Millar G. and Margaret Callander; educ Gordon Schools, Huntly and Kirkcaldy High 1966–73; University of Glasgow 1973–78 (BD), 1978–80 (DipMin); lic by Presb of Paisley 25 Jun 1980; asst Aberdeen Mastrick 1980–81; m 1 Jul 1981 Joan Janet Forsyth b 31 Jul 1959 d of Allan James F. and Ann Morrison Reid; Children: Jennifer Joan b 17 Jan 1987; ord and ind to Redgorton with Stanley 3 Jun 1981; trans to St Margaret's 26 Nov 1986; became minister of united charge with Ladyloan St Columba's 28 Jun 1990.

BARRY (FES IX, 541; X, 297)

1969 WALTER THOMAS ANDREW STEWART
(FES X, 189, 297), trans from Calderbank to Barry 18 Dec 1969; ret 28 Feb 1999; app Honorary Chaplain to the Forces 1998.

BRECHIN CATHEDRAL (FES X, 316, 317, 324)

Formed 4 Sep 1990 by union of Brechin Maison Dieu and Stracathro (linked from 11 Jan 1982) and Brechin Cathedral.

1951 WILLIAM GRAY BURNS
(FES IX, 557, 787; X, 324), ind to Stracathro 23 Aug 1951; became minister of linked charge with Logie-Pert 1 Aug 1957 and of linked charge with Glenesk 22 Sep 1977; ret 31 Dec 1981; died 18 Dec 1997.

1965 PETER MITCHELL GORDON
(FES X, 300, 316), trans from Dundee Camperdown to Brechin Cathedral 7 Jul 1965; trans to Airdrie West 5 Sep 1985.

1981 GEORGE FREDERICK ROBINSON HENDERSON
(FES X, 317), ord and ind to Maison Dieu 24 Aug 1960; ret 31 Jan 1981; died 6 Sep 1982.

1982 DAVID JAMES TAYLOR
ord and ind to Stracathro with Brechin Maison Dieu 13 Jul 1982; trans to Glasgow Colston Milton 10 Dec 1986.

1986 ROBERT KENNETH MACKENZIE
trans from Creich with Rosehall to Brechin Cathedral 20 Mar 1986; became minister of united charge with Brechin Maison Dieu with Stracathro 4 Sep 1990; trans to Strachur and Strachlachlan 17 Jun 1998.

1998 JAMES ALEXANDER SIMPSON
(FES X, 38, 176), Interim minister at Almondbank Tibbermore 1997–98; introd as Interim minister at Brechin Cathedral 15 Sep 1998; ret 30 Sep 1999; d Morag m Derek Macaskill; s Neil m Anne; s Graeme m Lorna; s Alistair m Laura; Addl publ: *Doubts Are Not Enough* (St Andrew Press, 1982); *Holy Wit* (Gordon Wright, 1986); *Laughter Lines* (Gordon Wright, 1987); *The Master Mind* (Handsel Press, 1989); *History of Dornoch Cathedral* (Pilgrim Press, 1989); *History of Royal Dornoch Golf Club* (Pilgrim Press, 1991); *Keywords of Faith* (St Andrew Press, 1991); *All About Christmas* (Gordon Wright, 1994); *The Laugh Shall Be First* (St Andrew Press, 1998).

BRECHIN GARDNER MEMORIAL (FES X, 317)

Brechin Gardner Memorial West and St Columba's renamed Brechin Southesk 1975. Name changed to Brechin Gardner Memorial 24 Aug 1997.

1948 ARTHUR McNAUGHTAN
(FES IX, 25, 47, 548; X, 317), [correction: McNaughtan, not McNaughton as in Vol X, 317]; trans from Edinburgh Lockhart Memorial to West and St Columba's 28 Nov 1948; ret 31 May 1971; died 15 Nov 1978.

1966 FRANCIS GEORGE BERNARD LIDDIARD
(FES X, 274, 317), trans from Dunfermline Townhill to Gardner Memorial and East 19 Apr 1966; dem 5 Oct 1971 to enter teaching profession; d Lucy m James Henderson.

1972 ANDREW MORRISON DOUGLAS
(FES X, 276, 317 (2), 325), trans from Aberdeen
Bon Accord St Paul's to Brechin Gardner Memorial
and East with West and St Columba's 15 Jun 1972;
became minister of united charge 5 Dec 1974; trans
to Aberdeen High Hilton 21 Dec 1977.

1978 JAMES POTTER REID DRYSDALE
(FES X, 265), trans from Fallin to Southesk 1 Jun
1978; ret 31 Jan 1999; d Fiona m Daniel Robertson;
d Jillian m Adrian Valentine.

1999 MOIRA HERKES
B 22 Jan 1947 at Edinburgh, d of Alasdair Mac-
Donald and Joan Colston Duncan; educ Lanark
Grammar and Broughton Senior Secondary 1952–
65; University of Edinburgh 1980–84 (BD); Medical
Research Council 1967–70; lic by Presb of Edin-
burgh 1 Jul 1985; asst Edinburgh Greenbank
1994–95; m 11 Mar 1967 David Herkes b 2 Jul
1935 s of David H. and Elizabeth Thompson;
Children: Lynn b 10 Jan 1970 m George Morrison;
Christin Louise b 17 Jan 1972; ord and ind to
Bedrule with Denholm with Minto 10 Jun 1985;
trans to Prestonpans Prestongrange 8 Nov 1988;
introd as Assoc at Dunblane Cathedral 24 Mar
1994; ind to Dunfermline St Andrew's Erskine 22
Mar 1998; trans to Gardner Memorial 20 Oct 1999.

CARMYLLIE (FES IX, 541; X, 317)

Linked 28 Dec 1983 with Arbirlot with Colliston.

1968 ALEXANDER SPENCE
(FES IX, 54, 574; X, 31, 156, 317), trans from
Glasgow Cranhill to Carmyllie 25 Sep 1968; ret 27
Dec 1983; introd as Assoc at Elgin St Giles' 1986;
ret 1989.

1983 DAVID SHEPHERD ALLAN GRIEVE
(FES X, 271, 350), ind to Arbirlot with Colliston 17
Aug 1982; became minister of linked charge with
Carmyllie 28 Dec 1983, see Arbirlot.

1991 KENNETH BROWN
ord and ind to Arbirlot with Carmyllie with Colliston
15 May 1991, see Arbirlot.

CARNOUSTIE (FES X, 298)

Formed 9 Dec 1969 by union of Carnoustie Old
and Carnoustie St Stephen's.

1951 ARCHIBALD MACKENZIE
(FES IX, 295, 320, 542; X, 298), trans from Blantyre
Old to Carnoustie Old 28 Mar 1951; ret 31 Dec
1968; died 8 Mar 1985.

1957 FRANCIS CLARK
(FES IX, 56, 189, 426; X, 253, 298 (2)), trans from
Perth Letham to St Stephen's 15 May 1957;
became minister of united charge with Old 9 Dec
1969; ret 28 Feb 1983; died 4 Nov 1983.

1983 JOHN COLIN CASKIE
B 17 Aug 1947 at Glasgow, s of John Robert C.
and Mary Anderson Bellingham; educ Knightswood
Secondary, Glasgow 1959–62; University of Strathclyde 1970–73 (BA); University of Glasgow 1973–
76 (BD); Catering 1962–67; lic by Presb of Glasgow
25 Jun 1976; asst Glasgow Cathcart South
1976–77; m 24 Feb 1978 Alison Edna McDougall
b 22 Nov 1955 d of Ronald Spence M. and Edna
Shearer; Children: Andrew McDougall b 28 Nov
1979; Eleanor Jane b 13 Nov 1981; Graham Colin
b 22 May 1985; ord and ind to Glasgow Penilee St
Andrew 1 Jul 1977; trans to Carnoustie 21 Oct
1983.

CARNOUSTIE PANBRIDE (FES X, 297)

1968 WILLIAM BLACK
(FES X, 297), ord and ind to Panbride 15 Aug 1968;
dem 30 Sep 1978; introd to Half Morton and
Kirkpatrick Fleming (term) 20 Feb 1980.

1979 JAMES ERIC STEWART LOW
(FES X, 12, 34, 250, 403, 421), res from term app
at Dairsie with Kemback and ind to Panbride 10
May 1979; introd to Rotterdam 31 Jul 1988.

1989 MATTHEW STEEL BICKET
B 24 Jun 1952 at Glasgow, s of Robert Weir B.
and Jane MacFarlane; educ King's Park
Secondary, Glasgow 1962–70; East of Scotland
College of Agriculture 1973–76 (HND AGRIC);
Wolverhampton Polytechnic 1984–85 (CEdAgr);
University of Glasgow 1985–88 (BD); Agricultural
Missionary, Bangladesh (Church of Scotland)
1976–84; lic by Presb of Glasgow 5 Jul 1988;
asst Glasgow Netherlee 1988–89; m 20 Nov
1980 Frances Helen Bulman b 19 Apr 1953 d of
William B. and Margaret Alice West; Children:
Andrew Robert b 16 Dec 1981; Helen Margaret
b 14 Oct 1984; ord and ind to Panbride 20 Jun
1989.

COLLISTON (FES IX, 542; X, 317)

Linked 8 Jan 1961 with Arbirlot. Further linked 28
Dec 1983 with Carmyllie.

1930 ALEXANDER MACKENZIE
(FES VII, 170; VIII, 320; IX, 385, 542; X, 317), trans
from North Bute St Colmac's and St Ninian's to
Colliston 6 Aug 1930; ret 8 Jan 1961; died 16 Jan
1982.

1961 JAMES JOHNSTON TURNBULL
(FES IX, 45, 205; X, 27, 314), trans from Kirknewton and East Calder to Arbirlot with Colliston
19 Aug 1961; ret 31 May 1981.

1982 DAVID SHEPHERD ALLAN GRIEVE
(FES X, 271, 350), ind to Arbirlot with Colliston 17
Aug 1982; became minister of linked charge with
Carmyllie 28 Dec 1983, see Arbirlot.

1991 KENNETH BROWN
ord and ind to Arbirlot with Carmyllie with Colliston 15 May 1991, see Arbirlot.

DUN (FES V, 387; VIII, 500; IX, 548; X, 318)

Linked 1 Aug 1955 with Hillside.

1955 WILLIAM JAMES SINCLAIR
(FES IX, 608, 801; X, 318), res as Warden of Simpson House, Edinburgh and ind to Dun with Hillside 6 Dec 1955; died 12 Dec 1976.

1977 ALAN FREW MUNRO DOWNIE
ord and ind to Dun with Hillside 19 Oct 1977; trans to Alloa St Mungo's 15 Feb 1997.

1997 CHRISTINE HOUGHTON
B 2 Aug 1945 at Dunfermline, d of Alexander Sharp Smith and Christina Anderson Milne; educ Queen Anne High, Dunfermline 1950–60; St Colm's College, Edinburgh 1987–89 (TLS), 1989–90 (NCH: Counselling Skills); University of Edinburgh 1991–95 (BD); Nursing 1962–80; lic by Presb of Kirkcaldy 30 Jun 1996; asst Kirkcaldy St Brycedale 1996–97; m 13 Jun 1963 Brian Houghton b 3 Jun 1944 s of Thomas H. and Jenny Roberts; Children: Bryn b 20 Nov 1973; Jillian b 16 Apr 1977; ord and ind to Dun with Hillside 20 Aug 1997.

DUNNICHEN, LETHAM AND KIRKDEN (FES IX, 532; X, 318)

1970 JOHN MILLER WILSON
(FES X, 318, 427), res from app with Overseas Council in India and ind to Dunnichen, Letham and Kirkden 26 Mar 1970; dem 6 Feb 1980 on app by Board of World Mission and Unity for service in Ghana.

1980 BRIAN HENRY OXBURGH
ord and ind to Dunnichen, Letham and Kirkden 9 Jul 1980; trans to Saltcoats St Cuthbert's South Beach 29 Jun 1988.

1990 ALLAN FREDERICK WEBSTER
B 13 Jan 1948 at Gainsborough, Lincolnshire, s of Charles Frederick W. and Agnes Fulton Barclay; educ John Neilson Institution, Paisley 1953–66; University of Glasgow 1966–70 (MA); Jordanhill College, Glasgow 1971–72 (PGCE); University of Glasgow 1974–77 (BD); Trainee Personnel Officer 1970–71; Teaching 1972–74; lic by Presb of Paisley 28 Jun 1977; asst Glasgow Newlands South 1977–78; m 25 Jun 1976 Kathleen Anne Sloss b 12 Mar 1953 d of James Smith S. and Isobel Rodger; Children: Joanne Carolyn b 7 Sep 1980, David James b 1 Oct 1982, Lucy Ruth b 28 Apr 1987; ord and ind to Glasgow Victoria Park 28 Jun 1978; trans to Dunnichen, Letham and Kirkden 11 Jan 1990.

EASSIE AND NEVAY (FES V, 259; VIII, 474; IX, 527; X, 311)

Linked 27 Feb 1966 with Newtyle.

1975 HARVEY LEIGHTON GRAINGER
(FES X, 311), ord and ind to Eassie and Nevay with Newtyle 12 Aug 1975; dem 16 Aug 1981 to take up social work app; ind to Aberdeen Kingswells 31 May 1989.

1982 ALEXANDER McALPINE KNOX
(FES X, 231 (2), 421), trans from Kingarth and Kilchattan Bay with Rothesay The High Kirk to Eassie and Nevay with Newtyle 14 Sep 1982; died 4 May 1992.

1992 CARLEEN JANE ROBERTSON
B 12 Jul 1960 at Aberfeldy, d of Charles R. and Elizabeth Angus Irvine; educ Breadalbane Academy 1965–78; University of Edinburgh 1985–90 (BD, CCEd); Secretary 1979–81; Shop Manageress 1981–83; lic by Presb of Dunkeld and Meigle 28 Jun 1990; asst Perth St John's 1990–92; ord and ind to Eassie and Nevay with Newtyle 25 Nov 1992.

EDZELL LETHNOT (FES IX, 549; X, 318)

Linked 1 Jul 1982 with Glenesk. Further linked 12 Jan 1997 with Fern Careston Menmuir.

1957 ARCHIBALD WATT
(FUF 327; FES IX, 250, 340, 419; X, 148, 318), trans from Rutherglen Stonelaw to Edzell and Lethnot 31 Jan 1957; ret 31 May 1969; died 1 Jan 1981.

1970 PENTLAND FRANCIS COLLEY BLACK
(FES IX, 446, 540, 685; X, 149, 318, 338, 389), trans from Glasgow Thornliebank Woodlands to Edzell and Lethnot 20 Feb 1970; ret 30 Jun 1982; died 6 Feb 1994.

1982 JOHN WILLIAM ARTHUR FORBES
(FES X, 352), res from the Charity Project Trust and ind to Edzell Lethnot with Glenesk 17 Nov 1982; became minister of linked charge with Fern Careston and Menmuir 12 Jan 1997; ret 5 Apr 1999; d Victoria m Alisdair Barlas; s Angus m Fiona Readman.

FARNELL (FES V, 392; VIII, 501; IX, 549; X, 318)

Linked 1 Jul 1990 with Montrose St Andrew's.

1959 JOHN WILLIAM FRASER
(FES IX, 586; X, 318, 339), trans from Banchory Ternan West to Farnell with Kinnell 7 Oct 1959; continued as minister of Farnell following termination of linkage 19 Oct 1967; ret 9 Oct 1983; d Christine m Iain Lang Cochrane; Addl publ: *Concerning Scandals* (Eerdmans, St Andrew Press, 1978).

1984 JOSEPH BALDWIN PERRY
(FES X, 133, 157, 302), dem from Greenock
Martyrs' and North 31 Jan 1983; introd on term
app to Farnell with Chaplaincy at Stracathro
Hospital 18 Oct 1984; ret 30 Sep 1989 from Farnell
and 31 Oct 1995 from Stracathro Hospital.

1990 IAIN MACKECHNIE DOUGLAS
(FES X, 418), ind to Montrose St Andrew's 3 Jul
1980; became minister of linked charge with Farnell
1 Jul 1990, see Montrose.

FERN, CARESTON MENMUIR (FES X, 318, 323)

Formed 17 Jun 1982 by union of Fern, Careston
and Menmuir. Linked 20 Jun 1982 with Oathlaw
Tannadice. Arrangement terminated 12 Jan 1997
in favour of linkage with Edzell Lethnot with
Glenesk.

1937 GEORGE ARTHUR SEFTON
(FES VIII, 585; FES IX, 549, 610; X, 318), trans
from Pitsligo to Fern and Careston 1 Oct 1937; ret
12 Jan 1966; died 2 Sep 1988.

1948 JOHN COCHRANE DORWARD
(FUF 549; IX, 554, 732; X, 323), res as Scottish
Secretary, Moukden Medical College and China
Christian Universities Assoc and ind to Menmuir
16 Dec 1948; ret 31 Dec 1957; died 18 Dec
1986.

1966 ALEXANDER WALLACE MACKINNON
(FES X, 448; X, 113, 265, 318, 383), trans from
Creich to Fern, Careston with Menmuir 29 Jun
1966; became minister of united charge 17 Jun
1982 and of linked charge with Oathlaw Tannadice
20 Jun 1982; Chaplain to Noranside Prison 1968–
86; ret 31 Oct 1986.

1989 ANDREW JOHN JOLLY
res from RAChD and ind to Fern Careston Menmuir
with Oathlaw Tannadice 19 Oct 1989; dem on app
by RAF Chaplains' Branch 8 Feb 1996.

1997 JOHN WILLIAM ARTHUR FORBES
(FES X, 352), ind to Edzell Lethnot with Glenesk
17 Nov 1982; became minister of linked charge
with Fern Careston and Menmuir 12 Jan 1997.

FORFAR EAST AND OLD (FES X, 319)

Formed 27 Sep 1977 by union of Forfar East and
Forfar Old.

1935 DAVID MATHIESON BELL
(FES VIII, 456; IX, 533; X, 319), trans from
Aberdeen Woodside South to Forfar Old 4 Jun
1935; ret 31 Oct 1976; died 1 Nov 1978.

1963 LEWIS POTTER GRAY HARDIE
(FES X, 319), ord and ind to Forfar East 28 Nov
1963; ret 1 Nov 1976; died 3 Apr 1984.

1978 GRAHAM NORRIE
(FES X, 261), trans from Alloa West to Forfar East
and Old 7 Jun 1978; Addl children: Alison Ruth b
12 Nov 1979; d Nicola m John Harry Ronald Wyllie.

FORFAR LOWSON MEMORIAL (FES V, 288; VIII,
481; IX, 533; X, 319)

1971 MALCOLM McGREGOR DOWIE
(FES X, 319), ord and ind to Lowson Memorial 18
Aug 1971; ret 31 Jan 1992; died 7 Apr 1993.

1992 ROBERT McCRUM
B 2 Oct 1949 at Hamilton, s of John Sutherland M.
and Margaret Maguire; educ St John's Grammar,
Hamilton 1962–66; University of Glasgow 1976–
82 (BD, CMin); Mechanical Engineering 1966–76;
lic by Presb of Hamilton 28 Jun 1981; asst Wishaw
Old 1977–79; Stonehouse St Ninian's 1979–81;
m 1 Apr 1977 Valerie Taylor b 10 May 1955 d of
Raymond T. and Elsie Owens; Children: Mark b 9
Jul 1980; Scott b 8 Feb 1982; Garry b 14 Nov 1983;
ord and ind to Auchtergaven and Moneydie 5 May
1982; dem on app by Royal Naval Chaplaincy
Service 20 Oct 1986; res and ind to Lowson
Memorial 5 Aug 1992.

FORFAR ST MARGARET'S (FES X, 319)

Formed 1 May 1977 by union of Forfar St James'
and Forfar West.

1940 DUNCAN DEWAR DUNCAN
(FES IX, 62, 308, 534; X, 319), trans from Glasgow
Sydney Place and East Campbell Street to Forfar
West 26 Sep 1940; ret 1 May 1977; died 25 Oct
1993.

1970 ROBERT HILL
(FES X, 319), trans from Belfast Broadway and
ind by mutual eligibility to St James' 10 Sep 1970;
became minister of united charge with West 1 May
1977; introd to Lisbon St Andrew's 3 Mar 1988.

1988 JOHN MAXWELL BIRRELL
trans from Carluke St Andrew's to St Margaret's
22 Sep 1988; dem 9 Dec 1996 on app as Chaplain
to Perth Royal Infirmary.

1998 JEAN BLANE MONTGOMERIE
(FES X, 337), trans from Peterculter Kelman
Memorial to St Margaret's 27 Aug 1998.

FRIOCKHEIM KINNELL (FES X, 320)

Formed 19 Oct 1967 by union of Friockheim and
Kinnell. Linked 21 Aug 1983 with Inverkeilor and
Lunan.

1929 STEWART BAILLIE
(FES VIII, 510; IX, 543; X, 319), ord and ind to
Friockheim 1 Aug 1929; ret 2 May 1967; died 1
May 1976.

1968 DUNCAN AINSLIE
(FES IX, 610; X, 279, 320, 351), trans from Auchtertool to Friockheim Kinkell 24 Apr 1968; ret 20 Aug 1983; died 30 Mar 1988.

1983 IAN LAWRIE FORRESTER
(FES X, 321, 419), ind to Inverkeilor and Lunan 11 Oct 1967; became minister of linked charge with Friockheim Kinnell 21 Aug 1983, see Inverkeilor and Lunan.

1996 DAVID JOHN TAVERNER
B 8 Apr 1958 at Edinburgh, s of Glyn Rees T. and Isobel Richardson Cowe; educ George Watson's, Edinburgh 1970–76; University of Edinburgh 1991–94 (BD); Banking 1976–91; lic by Presb of Melrose and Peebles 19 Jul 1994; asst Dalkeith St John's and King's Park 1994–96; ord and ind to Friockheim Kinnell with Inverkeilor and Lunan 25 Sep 1996.

GLAMIS, INVERARITY AND KINNETTLES (FES X, 320, 321)

Glamis linked 24 Mar 1982 with Inverarity and Kinnettles. Congregations united 6 Sep 1996.

1942 HUGH GOW MHUIR WATSON
(FES IX, 207, 534; X, 320), trans from Lamlash St George's to Glamis 15 Dec 1942; ret 31 Dec 1971; died 13 Mar 1982.

1959 DAVID GEORGE HAMILTON WHYTE
(FES IX, 175, 314, 593; X, 321, 341), trans from Keig with Tough to Inverarity and Kinnettles 16 Apr 1959; ret 24 Mar 1982; died 24 Oct 1990.

1972 DAVID CECIL HENDERSON
(FES X, 320), ind to Glamis 7 Jul 1972; ret 31 Jul 1982.

1982 JOHN ALFRED SHERRARD
(FES X, 72, 300, 313), trans from Galashiels St Ninian's to Glamis with Inverarity and Kinnettles 26 Oct 1982; ret 31 Oct 1989; died 26 May 1999; s Scott Rathman m Susan Clark.

1990 ANDREW TRELAWNEY GREAVES
ind to Glamis with Inverarity and Kinnettles 28 Sep 1990; became minister of united charge 6 Sep 1996; dem 31 Aug 1997 on app as Chaplain to Gordonstoun School.

1998 JOHN ALASTAIR HILTON MURDOCH
res as Chaplain to Aiglon College, Switzerland and ind to Glamis, Inverarity and Kinnettles 31 Mar 1998; dem 31 Aug 1999 and app Chaplain to St Leonards School, St Andrews 1 Sep 1999.

GLENESK (FES IX, 551; X, 320)

Linked with Logie-Pert and Stracathro 1977 until 1981. Linked 1 Jul 1982 with Edzell Lethnot. Further linked 12 Jan 1997 with Fern Careston Menmuir.

1959 DAVID STEVENS
(FES IX, 135, 434, 704, 706; X, 79, 320), trans from Kirtle to Glenesk 21 Jan 1959; ret 30 Jun 1972.

1972 JOHN THOMAS HERBERTSON TAYLOR
(FES IX, 506, 595; X, 213, 230, 300, 321), trans from Bute St Ninian's to Glenesk 1 Nov 1972; introd to Leslie Christ's Kirk on the Green 15 May 1977 (term).

1977 WILLIAM GRAY BURNS
(FES IX, 557, 787; X, 324), ind to Stracathro 23 Aug 1951; became minister of linked charge with Logie-Pert 1 Aug 1957 and of linked charge with Glenesk 22 Sep 1977; ret 31 Dec 1981; died 18 Dec 1997.

1982 JOHN WILLIAM ARTHUR FORBES
(FES X, 352), ind to Edzell Lethnot with Glenesk 17 Nov 1982, see Edzell Lethnot.

GLENISLA (FES IX, 527; X, 311)

Linked 5 Jun 1980 with Lintrathen with Kilry. Further linked 19 Jun 1994 with Airlie, Ruthven and Kingoldrum.

1970 ROBERT MAURICE KING
(FES IX, 475; X, 34, 281, 311), trans from Bo' ness Old to Glenisla with Kilry 6 Nov 1970; dem 31 Jul 1979 to take up app with United Church of Jamaica and Grand Cayman in Brownsville.

1980 IVAN CORRY WARWICK
ord and ind to Glenisla with Kilry with Lintrathen 21 Sep 1980; dem 6 Sep 1985 to take up app with RAChD.

1986 ROBERT JOHN RAMSAY
ord and ind to Glenisla with Kilry with Lintrathen 14 May 1986; became minister of linked charge with Airlie Kingoldrum and Ruthven 19 Jun 1994; trans to Invergowrie 3 Dec 1997.

1994 HELEN PERCY
introd as Assoc at Airlie Kingoldrum and Ruthven with Glenisla with Kilry with Lintrathen, see Airlie.

1999 LESLIE McEWEN BARRETT
introd as Interim minister at Airlie Ruthven and Kingoldrum with Glenisla with Kilry with Lintrathen 1 Mar 1999, see Airlie.

GUTHRIE AND RESCOBIE (FES IX, 535; X, 321)

Linked 17 Jun 1983 with Aberlemno.

1961 GEORGE ALEXANDER WATSON
(FES X, 321), ord and ind to Guthrie and Rescobie 6 Apr 1961; ret 31 May 1970; died 2 Sep 1994.

1970 RICHARD SAMUEL BISHOP
(FES IX, 461; X, 273, 315, 321), trans from Arbroath Inverbrothock to Guthrie and Rescobie 17 Sep 1970; ret 16 Jun 1983; died 1 Apr 1984.

1984 BRIAN RAMSAY
ind to Aberlemno with Guthrie and Rescobie 15 Mar 1984, see Aberlemno.

HILLSIDE (FES V, 398; VIII, 502; IX, 551; X, 321)

Linked 1 Aug 1955 with Dun.

1955 WILLIAM JAMES SINCLAIR
(FES IX, 608, 801; X, 318), ind to Dun with Hillside 6 Dec 1955, see Dun.

1977 ALAN FREW MUNRO DOWNIE
ord and ind to Dun with Hillside 19 Oct 1977; trans to Alloa St Mungo's 15 Feb 1997.

1997 CHRISTINE HOUGHTON
ord and ind to Dun with Hillside 20 Aug 1997, see Dun.

INCHBRAYOCK (FES X, 321)

Linked 22 Mar 1981 with Montrose Melville South.

1974 DAVID GRAHAM LEITCH
(FES X, 321), ord and ind to Inchbrayock Ferryden 15 Oct 1974; trans to Edinburgh Barclay 25 Oct 1980.

1981 PHILIP ROSS MACKINTOSH MALLOCH
trans from Uddingston Trinity to Inchbrayock with Montrose Melville South 17 Sep 1981; trans to Killearn 2 Dec 1993.

1994 DAVID STUART DIXON
B 8 Jun 1949 at Gatley, Cheshire, s of Francis Hope D. and Muriel Betty Ford; educ Caterham School, Surrey 1960–68; University of Dundee 1968–72 (MA); University of Aberdeen 1972–75 (BD); lic by Presb of Aberdeen 29 Jun 1975; asst Cumbernauld Kildrum 1975–77; m 19 Jul 1975 Helen Mary Cook b 7 Apr 1949 d of Alfred C. and Hilda Knight; Children: Jennifer Ruth b 27 Jan 1981; John Richard b 8 Jan 1984; ord by Presb of Falkirk during assistantship at Kildrum 2 Jun 1976; ind to Lybster and Bruan 23 Sep 1977; trans to Inchbrayock with Montrose Melville South 10 Aug 1994.

INVERKEILOR AND LUNAN (FES IX, 543; X, 321)

Linked 21 Aug 1983 with Friockheim Kinnell.

1967 IAN LAWRIE FORRESTER
(FES X, 321, 419), dem from Trinidad Greyfriars and ind to Inverkeilor and Lunan 11 Oct 1967; became minister of linked charge with Friockheim Kinnell 21 Aug 1983; ret 31 Dec 1995; m 30 Jun 1995 Mary Morris Davidson d of Peter Ramsay and May Smith.

1996 DAVID JOHN TAVERNER
ord and ind to Friockheim Kinnell with Inverkeilor and Lunan 25 Sep 1996, see Friockheim Kinnell.

KILRY (FES V, 265; IX, 528; X, 312)

Linked 19 Jun 1994 with Airlie, Kingoldrum and Ruthven with Lintrathen.

1970 ROBERT MAURICE KING
(FES IX, 475; X, 34, 281, 311), ind to Glenisla with Kilry 6 Nov 1970, see Glenisla.

1980 IVAN CORRY WARWICK
ord and ind to Glenisla with Kilry with Lintrathen 21 Sep 1980, see Glenisla.

1986 ROBERT JOHN RAMSAY
ord and ind to Glenisla with Kilry with Lintrathen 14 May 1986, see Glenisla.

1994 HELEN PERCY
introd as Assoc at Airlie Kingoldrum and Ruthven with Glenisla with Kilry with Lintrathen, see Airlie.

1999 LESLIE McEWEN BARRETT
introd as Interim minister at Airlie Ruthven and Kingoldrum with Glenisla with Kilry with Lintrathen 1 Mar 1999, see Airlie.

KIRRIEMUIR ST ANDREW'S (FES X, 322)

Linked 17 Nov 1996 with Oathlaw Tannadice.

1966 WILLIAM JONES
(FES IX, 479; X, 283, 322), res as Chaplain to Quarrier's Homes, Bridge of Weir and ind to St Andrew's 24 Feb 1966; ret 30 Apr 1987; s Norman m Walker; d Kirsteen m Shelley; s Stewart m Perkin; d Catriona m Clark.

1988 PETER YOUNGSON
(FES X, 165, 236, 281), trans from Jura to St Andrew's 14 Jan 1988; dem in interests of readjustment 17 Nov 1996; d Carolyn m Richard Ovenden; s Donald m Janet Pagulayan; Publ: *The Long Road: A Guide to Jura* (DGB Wright, 1983); *Ancient Hebridean Tales of Jura* (PYP, 1993).

1997 WILLIAM BOGLE McCULLOCH
B 3 Jul 1946 at Overtown, s of John M. and Isabella Bogle; educ Wishaw High 1951–62; Stow College of Engineering 1970 (HNC); Glasgow College of Engineering 1973–74 (HS); University of Edinburgh 1992–95 (BD); Mechanical Engineering 1962–65; Civil Engineering 1965–92; lic by Presb of Ardrossan 4 Jul 1995; asst Edinburgh St Andrew's and St George's 1995–97; m 2 Jul 1972 Jean Anne Wilson b 24 May 1952 d of Joseph W. and Jeannie Paterson; Children: Joanna b 7 May 1976; Jennifer b 18 Sep 1978; Alastair John b 6 Jan 1983; ord and ind to St Andrew's with Oathlaw Tannadice 24 Jul 1997.

LINTRATHEN (FES IX, 529; X, 312)

Union with Kingoldrum severed 5 Jun 1980. Linked same date with Glenisla with Kilry. Further linked 19 Jun 1994 with Airlie, Kingoldrum and Ruthven.

1956 JAMES ALAN ROBERTSON
(FES IX, 623, 708; X, 312, 361), trans from Port-knockie to Lintrathen and Kingoldrum 17 May 1956; ret 8 Jun 1980; died 25 Jun 1984.

1980 IVAN CORRY WARWICK
ord and ind to Glenisla with Kilry with Lintrathen 21 Sep 1980, see Glenisla.

1986 ROBERT JOHN RAMSAY
ord and ind to Glenisla with Kilry with Lintrathen 14 May 1986, see Glenisla.

1994 HELEN PERCY
introd as Assoc at Airlie Kingoldrum and Ruthven with Glenisla with Kilry with Lintrathen, see Airlie.

1999 LESLIE McEWEN BARRETT
introd as Interim minister at Airlie Ruthven and Kingoldrum with Glenisla with Kilry with Lintrathen 1 Mar 1999, see Airlie.

LOGIE-PERT (FES IX, 553; X, 323)

Congregation dissolved 30 Apr 1982.

1957 WILLIAM GRAY BURNS
(FES IX, 557, 787; X, 324), ind to Stracathro 23 Aug 1951; became minister of linked charge with Logie-Pert 1 Aug 1957, see Brechin Cathedral.

MONTROSE MELVILLE SOUTH (FES IX, 554; X, 323)

Linked 22 Mar 1981 with Inchbrayock.

1948 JAMES FERGUSON WILSON
(FES IX, 473, 554, 556; X, 323), trans from Cardenden to Montrose South 16 Nov 1948; became minister of united charge with Melville 11 Nov 1951; ret 31 Jul 1980; died 5 Jun 1998.

1981 PHILIP ROSS MACKINTOSH MALLOCH
trans from Uddingston Trinity to Inchbrayock with Montrose Melville South 17 Sep 1981; trans to Killearn 2 Dec 1993.

1994 DAVID STUART DIXON
ind to Inchbrayock with Montrose Melville South 10 Aug 1994, see Inchbrayock.

MONTROSE OLD (FES V, 409; VIII, 505; IX, 554; X, 323)

1969 JAMES LESLIE WEATHERHEAD
(FES X, 231, 323), trans from Rothesay Trinity to Montrose Old 17 Sep 1969; dem to take up app as Principal Clerk of General Assembly 1 Jul 1985.

1985 LAURENCE ARTHUR BROWN WHITLEY
(FES X, 141), trans from Busby East with Busby West to Montrose Old 24 Sep 1985; University of St Andrews 1986–93 (PhD); m 5 Sep 1981 Catherine MacLean MacFadyen b 27 Jul 1960 d of John M. and Jane MacFarlane Thompson Cameron; Children: Edward Cameron b 20 Jan 1987; Hilary Elizabeth Jane b 22 May 1989.

MONTROSE ST ANDREW'S (FES X, 323)

Formed 2 Mar 1977 by union of Montrose St Luke's and St John's and Montrose St George's and Trinity. Linked 1 Jul 1990 with Farnell.

1967 ROBERT TYRE
(FES X, 95, 323), trans from Mochrum to St Luke's and St John's 25 Oct 1967; trans to Aberdeen St Ninian's 17 Jun 1976.

1970 JOHN FRASER DAVIDSON
(FES X, 323), ord and ind to St George's and Trinity 11 Aug 1970; became minister of united charge with St Luke's and St John's 2 Mar 1977; dem 12 Jul 1980 to enter teaching profession; Dundee College of Education 1979–80 (PGCE); Northern College, Dundee 1987 (Dip Ed Tech); Teacher of Physics and RE, Montrose Academy 1980–86, Principal teacher of Computing, Craigie High, Dundee 1986–91, Forfar Academy 1991-; Society of Ordained Scientists (1992); d Susan m Kerwin William John Robertson.

1980 IAIN MACKECHNIE DOUGLAS
(FES X, 418), res as Principal teacher of RE, Morgan Academy, Dundee and ind to St Andrew's 3 Jul 1980; became minister of linked charge with Farnell 1 Jul 1990; m (2) 29 Dec 1995 Patricia Mary McAvoy b 26 Jul 1946 d of Thomas M. and May Robertson; Publ: *The Commentary on the Book of Ruth by Claudius of Turin* (*Sacris Erudiri*, Vol 22, 2, Bruges 1974–75); *Bede's de Templo and the Commentary on Samuel and Kings by Claudius of Turin* in *Famulus Christi* (SPCK, 1974); *Famulus Christi. Essays in Commemoration of the Thirteenth Centenary of the Birthday of the Venerable Bede* ed G Bonner.

NEWTYLE (FES IX, 530; X, 313)

Linked 27 Feb 1966 with Eassie and Nevay.

1975 HARVEY LEIGHTON GRAINGER
(FES X, 311), ord and ind to Eassie and Nevay with Newtyle 12 Aug 1975, see Eassie and Nevay.

1982 ALEXANDER McALPINE KNOX
(FES X, 231 (2), 421), ind to Eassie and Nevay with Newtyle 14 Sep 1982, see Eassie and Nevay.

1992 CARLEEN JANE ROBERTSON
ord and ind to Eassie and Nevay with Newtyle 25 Nov 1992, see Eassie and Nevay.

OATHLAW TANNADICE (FES X, 323, 324)

Formed 17 Jun 1982 by union of Oathlaw and Tannadice. Linked 20 Jun 1982 with Fern, Careston, Menmuir. Arrangement terminated 17 Nov 1996 in favour of linkage with Kirriemuir St Andrew's.

1965 JAMES DEMPSTER TAYLOR
(FES X, 323), ord and ind to Oathlaw with Tannadice 19 Feb 1965; ret 19 Jun 1982; died 17 Dec 1989.

1982 ALEXANDER WALLACE MACKINNON
(FES X, 448; X, 113, 265, 318, 383), ind to Fern, Careston with Menmuir 29 Jun 1966; became minister of united charge 17 Jun 1982 and of linked charge with Oathlaw Tannadice 20 Jun 1982, see Fern, Careston and Menmuir.

1989 ANDREW JOHN JOLLY
ind to Fern Careston Menmuir with Oathlaw Tannadice 19 Oct 1989, see Fern Careston Menmuir.

1997 WILLIAM BOGLE McCULLOCH
ord and ind to Kirriemuir St Andrew's with Oathlaw Tannadice 24 Jul 1997.

THE GLENS AND KIRRIEMUIR OLD (FES X, 321, 322)

Formed 14 Sep 1999 by union of The Glens and Kirriemuir Old (union 12 Jan 1972 of Barony and St Ninian's).

1959 JOHN MACDONALD SKINNER
(FES IX, 180, 488, 699; X, 108, 322 (2)), trans form Dreghorn and Pearston Old to Barony 28 May 1959; became minister of united charge with St Ninian's 12 Jan 1972; ret 30 Jun 1982; died 9 Mar 1986.

1960 STEWART COUPER
(FES IX, 83; X, 51, 321), trans from Penicuik St Mungo's to The Glens 18 Feb 1960; ret 31 Mar 1971; died 22 Aug 1990.

1971 DENNIS LEADBEATER
(FES IX, 361; X, 66, 216, 321), trans from Hawick Trinity to The Glens 24 Nov 1971; ret 31 May 1999.

1983 JOHN STEVENSON
(FES X, 154, 268), trans from Glasgow Cardonald to Kirriemuir Old 16 Feb 1983; dem on app as General Secretary, Dept of Education 1 Jan 1993.

1993 MALCOLM IAIN GRANT ROONEY
B 24 Mar 1952 at Glencoe, s of Arthur Grant R. and Mary Munro Downie; educ Larbert High 1963–70; Scottish School of Physical Education 1970–73 (DPE); Dunfermline College of Physical Education 1981–84 (BEd); University of Edinburgh 1989–92 (BD); Teaching (PE) 1973–89; lic by Presb of Stirling, Jun 1992; asst Alloa St Mungo's 1992–93; m 21 Dec 1974 Christine Fraser McGlashan b 3 Nov 1949 d of Thomas Fraser M. and Isobel Sinclair Stewart; Children: Alasdair Grant b 11 Mar 1978; Iain Fraser b 9 Apr 1980; Stewart Malcolm b 1 Aug 1983; ord and ind to Kirriemuir Old 13 May 1993; became minister of united charge with The Glens 14 Sep 1999.

PRESBYTERY OF ABERDEEN

FULL-TIME PRESBYTERY CLERK (FES X, 325)

1964 JOHN MOWAT
(FES IX, 347, 566; X, 325), dem from Newhills on app as Clerk to Presb of Aberdeen and Librarian, Christ's College, Aberdeen 31 Dec 1964; ret 30 Sep 1975; died 6 Sep 1989.

BEECHGROVE (FUF 410; FES IX, 558; X, 325)

1966 ERNEST GEORGE SANGSTER
(FES X, 325, 442), res as Chaplain of the St Andrews Colleges, Univ of St Andrews and ind to Beechgrove 5 Jan 1966; trans to Edinburgh Blackhall St Columba's 5 May 1976.

1977 THOMAS DOUGLAS ALLSOP
(FES X, 222, 322 (2)), trans from Glasgow Knightswood St Margaret's to Beechgrove 13 Jan 1977; dem on grounds of ill-health 30 Nov 1999.

BRIDGE OF DON OLDMACHAR

Church Extension 1993. New building dedicated Sep 1998.

1995 WALTER GRAHAM BLACK
B 13 Sep 1957 at Glasgow, s of John Lowe Hunter B. and Fionna Morag Oman; educ Kelvinside Academy, Glasgow 1969–75; University of Aberdeen 1975–79 (MA), 1979–82 (BD); lic by Presb of Aberdeen 28 Jun 1982; asst Bearsden New Kilpatrick 1982–85; m 9 Jul 1982 Hazel Anne Somerset Short b 30 Jan 1961 d of David Somerset S. and Joan Anne McLay; Children: Peter Jonathan b 27 Jan 1984; Lucy Jane b 26 Feb 1986; ord by Presb of Dumbarton during assistantship at New Kilpatrick 11 Sep 1983; ind to Newport-on-Tay 6 Oct 1985; introd as Assoc at Aberdeen St Columba's Bridge of Don 6 Dec 1993; ind to Bridge of Don Church Extension Charge 18 Jan 1995; dem 31 Aug 1999.

BUCKSBURN AND STONEYWOOD (FES X, 334, 338)

Formed 25 October 1989 by union of Bucksburn and Stoneywood.

1954 COLIN KIRKNESS JUNNER
(FES IX, 574, 611, 682; X, 334), trans from Savoch to Bucksburn 23 Jun 1954; ret 31 Jan 1978; died 29 Apr 1986.

1972 JAMES ANDREW McMULLIN
(FES X, 338), admitted by General Assembly and ind to Stoneywood 5 Apr 1972; trans to Blackbraes and Shieldhill 15 Jun 1988.

1978 WILLIAM McLEISH ALEXANDER
(FES X, 406), trans from Northmavine to Bucksburn 27 Jul 1978; became minister of united charge with Stoneywood 25 Oct 1989; trans to Berriedale and Dunbeath with Latheron 28 Oct 1993.

1994 NIGEL PARKER
B 7 Dec 1960 at Portchester, Fareham, Hampshire, s of Harry P. and Ivy Mary Wilkes; educ Price's Grammar, Fareham and Queen Anne High, Dunfermline 1972–78; University of Birmingham 1978–82; University of Aberdeen 1986–90 (BD), 1991–93 (MTh); Teaching 1982–83; Social Work 1984–86; lic by Presb of Dunfermline 1 Jul 1990; asst Aberdeen Beechgrove 1990–91; m 3 Sep 1988 Catherine Elspeth Foster b 4 Apr 1953 d of James F. and Elspet Christie Wilson; ord and ind to Bucksburn Stoneywood 18 Aug 1994.

COVE

New Charge 1997.

1998 FYFE BLAIR
B 6 Sep 1964 at Johnstone, s of Gordon Fyfe B. and Jeanette Millar Kerr; educ Johnstone High 1969–82; University of Aberdeen 1985–88 (BA); University of Aberdeen 1985–88 (BD); lic by Presb of Aberdeen 27 Jun 1988; asst Aberdeen Mannofield 1988–89; m 27 Jun 1987 Gillian Jeannie Pollock b 16 Jul 1964 d of Derek P. and Olive Larmour; Children: Rachel Catherine b 10 Jul 1990; Anna Coralie b 29 May 1993; ord and ind to Cellardyke with Kilrenny 26 Jun 1989; trans to Cove 1 Jan 1998.

CRAIGIEBUCKLER (FES VI, 49; VIII, 536; IX, 559; X, 325)

1942 HENRY MARTIN RICKETTS
(FES IX, 559; X, 325), ord and ind to Craigiebuckler 28 Jan 1942; ret 14 Nov 1981; died 26 Nov 1983.

1982 IAN PERCY DOUGLAS
(FES X, 27), trans from Edinburgh Viewforth to Craigiebuckler 3 Jun 1982; ret 31 May 1999 on grounds of ill-health; Addl children: Christopher Ian b 1 Mar 1975.

1999 KENNETH LINDSAY PETRIE
B 12 Sep 1958 at Dundee, s of David Lockhart P. and Marion Cant Whyte; educ Morgan Academy, Dundee 1970–76; University of Dundee 1976–80 (MA); University of Edinburgh 1980–83 (BD); lic by Presb of Dunfermline 3 Jul 1983; asst Skene 1983–85; m 27 Sep 1980 Patricia Jane Tait b 14 Aug 1958 d of William Goodwin T. and Jean Denholm Sorley; Children: Kathryn Ann b 7 Aug 1983; Stewart Ross b 14 Feb 1985; ord by Presb of Gordon during assistantship at Skene 15 May 1984; ind to Stonehaven South 11 Apr 1985; became minister of linked charge with Kinneff 13 Sep 1990; trans to Craigiebuckler 30 Sep 1999.

CULTS EAST (FUF 422; FES IX, 575; X, 334)

1928 JOHN ELDER
(FUF 422; FES XI, 575; X, 334), ord and ind to Cults East 1928; ret 17 Oct 1965; died 7 Mar 1989.

1966 JAMES DONALD SMITH
(FES X, 250, 251, 334), trans from Errol to Cults East 12 May 1966; trans to Auchtergaven 5 Dec 1973.

1974 DONALD BLAIR RENNIE
(FES X, 135, 150, 334), trans from Greenock St Ninian's to Cults East 6 Jun 1974; dem to take up app as Industrial Mission Organiser for North East Scotland 4 Sep 1991.

1993 FLORA JOHNSTON MUNRO
B 22 Mar 1945 at Kilmarnock, d of Alexander James Milne and Martha Young Muir Ward Smith; educ Drumgarth, Inchgarth and Kaimhill Secondary, Aberdeen 1950–60; College of Commerce 1960–61; University of Aberdeen 1985–86 (access course), 1986–91 (BD); Secretary 1962–67, 1969–72; lic by Presb of Aberdeen 27 Jun 1991; asst Aberdeen Kirk of St Nicholas 1991–93; m 4 Jun 1965 George Munro b 20 Mar 1945 s of George M. and Elizabeth Gray; Children: George b 4 May 1967; Stuart b 28 Sep 1972; Samuel b 31 May 1977; Rodger b 30 Mar 1981; Luke b 2 Jun 1983; ord and ind to Cults East 21 Oct 1993.

CULTS WEST (FES VI, 49; VIII, 536; IX, 575; X, 334)

1938 ALEXANDER RAE GRANT
(FES VI, 164; VIII, 267; IX, 575, 599; X, 334), trans from Keithhall and Kinkell to Cults West 17 Mar 1938; ret 31 Dec 1966.

1967 ANGUS WILSON MORRISON
(FES X, 97, 334), trans from Whithorn St Ninian's Priory to Cults West 15 Jun 1967; trans to Edinburgh Braid 30 Jun 1977.

1978 THOMAS CRAWFORD RICHARDSON
(FES X, 216), trans from Clydebank Radnor Park to Cults West 1 Feb 1978; Addl children: Joanne Marie b 18 Jul 1976; American Bible College 1977–78 (ThB).

DENBURN (FES X, 325, 326)

Formed 26 October 1976 by union of Bon-Accord St Paul's and Gilcomston St Colm's.

1972 JAMES THOMSON McNAY
(FES X, 156, 198, 325), trans from Glasgow Croftfoot to Bon-Accord St Paul's 7 Dec 1972; trans to Coatbridge Maxwell 24 Mar 1976.

1973 ARCHIBALD MACCALLUM CAMPBELL
(FES IX, 257, 444; X, 89, 151, 161, 278, 326), trans from Portmoak to Gilcomston St Colm's 21 Jun 1973; became minister of united charge with Bon-Accord St Paul's 26 Oct 1976; trans to Traquair 21 Jun 1979.

1980 ALASTAIR FERGUSON LAMONT
(FES X, 102, 421), trans from Girvan South to Denburn 16 Jan 1980; died 21 Jul 1998; Publ: *Antisemitism and Christian Responsibility* (Handsel Press, 1985).

1999 LESLEY RISBY
B 22 Nov 1950 at Glasgow, d of Colin Cox and Elizabeth Paton; educ Rothesay Academy 1962–69; Duncan of Jordanstone College of Art, Dundee 1969–71; University of Aberdeen 1989–93; lic by Presb of Aberdeen 29 Jun 1993; asst Aberdeen Rubislaw 1993–94; m 8 Feb 1988 Andrew Philip Risby b 6 May 1965 s of Philip R. and Mary Malcolm; Children: Rowan b 19 Aug 1977; ord and ind to Blairdaff with Chapel of Garioch 29 Nov 1994; trans to Denburn 28 Jul 1999.

DYCE (FES IX, 576; X, 335)

1966 JAMES FINLAY SCOTT
(FES X, 335, 357), trans from Clatt with Rhynie to Dyce 27 Jun 1966; ret 31 Aug 1997; s Robert m Alison Parkin; d Marie m Leslie Anderson.

1998 RUSSEL MOFFAT
B 28 Apr 1955 at Bo' ness, s of Thomas Hamilton M. and Margaret Helen Robertson Russell; educ Bo'ness Academy 1968–72; University of Aberdeen 1980–84 (BD), [part-time] 1989–92 (MTh); University of Edinburgh 1984–85 (CPS); Lothians and Borders Police 1972–76; lic by Presb of Edinburgh, 1986; asst Dyce 1985–86; m 10 Sep 1982 Brenda Margaret Hutchison d of Charles McKay H. and Ruth Sumner; Children: David Mark b 4 Jul 1986; Laura Michelle b 6 Oct 1988; Peter Kane b 14 Nov 1990; ord and ind to New Deer St Kane's 8 May 1986; trans to Dyce 19 Mar 1998.

FERRYHILL (FES X, 326)

Formed 2 October 1990 by union of Ferryhill South and Ferryhill North.

1929 JOHN HARRIS BURRY
(FES VI, 378; VIII, 526, 622; IX, 560, 639; X, 326), trans from Alves North to Ferryhill North 19 Dec 1929; dem 31 Mar 1953; died 4 Aug 1982.

1953 THOMAS SCOTT
(FES IX, 560, 706; X, 50, 85, 326, 425), trans from Orkney St Andrews to Ferryhill North 5 Nov 1953; dem 27 Aug 1959 to take up app with FMC at Kuala Lumpur, Malaya.

1960 PETER DAVIDSON
(FES IX, 53; X, 30, 83, 326), trans from Dumfries Lincluden to Ferryhill North 10 Mar 1960; ret 30 Sep 1983; died 20 Jan 1995.

1967 ROBERT STOCKBRIDGE WHITEFORD
(FES IX, 219, 630; X, 125, 126, 326), trans from Neilston Old to Ferryhill South 6 Dec 1967; trans to Shapinsay 3 Jun 1981.

1982 JOHN HUNTER ADDISON DICK
B 27 Dec 1945 at Dunfermline, s of John Rivers D. and Margaret Hamilton Addison; educ Dunfermline High 1957–63; University of Edinburgh 1963–67 (MA), 1972 (MSc), 1978–81 (BD); Research Asst, Dept of Geography, University of Edinburgh 1967–70; Senior Tutor, Dept of Geography, University of Queensland, Australia 1970–78; lic by Presb of Edinburgh 5 Jul 1981; asst Edinburgh Fairmilehead 1981–82; m 31 Jul 1970 Gillian Averil Ogle-Skan b 9 Apr 1949 d of Peter Henry O. and Pamela Moira Heslop; separated 1996; Children: Robin Peter Addison b 6 Feb 1974; Ewan James Addison b 9 Oct 1976; Stuart John Addison b 13 Jun 1978; ord and ind to Ferryhill South 15 Jun 1982; became minister of united charge with Ferryhill North 2 Oct 1990.

1984 ANDREW CORMACK CHRISTIE
(FES X, 357), dem from Clatt with Rhynie and introd on term app to Ferryhill North 18 Oct 1984; ind to Banchory-Devenick with Maryculter and Cookney 14 Jun 1990.

GARTHDEE (FES IX, 560; X, 326)

1975 WILLIAM HUNTER FRAME
(FES X, 326), ord and ind to Garthdee 9 Jul 1975; trans to Newmains Bonkle with Coltness Memorial 16 Jul 1980.

1981 ANGUS HALLEY HADDOW
(FES X, 295, 333), trans from Aberdeen Trinity to Garthdee 30 Apr 1981; trans to Methlick 22 Oct 1990.

1991 JAMES WEIR
B 27 Apr 1952 at Irvine, s of Robert Graham W. and Murray; educ Airdrie High 1964–67; University of Glasgow 1985–89 (BD), 1989–90 (CMin); Building 1967–89; lic by Presb of Hamilton 26 Jun 1990; asst Glasgow Shettleston Old 1990–91, St Paul's Provanmill 1991; m 16 Jul 1974 Mary Blades b 22 Apr 1948 d of John B. and Annie Mallen; Children: Anne b 16 Apr 1968 m Gardner; Morag b 13 Mar 1971; James b 4 Feb 1975; ord and ind to Garthdee 30 Oct 1991.

1999 SCOTT BLYTHE
B 2 Jan 1971 at Paisley, s of George Robert B. and Marilyn Murray; educ Claremont High, East Kilbride 1982–88; University of Strathclyde 1988–91 (BSc); University of Glasgow 1992–95 (BD); Iona Community 1991–92; lic by Presb of Hamilton 30 Jun 1995; asst Glasgow Wellington 1995–97; ord by Presb of Lorn and Mull and app Programme Worker, MacLeod Centre, Iona 5 Mar 1997; introd as Assoc (part-time) at Garthdee and Chaplain (part-time) to Robert Gordon University 15 Apr 1999.

GILCOMSTON SOUTH (FUF 413; FES IX, 561; X, 326)

1945 WILLIAM STILL
(FES IX, 561; X, 326), ind to Gilcomston South 7 Jun 1945; died 30 Jul 1997.

1998 DAVID DOMINIC SMART
B 18 Sep 1959 at Morley, Yorkshire, s of David Harry S. and Mary Annie Harper; educ Batley Boys' Grammar 1971–78; University of Aberdeen 1979–84 (BSc), 1984–87 (BD), 1989–92 (MTh); lic by Presb of Aberdeen 30 Jun 1987; asst Edinburgh St Giles' Cathedral 1987–88; m 24 Aug 1984 Marjorie Helen Robb d of Albert R. and Violet Ann Addison; Children: Meredith Rosemary b 19 Aug 1988; Stephanie Daniela b 6 Dec 1990; Melissa Olivia b 19 Apr 1994; ord and ind to Dundee Logie and St John's Cross 15 Jul 1988; trans to Gilcomston South 18 Jun 1998.

GREYFRIARS JOHN KNOX (FES X, 326, 327)

Formed 6 Jun 1996 by union of Greyfriars and John Knox (union 27 Aug 1987 of John Knox [Gerrard Street] and John Knox [Mounthooly]).

1952 JOHN EDWARD HILBERT BLAKE BIRKBECK
(FES IX, 556, 563, 765; X, 327), res from Colonial app to Iran Abadan and ind to John Knox Gerrard Street 28 Feb 1952; dem on app as Director of Drummond Press, Stirling 14 Feb 1970; died 23 Mar 1988.

1962 GEORGE DYMOCK GOLDIE
(FES IX, 42; X, 25 (2), 326), trans from Edinburgh Slateford Longstone to Greyfriars 25 Oct 1962; ret 15 Mar 1995; d Susan m Ogilvie.

1968 LAURIE YOUNG GORDON
(FES X, 275, 327), trans from Kelty Oakfield to John Knox (Mounthooly) 5 Sep 1968; became minister of united charge with Gerrard Street 27 Aug 1987; ret 31 Jul 1995.

1970 WILLIAM HALLIDAY THOMSON
(FES X, 30, 327), trans from Broxburn West to John Knox Gerrard Street 27 Aug 1970; trans to Glenrothes St Columba's 29 Jan 1976.

1977 CHARLES JOHN FERGUSON WATT
(FES IX, 752; X, 427, 439), res as Tutor, St Colm's College, Edinburgh and ind to John Knox Gerrard Street 20 Jan 1977; died 23 Oct 1977.

1978 HENRY RAMSAY MANN FRASER
(FES IX, 710; X, 49, 192, 247, 388, 404), trans from Coatbridge Coatdyke to John Knox Gerrard Street 6 Jul 1978; ret 31 Dec 1985; died 6 Nov 1987.

1997 IAN DENNIS
B 11 Oct 1962 at Larne, N Ireland, s of Francis D. and Eleanor Topping; educ Ballyclare High 1973–80; Ulster Polytechnic 1981–83 (HND); Queens University, Belfast 1985–89 (BD); University of Aberdeen 1989–90 (CPS); Computer Manager 1984–85; lic by Presb of Carrickfergus, Jun 1991; asst Joymount Presb Church, Carrickfergus 1990–94; m 13 Oct 1992 Susan Pope b 3 Sep 1964 d of Derek P. and Anne Hatrick; Children: Mark Connor b 20 Aug 1996; Helen Ruth b 6 May 1999; ord and ind to Second Keady and Drumhillery Presb Churches 7 Mar 1994; trans to Greyfriars John Knox 5 Sep 1997.

HIGH HILTON (FES IX, 562; X, 326)

1958 JAMES BROWN MIRRILEES
(FES IX, 341, 387; X, 326), dem from Mowbray Presb Church, Cape Town, S Africa and ind to High Hilton 11 Sep 1958; ret 30 Jun 1977; m 1 Jun 1937 Margaret Jane Murdoch b 25 Jul 1908, died 1998, d of William M. and Mary Johnstone; Children: Sheila b 25 Aug 1938 m Millar; Margaret b 7 Feb 1941 m Smillie; Christine b 4 Jul 1945 m Findlay; Kathleen b 21 Aug 1948 m Doherty.

1977 ANDREW MORRISON DOUGLAS
(FES X, 276, 317 (2); 325), trans from Brechin Southesk to High Hilton 21 Dec 1977; Minutes Clerk, Presb of Aberdeen 1981–90; Clerk 1990–93, 1996–; ret 18 Sep 1995.

1996 ARCHIBALD PETER DICKSON
B 21 Mar 1969 at Edinburgh, s of John Leslie D. and Vivienne Alison Richards; educ Merchiston Castle, Edinburgh 1980–87; University of Dundee 1987–90 (BSc); University of Aberdeen 1991–94 (BD); lic by Presb of St Andrews 7 Jul 1994; asst Gairloch and Dundonnell 1994–95; m 7 Aug 1993 Eleanor Mary Fraser b 14 May 1965 d of Malcolm F. and Margaret McDougal; Children: Esther Margaret b 23 Jun 1995; Leslie James 30 Nov 1996; ord and ind to High Hilton 27 Feb 1996.

HOLBURN CENTRAL (FES VI, 10; VIII, 527; IX, 562; X, 326)

1976 IAN GRAY SCOTT
(FES X, 262), trans from Bridge of Allan Holy Trinity to Holburn Central 11 Mar 1976; trans to Edinburgh Greenbank 26 Jan 1983.

1983 ALAN DOUGLAS McDONALD
res as Community minister at Drylaw, Muirhouse and the Old Kirk, Edinburgh and ind to Holburn Central 28 Jul 1983; trans to Cameron with St Andrews St Leonard's 27 Aug 1998.

1999 GEORGE STRACHAN COWIE
B 18 Nov 1963 at Dundee, s of Gordon Strachan C. and Angela Mary Whelband; educ Glasgow Academy and Jordanhill College School 1970–81; University of Glasgow 1981–85 (BSc), 1987–90 (BD); Civil Engineering 1985–87; lic by Presb of Glasgow 3 Jul 1990; asst Glasgow Temple Anniesland 1990–91; m 28 Jul 1989 Marian Edmiston b 31 Aug 1963 d of John Andrew E. and Marjory Ellen Aitken; Children: Graeme Strachan b 27 May 1991; Kirsty-Anne b 11 Apr 1994; ord and ind to Auchtertool with Kirkcaldy Linktown 21 Aug 1991; trans to Holburn Central 27 May 1999.

HOLBURN WEST (FUF 414; FES IX, 562; X, 327)

1951 ARCHIBALD GLEN HUTCHISON GRANT
(FES IX, 462, 562; X, 327), trans from Dunfermline St John's to Holburn West 15 Mar 1951; ret 31 Oct 1979; died 26 May 1985.

1980 MICHAEL VICTOR ALEXANDER MAIR
(FES X, 219), res as Community Worker, Coventry and ind to Holburn West 3 Sep 1980; trans to Dundee Craigiebank with Douglas and Angus 21 Oct 1998.

1996 ELIZABETH JEANIE BURNS ROSS
ord by Presb of Aberdeen and introd as Assoc at Holburn West 7 Mar 1996; app Chaplain (part-time) to Craiginches Prison, Aberdeen Jun 1997; ind to Edinburgh St Martin's 20 Oct 1999.

1999 DUNCAN CAMPBELL EDDIE
B 17 Feb 1963 at Fraserburgh, s of David E. and Evelyn Ingram; educ Mackie Academy, Stonehaven 1975–80; University of Aberdeen 1980–84 (MA); University of Edinburgh 1987–90 (BD); Student/Lecturer, S India Biblical Seminary, Bangalore 1984–85; Care Asst, Rehabilitation Centre for Drug Dependants 1985–87; lic by Presb of Kincardine and Deeside 1 Jul 1990; asst Edinburgh Old Kirk 1990–91; m 28 Apr 1995 Carol Buchanan b 2 Sep 1963 d of Keith B. and Maureen Bryans; Children: Callum James b 28 Jan 1997; ord and ind to Old Cumnock Crichton West with St Ninian's 16 Jan 1992; trans to Holburn West 14 Oct 1999.

KINGSWELLS (FUF 424; FES IX, 578; X, 336)

1965 JAMES McKERRON
(FES X, 336), ord and ind to Kingswells 7 Apr 1965; ret 31 Oct 1976; died 19 Jan 1987.

1977 RODERICK BENJAMIN HENDERSON
B 21 Jun 1915 at Inverness, s of Bartlett H. and Isabella MacLeod; educ Inverness Royal Academy 1926–29; Aberdeen Commercial College 1970–71; University of Aberdeen 1971–73; Senior Sales Management 1959–70; lic by Presb of Aberdeen 18 Jun 1972; asst Aberdeen Ferryhill South 1972–73; Dyce 1973–74; Aberdeen West Church of St Nicholas 1974–75; m 6 Aug 1941 Isabella Cameron Munro b 13 Nov 1917 d of Donald M. and Catherine Macdonald; Children: David Munro b 16 Jan 1943 m Anna Webster; Roy Bartlett b 28 Oct 1948 m Wilma Hepburn; ord by Presb of Aberdeen during assistantship at Dyce 21 Oct 1973; Asst Minister, City Presb Church, Salisbury, Rhodesia 1974–77; ind to Kingswells 12 May 1977; ret 29 Aug 1982.

1983 WILLIAM SUNTER
(FES X, 150, 264), trans from Dunblane St Blane's and introd to Kingswells (term) 17 Feb 1983; ret 1988; died 11 Dec 1998.

1989 HARVEY LEIGHTON GRAINGER
(FES X, 311), res as joint manager of 'Broomhill House', Aberdeen (social work with homeless children) and ind to Kingswells 31 May 1989; d Susan m Yule.

KIRK OF ST NICHOLAS (FES X, 331)

Formed 19 Jun 1980 by union of East of St Nicholas (name changed 1976 from North and East of St Nicholas) and West of St Nicholas.

1974 WILLIAM GERAINT EDWARDS
(FES X, 112, 332, 352, 445), trans from Fyvie to West of St Nicholas 29 Mar 1974; dem 31 Dec 1979 and introd to the English Reformed Church, Amsterdam.

1980 LANCE BERESFORD STONE
B 15 Apr 1953 at Mexico City, Mexico, s of John Edward Claude S. and Edith Maisie Beresford; educ Ardvreck School, Crieff and Merchiston Castle, Edinburgh 1962–70; University of Edinburgh 1971–76 (BD); Princeton Theological Seminary, USA 1976–77 (MTh); lic by Presb of Edinburgh 3 Jul 1977; asst Aberdeen West of St Nicholas 1977–78; m 3 Jul 1976 Sally Ann Oakley b 9 Apr 1953 d of Edwin Ernest O. and Isobel Joy Dick; ord by Presb of Aberdeen during assistantship at West of St Nicholas 10 Apr 1978; introd as Assoc 19 Jun 1980; dem 1 Aug 1984.

1980 JAMES CHARLES STEWART
(FES X, 218, 331), trans from St Andrew's Drumchapel to North and East of St Nicholas 21 Jun 1974; became minister of united charge with West of St Nicholas 19 Jun 1980; Honorary Chaplain to Robert Gordon University, Aberdeen; Publ: Contributor to *Getting the Liturgy Right* (SPCK, 1982); contributor to *The Word in Season* (Canterbury Press, 1988).

LANGSTANE KIRK (FES X, 327)

Congregation dissolved 4 Apr 1999.

1955 GEORGE THOMSON HENDERSON REID
(FES IX, 18, 87, 263; X, 155, 327, 330), trans from Glasgow Claremont to West of St Andrew 2 Jun 1955; became minister of united charge with St Nicholas Union Grove 15 Apr 1973; ret 31 Oct 1975; died 5 Jan 1991.

1973 GERALD BRIAN MACALLAN
(FES IX, 467; X, 276, 327, 331), trans from Lochgelly Macainsh to St Nicholas Union Grove 23 Nov 1961; became Assoc of united charge with West of St Andrew 15 Apr 1973; trans to Kintore 26 Sep 1978.

1976 ALASDAIR BOTHWELL GORDON
(FES X, 335), dem from Fintray with Kinellar and Blackburn 31 Dec 1975 and app Clerk to Presb of Aberdeen 1 Jan 1976; also Assoc at Langstane Kirk; ind to Aberdeen Summerhill 25 Aug 1977.

1979 ALEXANDER JOHN GEDDES
(FES X, 45, 129), trans from Paisley St John's to Langstane Kirk 6 Dec 1979; trans to Stewarton St Columba's 18 May 1989.

MANNOFIELD (FES VI, 12; VIII, 527; IX, 564; X, 327)

1975 JOHN FERGUSON ANDERSON
(FES X, 34, 328), trans from Bo'ness St Andrews to Mannofield 22 Oct 1975; s Duncan m Aine Currie.

MASTRICK (FES IX, 564; X, 328)

1960 JAMES WYLIE TYRRELL
(FES X, 328), ord and ind to Mastrick 29 Jun 1960; ret 30 Sep 1983; died 18 Oct 1983.

1984 FRED COUTTS
(FES X, 356), trans from Buckie North to Mastrick 22 Mar 1984; dem on app as Chaplain to Aberdeen Royal Hospitals 11 Sep 1989.

1985 GEORGE GAMMACK
ord and introd as Assoc at Mastrick 26 Sep 1985; ind to Dundee Whitfield 29 May 1991.

1990 BRIAN CRAIG RUTHERFORD
B 8 Jun 1947 at Glasgow, s of Eric Wallace R. and Margaret Craig; educ King's Park, Glasgow 1959–64; University of Glasgow 1964–68 (BSc); Edinburgh College of Commerce 1968–71 (DMS); University of Edinburgh 1973–76 (BD); Personnel/ Industrial Relations 1968–73; lic by Presb of Edinburgh, 1976; asst Edinburgh Carrick Knowe 1976–77; m 10 Jun 1972 Margaret Jean Walker b 11 Jun 1947 d of Horace W. and Anne Duncan; Children: Alasdair Craig b 4 Dec 1978; Andrew Stuart b 4 Jun 1981; ord and ind to Strathbrock 20

Jul 1977; dem on app by Board of World Mission to Greyfriars St Ann's, Trinidad, West Indies 8 Aug 1983; app General Treasurer, Blantyre Synod, Church of Central Africa Presb 1988; ind to Mastrick 5 Jul 1990.

MIDDLEFIELD (FES IX, 546; X, 328)

1961   JOHN LOGIE
(FES IX, 738; X, 328, 421), res from service with Overseas Council in Rajasthan and ind to Middlefield 29 Nov 1961; trans to Leslie-Premnay with Oyne 1 Jun 1976.

1977   JAMES BLAIKIE
(FES X, 408), trans from Fetlar with Yell to Middlefield 31 Mar 1977; trans to Aberluthnott with Laurencekirk 7 Jan 1980.

1980   ALAN SHARP
ord and ind to Middlefield 23 Sep 1980; trans to Corby St Ninian's 13 Jul 1989.

1991   WILLIAM FORSYTH HUNTER
res as Summer Mission Organiser/Youth Officer at St Ninian's, Crieff 20 Jun 1986 and ind to Middlefield 7 Aug 1991; trans to Glasgow Ruchazie 2 Mar 1999.

NEWHILLS (FES VI, 63; VIII, 539; IX, 580; X, 336)
1976   NORMAN MACIVER
B 9 Jan 1941 at Glasgow, s of Malcolm M. and Margaret Ann MacDonald; educ Woodside Secondary, Glasgow 1953–59; University of Glasgow 1970–73 (MA), 1973–76 (BD); Insurance Broker 1960–70; lic by Presb of Glasgow, Jun 1976; m 14 Jun 1963 Agnes Irene Murdoch b 8 Jul 1941 d of Joseph McKinlay M. and Agnes Kennedy McBride Porter; Children: Wendy Margaret b 13 Jun 1964 m Robert Dingwall; Irene Ann b 24 May 1967 m Michael Mearns; Margaret MacDonald b 14 May 1969 m Ian Roebuck; Joan MacDonald b 14 May 1969 m Michael Bowie; ord and ind to Newhills 26 Aug 1976; Publ: Contributor to *Ten Worshipping Churches* (Marc Europe, 1987); editor of *Clann Ag Urnaigh* (St Andrew Press, 1991); *God Still Moves in Revival* (Zivot Viry, Prague, 1994); *The Task of Church Growth* (BCGA, 1998); *From Bethlehem to Brussels* (BCGA, 1999); *From Barvas to Budapest* (BCGA, 1999); *Discipline in a Broad Church* (Rutherford Journal, 1999).

NIGG (FES VI, 69; VIII, 540; IX, 564; X, 328)

1964   LAURENCE JOHN MATTHEWS
(FES X, 328, 357), trans from Cairney to Nigg 3 Dec 1964; ret 31 Oct 1985; died 30 Sep 1999.

1986   DONALD MACLENNAN THOMSON
(FES X, 174), dem from Glasgow St Enoch's Hogganfield 9 Dec 1981; ind to Nigg 8 May 1986; dem 8 Sep 1999; Addl children: Susan Elizabeth b 20 Aug 1979.

NORTH OF ST ANDREW (FES X, 328)
Formed 3 Nov 1968 by union of Aberdeen King Street and Aberdeen North.

1954   DUNCAN GRAHAM LYLE
(FES IX, 80, 270, 322, 564; X, 327), trans from Cambuslang Rosebank to King Street 7 Oct 1954; ret 30 Sep 1967; died 14 Mar 1979.

1958   ALEXANDER ALBERT BOWYER
(FES IX, 319; X, 187, 328 (2)), trans from Bellshill West to Aberdeen North 25 Mar 1958; became minister of united charge with King Street 3 Nov 1968; ret 30 Jun 1976; died 3 Jun 1978.

1976   WILLIAM GORDON HAGGARTY
(FES X, 142), trans from Chryston to North of St Andrew 30 Sep 1976; resigned charge and status 1 May 1990.

1990   THOMAS FORRESTER WILSON
B 19 Nov 1954 at Glasgow, s of Thomas Jones Wright W. and Grace Peat; educ Uddingston Grammar 1960–70; University of Glasgow 1978–83 (BD); Northern College, Aberdeen 1995–96 (PGCE); lic by Presb of Glasgow, Jun 1983; asst Croftfoot 1983–84; m 27 Jun 1981 Alison Hamilton b 20 Jun 1954; Children: Craig b 27 Aug 1987; ord and ind to Garvock St Cyrus with Benholm and Johnshaven 14 Aug 1984; trans to North of St Andrew 17 Jan 1990; dem 19 Aug 1996 to enter teaching profession.

1997   GRAEME WATSON MACKINNON MUCKART
B 11 Dec 1943 at Dunfermline, s of William Douglas M. and Anne MacKinnon; educ Royal Naval School, Malta; Willesden County Grammar, London and Portsmouth Southern Grammar 1955–62; University of St Andrews 1978–82 (MTheol); University of Stirling 1989–92 (part-time), 1993 (MSc); Bank Officer 1962–64; Architectural trainee and appts 1964–76; Resident Group, Iona Abbey 1976–78; lic by Presb of St Andrews 27 Jun 1982; asst Edinburgh Carrick Knowe 1982–83; m (1) 30 Jul 1971 Mary Elspeth Small b 14 Jul 1946 d of Colin S. and Mary Taylor; Children: Elspeth Rona b 21 Apr 1974; Alasdair Douglas b 27 Dec 1975; marriage dissolved 1989; m (2) 23 Jan 1993 Elizabeth Macaskill Miller b 22 May 1951 d of William Beattie M. and Katie Macaskill; Children: Catriona Ruth b 30 Jul 1994; ord and ind to Falkirk Erskine 12 Jul 1983; loc ten Carriden 1 Sep 1990; app to St Andrew's, Colombo, Sri Lanka 22 Jun 1992; ind to North of St Andrew 6 Mar 1997; Publ: *Ceylon Churchman* (sermon, 1993); contributor to and editor of *A Response to the Devolution Proposals* ('Sri Lanka Assoc for Theology', 1996).

NORTHFIELD (FES IX, 565; X, 328)

1973   JAMES SCOTT
(FES X, 329), ord and ind to Northfield 8 Jun 1973; trans to Drumoak with Durris 13 Feb 1992.

1992 DAVID ANDERSON
(FES X, 264), trans from Aberlour to Northfield 12 Aug 1992; trans to Fordyce 22 Oct 1997.

1998 SCOTT CLELAND GUY
B 24 Jun 1955 at Stirling, s of John Cleland G. and Elizabeth Sneddon; educ Denny High 1967–73; Scottish College of Textiles 1973–76 (HND, LTI); University of Edinburgh 1984–88 (BD); Clothing Industry 1976–84; lic by Presb of Stirling 30 Jun 1988; asst Stirling Church of the Holy Rude with Allan Park South 1988–89; m 22 Jul 1978 Adrienne Landreth Duncanson b 19 May 1958 d of James Fraser D. and Janice Landreth Howey; Children: Rachel Elizabeth Landreth b 16 May 1979; Neil Cleland b 14 Feb 1981; Helen Janice b 13 Aug 1983; ord and ind to St Andrew's-Lhanbryd and Urquhart 9 Jun 1989; trans to Northfield 17 Dec 1998.

PETERCULTER (FES X, 337)

Formed 11 Mar 1999 by union of Kelman Memorial and St Peter's.

1948 THOMAS WILSON HOWIE
(FES IX, 159, 581; X, 337), trans from Glenluce Ladyburn to St Peter's 9 Nov 1948; ret 30 Jun 1981; died 14 Feb 1986.

1961 JOHN ANDREW
(FES X, 337), dem from Kelman Memorial to enter teaching profession (RE) 31 Aug 1972; ret 20 Apr 1995; Publ: *From Abraham to David* (Hulton, 1985); *The Life and Work of Jesus* (Hulton, 1985); *A Puzzle Pack of Bible Knowledge* (Stanley Thornes, 1989).

1973 JEAN BLANE MONTGOMERIE
(FES X, 337), ord and ind to Kelman Memorial 11 Jan 1973; trans to Forfar St Margaret's 27 Aug 1998.

1982 ALEXANDER GRAINGER STODDART
(FES X, 85), trans from Kirkconnel St Conal's with St Mark's to St Peter's 9 Dec 1982; trans to Meldrum and Bourtie 8 Jun 1988.

1991 WILLIAM G McKAIG
dem from Coatbridge Calder 30 Jun 1983; ind to St Peter's 26 Jun 1991; dem 5 Oct 1993.

1996 TREVOR CHARLES WILLIAMS
trans from Dunrossness with Sandwick, Cunningsburgh and Quarff to St Peter's 6 Mar 1996; trans to Kirtle-Eaglesfield with Middlebie with Waterbeck 12 Jan 1999.

1999 JOHN ALEXANDER FERGUSON
B 17 Jan 1963 at Dumbarton, s of William F. and Elspeth Violet Cameron; educ Vale of Leven Academy 1975–81; University of Glasgow 1981–87 (BD, DipMin); lic by Presb of Dumbarton 5 Jul 1987; asst Bearsden Westerton Fairlie Memorial 1987–88; m 14 Sep 1985 Christina McInnes b 3 Jun 1961 d of Robert M. and Margaret Beaton; Children: Euan b 17 Mar 1992; Callum b 24 Aug 1994; ord and ind to Kirkcaldy Old 16 Jun 1988; trans to Peterculter 2 Sep 1999.

QUEEN'S CROSS (FES X, 328, 329)

Formed 30 Mar 1989 by union of Melville Carden Place and Queen's Cross.

1965 EDMUND SAMUEL PHILIP JONES
(FES X, 329), ord by Presb of Dunfermline during assistantship at Dunfermline Abbey 9 Jul 1961; University of St Andrews 1962–64 (PhD); ind to Queen's Cross 3 Mar 1965; dem 20 Nov 1983 to take up app at New York Presb Church, Washington DC.

1968 ROBERT WILLIAM MONTGOMERY
(FES IX, 336; X, 200, 328, 423), res from service with Overseas Council in Calcutta and ind to Melville Carden Place 19 Dec 1968; ret 30 Sep 1988; died 22 Aug 1996.

1984 ROBERT FLEMING BROWN
(FES X, 159), trans from Ayr St Quivox to Queen's Cross 15 Nov 1984; became minister of united charge with Melville Carden Place 30 Mar 1989; Children: David Caldow b 23 Mar 1977; Craig Alexander b 1 Aug 1979.

ROSEMOUNT (FES X, 329)

Formed 3 Jul 1990 by union of Rosemount and Rutherford.

1949 SAMUEL BALLANTYNE
(FES IX, 567, 684; X, 329), trans from Wick Bridge Street to Rutherford 21 Apr 1949; ret 30 Jun 1982; m (2) 15 Apr 1968 Barbara Lobban Goodall b 25 Apr 1922 d of Charles G. and Margaret Jane Rhind; d June m John Tether; s David m Rosemary Masson; s Andrew m Dorothy Melvin; d Christine m (1) Brian Ritchie, m (2) Graeme Law.

1968 JOHN GREENLAW FRASER
(FES IX, 480; X, 284, 322, 329), trans from Laurencekirk to Rosemount 24 Oct 1968; ret 31 Aug 1989; died 21 Jan 1998.

1983 ALEXANDER DAVID MOORE GRAHAM
(FES X, 149), Warden of Iona Abbey 1980–83; introd to Rutherford 8 Mar 1983 (term); became minister of united charge with Rosemount 3 Jul 1990; Children: Patrick John Moore; Duncan David; Gillian Mary Elizabeth.

RUBISLAW (FES VI, 25; VIII, 531; IX, 566; X, 329)

1968 ALEXANDER SCOTT HUTCHISON
(FES X, 289, 329), trans from Ceres to Rubislaw 28 Feb 1968; dem on app as Chaplain to Aberdeen Hospitals 5 Sep 1986.

1987   ANDREW GORDON NIMMO WILSON
B 29 Jul 1952 at Glasgow, s of Andrew Harper W.
and Helen Lees; educ Hillhead High, Glasgow
1964–70; University of Glasgow 1970–73 (MA),
1973–76 (BD); lic by Presb of Glasgow 25 Jun
1976; asst Dundee St Mary's 1976–78; m 27 Jul
1979 Isabel Johnston Reid b 8 Feb 1956 d of
Charles R. and Winifred Fender Brown; Children:
Kenneth Charles McCallum b 22 Nov 1982; Kirsty
Helen b 30 Mar 1985; ord by Presb of Dundee
during assistantship at St Mary's 31 Mar 1977; ind
to Bridge of Weir Freeland 10 May 1978; trans to
Rubislaw 10 Dec 1987.

RUTHRIESTON SOUTH (FES VI, 25; VIII, 531;
IX, 567; X, 329)

1946   DAVID YUILLE HOWIE
(FES IX, 243, 567, 628; X, 329), trans from Keith
North to Ruthrieston South 25 Apr 1946; ret 7 Jul
1972; died 2 Nov 1995.

1972   KENNETH WAYLAND DUPAR
(FES X, 329), ind to Ruthrieston South 30 Nov
1972; Visiting Lecturer, Federal Theological
Seminary, S Africa Aug-Oct 1982; dem on app as
Director of Extension Education, Christ's College,
Aberdeen and Lecturer in Practical Theology (part-
time), King's College, Aberdeen 5 Sep 1984.

1985   HUGH FINDLAY KERR
(FES X, 63, 420), res from app at Lausanne and
ind to Ruthrieston South 28 Mar 1985; Addl
children: Andrew Duncan b 30 Jul 1977.

RUTHRIESTON WEST (FUF 417; FES IX, 567;
X, 329)

1972   WILLIAM CRAWFORD ANDERSON
(FES X, 330), ord and ind to Ruthrieston West 7
Sep 1972; dem 30 Jun 1980 on app as Chaplain
to Heriot-Watt University.

1981   JAMES LINDSAY KINNEAR WOOD
(FES X, 250), trans from Cargill-Burrelton with
Collace to Ruthrieston West 16 Jan 1981; ret 30
Apr 1995.

1996   SEAN SWINDELLS
B 22 Jul 1960 at Derby, s of Michael Charles S.
and Sayer; educ Homelands School, Derby 1971–
76; University of Edinburgh 1989–93 (BD); University of Aberdeen 1993–94 (DipMin); Chef 1978–
87; lic by Presb of Edinburgh 3 Jul 1994; m 9 Jun
1995 Alison Iris Wright b 28 Jan 1958 d of Robert
Ian W. and Marjory McHattie; ord and ind to
Ruthrieston West 20 Apr 1996.

ST CLEMENT'S (FES X, 330)
Congregation dissolved 31 May 1987.

1964   ARTHUR JOHN JONES
(FES X, 330), ord and ind to St Clement's 28 Feb
1964; dem 14 Jun 1985.

ST COLUMBA'S BRIDGE OF DON
New building dedicated 7 Sep 1983. Deed of
Constitution 1 Oct 1985.

1986   PETER DOUGLAS WILSON
B 2 Jun 1948 at Kirkcaldy, s of James Muir W. and
Jean Neilson Douglas; educ Kirkcaldy Old High
1960–64; Kirkcaldy Technical College 1969–72;
University of Edinburgh 1972–78 (LTh, CPS); lic
by Presb of Kirkcaldy 4 Jul 1978; asst Troon St
Meddan's 1978–79; m 3 Oct 1970 Karin Reston
Anderson b 16 Oct 1947 d of William Wilson A.
and Eleanor Reston Bell Davidson; Children:
Eleanor Jean b 29 Nov 1972; Ruth Davidson b 9
Aug 1976; Timothy Douglas b 9 Jun 1978; ord and
ind to Errol 9 May 1979; became minister of linked
charge with Kilspindie and Rait 28 May 1980; trans
to St Columba's Bridge of Don 6 Feb 1986; dem
29 Feb 1988; died 7 Dec 1998.

1989   MAXWELL DAVIDSON CRAIG
(FES X, 38, 183 (2)), trans from Glasgow Wellington to St Columba's Bridge of Don 21 Jan 1989;
dem on app as General Secretary, Action of
Churches Together in Scotland 1 Jan 1991.

1991   LOUIS KINSEY
B 11 Dec 1959 at Wingate, Co Durham, s of Louis
K. and Margaret West; educ Milton High School,
Bulawayo, Ellis Robins School, Harare and
Sandhurst; University of Edinburgh 1984–89 (BD,
DipMin); Army 1976–83; lic by Presb of Edinburgh
1 Oct 1989; asst Elgin St Giles' and St Columba's
1989–91; m 4 Apr 1987 Sally-Anne Stewart b
20 Mar 1962 d of Daniel S. and Pamla Fridge;
Children: Louis Daniel Stewart b 31 Jan 1990;
Harry Benjamin Stewart b 5 Jun 1993; ord and ind
to St Columba's Bridge of Don 20 Feb 1991.

1993   WALTER GRAHAM BLACK
dem from Newport-on-Tay and introd as Assoc at
St Columba's Bridge of Don 6 Dec 1993; ind to
Bridge of Don Church Extension Charge 18 Jan
1995.

ST GEORGE'S-TILLYDRONE (FES X, 330)

1968   NORMAN LIVINGSTONE FAULDS
(FES X, 330, 332), ord and ind to Tillydrone-Hayton
6 Sep 1968; became minister of united charge with
St George's-in-the-West 22 Jun 1969; trans to
Edinburgh Granton 28 Sep 1978.

1978   STEWART DUNCAN JEFFREY
(FES X, 113, 386), trans from Kilmarnock St
Kentigern's to St George's-Tillydrone 22 Nov 1978;
trans to Banff St Mary's 25 Oct 1991.

1992   SHIRLEY ANNE FRASER
B 3 Aug 1943 at Edinburgh, d of Donald MacIntosh
F. and Edith Hazel Smith; educ Mary Erskine
School for Girls, Edinburgh 1948–61; University
of Edinburgh 1961–64 (MA), 1987–90 (BD);

University of St Andrews 1964–65 (DSAdmin); University of Liverpool 1967–68 (DASocStud); Teaching (VSO, Zambia) 1965–66; Social Work 1966–71, 1976–78; Travelling Sec (Scotland) for Inter-Varsity Fellowship 1971–74; Asst Leader, Simpson House, Edinburgh (Church of Scotland) 1974–75; Women's Council Secretary, Board of Social Responsibility 1976–78; Church Social Worker, Edinburgh Holy Trinity 1978–87; loc ten Edinburgh Slateford Longstone 1991–92; lic by Presb of Edinburgh 1 Jul 1990; asst Edinburgh Juniper Green 1990–91; ord and ind to St George's-Tillydrone 17 Jun 1992; Publ: Chapter on house groups and church organizations in *Local Church Evangelism* (St Andrew Press, 1987); *The Origins of Scottish Interest in Missions to the Jews* (Didasko Press, 1990); *In the Footsteps of Ion Keith-Falconer* (private, 1998).

ST JOHN'S (FES X, 330)

for Deaf People.

1985   SARAH ELIZABETH CARMICHAEL NICOL
ord and ind to St John's Church for Deaf People 20 Mar 1985; introd as Assoc at Edinburgh Blackhall St Columba's 13 Sep 1987.

1991   JOHN ROBERT OSBECK
trans from Enzie with Rathven to St John's Church for Deaf People 1 Sep 1991; app Community minister for ministry among Deaf People in Aberdeen and North of Scotland 1 Jan 1998.

ST MACHAR'S CATHEDRAL (FES VI, 16; VIII, 528; IX, 569; X, 330)

1967   ANDREW STEWART TODD
(FES IX, 354; X, 13, 212, 330), trans from North Leith to St Machar's Cathedral 31 Aug 1967; ret 31 Mar 1993; DD (Aberdeen) 1982; Chaplain in Ordinary to the Queen in Scotland 1991–96; Extra Chaplain to the Queen in Scotland 1996–; Addl children: David William b 3 Dec 1956; Victoria Jane b 11 Aug 1958; Philip John b 7 May 1960; d Diana m Thurston Smith; Addl publ: Trans from German of *Old Testament Theology* by Koehler (Lutterworth Press, 1957) and of *Lord of the Temple* by Lohmeyer (Oliver & Boyd, 1961); numerous articles and pamphlets on liturgical and musical themes.

1979   MALCOLM MACLEOD
ord by Presb of Aberdeen and introd as Assoc at St Machar's Cathedral 30 Sep 1979; ind to Arbroath Old 9 Jul 1984.

1993   RICHARD ERNEST FRAZER
B 20 Nov 1957 at Stirling, s of William Archibald F. and Joan Hogg Rennie; educ Portobello Secondary and Doncaster Grammar 1969–76; University of Newcastle 1976–79 (BA); University of Edinburgh 1982–85 (BD); Housing 1979–80; Teaching (English as a Foreign Language, Italy) 1980–82;

lic by Presb of Edinburgh 30 Jun 1985; asst Edinburgh St Giles' Cathedral 1985–87; Schoharie, Breakabeen and N Blenheim, New York 1987–88; m 27 Jan 1990 Katherine Tullis Sinclair b 12 Jun 1963 d of Donald Matheson S. and Jean Stella Fleming-Bernard; Children: William Donald b 16 Dec 1990; Jean Bay b 27 Feb 1993; Thomas Richard b 21 Apr 1995; ord by Presb of Edinburgh during assistantship at St Giles' 14 Dec 1986; ind to Cargill-Burrelton with Collace 27 Nov 1988; trans to St Machar's Cathedral 14 Oct 1993; Publ: *A Collace Miscellany* (J Scott, 1992).

ST MARK'S (FES X, 331)

Formed 3 Jun 1981 by union of St Mark's (union 1 Apr 1973 of Aberdeen East and Belmont and Aberdeen South) and Trinity.

1953   JAMES STEWART LEGGE WOOD
(FES IX, 571, 598, 637, 757; X, 332), trans from Newtonmore to Aberdeen South 27 Oct 1953; ret 3 Mar 1973; died 1 Jan 1991.

1954   NORMAN MACDONALD
(FES IX, 572, 642, 664; X, 333), trans from Dyke to Aberdeen Trinity 5 May 1954; ret 23 Oct 1970.

1962   WALTER JAMES GORDON
(FES IX, 66, 359, 501; X, 41, 326, 331), trans from Larbert and Dunipace Old to East and Belmont 4 Mar 1962; became minister of united charge with South 1 Apr 1973; ret 31 Dec 1974; died 1 Nov 1998; d Carolyn m Steel.

1971   ANGUS HALLEY HADDOW
(FES X, 295, 333), trans from Largo St David's to Trinity 27 May 1971; trans to Aberdeen Garthdee 30 Apr 1981.

1975   HAMISH KIRKPATRICK FLEMING

(FES X, 113, 122, 331), trans from Kilmarnock St Marnock's to St Mark's 5 Jun 1975; became minister of united charge with Trinity 3 Jun 1981; trans to Banchory-Ternan East 4 Sep 1986.

1989   JOHN MUTCH WATSON
B 16 Apr 1944 at Glasgow, s of William Hector W. and Jean Hindle Wilson Chalmers; educ Bellahouston Academy, Glasgow 1956–61; University of Glasgow; Police Officer 1961–85; lic by Presb of Paisley 31 Aug 1988; m 15 Jul 1967 Jennifer Brown b 10 Dec 1945 d of Thomas B. and Violet McLoy; Children: William b 4 Apr 1969 m Donaldson; David b 28 Sep 1974; ord and ind to St Mark's 16 Jun 1989.

ST MARY'S (FES IX, 569; X, 331)

1967   MICHAEL SCOTT MURRAY CRAWFORD
(FES X, 331), ord by Presb of Edinburgh during assistantship at St George's West 20 Mar 1966; ind to St Mary's 26 Oct 1967.

ST NICOLAS SOUTH OF KINCORTH (FES IX, 570; X, 331)

1970	WILLIAM GEORGE WATT
(FES X, 331), ord and ind to St Nicholas South of Kincorth 1 May 1970; ret 31 Jul 1977; s Michael m Margaret Hyne; d Heather m (1) David Ross, m (2) David Bills; s Peter Jonathan m Sophia Ann Hunter.

1978	WILLIAM EDWARDS WILKIE
B 13 Feb 1935 at Dundee, s of James W. and Amelia McDonald; educ Logie Junior Secondary, Dundee 1940–50; University of Aberdeen 1974–78 (LTh); Landscape Gardner 1956–74; lic by Presb of Dundee 25 Jun 1978; m 19 Mar 1955 Agnes Crawford Millar b 4 Apr 1936 d of Alexander M. and Isabella McCorkindale; Children: Isabella b 9 Jan 1957 m Gordon Barbour; James b 17 Apr 1958; Garry Edwards b 28 Mar 1961; Linda Agnes Margaret b 20 May 1964 m David Chapman; ord and ind to St Nicholas South of Kincorth 26 Jul 1978.

ST NINIAN'S (FES VI, 30; VIII, 532; IX, 571; X, 332)

Linked 15 Nov 1995 with Stockethill. Arrangement terminated 31 Aug 1999.

1929	JOHN McILWRAITH
(FES V, 336; VIII, 489, 532; IX, 571; X, 332), trans from Dundee Maryfield to St Ninian's 20 Feb 1929; ret 31 Jan 1962; died 17 Jul 1977.

1962	JOHN (IAN) MANSON PATERSON
(FES IX, 745, 800; X, 295, 332), res as Candidates Secretary of FMC and ind to St Ninian's 4 Sep 1962; trans to St Andrews Hope Park 23 Aug 1966.

1967	ROBERT KELTIE
(FES IX, 87; X, 53, 332, 357, 420), res from app with Overseas Council in Kenya and ind to St Ninian's 24 Jan 1967; trans to Cabrach with Mortlach 20 Nov 1975.

1976	ROBERT TYRE
(FES X, 95, 323), trans from Montrose St Luke's and St John's to St Ninian's 17 Jun 1976; became minister of linked charge with Stockethill 15 Nov 1995; ret 10 Sep 1998.

ST STEPHEN'S (FES X, 325, 329)

Formed 1 Sep 1988 by union of Causewayend and Powis.

1947	GEORGE SCOTT SKAKLE
(FES IX, 566; X, 329), ind to Powis 29 Oct 1947; ret 31 May 1988.

1975	IAN DOUGLAS GRANT SUTHERLAND
(FES IX, 289, 655; X, 285, 325, 373), trans from Leslie Christ's Kirk on the Green to Causwayend

25 Sep 1975; ret 15 May 1985; Addl publ: *Meditations on a Harmony of the Gospels* (Berith Publ, 1999).

1986	ANDREW THOMSON BLAKE McGOWAN
trans from Mallaig and The Small Isles to Causewayend 20 Jun 1986; trans to Glasgow Trinity Possil and Henry Drummond 15 Sep 1988.

1989	JAMES McBRIDE DAVIES
B 10 Oct 1956 at Johnstone, s of James D. and Sarah McCalmont; University of St Andrews 1973–77 (BSc); University of Glasgow 1977–80 (BD); lic by Presb of Paisley 25 Jun 1980; asst Aberdeen Northfield 1980–82; m 17 Aug 1985 Audrey Storey; ord and ind to Glasgow Carmyle with Kenmuir Mount Vernon 25 Nov 1982; trans to St Stephen's 22 Feb 1989.

STOCKETHILL (FES IX, 571; X, 332)

Linked 15 Nov 1995 with St Ninian's. Congregation dissolved 31 Aug 1999.

1959	GEORGE PATON
(FES IX, 327; X, 193, 332), res as Asst at Glasgow Castlemilk West and ind to Stockethill 1 Oct 1959; pastoral tie dissolved 11 Mar 1973; died 15 Jan 1999.

1974	JAMES ALEXANDER IAIN MACEWAN
(FES X, 332), ord by Presb of Glasgow during assistantship at Lochwood 27 Mar 1973; ind to Stockethill 31 Jan 1974; trans to Abernethy with Cromdale and Advie 28 Feb 1980.

1980	ANDREW THOMAS MACLEAN
ord and ind to Stockethill 8 May 1980; dem on app as Chaplain to Students' Assoc, University of Strathclyde 1 Sep 1985.

1986	KENNETH WILLIAM DONALD
res from app as Assoc at Edinburgh Holy Trinity and ind to Stockethill 20 Mar 1986; dem 28 Feb 1995; ind to Wemyss 4 Mar 1999.

1995	ROBERT TYRE
(FES X, 95, 323), trans from Montrose St Luke's and St John's to Aberdeen St Ninian's 17 Jun 1976; became minister of linked charge with Stockethill 15 Nov 1995.

SUMMERHILL (FES X, 332)

Granted full status 1988.

1969	DAVID WISHART TORRANCE
(FES X, 31, 332), trans from Livingston to Summerhill 2 May 1969; trans to Earlston 30 Mar 1977.

1977	ALASDAIR BOTHWELL GORDON
(FES X, 335), res as Clerk to Presb of Aberdeen and ind to Summerhill 25 Aug 1977; dem 31 Dec 1980 to take up app as Senior Admin Asst,

Voluntary Service Aberdeen; app Lecturer in Law, Aberdeen College 18 Sep 1989; Jordanhill College, Glasgow 1993 (qualification to teach business studies); ret from Aberdeen College 24 Aug 1998 and app Tutor at Brain Injury Vocational Centre (Rehab Scotland), Aberdeen 1 Mar 1999; Publ: Co-author of *The Hope of Israel* (Gilcomston South Church, 1976); contributor to *Dictionary of Evangelical Biography* (Blackwell, 1995); *Elements of Scots Law* (Green, 1997); *Contract LawBasics* (Green, 1998); *Succession LawBasics* (Green, 1999); various articles in magazines and periodicals.

1981   IAN ALEXANDER McLEAN
B 26 Dec 1956 at Aberdeen, s of William Jamieson M. and Margaret Milne; educ Stockport Grammar and George Heriot's, Edinburgh 1968–74; University of Edinburgh 1974–77 (BSc), 1977–80 (BD); lic by Presb of Edinburgh 6 Jul 1980; asst Bearsden South 1980–81; m 2 Aug 1985 Elaine Margaret McLeish b 6 Nov 1960 d of Robert M. and Gladys Miller; Children: Gavin Alexander b 5 Oct 1987; Laura Margaret b 4 Sep 1990; ord and ind to Summerhill 27 May 1981.

TORRY ST FITTICK'S (FES X, 330, 332)

Formed 29 May 1991 by union of Torry and St Fittick's.

1957   JOHN CHISHOLM DICKSON
(FES IX, 576; X, 330, 335), trans from Echt to St Fittick's 13 Jun 1957; Chaplain to Craiginches Prison, Aberdeen 1958–68; Chaplain to TA and Army Cadet Force 1951–87; ret 31 Mar 1987; d Anne m Malcolm Kershaw; s John m Lynne Cuthill.

1967   NORMAN SWINBURNE
(FES X, 267, 333), ind to Torry 16 Aug 1967; trans to Sauchie 1 Jul 1975.

1976   DAVID JOHN TEMPLE
B 27 Jan 1947 at Belfast, s of David T. and Mary Lynd; educ Belfast Royal Academy 1959–66; Trinity College, Dublin 1966–70 (BA); University of Edinburgh 1971–74 (BD); Teaching 1970–71; lic by Presb of Edinburgh, Jul 1974; asst Cumbernauld St Mungo's 1974–75; Falkirk St Andrew's 1975–76; m 1 Aug 1974 Jennifer Janet Sheddon Oliver b 22 Oct 1950 d of Mr and Mrs Thomas O; Children: Andrew Hume b 20 Oct 1978; ord and ind to Torry 18 Mar 1976; dem 30 May 1980 to take up app at Third Portglenone Church, N Ireland.

1981   ARCHIE STEWART
B 20 May 1926 at Dundee, s of Archibald S. and Wilhelmina Edward; educ Rockwell Central School 1936–40; University of St Andrews 1972–75; lic by Presb of Dundee 8 Jan 1976; asst Dundee Mains of Fintry 1975–76; m 2 Jul 1949 Agnes Samson Cameron b 17 Nov 1927 d of William C.

and Anne Samson; Children: Anne Cameron b 12 Jul 1964; Carol Stephen b 6 Oct 1966; ord and ind to Kilmuir and Logie Easter 12 Aug 1976; trans to Torry 28 Jan 1981; died 6 Dec 1989.

1988   THOMAS YOUNG BELL
B 1 Aug 1929 at Falkirk, s of James B. and Helen Gray Young; educ Graeme High, Falkirk 1942–44; Falkirk Technical College 1967–69; Callendar Park College 1969–71; University of Glasgow 1978–82, 1984–86 (MA); National Savings Bank 1971–73; Social Work 1973–78; lic by Presb of Falkirk 4 Dec 1987; asst Bo'ness Old 1986–87; m 30 Jun 1962 Moyra Elizabeth Monk b 1 Jun 1929 d of Captain R J M. and Isabella Geidt; Children: Helen b 12 Apr 1963; Richard b 31 Jan 1966; ord and ind to St Fittick's 6 May 1988; ret 31 May 1990; died 25 Aug 1990.

1991   DAVID SCOTT HUTCHISON
B 2 Apr 1965 at St Andrews, s of Alexander Scott H. and Gillian Alice Curry; educ Aberdeen Grammar 1976–83; University of Loughborough 1983–86 (BSc); University of Edinburgh 1986–89 (BD); Princeton Seminary, USA 1989–90 (ThM); lic by Presb of Aberdeen 4 Jul 1989; asst Aberdeen Northfield 1990–91; m 15 Aug 1989 Hazel McNair b 1 Oct 1968 d of James M. and Muriel Eadie; Children: Caroline Gillian b 19 May 1995; ord and ind to Torry St Fittick's 14 Aug 1991; ret 30 Sep 1998.

1999   IAIN CAMERON BARCLAY
B 13 Sep 1947 at Giffnock, s of Thomas Mungo B. and Jane Scott Dobie Walker; educ Queen's Park, Glasgow 1959–65; University of Edinburgh 1970–75 (MA), 1970–75 (BD), 1992–94 (MTh); University of Glasgow 1994–96 (MPhil); lic by Presb of Glasgow, 1975; asst Edinburgh Holy Trinity 1975–76; m 2 Sep 1983 Carilon Dene Wilmot b 19 Oct 1937 d of Gerald Cursack W. and Sheelah Kathleen Jackson; ord by Presb of Edinburgh and app by RAChD, 1976; ind to Edinburgh New Restalrig 31 May 1979; trans to Kilfinan with Kyles 8 Nov 1988; dem to take up place as full-time student at University of Aberdeen 1996, also app Pastoral Asst at Beechgrove; Chaplain (TA) since 1982; app Chaplain (ACF) 1996; ind to Torry St Fittick's 7 Oct 1999.

WOODSIDE (FES X, 333)

Formed 13 May 1982 by union of Woodside North and Woodside South.

1955   ANDREW MONTGOMERY RUSSELL
(FES IX, 538; X, 314, 333), trans from Arbroath Erskine to Woodside North 8 Jun 1955; ret 30 Jun 1976; s Colln m Elizabeth Agnes Tough; s Brian m Margaret June Kingman; s Derek m Jean Allison Clark; s Kenneth m Elsy Florelia Velasquez.

1967   ROBERT WATT
(FES IX, 471; X, 265, 279, 333), trans from Kilmadock to Woodside South 24 Aug 1967; ret 13 May 1982 in interests of union; s Thomas m Susan Fiddes; s Ian m Isabella Emily Campbell.

1977   PETER WEBSTER
ord by Presb of Aberdeen and introd on term app to Woodside North 22 Jun 1977; ind to Greenock Cartsdyke 15 Sep 1981.

1982   JAMES GORDON MATHEW
(FES X, 51), trans from Penicuik North to Woodside 13 May 1982; trans to Glasgow Scotstoun 29 Jun 1989.

1990   ALISTAIR MURRAY
B 8 Apr 1953 at Belfast, s of John M. and Martha Harvey; educ Model Secondary, Belfast 1964–68; Bible Training Institute, Glasgow 1975–78 (Dip); University of Glasgow 1980–84 (BD); Plumber 1968–75; lic by Presb of Glasgow (UFC) 19 Jun 1984; asst Chryston UFC 1980–84; m 7 Jan 1978 Susanna Anderson b 21 Mar 1954 d of James A. and Isabella Bruce; Children: Alan Neil b 25 Sep 1986; ord by Presb of Glasgow (UFC) and ind to Ayr UFC 25 Aug 1984; ind to Woodside 22 Mar 1990.

PRESBYTERY OF KINCARDINE AND DEESIDE

ABERLUTHNOTT (FES IX, 545; X, 314)

Linked 1 Aug 1979 with Laurencekirk.

1958 ALEXANDER WHITE
(FES IX, 67; X, 42, 314), trans from Pardovan and Kingscavil to Aberluthnott 5 Feb 1958; ret 30 Sep 1978; died 22 Nov 1989.

1980 JAMES BLAIKIE
(FES X, 408), trans from Aberdeen Middlefield to Aberluthnott with Laurencekirk 7 Jan 1980; trans to St Andrew's with Wallace Green with Lowick 26 Sep 1986.

1987 ALEXANDER ROBERTSON
trans from Glasgow Scotstoun East to Aberluthnott with Laurencekirk 6 Nov 1987; trans to Canisbay with Keiss 1 Nov 1991.

1992 ROBERT JOHNSTON
(FES X, 300), trans from Edinburgh St Mary's with St Stephen's to Aberluthnott with Laurencekirk 18 Jun 1992; ret 30 Nov 1997; s Erik m Sheena Colquhoun; s Alan m Shelagh Moonie; s Colin m Frances Evans.

1999 PETER ALAN DUNCAN BERRILL
B 15 Nov 1951 at Wirksworth, Derbyshire, s of Alan Joseph B. and Sheila Rose McNab; educ Wirksworth Grammar and Kirkcudbright Academy 1962–69; University of Edinburgh 1969–72 (MA), 1973–76 (BD); Piano Teacher 1980–83; lic by Presb of Dumfries and Kirkcudbright 19 Jul 1976; asst East Kilbride Greenhills 1976–78; m 7 Jun 1976 Eileen Catherine Mairead McCann; Children: Naomi Claire b 10 Nov 1981; Matthew Joseph b 25 Aug 1983; John Paul Alan b 1 Dec 1985; Peter Harry Charles b 18 May 1989; ord and ind to Glenrothes Christ's Kirk on the Green 27 Oct 1983; dem 30 Apr 1987 to enter teaching profession (music); ind to Aberluthnott with Laurencekirk 3 Jun 1999.

ABOYNE-DINNET (FES X, 339, 341)

Linkage of Dinnet with Logie Coldstone and Migvie terminated 13 Jun 1984. Dinnet linked 31 Oct 1984 with Aboyne. Congregations united 20 Jun 1993.

1956 ANDREW GARDINER
(FES IX, 462; X, 273, 339), trans from Dunfermline St Leonard's to Aboyne 9 Sep 1956; ret 31 Oct 1984; died 19 Jul 1989.

1966 EUGEN WILFRED RUSHFORTH
(FES IX, 352, 602; X, 106, 341, 346), trans from Tarbolton to Dinnet with Logie Coldstone and Migvie 30 Nov 1966; ret 30 Nov 1983; died 29 Dec 1991.

1985 WILLIAM DOUGLAS WATT
B 14 Apr 1934 at Gourdon, s of Andrew Milne W. and Annabelle Moir; educ Inverbervie Secondary; Aberdeen College of Commerce 1974–75; University of Aberdeen 1975–78 (LTh); Fish Processor/Van Salesman 1949–61; Port Missionary, British Sailors' Society 1961–75; lic by Presb of Kincardine and Deeside 9 Jul 1978; m 24 Nov 1956 Anne Craig b 22 Feb 1935 d of James C. and Isabella McLeod; Children: Douglas b 22 Feb 1958 m Emily Henderson; Isobel b 27 Oct 1961 m Robert Cargill; Jaqueline b 9 Jan 1966 m Adrian Gibb; ord and ind to Ardrishaig with South Knapdale 29 Nov 1978; trans to Aboyne with Dinnet 21 Jun 1985; became minister of united charge 20 Jun 1993; ret on grounds of ill-health 30 Sep 1996; Publ: *250 Years Ministry. South Knapdale Church* (1984).

1997 DAVID JOHN DEVENNEY
B 15 Nov 1956 at Glasgow, s of Moses Alexander D. and Isobel Devenny; educ Garriochmill Secondary, Glasgow; University of St Andrews 1991–95; Police Officer 1976–80; Royal Marines 1980–91; lic by Presb of Kirkcaldy 9 Jul 1995; m 22 Nov 1975 Margaret Anne Keenan b 24 Mar 1958 d of Frederick K. and Isabel Hognet; Children: Julie Anne b 3 Dec 1978; David Scott b 22 Dec 1979; ord and ind to Aboyne-Dinnet 20 Feb 1997.

ARBUTHNOTT (FES V, 452; VIII, 516; IX, 545; X, 316)

Linked 1 Jan 1967 with Kinneff. Further linked 27 Aug 1987 with Bervie. Linkage with Kinneff terminated 13 Sep 1990.

1951 GILBERT WILLIAM MOORE
(FES IX, 377, 451, 545, 625, 710; X, 316), dem from Norrieston 30 Nov 1951; introd to Arbuthnott 1 Dec 1951; ret 30 Apr 1964; died 2 Jan 1978.

1965 GORDON RUSSELL McLEAN BLACK
(FES IX, 595; X, 316, 343, 361, 400), dem from Portknockie and introd to Arbuthnott 9 Mar 1965; ind to Birsay 12 Jan 1967.

1967 JOHN BELL DEANS
(FES IX, 564; X, 258, 316, 328, 445, 450), res from service with RAChD and ind to Arbuthnott with Kinneff 21 Apr 1967; dem 11 Mar 1974 on app as Chaplain to Aberdeen City Hospital.

1974 IAN GEORGE GOUGH
(FES X, 316), ord and ind to Arbuthnott with Kinneff 7 Aug 1974; trans to Glasgow St James' (Pollok) 17 Feb 1982.

1982 THOMAS FORREST SMITH
(FES X, 147, 274, 285), res from term app at Rosneath St Modan's and introd on term app to Arbuthnott with Kinneff 14 Apr 1982; res from app 30 Sep 1986; Publ: Articles in local and national newspapers.

1987 CONNIE PHILP
B 24 Jun 1930 at Greenlaw, d of Isabella Philp (adoptive mother); educ Darroch Secondary, Edinburgh 1942–44; St Colm's College, Edinburgh 1955–57; Falkirk Technical College 1973–74; University of Edinburgh 1974–78 (BD); Office and Library Work 1944–55; Deaconess 1957–73; lic by Presb of Falkirk 1 Sep 1978; asst Bo'ness Old 1978–79; ord and ind to Benholm and Johnshaven with Bervie 22 Oct 1980; became minister of Bervie 15 Apr 1984 and of linked charge with Arbuthnott with Kinneff 27 Aug 1987; became minister of Arbuthnott with Bervie 13 Sep 1990; ret 31 Jul 1995.

1995 ALASTAIR GARDINER McKILLOP
B 12 Jun 1961 at Lennoxtown, s of Daniel M. and Christina Alice Thomson; educ Lenzie Academy 1973–78; Glasgow Bible College 1987–91(BD); University of Glasgow 1992–94 (DipMin); Technical Foreman 1981–87; lic by Presb of Falkirk 16 Aug 1994; asst Cumbernauld Old 1994–95; m 22 Apr 1983 Lorraine Helen Richardson b 29 Dec 1957 d of David Lawson R. and Ann Watson Montgomery Henderson; Children: Kirsten Ann b 16 Mar 1984; Mark David b 17 Apr 1989; ord and ind to Arbuthnott with Bervie 23 Nov 1995.

BANCHORY-DEVENICK (FES IX, 573; X, 333)

Linked 30 Sep 1972 with Maryculter. Linkage continues following union of Maryculter and Cookney 1 Dec 1982.

1962 IAN APPLEBY AULD
(FES IX, 11, 74 (2), 83, 91; X, 7, 333), trans from Edinburgh Craigentinny St Christopher's to Banchory-Devenick 25 Jan 1962; ret 30 Sep 1972.

1973 THOMAS LITHGOW
(FES IX, 202, 485; X, 289, 333), trans from Auchtermuchty to Banchory-Devenick with Maryculter 19 Apr 1973; ret 31 May 1982.

1983 DAVID CHRISTIE ROBERTSON SIMPSON
B 1 Feb 1952 at Dufftown, s of Thomas S. and Margaret Annie Milne; educ Mortlach Secondary, Dufftown and Keith Grammar 1957–70; University of Aberdeen 1977–82 (BD, CPS); lic by Presb of Moray 29 Jun 1982; asst Dyce 1982–83; m 16 Apr 1984 Sylvia Gill Stevens b 22 Jul 1959 d of Peter Miller S. and Sarah Ann Gill; Children: Peter and James; ord and ind to Banchory-Devenick with Maryculter and Cookney 5 May 1983; dem 31 Dec 1989.

1990 ANDREW CORMACK CHRISTIE
(FES X, 357), res from term app at Aberdeen Ferryhill North and ind to Banchory-Devenick with Maryculter and Cookney 14 Jun 1990; s Andrew m Alison Murray.

BANCHORY-TERNAN EAST (FES VI, 79; VIII, 544; IX, 585; X, 339)

Linked 1981 until 1986 with Durris.

1969 WILLIAM NICHOLSON
(FES IX, 458; X, 19, 252, 271, 339), trans from Portobello St Philip's Joppa to Banchory-Ternan East 30 Jan 1969; became minister of linked charge with Durris 1981; ret 25 Feb 1986.

1986 HAMISH KIRKPATRICK FLEMING
(FES X, 113, 122, 331), trans from Aberdeen St Mark's to Banchory-Ternan East 4 Sep 1986.

BANCHORY-TERNAN WEST (FUF 428; FES IX, 586; X, 339)

1966 ALEXANDER MITCHELL STUART
(FES IX, 340, 623; X, 203, 340), trans from Uddingston Chalmers to Banchory-Ternan West 13 Jan 1966; ret 1 Nov 1979; died 20 Oct 1991.

1980 IAIN FERGUSON PATON
ord and ind to Banchory-Ternan West 29 May 1980; trans to Glasgow Newlands South 6 Oct 1985.

1986 GEORGE ANGUS CHALMERS
(FES X, 37, 61), trans from Denny Westpark to Banchory-Ternan West 10 Mar 1986; trans to Catrine with Sorn 15 Sep 1994.

1995 DONALD KENNETH WALKER
B 29 Jul 1949 at Livingstonia, Malawi, s of Robert Bernard William W. and Grace Brownlee Torrance; educ Lesmahagow Junior Secondary and Hamilton Academy 1961–68; Kirkcaldy Technical College 1968–70; University of Aberdeen 1970–71; University of St Andrews 1971–76 (BD); University of Edinburgh 1976–78; lic by Presb of Lanark 26 Nov 1978; asst Skene 1978–79; Nairn Old 1979–80; m 27 Jun 1980 Judith Veitch Anderson b 3 May 1946 d of Norman Veitch A. and Doreen Florence Lovell; Children: Ewan Donald b 26 Aug 1982; Hannah

Jane b 28 Jun 1985; ord by Presb of Inverness during assistantship at Nairn Old 14 Nov 1979; ind to St Margaret's United Church of Zambia, Kitwe 27 Sep 1981; trans to Trinity United Church of Zambia, Kalulushi, Jun 1986; Co-ordinator for Evangelism, United Church of Zambia; ind to Banchory-Ternan West 12 Jan 1995.

BERVIE (FES IX, 546; X, 316)

Linked 31 Mar 1980 with Benholm and Johnshaven. Linkage terminated 15 Apr 1984. Linked 27 Aug 1987 with Arbuthnott with Kinneff. Linkage with Kinneff terminated 13 Sep 1990.

1958 DONALD CAMPBELL
(FES IX, 621, 722; X, 316, 358), trans from Findochty to Bervie 26 Feb 1958; ret 31 Oct 1979; Publ: 'Happy of Heart' (private, 1987).

1980 CONNIE PHILP
ord and ind to Benholm and Johnshaven with Bervie 22 Oct 1980; became minister of Bervie 15 Apr 1984 and of linked charge with Arbuthnott with Kinneff 27 Aug 1987; became minister of Arbuthnott with Bervie 13 Sep 1990; ret 31 Jul 1995.

1995 ALASTAIR GARDINER McKILLOP
ord and ind to Arbuthnott with Bervie 23 Nov 1995, see Arbuthnott.

BIRSE AND FEUGHSIDE (FES X, 340, 341, 342)

Birse linked 1 Aug 1983 with Finzean with Strachan. Linkage terminated 1 Jun 1987 in favour of three-way union as Birse and Feughside.

1963 JOHN ALEXANDER PATERSON
(FES IX, 535, 718, 760; X, 77, 195, 340), trans from Hamilton Gilmour Memorial and Whitehill to Birse 26 Sep 1963; ret 31 May 1972; died 3 Jun 1986.

1970 ALFRED JAMES ARMOUR
(FES IX, 133, 204, 460, 568, 612, 620; X, 228, 341, 357), trans from Dunoon St Cuthbert's to Strachan with Finzean 21 Oct 1970; ret 30 Jun 1983; died 8 Jun 1986.

1973 ROBERT RIGG
(FES IX, 25, 601; X, 15, 33, 262, 340), trans from Balquhidder to Birse 14 Feb 1973; ret 5 Jul 1978; died 17 Dec 1978.

1979 ELIZABETH BAXTER FORBES KINNIBURGH
(FES X, 436), res as Lecturer in Religious Education, Dundee College of Education and introd to Birse (term) 23 Sep 1979; became minister of linked charge with Finzean with Strachan 1 Aug 1983; ret 31 Dec 1986 on grounds of ill-health.

1987 JOHN FERGUS FERGUSON
ord and ind to Birse and Feughside 3 Sep 1987; trans to Perth Kinnoull 1 Dec 1993.

1994 JACK HOLT
B 9 Jul 1958 at Greenock, s of Jack H. and Margaret McGowan; educ Greenock High 1970–75; James Watt College, Greenock 1975–77 (ONC); Paisley College of Technology 1977–81 (BSc); University of Glasgow 1981–84 (BD); Sponsored student with IBM 1975–81; lic by Presb of Greenock 27 Jun 1984; asst Broom 1984–86; m 30 May 1980 Sandra McMillan b 25 Mar 1959 d of James M. and Sarah Wilson Stewart Muir; Children: Jonathan b 14 Aug 1984; Adam b 30 Dec 1987; Sarah Grace b 23 Oct 1991; ord by Presb of Glasgow during assistantship at Broom 18 Apr 1985; ind to Kilmarnock Shortlees 16 Apr 1986; trans to Birse and Feughside 22 Sep 1994.

BRAEMAR (FUF 429; FES VI, 85; VIII, 545; IX, 586; X, 340)

Linked 1 Oct 1978 with Crathie.

1969 GILBERT ELLIOT ANDERSON
(FES IX, 653; X, 41, 340, 372), trans from Linlithgow St Ninian's Craigmailen to Braemar 13 Mar 1969; ret 28 Oct 1975; died 22 Feb 1990.

1978 DUNCAN PRIMROSE MACPHEE
(FES IX, 337; X, 225, 246, 283 (2)), dem from Fortingall with Glenlyon and introd on term app to Braemar 22 Apr 1976; introd as Assoc at Braemar with Crathie 6 Oct 1978; ret 31 Oct 1980.

1979 JAMES ALEXANDER KEITH ANGUS
(FES X, 78, 132), trans from Gourock Old to Braemar with Crathie 2 Apr 1979; ret 31 Dec 1995; Domestic Chaplain to the Queen in Scotland 1979–96; Extra Chaplain to the Queen 1996–; app Lieutenant of the Royal Victorian Order (LVO) 1990; Publ: *Crathie Parish Church* (Pilgrim Press).

1996 ROBERT PATERSON SLOAN
(FES X, 381), trans from Perth North to Braemar with Crathie 18 Apr 1996; s Andrew m Annette Elizabeth Gillies; s Peter m Inge Reiff Musgrove.

CRATHIE (FUF 429; FES VI, 91; VIII, 546; IX, 587; X, 340)

Linked 1 Oct 1978 with Braemar.

1972 THOMAS JAMES TRAIL NICOL
(FES IX, 505, 792; X, 340, 447), res from RAChD and ind to Crathie 3 May 1972; ret 31 Oct 1977; died 28 Jul 1998; d Janet m Parker; d Katherine m Ashe.

1978 DUNCAN PRIMROSE MACPHEE
(FES IX, 337; X, 225, 246, 283 (2)), introd as Assoc at Braemar with Crathie 6 Oct 1978, see Braemar.

1979   JAMES ALEXANDER KEITH ANGUS
(FES X, 78, 132), trans from Gourock Old to Braemar with Crathie 2 Apr 1979, see Braemar.

1996   ROBERT PATERSON SLOAN
(FES X, 381), ind to Braemar with Crathie 18 Apr 1996, see Braemar.

CROMAR (FES X, 340, 342)

Formed 31 Oct 1984 by union of Coull and Tarland with Logie Coldstone and Migvie.

1967   JOHN WIGHTMAN STIRLING BROWN
(FES X, 340 (2), 416), res from Church Training Centre, Ohafia, Nigeria and ind to Coull with Tarland 16 Nov 1967; became minister of united charge 7 Sep 1975 and of united charge with Logie Coldstone and Migvie 31 Oct 1984; ret 31 Mar 1995; Clerk to Presb of Kincardine and Deeside from 1 Feb 1983; University of Aberdeen (part-time) 1984–88 (BTh).

1996   REGINE URSULA CHEYNE
University of Aberdeen 1985–88 (BD); lic by Presb of Aberdeen, Jun 1988; ord and ind to Whalsay and Skerries 3 Sep 1988; trans to Cromar 2 May 1996.

DRUMOAK (FES IX, 575; X, 334)

Linked 1 Oct 1987 with Durris.

1959   WILLIAM SERLE
(FES X, 334), ord and ind to Drumoak 13 Aug 1959; ret 30 Sep 1987; died 7 Oct 1992.

1988   DAVID F PRENTIS
trans from Rousay to Drumoak with Durris 14 Apr 1988; dem 31 Jul 1991.

1992   JAMES SCOTT
(FES X, 329), trans from Aberdeen Northfield to Drumoak with Durris 13 Feb 1992; m 22 Sep 1973 Rosalind Ann Smith b 5 Jul 1947 d of William Shearer S. and Christina Herd Murray Williamson; Children: Graham Mark b 23 Nov 1976; Kenneth Andrew b 1 Jul 1980; Publ: *Windows into the Past* (Durris Church, 1997).

DURRIS (FES IX, 576; X, 335)

Linkage with Rickarton terminated 6 Nov 1979. Linked 1981–86 with Banchory-Ternan East. Linked 1 Oct 1987 with Drumoak.

1958   JAMES FORREST KELLAS
(FES VIII, 527; IX, 564; X, 327, 335), dem from Aberdeen Mannofield and introd on term app to Durris 1 Oct 1958; ret 31 Dec 1966; died 9 Jan 1977.

1968   WILLIAM ADAMSON SOUTHWELL
(FES X, 335), ord and ind to Durris with Rickarton 28 Mar 1968; ret 31 May 1979; died 24 May 1994.

1981   WILLIAM NICHOLSON
(FES IX, 458; X, 19, 252, 271, 339), ind to Banchory-Ternan East 30 Jan 1969; became minister of linked charge with Durris 1981, see Banchory-Ternan East.

1988   DAVID F PRENTIS
trans from Rousay to Drumoak with Durris 14 Apr 1988; dem 31 Jul 1991.

1992   JAMES SCOTT
(FES X, 329), ind to Drumoak with Durris 13 Feb 1992, see Drumoak.

GLENMUICK (BALLATER) (FES IX, 587; X, 341)

1943   WILLIAM MELVILLE KING
(FES IX, 35, 587; X, 341), trans from Edinburgh St Aidan's to Glenmuick (Ballater) 16 Sep 1943; ret 31 Dec 1972; died 30 Aug 1984.

1973   JAMES GEORGE STEWART BLYTH
(FES X, 292, 341), trans from Monimail to Glenmuick (Ballater) 6 Jun 1973; ret 31 May 1986; s James m Nathalie Gevrey; d Helen m Andrew Keating.

1986   ALASTAIR BROWN
B 14 Oct 1949 at Coatbridge, s of David B. and Mary McKenzie Boag; educ Clifton High, Coatbridge 1960–64; University of Aberdeen 1980–84 (BD), 1984–85 (CPS); Draughtsman 1965–80; lic by Presb of Gordon 8 Sep 1985; m 31 Oct 1970 Jennifer McCracken b 6 Nov 1947 d of John McC. and Janet Nugent; Children: Andrew b 4 Aug 1971; Colin b 5 Aug 1973; ord and ind to Glenmuick (Ballater) 25 Sep 1986; ret 28 Feb 1992.

1992   ALBERT CAIE
B 21 Jul 1932 at Aberdeen, s of Albert C. and Jane Allen Jenkins; educ Aberdeen Grammar 1944–48; Langside College 1972–73; University of Glasgow 1973–75, 1980–83 (LTh); Royal Navy 1950–52; Civil Engineering 1953–58; Industrial Estates Management Corporation for England 1959–66; Glasgow Western Infirmary 1966–69; lic by Presb of Glasgow 27 Jun 1983; m 2 Jul 1954 Helen Elizabeth Mitchell d of William James M. and Esther Scott; Children: William John b 6 Jul 1955 m Elizabeth Moore; Philip Albert b 3 Nov 1959 m Gillian Bell; Heather Elizabeth b 2 May 1965 m Alan Grieve; ord and ind to Fintray with Keithhall with Kinellar 11 Aug 1983; trans to Glenmuick (Ballater) 20 Oct 1992; ret 31 Jul 1997.

1999   ANTHONY WATTS
B 13 Oct 1948 at Chatham, Kent, s of Charles Edward W. and Alice Murrell; educ Chatham Technical High 1960–66; University of Aberdeen 1994–97 (BD); Naval Architect 1966–75; Teaching (Technical) 1977–94; lic by Presb of Gordon 19 Jun 1997; asst Methlick 1997–99; m 9 Oct 1982 Judith Ann Cain b 8 Oct 1957 d of Gerard Charles

C. and Joan Frances Appleton; Children: Sean Matthew Charles b 20 Nov 1983; Paul Edward Mark b 23 Aug 1985; ord and ind to Glenmuick (Ballater) 21 Jan 1999.

KINCARDINE O'NEIL (FES VI, 100; VIII, 549; IX, 588; X, 342)

Linked 6 May 1980 with Lumphanan.

1948 DONALD MACKELLAR LEITCH URIE (FES IX, 530, 588; X, 342), trans from Persie and Netherton to Kincardine O'Neil 22 Jun 1948; ret 30 May 1980.

1980 THOMAS JAMES GRANT SEATH ord and ind to Kincardine O'Neil with Lumphanan 25 Sep 1980; trans to Motherwell Manse Road 20 Dec 1985.

1986 JAMES WHITELAW ANDERSON B 19 Dec 1932 at Arbroath, s of George Nicholson A. and Elizabeth Liddle; educ Arbroath High 1944–48; Dundee College of Technology 1951–54 (HND); University of Manchester 1960–62 (AMCST: BSc); University of St Andrews 1983–85 (MTh); Engineering 1948–83; lic by Presb of Angus 14 Jul 1985; asst Forfar East and Old 1985–86; m 24 Aug 1957 Mary Graham Birse b 29 Dec 1934 d of George B. and Elizabeth Cable; Children: Rosemary Helen b 11 Jun 1959; Graeme James b 19 Oct 1963; ord and ind to Kincardine O'Neil with Lumphanan 26 Jun 1986; ret 31 Dec 1997.

1998 NORMA PEEBLES ROBERTSON B 8 Nov 1941 at Edinburgh, d of Alexander R. and Janet Harvey Naysmith Kerr; educ Portobello Secondary 1954–60; University of Edinburgh 1987–91 (BD); Standard Life 1960–87; lic by Presb of Edinburgh 7 Jul 1991; asst Edinburgh Greenbank 1991–93; ord by Presb of Hamilton and introd as Assoc at East Kilbride Moncreiff 8 Jun 1993; ind to Kincardine O'Neil with Lumphanan 11 Jun 1998.

KINNEFF (FES IX, 552; X, 321)

Linked 1 Jan 1967 with Arbuthnott. Further linked 27 Aug 1987 with Bervie. Linkage terminated 13 Sep 1990 in favour of linkage with Stonehaven South.

1974 IAN GEORGE GOUGH (FES X, 316), ord and ind to Arbuthnott with Kinneff 7 Aug 1974; trans to Glasgow St James' (Pollok) 17 Feb 1982.

1982 THOMAS FORREST SMITH (FES X, 147, 274, 285), introd to Arbuthnott with Kinneff 14 Apr 1982, see Arbuthnott.

1987 CONNIE PHILP ord and ind to Benholm and Johnshaven with Bervie 22 Oct 1980; became minister of Bervie 15 Apr 1984 and of linked charge with Arbuthnott with Kinneff 27 Aug 1987, see Arbuthnott.

1990 KENNETH LINDSAY PETRIE ind to Stonehaven South 11 Apr 1985; became minister of linked charge with Kinneff 13 Sep 1990; trans to Aberdeen Craigiebuckler 30 Sep 1999.

LAURENCEKIRK (FES X, 322)

Linked 1 Aug 1979 with Aberluthnott.

1969 ROBERT FYFE HOWAT (FES IX, 605; X, 98, 322, 348), trans from Annbank Old to Laurencekirk 30 Apr 1969; ret 31 Jul 1979; died 13 Aug 1981.

1980 JAMES BLAIKIE ind to Aberluthnott with Laurencekirk 7 Jan 1980, see Aberluthnott.

1987 ALEXANDER ROBERTSON ind to Aberluthnott with Laurencekirk 6 Nov 1987, see Aberluthnott.

1992 ROBERT JOHNSTON (FES X, 300), trans from Edinburgh St Mary's with St Stephen's to Aberluthnott with Laurencekirk 18 Jun 1992; ret 30 Nov 1997.

1999 PETER ALAN DUNCAN BERRILL ind to Aberluthnott with Laurencekirk 3 Jun 1999, see Aberluthnott.

LUMPHANAN (FES IX, 588; X, 342)

Linked 6 May 1980 with Kincardine O'Neil.

1972 SILVESTER SKINNER (FES IX, 701; X, 342, 353, 400, 411), trans from Gardenstown to Lumphanan 2 Mar 1972; ret 31 Oct 1979.

1980 THOMAS JAMES GRANT SEATH ind to Kincardine O'Neil with Lumphanan 25 Sep 1980, see Kincardine O'Neil.

1986 JAMES WHITELAW ANDERSON ord and ind to Kincardine O'Neil with Lumphanan 26 Jun 1986; ret 31 Dec 1997.

1998 NORMA PEEBLES ROBERTSON ind to Kincardine O'Neil with Lumphanan 11 Jun 1998, see Kincardine O'Neil.

MARYCULTER AND COOKNEY (FES X, 334, 336)

Formed 1 Dec 1982 by union of Maryculter and Cookney. Linkage with Banchory-Devenick continues after union.

1964 ROBERT INGRAM MITCHELL (FES IX, 90, 497, 610; X, 294, 336), trans from Kilconquhar and Colinsburgh to Maryculter 9 Oct 1964; ret 30 Jun 1971; died 26 Jul 1982.

1973 THOMAS LITHGOW
(FES IX, 202, 485; X, 289, 333), trans from Auchtermuchty to Banchory-Devenick with Maryculter 19 Apr 1973; ret 31 May 1982.

1983 DAVID CHRISTIE ROBERTSON SIMPSON
ord and ind to Banchory-Devenick with Maryculter and Cookney 05 May 1983; dem 31 Dec 1989.

1990 ANDREW CORMACK CHRISTIE
(FES X, 357), ind to Banchory-Devenick with Maryculter and Cookney 14 Jun 1990, see Banchory-Devenick.

MEARNS COASTAL (FES IX, 545; X, 316, 320)

Formed 12 Feb 1998 by union of Benholm and Johnshaven and Garvock St Cyrus. (Benholm and Johnshaven linked 31 Mar 1980 with Bervie. Linkage terminated 15 Apr 1984 in favour of linkage with Garvock St Cyrus).

1971 ARTHUR WILLIAM BRUCE
(FES IX, 62, 563; X, 84, 239, 320), trans from Kilninian and Kilmore with Tobermory to Garvock St Cyrus 22 Oct 1971; dem on grounds of ill-health 30 Sep 1974; ind to Fortingall with Glenlyon 26 Nov 1976.

1972 ALEXANDER DONALD MACLEOD
(FES X, 50, 186, 316), trans from Airdrie South Bridge Street to Benholm and Johnshaven 19 Jan 1972; ret 31 Mar 1979; died 18 Oct 1993.

1975 JAMES ALEXANDER WEMYSS SMITH
(FES IX, 62; X, 38, 320, 353), trans from King Edward to Garvock St Cyrus 19 Mar 1975; ret 31 Jul 1983; d Morag m Plenderleath.

1980 CONNIE PHILP
ord and ind to Benholm and Johnshaven with Bervie 22 Oct 1980; became minister of Bervie 15 Apr 1984.

1984 THOMAS FORRESTER WILSON
ord and ind to Garvock St Cyrus with Benholm and Johnshaven 14 Aug 1984; trans to Aberdeen North of St Andrew 17 Jan 1990.

1991 HARRY JAMES BROWN
ord and ind to Benholm and Johnshaven with Garvock St Cyrus 11 Jul 1991; trans to Dundee Menzieshill 18 Dec 1996.

1998 GEORGE IRVINE HASTIE
(FES X, 5), trans from Cowdenbeath Cairns to Mearns Coastal 12 Feb 1998; Publ: *Farm at Backyards* (private, 1994); *The Hastie Collection* (archive of pictures on Inverkeithing and Fife Towns 1964–94, lodged with Royal Commission on Ancient Monuments, Edinburgh, 1997).

NEWTONHILL (see FES X, 333)

New church at Newtonhill (to replace building at Bourtreebush) completed Jul 1987, dedicated Sep 1987. Linkage of Bourtreebush and Cookney terminated 1 Dec 1982. Bourtreebush linked same date with Portlethen. Arrangement terminated 7 Oct 1992.

1966 JAMES WELSH DUNCAN
(FES X, 64, 333), trans from Hawick Burnfoot to Bourtreebush with Cookney 5 May 1966; died 21 Feb 1982.

1982 KENNETH MACLEOD
(FES IX, 661; X, 226, 337, 378, 396), trans from Daliburgh to Portlethen 27 Apr 1967; became minister of linked charge with Bourtreebush 1 Dec 1982; ret 30 Sep 1986.

1987 JAMES DOUGLAS SIMPSON
ord and ind to Bourtreebush with Portlethen 7 May 1987; became minister of Newtonhill with Portlethen, Sep 1987 and of Portlethen 7 Oct 1992, see Portlethen.

1993 CHRISTINE CREEGAN
B 30 Aug 1944 at Ellon, d of Thomas William Milne and McLeod; educ Logie Junior Secondary, Dundee 1948–60; University of St Andrews 1988–92 (MTh); Secretary 1960–70; lic by Presb of Dundee 15 Nov 1992; asst Dundee High Kirk 1992–93; m 23 Apr 1966 Joseph Francis Creegan b 1 Jan 1941 s of Joseph C. and Mary Cairney; Children: Arlene b 14 Mar 1970; Grant b 15 Mar 1972; Martin b 21 Nov 1973; Stuart b 9 Oct 1975; ord and ind to Newtonhill 28 Aug 1993.

PORTLETHEN (FES VI, 73; VIII, 542; IX, 581; X, 337)

Linked with Bourtreebush 1 Dec 1982. Church at Bourtreebush replaced by new building at Newtonhill, Sep 1987. Linked with Newtonhill until 7 Oct 1992.

1967 KENNETH MACLEOD
(FES IX, 661; X, 226, 337, 378, 396), trans from Daliburgh to Portlethen 27 Apr 1967; became minister of linked charge with Bourtreebush 1 Dec 1982; ret 30 Sep 1986; s Alexander m Kate Flood; d Mary m Adrian Patterson; d Katherine m Joseph McGrane; s Iain m Margaret Jack.

1987 JAMES DOUGLAS SIMPSON
B 9 Nov 1960 at Hamilton, s of James S. and Elizabeth Gillespie Darroch; educ Garrion Academy, Wishaw 1973–79; University of Dundee 1980–83 (BSc); University of Aberdeen 1983–86 (BD); lic by Presb of Aberdeen 30 Jun 1986; asst Bellshill West; m 25 Jun 1983 Janice Mabel Robinson b 1 Jan 1956 d of John Little R. and Amy James Urquhart; Children: Jennifer Urquhart b 15 Jul 1986; James Andrew b 7 Dec 1987; ord and ind to

Bourtreebush with Portlethen 7 May 1987; became minister of Newtonhill with Portlethen, Sep 1987; became minister of Portlethen 7 Oct 1992; dem 31 Jul 1996 and emigrated to Atlanta, USA.

1997 JOHN RAE NOTMAN
B 10 May 1958 at Dumfries, s of John Rae N. and Elizabeth Brownridge Kirk; educ Dumfries Academy 1970–76; Heriot-Watt University 1976–81; University of Edinburgh 1986–89 (BD); Engineering 1982–86; lic by Presb of Edinburgh 2 Jul 1989; asst Edinburgh St Michael's 1989–90; m 15 Aug 1981 Frances Margaret Cooper b 28 Mar 1959 d of Francis Edmond C. and Margaret Ina Wardhoch; Children: Peter Ian b 12 Jul 1986; Ruth Anne b 5 Apr 1988; ord and ind to Dundee Douglas and Angus 13 Jun 1990; trans to Portlethen 6 Mar 1997.

RICKARTON (FES V, 480; VIII, 524; IX, 581; X, 337)

Linkage with Durris terminated 6 Nov 1979. Congregation dissolved 28 Feb 1980.

1961 JOHN WILSON BLAIR
(FES IX, 143, 237, 336, 713, 719; X, 85 (2), 337), trans from Glencairn with Moniaive to Rickarton 22 Sep 1961; ret 31 May 1967; died 28 Jan 1980.

1968 WILLIAM ADAMSON SOUTHWELL
(FES X, 335), ord and ind to Durris with Rickarton 28 Mar 1968; ret 31 May 1979; died 24 May 1994.

STONEHAVEN DUNNOTTAR (FES V, 459; VIII, 517; IX, 582; X, 337)

1974 JOHN RANKIN
(FES X, 337), ord and ind to Dunnottar 5 Jun 1974; trans to Perth Craigie 30 Nov 1988.

1989 JOHN DEAS WHITEFORD
ord and ind to Dunnottar 22 Jun 1989; trans to Glasgow Newlands South 27 Nov 1997.

1998 GORDON ALEXANDER FARQUHARSON
B 7 Feb 1942 at Dumfries, s of Norman F. and Henrietta Coltart; educ Dumfries Academy; University of Edinburgh 1960–66 (MA, DipEd), 1994–96 (BD); Moray House College, Edinburgh 1966–67 (CEd); Teaching 1966–94; Head Teacher 1984–94; lic by Presb of Lorn and Mull 27 Jun 1996; asst Edinburgh Greenside 1996–98; m 18 Jul 1970 Elizabeth Mary Naismith b 2 Jun 1943 d of Malcolm N. and Janet Box; Children: Alasdair Gordon b 13 May 1974; ord and ind to Dunnottar 25 Jun 1998.

STONEHAVEN FETTERESSO (FES V, 464; VIII, 520; IX, 583; X, 338)

1957 ROBERT GRAY
(FES IX, 53, 61; X, 37, 338), trans from Falkirk St John's Camelon to Fetteresso 18 Mar 1957; ret 30 Nov 1982; m 22 Feb 1946 Johanna Isabel Mackenzie Morison b 1 Oct 1921 d of William Mackenzie M. and Elizabeth Anne Jackson; Children: Isabel Anne b 17 Apr 1948 m David Hay; Robert Lindsay Morison b 1 Feb 1951 m Elaine Cunningham; Roderick Mackenzie b 25 Feb 1956 m Anne Tang.

1983 GRAHAM SOMERVILLE FINCH
trans from North Ronaldsay with Sanday to Fetteresso 21 Apr 1983; trans to Cadder 22 Sep 1999.

STONEHAVEN SOUTH (FUF 426; FES IX, 583; X, 338)

Linked 13 Sep 1990 with Kinneff.

1967 ROBERT HILL RICHMOND
(FES IX, 161; X, 96, 338), trans from Port Patrick to Stonehaven South 30 Nov 1967; ret 30 Sep 1984; died 13 Sep 1985.

1985 KENNETH LINDSAY PETRIE
ind to Stonehaven South 11 Apr 1985; became minister of linked charge with Kinneff 13 Sep 1990; trans to Aberdeen Craigiebuckler 30 Sep 1999.

TORPHINS (FES IX, 590; X, 342)

1971 GRAHAME RUSSELL WALKER
(FES X, 343, 353), trans from Macduff Doune to Torphins 18 Feb 1971; ret 28 Feb 1987; died 27 Nov 1999.

1987 PETER REYNOLDS TAYLOR
B 25 Sep 1936 at Aberdeen, s of William T. and Margaret Duffus Dalgarno; educ Aberdeen Grammar 1947–51; University of Aberdeen 1971–77 (BD); Northern Co-operative Society 1951–57; George Strathdee 1957–62; HM Forces 1962–71; lic by Presb of Aberdeen 21 May 1977; m 16 Aug 1958 Dorothy Anne Moonie b 23 Apr 1939 d of James Hutcheon M. and Violet Anne Douglas; Children: Peter John b 13 Jul 1959 m Mhairi Davidson; Michael Andrew b 23 Jun 1960; Dorothy-Anne b 30 Jul 1962 m Brian Scott; Nicholas Mark b 28 Mar 1971, died 2 May 1981; ord and ind to Culloden 21 Sep 1977; trans to Torphins 25 Sep 1987; app JP 1979.

WEST MEARNS (FES X, 319, 320)

New name adopted after union of Fettercairn, Fordoun and Glenbervie 17 Apr 1994 (congregations linked from 17 Jul 1980).

1949 EWEN MACLEAN
(FES IX, 494, 550; X, 319), trans from Anstruther Chalmers Memorial to Fettercairn 5 May 1949; became minister of linked charge with Fordoun with Glenbervie 17 Jul 1980; ret 31 Mar 1983; died 9 Jun 1993.

1970   GEORGE WILLIAM LOW PARKINSON
(FES IX, 313, 623; X, 218, 319), trans from
Drumchapel St Mark's to Fordoun with Glenbervie
25 Feb 1970; ret 31 Oct 1979; died 23 Nov 1982.

1983   KENNETH E W TYSON
trans from Corby St Ninian's to Fettercairn with
Fordoun with Glenbervie 11 Aug 1983; ret 31 Dec
1987; died 15 Jul 1996.

1988   DAVID JACK
B 22 Jan 1936 at Cowdenbeath, s of James Park
J. and Margaret Craig Kirk; educ Kirkcaldy High
1947–51; University of Glasgow 1985–88 (LTh);
Sub Postmaster 1958–63, 1973–85; Insurance
1963–73; lic by Presb of Kincardine and Deeside
8 Sep 1983; asst Banchory Ternan East with Durris
1983–84; m 6 Oct 1958 Helen Scott b 29 Dec 1936
d of William Wallace Geddes S. and Helen Jessie
MacCrae Christie; Children: Margaret Kirk b 9 Mar
1963 m Iain MacLeod; Helen MacCrae b 25 Sep
1965 m Douglas Whyte; Elizabeth Jean b 17 Apr
1969 m Scott Gardner; ord as Aux by Presb of
Kincardine and Deeside and assgnd to Banchory
Ternan East with Durris 8 Jul 1984; ind to
Fettercairn with Fordoun with Glenbervie (full-time
ministry) 4 Aug 1988; became minister of united
charge 17 Apr 1994; ret 1 Nov 1999.

PRESBYTERY OF GORDON

BARTHOL CHAPEL (FES VI, 186; VIII, 572; IX, 573; X, 333)

Linked 8 Oct 1958 with Tarves.

1963 ALASDAIR WILLIAM MACDONELL
(FES X, 202, 333), trans from Uddingston Burnhead to Barthol Chapel with Tarves 27 Jul 1963; trans to Haddington St Mary's 26 Sep 1979.

1980 WILLIAM M MURDOCH
ord and ind to Barthol Chapel with Tarves 29 May 1980; dem 31 Mar 1991 on app as Chaplain to University of Aberdeen.

1991 LESLIE McEWEN BARRETT
ord and ind to Barthol Chapel with Tarves 27 Jun 1991; introd as Interim minister at Airlie Ruthven and Kingoldrum with Glenisla with Kilry with Lintrathen 1 Mar 1999.

1999 ALAN THOMSON McKEAN
B 6 Sep 1950 at Glasgow, s of George M. and Margaret Davidson Thomson; educ Glasgow Academy 1955–67; Langside College 1968–70; University of Glasgow 1976–81 (BD); Butchery Manager 1972–74; Engineering 1974–75; Police 1975–76; lic by Presb of Glasgow, 1980; asst Loanhead 1981–82; m 7 Sep 1974 Kathleen Stephen b 11 Apr 1951 d of David S. and Jessie Anderson; ord and ind to Kirkmichael, Straloch and Glenshee 3 Sep 1982; trans to Fauldhouse St Andrew's 23 Mar 1994; trans to Barthol Chapel with Tarves 14 Oct 1999.

BELHELVIE (FES IX, 573; X, 333)

1953 DAVID STUART FORSYTH
(FES IX, 573 (2); X, 333), ord and ind to Belhelvie North 8 Sep 1948; became minister of united charge with South 15 Feb 1953; ret 31 Aug 1992; Publ: *The Minister's Gun* (*The Scots Magazine*, 1995).

1993 DOUGLAS WILLIAM CLARK
ord and ind to Bellhelvie 25 May 1993; trans to East Kilbride Old 16 Feb 1998.

1998 DANIEL HAWTHORN
B 8 Sep 1939 at Ballantrae, s of Gavin H. and Martha Louisa Henderson; educ Jordanhill College School, Glasgow 1952–58; University of Glasgow 1958–64 (MA, BD); lic by Presb of Glasgow 21 Apr 1964; asst Glasgow Cardonald 1964–66; m 28 Jun 1961 Carole Margaret Jensen b 12 Oct 1941 d of Carl Gustavson J. and Marjory Will; Children: Eric Gordon b 10 Jun 1963; Douglas Henderson b 5 Mar 1965; Carl Stewart b 23 Mar 1967; Kenneth Daniel b 2 Oct 1969; ord by Presb of Glasgow during assistantship at Cardonald 31 Aug 1965; Staff Secretary, Student Christian Movement 1966–68; Lecturer in Religious Education, Callendar Park College of Education, Falkirk 1968–73 and Aberdeen College of Education (now Northern College of Education) 1973–94; ind to Belhelvie 16 Sep 1998; Publ: Contributor to *Religious and Moral Education* (Scottish Consultative Council on Curriculum, 1994); main contributor to and editor of *5–14 Catalogue, Religious and Moral Education* (SCCC, 1994).

BLAIRDAFF (FES IX, 596; X, 344)

Linkage with Monymusk terminated 11 May 1982 in favour of linkage with Chapel of Garioch.

1972 WILLIAM ANGUS SMITH
(FES X, 344), ord and ind to Blairdaff with Monymusk 20 Jan 1972; dem 31 Jul 1978.

1979 IAN ADAIR MUIRHEAD
(FES IX, 334, 533; X, 198, 437), introd on term app to Blairdaff with Monymusk 10 May 1979; ret 13 May 1982; died 21 May 1983.

1982 JAMES PARKER SERVICE
(FES IX, 176; X, 102, 113), trans from Kilmarnock Shortlees to Chapel of Garioch 11 Aug 1976; became minister of linked charge with Blairdaff 11 May 1982; ret 31 Aug 1983; died 17 Jan 1989.

1984 ERIC GORDON MILTON
(FES X, 151, 351), res as Chaplain to Queen Victoria School, Dunblane and ind to Blairdaff with Chapel of Garioch 13 Apr 1984; ret 13 Apr 1994.

1994 LESLEY RISBY
ord and ind to Blairdaff with Chapel of Garioch 29 Nov 1994; trans to Aberdeen Denburn 28 Jul 1999.

CHAPEL OF GARIOCH (FES IX, 596; X, 344)

Linked 11 May 1982 with Blairdaff.

1971 GEORGE LESLIE PARKINSON
(FES X, 344, 401 (2)), trans from Kirkwall East to Chapel of Garioch 31 Mar 1971; dem 6 Nov 1973; died 2 Mar 1981.

1974 JOHN MUIR HADDOW
(FES IX, 534, 723; X, 213, 321, 344), trans from Bonhill Old with Alexandria Bridge Street to Chapel of Garioch 28 Aug 1974; died 26 Jan 1975.

1976 JAMES PARKER SERVICE
(FES IX, 176; X, 102, 113), trans from Kilmarnock Shortlees to Chapel of Garioch 11 Aug 1976; became minister of linked charge with Blairdaff 11 May 1982; ret 31 Aug 1983; died 17 Jan 1989.

1984 ERIC GORDON MILTON
(FES X, 151, 351), ind to Blairdaff with Chapel of Garioch 13 Apr 1984, see Blairdaff.

1994 LESLEY RISBY
ord and ind to Blairdaff with Chapel of Garioch 29 Nov 1994, see Blairdaff.

CLUNY (FES IX, 597; X, 344)

Linked 13 May 1982 with Monymusk.

1970 THOMAS EDWARD BROWN
(FES X, 344), trans by mutual eligibility from Liverpool Maghull St George's (Presb Church of England) to Cluny 5 Nov 1970; ret 7 Nov 1981; died 14 Sep 1997; m (2) 31 Mar 1990 Margaret Small Donaldson b 23 Mar 1915 d of Ebeneezer D. and Maggie Jane Craik Small.

1982 JOHN DONALD HENDERSON
(FES IX, 564; X, 88, 290, 328, 356), trans from Makerstoun with Smailholm with Stichill, Hume and Nenthorn to Cluny with Monymusk 18 Nov 1982; ret 5 Jan 1992; d Janis m Ian Anderson White Fulton.

1992 GEORGE EUAN DARGIE GLEN
B 5 Nov 1958 at Dundee, s of George Smith G. and Williamina Reid Francis; educ Kirkton High, Dundee 1970–76; Dundee College of Commerce 1976–77; Dundee College of Technology 1977–82 (BSc); University of Aberdeen 1987–90 (BD); Quantity Surveying 1982–87; lic by Presb of Dundee 26 Aug 1990; asst Aberdeen Rubislaw 1990–92; m 27 Jul 1990 Anne Hamilton Fawkes b 31 Jul 1967 d of George Miller Allan F. and Beatrice Betty Anne Forbes; Children: Andrew James George b 26 Mar 1994; ord and ind to Cluny with Monymusk 27 May 1992.

CULSALMOND AND RAYNE (FES X, 344, 346)

Linkage of Culsalmond and Rothienorman terminated 27 Aug 1985. Culsalmond linked same date with Daviot with Rayne. Culsalmond and Rayne united 3 Nov 1989. Linkage with Daviot continues.

1951 RODNEY MILLIGAN
(FES IX, 597; X, 344), ind to Culsalmond 29 Nov 1951; became minister of linked charge with Rothienorman 18 May 1958; ret 27 Aug 1985.

1973 JOHN WILFRED MOORE
(FES IX, 743; X, 244, 345), ind to Daviot 18 Apr 1963; became minister of linked charge with Rayne 25 Oct 1973, see Daviot.

1984 ALLAN DAVIDSON SCOTT
introd to Daviot with Rayne (term) 14 Jun 1984; became minister of linked charge with Culsalmond 27 Aug 1985, see Daviot.

1989 MARY MONICA CRANFIELD
B 8 Jun 1962 at Durham, d of Charles Ernest Burland C. and Ruth Elizabeth Gertrude Bole; educ Durham High 1973–80; University of Aberdeen 1980–84 (BD); University of St Andrews 1985 (DipPTh), 1985–87 (MA); lic by Presb of Aberdeen 30 Jun 1986; asst Glasgow Netherlee 1987–88; Bishopbriggs Cadder 1989; ord and ind to Culsalmond and Rayne with Daviot 28 Nov 1989.

DAVIOT (FES VI, 155; VIII, 564; IX, 598; X, 344)

Linked 25 Oct 1973 with Rayne. Further linked 27 Aug 1985 with Culsalmond. Culsalmond and Rayne united 3 Nov 1989. Linkage with Daviot continues.

1963 JOHN WILFRED MOORE
(FES IX, 743; X, 244, 345), trans from Kilmonivaig to Daviot 18 Apr 1963; became minister of linked charge with Rayne 25 Oct 1973; ret 30 Sep 1983; s Keith m Lise Patricia Howe.

1984 ALLAN DAVIDSON SCOTT
B 7 Jul 1924 at New Aberdour, s of Samuel S. and Christina Whyte; Gamekeeper 1938–42; Navigator, RAF 1942–46; Fisherman 1946–47; Police 1948–73; educ Inverurie Academy (further educ evening classes) 1967–72; University of Aberdeen 1973–77 (BD); lic by Presb of Gordon, Apr 1977; m 26 Mar 1952 Laura Beattie b 1 Jan 1928 d of William B. and Catherine Brockie; Children: Michael Laurence; Douglas Neil; ord and ind to Humbie with Yester 26 Oct 1977; became minister of linked charge with Bolton and Saltoun 17 Oct 1979; introd to Daviot with Rayne (term) 14 Jun 1984; became minister of linked charge with Culsalmond 27 Aug 1985; ret 1 Nov 1989.

1989 MARY MONICA CRANFIELD
ord and ind to Culsalmond and Rayne with Daviot 28 Nov 1989, see Culsalmond and Rayne.

DRUMBLADE (FES IX, 625; X, 357)

Linked 21 Sep 1975 with Huntly Strathbogie.

1975 GEORGE COMPTON STEWART
(FES IX, 458; X, 271, 359), trans from Cowdenbeath West to Huntly Strathbogie 20 Dec 1962; became minister of linked charge with Drumblade

21 Sep 1975; ret 28 Feb 1995; m (2) 18 Oct 1993 Jenny Fordyce Isaac b 14 May 1948 d of Alexander Riddoch I. and Helen Beattie Fordyce; s Fraser m Anna MacLean; d Heather m Colin Fettes; s Keith m Lorraine Mitchell; d Gail m Paul O' Brien.

1995 NEIL IAIN MACKAY MACGREGOR
B 4 May 1954 at Glasgow, s of Iain M. and Peggy MacKay; educ Woodside Senior Secondary, Glasgow; Glasgow School of Art and Mackintosh School of Architecture 1975–79 (CArch); University of Glasgow 1989–93 (BD); Architectural Asst 1972–88; Project Manager 1988–89; lic by Presb of Glasgow 1 Jul 1993; asst Bearsden New Kilpatrick 1993–94; m 18 Aug 1979 Linda Elizabeth Niven b 28 Mar 1959 d of William N. and Mary Carruthers; ord and ind to Drumblade with Huntly Strathbogie 30 Aug 1995.

ECHT (FES VI, 95; VIII, 574; IX, 576; X, 335)

Linked 31 Dec 1965 with Midmar.

1971 CHARLES HENRY STUART
(FES IX, 92, 583; X, 8, 333, 335, 338), trans from Edinburgh Duddingston to Echt with Midmar 2 Sep 1971; ret 31 Jul 1982; died 27 Jun 1995.

1983 GEORGE KLEMENS ROBSON
ord and ind to Echt with Midmar 12 May 1983; trans to Dundee Balgay 23 Sep 1987.

1988 JAMES STENHOUSE DICK
ord and ind to Echt with Midmar 17 May 1988; trans to Glasgow Ruchazie 1995.

1996 DAVID IAIN SOUTER
B 28 Dec 1945, University of St Andrews (BD); asst Perth St Leonard's-in-the-Fields and Trinity 1994–96; ord and ind to Echt with Midmar 27 Feb 1996.

ELLON (FES X, 335, 336)

Formed 1 Aug 1977 by union of Ellon and Slains and Logie Buchan.

1939 CHARLES McPHERSON
(FES IX, 578; X, 336), ord and ind to Logie Buchan 28 Sep 1939; died 21 Nov 1976.

1947 JOHN MURRAY
(FES IX, 582, 596, 711; X, 337), trans from Blairdaff to Slains and Forvie 3 Apr 1947; ret 30 Nov 1972.

1962 STANLEY JAMES RAFFAN
(FES IX, 601; X, 133, 335 (2), 346), trans from Greenock Martyrs' and North to Ellon 5 Dec 1962; became minister of united charge with Slains and Forvie 4 Mar 1973; dem 14 Jul 1977 on app as Chaplain to Crichton Royal Hospital, Dumfries.

1978 MATTHEW ANDERSON RODGER
B 19 Jun 1936 at Glasgow, s of Matthew R. and Jeannie Yorke; educ Queen's Park Senior Secondary 1948–54; University of Glasgow 1973–77 (BD); CA Apprenticeship 1954–58; Company Accountant and Director 1959–72; Secretary and General Manager Charitable Housing Assoc 1972–73; lic by Presb of Irvine and Kilmarnock 29 Jun 1977; m 1 Jun 1961 Mary Orr Scrivener b 23 Mar 1935, died 28 Sep 1998, d of Alan S. and Christina Harper; Children: Elaine Anderson b 4 Sep 1963 m Graham Douglas Ward; Alastair Alan b 5 Mar 1968 m Janet Waugh; Graeme Andrew b 7 Mar 1968; ord and ind to Ellon 19 Jan 1978; ret 3 Jan 1999.

1980 ANDREW ELLIOT LAMBIE
(FES X, 216, 406), trans from Lerwick and Bressay and introd as Assoc at Ellon 25 Sep 1980; ind to Carmichael with Covington and Thankerton with Pettinain 12 Jun 1985.

1985 MICHAEL JOHN ERSKINE
ord by Presb of Gordon and introd as Assoc at Ellon, 1985; ind to Inverkip 25 Nov 1987.

1988 ALISON JANE SIMPSON
ord by Presb of Gordon and introd as Assoc at Ellon 25 Sep 1988; trans to Maud with Savoch 20 Mar 1991.

1994 ELEANOR ELIZABETH MACALISTER
B 5 Feb 1952 at Kilmacolm, s of William Kilgour Smart Jamieson and Eleanor Wright; educ John Neilson Institute, Paisley; Jordanhill College, Glasgow 1970–73 (DCEd); University of Aberdeen 1989–93 (BD); Teaching 1973–79; lic by Presb of Gordon 27 Jun 1993; asst Ellon 1993–94; m 18 Apr 1974 Gary Macalister b 27 Feb 1952 s of John M. and Margaret Susan Murray; Children: Euan Gary b 10 Apr 1979; Rhona Susan b 7 Jan 1983; ord by Presb of Gordon and introd as Assoc at Ellon 10 May 1994; ind to same charge 27 Apr 1999.

FINTRAY AND KINELLAR (FES X, 335, 336)

Formed 7 Mar 1993 by union of Fintray and Kinellar. Linkage with Keithhall continues.

1958 GEORGE WILLIAM ANDERSON
(FES IX, 589, 663, 679; X, 336, 342), trans from Strachan to Kinellar and Blackburn 14 Mar 1958; ret 30 Jun 1969; died 20 Jun 1979.

1961 THOMAS CRAWFORD
(FES IX, 571, 623, 644; X, 335, 367), trans from Forres High to Fintray 7 Jun 1961; ret 31 Dec 1969; died 2 May 1978.

1970 ALASDAIR BOTHWELL GORDON
(FES X, 335), ord and ind to Fintray with Kinellar and Blackburn 17 Jun 1970; dem 31 Dec 1975 and app Clerk to Presb of Aberdeen 1 Jan 1976.

1976 JAMES KINCAID
(FES X, 277, 421), res from app with Overseas Council in S Africa and ind to Fintray with Keithhall with Kinellar 21 Dec 1976; dem 30 Sep 1982.

1983 ALBERT CAIE
ord and ind to Fintray with Keithhall with Kinellar 11 Aug 1983; trans to Glenmuick (Ballater) 20 Oct 1992.

1993 MARGARET JAY GARDEN
B 15 Jun 1943 at Aberdeen, d of William Smith G. and Christina Margaret Reekie; educ Mackie Academy, Stonehaven 1955–61; Edinburgh Royal Infirmary and Western General Hospital 1961–64 (Qualification in Radiography and Radiotherapy); Robert Gordon's Technical College 1972–74 (CQSW); University of Aberdeen 1982–86 (BD); Radiotherapy Radiographer 1964–72; Social Work 1974–82; lic by Presb of Kincardine and Deeside 29 Jun 1986; asst Dyce 1987–88; locum minister in Aberdeen and Aberdeenshire 1988–93; ord and ind to Fintray and Kinellar with Keithhall 23 Aug 1993.

FOVERAN (FES IX, 577; X, 336)

1972 ROBERT JAMES STUART WALLACE

(FES IX, 131; X, 77, 288, 336), trans from Carlisle to Foveran 22 Sep 1972; ret 30 Jan 1986.

1986 JOHN ALEXANDER COOK
B 8 Jun 1958 at Kirkcaldy, s of Roy James Alexander C. and Jean Andrew Callander; educ Kirkcaldy High 1970–76; University of Edinburgh 1976–80 (MA); University of Aberdeen 1982–85 (BD); Care Asst 1980–81; Teaching 1981–82; lic by Presb of Kirkcaldy 2 Jul 1985; asst Dundee Ogilvie and Stobswell 1985–86; m 7 Aug 1992 Alison Mary Mutch b 10 Jul 1958 d of William Watson M. and Isabella Christian Cantlay; Children: Isabella Jean b 23 Dec 1993; Roy William b 27 Jun 1995; ord and ind to Foveran 21 Jul 1986.

HOWE TRINITY (FES X, 339, 341, 343)

Alford with Tullynessle and Forbes linked 1 Feb 1977 with Keig. Congregations united 4 Jul 1999.

1966 JAMES SIDNEY ALLISON SMITH
(FES X, 224, 339, 404), trans from Stromness St Peter's Victoria Street to Alford with Tullynessle and Forbes 28 Sep 1966; became minister of linked charge with Keig 1 Feb 1977; trans to Drongan The Schaw Kirk 30 Apr 1980.

1967 JOHN BLACKBURN CLARKE
(FES X, 341, 383), trans from Clyne to Keig with Tough 5 Apr 1967; pastoral tie severed 31 Aug 1972; died 18 May 1992.

1974 JOHN McKENDRICK PATERSON
(FES IX, X, 242, 319, 321, 336, 341), trans from Inchbrayock to Keig with Tough 1 May 1974; ret 31 Aug 1976; died 9 Oct 1991.

1980 JOYCE P COLLIE
ind to Alford with Keig with Tullynessle and Forbes 17 Nov 1980; trans to Corgarff and Strathdon with Glenbuchat-Towie 19 Jun 1986.

1987 ALFRED BOWIE
(FES X, 156), trans from Glasgow Colston Wellpark to Alford with Keig with Tullynessle and Forbes 30 Sep 1987; ret 22 Jul 1998.

HUNTLY CAIRNIE GLASS (FES X, 357, 359)

Formed 6 Mar 1994 by union of Huntly and Cairnie-Glass. (Congregations linked from 13 Jan 1983).

1967 DAVID WHITE McCREADIE
(FES X, 167, 359), trans from Glasgow Netherton St Matthew's to Huntly 22 Jun 1967; trans to Callander St Kessog's 27 May 1982.

1970 ROBERT SMITH McLEISH
(FES X, 357), ord and ind to Cairnie-Glass 14 May 1970; trans to Duffus, Spynie and Hopeman 29 Feb 1980.

1980 DONALD ROBERTSON FRASER
(FES IX, 83, 505 (2); X, 262, 299, 367), trans from Balquhidder to Cairnie-Glass 19 Sep 1980; trans to Kinloss and Findhorn 20 Apr 1983.

1983 ALLAN S MACPHERSON
ind to Cairnie-Glass with Huntly 1 Sep 1983; dem 31 Aug 1993 on app as Chaplain to Merchiston Castle School, Edinburgh.

1994 THOMAS RANKINE CALDER
B 25 Sep 1958 at Edinburgh, s of James Moray C. and Aileen Mary Alexander Rankine; educ George Watson's, Edinburgh and Trinity College, Glenalmond 1969–76; University of Dundee 1976–79 (LLB); University of Edinburgh 1990–93 (BD); Writer to the Signet 1983–90; lic by Presb of Edinburgh 4 Jul 1993; asst Edinburgh Cluny; m 9 Oct 1987 Catriona Mary MacLean b 20 Aug 1959 d of Donald Watt M. and Sheila Scott Hume; Children: Hugh James Donald b 5 Jun 1989; Lachlan Thomas Michael b 18 Jul 1991; Marsaili Elspeth Siobhan b 2 May 1994; ord and ind to Huntly Cairnie-Glass 25 Aug 1994.

HUNTLY STRATHBOGIE (FUF 455; FES IX, 627; X, 359)

Linked 21 Sep 1975 with Drumblade.

1962 GEORGE COMPTON STEWART
(FES IX, 458; X, 271, 359), ind to Huntly Strathbogie 20 Dec 1962; became minister of linked charge with Drumblade 21 Sep 1975, see Drumblade.

1995 NEIL IAIN MACKAY MACGREGOR
ord and ind to Drumblade with Huntly Strathbogie 30 Aug 1995, see Drumblade.

INSCH-LESLIE-PREMNAY-OYNE (FES X, 345, 346)

Formed 30 Nov 1983 by union of Insch, Leslie-Premnay and Oyne.

1960 PATRICK HUGH ROBSON MACKAY
(FES IX, 55 (2); X, 32, 346), trans from Torphichen to Leslie and Waulkmill with Premnay 30 Mar 1960; ret 30 Sep 1972; died 11 Jan 1994.

1964 ERIC McCABE RULE
(FES IX, 89, 763; X, 346, 425), res from app with Overseas Council at Demerara Georgetown St Andrew's, British Guiana and ind to Oyne and Rayne 19 Nov 1964; became minister of linked charge with Leslie-Premnay 23 Oct 1973; ret 1 Aug 1975; died 22 Mar 1983.

1967 RODERICK MACDONALD
(FES IX, 699; X, 345, 398), trans from Stornoway St Columba's and ind to Insch 21 Dec 1967; ret 30 Nov 1983; died 10 Jun 1998; Addl publ: *Leth-Cheud Bliadhna* (Gairm, 1978); *Laoidhean Molaidh* (Cruisgean, 1983).

1976 JOHN LOGIE
(FES IX, 738; X, 328, 421), trans from Aberdeen Middlefield to Leslie-Premnay with Oyne 1 Jun 1976; ret 30 Sep 1983; died 2 Apr 1986.

1984 ROBERT SMITH McLEISH
(FES X, 357), trans from Duffus, Spynie and Hopeman to Insch-Leslie-Premnay-Oyne 31 May 1984; Children: Kirsteen Mary b 5 Sep 1973; Mungo James b 5 Oct 1975.

INVERURIE ST ANDREW'S (FES VI, 160; VIII, 566; IX, 598; X, 345)

1967 JAMES MELDRUM DAVIDSON
(FES IX, 476, 533; X, 199, 282, 345), trans from Motherwell Dalziel High to St Andrew's 23 Aug 1967; ret 31 Dec 1988.

1989 IAIN JAMES McINTOSH TELFER
B 4 Jan 1953 at Aberfeldy, s of John McIntosh and Joan Alice T.; educ Grove Academy, Broughty Ferry 1965–71; University of Edinburgh 1971–75 (BD); University of Aberdeen 1975–77 (DPS); lic by Presb of Dundee, Jun 1977; asst Elgin St Giles' 1977–79; m 25 Jun 1983 Hazel Margaret Tullo b 22 May 1950; Children: Colin William b 11 May 1984; Alison Joan b 1 May 1987; Kirsty Elizabeth Janet b 29 Apr 1990; ord by Presb of Moray during assistantship at Elgin St Giles' 17 Feb 1978; ind to Bearsden Westerton Fairlie Memorial 20 Jun 1979; became minister of linked charge with Dalmuir Overtoun 9 Sep 1984; trans to St Andrew's 3 Jul 1989.

1990 DUGALD JAMES RADCLIFFE CAMERON
ord by Presb of Gordon and introd as Assoc at St Andrew's 23 Aug 1990; ind to Edinburgh St Martin's 19 Aug 1992.

1993 LINDA J WILLIAMS
ord by Presb of Gordon and introd as Assoc at St Andrew's 29 Aug 1993; res 29 Feb 1996.

INVERURIE WEST (FUF 434; FES IX, 598; X, 345)

1959 COLIN CAMPBELL REITH MACPHERSON
(FES X, 274, 345), ord by Presb of Ayr during assistantship at The Auld Kirk 18 Jul 1958; ind to Inverurie West 3 Jun 1959; trans to Dunfermline St Margaret's 3 Feb 1966.

1966 JOHN LEONARD SCOTT
(FES X, 38, 345), trans from Falkirk Graham's Road to Inverurie West 1 Sep 1966; ret 14 Sep 1989; d Isobel m Chris Humble; d Mary m Andrew Parkinson.

1989 IAN BULLOCH GROVES
B 17 Jul 1951 at Fyvie, s of George Walker Faulds G. and Mary Cook Bulloch; educ Aberdeen Grammar 1963–68; University of Aberdeen 1983–88 (BD, CPS); Hotel Management and Admin 1970–73; Tourist Promotion 1973–81; Warden of Residential Centre 1981–83; lic by Presb of Moray 26 Jun 1988; asst Ayr Castlehill 1988–89; m 26 Aug 1972 Anne Jeanette Tarburn b 26 Feb 1950 d of Gavin McLean T. and Jeannie Milne; Children: Paul; David; ord and ind to Inverurie West 28 Nov 1989.

KEITHHALL (FES VI, 162; VIII, 566, 567; IX, 599; X, 345)

Keithhall-Kinkell linked 1 Jul 1976 with Fintray with Kinellar-Blackburn as Fintray with Keithhall with Kinellar. Linkage continues following union of Fintray and Kinellar 7 Mar 1993.

1976 JAMES KINCAID
(FES X, 277, 421), ind to Fintray with Keithhall with Kinellar 21 Dec 1976, see Fintray and Kinellar.

1983 ALBERT CAIE
ord and ind to Fintray with Keithhall with Kinellar 11 Aug 1983; trans to Glenmuick (Ballater) 20 Oct 1992.

1993 MARGARET JAY GARDEN
ord and ind to Fintray and Kinellar with Keithhall 23 Aug 1993, see Fintray and Kinellar.

KEMNAY (FES IX, 599; X, 345)

1973 JOHN MILLAR SHIELDS
(FES X, 345), ord by Presb of Aberdeen 30 Jan 1972 and app Senior Asst at West Church of St Nicholas; ind to Kemnay 30 Mar 1973; dem 2 Sep 1976 to take up app with RAChD.

1977   IAN MACKENZIE FORBES
(FES IX, 243; X, 142, 184, 200), trans from Motherwell South Dalziel to Kemnay 12 Jan 1977; ret 18 May 1990; died 27 Jun 1994.

1990   JOHN PATON RENTON
B 10 Jan 1946 at Glasgow, s of John Paton and Helen R; educ Kingsridge Secondary 1957–61; University of Aberdeen 1972–75 (LTh); Open University 1994 (BA); lic by Presb of Dumbarton 29 Jun 1975; asst Aberdeen St Nicholas South of Kincorth 1976–77; m Morag McCurrach b 10 May 1953 d of James Harris M. and Florence Evelyn Finlayson; Children: David Paton b 10 May 1979; Gillian Hay b 22 Jul 1982; ord and ind to Paisley Greenlaw 24 Jun 1976; trans to Kemnay 18 Oct 1990.

KINTORE (FUF 436; FES VI, 168; VIII, 568; IX, 599; X, 345)

1973   ERIC VALLANCE HUDSON
(FES X, 346), ind to Kintore 18 May 1973; dem 12 Mar 1978 on app as Religious Programmes Officer for Scottish Television.

1978   GERALD BRIAN MACALLAN
(FES IX, 467; X, 276, 327, 331), trans from Aberdeen Langstane Kirk to Kintore 26 Sep 1978; ret 10 Mar 1992; s David m Kevon Arthur; d Margaret m Gilbert Milan; s Paul m Fiona Douglas.

1992   ALAN GREIG
B 19 Nov 1951 at Helensburgh, s of Robert Alexander G. and Mary Bryson McCulloch; educ Coatbridge High 1963–69; University of Strathclyde 1969–73 (BSc); University of Edinburgh 1973–76 (BD); lic by Presb of Dumbarton 27 Jun 1976; asst Aberdeen Northfield 1976–77; m 16 Jul 1976 Ruth Dykes Evans d of John Douglas E. and Winifred Mounsey; Children: Colin Alan b 16 Jun 1978; Ross David b 1 May 1981; ord and ind to Hurlford Reid Memorial 28 Jul 1977; dem on app by Board of World Mission and Unity for service in Zambia 21 Sep 1983; ind to Kintore 16 Jul 1992.

LEOCHEL CUSHNIE AND LYNTURK (FES IX, 594; X, 342)

Linked 1 Feb 1977 with Tough.

1974   HENRY McFARLANE SMITH
(FES IX, 324; X, 145, 191, 342), trans from Kilsyth Old to Leochel Cushnie and Lynturk 26 Feb 1974; became minister of linked charge with Tough 1 Feb 1977; died 21 Feb 1983.

1983   JAMES BENJAMIN RENNIE
(FES X, 244, 258), trans from Blackford to Leochel Cushnie and Lynturk with Tough 1 Dec 1983; ret 30 Apr 1992; w Margaret died 15 Jul 1999; s Brian m (2) Jacqueline Mary Semple.

1992   GEORGE ALAN SIMPSON STIRLING
(FES X, 372, 426), [correction: ord 14 Sep 1960, not 1961 as in Vol X, 372]; trans from Inverness Hilton to Leochel Cushnie and Lynturk with Tough 6 Nov 1992; ret 11 Oct 1999; d Shona m Brian Fraser; d Julie m Elie Diab.

MELDRUM AND BOURTIE (FES IX, 600; X, 346)

1958   ROBERT WYLLIE URQUHART
(FES IX, 149, 583; X, 338, 346), trans from Stonehaven South to Meldrum and Bourtie 24 Sep 1958; ret 1 Dec 1980; died 8 Apr 1984.

1981   ROBERT I JOHNSTONE
ord and ind to Meldrum and Bourtrie 1 Jun 1981; trans to Kilmarnock St John's Onthank 19 Oct 1987.

1988   ALEXANDER GRAINGER STODDART
(FES X, 85), trans from Peterculter St Peter's to Meldrum and Bourtie 8 Jun 1988; s Mark m Anne Brash; s Iain m Valerie Bruce.

METHLICK (FES IX, 579; X, 336)

1959   EBENEZER CRAIGIE PURVIS HOOD
(FES IX, 573; X, 333, 336), trans from Banchory-Devenick to Methlick 19 Aug 1959; ret 1 Jun 1989; Clerk to Synod of Grampian 1986–92.

1990   ANGUS HALLEY HADDOW
(FES X, 295, 333), trans from Garthdee to Methlick 22 Oct 1990; ret 28 Feb 1999; d Alison m James Barbour; d Jill m Paul Skinner; Publ: Co-author of *The Paranormal in Holy Scripture* (Churches' Fellowship for Psychical and Spiritual Studies, 1988); *The History of Methlick Parish Church* (private, 1995); *Psychical Studies and the Bible* (Churches' Fellowship for Psychical and Spiritual Studies, 1997).

1999   ALBERT EDWARD SMITH
B 21 Feb 1941 at Paisley, s of William S. and Mary Cherry; educ Paisley West Secondary 1952–56; Langside College, Glasgow 1975–76; University of Glasgow 1978–82 (BD); Salvation Army Officer 1960–73; Residential Social Work 1973–78; lic by Presb of Greenock, Jun 1982; asst West Kilbride St Andrew's 1982–83; m 5 Oct 1963 Janet Rose Farmer b 30 Aug 1938 d of William James F. and Edna Mae Bloodworth; Children: Yvonne b 7 Sep 1964; Valerie Ann b 1 Nov 1965; Julie b 29 Nov 1967; ord and ind to Johnstone High 2 Jun 1983; trans to Dunkeld 14 Nov 1990; trans to Methlick 19 Oct 1999.

MIDMAR (FES IX, 580; X, 336)

Linked 31 Dec 1965 with Echt.

1952   WILLIAM BUCHANAN
(FES V, 409; VIII, 257, 504; IX, 335, 573, 580; X, 336), trans from Belhelvie South to Midmar 8 Feb 1952; ret 31 Dec 1965; died 6 Oct 1978.

1965 SYDNEY EDWIN PEEBLES BEVERIDGE
(FES X, 287, 335), ind to Echt 6 Jul 1964; became minister of linked charge with Midmar 31 Dec 1965; trans to Scoonie (Leven) 11 Feb 1971.

1971 CHARLES HENRY STUART
(FES IX, 92, 583; X, 8, 333, 335, 338), trans from Edinburgh Duddingston to Echt with Midmar 2 Sep 1971; ret 31 Jul 1982; died 27 Jun 1995.

1983 GEORGE KLEMENS ROBSON
ord and ind to Echt with Midmar 12 May 1983; trans to Dundee Balgay 23 Sep 1987.

1988 JAMES STENHOUSE DICK
ord and ind to Echt with Midmar 17 May 1988; trans to Glasgow Ruchazie 1995.

1996 DAVID IAIN SOUTER
ord and ind to Echt with Midmar 27 Feb 1996.

MONYMUSK (FES VI, 175; VIII, 569; IX, 601; X, 346)

Linkage with Blairdaff terminated 11 May 1982. Linked 13 May 1982 with Cluny.

1972 WILLIAM ANGUS SMITH
(FES X, 344), ord and ind to Blairdaff with Mony-musk 20 Jan 1972; dem 31 Jul 1978.

1979 IAN ADAIR MUIRHEAD
(FES IX, 334, 533; X, 198, 437), introd on term app to Blairdaff with Monymusk 10 May 1979; ret 13 May 1982; died 21 May 1983.

1982 JOHN DONALD HENDERSON
(FES IX, 564; X, 88, 290, 328, 356), ind to Cluny with Monymusk 18 Nov 1982, see Cluny.

1992 GEORGE EUAN DARGIE GLEN
ord and ind to Cluny with Monymusk 27 May 1992, see Cluny.

NEW MACHAR (FES IX, 580; X, 336)

1968 WILLIAM ALBERT CLAYDON
(FES X, 337), ord and ind to New Machar 25 Sep 1968; ret 31 Oct 1987; died 21 May 1990.

1988 IAN DRYDEN
B 4 Nov 1935 at Dundee, s of John D. and Georgina Phillip; educ Morgan Academy, Dundee 1947–53; University of St Andrews 1953–56 (MA), 1985–87 (non-grad Divinity Studies); Dundee Teacher Training College 1956–57 (DEd); Teaching 1957–85; lic by Presb of Dundee 28 Jun 1987; m 5 Jul 1960 Isobel Anderson b 7 Feb 1938 d of Thomas A. and Elizabeth McGavin; Children: Michael b 1 Jul 1961 m Leslie Bell; Shirley b 31 Jul 1963; Shona b 14 Feb 1967 m Michael Webster; ord and ind to New Machar 23 Jun 1988.

NOTH (FES X, 357, 359)

Formed 28 Mar 1985 by union of Clatt with Rhynie and Gartly with Kennethmont.

1956 THOMAS MAXWELL McAUSLANE
(FES IX, 320, 458, 563, 625; X, 356, 359), trans form Cabrach to Gartly with Kennethmont 16 Apr 1956; ret 30 Jun 1972; died 28 Jan 1992.

1967 JOHN HONEYMAN
(FES X, 357, 405, 407), trans from Sandwick and Cunningsburgh with Quarff to Clatt with Rhynie 18 May 1967; ret 3 Sep 1974; died 25 Feb 1991.

1973 ROBERT LIDDEL
(FES IX, 789; X, 359, 446), [correction: res from RAChD 22 Jan 1967, not 31 Dec 1970; app by Overseas Council to Cyprus 29 Mar 1967, not Bahamas 1 Jan 1971; and thereafter to Grand Bahama, not Amsterdam as in Vol X, 446]; Interim minister in Amsterdam 1971–72; ind to Gartly with Kennethmont 10 May 1973; ret 22 Jan 1985; died 19 Oct 1991.

1975 ANDREW CORMACK CHRISTIE
(FES X, 357), ord and ind to Clatt with Rhynie 8 May 1975; introd on term app to Aberdeen Ferryhill North 18 Oct 1984.

1985 KEITH BURTON
ord and ind to Noth 29 Aug 1985; dem 22 Aug 1988.

1989 JOHN McCALLUM
B 29 Jun 1954 at Kilbirnie, s of Alexander M. and Margaret Howard Marshall; educ Dalry High and Garnock Academy 1966–72; Royal Scottish Academy of Music and Drama 1975–76; University of St Andrews 1983–87 (BD), 1987–88 (DPTh); Clerk and Trainee Manager 1972–75; Sales Rep and Manager 1976–83; lic by Presb of Ardrossan, 1988; asst Dundee Roseangle Ryehill 1988–89; m 20 Jun 1987 Ann McCormack b 12 Jul 1962, adoptive parents George M. and Sarah Jane McEvoy; Children: Ross Matthew b 27 Aug 1988; Struan Alexander b 2 Jan 1991; divorced 16 Apr 1996; ord and ind to Noth 1 Jun 1989.

SKENE (FES IX, 582; X, 337)

1972 IAIN URQUHART THOMSON
(FES X, 337), ord by Presb of Ayr during assistantship at Castlehill 10 Nov 1970; ind to Skene 23 Mar 1972; app Clerk (part-time) to Presb of Gordon 1 Jan 1988; Addl children: Elizabeth Stewart b 18 Sep 1978; Andrew Freeland b 11 Jan 1981; Fiona Urquhart b 25 Nov 1983.

1981 JAMES GLADSTONE MACDONALD PURVES
ord by Presb of Gordon and app Asst at Skene 8 Mar 1981; ind to Glenrothes St Ninian's 28 Jan 1982.

1988　GORDON KIRKWOOD
ord by Presb of Glasgow during assistantship at Greenbank 3 Dec 1987; introd as Assoc at Skene 12 Apr 1988; ind to Paisley Castlehead 27 Mar 1990.

TARVES (FES VI, 203; VIII, 576; IX, 583; X, 338)
Linked 8 Oct 1958 with Barthol Chapel.

1963　ALASDAIR WILLIAM MACDONELL
(FES X, 202, 333), trans to Barthol Chapel with Tarves 27 Jul 1963, see Barthol Chapel.

1980　WILLIAM M MURDOCH
ord and ind to Barthol Chapel with Tarves 29 May 1980; dem 31 Mar 1991 on app as Chaplain to University of Aberdeen.

1991　LESLIE McEWEN BARRETT
ord and ind to Barthol Chapel with Tarves 27 Jun 1991, see Barthol Chapel.

1999　ALAN THOMSON McKEAN
ind to Barthol Chapel with Tarves 14 Oct 1999, see Barthol Chapel.

TOUGH (FES VI, 140; VIII, 560; IX, 594; X, 343)
Linkage with Keig terminated 1 Feb 1977. Linked same date with Leochel Cushnie and Lynturk.

1967　JOHN BLACKBURN CLARKE
(FES X, 341, 383), trans from Clyne to Keig with Tough 5 Apr 1967; pastoral tie severed 31 Aug 1972; died 18 May 1992.

1974　JOHN McKENDRICK PATERSON
(FES IX, X, 242, 319, 321, 336, 341), trans from Inchbrayock to Keig with Tough 1 May 1974; ret 31 Aug 1976; died 9 Oct 1991.

1977　HENRY McFARLANE SMITH
(FES IX, 324; X, 145, 191, 342), trans from Kilsyth Old to Leochel Cushnie and Lynturk 26 Feb 1974; became minister of linked charge with Tough 1 Feb 1977; died 21 Feb 1983.

1983　JAMES BENJAMIN RENNIE
(FES X, 244, 258), trans from Blackford to Leochel Cushnie and Lynturk with Tough 1 Dec 1983, see Leochel Cushnie.

1992　GEORGE ALAN SIMPSON STIRLING
(FES X, 372, 426), trans from Inverness Hilton to Leochel Cushnie and Lynturk with Tough 6 Nov 1992.

UDNY AND PITMEDDEN (FES IX, 584; X, 338)
1964　KENNETH NORMAN MACRAE
(FES IX, 58, 711; X, 338, 405, 406), trans from Lerwick and Bressay to Udny and Pitmeddan 19 Mar 1964; ret 31 Aug 1977; died 6 Nov 1983.

1978　CHESTER D ARMISTEAD
ord and ind to Udny and Pitmedden 18 May 1978; dem 31 Jan 1985.

1985　GEORGE RITCHIE ROBERTSON
B 4 Oct 1939 at Port Seton, s of Hugh Cameron R. and Jean Jarron Ritchie; educ Preston Lodge High, Prestonpans 1944–54; University of Edinburgh 1981–84 (LTh); Radio and Television Engineer 1955–81; lic by Presb of Lothian 1 Apr 1984; asst Musselburgh St Ninian's 1984–85; m 30 Sep 1961 Margaret Cleghorn Flanders b 17 Feb 1937 d of Thomas F. and Agnes Redpath; Children: Stuart George b 29 Jul 1962; Andrew Hugh b 23 Feb 1967; ord and ind to Udny and Pitmedden 4 Jul 1985.

UPPER DONSIDE (FES X, 340, 341)
Formed 22 Mar 1996 by union of Auchindoir Kildrummy, Corgarff Strathdon and Glenbuchat-Towie.

1942　ALEXANDER MACLAGGAN SMEATON
(FES IX, 591, 711; X, 339), trans from Burra Isle to Auchindoir 25 Nov 1942; became minister of linked charge with Kildrummy 18 Nov 1956; ret 31 Oct 1963; died 16 May 1980.

1964　DAVID REID
(FES X, 339, 448), ind to Auchindoir and Kildrummy 29 Jul 1964; dem 11 Apr 1967 on app by RAChD.

1967　JAMES McLAREN RITCHIE
(FES IX, 747; X, 16, 339, 424), res from service with Overseas Council in Kenya and ind to Auchindoir and Kildrummy 26 Sep 1967; introd to term app at Edinburgh McDonald Road 21 Oct 1970.

1969　HADDEN MONTGOMERY GILMOUR
(FES IX, 417, 470; X, 247, 341), trans from Logie-rait to Glenbuchat-Towie 28 Feb 1969; ret 19 Apr 1976; died 14 Mar 1998.

1971　WILLIAM MURRAY GALBRAITH EDGAR
(FES IX, 388, 501, 630, 671; X, 335, 339, 370, 384), trans from Ardersier with Petty to Auchindoir and Kildrummy 22 Apr 1971; ret 13 Dec 1975.

1973　WILLIAM WALLACE
(FES IX, 589; X, 115, 340, 342), trans from Brodick to Corgarff and Strathdon 28 Nov 1973; ret 31 Mar 1977; died 17 Aug 1989.

1977　WILLIAM ANDERSON BRYDEN
ord and ind to Corgarff-Strathdon with Glenbuchat-Towie 21 Sep 1977; trans to Glasgow Yoker Old with St Matthew's 1 Jun 1981.

1977　COLIN DOUGLAS WALKER
B 11 Nov 1915 at London, s of Robert Russell and Charlotte Elizabeth W; educ UCS Frognal, London 1928–32; University of Aberdeen 1974–76; Tea

Taster 1932–70; lic by Presb of Gordon, 1976; m 18 Apr 1947 Betty Simpson b 11 Dec 1923; ord and ind to Auchindoir and Kildrummy 1 Jul 1977; ret 30 Jun 1982.

1981 RONALD MICHAEL LEEMAN CHILTON
(FES X, 390), trans from Hamilton Burnbank to Corgarff and Strathdon with Glenbuchat-Towie 15 Dec 1981; dem 31 Mar 1986; 'Grey Cells Books' (self-employed) 1 May 1988; Open University 1995 (Dip Eur Hum); Open University 1992–96 (BA); University of Hull 1996–98 (MA); Addl children: Thomas Martin James b 10 Jan 1980; Colin Michael b 1 Oct 1981; d Fiona m Andrew Rawlinson; w Jennifer died 2 Jul 1991; m (2) 26 Mar 1994 Marion Smith b 13 Apr 1941 d of John William and Betty S; Publ: Contributor to *Reformed Book of Common Order* (National Church Assoc, 1977); *The Life and Ministry of Geert Groote of Deventer 1340–1384* (forthcoming).

1983 ERIC RALPH LACEY
(FES X, 209 (2)), dem from Forth St Paul's 30 Sep 1975 to enter teaching profession (RE); ind to Auchindoir and Kildrummy 24 Feb 1983; trans to Creich with Rosehall 23 Oct 1986.

1986 JOYCE P COLLIE
trans from Alford with Keig with Tullynessle and Forbes to Corgarff and Strathdon with Glenbuchat-Towie 19 Jun 1986; ret 31 Aug 1994.

1989 AGNES ALEXANDER REID
B 12 May 1929 at Dalry, d of David McKenzie and Christina R; educ Dalry High 1934–46; Victoria Infirmary, Glasgow 1954 (RGN); Simpson Memorial Maternity Pavilion, Edinburgh 1955 (SCM); Post-Registration Ophthalmic Training, Moorfields Eye Hospital, London 1957 (OND); Ophthalmic Nursing 1957–71; Divisional Nursing Officer, Glasgow Western Infirmary 1971–84; lic by Presb of Paisley 27 Jun 1985; ord by Presb of Lanark and introd as Assoc at Douglas Water and Rigside 30 Oct 1985; ind to Auchindoir and Kildrummy 18 Apr 1989; ret 31 Aug 1994.

1996 JOHN CHRISTOPHER LEDGARD
B 3 Jun 1941 at Huddersfield, s of Alan Evans L. and Nora Bennett; educ Scarborough High 1952–59; Wesley College, Headingley 1963–67 (CTh); Open University 1973–76 (BA); Banking 1959–62; Horticulture 1962–63; lic by Presb of Melrose and Peebles 30 Jun 1992; asst Lerwick and North Isles, Shetland (Methodist Church) 1967–69; m (2) 12 Jan 1991 Elizabeth Esplin Wilkie b 28 Jul 1941 d of John W. and Lilian Cooke; Children from previous marriage; Ian Mark b 19 Aug 1966; Paul Jonathan b 13 Feb 1968; David Magnus b 28 Jul 1970; ord by Methodist Church during assistant-ship at Lerwick and North Isles, Shetland 7 Jul 1969; Church of Scotland and Free Churches Chaplain to RAF 1970–86; Methodist minister, Whitby 1986–89; app Secretary of Bield Housing Trust, Edinburgh 29 Jan 1990; app Hon Asst at St Giles' Cathedral, Edinburgh 2 Jun 1991; ind to Boyndie with Ordiquhill and Cornhill 6 Nov 1992; trans to Upper Donside 22 Mar 1996; ret on grounds of ill-health 30 Nov 1998; Publ: *History of Sherburn Methodist Circuit* (private, 1968); series of articles on History of origins of Chaplaincy within the RAF (RAF, 1985–87).

1999 RICHARD JOHN GILMOUR DARROCH
B 17 Jun 1955 at Irvine, s of Richard McCloy D. and Margaret Hopkirk Gilmour; educ Ardrossan Academy 1967–73; Ayr College 1975–76; Open University 1987–88; University of Glasgow 1988–91 (BD, MTh), 1991–94 (MTh); Postman 1973, 1974–75; Newspaper Reporter 1975–76; Shop Asst 1977–78; Mineral Sampler 1979–88; Driving Instructor 1986–88; lic by Presb of Ardrossan 9 Sep 1992; m 29 Dec 1982 Margaret Crawford Orr b 31 Mar 1935 d of Crawford O. and Margaret Cochran Bain; ord and ind to Motherwell Manse Road 21 Sep 1993; trans to Upper Donside 2 Jul 1999; Publ: Various articles for *Vision*, Bulletin of Glasgow Theological Forum; editor 1993–94.

PRESBYTERY OF BUCHAN

ABERDOUR (FUF 442; FES VI, 209; VIII, 578; IX, 603; X, 347)

Linkage with Tyrie terminated 19 Jul 1995. Linked 20 Jul 1995 with New Pitsligo.

1954 WILLIAM MENZIES HANNAH
(FES IX, 101, 603, 610, 647; X, 347), trans from Peterhead West Associate to Aberdour 25 Jun 1954; ret 31 Oct 1969; died 22 Oct 1987.

1970 GAVIN McCALLUM
(FES X, 347), ord and ind to Aberdour with Tyrie 25 Jun 1970; dem 31 Jul 1974.

1975 GEOFFREY LEE
(FES X, 347), ord and ind to Aberdour with Tyrie 26 Jun 1975; trans to Dumbarton Knoxland 27 Feb 1980.

1982 CHARLES JOHN BIRNIE
(FES X, 98), trans from Annbank to Aberdour with Tyrie 6 May 1982; ret 19 Jul 1995; d Jeananne m Wells; s Norman m Elizabeth Smith; s Robin m Karen Morrison; Publ: Editor of *Makars' Quhair* (private, 1968); *A Dizzen Sangs* (private, 1996); various articles and poems.

1995 ROBERT WILLIAM MASSIE
ord and ind to New Pitsligo 25 Aug 1989; became minister of linked charge with Aberdour 20 Jul 1995; trans to Monifieth St Rule's 20 Oct 1999.

AUCHABER UNITED (FES X, 352, 354)

Formed 12 May 1992 by union of Forgue Inverkeithny and Ythanwells Auchaber (linked 1 Jan 1982). Linked 20 Sep 1993 with Auchterless as Auchaber United with Auchterless.

1962 DAVID BEEDIE
(FES X, 352), ord and ind to Forgue Inverkeithny 29 Aug 1962; dem 31 Aug 1981.

1962 IAN CAMERON SCOULAR THOMSON
(FES IX, 681; X, 354, 387), trans from Latheron Old to Ythanwells Auchaber 18 Jan 1962; ret 1 Jan 1982; died 19 Aug 1983.

1982 FRANK C COLLIER
ind to Forgue Inverkeithny with Ythanwells Auchaber 25 Mar 1982; dem 30 Nov 1990.

1994 IRENE ANNE CHARLTON
ord and ind to Auchaber United with Auchterless 23 Feb 1994; trans to Whalsay and Skerries 17 Aug 1997.

1999 ALISON JAFFREY
B 18 Apr 1963 at Paisley, d of Alasdair Gunn and Anna Roxburgh McInnes; educ Victoria Drive, Glasgow and John Southland's, New Romney, Kent 1975–81; Central College of Commerce, Glasgow 1981–82; University of Glasgow 1982–86 (MA), 1986–89 (BD); lic by Presb of Glasgow 3 Jul 1989; asst Kirkwall St Magnus Cathedral 1989; Barrhead South and Levern 1990; m 4 Aug 1989 Andrew Jaffrey b 9 Nov 1964 s of Donald J. and Catherine Ferguson; Children: Duncan Gunnar b 4 Mar 1999; ord and ind to Forth St Paul's 27 Sep 1990; ret on grounds of ill-health 25 Oct 1995; introd to Auchaber United with Auchterless (shared ministry, 50%) 27 Sep 1999.

1999 MARGARET MURIEL McKAY
B 9 Oct 1938 at Cardiff, d of Eric Millard Fillmore and Florence Mary Tear; educ North London Collegiate School and County Grammar School, Sale 1949–56; University of Edinburgh 1958–62 (MA); University of Cambridge (Westminster College) 1987–91 (BD London); University of London 1991–93 (MTh); Teaching 1962–66; Admin Officer 1972–76; Violincello Teacher 1980–87; m 28 Dec 1962 William Robert McKay b 18 Apr 1939 s of William Wallace M. and Margaret Halley Adamson Foster; Children: Catriona b 4 Mar 1967 m Benedict James Curtis; Elspeth b 4 Mar 1967; ord by URC (Cambridge District) and ind to Abbey Lane, Saffron Walden and Stansted Group, Essex 21 Jun 1991; ind to Auchaber United with Auchterless (shared ministry, 50%) 27 Sep 1999; Publ: Editor of *Rev Dr John Walker's Report on the Hebrides 1764 and 1771* (John Donald, 1980).

AUCHTERLESS (FES VI, 248; VIII, 588; IX, 613; X, 352)

Linked 27 Aug 1985 with Rothienorman. Arrangement terminated 20 Sep 1993 to allow for linkage with Auchaber United.

1957 ALEXANDER TAYLOR MACKENZIE
(FES IX, 92, 764; X, 352), res from app at St Andrew's Scots Church, Colombo, Ceylon and ind to Auchterless 11 Apr 1957; ret 30 Sep 1963; died 18 Jan 1999.

1964 ROBERT ARBUCKLE BARR
(FES IX, 233, 636; X, 352, 363 (2)), ind to Auchterless 9 Apr 1964; died 6 Oct 1972.

1973 JOHN WILLIAM ARTHUR FORBES
(FES X, 352), ord and ind to Auchterless 6 Apr 1973; dem on app to Scottish Churches Action for World Development Jun 1979.

1979 GEORGE ROBERTSON FIDDES
ord and ind to Auchterless 2 Aug 1979; trans to Prestwick St Nicholas' 19 Jun 1985.

1986 HAMISH GAULT SMITH
(FES X, 186, 407), trans from Burra Isle with Tingwall to Auchterless with Rothienorman 17 Apr 1986; ret on grounds of ill-health, Dec 1992.

1994 IRENE ANNE CHARLTON
ord and ind to Auchaber United with Auchterless 23 Feb 1994; trans to Whalsay and Skerries 17 Aug 1997.

1999 ALISON JAFFREY
introd to Auchaber United with Auchterless (part-time) 27 Sep 1999, see Auchaber.

1999 MARGARET MURIEL McKAY
ind to Auchaber United with Auchterless (50%) 27 Sep 1999, see Auchaber.

BANFF (FES X, 355)

Formed 14 Sep 1994 by union of Banff St Mary's and Banff Trinity and Alvah. Linkage with King Edward continues.

1967 ALEXANDER SLATER GEDDES
(FES IX, 208, 294, 481, 555; X, 174, 355, 359), trans from Huntly to St Mary's 11 Jan 1967; ret 3 Mar 1985; died 25 Sep 1998.

1971 HAROLD ANDREW MACLEAN STEVEN
(FES X, 355), ord by Presb of Dumbarton during assistantship at New Kilpatrick 12 Apr 1970; ind to Banff Trinity and Alvah 7 Oct 1971; became minister of linked charge with King Edward 29 Jun 1993; trans to Baldernock 20 Apr 1994.

1986 AUSTIN URQUHART ERSKINE
ord and ind to St Mary's 13 Jun 1986; trans to Anwoth and Girthon with Borgue 25 Jul 1990.

1991 STEWART DUNCAN JEFFREY
(FES X, 113, 386), trans from Aberdeen St George's-Tillydrone to St Mary's 25 Oct 1991; became minister of united charge with Trinity and Alvah 14 Sep 1994; ret 18 Aug 1997; d Ruth m Duncan; d Shirley m Wiseman; d Laura m McCheyne.

1996 SEORAS LACHIE MACKENZIE
ord by Presb of Buchan and introd as Assoc at Banff with King Edward 1 May 1996; res 14 Jun 1998 on app by RAChD.

1998 ALAN MACGREGOR
B 7 Jul 1947, lic by Presb of Lanark 7 Jul 1991; ord and ind to Kirkconnel 2 Oct 1992; trans to Banff with King Edward 27 Mar 1998.

CRIMOND (FES VI, 212; VIII, 578; IX, 604; X, 348)

Linked 19 Mar 1959 with St Fergus.

1959 DAVID ALEXANDER DUNCAN
(FES VIII, 398; IX, 449; X, 265, 351), trans from Kilmadock East to St Fergus 6 Jun 1957; became minister of linked charge with Crimond 19 Mar 1959; ret 30 Sep 1962; died 13 Apr 1977.

1963 OLIVER URIAH SPRINGER
(FES X, 279, 348), ord and ind to Crimond with St Fergus 10 Jul 1963; introd to term app at Buckhaven St Andrew's 30 Sep 1969.

1971 JOHN MAIR
(FES X, 236, 348), trans from Jura to Crimond with St Fergus 21 Jan 1971; dem 31 Aug 1972 to enter teaching profession; app Teacher of RE and Science, St Martin's School, Northwood, Middlesex 1 Sep 1972; app Careers Master and Head of Biology, Keil School, Dumbarton 1 Jan 1975; ret 2 Sep 1997.

1972 GEORGE WILSON BAIRD
(FES IX, 137, 636; X, 81, 200, 348), [correction: Crimond, not Grimond as in Vol X, 200]; trans from Motherwell St Andrew's to Crimond with St Fergus 25 Oct 1972; ret 31 May 1984.

1985 ALEXANDER McGHEE
B 11 Sep 1929 at Port Glasgow, s of James Stevens Gardner M. and Annie McGovern; educ Port Glasgow High 1941–44; University of Glasgow 1965–66; Salvation Army Officer 1958–65; Congregational Minister 1970–77; Glasgow Division Education Dept 1978–85; m 3 May 1990 Irene Fraser d of Alexander and Jessie F; ord by Congregational Church, Jun 1970; admitted by General Assembly 1977; ind to Crimond with St Fergus 17 Jan 1985; died 20 Oct 1992.

1993 JAMES (HAMISH) EDWARD LYALL
B 25 Dec 1948 at Halkirk, s of William L. and Johan MacLeod; educ Halkirk Junior Secondary 1953–64; Glasgow Bible College 1985–86 (Dip); University of Glasgow 1986–90 (BD); Instrument Mechanic 1966–77; Technician 1977–85; loc ten Wick Central 1989–90; lic by Presb of Caithness 17 Sep 1990; asst Elgin St Giles' and St Columba's 1990–92; m 4 Apr 1975 Patricia Cormack McAllan b 1 May 1951 d of Peter Cormack M. and Margaret Simpson; ord and ind to Crimond with St Fergus 4 May 1993; app Chaplain (part-time) to Peterhead Prison 1 Dec 1994.

CRUDEN (FES X, 334)

1974 RODGER NEILSON
(FES X, 334), ord by Presb of Stirling during assistantship at St Mungo's 30 Apr 1972; ind to Cruden 24 Jan 1974; Publ: Co-author of *Searchlight* Vol 1 (Boys' Brigade, 1981); *Ornithology* (Boys' Brigade, 1995).

DEER (FES X, 348)

1954 ANTHONY JAMES GRUBB
(FES IX, 231, 550, 604; X, 348 (2)), trans from Greenock St Andrew's to Deer 13 May 1954; became minister of united charge with Ardallie and Deer Clola 4 May 1975; ret 31 Mar 1986; w Mary died 1998; d Rosemary m Sell.

1968 ALEXANDER HARRISON MACKENZIE
(FES IX, 53, 134, 605; X, 30, 330, 347), trans from Aberdeen St George's-in-the-West to Ardallie with Deer Clola 18 Jan 1968; ret 31 Jul 1974; died 1 Apr 1987.

1986 JAMES WISHART
B 26 Dec 1944 at South Ronaldsay, s of James William Stanley W. and Margaret Helen Sinclair; educ Kirkwall Grammar 1950–60; Craibstone Agricult College 1962–63 (CAg); University of Aberdeen 1980–85 (BD); Farming 1960–80; lic by Presb of Gordon 8 Sep 1985; asst Ellon 1985–86; m 10 Jun 1972 Helen Donaldson b 27 Feb 1954 d of George Cooper D. and Beatrice Joyce Swift; Children: Joyce Helen b 2 Jun 1973; James Donaldson b 1 Feb 1977; ord and ind to Deer 20 Aug 1986.

FORDYCE (FES X, 358)

1955 ROBERT AITKEN MONTGOMERY
(FES X, 358, 361), ord and ind to Portsoy 28 Sep 1955; became minister of united charge with Fordyce 2 Jan 1972; dem on app as Chaplain to Quarrier's Homes 28 Mar 1978.

1962 JAMES HUME
(FES IX, 425, 613, 765; X, 352, 358, 404), trans from Stromness to Fordyce 26 Jul 1962; ret 31 Oct 1971; died 9 Apr 1976.

1978 JAMES MORTON COWIE
ord by Presb of Perth during assistantship at Crieff St Michael's and St Ninian's 4 May 1977; ind to Fordyce 5 Oct 1978; trans to Hawick Burnfoot 17 May 1984.

1984 ROBERT LYNN
ord and ind to Fordyce 1 Nov 1984; trans to Ayr St Leonard's 8 Nov 1989.

1990 RAMSAY BAXTER SHIELDS
ord and ind to Fordyce 9 May 1990; trans to Milngavie St Luke's 9 Apr 1997.

1997 DAVID ANDERSON
(FES X, 264), trans from Aberdeen Northfield to Fordyce 22 Oct 1997; dem 30 Nov 1999.

FRASERBURGH OLD (FES VI, 220; VIII, 581; IX, 605; X, 348)

1945 ANDREW ALEXANDER SMITH MITCHELL
(FES IX, 605, 679; X, 348), trans from Bruan Thrumster to Fraserburgh Old 12 Dec 1945; ret 30 Sep 1972; died 31 Jan 1991.

1973 DOUGLAS ROY CLYNE
(FES X, 348), ord and ind to Fraserburgh Old 16 May 1973; s Timothy m Jane Purves.

FRASERBURGH SOUTH (FUF 441; FES IX, 605; X, 348)

Linked 11 Dec 1983 with Inverallochy and Rathen East.

1971 THOMAS ALAN WHITEWAY GARRITY
(FES X, 348), ord by Presb of Dundee during assistantship at St Mary's 27 Mar 1969; ind to Fraserburgh South 25 Aug 1971; trans to the Auld Kirk of Ayr 24 Feb 1982.

1982 RONALD FRASER YULE
ord and ind to Fraserburgh South 28 Sep 1982; became minister of linked charge with Inverallochy and Rathen East 11 Dec 1983.

FRASERBURGH WEST (FES VI, 224; IX, 606; X, 349)

1962 WALTER GORDON BEATTIE
(FES X, 96, 349), trans from Sorbie to Fraserburgh West 20 Nov 1962; trans to Arbroath Abbey 17 May 1977.

1978 BERTRAM ANDREW LYON
(FES X, 31), trans from Harthill St Andrew's to Fraserburgh West 9 Mar 1978; Addl children: Holly Jane b 6 Jan 1977.

FYVIE (FES X, 352)

Linked 20 Sep 1993 with Rothienorman.

1975 CHARLES IAN GRAHAM STOBIE
(FES IX, 222, 716, 717; X, 128, 250, 352), ind to Fyvie 25 Feb 1975 having resigned from service with Presb Church of Canada, Newfoundland; ret 8 Sep 1986.

1987 DAVID MURRAY McKAY
trans from Balmaclellan with Balmaghie with Kells to Fyvie 13 Mar 1987; trans to Largs St Columba's 2 Apr 1992.

1994 ROBERT MASSON LAWRIE
B 2 Aug 1966 at Johnstone, s of Robert L. and Jean Bannerman Blakely Masson; educ Kelvinside

Academy, Glasgow 1970–84; University of Glasgow 1984–85, 1987–90 (BD); 1990–92 (DipMin); London College of Music 1986 (LLCM); Piano Teacher 1986–87; lic by Presb of Greenock 28 Jun 1992; asst Dundee St Mary's 1992–94; ord and ind to Fyvie with Rothienorman 28 Sep 1994; dem 30 Sep 1998; University of Strathclyde 1998–99 (MSc).

1999 ALEXANDER BUCHAN NOBLE
B 23 May 1955 at Fraserburgh, s of George Strachan N. and Mary Kinsman Addison; educ Fraserburgh Academy and Dalziel High, Motherwell 1967–73; University of Glasgow 1973–76 (MA); University of Aberdeen 1976–79 (BD); Princeton Theological Seminary, USA 1979–80 (ThM); lic by Presb of Hamilton 28 Jun 1979; asst Edinburgh St Ninian's Corstorphine 1980–81; m 28 Jun 1991 Patricia Anne West b 11 Nov 1964 d of Andrew West and Jessie Bruce; ord and ind to Stirling St Mark's 6 Jan 1982; trans to Dunbar 16 Sep 1993; trans to Fyvie with Rothienorman 23 Sep 1999.

GAMRIE (FES IX, 614; X, 353)

Linked 1 Jun 1978 with King Edward. Linkage terminated and congregation dissolved 25 Oct 1992.

1971 JOHN KENNETH HOLMES
(FES X, 342, 353), trans from Lumphanan to Gamrie 2 Sep 1971; ret 31 May 1978; died 9 Mar 1995.

1978 ADAM McCALL BOWIE
ind to King Edward 30 Jul 1976; became minister of linked charge with Gamrie 1 Jun 1978, see King Edward.

1982 GEORGE MABON BAIN
(FES X, 240), trans from Kilninian and Kilmore with Tobermory with Salen and Ulva with Torosay and Kinlochspelvie to Gamrie with King Edward 30 Mar 1982; died 9 Jan 1987.

1988 ALAN JAMES BYERS
(FES X, 348, 416), trans from Boddam to Gamrie with King Edward 12 Feb 1988; ret 31 Aug 1992; s Calum m Sally Duthie; s David m Rachel Halstead; d Mary m Norman Craik; s Andrew m Linda Cheesewright.

GARDENSTOWN (FES IX, 614; X, 353)

1972 ANDREW SHAW
(FES X, 276, 353), trans from Lochcraig to Gardenstown 15 Dec 1972; ret 30 Nov 1985; d Jenny m John Magnus Tait; d Elizabeth m William Neil Farquhar.

1986 ROBERT McINTYRE WALKER
B 25 Sep 1954 at Glasgow, s of Robert McIntyre W. and Elizabeth Rooney; educ Whitehill

Secondary, Glasgow 1966–71; University of Glasgow 1971–77 (MA, BD); lic by Presb of Glasgow, 1977; asst Bellshill West 1977–78; m 17 Sep 1975 Aileen Ellis McCracken b 29 Jun 1954 d of Charles Dobbie M. and Christina McLuskie Ellis; Children: Richard Jonathan b 19 Jun 1979; Evelyn Ruth b 22 May 1981; David Martin b 3 Jul 1988; ord and ind to Lochranza and Pirnmill with Shiskine 22 Jun 1978; dem 31 Jul 1983 on app to Samuel Bill Theological College, Abak, Nigeria; ind to Gardenstown 25 Apr 1986; dem charge and status 6 Sep 1995.

1996 DONALD NORMAN MARTIN
B 20 Jan 1953 at Stornoway, s of Donald M. and Johanna Maciver; educ Nicolson Institute, Stornoway 1965–69; University of Aberdeen 1990–94 (BD); Manager, Co-operative Wholesale Society 1976–86; Wholsale Fruiterer (self-employed) 1986–89; lic by Presb of Lewis 29 Jun 1994; asst Aberdeen Mannofield 1994–95; m 10 Sep 1982 Suzanne Margaret b 10 Jan 1962 d of Donald M. and Margaret Morrison; Children: Gillian b 8 Dec 1983; James b 3 May 1986; Douglas b 13 Aug 1989; ord and ind to Gardenstown 31 May 1996.

INVERALLOCHY AND RATHEN EAST (FES IX, 606; X, 349)

Linked 11 Dec 1983 with Fraserburgh South.

1947 JAMES DONALD FRASER
(FES IX, 606; X, 349), ind to Inverallochy and Rathen East 7 Apr 1947; ret 30 Nov 1983; died 24 Jan 1988.

1982 RONALD FRASER YULE
ord and ind to Fraserburgh South 28 Sep 1982; became minister of linked charge with Inverallochy and Rathen East 11 Dec 1983.

KING EDWARD (FES VI, 264; VIII, 593; IX, 615; X, 353)

Linked 1 Jun 1978 with Gamrie. Linkage terminated 25 Oct 1992. Linked 29 Jun 1993 with Banff Trinity and Alvah. Linkage continues following union of Banff St Mary's and Banff Trinity and Alvah 14 Sep 1994.

1976 ADAM McCALL BOWIE
ord and ind to King Edward 30 Jul 1976; became minister of linked charge with Gamrie 1 Jun 1978; trans to Dull and Weem with Fortingall and Glenlyon 23 Aug 1981.

1982 GEORGE MABON BAIN
(FES X, 240), ind to Gamrie with King Edward 30 Mar 1982, see Gamrie.

1988 ALAN JAMES BYERS
(FES X, 348, 416), trans from Boddam to Gamrie with King Edward 12 Feb 1988, see Gamrie.

1993   HAROLD ANDREW MACLEAN STEVEN
(FES X, 355), ind to Banff Trinity and Alvah 7 Oct 1971; became minister of linked charge with King Edward 29 Jun 1993, see Banff.

1994   STEWART DUNCAN JEFFREY
(FES X, 113, 386), ind to Banff St Mary's 25 Oct 1991; became minister of united charge with Trinity and Alvah linked with King Edward 14 Sep 1994, see Banff.

1996   SEORAS LACHIE MACKENZIE
introd as Assoc at Banff with King Edward 1 May 1996, see Banff.

1998   ALAN MACGREGOR
trans from Kirkconnel to Banff with King Edward 27 Mar 1998.

KINNIMONTH AND NEW LEEDS (FES IX, 606; X, 349)

Congregation dissolved 31 Oct 1978.

1954   JOHN MACGILBERT
(FES IX, 279, 280, 606; X, 349), trans from Glasgow Macgregor Memorial to Kinnimonth and New Leeds 2 Dec 1954; ret 31 May 1978; died 19 Apr 1983.

LONGSIDE (FES X, 349)

Formed 1 Apr 1970 by union of Longside and Blackhill.

1947   HAMILTON ALLAN HENRY
(FES IX, 603, 708; X, 347), trans from South Ronaldsay to Blackhill 13 Feb 1947; ret 31 Mar 1970; died 19 Aug 1985.

1968   HARRY GREENWOOD
(FES X, 30, 349 (2)), trans from Fauldhouse Crofthead with Longridge and Breich to Longside 5 Dec 1968; became minister of united charge with Blackhill 1 Apr 1970; trans to Madderty with Trinity Gask and Kinkell 19 Apr 1978.

1978   WILLIAM NEILSON THOMSON HODGE
(FES X, 31, 358), trans from Fauldhouse St Andrew's with Longridge and Breich to Longside 7 Sep 1978; ret 31 Aug 1995; s John m Hunter; s David m Gruer.

1995   NEIL MACKINNON
trans from Coll with Tiree to Longside 23 Nov 1995; dem 31 Jul 1996.

1997   NORMAN ANGUS SMITH
B 10 Jul 1971 at Stornoway, s of Robert S. and Jessie Mary Carmichael; educ Nicolson Institute, Stornoway 1982–89; University of Aberdeen 1989–92 (MA), 1992–95 (BD); lic by Presb of Lewis 30 Jun 1995; asst Macduff 1995–97; ord and ind to Longside 27 Feb 1997.

LONMAY (FES VI, 228; VIII, 583; IX, 607; X, 349)

Linked 6 Dec 1958 with Rathen West.

1949   DANIEL MURRAY STEWART
(FES VIII, 319; IX, 72, 384, 409, 546, 607; X, 349), dem from Benholm and Johnshaven and ind to Lonmay 30 Sep 1949; became minister of linked charge with Rathen West 6 Dec 1958; ret 31 Aug 1967; died 15 Oct 1987.

1967   JAMES CARSON STRACHAN
(FES IX, 421, 793; X, 93, 349, 448), trans from Colmonell to Lonmay with Rathen West 22 Nov 1967; trans to Mossgreen and Crossgates 25 Oct 1978.

1979   GEORGE MILLER ALLAN FAWKES
B 20 Mar 1935 at Glasgow, s of George Wannop F. and Euphemia Allan Scott; educ Irvine Royal Academy 1945–52; University of Glasgow 1952–57 (BSc); Open University 1973–76 (BA); University of Aberdeen 1977–79; Statistician 1957–58, 1961–64; Lecturer, Inverness Tech College 1964–77; Education Officer 1958–61; lic by Presb of Inverness 12 Jun 1979; m 2 Apr 1965 Beatrice Betty Anne Forbes b 6 May 1939 d of James Ramsay F. and Beatrice Deans Low; Children: Anne Hamilton b 29 Jul 1967 m Euan Glen; David George Forbes b 5 Feb 1971; ord and ind to Lonmay with Rathen West 29 Aug 1979; Chaplain (part-time) to Peterhead Prison; JP.

MACDUFF (FES X, 353, 354)

Formed 1 Aug 1989 by union of Macduff Doune and Macduff Gardner.

1971   DAVID JAMES RANDALL
(FES X, 353), ord and ind to Macduff Doune 30 Jul 1971; became minister of united charge with Gardner 1 Aug 1989; Addl children: Alison b 15 Sep 1984; s David m Linnea Swinson; s Colin m Laura Malcolm; s Andrew m Kay Murray.

1973   LESLIE McMILLAN STEELE
(FES X, 354), ord and ind to Gardner 29 Jun 1973; trans to Galashiels Old and St Paul's 19 Feb 1988.

MARNOCH (FES IX, 629; X, 360)

1959   EDWARD WILLIAM WALKER
(FES IX, 151, 752; X, 360), trans from Auchencairn to Marnoch 13 May 1959; ret 6 Jan 1985; died 22 Aug 1990.

1985   ROBERT ALEXANDER JONES
(FES X, 262), trans from Bannockburn Allan to Marnoch 9 May 1985; ret 31 Jan 1997; d Ann m Kevin Neary.

1997   ROSEMARY LEGGE
B 29 May 1953 at Leamington Spa, d of David Ralph Haines and Barbara Walton; educ Coundon Court Comprehensive 1964–71; Imperial College,

London 1971–74 (BSc); Northumbria Bible College, Berwick-on-Tweed 1984–88 (BD); University of Aberdeen 1988–90 (MTh); Building Services Engineering 1972–84; lic by Presb of Gordon 16 Jun 1991; m 1 Jul 1995 William John Legge b 21 Apr 1953 s of William George L. and Mary Isabella Kiloh; ord and ind to Enzie with Rathven 8 May 1992; trans to Marnoch 18 Sep 1997.

MAUD AND SAVOCH (FES X, 349, 351)

Formed 23 Feb 1996 by union of Maud and Savoch. Linked 16 Apr 1999 with New Deer St Kane's.

1964   JAMES MOORE
(FES X, 351, 400, 402), trans from Orphir to Savoch 20 Feb 1964; ret 30 Nov 1969; died 16 May 1986.

1970   WILLIAM DEREK SCOTT
(FES X, 266, 349, 400 (2)), trans from Menstrie to Maud 3 Dec 1970; became minister of linked charge with Savoch 8 Jun 1975; ret 31 Dec 1989.

1971   JAMES CORDINER
(FES IX, 330, 604; X, 149, 195, 265, 351), trans from Twechar to Savoch 25 Feb 1971; ret 31 Dec 1974; died 5 Aug 1999.

1991   ALISON JANE SIMPSON
B 15 Sep 1960 at Dumfries, d of George Fazakerley and Daisy Clark; educ Cargenbridge Secondary and Dumfries Academy 1972–78; University of St Andrews 1980–86 (BSc, BD); Princeton Theological Seminary, USA 1986–87 (ThM); Chemical Technician 1978–80; lic by Presb of St Andrews 29 Jun 1986; asst Glasgow Cathcart Old 1987–88; m 10 Oct 1992 Stephen Simpson b 21 May 1966 s of William S. and Aileen Park; ord by Presb of Gordon and introd as Assoc at Ellon 25 Sep 1988; ind to Maud with Savoch 20 Mar 1991; became minister of united charge 23 Feb 1996; dem 30 Sep 1997; ord as Priest in Scottish Episcopal Church 14 Dec 1999.

1999   ALISTAIR PATRICK DONALD
B 12 Sep 1956 at Giffnock, s of Patrick Dunlop D. and Catherine Gilchrist Robertson; educ Glasgow Academy 1966–74; University of St Andrews 1974–78 (MA); University of Wales 1978–81 (PhD); University of Edinburgh 1994–97 (BD); Environmental Scientist 1981–94; lic by Presb of Dunfermline 28 Jun 1997; asst Dunfermline Gillespie Memorial 1997–99; m 27 Jun 1980 Nicola Clare Shepherd b 2 Mar 1956 d of Melville Ogilvy S. and Pamela Macmillan; Children: James Patrick b 1 Feb 1984; Ewan Rhodri b 4 Apr 1989; Calum Ogilvy b 16 Feb 1991; ord and ind to Maud and Savoch with New Deer St Kane's 16 Apr 1999.

MONQUHITTER AND NEW BYTH (FES VI, 268; VIII, 594; IX, 616; X, 354)

Formed 28 Mar 1996 by union of Monquhitter and New Byth.

1971   ALEXANDER AYTON FAIRWEATHER
(FES X, 354), res from service with RAF Chaplains' Branch and ind to Monquhitter with New Byth 31 Oct 1971; trans to Edinburgh Pilrig and Dalmeny Street 20 Dec 1978.

1979   BRIAN STUART COOPER DONALD
(FES X, 147, 418), trans from Rutherglen East to Monquhitter with New Byth 28 Sep 1979; became minister of united charge 28 Mar 1996; ret 30 Jun 1998; died 5 Aug 1999; d Louise m James Clayton Murray Andrews.

NEW DEER ST KANE'S (FES X, 350)

Linked 16 Apr 1999 with Maud and Savoch.

1924   MATTHEW WELSH NEILSON
(FUF 175; FES VIII, 490, 581; IX, 608; X, 350 (2)), trans from Dundee St Matthew's to New Deer South 16 May 1924; became minister of united charge with Maud and North Trinity 27 Mar 1958; ret 30 Sep 1958; died 13 May 1981.

1959   DONALD MALCOLM MACLEOD
(FES IX, 338, 367; X, 201, 350), trans from Kirk o' Shotts to New Deer St Kane's 2 Apr 1959; died 15 Feb 1985.

1986   RUSSEL MOFFAT
ord and ind to New Deer St Kane's 8 May 1986; trans to Dyce 19 Mar 1998.

1999   ALISTAIR PATRICK DONALD
ord and ind to Maud and Savoch with New Deer St Kane's 16 Apr 1999, see Maud and Savoch.

NEW PITSLIGO (FES IX, 608; X, 350)

Linked 20 Jul 1995 with Aberdour.

1959   ISAAC RALPH
(FES IX, 715; X, 350, 407), trans from Tingwall to New Pitsligo 6 Mar 1959; died 6 Aug 1988.

1989   ROBERT WILLIAM MASSIE
ord and ind to New Pitsligo 25 Aug 1989; became minister of linked charge with Aberdour 20 Jul 1995; trans to Monifieth St Rule's 20 Oct 1999.

ORDIQUHILL AND CORNHILL (FES X, 360)

Linked 29 Jan 1988 with Boyndie (Ord dropped from name). Name changed 1999 from Boyndie to Whitehills.

1969   ALLAN TAYLOR WHYTE
(FES IX, 753; X, 133, 360, 363, 427), trans from Kirkmichael and Tomintoul to Ordiquhill, Cornhill and Ord 6 Aug 1969; died 10 Jul 1986.

1988 GEORGE TODD POUSTIE
(FES X, 356), ord and ind to Boyndie 17 Jun 1966; became minister of linked charge with Ordiquhill and Cornhill 29 Jan 1988; ret 30 Jun 1992.

1992 JOHN CHRISTOPHER LEDGARD
ind to Boyndie with Ordiquhill and Cornhill 6 Nov 1992; trans to Upper Donside 22 Mar 1996.

1997 GORDON HENIG
ord and ind to Boyndie with Ordiquhill and Cornhill 28 Aug 1997.

PETERHEAD OLD (FES VI, 230; VIII, 583; IX, 609; X, 350)

1915 HUGH DOUGLAS SWAN
(FES VI, 233; VIII, 584; IX, 609), [correction: ind to Peterhead 1915, not 1918 as in Vol IX, 609]; trans from Redgorton to Peterhead 6 Oct 1915; dem 15 Nov 1951; died 9 Nov 1981.

1974 JAMES FERGUS MILLER
(FES X, 350), res as Asst Chaplain to University of Glasgow and ind to Peterhead Old 28 Mar 1974; trans to Dumbarton Riverside 30 May 1978.

1978 DAVID SINCLAIR ROSS
B 24 Jul 1945 at Aberdeen, s of William Frederick Slade R. and Elspeth Black; educ Aberdeen Academy 1950–63; University of Aberdeen 1963–68 (BSc, MSc); University of Glasgow 1968–71 (PhD); University of Aberdeen 1974–77 (BD); Research Chemist, Aachen, Germany 1971–74; lic by Presb of Aberdeen 29 Jun 1978; asst Aberdeen Northfield 1977–78; m (1) 6 Jul 1968 Heather Watt b 4 May 1947 d of William and Thelma W; Children: Fraser Graeme b 5 May 1971; Stephen Andrew b 7 Sep 1973; m (2) 27 Sep 1996 Pamela Ann Anderson Nimmo b 4 Nov 1958 d of James N. and Elizabeth Anderson; Children: Lisa Miriam b 10 Aug 1997; Ewan James b 8 Jul 1999; ord and ind to Peterhead Old 20 Sep 1978.

PETERHEAD ST ANDREW'S (FES X, 350)

1968 WILLIAM HAY BROWN
(FES X, 15, 351), trans from Edinburgh Lochend to St Andrew's 20 Feb 1968; ret 9 Sep 1990; d Elizabeth m Noble.

1991 WILLIAM MICHAEL BECKET DUNLOP
B 4 May 1951 at Glasgow, s of William Beckett D. and Charmain Katherine Chauncy Speirs; educ Rugby School 1964–69; University of Edinburgh 1970–73 (LLB); Trinity Theological College, Bristol 1974–75; University of Glasgow 1978–80; Trainee Social Worker 1974; Scottish Secretary to Universities and Colleges Christian Fellowship 1975–78; lic by Presb of Glasgow 26 Jun 1980; asst Glasgow St George's Tron 1980–82; m 7 Apr 1979 Margaret Jennifer Marwick b 29 Aug 1952 d of John George M. and Elizabeth Munro Forbes:

Children: John William b 23 Mar 1981; Stephen James b 23 Jun 1983; Alasdair Graham b 31 Oct 1986; ord by Presb of Glasgow during assistantship at St George's Tron 29 Jan 1981; app by Board of World Mission to Sefula Church, United Church of Zambia 26 Aug 1984; app to Livingstone, UCZ 21 May 1986; ind to St Andrew's 6 Jun 1991; ret 30 Sep 1995 on grounds of ill-health.

1996 DAVID GEORGE PITKEATHLY
B 26 Mar 1965 at Manchester, s of Denis Aitken P. and Isabel Gilmour Crerar; educ Glasgow Academy 1973–82; University of Dundee 1982–86 (LLB, DipLP); University of St Andrews 1991–94 (BD); Solicitor 1986–91; lic by Presb of Glasgow 1 Jul 1994; asst Stonehaven Fetteresso 1994–96; m Pauline Steenbergen b 2 Mar 1969 d of Henry Dick Cummings S. and Margarete Montgomery; ord and ind to St Andrew's 3 Apr 1996.

PETERHEAD TRINITY (FES X, 347, 351)

Formed 11 Oct 1991 by union of Boddam and Peterhead West Associate.

1944 JOHN ALEXANDER ROSIE
(FES IX, 603, 609), trans from Ardallie to Peterhead West Associate 14 Jun 1944; trans to West Kirby Presb Church 21 Apr 1950; died 20 Oct 1997.

1950 WILLIAM MENZIES HANNAH
(FES IX, 101, 603, 610, 647; X, 347), trans from Rothes to Peterhead West Associate 4 Oct 1950; trans to Aberdour 25 Jun 1954.

1954 GEORGE IRVINE FRANCIS
(FES IX, 56, 572, 610; X, 201, 351), trans from Aberdeen Woodside North to Peterhead West Associate 24 Nov 1954; trans to Shotts Calderhead 31 Jul 1963.

1964 JOHN PAUL TIERNEY
(FES IX, 478; X, 104, 283, 351), trans from Muirkirk to Peterhead West Associate 5 Mar 1964; ret 31 Dec 1985.

1971 ALAN JAMES BYERS
(FES X, 348, 416), res from service with Overseas Council in Ghana and ind to Boddam 15 Sep 1971; trans to Gamrie with King Edward 12 Feb 1988.

1986 PHILIPPA MARGARET BAKER OTT
ord and ind to Peterhead West Associate 24 Jun 1986; became minister of linked charge with Boddam 17 Feb 1988 and of united charge 11 Oct 1991; dem 30 Apr 1995 on app to Jerusalem St Andrew's.

1996 LEONARD PAUL McCLENAGHAN
B 27 Nov 1946 at Belfast, s of Harold Robert M. and Annie McDowell; educ Grosvenor High School, Belfast 1958–65; Magee University College, Londonderry 1965–67; Trinity College, Dublin 1967–69 (BA); Assembly's College, Belfast 1969–72; lic

by Presb of East Belfast, Jun 1972; asst Hamilton Road Presb Church, Bangor 1971–75; m 26 Jul 1972 Shirley Joy Lockhart b 13 Jan 1948 d of William John L. and Eveline Heasty; Children: Christopher Simon b 14 Oct 1977; Philip Jeffrey b 26 Sep 1980; ord by Presb Church in Ireland and ind to Hamilton Road Church, Bangor 13 Jan 1973; minister of Presb Church in Ireland 1973–96; ind to Trinity 28 Jun 1996.

PITSLIGO (FES IX, 610; X, 351)

Linked 29 Aug 1985 with Sandhaven and Pitullie (Pitullie dropped from name).

1975 MALCOLM McINTOSH REW
(FES X, 351), ord by Presb of Edinburgh during assistantship at South Leith 23 Jun 1974; ind to Pitsligo 14 Aug 1975; dem 30 Jun 1980 and app Asst at Albany Deaf Church of Edinburgh.

1981 ROBERT HUGH DRUMMOND
(FES X, 77, 287, 381), trans from Thornton to Pitsligo 13 Aug 1981; became minister of linked charge with Sandhaven 29 Aug 1985; trans to Balmaclellan with Kells 29 Sep 1988.

1990 IAN GEORGE THOM
B 14 May 1955 at Perth, s of George Burns T. and Mary Girdwood Anderson Drummond; educ Crieff Secondary and Morrison's Academy, Crieff 1967–74; University of Strathclyde 1974–78 (BSc), 1978–81 (PhD); University of Glasgow 1986–89 (BD); Research Chemist 1981–85; lic by Presb of Glasgow 3 Jul 1989; asst Chryston 1989–90; m 25 Mar 1983 Wendy Elizabeth Speed b 4 Jun 1958 d of Alexander Matthew McAslan S. and Iris May McDonald; Children: Jennifer Ruth b 28 Sep 1984; Flora Louise b 8 Jan 1986; Mairi Susan b 16 Aug 1988; ord and ind to Pitsligo with Sandhaven 27 Jun 1990.

RATHEN WEST (FES VI, 238; VIII, 585; IX, 610; X, 351)

Linked 6 Dec 1958 with Lonmay.

1958 DANIEL MURRAY STEWART
(FES VIII, 319; IX, 72, 384, 409, 546, 607; X, 349), dem from Benholm and Johnshaven and ind to Lonmay 30 Sep 1949; became minister of linked charge with Rathen West 6 Dec 1958; ret 31 Aug 1967; died 15 Oct 1987.

1967 JAMES CARSON STRACHAN
(FES IX, 421, 793; X, 93, 349, 448), trans from Colmonell to Lonmay with Rathen West 22 Nov 1967; trans to Mossgreen and Crossgates 25 Oct 1978.

1979 GEORGE MILLER ALLAN FAWKES
ord and ind to Lonmay with Rathen West 29 Aug 1979, see Lonmay.

ROTHIENORMAN (FES IX, 602; X, 346)

Linkage with Culsalmond terminated 27 Aug 1985. Linked same date with Auchterless. Arrangement terminated 20 Sep 1993 to allow linkage with Fyvie.

1948 THOMAS SMITH CRICHTON
(FUF 177; FES IX, 272, 318, 602), trans from Glasgow High Carntyne to Rothienorman 5 Feb 1948; dem 1954; died 30 Sep 1983.

1958 RODNEY MILLIGAN
(FES IX, 597; X, 344), ind to Culsalmond 29 Nov 1951; became minister of linked charge with Rothienorman 18 May 1958; ret 27 Aug 1985.

1986 HAMISH GAULT SMITH
(FES X, 186, 407), trans from Burra Isle with Tingwall to Auchterless with Rothienorman 17 Apr 1986; ret on grounds of ill-health, Dec 1992.

1994 ROBERT MASSON LAWRIE
ord and ind to Fyvie with Rothienorman 28 Sep 1994; dem 30 Sep 1998.

1999 ALEXANDER BUCHAN NOBLE
ind to Fyvie with Rothienorman 23 Sep 1999, see Fyvie.

SANDHAVEN (see FES IX, 610 (Pitsligo))

Former Mission Station. Linked 29 Aug 1985 with Pitsligo.

1985 ROBERT HUGH DRUMMOND
(FES X, 77, 287, 381), trans from Thornton to Pitsligo 13 Aug 1981; became minister of linked charge with Sandhaven 29 Aug 1985; trans to Balmaclellan with Kells 29 Sep 1988.

1990 IAN GEORGE THOM
ord and ind to Pitsligo with Sandhaven 27 Jun 1990, see Pitsligo.

ST FERGUS (FES VI, 240; VIII, 586; IX, 610; X, 351)

Linked 19 Mar 1959 with Crimond.

1957 DAVID ALEXANDER DUNCAN
(FES VIII, 398; IX, 449; X, 265, 351), trans from Kilmadock East to St Fergus 6 Jun 1957; became minister of linked charge with Crimond 19 Mar 1959; ret 30 Sep 1962; died 13 Apr 1977.

1963 OLIVER URIAH SPRINGER
(FES X, 279, 348), ord and ind to Crimond with St Fergus 10 Jul 1963; introd to term app at Buckhaven St Andrew's 30 Sep 1969.

1971 JOHN MAIR
(FES X, 236, 348), ind to Crimond with St Fergus 21 Jan 1971, see Crimond.

1972 GEORGE WILSON BAIRD
(FES IX, 137, 636; X, 81, 200, 348), trans from Motherwell St Andrew's to Crimond with St Fergus 25 Oct 1972, see Crimond.

1985 ALEXANDER McGHEE
ind to Crimond with St Fergus 17 Jan 1985, see Crimond.

1993 JAMES (HAMISH) EDWARD LYALL
ord and ind to Crimond with St Fergus 4 May 1993, see Crimond.

STRICHEN (FES IX, 611; X, 351)

Linked 19 Jul 1995 with Tyrie.

1960 FRANCIS GORDON McLAREN
(FES IX, 536; X, 322, 351), trans from Kirriemuir Livingstone to Strichen 27 Apr 1960; ret 30 Sep 1975; died 23 Mar 1999.

1976 ROBERT COLQUHOUN WOTHERSPOON
ord and ind to Strichen 24 Jun 1976; trans to Glasgow Castlemilk West 13 Mar 1980.

1980 BRIAN BAIN
ord and ind to Strichen 3 Jul 1980; trans to Gask with Methven 9 Apr 1986.

1986 JAMES LYNCH WILSON
ord and ind to Strichen 24 Sep 1986; trans to Dundee Trinity 20 Oct 1993.

1994 STEPHEN ALASTAIR BLAKEY
B 5 Jul 1953 at Dumfries, s of William Merriet B. and Elizabeth Russell Burnet; educ Madras College, St Andrews 1964–71; University of St Andrews 1971–74 (BSc); University of Edinburgh 1974–77 (BD); lic by Presb of St Andrews; m 5 Sep 1975 Christine Anne Lauritsen b 8 Mar 1953 d of Einer L. and Margaret Lothian Small; Children: Barbara Elizabeth b 30 Jan 1977; Malcolm Alastair William b 16 Jun 1978; Caroline Margaret b 16 May 1980; Graham Andrew Stewart b 13 Apr 1982; ord by Presb of St Andrews and app by RAChD 28 Aug 1977; ret 31 Aug 1993 to take up app with Assoc of Vineyard Churches; ind to Strichen 22 Sep 1994; became minister of linked charge with Tyrie 19 Jul 1995; dem 31 Dec 1999.

TURRIFF ST ANDREW'S (FUF 499; FES IX, 616; X, 354)

1947 THOMAS LEAN WARK
(FES IX, 616; X, 354), ord and ind to St Andrew's 20 Aug 1947; ret 30 Jun 1982; died 18 Jul 1993.

1983 DONALD BAIN CARRICK INGLIS
B 17 Dec 1941 at Aberdeen, s of William Carrick I. and Margaret Alexandra Collie Bain; educ Aberdeen Grammar 1952–60; University of Aberdeen

1960–63 (MA), 1964–68 (MEd); Aberdeen College of Education 1963–64; University of Glasgow 1970–73 (BD); Jordanhill College, Glasgow 1976; Teaching 1964–68; Educational Psychologist 1968–72, 1977–83; lic by Presb of Glasgow 26 Jun 1975; asst Bathgate High 1975–77; m 24 Sep 1974 Yvonne Mary Sunderland Cook b 7 Jan 1943 d of James Darroch C. and Edith Ellen Noble Ritchie; Children: Fraser Graeme b 28 May 1977; Rosemary Anne b 4 Apr 1979; Sandra Elizabeth b 16 Oct 1980; ord by Presb of Livingston and Bathgate during assistantship at Bathgate High 1975; res as Senior Educational Psychologist with Fife Regional Council and ind to St Andrew's 18 May 1983; Chairman, Turriff Academy School Board 1995–97.

TURRIFF ST NINIAN'S AND FORGLEN (FES X, 354)

Formed 28 Mar 1971 by union of Turriff St Ninian's and Forglen.

1927 PETER CRAIK MACQUOID
(FES VIII, 595; IX, 616; X, 354), trans from Bothkennar to St Ninian's 20 Apr 1927; ret 30 Apr 1966; died 17 Feb 1983.

1964 ARTHUR AUGUSTUS MULLO WEIR
(FES IX, 552; X, 244, 322, 352), trans from Nether Lochaber to Forglen 26 Mar 1964; ret 31 Oct 1969; died 22 May 1995.

1966 DAVID PATRICK LOW CUMMING
(FES X, 102, 354 (2), 366), trans from Girvan South to Turriff St Ninian's 19 Oct 1966; became minister of united charge with Forglen 28 Mar 1971; trans to Elgin St Giles' 27 Jun 1973.

1974 DAVID BUTTERS
(FES X, 266, 354), trans from Kincardine-in-Menteith with Norrieston to St Ninian's and Forglen 31 Jan 1974; ret 31 Jan 1998; d Carol m Keith Harper; s Colin m Michaela Carson.

1998 BRUCE KNIGHT GARDNER
B 7 Sep 1948 at Aberdeen, s of Alexander Mac-Murray G. and Myra Craig; educ Aberdeen Grammar 1961–67; University of Aberdeen 1967–71 (MA), 1984–87 (BD), 1993–94, 1996–98 (PhD); Jordanhill College, Glasgow 1971–72 (PGCE); Basil Paterson College, Edinburgh 1994 (CTEFLA); Teaching 1972–84; lic by Presb of Aberdeen 30 May 1987; asst Kemnay 1987–88; m 21 Aug 1970 Christine McColl Hogg b 8 Nov 1947 d of James Torrance H. and Jessie (or Janet) Garlick; Children: Alan Craig b 27 Jul 1975; Ailsa McColl b 3 Aug 1977; Catriona Knight b 9 Jan 1979; Eilidh Hogg b 11 Oct 1981; ord and ind to Carloway 21 Oct 1988; dem 15 May 1994 on app by Free Church of Scotland as Missionary in Peru; service in Colegio San Andres, Lima 1994–96; Assoc at Newhills 1996–98; ind to St Ninian's and Forglen 28 Aug 1998; Publ: *The Ancient Mystery of Foggieloan*

(Leopard Magazine, 1979); *The Genesis Calendar: The Synchronistic Tradition in Genesis 1–11* (Univ of Aberdeen, 1998); *The Genesis Calendar* (forthcoming).

TYRIE (FES VI, 245; VIII, 587; IX, 612; X, 351)

Linkage with Aberdour terminated in favour of linkage with Strichen 19 Jul 1995.

1975 GEOFFREY LEE
(FES X, 347), ord and ind to Aberdour with Tyrie 26 Jun 1975; trans to Dumbarton Knoxland 27 Feb 1980.

1982 CHARLES JOHN BIRNIE
(FES X, 98), trans from Annbank to Aberdour with Tyrie 6 May 1982, see Aberdour.

1995 STEPHEN ALASTAIR BLAKEY
ind to Strichen 22 Sep 1994; became minister of linked charge with Tyrie 19 Jul 1995, see Strichen.

WHITEHILLS (FES IX, 618; X, 356)

Boyndie linked 29 Jan 1988 with Ordiquhill, Cornhill and Ord (Ord dropped from name). Name changed 1999 to Whitehills.

1957 ALEXANDER WILSON GREIG
(FES IX, 14, 83; X, 9, 356), trans from Edinburgh Fountainbridge to Boyndie 8 Nov 1957; ret 31 Oct 1965; died 14 Sep 1991.

1966 GEORGE TODD POUSTIE
(FES X, 356), ord and ind to Boyndie 17 Jun 1966; became minister of linked charge with Ordiquhill and Cornhill 29 Jan 1988; ret 30 Jun 1992.

1992 JOHN CHRISTOPHER LEDGARD
ind to Boyndie with Ordiquhill and Cornhill 6 Nov 1992; trans to Upper Donside 22 Mar 1996.

1997 GORDON HENIG
B 14 Apr 1951 at Whitburn, educ Lindsay High School, Bathgate and Whitburn Academy 1963–67; Open University 1982–88 (BSc); University of Edinburgh 1992–95 (BD); lic by Presb of Melrose and Peebles 4 Jul 1995; ord and ind to Boyndie with Ordiquhill and Cornhill 28 Aug 1997.

PRESBYTERY OF MORAY

ABERLOUR (FUF 450; FES VI, 334; VIII, 611; IX, 639; X, 365)

1975 ANN FRANCES JACKSON
(FES X, 365), ord by Presb of Edinburgh during assistantship at Currie 18 May 1974; ind to Aberlour 12 Dec 1975; dem 15 Oct 1982.

1983 DAVID ANDERSON
(FES X, 264), trans from Cowie with Plean to Aberlour 2 Aug 1983; trans to Aberdeen Northfield 12 Aug 1992.

1993 KENNETH J WALKER
ord and ind to Aberlour 8 Jan 1993; dem 3 Sep 1996.

1998 ELIZABETH MARSHALL CURRAN
B 28 Apr 1943 at Dunfermline, d of William John C. and Ellen Wyles Allan; educ Beath High, Cowdenbeath 1948–61; Moray House College, Edinburgh 1961–64 (DPEd), 1967–68 (DSEd); University of Edinburgh 1990–93 (BD); Teaching 1964–67 (primary), 1968–90 (special needs); lic by Presb of Edinburgh 4 Jul 1993; asst Edinburgh Kaimes Lockhart Memorial 1993–94; ord by Presb of Edinburgh and introd as Assoc at St George's West 2 Feb 1995; ind to Aberlour 7 May 1998.

ALVES AND BURGHEAD (FES X, 365)

Formed 31 May 1982 by union of Alves and Burghead. Linked 13 Jan 1995 with Kinloss and Findhorn.

1956 JAMES McLEMAN
(FES IX, 332; X, 197, 365), trans from Holytown to Burghead 31 May 1956; became minister of linked charge with Alves 8 Nov 1963; ret 30 Nov 1981; died 26 Jul 1998; Addl publ: *The Genesis of John* (St Andrew Press, 1980).

1982 ROY MACKENZIE
ord and ind to Alves and Burghead 22 Oct 1982; trans to Dundee Lochee Old and St Luke's 2 Oct 1985.

1987 JAMES ALEXANDER MUNRO
trans from South Uist to Alves and Burghead 18 Aug 1987; trans to Kilmallie 23 Feb 1994.

1995 JOHN CAIRNS BECK
(FES X, 387), trans from Glasgow Dennistoun Central to Alves and Burghead with Kinloss and Findhorn 28 Jun 1995.

BELLIE (FES IX, 640; X, 365)

Linked 1 Mar 1959 with Speymouth.

1959 ALICK HUGH MACAULAY
(FES IX, 664; X, 365, 379, 380), trans from Lochbroom and Ullapool to Bellie with Speymouth 22 Jul 1959; ret 30 Jun 1981; d Margaret m Robert MacDonald; s Roderick m Margaret MacIntosh; s Donald m Morag Paterson; d Mary m John Keenan; d Anne m Richard Melville; d Ruth m Mark Graham; d Clare m Shane Voss.

1983 DAVID JAMES FERGUSON
(FES X, 199, 407), trans from Motherwell Crosshill to Bellie with Speymouth 26 Mar 1982; became minister of united charge with Garmouth 14 Nov 1988; app Clerk to Presb of Moray 1997.

BIRNIE (FES VI, 378; VIII, 622; IX, 640; X, 365)

Linked 1 Oct 1972 with Pluscarden.

1956 ADAM RONALD RENTOUL TORRIE
(FES IX, 396, 726; X, 365, 413), res from app at Gibraltar St Andrew's and ind to Birnie 7 Sep 1956; became minister of linked charge with Pluscarden 1 Oct 1972; ret 31 Oct 1986; died 26 Jun 1996.

1986 GORDON STRACHAN COWIE
B 10 Jun 1933 at Aberdeen, s of George Strachan C. and Edna Marion Littlechild; educ Aberdeen Grammar 1937–51; University of Aberdeen 1951–55 (MA), 1955–58 (LLB); Lecturer, University of St Andrews 1960–67; Professor of Public Law, University of Glasgow 1967–86; lic by Presb of Glasgow 1 Jul 1985; asst Glasgow Temple Anniesland 1984–85; Milngavie Cairns 1985–86; m 11 Aug 1961 Angela Mary Whelband b 28 Nov 1942 d of Rowland George W. and Marjory Pearse; Children: Rosemary Anne b 15 May 1962 m Jeremy Farr; George Strachan b 18 Nov 1963 m Marian Edmiston; David Gordon b 21 Aug 1968 m Lisa Burton; Andrew Graeme b 11 Jul 1973; ord and ind to Birnie with Pluscarden 2 Nov 1986; ret 31 Dec 1992.

1993 RONALD JOHN SCOTLAND
B 18 Jul 1938 at Edinburgh, s of John William Bews S. and Edith Forbes; educ George Heriot's, Edinburgh 1943–56; University of Edinburgh 1989–92; Quantity Surveying and Building Management 1956–89; lic by Presb of Edinburgh 5 Jul 1992; asst Edinburgh St Nicholas' Sighthill 1992–93; m 2 Apr 1964 Jill Robertson Dawson b 10 Oct 1940 d of Robert Robertson D. and Helen Whall; Children: Andrew John Kenneth b 4 Dec 1965; Wendy May b 1 Jul 1967; Roderick James Dawson b 28 Nov 1973; ord and ind to Birnie with Pluscarden 3 Sep 1993.

BUCKIE NORTH (FES VI, 280; VIII, 596; IX, 619; X, 356)

Linkage with Rathven terminated 7 Dec 1980.

1974 FRED COUTTS
(FES X, 356), ind to Buckie North 29 Mar 1974; became minister of linked charge with Rathven 11 Apr 1975; trans to Aberdeen Mastrick 22 Mar 1984.

1984 WILLIAM TAYLOR
B 22 Jan 1931 at New York, s of William T. and Margaret Skelton McGee; educ Peterhead Academy 1943–49; University of Aberdeen 1949–53 (MA), 1955–58 (MEd); Aberdeen College of Education 1955–56 (PGCE); University of Glasgow 1983–84; Teaching 1956–65; PT Classics 1965–83; lic by Presb of Paisley 28 Jun 1984; m 5 Jul 1958 Elizabeth Bruce Buchan b 2 Aug 1932 d of John Bruce B. and Annie Bruce Cordiner; Children: Margaret Anne b 28 Feb 1960 m Ian Tannahill; William b 17 Jun 1963; ord and ind to Buckie North 28 Sep 1984; ret 22 Jan 1996.

1996 ROBERT PATTERSON BOYLE
B 21 Jun 1945 at Dundee, s of Patrick Joseph B. and Jessie Patterson; educ Logie Secondary, Dundee 1957–60; Dundee College of Commerce 1982–84; University of Aberdeen 1984–89 (LTh, CPS); Motor Mechanic 1972–74; Machine/Bench Operator 1972–74; Tool Setter 1976–79; Machine Technician 1975–76, 1979–80; Motor Mechanic 1980–82; Care Asst 1982; lic by Presb of Dundee 13 Aug 1989; asst Aberdeen St Mary's King Street 1989–90; m 18 Mar 1967 Elaine Ryan Glancy Taylor b 18 Dec 1947 d of William Dick T. and Alice Barton Glancy; Children: Elaine Taylor b 13 Apr 1970 m Michael Watson; Matthew Robert b 26 May 1989; ord and ind to Perth Letham St Mark's 28 Nov 1990; trans to Buckie North 9 Aug 1996; app Chaplain to Tayside Fire Brigade 1994.

BUCKIE SOUTH AND WEST (FES X, 356)

Linked 4 Apr 1997 with Enzie.

1957 DANIEL HARPER GERRARD
(FES IX, 788; X, 356, 445), ret from RAF Chaplains' Branch and ind to Buckie West 17 Feb 1957; dem on app by Presb Church of Albany, W Australia 15 Mar 1961; died 16 May 1995.

1968 GEORGE WEST DUNCAN
(FES X, 356 (2)), ord and ind to Buckie South 12 Jun 1968; became minister of united charge with West 10 May 1970; died 17 Feb 1979.

1980 THOMAS NELSON JOHNSTON
(FES X, 402), trans from Rousay to Buckie South and West 30 Jan 1980; trans to Edinburgh Priestfield 26 Apr 1990.

1991 ERIC WALTER FOGGITT
B 13 May 1955 at Paris, s of George Bernard F. and Jacqueline Angèle Merlet; educ Watford Grammar and Mortimer Wilson Comprehensive, Alfreton 1966–73; University of Edinburgh 1973–77 (MA); Queen Margaret College, Edinburgh 1980–83 (BSc); University of Glasgow 1987–90 (BD); Teaching 1977–83; Speech Therapy 1983–89; lic by Presb of Glasgow, Sep 1990; asst Kirkintilloch St David's Memorial 1990–91; m 30 Jul 1983 Jacqueline Elizabeth Bryan b 29 Jun 1962 d of Ian B. and Joyce Robertson; Children: Peter Ian b 4 Oct 1984; Ashley Jacqueline b 14 Feb 1987; David Hareau b 1 Aug 1992; ord and ind to Buckie South and West 21 Jun 1991; became minister of linked charge with Enzie 4 Apr 1997.

CULLEN AND DESKFORD (FES X, 357)

Formed 27 Jun 1986 by union of Cullen and Deskford.

1937 JOHN TENNYSON GUTHRIE
(FES IX, 620 (2); X, 357), ord and ind to Cullen Old 14 Apr 1937; became minister of united charge with Seafield 22 Dec 1946 and of linked charge with Deskford 1 Oct 1967; died 21 Jan 1986.

1987 ALEXANDER JAMES MACPHERSON
ord by Presb of Dumbarton during assistantship at Milngavie St Paul's 4 Jun 1986; ind to Cullen and Deskford 1 May 1987; trans to Buchanan with Drymen 16 Jan 1997.

1997 GEORGE MELVYN WOOD
B 13 May 1956 at Banff, s of George Andrew W. and Edna Mair Watt; educ Banff Academy 1968–74; University of Aberdeen 1974–78 (MA), 1978–81 (BD); lic by Presb of Buchan 5 Jul 1981; asst London Crown Court 1981–83; m 26 Sep 1981 Doreen Mary Gillies b 27 Nov 1952 d of Finlay G. and Johan Fraser; Children: Calum George Daniel b 10 Feb 1989; ord by Presb of England during assistantship at Crown Court 20 Jun 1982; ind to Largs Clark Memorial 12 Jul 1983; trans to Cullen and Deskford 5 Dec 1997; app Clerk to Presb of Moray 30 Jun 1999.

DALLAS (FES X, 365)

Linked 6 Aug 1961 with Rafford. Further linked 30 Nov 1987 with Forres St Leonard's.

1961 JOHN CAMERON CORDINER
(FES IX, 646; X, 368), ord and ind to Rafford 13 Nov 1942; became minister of linked charge with Dallas St Michael's 6 Aug 1961; died 16 May 1986.

1988 PETER ROBERTSON
ord and ind to Dallas with Forres St Leonard's with Rafford 3 Jun 1988; dem 31 Dec 1998.

DUFFUS, SPYNIE AND HOPEMAN (FES X, 366, 367)

Formed 20 Jul 1979 by union of Duffus, Spynie and Hopeman.

1954 BENJAMIN SIBBALD
(FUF 169; FES IX, 223, 437, 641, 749; X, 366), trans from Glendevon to Duffus 10 Nov 1954; became minister of linked charge with Spynie 24 Aug 1958; ret 1 May 1963; died 17 Dec 1976.

1963 GEORGE KENNETH GARDNER DONAGHY
(FES IX, 217; X, 74, 125, 366), trans from Selkirk Lawson Memorial to Duffus with Spynie 29 Nov 1963; ret 30 Nov 1977; died 24 Jul 1983.

1967 JOHN LUMSDEN PORTEOUS
(FES X, 367), ord and ind to Hopeman 28 Apr 1967; ret 31 Jan 1979; died 20 Jun 1979.

1980 ROBERT SMITH McLEISH
(FES X, 357), trans from Cairnie-Glass to Duffus, Spynie and Hopeman 29 Feb 1980; trans to Insch-Leslie-Premnay-Oyne 31 May 1984.

1984 JOHN THOMSON STUART
(FES X, 150, 448), trans from Bedrule with Denholm with Minto to Duffus, Spynie and Hopeman 23 Nov 1984; ret 4 Dec 1993; w Audrey died 17 Jun 1973; m (2) 23 Mar 1978 Elsie Mary Ogilvie b 7 Nov 1930 d of John Wink O. and Isabella Mackay; spouse's children from previous marriage: Alison b 16 Oct 1957; Simon b 13 May 1959; Alexander b 27 Aug 1960; Sarah b 5 Jun 1965.

1994 ARCHIBALD ROBERT HALLIDAY
B 17 Feb 1934 at Glasgow, s of Archibald H. and Mary Jane Henderson; educ Coatbridge High 1946–51; University of London 1960–64 (BD); Baptist Theological College of Scotland 1960–64; RAF 1953–54; Quantity Surveying 1954–60; asst Cadder 1993–94; m 19 Aug 1960 Claire Smith b 24 May 1937 d of Alexander S. and Mary Reid Lindsay; Children: Paul b 4 Nov 1961; Mark b 23 Jan 1964; Philip b 30 Mar 1965; Simon b 29 Jul 1966; ord by Baptist Union of Scotland and ind to Keiss Baptist Church 25 Sep 1964; Arbroath Baptist Church 1968–78; Totteridge Baptist Church 1978–82; Shettleston Baptist Church 1982–93; ind to Duffus, Spynie and Hopeman 25 Feb 1994; ret 30 Apr 1999.

DYKE (FES IX, 642; X, 366)

Linked 30 Nov 1979 with Edinkillie.

1960 THOMAS FERGUSON NEILL
(FES IX, 264, 352; X, 156, 366), trans from Glasgow Cranhill to Dyke 18 May 1960; ret 31 Jan 1975; died 2 Jan 1996.

1975 THOMAS WILLIAMSON
(FES IX, 201, 475; X, 115, 165 (2), 366), trans from Glasgow Lansdowne to Dyke 25 Jun 1975; became minister of linked charge with Edinkillie 30 Nov 1979; ret 31 Oct 1982; Publ: Editor of *Dyke Church Bicentenary Book* (1981).

1983 ANN McCOLL POOLE
B 25 Jan 1938 at New Stevenston, d of John McEwan and Janet McConnell; educ Bellshill Academy 1949–51; Hamilton College 1972–76 (DipEd, ACE); University of Glasgow 1980–83 (LTh); Teaching 1976–80; lic by Presb of Stirling 3 Jul 1983; m 16 Mar 1956 Alexander McColl Poole b 22 Jul 1937, died 17 May 1977, s of Thomas Peat P. and Barbara McColl; Children: Alexander John Graeme b 28 Aug 1957 m Frances Morgan; Heather Ann Elizabeth b 20 Dec 1964 m Steven Gray; ord and ind to Dyke with Edinkillie 9 Sep 1983.

EDINKILLIE (FES IX, 642; X, 366)

Linked 30 Nov 1979 with Dyke.

1968 JAMES DOUGLAS DUFF
(FES IX, 139, 518, 519; X, 82, 290, 332, 366), trans from Aberdeen Summerhill to Edinkillie 7 Nov 1968; ret 31 Aug 1978; died 20 Mar 1994.

1979 THOMAS WILLIAMSON
(FES IX, 201, 475; X, 115, 165 (2), 366), ind to Dyke 25 Jun 1975; became minister of linked charge with Edinkillie 30 Nov 1979, see Dyke.

1983 ANN McCOLL POOLE
ord and ind to Dyke with Edinkillie 9 Sep 1983, see Dyke.

ELGIN HIGH (FUF 463; FES IX, 642; X, 366)

1951 JOHN WALTER EVANS
(FES IX, 98, 642; X, 366), trans from Chirnside North to Elgin High 10 Apr 1951; ret 31 Oct 1984.

1985 ALISTAIR HOGARTH MORRISON
ord and ind to Elgin High 31 May 1985; trans to Paisley St Mark's Oldhall 27 Sep 1989.

1991 CHARLES DOUGLAS McMILLAN
B 31 May 1939 at Crosshouse, Kilmarnock, s of Charles Douglas M. and Flora Elizabeth McKechnie Thomson; educ Crosshouse Secondary; University of Glasgow 1973–78 (LTh); Retail Industry and National Service (RAF) 1954–61; Factory Work/Production Control 1961–73; lic by

Presb of Irvine and Kilmarnock 29 Jun 1978; asst Troon Portland 1978–79; m 14 Apr 1962 Mary Isobel McDonald b 28 Jan 1939 d of Donald John M. and Mary Isobel Adam; Children: Donald John b 25 Nov 1963 m Fiona Bennie; Charles Alexander b 11 Jun 1966; Mairi Elizabeth b 29 Jun 1970 m John Brown; ord and ind to Bannockburn Ladywell 31 May 1979; trans to Elgin High 2 Nov 1991.

ELGIN ST GILES' AND ST COLUMBA'S SOUTH
(FES X, 366, 367)

Formed 1 Oct 1999 by union of Elgin St Giles' and Elgin South.

1956   PETER DIACK
(FES IX, 574; X, 333, 367), trans from Bour-treebush to Elgin South 22 Nov 1956; ret 31 Dec 1994.

1973   DAVID PATRICK LOW CUMMING
(FES X, 102, 354 (2), 366), trans from Turriff St Ninian's to Elgin St Giles' 27 Jun 1973; dem 31 Aug 1985 on app as Secretary Depute, Dept of Ministry and Mission.

1983   ANDREW J WILSON
introd as Assoc at Elgin St Giles' 1 Jul 1983; ind to Dundee Downfield South 28 May 1986.

1986   GEORGE BRYAN ROLLO
(FES X, 316), trans from Arbroath St Margaret's to Elgin St Giles' 7 May 1986; Addl children: Paul William b 10 Feb 1976; Sarah Elizabeth b 7 Apr 1978; Andrew George b 8 Jun 1985.

1986   ALEXANDER SPENCE
(FES IX, 54, 574; X, 31, 156, 317), introd as Assoc at Elgin St Giles' 1986; ret 1989.

1992   JAMES MERCIER THOMSON
(FES IX, 199; X, 114, 218), [correction: Mercier, not Mercer as in Vol IX, X]; dem from Dumbarton The West Kirk and introd as Assoc at Elgin St Giles' 31 Jul 1992.

ENZIE (FES IX, 621; X, 358)

Linked 7 Dec 1980 with Rathven. Arrangement terminated 4 Apr 1997. Linked same date with Buckie South and West.

1972   DONALD MACDONALD
(FES X, 358), ord and ind to Enzie 12 May 1972; dem 30 Jun 1980; died 29 Jan 1994.

1981   JOHN ROBERT OSBECK
ord by Presb of Aberdeen during assistantship at Dyce 3 Jul 1979; ind to Enzie with Rathven 9 May 1981; ind to Aberdeen St John's Church for Deaf People 1 Sep 1991.

1992   ROSEMARY LEGGE
ord and ind to Enzie with Rathven 8 May 1992; trans to Marnoch 18 Sep 1997.

1997   ERIC WALTER FOGGITT
ord and ind to Buckie South and West 21 Jun 1991; became minister of linked charge with Enzie 4 Apr 1997.

FINDOCHTY (FUF 454; FES IX, 621; X, 358)

Linked 22 Nov 1970 with Portknockie. Further linked 17 Apr 1997 with Rathven.

1974   DAVID KEITH PATTERSON BENNETT
(FES X, 358), ord and ind to Findochty with Portknockie 20 Sep 1974; trans to Kirkpatrick-Irongray with Lochrutton 30 Aug 1987.

1988   WILLIAM BROWN ROSS
ord and ind to Findochty with Portknockie 7 Oct 1988; trans to Alvie and Insh and app Warden of Badenoch Centre 13 Dec 1995.

1997   GRAHAM AUSTIN
B 1 May 1960 at Duns, s of Charles A. and Agnes Fraser Shand; educ Earlston High 1972–76; Glasgow Bible Training Institute 1980–83 (DBTI); St Colm's College, Edinburgh 1986–78 (CChCS); University of Edinburgh 1992–96 (BD); Youth Work 1983–86; Deacon 1987–92; lic by Presb of Lothian 4 Jul 1996; asst Penicuik North 1996–97; m 25 Aug 1984 Denise Linda Buchanan b 23 Jan 1962 d of Malcolm B. and Estelle Hedges; ord and ind to Findochty with Portknockie with Rathven 6 Jun 1997.

FORRES ST LAURENCE (FES VI, 420; VIII, 644; IX, 644; X, 367)

1974   WILLIAM McEWIN REID
(FES X, 109, 367), trans from Hurlford Kirk to St Laurence 4 Jan 1974; dem 31 Dec 1992 on app to the Scots Kirk, Paris.

1993   BARRY JAMES BOYD
B 29 Jan 1954 at Glasgow, s of Joseph Barr B. and Christina Ballantyne; educ Ruthrieston Secondary, Aberdeen 1966–71; University of Aberdeen 1987–92 (LTh, DPS); North East Scotland Water Board 1971–73; Trainee Retail Manager 1973–75; British Telecom 1975–87; lic by Presb of Aberdeen 25 Jun 1992; ord and ind to St Laurence 27 Aug 1993.

FORRES ST LEONARD'S (FES X, 367)

Linked 30 Nov 1987 with Dallas with Rafford.

1960   DAVID LESLIE SCOTT
(FES IX, 748; X, 367, 425), res from service with FMC and ind to Forres Castlehill 18 Nov 1960; ret 30 Jun 1972; died 16 Oct 1980.

1961   ANDREW KIRKWOOD FAIRLIE
(FES IX, 205, 329, 683 (2); X, 194, 367), trans from Hamilton Avon Street to Forres High 13 Dec 1961; ret 4 Dec 1970; died 13 Feb 1988.

1972 JOHN CLARKE PORTER
(FES X, 281, 367 (2)), trans from Dysart St Serf's to Forres High 22 Mar 1972; became minister of united charge with Castlehill 30 Jun 1972; ret 30 Apr 1987 on grounds of ill-health; s Donald m Julia Coutts; d Marion m Alan McCaig.

1988 PETER ROBERTSON
ord and ind to Dallas with Forres St Leonard's with Rafford 3 Jun 1988; dem 31 Dec 1998.

GRANGE (FES IX, 627; X, 359)

Linked 13 Jul 1975 with Rothiemay.

1963 ALISTAIR ANDREW BENVIE DAVIDSON
(FES X, 359), ind to Grange 24 Jan 1963; became minister of linked charge with Rothiemay 13 Jul 1975; ret 30 Jun 1997.

KEITH NORTH NEWMILL AND BOHARM (FES X, 355, 360)

Formed 23 Jun 1983 by union of Keith North and Newmill and Boharm.

1961 JOHN THOMAS ROBERTSON
(FES X, 359, 360), ord and ind to Keith North 13 Sep 1961; became minister of united charge with Newmill 7 Jun 1970 and with Boharm 23 Jun 1983; ret 13 Oct 1993; d Marion m Bethune.

1993 MICHAEL GERRARD LYALL
B 28 Mar 1958 at Edinburgh, s of John Roberston L. and Elizabeth McGregor Brown; educ Lesmahagow High and Dumbarton Academy 1970–76; University of Glasgow 1987–92 (BD, CMin); Principal Asst of Accounts 1976–87; lic by Presb of Dumbarton 28 Jun 1992; asst Bonhill 1992–93; m 11 Oct 1980 Maureen Gordon b 29 Sep 1961 d of George G. and Jean Morrison Livingstone; Children: Jonathan Michael b 10 Mar 1984; Ian Gordon b 6 Jul 1986; Stuart David b 12 Feb 1990; ord and ind to Keith North, Newmill and Boharm 11 May 1993.

KEITH ST RUFUS AND BOTRIPHNIE (FES X, 355, 360)

Formed 16 Jun 1983 by union of Keith St Rufus and Botriphnie.

1962 JAMES SOUTER STEPHEN
(FES IX, 630; X, 355, 360), trans from Mortlach to Botriphnie 24 Jan 1962; became minister of linked charge with Boharm 29 Nov 1970; ret 15 Jul 1983; died 29 Apr 1997.

1976 JOHN ANGUS MACLEOD
(FES X, 38, 271), trans from Cowdenbeath Cairns to St Rufus 14 May 1976; became minister of united charge with Botriphnie 16 Jun 1983; ret 24 May 1995.

1995 RANALD STUART ROBERTSON GAULD
B 18 Mar 1956 at Aberdeen, s of William Robertson G. and Vivian Vernon-Jarvis; educ Aberdeen Grammar 1961–74; University of Aberdeen 1974–77 (LLB), 1977–79 (MA), 1986–90 (BD); Solicitor 1979–85; Administrator, Tiberias, Israel 1985–86; lic by Presb of Aberdeen 27 Jun 1990; asst Aberdeen Holburn West 1990–91; m 5 Jan 1993 Kay Frances Chalmers b 6 Aug 1959 d of James Dawson Smith C. and Frances Mary Grant; ord by Presb of West Lothian and introd as Assoc at Linlithgow St Michael's 25 Sep 1991; trans to St Rufus and Botriphnie 5 Oct 1995.

1999 KAY FRANCES GAULD
B 6 Aug 1959 at Buckie, d of James Dawson Smith Chalmers and Frances Mary Grant; educ Banff Academy 1971–76; University of Aberdeen 1988–92 (BD); Union Theological Seminary and Jewish Theological Seminary, New York 1992–93 (STM); University of Aberdeen 1995–98 (PhD); Clydesdale Bank 1976–88; lic by Presb of Gordon 27 Jun 1993; asst Rosyth 1993; Mid Calder 1994; m 5 Jan 1993 Ranald Stuart Robertson Gauld b 18 Mar 1956 s of William Robertson G. and Vivian Vernon-Jarvis; ord by Presb of Moray and introd as Assoc (part-time) at St Rufus and Botriphnie 1 Jul 1999.

KINLOSS AND FINDHORN (FES IX, 645; X, 368)

Continued vacancy from 1985 until 1995. Linked 13 Jan 1995 with Alves and Burghead.

1937 DAVID MARTIN GALLOWAY
(FES IX, 645; X, 368), ord and ind to Kinloss and Findhorn 10 Mar 1937; ret 30 Apr 1981; died 21 Oct 1987.

1983 DONALD ROBERTSON FRASER
(FES IX, 83, 505 (2); X, 262, 299, 367), trans from Huntly Cairnie-Glass to Kinloss and Findhorn 20 Apr 1983; ret 31 Jul 1985.

1995 JOHN CAIRNS BECK
(FES X, 387), trans from Glasgow Dennistoun Central to Alves and Burghead with Kinloss and Findhorn 28 Jun 1995.

KNOCKANDO, ELCHIES AND ARCHIESTOWN (FES X, 368)

Linked 17 Jan 1982 with Rothes.

1932 LEWIS DAVIDSON ROSS
(FES IX, 642 (2); X, 366), ord and ind to Elchies 24 Aug 1932; became minister of united charge with Archiestown 7 Jan 1934; ret 30 Jun 1968; died 26 Apr 1988.

1940 ROBERT PRENTICE
(FES IX, 645; X, 368 (2)), ord and ind to Knockando 30 Oct 1940, became minister of united charge with Elchies and Archiestown 30 Jun 1968; ret 30 Apr 1981; died 2 Mar 1999.

1982 ROBERT JAMES MELLIS
ord and ind to Knockando, Elchies and Archiestown with Rothes 2 Jul 1982; trans to Tarbat 24 Mar 1988.

1989 IVAN CORRY WARWICK
ret from RAChD and ind to Knockando, Elchies and Archiestown with Rothes 30 Aug 1989; trans to Fodderty and Strathpeffer 23 Jul 1999.

LOSSIEMOUTH ST GERARDINE'S HIGH (FES X, 368)

Formed 7 Aug 1960 by union of Lossiemouth High and Drainie St Gerardine's.

1933 NORMAN WALLIS SAMMON
(FUF 541; FES IX, 645, 748; X, 368), res from service with FMC in Nagpur, India and ind to Lossiemouth High 23 Mar 1933; ret 7 Aug 1960; died 14 May 1978.

1961 HENDRY FORBES WATT
(FES IX, 489; X, 12, 291, 368), trans from Edinburgh Juniper Green St Margaret's to St Gerardine's High 3 Mar 1961; ret 30 Sep 1976 on grounds of ill-health; w Evelyn died 1 Nov 1983.

1977 DAVID JAMES HEPBURN LAING
ord by Presb of Aberdeen during assistantship at West of St Nicholas 15 Mar 1976; introd to St Gerardine's High (term) 15 Jun 1977 and ind to same charge Jun 1980; trans to Dundee Craigiebank 9 Nov 1982.

1983 RODERICK G SANGSTER
ord and ind to St Gerardine's High 19 May 1983; dem 31 Dec 1986.

1986 DUNCAN MURRAY
B 11 Feb 1937 at Dundee, s of Wilfred David and Lavinia Duncan M; educ Rockwell Junior Secondary, Dundee 1949–52; Dundee Technical College 1962 (HNC); University of Aberdeen 1982–85 (BTh); Marine Eng (Ben Line) 1958–62; Plant Eng Draughtsman 1962–77; Sen Eng (Hospital) 1977–82; lic by Presb of Dundee 30 Jun 1985; asst Dundee Roseangle Ryehill 1985–86; m 6 Dec 1958 Elizabeth Gourlay Hastie Cairns b 27 Aug 1937 d of William C. and Elizabeth Hastie; Children: Jacqueline Elizabeth b 8 Oct 1960 m Richard Callison; Neil David b 28 Aug 1963 m Janice Nimmo; ord and ind to St Gerardine's High 9 Jul 1986.

LOSSIEMOUTH ST JAMES' (FUF 466; FES IX, 645; X, 368)

1973 GEORGE LAMB CORDINER
(FES X, 368), ord and ind to St James' 11 May 1973.

MORTLACH AND CABRACH (FES X, 356, 360)

Formed 21 Mar 1982 by union of Mortlach and Cabrach.

1975 ROBERT KELTIE
(FES IX, 87; X, 53, 332, 357, 420), trans from Aberdeen St Ninian's to Cabrach with Mortlach 20 Nov 1975; ret 31 Dec 1981.

1982 HUGH MACCOMMACH CROLL SMITH
(FES X, 388), trans from Reay to Mortlach and Cabrach 11 Aug 1982.

PLUSCARDEN (FUF 466; FES IX, 646; X, 368)

Linked 1 Oct 1972 with Birnie.

1959 KEITH NORMAN PATERSON
(FES VIII, 714; IX, 745; X, 368, 424), res from service with Overseas Council in Punjab, India and ind to Pluscarden 26 Jun 1959; ret 30 Sep 1972; died 3 Nov 1994.

1972 ADAM RONALD RENTOUL TORRIE
(FES IX, 396, 726; X, 365, 413), ind to Birnie 7 Sep 1956; became minister of linked charge with Pluscarden 1 Oct 1972, see Birnie.

1986 GORDON STRACHAN COWIE
ord and ind to Birnie with Pluscarden 2 Nov 1986, see Birnie.

1993 RONALD JOHN SCOTLAND
ord and ind to Birnie with Pluscarden 3 Sep 1993, see Birnie.

PORTKNOCKIE (FES IX, 623; X, 361)

Linked 22 Nov 1970 with Findochty. Further linked 17 Apr 1997 with Rathven.

1965 ALEXANDER CURRIE HILL
(FES X, 361), ord and ind to Portknockie 17 Nov 1965; ret 7 Apr 1970; died 16 Mar 1983.

1972 THOMAS ALEXANDER BERTRAM
(FES X, 358), ord and ind to Findochty with Portknockie 14 Jan 1972; dem 16 Sep 1973 to return to teaching.

1974 DAVID KEITH PATTERSON BENNETT
(FES X, 358), ord and ind to Findochty with Portknockie 20 Sep 1974; trans to Kirkpatrick-Irongray with Lochrutton 30 Aug 1987.

1988 WILLIAM BROWN ROSS
ord and ind to Findochty with Portknockie 7 Oct 1988, see Findochty.

1997 GRAHAM AUSTIN
ord and ind to Findochty with Portknockie with Rathven 6 Jun 1997, see Findochty.

RAFFORD (FES IX, 646; X, 368)

Linked 6 Aug 1961 with Dallas. Further linked 30 Nov 1987 with Forres St Leonard's.

1942 JOHN CAMERON CORDINER
(FES IX, 646; X, 368), ord and ind to Rafford 13 Nov 1942; became minister of linked charge with Dallas St Michael's 6 Aug 1961; died 16 May 1986.

1988 PETER ROBERTSON
ord and ind to Dallas with Forres St Leonard's with Rafford 3 Jun 1988; dem 31 Dec 1998.

RATHVEN (FES VI, 294; VIII, 601; IX, 623; X, 361)

Linkage with Buckie North terminated 7 Dec 1980. Linked same date with Enzie. Linkage terminated 4 Apr 1997. Linked 17 Apr 1997 with Findochty with Portknockie.

1959 THOMAS SUGDEN HOWIESON
(FES IX, 712; X, 361, 405), trans from Delting Brae to Rathven 8 Apr 1959; ret 1 Jul 1974; died 14 Aug 1994.

1975 FRED COUTTS
(FES X, 356), ind to Buckie North 29 Mar 1974; minister of linked charge with Rathven 11 Apr 1975 until 7 Dec 1980; trans to Aberdeen Mastrick 22 Mar 1984.

1981 JOHN ROBERT OSBECK
ind to Enzie with Rathven 9 May 1981, see Enzie.

1992 ROSEMARY LEGGE
ord and ind to Enzie with Rathven 8 May 1992; trans to Marnoch 18 Sep 1997.

1997 GRAHAM AUSTIN
ord and ind to Findochty with Portknockie with Rathven 6 Jun 1997, see Findochty.

ROTHES (FES IX, 647; X, 368)

Linked 17 Jan 1982 with Knockando, Elchies and Archiestown.

1956 DANIEL EDWARD GUNN
(FES IX, 603; X, 347, 368), trans from Ardallie to Rothes 13 Jan 1956; ret 31 May 1980; died 28 Apr 1995.

1982 ROBERT JAMES MELLIS
ord and ind to Knockando, Elchies and Archiestown with Rothes 2 Jul 1982; trans to Tarbat 24 Mar 1988.

1989 IVAN CORRY WARWICK
ind to Knockando, Elchies and Archiestown with Rothes 30 Aug 1989, see Knockando.

ROTHIEMAY (FES IX, 631; X, 361)

Linked 13 Jul 1975 with Grange.

1966 ERNEST WOOD BURNETT
(FES IX, 461, 618, 730; X, 5, 273, 361), trans from Edinburgh Bruntsfield to Rothiemay 16 Mar 1966; ret 15 May 1975; died 2 Sep 1982.

1975 ALISTAIR ANDREW BENVIE DAVIDSON
(FES X, 359), ind to Grange 24 Jan 1963; became minister of linked charge with Rothiemay 13 Jul 1975; ret 30 Jun 1997.

SPEYMOUTH (FES VI, 401; VIII, 638; IX, 647; X, 369)

Union of Speymouth and Garmouth severed 1 Mar 1959. Speymouth linked same date with Bellie. Linkage continues following union of Speymouth and Garmouth 14 Nov 1988.

1959 ALICK HUGH MACAULAY
(FES IX, 664; X, 365, 379, 380), trans from Lochbroom and Ullapool to Bellie with Speymouth 22 Jul 1959; ret 30 Jun 1981.

1983 DAVID JAMES FERGUSON
(FES X, 199, 407), trans from Motherwell Crosshill to Bellie with Speymouth 26 Mar 1982; became minister of united charge with Garmouth 14 Nov 1988; app Clerk to Presb of Moray 1997.

ST ANDREW'S-LHANBRYD AND URQUHART (FES X, 368, 369)

Formed 14 Nov 1988 by union of St Andrew's-Lhanbryd and Urquhart (linkage of Urquhart and Garmouth terminated same date).

1944 STANLEY FORSYTH
(FES IX, 648; X, 369), ord and ind to Urquhart 26 Jan 1944; became minister of linked charge with Garmouth 5 Apr 1959; ret 14 Nov 1988; died 9 Apr 1989.

1962 JAMES ALLAN LAING
(FES IX,13, 96; X, 8, 368), trans from Edinburgh Duddingston to St Andrew's-Lhanbryd 8 Jun 1962; ret 30 Jun 1975; died 13 Jul 1985.

1975 DAVID WARD LUNAN
(FES X, 153, 368), trans from Calton New to St Andrew's-Lhanbryd 10 Oct 1975; trans to Glasgow Renfield St Stephen's 18 Sep 1987.

1989 SCOTT CLELAND GUY
ord and ind to St Andrew's-Lhanbryd and Urquhart 9 Jun 1989; trans to Aberdeen Northfield 17 Dec 1998.

PRESBYTERY OF ABERNETHY

ABERNETHY (FES IX, 632; X, 362)

Linked 17 Feb 1972 with Cromdale and Advie.

1966 JAMES HENDERSON TAYLOR BOYD (FES IX, 326, 708; X, 45, 353, 362, 403), trans from Gamrie with New Byth to Abernethy 30 Nov 1966; became minister of linked charge with Cromdale and Advie 17 Feb 1972; ret 13 Oct 1979; died 24 Jul 1992.

1980 JAMES ALEXANDER IAIN MACEWAN (FES X, 332), trans from Aberdeen Stockethill to Abernethy with Cromdale and Advie 28 Feb 1980; Addl children: Inga Aileen b 12 Nov 1977.

ALVIE AND INSH (FES IX, 632; X, 362)

Continued vacancy from 1998.

1960 ALEXANDER HUTCHISON (FES IX, 35, 169, 466, 467; X, 99, 362), trans from Ayr Darlington New to Alvie and Insh 4 Nov 1960; ret 31 Mar 1978; died 6 Apr 1994.

1978 JOHN ROBERTSON LYALL (FES X, 210, 454), res as Field Officer for Christian Education and ind to Alvie and Insh 27 Oct 1978; also app Warden of Badenoch Christian Centre; died 12 Mar 1995; Publ: Contributor to *Ten Rural Churches Britain* (Marc, 1988).

1995 WILLIAM BROWN ROSS trans from Findochty with Portknockie to Alvie and Insh and app Warden of Badenoch Centre 13 Dec 1995; trans to Kilmory with Lamlash 30 Sep 1998.

BOAT OF GARTEN AND KINCARDINE (FES IX, 632; X, 362)

Linked 26 Mar 1969 with Duthil.

1969 IVAN FRANCIS TIBBS (FES IX, 227, 353, 801; X, 233, 362), trans from Campeltown Longrow to Boat of Garten and Kincardine with Duthil 23 Oct 1969; ret 31 Aug 1981; died 8 Sep 1998.

1981 MATTHEW SMITH STEWART B 10 Jan 1931 at Bellshill, s of Charles S. and Margaret Smith; educ Bellshill Academy; University of Strathclyde 1975 (DMS); University of Glasgow 1981 (LTh); Engineering 1946–52; RAF Navigation Officer 1952–56; Probation Officer 1956–57; Boys' Brigade Organiser, Ghana 1957–61, UK 1962–66; Personnel Officer 1966–78; lic by Presb of Hamilton 28 Jun 1981; m 15 Aug 1959 Christina Crawford Johnson b 1 Oct 1937 d of Robert Thomas J. and Elizabeth Brown Kirk Crawford; Children: Fraser Crawford b 14 Aug 1960; Alastair Robert b 14 Aug 1960 m Abigail Louise Wilman; Fiona Elizabeth Margaret b 30 Oct 1965; ord and ind to Boat of Garten and Kincardine with Duthil 23 Oct 1981; ret 30 Sep 1998.

1999 DAVID WILLIAMSON WHYTE B 17 Jul 1946 at Glasgow, s of Harry Cowie W. and Annie Gray Williamson; educ Albert Secondary, Glasgow; University of Aberdeen 1989–91 (LTh); Compositor-Printing 1961–88; lic by Presb of Moray 27 Sep 1991; asst Glasgow Renfield St Stephen's 1991–92; m 18 May 1968 Janet Simpson Thompson d of James Howatt T. and Alice Armour; Children: Mark David b 6 Sep 1969; Martin Thompson b 9 May 1972; ord and ind to Culross and Torryburn 12 Feb 1993; trans to Boat of Garten and Kincardine with Duthil 5 Mar 1999.

CROMDALE AND ADVIE (FES X, 362)

Linked 17 Feb 1972 with Abernethy.

1937 JOSEPH GRANT (FES IX, 630, 633; X, 362), trans from Rhynie to Cromdale 16 Jun 1937; became minister of linked charge with Advie 6 Oct 1959; ret 30 Jun 1971; died 25 Jul 1990.

1972 JAMES HENDERSON TAYLOR BOYD (FES IX, 326, 708; X, 45, 353, 362, 403), ind to Abernethy 30 Nov 1966; became minister of linked charge with Cromdale and Advie 17 Feb 1972, see Abernethy.

1980 JAMES ALEXANDER IAIN MACEWAN (FES X, 332), ind to Abernethy with Cromdale and Advie 28 Feb 1980, see Abernethy.

DULNAIN BRIDGE (FES IX, 633; X, 362)

Linked 16 Mar 1976 with Grantown-on-Spey.

1956 HERBERT GEORGE JACKSON (FES X, 362), ord and ind to Dulnain Bridge 19 Dec 1956; ret 8 Aug 1975; died 16 Mar 1977.

1976 GEORGE BAIN JOHNSTON
(FES IX, 102, 635; X, 363 (2)), ind to Inverallan 27 Mar 1952; became minister of united charge with Grantown South 2 Jun 1960 and of linked charge with Dulnain Bridge 16 Mar 1976, see Grantown-on-Spey.

1980 COLIN MATHIESON ALSTON
ind to Dulnain Bridge with Grantown-on-Spey 15 Dec 1980; dem 30 Nov 1987 on app by Board of World Mission and Unity to Trinidad.

1988 MORRIS SMITH
B 8 Dec 1948 at Edinburgh, s of Alister Cowan S. and Mary Walker Bryce; educ Portobello High 1953–66; University of Edinburgh 1982–87 (BD, CCE); Apprentice GPO Telephones 1966–69; Telephone Engineer 1969–82; lic by Presb of Lothian 2 Jul 1987; asst Edinburgh Fairmilehead 1987–88; m 17 Apr 1970 Janette Tenn Ireland b 20 Aug 1949 d of Hugh Carson I. and Janet Macalpine Buchan; Children: Jennifer Ireland b 27 May 1971; Kirsty Miller b 1 May 1974 m Stephen George; ord and ind to Dulnain Bridge with Grantown-on-Spey 16 May 1988.

DUTHIL (FES VI, 359; VIII, 616; IX, 634; X, 363)

Linked 26 Mar 1969 with Boat of Garten and Kincardine.

1945 THOMAS MACKENZIE DONN
(FES IX, 634, 674, 699; X, 363), trans from Stornoway Martin's Memorial to Duthil 15 Mar 1945; ret 20 Mar 1969.

1969 IVAN FRANCIS TIBBS
(FES IX, 227, 353, 801; X, 233, 362), ind to Boat of Garten and Kincardine with Duthil 23 Oct 1969, see Boat of Garten.

1981 MATTHEW SMITH STEWART
ord and ind to Boat of Garten and Kincardine with Duthil 23 Oct 1981, see Boat of Garten.

1999 DAVID WILLIAMSON WHYTE
ind to Boat of Garten and Kincardine with Duthil 5 Mar 1999, see Boat of Garten.

GRANTOWN-ON-SPEY (FES X, 363)

Linked 16 Mar 1976 with Dulnain Bridge.

1953 DONALD ROSS
(FUF 321; FES IX, 27, 524, 634; X, 363), trans from Edinburgh Mayfield North to Grantown South 12 Nov 1953; ret 16 Nov 1959; died 12 May 1988.

1960 GEORGE BAIN JOHNSTON
(FES IX, 102, 635; X, 363 (2)), trans from Greenlaw Old to Inverallan 27 Mar 1952; became minister of united charge with Grantown South 2 Jun 1960 and of linked charge with Dulnain Bridge 16 Mar 1976; ret 23 Aug 1980; died 3 Feb 1996.

1980 COLIN MATHIESON ALSTON
ind to Dulnain Bridge with Grantown-on-Spey 15 Dec 1980, see Dulnain Bridge.

1988 MORRIS SMITH
ord and ind to Dulnain Bridge with Grantown-on-Spey 16 May 1988, see Dulnain Bridge.

INVERAVEN AND GLENLIVET (FES IX, 635; X, 363)

1950 WILLIAM MENZIES MALCOLM
(FES IX, 448, 635 (2); X, 363), trans from Fallin to Inveraven 12 Dec 1950; became minister of united charge with Glenlivet and Craggan 30 Apr 1953; ret 31 Jul 1976; died 13 Nov 1981.

1977 DONALD ANGUS MACLEOD
(FES X, 123, 155, 189, 236), res from Bothwell Kirkfield and Wooddean (term) and ind to Inveraven and Glenlivet 31 Mar 1977; ret 22 Apr 1987; died 3 Sep 1999.

1987 CHRISTINA ANNE MACDONALD DOUGLAS
B 4 May 1923 at Ardclach, d of Donald Kinnaird and Anne MacDonald-Stewart; educ Nairn Academy 1935–39; University of Glasgow (CSW); Moray House College, Edinburgh; Social Work 1969–86; lic by Presb of Falkirk 19 Jun 1987; m 14 Jun 1946 Ian Douglas s of William D. and Barker; ord and ind to Ineraven and Glenlivet 21 Aug 1987; ret 31 Mar 1993.

1993 MARGARET ALISON MUIR
B 13 Mar 1950 at Aberfeldy, d of Thomas M. and Catherine Lees Thomson; educ Pitlochry High and Breadalbane Academy, Aberfeldy 1955–68; University of Edinburgh 1968–71 (MA), 1971–73 (LLB), 1985–88 (BD); Solicitor 1973–85; lic by Presb of Edinburgh 3 Jul 1988; asst Edinburgh Fairmilehead 1988–90; ord by Presb of Edinburgh during assistantship at Fairmilehead 28 May 1989; ind to Inveraven and Glenlivet 17 Aug 1993.

KINGUSSIE (FES X, 363)

1959 NINIAN BLUNDELL WRIGHT
(FES IX, 174, 714; X, 352, 363), trans from Fyvie to Kingussie 21 Jul 1959; ret 3 Mar 1973; died 18 Jun 1993.

1973 ALBERT JENNER
(FES IX, 535; X, 124, 163, 322, 363), trans from Johnston St Andrew's Trinity to Kingussie 5 Oct 1973; died 3 Jul 1990.

1991 NORMAN ROY MACASKILL
(FES X, 277), trans from Lochgelly Macainsh to Kingussie 9 Apr 1991.

KIRKMICHAEL AND TOMINTOUL (FES X, 363)

1969 KENNETH ROSS
(FES X, 233, 234, 240, 276, 363), trans from Gigha and Cara to Kirkmichael and Tomintoul 17 Dec 1969; dem 1 Feb 1977; ind to Northmavine 4 Nov 1978.

1977 GORDON ROSS MACKENZIE
ord and ind to Kirkmichael and Tomintoul 26 Oct 1977; trans to Monikie and Newbigging 14 Feb 1985.

1985 DONALD ALICK MACLEAN
B 21 Jun 1923 at Hougharry, North Uist, s of Angus M. and Johana Maclean; educ Bayhead Secondary, N Uist and Skerry's College, Glasgow; University of Glasgow (MA); Jordanhill College, Glasgow; Free Presb Church (Divinity); Crofting; Army Service; lic by Presb of Glasgow (Free Presb Church) 3 Jun 1953; m 24 Jun 1953 Jessie Fraser d of John and Marjorie F; ord by Presb of Glasgow (Free Presb Church) and app for service in Zimbabwe 6 Jun 1953; ind to Bracadale (FPC) Oct 1957; Halkirk and Thurso (FPC) Nov 1967; ind to Carloway 2 Dec 1983; trans to Kirkmichael and Tomintoul 25 Sep 1985; ret 31 Oct 1989; died 1 Apr 1999.

1992 SVEN (SVEINBJÖRN) SESSELIUS BJARNASON
B 19 Aug 1941 at Reykjavik, Iceland, s of Bjarni B. and Ösk Sveinbjarnardóttir; educ Reykjavik Eastern Junior High and Reykjavik Grammar 1954–62; Heriot-Watt University 1962–64; University of Iceland 1966–73 (Cand Theol); University of Edinburgh 1970–71 (CPS); Office of Civil Defence, Iceland 1964–73; Ministry of Justice, Iceland; m 12 Sep 1967 Catherine MacDonald b 16 Jun 1934 d of Angus M. and Christina McCuish; Children: Angus Gudmundur b 31 Dec 1970; Kristine b 19 Dec 1973; ord by the Bishop of Iceland 1 Jul 1973; ind to Cowdenbeath Cairns 24 Nov 1976; dem 31 Aug 1987; various locums 1987–90; loc ten Kirkmichael and Tomintoul 22 Apr 1990; ind to same charge 26 May 1992.

LAGGAN (FES IX, 636; X, 364)

Linked 17 Mar 1975 with Newtonmore.

1975 DAVID LEWIS STODDART
(FES X, 196, 364), trans from Hamilton South with Quarter to Newtonmore with Laggan 17 Mar 1975; ret 7 Oct 1987.

1988 GORDON S LENNOX
ind to Laggan with Newtonmore 10 May 1988; dem 31 Jan 1991.

1991 IRENE CAMERON GILLESPIE
B 21 Jul 1946 at Alloa, d of David McAllister and Jessie Leonard Cameron Stewart; educ Grange Secondary and Alloa Academy 1958–62; University

of Glasgow 1985–89 (BD); Library Asst 1962–72; lic by Presb of Stirling 29 Jun 1989; asst Bridge of Allan Holy Trinity 1989–90; m 11 Oct 1972 Duncan Gillespie b 11 Feb 1928 s of David G. and Barbara Janet Geddes McIntyre; Children: Alison Irene b 12 Dec 1975; Ailsa Helen Stewart b 13 Jun 1977; ord and ind to Laggan with Newtonmore 24 Jun 1991.

NEWTONMORE (FES IX, 637; X, 364)

Linked 17 Mar 1975 with Laggan.

1962 JAMES MURRAY
(FES VIII, 577; IX, 232, 583; X, 135 (2), 364), trans from Greenock St Mark's Greenbank to Newtonmore 6 Sep 1962; ret 29 Sep 1974; died 18 Jul 1993.

1975 DAVID LEWIS STODDART
(FES X, 196, 364), trans from Hamilton South with Quarter to Newtonmore with Laggan 17 Mar 1975; ret 7 Oct 1987.

1988 GORDON S LENNOX
ind to Laggan with Newtonmore 10 May 1988; dem 31 Jan 1991.

1991 IRENE CAMERON GILLESPIE
ord and ind to Laggan with Newtonmore 24 Jun 1991, see Laggan.

ROTHIEMURCHUS AND AVIEMORE (FES IX, 637; X, 364)

1961 FREDERICK HAROLD SALTER
(FES IX, 604; X, 166, 347, 364), trans from Glasgow Martyrs' to Rothiemurchus and Aviemore 4 Oct 1961; ret 1 Oct 1974; died 17 Nov 1997.

1975 JAMES WILLIAM BENSON
(FES X, 364), ord and ind to Rothiemurchus and Aviemore 18 Jun 1975; trans to Balquhidder 25 Aug 1982.

1982 WILLIAM WALLACE NIVEN
ord and ind to Rothiemurchus and Aviemore 24 Nov 1982; trans to Alness 26 Oct 1989.

1990 RON CHRISTIE WHYTE
B 17 Oct 1947 at Arbroath, s of John Yeaman W. and Annie Watt Smith; educ Arbroath High 1953–63; Dundee Tech College 1963–66; University of Aberdeen 1983–88 (BD, CPS); Electrician 1963–72; Oil Industry 1972–74, 1976–83; Royal Navy Aux Service 1974–76; lic by Presb of Lochcarron and Skye 14 Jul 1989; asst Gairloch and Dundonnell 1989–90; m 6 Jun 1969 Patricia Ann Ohren b 23 Jun 1947 d of Fredric George O. and Doris Duke; Children: James Alexander b 10 Nov 1974; Iain Ron b 23 Feb 1976 m Laura Mowat; Naomi Elizabeth b 8 Jun 1984; Paul David b 25 Aug 1986; ord and ind to Rothiemurchus and Aviemore 9 May 1990.

PRESBYTERY OF INVERNESS

ARDCLACH (FES IX, 649; X, 370)

Linked 3 Apr 1963 with Auldearn and Dalmore.

1963 DAVID WILLIAM DOUGLAS JOHNSTON
(FES IX, 582; X, 337, 370), trans from Skene to
Ardclach with Auldearn and Dalmore 4 Sep 1963;
died 28 Nov 1976.

1977 ANDREW D M REID
ord and ind to Ardclach with Auldearn and Dalmore
9 Jun 1977; dem 19 Oct 1983.

1984 ALEXANDER JAMES SHAW
(FES X, 271), trans from Cowdenbeath West to
Ardclach with Auldearn and Dalmore 20 Dec 1984;
dem 19 May 1992.

1993 JOHN LITTLE WAUGH
(FES X, 400), trans from Birsay to Ardclach with
Auldearn and Dalmore 15 Apr 1993.

ARDERSIER (FES X, 370)

Linked 2 Apr 1963 with Petty.

1971 GARDEN WILLIAM MURRAY RITCHIE
(FES X, 244, 370, 388), trans from Knoydart with
Mallaig to Ardersier with Petty 2 Sep 1971; ret 31
Aug 1995.

1996 ALEXANDER WHITEFORD
B 14 Jun 1948 at Houston, s of James W. and
Annie Orr Kerr; educ Carrick Academy, Maybole
1960–64; University of St Andrews 1991–94 (LTh);
Farming 1964–88; lic by Presb of St Andrews 7
Jul 1994; asst Largo and Newburn with Largo St
David's 1994–96; m 4 Feb 1971 Marion Sloan
Wilson b 21 Jul 1949 d of Robert W. and Maggie
Jamieson; Children: Janice Margaret b 4 Oct 1972
m John Douglas; Catriona Anne b 21 Jul 1977;
Gordon James b 21 Dec 1980; ord and ind to
Ardersier with Petty 9 Aug 1996.

AULDEARN AND DALMORE (FUF 468; FES VI,
435; VIII, 647; IX, 650; X, 370)

Linked 3 Apr 1963 with Ardclach.

1963 DAVID WILLIAM DOUGLAS JOHNSTON
(FES IX, 582; X, 337, 370), trans from Skene to
Ardclach with Auldearn and Dalmore 4 Sep 1963;
died 28 Nov 1976.

1977 ANDREW D M REID
ord and ind to Ardclach with Auldearn and Dalmore
9 Jun 1977; dem 19 Oct 1983.

1984 ALEXANDER JAMES SHAW
(FES X, 271), ind to Ardclach with Auldearn and
Dalmore 20 Dec 1984, see Ardclach.

1993 JOHN LITTLE WAUGH
(FES X, 400), trans from Birsay to Ardclach with
Auldearn and Dalmore 15 Apr 1993.

CAWDOR (FES IX, 650; X, 370)

Linked 5 Jan 1967 with Croy and Dalcross.

1957 WILLIAM MOORE
(FES IX, 152, 639, 708; X, 89, 370), trans from
Borgue to Cawdor 16 Oct 1957; minister of linked
charge with Ardclach 6 Jan 1960 until 3 Apr 1963;
ret 31 Dec 1966; died 30 Jun 1990.

1967 DAVID JOHNSTON
(FES IX, 488; X, 220, 291, 371), trans from Edenshead to Croy and Dalcross 3 Jun 1965; became
minister of linked charge with Cawdor 5 Jan 1967;
trans to Fintry 6 Dec 1972.

1973 WILLIAM BEATTIE MILLER
(FES IX, 760; X, 108, 188, 370), trans from
Crosshouse to Cawdor with Croy and Dalcross
16 May 1973; ret 30 Oct 1987; d Elizabeth m
Graeme Muckart; s James m Mary Margaret
Johnston.

1988 IAN MUNRO WILSON
B 10 Feb 1928 at Aberdeen, educ Robert Gordon's
College, Aberdeen 1939–44; University of Aber-
deen 1985–86, 1986–87; Accountancy 1944–85;
lic by Presb of Aberdeen 30 Jun 1987; asst
Aberdeen St Mary's 1987–88; m 11 Mar 1967 Ann
Forbes Aitken b 18 Jul 1930; Children: Graeme
Ian b 21 May 1969; Catriona Ann b 2 Jan 1975;
ord and ind to Cawdor with Croy and Dalcross 18
May 1988; ret 30 Jun 1993.

1994 MATTHEW ROBERTSON
(FES X, 448), ret from RAChD 31 Aug 1993 and
ind to Cawdor with Croy and Dalcross 20 Feb 1994;
d Alison Mary m Donald McKill; s John m Jane
Anne Lessels.

CROY AND DALCROSS (FES IX, 651; X, 370)

Linked 5 Jan 1967 with Cawdor.

1973 WILLIAM BEATTIE MILLER
(FES IX, 760; X, 108, 188, 370), trans from Cross-house to Cawdor with Croy and Dalcross 16 May 1973; ret 30 Oct 1987.

1988 IAN MUNRO WILSON
ord and ind to Cawdor with Croy and Dalcross 18 May 1988, see Cawdor.

1994 MATTHEW ROBERTSON
(FES X, 448), ret from RAChD 31 Aug 1993 and ind to Cawdor with Croy and Dalcross 20 Feb 1994.

CULLODEN, THE BARN CHURCH

Church Extension 1975. Became Culloden The Barn on achieving full status 1990.

1977 PETER REYNOLDS TAYLOR
ord and ind to Culloden 21 Sep 1977; trans to Torphins 25 Sep 1987.

1988 R GRAEME DUNPHY
ord and ind to Culloden 2 Sep 1988; dem 30 Sep 1993 to take up app in Germany.

1994 JAMES HENRY ROBERTSON
(FES X, 135), trans from Thornliebank to Culloden The Barn 19 Aug 1994; Addl children: Daniel b 26 Mar 1977; Charis b 3 Jun 1982.

DAVIOT AND DUNLICHITY (FES VI, 447; VIII, 650; IX, 651; X, 371)

Linked 30 Dec 1970 with Moy, Dalarossie and Tomatin.

1943 JOHN MACPHERSON
(FES VIII, 336, IX, 401, 651; X, 371), trans from Muckairn to Daviot and Dunlichity 24 Feb 1943; ret 31 Oct 1970; died 30 Jan 1980.

1971 IAN WILLIAM MACBAIN
(FES X, 371), ord and ind to Daviot and Dunlichity with Moy, Dalarossie and Tomatin 29 Sep 1971; dem 30 Sep 1976; ind to Coatbridge Coatdyke 29 Feb 1979.

1979 MATTHEW NOEL PATTERSON
(FES X, 77, 156, 253, 284), trans from Kirkcaldy Viewforth to Daviot and Dunlichity with Moy, Dalarossie and Tomatin 17 Oct 1979; ret 30 Nov 1985; died 13 Mar 1991.

1986 LILIAN MARGARET BRUCE
(FES X, 74), res from app with Overseas Council in Tanzania 1985; ind to Daviot and Dunlichity with Moy, Dalarossie and Tomatin 17 Mar 1986.

DORES AND BOLESKINE (FES X, 371)

1967 JOHN McEWAN
(FES X, 371, 375), ord and ind to Stratherrick and Boleskin 12 Jul 1967; became minister of united charge with Dores 30 Jun 1973; ret 5 Sep 1982; died 23 Aug 1990.

1983 NICHOLAS DOUGLAS CHETWYND ARCHER
(FES X, 415), ind to Dores and Boleskin 19 May 1983; dem 31 May 1992 to enter teaching profession.

1993 JAMES CHRISTIE
B 5 Jan 1936 at Aberdeen, s of James C. and Frances Macaulay; educ Central School, Aberdeen 1948–52; University of Aberdeen 1988–91 (LTh); Local Government (law and admin) 1952–88; lic by Presb of Buchan 26 Jun 1991; asst Marnoch 1991–92; m 20 Aug 1965 Ann White Cattanach b 22 Mar 1941 d of James Stephen Pirie C. and Christina Sutherland White; Children: Neil and Ewan b 13 Sep 1971; ord and ind to Dores and Boleskine 15 Jan 1993.

INVERNESS CROWN (FUF 473; FES IX, 652; X, 371)

1970 ROBERT JAMES VICTOR LOGAN
(FES X, 51, 371), trans from Newton to Inverness Crown 7 Oct 1970; trans to Abdie and Dunbog with Newburgh 19 Mar 1998.

1998 PETER HARRY DONALD
B 3 Feb 1962 at Edinburgh, s of David James D. and Muriel Audrey Brown; educ George Watson's, Edinburgh 1967–80; University of Cambridge 1980–83 (BA), 1983–86 (PhD); University of Edinburgh 1987–90 (BD); Research Fellow, Institute of Historical Research, University of London 1986–87; lic by Presb of Edinburgh 1 Jul 1990; asst Edinburgh St Michael's 1990–91; m 5 Sep 1987 Brigid Mary McNeill b 11 Jan 1957 d of Peter M. and Maureen MacIlwaine; Children: David Peter b 22 Feb 1992; Hannah Maureen b 26 Jul 1993; ord and ind to Edinburgh Leith St Serf's 5 Sep 1991; trans to Inverness Crown 10 Dec 1998; Publ: *An Uncounselled King: Charles I and the Scottish Troubles 1637–41* (CUP, 1990); various articles.

INVERNESS DALNEIGH AND BONA (FES X, 372)

1972 FERGUS ALEXANDER ROBERTSON
(FES X, 372 (2)), ind to Dalneigh 28 Jul 1972; became minister of united charge with Bona 30 Jun 1973; trans to Edinburgh New Restalrig 22 Jun 1989.

1990 ROBERT CARL NELSON
B 3 Sep 1949 at Waukegan, Illinois, USA, s of Herman Nils N. and Elizabeth Marie Nilsson; educ Lake Forest High 1963–67; Trinity International

University 1972–75 (BA); University of Aberdeen 1975–78 (BD); Non-commissioned Officer, US Air Force 1968–72; lic by Presb of Aberdeen 29 Jun 1978; asst Largs St Columba's 1978–80; m 22 Aug 1972 Kathleen Bruce Cameron b 26 Apr 1949 d of Lewis C. and Lilly Mae Bruce; Children: Sarah Elizabeth b 10 May 1976 m Scott MacKay; David Bruce b 24 Mar 1978; Stephen Carl b 16 May 1984; ord and ind to Caldercruix, Longriggend and Meadowfield 28 May 1980; trans to Dalneigh and Bona 31 May 1990; dem 30 Jun 1998.

1999 FERGUS ALEXANDER ROBERTSON (FES X, 372 (2)), trans from Edinburgh New Restalrig to Dalneigh and Bona 10 Aug 1999; Children: Lois Alexandra b 29 Nov 1977; Eleanor Anne b 12 May 1980; Lucy Marjorie b 25 Oct 1986.

INVERNESS EAST (FUF 473; FES IX, 653; X, 372)

1955 DONALD MACFARLANE (FES IX, 269, 580, 686; X, 160, 372), trans from Glasgow Gilmorehill to Inverness East 14 Sep 1955; ret 30 Sep 1980.

1981 AONGHAS IAN MACDONALD (FES X, 390, 397), trans from Barvas to Inverness East 2 Apr 1981; s Donald m Jennifer Elane MacKenzie; s Iain m Maria Mearns.

INVERNESS HILTON (FES X, 372)

1965 GEORGE ALAN SIMPSON STIRLING (FES X, 372, 426), res from service with Overseas Council in Rajasthan, India and ind to Hilton 29 Sep 1965; trans to Leochel Cushnie and Lynturk with Tough 6 Nov 1992.

1994 DUNCAN MACPHERSON B 7 Jul 1963 at Uig, Skye, s of Andrew M. and MacLennan; educ Portree High 1975–81; University of Aberdeen 1981–85 (LLB); University of Glasgow 1985–86 (DipLP), 1988–91 (BD); Solicitor 1986–88, 1989–91 (part-time); Youthshare Volunteer, Tiberias, Israel 1988–89; lic by Presb of Skye and Lochcarron 27 Sep 1991; asst Inverness Dalneigh and Bona 1992–93; m 16 Aug 1990 Shona Fraser Campbell b 10 Mar 1967 d of John William C. and MacIntyre; Children: Eilidh Grace b 21 Sep 1993; Rory Fraser b 18 Dec 1994; Peter Andrew John b 25 Jun 1998; ord and ind to Hilton 11 Mar 1994.

INVERNESS KINMYLIES

Church Extension 3 Nov 1992.

1992 FRASER METHVEN COMPTON STEWART B 24 May 1955 at Cowdenbeath, s of George Compton S. and Jane (Jean) Greenhorn Ballantyne; educ The Gordon Schools, Huntly; University

of Edinburgh 1973–76 (BSc), 1976–79 (BD); lic by Presb of Gordon 5 Jul 1979; asst Rosyth 1979–80; m 13 Jul 1979 Anna Macleod MacLean b 9 Jun 1958 d of Colin Ian M. and Mary Margaret Ross Nicolson; Children: Ewan MacLean b 10 Jan 1982; Iain MacLean b 26 Sep 1983; Calum MacLean b 29 Oct 1985; ord and ind to Cumbernauld Abronhill 12 Jun 1980; trans to Ardler, Kettins and Meigle 12 Mar 1986; trans to Kinmylies 3 Nov 1992.

INVERNESS NESS BANK (FUF 474; FES IX, 653; X, 372)

1974 ARCHIBALD TEARLACH BLACK (FES X, 207, 372, 416), trans from Carstairs with Carstairs Junction to Ness Bank 28 Aug 1974; ret 31 Aug 1997.

1998 (SAMUEL) JOHN CHAMBERS B 3 Apr 1944 at Banbridge, Co Down, N Ireland, s of Samuel George C. and Anna Dorothy Wilkinson; educ Banbridge Academy, Co Down and Annadale Grammar, Belfast 1959–63; Queens University, Belfast 1969 (BSc); Presb College, Belfast 1969–72; lic by Presb of Belfast East 26 Dec 1971; asst Belfast McQuiston Memorial 1971–73; m 16 Jul 1971 Anne Christine Whitelaw b 10 Dec 1949 d of Thomas W. and May Calder; Children: Rachel b 12 Feb 1975; Peter b 28 Apr 1976; David b 18 Apr 1980; ord by Presb of Belfast East during assistantship at McQuiston Memorial 25 Jun 1972; ind to Ballindrait and Raphoe (Presb Church in Ireland) 1 Jul 1973; trans to Second Presb Church, Comber 24 Apr 1979; app Chief Executive of Relate, N Ireland 1 Nov 1984; Chairman of International Commission on Marriage and Interpersonal Relationships 1994–98; ind to Ness Bank 25 Sep 1998; OBE 1995; Publ: Conference reports in *Sexual and Family Therapy* (Carfax), *Who Pays?* (Vol 11, 1996), *Values and Families* (Vol 12, 1997), *Rights of Children* (Vol 13, 1998), *Vive la Difference: Men and Women in Relationships* (Vol 13 No 4, 1998).

INVERNESS ST COLUMBA HIGH (FUF 474; FES IX, 654; X, 372)

1953 STEPHEN FREW (FES IX, 336, 547, 654; X, 372), trans from Motherwell South Dalziel to St Columba High 25 Nov 1953; ret 14 Sep 1975; died 14 Jan 1991.

1976 ALASTAIR STEWART YOUNGER (FES X, 279), trans from Auchterderran to St Columba High 28 Apr 1976.

INVERNESS ST STEPHEN'S (FES VI, 467; VIII, 652; IX, 654; X, 373)

Linked 6 Jan 1971 with The Old High (First Charge).

1971   IAN FINDLAY McINTOSH
(FES X, 373), admitted by General Assembly 1971 and ind to St Stephen's with The Old High (First Charge) 28 Oct 1971; died 6 Oct 1992.

1994   COLIN MACEWEN ANDERSON
(FES X, 18, 452), [correction: MacEwen, not Mac-Ewan as in Vol X, 18]; res as Chaplain to University of Glasgow and ind to St Stephen's with The Old High 29 Nov 1994; Chaplain (part-time) to Inverness Prison.

INVERNESS THE OLD HIGH (FES VI, 454; VIII, 651; IX, 654; X, 373)

Linked 6 Jan 1971 with St Stephen's.

1963   THOMAS NICOLL FRASER
(FES IX, 788; X, 373, 445), res from RAChD 3 Nov 1962; ind to Inverness The Old High 20 Mar 1963; ret 15 Feb 1969; died 23 Jul 1979.

1971   IAN FINDLAY McINTOSH
(FES X, 373), admitted by General Assembly 1971 and ind to St Stephen's with The Old High (First Charge) 28 Oct 1971; died 6 Oct 1992.

1994   COLIN MACEWEN ANDERSON
(FES X, 18, 452), ind to St Stephen's with The Old High 29 Nov 1994, see St Stephen's.

INVERNESS TRINITY (FES X, 373)

Formed 14 Apr 1971 by union of Merkinch (St Mark's) and Queen Street. Name changed from St Mark's (Queen Street and Merkinch) to Trinity.

1955   IAN FIFE MONTGOMERY
(FES IX, 409, 564, 663; X, 243, 372), trans from Glengarry to Queen Street 4 May 1955; ret 31 Jan 1970; died 6 Nov 1981.

1966   NORMAN IAIN MACRAE
(FES X, 372, 373), ord and ind to Merkinch (St Mark's) 27 Apr 1966; became minister of united charge with Queen Street 14 Apr 1971; Chaplain to Porterfield Prison 1968–78; d Ethel m Richard Taylor; d Catriona m David Paterson.

INVERNESS WEST (FES VI, 460; VIII, 652; IX, 654; X, 373)

Second Charge.

1971   THOMAS SWANSTON
(FES X, 197, 373), trans from Holytown to Inverness West (Second Charge) 22 Sep 1971; died 16 Feb 1991.

1992   ALISTAIR MALCOLM
B 6 Jul 1947 at Meikelour, s of William M. and Annie Greenhill; educ Bellshill Academy; University of Aberdeen 1969–75 (BD, DPS); Music Tutor 1967–68; lic by Presb of Aberdeen 29 Jun 1975;

asst Dunblane 1975–76; m 28 Dec 1970 Ann Stodart Lyon Russell d of Robert R. and Elizabeth Whyte; Children: Gary; Jason; Mark; Laura m Randall; ord and ind to Bargeddie 16 Oct 1976; trans to Inverness West 7 Nov 1992.

KILMORACK AND ERCHLESS (FES X, 371, 379)

Formed 21 Jun 1979 by union of Kilmorack and Erchless.

1965   THOMAS DRYSDALE LIND
(FES X, 379), ord and ind to Kilmorack 2 Dec 1965; became minister of united charge with Erchless 21 Jun 1979; trans to Ballantrae 12 Jan 1983.

1975   DUNCAN GORDON McPHERSON
(FES X, 42, 371), [correction: Duncan Gordon, not Duncan George as in Vol X, 42]; trans from Muiravonside to Erchless 11 Jun 1975; ret 30 Apr 1978; died 22 Feb 1981.

1983   PHILIP TAYLOR
ord and ind to Kilmorack and Erchless 21 Jul 1983; dem 5 Apr 1986; ind to Edinburgh St Andrew's Clermiston 24 Mar 1988.

1987   ALEXANDER AYTON FAIRWEATHER
(FES X, 354), trans from Edinburgh Pilrig and Dalmeny Street to Kilmorack and Erchless 11 Jun 1987; ret 31 Jan 1998; died 12 May 1999.

1998   GEORGE DUTHIE
B 8 Jan 1947 at Sandhaven, s of George D. and Margaret McPherson Taylor; educ Fraserburgh Academy 1959–62; Fraserburgh FEC 1962–67 (ONC); Aberdeen Tech 1966–68 (OS); Robert Gordon's College, Aberdeen 1968–70 (HNC); University of Strathclyde 1970–72 (BSc), 1973–74 (MSc), 1974–76 (PhD); University of St Andrews 1993–96 (BD); Mechanical Engineering 1962–73; Engineering Research 1976–86; Engineering Management 1986–93; lic by Presb of St Andrews 3 Jul 1996; asst Troon St Meddan's 1996–98; m 21 Apr 1973 Mari Brabender b 12 Jun 1953 d of Alexander B. and Isobell Murphy; Children: Pamela b 16 Jan 1974; Dawn b 27 Aug 1976; ord and ind to Kilmorack and Erchless 3 Jul 1998.

KILTARLITY (FES IX, 655; X, 373)

Linked 24 Sep 1982 with Kirkhill.

1966   ROBERT MACBEAN GILMOUR
(FES IX, 417, 788; X, 373, 445), res from RAChD and ind to Kiltarlity 29 Jun 1966; ret 31 Aug 1981.

1982   CAMPBELL MACKINNON
B 9 Sep 1954 at Inverness, s of Hector Norman M. and Ishbel Campbell; educ Inverness High 1966–72; Heriot-Watt University 1972–77 (BSc); University of Edinburgh 1978–81 (BD); lic by Presb of Inverness; asst Glasgow Rutherglen Stonelaw

1981–82; m 25 Jul 1985 Janice Campbell McGill b 28 Aug 1960 d of Walter Buchanan M. and Dorothea Myrtle Woollard; ord and ind to Kiltarlity with Kirkhill 23 Sep 1982.

KIRKHILL (FES IX, 656; X, 373)

Linked 24 Sep 1982 with Kiltarlity.

1975 COLIN NORMAN MACKENZIE
(FES IX, 695; X, 118, 373, 396), trans from Kilwinning Erskine with Fergushill to Kirkhill 12 Feb 1975; trans to Carinish 4 Jun 1982.

1982 CAMPBELL MACKINNON
ord and ind to Kiltarlity with Kirkhill 23 Sep 1982, see Kiltarlity.

MOY, DALAROSSIE AND TOMATIN (FUF 475; FES VI, 475; VIII, 653; IX, 656; X, 374)

Linked 30 Dec 1970 with Daviot and Dunlichity.

1971 IAN WILLIAM MACBAIN
(FES X, 371), ord and ind to Daviot and Dunlichity with Moy, Dalarossie and Tomatin 29 Sep 1971; dem 30 Sep 1976; ind to Coatbridge Coatdyke 29 Feb 1979.

1979 MATTHEW NOEL PATTERSON
(FES X, 77, 156, 253, 284), ind to Daviot and Dunlichity with Moy, Dalarossie and Tomatin 17 Oct 1979, see Daviot.

1986 LILIAN MARGARET BRUCE
(FES X, 74), ind to Daviot and Dunlichity with Moy, Dalarossie and Tomatin 17 Mar 1986, see Daviot.

NAIRN OLD (FES VI, 442; VIII, 649; IX, 657; X, 374)

1968 ALEXANDER CAMERON GIBSON
(FES X, 109, 374), trans from Fenwick to Nairn Old 8 Sep 1968; trans to Eskdalemuir with Hutton and Corrie 9 Sep 1980.

1981 THOMAS P HEGGIE
trans from Forth St Paul's to Nairn Old 26 Mar 1981; dem 30 Nov 1985.

1986 IAN WILLIAM FINLAY HAMILTON
B 29 Nov 1946 at Glasgow, s of John H. and Anne McFarlane Hill; educ Victoria Drive Secondary, Glasgow 1958–63; London College of Music (external) 1972 (ALCM); University of Glasgow 1972–77 (LTh); Victoria College of Music, London (external) 1976 (AVCM); Central School of Religion, London (external) 1986 (BD); Banking 1963–69; Music Publishing 1969–72; lic by Presb of Glasgow 30 Jun 1977; asst Bearsden South 1977–78; m 10 Sep 1971 Margaret McLaren Moss b 11 Jan 1950 d of Charles Stewart M. and Janet Todd Begg; Children: David Finlay b 30 Jul 1979; Gillian Margaret and Jennifer Anne b 1 Feb 1982; ord and ind to Alloa North 3 Oct 1978; trans to

Nairn Old 3 Oct 1986; Publ: *Reflections from the Manse Window* (Moravian Press, 1992); *Second Thoughts* (Moravian Press, 1994); *They're Playing My Song!* (Moravian Press, 1996); *A Century of Christian Witness* (Nairn Old, 1997); *Take Four!* (Moravian Press, 1998); contributor to *Expository Times* and *People's Friend*.

NAIRN ST NINIAN'S (FES X, 374)

Formed 1 Aug 1974 by union of Nairn High and Nairn Rosebank.

1961 JOHN ARCHIBALD TAYLOR
(FES IX, 50, 88; X, 28, 374), trans from Bathgate High to Rosebank 28 Sep 1961; ret 31 Oct 1973; died 2 Oct 1987.

1975 WILLIAM BUCHANAN WHYTE
(FES X, 254, 374), ord by Presb of Perth during assistantship at St John's 5 Jun 1974; ind to St Ninian's 5 Mar 1975; Addl children: Susan b 23 Mar 1976.

PETTY (FES IX, 658; X, 374)

Linked 2 Apr 1963 with Ardersier.

1971 GARDEN WILLIAM MURRAY RITCHIE
(FES X, 244, 370, 388), trans from Knoydart with Mallaig to Ardersier with Petty 2 Sep 1971; ret 31 Aug 1995.

1996 ALEXANDER WHITEFORD
ord and ind to Ardersier with Petty 9 Aug 1996, see Ardersier.

URQUHART AND GLENMORISTON (FES X, 371, 375)

Formed 27 Aug 1992 by union of Urquhart and Glenmoriston. Congregations linked from 30 Apr 1980.

1949 PETER FRASER
(FES IX, 652, 734; X, 371), res as Chaplain to Prince of Wales College, Achimota, W Africa and ind to Glenmoriston 7 Jul 1949; ret 30 Apr 1980; died 22 Nov 1993.

1956 JOHN CAMPBELL
(FES IX, 634, 689, 694; X, 362, 375), trans from Dulnain Bridge to Urquhart 6 May 1956; ret 30 Sep 1978; s Neil m Carole Adams; d Helen m Stewart MacDonald.

1980 FRARY BARTON BUELL
B 16 Feb 1930 at Great Falls, Montana, USA, s of Frary Barton B. Sr and Minna Leah Kingsbury; educ Conrad High, Montana 1936–48; University of Montana 1949–52 (BA); US Army 1952–54; Fuller Theological Seminary, California 1954–58 (MDiv); University of Edinburgh 1978–79; Missionary 1958–78; lic by Presb of Edinburgh 1 Jul 1979;

asst Edinburgh Tron Kirk Moredun 1978–79; m 18 May 1961 Margaret Elizabeth Aitken b 20 Sep 1930, died 23 Dec 1997 d of David Alexander A. and Margaret Mitchell; Children: Mary Margaret b 3 Mar 1963 m James Fairley; Susan Elizabeth b 13 Dec 1966; Helen Louise b 2 Mar 1968; ord and ind to Urquhart with Glenmoriston 27 May 1980; became minister of united charge 27 Aug 1992; ret 17 Mar 1995.

1996 HUGH FINDLAY WATT
B 10 Jun 1957 at Glasgow, s of Robert Rodger W. and Jean Greig Sweeney; educ Douglas Academy, Milngavie 1969–75; University of Aberdeen 1975–80 (BD), 1982–84 (DPS); UCCF Travelling Secretary 1980–82; lic by Presb of Aberdeen 28 Jun 1984; asst Montrose Melville South with Inchbrayock 1984–85; m 14 Aug 1982 Ann Elizabeth Wilkin b 1 Dec 1957 d of Peter W. and Elizabeth Allen; Children: Shirley Ann b 12 Sep 1985; Lisa Marie b 13 Dec 1986; Karen Elizabeth b 27 Jan 1988; Emma Jill b 18 Mar 1993; Robert Rodger Allen b 10 Feb 1995; ord and ind to Glasgow Lochwood 13 Jan 1986; trans to Urquhart and Glenmoriston 11 Jan 1996.

PRESBYTERY OF LOCHABER

ACHARACLE (FUF 300; FES IV, 104; IX, 408; X, 242)

Linked 6 Apr 1977 with Ardnamurchan.

1958 MURDANIE MACRITCHIE
(FES X, 242), ord and ind to Acharacle 1 May 1958; ret 30 Aug 1969; w Annie died 22 Oct 1987; d Chrissie m Angus Kenneth MacLeod; s Angus m Anne Murray.

1970 ANDREW HALL MACKENZIE
(FES X, 236, 242), trans from Kilchoman with Portnahaven to Acharacle 1 Dec 1970; became minister of linked charge with Ardnamurchan 6 Apr 1977; ret 31 Mar 1978.

1980 SAMUEL GERARD VICTOR CRAWFORD ord and ind to Acharacle with Ardnamurchan 19 Aug 1980; trans to Glasgow Calton Parkhead 28 Jan 1987.

1987 THOMAS MOFFAT
B 27 Apr 1943 at Bellshill, s of Thomas M. and Isabella Foster; educ Lasswade High 1954–61; University of Edinburgh 1961–65 (BSc), 1965–68 (BD); Teaching, The Grammar School, Stockton-on-Tees 1968–71; Lecturer, Sunderland College of Education 1971–76; Lecturer, Sunderland Polytechnic 1976–87; lic by Presb of Dalkeith 3 May 1968; m (1) 27 Jul 1967 Carole Georgene Davies b 28 Jul 1943; divorced 1994; m (2) 24 Sep 1996 Christina MacDonald Hunter b 27 Jul 1949 d of Gordon Austral H. and Christina Ann MacMillan; ord by Presb of England 1976; ind to Acharacle with Ardnamurchan 28 Aug 1987.

ARDGOUR (FES IV, 126; VIII, 343; IX, 408; X, 242)

Linking arrangement with Strontian confirmed 28 Aug 1959.

1963 SAMUEL EATON
(FES IX, 83, 97, 222; X, 51, 242), trans from Newton to Ardgour with Strontian 15 Nov 1963; ret 30 Apr 1971; died 29 Jan 1984.

1972 MUNGO CARRICK
(FES IX, 730, 756; X, 228, 242, 285), trans from Kirkcaldy Victoria Road to Ardgour with Strontian 29 Mar 1972; ret 8 Sep 1975; died 22 May 1997.

1976 JAMES ALEXANDER CARMICHAEL
B 4 Feb 1936 on Isle of Islay, s of Archibald C. and Ann MacTaggart; educ Islay High 1948–51; University of Glasgow 1969–74; Army 1954–56; Distilling 1956–69; lic by Presb of Islay 9 Jul 1974; asst Dundee Douglas and Angus 1974–76; m 1 Dec 1984 Elizabeth Watt b 5 Feb 1946 d of George W. and Elizabeth Irvine; ord and ind to Ardgour with Strontian 21 Jan 1976.

ARDNAMURCHAN (FES IV, 105; VIII, 337; IX, 404; X, 242)

Linked 6 Apr 1977 with Acharacle.

1968 HAROLD GEORGE CREIGHTON FERRIE
(FES X, 242), ind to Ardnamurchan 10 Jan 1968; ret 1 Nov 1975; died 7 May 1980.

1977 ANDREW HALL MACKENZIE
(FES X, 236, 242), trans from Kilchoman with Portnahaven to Acharacle 1 Dec 1970; became minister of linked charge with Ardnamurchan 6 Apr 1977, see Acharacle.

1980 SAMUEL GERARD VICTOR CRAWFORD ind to Acharacle with Ardnamurchan 19 Aug 1980, see Acharacle.

1987 THOMAS MOFFAT
ind to Acharacle with Ardnamurchan 28 Aug 1987, see Acharacle.

ARISAIG AND THE SMALL ISLES (FES X, 242, 244)

Formed 3 Sep 1991 by union of Arisaig and The Small Isles (Moidart dropped from name). Continued vacancy from 1994.

1964 THOMAS CHALMERS URQUHART
(FES X, 77, 242), trans from Carlisle Chapel Street to Arisaig and Moidart 1 Jul 1964; ret 31 Oct 1991; died 26 Aug 1998.

1992 JOHN MELVYN COOGAN
ord and ind to Arisaig and The Small Isles 9 May 1992; dem 2 Feb 1994; ind to Carstairs with Carstairs Junction 14 Nov 1996.

DUROR (FES IV, 84; VIII, 332; IX, 399; X, 238)

Linked 26 Jan 1960 with Glencoe St Munda's.

1960 HECTOR ANGUS MACINTOSH MACLEAN
(FES IX, 229, 677; X, 133, 238), trans from Greenock Gaelic to Duror with Glencoe St Munda's 21 Dec 1960; ret 31 Oct 1978; d Margaret m Alister MacKenzie; d Patricia m Finlay Maclennan; m (2) 3 Oct 1992 Ida MacLellan b 1 Nov 1918 d of Donald Archibald M. and Sarah Jane Shepherd.

1979 ARCHIBALD RUSSELL
(FES IX, 17; X, 11, 149, 177, 218), res as Community minister at Drumchapel and ind to Duror with Glencoe St Munda's 7 Sep 1979; ret 30 Nov 1990; Publ: *The History of St Munda, Glencoe* (private, 1990); *A History of Mission in Lochaber* (Presb of Lochaber, 1992); *Abertarff/Lochaber— A History* (private, 1995).

1991 ROBERT JAMES MALLOCH
ret from RAChD and ind to Duror with Glencoe St Munda's 1 May 1991; trans to North Knapdale 1 Mar 1997.

1998 ANNE MURRAY JONES
B 24 Aug 1950 at Edinburgh, d of William Young and Helen Grieg Cunningham; educ Preston Lodge, Prestonpans 1961–64; University of Edinburgh 1988–90 (Access), 1990–94 (BD); lic by Presb of Lothian 10 Apr 1997; asst Prestonkirk 1997–98; Belhaven 1998; m 26 Nov 1969 Henry Melrose Jones b 1 Mar 1948 s of Henry and Janet J; Children: Keith b 4 Dec 1970 m Caroline; Sean b 5 Sep 1964 (adopted) m Susan; ord and ind to Duror with Glencoe St Munda's 23 Oct 1998.

FORT AUGUSTUS (FES IX, 408; X, 243)

Linked 26 Mar 1987 with Glengarry.

1939 HUGH MALCOLM GILLIES
(FES IX, 409; X, 243), ord and ind to Fort Augustus 26 Sep 1939; ret 30 Jun 1980; JP for Inverness-shire.

1980 GILBERT STUART CAMERON
(FES IX, 391; X, 233, 300, 417), res from app at Nassau St Andrew's, Bahamas and ind to Fort Augustus 13 Jul 1980; ret 1 Apr 1986; died 24 Oct 1992.

1987 GEORGE WILSON CHARLTON
(FES IX, 397; X, 51, 269), trans from Musselburgh St Ninian's to Fort Augustus with Glengarry 18 Sep 1987; ret 30 Sep 1992; app Chaplain (part-time) to Inverness Prison 1995; d Dorothy (died 11 Mar 1980) m Andrew Hall; s Paul m Rachel Nelson; d Margaret m Ian Patterson (divorced 1991–92); d Frances m Andres Leslie.

1992 ALAN HENRY WORBEY LAMB
B 4 Mar 1931 at Croydon, s of Henry Charles L. and Marjorie Elsie Worbey; educ Horsenden School, Greenford 1943–44; Western College, Bristol 1953–59; University of Bristol 1955–58 (BATh); University of Aberdeen 1991–94 (MTh); Post Office Savings Bank 1944–48; Instrument Mechanic (RAF) 1948–53; m (1) 9 Aug 1958 Patricia Rita Ivatts b 30 Nov 1933 d of Ivan I. and Gertrude Lee; Children: Deborah Claire b 17 Jul 1959; Judith Margaret b 8 Jun 1962; m (2) 14 Feb 1991 Helen Shiela Sudol b 7 May 1942 d of Andrew S. and Margaret Robertson Mowat; ord by Congregational Union and ind to Edmonton, London 20 Jun 1959; Muswell Hill URC 1963–73; Brislington URC 1973–83; Sidmouth Group URC 1983–85; Letting Secretary, The Dell Estate, Whitebridge, Inverness 1985–92; introd as Assoc at Fort Augustus with Glengarry 2 Jun 1992.

1993 MOSES DONALDSON
(FES X, 239), trans from Duneaton to Fort Augustus with Glengarry 15 Oct 1993; d Jun m MacLennan; s Brian m MacPherson; d Ann m Sandie; d Karen m Millar.

FORT WILLIAM DUNCANSBURGH (FES IV, 129; VIII, 343; IX, 409; X, 243)

Linked 21 Jul 1987 with Kilmonivaig.

1966 ALASTAIR KENNETH ROBERTSON
(FES IX, 103, 409; X, 61, 193, 243), trans from Coatbridge Trinity to Duncansburgh 25 Oct 1966; ret 30 Apr 1981; died 17 Apr 1995.

1983 JOHN PATRICK WRIGHT
dem from Kildalton and Oa and introd to Duncansburgh (term) 14 Apr 1983; res from app 31 Jul 1986; ind to Glasgow New Govan 20 Jun 1989.

1987 JOHN LEANDER MILLAR
B 18 Aug 1952 at Irvine, s of John Forsyth M. and Margaret McDonald Allan; educ High School of Glasgow 1964–70; University of Glasgow 1973–78 (BD), 1978–80 (MA); Trainee Accountant 1970–73; lic by Presb of Glasgow 26 Jun 1980; asst Glasgow Stonelaw 1980–81; m (1) 18 Jun 1976 Isobel Margaret McQuaker b 19 Jan 1955 d of Alistair M. and Isabella Gaul Gibb; Children: Cameron Leander b 1 Apr 1983; Alistair John b 21 Jan 1985; Fraser Duncan b 8 Aug 1988; m (2) 13 Aug 1994 Sandra McLeod b 20 Nov 1954 d of Stanley John Kemp M. and Olive Duguid; ord and ind to Glasgow Lansdowne 24 Oct 1981; trans to Duncansburgh with Kilmonivaig 24 Sep 1987; ret on grounds of ill-health 30 Jun 1990.

1990 DONALD ARCHIBALD MACQUARRIE
B 21 Oct 1946 at Glasgow, s of Malcolm M. and Mary MacVicar; educ Balshagray Victoria Drive, Glasgow 1959–65; Paisley College 1965–69 (BSc); University of Glasgow 1975–78 (BD); Electrical

Engineering 1969–75; lic by Presb of Dumbarton 29 Jun 1978; asst Glasgow Cardonald 1978–79; m 1 Aug 1972 Patricia Davida Barr b 12 Apr 1947 d of Barr and Harbinson; Children: Alastair b 31 Dec 1973; Fiona and Stuart b 17 Jun 1975; ord and ind to Jamestown 28 Aug 1979; trans to Duncansburgh with Kilmonivaig 22 Aug 1990.

FORT WILLIAM MACINTOSH MEMORIAL (FUF 298; FES IX, 409; X, 243)

1967 ALAN RAMSAY
(FES X, 243), ord and ind to MacIntosh Memorial 3 Sep 1967; Clerk to Presb of Lochaber 1977–82 and from 1990; d Ruth m Edwards; d Lesley m Ballantyne.

GLENCOE ST MUNDA'S (FES IV, 84; VIII, 333; IX, 399; X, 238)

Linked 26 Jan 1960 with Duror.

1960 HECTOR ANGUS MACINTOSH MACLEAN
(FES IX, 229, 677; X, 133, 238), ind to Duror with Glencoe St Munda's 21 Dec 1960, see Duror.

1979 ARCHIBALD RUSSELL
(FES IX, 17; X, 11, 149, 177, 218), ind to Duror with Glencoe St Munda's 7 Sep 1979, see Duror.

1991 ROBERT JAMES MALLOCH
ret from RAChD and ind to Duror with Glencoe St Munda's 1 May 1991; trans to North Knapdale 1 Mar 1997.

1998 ANNE MURRAY JONES
ord and ind to Duror with Glencoe St Munda's 23 Oct 1998, see Duror.

GLENGARRY (FES IV, 133; VII, 344; IX, 409; X, 243)

Linkage with Kilmonivaig terminated 26 Mar 1987 in favour of linkage with Fort Augustus.

1974 GRAHAME McLAREN HENDERSON
(FES X, 243), ord and ind to Glengarry with Kilmonivaig 27 Aug 1974; trans to Dingwall Castle Street 19 Mar 1987.

1987 GEORGE WILSON CHARLTON
(FES IX, 397; X, 51, 269), ind to Fort Augustus with Glengarry 18 Sep 1987, see Fort Augustus.

1992 ALAN HENRY WORBEY LAMB
introd as Assoc at Fort Augustus with Glengarry 2 Jun 1992, see Fort Augustus.

1993 MOSES DONALDSON
(FES X, 239), trans from Duneaton to Fort Augustus with Glengarry 15 Oct 1993.

KILMALLIE (FUF 299; FES IV, 134; VIII, 344; IX, 410; X, 243)

1967 ROBERT JOHN McDOUGALL ANDREW
(FES X, 243, 315, 364), trans from Arbroath St Margaret's to Kilmallie 23 Nov 1967; trans to Uddingston Old 27 Jan 1983.

1983 DONALD HENDRY SCOTT
ord and ind to Kilmallie 28 Jun 1983; dem 18 Jun 1987; loc ten Delting with Lunnasting and Nesting 11 Jun 1987.

1988 KENNETH JOHN MACPHERSON
ord and ind to Kilmallie 7 May 1988; trans to Cross, Ness 9 Jun 1993.

1994 JAMES ALEXANDER MUNRO
B 27 Jan 1948 at Tain, s of James Alexander M. and Margaret Livingstone Graham; educ McLaren High 1955–66; University of Edinburgh 1971–76 (BD, Dip Missionary Studies); Banking 1966–69; Social Work 1969–71; lic by Presb of Edinburgh 3 Jul 1976; asst Dyce 1976–77; Greenock Cartsburn Augine 1977–78; m 22 Sep 1973 Irene Hay b 28 Feb 1952 d of William Abel H. and Edith Evelyn Lampon; Children: Eilidh b 13 Feb 1975; Dolina b 16 Jun 1978; Ishbel b 13 Aug 1980; Anna b 7 Mar 1984; Kirsteen b 22 Apr 1987; ord and ind to Tiree and Coll 12 Jul 1979; trans to South Uist 15 Sep 1983; trans to Alves and Burghead 18 Aug 1987; trans to Kilmallie 23 Feb 1994.

KILMONIVAIG (FES IV, 136; VIII, 344; IX, 410; X, 244)

Linkage with Glengarry terminated 26 Mar 1987 in favour of linkage 21 Jul 1987 with Fort William Duncansburgh.

1974 GRAHAME McLAREN HENDERSON
(FES X, 243), ord and ind to Glengarry with Kilmonivaig 27 Aug 1974; trans to Dingwall Castle Street 19 Mar 1987.

1987 JOHN LEANDER MILLAR
ind to Duncansburgh with Kilmonivaig 24 Sep 1987, see Fort William Duncansburgh.

1990 DONALD ARCHIBALD MACQUARRIE
ord and ind to Jamestown 28 Aug 1979; trans to Duncansburgh with Kilmonivaig 22 Aug 1990.

KINLOCHLEVEN (FUF 299; FES IX, 410; X, 244)

Linked 13 Aug 1981 with Nether Lochaber.

1968 DAVID WILLIAM BLACK
(FES X, 244), ord and ind to Kinlochleven 8 Aug 1968; dem 19 Apr 1976 on app for service with United Church of Jamaica and Grand Cayman.

1977   EDGAR JOHN OGSTON
ord by Presb of Moray during assistantship at Elgin St Giles' 15 Feb 1976; ind to Kinlochleven 8 Jun 1977; became minister of linked charge with Nether Lochaber 13 Aug 1981; app by Board of World Mission for service with United Church of Jamaica and Grand Cayman 25 Jan 1984.

1984   KLAUS OTTO FRITZ BUWERT
ord and ind to Kinlochleven with Nether Lochaber 30 May 1984; trans to Wishaw Thornlie 25 Aug 1999.

MALLAIG ST COLUMBA AND KNOYDART (FES X, 244)

Union of Mallaig and The Small Isles dissolved 3 Sep 1991.

1972   IAN GORDON FORBES
(FES IX, 147, 371; X, 67, 222, 244), trans from Jedburgh Old to Mallaig 1 Mar 1972; became minister of united charge with The Small Isles 1 Jun 1972; ret 30 Sep 1979; died 26 Nov 1983.

1980   ANDREW THOMSON BLAKE McGOWAN
ind to Mallaig and The Small Isles 29 Feb 1980; trans to Aberdeen Causewayend 20 Jun 1986.

1987   ROBERT ALAN KNOX
(FES X, 120, 221, 446), ret from service with RAChD and ind to Mallaig and The Small Isles 20 Mar 1987; dem 30 Jun 1989.

1989   BENJAMIN JOHNSTONE
(FES X, 196), trans from Hamilton South with Quarter to Mallaig and The Small Isles 22 Sep 1989; became minister of Mallaig St Columba and Knoydart 3 Sep 1991; Children: Laura MacPherson b 28 Mar 1983.

MORVERN (FES IV, 116; VIII, 340; IX, 405; X, 240)

1931   HECTOR ANGUS MACSWEEN
(FES IX, 406; X, 240), ord and ind to Morvern 8 Jul 1931; ret 15 Jul 1971; died 8 Dec 1980.

1972   NORMAN MACSWEEN
(FES IX, 693; X, 232, 240, 395, 396), trans from Manish Scarista to Morvern 25 Oct 1972; trans to Kinloch 16 Nov 1977.

1978   DUNCAN FINLAYSON
(FES IX, 320, 799; X, 50, 308, 435), res as Principal of St Colm's College, Edinburgh and ind to Morvern 15 Sep 1978; ret 31 Jan 1983; d Patricia

m Tor Robin Justad; s Duncan m Marlene Hendron; s Edward m Jacqueline Ann Creed; d Iona m (1) Ian Findlay, divorced, m (2) Iain Sarjeant; Publ: *Aspects of the Life and Influence of Thomas Erskine of Linlathen 1788–1870* (Scottish Church History Society, 1978).

1984   ALICIA ANN WINNING
B 1 Dec 1940 at Edinburgh, d of Thomas Girdwood W. and Katharine Charles Maclagan; educ George Watson's Ladies' College 1945–58; University of Edinburgh 1959–63 (MA), 1964–65 (DipEd), 1981–84 (BD); Moray House College, Edinburgh 1963–64; Teaching 1965–81; lic by Presb of Dunkeld and Meigle 3 Jul 1983; asst Edinburgh Palmerston Place 1983–84; ord and ind to Morvern 10 Oct 1984.

NETHER LOCHABER (FUF 297; FES IV, 128; VIII, 343; IX, 411; X, 244)

Linked 13 Aug 1981 with Kinlochleven.

1965   JAMES HARVEY KERR
(FES IX, 385; X, 230, 244, 322), trans from Kirriemuir St Ninian's to Nether Lochaber 15 May 1965; ret 31 Jul 1981; died 21 May 1993.

1981   EDGAR JOHN OGSTON
ind to Kinlochleven 8 Jun 1977; became minister of linked charge with Nether Lochaber 13 Aug 1981, see Kinlochleven.

1984   KLAUS OTTO FRITZ BUWERT
ord and ind to Kinlochleven with Nether Lochaber 30 May 1984; trans to Wishaw Thornlie 25 Aug 1999.

STRONTIAN (FES IV, 138; VIII, 345; IX, 411; X, 244)

Linking arrangement with Ardgour confirmed 28 Aug 1959.

1963   SAMUEL EATON
(FES IX, 83, 97, 222; X, 51, 242), trans from Newton to Ardgour with Strontian 15 Nov 1963; ret 30 Apr 1971; died 29 Jan 1984.

1972   MUNGO CARRICK
(FES IX, 730, 756; X, 228, 242, 285), trans from Kirkcaldy Victoria Road to Ardgour with Strontian 29 Mar 1972; ret 8 Sep 1975; died 22 May 1997.

1976   JAMES ALEXANDER CARMICHAEL
ord and ind to Ardgour with Strontian 21 Jan 1976, see Ardgour.

PRESBYTERY OF ROSS

ALNESS (FUF 480; FES VII, 25; VIII, 658; IX, 659; X, 377)

1967 GORDON MATTHEW REID BENNETT
(FES IX, 786; X, 377, 444), res from RAChD and ind to Alness 19 Sep 1967; ret 30 Sep 1972; died 8 Dec 1989.

1973 JAMES SMITH LEISHMAN
(FES X, 216, 377), trans from Clydebank Linnvale to Alness 31 May 1973; trans to Patna Waterside 22 Oct 1980.

1981 GEORGE GEMMELL CRINGLES
ord and ind to Alness 29 May 1981; trans to Dunblane St Blane's 1 Nov 1988.

1989 WILLIAM WALLACE NIVEN
B 7 Feb 1928 at Edinburgh, s of David N. and Jean Hearty Cockburn; educ Mortlach Academy, Dufftown, Saughton Secondary and Boroughmuir High, Edinburgh 1939–46; University of Aberdeen 1979–82 (BTh); Civil Service 1946–79; lic by Presb of Inverness 26 Jun 1982; m 28 Feb 1953 Agnes Ellen Sheppard b 28 Nov 1925 d of Thomas Marshall S. and Ellen Mitchell Tennent; Children: Elinor Sheppard b 3 Aug 1957; Wilma Wallace b 19 Nov 1962; ord and ind to Rothiemurchus and Aviemore 24 Nov 1982; trans to Alness 26 Oct 1989; ret 31 Mar 1995.

1996 RANALD MORRISON
B 29 Dec 1952 at Inverness, s of John M. and Winniefred Jessie Nicolson; educ Glenurquhart Senior Secondary and Inverness Royal Academy 1965–71; The Bradford College 1972–74 (Dip Trans and Interp); University of Aberdeen 1989–93 (BD); Admin and Sales 1975–89; loc ten Peterhead St Andrew's 1995–96; lic by Presb of Inverness 2 Sep 1993; asst Aberdeen Mannofield 1993–94; m 15 Apr 1988 Margaret MacLeod b 21 May 1962 d of Donald M. and Catherine Isabella Graham; Children: Iain MacLeod b 7 Apr 1995; ord and ind to Alness 2 Feb 1996.

AVOCH (FUF 477; FES VII, 1; VIII, 655; IX, 659; X, 377)

Linked 3 May 1978 with Fortrose and Rosemarkie.

1967 FINLAY MACLEOD
(FES IX, 673; X, 377, 385), trans from Lairg to Avoch 11 May 1967; ret 30 Mar 1978; died 23 Apr 1990.

1978 JAMES FORSYTH
(FES X, 187, 378), trans from Bellshill St Andrew's to Fortrose and Rosemarkie 30 May 1975; became minister of linked charge with Avoch 3 May 1978, see Fortrose and Rosemarkie.

1981 NICHOLAS W M SIMPSON
ind to Avoch with Fortrose and Rosemarkie 16 Feb 1981; dem 30 Jun 1994 and emigrated to USA.

1995 SAMUEL ALEXANDER REID TORRENS
B 12 Oct 1960 at Ballymoney, N Ireland, s of Arthur Edwin T. and Sarah Matilda Reid; educ Dalriada Grammar and Ballymena College 1972–79; Ulster Polytechnical College 1979–83 (BSc); University of Edinburgh 1990–93 (BD); Engineering 1983–87; Lecturer in Information Technology 1987–88; Electronics and Instrumentation Technician 1988–90; lic by Presb of Lothian 4 Jan 1993; asst Edinburgh New Restalrig 1993–94; m 1 Jul 1989 Minnie Jane Christie d of James C. and Mary Ann Taggart; Children: Rebecca b 3 Aug 1997; ord and ind to Avoch with Fortrose and Rosemarkie 6 Jan 1995.

CONTIN (FES X, 377, 379)

Formed 1 Aug 1989 by union of Contin-Strathconon and Kinlochluichart and Strathgarve.

1969 FINLAY MACDONALD
(FES IX, 676, 692; X, 341, 379, 387), trans from Keiss to Kinlochluichart and Strathgarve 22 Oct 1969; ret 31 Jul 1989; died 30 Nov 1996.

1970 ALEXANDER MACDONALD
(FES X, 377, 390, 396), trans from Applecross to Contin-Strathconon 23 Oct 1970; trans to Cross, Ness 6 Jul 1982.

1983 JAMES FORSYTH
(FES X, 187, 378), res as Director of Resource Centre for World Development, Glenrothes and introd to Contin-Strathconon (term) 1 Jun 1983; ind to Kilchrenan and Dalavich with Muckairn 6 Jan 1986.

1986 JOHN HARKESS OSTLER
(FES X, 247), res from RAF Chaplains' Branch and ind to Contin-Strathconon 31 Oct 1986; dem 30 Jun 1987; Addl children: Duncan William b 4 Aug 1976.

1987 MARGARET LIDDELL
B 7 Jun 1932 at Wishaw, d of Robert Robertson L. and Helena Mary Symon; educ Wishaw High 1944–47; St Colm's College, Edinburgh 1962–64; University of Aberdeen 1981–85 (BD); University of St Andrews 1985–86 (DipPTh); Florist 1947–62; Service with Overseas Council in Zambia 1964–80; lic by Presb of Hamilton 27 Jun 1985; asst Kirriemuir Old 1986–87; ord and ind to Contin-Strathconon 27 Nov 1987; became minister of united charge with Kinlochluichart and Strathgarve 1 Aug 1989; ret 28 Feb 1997.

1997 THOMAS MATHIESON McWILLIAM
(FES X, 143, 305), trans from Paisley Lylesland to Contin, Apr 1997.

CROMARTY (FES IX, 660; X, 377)

1962 JAMES MACARTHUR EWING
(FES IX, 82, 261, 540; X, 51, 377), trans from Newbattle to Cromarty 10 Jan 1962; ret 7 Jul 1975; died 14 Feb 1994.

1975 ROBERT WOOD CLARK GALLOWAY
(FES X, 117, 377), trans from Kilbirnie St Columba's to Cromarty 18 Dec 1975; ret 1 Sep 1998.

1999 JOHN MURDO TALLACH
B 17 Jan 1945 at Kames, s of James Andrew T. and Elizabeth Duff Fraser; educ Nicolson Institute, Stornoway and Dingwall Academy 1957–64; University of Edinburgh 1964–67 (MA); University of Aberdeen 1981–83 (DipPhil), 1986–90 (MLitt); lic by Northern Presb (FPC), 1970; m 7 Jul 1971 Isobel Helen Fraser b 9 Jun 1949 d of James Samuel F. and Finlayson; Children: David James b 13 Oct 1974; Irene Elizabeth b 12 Dec 1977; ord by Northern Presb (FPC) and ind to Kinlochbervie and Scourie 20 Nov 1970; trans to Aberdeen FPC 27 Jul 1979 (became Aberdeen Congregation of the Associated Presb Churches May 1989); ind to Cromarty 27 Aug 1999; Publ: *God Made Them Great* (Banner of Truth Trust, 1973); *They Shall Be Mine* (Banner of Truth Trust, 1981); *Walking in the Way* (Christian Focus, 1983); editor of *I Shall Arise* [sermons of Rev D A Macfarlane] (Faro Publs, 1984); *A Plea Against Extremism* (Christian Focus, 1989); *Give me that Joy* (Christian Focus, 1997).

DINGWALL CASTLE STREET (FUF 480; FES IX, 660; X, 377)

1952 MALCOLM BUCHANAN
(FES IX, 580, 629, 661; X, 377), trans from Marnoch to Castle Street 10 Jan 1952; ret 31 Jul 1972; died 6 Feb 1990.

1973 ARCHIBALD MACVICAR
(FES IX, 405; X, 239, 378, 394), trans from Strath to Castle Street 15 Feb 1973; ret 31 Mar 1986; died 31 Aug 1996.

1987 GRAHAME McLAREN HENDERSON
(FES X, 243), trans from Kilmonivaig with Glengarry to Castle Street 19 Mar 1987.

DINGWALL ST CLEMENT'S (FES VII, 32; VIII, 659; IX, 661; X, 378)

1971 JOHN DRON
(FES X, 378), ord and ind to St Clement's 13 May 1971; died 16 Sep 1978.

1979 GORDON HOLROYD
(FES X, 239, 385, 407, 454), trans from Isle of Mull Parish Churches to St Clement's 11 Dec 1979; ret 30 Oct 1993.

1994 RUSSEL SMITH
B 4 Jul 1948 at Newcastle/Tyne, s of Sidney Clifford S. and Jessie Turner; educ Manor Park Grammar, Newcastle 1960–64; Newcastle Polytechnic 1964–72 (MIWM); Sunderland Polytechnic 1979 (Cert in Hum); University of Glasgow 1988–92 (BD); Industrial Chemist 1964–76; Senior Sales Executive 1976–88; lic by Presb of Irvine and Kilmarnock 30 Jun 1992; asst Stewarton St Columba's 1992–94; m 24 Jun 1978 Ann Catherine Shaw b 9 Sep 1947 d of Eric S. and Lena Bennett; Children: Russel Andrew b 8 Jul 1981; Kenneth Frazer b 6 Apr 1983; James Cameron Christopher b 23 Dec 1987; ord and ind to St Clement's 14 Jan 1994.

FEARN ABBEY AND NIGG CHAPELHILL (FES X, 381, 382)

Formed 27 Jun 1978 by union of Fearn Abbey and Nigg Chapelhill.

1934 KENNETH MACLEOD
(FES IX, 668; X, 382), ord and ind to Nigg Chapelhill 6 Jul 1934; ret 17 Nov 1965; died 29 May 1992.

1954 JOHN ROBSON MARTIN
(FUF 563; FES IX, 69, 267, 668, 742; X, 382), trans from Glasgow Eglinton-Elgin to Nigg Old 8 Oct 1954; ret 3 Feb 1966; died 12 Jul 1979.

1963 KENNETH MACFARLANE
(FES X, 381), ord and ind to Fearn 3 Apr 1963; became minister of united charge with Nigg Chapelhill 27 Jun 1978; ret 31 Jan 1993; Publ: *From Scenes Like These . . .*; *The Reverend John Ross, DD, Remembered*.

1966 JAMES KEILLOR
(FES IX, 64, 721; X, 87, 157, 382, 412), ind to Nigg 26 Aug 1966; dem charge and status 12 Dec 1969.

1970 WILLIAM CAMPBELL
(FES IX, 633, 654, 659, 669; X, 303 (2), 362, 382), trans from Dundee Maryfield Victoria Street to Nigg 21 Aug 1970; ret 1 Oct 1977; died 31 Aug 1990.

1994 JAMES FORSYTH
(FES X, 187, 378), dem from Kilchrenan and Dalavich with Muckairn 31 Oct 1988; ind to Fearn Abbey and Nigg Chapelhill 6 Aug 1994.

FERINTOSH (FES X, 378)

1961 DONALD RODERICK MACLEOD
(FES IX, 410; X, 79, 243, 378), trans from Johnstone and Hope Memorial to Ferintosh 14 Dec 1961; ret 31 Dec 1986.

1988 THOMAS CLIFFORD KELLY
(FES X, 230), trans from Cargill-Burrelton with Collace to Ferintosh 3 May 1988; ret 30 Nov 1993; s Blair m Carol Morgan; d Susan m Dan Gibson; d Kathleen m Jaffrey Weir.

1994 DANIEL JOHN McLEISH CARMICHAEL
B 6 Jul 1968 at Glasgow, s of Neil Carswell C. and Jane Smith McLeish; educ Glasgow Academy 1973–85; University of Glasgow 1985–89 (MA); University of Aberdeen 1989–92 (BD); lic by Presb of Glasgow 26 Jun 1992; asst Aberdeen Mannofield 1992–93; m 4 Feb 1995 Joanne Elizabeth Souter b 10 Oct 1970 d of Ian Souter and Ruth Ledger; Children: Matthew Daniel b 9 Jan 1999; ord and ind to Ferintosh 18 Feb 1994.

FODDERTY AND STRATHPEFFER (FES IX, 661; X, 378)

1962 JOHN MACINTYRE
(FES IX, 35, 391, 401; X, 21, 378), trans from Edinburgh Rosehall to Fodderty and Strathpeffer 20 Dec 1962; died 19 Jun 1977.

1978 JOHN BUCHAN
(FES X, 161), trans from Glasgow Hamilton Crescent to Fodderty and Strathpeffer 14 Mar 1978; ret 31 Dec 1993.

1994 MORAG McLEOD THOMSON
B 6 Sep 1946 at Forth, d of Thomas Alexander and Joanna McLeod; educ Lanark Grammar 1958–63; David Dales, Allan Glen's, Glasgow 1967–69 (FIMLS); University of Edinburgh 1990–93 (BD); Blood Transfusion Service 1964–90; Bangour General Hospital 1969–76; lic by Presb of Lanark 29 Jun 1993; asst Biggar 1993–94; m 14 Sep 1968 George Green Thomson s of George T. and Jessie McLeod; ord and ind to Fodderty and Strathpeffer 28 Jul 1994; died 15 Mar 1998.

1999 IVAN CORRY WARWICK
B 20 Oct 1953 at Bangor, N Ireland, s of James Steuart Corry W. and Eileen Alice Kathleen Smiley; educ Bangor Grammar 1965–72; University of Edinburgh 1973–77 (BD); University of St Andrews 1977–78 (DPS); Irish School of Ecumenics 1978–79 (DEcum); lic by Presb of Edinburgh 1 Jul 1979; asst Glasgow Easterhouse St George's and St Peter's 1979–80; m 30 Sep 1989 Jocelyn Lydia

Cromarty Rose b 10 Sep 1962 d of William R. and Aileen Laird Sinclair; Children: Catriona Sinclair b 21 May 1991; Corrie Anna b 18 Apr 1993; Jennifer Olivia Smiley b 16 Dec 1994; ord and ind to Glenisla with Kilry with Lintrathen 21 Sep 1980; dem 6 Sep 1985 to take up app with RAChD; ind to Knockando, Elchies and Archiestown with Rothes 30 Aug 1989; trans to Fodderty and Strathpeffer 23 Jul 1999.

FORTROSE AND ROSEMARKIE (FES X, 378)

Linked 3 May 1978 with Avoch.

1959 ALEXANDER MACRAE
(FES IX, 474; X, 281, 378, (2)), trans from East Wemyss St George's to Fortrose 24 Sep 1959; became minister of united charge with Rosemarkie 3 May 1967; ret 7 Nov 1974; died 29 Nov 1978.

1975 JAMES FORSYTH
(FES X, 187, 378), trans from Bellshill St Andrew's to Fortrose and Rosemarkie 30 May 1975; became minister of linked charge with Avoch 3 May 1978; dem to take up app as Director of Resource Centre for World Development, Glenrothes 10 Sep 1980.

1981 NICHOLAS W M SIMPSON
ind to Avoch with Fortrose and Rosemarkie 16 Feb 1981; dem 30 Jun 1994 and emigrated to USA.

1995 SAMUEL ALEXANDER REID TORRENS
ord and ind to Avoch with Fortrose and Rosemarkie 6 Jan 1995, see Avoch.

INVERGORDON (FUF 483; FES IX, 666; X, 381)

1968 ROBERT PATERSON SLOAN
(FES X, 381), ord and ind to Invergordon 20 Jun 1968; trans to Perth North 1 Feb 1978.

1978 GRAHAM WATSON FOSTER
(FES X, 39), trans from Falkirk St Modan's to Invergordon 11 Aug 1978; trans to Dundee The Steeple 18 Nov 1986.

1987 DAVID SINCLAIR SCOTT
ord and ind to Invergordon 26 Jun 1987; trans to Dundee Logie and St John's Cross 20 Aug 1999.

KILLEARNAN (FES VII, 10; VIII, 656; IX, 662; X, 379)

Linked 25 Apr 1999 with Knockbain.

1956 RICHARD FREDERICK BOLSTER
(FES X, 379), ord and ind to Killearnan 22 Nov 1956; ret 30 Apr 1984; w Doreen died 26 Feb 1998.

1985 SUSAN MARJORY BROWN
ord and ind to Killearnan 18 Sep 1985; trans to Dornoch Cathedral 20 Feb 1998.

KILMUIR AND LOGIE EASTER (FES X, 381, 382)

Formed 15 Apr 1976 by union of Kilmuir-Easter and Logie Easter.

1964 ALAN GRANT SMITH
(FUF 470; FES IX, 644; X, 276, 367, 382), trans from Kinross East to Logie Easter 23 Apr 1964; ret 15 Apr 1976; died 30 Aug 1989.

1972 JAMES OSWALD WELSH
(FES IX, 320, 407; X, 188, 381, 427), res from app with Overseas Council at Kikuyu, Kenya and ind to Kilmuir-Easter 30 Mar 1972; ret 15 Apr 1976; died 14 Dec 1985.

1976 ARCHIE STEWART
ord and ind to Kilmuir and Logie Easter 12 Aug 1976; trans to Aberdeen Torry 28 Jan 1981.

1981 RODERICK MACLEAN MACKINNON
(FES X, 396), trans from South Uist to Kilmuir and Logie Easter 26 Aug 1981; ret 30 Apr 1995; app Clerk to Presb of Uist 20 Jan 1971; app Clerk to Presb of Ross 6 Sep 1988; app Clerk to Synod of Ross, Sutherland and Caithness 1 Jan 1983 (Synod abolished 1992), ret as Presb Clerk Jun 2000; Publ: Various book reviews for *West Highland Free Press*; sermons and articles for *Gaelic Supplement* and *Life & Work*.

1996 KENNETH JOHN PATTISON
B 22 Apr 1941 at Glasgow, s of John P. and Eliza Bryce Philp; educ Lenzie Academy 1953–58; University of Glasgow 1958–62 (MA), 1962–65 (BD); Union Theological Seminary, New York, 1965–66 (STM); lic by Presb of Linlithgow and Falkirk 20 Apr 1965; m 13 Jan 1968 Susan Jennifer Brierley Jenkins b 4 Jan 1943 d of Philip Edward Aveling J. and Cicely Maud Brierley; Children: Helen Amelia b 18 Jan 1969 m Stephen Alexander Howie; Catherine Margaret b 4 Nov 1970; Stephen John b 21 Oct 1972; ord by Church of Central Africa Presb and introd as Assoc at the Cathedral Church of St Michael and All Angels, Blantyre, Malawi 7 Jun 1967; various apps as minister, chaplain, tutor and principal in Malawi 1967–77; ind to Ardrossan Park 27 Oct 1977; app as Chaplain to Glasgow Royal Infirmary Jun 1984; introd as Assoc at Edinburgh St Andrew's and St George's Aug 1990; ind to Kilmuir and Logie Easter 12 Jan 1996; Publ: Bible knowledge correspondence course on Luke and Acts (Malawi Correspondence College, 1974).

KILTEARN (FES VII, 40; VIII, 661; IX, 662; X, 379)

1965 CHARLES ROBERTSON
(FES X, 379), ord and ind to Kiltearn 21 Oct 1965; trans to Edinburgh Canongate 16 Jun 1978.

1979 ANTHONY LIVESLEY
B 13 Apr 1932 at Hale, Altrincham, s of Arthur William L. and Nina Smyth Clifford; educ Kirkby Lonsdale Grammar 1942–49; World Evangelical Crusade College 1957–59; University of Aberdeen 1969 (Lay Missionary Course); University of Glasgow 1976–79 (LTh); Horticulture 1949–57; World Evangelical Crusade International 1959–69; Lay Missionary with Home Board 1969–76; lic by Presb of Paisley, Jun 1979; asst Johnstone St Andrew's Trinity; m 21 Dec 1963 Noreen Wyard-Scott b 29 Jul 1935 d of Percy W. and Dorothy Aubin; Children: Iain b 17 Nov 1964 m Shelagh Laing; Lynda b 7 Mar 1966 m Neil Thomson; Heather b 8 Sep 1971 m Alistair Board; ord and ind to Kiltearn 9 Oct 1979; ret 9 Oct 1997.

1998 DONALD ALEXANDER MACSWEEN
B 18 Dec 1955 at Inverness, s of Johan M; educ Sir E Scott School, Tarbert and Inverness High 1961–73; University of Glasgow 1985–90 (BD); Retail Management 1974–82; Insurance Salesman 1982–85; lic by Presb of Glasgow, 1990; asst Stornoway High 1990–91; m 14 Aug 1991 Sandra MacLean Smith 23 Feb 1964 d of William S. and Christina MacLean; Children: William Alexander b 21 Feb 1993; Innes John b 7 Mar 1996; ord and ind to Durness and Kinlochbervie 11 Oct 1991; trans to Kiltearn 16 Jan 1998.

KNOCKBAIN (FES IX, 663; X, 379)

Linked 25 Apr 1999 with Killearnan.

1952 JOHN MACKAY
(FES IX, 399, 663; X, 379), trans from Glencoe to Knockbain 18 Dec 1952; ret 15 Sep 1979; died 30 Jul 1998; w Jean died 24 Dec 1996; s Ian m Marion McCallum.

1980 WALTER CAMPBELL CAMPBELL-JACK
ord by Presb of Inverness during assistantship at Nairn Old; ind to Knockbain 20 Mar 1980; trans to Dumfries Greyfriars 12 Mar 1999.

LOCHBROOM AND ULLAPOOL (FES X, 379)

1960 WILLIAM MACLENNAN
(FES IX, 693; X, 379, 395, 396), trans from Carinish to Lochbroom and Ullapool 18 Aug 1960; ret 30 Sep 1981.

1982 PHILIP ROBERTSON HAIR
ord by Presb of Glasgow during assistantship at Chryston 5 Mar 1980; ind to Lochbroom and Ullapool 4 Jun 1982; trans to Edinburgh Holyrood Abbey 12 Jun 1998.

1999 JAMES GEMMELL
B 1 Mar 1960 at Glasgow, s of James G. and Jessie Donald; educ Cathkin High and John Street Secondary 1972–76; University of Glasgow 1992–96 (BD); University of Edinburgh 1996–97 (MTh); Electrical Engineer 1976–84; Service Engineer 1984–92; lic by Presb of Glasgow 30 Oct 1997; m 22 Sep 1984 Kathrine Smith b 18 Jun 1962 d of Robert S. and Kathleen Todd; Children: James Robert b 11 May 1987; Jennifer b 1 Oct 1989; ord and ind to Lochbroom and Ullapool 19 Feb 1999.

RESOLIS AND URQUHART (FES X, 378, 380)

Re-adjustment of the bounds of the Parishes of Resolis and Urquhart took place 1 Jan 1977. The enlarged Parish of Resolis became known as Resolis and Urquhart.

1959 JOHN ANGUS NEWALL
(FES IX, 660, 675; X, 377, 380), trans from Carnoch Strathconnon to Resolis 23 Apr 1959; ret 31 Oct 1971; died 27 Dec 1996.

1973 ALEXANDER MACKENZIE SUTHERLAND
(FES IX, 112, 583, 667, 685; X, 23, 45, 69, 380, 382), trans from Peebles Leckie Memorial to Resolis 9 Feb 1973; ret 31 Oct 1976; died 1 Mar 1993.

1977 WILLIAM GALBRAITH YOUNG
(FES IX, 754), res from service with Overseas Council in Pakistan and ind to Resolis and Urquhart 25 Nov 1977; ret 31 Mar 1986; died 20 Nov 1995.

1986 JOHN McLEOD
(FES X, 31, 422), trans from Livingston St Paul's to Resolis and Urquhart 27 Feb 1986; ret 30 Jun 1993.

1994 ALASDAIR JOHN MACLENNAN
B 15 Mar 1937 at Inverness, s of Roderick M. and Jean Dingwall; educ Inverness Royal Academy 1942–54; Jordanhill College, Glasgow 1963–66 (DipComEd); University of Aberdeen 1974–78 (BD); Military Service 1956–59; Electrical Surveying 1959–63; Community Education 1966–73; lic by Presb of Inverness 19 Jul 1978; m 21 Sep 1974 Elizabeth Flora MacKenzie b 18 Mar 1941 d of James M. and Catherine Horne; ord and ind to Clyne 31 Jan 1979; dem 31 Jan 1987 to take up app with Dept of National Mission as Organiser for Evangelism, Highlands and Islands; res Feb 1993 and ind to Resolis and Urquhart 7 Jan 1994.

ROSSKEEN (FES IX, 669; X, 382)

1943 DUNCAN MACDIARMID
(FUF 403; FES IX, 268, 547, 669; X, 382), trans from Glasgow Gairbraid to Rosskeen 7 Jul 1943; ret 30 Sep 1968; died 14 Mar 1993.

1969 ANDREW YOUNGSON HOWE
(FES X, 382, 384), trans from Farr to Rosskeen 23 Apr 1969; ret 31 Dec 1989 on grounds of ill-health.

1990 ROBERT JONES
B 21 Sep 1952 at Sheffield, s of Jack Baldwin J. and Mary Snowden; educ King James' Grammar, Huddersfield 1963–70; University of Edinburgh 1970–74 (BSc), 1986–89 (BD); Forestry Work 1974–85; lic by Presb of Edinburgh 2 Jul 1989; asst Edinburgh Greenbank 1989–90; m 21 Jun 1975 Joanne Ross b 2 Apr 1953 d of John

Corstorphine R. and Annie Hardman Brown; Children: Sara Catherine b 3 Aug 1976; Marc Ross b 25 Jan 1979; Aileen Ruth b 7 Jul 1982; Benjamin David b 20 May 1993; ord and ind to Rosskeen 31 Aug 1990.

TAIN (FES IX, 669; X, 382)

1953 ALEXANDER GILLON MACALPINE
(FES IX, 35, 162, 669; X, 382), trans from Edinburgh Rosehall to Tain 7 May 1953; ret 31 Mar 1975.

1977 DOUGLAS ANDERSON HORNE
B 31 Aug 1939 at Cockenzie, s of John James H. and Jean Jarron; educ Preston Lodge 1951–57; University of Glasgow 1972–73; University of Edinburgh 1973–76 (BD); Apprentice Engineer 1954–57; Shop Asst 1957–60; Fishermen's Mission 1960–66; Minister of Bo' ness Baptist Church 1966–69; Rubber Company 1969–72; lic by Presb of West Lothian, Jun 1976; asst Falkirk St Modan's 1976–77; m 12 Aug 1961 Christina McLeod b 14 Apr 1941 d of John M. and Christina Moodie; Children: Julia Christine b 28 Jun 1962 m Steven Meek; Angela Jean b 9 Apr 1964 m Andrew Mein; Deborah b 8 Jul 1965; Stephanie b 17 Apr 1967 m Iain Nicol; ord and ind to Tain 6 May 1977.

TARBAT (FES IX, 669; X, 382)

1972 WILLIAM ORR
(FES X, 382), ord and ind to Tarbat 9 Jun 1972; ret 4 Aug 1987.

1988 ROBERT JAMES MELLIS
trans from Knockando, Elchies and Archiestown with Rothes to Tarbat 24 Mar 1988; trans to Shapinsay 30 Mar 1992.

1993 JAMES ERIC STEWART LOW
(FES X, 12, 34, 250, 403, 421), res from app in Rotterdam 1991 and ind to Tarbat 26 Feb 1993; ret 30 Nov 1997; Children: Lindesay Matheson b 6 Feb 1967 [omitted from FES X, 403].

1998 IAIN MACKENZIE
(FES X, 138, 152), trans from Canonbie with Langholm Ewes and Westerkirk to Tarbat 29 Jul 1998; m (2) 21 Apr 1990 Grace Dunlop b 15 Aug 1940 d of Thomas D. and Annie Dunnachie.

URRAY AND KILCHRIST (FES IX, 665; X, 380)

1949 GEORGE VICTOR ROWLAND GRANT
(FES IX, 665; X, 380), ord and ind to Urray and Kilchrist 9 Jun 1949; ret 31 Oct 1982; Clerk to Presb of Dumfries and Kirkcudbright 1983–87; Addl publ: Co-author of *Urray Parish* in *The Third Statistical Account of Scotland* (Scottish Academic Press, 1987); *The '45: A Disastrous Mistake* in *The '45:*

To Gather an Image Whole ed Lesley Scott-Moncrieff (Mercat Press, 1988); *Urray and Kilchrist: The Parish, Churches and Ministers from the earliest times to 1982* (Gospel Truth, 1999).

1983 IAIN CAMPBELL LAW
B 22 Feb 1957 at Edinburgh, s of James L. and Evelyn Robertson Paterson; educ George Heriot's, Edinburgh 1964–75; University of St Andrews 1975–79; University of Edinburgh 1978–82 (BD); lic by Presb of Edinburgh, Jun 1982; asst Hamilton Old; m 26 Jun 1982 Jill Ross Aitchison d of Ian A. and Alice Mill; ord and ind to Urray and Kilchrist 9 Jun 1983; dem 30 Mar 1988.

1989 CHARLES MACDONALD MACKINNON
ord and ind to Urray and Kilchrist 10 Aug 1989; trans to Kilsyth Anderson 25 Aug 1999.

PRESBYTERY OF SUTHERLAND

ALTNAHARRA AND FARR (FES X, 383, 384)

Formed 26 Sep 1982 by union of Altnaharra and Farr.

1974 CLIFFORD ALFRED JOHN RENNIE
(FES X, 383), ind to Altnaharra and Farr 14 Jun 1974; trans to Larbert Old 23 Aug 1985.

1986 JOHN LINCOLN
ord and ind to Altnaharra and Farr 3 Jun 1986; trans to Balquhidder with Killin and Ardeonaig 19 Jun 1997.

1998 JOHN MILLER WILSON
(FES X, 318, 427), trans from Bolton and Saltoun with Humbie with Yester to Altnaharra and Farr 14 Aug 1998; Addl children: Alison Mary Isabella b 17 Mar 1975.

ASSYNT AND STOER (FES IX, 670; X, 383)

1971 FREDERICK ROSS HURST
(FES X, 236, 383), trans from Colonsay and Oronsay to Assynt and Stoer 3 Dec 1971.

CLYNE (FES IX, 670; X, 383)

1967 CHARLES ABEL
(FES X, 383, 401), trans from Orkney The South Isles to Clyne 22 Nov 1967; dem 31 Aug 1978.

1979 ALASDAIR JOHN MACLENNAN
ord and ind to Clyne 31 Jan 1979; dem 31 Jan 1987 on app by Dept of National Mission as Organiser for Evangelism, Highlands and Islands.

1987 IAN WILLIAM McCREE
(FES X, 29), trans from Glenrothes St Margaret's to Clyne 3 Jul 1987; Addl children: Mark Thomas b 26 Apr 1977.

CREICH (FES IX, 671; X, 383)

Linked 1 Jun 1973 with Rosehall.

1971 EUGENE JOHN DUPUY
(FES X, 383), ord and ind to Creich 18 Nov 1971; became minister of linked charge with Rosehall 1 Jun 1973; ret on grounds of ill-health 31 Jul 1979; died 14 Jun 1994.

1980 ROBERT KENNETH MACKENZIE
ord by Presb of Hamilton during assistantship at Old and Auchingramont 9 May 1976; ind to Creich with Rosehall 30 Apr 1980; trans to Brechin Cathedral 20 Mar 1986.

1986 ERIC RALPH LACEY
(FES X, 209 (2)), [correction: w Mary d of Margaret McLean Hanton, not Margaret McLeary Hanton as in Vol X, 209]; trans from Auchindoir and Kildrummy to Creich with Rosehall 23 Oct 1986; ret 2 Apr 1992; s Robert m Marion Martin.

1992 ALASTAIR FLEMING McCORMICK
(FES X, 123, 230), res from World Mission app in Nassau, Bahamas and ind to Creich with Rosehall 30 Nov 1992; ret 31 Dec 1998.

1999 HEATHER CLAIRE OLSEN
B 23 Apr 1943 at Glasgow, d of Olaf Sinclair O. and Grace Hay; educ Jordanhill College School, Glasgow 1949–60; University of Glasgow (BD); ord and ind to Windygates and Balgonie 16 Aug 1978; dem 30 Sep 1996; ind to Creich with Rosehall 11 Jun 1999.

DORNOCH CATHEDRAL (FES IX, 671; X, 384)

1976 JAMES ALEXANDER SIMPSON
(FES X, 38, 176), trans from Glasgow St John's Renfield to Dornoch Cathedral 21 Apr 1976; Moderator of General Assembly 1994–95; dem from Dornoch and introd as Interim minister at Almondbank Tibbermore 7 May 1997.

1998 SUSAN MARJORY BROWN
B 12 Dec 1958 at Edinburgh, d of James Storie Callender Attwell and Margaret Reid Brown; educ Penicuik High 1971–77; University of Edinburgh 1977–83 (BD, DipMin); lic by Presb of Lothian 3 Jul 1983; asst Edinburgh St Giles' Cathedral 1983–85; m 4 Apr 1981 Derek Gordon Brown b 25 Sep 1959 s of John B. and Gwyneth Louise Bannerman; Children: Simon Kenneth b 10 Jan 1987; Hannah Rachel b 16 Apr 1990; ord and ind to Killearnan 18 Sep 1985; trans to Dornoch Cathedral 20 Feb 1998.

DURNESS AND KINLOCHBERVIE (FES X, 384, 385)

Formed 6 Aug 1990 by union of Kinlochbervie and Durness.

1972 WILLIAM BROAD BLACK
(FES X, 384), ind to Durness with Kinlochbervie 19 May 1972; dem 15 Dec 1981 on app as Missionary with OMF International in Korea.

1982 ANTHONY JOHN ROBERT FOWLER
ord and ind to Durness with Kinlochbervie 14 Jul 1982; trans to Paisley St Columba Foxbar 28 Nov 1985.

1986 WILLIAM BLACK
(FES X, 297), trans from Kirkinner with Sorbie to Durness with Kinlochbervie 29 May 1986; ret 30 Sep 1989.

1991 DONALD ALEXANDER MACSWEEN
ord and ind to Durness and Kinlochbervie 11 Oct 1991; trans to Kiltearn 16 Jan 1998.

1998 JOHN THOMAS MANN
B 29 Apr 1960 at Belfast, s of John M. and Elizabeth Mary Brittain; educ American Community School, Beirut, Lebanon and Portora Royal School, Enniskillen 1971–78; University College of Swansea 1979–82 (BSc); University of Edinburgh 1985–88 (BD); Accountancy 1982–85; lic by Presb of England 24 Jul 1988; asst Edinburgh Braid 1988–89; m 4 Apr 1997 Julia Ann Thom b 28 Oct 1965 d of Gordon James T. and Ann Gairn Livingstone; ord and ind to Fortingall and Glenlyon with Kenmore and Lawers 5 Dec 1990; trans to Durness and Kinlochbervie 23 Nov 1998.

EDDRACHILLIS (FUF 502; FES VII, 104; VIII, 674; IX, 675; X, 384)

1967 THOMAS SUTER SINCLAIR
(FES X, 384), ord by Presb of Aberdeen during assistantship at Holburn Central 26 Jun 1966; ind to Eddrachillis 8 Dec 1967; trans to Stornoway Martin's Memorial 16 Jun 1976.

1977 JOHN GARDNER OLIVER
(FES X, 170, 188, 411), ind to Eddrachillis 18 May 1977; died 27 Apr 1985.

1986 JOHN SELFRIDGE
B 10 Aug 1921 at Craigs, Cullybacken, N Ireland, s of William Miller S. and Margaret Blackley McKibben; educ Ballymena Technical School 1926–36; Metropolitan Bible College 1937–43; American Bible College, Florida 1975–79 (BTh, BREd); Missionary School of Medicine 1962; Missionary in Africa 1948–86; lic by Metropolitan Church Assoc, Wisconsin, USA 1948; m 18 Nov 1952 Isabella MacMillan MacKenzie b 30 Jul 1923 d of William M. and Catherine MacMillan; Children: Ruth Catherine Margaret b 9 Apr 1961 m Cook; ord by Emmanuel Missionary Society, Birkenhead, England 30 Jul 1963; cont with missionary work in Africa following ord; app Organising Secretary, Programme for Evangelism, Evangelical Assoc of Malawi 1 Mar 1970; service with Church of Central Africa Presb in Malawi and S Africa 1974–86; ind to Eddrachillis 10 Oct 1986; ret 9 Sep 1991; Publ: *Following Jesus* (Evangel Publishing House, Kenya, 1975); *How to be a Happy Christian* (Biblecor, 1980); *The Church's First 30 years in Malawi* (private, 1981); *Joseph Booth and John Chilembwe* (private, 1982); *Effective Christian Living* (Christian Focus, 1994); *Jack of All Trades Mastered by One* (Christian Focus, 1996); *Life of Margaret Benzies* (Lewis Recordings, 1999).

1993 JOHN MACPHERSON
B 8 Feb 1955 at Inverness, s of John M. and Lenore Marie Brown; educ Millburn Secondary, Inverness and Inverness High 1967–73; University of St Andrews 1973–77 (BSc); University of Aberdeen 1987–90 (BD); Civil Service 1978–85; lic by Presb of Inverness 30 Aug 1991; asst Kilmacolm St Columba 1991; Paisley Sherwood 1991–92; ord and ind to Eddrachillis 22 Jan 1993.

GOLSPIE (FES IX, 671; X, 384)

1946 CECIL ALEXANDER DODDS
(FES IX, 672), ord and ind to Golspie 14 Jul 1946; dem 23 Aug 1953 on app to Espanola, Ontario; died 11 Apr 1999.

1954 ROBERT CRAWFORD ALSTON
(FES IX, 366, 688, 672; X, 362, 384, 385), trans from Nigg Old to Golspie 13 Jan 1954; trans to Boat of Garten and Kincardine 26 Sep 1965.

1966 JOHN MARSHALL MILLAR CRAIG
(FES X, 76, 384), trans from Annan Erskine to Golspie 27 Apr 1966; died 25 Jun 1982.

1983 EDWARD JOSEPH THOMPSON
ord by Presb of Edinburgh during assistantship at St George's West 6 Jun 1982; ind to Golspie 21 Apr 1983; trans to Troon Portland 1 Jun 1988.

1989 GEORGE MITCHELL DONALDSON
B 25 Jan 1950 at Edinburgh, s of Charles Noble D. and Nettie Irene Grant; educ Knox Academy, Haddington 1961–67; University of Edinburgh 1967–71 (MA), 1980–83 (BD); Teaching 1972–76; lic by Presb of Edinburgh 3 Jul 1983; asst Edinburgh St Nicholas' Sighthill 1983–84; m 24 Sep 1977 Margaret Mary Easton d of William E. and Margaret Mary McInally; Children: Andrew Grant; ord and ind to Tiree and Coll 15 Jun 1984; became minister of linked charge 29 Aug 1986; trans to Golspie 4 Mar 1989.

KILDONAN AND LOTH HELMSDALE (FES IX, 672; X, 385)

1948 JOHN SCOTT FULTON
(FES IX, 210, 240, 672; X, 385), trans from Busby East to Kildonan and Loth Helmsdale 1 Dec 1948; ret 7 Jun 1977; died 18 Jun 1984.

1978 GRAHAM RICHARD HOUSTON
ord and ind to Kildonan and Loth Helmsdale 17 Feb 1978; trans to Perth Letham St Mark's 6 May 1982.

1983 JOHN RUSHTON
B 25 Apr 1947 at Llansadryn, Anglesey, N Wales, s of James Henry and Olive R; educ Hutton Grammar 1958–65; University of Glasgow 1965–70 (BVMS); University of Edinburgh 1979–82 (BD); lic by Presb of Lothian 4 Jul 1982; asst Musselburgh St Ninian's 1982–83; m 26 Aug 1972 Susan Margaret Hamilton b 10 Apr 1948 d of John Harris H. and Gwyneth Doreen Truscott; Children: David Ian b 17 Jan 1974; Moira Anne b 20 Oct 1975; Mark James b 8 Sep 1977; Sarah Margaret b 19 Mar 1980; ord and ind to Kildonan and Loth Helmsdale 24 Jun 1983; dem 31 Jan 1996 on app as Scottish Director of Overseas Missionary Fellowship.

1996 MELVYN JAMES GRIFFITHS
B 29 Jul 1951 at Bloemfontein, Republic of S Africa, s of Leslie Norman G. and Elizabeth Joyce Searle; educ J.G. Meiring High, Goodwood, S Africa 1957–69; Bible Institute of S Africa 1972–75 (Dip); London University 1972–75 [extra mural] (DipTh); Rhodes University 1976–78 (BA); Bank Clerk 1970–72; m 31 May 1975 Hazel Mary Lambert b 11 Sep 1954 d of Harold John L. and Edith Myrl Worth; Children: Angelene Mary b 31 Dec 1975; Brenda Laurel Zietsman b 13 Aug 1977; Melodee Grace b 14 Aug 1980; Jonathan James b 17 Jun 1982; ord in Cape Town, S Africa 14 Dec 1978; ind to Randparkridge Ecumenical Church 30 Jan 1979; ind to Stutterheim and District Presb Church 1 Jan 1981; ind to St Paul's, East London 30 Apr 1986; app Chaplain to Military Hospital, Pretoria, S Africa 1 Jan 1989; ind to Kildonan and Loth Helmsdale 29 Aug 1996.

KINCARDINE CROICK AND EDDERTON (FES X, 381, 382)

Formed 5 Dec 1976 by union of Kincardine, Croick and Edderton.

1961 AMBROSE SHEPHERD RUSSELL
(FES IX, 545, 703, 758; X, 381), res from service with Overseas Council at Demerara Georgetown St Andrew's, British Guiana and ind to Edderton 26 Jan 1961; ret 31 Mar 1974; died 24 Sep 1983.

1968 ROBERT McMILLAN
(FES IX, 629; X, 101, 289, 360, 382), trans from Crosshill to Kincardine and Croick 7 Aug 1968; ret 1 Sep 1975; died 15 Jun 1998.

1975 DOUGLAS BRIAN THOMPSON
(FES IX, 559; X, 7, 306, 325, 381), trans from Edinburgh Corstorphine Old to Edderton with Tain 29 Aug 1975; died 23 Jun 1976.

1976 ALISTAIR McRAE RENNIE
(FES IX, 335, 556; X, 199, 424), res from service with Board of World Mission in Malawi and ind to Kincardine and Croick 30 Jan 1976; became minister of united charge with Edderton 5 Dec 1976; ret 2 Nov 1986; s (John) Keith m (1) J Dilys Barker, (2) M S Muntemba; d Helen m Derry Kingston; s Douglas m Sarah Acheson; s Graham m Rosemary Goldsworthy.

1986 FREDERICK WILLIAM HIBBERT
ord and ind to Kincardine, Croik and Edderton 12 Dec 1986; dem to take up app as Director of Sea of Galilee Centre, Tiberias, Israel 1 Oct 1995.

1996 ALAN GRANT NAPIER WATT
B 7 Jun 1944 at Dundee, s of Alexander Cameron W. and Flora Napier; educ Grove Academy, Broughty Ferry 1956–62; Jordanhill College, Glasgow 1968–70 (DYCS); Dundee College 1976–78 (CQSW); University of St Andrews 1992–95 (MTh); Retail Trade 1962–68; Community Education and Social Work 1970–92; lic by Presb of Angus 25 Jun 1995; asst Aberlemno with Guthrie and Rescobie 1995–96; m (1) 15 Apr 1972 Elsie Dollin b 1 Apr 1937, died 26 Feb 1973 d of Walter D. and Catherine McPhail; Children: Cameron McPhail b 26 Feb 1973; m (2) 17 Jul 1992 Isobel Anne Mackenzie b 18 Oct 1943 d of Lyall M. and Margaret Joiner; ord and ind to Kincardine, Croick and Edderton 31 May 1996.

LAIRG (FUF 500; FES VII, 92; VIII, 673; IX, 672; X, 385)

Linked 1 Jul 1970 with Rogart.

1968 JOHN LESLIE GOSKIRK
(FES X, 385), ord and ind to Lairg 19 Jun 1968; became minister of linked charge with Rogart 1 Jul 1970; Addl children: Christian Lesley Cranstoun b 8 Jan 1976; Mairead Sutherland b 22 Apr 1980; s Alexander m Elizabeth Maclean MacLeod; s Calum m Kirsteen Anne Peters.

MELNESS AND TONGUE (FES X, 385)

Formed 21 Nov 1998 by union of Melness, Eriboll and Tongue.

1957 DOUGLAS FLEMING BAXTER
(FES IX, 786; X, 385, 444), ret from RAChD and ind to Tongue 6 Feb 1957; ret 31 Oct 1963.

1967 ALFRED McCLINTOCK
(FES IX, 203, 217, 333; X, 198, 385), trans from Larkhall St Machan's to Melness and Eriboll with Tongue 27 Jul 1967; ret 14 Nov 1984; died 23 May 1998; s Andrew m Ann Miller; s Alfred m Dorothy Black; d Margaret m Ken Muir Mackie; s Robert m Gillian Coull; Publ: *Something for the Eye to See* (Frank Foster, 1979).

1984 JAMES ALEXANDER RETTIE
B 5 Apr 1935 at Aberdeen, s of William R. and Elizabeth Wood; educ Bankhead Junior Secondary, Aberdeen 1947–50; University of Aberdeen 1978–81 (BTh); m 4 Jul 1959 Margaret Farmer b 14 Feb 1938 d of David and Annabella F; Children: June Allison b 2 Oct 1962 m Raymond Murray; Angela b 7 Mar 1969 m Callum Sutherland; ord by Presb of Lanark and introd as Assoc at Douglas Water and Rigside 20 Aug 1981; trans to Melness and Eriboll with Tongue 29 Nov 1984; became minister of united charge 21 Nov 1998; ret 31 Aug 1999.

ROGART (FES IX, 673; X, 385)

Linked 1 Jul 1970 with Lairg.

1970 JOHN LESLIE GOSKIRK
(FES X, 385), ord and ind to Lairg 19 Jun 1968; became minister of linked charge with Rogart 1 Jul 1970.

ROSEHALL (FUF 501; FES IX, 673; X, 385)

Linked 1 Jun 1973 with Creich.

1957 JOHN MACKAY
(FES X, 385), ord by Presb of Skye May 1957 and ind to Rosehall 7 Aug 1957; ret 31 Oct 1967; died 5 Feb 1982.

1968 ROBERT CRAWFORD ALSTON
(FES IX, 366, 688, 672; X, 362, 384, 385), trans from Boat of Garten and Kincardine to Rosehall 25 Sep 1968; ret 31 May 1973; died 27 Feb 1985.

1973 EUGENE JOHN DUPUY
(FES X, 383), ind to Creich 18 Nov 1971; became minister of linked charge with Rosehall 1 Jun 1973, see Creich.

1980 ROBERT KENNETH MACKENZIE
ind to Creich with Rosehall 30 Apr 1980, see Creich.

1986 ERIC RALPH LACEY
(FES X, 209 (2)), ind to Creich with Rosehall 23 Oct 1986, see Creich.

1992 ALASTAIR FLEMING McCORMICK
(FES X, 123, 230), res from World Mission app in Nassau, Bahamas and ind to Creich with Rosehall 30 Nov 1992; ret 31 Dec 1998.

1999 HEATHER CLAIRE OLSEN
ind to Creich with Rosehall 11 Jun 1999, see Creich.

PRESBYTERY OF CAITHNESS

BERRIEDALE AND DUNBEATH (FES IX, 678; X, 386)

Linked 6 Nov 1969 with Latheron.

1969   ROBERT WILLIAM BLACKWOOD
(FES X, 386), ord and ind to Berriedale and Dunbeath Ross with Latheron 6 Nov 1969; dem 23 Jun 1992.

1993   WILLIAM McLEISH ALEXANDER
(FES X, 406), trans from Bucksburn Stoneywood to Berriedale and Dunbeath with Latheron 28 Oct 1993; ret 31 Aug 1998; d Elizabeth m Alexander West; s James m Gillian Statham.

BOWER (FES IX, 678; X, 386)

Linked 29 Jun 1970 with Watten.

1960   DOUGLAS BRIGGS
(FES IX, 182, 382, 511, 682, 684; X, 386, 387), trans from Lybster to Bower 1 Nov 1960; ret 31 Mar 1970; died 23 Oct 1984.

1970   MICHAEL GRAEME MAPPIN
(FES X, 386), ind to Bower with Watten 29 Jun 1970; Clerk to Presb of Caithness from 1975; ret 31 Jan 1998; Addl children: Elizabeth Ann b 20 Oct 1975.

1999   GRANT BELL
ind to Bower with Watten 30 Jul 1999.

CANISBAY (FES IX, 679; X, 386)

Linked 30 Apr 1980 with Keiss.

1958   GEORGE BELL
(FES IX, 53, 434, 442; X, 257, 386), trans from Blackford to Canisbay 7 Nov 1958; ret 31 Oct 1979; died 2 May 1982.

1982   ALEXANDER MUIR
ord and ind to Canisbay with Keiss 24 Feb 1982; trans to Carinish 2 Jul 1991.

1991   ALEXANDER ROBERTSON
B 26 Oct 1941 at Dundee, s of Alexander R. and Isabella Ritchie; educ Logie Secondary, Dundee 1953–57; University of Glasgow 1965–66; Glasgow Baptist College 1966–69; lic by Baptist Union of Scotland 9 Aug 1969; m 26 Jul 1969 Kathleen Gibb Alexander b 24 Aug 1943 d of James and Kathleen A; Children: Fiona Kathleen b 27 May 1972; Morag Alexander b 6 Aug 1975; ord by Baptist Union and ind to Wick Baptist Church 9 Aug 1969; Trinidad Baptist Union 1975–79; Baptist Missionary Society 1979–80; admitted by General Assembly 1980 and app as Asst at Strathfillan; ind to Glasgow Scotstoun East 27 Aug 1981; trans to Aberluthnott with Laurencekirk 6 Nov 1987; trans to Canisbay with Keiss 1 Nov 1991; died 9 Aug 1996.

1998   IAIN MACNEE
B 23 Apr 1946 at Glasgow, s of Ian M. and Margaret Donald; educ Hutchesons' Grammar, Glasgow 1958–64; University of Aberdeen 1969–74 (LTh); Greenwich School of Theology 1991 (BD), 1995 (PhD); Trinity Theological Seminary, USA 1993 (MA); Industrial Management Training 1964–65; Youth Work Secretary 1965–69; lic by Presb of Glasgow 27 Jun 1974; asst Port Glasgow Hamilton Bardrainney 1974–76; m 19 Mar 1988 Anthea Lynne Reeves b 26 May 1955 d of Leonard Thomas R. and Hazel Jessie Joan Brown; ord by Presb of Greenock during assistantship at Port Glasgow Hamilton Bardrainney 30 May 1975; ind to Glasgow South Carntyne 27 May 1976; trans to Newbattle 20 Jun 1985; trans to Girvan South 18 May 1988; trans to Canisbay with Keiss 17 Feb 1998.

DUNNET (FES IX, 680; X, 386)

Linked 1 Jul 1970 with Olrig.

1967   GEORGE BALLINGAL
(FES IX, 662; X, 311, 379, 386), trans from Glenshee and Glenericht to Dunnet 12 Apr 1967; ret 30 Jun 1970; died 8 Dec 1978.

1970   WILLIAM DUNGAVEL
(FES X, 386), ord and ind to Dunnet with Olrig 1 Jul 1970; dem 29 Apr 1987.

1989   DAVID DEAS MELVILLE
ord and ind to Dunnet with Olrig 1 Sep 1989; trans to Kirkconnel 22 Jan 1999.

HALKIRK AND WESTERDALE (FES X, 387, 388)

Formed 1 Apr 1986 by union of Halkirk and Westerdale and Halsary.

1940   ANGUS STUART MACIVER
(FES IX, 684; X, 388), ord and ind to Westerdale and Halsary 5 Nov 1940; ret 11 Nov 1970; died 9 Sep 1984.

1970   ANDREW FERGUSON ANDREW
(FES IX, 453, 678; X, 386, 387), trans from Berriedale and Dunbeath Ross to Halkirk 3 Jul 1956; became minister of linked charge with Westerdale and Halsary 11 Nov 1970; ret 12 Jan 1975; died 21 May 1982.

1975   JOHN CAIRNS BECK
(FES X, 387), ord and ind to Halkirk with Westerdale and Halsary 15 May 1975; trans to Glasgow Dennistoun Central 10 Jul 1980.

1981   KENNETH WARNER
B 10 Dec 1938 at Glasgow, s of Graham Nicol W. and Sheila Lyall Guthrie MacAulay; educ George Watson's, Edinburgh 1951–57; Edinburgh College of Art 1957–63 (DArch); 1963–65 (DTP); University of St Andrews 1978–81 (BD); RIBA 1965–81; MRTPI 1970–81; Chartered Architect and Town Planner 1965–78; lic by Presb of St Andrews 29 Jun 1981; m 5 Oct 1966 Ann Brown b 5 Aug 1947 d of Robert Maule-Brown and Netta Harvey Sangster; Children: David Robert Bruce b 6 Jun 1972; Robert Sangster b 12 Mar 1976; ord and ind to Halkirk with Westerdale and Halsary 3 Sep 1981; became minister of united charge 1 Apr 1986.

KEISS (FES IX, 680; X, 387)

Linked 30 Apr 1980 with Canisbay.

1963   DAVID RANKINE BELL
(FES IX, 1, 301, 311, 704; X, 28, 387), trans from Addiewell to Keiss 27 Mar 1963; ret 2 Oct 1967; died 20 Aug 1981.

1971   NEIL ALEXANDER DUNCAN
(FES X, 387), ord and ind to Keiss 14 May 1971; dem 21 May 1979.

1982   ALEXANDER MUIR
ord and ind to Canisbay with Keiss 24 Feb 1982; trans to Carinish 2 Jul 1991.

1991   ALEXANDER ROBERTSON
ind to Canisbay with Keiss 1 Nov 1991, see Canisbay.

1998   IAIN MACNEE
trans from Girvan South to Canisbay with Keiss 17 Feb 1998, see Canisbay.

LATHERON (FES IX, 681; X, 386)

Linked 6 Nov 1969 with Berriedale and Dunbeath.

1989   ROBERT WILLIAM BLACKWOOD
(FES X, 386), ord and ind to Berriedale and Dunbeath Ross with Latheron 6 Nov 1969; dem 23 Jun 1992.

1993   WILLIAM McLEISH ALEXANDER
(FES X, 406), trans from Bucksburn Stoneywood to Berriedale and Dunbeath with Latheron 28 Oct 1993; ret 31 Aug 1998.

LYBSTER AND BRUAN (FES X, 387)

1971   ALAN CAMERON RAEBURN
(FES X, 387), ord and ind to Lybster and Bruan 30 Jul 1971; trans to Glasgow Battlefield East 16 Mar 1977.

1977   DAVID STUART DIXON
ord by Presb of Falkirk during assistantship at Kildrum 2 Jun 1976; ind to Lybster and Bruan 23 Sep 1977; trans to Inchbrayock with Montrose Melville South 10 Aug 1994.

1996   IAIN ALEXANDER SUTHERLAND
B 5 Aug 1968 at Edinburgh, s of Donald S. and Mary Sheila Findlay; educ Queensferry High 1980–86; University of Edinburgh 1986–90 (BSc); University of Aberdeen 1991–94 (BD); Agriculture 1986–90; Fish Farming 1990–91; lic by Presb of Edinburgh 3 Jul 1994; asst Banff 1994–95; m 9 Jul 1994 Heather Edith Ogston b 16 Mar 1970 d of Douglas Archibald O. and Irene Edith Watt; ord and ind to Lybster and Bruan 11 Jan 1996.

OLRIG (FES IX, 682; X, 387)

Linked 1 Jul 1970 with Dunnet.

1970   WILLIAM DUNGAVEL
(FES X, 386), ord and ind to Dunnet with Olrig 1 Jul 1970; dem 29 Apr 1987.

1989   DAVID DEAS MELVILLE
ord and ind to Dunnet with Olrig 1 Sep 1989; trans to Kirkconnel 22 Jan 1999.

REAY (FES X, 387)

Linked 28 Oct 1994 with Strathy and Halladale.

1973   HUGH MACCOMMACH CROLL SMITH
(FES X, 388), ord and ind to Reay 17 May 1973; trans to Mortlach and Cabrach 11 Aug 1982.

1983   JAMES STEWART DEWAR
B 5 Oct 1957 at Lanark, s of George D. and Betty Stewart; educ Lanark Grammar 1969–75; University of Edinburgh 1975–79 (MA), 1979–82 (BD); lic by Presb of Lanark 1 Jul 1982; asst Edinburgh Sighthill St Nicholas' 1982–83; m 9 Aug 1980 Jean Kathryn Fraser b 19 May 1957 d of Alistair William F. and Jean Sinclair Robb; Children: Alistair Stewart b 8 Mar 1985; Fiona Anne b 5 Mar 1988; Kirsty Fraser b 5 Mar 1988; ord and ind to Reay 24 Jun 1983; became minister of linked charge with Strathy and Halladale 28 Oct 1994; Publ: *The Old White House of God* (private, 1989).

STRATHY AND HALLADALE (FES IX, 676; X, 385)

Linked 28 Oct 1994 with Reay.

1968 WALTER JOHNSTONE
(FES IX, 327, 619, 680; X, 193, 385), trans from Coatbridge Old Monkland to Strathy and Halladale 18 Dec 1968; ret 15 Nov 1977; died 11 Feb 1988.

1978 ROBERT MAULE-BROWN
(FES IX, 142, 182; X, 56 (2), 189, 241, 342, 400, 423), trans from Strathfillan to Strathy and Halladale 6 Jun 1978; ret 30 Jun 1985.

1987 FRANCIS DENTON BARDGETT
ord and ind to Strathy and Halladale 11 Aug 1987; introd as Community minister, Orkney 1 Sep 1993.

1994 JAMES STEWART DEWAR
ord and ind to Reay 24 Jun 1983; became minister of linked charge with Strathy and Halladale 28 Oct 1994.

THURSO ST PETER'S AND ST ANDREW'S (FES IX, 683; X, 388)

1965 DONALD STEWART RIACH
(FES X, 388), ord by Presb of Dalkeith during assistantship at Newbattle 15 May 1964; ind to St Peter's and St Andrew's 28 Apr 1965; dem 6 Sep 1988.

1989 KENNETH SAMUEL BORTHWICK
B 27 Sep 1958 at Bearsden, s of George Williamson B. and Margaret Agnes Russell MacLachlan; educ Kelvinside Academy, Glasgow 1963–76; University of Glasgow 1979 (MA), 1982 (BD); lic by Presb of Glasgow, 1982; asst Linlithgow St Michael's 1982–84; m 5 Jul 1982 Morag Matheson b 21 Feb 1958 d of Donald M. and Violet Hamill; Children: Sarah Abigail b 15 Nov 1984; David Samuel b 20 Apr 1987; ord by Presb of West Lothian during assistantship at Linlithgow St Michael's 29 May 1983; ind to Eday with Stronsay Moncur Memorial 6 Apr 1984; trans to St Peter's and St Andrew's 6 Jul 1989.

THURSO WEST (FUF 509; FES IX, 683; X, 388)

1961 GORDON WILLIAM JAMES MORTIMER
(FES X, 388), ord and ind to Thurso West 20 Apr 1961; dem 3 Nov 1964 to enter teaching profession; died 31 Aug 1995.

1965 ANDREW DENIS WILLIAMS
(FES X, 305, 388), ord and ind to Thurso West 25 Mar 1965; dem 10 Apr 1968 to take up app as Asst at Grangemouth Kerse.

1968 GEORGE STEWART SHARP
(FES X, 251, 388), ord and ind to Thurso West 27 Jun 1968; trans to Forgandenny with Forteviot 17 Apr 1974.

1974 JOHN BRUCE THOMSON
(FES X, 388), ind to Thurso West 10 Sep 1974; trans to Scone Old 22 Jun 1983.

1984 RONALD JOHNSTONE
B 11 Nov 1945 at Glasgow, s of Daniel McCallum J. and Christina Cameron; educ Woodside Secondary, Glasgow 1957–63; University of Glasgow 1971–76 (BD); Civil Service 1963–71; lic by Presb of Glasgow 25 Jun 1976; asst New Erskine 1976–77; m 11 Sep 1970 Freda Qualter b 10 Mar 1947 d of Alfred Q. and Ethel Pullin; Children: Pauline Joy b 13 Mar 1974; Rachael Lorna b 22 Dec 1977; ord and ind to Glasgow Pollokshaws 10 May 1977; trans to Thurso West 10 May 1984.

WATTEN (FES IX, 684; X, 388)

Linked 29 Jun 1970 with Bower.

1970 MICHAEL GRAEME MAPPIN
(FES X, 386), ind to Bower with Watten 29 Jun 1970, see Bower.

1999 GRANT BELL
ind to Bower with Watten 30 Jul 1999.

WICK BRIDGE STREET (FUF 510; FES IX, 684; X, 388)

1955 ALISTAIR ANDERSON ROY
(FES X, 388), ord and ind to Bridge Street 23 Mar 1955.

WICK OLD (FES VII, 140; VIII, 679; IX, 685; X, 389)

1971 THOMAS GRAY McCALLUM ROBERTSON
(FES X, 389), ord and ind to Wick Old 3 Sep 1971; trans to Edenshead and Strathmiglo 24 May 1984.

1986 JAMES WATSON
(FES X, 10 (2)), res as Environmental Health Officer for Stonehaven and Caithness and ind to Wick Old 12 Jan 1986; trans to Bowden with Lilliesleaf 6 Apr 1988.

1988 ROBERT STEWART FRIZZELL
(FES X, 150, 169), trans from Glasgow Balshagray to Wick Old 29 Dec 1988; app by RAChD to Army Cadet Force 16 Jul 1993; ret 6 Mar 2000; d Lydia m Michelet; d Judith m Burns.

WICK PULTNEYTOWN AND THRUMSTER (FES X, 389)

Formed 23 Oct 1990 by union of Wick Central and Wick St Andrew's and Thrumster.

1968 JAMES SINCLAIR CORMACK
(FES X, 5, 389), trans from Edinburgh Buccleuch to Wick Central 14 Feb 1968; ret 18 Jan 1988; died 7 Sep 1997.

1974 WILLIAM FITCH WALLACE
(FES X, 389), Interdenominational Church, Addis Ababa, Ethiopia 1971–73; ind to St Andrew's and Thrumster 8 Jun 1974; became minister of united charge with Wick Central 23 Oct 1990; Addl children: Katherine Jean b 18 May 1977; Ruth Margaret b 12 Sep 1979; Publ: Articles for various newspapers and journals.

PRESBYTERY OF LOCHCARRON-SKYE

APPLECROSS LOCHCARRON AND TORRIDON
(FES X, 390, 391, 392)

Formed 17 Jul 1998 by union of Applecross with
Lochcarron and Shieldaig with Torridon and Kinlochewe.

1960 JOHN MACDONALD
(FES IX, 398, 667; X, 381, 391), trans from Kilmuir
Easter to Lochcarron with Shieldaig 9 Dec 1960;
ret 30 Apr 1966; died 25 Aug 1986.

1966 THOMAS BIRNIE NOBLE
(FUF 152; FES IX, 207; X, 391), dem from Largs
St John's 29 Oct 1932 to take up app in journalism;
introd as Assoc at Lochcarron with Shieldaig with
Torridon and Kinlochewe 10 Jul 1966; ret 31 Oct
1973; died 26 Jul 1984.

1967 JOHN MACLEOD
(FES IX, 17, 236; X, 10 (2), 391), trans from
Edinburgh Highland Tolbooth St John's to Lochcarron with Shieldaig with Torridon and Kinlochewe 16 Feb 1967; ret 6 Oct 1972; died 12 Nov
1988.

1972 RONALD MICHAEL LEEMAN CHILTON
(FES X, 390), ord and ind to Applecross 13 Sep
1972; trans to Hamilton Burnbank 2 Mar 1978.

1973 WILLIAM PETER FINLAY
(FES X, 391, 419), res from service with Overseas
Council in Kasama, Zambia and introd as Assoc
at Lochcarron and Shieldaig with Torridon and
Kinlochewe 30 Jun 1973; introd as Assoc to Paisley
St Ninian's Ferguslie (term) 1 Apr 1978.

1973 ALLAN IAN MACARTHUR
(FES X, 391), ord and ind to Lochcarron and
Shieldaig with Torridon and Kinlochewe 9 Aug
1973; became minister of linked charge with
Applecross 21 Dec 1978; ret 30 May 1998; d
Anne m Roger Bamfield; d Rosemary m Ronald
Calder; d Grace m John Marston; d Donella m
Graham Lawson; s Allan m Victoria Willimot; d Ruth
m Angus MacDonald; d Heather m Brian
Beckmann.

1978 KENNETH MACDONALD
(FES X, 394), dem from Snizort North and introd
as Assoc at Applecross with Lochcarron and
Shieldaig with Torridon and Kinlochewe 21 Dec
1978; ret 31 Dec 1992.

1994 DAVID VAUGHAN SCOTT
B 15 Oct 1949 at New York, USA, s of Charles S.
and Megan Currie; educ Fettes College, Edinburgh
1963–66; University of Aberdeen 1988–92 (BTh);
Shepherd/Crofter/Farmer 1967–87; lic by Presb of
Sutherland 2 Jul 1992; asst Auchterderran with St
Fothad's with Kinglassie 1992–94; m 2 Oct 1993
Fena Harris b 31 May 1952 d of Frank H. and Ann
Forret; Children: Skye b 13 Sep 1980 (from
previous marriage); ord by Presb of Lochcarron
and Skye and introd as Assoc at Applecross with
Lochcarron and Shieldaig with Torridon and
Kinlochewe 3 Jun 1994.

BRACADALE AND DUIRINISH (FES X, 393)

Formed 1 May 1998 by union of Bracadale and
Duirinish.

1962 JOHN MACNAUGHTON
(FES IX, 697; X, 393, 397), trans from Barvas to
Bracadale 6 Jul 1962; died 9 Jun 1980.

1968 KENNETH JOHN MACPHERSON
(FES IX, 189, 328; X, 393 (2)), trans from Dalserf
to Duirinish 27 Sep 1968; became minister of united
charge with Waternish 1 Sep 1974; ret 31 Mar
1984; died 19 Mar 1993.

1981 DONALD ANGUS MACKAY
(FES X, 396), trans from Kilmuir with Stenscholl to
Bracadale 14 Apr 1981; trans to Bernera 17 Aug
1990.

1984 MICHAEL JAMES LIND
ord and ind to Duirinish 12 Oct 1984; trans to
Campbeltown Highland 26 Sep 1997.

1994 RODERICK ALEXANDER RANDLE
MACLEOD
ord and ind to Bracadale 28 Jan 1994; dem on
app by Royal Naval Chaplaincy Service 20 Feb
1998.

GAIRLOCH AND DUNDONNELL (FES X, 378,
390)

Formed 4 Oct 1983 by union of Gairloch and
Dundonnell.

1973 STEPHEN PALIT
(FES X, 378), trans from Aberdeen North and East of St Nicholas to Dundonnell 26 Jan 1973; ret 13 Jun 1983.

1975 JOHN SMITH
(FES X, 91, 180, 390), trans from Glasgow South Carntyne to Gairloch 15 May 1975; died 19 Feb 1983.

1984 WILLIAM JOHN MACDONALD
trans from Newbattle to Gairloch and Dundonnell 10 Aug 1984; dem 31 Jul 1999 on app by Dept of National Mission.

GLENELG AND KINTAIL (FES X, 390,391)

Formed 23 Mar 1987 by union of Glenelg, Glenshiel and Kintail.

1967 ALEXANDER DUNCAN MACRAE
(FES IX, 406, 520, 633; X, 120, 238, 307, 360, 390), trans from Shiskine to Glenelg 16 Feb 1967; became minister of linked charge with Glenshiel 30 Jun 1968; ret 30 Nov 1971; died 12 May 1979.

1972 ALASDAIR IAN MACKENZIE
(FES IX, 379, 478, 623; X, 169 (2), 361, 390), trans from Glasgow Parkhead to Glenelg with Glenshiel with Kintail 1 Nov 1972; ret 20 Jan 1986.

1973 BRIAN CONLAN
(FES X, 390), introd as Assoc at Glenelg with Glenshiel with Kintail 31 Aug 1973; res from app 31 Oct 1980.

1988 DONALD BEATON
(FES X, 133, 444), trans from Kilmuir and Stenscholl to Glenelg and Kintail 21 Apr 1988; d Catriona m Patrick John Mercer.

KILMUIR AND STENSCHOLL (FES X, 393, 394)

Formed 26 Oct 1981 by union of Kilmuir and Stenscholl.

1948 ANGUS MACKAY
(FES IX, 689, 694; X, 393), trans from Carinish to Kilmuir 27 Apr 1948; became minister of linked charge with Stenscholl 26 Apr 1974; ret 31 May 1977; died 26 Feb 1986.

1949 DONALD JOHN MACKINNON
(FES IX, 691, 692, 694; X, 394), trans from Waternish to Stenscholl 5 Apr 1949; ret 30 Jun 1971; died 15 Sep 1976.

1974 JOHN ROSS MACLEAN
(FES IX, 403; X, 241, 373, 384, 393), dem from Kirkhill and introd as Assoc at Kilmuir with Stenscholl 27 Apr 1974; ret 10 Dec 1977; died 16 Sep 1985.

1979 DONALD ANGUS MACKAY
(FES X, 396), trans from Manish-Scarista to Kilmuir with Stenscholl 27 Feb 1979; trans to Bracadale 14 Apr 1981; m 5 Apr 1979 Catherine Buchanan b 8 Mar 1944 d of Murdo B. and Peggy Macritchie; Children: Margaret Elizabeth b 5 Mar 1980.

1982 DONALD BEATON
(FES X, 133, 444), ret from RAChD and ind to Kilmuir and Stenscholl 17 Feb 1982; trans to Glenelg and Kintail 21 Apr 1988.

1990 ALEN JOHN RONALD McCULLOCH
ord and ind to Kilmuir and Stenscholl 16 Feb 1990; dem 11 Jun 1995 on app by RAChD.

1996 NORMAN WALKER DRUMMOND
B 1 Apr 1952 at Greenock, s of Edwin Payne D. and Jean Walker; educ Merchiston Castle, Edinburgh 1956–70; University of Cambridge 1970–73 (MA); University of Edinburgh 1973–76 (BD); lic by Presb of Greenock 25 Jun 1976; m 1 Jul 1976 Elizabeth Helen Kennedy b 23 Feb 1955 d of David K. and Mary Burn; Children: Andrew Edwin b 29 May 1977; Margaret Elizabeth b 11 Jan 1980; Marie Clare b 2 Oct 1981; Christian Henry b 14 Sep 1986; Ruaraidh Walker b 7 May 1993; ord by Presb of Greenock and app by RAChD 15 Aug 1976; Chaplain to Fettes College, Edinburgh 1982–84; Headmaster, Loretto School, Edinburgh 1984–95; ind to Kilmuir and Stenscholl 12 Jul 1996; dem 31 Dec 1998; Founder and Chairman of Columba 1400 Community and International Leadership Centre, Isle of Skye; BBC National Governor for Scotland 1994–99; Publ: *The First 25 Years: History of the Kirk Session of the Black Watch* (private, 1979); *Mothers' Hands* (Tantallon Press, 1994).

LOCHALSH (FES X, 391)

Formed 22 Jun 1990 by union of Lochalsh and Stromeferry and Plockton and Kyle.

1970 DONALD ROBERTSON
(FES IX, 404; X, 238, 244, 347, 391, 408), trans from Ardallie with Deer Clola to Lochalsh and Stromeferry 8 Oct 1970; ret 31 Mar 1976; died 16 Jun 1995.

1973 DUNCAN MACKINNON
(FES X, 392, 393, 397), trans from Cross Ness to Plockton and Kyle 21 Jun 1973; ret 30 May 1989; s Alister m Catherine Morrison.

1976 JOHN STIRLING GREIG
B 7 Jul 1915 at Elphinstone, s of John G. and Margaret Dickson; educ Preston Lodge Secondary 1927–29; University of Glasgow 1975–76; Business directorships in Scottish co-operative and international co-operative organisations; lic by Presb of Irvine and Kilmarnock 9 Jun 1976; m 31 Oct 1942 Marion Finlayson b 29 Aug 1919;

Children: Ian Finlay Stirling b 23 Mar 1945 m Barbara Ann Munns; ord and ind to Lochalsh and Stromeferry 23 Sep 1976; ret 17 Sep 1983; died 12 Oct 1988.

1984   EWEN SINCLAIR NICOLL
(FES X, 303), trans from Carlisle with Longtown to Lochalsh and Stromeferry 3 Feb 1984; trans to Arrochar with Luss 2 Oct 1986.

1990   HECTOR MORRISON
trans from Barvas to Lochalsh 30 Nov 1990; dem on app as Lecturer in Biblical Studies, Highland Theological Institute 1 Aug 1994.

1995   ALLAN BRYCE BROWN
B 28 Jun 1959 at Broxburn, s of Allan Bryce B. and Mary Ferguson; educ Caldervale High, Airdrie 1971–76; West Lothian College of Further Education 1976–77 (SNCCO); Bell College of Technology, Hamilton 1977–79 (DCDP); University of Edinburgh 1989–93 (BD, MTh); Computer Operator 1979–86; Senior Computer Operator 1986–89; lic by Presb of West Lothian 14 Oct 1993; asst Chryston 1989–95; m 21 Aug 1982 Mae Hume Swan b 4 Jul 1962 d of Frank Dorian Dobson S. and Janet Joyce Hume; Children: Stephen b 2 Oct 1990; ord and ind to Lochalsh 24 Feb 1995.

PORTREE (FES IX, 690; X, 393)

1973   JAMES GUNN MATHESON
(FES IX, 4; X, 393, 455), res as Secretary of Stewardship and Budget Committee and ind to Portree 28 Sep 1973; Moderator of General Assembly 1975–76; ret 30 Sep 1979.

1980   JOHN FERGUSON
(FES X, 397), trans from Cross, Ness to Portree 20 Mar 1980; DD (Canada Christian College) 1996; Addl children: Agnes b 14 Feb 1978; Publ: Gaelic trans of *The Pilgrim's Progress* (children's ed, Cruisgean, 1979); *Slainte Mhath* (Skye Graphics, 1983).

SNIZORT (FES X, 393, 394)

Formed 24 Apr 1979 by union of Snizort South (linked with Waternish 1 Dec 1961 until 19 Sep 1972) and Snizort North.

1950   DONALD WILLIAM MACDONALD
(FES IX, 688, 691; X, 394), trans from Torridon to Snizort South 4 May 1950; became minister of linked charge with Waternish 1 Dec 1961; ret 31 Dec 1978; died 28 Jan 1980.

1965   KENNETH MACDONALD
(FES X, 394), ord and ind to Snizort North 21 Sep 1965; introd as Assoc at Applecross with Lochcarron and Shieldaig with Torridon and Kinlochewe 21 Dec 1978.

1979   JOHN EWEN MACINNES
(FES X, 234, 393), dem from Saddell and Carradale 30 Sep 1978; ind to Snizort 21 Dec 1979; ret 30 Jun 1987; died 19 Sep 1997.

1988   DONALD MACLEOD
B 5 Dec 1946 at Stornoway, s of Archibald M. and Peggy MacDonald; educ Nicolson Institute, Stornoway 1950–62; University of Aberdeen 1983–88 (LTh, DPS); Electronics Engineering 1962–83; lic by Presb of Lewis 6 Jul 1988; m 7 Mar 1973 Margaret MacKenzie b 13 Jan 1947 d of John Findlay M. and Alina Murray; Children: David b 16 May 1974; Aileen b 14 Nov 1976; Mairi b 1 Apr 1981; ord and ind to Snizort 2 Nov 1988.

STRATH AND SLEAT (FES X, 393, 394)

Formed 22 Mar 1983 by union of Strath and Sleat.

1950   ANGUS MACDOUGALL
(FES IX, 400, 690; X, 393), trans from Kilbrandon and Kilchattan to Sleat 26 Oct 1950; ret 31 Jul 1982.

1974   GIRVAN CHRISTIE McKAY
(FES X, 394, 422), res from service with Overseas Council in Argentina and ind to Strath 31 Jan 1974; dem on app by Presb Church in Ireland to Waterford Presb Church 9 Jun 1977; ind to Tullamore and Mountmellick (PCI) 1983; ret 31 Aug 1996; Publ: Various articles, short stories and sermons in Gaelic pages of *Life & Work* and in *Gairm* (Gaelic Literary Magazine) since 1960; regular contributor to *Monato* (International news magazine, publ in Esperanto, Antwerp).

1977   JOHN ARCHIBALD ROBERTSON
(FES IX, 685; X, 34, 327, 389), dem from York Memorial Presb Church, Toronto, Canada and ind to Strath 28 Nov 1977; dem 8 Oct 1978 and returned to Canada.

1979   JOHN MURDO MACLEOD MACARTHUR
(FES X, 384, 397), trans from Carloway to Strath 15 Mar 1979; became minister of united charge with Sleat 22 Mar 1983; dem 2 Dec 1984; ind to Glasgow St Columba 4 Apr 1989.

1984   NORMAN HILL
B 5 Sep 1950 at Falkirk, s of Thomas H. and Williamina MacIntosh; educ Falkirk High 1962–68; University of Aberdeen 1978–83 (BD, CPS); lic by Presb of Falkirk 26 Jun 1983; asst Aberdeen Northfield 1983–84; m 12 Dec 1979 Jane Agnes Scott b 22 Dec 1954 d of Leslie and Mary S; Children: David b 9 Oct 1980; Kenneth b 4 Aug 1982; ord by Presb of Lochcarron-Skye and introd as Assoc at Strath and Sleat 30 Nov 1984; dem 31 Aug 1990.

1986 DONALD ANGUS MACLENNAN
admitted by General Assembly 1986; ind to Strath and Sleat 28 Aug 1986; trans to Kinloch 24 Apr 1989.

1990 IAIN MICHAEL ALEXANDER REID
B 26 Jun 1951 at Stirling, s of John McColl R. and Elizabeth Alexander; educ Stirling High 1963–71; Dundee College of Further Education 1972–75; University of Glasgow 1985–89 (BD, CQSW, DSW); lic by Presb of Stirling 29 Jun 1989; asst Bearsden New Kilpatrick 1989–90; Margaret Taylor Benny b 9 Jul 1952 d of Henry Cowie B. and Margaret Johnston; Children: Jennifer b 29 Aug 1973; Craig b 8 Sep 1977; ord and ind to Strath and Sleat 7 Sep 1990.

1991 JAMES GRIER
ord by Presb of Lochcarron-Skye and introd as Assoc at Strath and Sleat 26 Apr 1991; ind to Coatbridge Middle 16 May 1996.

1997 JOHN MURDO NICOLSON
B 10 Feb 1962 at Stornoway, s of Alexander Donald N. and Catherine Duncanson; educ Nicolson Institute, Stornoway 1989–91; University of Aberdeen 1995 (BD), 1996 (DipMin); Carpet Fitter 1978–84; Material Controller 1984–88; Undertaker 1988–96; lic by Presb of Lewis 5 Jul 1996; m 26 Jun 1985 Marina Hughson b 11 Nov 1962 d of Robert Andrew H. and Henrietta Mackenzie Ross; Children: David b 5 Oct 1986; Amy b 3 Jul 1991; ord by Presb of Lochcarron-Skye and introd as Assoc at Strath and Sleat 5 Sep 1997.

PRESBYTERY OF UIST

BARRA (FUF 494; FES VII, 185; VIII, 688; IX, 693; X, 395)

1970 RODERICK MACKINNON
(FES IX, 565, 668 (2), 758, 765; X, 377, 391, 395), trans from Contin-Strathconon to Barra 5 Feb 1970; ret 15 Apr 1978; died 8 Mar 1988.

1982 IAIN ROSS MUNRO
(FES X, 110, 257), trans from Kilarrow with Kilmeny to Barra 24 Mar 1982; ret 31 Oct 1985; died 3 Sep 1996.

1986 JAMES BISHOP MACLEAN
ord and ind to Barra 5 Jun 1986; dem to take up app with RAChD 8 May 1990.

1993 ARTHUR DAVID COURTENAY GREER
(FES X, 163 (2), 419), trans from Dunscore with Glencairn and Moniaive to Barra 29 Jul 1993; ret 31 Aug 1996; New York Theological Seminary 1985 (DMin); d Elizabeth m John Strachan; d Janet m Alan Kenneth Denniss; d Kathleen m David Smith; s David m Sophie Noussier.

BENBECULA (FUF 493; FES VII, 186; VIII, 688; IX, 693; X, 395)

1975 IAIN MACDONALD FORBES
(FES X, 395, 419, 453), res as Home Organisation Secretary, Overseas Council and ind to Benbecula 17 Jan 1975; trans to Howe of Fife 17 Feb 1983.

1983 ADRIAN PETER JOHN VARWELL
ord and ind to Benbecula 24 Aug 1983; dem to take up app as Director of St Ninian's Centre, Crieff 1 Oct 1997.

1998 KENNETH JOHN MACPHERSON
B 17 Jul 1950 at North Uist, s of Donald John M. and Johann Morrison; educ Bayhead Secondary, N Uist and Nicolson Institute, Stornoway; University of Glasgow 1982–87 (BD, CMin); Storeman 1965–68; Fisherman 1968–78; lic by Presb of Uist 23 Mar 1988; m 27 Oct 1972 Christine Anne Stewart b 20 Aug 1953 d of Donald S. and Lexy MacAskill; Children: Bryan Stewart b 29 Jun 1973 m Roslyn; Marilyn Anne b 27 Apr 1980; ord and ind to Kilmallie 7 May 1988; trans to Cross, Ness 9 Jun 1993; trans to Benbecula 23 Sep 1998.

BERNERA (FUF 493; FES VII, 188; VIII, 688; IX, 693; X, 395)

Vacant from 1985 until 1990.

1966 RODERICK MACLEOD
(FES X, 395), ord and ind to Bernera 12 Jul 1966; trans to Cumlodden, Lochfyneside and Lochgair 20 Sep 1985; Clerk to Presb of Uist 1981–85; Member, Western Isles Islands Council 1974–82; Visiting Scholar, Harvard Divinity School, 1979.

1990 DONALD ANGUS MACKAY
(FES X, 396), trans from Bracadale to Bernera 17 Aug 1990; ret 31 Oct 1993; died 25 May 1999.

CARINISH (FUF 493; FES IX, 694; X, 396)

Vacant from 1985 until 1991.

1966 NORMAN MACDONALD
(FES IX, 396, 687, 693; X, 236, 375, 396), trans from Stratherrick and Boleskine to Carinish 22 Dec 1966; ret 30 Apr 1972; died 14 Dec 1978.

1974 RODERICK MORRISON
(FES X, 396), ord and ind to Carinish 5 Jun 1974; trans to Stornoway High 23 Jun 1981.

1982 COLIN NORMAN MACKENZIE
(FES IX, 695; X, 118, 373, 396), trans from Kirkhill to Carinish 4 Jun 1982; ret 28 Aug 1985; died 30 Jan 1994.

1991 ALEXANDER MUIR
B 26 Dec 1940 at Rutherglen, s of John M. and Ann Buchan; educ Rutherglen Academy 1953–58, 1959–60; University of Glasgow 1960–63 (MA), 1977–80 (BD); Jordanhill College, Glasgow 1963–64 (Teaching Dip); Insurance Clerk 1958–59; Teaching 1964–66, 1967–77; Voluntary Missionary Work, Nigeria 1966–67; lic by Presb of Glasgow, Jun 1980; asst Largs St Columba's 1980–81; m 9 Jul 1971 Catriona Kinloch Male b 9 Oct 1949 d of John Patrick M. and Helen Leitch Kinloch; Children: Kenneth John MacGregor b 30 Sep 1973; Graham Alexander Kinloch b 15 Apr 1976; Alistair James Buchan b 26 May 1982; Ian Hector Bruce b 18 Jul 1986; ord and ind to Canisbay with Keiss 24 Feb 1982; trans to Carinish 2 Jul 1991; ret 31 Dec 1996 on grounds of ill-health; Publ: *Revivals and the Charismatic Controversy* (Handsel Press, 1988);

God Has Given us a Dream (Cleat Recordings, 1985); *Pray for Scotland* (Harp Recordings, 1987); *Pensacola: Genuine Revival or Toronto Repackaged?* (St Matthew Publ, 1997).

1998 THOMAS JOSEPH REEVES MACKINNON
B 16 Jul 1953 on Skye, s of Roderick MacLeod M. and Flora Charlotte Reeves; educ Portree High; University of Aberdeen 1991–95 (LTh, DipMin); Engraver 1968–70; Welder/Fitter 1971–90; lic by Presb of Lochcarron-Skye, 1995; m 15 Nov 1975 Julia Alexina MacLeod d of John and Peggy Ann M; Children: Ruairidh MacLeod; Margaret Ann; Angus John; ord and ind to Glassary and Kilmartin 7 Jun 1996; trans to Carinish 11 Sep 1998.

KILMUIR AND PAIBLE (FES IX, 694; X, 396)

Vacant from 1988 until 1993.

1966 WILLIAM MACKENZIE MACDONALD
(FES IX, 698; X, 396, 398), trans from Lochs-in-Bernera to Kilmuir and Paible 24 Mar 1966; ret 31 Jul 1972 on grounds of ill-health; died 21 Feb 1993.

1976 NORMAN MACIVER
ord and ind to Kilmuir and Paible 16 Apr 1976; trans to Tarbert (Harris) 28 Oct 1988.

1993 DAVID MACINNES
(FES X, 397), trans from Glasgow Gardner Street to Kilmuir and Paible 3 May 1993; ret 15 Jul 1999.

LOCHMADDY AND TRUMISGARRY (FES IX, 694; X, 396)

1963 JOHN MURDO SMITH
(FES X, 396 (2)), trans from South Uist Howmore to Lochmaddy and Trumisgarry 2 Jul 1963; ret 31 Aug 1992; d Fiona m John Crooks; s Alasdair m Angela Macleod.

1995 ANGUS JOHN MACDONALD
B 24 Feb 1940 at Stornoway, s of Angus M. and Kate MacLennan; educ Laxdale Junior Secondary and Nicolson Institute, Stornoway 1945–56; Nurse Training School, Inverness 1958–61 (RMN); London 1961–64 (RGN); Dundee 1964–65 (RNMH); Manchester Business School 1979–80; Pacific Western University, USA 1988–89 (BSc); University of Aberdeen 1991–94 (BD); Director of Nursing 1974–86; Hospital Management Consultant, British Government Overseas (ODA) 1986–90; lic by Presb of Lewis 29 Jun 1994; asst Stornoway Martin's Memorial 1994–95; m 30 Jul 1974 Jennifer Christine Bailey b 7 Jun 1949 d of John B. and Anne; Children: Ian Angus b 6 May 1975; Karina Mary b 14 Jan 1977; Andrew Lewis b 30 Nov 1978; ord and ind to Lochmaddy and Trumisgarry 4 Jul 1995.

MANISH-SCARISTA (FES IX, 695; X, 396)

Vacant from 1979 until 1988.

1973 DONALD ANGUS MACKAY
(FES X, 396), ord and ind to Manish-Scarista 8 Aug 1973; trans to Kilmuir with Stenscholl 27 Feb 1979.

1988 MURDO SMITH
B 20 Jul 1947 at Shader, Isle of Lewis, s of John S. and Johanna Murray; educ Nicolson Institute, Stornoway 1959–66; University of Edinburgh 1982–87 (MA, BD); lic by Presb of Edinburgh 5 Jul 1987; asst Stornoway High 1987–88; m 1 Sep 1982 Alice Mary MacLean b 28 Feb 1951 d of John and Georgina M; Children: Iain b 9 Oct 1985; Gordon b 16 Feb 1988; Siobhan b 23 Jun 1989; ord and ind to Manish-Scarista 23 Sep 1988.

SOUTH UIST (FES VII, 194; VIII, 690; IX, 695; X, 396)

Formed 31 May 1978 by union of Daliburgh and South Uist Howmore.

1968 RODERICK MACLEAN MACKINNON
(FES X, 396), ord and ind to Daliburgh 3 Jul 1968; became minister of united charge with South Uist Howmore 31 May 1978; trans to Kilmuir and Logie Easter 26 Aug 1981.

1983 JAMES ALEXANDER MUNRO
trans from Tiree and Coll to South Uist 15 Sep 1983; trans to Alves and Burghead 18 Aug 1987.

1989 GAVIN JOHN ELLIOTT
res as Mission Partner with United Church of Zambia, Lusaka and ind to South Uist 29 Aug 1989; trans to Biggar 29 Nov 1995.

1998 JAMES BARBOUR LAWSON
(FES X, 446), trans from Prestonkirk with Stenton with Whittingehame to South Uist 25 Mar 1998.

TARBERT (FUF 494; FES IX, 695; X, 396)

1947 MURDO MACLEOD
(FES IX, 689, 696; X, 396), dem from Tarbert 29 Feb 1956 on app by Home Board to act as loc ten in vacant charges in the Highlands and Islands; died 15 Feb 1985.

1956 DONALD ANGUS MACRAE
(FES IX, 690, 693; X, 395, 396), trans from Benbecula to Tarbert 30 Aug 1956; ret 2 Apr 1988.

1988 NORMAN MACIVER
B 13 Jul 1945 on Lewis, s of Malcolm M. and Johanna MacKinnon; educ Aird J S School, Lewis 1950–60; University of Glasgow 1969–74 (BD); Sales/Clerk 1963–68; lic by Presb of Glasgow 27 Jun 1974; asst Linlithgow St Michael's 1974–76; m 24 Jul 1974 Catherine Mary MacKay b 17 Nov 1948 d of Angus M. and Katie Ferguson; Children: Iain b 20 Jul 1975; Caitriona b 27 May 1978; David Angus b 14 Sep 1980; ord and ind to Kilmuir and Paible 16 Apr 1976; trans to Tarbert 28 Oct 1988.

PRESBYTERY OF LEWIS

BARVAS (FUF 495; FES VII, 199; VIII, 692; IX, 697; X, 397)

1966 ALEXANDER MORRISON
(FES IX, 695; X, 396 (2), 397), trans from Carinish to Barvas 11 May 1966; ret 30 Jun 1973.

1973 AONGHAS IAN MACDONALD
(FES X, 390, 397), trans from Gairloch to Barvas 30 Oct 1973; trans to Inverness East 2 Apr 1981.

1981 HECTOR MORRISON
ord and ind to Barvas 9 Dec 1981; trans to Lochalsh 30 Nov 1990.

1993 IVOR MACDONALD
B 27 Jan 1960 at St Andrews, s of Murdo M. and Mairi Todd MacRaild; educ Hutchesons' Grammar, Glasgow 1971–76; University of Aberdeen 1976–80 (BSc), 1989–90, 1991–92 (BD); University of Reading 1980–81 (MSc); Westminster Theological Seminary, Philadelphia, USA 1990–91; Agricultural Adviser 1981–89; lic by Presb of Ross 17 Jul 1992; asst Aberdeen Ferryhill 1992–93; m 11 Apr 1986 Rosemary Jane Fraser MacLeod b 2 Jul 1960 d of Donald Kenneth M. and Christina Catherine MacDonald; Children: Grace Mairi b 25 May 1989; Esther Catherine b 25 Aug 1991; Jonathan Donald Murdo b 19 May 1995; Euan Fraser b 20 Dec 1997; ord and ind to Barvas 12 Nov 1993.

CARLOWAY (FUF 495; FES IX, 697; X, 397)

1971 JOHN MURDO MACLEOD MACARTHUR
(FES X, 384, 397), trans from Durness with Kinlochbervie to Carloway 8 Dec 1971; trans to Strath 15 Mar 1979.

1983 DONALD ALICK MACLEAN
ind to Carloway 2 Dec 1983; trans to Kirkmichael and Tomintoul 25 Sep 1985.

1988 BRUCE KNIGHT GARDNER
ord and ind to Carloway 21 Oct 1988; dem 15 May 1994 on app by Free Church of Scotland as Missionary in Peru.

1997 MURDO MACDONALD CAMPBELL
B 13 May 1960 at Stornoway, s of Norman C. and Christina MacLeod; educ Bayble Secondary, Lewis 1960–76; University of Aberdeen 1991–96 (BD, DipMin); Shop Manager 1976–90; lic by Presb of Lewis 5 Jul 1996; asst Stornoway Martin's Memorial 1996–97; m 19 May 1982 Lorraine Anne MacLeod b 19 Aug 1964 d of Donald M. and Catherine Christina Macritchie; Children: Stuart b 27 Sep 1982; Lewis b 7 Apr 1985; ord and ind to Carloway 14 Oct 1997.

CROSS, NESS (FES IX, 697; X, 397)

1973 JOHN FERGUSON
(FES X, 397), ord and ind to Cross, Ness 3 Oct 1973; trans to Portree 20 Mar 1980.

1982 ALEXANDER MACDONALD
(FES X, 377, 390, 396), trans from Contin-Strathconon to Cross, Ness 6 Jul 1982; ret 30 Jun 1991; d Anna m Roberts; d Margaret m Afrin.

1993 KENNETH JOHN MACPHERSON
trans from Kilmallie to Cross, Ness 9 Jun 1993; trans to Benbecula 23 Sep 1998.

KINLOCH (FES X, 397, 398)

Formed 7 Mar 1995 by union of Kinloch and Park.

1959 RODERICK MURRAY
(FES X, 392, 397), trans from Torridon and Kinlochewe to Kinloch, Lewis 8 Apr 1959; ret 31 Aug 1967; died 3 Sep 1989.

1968 DONALD MACAULAY
(FES X, 398), ord and ind to Park 28 Aug 1968; ret 31 Dec 1991.

1968 DAVID MACINNES
(FES X, 397), ord and ind to Kinloch 16 Apr 1968; trans to Glasgow Gardner Street 8 Apr 1977.

1977 NORMAN MACSWEEN
(FES IX, 693; X, 232, 240, 395, 396), trans from Morvern to Kinloch 16 Nov 1977; ret 31 May 1986; Chaplain (part-time) to Western Isles Hospital 1989–91, 1995–97, locum Chaplain 1997–99; s Calum m Margaret Simpson; d Christine m Murdo MacKenzie.

1989 DONALD ANGUS MACLENNAN
B 6 Feb 1941 at Harris, s of Alexander M. and Anne MacLeod; educ Leverhulme Memorial School, Harris and Edinburgh College of Commerce 1953–70; Free Presb College, Glasgow 1970–75; Sales Supervision 1960–69; lic by Presb

of Outer Isles (Free Presb Church) 5 Jun 1975; m 7 Sep 1965 Rachel Morrison b 12 Jan 1936 d of Roderick and Marion M; ord by Free Presb Church (Outer Isles Presb) and ind to Uig 5 Aug 1975; admitted by General Assembly 1986; ind to Strath and Sleat 28 Aug 1986; trans to Kinloch 24 Apr 1989; became minister of united charge with Park 7 Mar 1995.

KNOCK (FUF 496; FES VII, 202; IX, 698; X, 397)

1964   WILLIAM MACDONALD
(FES IX, 686; X, 390, 396, 398), trans from Manish-Scarista to Knock 18 Mar 1964; ret 31 Jul 1982.

1984   JAMES MACDONALD
B 9 May 1943 at Stornoway, s of Murdo M. and Johanna Smith; educ Lionel Secondary and Nicolson Institute, Stornoway; University of Aberdeen 1979–83 (LTh, CPS); Merchant Navy 1960–74; lic by Presb of Lewis 27 Jun 1983; asst Stornoway High 1983–84; m 30 Jul 1971 Mary Ann MacLeod b 4 Apr 1941 d of John M. and Annie MacKay; Children: Iain Ivor b 28 Mar 1964; James Murdo b 28 Aug 1972; Janice Ann b 2 Apr 1975; Donald MacLeod b 8 Sep 1979; ord and ind to Knock 29 Jun 1984.

LOCHS-CROSSBOST (FUF 496; FES IX, 698; X, 398)

Vacant from 1982 until 1993.

1950   NEIL MURDO MACDONALD
(FES IX, 698; X, 398), ord and ind to Lochs-Crossbost 7 Jun 1950; ret 31 Jul 1982; died 30 Jan 1986.

1993   ANDREW WILLIAM FRANCIS COGHILL
B 20 Jan 1965 at Paisley, s of Ian George C. and Isabelle Martin Baxter; educ Cults Academy 1977–82; Aberdeen Technical College 1984–86 (ONC); University of Aberdeen 1986–92 (BD, DPS); Lab Technician 1983–85; Warehouse Asst 1985–86; lic by Presb of Aberdeen 25 Jun 1992; m 19 Jun 1992 Deborah Mary Hunt b 8 Jun 1969 d of Trevor George H. and Pauline Hazel Keen; Children: Joshua Andrew b 24 Jun 1994; Philip David b 30 Apr 1996; Naomi Deborah b 9 Feb 1998; ord and ind to Lochs-Crossbost 16 Jul 1993.

LOCHS-IN-BERNERA (FES VII, 203; VIII, 692; IX, 698; X, 398)

Vacant from 1979 until 1989.

1967   DUNCAN MACASKILL
(FES IX, 674, 688; X, 371, 385, 393, 398), trans from Erchless to Lochs-in-Bernera 22 Aug 1967; ret 31 Jul 1974; d Mary m Tony Spender; s Donald m Nancy Urquhart; d Aileen m Charles MacKenzie; Publ: *Bean Mo Ruin* (Cruisgean Argyll, 1987); *An Dochas Beo* (Cruisgean Argyll, 1990); *The Central Christ* (Cruisgean Argyll, 1994).

1975   RODERICK STEWART
(FES IX, 313, 694; X, 184, 217, 353, 398), trans from Dalmuir Ross Memorial with Duntocher West to Lochs-in-Bernera 4 Jun 1975; ret 22 Nov 1979; died 19 Dec 1983.

1989   KENNETH DONALD MACLEOD
B 2 Nov 1954 at Stornoway, s of Donald Malcolm M. and Dolina Morrison; educ Nicolson Institute, Stornoway 1981–83 (mature student); University of Glasgow 1983–87 (BD); Shopkeeper (self-employed) 1970–81; lic by Presb of Lewis 28 Sep 1988; asst Stornoway High 1988–89; m 27 Aug 1986 Kathleen Margaret Morrison b 19 Nov 1960 d of George Hugh M. and Henrietta MacDonald; Children: David Malcolm b 24 Nov 1989; Mairi Morrison b 24 May 1992; Ruth b 24 Jan 1995; ord and ind to Lochs-in-Bernera 29 Nov 1989.

STORNOWAY HIGH (FUF 497; FES IX, 699; X, 398)

1950   ANGUS MACCUISH
(FES IX, 206, 357, 699; X, 398), trans from Arrochar to Stornoway High 6 Dec 1950; ret 31 Dec 1980; died 5 Oct 1992.

1981   RODERICK MORRISON
(FES X, 396), trans from Carinish to Stornoway High 23 Jun 1981; trans to Glasgow Gardner Street 7 Oct 1994.

1998   WILLIAM BROAD BLACK
(FES X, 384), res from service with OMF International in Korea and ind to Stornoway High 30 Jan 1998; Addl children: Mary Catriona b 13 Dec 1977; d Rhoda m Andrew Schofield; Publ: *Light Where We Walk* (SU, 1998).

STORNOWAY MARTIN'S MEMORIAL (FUF 497; FES IX, 699; X, 398)

1976   THOMAS SUTER SINCLAIR
(FES X, 384), [correction: m 5 Jul 1969, not 9 May 1969 as in Vol X, 384]; trans from Eddrachillis to Martin's Memorial 16 Jun 1976; Clerk to Presb of Lewis from 1981; Chairman, Western Isles Children's Panel 1977–83; University of Edinburgh 1992 (BD); Addl children: Andrew b 1 Oct 1972, adopted 23 May 1977.

STORNOWAY ST COLUMBA (FES VII, 205; VIII, 692; IX, 699; X, 398)

1969   KENNETH MACLEOD
(FES X, 291, 390, 392, 398), trans from Dairsie to St Columba 10 Jul 1969; ret 31 Mar 1985; died 28 Dec 1991.

1986   DAVID LIVINGSTON WRIGHT
(FES X, 53, 65, 319), trans from Hawick Old with Teviothead to St Columba 18 Feb 1986; ret 31

Oct 1998; d Fiona m Neil Bell; Addl publ: *Reformed and Evangelical* (National Church Assoc, 1992); *The Difference Christ Makes* (Pentland Press, 1997).

UIG (FES X, 398, 399)

Formed 5 Sep 1979 by union of Uig Baile-na-cille and Uig, Uigen.

1951 ANGUS MACFARLANE
(FES IX, 700; X, 399), ord and ind to Uig Baile-na-cille 4 Jul 1951; ret 31 Mar 1979; died 7 Feb 1998.

1964 WILLIAM MACLEOD
(FES X, 395, 399), trans from Benbecula to Uig, Uigen 26 Feb 1964; became minister of united charge with Uig Baile-na-cille 5 Sep 1979; s Murray m Janet Hay.

PRESBYTERY OF ORKNEY

BIRSAY (FES X, 400)

Linked 31 Jul 1993 with Rousay. Arrangement terminated 30 Aug 1998 to allow for linkage with Harray and Sandwick.

1967 GORDON RUSSELL McLEAN BLACK
(FES IX, 595; X, 316, 343, 361, 400), dem from Arbuthnott and ind to Birsay 12 Jan 1967; ret 31 Jan 1973; died 22 Sep 1978.

1973 JOHN LITTLE WAUGH
(FES X, 400), ord and ind to Birsay 19 Jul 1973; trans to Ardclach with Auldearn and Dalmore 15 Apr 1993.

1994 ROBIN GRAEME BROWN
(FES X, 416), res as Principal of St Colm's College, Edinburgh and ind to Birsay with Rousay 30 Mar 1994; ret 30 Aug 1998; Publ: Editor of *Coracle* (Iona Community, 1974–80).

1998 LYNN BRADY
ord and ind to Harray with Sandwick 29 May 1996; became minister of linked charge with Birsay 30 Aug 1998.

DEERNESS (FUF 512; FES VII; 213; VIII, 693; IX, 701; X, 400)

Linked 31 Oct 1974 with St Andrews. Further linked 30 Sep 1992 with Holm.

1929 HARALD LAMB MOONEY
(FES VIII, 693; IX, 702; X, 400), ord and ind to Deerness 23 Jul 1929; became minister of linked charge with St Andrews 31 Oct 1974; ret 31 Aug 1984; died 2 Sep 1989.

1985 IAN J M McDONALD
ord by Presb of Edinburgh and app Asst at St George's West 6 May 1984; ind to Deerness with St Andrews 3 Jul 1985; trans to Bannockburn Ladywell 30 Sep 1992.

1993 JOAN HOWIE CRAIG
B 13 May 1940 at Ayr, d of John Hilston C. and Jean Pryde Howie; educ Ayr Academy 1952–57; Jordanhill College, Glasgow 1961–64 (DCE); St Colm's College, Edinburgh 1968–70; University of Edinburgh 1968–70 (CPS); University of St Andrews 1975–77 (MTheol); Civil Service 1957–59; Teaching (primary) 1964–68; Deaconess

1970–77 (Probationer, Hamilton Laighstonehall [now Trinity] 1970–71, commissioned by Presb of Stirling 4 Oct 1971); Asst Warden, Scottish Churches' House, Dunblane 1971–74; Teaching 1974–75; Scottish Sec, Christian Education Movement 1979–86; lic by Presb of Perth 29 Jun 1977; asst Edinburgh Palmerston Place 1977–78; ord by Presb of Perth 17 Sep 1986; app by Board of World Mission to St Columba's, Dar-es-Salaam, Tanzania (PCEA) 26 Oct 1986; app Lecturer, St Mark's Anglican Theological College, Dar-es-Salaam 1 Sep 1989; app by Christian Study Centre, Rawalpindi, Pakistan 10 Apr 1992; ind to Deerness with Holm with St Andrews 1 Apr 1993; Publ: Various articles on Religious Education (Christian Education Movement, 1979–86); *Into Africa* (diary extracts with Joy Billington, *The Scotsman*, 1987); various articles for Board of World Mission (1986–93); *Causeways to Community* (poem, *The Orkney View*, 1995).

EDAY (FES IX, 702; X, 400)

Linked 2 Jun 1960 with Stronsay.

1950 EDWARD PHILIPS GRIEVE FOX
(FES IX, 710; X, 404), ord and ind to Stronsay 28 Jun 1950; became minister of linked charge with Eday 2 Jun 1960; ret 30 Sep 1983; Addl publ: Numerous articles and booklets (*The Orcadian*, 1950–97).

1984 KENNETH SAMUEL BORTHWICK
ord by Presb of West Lothian during assistantship at Linlithgow St Michael's 29 May 1983; ind to Eday with Stronsay Moncur Memorial 6 Apr 1984; trans to Thurso St Peter's and St Andrew's 6 Jul 1989.

1990 KENNETH HAROLD FISHER
(FES X, 406), res as Assoc at Douglas St Bride's with Douglas Water with Rigside 16 Apr 1980; ind to Eday with Stronsay Moncur Memorial 3 Jul 1990; ret 30 Jun 1994.

1996 JOYCE ANNE KEYES
B 2 Aug 1949 at Glasgow, d of Albert and Mary Goswell; educ Stevenson High, Glasgow 1960–63; University of Glasgow 1991–94 (BD); asst Glasgow St Paul's Provanmill 1994–95; Cumbernauld Old 1995–96; m 14 Aug 1968 Charles Grant Keyes b 18 Sep 1941; Children: Marie b 24 Feb 1969 m Peter Carson; Rory b 19 Sep 1970 m Julie

Rogers; Glen b 22 Feb 1976 m Emma Barr; Gillan b 24 Oct 1982; ord and ind to Eday with Stronsay Moncur Memorial 11 Sep 1996.

EVIE (FUF 513; FES VII, 214; VIII, 693; IX, 702; X, 400)

Evie with Rendall linked 31 Jan 1979 with Firth.

1965 THOMAS GARRIOCH TAIT
(FES IX, 705; X, 402), ord and ind to Rendall 20 Jan 1938; became minister of linked charge with Evie 2 Aug 1965; ret 31 Jan 1979; died 24 Jun 1986.

1979 PETER E WRIGHT
ind to Evie with Firth with Rendall 22 Oct 1979; dem 1 Dec 1980; ind to Muiravonside 27 Apr 1982.

1981 ALLAN R COWIESON
ord and ind to Evie with Firth with Rendall 28 May 1981; dem 31 Jul 1985.

1986 TREVOR GEORGE HUNT
B 28 Mar 1942 at Deal, Kent, s of Albert Edwin H. and Doreen Annie Goddard; educ Matthew Arnold, Staines 1955–57; Open University 1978, 1991–93 (BA); University of Aberdeen 1979–83 (BD); lic by Presb of Aberdeen 28 Jun 1984; asst Aberdeen Dyce 1984–85; m 14 Mar 1964 Pauline Hazel Keen b 1 May 1942 d of John K. and Emily Elsie Crook; Children: Elizabeth Ann b 20 Jan 1965; Matthew John b 13 Oct 1966 m Rachel Marie Montgomery; Deborah Mary b 8 Jun 1969 m Andrew William Francis Coghill; ord and ind to Evie with Firth with Rendall 30 Jan 1986; Asst Clerk to Presb of Orkney 1989–91; Depute Clerk 1991–94; Clerk 1994–97 and from 1998.

FIRTH (FES IX, 702; X, 400)

Vacant from 1961 until 1979. Linked 31 Jan 1979 with Evie with Rendall.

1979 PETER E WRIGHT
ind to Evie with Firth with Rendall 22 Oct 1979, see Evie.

1981 ALLAN R COWIESON
ord and ind to Evie with Firth with Rendall 28 May 1981; dem 31 Jul 1985.

1986 TREVOR GEORGE HUNT
ord and ind to Evie with Firth with Rendall, see Evie.

FLOTTA (FES VII, 238; IX, 703; X, 401)

Linked 16 Mar 1986 with Hoy and Walls.

1969 EWEN GORDON SINCLAIR TRAILL
(FES IX, 530; X, 71, 313, 401, 426), trans from Ashkirk with Lilliesleaf to Flotta and Fara with Hoy and Graemsay with Walls Old 16 May 1969; ret 29 Feb 1984; died 31 Oct 1987.

1985 WILLIAM GRAHAM MONTEITH
(FES X, 59), trans from Berwick-on-Tweed Wallace Green with Lowick to Flotta and Fara with Hoy and Graemsay with Walls Old 15 May 1985; became minister of Flotta and Fara with Hoy and Walls 16 Mar 1986; dem 30 Sep 1994.

1995 FIONA LINDSAY LILLIE
ord and ind to Flotta with Hoy and Walls 4 May 1995; dem 30 Sep 1998; ind to Stromness 15 Jun 1999.

HARRAY (FES IX, 703; X, 401)

Linked 4 Apr 1967 with Sandwick. Further linked 30 Aug 1998 with Birsay.

1956 DOUGLAS MATHESON ROSS
(FUF 519; FES IX, 443, 613, 682, 709; X, 352, 401), trans from Forglen to Harray 7 Jun 1956; ret 4 Apr 1967; died 5 May 1980.

1967 ALEXANDER NICOL JAMIESON
(FES IX, 143; X, 85, 401), res as Chaplain to Queen Victoria School, Dunblane and ind to Harray with Sandwick 29 Sep 1967; died 29 Nov 1983.

1984 ROBERT FRASER PENNY
ord and ind to Harray with Sandwick 13 Jun 1984; trans to Airdrie New Wellwynd 31 May 1995.

1996 LYNN BRADY
B 25 Oct 1963 at Glasgow, d of George Restrick B. and Ann MacGoldrick B; educ Knightswood Secondary, Glasgow 1975–79; University of Edinburgh 1989–93 (BD); University of Aberdeen 1993–94 (DipMin); lic by Presb of Edinburgh 3 Jul 1993; asst Aberdeen Holburn Central 1994–96; ord and ind to Harray with Sandwick 29 May 1996; became minister of linked charge with Birsay 30 Aug 1998.

HOLM (FUF 514; FES VII, 217; VIII, 694; IX, 703; X, 401)

Linked 30 Sep 1992 with Deerness with St Andrews.

1958 THOMAS JOHN COULTER
(FES IX, 446, 454, 760; X, 401), dem from Stirling St Ninian's St George's 30 Apr 1953; ind to Holm 9 Oct 1958; ret 31 Oct 1968; died 25 Dec 1986.

1970 JAMES GRANT
(FES X, 83, 87, 401, 403), trans from Dumfries Lochside to Holm 4 Aug 1970; trans to Penpont and Keir 13 Jun 1974.

1975 ALAN HUNTER STUART TAYLOR
(FES X, 80, 365, 401), trans from Aberlour to Holm 31 Jul 1975; trans to Brydekirk with Hoddam 14 Oct 1987.

1989 PETER BROWN
(FES IX, 786; X, 229, 270, 444), dem from Kilfinan with Kyles 30 Apr 1987; ind to Holm 30 Apr 1989; ret 1 Jun 1992; University of Aberdeen 1981–84 (MA); FSA(Scot) 1985; s Peter m Alison Mendez; s Jonathan m Jane Elizabeth Emslie; s Christopher m Patricia Shiels; s Paul m Alison Millar.

1993 JOAN HOWIE CRAIG
ind to Deerness with Holm with St Andrews 1 Apr 1993, see Deerness.

HOY AND WALLS (FES X, 401, 404)

Formed 16 Mar 1986 by union of Hoy and Walls Old. Linked same date with Flotta and Fara.

1969 EWEN GORDON SINCLAIR TRAILL
(FES IX, 530; X, 71, 313, 401, 426), ind to Flotta and Fara with Hoy and Graemsay with Walls Old 16 May 1969, see Flotta.

1985 WILLIAM GRAHAM MONTEITH
(FES X, 59), ind to Flotta and Fara with Hoy and Graemsay with Walls Old 15 May 1985; became minister of Flotta and Fara with Hoy and Walls 16 Mar 1986, see Flotta.

1995 FIONA LINDSAY LILLIE
ord and ind to Flotta with Hoy and Walls 4 May 1995; dem 30 Sep 1998; ind to Stromness 15 Jun 1999.

KIRKWALL EAST (FES X, 401)

1971 DAVID JAMES INNES
(FES X, 382, 401), trans from Tarbat to Kirkwall East 15 Oct 1971; dem 31 Jul 1982.

1983 HELEN JUNE RUTH ALEXANDER
ord by Presb of Edinburgh during assistantship at St Giles' 21 Jun 1981; ind to Kirkwall East 26 Aug 1983; dem on app as Assoc Chaplain to University of Edinburgh 23 Jun 1986.

1987 WILLIAM BRIAN WILKINSON
(FES X, 240, 271), trans from Kilmore and Oban to Kirkwall East 11 Nov 1987; trans to Glenaray and Inveraray 23 Mar 1993.

1993 ALLAN McCAFFERTY
B 19 Jan 1967 at Motherwell, s of Frank M. and Mary Johnston Donaldson; educ Garrion Academy, Wishaw 1978–84; University of Glasgow 1984–87 (BSc); University of Edinburgh 1988–91 (BD); Volunteer, Church of Scotland Centre, Tiberias 1987–88; lic by Presb of Hamilton 2 Jul 1991; asst Bridge of Allan Holy Trinity 1991–93; ord and ind to Kirkwall East 3 Nov 1993.

KIRKWALL ST MAGNUS CATHEDRAL (FES VII, 220; VIII, 694; IX, 704; X, 402)

1968 HARRY WILLIAM McPHAIL CANT
(FES IX, 448; X, 14, 265, 402), trans from Edinburgh Leith St Thomas' to St Magnus Cathedral 30 Aug 1968; ret 30 Sep 1990; d Elizabeth m Michael Tyrie Austin; d Alison m John Philip Newell; s Andrew m Alice Rachel Flett; Publ: *Preaching in a Scottish Parish* (*Kirkwall Press*, 1970); *Springs of Renewal in Congregational Life* (*Kirkwall Press*, 1980); joint-editor of *Light in the North—St Magnus Cathedral through the Centuries* (*Orkney Press*, 1989).

1990 RONALD FERGUSON
(FES X, 158), Leader of Iona Community 12 Mar 1982–84 Aug 1989; Biographer (full-time) of George MacLeod Aug-Dec 1989; ind to St Magnus Cathedral 12 Dec 1990; Addl children: Alasdair Geoffrey b 8 May 1979; Publ: *Geoff* (Famedram, 1979); *Grace and Dysentery* (Wild Goose Publs, 1985); editor of *The Whole Earth Shall Cry Glory* (Wild Goose Publs, 1986); *Chasing the Wild Goose* (Collins, 1988); *George MacLeod* (Collins, 1990); editor of *Daily Readings by George MacLeod* (Collins, 1991); *Black Diamonds and Blue Brazil* (Famedram, 1993); *Technology at the Crossroads* (St Andrew Press, 1994); *Every Blessed Thing* (St Magnus Festival, 1993); *Orkneyinga* (St Magnus Festival, 1997); *Love Your Crooked Neighbour* (St Andrew Press, 1999); *Donald Dewar Ate My Hamster* (Famedram, 1999).

NORTH RONALDSAY (FUF 515; FES VII, 266; VIII, 699; IX, 704; X, 402)

Linked 9 Oct 1978 with Sanday.

1969 THOMAS ARTHUR TULLOCH
(FE IX, 574, 597; X, 58, 344, 402), trans from Whitekirk and Tyninghame to North Ronaldsay 13 Jun 1969; ret 31 Jul 1978; died 28 Feb 1988.

1978 GRAHAM SOMERVILLE FINCH
ord and ind to Sanday 20 Jul 1977; became minister of linked charge with North Ronaldsay 9 Oct 1978; trans to Stonehaven Fetteresso 21 Apr 1983.

1986 WALTER M MACINTYRE
ord and ind to North Ronaldsay with Sanday 14 May 1986; dem 14 Aug 1987 to take up app at University of Massachusets, USA.

1989 ALEXANDER BUCHAN
(FES X, 188), Jordanhill College, Glasgow 1987–88; dem from Kennoway 30 Jun 1985; ind to North Ronaldsay with Sanday 28 Nov 1989; ret 30 Sep 1992.

1994 JAMES DANIEL MACGHEE GIBB
B 16 Nov 1940 at Glasgow, s of James Alexander Morrison G. and Alexandrina MacLeod McGhee G; educ Eastbank Academy, Glasgow 1952–55;

Open University 1975–79 (BA); University of Glasgow 1989–92 (LTh); Coach Painter 1956–63; Prison Officer 1963–67; Police Officer 1967–84; Asst Warden, Probation Hostel 1984–85; Director, Aycliffe Security 1985–88; County Organiser, Durham County Assoc for the Disabled 1986–88; Counsellor 1986–88; lic by Presb of Glasgow 26 Jun 1992; asst Cambuslang St Andrew's 1992–93; m 24 Mar 1962 Agnes Greenshields Bell Davis b 29 Jan 1942 d of John D. and Margaret Bell; Children: James b 11 Dec 1963; John b 31 Oct 1965; David b 25 Sep 1967; Margaret b 17 Apr 1971 m Julian Anthony Lenahan; Daniel Robert b 23 Dec 1975; ord and ind to North Ronaldsay with Sanday 27 Jul 1994.

ORPHIR (FES IX, 705; X, 402)

Linked 7 May 1964 with Stenness.

1964   DAVID ALBERT WILLIAMS
(FES IX, 709; X, 404), ord and ind to Stenness 28 Apr 1944; became minister of linked charge with Orphir 7 May 1964; ret 31 Oct 1984; died 20 Mar 1994.

1967   WILLIAM DOUGLAS DRYSDALE
(FES IX, 212, 360, 529; X, 122, 402), dem from Bishopton Old Erskine 30 Sep 1966; introd as Assoc at Orphir with Stenness 1 Jan 1967; ret 30 Nov 1977; died 28 Nov 1979.

1985   THOMAS LEGERWOOD CLARK
B 29 Jul 1943 at Edinburgh, s of Thomas Noel C. and Betsy Martin; educ Lasswade Secondary and Inverness Royal Academy; University of Aberdeen 1979–83 (BD); Police Service 1963–79; lic by Presb of Dundee 26 Jun 1983; asst Dundee Roseangle Ryehill 1983–84; m 30 Aug 1968 Margaret Wilson Rough b 1 May 1944 d of Robert R. and Helen Skinner; Children: Karen Helen b 18 Dec 1970; Martin Thomas b 12 May 1972; ord and ind to Orphir with Stenness 12 Jun 1985.

PAPA WESTRAY (FUF 516; FES IX, 705; X, 402)

Linked 15 Mar 1960 with Westray.

1971   ALEXANDER CRAWLEY DOW
(FES IX, 465, 568, 788; X, 338, 402, 445), trans from Aberdeen Stoneywood to Papa Westray with Westray 13 May 1971; ret 31 Mar 1979; died 8 Apr 1986.

1980   DAVID WILLIAM DUTTON
ind to Guisborough and Lingdale (URC) 30 Apr 1977; ind to Papa Westray with Westray 1 Feb 1980; trans to Stranraer The High Kirk 12 Mar 1986.

1986   MARY GORDON SPOWART
B 5 Jul 1929 at Glasgow, d of John Elliot and Helen McSeveney; educ Coatbridge Senior Secondary 1941–46; Jordanhill College, Glasgow 1946–49;

University of Edinburgh 1972–76; Teaching 1949–52, 1965–72; lic by Presb of Falkirk, Jun 1976; asst Carriden 1976–77; Grangemouth Old 1977–78; m 5 Jul 1952 David Spowart b 29 Apr 1915 (deceased) s of David S. and Helen Eason; Children: David Elliot b 15 Jun 1953 m Pamela Kerr; Helen Gordon b 3 Feb 1955 m Pasquale Glave; Nan Wilson b 13 Jul 1960 m James MacFarlane; ord and ind to Richmond Craigmillar with Newcraighall 2 Feb 1978; became minister of united charge 4 Dec 1983; trans to Papa Westray with Westray 3 Dec 1986; ret 1 Jul 1991.

1993   IAIN DONALD MACDONALD
B 25 Oct 1964 at Glasgow, s of John Angus and Ina M; educ Williamwood High, Glasgow 1976–82; Moray House College, Edinburgh 1983–86 (DipChEd); University of Edinburgh 1989–92 (BD); lic by Presb of Edinburgh 5 Jul 1992; asst Edinburgh Viewforth 1992–93; m 1 Sep 1989 Joanna Catherine Burn b 31 Oct 1962 d of Neil and Katie B; Children: Hannah Chirsty b 1 Feb 1995; Angus Neil b 18 Mar 1998; ord and ind to Papa Westray with Westray 2 Sep 1993.

RENDALL (FUF 520; FES VII, 228; VIII, 694; IX, 705; X, 402)

Linked 2 Aug 1965 with Evie. Further linked 31 Jan 1979 with Firth.

1938   THOMAS GARRIOCH TAIT
(FES IX, 705; X, 402), ord and ind to Rendall 20 Jan 1938; became minister of linked charge with Evie 2 Aug 1965; ret 31 Jan 1979; died 24 Jun 1986.

1979   PETER E WRIGHT
ind to Evie with Firth with Rendall 22 Oct 1979, see Evie.

1981   ALLAN R COWIESON
ord and ind to Evie with Firth with Rendall 28 May 1981; dem 31 Jul 1985.

1986   TREVOR GEORGE HUNT
ord and ind to Evie with Firth with Rendall, see Evie.

ROUSAY (FUF 516; FES VII, 267; VIII, 700; IX, 705; X, 402)

Linked 31 Jul 1993 with Birsay. Arrangement terminated 30 Aug 1998. Continued vacancy from 1998.

1967   JOHN FRASER GILLAN
(FES IX, 707; X, 252, 279, 402, 403), trans from Buckhaven St Andrew's to Rousay 18 Aug 1967; ret 31 Oct 1971; died 7 Feb 1981.

1972   THOMAS NELSON JOHNSTON
(FES X, 402), ord and ind to Rousay 28 Jul 1972; trans to Buckie South and West 30 Jan 1980.

1982   DAVID F PRENTIS
admitted by General Assembly and ind to Rousay 8 Dec 1982; trans to Drumoak with Durris 14 Apr 1988.

1989   COLIN ALEXANDER STRONG
ord and ind to Rousay 16 Jun 1989; trans to Dundee Mid Craigie 15 Jan 1992.

1994   ROBIN GRAEME BROWN
(FES X, 416), ind to Birsay with Rousay 30 Mar 1994, see Birsay.

SANDAY (FES X, 402)

Linked 9 Oct 1978 with North Ronaldsay.

1972   KENNETH THOMAS THOMSON
(FES X, 319, 402), ind to Sanday 25 Aug 1972; dem 24 Feb 1977 and introd on term app to Newtown.

1977   GRAHAM SOMERVILLE FINCH
ord and ind to Sanday 20 Jul 1977; became minister of linked charge with North Ronaldsay 9 Oct 1978; trans to Stonehaven Fetteresso 21 Apr 1983.

1986   WALTER M MACINTYRE
ord and ind to North Ronaldsay with Sanday 14 May 1986; dem 14 Aug 1987 to take up app at University of Massachusets, USA.

1989   ALEXANDER BUCHAN
(FES X, 188), Jordanhill College, Glasgow 1987–88; dem from Kennoway 30 Jun 1985; ind to North Ronaldsay with Sanday 28 Nov 1989; ret 30 Sep 1992.

1994   JAMES DANIEL MACGHEE GIBB
ord and ind to North Ronaldsay with Sanday 27 Jul 1994, see North Ronaldsay.

SANDWICK (FES IX, 707; X, 403)

Linked 4 Apr 1967 with Harray. Further linked 30 Aug 1998 with Birsay.

1967   ALEXANDER NICOL JAMIESON
(FES IX, 143; X, 85, 401), ind to Harray with Sandwick 29 Sep 1967, see Harray.

1984   ROBERT FRASER PENNY
ord and ind to Harray with Sandwick 13 Jun 1984; trans to Airdrie New Wellwynd 31 May 1995.

1996   LYNN BRADY
ord and ind to Harray with Sandwick 29 May 1996, see Harray.

SHAPINSAY (FES IX, 708; X, 403)

1962   NORMAN FENWICK
(FES X, 403), ind to Shapinsay 28 Sep 1962; ret 6 May 1980; died 2 Dec 1985.

1981   ROBERT STOCKBRIDGE WHITEFORD
(FES IX, 219, 630; X, 125, 126, 326), trans from Aberdeen Ferryhill South to Shapinsay 3 Jun 1981; also Assoc at Kirkwall St Magnus Cathedral; ret 30 Nov 1986; d Elizabeth m Alan Garrity; s John m Rosemarie Edholm; s Robert m Linda Mackay; s William m Linda Lowe.

1988   IAN SUTCLIFFE
ind to Shapinsay 6 May 1988 (following several years as locum at Westray and Shapinsay); ret 31 May 1991.

1992   ROBERT JAMES MELLIS
B 20 May 1933 at Lhanbryde, s of Robert M. and Johanna Cran Knight; educ Bridge of Don Junior Secondary and Central School, Aberdeen 1945–50; University of Aberdeen 1951–54 (CA), 1978–81 (BTh); Accountancy 1950–78; lic by Presb of Gordon 6 Oct 1981; asst Aberdeen Dyce 1981–82; m 4 Jun 1960 Agnes Christina Allan b 24 Nov 1936 d of George A. and Christina Dollinson; Children: Christine Johanna b 2 Apr 1961 m Stanley Clark; Fiona Mary b 31 Aug 1963 m David Coltherd; Robert George b 12 May 1966 m Tracy Weir; ord and ind to Knockando, Elchies and Archiestown with Rothes 2 Jul 1982; trans to Tarbat 24 Mar 1988; trans to Shapinsay 30 Mar 1992; ret 20 May 1998.

1998   JOYCE LYNN
trans from Dundee Roseangle Ryehill to Shapinsay 25 Nov 1998.

SOUTH RONALDSAY AND BURRAY (FES X, 403)

1967   STUART DONALD BLAIR PICKEN
(FES X, 400, 403), ord and ind to Burray with South Ronaldsay 1 May 1967; became minister of united charge 1 Jan 1969; dem 31 Aug 1972 to take up app at International Christian University, Tokyo, Japan; m (2) 8 Jul 1996 Hongwen Guo b 5 Jul 1966 d of Daoyuan G; Children: William Daoyuan Blair b 21 May 1998; Addl publ: *Buddhism: Japan's Cultural Identity* (Kodansha, 1980); *Christianity and Japan* (Kodansha, 1981); *The Essentials of Shinto* (Greenwood, 1994).

1973   JAMES ERIC STEWART LOW
(FES X, 12, 34, 250, 403, 421), trans from Edinburgh Kirk o' Field to South Ronaldsay and Burray 13 Nov 1973; introd to Dairsie with Kemback (term) 2 Oct 1977.

1978   MORRIS GLYNDWR McKENZIE
B 10 Feb 1928 at Invercargill, New Zealand, s of Duncan Norman M; educ John McGlashan College, Dunedin, New Zealand 1939–46; Victorian University College, 1949–56 (BA); University of Otago 1956–59 (LLB); University of St Andrews 1974–76; Civil Service (New Zealand) 1947–55; Solicitor 1960–74; lic by Presb of St Andrews 30

Jun 1976; asst Forfar St James' 1975–76; m 18 Jan 1964 Janette Zena Lewis d of John L. and Zena May Glenny; ord and ind to South Ronaldsay and Burray 4 Sep 1978; ret 4 Sep 1993.

1994 MARIA ANNETTE GEERTRUDIS PLATE
B 19 Oct 1935 at Utrecht, The Netherlands, d of Johannes Burchardus Plate and Geertrudis Dina Van Oorschot; University of Glasgow 1964–65 (Social Work), 1976–77 (CQSW, DSW); St Colm's College, Edinburgh 1965–67 (Deaconess Training); University of Edinburgh 1970–72 (CPS), 1980–82 (LTh); Open University 1978–82 (BA); Deaconess 1967–69 (Glasgow St Francis-in-the-East), 1969–72 (Edinburgh Muirhouse); Asst Leader, Simpson House, Edinburgh 1972–74; Social Work 1974–80; lic by Presb of Edinburgh 4 Jul 1982; asst Edinburgh Blackhall St Columba's 1982–83; ord and ind to Cardenden St Fothad's 5 Jul 1983; introd as Assoc at Edinburgh Kaimes Lockhart Memorial 14 Nov 1989; ind to same charge 28 Nov 1990; trans to South Ronaldsay and Burray 25 Aug 1994.

ST ANDREWS (FES IX, 706; X, 402)

Linked 31 Oct 1974 with Deerness.

1954 JAMES JOHNSON DAVIDSON
(FES IX, 706, 714; X, 402), trans from Nesting to St Andrews 20 Aug 1954; ret 31 Oct 1974; died 5 Sep 1984.

1974 HARALD LAMB MOONEY
(FES VIII, 693; IX, 702; X, 400), ord and ind to Deerness 23 Jul 1929; became minister of linked charge with St Andrews 31 Oct 1974, see Deerness.

1985 IAN J M McDONALD
ind to Deerness with St Andrews 3 Jul 1985, see Deerness.

1993 JOAN HOWIE CRAIG
ind to Deerness with Holm with St Andrews 1 Apr 1993, see Deerness.

STENNESS (FUF 520; FES VII, 250; VIII, 697; IX, 709; X, 404)

Linked 7 May 1964 with Orphir.

1944 DAVID ALBERT WILLIAMS
(FES IX, 709; X, 404), ord and ind to Stenness 28 Apr 1944; became minister of linked charge with Orphir 7 May 1964; ret 31 Oct 1984; died 20 Mar 1994.

1967 WILLIAM DOUGLAS DRYSDALE
(FES IX, 212, 360, 529; X, 122, 402), introd as Assoc at Orphir with Stenness 1 Jan 1967, see Orphir.

1985 THOMAS LEGERWOOD CLARK
ord and ind to Orphir with Stenness 12 Jun 1985, see Orphir.

STROMNESS (FES X, 404)

1960 JOHN ALEXANDER ROBSON WATT
(FES IX, 622, 753, 802; X, 404), res as Field Secretary, Overseas Council and ind to Stromness North 14 Jul 1960; ret 31 Aug 1970; died 16 Feb 1995.

1967 GREGOR MACGREGOR
(FES X, 404 (2)), [correction: Gregor, not George as in Vol X, 404]; ord and ind to St Peter's and Victoria Street 13 Jun 1967; became minister of united charge with North 1 Feb 1971; dem 30 Sep 1973.

1974 DEREK GAVIN CHITTICK
(FES X, 404), ord and ind to Stromness 28 Mar 1974; dem 15 May 1985.

1986 PHILLIP EARNSHAW
ord and ind to Stromness 5 Jun 1986; trans to Glasgow Pollokshields 5 Jun 1991.

1992 MARJORY ANNE MACLEAN
ind to Stromness 26 Mar 1992; dem 6 Nov 1998 on app as Depute Clerk of General Assembly.

1997 ANDREA ELISABET PRICE
B 22 Apr 1960 at Stuttgart-Möhringen, Germany, d of Hans-Otto Helfritz and Jutta Elisabet Kleinmann; educ Ernst-Barlach Gymnasium, Dinslaken 1972–79; University of Bonn 1979–81; University of St Andrews 1981–82; University of Tübingen 1982–84; University of Wuppertal 1984–86; lic by Presb of Orkney 14 May 1995; m 5 Apr 1986 Neil Price b 30 Oct 1951 s of Hugh and Nora P; Children: Catriona Elizabeth b 27 Jun 1987; Julia Frances b 1 Dec 1988; Marcus Alexander b 9 Nov 1990; ord by Presb of Orkney 29 Jan 1997; Asst at Stromness Jan 1997 until Jun 1999, thereafter supply work.

1999 FIONA LINDSAY LILLIE
B 19 Oct 1951 at Grimsby, d of Archibald Girvan Ross and Audrey Lindsay; educ Collegiate High School for Girls, St Dominic's Priory, Port Elizabeth, S Africa 1963–67; University of Natal 1969–72 (BA); University of St Andrews 1989–93 (BD, MLitt); lic by Presb of St Andrews 1 Jul 1992; asst St Andrews St Leonard's 1993–94; m 3 Jul 1981 John Patrick Lillie b 4 Dec 1948 s of John L. and Barbara Barrow; Children: Sarah Catherine b 30 Aug 1982; Angus John b 15 Apr 1986; ord and ind to Flotta with Hoy and Walls 4 May 1995; dem 30 Sep 1998; ind to Stromness 15 Jun 1999.

STRONSAY MONCUR MEMORIAL (FUF 519; FES VII, 272; VIII, 700; IX, 710; X, 404)

Linked 2 Jun 1960 with Eday.

1950 EDWARD PHILIPS GRIEVE FOX
(FES IX, 710; X, 404), ord and ind to Stronsay 28 Jun 1950; became minister of linked charge with Eday 2 Jun 1960; ret 30 Sep 1983; Addl publ: Numerous articles and booklets (*The Orcadian*, 1950–97).

1984 KENNETH SAMUEL BORTHWICK
ind to Eday with Stronsay Moncur Memorial 6 Apr 1984, see Eday.

1990 KENNETH HAROLD FISHER
(FES X, 406), ind to Eday with Stronsay Moncur Memorial 3 Jul 1990, see Eday.

1996 JOYCE ANNE KEYES
ord and ind to Eday with Stronsay Moncur Memorial 11 Sep 1996, see Eday.

WESTRAY (FUF 519; FES VII, 276; VIII, 700; IX, 710; X, 404)

Linked 15 Mar 1960 with Papa Westray.

1971 ALEXANDER CRAWLEY DOW
(FES IX, 465, 568, 788; X, 338, 402, 445), trans from Aberdeen Stoneywood to Papa Westray with Westray 13 May 1971; ret 31 Mar 1979; died 8 Apr 1986.

1980 DAVID WILLIAM DUTTON
ind to Papa Westray with Westray 1 Feb 1980, see Papa Westray.

1986 MARY GORDON SPOWART
ind to Papa Westray with Westray 3 Dec 1986, see Papa Westray.

1993 IAIN DONALD MACDONALD
ord and ind to Papa Westray with Westray 2 Sep 1993, see Papa Westray.

PRESBYTERY OF SHETLAND

BURRA ISLE (FUF 521; FES IX, 711; X, 405)

Linked 3 Oct 1975 with Tingwall.

1975 HAMISH GAULT SMITH
(FES X, 186, 407), trans from Airdrie St Columba's
to Tingwall 29 Sep 1972; became minister of linked
charge with Burra Isle 3 Oct 1975; trans to Auchterless with Rothienorman 17 Apr 1986.

1986 JAMES HOSIE
(FES X, 134, 163, 257), trans from Ayr St Andrew's
to Burra Isle with Tingwall 26 Jul 1986; trans to
Ardrishaig with South Knapdale 27 Mar 1992.

1995 NORMAN ROSS WHYTE
B 2 Dec 1956 at Johnstone, s of Thomas Wilson
W. and Isabella Gowans Fairbairn; educ Barrhead
High and Paisley Grammar 1968–74; University
of Glasgow 1974–80 (BD, DipMin); lic by Presb of
Paisley 26 Jun 1980; asst Largs Clark Memorial
1980–82; ord and ind to Glassary and Kilmartin 25
Aug 1982; trans to Burra Isle with Tingwall 3 Jun
1995.

DELTING (FUF 522; FES IX, 712; X, 405)

Linked 27 Nov 1977 with Nesting and Lunnasting.

1960 WILLIAM MARSHALL
(FES X, 94, 405), trans from Inch to Delting 27
Oct 1960; dem 31 Jul 1963; died 18 Aug 1995.

1964 JAMES MACRURIE
(FES IX, 742; X, 164, 241, 405, 422), trans from
Glasgow Kinning Park to Delting 6 Jan 1964; trans
to Salen and Ulva with Torosay and Kinlochspelvie
21 Oct 1966.

1968 WILLIAM CLEMENT ROBB
(FES X, 405), ord and ind to Delting 17 Jun 1968;
dem 31 Oct 1976; ind to Glasgow Househillwood
St Christopher's 25 Mar 1981.

1979 GEORGE COOPER
B 14 Jan 1916 at Coventry, s of Tom C. and Lillian
Ravenhall Ward; educ College of Art, Coventry
1921–31; University of London 1937–43 (BD); Selly
Oak Colleges, Birmingham 1945–46; Lithographic
Printer 1933–37; m 8 Jul 1943 Mary Olivia Munn b
11 Jun 1921 d of Denis Smith M. and Lucy Lavinia
Randall; Children: Simon b 18 Sep 1944; Olivia b
6 Jun 1956 m McGuinness; Clare b 3 Jan 1958;

ord by Congregational Church of England and
Wales and ind to John Robinson Memorial, Gains-
boro 3 Sep 1943; service with London Missionary
Society in N Rhodesia 1945–50; Government
Advisor on Rural Crafts, N Rhodesia 1950–52;
administrator for British Leprosy Relief Assoc,
Tanzania 1952–66; Presb Church of E Africa,
Mombasa, Kenya 1966–72; St Columba's, Dar-es-
Salaam, Tanzania 1972–79; admitted by General
Assembly 1976; ind to Delting with Nesting and
Lunnasting 25 Aug 1979; dem 31 Aug 1980;
Rural Development Advisor with Presb Church of
E Africa 1980–86; ret 30 Sep 1986; Publ: *Village
Crafts of Barotseland* (Rhodes Livingston Institute,
1951).

1981 GILBERT SIM
ord and ind to Delting with Nesting and Lunnasting
4 Jul 1981; dem 31 Aug 1986.

1988 ELINOR JANET GORDON
ord and ind to Delting with Nesting and Lunnasting
13 Aug 1988; trans to Muthill with Trinity Gask and
Kinkell 11 Apr 1994.

1996 WINIFRED MUNSON
B 7 Sep 1939 at Edinburgh, d of Wilfred Arthur
Barnes Smith and Henrietta McKigen; educ Kelso
High and Lasswade Secondary 1950–54; Lebanon
Missionary Bible College 1980–83 (DTh Missionary
Studies and Cambridge Diploma); University of
Edinburgh 1990–93 (BD); Secondary School
Welfare Work 1970–74; Secretary 1983–86; lic by
Presb of Lothian 5 Sep 1993; asst Edinburgh
London Road 1993–95; divorced; Children: Janet
b 4 Nov 1962; Susan b 14 Apr 1966; ord and ind
to Delting with Nesting and Lunnasting 11 May
1996.

**DUNROSSNESS AND ST NINIAN'S INC. FAIR
ISLE** (FUF 522; FES VII, 282; VIII, 702; IX, 712;
X, 406)

Linked 17 Feb 1980 with Sandwick, Cunningsburgh
and Quarff.

1960 JOHN MOFFAT
(FES IX, 254, 743; X, 406, 423), res from service
with Overseas Council at Ajmer, Rajputana and
ind to Dunrossness 18 Feb 1960; ret 22 Jul 1965;
died 6 Jan 1997.

1966 IAIN TAYLOR CAMPBELL
(FES X, 406), ord and ind to Dunrossness 25 Aug 1966; dem 31 Apr 1969.

1969 KENNETH HAROLD FISHER
(FES X, 406), ord and ind to Dunrossness 14 Aug 1969; dem 9 May 1979 and introd as Assoc at Douglas St Bride's with Douglas Water with Rigside.

1981 EDITH F McMILLAN
ord and ind to Dunrossness with Sandwick, Cunningsburgh and Quarff 10 Apr 1981; dem 4 Apr 1990; introd as Assoc at Dundee Craigiebank with Douglas and Angus 4 Aug 1999.

1990 TREVOR CHARLES WILLIAMS
ord and ind to Dunrossness with Sandwick, Cunningsburgh and Quarff 26 Sep 1990; trans to Peterculter St Peter's 6 Mar 1996.

1997 CHARLES HUGH MOAR GREIG
B 2 Jul 1951 at Lerwick, s of James G. and Robina Janet Sinclair; educ Lerwick Central School and Anderson Educational Institute 1962–70; University of Aberdeen 1970–73 (MA), 1973–76 (BD); lic by UFC 7 Jul 1976; m 28 Jul 1979 Diane Margaret Boyd Barbour b 22 Dec 1952 d of David Bell B. and Ann Wilson White; ord by UFC and ind to Edinburgh Blackhall 24 Jul 1976; ind to Bellshill Orbiston with St Andrew's 6 May 1981; trans to Kinghorn 26 Oct 1988; trans to Dunrossness and St Ninian's inc Fair Isle with Sandwick Cunningsburgh and Quarff 18 Jan 1997.

FETLAR (FES IX, 713; X, 406)

Linked 26 Oct 1975 with Yell.

1975 JAMES BLAIKIE
(FES X, 408), ord and ind to Yell 27 Apr 1972; became minister of linked charge with Fetlar 26 Oct 1975; trans to Aberdeen Middlefield 31 Mar 1977.

1977 ERNEST CHAPMAN
ord and ind to Fetlar with Yell 22 Oct 1977; dem 31 Jan 1980.

1982 MAGNUS JAMES CAMERON WILLIAMSON
B 9 Sep 1934 at Nesting, Shetland, s of John Henry W. and Roby Elizabeth Pearson; educ Lerwick Central Public School 1941–50; University of Aberdeen 1963–65 (lay missionary course), 1981–82 (ministry course); Building/General Labourer 1955–63; Lay Missionary 1965–81; lic by Presb of Shetland 1 Jun 1982; m 28 Dec 1963 Eunice Winifred Mary Williamson b 21 Aug 1931 d of Laurence Arthur W. and Mary Nicolson Barclay Houston; Children: John Laurence b 28 Jan 1965 m Edna Johnson; Robert Arthur b 12 Oct 1966 m Shella McWhirter; Maria Kathleen b 16 Mar 1968 m James Lewis; Magnus Christie b 14 Jul 1976; ord and ind to Fetlar with Yell 19 Jun 1982; ret 30 Sep 1999.

LERWICK AND BRESSAY (FES X, 406)

1964 ANDREW ELLIOT LAMBIE
(FES X, 216, 406), trans from Clydebank Linnvale to Lerwick and Bressay 28 Oct 1964; introd as Assoc at Ellon 25 Sep 1980.

1981 JAMES WYLIE MACDONALD
trans from Glasgow Barlanark Greyfriars to Lerwick and Bressay 6 Jul 1981; dem on app as Principal Chaplain to British and International Sailors' Society Aug 1990.

1991 JAMES ADRIAN MILLER DOWSWELL
B 27 Aug 1936 at Glasgow, s of Allen Edward D. and Harriet Helen Miller Scotland; educ Airdrie Academy 1947–55; University of St Andrews 1986–89; Data Processing 1955–86; lic by Presb of England, Jul 1989; asst London Crown Court 1989–90; m 5 Aug 1962 Janet Grindlay Laird b 21 Jul 1939 d of Joseph L. and Jean Kennedy; Children: Morag Laird Livingstone b 12 Jan 1964 m Wallis; Fiona Scotland b 29 Apr 1966; ord and ind to Lerwick and Bressay 17 Jan 1991.

NESTING AND LUNNASTING (FES VII, 309; VIII, 706; IX, 714; X, 406)

(Lunnasting was formerly a Mission Station). Linked 27 Nov 1977 with Delting.

1968 ANDREW GORDON RIDDELL
(FES IX, 134; X, 79, 175, 406), res as teacher and lay missionary, Orkney and ind to Nesting 12 Jul 1968; trans to Walls 2 Mar 1977.

1979 GEORGE COOPER
ind to Delting with Nesting and Lunnasting 25 Aug 1979, see Delting.

1981 GILBERT SIM
ord and ind to Delting with Nesting and Lunnasting 4 Jul 1981; dem 31 Aug 1986.

1988 ELINOR JANET GORDON
ord and ind to Delting with Nesting and Lunnasting 13 Aug 1988, see Delting.

1996 WINIFRED MUNSON
ord and ind to Delting with Nesting and Lunnasting 11 May 1996, see Delting.

NORTHMAVINE (FES VII, 312; VIII, 706; IX, 714; X, 406)

1971 WILLIAM McLEISH ALEXANDER
(FES X, 406), ord and ind to Northmavine 16 Jun 1971; trans to Aberdeen Bucksburn 27 Jul 1978.

1978 KENNETH ROSS
(FES X, 233, 234, 240, 276, 363), dem from Kirkmichael and Tomintoul 1 Feb 1977; ind to Northmavine 4 Nov 1978; ret 31 Oct 1980; died 29 Dec 1990.

1982 IAIN RICHARD TORRANCE
ord and ind to Northmavine 23 Jan 1982; dem 31 Aug 1985 to take up app as Lecturer in New Testament and Christian Ethics, Queen's College, Birmingham 1 Sep 1985.

1987 ALICE H KIRKPATRICK
ord and ind to Northmavine 5 Sep 1987.

SANDSTING AND AITHSTING (FES VII, 314; VIII, 706; IX, 714; X, 407)

Linked 23 Mar 1980 with Walls.

1963 MAGNUS CHEYNE
(FES X, 407), ord and ind to Sandsting and Aithsting 12 Jun 1963; dem 31 Dec 1979; app Community minister for oil workers and their families, Shetland 1980.

1980 JAMES NEILSON BLAIR
(FES X, 405), trans from Sandwick with Cunningsburgh with Quarff to Sandsting and Aithsting with Walls 1980; ret 12 Jul 1986; Publ: *Through Cloud and Sunshine* (Nelson Smith, 1988); *I Remember* (*Shetland Times*, 1991); *Confessions of a Parish Minister* (*Shetland Life Magazine*, 1996).

1988 JOHN GROOM MILLER
ret from RAF Chaplains' Branch and ind to Sandsting and Aithsting with Walls 5 Nov 1988; trans to Eskdalemuir with Hutton and Corrie with Tundergarth 13 Feb 1991.

1991 BARRY KNIGHT
ord and ind to Sandsting and Aithsting with Walls 4 Jul 1991; trans to Colvend, Southwick and Kirkbean 2 Jul 1996.

1997 WILLIAM JOHNSTONE McMILLAN
(FES X, 41), trans from New Erskine to Sandsting and Aithsting with Walls and Sandness 8 Mar 1997; Publ: Booklet on History of St Ninian's Craigmailen (private, 1976).

SANDWICK, CUNNINGSBURGH AND QUARFF (FES X, 405, 407)

Formed 12 Feb 1980 by union of Cunningsburgh, Quarff and Sandwick. Linked 17 Feb 1980 with Dunrossness and St Ninian's inc. Fair Isle.

1967 JAMES NEILSON BLAIR
(FES X, 405), trans from Mid Yell to Sandwick with Cunningsburgh with Quarff 14 Dec 1967; trans to Sandsting and Aithsting with Walls 1980.

1981 EDITH F McMILLAN
ord and ind to Dunrossness with Sandwick, Cunningsburgh and Quarff 10 Apr 1981, see Dunrossness.

1990 TREVOR CHARLES WILLIAMS
ind to Dunrossness with Sandwick, Cunningsburgh and Quarff 26 Sep 1990, see Dunrossness.

1997 CHARLES HUGH MOAR GREIG
ind to Dunrossness and St Ninian's inc Fair Isle with Sandwick Cunningsburgh and Quarff 18 Jan 1997, see Dunrossness.

TINGWALL (FES X, 407)

1972 HAMISH GAULT SMITH
(FES X, 186, 407), ind to Tingwall 29 Sep 1972; became minister of linked charge with Burra Isle 3 Oct 1975, see Burra Isle.

1986 JAMES HOSIE
(FES X, 134, 163, 257), ind to Burra Isle with Tingwall 26 Jul 1986, see Burra Isle.

1995 NORMAN ROSS WHYTE
ind to Burra Isle with Tingwall 3 Jun 1995, see Burra Isle.

UNST (FES IX, 715; X, 407)

1974 SINCLAIR BUCHANAN FERGUSON
(FES X, 407), ord by Presb of Glasgow during assistantship at St George's Tron 29 Sep 1971; ind to Unst 4 Apr 1974; dem 4 Apr 1976 on app as Editor, Banner of Truth Trust.

1976 SCOTT MACKENZIE RAE
ord and ind to Unst 23 Jun 1976; dem to take up app with Royal Naval Chaplaincy Service 1 Feb 1981.

1982 KENNETH RANKIN ROSS
ord and ind to Unst 18 Sep 1982; dem to take up app as Lecturer in Theology, University of Malawi 1 Aug 1988.

1989 GILLIAN MUNRO
ord and ind to Unst 12 Aug 1989; dem on app as Chaplain's Asst, Aberdeen Royal Infirmary 2 Jul 1995.

1997 JOHN LAMONT McNAB
B 23 Apr 1954 at Glasgow, s of Duncan Lamont M. and Anne Aitkenhead Howatt; educ Dollar Academy 1966–72; University of Glasgow 1972–76 (MA); University of Edinburgh 1988–92 (BD); Social Work 1977–88; lic by Presb of Edinburgh, Jul 1992; asst Falkirk Grahamston 1992–94; ord and ind to Unst 1 Feb 1997.

WALLS AND SANDNESS (FUF 525; FES VII, 317; VIII, 707; IX, 716; X, 407)

Linked 23 Mar 1980 with Sandsting and Aithsting.

1965 JOHN FIRTH
(FES IX, 715; X, 407 (2)), trans from Unst to Walls 24 Mar 1965; ret 30 Apr 1974; died 30 Aug 1979.

1977   ANDREW GORDON RIDDELL
(FES IX, 134; X, 79, 175, 406), trans from Nesting and Lunnasting to Walls 2 Mar 1977; died 14 Nov 1978.

1980   JAMES NEILSON BLAIR
(FES X, 405), ind to Sandsting and Aithsting with Walls 1980, see Sandsting and Aithsting.

1988   JOHN GROOM MILLER
ind to Sandsting and Aithsting with Walls 5 Nov 1988, see Sandsting and Aithsting.

1991   BARRY KNIGHT
ord and ind to Sandsting and Aithsting with Walls 4 Jul 1991, see Sandsting and Aithsting.

1997   WILLIAM JOHNSTONE McMILLAN
(FES X, 41), trans from New Erskine to Sandsting and Aithsting with Walls and Sandness 8 Mar 1997.

WHALSAY AND SKERRIES (FES X, 408)

Vacant from 1978 until 1983.

1950   ANDREW COPLAND MEIKLE
(FES IX, 717; X, 408), ord and ind to Whalsay 8 Dec 1950; ret 31 Mar 1955; died 1 Jun 1989.

1974   DAVID COWAN
(FES X, 408), ind to Whalsay and Skerries 15 Jun 1974; trans to Clydebank St Andrew's 31 May 1976.

1977   ALEXANDER BUCHAN
(FES X, 188), trans from Blanytre St Andrew's to Whalsay and Skerries 19 Mar 1977; dem 12 Aug 1978 to take up app at Ithaca Pastoral Charge, Brisbane, Australia.

1983   STEWART McMILLAN
ord and ind to Whalsay and Skerries 15 Jan 1983;

dem 15 Jan 1988; ind to Dundee Strathmartine 5 Apr 1990.

1988   REGINE URSULA CHEYNE
ord and ind to Whalsay and Skerries 3 Sep 1988; trans to Cromar 2 May 1996.

1997   IRENE ANNE CHARLTON
B 18 Apr 1953 at Edinburgh, d of Thomas Blair Wark and Margaret Mitchell Ramsay Weir; educ Knox Academy, Haddington 1965–71; University of Aberdeen 1985–91 (BTh, CPS); Accountancy 1972–74; Dressmaking 1978–85; lic by Presb of Aberdeen 27 Jun 1991; asst Aberdeen St Mary's 1991–93; m 4 Aug 1972 Richard Malcolm Charlton b 28 Dec 1951 s of Thomas Malcolm C. and Valerie McCulloch; Children: Gordon Malcolm b 14 Aug 1974 m Susan Georgea Wyness; Iain Andrew b 2 Aug 1977; ord and ind to Auchaber United with Auchterless 23 Feb 1994; trans to Whalsay and Skerries 17 Aug 1997.

YELL (FES X, 408)

Linked 26 Oct 1975 with Fetlar.

1972   JAMES BLAIKIE
(FES X, 408), ord and ind to Yell 27 Apr 1972; became minister of linked charge with Fetlar 26 Oct 1975; trans to Aberdeen Middlefield 31 Mar 1977.

1977   ERNEST CHAPMAN
ord and ind to Fetlar with Yell 22 Oct 1977; dem 31 Jan 1980.

1982   MAGNUS JAMES CAMERON WILLIAMSON
ord and ind to Fetlar with Yell 19 Jun 1982, see Fetlar.

PRESBYTERY OF ENGLAND

CORBY DANESHOLME AND KINGSWOOD

Ecumenical parish sponsored by the Baptist Union, the Methodist Church, the United Reformed Church and the Church of Scotland.

1987 JAMES AIRD TREVORROW
(FES X, 409), dem from Kilarrow with Kilmeny 31 Oct 1987; app to Danesholme and Kingswood Ecumenical Experiment, Corby 13 Nov 1987; ind to Glasgow Cranhill 11 Apr 1994.

CORBY ST ANDREW'S (FES IX, 719; X, 409)

1973 JAMES AIRD TREVORROW
(FES X, 409), ord by Presb of Edinburgh 1971; ind to St Andrew's 15 Jan 1973; trans to Kilarrow with Kilmeny 7 Nov 1982.

1983 JOHN FORBES MACKIE
B 4 Apr 1944 at Edinburgh, s of Charles Wright M. and Margaret Archibald Forbes; educ George Heriot's, Edinburgh 1949–59; Telford College, Edinburgh 1971–73; University of Edinburgh 1973–78 (BD, CPS); Electrician (Royal Navy) 1961–71; lic by Presb of Edinburgh 2 Jul 1978; asst Edinburgh Tron Kirk Moredun 1978–79; ord by Presb of Edinburgh and app by Royal Naval Chaplaincy Service 22 Apr 1979; ind to St Andrew's 7 Jul 1983.

CORBY ST NINIAN'S (FES X, 409)

1964 JOHN SCOTT DRUMMOND
(FES IX, 733; X, 95, 409, 418), trans from Newton Stewart St John's to St Ninian's 14 May 1964; ret 1 Apr 1978; Addl publ: *Here's tae Melrose and Other Poems* (Meigle Printers, 1983).

1978 KENNETH E W TYSON
ord and ind to St Ninian's 4 Oct 1978; trans to Fettercairn with Fordoun with Glenbervie 11 Aug 1983.

1984 DAVID COWAN
(FES X, 408), res from term app at Motherwell Manse Road and ind to St Ninian's 1 Mar 1984; dem 8 Jun 1988.

1989 ALAN SHARP
B 18 May 1954 at Kirkcaldy, s of Alexander Thomson S. and Catherine S; educ Kirkcaldy High 1966–72; University of Edinburgh 1972–76 (BSc);

University of St Andrews 1976–79 (BD); lic by Presb of Kirkcaldy, 1979; asst West Kilbride St Andrew's 1979–80; m 4 Aug 1979 Linda May Woods b 3 Feb 1956 d of Bryan and Margaret W; ord and ind to Aberdeen Middlefield 23 Sep 1980; trans to St Ninian's 13 Jul 1989.

GILLINGHAM ST MARGARET'S (FES IX, 729; X, 409)

Congregation dissolved 3 Apr 1988.

1965 HECTOR GILBERT ROSS
(FES IX, 226, 709; X, 217, 404, 409), trans from Dalmuir to St Margaret's 29 Jun 1965; ret 3 Apr 1988; died 28 Oct 1999.

GUERNSEY ST ANDREW'S IN THE GRANGE (FES X, 409)

1969 OWAIN TUDOR HUGHES
(FES X, 409), dem from St George's (Presb Church of England) and ind to St Andrew's 18 Jul 1969; admitted by General Assembly 1972; ret 30 Jun 1976.

1976 CHARLES FYFE DAVISON
B 7 Aug 1921 at Winnipeg, Manitoba, Canada, s of Charles D. and Isabel Fyfe; educ Larne Grammar, Co Antrim, N Ireland 1932–39; Trinity College, Dublin 1939–43 (MA); Assemblies Theological College, Belfast 1943–45; lic by Presb of Carrickfergus, 1945; asst Windsor Church, Belfast 1945–47; m 11 Jun 1947 Dorothy Maureen Paterson b 22 Dec 1921 d of James Morrow P; Children: Gael, Paul, Timothy, Peter; ord by Presb of Carrickfergus and app by RAF Chaplains' Branch 1 Jul 1947; res from RAF Chaplains' Branch 7 Aug 1976 and ind to St Andrew's in the Grange 28 Oct 1976; ret 1 Oct 1987.

1987 GEORGE LOCKHART LUGTON
(FES X, 213, 224, 454), res as Joint Secretary, Ministry and Mission Dept and ind to St Andrew's in the Grange 3 Sep 1987; ret 31 Oct 1997.

1998 ALEXANDER EWING STRACHAN
(FES X, 265), trans from Musselburgh St Michael's Inveresk to St Andrew's in the Grange 27 Mar 1998; app Healthcare Chaplain (full-time) to Dumfries Hospitals 17 Jun 1999.

JERSEY ST COLUMBA'S (FES X, 410)

1967 WILLIAM TYRELL YATES BROWNE
(FES IX, 681, 787; X, 262, 410, 444), dem from Balquhidder 4 Jan 1967 and ind to St Columba's (Presb Church of England); resumed status as minister of Church of Scotland when congregation was admitted to Church of Scotland 25 May 1972; ret 1976; died 2 Apr 1996.

1976 ERIC GORDON MILTON
(FES X, 151, 351), trans from Glasgow Battlefield East to St Columba's 27 Jul 1976; dem 14 Apr 1982 on app as Chaplain to Queen Victoria School, Dunblane.

1982 PAUL STEPHEN KIRBY
B 3 Mar 1947 at Rochester, s of Leslie Dennis K. and Muriel Mary Avery; educ Sir Joseph Williamson's Mathematical School, Rochester 1958–64; All Nations Missionary College Diploma in Missionary Studies 1965–68; Université d' Aix-Marseille 1968–69 (Diplome de la Langue Française); Univer-sity of Edinburgh 1970–72 (CPS), 1972–75 (BD); University of Southampton 1990–91 (PGCE); ord by French Protestant Church 1968; assistantships in Pas de Calais and Marseille 1968–70; lic by Presb of Edinburgh 9 Jul 1975; asst London St Columba's, Pont Street 1975–77; m 13 Aug 1970 Helen Grace Lorraine Ross b 1 Oct 1948 d of Alex-ander R. and Isobel Stuart; divorced 1997; Children: Harriet Jane Louisa b 28 Jul 1987; ord by Presb of England during assistantship at St Columba's, Pont Street 18 Jan 1976; app by RAF Chaplains' Branch 15 May 1977; ind to St Columba's 6 Jul 1982; dem 1 Jul 1990; app Head of Philosophy and Religion, Hautlieu School, Jersey 10 Sep 1992.

1991 ROBERT MORRISON NICOL
B 16 Jul 1929 at Bathgate, s of Robert N. and Margaret Morrison; educ Bathgate Academy 1934–45; University of Edinburgh 1983–84; Tailoring (Cutter/Designer) 1945–63; Clothing Industry (Factory Management) 1963–83; lic by Presb of West Lothian 28 Jun 1984; m 2 Apr 1955 Margaret Gardner Livingston b 23 Apr 1931 d of Peter L. and Susan Findlay; Children: Catriona b 5 Feb 1959 m Alistair Buxton; Valerie b 17 Sep 1961 m Russell Brodie; ord and ind to Cum-mertrees with Mouswald with Ruthwell 16 Aug 1984; trans to St Columba's 28 Feb 1991; ret 30 Oct 1996.

1997 JAMES GAULT MACKENZIE
B 15 Jun 1940 at Glasgow, s of Kenneth M. and Elizabeth Gault; educ Allan Glen's, Glasgow 1945–53; Open University 1970–74 (BA); University of Aberdeen 1976–79 (BD); Design Engineer 1953–76; lic by Presb of Inverness 27 Jun 1979; m 21 Aug 1962 Jean Miller Sinclair b 20 Jan 1935 d of Donald S. and Helen MacLeod; Children: Andrew b 23 Dec 1967; Jacqueline b 7 Sep 1970

(deceased); Eleanor b 29 Sep 1971; ord and ind to Hamilton Hillhouse 29 Feb 1980; trans to St Columba's 7 Mar 1997.

LIVERPOOL ST ANDREW'S (FES VII, 465; VIII, 724; IX, 719; X, 410)

Vacant from 1985. Continued vacancy declared.

1962 ERNEST JOHN BRAIN
(FES X, 170, 410), trans from Glasgow Pollok Street to St Andrew's 11 May 1962; ret 30 Sep 1985.

LONDON CROWN COURT (FES VII, 467; VIII, 724; IX, 719; X, 410)

1963 JOHN ALEXANDER MILLER SCOTT
(FES IX, 503; X, 121, 299, 410), trans from Steven-ston High to Crown Court 31 Jan 1963; dem 9 Jun 1985 and introd to Jerusalem St Andrew's 15 Jul 1985.

1986 KENNETH GRANT HUGHES
(FES X, 31, 57, 137), trans from Stenton with Whittingehame with Prestonkirk to Crown Court 16 Apr 1986; ret 1 Nov 1990.

1991 HENRY STANLEY COWPER HOOD
(FES X, 17, 420), trans from Glasgow Anderston Kelvingrove to Crown Court 7 Nov 1991.

LONDON ST COLUMBA'S (FES X, 410)

Linked 20 Nov 1983 with Newcastle St Andrew's.

1960 JAMES FRASER McLUSKEY
(FES IX, 504, 783; X, 223, 299, 410 (2)), trans from Bearsden New Kilpatrick to St Columba's, Pont Street 9 Dec 1960; became minister of linked charge with Dulwich East (St James') 1 Feb 1970 and of united charge 9 Jul 1972; became minister of linked charge with Newcastle St Andrew's 20 Nov 1983; Moderator of General Assembly 1983–84; ret 31 Oct 1986.

1970 GEORGE GORDON CAMERON
(FES IX, 276 (2), 515; X, 127, 305, 410), dem from Paisley Glenburn 31 Dec 1969 and introd as Assoc at St Columba's 5 Feb 1970; ret 30 Apr 1975; died 20 Nov 1980.

1980 WILLIAM ALEXANDER CAIRNS
B 23 Dec 1945 at London, s of William C. and Isobel Margaret Thom; educ Sutton Valence School, Kent 1959–64; University of St Andrews 1972–77 (BD); Paper Making Industry 1964–69; lic by Presb of Lothian 30 Oct 1977; asst London St Columba's, Pont Street 1977–80; ord by Presb of England during assistantship at St Columba's, Pont Street 9 Apr 1978; introd as Assoc at St Columba's 1 Aug 1980.

1988   JOHN HEDLEY McINDOE
(FES X, 211, 304), trans from Lanark St Nicholas'
to St Columba's with Newcastle St Andrew's 12 Feb
1988; Moderator of General Assembly 1996–97; d
Margot m Fergusson; d Jennifer m Ballantyne.

1996   CALUM IAIN MACLEOD
B 28 Dec 1967 at Glasgow, s of Malcolm John M.
and Christina MacLeod MacLean; educ Williamwood High, Glasgow 1979–85; University of
Strathclyde 1985–89 (BA); University of Glasgow
1991–94 (BD); Health Care Management 1989–
91; lic by Presb of Glasgow; asst London St
Columba's, Pont Street 1994–96; ord by Presb of
England and app Asst at St Columba's, Pont Street
31 Mar 1996; app Interim Assoc Pastor, Fourth
Presb Church of Chicago 26 Sep 1997.

NEWCASTLE ST ANDREW'S (FES VII, 462; VIII,
723; IX, 720; X, 411)

Vacant from 1970 until 1983. Linked 20 Nov 1983
with London St Columba's.

1983   JAMES FRASER McLUSKEY
(FES IX, 504, 783; X, 223, 299, 410 (2)), ind to
London St Columba's, Pont Street 9 Dec 1960;
became minister of linked charge with St Andrew's
20 Nov 1983, see St Columba's.

1988   JOHN HEDLEY McINDOE
(FES X, 211, 304), trans from Lanark St Nicholas'
to London St Columba's with St Andrew's 12 Feb
1988.

PRESBYTERY OF EUROPE

AMSTERDAM (FES VII, 537; VIII, 727; IX, 721; X, 412)

1980 WILLIAM GERAINT EDWARDS
(FES X, 112, 332, 352, 445), dem from Aberdeen West of St Nicholas 31 Dec 1979 and introd to the English Reformed Church, Amsterdam; res 31 Aug 1989 and ind to St Andrew's (URC), Bournemouth; ret 31 Aug 1999.

1990 JOHN ALEXANDER COWIE
B 11 Jan 1954 at Birmingham, s of Alexander Grant C. and Olive Joyce Wheeler; educ Royal High, Edinburgh 1966–72; University of Edinburgh 1972–76 (BSc), 1978–81 (BD); Teacher and House Parent, Murree Christian School, Pakistan 1976–78, 1981–82; lic by Presb of Edinburgh 28 Jun 1982; asst Edinburgh Palmerston Place 1982–83; m 29 Dec 1982 Gillian Dorothy More b 12 Nov 1948 d of John Taylor and Daphne Elizabeth M; Children: Matthew John b 11 Sep 1983; Sarah Elizabeth b 4 Jun 1985; Ruth Gillian b 8 Jun 1988; ord and ind to Kirkcaldy Invertiel 23 Jun 1983; became minister of linked charge with Auchtertool 31 Mar 1987; dem 31 Dec 1989 and introd to the English Reformed Church, Amsterdam 1990.

BRUSSELS (FES VII, 534; VIII, 727; IX, 721; X, 412)

1959 ALEXANDER JOHN MACLEOD
(FES IX, 690, 765; X, 412), res as Chaplain to Iraq Petroleum Co, Iraq and introd to Brussels St Andrew's 1 Feb 1959; ret 3 Apr 1974.

1974 ANGUS THOW MACKNIGHT
(FES X, 412), introd to Brussels St Andrew's 22 Aug 1974; dem 28 Feb 1984 on app by Board of World Mission to Sri Lanka Colombo St Andrew's.

1984 CHARLES CECIL MACNEILL
(FES X, 447), res from RAF Chaplains' Branch and introd to Brussels St Andrew's 9 May 1984; ret 30 Sep 1991; OBE 1983; s Alan m Rosemary.

1991 THOMAS CAMPBELL PITKEATHLY
B 11 Jul 1939 at St Andrews, s of John William P. and Dora Campbell; educ Buckhaven High 1950–56; University of St Andrews 1956–59; University of Edinburgh 1980–83 (BD); Accountancy 1959–80; lic by Presb of Lothian 3 Jul 1983; asst Haddington St Mary's 1983–84; m 28 Sep 1963 Patricia Anne Miller b 29 May 1940 d of Ernest Craig Bell M. and Sheila Lindsay Currie; Children: Maureen Campbell b 1 Aug 1966 m Philip Atherton; Laura b 2 Sep 1968 m William Burnside; Valerie Jane b 6 May 1971; ord and ind to Bridge of Weir St Machar's Ranfurly 25 Sep 1984; introd to Brussels St Andrew's 25 Oct 1991.

BUDAPEST

Scottish Mission, then St Columba's Church of Scotland.

1978 BERTALAN TAMAS
Minister of the Hungarian Reformed Church; app by Overseas Council as Asst minister of Scottish Mission, Budapest 1 Dec 1976; app Minister of same 1 Apr 1978; continued at Scottish Mission following app by Hungarian Reformed Church as Head of Ecumenical and International Department; ret from Scottish Mission, Mar 1999 but continues as mission partner to Church of Scotland.

1991 ALISON PATERSON McDONALD MATHESON
introd to Scottish Mission, Budapest 1 Mar 1991; ord by Presb of Europe 16 Jun 1991; introd as Assoc at Edinburgh Mayfield Salisbury 1 Dec 1994.

1994 SUSAN GAZARD COWELL
B 14 Oct 1943 at Glasgow, d of Thomas C. and Kate Simpson; educ St George's, Edinburgh 1948–61; Froebel Educational Institute, London 1962–65; Moray House College, Edinburgh; University of Edinburgh; Teaching 1965–71; Home Mission Board—Travelling Families 1971–73; YWCA—Training 1973–74; Mental Handicap Education 1974–82; lic by Presb of Lothian, Jun 1985; asst Edinburgh Greenbank 1985–87; ord by Presb of Edinburgh during assistantship at Greenbank 25 May 1986; ind to Culter with Libberton and Quothquan with Symington 23 Apr 1987; introd to Budapest St Columba's 20 Jun 1994.

CLUJ

1998 CELIA GRACE KENNY
B 26 Mar 1947 at Kirkcaldy, d of James Young Thomson and Grace Robertson; educ Kirkcaldy High 1959–65; Royal Scottish Academy of Music 1965–68 (DRSAM); Trinity College, Dublin 1982–

86 (BA); University of Edinburgh 1991–92 (MTh); lic by Presb of Edinburgh 10 Jan 1993; m 13 Jun 1973 Kevin Anthony Kenny b 11 Jun 1947 s of Edward K. and Eibhlin Nicholson; Children: Joanne Elizabeth b 6 Nov 1974; Stephen Edward James b 5 Nov 1976; Heather Dorothy b 20 Apr 1978; Matthew Kevin b 3 May 1979; ord by Presb of Edinburgh and app Asst at St George's West 1 Mar 1994; app Asst at St Giles' Cathedral 20 Aug 1995; app by Protestant Theological Institute, Cluj, Romania 1998.

COSTA DEL SOL

Shared ministry with Gibraltar St Andrew's from 1978. Charges linked 1996.

1978 DAVID STUART PHILIP
(FES IX, 463; X, 86, 274, 284), dem from Kirkcaldy St Brycedale 22 Oct 1978 and app by Board of World Mission to Costa del Sol with Gibraltar St Andrew's; Officiating Chaplain to Navy, Army and Air Force; ret 30 Jun 1990; d Wendy m Pepper; d Candice m Deas.

1993 JAMES MURDOCH ROGERS
(FES X, 304), dem from Dundee Roseangle Ryehill and app to Gibraltar St Andrew's with Costa del Sol 29 Sep 1993; ret 31 Jul 1996.

1996 JOHN ROBERT PAGE
B 11 Oct 1937 at Upper Norwood, London, s of Clifford Lionel P. and Rhoda Irene Noble; educ Bec Grammar, London 1949–56; University of Bristol/London 1967–70 (DipMin); University of Edinburgh 1984–87 (BD); Energy Marketing 1963–73 (Shell UK), 1973–83 (EEC Brussels); lic by Presb of Edinburgh 5 Jul 1987; asst Edinburgh St David's Broomhouse 1987–88; m 19 Jul 1958 Janet Dilys Spencer b 31 Dec 1938 d of Gordon Kenneth S. and Olive Price; Children: Andrew Philip b 16 Feb 1960; Deborah Frances b 3 Jul 1963; ord and ind to Dunlop 9 Jun 1988; app by Board of World Mission to Costa del Sol with Gibraltar St Andrew's 3 Mar 1996.

GENEVA (FES VII, 556; VIII, 729; IX, 721; X, 412)

1951 ROBERT CUTHBERT MACKIE
(FES IX, 722; X, 412), Assoc General Secretary, WCC 1948–56 and minister of Scots Kirk, Geneva 1951–55; died 13 Jan 1984.

1971 JOHN BOOKLESS HOOD
(FES IX, 34, 138, 438; X, 257, 260, 412), dem from Auchterarder St Andrew's and West and introd to Geneva 10 Mar 1971; ret 1977; died 4 May 1979.

1977 PATRICK DOUGLAS GORDON CAMPBELL
(FES IX, 434; X, 258, 269), dem from Tillicoultry 9 Oct 1977 on app to Geneva; ret 6 Apr 1984; d Alison m Andrew Kinghorn; s Andrew m Christine Liddle.

1984 WILLIAM DAVID RANALD CATTANACH
(FES IX, 230; X, 23, 135, 325), dem from Edinburgh St George's West on app to Geneva 3 May 1984; ret 1 Nov 1989.

1989 ARTHUR RAYMOND CHARLES GASTON
(FES X, 264, 267), dem from Dollar with Muckhart with Glendevon 21 Sep 1989 and introd to Geneva; dem on app as Staffing Secretary, Board of World Mission 1 Nov 1993.

1994 JAMES WILSON McLEOD
B 20 Dec 1935 at Edinburgh, s of James M. and Catherine Wilson; educ James Clark School, Edinburgh 1944–50; University of Edinburgh 1960–63 (MA); Baptist Theological College of Scotland 1963–65 (DTh); RAF 1953–57; m 4 Jul 1959 Marjorie Ferguson b 9 Apr 1935 d of James F. and Barbara Mackie; ord by Baptist Union of Scotland and ind to Pollock Baptist Church 7 Aug 1965; app Christian Education/Youth Director, Baptist Union of Scotland 30 Jan 1969; app Warden, Scottish Churches' House, Dunblane 20 Oct 1974; admitted by General Assembly 1978; ind to Bellshill West 15 May 1982; introd to Geneva 11 Jan 1994.

GENOA (FUF 526; FES IX, 724; X, 412)

Removed from the list of Presb.

1971 HENRY DANE SHERRARD
(FES X, 413), introd to Genoa 31 May 1971; ind to Buckhaven 21 Dec 1976.

GIBRALTAR ST ANDREW'S (FUF 529; FES IX, 726; X, 413)

Shared ministry with Costa del Sol from 1978. Charges linked 1996.

1973 NORMAN MACLEAN
(FES IX, 225, 791; X, 320, 413, 447), res from RAChD and app by Overseas Council to Gibraltar St Andrew's 1 Nov 1973; ret 1975; died 30 Nov 1982.

1975 ALLAN MACINNES MACLEOD
(FES IX, 64, 791; X, 447), ret from RAF Chaplains' Branch and introd to Gibraltar St Andrew's Jun 1975; res from app 1978 and ind to Gordon St Michael's with Legerwood with Westruther 13 Dec 1979.

1978 DAVID STUART PHILIP
(FES IX, 463; X, 86, 274, 284), dem from Kirkcaldy St Brycedale 22 Oct 1978 and app by Board of World Mission to Costa del Sol with Gibraltar St Andrew's, see Costa del Sol.

1990 JOHN ALASTAIR HILTON MURDOCH
introd to Gibraltar St Andrew's 26 Aug 1990; app Chaplain to Christ's Hospital, Sussex 16 Oct 1992.

1993 JAMES MURDOCH ROGERS
(FES X, 304), dem from Dundee Roseangle Ryehill and app to Gibraltar St Andrew's with Costa del Sol 29 Sep 1993; ret 31 Jul 1996.

1996 JOHN ROBERT PAGE
app by Board of World Mission to Costa del Sol with Gibraltar St Andrew's 3 Mar 1996, see Costa del Sol.

LAUSANNE (FUF 526; FES IX, 722; X, 413)

1974 WILLIAM MAURICE ISHERWOOD
(FES X, 412, 413), res from service with Overseas Council at Nicosia, Cyprus and introd to Lausanne 14 Jul 1974; res from app 1980; introd to Rotterdam 1981.

1980 HUGH FINDLAY KERR
(FES X, 63, 420), dem from Coldstream and introd to Lausanne 28 Apr 1980; trans to Aberdeen Ruthrieston South 28 Mar 1985.

1985 CHARLES MURRAY STEWART
(FES IX, 84; X, 26, 52), dem from Edinburgh Gorgie and introd to Lausanne 29 Apr 1985; ret 1 Feb 1994; died 21 Aug 1994.

1994 DOUGLAS RAMSAY MURRAY
B 29 May 1939 at Glasgow, s of Alexander Rothnie M. and Agnes Seaton Douglas; educ Shawlands Academy and Allan Glen's, Glasgow 1952–58; University of Glasgow 1958–61 (MA); Scottish Congregational College 1961–64; Andover Newton Theological School, Massachusetts 1964–65 (BD); m 5 Jul 1963 Sheila Berrie b 16 Aug 1940 d of John B. and Margaret Dykes; Children: Eric Douglas b 25 Sep 1965; Allan Stewart b 27 Apr 1967; Eleanor Susan b 12 May 1971; ord by Congregational Union of Scotland and ind to Drumchapel Congregational Church 30 Sep 1965; trans to Duke Street Congregational Church, Leith Sep 1969; admitted by General Assembly and ind to Wishaw Cambusnethan Old 14 Feb 1980; introd to Lausanne 4 Feb 1994.

LISBON (FUF 529; FES IX, 726; X, 413)

Vacant from 1980 until 1988.

1959 KENNETH HOPE TYSON
(FES IX, 722; X, 413 (2)), res from app at Lausanne on app by Overseas Council to Lisbon St Andrew's 30 Apr 1959; ret 31 Aug 1971; died 13 Feb 1979.

1974 DAVID WILLIAM NORWOOD
(FES IX, 593, 719; X, 144 (2), 410, 413), dem from Glasgow Orchard Park Giffnock and introd to Lisbon St Andrew's 28 Feb 1974; ret 30 Mar 1980; w Elsie died 1991.

1988 ROBERT HILL
(FES X, 319), dem from Forfar St Margaret's and introd to Lisbon St Andrew's 3 Mar 1988; ret 30 Jun 1997.

1998 GORDON OLIVER
B 21 Jul 1950 at Edinburgh, s of David O. and Sarah Margaret Isobel Prior; educ Leith Academy 1962–66; University of Edinburgh 1973–78 (BD); Civil Service 1966–72; lic by Presb of Edinburgh, Jun 1977; asst East Kilbride Greenhills 1978–80; m 28 Oct 1972 Jennifer Ann Darling b 13 Sep 1953 d of David D. and Sarah Muncaster; Children: Nicholas David b 2 May 1973; Sarah Naomi b 15 Aug 1978; ord by Presb of Hamilton during assistantship at Greenhills, Sep 1979; introd as Community minister at Hamilton Trinity 23 Jun 1980; ind to Alyth 24 Oct 1985; introd to Lisbon St Andrew's 18 Jan 1998.

MALTA ST ANDREW'S (FUF 527; FES IX, 724; X, 413)

1964 JOHN MITCHELL MILNE
(FES IX, 719, 792; X, 413, 447), res from RAF Chaplains' Branch and app by Overseas Council to Malta 30 Jun 1964; ret 30 Jun 1974; died 27 Jul 1987.

1975 COLIN ANDREW WESTMARLAND
(FES X, 165, 413), res from term app at Glasgow Langside Old and app to Malta St Andrew's 28 Mar 1975.

PARIS (FES VII, 535; VIII, 727; IX, 722; X, 413)

1969 WILLIAM MACDONALD DEMPSTER
(FES IX, 46, 482, 798; X, 414), res as Secretary of Committee for Huts and Canteens (HM Forces) and introd to the Scots Kirk, Paris 1 Apr 1969; ret 30 Sep 1975; died 24 Sep 1991.

1975 DAVID McKEAN
(FES IX, 790; X, 6, 414, 447), dem from Edinburgh Colinton Mains 30 Sep 1975 and introd to the Scots Kirk, Paris 31 Oct 1975; ret 31 Oct 1982; loc ten Edinburgh Craigmillar Park 1983; Chaplain (part-time) to Port of Leith 1983–89.

1982 BRUCE ROBERTSON
(FES IX, 662; X, 246, 379), dem from Cockburnspath with Innerwick with Oldhamstocks 30 Sep 1982 and introd to the Scots Kirk, Paris; ret 30 Nov 1992.

1993 WILLIAM McEWIN REID
(FES X, 109, 367), dem from Forres St Laurence 31 Dec 1992 on app to the Scots Kirk, Paris.

ROME ST ANDREW'S (FUF 527; FES IX, 725; X, 414)

1956 ALEXANDER JOHN MACLEAN
(FES IX, 409; X, 243, 414), dem from Fort William Duncansburgh and introd to Rome St Andrew's 10 Jun 1956; ret 31 Dec 1975; died 14 Jun 1988.

1976 JAMES WILLIAM FULLER
(FES X, 208), dem from Culter with Libberton and Quothquan and introd to Rome St Andrew's 16 Jun 1976; ret 1978; died 23 Feb 1996.

1978 JAMES NEIL STEWART ALEXANDER
(FES IX, 322; X, 434), res as Senior Lecturer in New Testament, University of Glasgow and introd to Rome St Andrew's 3 Oct 1978; res from app 1983; introd to Crieff St Andrew's (term) 12 Apr 1984.

1983 COLIN IAN MACLEAN
(FES X, 385, 398, 422), dem from Glasgow Barony Ramshorn and introd to Rome St Andrew's 30 Sep 1983; ret 31 Dec 1988; died 30 Oct 1990.

1988 JOHN DURHAM ROSS
(FES X, 151, 164), res as Industrial Chaplain for Dundee and introd to Rome St Andrew's 11 Oct 1988; died 12 Jul 1991.

1991 DAVID FERGUSON HUIE
(FES X, 420, 446), ret from Royal Naval Chaplaincy Service 5 Apr 1990; app locum at Rome St Andrew's 28 Mar 1990; app to same charge 1 Sep 1991 (service of introd 8 Mar 1992); d Rosalyn m Armand Georges Paul Renucci; d Ann m Federico Albizzati.

ROTTERDAM (FES VII, 549; VIII, 729; IX, 722; X, 414)

1972 JAMES GILBERT MORRISON
(FES IX, 792; X, 412, 414, 447), res as Community minister, Nicosia, Cyprus and introd to Rotterdam 29 Jun 1972; ret 23 Nov 1980; MBE 1980; s Hugh m Cornelia Ziock; s Allister m Vicki Ledsam; s Graham m Winnie Siu.

1981 WILLIAM MAURICE ISHERWOOD
(FES X, 412, 413), res from app at Lausanne 1980 and introd to Rotterdam 1981; ret 1983; died 24 Feb 1991.

1983 DUNCAN MACGILLIVRAY
dem from Peebles St Andrew's Leckie 31 May 1983 and introd to Rotterdam; ind to Kirkmaiden with Stoneykirk 16 May 1988.

1988 JAMES ERIC STEWART LOW
(FES X, 12, 34, 250, 403, 421), dem from Carnoustie Panbride and introd to Rotterdam 31 Jul 1988; res from app 1991; ind to Tarbat 26 Feb 1993.

1992 ALEXANDER C WARK
dem from Larkhall St Machan's 30 Jun 1992 on app to Rotterdam; ind to Methil 13 Feb 1994.

1995 ROBERT ALASDAIR CALVERT
B 22 Sep 1955 at Portsmouth, s of Thomas C. and Elizabeth Laura Ann; educ Bishop's Stortford College, Hertfordshire 1967–74; University of Dundee 1974–77 (BSc); University of Edinburgh 1979–82 (BD); Social Work and Salvation Army 1978–79; lic by Presb of Edinburgh, Jul 1982; asst Loanhead 1982–83; m 13 Jul 1982 Lesley-Ann Barr Thomson b 5 Aug 1960 d of Fred and Elizabeth T; Children: Simeon Craig b 28 Jul 1983; Zoe Elizabeth b 23 Jan 1985; Benjamin Scott b 3 Oct 1986; Daniel Bruce b 1 Dec 1988; ord and ind to Drumchapel St Mark's 11 Aug 1983; introd to Rotterdam 1 Aug 1995; Publ: *From Membership to Discipleship* (Rutherford House, 1990); *Hi-tech/Lo-jobs* (Rutherford House, 1996).

VIENNA (FES X, 414)

Removed from the list of Presb.

1973 WILLIAM MACLEOD MACARTNEY
(FES IX, 214, 643, 738; X, 61, 330, 366, 414), dem from Hutton and Fishwick with Paxton on app by Overseas Council to Vienna Community Church 30 Jun 1973; ret 31 Aug 1978; d Margaret m Iain Macdonald Forbes; d Elizabeth m Colin Crabbie.

PRESBYTERY OF JERUSALEM

JERUSALEM ST ANDREW'S

1966 WILLIAM GARDINER-SCOTT
(FES IX, 793; X, 362, 425), app by Overseas
Council to St Andrew's Church and Hospice,
Jerusalem 1 May 1966; ret 23 Feb 1976; died 27
May 1998.

1975 THOMAS CALDWELL HOUSTON
(FES X, 420), ind to Milford and Fanad, Presb of
Donegal, Ireland Apr 1971; app to Jerusalem St
Andrew's 2 Jan 1975; ind to Baillieston St Andrew's
30 Apr 1980.

1980 ROBERT CRAIG
(FES IX, 787; X, 429), res as Principal and Vice-
Chancellor, University of Zimbabwe and ind to
Jerusalem St Andrew's 1980; LLD (Witswaters-
rand) 1979; LLD (Birmingham) 1980; LLD (Natal)
1981; DLitt (Zimbabwe) 1981; ret 1985; Moderator
of General Assembly 1986–87; died 30 Jan 1995;
s John Michael Robert m Sara Reid; Addl publ:
The Task of the Church in Today's World (*Orkney
Press*, 1989).

1985 JOHN ALEXANDER MILLER SCOTT
(FES IX, 503; X, 121, 299, 410), dem from London
Crown Court 9 Jun 1985 and introd to Jerusalem
St Andrew's 15 Jul 1985; Chairman of Israel
Council of Church of Scotland 1985–88; DD
(Glasgow) 1986; ret 31 Aug 1988; s Peter m
Katharine Mary Comber; s Stephen m Eilean
Shona Mudie; d Elspeth m William John Salter.

1988 ROBERT COLIN MAXWELL MORTON
(FES X, 57, 125), dem from Prestonpans Preston
and introd to Jerusalem St Andrew's 14 Jul 1988;
ret 21 Jun 1998.

1995 PHILIPPA MARGARET BAKER OTT
B 11 Jul 1961 at Swansea, S Wales, d of Leonard
Baker Short and Margaret Mary Smith; educ Bishop
Gore Senior Comprehensive, Swansea 1974–77;
University of Wales 1978–79; University of Aberdeen 1979–84 (BD, CPS); lic by Presb of Aberdeen
28 Jun 1984; asst Cults East 1984–85; m 4 Aug
1981 David Hemphill Ott b 19 Jun 1944 s of Elmer
Barchfield O. and Margaret Hemphill; ord and ind
to Peterhead West Associate 24 Jun 1986; became
minister of linked charge with Boddam 17 Feb 1988
and of united charge 11 Oct 1991; dem 30 Apr
1995 on app to Jerusalem St Andrew's; dem 31
Jul 1997.

1997 IAIN FERGUSON PATON
dem from Glasgow Newlands South and introd
to Jerusalem St Andrew's 1 Mar 1997; ind to
Elie with Kilconquhar and Colinsburgh 7 Dec
1998.

TIBERIAS ST ANDREW'S

1983 ROBIN ALASDAIR ROSS
dem from Denny Old 10 Oct 1982 and app to
Tiberias 2 Feb 1983; app Middle East Secretary,
Board of World Mission and Unity 8 Aug 1988.

1995 FREDERICK WILLIAM HIBBERT
B 7 Apr 1939 at Isleworth, Middlesex, s of William
John H. and Sarah Jane Holt; educ Hampton
Grammar 1950–57; University of London 1980–
83 (BD); University of Edinburgh (DipMin); Air
Conditioning Contractor 1971–79; lic by Presb of
Jedburgh; asst Edinburgh Cluny 1985–86; m (1)
12 Aug 1961 Jeanne Capon b 15 Feb 1939 d of
Robert C. Children: Matthew b 20 Feb 1966;
Thomas b 30 May 1967; Luke b 3 May 1969 m
Catherine Montgomery; m (2) 5 Mar 1977 Diana
Patricia Mary Hall b 18 Dec 1940; ord and ind to
Kincardine, Croik and Edderton 12 Dec 1986; dem
to take up app as Director of Sea of Galilee Centre,
Tiberias, Israel 1 Oct 1995.

AUXILIARY MINISTERS

In alphabetical order

1986 IAIN THOMAS ARTHUR CARPENTER ADAMSON
B 17 Jun 1928 at Dundee, s of Alexander A. and Margaret Marian Abel; educ Morgan Academy, Dundee 1939–45; University of St Andrews 1945–49 (BSc), 1980–81 (MSc); Princeton University, USA 1949–52 (AM, PhD); University Lecturer (Maths and Computer Science) 1952–93; lic by Presb of Dundee 29 Sep 1985; asst Abernyte with Inchture and Kinnaird with Longforgan 1985–86; m 26 Aug 1967 Robin Andison b 30 Mar 1938 d of Reginald Thomas A. and Nellie Hawthorn Jolly; Children: Margaret Harhorn Mary b 18 Sep 1969; ord by Presb of Dundee and assgnd to Abernyte with Inchture and Kinnaird with Longforgan 21 Sep 1986; ret 30 Jun 1993; Publ: *Introduction to Field Theory* (Oliver & Boyd, 1964, CUP, 1982); *Rings, Modules and Algebras* (Oliver & Boyd, 1971); *Elementary Rings and Modules* (Oliver & Boyd, 1972); *Elementary Mathematical Analysis* (Longman, 1975); *Data Structures and Algorithms: A First Course* (Springer, 1996); *A General Topology Workbook* (Birkhäuser, 1996); *A Set Theory Workbook* (Birkhäuser, 1998); tr of *The Theory of Algebraic Number Fields* by David Hilbert (Springer, 1998).

1984 DAVID MOORE ANDERSON
B 4 Oct 1948 at Forfar, s of Alexander Moore A. and Janet Scott Kinnear Robertson; educ Mackie Academy, Stonehaven and Alloa Academy 1960–66; Stow College, Glasgow 1966–69 (FCOptom); Aston University, Birmingham 1970–71 (MSc); Lecturer in Optometry 1972–76; Optometrist 1976-present; lic by Presb of Lochaber 25 Sep 1983; asst Fort William Duncansburgh 1983–84; m 15 Jul 1972 Maureen Janet Campbell b 9 Feb 1948 d of David C. and Margaret McTurk; Children: Shirley b 22 Sep 1975; Jillian b 9 Dec 1977; ord by Presb of Lochaber and assgnd to Kilmallie 20 Aug 1984; assgnd to Fort William Duncansburgh, Oct 1988; assgnd as Elder Trainer 1995; assgnd as Interim Moderator at Kinlochleven with Nether Lochaber Jul 1999.

1996 ELIZABETH STEWART BROWN
B 30 Sep 1942 at Glasgow, d of William Robertson and Kerr; educ Hutchesons' Girls' Grammar, Glasgow 1947–59; Nursing 1961–78; lic by Presb of Perth 25 Sep 1995; asst Perth St John's 1995–96; m 3 Aug 1964 Iain Brown b 30 Mar 1940 s of Thomas B. and Docherty; Children: David b 20 May

1965 m Denise; Susan b 29 Jun 1967 m Frank; Morag b 1 Jul 1970 m Adam; ord by Presb of Perth and assgnd to Perth St John's 25 Sep 1996.

1985 IAN H CALDER
lic 2 Oct 1984; ord by Presb of Gordon 7 Jul 1985 and assgnd to Huntly Strathbogie; died 6 Aug 1992.

1997 JUNE CLOGGIE
B 22 Jun 1936 at Glasgow, d of James Hamilton Hendry and Catherine Shields; educ King's Park Senior Secondary, Glasgow 1941–52; lic by Presb of Stirling 3 Oct 1996; asst Callander 1996–97; m 24 Mar 1959 David Cloggie b 30 Aug 1931 s of Robert Wood C. and Elizabeth Rankin Davis; Children: Andrew b 17 Jun 1964 m Susan Kemplay; Sharon b 2 May 1967 m Douglas Telfer; ord by Presb of Stirling and assgnd to Stirling St Mark's 28 Aug 1997; assgnd to Callander Nov 1998.

1997 SHEILA ANN CRAGGS
B 21 Feb 1946 at Alnwick, d of James Thompson Kirkup and Lilian Elizabeth Smith; educ Duchess's Grammar, Alnwick 1950–65; Clerical Asst 1992–99; lic by Presb of Gordon 19 Sep 1996; m 20 Sep 1969 Thomas Edward Craggs b 27 Mar 1947 s of Charles Ronald C. and Sanderson; Children: Trudi b 1 Feb 1974; Jill b 10 Jul 1979; ord by Presb of Gordon and assgnd to Ellon 15 Sep 1997.

1991 ALISTAIR BOOTH CRUICKSHANK
B 3 Aug 1931 at Dumfries, s of William C. and Alexina Wilson Tinning; educ Stirling High 1943–50; University of Glasgow 1950–54 (MA); Jordanhill College, Glasgow 1954–55 (PGCE); University of Georgia, USA 1955–56; Director of Royal Scottish Geographical Society 1986–96; lic by Presb of Stirling 28 Nov 1989; m 4 Sep 1957 Sheena Carlin Brown b 26 Mar 1936 d of David B. and Janet Cameron Carlin; Children: Alexander Brown b 8 Dec 1958 m Julie Foster; Gillean Jane Booth b 8 Feb 1961 m Jeff Atkins; Neil Fraser b 8 Mar 1963 m Merrideth Wells; ord by Presb of Stirling Jan 1991 and assgnd to Stirling St Mark's and Viewfield; assgnd to Glendevon Oct 1993; assgnd to Kilmadock May 1994; Interim minister Montclair Heights Church, Montclair, USA (Reformed Church of America) 1997–98.

1987 DAVID WALLACE DAVIDSON
B 23 Jan 1930 at Glasgow, s of William Harold D. and Agnes Wallace McCrone; educ King's Park, Glasgow 1935–47; Marine, Industrial and Auto-

motive Engineering 1947–84; High School Janitor 1984–95; lic by Presb of South Argyll 3 Oct 1986; asst Kilarrow with Kilmeny 1986–87; m 17 Jul 1953 Annie McCulloch Hughes b 24 Jan 1925 d of Thomas H. and Elizabeth Adams; Children: Alan William b 24 Feb 1955; Islay Elizabeth b 28 Jan 1958; Christine Agnes b 28 Apr 1962; ord by Presb of South Argyll and assgnd to Kilarrow with Kilmeny 2 Oct 1987; app Chaplain to Islay Hospital 1 Jul 1995; loc ten Kilarrow with Kilmeny on retirement of minister 1 Oct 1995; assgnd to Kildalton and Oa, Islay 1 Jul 1996; assgnd by Presb of South Argyll 1 Oct 1998 to work throughout the area of Presb but normally in parishes on Islay and Jura.

1986 HENRY DAVID MITCHELL DUTCH
B at Montrose, educ Montorse Academy; University of Edinburgh (MTh); Journalism (*Montrose Review, Glasgow Herald*); Director of Public Relations, Strathclyde Regional Council 1974–93; ord by Presb of Dumbarton 14 Sep 1986; assgnd to Dumbarton Riverside and Bonhill; trans to Presb of Glasgow and assgnd to Glasgow Cathedral 1997; died 8 Apr 1997.

1991 JANICE MARY FARIS
B 16 Jun 1956 at Birmingham, d of Henry Foreman and Janet Marjorie Gadge; educ Sutton Coldfield Girls' High and Wellington Girls' High 1967–74; University of Southampton 1974–77 (BSc); Moray House College, Edinburgh 1977–78 (Cert Sec Ed); University of Edinburgh 1996–99 (BD); Teaching 1978–82 (Biology, Chemistry, General Science), 1990 (RE); lic by Presb of West Lothian 23 Sep 1990; asst Bathgate Boghall 1990–91; m 30 Jul 1977 Paul Samuel Alexander Faris b 14 Oct 1954 s of John Acheson F. and Mary Josephine Campbell; Children: Susan Helen b 27 Apr 1982; Richard Samuel b 22 Jul 1984; ord by Presb of West Lothian and assgnd to Armadale 6 Oct 1991; Chaplain (part-time) to St John's Hospital, Livingston 1992–97; assgnd to Kirk of Calder 1995–1997; studying for full-time ministry; Asst at Bathgate St John's (full-time) 1999.

1988 ARCHIBALD McINTYRE FERGUSON
B 19 Oct 1930 at Glasgow, s of Archiblad F. and Anne Miller Rankin; educ Hermitage Academy, Helensburgh 1935–45; Royal College of Science and Technology, Glasgow 1955–58 (HNC); University of Glasgow 1968–70 (MSc), 1974–76 (PhD); Naval Architect 1946–62 (RAF Air Crew 1952–54); Senior Academic, University of Glasgow 1962–88; lic by Presb of Dumbarton 13 Sep 1987; m 4 Apr 1958 Margaret Crawford Colquhoun b 20 Jan 1936 d of Walter C. and Agnes Clark Bowie; Children: Lorna Jane b 13 Mar 1963 m Alan Nimmo; Douglas Archibald Walter b 9 Jun 1965 m Alison Margaret Dick; ord by Presb of Dumbarton and assgnd to Dumbarton West Kirk 9 Oct 1988; assgnd to Rosneath and Craigrownie 1 Oct 1993; assgnd to Alexandria 1 Dec 1997.

1998 TIMOTHY EDWARD GEORGE FLETCHER
B 27 Sep 1947 at Winchester, s of Kenneth Ernest John F. and Georgina Hall; educ Dean Close School, Cheltenham 1961–65; Thames Valley University, London; Commercial Director (Engineering) 1989–97; Finance Manager (Charity Sector) 1998-present; lic by Presb of England 2 Nov 1997; asst London St Columba's 1997–98; m 24 Oct 1970 Sheilah Wright b 10 Jul 1950 d of Douglas W. and Gladys Moonie; Children: Andrew Douglas Kenneth b 21 Sep 1976; ord by Presb of England and assgnd to London Crown Court 27 Sep 1998.

1999 ALEXANDER GLASS
B 1 Jun 1932 at Dunbar, s of Alexander G. and Frances Robertson; educ Dunbar Grammar 1937–49; University of Edinburgh 1949–53, 1953–55 (MA), 1955–56 (DipEd); National Service 1956–58; Teaching 1958–97; lic by Presb of Ross 16 Sep 1993; asst Alness 1993–94; m 1 Aug 1959 Edith Margaret Duncan Baxter b 9 Sep 1932 d of Andrew Ritchie B. and Helen Brown Geddes; Children: Eleanor Frances b 13 Sep 1961; Muriel Edith b 8 Jun 1963 m Nicholas Brennan; Louise Alison b 29 Nov 1969; ord by Presb of Ross and assgnd to Fortrose and Rosemarkie 15 Jan 1999.

1986 CHARLOTTE McKENZIE HENDERSON
B 23 Mar 1926 at Edinburgh, d of William Fingzies Clunie and Charlotte McKenzie; educ James Gillespie's School for Girls, Edinburgh 1935–42; University of London 1950 (Cert Bibl Studies); St Colm's College, Edinburgh 1949–51 (Deaconess Studies); University of Edinburgh 1970 (CPS); Civil Service 1942–48; Deaconess 1952–64; Staff Member, St Colm's College, Edinburgh 1965–70; Asst Chaplain to Royal Edinburgh Hospital 1971–83; Chaplain (part-time) to Saughton Prison, Edinburgh 1984; lic by Presb of Edinburgh 3 Jul 1983; m 21 Jun 1983 Robert John Henderson b 5 May 1925 s of Robert James H. and Grace Amelia Wright; ord by Presb of Dunfermline and assgnd to Cairneyhill with Limekilns 12 Oct 1986; app Chaplain (part-time) to Shotts Prison 1988; app Chaplain (part-time) to Longmore Hospital 1991; Asst, Edinburgh Liberton 1991; loc ten South Leith 1995; app Chaplain (part-time) to City Hospital, Edinburgh 1995; loc ten Granton 1997; Pastoral Asst, Edinburgh Viewforth 1998; Pastoral Asst/loc ten, Leith St Thomas' Junction Road 1999; Officiating Chaplain, Army Headquarters Scotland 1999.

1984 THOMAS H HOWAT
ord by Presb of Melrose and Peebles and assgnd to Broughton, Glenholm and Kilbucho 25 Jul 1984; assgnd to Upper Tweedale 1989; died 1 Oct 1992.

1992 MARION LORRAINE KIRKWOOD HOWIE
B 26 Jul 1948 at Stevenston, d of Thomas Dillen and Rachel Smith; educ Stevenston High and Dalry High 1953–66; University of Glasgow 1967–69

(MA); Jordanhill College, Glasgow 1969–70 (CSE); University of Strathclyde 1983–84 (ACRS); Teaching (to present); lic by Presb of Ardrossan, 1991; m 19 Jul 1971 William Howie b 30 Sep 1948 s of James H. and Janet Johnston; Children: Graeme John b 13 Oct 1978; Iain Dillen b 24 Apr 1986; ord by Presb of Ardrossan and assgnd to Ardrossan Park 1 Jul 1992.

1988   ELLA DUNCAN HUTCHISON
B 18 Apr 1931 at Clydebank, d of James McLaughland and Isabella Forsyth; educ Hyndland Secondary, Glasgow 1943–49; University of Glasgow 1949–52 (MA), 1961–65 (MEd), 1974–76 (DEP); Teaching 1952–62; Educational Psychology 1972–91; admitted to Office of Reader by Presb of Glasgow 24 Nov 1980; lic by Presb of Glasgow 4 Oct 1988; m 15 Mar 1963 William McPhee Hutchison b 2 Jul 1924 s of William H. and Ann McPhee; Children: Bruce b 7 Aug 1964; Leslie b 31 Aug 1966; ord by Presb of Glasgow and assgnd to Calton Parkhead and the Dalmarnock Centre 4 Oct 1988; assgnd to Mount Zion, Quarrier's, Bridge of Weir 30 Sep 1989; ret 30 May 1993.

1991   JOHN HARLEY JENKINSON
B 16 Feb 1940 at Falkirk, s of Gordon Hardie J. and Agnes McKay Harley; educ Larbert High, 1945–56; Trinity College, London (LTCL); London College of Music (ALCM); Callendar Park College (DipCE); Moray House College, Edinburgh (DipSEN); Teaching 1966–87; Head Teacher, Special Educ 1987–93; lic by Presb of Falkirk 11 Sep 1990; m 28 Jul 1973 Morag McGuffie b 17 Feb 1950 d of James M. and Janet Sharp; Children: Fiona b 26 Mar 1976; Karen b 14 Sep 1978; ord by Presb of Falkirk and assgnd to Bo'ness Old 11 Sep 1991; assgnd to Bainsford 16 Aug 1994; assgnd to Carriden and Blackness 15 Oct 1997; Publ: *Gless Doors and Jeely Pieces* (Falkirk Library, 1984).

1999   ELIZABETH KAY
ord by Presb of Dundee and assgnd to Abernyte with Inchture and Kinnaird with Longforgan 17 Feb 1999.

1993   WILLIAM HUGH LAIDLAW
B 1 Sep 1944 at Chipping Norton, s of Stewart L. and Kathleen Myfanwy Roberts; educ Wycliffe College, Stonehouse, Glos 1954–63; University of Cambridge 1963–66 (MA); Electronic Engineering 1966–91; Lecturing 1992–present; lic by Presb of St Andrews 29 Oct 1991; m 12 Apr 1969 Patricia Elizabeth Gerono b 9 Sep 1948 d of Mickolaj G. and Elizabeth Davie; Children: Carol Judith b 1 May 1972; ord by Presb of St Andrews and assgnd to Dairsie and Kemback and Strathkinness 30 Nov 1993; ret 31 Jul 1998.

1995   ANNE MARION MACFADYEN
B 8 Sep 1933 at Glasgow, d of Dugald Brown MacNeill and Marion McIsaac; educ Hyndland

Secondary, Glasgow 1938–50; University of Glasgow 1955 (BSc), 1988 (BD); West of Scotland College of Agriculture 1955 (SDDH), FSA (Scot); Asst Experimental Officer, DOAS 1956–60; lic by Presb of Glasgow 25 Oct 1993; m 5 Mar 1960 John Dale Macfadyen b 10 Aug 1933 s of William Loudon M. and Matilda Blair Young; Children: Marion Blair b 18 Jun 1962 m Graeme MacDonald; Alan Loudon b 27 Mar 1964; Gordon Ross b 17 Jun 1967; Jane Anne b 20 Jul 1969; ord by Presb of Glasgow and assgnd to Pollokshaws 11 Jan 1995.

1994   ELIZABETH ANNE MACK
B 15 Sep 1939 at Lanark, d of William M. and Frances Sanderson Veitch; educ Lanark Grammar 1952–58; Dunfermline College of Physical Education 1958–61 (DipPE); Teaching 1961–90; RAF Officer 1970–73; lic by Presb of Dumfries and Kirkcudbright 24 Sep 1993; ord by Presb of Dumfries and Kirkcudbright and assgnd to Colvend, Southwick and Kirkbean 26 Aug 1994; assgnd to Kirkmichael and Torthorwald Apr 1999.

1985   JOHN CLUNIE MACK
ord 2 Jul 1985 and assgnd to Insch-Leslie-Premnay-Oyne; assgnd to Upper Donside 1996.

1996   COLIN McLACHLAN MAILER
B 12 Jan 1939 at Falkirk, s of William Paterson M. and Elizabeth Currie McLachlan; educ Falkirk High 1950–56; Newspaper Editor 1973–99; lic by Presb of Falkirk 19 Sep 1995; asst Grangemouth Zetland 1995–96; m 1 Dec 1962 Jessie Young Leigh Sadler b 16 Feb 1939 d of Gavin S. and Christina Robertson Bald; ord by Presb of Falkirk and assgnd to Grangemouth Kerse 3 Oct 1996; assgnd to Grangemouth Zetland 3 Oct 1999; ret from Journalism 8 Jan 1999.

1994   KENNETH IAN MALCOLM
B 19 Mar 1936 at Dundee, s of Alexander M. and Flora Easson; educ Morgan Academy, Dundee 1941–51; University of St Andrews 1989–92 (BD); Bank Manager 1956–89; lic by Presb of Dundee 19 Sep 1993; asst Dundee St Andrew's; m 22 Sep 1962 Marjory Harris b 13 Jun 1941 d of William H. and Ina Lilburn; Children: Fiona Isobel b 15 Oct 1963 m Gill; Katrina Anne b 5 Jun 1965; Ian Alexander b 13 Oct 1966; ord by Presb of Dundee during assgn at Craigiebank 23 Sep 1994; assgnd to Fowlis and Liff with Lundie and Muirhead of Liff 17 May 1995.

1994   EILEEN MANSON
B 6 Dec 1942 at Greenock, d of John Williamson and Agnes Calderhead Nimmo; educ Greenock High 1947–59; Jordanhill College, Glasgow 1959–62 (DipCEd); Teaching 1962–75; lic by Presb of Greenock 10 Oct 1993; m 24 Dec 1964 Rodger Manson b 4 Jul 1943 s of Alex M. and Agnes Hamilton; Children: Russell b 21 Jan 1969 m Jeanie Collins; Sandy b 7 Mar 1971 m Karen O'Hagan; ord by Presb of Greenock and assgnd to the Greenock Old West Kirk 30 Jun 1994.

1988 JOHN McALPINE
B 18 Dec 1925 at Cambuslang, s of Arthur M. and Isabella McLeish McBride; educ Dalmellington High and Ayr Academy 1931–43; University of Glasgow 1943–46 (BSc); Moray House College, Edinburgh 1948–49 (PGCE); Teaching 1949–56; Educational Admin 1956–63; Civil Service 1963–86; lic by Presb of Hamilton 23 Sep 1988; m 24 Mar 1951 Margaret Edwina Evans b 4 May 1927 d of William John and Elizabeth Jane E; Children: William Arthur b 29 Nov 1954 m Elaine Beatrice Hugil; Alison Jane b 4 Mar 1956; Carol Ann b 21 Sep 1967 m Alastair Marcus Hull; Pamela Margaret b 18 Oct 1969 m William Gray; ord by Presb of Hamilton and assgnd to Newarthill with Carfin 28 Sep 1988; assgnd to Newmains Coltness Memorial with Bonkle 3 Mar 1998.

1994 GEORGE McDONALD McCANN
B 15 Oct 1935 at Glasgow, s of Samuel M. and Donella McKay McDonald; educ Possil Senior Secondary, Glasgow 1947–52; University of Strathclyde (Royal College of Science and Technology) 1952–58 (BSc, PGD); Jordanhill College, Glasgow 1968 (PGCFE); Aux Ministry Training 1991–93; National Service 1958–60; British Nylon Spinners 1960–64; Lecturer and Textile Technician, Lauder Technical College 1964–69; Lecturer and Head of Dept, Scottish College of Textiles 1969–93; lic by Presb of Melrose and Peebles 22 Sep 1993; m 19 Sep 1962 Barbara Mather b 9 Mar 1933 d of William M. and Barbara Thomson; Children: Barbara b 30 Oct 1963 m Bruce Mackie; Donella b 21 Jun 1965; Ruth b 24 Aug 1970; Samuel b 24 Aug 1970, died 27 Jan 1989; ord by Presb of Melrose and Peebles and assgnd to Ashkirk with Selkirk 20 Jun 1994.

1993 MARY MUNRO
B 26 Sep 1932 at Belfast, d of Patrick Hughes and Aida Bird; educ St Louis High, Kilkeel, N Ireland 1943–47; Open University 1981–87 (BA); Office Work 1973–92; lic by Presb of Wigtown and Stranraer 13 Oct 1992; m 27 Feb 1954 Charles Munro b 27 Apr 1928 s of David M. and Elsie Mackie; Children: Ann b 29 Feb 1956 m MacLeod; David b 21 Aug 1957 m Ross; William b 29 Dec 1958, died 20 Dec 1976; Neil b 4 Jan 1961 m Newcombe; Sheila b 23 May 1963; Elspeth b 13 Jun 1969 m Nawrocki; ord by Presb of Wigtown and Stranraer and assgnd to Stoneykirk with Kirkmaiden 13 Oct 1993.

1994 ANDREW EADIE PATERSON
B 26 Sep 1953 at Dunfermline, s of William P. and Christina Fairgreave Elliot; educ Hemsworth Grammar, West Yorkshire 1964–69; Church of Scotland Aux Ministers Training Certificate; Lothian and Borders Fire Brigade 1978–; lic by Presb of Dunfermline 19 Sep 1993; ord by Presb of Dunfermline and assgnd to Dunfermline St Leonard's 8 Sep 1994.

1992 MAUREEN ELIZABETH PATERSON
B 17 May 1942 at Rosyth, d of James Linton McIlree and Dolina Gregson; educ Dunfermline High 1954–60; University of Edinburgh 1960–64 (BSc); Research Scientist 1964–67; Lecturer (part-time) 1978-present; lic by Presb of Kirkcaldy 8 Sep 1991; m 16 Jul 1966 John Maver Paterson b 6 Mar 1935 s of Thomas Maver P. and Agnes Campbell Bowden; Children: Gillian Anne b 29 Nov 1967 m Mark Davison; Lesley Seonaid b 13 Jan 1970 m David Williams; Morag Elizabeth b 22 May 1972; ord by Presb of Kirkcaldy and assgnd to Glenrothes St Ninian's 24 Jun 1992; assgnd to Kirkcaldy Pathhead 14 Sep 1993.

1992 JOOST POT
B 14 Aug 1929 at Nieuw-Lekkerland, The Netherlands, s of Johan P. and Boukje Johanna; educ RHBS Schiedam, Holland 1945–50; HTS Dordrecht, Holland (ING/BSc); Senior Engineer in Teaching Hospital, Rotterdam 1960–89; lic by Presb of Europe (in Amsterdam) 29 Sep 1991; asst Geneva (Church of Scotland) 1992; m 7 Apr 1961 Marion Davidson b 31 Dec 1928 d of James D. and Annie Robertson; ord by Presb of Europe in Rome and assgnd to Rotterdam 8 Mar 1992; also short-term interim posts in Gibraltar, Paris and Lausanne; Publ: *On Safety in Hospitals* (in Dutch).

1996 ALASTAIR EDWARD RAMAGE
B 14 Oct 1939 at Worcester Park, Surrey, s of Archibald McAllister R. and Margaret Evelyn Winifred Mathias; educ Solihull School, Warwickshire 1943–58; University of Oxford 1958–59; University of Birmingham 1959–61 (CertEd); Rose Bruford Drama School 1961–62 (ADB); University of London 1971–74 (BA); Theatre 1962–69; Teaching 1970–93; lic by Presb of Dumbarton 18 Oct 1995; asst Baldernock 1995–96; m 7 Dec 1968 Susan Ross Towill b 14 May 1947 d of Edwin T. and Catherine Ross; Children: Magnus Alastair b 26 Nov 1970; Roderick Ewan b 1 Feb 1973; ord by Presb of Dumbarton 25 Sep 1996; assgnd to Bearsden Westerton Fairlie Memorial 1 Oct 1996.

1993 THOMAS SPENCE RIDDELL
B 23 Jun 1953 at Airdrie, s of Archibald R. and Rebecca Calderwood Girdwood; educ Airdrie Academy 1965–70; University of Strathclyde 1970–74 (BSc); Chemical Engineering 1974-present; lic by Presb of West Lothian 15 Sep 1992; m 13 Aug 1977 Joyce Gladstone Kerr b 28 May 1956 d of Hamilton Reid K. and Mary Fawcett; Children: Victoria Rebecca b 18 Mar 1980; Graeme Hamilton Archibald b 8 Aug 1982; ord by Presb of West Lothian and assgnd to Livingston Old 9 Sep 1993; assgnd to Linlithgow St Michael's 20 Nov 1994.

1998 CATHERINE ANNIE McQUATER SHAW
B 26 Sep 1935 at Glasgow, d of William Carruthers and Janet Litster Ramsay; educ Bellahouston Senior Secondary, Glasgow 1947–53; University of Glasgow 1953–57 (MA); Jordanhill College,

Glasgow 1957–58 (DCE), 1976–78 (ITQ); Aux Ministry Training 1994–98; Teaching (primary) 1958–91; lic by Presb of Irvine and Kilmarnock 2 Oct 1997; asst Kilmarnock Grange 1997–98; m 18 Aug 1962 Herbert Cleveland Shaw b 18 Mar 1927 s of Victor S. and Dora Cleveland; Children: Janet Catherine b 2 Oct 1963 m Cameron Boyd; Carol Anne b 30 Aug 1965; Ian Stuart b 2 Aug 1967; Malcolm Robert b 23 Aug 1969; ord by Presb of Irvine and Kilmarnock and assgnd to Kilmarnock St John's Onthank 17 Sep 1998.

1996 JAMES HALBERT SIMPSON
B 20 Nov 1939 at Edinburgh, s of Robert McDiarmid S. and Clara Eastop Crichton; educ Leith Academy 1951–55; University of Strathclyde 1973–76 (BSc); Chief Building Services Engineer 1961–93; lic by Presb of Dundee 18 Oct 1995; m 29 Sep 1962 Helen Millar Urquhart Kinnoch b 9 Oct 1939 d of William Urquhart K. and Elspeth Dean McLean; Children: Hamish Crichton b 26 Jan 1966 m Iona McLaren; Murray Kinnoch b 24 Mar 1967 m Lesley Cameron; Fiona McLean b 12 Jul 1972 m Michael Bolik; ord by Presb of Dundee and assgnd to Dundee Trinity 4 Nov 1996; assgnd to Camperdown 11 Aug 1999.

1984 ROBERT McKENZIE SMITH
ord by Presb of Glasgow 30 Aug 1984 and assgnd to Balornock North with Barmulloch; died 30 Oct 1994.

1986 WILLIAM G TAIT
ord by Presb of Dunfermline 28 Sep 1986 and assgnd to Culross and Torryburn; assgnd to Cowdenbeath West with Mossgreen and Crossgates 1987; died 24 Dec 1993.

1996 DIANA ELIZABETH TOWNSEND
B 15 Nov 1940 at Rhyl, Wales, d of Francis William Harris and Ruth Elizabeth Nelson Chaudoir; educ Queen Elizabeth's Girls' Grammar, Barnet and Kings High, Warwick 1951–59; University of Oxford 1959–63 (MA, DEd); Teaching 1963–94; lic by Presb of Europe 24 Sep 1995; asst London Crown Court (part-time) 1995–96; m 10 Sep 1966 Malcolm Townsend b 20 Feb 1938 s of William T. and Emily Bingham; Children: Neil William b 25 Mar 1969; Christopher Francis b 7 Mar 1971; ord by Presb of Europe and assgnd to Brussels 24 Jun 1996.

1993 DAVID WANDRUM
B 16 Mar 1950 at Greenock, educ Greenock High; College of Commerce, Glasgow; Police Officer, Strathclyde Police (to present); lic by Presb of Falkirk 20 Sep 1991; asst Stenhouse and Carron 1991–92; ord by Presb of Falkirk and assgnd to Stenhouse and Carron 20 Jan 1993; assgnd to Cumbernauld Old Aug 1995; assgnd to Bonnybridge St Helen's Oct 1998.

1993 JEAN STEWART WATSON
B 23 Jul 1928 at Kirkcowan, d of Louis Herbert W. and Elizabeth Mitchell Stewart; educ Hamilton Academy and Mary Erskine School, Edinburgh 1940–46; University of Edinburgh 1946–50 (MA); Moray House College, Edinburgh 1950–51; Teaching 1951–89 (Asst Rector, Dollar Academy 1979–89); Aux Ministry Training Course 1989–91; lic by Presb of Stirling 25 Mar 1992; asst Menstrie 1992; assgnd to Alva 10 Jun 1993; ord by Presb of Stirling 16 Sep 1993; assgnd to Dollar 1 Mar 1998.

1990 MARY DALLAS WILSON
B 11 May 1933 at Southampton, Ontario, Canada, d of George Hepburn Nicol and Mary Gibson Dallas; educ Buckhaven High 1946–51; Edinburgh Southern Group Nursing School 1952–55 (RGN); Royal Maternity Hospital, Glasgow 1955–56 (SCM); Liverpool School of Medicine 1963 (Dip Tropical Nursing); Church of Scotland Cert for Aux Ministry; Nursing 1958–68; lic by Presb of Lothian 22 Oct 1989; asst Haddington St Mary's 1989–90; m 2 Nov 1968 John Miller Wilson b 28 Oct 1939 s of John Russell W. and Isabella Carlaw Duncan Robertson; Children: John Nicol b 13 Apr 1973; Alison Mary Isabella b 17 Mar 1975; ord by Presb of Lothian and assgnd to Bolton and Saltoun with Humbie with Yester 20 Sep 1990; assgnd to pulpit supply throughout Presb of Sutherland Nov 1998.

1986 ROBERT (ROY) WILSON
B 19 Nov 1929 at Glasgow, s of John W. and Wilhelmina Crawford Allan; educ Glasgow Academy 1935–45; Glasgow School of Art; Royal Technical College, Glasgow (DA, ARIBA, ARIAS); Architect 1945–96 (Senior Partner 1978–96); lic by Presb of Dumbarton, Sep 1985; m (1) 19 Feb 1958 Sheila MacGregor Watt b 5 Jun 1927, died 17 Oct 1994, d of Watt and Bell; Children: Robert Douglas b 23 Mar 1964 m Lesley Fleming; Lyndsey Catherine b 17 Oct 1968 m Alexander Hamilton; m (2) 22 Aug 1996 Christina Ogilvie Alexander b 15 Dec 1930 d of McFadyen and Jarvie; ord by Presb of Dumbarton and assgnd to Renton Trinity and to Clerk of Dumbarton Presb, Sep 1986; assgnd to Bearsden North Sep 1987 and continued assgn with Presb Clerk; assgnd to Vale of Leven Oct 1996; assgnd to Clydebank Nov 1997.

1997 JAMES ZAMBONINI
B 2 Jun 1952 at Hamilton, s of James Z. and Isabella McSherry; educ Hassenbrook High, Essex and Danforth Technical College, Toronto, Canada 1957–67; Sales Manager (to present); lic by Presb of Hamilton 18 Oct 1995; m 30 Jul 1971 Sheena Reid b 13 Aug 1947 d of Alexander R. and Margaret Rankin; Children: Caroline b 13 Apr 1973; Rosa b 19 Dec 1981; ord by Presb of Hamilton and assgnd to Shotts Calderhead Erskine 4 May 1997.

COMMUNITY MINISTERS

In alphabetical order

1986 WILLIAM JOHN AINSLIE
ord by Presb of Glasgow and introd as Community minister at Easterhouse 4 Jun 1986; ret 30 Sep 1991.

1993 FRANCIS DENTON BARDGETT
dem from Strathy and Halladale and introd as Community minister, Orkney 1 Sep 1993; dem to take up app as Secretary-Depute, Dept of National Mission 20 Oct 1997.

1990 ALISON HELEN BURNSIDE
ord by Presb of Hamilton and introd as Community minister at Motherwell North and Motherwell St Andrew's; ind to Kilmarnock St Ninian's Bellfield 21 Sep 1995.

1980 MAGNUS CHEYNE
(FES X, 407), dem from Sandsting and Aithsting 31 Dec 1979; app Community minister for oil workers and their families, Shetland 1980; Assoc at Burra with Tingwall and at Fetlar with Yell 1984; app Community minister, Shetland 1988; ret 31 May 1996.

1996 JAMES MORTON COWIE
B 17 Jul 1948 at Aberdeen, s of Arthur C. and Margaret Grey Morton; educ Aberdeen Academy 1960–66; University of Aberdeen 1970–74 (BD); United Theological Seminary, New Brighton, USA 1974–75 (Family Studies); University of Edinburgh 1975–76 (CCE); Accountancy 1966–70; lic by Presb of Aberdeen 30 Jun 1976; asstshp Crieff St Michael's and St Ninian's 1976–78; m 18 Jul 1972 Margaret Davidson b 10 Sep 1948 d of Robert D. and Marion Brebber; Children: Gayla b 28 Dec 1978; Calvin b 25 Sep 1980; ord by Presb of Perth during assistantship at Crieff St Michael's and St Ninian's 4 May 1977; ind to Fordyce 5 Oct 1978; trans to Hawick Burnfoot 17 May 1984; introd as Community minister at Edinburgh Craigmillar and app Chaplain to Thistle Foundation 1 Sep 1996.

1982 MARGARET FORSYTH CURRIE
res as Asst at Renfrew Old and introd as Community minister at Greenock Cartsdyke 23 Mar 1982; ind to Airdrie St Columba's 17 Dec 1987.

1984 ROBERT CURRIE
(FES X, 158, 215), dem from Glasgow Dowanhill and introd as Community minister at Glasgow Partick 25 Jun 1984; ret 31 Dec 1989; Chaplain

(part-time) to Queen Mother's Hospital, Glasgow 1978–94; app Hon Assoc at Paisley Abbey Jan 1990; d Gillian m Brian Thomson; Publ: Reviews for *Coracle* (Iona Community) and other publs; *Pastoral Guidelines on Handling Cot Deaths* (OUP) for Committee on Aids to Worship.

1973 RONALD FERGUSON
(FES X, 158), ord by Presb of Glasgow during assistantship at Easterhouse St George's and St Peter's 14 Apr 1972; app Community minister in Easterhouse 1 Dec 1973; res 1979; Exchange minister with United Church of Canada 1979–80; app Deputy Warden, Iona Abbey 1 Sep 1980.

1982 IAN COLIN FRASER
ord by Presb of Greenock and introd as Community minister at Greenock Cartsdyke, Jul 1982; ind to Glasgow St Luke's and St Andrew's 22 Feb 1995.

1980 ROBERT H KERR
ord by Presb of Edinburgh during assistantship at Craigsbank 1979; introd as Community minister at Edinburgh Corstorphine 1980; dem 31 May 1983 and emigrated to Canada.

1980 JOHN T LAMB
introd as Community minister at Stirling St Ninians Old 3 Sep 1980; res from app 1 Aug 1995.

1978 MAUDEEN I MACDOUGALL
ord by Presb of West Lothian and ind to Livingston New Town as Community minister 4 Oct 1978; ind to Dundee Meadowside St Paul's 25 Sep 1984.

1982 AILSA GAIL MACLEAN
ord by Presb of Edinburgh during assistantship at Fairmilehead 8 May 1979; loc ten Currie Kirk 1 Oct 1981; introd as Community minister at Cumbernauld Condorrat 28 May 1982; app Asst Warden at Carberry Tower 1 Aug 1984.

1984 ALEXANDER SCOTT MARSHALL
ord by Presb of Edinburgh and introd as Community minister at Drylaw, Muirhouse and The Old Kirk 30 Aug 1984; ind to Pardovan Kingscavil and Winchburgh 30 Jun 1998.

1979 ALAN DOUGLAS McDONALD
ord by Presb of Edinburgh and introd as Community minister at Drylaw, Muirhouse and the Old Kirk 25 Oct 1979; ind to Aberdeen Holburn Central 28 Jul 1983.

1976   MARY OLIVER McKENZIE
ord by Presb of Glasgow and introd as Assoc
Community minister, Drumchapel 15 Oct 1976;
introd as Community minister, Drumchapel 19 Jun
1980; ind to Edinburgh Richmond Craigmillar 12
Jun 1987.

1984   MARGARET GILCHRIST McLEAN
B 21 Aug 1921 at Glasgow, d of Neil Smith M. and
Elizabeth Kilday Herd; educ Hyndland Secondary,
Glasgow 1932–37; St Colm's College, Edinburgh
1947–49; University of Glasgow 1972–76 (BD);
Jordanhill College, Glasgow 1976–77; Deaconess,
Glasgow Partick St Bride's 1950–53; Field Sec,
Scottish Sunday School Union for Christian
Education 1953–72; lic by Presb of Glasgow 30
Jun 1977; asstshp Greenock St Margaret's 1949–
50; ord by Presb of Lorn and Mull and introd as
Assoc to Isle of Mull parishes 3 Oct 1978; introd
as Community minister, Annandale and Eskdale
23 Aug 1984; ret 23 Aug 1991.

1980   GORDON OLIVER
ord by Presb of Hamilton during assistantship at
Greenhills Sep 1979; introd as Community minister
at Hamilton Trinity 23 Jun 1980; ind to Alyth 24
Oct 1985.

1998   JOHN ROBERT OSBECK
B 15 Sep 1946 at Glasgow, s of John O. and
Davina Winton; educ Whitehill Secondary, Glasgow
1951–66; University of Glasgow 1973–78 (BD);
Nursing 1967–73; lic by Presb of Glasgow 29 Jun
1978; asstshp Dyce 1978–81; m 18 Sep 1976
Johanna Stewart b 10 Dec 1949 d of Thomas S.

and Margaret Black; Children: Deborah Stewart b
31 May 1979; ord by Presb of Aberdeen during
assistantship at Dyce 3 Jul 1979; ind to Enzie with
Rathven 9 May 1981; ind to Aberdeen St John's
Church for Deaf People 1 Sep 1991; app Community minister for ministry among Deaf People in
Aberdeen and North of Scotland 1 Jan 1998.

1981   ALASTAIR OSBORNE
(FES X, 130), res from term app at Paisley St
Ninian's Ferguslie Park 30 Sep 1980; introd as
Community minister at Ayr St Quivox 1 Sep 1981;
res from app 10 Mar 1989.

1995   DOUGLAS STUART PATERSON
dem from Cumbernauld St Mungo's and introd as
Community minister, Kilwinning 26 Sep 1995; ind
to Kilwinning Mansefield Trinity 21 Apr 1999.

1973   ARCHIBALD RUSSELL
(FES IX, 17; X, 11, 149, 177, 218), trans from
Glasgow Anderston and introd as Community
minister at Drumchapel 31 Jan 1973; ind to Duror
and Glencoe 7 Sep 1979; Editor of *Drumchapel
News* 1974–76.

1992   ROBERT CAMBRIDGE SYMINGTON
(FES X, 19, 250), dem from Killearn and introd as
Community minister, Lorn and Mull 5 May 1992;
ret 5 Aug 1997.

1982   PETER HEATLIE WELSH
ord and introd as Community minister at Glasgow
Easterhouse 3 Sep 1982; res from app 31 Aug
1985.

CHAPLAINS TO FORCES

In alphabetical order

1997 CLIFFORD ROBERT ACKLAM
B 9 Nov 1962 at Edinburgh, s of Robert A. and Elizabeth Birnie Henderson; educ Penicuik High 1975–81; Capernwray Bible School 1986–87; Telford College, Edinburgh 1987–88 (SVEC PECS); University of St Andrews 1990–94 (BD); University of Edinburgh 1994–95 (MTh); Physical Recreation 1988–90; lic by Presb of Edinburgh, Nov 1995; asstshp Falkirk Old and St Modan's 1995–97; m 30 Sep 1995 Ann Marie Boyle b 17 May 1963 d of Thomas B. and Kathleen Flynn; ord by Presb of Falkirk during assistantship at Falkirk Old and St Modan's 5 Jun 1997; app by RAChD 16 Jun 1997.

1993 JAMES WILLIAM AITCHISON
B 5 Aug 1958 at Kinghorn, s of James A. and Mary Patterson Allan; educ Seleter Secondary, Singapore, Forres Academy and Kirkcaldy High 1970–76; Glasgow Bible Training Institute 1981–84 (DipTheol); University of Aberdeen 1987–91 (BD); lic by Presb of Aberdeen 27 Jun 1991; asstshp Aberdeen Dyce 1991–93; m 31 Mar 1984 Marion Elizabeth Gillon b 12 May 1960 d of Alexander G. and Alexandra Cochrane; Children: Jamie Alexander b 3 Jan 1985; David Jonathan b 19 Aug 1986; Peter John Douglas b 26 Feb 1989; ord by Presb of Aberdeen and app by RAChD 21 Jan 1993.

1963 EUSTACE ANNESLEY
ord and ind to Cranshaw Presb Church, N Ireland 7 Jul 1957; Chaplain to HM Forces 1963–86; Deputy Asst Chaplain General, Dusseldorf 1977–80; Asst Chaplain General Scotland 1981–86; ind to Langbank 12 Mar 1986.

1996 IAIN CAMERON BARCLAY
ord by Presb of Edinburgh and app by RAChD, 1976; ind to Edinburgh New Restalrig 31 May 1979.

1965 DONALD BEATON
(FES X, 133, 444), dem from Greenock Gaelic on app by RAChD 1 Mar 1965; ind to Kilmuir and Stenscholl 17 Feb 1982.

1969 JOHN McLACHLAN BLACK
(FES X, 318, 444), dem from Dunnichen, Letham and Kirkden on app by RAF Chaplains' Branch 19 Oct 1969; ind to Coatbridge Blairhill Dundyvan 21 Mar 1991.

1977 STEPHEN ALASTAIR BLAKEY
ord by Presb of St Andrews and app by RAChD 28 Aug 1977; ret 31 Aug 1993 to take up app with Assoc of Vineyard Churches.

1955 ALEXANDER GLEN BOWIE
(FES X, 444), ord by Presb of Ardrossan 30 Dec 1954 and app by RAF Chaplains' Branch 7 Jan 1955; Principal Chaplain to RAF 1980–84; ret 22 Oct 1984; Hon Chaplain to the Queen 1980–84; Hon Chaplain, Royal Scottish Corp 1981-; CBE 1984; w Mary died 26 Jul 1991; d Alexandra m Cox; Publ: Editor *Scottish Forces Bulletin* 1986–96.

1954 WILLIAM HENRY GREENWAY BRISTOW
(FES IX, 150, 786; X, 444), ret from RAChD 30 Sep 1970; app teacher (English) Harlaw Academy, Aberdeen 18 Aug 1974; app Head teacher, Meadowns School, Campbeltown 4 Feb 1979; ret 1 Mar 1991; app Chaplain (part-time) to Campbeltown Hospital 1 Apr 1990; Addl children: Wendy b 6 Apr 1954; d Mairi m Johnstone.

1993 SCOTT JAMES BROWN
B 16 May 1968 at Bellshill, s of James B. and Margaret Bell Bryson; educ Hamilton Grammar 1980–85; Bell College of Technology, Hamilton 1985–88 (HND); University of Aberdeen 1988–92 (BD); lic by Presb of Hamilton, Jun 1992; asstshp Falkirk St Andrew's West 1992–93; ord by Presb of Hamilton and app by Royal Naval Chaplaincy Service 13 Apr 1993; Chaplain to Moderator of General Assembly 1999–2000.

1963 PETER BROWN
(FES IX, 786; X, 229, 270, 444), dem from Ballingry on app by Royal Naval Chaplaincy Service 29 Jun 1963; res 20 May 1981 and app as Asst at Banchory-Ternan East with Durris; ind to Kilfinan with Kyles 8 Apr 1984.

1985 ROBERT NEIL CAMERON
B 3 Jul 1940 at Liverpool, s of Kenedy C. and Eva Fleming; educ Royal Belfast Academical Institution 1951–58; Assembly's College, Belfast 1971–75; Trainee Accountant 1958–61; employment: various (inc family business) 1961–71; lic by Presb of Belfast South 8 Jun 1975; asstshp Belfast St John's Presb Church 1975–77; m 3 Aug 1965 Wilhelmina Ethel Patterson b 12 Jul 1940 d of Samuel Herbert P. and Isobel Graham; Children: Fiona Elizabeth

b 23 Mar 1967 m Weir; Graham Fleming Neil b 9 Dec 1968; ord by Presb of Belfast East during assistantship at St John's 11 Jan 1976; ind to Millisle and Ballycopeland Presb Church 22 Mar 1977; app by RAChD 1 Nov 1979; app Community Chaplain, Rheindahlen Area 1 Nov 1985.

1999   DANIEL CONNOLLY
B 21 Apr 1955 at Glasgow, s of Daniel and Mary C; educ St Thomas Aquinas, Glasgow 1967–71; University of Edinburgh 1992–94 (BD); Scottish Baptist College 1986–88 (DipMin); Glasgow Bible College 1979–81 (DipTh, CRT); Dental Technician 1971–73; Credit Controller 1973–79; lic by Scottish Baptist Union, 1983; m 25 Feb 1978 Karen Dawn Garrett b 26 Jun 1956 d of John and Joyce G; Children: Nicola Louise b 2 May 1979; Leigh Allan b 3 Aug 1981; ord by Scottish Baptist Union and ind to Shevington Moor, Jun 1983; admitted by General Assembly and ind to Kirkcaldy Viewforth with Thornton 10 Jan 1995; dem 14 Feb 1999 on app by RAChD.

1994   DAVID GEORGE COULTER
B 29 Dec 1957 at Belfast, s of George Albert C. and Elizabeth Nulty; educ Regent House School, Newtownards, Co Down, N Ireland 1962–76; Queen's University, Belfast 1976–80 (BA); University of St Andrews 1985–88 (BD); University of Edinburgh 1992–97 (PhD); Army Officer 1980–85; lic by Presb of St Andrews 4 Jul 1988; asstshp St Andrews Hope Park 1988–89; m 21 Aug 1981 Grace Frances Woods b 10 May 1958 d of Alexander Jamison W. and Frances Mary Haslett; Children: Andrew David b 2 Oct 1990; Thomas Alexander b 15 Jun 1993; ord by Presb of St Andrews and app by RAChD 2 Apr 1989; app Chaplain to Loretto School, Musselburgh 20 Mar 1992; app by RAChD 21 Mar 1994.

1988   GORDON THOMAS CRAIG
B 16 Sep 1959 at Glasgow, s of John C. and Strachan; educ Castlehead High, Paisley and Paisley Grammar 1964–77; University of Glasgow 1981–87 (BD, DipMin); Trainee Site Manager 1977–81; lic by Presb of Paisley 29 Jun 1987; asstshp Paisley Martyrs 1987–88; m 7 Jul 1984 Rhona McLennan b 19 May 1963 d of Louis M. and Marion Jamieson; Children: Gemma b 22 Jan 1991; Lauren b 27 Sep 1993; Mark b 17 Aug 1996; ord by Presb of Paisley and app by RAChD 5 Apr 1988.

1974   GORDON WILLIAM CRAIG
(FES X, 296, 444), dem from St Monans on app by Royal Naval Chaplaincy Service 9 Sep 1974; ret from RN 31 Oct 1999; College of St Mark and St John, Plymouth 1978–79 (PGCE); MBE; d Sally m Sean Witheford.

1968   KEITH DALLAS CROZER
(FES X, 257, 444), dem from Aberuthven with Gask 7 Oct 1968 on app by RAChD; ret 1981; died 7 Sep 1995.

1979   J R DAILLY
ord 1979 and app by RAChD.

1982   THOMAS ALEXANDER DAVIDSON KELLY
dem from Kilberry with Tarbert on app by RAChD 5 Jul 1982; ind to Govan Old 22 Jun 1989.

1976   NORMAN WALKER DRUMMOND
ord by Presb of Greenock and app by RAChD 15 Aug 1976; app Chaplain to Fettes College, Edinburgh 1982.

1982   MICHAEL STANLEY EDWARDS
ord by Presb of Glasgow and app by RAF Chaplains' Branch 26 Apr 1982; introd as Assoc at Govan Old 7 Feb 1996.

1991   NEIL NORMAN GARDNER
ord by Presb of Dumbarton and app by RAChD 29 May 1991; ind to Alyth 23 Sep 1998.

1972   BEVERLY GILBERT DOUGLAS DAVIDSON GAULD
(FES X, 445), ord by Presb of Edinburgh and app by RAChD 31 Dec 1972; ind to Carnwath 27 Jun 1978.

1972   JAMES HAMILTON
(FES X, 445), app by RAChD 6 Jun 1972; ind to Bo'ness St Andrew's 26 May 1976.

1961   JAMES HARKNESS
(FES X, 445), app Depute Chaplain General to HM Forces 1 Nov 1984; app Chaplain General 1 Jan 1987; ret 9 Apr 1995; Moderator of General Assembly 1995–96; QHC 31 Dec 1982; Chaplain in Ordinary to the Queen from 1996; Dean of the Chapel Royal 1996; OBE 1978; CB 1993; s Paul m Jaqueline Foster.

1961   BRUCE JOHN LAIRD HAY
(FES X, 226, 445), dem from Lochgilphead 17 Sep 1961 to take up app with RAChD; ind to Makerstoun with Smailholm with Stichill, Hume and Nenthorn 1 Nov 1983.

1968   DAVID FERGUSON HUIE
(FES X, 420, 446), res from service with Overseas Council in Israel on app by Royal Naval Chaplaincy Service 18 Jun 1968; app locum at Rome St Andrew's 28 Mar 1990.

1961   JOSEPH ROSS INGRAM
(FES IX, 329; X, 194, 446), dem from Greengairs to take up app with RAF Chaplains' Branch 26 Apr 1961; ret 26 Apr 1977; s Bruce m Christine; s Scott m Nina; s Douglas m Annie; Publ: *Whither Wings?* (Canon, 1998).

1996   ANDREW JOHN JOLLY
B 14 Apr 1956 at Aberdeen, s of John J. and Elizabeth Walker Cruikshank; educ Hillhead High, Glasgow 1968–73; University of Glasgow 1977–82 (BD, CMin); Electrical Engineering 1973–75;

Product Design 1975–76; lic by Presb of Glasgow 28 Jun 1982; asstshp Glasgow Knightswood St Margaret's 1982–84; m 2 Oct 1989 Christine Susan Wheeler Hobbins b 3 Dec 1956 d of Kenneth Albert Wheeler H. and Glynis; Children: Sarah Christine b 10 Oct 1990; Alexander Jane b 22 Mar 1993; ord by Presb of Glasgow during assistantship at St Margaret's 21 Apr 1983; app by RAChD 1 Jun 1984; ind to Fern Careston Menmuir with Oathlaw Tannadice 19 Oct 1989; dem on app by RAF Chaplains' Branch 8 Feb 1996.

1971 WILLIAM OWEN JONES
(FES X, 446), app by RAChD 1 Mar 1965 during service with Presb Church of England; admitted by General Assembly 1971 and continued with RAChD.

1977 DONALD KEITH
(FES IX, 123), dem from Elderslie Kirk on app by Royal Naval Chaplaincy Service 14 Apr 1977; res from app 14 Apr 1981 and ind to Glasgow Mosspark 7 Jun 1981; dem 14 May 1984 and re-app by RNCS; Addl children: Donald Angus Alexander b 9 Jun 1975.

1984 ANGUS KERR
app by RAChD 1 Jun 1984; ind to Kirkcaldy View-forth 1 May 1987.

1993 DAVID VANCE FOX KINGSTON
B 1 Jan 1964 at Edinburgh, s of Dennis Sidney K. and Mary Vance Fox Smith; educ Dalkeith High 1976–81; University of St Andrews 1986–91 (BD, DipPT); Civil Service 1982–86; lic by Presb of Lothian 1 Aug 1991; asstshp Hamilton Old 1991–93; ord by Presb of Hamilton and app by RAChD 18 Feb 1993.

1977 PAUL STEPHEN KIRBY
ord by Presb of England during assistantship at St Columba's, Pont Street 18 Jan 1976; app by RAF Chaplains' Branch 15 May 1977; res and ind to Jersey St Columba's 6 Jul 1982.

1980 ROBERT ALAN KNOX
(FES X, 120, 221, 446), dem from Helensburgh St Bride's 17 Feb 1980 on app by RAChD; ind to Mallaig and The Small Isles 20 Mar 1987.

1966 JAMES BARBOUR LAWSON
(FES X, 446), app by RAChD 11 Oct 1966; ret on app as Officer-in-Charge, Simpson House, Edinburgh Sep 1982.

1970 JOHN CHRISTOPHER LEDGARD
Church of Scotland and Free Churches Chaplain to RAF 1970–86; Methodist minister, Whitby 1986–89.

1970 PETER THOMAS MACFARLANE
(FES X, 446), ord by Presb of Edinburgh 26 Apr 1970 and app by RAChD; Open University 1978–81 (BA); Central School of Religion 1985–87 (ThD); ret 7 Aug 1994.

1998 SEORAS LACHIE MACKENZIE
B 10 Mar 1963 at Helensburgh, s of Hector Lachie M. and Rebecca Mary Ross; educ Inverness High School 1975–79; Bible Training Institute, Glasgow 1984–87; University of Aberdeen 1990–95 (BD, DipMin); lic by Presb of Inverness 31 Aug 1995; asstshp New Deer St Kane's 1995–96; m 11 Jun 1983 Elizabeth Riddle b 21 Oct 1959 d of Murdoch R. and Agnes MacKechnie MacQueen; ord by Presb of Buchan and introd as Assoc at Banff with King Edward 1 May 1996; res 14 Jun 1998 on app by RAChD.

1979 JOHN FORBES MACKIE
ord by Presb of Edinburgh and app by Royal Naval Chaplaincy Service 22 Apr 1979; ind to Corby St Andrew's 7 Jul 1983.

1928 KENNETH MACKINTOSH
(FES VIII, 732; IX, 740, 791; X, 447), ret from RAChD 15 Aug 1947; Teaching (English, RE) 1951–68; died 4 Oct 1985.

1990 JAMES BISHOP MACLEAN
dem from Barra 8 May 1990 to take up app with RAChD; ind to Eddleston with Peebles Old 14 Nov 1997.

1992 RODERICK N MACLEOD
ord by Presb of Gordon and app Asst at Skene 1 Jun 1986; app by RAChD 1992.

1996 CHARLES ANGUS MACLEOD
B 5 Jan 1963 at Edinburgh, s of Norman M. and Sheila Mary Gorrie; educ Strathallan School, Forgandenny 1975–80; University of St Andrews 1981–85 (MA), 1991–94 (BD); University of Cambridge 1986–87 (PGCE); Advertising and Marketing 1987–89; Teaching 1989–91; lic by Presb of Lochcarron and Skye, Sep 1994; asstshp Bethesda Presb Church, Aberdeen, N Carolina 1994–95; Glasgow Newlands South 1995–96; ord by Presb of Glasgow and app by RAChD, Oct 1996;

1998 RODERICK ALEXANDER RANDLE MACLEOD
B 16 Feb 1965 at Edinburgh, s of Donald Alexander M. and Rosemary Lillian Abel Randle; educ Fettes College, Edinburgh 1978–83; University of Cambridge 1984–87 (BA); University of Edinburgh 1988–89 (MBA); University of St Andrews 1989–92 (BD); 2 Lt Queen's Own Highlanders 1984; Schoolmaster, Loretto School, Edinburgh 1987–88; Labourer, MacLeod Estates, Dunvegan 1988; lic by Presb of Lochcarron and Skye 27 Nov 1992; asstshp Portree 1992–93; m 15 Oct 1996 Annice Macdonald b 5 Jan 1967 d of Alastair Macdonald and Peggy Mackenzie; Children: Christina Margaret b 20 Jan 1998; ord and ind to Bracadale 28 Jan 1994; dem on app by Royal Naval Chaplaincy Service 20 Feb 1998.

1962 CHARLES CECIL MACNEILL
(FES X, 447), ord by Presb of Glasgow 4 Jun 1962 and app by RAF Chaplains' Branch 6 Jun 1962; introd to Brussels St Andrew's 9 May 1984.

1960 ADAM ALEXANDER MACPHERSON
(FES IX, 449; X, 265), ret from Kilmadock West 8 Apr 1958; app Officiating Chaplain to Forces, Aldershot District 2 Feb 1960; ret 1 Sep 1970; died 7 Mar 1987.

1987 PHILIP LUDWIK MAJCHER
B 23 Sep 1953 at Perth, s of Joseph M. and Minnie; educ Perth High 1966–72; University of St Andrews 1973–78 (BD), University of Edinburgh 1978–80; lic by Presb of Perth 6 Jan 1980; asstshp Linlithgow St Michael's 1980–82; m 4 Aug 1979 Linda Elizabeth Clare b 28 Apr 1955 d of Raymond C. and Asta Elizabeth Nimmerfeldt; Children: Sarah Jane Elizabeth b 9 Nov 1982; Christopher Philip Stuart b 8 Jul 1984; Iain Malcolm Thomas b 21 Mar 1987; ord and ind to Kirkcowan with Wigtown 23 Jun 1982; dem on app by RAChD 7 Sep 1987; app Staff Chaplain 5 Aug 1993; app Senior Chaplain 17 Apr 1996.

1987 ROBERT JAMES MALLOCH
ord by Presb of Hamilton and app by RAChD 1 Apr 1987; ind to Duror with Glencoe St Munda's 1 May 1991.

1989 ANTHONY MYLES MARTIN
B 14 Sep 1957 at Waipawa, New Zealand, s of David Christopher M. and Sybil Bertha West; educ Hastings Boys' High, Hawkes Bay, NZ 1970–74; Massey University 1976–78 (BA); Otago University 1979–82 (BD); Fuller Theological Seminary 1999 (DMin); Aerial Navigating; Aerial Mapping; lic by Presb of Hawkes Bay (Presb Church of NZ), Nov 1982; asstshp North Invercargill Presb Church, NZ 1982–85; m 17 Jan 1981 Katherine Mary Craig b 17 Apr 1958 d of Wilfred James Gunn C. and Nancy Craig; Children: David James b 9 Jul 1984; Sarah Elizabeth b 16 Dec 1985; Rachel Mary b 20 May 1988; Jonathan Andrew b 25 Nov 1991; ord by Southland Presb, Presb Church of NZ and introd as Asst, North Invercargill 12 Dec 1982; introd as Assoc at North Invercargill 5 Feb 1985; ind to Te Anau, Mossburn 6 May 1986; app by RAChD (Parachute Regiment) 3 Jul 1989; app Chaplain to Army Training Regiment, Glencorse 12 Jun 1993; app Senior Chaplain 4 May 1995; app Chaplain NATO ARRC 4 Feb 2000; Publ: *Christian Foundation Seminar* (Eagle Publ, 1991); *Managing Stress* (Ministry of Defence, 1992); *Coping with Disaster* (Ministry of Defence, 1994); Doctorate: 'Pastoral care strategy for British Army chaplains ministering to soldiers suffering crisis and trauma'.

1986 ROBERT McCRUM
dem from Auchtergaven and Moneydie on app by Royal Naval Chaplaincy Service 20 Oct 1986; res and ind to Forfar Lowson Memorial 5 Aug 1992.

1995 ALEN JOHN RONALD McCULLOCH
B 4 Feb 1963 at Helensburgh, s of Ian Norman M. and Vera Levina Viljoen; educ Glasgow Academy 1973–80; University of St Andrews 1980–85 (MA); University of Edinburgh 1985–88 (BD); lic by Presb of Dumbarton 9 Oct 1988; asstshp Edinburgh Cluny 1988–89; m 19 Mar 1988 Sheena Margaret Una MacKay b 7 Aug 1964 d of Duncan M. and Mary Ann MacDonald; Children: Eilidh Kathleen Ann b 24 Dec 1988; Mairi Elizabeth Vera b 4 Jan 1991; Rachel Elsie Margaret b 24 May 1999; ord and ind to Kilmuir and Stenscholl 16 Feb 1990; dem 11 Jun 1995 on app by RAChD (Chaplain to 1 RHF, Fallingbostel, Germany 1995–98; Chaplain to 1 BW, Fort George, Inverness from 1998).

1988 IAIN McFADZEAN
B 18 May 1962 at Johnstone, s of Melville M. and Annie McLeish; educ Castlehead High, Paisley 1974–78; Reid Kerr College, 1978–80; University of Glasgow 1982–86 (BD), 1986–88 (MA); Chemical Technician 1978–82; lic by Presb of Paisley 7 Aug 1988; asstshp Beith High 1988–89; m 27 Aug 1982 Joy Marion Smart b 13 Sep 1962 d of Angus S. and Marion Miller; Children: Lisa Claire b 12 Mar 1984; Mark Iain b 6 Aug 1988; Johanna Louise b 7 Jan 1994; Lindsay Joy b 4 Oct 1996; ord by Presb of Ardrossan and app by RAF Chaplains' Branch 15 Apr 1988; trans to Royal Naval Chaplaincy Service Jul 1999.

1961 HAMISH NORMAN MACKENZIE McINTOSH
(FES IX, 247, 342; X, 105, 118, 447), dem from Old Cumnock St Ninian's on app by RAF Chaplains' Branch 22 Mar 1961; ind to Fintry 25 Nov 1982.

1970 PETER MEAGER
(FES X, 447), ord by Presb of Edinburgh and app by RAChD 16 Dec 1970; ind to Elie with Kilconquhar and Colinsburgh 17 Dec 1986.

1983 JOHN GROOM MILLER
ord by Presb of Irvine and Kilmarnock and app by RAF Chaplains' Branch 17 Jun 1983; ind to Sandsting and Aithsting with Walls 5 Nov 1988.

1984 PETER WATSON MILLS
B 9 Feb 1955 at Arbroath, s of Peter Watson M. and Janet Lonsdale; educ Arbroath High 1967–73; University of Aberdeen 1978–83 (BD, CPS); Police Constable 1974–78; lic by Presb of Aberdeen 30 Nov 1983; asstshp Montrose Melville South with Inchbrayock 1983–84; m 11 Jul 1979 Sheila Anderson b 11 Jul 1959 d of George Mark A. and Sheila McAteer; Children; Katie b 23 Oct 1982; Alison b 12 Jan 1984; ord by Presb of Angus 22 Apr 1984; and app by RAF Chaplains' Branch 13 May 1984; app Staff Chaplain, Chaplaincy Service 5 Jan 1998.

1953 PATRICK JOHNSTON MOFFETT
(FES IX, 14, 792; X, 447), dem from Edinburgh Gilmerton to take up app with Royal Naval Chaplaincy Service 4 Jun 1953; ret 1977; died 25 Feb 1986.

1978 ALEXANDER WILLIAM MUNRO
ord by Presb of Aberdeen and app by RAF Chaplains' Branch 16 Apr 1978; ret from RAF 11 Jun 1994; app Chaplain and Head of Religious Studies, The Licensed Victuallers' School, Ascot 1 Apr 1994.

1979 JOHN ALASTAIR HILTON MURDOCH
ord by Presb of Edinburgh and app by RAChD 17 Jun 1979; app Chaplain to Strathallan School 1 Sep 1982; app by RAChD 1 Sep 1983; app Chaplain to Fettes College 1 Sep 1986.

1999 JOHN MURNING
B 14 Nov 1958 at Airdrie, s of Richard M. and Janet Tweedie Saunders Hill; educ Airdrie Academy 1970–74; University of Aberdeen 1982–86 (BD); University of Edinburgh 1986–87 (CPS); Engineering 1975–79; Civil Service 1980–82; lic by Presb of Hamilton 27 Aug 1987; asstshp Lanark St Nicholas' 1987–88; m 7 Jul 1988 Linda Mary Mason McGregor b 2 Sep 1964 d of Ian M. and June Mason; Children: Sally Margaret b 20 Mar 1992; Jack Richard b 27 Jun 1994; ord and ind to Glasgow New Cathcart 31 Aug 1988; dem 13 Jun 1999 on app by RAChD.

1971 BRUCE FERGUSON NEILL
(FES X, 274, 447), dem from Dunfermline Townhill to take up app with Royal Naval Chaplaincy Service 27 Dec 1971; ind to Maxton and Mertoun with St Boswells 26 Jan 1996.

1992 ALISON ESTHER PHYLLIS NORMAN
B 11 Nov 1961 at Dundee, d of Gordon Rankine N. and Mary Watt Morrice; educ Harris Academy, Dundee 1973–79; University of Aberdeen 1979–82 (MA); University of St Andrews 1982–86 (BD); lic by Presb of Hamilton 26 Jun 1986; asstshp Hamilton Old 1985–87; ord by Presb of Hamilton during assistantship at Hamilton Old 1 Mar 1987; ind to Culross and Torryburn 10 Sep 1987; dem on app by Royal Naval Chaplaincy Service 1 Oct 1992.

1980 JOHN HARKESS OSTLER
(FES X, 247), dem from Grantully, Logierait and Strathtay 31 Aug 1980 on app by RAF Chaplains' Branch; ind to Contin-Strathconon 31 Oct 1986.

1992 DONALD KERR PRENTICE
B 15 Mar 1954 at Elgin, s of Robert P. and Mary Thomson; educ Elgin Academy; University of Aberdeen 1974–77 (BSc); University of St Andrews 1985–88 (BD); Civil Service 1977–80; Teaching 1980–85; lic by Presb of Moray 26 Jun 1988; asstshp Anstruther 1988–89; m 12 Aug 1985 Alison Cunningham b 24 Aug 1956 d of John C. and

Agnes Jamieson Ritchie; Children: Rebecca b 5 May 1988; Ruth b 27 Mar 1990; Sophie b 17 Feb 1993; ord and ind to Iona and Ross of Mull with Kilfinichen and Kilvickeon 20 Jul 1989; dem on app by RAChD 1 May 1992; Publ: *Columba: Soldier or Saint* (Rainbow Press, 1990).

1981 SCOTT MACKENZIE RAE
B 30 Apr 1951 at Irvine, s of Joseph Colvin R. and Thomasina Hunter Mackenzie; educ Kilmarnock Academy 1956–69; University of Glasgow 1969–73 (BD), 1973–75 (CPS); lic by Presb of Irvine and Kilmarnock, 1975; asstshp Dundee Camperdown 1975–76; m 11 Sep 1973 Catherine MacPherson b 16 Mar 1953 d of Neil M. and Eliza Jane Lauchlan; Children: Joanne MacPherson b 28 Oct 1974; Susan Jane b 11 Jan 1977; Rebecca Thomson b 12 Sep 1980; Samantha Ella b 8 Dec 1990; ord and ind to Unst, Shetland 23 Jun 1976; dem to take up app with Royal Naval Chaplaincy Service 1 Feb 1981.

1978 JAMES REID
(FES IX, 376; X, 20, 142, 224), res from service with Presb Church of W Australia in Manly and app Air Commodore Principal Air Chaplain 12 Mar 1978; ret 5 Feb 1987; d Coralie m Steven Steward; Publ: *The First Hundred Years* (Singapore Press, 1984).

1967 DAVID REID
(FES X, 339, 448), dem from Auchindoir and Kildrummy on app by RAChD 11 Apr 1967; app Senior Chaplain, Osnabrück 1975; ind to Largoward with St Monans 22 Nov 1983.

1968 MATTHEW ROBERTSON
(FES X, 448), app by RAChD 1 Jul 1968; app Senior Chaplain to Army in Scotland Jun 1991; ret 31 Aug 1993 and ind to Cawdor with Croy and Dalcross 20 Feb 1994.

1992 MICHAEL DAVID SCOULER
ord by Presb of Aberdeen and app by RAChD 27 Jun 1988; ind to Earlston 19 Mar 1992.

1993 SCOTT JAMES SINCLAIR SHACKLETON
B 30 Aug 1964 at Glasgow, s of William S. and Margaret Brown; educ Stonelaw High, Rutherglen 1976–82; Glasgow College of Technology 1982–87 (BA): University of St Andrews 1989–92 (BD); Social Work (Child Care) 1987–88; Advertising Exec (*The Scotsman*) 1988–89; lic by Presb of Greenock 16 Jun 1992; asstshp St Andrews St Leonard's 1992–93; m 26 Sep 1987 Gillian Fiona Smillie b 20 Mar 1965 d of John S. and Irene Watt; Children: Adam William McPherson b 5 Jul 1988; Cameron John McKenzie b 11 Nov 1990; ord by Presb of St Andrews 15 Apr 1993; app by Royal Naval Chaplaincy Service 20 Apr 1993.

1984 DUNCAN SHAW
B 3 Dec 1952 at Inverness, s of Duncan S. and Alexandrena Mackenzie; educ Daniel Stewart's,

Edinburgh 1964–71; University of Edinburgh 1979–83 (LTh, CPS); Social Work 1974–79; lic by Presb of Stirling, Apr 1984; asstshp Dunblane Cathedral 1983–84; m 20 Dec 1980 Dorothy Dunn b 31 Dec 1951 d of Alan D. and Madge Tarren; ord by Presb of Stirling 24 Apr 1984; and app by RAF Chaplains' Branch 15 May 1984.

1977   JOHN SHEDDEN
(FES X, 88), dem from Thornhill on app as Social Welfare Officer, Salisbury, Rhodesia 12 Jul 1975; app by RNChS 12 Jan 1977; ind to Moose Jaw Presb Church, Saskatchewan 1 Mar 1984; dem to take up app with RAF Chaplains' Branch 3 Mar 1986; ind to Hawick Wilton with Teviothead 29 May 1998.

1976   JOHN MILLAR SHIELDS
(FES X, 345), dem from Kemnay 2 Sep 1976 to take up app with RAChD; ind to Channelkirk with Lauder Old 22 Aug 1997.

1972   ANGUS SMITH
(FES X, 395, 448), dem from Benbecula to take up app with RAChD 23 Oct 1972; app Chaplain to Oil Industry, Aberdeen 1 Sep 1991.

1976   CHARLES EDWARD STEWART
B 10 Jun 1946 at Glasgow, s of Charles S. and Mary McDougall; educ Govan High 1958–61; University of Strathclyde 1970–72 (BSc), 1981–85 (PhD); University of Glasgow 1972–75 (BD); University of Edinburgh 1994–96 (MTh); Marine Design Engineering 1966–70; lic by Presb of Glasgow 26 Jun 1975; asstshp Bearsden South 1974–76; m 20 Jun 1970 Margaret Marion Smith b 20 Apr 1950 d of James S. and Elizabeth MacIntyre; Children: Stephen Charles b 18 Jun 1972; Sarah-Jane b 7 Oct 1975; Alasdair James b 6 Feb 1978; ord by Presb of Dumbarton and app by Royal Naval Chaplaincy Service 28 Feb 1976; app Director General, Naval Chaplaincy Service 1996; app Chaplain of the Fleet 1998; Hon Chaplain to the Queen from 1996.

1961   JOHN THOMSON STUART
(FES X, 150, 448), dem from Glasgow Auldfield on app by RAChD 16 Sep 1961; ind to Bedrule with Denholm with Minto 30 Aug 1978.

1990   KENNETH ROBERT THOM
B 6 Sep 1954 at Ayr, s of Gordon James T. and Ann Cairn Livingstone; educ Prestwick High and Ayr Academy 1959–72; University of Glasgow 1979–84 (BD); lic by Presb of Ayr 28 Jun 1984; asstshp Troon St Meddan's 1984–85; m 18 Aug 1979 Janice Mary Dunlop b 9 Apr 1957 d of James Stuart D. and Georgina Mary Garrard; Children: Andrew Jonathan Samuel b 23 Jul 1988; ord and ind to Dundee Mains 25 Sep 1985; dem 18 Nov 1990 on app by RAF Chaplains' Branch; ind to Brislington URC, Bristol 6 Oct 1994.

1985   IVAN CORRY WARWICK
dem from Glenisla with Kilry with Lintrathen to take up app with RAChD 6 Sep 1985; ind to Knockando, Elchies and Archiestown with Rothes 30 Aug 1989.

1977   JOHN PATERSON WHITTON
B 19 Mar 1952 at Glasgow, s of John Morrison W. and Jessie Shaw Thomson; educ Rutherglen Academy 1964–70; University of Glasgow 1970–73 (MA), 1973–76 (BD); lic by Presb of Glasgow, 1976; asstshp Glasgow King's Park 1976–77; m 21 Jul 1978 Marion Black Syme b 2 Aug 1956 d of Robert Walker S. and Marion Murray; Children: David Peter b 19 Sep 1980; Susan Margaret b 14 Aug 1982; ord by Presb of Glasgow and app by RAChD 2 Jun 1977; app Senior Chaplain 19 Sep 1989; app Staff Chaplain HQ Southern District 1 Sep 1991; app Deputy Warden RAChD Centre 2 Jun 1993; app Warden RAChD Centre 3 May 1997; app Asst Chaplain General, Army Headquarters Scotland 1 Mar 1999.

1953   WILLIAM GEORGE AUGUSTUS WRIGHT
(FES IX, 719, 794; X, 449), dem from Liverpool St Andrew's on app by RAChD 25 Aug 1953; app Senior Chaplain Scotland May 1972; ret 31 Dec 1974; died 11 Feb 1997.

CHAPLAINS TO HOSPITALS

In alphabetical order

1989 JOHN BANKS
B 13 Apr 1937 at Edinburgh, s of George B. and Catherine Farquhar; educ Trinity Academy, Edinburgh 1942–53; University of Glasgow 1974–79 (BD); Letterpress Printer 1953–63; lic by Presb of Edinburgh (UFC) 10 May 1968; m 6 Sep 1958 Moira Jean Smith b 9 Sep 1936 d of Robert S. and Marion Grierson; Children: Alison Katharine b 2 Jul 1968; ord by Presb of Glasgow (UFC) and ind to Cathcart (UFC) 9 Sep 1968; General Secretary of UFC 1977–80; admitted by General Assembly 1980 and ind to Greenock Old West Kirk 19 Oct 1980; dem 31 Dec 1988 on app as Chaplain to Ailsa Hospital, Ayr.

1959 THOMAS DONALDSON BARR
(FES IX, 104, 180, 275; X, 159, 162, 450), dem from Glasgow Garthamlock on app as Chaplain to Gartnavel Hospital, Glasgow 1 Oct 1959; died 12 Apr 1977.

1962 DAVID BARR
(FES IX, 247, 300; X, 177, 450), dem from Glasgow St Mary's Partick and app Chaplain to Glasgow Royal Infirmary 6 Sep 1962; ret 30 Jun 1984; Publ: *Hospital Chaplaincy* (National Assoc of Whole Hospital Chaplains, 1980); review of *Hospital Chaplaincy* by Denis Duncan (*British Weekly*, 1981).

1996 JOHN MAXWELL BIRRELL
B 14 Apr 1946 at Edinburgh, s of John Frederick B. and Hilary Mary Granger; educ Trinity College, Glenalmond 1959–64; University of St Andrews 1965–68 (MA); University of Edinburgh 1970–73 (LLB), 1970–73 (BD); lic by Presb of Edinburgh; m 23 Mar 1978 Isobel Ritchie Wilson b 26 Sep 1950 d of James Cant W. and Esther Kellock; Children: Gillian Ruth b 8 Aug 1979; Claire Elizabeth b 24 Jun 1981; Nicola Rachel b 14 Mar 1985; ord by Presb of Edinburgh 19 Jan 1975; Project Co-ordinator, Calton Youth Ministry, Edinburgh 1973–76; Deputy Leader, Simpson House, Edinburgh 1976–77; Warden, Stroove House, Skelmorlie 1977–80; ind to Carluke St Andrew's 26 Nov 1980; trans to Forfar St Margaret's 22 Sep 1988; dem 9 Dec 1996 on app as Chaplain to Perth Royal Infirmary.

1994 ISOBEL RITCHIE BIRRELL
ord by Presb of Angus and app Chaplain to Forfar Infirmary 4 Jul 1994; app Chaplain to Stracathro Hospital 1 Oct 1995 and to Sunnyside Royal 1 Feb 1996; app Chaplain to Murray Royal, Perth 1 Apr 1998; ind to Craigend Moncreiffe with Rhynd (part-time) with Chaplaincy, HM Prison, Perth 24 Mar 1999.

1997 SANDRA BLACK
B 31 Jul 1959 at Glasgow, d of James Anderson and Margaret Murray; educ Whitburn Academy 1971–77; University of St Andrews 1977–81 (BSc); University of Edinburgh 1983–86 (BD); Cook, St Ninian's Centre, Crieff 1982–83; lic by Presb of West Lothian 29 Jun 1986; asstshp Edinburgh Murrayfield 1986–87; m 14 Jun 1986 David Robert Black b 7 Jun 1960 s of Robert B. and Josephine Stewart; Children: Lucy b 30 Apr 1995; ord by Presb of Dumfries and Kirkcudbright and app Chaplain to Dumfries and Galloway Royal Infirmary 31 Jul 1988; introd as Assoc at Carlisle Chapel Street with Longtown St Andrew's and at Gretna Old, Gretna St Andrew's and Half Morton and Kirkpatrick Fleming 30 Apr 1992; app by Yorkhill NHS Trust, Glasgow, as Hospital Chaplain 8 Sep 1997.

1994 DEREK GORDON BROWN
B 25 Sep 1959 at Paisley, s of John B. and Gwyneth Louise Bannerman; educ Penicuik High 1971–76; University of Edinburgh 1980–86 (BD, DipMin); Banking 1976–80; lic by Presb of Lothian 3 Jul 1986; asstshp Inverness Trinity 1986–87; m 4 Apr 1981 Susan Marjory Attwell b 12 Dec 1958 d of James Storie Callendar A. and Margaret Reid Brown; Children: Simon Kenneth b 10 Jan 1987; Hannah Rachel b 16 Apr 1990; ord by Presb of Inverness 23 Nov 1989; app Asst Chaplain to Inverness Hospitals 1 Aug 1987; app Chaplain to Raigmore Hospital and Highland Hospice 1 Apr 1994.

1986 WILLIAM MURDOCH MACLEAN CAMPBELL
(FES X, 243, 245), dem from Lundie and Muirhead of Liff on app as Chaplain to Royal Cornhill and Woodlands Hospitals, Aberdeen 18 Aug 1986; Chaplain, Royal Naval Reserve 1981–92; Publ: Meditations (Methodist Publishing House, from 1994); article on liturgy with people with learning difficulties (Church Service Society, 1995).

1991 MURRAY CHALMERS
(FES X, 9, 41), dem from Edinburgh Fairmilehead on app as Chaplain to Royal Edinburgh Hospital 1

Aug 1991; s Ewan m Kay Byrne; d Elspeth m James Traynor.

1989 FRED COUTTS
(FES X, 356), dem from Aberdeen Mastrick on app as Chaplain to Aberdeen Royal Hospitals 11 Sep 1989; Addl children: Rosemary Anne b 30 Jul 1976; David Stefan b 18 Feb 1979.

1989 THOMAS CRICHTON
(FES X, 32), dem from Avonbridge with Torphichen on app as Chaplain to St John's Hospital, Livingston 1 Oct 1989.

1996 ELIZABETH ANNE CRUMLISH
B 6 Feb 1962 at Greenock, d of Hugh Stewart and Catherine Spark; educ Port Glasgow High 1966–79; University of Glasgow 1989–93 (BD), 1993–94 (CMin), 1995–97 (Dip Palliative Care); Medical Lab Scientific Officer 1979–89; lic by Presb of Greenock 17 Aug 1994; asstshp Bishopton 1994–95; m 31 Jul 1981 Idris Bryn Johns Crumlish b 23 Aug 1951 s of Peter C. and June Blackmore; Children: Ruaridh b 21 Sep 1993; Zara b 15 Sep 1998; ord by Presb of Greenock and introd as Assoc at Greenock St Luke's 30 Aug 1995; app by Inverclyde Royal NHS Trust as Hospital Chaplain 1 Oct 1996.

1974 JOHN BELL DEANS
(FES IX, 564; X, 258, 316, 328, 445, 450), dem from Arbuthnott with Kinneff on app as Chaplain to Aberdeen City Hospitals 11 Mar 1974; ret 18 Aug 1986.

1997 JAMES RONALD DICK
(FES X, 118), dem from Edinburgh Oxgangs on app as Chaplain to Borders General Hospital 15 Sep 1997; Children: Neil Ronald b 1 Feb 1977; Jane Margaret b 1 May 1981.

1971 JOHN LEONARD DOUGLAS
(FES VIII, 118; IX, 28, 107; X, 17, 450), dem from Newhaven-on-Forth 30 Sep 1958 on app as Chaplain to Edinburgh Northern Hospitals; ret 30 Jun 1971; died 24 Oct 1983.

1991 JAMES BELL FALCONER
B 20 Jun 1953 at Banff, s of David F. and Robina Mary Bell; educ Morton Academy, Thornhill 1958–69; University of Glasgow 1976–81 (BD, CMin); Apprentice Instrument Mechanic 1969–70; Dept of Clinical Physics and Bio Engineering, University of Glasgow 1970–72; Nursing 1972–76; lic by Presb of Hamilton 28 Jun 1981; asstshp Broom 1981–84; m 18 Aug 1979 Aileen Primrose b 21 Sep 1957 d of William Christie P. and Lily Wright; Children: Rachel Eleanor b 15 Jun 1987; Esther Lauren b 11 Jan 1990; ord by Presb of Glasgow during assistantship at Broom Church 31 Mar 1982; introd as Assoc at East Kilbride Moncreiff 4 Apr 1984; app Chaplain to Kingseat and House of Daviot Hospitals 30 Oct 1989; app Chaplain to Aberdeen Royal Hospitals 18 Nov 1991.

1959 JOHN HERON GIBSON
(FES IX, 21, 216, 364; X, 13, 450), dem from Edinburgh North Leith on app as Chaplain to Crichton Royal Infirmary, Dumfries 3 Sep 1959; ret 1977; died 19 Oct 1988.

1999 KAY GILCHRIST
B 27 May 1961 at Airdrie, d of David Adams G. and Margaret Edgar; educ Caldervale High, Airdrie 1966–78; Coatbridge College 1978–79; Lanarkshire School of Nursing 1979–82 (RGN); Glasgow Royal Maternity College 1982–84; University of Glasgow 1988–92 (BD), 1992–93 (CMin); Nursing and Midwifery 1983–88; lic by Presb of Hamilton 29 Jun 1993; asstshp Cumbernauld St Mungo's 1993–94; ord by Presb of Glasgow and introd as Assoc at Drumchapel St Andrew's 15 Feb 1996; dem 24 Jan 1999 on app as Chaplain to Rachel House Children's Hospice, Kinross.

1994 THOMAS JOHN GORDON
(FES X, 18), dem from Edinburgh Viewforth to take up app as Chaplain and Adviser in Spiritual Care, Marie Curie Centre, Edinburgh 1 Oct 1994; Children: Mairi Jean b 6 Jul 1976; Kathryn Anne b 19 May 1978; James William Thomas b 20 Jan 1980.

1977 DEREK HALEY
B 23 Aug 1934 at Bradford, s of Harold Dixon H. and Annie Pearson; educ Carlton Grammar, Bradford 1945–50; Yorkshire United Independent College, Bradford 1955–58; Northern Congregational College, 1958–60; University of Manchester 1958–60 (CTh); University of Edinburgh 1971 (DPS), 1975 (BD); Family Business 1950–52, 1954–55; National Service RAF 1952–54; lic by Congregational Union of England and Wales, Sep 1955; m 31 Dec 1960 Janet Frances Dunstone b 17 Jul 1934 d of David Walter D. and Mervyn Frances May Swift; Children: Christopher Nicholas b 12 Dec 1963; Claire Charlotte b 17 Aug 1965; ord by Congregational Union of England and Wales 5 Jul 1960; ministry in Congregational Church 1960–77; admitted by General Assembly 1977 and app Chaplain to Gartnavel Royal Hospital, Glasgow 1 Sep 1977; ret 23 Aug 1999.

1990 ANNE JESSIE McINROY HARPER
B 31 Oct 1949 at Glasgow, d of Daniel H. and Margaret Craig Wales; educ Camphill Secondary, Paisley 1961–67; University of Glasgow 1970–74 (BD), 1975–78 (MTh); Union Theological Seminary, New York 1974–75 (STM); Open University 1988–89 (CSP); Social Work 1967–70; Asst Minister, Second Presb Church, New York 1974–75; lic by Presb of Paisley, Jul 1978; asstshp Cumbernauld Abronhill 1978–79; ord by Presb of Paisley 28 Nov 1979; app Education Field Officer, Dept of Education 1 Aug 1979; ind to Glasgow Linthouse St Kenneth's 6 Jun 1984; dem on app as Chaplain to Glasgow Royal Infirmary 1 Dec 1990.

1997 YVONNE HIBBERT HENDRIE
B 7 Apr 1966 at Stranraer, d of George Barron Jamieson and Sarah Denham Reid Brown; educ Stranraer Academy 1978–84; University of Glasgow 1984–87 (MA), 1987–90 (BD); lic by Presb of Wigtown and Stranraer 22 Aug 1990; asstshp Ayr Castlehill 1990–91; Falkirk Grahamston United 1991–92; m 30 Jul 1989 Brian Robert Hendrie b 21 Sep 1962 s of Robert Woods H. and Sarah Wilson Merry; Children: Chloe Christine b 2 Jul 1997; ord by the Congregational Federation and ind to Hawick Congregational Church 21 Sep 1995; app Chaplain (part-time) to Falkirk and District Royal Infirmary 8 Dec 1997; app Chaplain (part-time) to Strathcarron Hospice 1 May 1999.

1998 JUDITH ANNE HUGGETT
B 24 Mar 1960 at Dunfermline, d of James William H. and Mary Lothian Boyce; educ Queen Anne High, Dunfermline and Price's Sixth Form College, Fareham 1972–78; University of Sheffield 1978–81 (BA); University of Glasgow 1985–88 (BD); Museum Curator 1982–85; lic by Presb of Dunfermline 3 Jul 1988; ord and ind to Gorebridge 16 Aug 1990; app Chaplain (part-time) to Herdmanflat Hospital, Haddington 1 Apr 1997; dem from Gorebridge 15 Nov 1998 on app as Chaplain to Crosshouse Hospital.

1984 MARY LAWSON HUTCHISON
ord and ind to Dumfries Lincluden with Holywood 20 Jan 1982; app Chaplain to Cresswell Maternity Hospital 1984 and to Dumfries and Galloway Royal Infirmary 1995.

1986 ALEXANDER SCOTT HUTCHISON
(FES X, 289, 329), dem from Aberdeen Rubislaw on app as Chaplain to Aberdeen Hospitals 5 Sep 1986; ret 22 Jul 1991; DD (St Andrews) 1982; d Elizabeth m Hall; d Sally m Kelly; d Gillian m Bradshaw; d Wendy m Rankin; w Gillian died 22 May 1989; m (2) 30 Sep 1990 Alison Margaret Hogg b 17 Jan 1962 d of Alastair Blaikie H. and Agnes Helen Rome Duncan; Children: Anna Helen b 24 Jul 1992; Chloe Alison b 9 May 1994.

1988 ALISON MARGARET HUTCHISON
B 17 Jan 1962 at Edinburgh, d of Alastair Blaikie Hogg and Agnes Helen Rome Duncan; educ Penicuik High 1974–80; University of Edinburgh 1980–84 (BD), 1985–87 (DipMin); S African Council of Churches 1984–85; lic by Presb of Lothian 2 Jul 1987; asstshp Loanhead 1987–88; m 30 Sep 1990 Alexander Scott Hutchison b 22 Jul 1926 s of James H. and Jean Wilson Scott; Children: Anna Helen b 24 Jul 1992; Chloe Alison b 9 May 1994; spouse's children from previous marriage: Elizabeth b 3 Nov 1957 m Iain Hall; Sally b 30 Jul 1959 m Alan Kelly; Ruth b 3 Feb 1961 m Benjamin Bradshaw; Wendy b 16 Mar 1963 m David Rankin; David b 2 Apr 1965 m Hazel; Andrew b 7 Oct 1967; ord by Presb of Aberdeen and app Chaplain to Aberdeen General Hospitals 5 Jun 1988.

1987 JOHN JOHNSTON
(FES X, 152), dem from Saltcoats St Cuthbert's South Beach on app as Chaplain to the Dumfries Hospitals 1 Nov 1987; app Dumfries Health Care Chaplain 1 Nov 1993; ret 12 Apr 1999; w Flora died 1982; m (2) 18 Oct 1989 Marion Young Paterson; d Eleanor m Duncan Wilson Turnbull.

1998 EWAN ROBERT KELLY
B 5 Jun 1965 at Bangour, West Lothian, s of James Miller K. and Elizabeth Ann Cook; educ Firrhill High, Edinburgh 1970–82; University of St Andrews 1982–85 (BSc); University of Manchester 1985–88 (MBChB); University of Edinburgh 1989–92 (BD); Junior Doctor 1988–89; lic by Presb of Edinburgh 6 Jul 1992; asstshp Leith St Andrew's 1992–93; m 15 Jul 1988 Julia Miller Ferguson b 9 Aug 1965 d of Duncan F. and Lorraine McCracken; Children: Stuart b 9 Aug 1992; Alastair b 1 Apr 1995; Fraser b 14 May 1997; ord by Presb of Edinburgh and introd as Assoc at Currie 13 Jan 1994; introd as Chaplain to Glasgow Southern General Hospital Jun 1995; introd as Chaplain to Edinburgh Royal Infirmary 12 May 1998.

1999 CAMERON HUNTER LANGLANDS
B 31 Dec 1965 at Edinburgh, s of George William L. and Catherine Falconer Gibson; educ Daniel Stewart's and Melville College, Edinburgh 1977–83; University of Edinburgh 1988–92 (BD), 1992–93 (MTh), Princeton Theological Seminary, USA 1993–94 (ThM); Personnel Officer 1983–86; Insurance Underwriter 1986–88; lic by Presb of Lothian 21 Jul 1994; asstshp Bonhill 1994–95; ord and ind to Renton Trinity 28 Jun 1995; dem 20 Sep 1999 on app as Health Care and Co-ordinating Chaplain, Greater Glasgow Primary Care NHS Trust.

1998 CHRISTOPHER LEON LEVISON
(FES X, 201), dem from Oakshaw Trinity on app as Chaplain to Victoria Hospital 4 Oct 1998; Addl children: Rosemary Celia Mackay b 3 Dec 1977.

1971 DAVID LYALL
(FES X, 115, 450), dem from Ardrossan Park on app as Chaplain to Edinburgh Northern Hospitals 1 Oct 1971; also app part-time Lecturer, University of Edinburgh 1 Oct 1971; res on app as Lecturer in Practical Theology, University of St Andrews 1 Oct 1987.

1961 MURDOCH MACBETH MACKAY
(FES IX, 564, 739; X, 328, 451), dem from Aberdeen Middlefield 31 May 1961 on app as Chaplain to Cornhill Hospital; app Hon Lecturer in Mental Health, University of Aberdeen 1 Oct 1973; ret 31 Aug 1986; Publ: *Good Health* (Tabb House, Cornwall, 1993).

1992 JANET PHILLIPS HOTCHKIES MACMAHON
B 31 May 1944 at Glasgow, d of Thomas Alexander Gallacher and Isabel Armstrong; educ Glasgow High School for Girls 1956–62; Glasgow School of

Speech Therapy 1962–65 (LCST); University of Glasgow 1982–85 (MSc), 1986–89 (BD); Speech and Language Therapist 1965–82, 1983–86; Research and Development Officer in Special Educational Needs, Church of Scotland 1990–92; lic by Presb of Dumbarton 9 Jul 1989; asstshp Milngavie Cairns 1989–90; Govan Old 1990; m 4 Sep 1968 Michael Kenneth Cowan MacMahon b 7 Aug 1943 s of Kenneth Austin M. and Alice Cowan; Children: Caroline Alice Isabel b 25 Jul 1970 m Jozsef Balazs Geller; Kenneth Michael Alexander b 18 Jul 1973; ord by Presb of Glasgow and app Chaplain to Glasgow Southern General Hospital 7 Oct 1992; Publ: *Walk in God's Ways* (Church of Scotland, 1993).

1998 IAIN AULAY MACLEOD MACRITCHIE
B 6 Feb 1963 at Kirkintilloch, s of Donald and Christina Annie M; educ Dumbarton Academy and Douglas Academy, Milngavie 1974–79; University of Glasgow 1979–83 (BSc); University of Aberdeen 1983–86 (BD), 1992–97 (PhD); Union Theological Seminary, New York 1993–94 (STM); lic by Presb of Dumbarton 27 Jun 1986; asstshp Ayr Castlehill 1986–87; m 27 Aug 1993 Morag Elizabeth Beautyman b 25 Oct 1961 d of Harry B. and Anna Rowan; Children: Eilidh Rowan b 18 Jan 1996; Calum Maclean b 20 Mar 1998; ord and ind to Stirling Viewfield 24 Jun 1987; introd as Pastoral Asst, Aberdeen Beechgrove and app Teaching Asst, Christ's College, University of Aberdeen 1 Oct 1992; loc ten Portlethen 1 Oct 1996; loc ten Dyce 15 Sep 1997; app Chaplain to Raigmore Hospital, Inverness 13 Apr 1998; Publ: *Calvinism and Celtic Culture* (*Journal of Religion and Health*, 1994); *The Shadow of Dunblane* (*Journal of Religion and Health*, 1996); Review of *Theology and Pastoral Counselling* by Deborah Hunsinger (*Scottish Journal of Theology*, 1998).

1986 ROBERT LAWSON MANSON
(FES X, 25, 423), dem from Edinburgh Slateford Longstone 31 Jan 1986 and app Asst Chaplain to Royal Edinburgh Hospital and Gogarburn Hospital; app Chaplain 1 Feb 1988; ret 30 Jul 1991; s Andrew m Hazel Ann Flitter; s Peter m Sylvia Ann Creed.

1996 IAN J M McDONALD
dem from Bannockburn Ladywell on app as Chaplain to Kirkcaldy Acute Hospitals 31 Jul 1996.

1970 THOMAS STEWART McGREGOR
(FES X, 36, 450), dem from Cumbernauld Kildrum to take up app as Chaplain to Edinburgh Royal Infirmary 16 Apr 1970; Senior Lecturer in Christian Ethics and Practical Theology, University of Edinburgh 1970–98; ret 8 Apr 1998; MBE 1994; Publ: Contributor to *Dictionary of Medical Ethics* (DLT, 1977 [1st ed] and 1981 [2nd ed]); contributor to *Dictionary of Pastoral Care* (SPCK, 1987); *The Whole Person and Suffering* (Strathcarron Hospice,

1991); contributor to *Dictionary of Medical Ethics* ed K M Boyd et al (BMJ, 1997); contributor to *Religions and Cultures* (Edinburgh and Lothians Racial Equality Council, 1999).

1997 RODERICK HOUSTON McNIDDER
B 11 May 1949 at Bothkennar, s of Henry William M. and Lilias Alison McGregor Houston; educ Larbert High 1954–67; Darlington College of Education 1971–74 (DCE); University of Glasgow 1982–86 (BD); Civil Service 1969–71; Teaching 1974–82; lic by Presb of Dumbarton 27 Jun 1986; asstshp Milngavie Cairns 1986–87; m 18 Oct 1975 Jennifer Wilkie Cochrane b 3 Nov 1947 d of John Campbell C. and Isabel Wilkie Leitch; Children: Fiona Alison b 23 Nov 1983; Mhairi Isabel b 5 Jun 1985; ord and ind to Southend 5 Jun 1987; dem to take up app as Hospital Chaplain (full-time), South Ayrshire NHS Trust 1 Apr 1997.

1996 JENNIFER MARGARET MILLAR
B 4 Sep 1956 at Glasgow, d of James Selkirk Davie and Jane Lang McAlpine; educ Bellshill Academy 1969–74; University of Edinburgh 1974–78 (BD); Moray House College, Edinburgh 1978–79 (PGCE); University of Glasgow 1981–83 (DipMin); Teaching 1979–81; lic by Presb of Hamilton, Dec 1983; asstshp Hamilton Cadzow 1983–84; m 17 Jul 1980 Alexander McKenzie Millar b 4 Jun 1953 s of James M. and Sarah Noble Arthurs; Children: Rhona Jane Sarah b 24 Feb 1991; ord by Presb of Glasgow during assistantship at Mearns 26 Aug 1986; dem on app as Chaplain (part-time) to Hillside Hospital, Perth Jan 1988; also app teacher (part-time) of Religious and Moral Educ, Auchterarder High School 30 Aug 1988; app teacher (full-time) of Religious and Moral Educ, Auchterarder High School 17 Aug 1996.

1998 DAVID MITCHELL
B 7 Nov 1958 at Greenock, s of Jessie Bowie Hunter; educ Greenock High 1970–76; University of St Andrews 1982–86 (BD), 1986–87 (DipPTh); University of Glasgow 1998 (MSc); Shop Asst 1976–80, 1980–82; lic by Presb of Greenock, Nov 1987; asstshp Ayr Castlehill 1987–88; m 15 Sep 1984 Elizabeth Miller McCallum b 2 Nov 1965 d of Daniel M. and Martha Watt Guiller; Children: David Davidson b 30 Mar 1986; Heather b 26 Feb 1989; ord and ind to Glasgow Colston Wellpark 23 Jun 1988; dem 1 Aug 1998 on app as Chaplain to Marie Curie Hospice, Huntershill.

1984 ALASTAIR RAMSAY MOODIE
(FES X, 177), res as Chaplain to Crosshouse Hospital and demitted status 30 Jun 1998; Publ: *Dead Ends and New Ways* (Iona Community, 1978).

1983 GILLIAN MARGARET MORTON
B 19 Jun 1936 at Dudley, Worcs, d of Benjamin Thomas Richards and Marjorie Winifred Turner; educ Dudley Girls' High and Edgehill College, Bideford 1940–55; University of St Andrews 1955–

59 (MA); Freie Universitaet, Berlin 1957–58; University of Zambia 1967–68 (PCE London); University of Edinburgh 1980–84 (BD); Teaching, Zambia, 1966–69; Lecturer at Teacher Training College, Livingstone, Zambia 1969–71; Short Courses Secretary, Scottish Pre-school Playgroups Assoc 1978–80; lic by Presb of Edinburgh 4 Jul 1982; m 20 Aug 1959 Alexander James Morton b 8 Jun 1934 s of James M. and Margaret Craig Kent; Children: Catriona Margaret b 30 Sep 1961 m Anand Michel Ramkissoon; Karen Elspeth b 25 Nov 1962 m Manikumarian Krishnan; David Craig and Callum Stewart b 6 Feb 1971; ord by Presb of Edinburgh and introd as Chaplain to Western General Hospital, Edinburgh 29 Jan 1983; app Chaplain to Borders General Hospital 20 Jun 1988; ret 15 Sep 1996; Publ: *Das Leben in Gemeinschaft teilen und Heil machen* (Una Sancta, 1983); *From Captivity to Liberation* (Univ of Edinburgh Occasional Paper, 1984); *Aids and the Scottish Churches* (*Contact*, 1987); *Captive and Free* (*Palliative Medicine*, Vol 2 No 2, 1988); *The Search for Personal Freedom in Chronic Illness* (*European Renal Care Assoc Journal*).

1995   GILLIAN MUNRO
B 26 Sep 1952 at Perth, d of David Mitchell M. and Isabella Neish Gordon; educ Perth Academy 1964–70; University of Aberdeen 1970–74 (BSc); Dundee College of Education 1974–75 (CEd); University of Edinburgh 1986–89 (BD); Teaching 1975–80; Church of Scotland Deaconess 1981–86; lic by Presb of Jedburgh, Jul 1989; ord and ind to Unst 12 Aug 1989; dem on app as Asst Chaplain, Aberdeen Royal Hospitals 2 Jul 1995; app Chaplain 1 Nov 1997.

1995   GEORGINA NELSON
B 19 Oct 1957 at Edinburgh, educ St Mary's Academy, Bathgate 1962–75; University of St Andrews 1975–84 (MA, PhD); University of Glasgow 1987–89 (BD), 1996–98 (Dip Palliative Care); University of Dundee 1982–83 (DipEd); lic by Presb of Hamilton 27 Jun 1989; asstshp Airdrie West 1989–90; ord and introd as Assoc at Cumbernauld Condorrat 22 Aug 1990; app Chaplain to St John's Hospital, Livingston 1 Oct 1995.

1984   KENNETH JOHN PATTISON
dem from Ardrossan Park on app as Chaplain to Glasgow Royal Infirmary Jun 1984; introd as Assoc at Edinburgh St Andrew's and St George's Aug 1990.

1983   ROBERT RAE
(FES X, 13, 265), dem from Leith St Andrew's on app as Chaplain to Dundee Teaching Hospitals 1 Apr 1983.

1977   STANLEY JAMES RAFFAN
(FES IX, 601; X, 133, 335 (2), 346), dem from Ellon and Slains 14 Jul 1977 on app as Chaplain to Crichton Royal Hospital, Dumfries; ret 14 Nov 1987; died 21 Feb 1997.

1998   BLAIR ROBERTSON
B 3 Mar 1964 at Edinburgh, s of William Brian R. and Mabel Fullerton Hardie; educ Daniel Stewart's and Melville College, Edinburgh 1969–82; University of Edinburgh 1982–85 (MA); University of Glasgow 1985–88 (BD); Princeton Theological Seminary, USA 1988–89 (ThM); lic by Presb of Edinburgh 3 Jul 1988; asstshp Hamilton Old 1989–90; ord and ind to Falkirk Erskine 23 Oct 1990; dem 20 Jul 1998 to take up app as Chaplain to Glasgow Southern General Hospital; Publ: *Storytelling in Pastoral Counselling: A Narrative Pastoral Theology* (*Pastoral Psychology*, 1990); *In My End Is My Beginning* (*Theology in Scotland*, 1995); *Touch Awe, Touch A* (sermon in *Journal of Health Care Chaplaincy*, Jun 1999).

1999   KEITH SAUNDERS
B 2 Oct 1953 at Berwick-on-Tweed, s of William Arthur S. and Doreen Gilchrist; educ Berwick Grammar 1964–69; Stevenson College, Edinburgh 1976–77 (SCE:H); University of Edinburgh 1977–82 (BD, CPS); Banking 1970–76; lic by Presb of Lothian 4 Jul 1982; asstshp Dalkeith St Nicholas' Buccleuch 1982–83; m 24 Apr 1982 Isabel Connell Purdon b 16 Jun 1950 d of Malcolm Grieve P. and Janet Bain Fingland; Children: Ross Malcolm b 13 Mar 1984; Rona Janeen b 4 Mar 1985; ord and ind to Coatbridge Calder 21 Dec 1983; dem 19 Sep 1999 to take up app as Chaplain to Glasgow Western Infirmary.

1988   MELVILLE FREDERICK SCHOFIELD
(FES X, 111, 126), dem from Kilmarnock Laigh to take up app as Chaplain to Edinburgh Northern Hospitals Group (based at Western General Hospital) 1 Mar 1988.

1999   DOUGLAS FREW STEVENSON
B 9 Aug 1959 at Ayr, s of John Crilley S. and Agnes Douglas Frew; educ Mainholm Academy, Ayr 1971–75; St Colm's College, Edinburgh 1983–84 (CCS); University of Edinburgh 1984–89 (BD, DipMin); Maintenance Electrician 1975–80; Maintenance Worker, Iona Community, Iona 1981–82; Counsellor 1990–91; lic by Presb of Edinburgh 1 Oct 1989; asstshp Edinburgh Old Kirk 1989–90; m (1) 1 Sep 1984 Kathryn Mary Law b 21 May 1959 d of John and Margaret L; Children: Graeme David Lawrie b 30 Nov 1988; m (2) 6 Apr 1994 Jacqueline Robertson b 5 Feb 1964 d of Jack R. and Alice Anderson; Children: Meghann Rose b 24 Feb 1995; Rory Douglas b 7 Mar 1999; ord by Presb of Edinburgh and introd as Assoc at Kaimes Lockhart Memorial 2 Jul 1991; ind to Musselburgh St Andrew's High 9 Jun 1994; dem 1 Feb 1999 on app as Chaplain to Edinburgh Royal Infirmary 18 Feb 1999.

1998   ANNE ELEANOR STEWART
B 22 Dec 1965 at Glasgow, d of Alexander Cunningham and Eleanor Janet Irvine; educ Hutchesons' Grammar, Glasgow 1977–83; University of Glasgow 1990–95 (BD, CMin); Care Asst

(part-time) 1986; Civil Service (Exec Officer, DSS) 1986–90; lic by Presb of Hamilton 30 Aug 1995; asstshp Hamilton St John's 1996–97; m 12 Jul 1993 James Stewart b 22 Mar 1968 s of William S. and Elizabeth Hazel Montgomery; Children: Hannah Joy b 10 Jul 1995; Adam James b 16 Aug 1997; Ruth Grace b 10 Aug 1999; ord by Presb of Perth 25 Feb 1998 and introd as Chaplain (part-time) to MacMillan House, Perth 1 Mar 1998.

1999   ALEXANDER EWING STRACHAN
(FES X, 265), dem from Guernsey St Andrew's in the Grange on app as Healthcare Chaplain (full-time) to Dumfries Hospitals 17 Jun 1999; Children: Matthew b 11 Feb 1975; Richard b 26 Oct 1977.

1997   ALISON IRIS SWINDELLS
B 28 Jan 1958 at Aberdeen, d of Robert Ian Wright and Marjory McHattie; educ Paisley Grammar 1970–75; University of Glasgow 1975–78 (LLB); University of Aberdeen 1992–95 (BD); Solicitor 1978–92; lic by Presb of Aberdeen 28 Jun 1995; asstshp Aberdeen Rubislaw 1995–97; m 9 Jun 1995 Sean Swindells b 22 Jul 1960 s of Michael Charles Roland S. and Molly Sayers; app Youth minister (part-time) at Rubislaw 1 Feb 1997; app Asst Chaplain (part-time) to Aberdeen Royal Infirmary 1 Dec 1997; ord by Presb of Aberdeen 15 Jan 1998.

1971   ALAN CHRISTIE SWINTON
(FES IX, 259; X, 36, 153, 192, 451), dem from Cumbernauld St Mungo's to take up app as Chaplain to Aberdeen Hospitals 30 Sep 1971; ret 22 Nov 1991 and dem status 7 Apr 1992.

1999   WILLIAM COLVILLE THOMAS
(FES X, 9, 62), res as Assoc at St Luke's URC, Eastbourne 1992 on app as Chaplain to Herd-manflat Psychiatric Hospital, Haddington 8 Feb 1999; s Robert m Suzanne Roberts; d Fiona m Rahid Amin; d Joan m Colin Saywood; d Catriona m Simon Withey; m (2) 2 Nov 1997 Tessa Mary Pyne b 16 Jun 1956 d of Peter P. and Grace Coup; Publ: *My Lessons in Prayer* (*Life & Work*, 1994).

1996   JAMES WATSON
(FES X, 10 (2)), ret from Bowden with Lilliesleaf 30 Jun 1994; app Chaplain (part-time) to Dunoon General Hospital 1 Jun 1996; Addl children: Yvonne b 14 Jul 1971 m Gordon Marr; s Douglas m Julie Lusk; d Elizabeth m Mark Leslie.

1993   ISABELLA HELEN WHYTE
B 4 May 1943 at Glasgow, d of John Martin and Margaret Reid Munro; educ Lenzie Academy 1955–61; Jordanhill College, Glasgow 1961–64 (DCE); University of Glasgow 1987–91 (BD); Teaching 1964–68, 1983–87; lic by Presb of Edinburgh 7 Jul 1991; asstshp Edinburgh St Andrew's and St George's 1991–93; m 31 Jul 1968 Iain Alexander Whyte b 3 Sep 1940 s of William Le Normand W. and Elizabeth Clark Alexander; Children: David Alexander b 10 Jun 1968; Margaret Iona b 19 Aug 1971; Jason John b 27 May 1974; ord by Presb of Dunfermline and app Chaplain to Queen Margaret Hospital, Dunfermline 30 Apr 1993.

1945   JAMES YOUNGSON
(FUF 564; FES IX, 567, 621, 755, 797; X, 451), dem from Aberdeen Ruthrieston South on app as Chaplain to Aberdeen Royal Infirmary 11 Nov 1945; ret 30 Apr 1971; died 24 Dec 1984.

INDUSTRIAL CHAPLAINS

In alphabetical order

1975 COLIN MACEWEN ANDERSON
(FES X, 18, 452), dem from Edinburgh Old Kirk on app as Industrial Chaplain on lower reaches of the Clyde 3 Mar 1975; ind to Greenock St Margaret's 12 Apr 1984.

1989 WILLIAM CRAWFORD ANDERSON
(FES X, 330), res as Chaplain to Heriot-Watt University on app as Chaplain to Oil Industry, Aberdeen 1989; res 1991.

1989 ERIK McLEISH CRAMB
(FES X, 178), dem from Glasgow Yoker Old with St Matthew's on app as Industrial Chaplain (Tayside) and National Co-ordinator 21 Jun 1989; Addl children: Fiona Elizabeth b 25 Aug 1976; Donald Henry b 22 Jun 1978; Colin McLeish b 14 Jul 1984; Pamela Helen b 19 Jan 1987; Publ: *Lifestyle* (Iona Community, 1976); *The Contribution of Liberation Theology to a Christian Response to Mass Unemployment* (Scottish Churches' Industrial Mission, 1980); *Scotland: A Struggle on the Periphery* (Scottish Churches' Industrial Mission, 1986); *Parables and Patter* (Wild Goose Publs, 1989); *A Parliament that Protects?* (SCM, 1999).

1987 ALISTER JOHN GOSS
(FES X, 271), dem from Edinburgh St Andrew's Clermiston on app as Industrial Chaplain for Inverclyde and West Coast 4 Oct 1987; app Industrial Chaplain for Glasgow 17 Nov 1998; m (2) 21 Jan 1982 Dorothy May Myles b 21 Jan 1953 d of James M. and Anderson; Children: Fiona Louise b 17 Mar 1986.

1980 HUGH CHARLES ORMISTON
(FES X, 306), dem as Assoc, Isle of Mull on app as Industrial Chaplain in the Forth Valley 1 Nov 1980; ind to Kirkmichael Straloch and Glenshee with Rattray 30 Apr 1998.

1981 NORMAN BENNIE ORR
(FES X, 137, 442), res as Chaplain to University of Dundee to take up employment outwith Church 1973; app Industrial Chaplain for Glasgow 1981; ret 1990; died 5 Oct 1991.

1991 DONALD BLAIR RENNIE
(FES X, 135, 150, 334), dem from Cults East to take up app as Industrial Mission Organiser for North East Scotland 4 Sep 1991; ret 7 Mar 1996; s Graeme m Caitlan Orr; d Ruth m Ronald Smith.

1985 JOHN DURHAM ROSS
(FES X, 151, 164), dem from Glasgow Langside and Battlefield Erskine on app as Industrial Chaplain for Dundee 31 Jan 1985; introd to Rome St Andrew's 11 Oct 1988.

1967 DONALD MACIVER ROSS
(FES X, 44, 147, 452), app Industrial Chaplain for Glasgow 31 Aug 1967; app Industrial Mission Organiser 1 May 1980; ret 11 Nov 1993; Chairman of Employee Counselling service 1976–95; Vice-chairman of Glasgow Council for the Voluntary Sector 1994–95; Vice-chairman of Unity Enterprise 1994–95; s Neil m Lisa MacDonald; s Alastair m Ruth Robertson Wilson; Publ: Editor of *Newsletter for Christians in Industry* (1980–82); *Christian Mission in Scotland* (Scottish Churches Industrial Mission Blue Paper, 1981); editor of *Newsletter of Scottish Churches Industrial Mission* (1982–87); *Scottish Churches and the Political Process Today* (CTPI, 1986); *The MSC and the Church* (Edinburgh Univ Press, 1989); co-editor of *New Patterns of Work* (Scottish Churches Industrial Mission, 1990); *God it's Monday* (St Andrew Press, 1997).

1991 ANGUS SMITH
(FES X, 395, 448), ret from RAChD on app as Chaplain to Oil Industry, Aberdeen 1 Sep 1991; s William m Brenda Deayton; s Cameron m Dawn Ritchie.

1990 ANGUS TURNER
B 25 Nov 1933 at Glasgow, s of Alexander T. and Christian Flockhart Rutherford; educ Allan Glen's School, Glasgow 1945–51; Royal College of Science and Technology 1954–58 (HNC); University of Glasgow 1971–75 (BD); Jordanhill College, Glasgow 1960; St Colm's College, Edinburgh 1961–62; Polymer Technician 1954–56; Polymer Chemist 1956–60; Church of Scotland Missionary, Zambia 1962–71; lic by Presb of Glasgow, Jun 1975; asstshp Glasgow Renfield St Stephen's 1975–76; m (1) 30 Mar 1961 Jane Shiela Clark McInnes b 14 Aug 1937, died 23 Apr 1984 d of John McDonald M. and Margaret Stirling; Children: Fiona b 23 Feb 1962 m Scott John; Deirdre b 29 Sep 1964; Innes Malcolm b 9 Oct 1966 m Darah; Lindsay Jane b 5 Nov 1976; m (2) 30 Aug 1986 Susan Alexander b 9 Jan 1956 d of Claud A. and Maisie Barbour; Children: Lewis b 24 Jul 1978; Ralph b 7 Oct 1980; Aelrid b 20 Mar 1988; ord by

Presb of Glasgow and introd as Assoc at Renfield St Stephen's 22 Jun 1976; res 31 Jul 1990 and app Industrial Chaplain for Glasgow Sep 1990; ret 25 Nov 1998.

1985   WILLIAM ANDREW WYLIE
(FES IX, 251; X, 21, 148, 413, 456), dem from Edinburgh St Andrew's and St George's on app as Industrial Chaplain for Inverclyde 20 Jun 1985; app Chaplain to Offshore Oil Industry 1 May 1986; ret 1 Nov 1991; m (2) 25 Jun 1988 Jennifer Barclay Geekie b 12 Jul 1949 d of Gordon G. and Sarah Culley; d Fiona m Horbye; d Heather m Torra.

UNIVERSITY CHAPLAINS

In alphabetical order

1986   HELEN JUNE RUTH ALEXANDER
B 1 Jun 1949 at Edinburgh, d of David A. and Jessie Paton McMillan; educ St Denis', Edinburgh 1954–67; Moray House College, Edinburgh 1969–72 (DSW); University of Glasgow 1975–80 (BD); Social Work 1972–75; lic by Presb of Glasgow 26 Jun 1980; asstshp Edinburgh St Giles' Cathedral 1980–83; ord by Presb of Edinburgh during assistantship at St Giles' Cathedral 21 Jun 1981; ind to Kirkwall East 26 Aug 1983; dem on app as Assoc Chaplain to University of Edinburgh 23 Jun 1986; res to take up post in social work Apr 1990.

1980   WILLIAM CRAWFORD ANDERSON
(FES X, 330), dem from Aberdeen Ruthrieston West 30 Jun 1980 on app as Chaplain to Heriot-Watt University; app Chaplain to Oil Industry, Aberdeen 1989.

1989   COLIN MACEWEN ANDERSON
(FES X, 18, 452), dem from Greenock St Margaret's on app as Chaplain to University of Glasgow 2 Oct 1989; ind to Inverness St Stephen's with The Old High 29 Nov 1994.

1989   ROBERT ALEXANDER ANDERSON
dem from Overtown on app as Chaplain to University of Edinburgh 1 Apr 1989; res from app 31 Jul 1994 and app Development Officer, Carberry Tower 1 Sep 1994.

1986   GEORGINA MARTHA BAXENDALE
dem from Coatbridge Blairhill Dundyvan 30 Sep 1986 on app as Assoc Chaplain to University of Glasgow; ind to Houston and Killellan 28 Jun 1989.

1983   GRAHAM KEITH BLOUNT
trans from Glasgow Linthouse St Kenneth's to Chalmers and also app Chaplain (part-time) to University of Stirling 12 Oct 1983; trans to Falkirk Old and St Modan's (joint ministry) 22 Jun 1990.

1999   SCOTT BLYTHE
introd as Assoc (part-time) at Garthdee and Chaplain (part-time) to Robert Gordon University 15 Apr 1999.

1997   FIONA CAROL DOUGLAS
B 11 Dec 1962 at Hamilton, d of Allan D. and Isobel Summers Anderson; educ Hamilton Grammar 1972–78; University of Glasgow 1978–82 (MA); University of Edinburgh 1982–85 (BD), 1990–96 (PhD); lic by Presb of Hamilton, 1988;

asstshp Edinburgh St Giles' Cathedral 1988–90; ord by Presb of Edinburgh during assistantship at St Giles' Cathedral 19 May 1989; app Warden of Hall of Residence, University of Edinburgh 1 Sep 1990; loc ten Duke St Congregational Church, Leith 4 Jan 1992; app Tutor in Practical Theology, University of Edinburgh 1 Oct 1992; BBC Religious Broadcasting 1 Apr 1997; app Chaplain to University of Dundee 1 Sep 1997.

1993   ALAN LINKLATER DUNNETT
app Chaplain to University of Strathclyde 1 Oct 1993; ind to Glasgow Partick South 11 Dec 1997.

1987   DAVID DOUGLAS GALBRAITH
(FES X, 21), Chaplain to University of St Andrews 1 Sep 1987–31 Aug 1993; Visiting Scholar, Parkin-Wesley College, Adelaide, Australia 1 Jun 1994–31 Dec 1994; app Admin Secretary, Panel on Worship, Panel on Doctrine, Committee on Artistic Matters 1 Mar 1995.

1992   CHRISTINE MARGARET GOLDIE
dem from Clydebank St Cuthbert's on app as Chaplain to Glasgow Polytechnic 17 Feb 1992 (now Glasgow Caledonian University); ind to Glasgow Colston Wellpark 8 Apr 1999.

1990   GRAHAM RICHARD HOUSTON
B 3 May 1950 at Glasgow, s of Campbell H. and Gertrude Dawson; educ Hutchesons' Grammar, Glasgow 1959–68; University of Strathclyde 1968–72 (BSc); University of Aberdeen 1973–76 (BD), 1979–83 (MTh); Heriot-Watt University 1991–96 (PhD); Architectural Asst 1972–73; lic by Presb of Aberdeen 26 Jun 1976; asstshp Edinburgh Palmerston Place 1976–77; m 19 Jan 1978 Irene Elizabeth Robertson b 9 Feb 1955 d of David R. and Elizabeth Dick; Children: Rachel Anna b 25 Feb 1979; Rhoda Susan b 11 Oct 1982; Stephen John b 5 May 1985; ord and ind to Kildonan and Loth Helmsdale 17 Feb 1978; dem from Perth Letham St Mark's 30 Jun 1990 to take up app as Chaplain to Heriot-Watt University 1 Jul 1990; Publ: *Prophecy Now* (Inter-Varsity Press, 1989); *Virtual Morality* (Inter-Varsity Press, 1998).

1975   EVERARD WILLIAM KANT
(FES IX, 364; X, 28, 55 (2), 85, 217, 441), dem from Kirkconnel St Mark's with Kirkconnel St Conal's and app Chaplain to International Students,

University of Glasgow 2 Feb 1975; ind to Kinghorn 13 Apr 1978.

1978 CHRISTOPHER LEON LEVISON
(FES X, 201), dem from Newmains Coltness Memorial on app as Assoc Chaplain to University of Aberdeen 20 Aug 1978; ind to Paisley High 30 Aug 1983.

1975 JOHN STEWART LOCHRIE
(FES X, 101, 441), dem from Dailly on app as Chaplain to the Students' Assoc, University of Strathclyde 10 Nov 1975; res 1987; ind to Arnsheen Barrhill with Colmonell 23 Mar 1999.

1998 MARJORY MACASKILL
B 30 Nov 1963 at Rutherglen, d of David Proctor Adams and Nancy Edmiston McBeth; educ Lanark Grammar 1975–81; University of Glasgow 1981–85 (LLB), 1985–88 (BD); lic by Presb of Lanark 3 Jul 1988; asstshp Glasgow Wellington 1988–89; m 16 Aug 1989 Donald Macaskill b 25 Feb 1965 s of Malcolm M. and Mary Campbell; Children: Rachael b 16 May 1992; ord and ind to Avonbridge with Torphichen 29 May 1990; dem 12 Jul 1998 on app as Chaplain to University of Strathclyde.

1996 GILLEAN PATRICIA MACLEAN
B 15 Nov 1955 at Glasgow, d of Kenneth MacDonald M. and Patricia Anne Green; educ Lockerbie Academy and Strathaven Academy; Eastern District College of Nursing 1973–77; University College, Cardiff 1989–90; University of Aberdeen 1990–93 (BD); Nursing 1977–92; Social Work 1987–89; lic by Presb of Gordon; asstshp Aberdeen Middlefield 1993–94; m 29 Nov 1975 James Pullar Moncur b 6 Oct 1955 s of James Anderson M. and Jean Pullar; Children: Fiona b 7 May 1977; Patricia b 2 Dec 1979; Rosemary b 18 Feb 1983; ord by Presb of Aberdeen and app Asst Chaplain to University of Aberdeen 1 Dec 1994; app Chaplain 1 Sep 1996.

1985 ANDREW THOMAS MACLEAN
dem from Aberdeen Stockethill on app as Chaplain to Students' Assoc, University of Strathclyde 1 Sep 1985; ind to Port Glasgow St Andrew's 30 Mar 1993.

1991 GORDON FRASER HAY MACNAUGHTON
dem from Fenwick on app as Chaplain to University of Dundee 1 Apr 1991; ind to Bearsden Killermont 26 Feb 1998.

1966 MAXWELL MAGEE
(FES IX, 233, 742; X, 135, 441), res as Chaplain to Overseas Students on app as Chaplain to University of Strathclyde 1 Jun 1966; ret 1975; died 3 May 1991.

1970 ALAN MAIN
(FES X, 344, 441), dem from Chapel of Garioch on app as Chaplain to University of Aberdeen 1 Sep 1970; res on app as Professor of Practical Theology, University of Aberdeen 1 Jan 1980.

1995 FIONA McDOUGALL MATHIESON
B 28 Dec 1962 at Lennoxtown, d of James McLaws Buchan and Marion McDougall; educ Williamwood High, Clarkston and Mearns Castle High, Newton Mearns 1974–80; Jordanhill College, Glasgow 1980–84 (BEd); University of Edinburgh 1984–87 (BD); Heriot-Watt University 1990–92 [part-time] (PGCEd); lic by Presb of Glasgow 2 Jul 1987; asstshp Edinburgh Greenbank 1987–88; m 1 Jul 1999 Angus Rankin Mathieson b 7 Feb 1961 s of James Rankin M. and Agnes Patrick Boyd; ord by Presb of Edinburgh during assistantship at Greenbank 19 Jun 1988; app Church of Scotland Youth Adviser 1 Sep 1988; app Chaplain to University of Glasgow 1 Apr 1995.

1964 DAVID ALEXANDER RAMAGE MILLAR
(FES X, 20, 437, 442), dem from Edinburgh Richmond Craigmillar on app as Chaplain to University of Glasgow 20 Oct 1964; app Lecturer in Practical Theology, University of Glasgow 1 Oct 1970; held both posts until ret as Chaplain 30 Sep 1989, ret as Lecturer 30 Sep 1990.

1977 JOHN PRINGLE LORIMER MUNRO
ord by Presb of Stirling, Oct 1977 and app Chaplain to University of Stirling; res on app by Overseas Council as Lecturer at St Paul's United Theological College, Limuru, Kenya Sep 1982.

1991 WILLIAM M MURDOCH
dem from Barthol Chapel with Tarves 31 Mar 1991 on app as Chaplain to University of Aberdeen; ret 1996.

1973 JOHN LOVE PATERSON
(FES X, 424, 442), res from service with Overseas Council in Kenya on app as Chaplain to University of Stirling 8 Jan 1973; ind to Linlithgow St Michael's 17 Mar 1977.

1978 JOHN PETER SANDISON PURVES
ord by Presb of Aberdeen 26 Oct 1978 and app Asst Chaplain to University of Aberdeen; res on app by Board of World Mission for service in Jamaica and Grand Cayman 1 Mar 1983.

1981 ALAN ANDERSON STUART REID
(FES X, 206, 220), res as Chaplain to Strathallan School, Forgandenny on app as Chaplain to University of Aberdeen, Jan 1981; ind to Bridge of Allan Chalmers 9 Jan 1990.

1971 LIONEL ALEXANDER RITCHIE
(FES IX, 297, 370; X, 221), res as Chaplain to Victoria School, Dunblane on app as Chaplain to University of Glasgow 1971; ret 1982; died 30 Dec 1996.

1966 THOMAS HARDY SCOTT
(FES X, 35, 442), dem from Bonnybridge to take up app as Chaplain to Heriot-Watt University 30 Sep 1966; ret 30 Sep 1979; died 20 May 1997.

1983 NORMAN JAMES SHANKS
ord by Presb of Edinburgh 14 Oct 1983; app Assoc
Chaplain to University of Edinburgh 26 Jun 1983;
app Chaplain 1 Sep 1985; app Lecturer in Practical
Theology, University of Glasgow 1 Dec 1988.

1998 HOWARD GEORGE TAYLOR
B 6 Jun 1944 at Stockport, s of Norman and
Dorothy T; educ Gravesend Technical School
1955–62; University of Nottingham 1962–65;
University of Edinburgh 1967–70; University of
Aberdeen 1998 (MTh); Lecturer, University of
Malawi 1965–67; lic by Presb of Edinburgh; asst
Zomba, Malawi 1971; m 22 Mar 1969 Eleanor Clark
b 3 Apr 1939 d of Nelson C. and Janet Turner;
Children: Douglas b 31 Jan 1970; Keith b 15 Feb
1972 m Nina; Ian b 11 Jul 1975; ord by Church of
Central Africa Presb and ind to Zomba, Malawi 13
May 1971; ind to Innellan with Inverchaolain and
Toward 27 Oct 1981; trans to Glasgow St David's
Knightswood 25 Sep 1986; dem 22 Sep 1998
to take up app as Chaplain and Lecturer, Heriot-
Watt University; Lecturer at International Christian
College, Glasgow from 1987; Publ: *Faith Seeks
Understanding* (CLAIM, Malawi, 1981); *Pray Today
1982–83* (Church of Scotland, 1982); *In Christ All
Things Hold Together* (Collins [UK] Eerdmans,
[USA], 1983); *World Hope in the Middle East*
(Handsel Press, 1985); *Delusion of Unbelief in a
Scientific Age* (Handsel Press, 1988); *Faith and
Understanding* (Rutherford House, 1990, 1998);
Israel The People of God (PWM, 1991); *The
Uniqueness of Christ in a Pluralist World* (Ruther-
ford House, 1994); *Is the New Testament the
Source of Anti-Semitism?* (CFI, 1995); *The Mystery
of Israel* (CFI); contributor to *God, Family and
Sexuality* (Order of Christian Unity, 1997); MTh
thesis: 'The Gospel and the Open Frontiers of
Science'; various articles and book reviews.

1993 JAMES BERNARD WALKER
(FES X, 304), res as Principal of Queen's College,
Birmingham on app as Chaplain to University of
St Andrews 1 Sep 1993; University of Oxford 1981
(DPhil); Addl children: Peter Donald b 12 Sep 1978;
Publ: *Athanasius of Alexandria* in *New Dictionary
of Christian Thought* (ed Ferguson and Wright,
Leicester, 1988); *Homosexuality—Predisposing
Factors* in *God, Family and Sexuality* (ed Torrance,
Handsel Press, 1997); *Israel—Covenant and Land*
(Handsel Press, 1988); various book reviews.

1981 IAIN ALEXANDER WHYTE
(FES X, 427), dem from Paisley Merksworth to take
up app as Chaplain to University of St Andrews 1
Oct 1981; ind to Coatbridge Blairhill Dundyvan 15
Jun 1987.

1994 IAIN ALEXANDER WHYTE
(FES X, 427), res as National Secretary, Christian
Aid Scotland to take up app as Chaplain to
University of Edinburgh 1 Oct 1994.

UNIVERSITIES AND COLLEGES

In alphabetical order

1973 JAMES STEWART ALEXANDER
(FES X, 434), app Lecturer in Eccl History, University of St Andrews 1973.

1966 HUGH ANDERSON
(FES IX, 310; X, 182, 428), app Professor of New Testament Language, Literature and Theology, University of Edinburgh 1 Oct 1966; ret 1985; Addl publ: *Gospel of Mark* (Westminster, 1974, Eerdmans, 1976); *Maccabees III and IV* (Doubleday, 1987).

1995 ALAN GRAEME AULD
(FES X, 434), app as Lecturer in Hebrew and Old Testament Studies, University of Edinburgh 1 Oct 1972; app Professor of Hebrew Bible, University of Edinburgh 1 Oct 1995; Dean of Divinity 1993–96; University of Aberdeen 1994 (DLitt); Publ: *Joshua, Moses and the Land* (T&T Clark, 1980); *Joshua, Judges and Ruth* (St Andrew Press and Westminster Press, Philadelphia, 1984); *Kings* (St Andrew Press and Westminster Press, 1986); *Amos* (Sheffield Academic Press, 1986); *Kings without Privilege* (T&T Clark, 1994); *Joshua Retold: Synoptic Perspectives* (T&T Clark, 1998).

1982 ROBERT ALEXANDER STEWART BARBOUR
(FES IX, 738; X, 428, 434), app Professor of New Testament Studies (part-time), University of Aberdeen 1 Sep 1982; Moderator of General Assembly 1979–80; ret 31 Aug 1986; s George Freeland m Charlotte Mackintosh; s David m Alexandra Howarth; s Andrew m Seonag MacDonald; Addl publ: Editor of *The Kingdom of God and Human Society* (T&T Clark, 1993); various articles.

1963 WILLIAM BARCLAY
(FES IX, 227, 778; X, 428), app Professor of Divinity and Biblical Criticism, University of Glasgow 1 Oct 1963; ret 30 Sep 1974; died 24 Jan 1978.

1974 ERNEST BEST
(FES X, 428), app Professor of Divinity and Biblical Criticism, University of Glasgow 1974; Dean of Faculty of Divinity 1978–80; ret 30 Sep 1982; Visiting Professor of New Testament, University of Otago 1983; Sprunt Lecturer, Union Theological Seminary, Richmond 1985; Fellowship, New College, University of Edinburgh 1995; DD

(Glasgow) 1997; d Sheila m Peter Malcolm Cannell; d Mary m (2) Andrew Denis Popple; Publ: *Disciples and Discipleship* (T&T Clark, 1978); co-editor of *Text and Interpretation* (CUP, 1979); *From Text to Sermon* (John Knox, 1979; T&T Clark, 1990); *Following Jesus* (1981); *Mark: The Gospel as Story* (T&T Clark, 1982); *Paul and His Converts* (T&T Clark, 1988); *II Corinthians* (Westminster, John Knox, 1987, 2nd ed 1990); *Ephesians* Study Guide (Sheffield Academic Press, 1993); *Interpreting Christ* (T&T Clark, 1993); *Essays on Ephesians* (T&T Clark, 1997); *Ephesians International Critical Commentary* (T&T Clark, 1998).

1954 MATTHEW BLACK
(FES IX, 422, 767, 768, 778; X, 429), ret as Professor of Biblical Criticism and Principal of St Mary's College, University of St Andrews 1978; died 2 Oct 1994.

1992 IAN CAMPBELL BRADLEY
B 28 May 1950 at Berkhamstead, Hertfordshire, s of William Ewart B. and Mary Campbell Tyre; educ Tonbridge School 1963–68; University of Oxford 1968–71 (MA), 1971–74 (DPhil); University of St Andrews 1986–89 (BD); Journalism 1975–82; Teaching and Writing 1982–85; lic by Presb of St Andrews 2 Jul 1989; asst St Andrews St Leonard's 1989–90; m 20 Jul 1985 Lucy Patricia Blackburn 24 Feb 1956 d of Robert B. and Esther Archer; Children: Mary Esther b 15 May 1986; Andrew David b 4 Aug 1988; ord by Presb of St Andrews during assistantship at St Leonard's 29 Apr 1990; app Head of Religious Broadcasting, BBC Scotland 1 May 1990; app Lecturer in Divinity, University of Aberdeen 1 Sep 1992; app Senior Lecturer in Practical Theology, University of St Andrews 1 Feb 1999; Publ: *The Penguin Book of Hymns* (Penguin, 1986); *God is Green: Christianity and the Environment* (DLT, 1990); *O love that wilt not let me go* (Collins, 1991); *Maring to the Promised Land: Has the Church a Future?* (John Murray, 1992); *The Celtic Way* (DLT, 1993); *The Power of Sacrifice* (DLT, 1994); *Columba, Pilgrim and Penitent* (Wild Goose Publs, 1996); *Abide with me: The World of Victorian Hymns* (SCM, 1997); *Celtic Christianity: Making Myths and Chasing Dreams* (Edinburgh Univ Press, 1999); *The Penguin Book of Hymns* (Penguin, 1999); *Colonies of Heaven: Celtic Models for the Church Today* (DLT, 2000).

1981   ROBIN GRAEME BROWN
(FES X, 416), app Leader of Iona Community 1 Nov 1974; app by Dept of Education, St Colm's, Edinburgh 1981; app Principal of College 1984; app Deputy General Secretary of Board of Parish Education 1993; ind to Birsay with Rousay 30 Mar 1994.

1931   JOHN HENDERSON SEAFORTH BURLEIGH
(FES VI, 259; VIII, 489; IX, 514, 769; X, 429), app Professor of Eccl History, University of Edinburgh Oct 1931; app Principal of New College and Dean of Faculty of Divinity 1 Oct 1956; ret 30 Sep 1964; died 22 Mar 1985.

1947   DAVID CAIRNS
(FES IX, 443, 769; X, 429), ret from Chair of Practical Theology, University of Aberdeen 30 Sep 1972; died 17 Oct 1992.

1970   JAMES KERR CAMERON
(FES X, 429, 434), app Professor of Eccl History, University of St Andrews 1 Sep 1970; ret 30 Sep 1989; s Euan m Ruth Tonkiss; Addl publ: Various publs for Eccl History Society (Basil Blackwell, 1990–97); contributor to *Theologische Realenzyklopädie* ed G Müller (Walter de Gruyter, Berlin, Vols 9–30, 1982–99); contributor to *New Dictionary of National Biography* ed C Matthew (OUP).

1987   PETER S CAMERON
dem from Edinburgh Portobello St Philip's Joppa 30 Sep 1987 on app as Lecturer in New Testament, University of Edinburgh; res 1991 and moved to Australia.

1999   STEPHEN JOHN CHESTER
B 7 May 1967 at Liverpool, s of John Edward C. and Valerie Ann Whitaker; educ Holywell High, Flintshire 1978–85; University of York 1985–88 (BA); University of Glasgow 1991–94 (BD), 1995–99 (PhD); Housing Officer 1989–91; lic by Presb of Glasgow 24 Oct 1994; asstshp Glasgow Burnside 1994–95; m 23 Mar 1991 Betsy May Benson b 1 May 1956 d of Edward Barrington B. and Mary Thomson Anderson; Children; Ian Edward b 1 Jan 1993; Mark Stephen b 26 Jan 1996; ord by Presb of Glasgow 16 Jun 1999; app Lecturer in New Testament, International Christian College, Glasgow 1 Apr 1999.

1964   ALEXANDER CAMPBELL CHEYNE
(FES X, 429, 434), app Professor of Eccl History, University of Edinburgh 1 Oct 1964; app Principal of New College, 1 Oct 1984; ret 30 Sep 1986; Hon DLitt (Memorial University, Newfoundland) 1983; Addl publ: *The Transforming of the Kirk* (St Andrew Press, 1983); *The Ten Years Conflict and the Disruption: An Overview* (Scottish Academic Press, 1993); *Studies in Scottish Church History* (T&T Clark, 1999); numerous articles.

1963   ROBERT CRAIG
(FES IX, 787; X, 429), res as Professor of Religion, Smith College, Northampton, Mass, USA on app as Professor of Theology, University of Zimbabwe 1963; app Principal and Vice-Chancellor 1969; ind to Jerusalem St Andrew's 1980.

1947   ARCHIBALD CAMPBELL CRAIG
(FUF 227; FES IX, 269, 778, 783; X, 434), Lecturer in Biblical Studies, University of Glasgow 1947 60; Moderator of General Assembly 1961–62; died 26 Aug 1985.

1982   ROBERT DAVIDSON
(FES X, 429, 434), app Principal of Trinity College, University of Glasgow 1 Oct 1982; Moderator of General Assembly 1990–91; ret 31 Oct 1991; Addl children: Scott Davidson b 8 Mar 1973; d Joyce m David Hughes; d Olive m Andrew Pascoe; d Denise m Stephen Brooks; Addl publ: *Genesis 12–50* (Cambridge Bible Commentary, 1979); *The Bible in Religious Education* (Handsel Press, 1979); *Jeremiah 1–20* (Daily Study Bible, St Andrew Press, Westminster USA, 1983); *Jeremiah II/Lamentations* (Daily Study Bible, St Andrew Press, Westminster, 1986); *Song of Songs/Ecclesiastes* (Daily Study Bible, St Andrew Press, Westminster, 1986); *The Courage to Doubt* (SCM, 1983); *Wisdom and Worship* (SCM, 1990); *A Beginners Guide to the Old Testament* (St Andrew Press, 1992); *Go by the Book* (St Andrew Press, 1996); *The Vitality of Worship: A Commentary on the Psalms* (Eerdmans and Handsel Press, 1998).

1935   EDGAR PRIMROSE DICKIE
(FUF 99; FES IX, 10, 135, 769; X, 430), dem from Edinburgh Corstorphine St Anne's on app as Chair of Divinity, University of St Andrews 30 Sep 1935; ret 30 Sep 1967; died 28 Jun 1991.

1984   KENNETH WAYLAND DUPAR
(FES X, 329), dem from Aberdeen Ruthrieston South on app as Director of Extension Education, Christ's College, Aberdeen and Lecturer in Practical Theology (part-time), King's College, Aberdeen 5 Sep 1984; Visiting Fellow, Princeton Theological Seminary, New Jersey 15 Sep 1990; app Chaplain to City Hospital Group, Aberdeen 1 Jul 1992; ret 15 Apr 1993; d Mairi m Jamal Gore; Publ: Contributor to *Children of the Way—Juniors* (St Andrew Press, 1979); *Holiday Club* (Harlaw House, 1982); *Visiting the Parish* (Christ's College, 1989); *Visiting the Hospital* (Christ's College, 1989).

1964   IAN COUTTS MACINTYRE FAIRWEATHER
(FES IX, 199, 733; X, 114, 435), app Lecturer in Religious Education, Jordanhill College, Glasgow 1 Jun 1964; recognised as University Lecturer in Religious Studies 1 Sep 1967; Secondary Teaching Qualification 17 Oct 1973; ret 30 Apr 1982; Publ: *Play Fair* [8 Teachers' Handbooks to accompany TV series] (Scottish Television, 1973–80);

contributor to *A Dictionary of Religious Educa-tion* (SCM, 1984); co-author of *The Quest for Christian Ethics* (Handsel Press, 1984); co-author of *Religious Education* (Scottish Academic Press, 1992).

1982 SINCLAIR BUCHANAN FERGUSON
(FES X, 407), res as Editor, Banner of Truth Trust on app as Professor of Systematic Theology, Westminster Theological Seminary, Philadelphia, USA 1 Jul 1982; ind to Glasgow St George's Tron 1 Jul 1998.

1990 DAVID ALEXANDER SYME FERGUSSON
B 3 Aug 1956 at Glasgow, s of Thomas Edgar Syme F. and Charis Wilson Boyle; educ Kelvinside Academy, Glasgow 1961–73; University of Glas-gow 1973–77 (MA); University of Edinburgh 1977–80 (BD); University of Oxford 1980–83 (DPhil); lic by Presb of Edinburgh 6 Jul 1980; asst Lanark St Nicholas' 1983–84; m 5 Sep 1985 Margot Evelyn McIndoe b 13 May 1962 d of John Hedley M. and Evelyn Kennedy Johnstone; Children: Mark John b 5 May 1989; Calum Thomas b 6 May 1993; ord by Presb of Falkirk and introd as Assoc at Cum-bernauld St Mungo's 19 Nov 1984; app Lecturer in Systematic Theology, University of Edinburgh 1 Oct 1986; app Professor of Systematic Theology, University of Aberdeen 1 Apr 1990; Publ: *Bultmann* (Chapman, 1992); *Christ, Church and Society* (T&T Clark, 1993); *The Cosmos and the Creator* (SPCK, 1998); *Community, Liberalism, and Christian Ethics* (CUP, 1998).

1968 JOHN ROBB FLEMING
(FES IX, 734; X, 419, 435), app Senior Lecturer in Divinity, University of St Andrews Sep 1968; ret 30 Sep 1976; died 27 Jun 1999; w Pearl died 1993; Addl publ: *The Growth of the Chinese Church in the New Villages of the State of Johore, Malaya 1950–60* (ThD Thesis, UTS Library, New York, 1961).

1978 DUNCAN BAILLIE FORRESTER
(FES X, 419), Chaplain and Lecturer (Political and Religious Studies), University of Sussex 1970–78; app Professor of Christian Ethics and Practical Theology, University of Edinburgh 1 Oct 1978; Dean of Faculty of Divinity from 1996; Principal of New College 1986–96; Director of Edinburgh University Centre for Theology and Public Issues from 1984; University of Sussex 1976 (DPhil); ThD (Univ of Iceland) 1997; DD (Glasgow) 1999; Tem-pleton Prize (UK) 1999; Addl publ: *Caste and Christianity* (Curzon, 1980); co-author of *Encounter with God* (T&T Clark, 1983); co-editor of *Studies in the History of Worship in Scotland* (T&T Clark, 1984); *Christianity and the Future of Welfare* (Epworth, 1985); *The Scottish Churches and the Political Process Today* (CPTI, 1986); *Theology and Politics* (Blackwell, 1988); co-editor and co-author of *Just Sharing* (Epworth, 1988); co-editor of *Worship Now II* (St Andrew Press, 1989); *Beliefs, Values and Policies* (Clarendon Press, 1989);

editor of *Theology and Practice* (Epworth, 1990); *Christian Justice and Public Policy* (CUP, 1997); *The True Church and Morality* (WCC, 1997); numerous articles (esp Indian politics and religion, ethics and political theology).

1980 DAVID DOUGLAS GALBRAITH
(FES X, 21), dem from Strathkinness on app as Lecturer (temp) in Practical Theology, University of St Andrews 1 Aug 1980; app Professor of Ministry and Mission, Trinity Theological College, Brisbane, Australia 1 Jun 1981; res Dec 1986; app Chaplain to University of St Andrews 1 Sep 1987.

1969 ALLAN DOUGLAS GALLOWAY
(FES IX, 502; X, 430, 435), app Professor of Divinity, University of Glasgow 1 Oct 1969; Prin-cipal of Trinity College, Glasgow 1975–80; Henley Henson Lecturer, Oxford 1978; ret 1 Oct 1980; Gifford Lecturer, Glasgow 1984; s John m Juanita; Addl publ: *The History of Christian Theology* (Eerdmans, 1986).

1987 JOHN CLARK LOVE GIBSON
(FES X, 336, 435), app Professor of Hebrew and Old Testament, University of Edinburgh 1 Oct 1987; ret 30 Sep 1994; s Herbert m Patricia Blyde; d Jane m Arthur Weatherly (divorced); s Robert m Juliet Curtis; s Peter m Christine Stevenson (divorced); Addl publ: *Canaanite Myths and Legends* (T&T Clark, 1978); *Daily Study Bible: Genesis Vol 1 and 2* (St Andrew Press, 1981, Westminster Press, 1982); *Textbook of Phoenician Inscriptions* (Clarendon Press, 1985); *Daily Study Bible: Job* (St Andrew Press, Westminster Press, 1986); *Davidson's Introduc-tory Hebrew Grammar/Syntax* [new ed] (T&T Clark, 1994); *Language and Imagery in the Old Testament* (SPCK, 1998); various articles on Semitic Languages and Old Testament subjects in journals from 1965.

1937 JOHN MACDONALD GRAHAM
(FES IX, 362, 771; X, 430), ret from Chair of Systematic Theology, University of Aberdeen 30 Sep 1971; died 7 Apr 1982.

1966 JOHN GRAY
(FES IX, 204, 779; X, 435), app Lecturer in Christian Ethics and Practical Theology, University of Edinburgh 1966; app Senior Lecturer 1969; app Assoc Dean of New College 1976; ret 30 Sep 1977; died 8 Apr 1999.

1962 JOHN GRAY
(FES IX, 206, 760, 779; X, 430), ret as Professor of Hebrew and Semitic Languages, University of Aberdeen Jun 1980.

1975 JAMES GREEN
(FES IX, 453; X, 111, 268), app Chair of Division of Religion and Philosophy, Sunderland Poly-technic 1 Apr 1975; died 1 Mar 1989.

1984 DAVID SAGE MILLEN HAMILTON
(FES X, 23, 223, 290, 331), dem from Bearsden New Kilpatrick on app as Lecturer in Practical Theology, University of Glasgow 1 Aug 1984; ret 30 Sep 1996; Publ: *Through the Waters: Baptism and the Christian Life* (T&T Clark, 1989); editor of *The Reading for Today* (Trinity St Mungo Press, 1995).

1981 ALASDAIR IAIN CAMPBELL HERON
(FES X, 435), app Professor of Reformed Theology, University of Erlangen 1 Oct 1981; Kerr Lecturer, University of Glasgow 1978; Henson Lecturer, University of Oxford 1999; Addl publ: Editor of *Scottish Journal of Theology* (Scottish Academic Press, T&T Clark, 1974–97); monographs: *Two Churches, One Love* (APCK, Dublin 1977); *A Century of Protestant Theology* (Lutterworth, Westminster, 1980); *The Holy Spirit* (Marshall, Morgan & Scott, Westminster 1983); *Table and Tradition* (Handsel Press, Westminster, 1983); edited works: *The Westminster Confession in the Church Today* (St Andrew Press, 1982); *Agreement and Disagreement between the Church of Scotland and the Roman Catholic Church* (Handsel Press, 1984); *The Forgotten Trinity* (BCC, 1991); numerous articles and essays.

1980 ALASTAIR GILBERT HUNTER
B 23 Jan 1943 at Glasgow, s of Gilbert H. and Isabella Sneddon Donald Cormack; educ Hutchesons' Grammar, Glasgow 1955–61; University of Glasgow 1961–65 (BSc), 1965–67 (MSc), 1972–75 (BD); Jordanhill College, Glasgow 1971 (DSEd); Asst Lecturer, University of Glasgow 1966–67; Church of Scotland Missionary in Pakistan 1968–71; Teaching 1971–72; lic by Presb of Glasgow 30 Jun 1975; asst Glasgow Cardonald 1975–76; m 30 Jun 1967 Dorothy Eleanore Petrie b 17 Apr 1943 d of George P. and Dorothy MacKay; Children: Jennifer Moira b 27 Mar 1968; Mark David b 17 Jan 1970; m (2) 8 Jun 1990 Margaret Elizabeth Whittaker b 1 Mar 1948 d of Alfred Joseph Haddleton W. and Jessie Croal Henderson; ord and ind to Stirling Viewfield 27 May 1976; dem 31 Dec 1979 on app as Lecturer in Hebrew and Old Testament, University of Glasgow; Publ: *Christianity and Other Faiths in Britain* (SCM, 1985); co-author of *A National Church in a Multi-Racial Scotland* (Scottish Churches' Council, 1986); contributor to *A Dictionary of Biblical Interpretation* (SCM, 1990); *Reading the Old Testament: The Psalms* (Routledge, 1999); articles for *Scottish Journal of Theology*; editor of *Trinity College Bulletin* 1984–93 (University of Glasgow); articles for CTBI and Church of Scotland publs; numerous articles and papers, esp. Jewish/Christian relations.

1958 ARCHIBALD MACBRIDE HUNTER
(FES IX, 126, 131, 771; X, 130), Professor of New Testament Exegesis and Master of Christ's College, University of Aberdeen; ret 30 Sep 1971; died 14 Sep 1991.

1980 WILLIAM JOHNSTONE
(FES X, 436), app Professor of Hebrew and Semitic Languages, University of Aberdeen 1 Nov 1980; DLitt (Glasgow) 1998; Addl publ: *Exodus* (Sheffield Academic Press, 1990); editor of *William Robertson Smith: Essays in Reassessment* (Sheffield Academic Press, 1995); *Chronicles* [2 vols] (Sheffield Academic Press, 1997); *Chronicles and Exodus* (Sheffield Academic Press, 1998); various chapters, articles and reviews in journals.

1970 ALBERT JOHN LANGDON
(FES X, 421, 436), res as Principal Lecturer in Religious Education at Hamilton College of Education on app as Principal Lecturer in RE at Moray House College, Edinburgh 1 Oct 1970; died 23 Sep 1985.

1953 WILLIAM LILLIE
(FES VIII, 740; FES IX, 634, 738, 779; X, 436), dem from Dulnain Bridge on app as Lecturer in Biblical Studies, University of Aberdeen 1 Oct 1953; ret 30 Jun 1969; died 29 Dec 1982.

1987 DAVID LYALL
(FES X, 115, 450), res as Chaplain to Edinburgh Northern Hospitals and app Lecturer in Practical Theology, University of St Andrews 1 Oct 1987; app Lecturer in Christian Ethics and Practical Theology, University of Edinburgh 1 Oct 1990; app Principal of New College 1 Oct 1999; University of Edinburgh 1974–79 (PhD); Publ: Co-author of *Helping the Helpers* (SPCK, 1988); *Counselling in the Pastoral and Spiritual Context* (Open Univ Press, 1995).

1994 DONALD MACASKILL
B 25 Feb 1965 at Glasgow, s of Malcolm M. and Mary Campbell; educ Hillhead High School, Glasgow 1976–82; University of Glasgow 1982–85 (MA), 1985–88 (BD), 1999 (PhD); lic by Presb of Glasgow 5 Jul 1988; asst St Magnus Cathedral, Orkney 1988–89; m 16 Aug 1989 Marjory Adams b 30 Nov 1963 d of David A. and Nancy McBeth; Children: Rachael b 16 May 1992; ord by Presb of West Lothian 3 Nov 1994; app Tutor and Director of Human Relations, Board of Parish Education 1 Apr 1994; app Vice-Principal, Scottish Churches Open College and Secretary for Readership 1998; Publ: Founding Editor of *Didache* [European Journal of Christian Education] (EAEE, 1997–); Co-editor of *British Journal of Theological Education* (Sheffield Academic Press, 1998-); various articles and contributions to volumes, various educational packs.

1964 MURDO EWEN MACDONALD
(FES IX, 39, 285, 690; X, 23, 430), dem from Edinburgh St George's West on app as Professor of Practical Theology, University of Glasgow 7 Jan 1964; ret 1984.

1974 STEVEN GABRIEL MACKIE
(FES X, 437), app Lecturer in Practical Theology and Ethics, University of St Andrews 1 Oct 1974;

ret 30 Sep 1993; s James m Sylvain Bayens; s Robert m Susan Bischofberger; s Alexander m Pamela Tresise; Addl publ: Co-author of *A National Church in a Multi-Racial Scotland* (Scottish Churches' Council, 1985).

1980   ALAN MAIN
(FES X, 344, 441), res as Chaplain to University of Aberdeen on app as Professor of Practical Theology, University of Aberdeen 1 Jan 1980; app Master of Christ's College, University of Aberdeen Oct 1992; Moderator of General Assembly 1998–99; d Katherine m James Burke; d Lesley m Ian Cook; Publ: Editor of *Worship Now II* (St Andrew Press, 1989); editor of *But Where Shall Wisdom be Found* (Aberdeen Univ Press, 1995).

1934   JOHN MAUCHLINE
(FES VIII, 257; IX, 336, 767, 773; X, 431), ret from Chair of Old Testament Language and Literature, University of Glasgow 39 Jun 1972; died 7 Jan 1984.

1980   JAMES IAN HAMILTON McDONALD
(FES X, 125, 436), app Lecturer in Christian Ethics, University of Edinburgh 1 Oct 1980; app Senior Lecturer in Christian Ethics and New Testament 1 Oct 1989; app Reader in Christian Ethics and New Testament 1 Oct 1992; ret 30 Sep 1998; Educational Institute of Scotland 1986 (FEIS); app Hon Fellow, University of Edinburgh 1 Oct 1998; Addl publ: *Kerygma and Didache* (CUP, 1980); *Resurrection* (SPCK, 1989); *Biblical Interpretation and Christian Ethics* (CUP, 1993); *The Crucible of Christian Morality* (Routledge, 1998).

1958   JAMES STEVENSON McEWEN
(FES IX, 116, 519, 610, 779; X, 430), app Professor of Church History, University of Aberdeen 1 Oct 1958; ret 30 Sep 1977; died 4 May 1993.

1951   DONALD MAITLAND McFARLAN
(FES IX, 739, 779; X, 436), res from service with FMC in Calabar on app as Lecturer in RE, Jordanhill College, Glasgow Sep 1951; ret 1981; died 2 Dec 1990.

1956   JOHN McINTYRE
(FES IX, 190; X, 430), app Professor of Divinity, University of Edinburgh 1 Oct 1956; Principal Warden of Pollock Halls of Residence 1960–71; Acting Principal and Vice-Chancellor, University of Edinburgh 1973–74; ret 30 Sep 1986; Dean of the Order of the Thistle and Chaplain to the Queen in Scotland 1974–89; Extra Chaplain to the Queen from 1989; Moderator of General Assembly 1982–83; DD (Glasgow) 1961; FRSE 1977; DHL (Worcester) 1983; CVO 1985; Dr *hr* (Edinburgh); Addl publ: *Faith, Theology and Imagination* (Handsel Press, 1987); *The Shape of Soteriology* (T&T Clark, 1992); *Theology after the Storm* (Eerdmans, 1997); *The Shape of Pneumatology* (T&T Clark, 1997); *The Shape of Christology* (2nd ed, T&T Clark, 1998).

1966   JAMES AINSLIE McINTYRE
(FES X, 436), app Lecturer in New Testament, University of Glasgow 1 Oct 1966; res from app 30 Sep 1984; Assoc at Bearsden New Kilpatrick 1990–97; m (2) 7 Sep 1983 Inez Margaret Hamilton b 5 Aug 1938 d of Daniel Murray H. and Agnes Gibson Dunn.

1968   WILLIAM McKANE
(FES X, 431), app Professor of Hebrew and Oriental Languages, University of St Andrews Jan 1968; app Dean of Faculty of Divinity 1973; Principal of St Mary's College 1982–86; ret 30 Sep 1990; Publ: *Studies in the Patriarchal Narratives* (Handsel Press, 1979); *Jeremiah* (T&T Clark, Vol I, 1984; Vol II, 1996); *Selected Christian Hebraists* (CUP, 1989); *A Late Harvest* (T&T Clark, 1995); *Micah* (T&T Clark, 1998).

1965   ROBERT PATON McKECHNIE
(FES IX, 342; X, 136, 204, 412), dem from Greenock Trinity 31 Dec 1965 to take up app as Lecturer (RE), Saffron Walden College of Education; died 21 Sep 1985.

1951   STEWART MECHIE
(FUF 473; FES IX, 10, 652, 780; X, 437), ret as Lecturer in Eccl History, University of Glasgow 30 Sep 1964; Librarian of Trinity College 1964–74; died 3 Mar 1981.

1970   DAVID ALEXANDER RAMAGE MILLAR
(FES X, 20, 437, 442), dem from Edinburgh Richmond Craigmillar on app as Chaplain to University of Glasgow 20 Oct 1964; app Lecturer in Practical Theology, University of Glasgow 1 Oct 1970; held both posts until ret as Chaplain 30 Sep 1989, ret as Lecturer 30 Sep 1990.

1961   IAN ALEXANDER MOIR
(FES IX, 432, 442; X, 262, 437), app Senior Lecturer in New Testament, University of Edinburgh 1 Oct 1974; ret 1981; died 5 Jun 1993.

1990   WILLIAM GORMAN MORRICE
(FES X, 198, 257), introd as Assoc at London Crown Court 13 Sep 1971; app Lecturer in New Testament, New College, University of London 1 Aug 1972; app New Testament Tutor and Librarian, St John's College, University of Durham 1 Aug 1975 [not 1972, as in Vol X, 198]; app Lecturer in New Testament Greek, University of Durham 1 Oct 1990; app Asst at Newcastle St Andrew's Mar 1989; ret 1 Aug 1995; Addl publ: *We Joy in God* (SPCK, 1977); *The New Beginning: Studies in the Fourth Gospel* (St Andrew Press, 1981); *Joy in the New Testament* (Paternoster Press, Eerdmans, 1984); *The Durham New Testament Greek Course: a Three Month Introduction* (Paternoster Press, 1993); *Hidden Sayings of Jesus* (SPCK, Hendrickson, 1997); sermons, articles and reviews in various journals.

1994 HECTOR MORRISON
B 13 Mar 1955 at Stornoway, s of Hector M. and Christina Ann Macritchie; educ Nicolson Institute, Stornoway 1967–73; University of Glasgow 1973–76 (BSc), 1976–80 (BD), 1989–94 part-time (MTh); lic by Presb of Lewis 24 Jun 1980; m 13 Apr 1981 Annice Catherine Maclennan b 11 Jul 1955 d of Murdani M. and Catherine Macdonald; Children: Neil Hector b 20 May 1982; Ruaraidh Allan b 23 Sep 1985; Cailean Maclennan b 11 Feb 1993; ord and ind to Barvas 9 Dec 1981; trans to Lochalsh 30 Nov 1990; dem on app as Lecturer in Biblical Studies, Highland Theological Institute 1 Aug 1994.

1989 DOUGLAS MILLAR MURRAY
B 25 Sep 1946 at Edinburgh, s of James Pettie M. and Georgina Helen Fowler; educ George Watson's, Edinburgh 1958–64; University of Edinburgh 1964–71 (MA, BD); University of Cambridge 1971–74 (PhD); lic by Presb of Edinburgh 16 Jun 1971; asst Glasgow King's Park 1975–76; m 16 Sep 1983 Freya Marion Smith b 1 May 1954 d of Innes S. and Christina Marion Lawrie; ord and introd to Callander St Bride's (term) 4 Aug 1976; ind to Edinburgh John Ker Memorial in deferred union with Candlish 29 May 1980; became minister of united charge 29 Nov 1981; app Lecturer in Eccl History, University of Glasgow 1 Oct 1989; app Principal of Trinity College, University of Glasgow 21 Oct 1997; Publ: Co-editor of *Studies in the History of Worship in Scotland* (T&T Clark, 1984, 2nd ed 1996); *Freedom to Reform;* Chalmers Lectures (T&T Clark, 1993).

1986 GEORGE McLEOD NEWLANDS
(FES X, 437), app Fellow and Dean, Trinity Hall, University of Cambridge 1 Oct 1982; app Professor of Divinity, University of Glasgow 1 Apr 1986; Principal of Trinity College, Glasgow 1991–97; Addl children: Craig b 22 May 1977; Publ: *Hilary of Poitiers* (Peter Lang, 1978); *Theology of the Love of God* (Collins, 1980); *The Church of God* (Marshall, Morgan & Scott, 1984); *Making Christian Decisions* (Mowbray, 1985); *God in Christian Perspective* (T&T Clark, 1994); *Generosity and the Christian Future* (SPCK, 1997).

1985 JOHN COCHRANE O'NEILL
B 8 Dec 1930 at Melbourne, Australia, s of John Archibald O. and Beni Alberta Cochrane; educ Melbourne Church of England Grammar 1944–47; University of Melbourne 1948–51 (BA); Ormond College Theological Hall, Melbourne 1952–54 (BD); Georg-Augustus Universität, Göttingen, Germany 1956; University of Cambridge 1956–59 (PhD); Tutor (History), University of Melbourne 1952; Senior Tutor 1953–55; Lecturer (Church History), Ormond College, Melbourne 1955; lic by Presb of Melbourne North (Presb Church of Australia) 1 Dec 1954; m 17 Apr 1954 Judith Beatrice Lyall b 30 Jun 1930 d of John Ramsden L. and Beatrice Campbell McDonald; Children: Rachel Margaret b 23 Apr 1957; Catherine Judith

b 26 Jan 1959 m (1) Michael Mulligan, (2) Benjamin Jerome Pritchard; Philippa Mary b 15 Sep 1961; ord by Presb of Melbourne West and app Lecturer in New Testament Studies, Ormond College 22 Nov 1960; app Dunn Professor of New Testament Language, Literature and Theology, Westminster College, Cambridge 7 Oct 1964; app Professor of New Testament Language, Literature and Theology, University of Edinburgh 3 Oct 1985; ret 30 Sep 1996; Publ: *The Theology of Acts in its Historical Setting* (SPCK, 1961); *The Puzzle of 1 John* (SPCK, 1966); *The Recovery of Paul's Letter to the Galatians* (SPCK, 1972); *Paul's Letter to the Romans* (Penguin, 1975); *Messiah: Six Lectures on the Ministry of Jesus. The Cunningham Lectures 1975–76* (Cochrane, 1980); *The Bible's Authority: A Portrait Gallery of Thinkers from Lessing to Bultmann* (T&T Clark, 1991); *Who did Jesus think he was?* (Brill, 1995); *The Point of it All: Essays on Jesus Christ* (Deo, 1999).

1996 RUTH PAGE
B 15 Sep 1935 at Dundee, d of Walter Westwood P. and Joan Sutherland Miller; educ Harris Academy, Dundee and The High School, Stirling 1947–52; University of St Andrews 1952–56 (MA); University of Otago 1969–71 (BD); University of Oxford 1972–75 (DPhil); Teaching 1957–68; lic by Presb of The Bay of Plenty, New Zealand, Dec 1971; ord by Presb of Dunedin, New Zealand, Jan 1975; Lecturer, Theological Hall, University of Otago 1975–79; app Lecturer (1979), then Senior Lecturer (1988), University of Edinburgh; app Principal of New College Oct 1996; Publ: *Ambiguity and the Presence of God* (SCM, 1985); *The Incarnation of Freedom and Love* (SCM, 1990); *God and the Web of Creation* (SCM, 1996); *God with us: Synergy in the Church* (SCM, 2000).

1972 IAN ROBERTSON PITT-WATSON
(FES IX, 784; X, 223, 319, 431, 442), dem from Bearsden New Kilpatrick on app as Professor of Practical Theology, University of Aberdeen 1 Oct 1972; ret 1981; died 11 Jan 1995.

1964 NORMAN WALKER PORTEOUS
(FUF 347; FES IX, 459, 774; X, 431), app Professor of Hebrew and Semitic Languages, University of Edinburgh 1937; app Principal of New College 8 Oct 1964; ret 30 Sep 1968.

1997 IAIN WILLIAM PROVAN
B 6 May 1957 at Johnstone, s of William P. and Rena Jamieson Dobie; educ Paisley Grammar 1969–74; University of Glasgow 1974–77 (MA); London Bible College 1977–80 (BA); University of Cambridge 1982–86 (PhD); Lecturer, Kings College, London 1986–88; Lecturer, New College, Edinburgh 1989–97; lic by Presb of Dunfermline; m 9 May 1981 Lynette Elizabeth McKee b 17 Nov 1956 d of Henry Andrew M. and Christina Duffus; Children: Andrew Iain b 13 May 1985; Kirsty Margaret b 3 Dec 1987; Duncan William b 25 Jun

1990; Catherine Emma b 5 Mar 1993; ord by Presb of Edinburgh 1991; res from New College to take up app as Marshall Sheppard Professor of Biblical Studies, Regent College, Vancouver, BC, Canada 1 Aug 1997; Publ: *Hezekiah and the Books of Kings* (De Gruyter, Berlin, 1988); *Lamentations* (Marshall Pickering, 1991); *1–2 Kings* (Hendrickson, 1995); *1–2 Kings* (Sheffield Academic Press, 1997).

1961 JOHN KELMAN SUTHERLAND REID
(FES IX, 11; X, 431), res as Professor of Theology, University of Leeds on app as Professor of Systematic Theology, University of Aberdeen 1 Oct 1961, ret 1976.

1972 JAMES RICHMOND
(FES X, 197), app Reader in Religious Studies, University of Lancaster 1972; Kerr Lecturer, University of Glasgow 1972–75; Resident Research Fellow, Theological Faculty, University of Göttingen 1973, 1975, 1978, 1981; app Professor of Systematic Theology, University of Lancaster 1980; ret as Professor Emeritus and Hon Life-Member, University of Lancaster 1995; Addl publ: Co-editor of *Reader in Contemporary Theology* (London, Philadelphia, 1967; London, New York, 1971; Spanish ed 1969; Italian ed, 1972); *Theology and Metaphysics* (London, 1970, New York, 1971, Chinese ed, Sichuan People's Publ House, 1990, 1997); *Ritschl: A Reappraisal—A Study in Systematic Theology* (The Kerr Lectures for 1975, University of Glasgow, Collins, 1978), German ed *Albrecht Ritschl: Eine Neubewertung* (Vandenhoeck und Rupprecht, Göttingen, 1982); numerous articles and essays in various publs.

1983 NIGEL JAMES ROBB
ord by Presb of Edinburgh 29 Apr 1981; app Lecturer in Pastoral Theology,Theological Hall, Perth, Australia 1 Jan 1983; res on app as Lecturer in Practical Theology and Christian Ethics, University of St Andrews 1 Sep 1990; res to take up app as Director of Educational Services, Dept of Ministry 1 Jan 1998.

1928 JAMES ROBSON
(FUF 276; FES IX, 375; X, 432), dem from Shandon 30 Sep 1928 on app as Lecturer in Arabic, University of Glasgow; app Professor of Arabic, University of Manchester 1949; died 9 Jan 1981.

1966 ANDREW CHRISTIAN ROSS
(FES X, 425, 438), res from service with FMC in Malawi on app as Lecturer in Church History, University of Edinburgh 31 Mar 1966; University of Edinburgh 1998 (DLitt); ret 30 Sep 1998; s Gavin m Marilyn Elliot; s Malcolm m Susan Buckley; s Neil m Margaret Carson; Addl publ: *John Philip: Missions, Race and Politics in South Africa 1775–1851* (Aberdeen Univ Press, 1986); *A Vision Betrayed: The Jesuit Mission in Japan and China*

1549–1742 (Edinburgh Univ Press, 1994); *Blantyre Missions and the Development of Modern Malawi* (VKW, 1996).

1993 ROBERT BASIL SALTERS
(FES X, 438), app Lecturer in Hebrew and Old Testament, University of St Andrews 1 Oct 1971; app Senior Lecturer 1 Oct 1993; Addl publ: *The Commentary of R Samuel ben Meir on Qoheleth* (Magnus Press, Jerusalem and Brill, Leiden, 1985); *Jonah and Lamentations* (Sheffield Academic Press, 1994).

1972 HENRY REAY SEFTON
(FES X, 51, 438, 455), app Lecturer in Church History, University of Aberdeen 1 Mar 1972; app Senior Lecturer 1 Jan 1991; app Master of Christ's College, Aberdeen 1 Oct 1982; ret 30 Sep 1992; app Clerk to Presb of Aberdeen 1 Sep 1993; Alexander Robertson Lecturer, University of Glasgow 1995; Chairman, Assoc of University Teachers (Scotland) 1982–84; Addl publ: *John Knox* (St Andrew Press, 1993); advisory editor *Dictionary of Scottish Church History and Theology* (T&T Clark, 1993); numerous articles in dictionaries and learned journals.

1988 NORMAN JAMES SHANKS
res as Chaplain to University of Edinburgh and app Lecturer in Practical Theology, University of Glasgow 1 Dec 1988; app Leader of Iona Community 5 Aug 1995.

1979 DOUGLAS WILLIAM DAVID SHAW
(FES X, 438), app Professor of Divinity, University of St Andrews 1 Sep 1979; app Principal of St Mary's College 1 Sep 1986; DD (Glasgow) 1992; ret 31 Aug 1993; Addl publ: *The Dissuaders* (SCM Press, 1978); editor of *In Divers Manners* (Univ of St Andrews, 1990); editor of *Dimensions: Literary and Theological* (Univ of St Andrews, 1992); editor *Theology in Scotland* (Univ of St Andrews, from 1994).

1944 JAMES WALTER DICKSON SMITH
(FES IX, 117, 781; X, 438), Principal Lecturer in, and Head of Dept of, Religious Education, Jordanhill College, Glasgow; ret 30 Sep 1967; died 4 Sep 1987.

1965 JAMES FINLAY ROBERTSON SQUIRES
(FES X, 439), app Lecturer in RE at Aberdeen College of Education 1 Apr 1965; app Principal Lecturer 1967; ret 1987; s Neil Paton b 1965.

1948 DAVID MUIR GIBSON STALKER
(FES IX, 201, 456, 781), dem from Aberdour and Dalgety 31 Jul 1948 on app as Lecturer in Biblical Studies, University of Edinburgh 1 Oct 1948; ret 1981; died 14 Dec 1988.

1999 JOHN SWINTON
ord by Presb of Aberdeen 24 Jun 1999; Lecturer in Practical Theology, University of Aberdeen.

1952 THOMAS FORSYTH TORRANCE
(FES IX, 524, 558, 775; X, 432), app to Chair of Christian Dogmatics, University of Edinburgh 1952; ret 30 Sep 1978; Moderator of General Assembly 1976–77; DSc (Heriot-Watt) 1983, DrTh (Reformed College, Debrecen) 1988, DD (Edinburgh) 1996; Fellow of Royal Society of Edinburgh 1979, Fellow of British Academy of London 1982; Cross of Thyateira 1977, Templeton Prize 1978; s Iain m Morag Ann MacHugh; Addl publ: *The Centrality of Christ* (1976); *Space, Time and Resurrection* (1976); *The Ground and Grammar of Theology* (1980); *Christian Theology and Scientific Culture* (1980); *Divine and Contingent Order* (1981); *Reality and Evangelical Theology* (1982); *Juridical Law and Physical Law* (1982); *The Mediation of Christ* (1983, 1992); *Transformation and Convergence in the Frame of Knowledge* (1984); *The Christian Frame of Mind* (1985, 1989); *Reality and Scientific Theology* (1985); *The Trinitarian Faith* (T&T Clark, 1988); *The Hermeneutics of John Calvin* (1988); *Karl Barth* (1990); *Science Théologique* (tr. by Lacoste, Paris, 1990); *Senso del divino e scienza moderna* (tr. by Del Re, 1992); *Preaching Christ Today* (Handsel Press, 1993); *Trinitarian Perspectives* (1994); *Divine Meaning* (1995); *The Christian Doctrine of God* (T&T Clark, 1996); *Scottish Theology from John Knox to John McLeod Campbell* (T&T Clark, 1996); co-author of *The Person of Jesus Christ* (1999); co-author of *A Passion for Christ: The Vision that Ignites Ministry* (Handsel Press, 1999); editor of numerous journals and other publications.

1999 IAIN RICHARD TORRANCE
B 13 Jan 1949 at Aberdeen, s of Thomas Forsyth T. and Margaret Edith Spear; educ Edinburgh Academy and Monkton Combe School, Bath 1954–66; University of Edinburgh 1967–71 (MA); University of St Andrews 1971–74 (BD); University of Oxford 1974–80 (DPhil); lic by Presb of Edinburgh 10 Jul 1974; m 27 Sep 1975 Morag Ann MacHugh b 9 Sep 1952 d of Francis John M. and Wendy Anne Lang; Children: Hew David Thomas b 22 Aug 1983; Robyn Alison Meta b 12 Feb 1985; ord and ind to Northmavine 23 Jan 1982; dem 31 Aug 1985 to take up app as Lecturer in New Testament and Christian Ethics, Queen's College, Birmingham 1 Sep 1985; app Lecturer in Patristics and NT, University of Birmingham 1 Sep 1989; app Lecturer in Systematic and Practical Theology, University of Aberdeen 1 Apr 1993; app Senior Lecturer 1 Sep 1997; app Professor in Patristics and Christian Ethics 1 Jun 1999; Chaplain (TA) 1982–97; TD 1995; Publ: Co-editor of *Scottish Journal of Theology* from 1982; *Christology after Chalcedon* (Canterbury Press, 1988); co-author of *Human Genetics: A Christian Perspective* (St Andrew Press, 1995); *Ethics and the Military Community* (MOD, 1998); co-editor of *In Praise of God: Essays on Modern Reformed Liturgy* (T&T Clark, 1999); articles, reviews and translations in various journals.

1977 JAMES BRUCE TORRANCE
(FES IX, 519; X, 307, 439), res as Senior Lecturer in Christian Dogmatics, University of Edinburgh on app as Professor of Systematic Theology, University of Aberdeen 1 Jan 1977; ret 1989.

1963 EDWIN SPROTT TOWILL
(FES IX, 29, 506; X, 18, 439), res as teacher (RE) at Dunfermline High School on app as Lecturer in RE at Dundee College of Education 1963; app Principal 1966; ret 1976; died 1 Jun 1989.

1987 JAMES BERNARD WALKER
(FES X, 304), dem from Galashiels Old and St Paul's to take up app as Principal of Queen's College, Birmingham 7 Apr 1987; res to take up app as Chaplain to University of St Andrews 1 Sep 1993.

1984 IAN WALKER
B 28 Nov 1941 at Aberdeen, s of George W. and Elizabeth Nicol Stewart; educ Aberdeen Grammar 1953–57; Robert Gordon's College, Aberdeen 1957–58; University of Aberdeen 1968–72 (BD); University of Edinburgh 1972–73 (DMS), 1989–92 (MEd); Merchant Navy 1958–67; lic by Presb of Aberdeen 25 Apr 1973; m 20 Aug 1962 Shona Maureen Cook b 16 May 1942 d of James Albert C. and Janet Bruce; Children: Fiona Lois b 1 Aug 1964 m Alasdair Graeme Knox; Nicola Elizabeth b 27 Dec 1967 m John William Forsyth Macartney; Gavin James b 24 May 1971; ord by United Church of Zambia in Kafue 1 Aug 1973; app to Chingola and Chililabombwe, Copperbelt Presb, Zambia 15 Feb 1976; ind to Garvald and Morham 15 Aug 1979; became minister of linked charge with Haddington West 13 Nov 1980; dem on app by Board of Education as Tutor, St Colm's College, Edinburgh 16 Sep 1984.

1987 AINSLIE WALTON
(FES X, 163, 356), dem from Buckie North to enter teaching profession 30 Sep 1973; app Lecturer in Practical Theology, University of Aberdeen 1987; ret 1995; s Bruce m Miranda Jane Chamers-Park; d Pamela m David Andison; Addl publ: *Living the Faith* (1993); *Sharing the Faith* (1994); *Care of the Sick, the Old and the Bereaved* (1995); *Ecumenism* (1996)—all publ by Univ of Aberdeen.

1937 CECIL JAMES MULLO WEIR
(FES IX, 469, 776; X, 433), ret from Chair of Hebrew and Semitic Languages, University of Glasgow 31 Sep 1968; died 4 Mar 1995.

1958 JAMES AITKEN WHYTE
(FES IX, 27, 402; X, 16 (2), 433), app Chair of Practical Theology and Christian Ethics, University of St Andrews 1 Oct 1958; ret 30 Sep 1987; Principal of St Mary's College 1978–82; Moderator of General Assembly 1988–89; Assoc (part-time) at St Andrews Hope Park 1987–96; LLD (Dundee) 1981; DD (St Andrews) 1989; DUniv (Stirling) 1994; Margaret Harris Lecturer, University of Dundee,

1990; Hon President, Christian Education Movement in Scotland 1971–94; Hon Vice-President, Scottish Assoc for Counselling 1977–87; President, Society for the Study of Theology 1983–84; w Elisabeth Wilson Mill died 25 Jul 1988; m (2) 26 Jun 1993 Ishbel Christina Rathie (nee Macaulay); s David m Rhona Winifred Peacock; stepdaughter Sheena Mary Rathie m John McRobert; Addl publ: Contributor to *Towards a Church Architecture* (Architectural Press, 1962); co-editor of *Worship Now* (St Andrew Press, 1972); co-editor *Worship Now II* (St Andrew Press, 1989); contributor to *A Dictionary of Christian Spirituality* (SCM, 1983); *Studies in the History of Worship in Scotland* (T&T Clark, 1984, 2nd ed 1996); *A New Dictionary of Christian Ethics* (SCM, 1986); *A New Dictionary of Liturgy and Worship* (SCM, 1986); *A Dictionary of Pastoral Care* (SPCK, 1987); *In Divers Manners* (St Mary's College, 1990); *Encyclopedia of the Reformed Faith* (St Andrew Press, 1992); *Community, Normality and Difference* (Aberdeen Univ Press, 1992); *Capital—a Moral Instrument?* (St Andrew Press, 1992); *The Risks of Freedom* (Pastoral Care Foundation, 1993); *Hugh Douglas, One Man's Ministry* (St Andrew Press, 1993); *Christ, Church and Society* (T&T Clark, 1993); *Laughter and Tears* (St Andrew Press, 1993).

1979   JOHN CHRISTOPHER WIGGLESWORTH app Lecturer, University of Aberdeen 1 Aug 1979; res on app as General Secretary, Board of World Mission and Unity 1 Jan 1987.

1977   ROBERT McLACHLAN WILSON (FES IX, 339, 781; X, 433), app Professor of Biblical Criticism, University of St Andrews 1977; Fellow of British Academy (FBA) 1977; DD (Aberdeen) 1982; ret 30 Sep 1983; s Andrew m Fiona Bradbury; s Peter m Ella Seymour; Addl publ: *Commentary on Hebrews* (Marshall Morgan & Scott, 1987); editor *Nag Hammadi and Gnosis* and *The Future of Coptology* (Brill, 1978); co-editor *Text and Interpretation* (CUP, 1979); translation editor, *Gnosis* by Rudolph (T&T Clark, 1983); assoc editor *New Testament Studies* 1967–77, editor 1977–83; numerous articles and reviews in various journals.

OVERSEAS APPOINTMENTS

In alphabetical order

1987   WILLIAM MACRAE AITKEN
(FES IX, 803), res as Asst Chaplain to Charterhouse School, Surrey and app by Board of World Mission as teacher and headmaster of St Andrew's High School, Ndola, Zambia 1987; ret 31 Oct 1990; died 11 Aug 1994.

1987   COLIN MATHIESON ALSTON
dem from Dulnain Bridge with Grantown-on-Spey 30 Nov 1987 on app by Board of World Mission and Unity to Greyfriars St Ann's, Port of Spain, Trinidad; app to Hunter Baillie Memorial Church, Annandale and The Welsh Church, Sydney, Australia 6 Sep 1990.

1980   ROBERT ALEXANDER ANDERSON
app by Board of World Mission as Tutor at St Paul's College, Limuru, Kenya 1980; ord by Presb of Kiambu, Presb Church of E Africa, Kenya 5 Aug 1984; res from service with Overseas Council and ind to Overtown 15 Dec 1986.

1978   KENNETH GEORGE ANDERSON
(FES X, 74, 415), dem from Selkirk Lawson Memorial 15 Jan 1978 on app by Union Church, Hong Kong; ind to Abernethy and Dron with Arngask 14 Jan 1988.

1971   NICHOLAS DOUGLAS CHETWYND ARCHER
(FES X, 415), dem from Ayr Castlehill on app by Overseas Council for service in Livingstonia, Malawi 1971; res from service 1977 and ind to Brydekirk with Hoddam 27 Apr 1978.

1955   ANDREW BAILLIE
(FES IX, 215; X, 416), res as Chaplain to Calcutta Mills and Docks and introd to Colombo St Andrew's 1 Oct 1955; ret 1984; died 10 Sep 1988.

1970   JOHN CAMPBELL BECKE
(FES IX, 197; X, 112, 413, 416), app to Sailors' Rest, Genoa 1 Jul 1970; dem on grounds of ill-health 31 Mar 1971; became teacher 31 May 1971; Publ: *Now the Day is Over* (Minerva, 1997).

1976   DAVID WILLIAM BLACK
(FES X, 244), dem from Kinlochleven 19 Apr 1976 and app for service with United Church of Jamaica and Grand Cayman in New Broughton and Mandeville; ind to Strathbrock 9 Jan 1984.

1982   WILLIAM BROAD BLACK
(FES X, 384), dem from Durness with Kinlochbervie 15 Dec 1981 on app as Missionary with OMF International in Korea; ind to Stornoway High 30 Jan 1998.

1979   ROBERT THOMSON BONE
(FES X, 162), dem from Glasgow Ibrox 1 Sep 1979 on app by Overseas Council for service at Livingstonia, Malawi; ret 1984; died 10 Jun 1998.

1976   FREDERICK MINTY BOOTH
(FES X, 268), dem from Stirling St Mark's 13 Apr 1976; app by Board of World Mission for service with United Church of Jamaica and Grand Cayman in Brownsville 14 Aug 1976; app Youth and Development Worker, Grand Cayman 12 May 1980; ind to Helensburgh St Columba 6 Nov 1982.

1938   ALEXANDER JOHN BOYD
(FUF 542; FES IX, 729; X, 416), ret as Principal of Madras Christian College 30 Jun 1957; died 27 Jan 1980.

1981   DENNIS GEORGE BRICE
B 21 Sep 1948 at London, s of Dennis Frank B. and Joy Vera Smith; educ Buckhurst Hill County High 1961–68; University of Aberdeen 1968–71 (BSc); University of Edinburgh 1971–74 (BD); Campus Chaplain, Philadelphia, USA 1975–81; lic by Presb of Edinburgh, Nov 1975; asstshp Rutherglen Stonelaw 1974–75; m 22 Dec 1979 Claudia Damaris Kraftson b 15 Aug 1956 d of Harry Aaron K. and Elizabeth Hallstrom; Children: Nathanael b 14 Jan 1981; Mark b 4 Jul 1983; Abigail b 31 Mar 1985; Peter b 9 Sep 1989; ord by Presb of Glasgow and app by Board of World Mission and Unity for service with Presb Church in Taiwan, Jan 1981; app Candidate Director, Arab World Ministries May 1996.

1980   LILIAN MARGARET BRUCE
(FES X, 74), dem from St Boswells on app with Overseas Council for service at St Columba's, Dar-es-Salaam, Tanzania 24 Jul 1980; res 1985 and ind to Daviot and Dunlichity with Moy, Dalarossie and Tomatin 17 Mar 1986.

1960   GEORGE BUCHANAN
(FES IX, 363, 730; X, 217), dem from Craigrownie and introd to Bermuda Christ Church 8 Dec 1960; ret 1977.

1994 PAUL CHRISTOPHER JAMES BURGESS
B 7 May 1941 at Bude, Cornwall, s of Henry James
B. and Dora; educ St Lawrence College, Ramsgate
1953–59; University of Cambridge 1960–64 (MA);
London College of Divinity 1966–68; VSO Pakistan
1964–66; m 19 Jul 1968 Catherine Duthie Chap-
man b 29 Apr 1933 d of James Simpson C. and
Margaret Harrison Hamilton; Children: Alastair
James b 15 Dec 1972; Graham MacPherson b 7
Jan 1978; ord as Deacon in the Church of England,
1968; priested 1970; Curate of St Stephen's,
Islington 1968–72; training with Church Missionary
Society, Selly Oak Colleges, Birmingham 1972–
73; Curate of St Lawrence's, Church Stretton
1973–74; Missionary with Church Missionary
Society in Pakistan 1974–83; Warden of Carberry
Tower 1984–86; Programme Co-ordinator, Car-
berry Tower 1986–88; Adult Education Adviser for
Livingston Ecumenical Parish (Episcopal Church)
1988–92; admitted by General Assembly 1992;
loc ten East Calder with Kirknewton 1992–93,
Fauldhouse 1993; service with Board of World
Mission from 1994; app Professor and Librarian,
Gujranwala Theological Seminary, Pakistan
1994; Publ: Contributor to *The Message of the
Bible* (Lion, 1988), re-issued as *The Bible for
Everyday Life* (1994); *Curriculum for Theological
Education* (Gujranwala Theological Seminary,
1995–97).

1968 JOHN BAIN BURNETT
(FES X, 405, 416), ord and ind to Burra Isles,
Shetland 30 May 1964; dem on app by Board of
World Mission to Buenos Aires 31 Dec 1968; ind
to Glasgow Priesthill 1 Oct 1976.

1966 JAMES EWEN ROSS CAMPBELL
(FES X, 417), app by FMC for service in S Africa
19 Apr 1966; ind to Auchterderran 28 Apr 1977.

1931 DUNCAN CAMPBELL
(FES IX, 730), ord by Presb of Glasgow and app
by FMC for service at Ekwendeni, Livingstonia 11
Oct 1931; dem 1949; died 15 Sep 1992.

1987 THOMAS STEVENSON COLVIN
(FES X, 417), service with Presb Church of Ghana
in Tamale 1959–64; service with Church of Central
Africa Presb, Blantyre, Malawi 1964–76; ret from
service with FMC and transferred to URC, London;
re-app by Board of World Mission for service
with Church of Central Africa Presb, Blantyre,
Malawi 1987; ret 16 Apr 1990; Publ: *Free to Serve*
(Iona Community, 1964); *Leap, Leap my soul* (Iona
Community, 1967); *Fill us with your love* (Hope
Publ, USA, 1983); *Come let us walk this road
together* (Hope Publ, USA, 1997).

1986 JOAN HOWIE CRAIG
ord by Presb of Perth 17 Sep 1986 and app by
Board of World Misison to St Columba's, Dar-es-
Salaam, Tanzania (PCEA) 26 Oct 1986; app
Lecturer, St Mark's Anglican Theological College,
Dar-es-Salaam 1 Sep 1989; app by Christian

Study Centre, Rawalpindi, Pakistan (research on
Christian-Muslim relations) 10 Apr 1992; ind to
Deerness with Holm with St Andrews 1 Apr 1993.

1981 ERIK McLEISH CRAMB
(FES X, 178), dem from Glasgow St Thomas'
Gallowgate 19 Apr 1981 on app by Overseas
Council for service in Kingston, Jamaica; ind to
Glasgow Yoker Old with St Matthew's 29 Aug
1984.

1958 WILLIAM DEMPSTER
(FES IX, 732; X, 418), app by Overseas Council
for service in Sulenkawa, S Africa 1 Apr 1958; ret
30 Apr 1959; died 20 Nov 1984.

1947 WALTER SCOTT DICKSON
(FES IX, 732; X, 418), res from service with
Overseas Council in Kenya and app teacher of RE,
Kirkcaldy High 6 Jan 1955; died 27 Feb 1984.

1988 IAN CUNNINGHAM DOUGALL
(FES X, 418), res as Chaplain to George Heriot's,
Edinburgh 1987 and app Headmaster of Mwambiti
High School, Voi, Kenya 1988; Lecturer at the
Pastoral Institute (Presb Church of E Africa),
Kikuyu, Kenya 1989–90; ret 30 Jun 1991; Publ:
Uria Njitikitie (1967); *Thiii* (1968); *Kanitha wa
Kristo* (1969); *What I Believe* (1989)—all jointly with
C Kiongo and J Oswald Welsh and publ by Presb
Church of E Africa.

1988 ELSPETH GILLIAN DOUGALL
app Chaplain at Alliance Girls' High School, Kikuyu,
Kenya 31 Aug 1988; ord in Kikuyu by Presb Church
of E Africa 29 Jan 1989; ind to Edinburgh Marmont
St Giles' (joint ministry) 5 Dec 1991.

1985 THOMAS MALCOLM FULLARTON DUFF
ord by Presb of Aberdeen 26 Jun 1985 and app
for service with Presb Church of E Africa in Dar-
es-Salaam, Tanzania; ind to Fergushill with
Kilwinning Erskine 9 Jan 1987.

1998 GRAHAM ALEXANDER DUNCAN
B 15 Jun 1949 at Aberdeen, s of James D. and
Edith Ferret Bond; educ Hilton Secondary and
Aberdeen Academy 1961–67; University of
Aberdeen 1967–71 (BEd), 1974–77 (BD); Univer-
sity of S Africa 1995–97 (MTh); Aberdeen
Education Authority 1971–74; lic by Presb of
Aberdeen 30 Jun 1977; m 6 Apr 1973 Sandra
Harper Todd b 13 Jul 1949 d of Robert T. and
Doris Harper; Children: Michael and David b 15
Feb 1975; Susan Noluthando b 9 Apr 1979; ord by
Ciskei Reformed Presb Church, S Africa and app
to Lovedale District/Institution 12 Mar 1978; app
Tutor at Federal Theological Seminary of S Africa
16 Jun 1982; ind to Cumbernauld Old 31 Aug 1988;
dem 5 May 1998 to take up app with Board of World
Mission as Lecturer, University of Fort Hare, S
Africa (under secondment by Reformed Presb
Church of S Africa); Publ: *Faith Apart from Works
is Dead* (*Journal of Theology of S Africa*, 1985).

1984 WILLIAM MICHAEL BECKET DUNLOP
ord by Presb of Glasgow during assistantship at St George's Tron 29 Jan 1981; app by Board of World Mission to Sefula Church, United Church of Zambia 26 Aug 1984; app to Livingstone, UCZ 21 May 1986; ind to Peterhead St Andrew's 6 Jun 1991.

1983 GAVIN JOHN ELLIOTT
dem from Glasgow Carntyne on app as Mission Partner with United Church of Zambia, Lusaka, Mar 1983; ind to South Uist 29 Aug 1989.

1971 IAN DONALD FAUCHELLE
(FES X, 169, 418), dem from Glasgow Partick Anderson 13 Apr 1971; Minister at Luanshya, Copperbelt (United Church of Zambia) 1971–76; Lecturer, Zomba Theological College, Malawi 1980–84 (Acting Principal 1983); Admin Asst to General Secretary, World Mission and Unity 1990; Minister at Trinity Church, Gweru, (Presb Church of S Africa) 1991–94; Lecturer, United Theological College, Harare, Zimbabwe and Minister, City Presb Church, Harare (PCSA) 1995–99; Chaplain and Minister (part-time), Conifer Grove, Auckland (Presb Church of New Zealand) 1999– .

1993 IAIN MACDONALD FORBES
(FES X, 395, 419, 453), [correction: ord by Presb of Inverness as missionary in training, not as 'asst at Cawdor' as in FES X, 395]; dem from Howe of Fife on app by Board of World Mission to the Evangelical Church of Christ in Mozambique 31 Oct 1993; d Catriona m David Milligan; s Fraser m Carey Smith; d Janet m David Hood; s Raeburn m Julie Anne Wright; s Donald m Kathleen Bamforth.

1999 THOMAS ALAN WHITEWAY GARRITY
(FES X, 348), dem from Ayr the Auld Kirk 28 Feb 1999 on app by Board of World Mission to Christ Church, Bermuda; d Caroline m Calvert.

1967 JAMES MARCUS GOSSIP
(FES IX, 735; X, 195, 419), dem from Hamilton Hillhouse 31 May 1967 to take up app with Overseas Council at Rajasthan; transferred to S Africa as permit to enter India was not granted; service with Bantu Presb Church of S Africa, Gordon Memorial; ret 1977; died 17 Nov 1985.

1983 ALAN GREIG
dem from Hurlford Reid Memorial on app by Board of World Mission and Unity for service in Zambia 21 Sep 1983; ind to Kintore 16 Jul 1992.

1996 JANE METHVEN HOWITT
B 19 Sep 1968 at Bellshill, d of Peter Murdoch H. and Myra Methven; educ Craigholme School, Glasgow 1974–86; University of Glasgow 1986–91 (MA); University of Aberdeen 1991–94 (BD); lic by Presb of Glasgow, Jul 1994; asstshp Glasgow Carnwadric 1994–96; ord by Presb of Glasgow 1 Feb 1996; app by Scripture Union to Baltic

Republics, Apr 1996; Publ: *Piezimes Bibeli Lasot* (Scripture Union Latvia, 1997–99).

1952 PETER INNES
(FES IX, 539, 736, 764; X, 314, 420), app Chaplain to Indian Tea Assoc, Assam 21 Apr 1952; ret 28 Feb 1974; died 8 May 1989.

1993 COLIN DAVID JOHNSTON
B 26 Mar 1960 at Auchinleck, s of Charles Livingstone Johnston and Jane Elizabeth Highet; educ Auchinleck Academy 1972–78; University of St Andrews 1978–81 (MA); University of Edinburgh 1982–85 (BD); lic by Presb of Ayr 27 Jun 1985; asstshp Netherlee 1985–86; ord and ind to Larkhall Trinity 21 Aug 1986; dem on app by Board of World Mission as Mission Partner with United Church of Zambia in Sefula, Maamba, Choma and Lusaka Central, Sep 1993.

1989 HELEN GIBSON JOHNSTONE
B 11 Sep 1930 at Glasgow, d of James Wallace McCrone and Margaret Gibb Lochhead; educ Hutchesons' Grammar, Glasgow and Clarendon School, Abergele, Denbighshire 1935–48; Univer-sity of St Andrews 1948–51 (MA), 1980–83 (BD); Asst Secretary, Woman's Guild 1965–67; Teaching (RE) 1968–78; lic by Presb of St Andrews 27 Jun 1982; m 27 Jul 1954 Robert Inch Johnstone b 25 Aug 1927 s of Robert Rutherford J. and Alexandra Davison White Inch; Children: Elizabeth Ann b 9 Jul 1956 m Michael John Bates; Alexandra Margaret b 29 May 1959; Andrew Robert James b 11 Sep 1960; ord and ind to Auchterhouse with Murroes and Tealing 28 Sep 1983; dem 16 Feb 1989 to take up app with Board of World Mission in Kitwe, Zambia; ret 1995.

1979 ROBERT MAURICE KING
(FES IX, 475; X, 34, 281, 311), dem from Glenisla with Kilry 31 Jul 1979 to take up app with United Church of Jamaica and Grand Cayman in Brownsville; returned 1982; ret 1983; died 4 Sep 1998; d Carol m David Hamilton; s John m Nicola McLeland.

1941 ALLAN DONALD LAMONT
(FES IX, 737; X, 421), res from service with Overseas Council in Nakuru, Kenya 31 Dec 1974; Asst (part-time) at Edinburgh St Martin's 1976–93; s (John) Graham m Annette Doran, divorced, m (2) Shirley Jardine.

1981 BRUCE BAIRNSFATHER LAWRIE
(FES X, 125), dem from Levern and Nitshill on app by Board of World Mission for service with Lucaya Presb Church, Freeport, Bahamas 29 Sep 1981; ind to Ettrick with Yarrow 15 Jan 1986.

1954 ROBERT MALCOLM MACDONALD
(FUF 559; FES IX, 739; X, 421), ret from service with Overseas Council in Calabar 1968; ret from Overseas Council 1970.

1959 MARGARET STEVENTON MACGREGOR
B 19 Aug 1933 at Irvine, d of John Dick M. and Elizabeth Grey Ferguson Anderson; educ Irvine Royal Academy 1938–51; University of Glasgow 1951–55 (MA); Jordanhill College, Glasgow, and University of Glasgow 1955–56 (DipEd); St Colm's College, Edinburgh 1958–59; Senate of Serampore College (external) 1962–68 (BD); Teaching 1956–58; Missionary with United Church of N India 1959 (became Church of North India 1970); app to Bishop's College, Calcutta 1972; asstshp Bhowanipore, Calcutta 1985–89; Osmond Memorial, Calcutta 1989–94; ord as Deacon by Church of N India 3 Feb 1985; ord as Presbyter 10 Dec 1985; ret 25 Oct 1994.

1984 ANGUS THOW MACKNIGHT
(FES X, 412), res from app at Brussels 28 Feb 1984 on app by Board of World Mission to Sri Lanka Colombo St Andrew's; ret 1986; died 30 Jan 1997.

1975 COLIN IAN MACLEAN
(FES X, 385, 398, 422), dem from Stornoway St Martin's Memorial on app by Overseas Council to Greyfriars St Ann's, Port of Spain, Trinidad 30 Nov 1975; ind to Glasgow The Barony 24 Oct 1979.

1993 DUNCAN JAMES MACPHERSON
ord by Presb of Dumbarton during assistantship at Cairns 6 Oct 1993; introd as Assoc and Youth minister, Christ Church, Bermuda 10 Oct 1993; app Asst (part-time) Canonbie with Langholm, Ewes and Westerkirk 22 Oct 1995.

1949 JOHN STRACHAN MALLOCH
(FES IX, 251, 742; X, 423), res from service with FMC at Akropong, Gold Coast and entered teaching profession 1963; died 18 Feb 1991.

1981 FREDERICK JOHN MARSHALL
(FES X, 137, 218), dem from Kilmacolm St Columba and introd to Christ Church, Bermuda 31 Dec 1981; ret 31 Dec 1992.

1991 IAIN GUNN MATHESON
dem from Hamilton Trinity 28 Feb 1991 on app by Board of World Mission to Prague; returned Dec 1992; teaching (music) from 1996.

1977 IAN DOUGLAS MAXWELL
ord by Presb of Edinburgh, Oct 1977 and app for service with Church of Pakistan at Sindh; app Chaplain to Sefula School, Zambia Jun 1979; introd as Assoc at Paisley St Ninian's Ferguslie 28 Oct 1982.

1989 ALASTAIR FLEMING McCORMICK
(FES X, 123, 230), dem from Perth St Andrew's 15 Feb 1989 and app by Board of World Mission to Nassau, Bahamas; ind to Creich with Rosehall 30 Nov 1992.

1997 ELAINE WRIGHT McKINNON
B 17 Dec 1955 at Glasgow, d of Malcolm Wright M. and Alice Plummer Nicol; educ Whitehill Secondary, Glasgow 1967–72; University of Glasgow 1972–75 (MA), 1984–87 (BD); University of London (external) 1978–81 (BA); Computer Tape Librarian; lic by Presb of Glasgow 8 Jul 1987; asstshp Glasgow Shettleston Old 1987–88; ord and ind to Grangemouth Grange 18 Nov 1988; loc ten Edinburgh Slateford Longstone 1991; app by Board of World Mission as Chaplain to Alliance Girls' High School, Kenya 11 Jan 1992; app Director of 'Create' Programme, Presb Church of E Africa 1 Jul 1995; app Lecturer in Old Testament and Greek, Pastoral Institute, Kikuyu, Kenya 1 Sep 1997.

1977 PETER WILLIAM MILLAR
(FES X, 157), dem from Glasgow Dalmarnock Old 31 Aug 1976 and app by Overseas Council for service in S India 4 Jan 1977; res from app to become Director, Columban House, Newtonmore 1 Jul 1989.

1977 MARGARET ROBB McRAE MILLAR
ord by United Church of Zambia 1 May 1977; Deaconess Tutor, United Church of Zambia 1975–90; Moderator, North Western Presb, Zambia 1991–95; ind to Kilchrenan and Dalavich with Muckairn 1 Nov 1996.

1995 ALEXANDER LESLIE MILTON
B 21 Jul 1961 at Uddingston, s of Ralph Clark M. and Elaine Lorimar Angus Honeyman; educ Airdrie Academy 1973–79; University of Glasgow 1979–84 (MA), 1984–87 (BD), 1987–95 (PhD); Lecturer, St Bedes Theological College, S Africa 1988–89; lic by Presb of Glasgow 5 Jul 1987; asstshp Edinburgh St Michael's 1987–88; Glasgow Jordanhill 1992–94; ord by Igreja Evangelica de Mozambique, Nampula 18 Aug 1996; app as Mission Partner in area of Theological Education, Mozambique 10 Dec 1995; Publ: Editor of *An African Challenge to the Church in the 21st Century* (SACC, 1997).

1935 ALEXANDER KING MINCHER
(FES IX, 743; X, 423), ret from service with Overseas Council at Calabar, Nigeria 6 Jul 1971; died 30 Dec 1996.

1947 GEORGE MORE
(FES IX, 743; X, 423), ord by Presb of St Andrews 30 Jun 1947 and app by FMC as missionary at Nagpur; transferred to ministry of United Church of N India 1948 and ind to Wardha 25 Oct 1949; ret 1977; died 12 Nov 1986.

1971 CHARLES SMITH MORRICE
(FES X, 200, 423), dem from Newarthill to take up app with Board of World Mission in Buenos Aires, Argentina 5 Sep 1971; ind to Mauchline 23 Jun 1976; dem to take up app with Board of World Mission as Lecturer in New Testament at St Paul's

United Theological College, Limuru, Kenya 1 Sep 1990; ret 31 Dec 1997; s Michael m Anne Forbes Dryden; s Kenneth m Naomi Ann Wood; d Elizabeth m Steven John Evans.

1979 GORDON CUMMING MORRIS
(FES IX, 744; X, 423), res from service with FMC in N Rhodesia (now Zambia) and app by Board of World Mission for service in Buenos Aires, Argentina 1 Jan 1979; ret 30 Jun 1984; Addl children: Peter Graham Cumming b 30 Aug 1956; d Pamela m Crews.

1992 GRAEME WATSON MACKINNON MUCKART
app to St Andrew's, Colombo, Sri Lanka 22 Jun 1992; ind to Aberdeen North of St Andrew 6 Mar 1997.

1982 JOHN PRINGLE LORIMER MUNRO
res as Chaplain to University of Stirling on app by Overseas Council as Lecturer at St Paul's United Theological College, Limuru, Kenya Sep 1982; ind to Arbroath Knox's with St Vigean's 11 May 1986.

1972 ANDREW MUNRO
ord by Presb of Strathbogie and Fordyce, Sep 1972 and app by Overseas Council for service in Ghana; res on app as Principal teacher, Elgin Academy 1976.

1973 JOHN MURRIE
(FES IX, 783; X, 423), app Warden and Minister of Church of Scotland Centre, Tiberias, Israel 1973; ind to Kirkliston 27 Oct 1976.

1966 CLARENCE WILLIAM MUSGRAVE
ord by Presb of Edinburgh and app by Overseas Council for service with United Church of Zambia 27 Nov 1966 (service in Livingstone, Mongu, Sefula and Lusaka); returned from Zambia and ind to Edinburgh Murrayfield 29 Oct 1980.

1982 THOMAS SINCLAIR NICHOLSON
ord by Presb of Orkney and app as Missionary with Presb Church in Taiwan 9 Jun 1982; ind to Gordon St Michael's, Greenlaw, Legerwood and Westruther 1 May 1995.

1991 SARAH ELIZABETH CARMICHAEL NICOL
trans from Edinburgh Blackhall St Columba's and introd as Assoc at Christ Church, Bermuda 1 Sep 1991; ind to Edinburgh Craigmillar Park 20 Apr 1994.

1940 ANDREW BRYCE NISBET
(FES IX, 724, 762), app to Aden 5 Mar 1940; app Chaplain to Palestine Police 1945; died 14 Jun 1983.

1988 THOMAS O'LEARY
dem from Inch with Stranraer St Andrew's to take up app with Board of World Mission in Colombo, Sri Lanka Jan 1988; ind to Lochwinnoch 2 Sep 1992.

1984 EDGAR JOHN OGSTON
dem from Kinlochleven with Nether Lochaber on app by Board of World Mission to Elmslie Memorial United Church, Georgetown, Grand Cayman (United Church of Jamaica and Grand Cayman) 25 Jan 1984; ind to Leven Scoonie Kirk 21 Dec 1987.

1977 STEPHEN ANTON PACITTI
(FES X, 170, 378), dem from Glasgow Pollok-shields Glencairn on app by Board of World Mission for service with Presb Church in Taiwan 28 Sep 1977; app Assoc Professor at Yu Shan Theological College, Hualien 21 May 1979; ind to Culter with Libberton and Quothquan 27 Feb 1997.

1967 KENNETH JOHN PATTISON
ord by Church of Central Africa Presb and introd as Assoc at the Cathedral Church of St Michael and All Angels, Blantyre, Malawi 7 Jun 1967; various apps as minister, chaplain, tutor and principal in Malawi 1967–77; ind to Ardrossan Park 27 Oct 1977.

1935 PATRICK WILLIAM ROBERTSON PETRIE
(FES IX, 745), ord by Presb of Dalkeith 24 Nov 1935; service at Keith-Falconer Memorial Church, Aden and Chaplain to Forces, Aden; died 22 Apr 1986.

1983 JOHN PETER SANDISON PURVES
res as Asst Chaplain to University of Aberdeen on app by Board of World Mission as Missionary with United Church of Jamaica and Grand Cayman 1 Mar 1983; ind to Dollar with Glendevon with Muckhart 27 Feb 1990.

1955 DAVID LIONEL RAE
B 1 Apr 1923 at Glasgow, s of David McGregor R. and Irene Muriel Crippen; educ Stirling High; University of Glasgow 1947–50 (MA), 1951–55 (BD); Post Office Sorting Clerk 1940–41; RAF 1941–45; lic by Presb of Glasgow; asstshp Glasgow Wellington 1955–56; m 27 Dec 1952 Margaret Marshall b 9 Dec 1925 d of James M. and Elizabeth Mary Ballantyne; Children: Gareth Barclay b 21 Jul 1959 m Alan Baker; Morven Elizabeth Howie b 16 Jul 1961 m Milind Kolhatkar; ord by Presb of Glasgow and app for service with Church of Scotland Mission in Poona 4 May 1955; ind to St Paul's, Church of N India, Poona 10 Oct 1976; ret 30 Jan 1990.

1994 ALEXANDER MALCOLM RAMSAY
dem from Bargrennan with Monigaff 31 Dec 1993 on app by Board of World Mission for service in Guatemala; Selly Oak Colleges, Birmingham Jan-Mar 1994, departed for Guatemala 15 Apr 1994; ind to Pitlochry 2 Jul 1998.

1961 SIMEON RATHBONE
(FES IX, 633, 637, 712; X, 78, 424), dem from Gretna Old to take up app at Buenos Aires St Andrew's 9 Oct 1961; ret 31 Mar 1970; died 9 Feb 1996.

1977 WILLIAM SCRYMGOUR RHODES
(FES IX, 746; X, 86), res from service with Overseas Council at Serampore College, India and ind to Lochrutton with Terregles 10 Apr 1975; dem 31 Jul 1977 and re-app by Overseas Council to Serampore; ret 1981.

1947 WILLIAM ALEXANDER DRAGE RIACH
(FES IX, 747; X, 424), res from service with FMC in Kenya and app Principal of Teacher Training College, Thika 1 Oct 1956; died 4 Sep 1999.

1978 WALTER RIGGANS
ord by Presb of Glasgow during assistantship at Garthamlock 15 Dec 1977; app to Church of Scotland Centre, Tiberias, Israel 1 Jan 1978; app Minister with the Israel Trust of the Anglican Church 1 Jan 1981; app Tutor in Biblical and Jewish Studies, All Nations Christian College, Ware, Herts 1 Aug 1986.

1974 JAMES McLAREN RITCHIE
(FES IX, 747; X, 16, 339, 424), res from Edinburgh McDonald Road (term) and app by Overseas Council for service in Yemen Arab Republic 1 Apr 1974; ind to Coalsnaughton 28 Sep 1977.

1925 DAVID MAXWELL ROBERTSON
(FUF 564; IX, 747), ord by Presb of Glasgow 20 Sep 1925 and app to Livingstonia Mission; ret from Lubwa 31 Mar 1939; died 12 Sep 1985.

1988 KENNETH RANKIN ROSS
dem from Unst to take up app as Lecturer in Theology, University of Malawi 1 Aug 1988; app Professor of Theology 10 Dec 1987; also app Parish minister, Nkanda 4 Jun 1989; dem charge and res University Chair 14 Oct 1998; app General Secretary, Board of World Mission 30 Nov 1998.

1983 BRIAN CRAIG RUTHERFORD
dem from Strathbrock on app by Board of World Mission to Greyfriars St Ann's, Trinidad, West Indies 8 Aug 1983; app General Treasurer, Blantyre Synod, Church of Central Africa Presb 1988; ind to Aberdeen Mastrick 5 Jul 1990.

1980 GEORGE BROWN CAMERON SANGSTER
(FES IX, 435, 566; X, 17, 329), dem from Edinburgh Murrayfield and introd as Assoc at Nairobi St Andrew's, Kenya 30 Apr 1980; ret 1983; died 16 Feb 1990; s David died 23 Apr 1976.

1993 HENRY ARTHUR SHEPHERD
(FES X, 329, 456), dem from Balerno on app to Christ Church, Bermuda 6 Feb 1993; ret 27 May 1998; d Lesley m Grant Thomas Laing.

1971 ALEXANDER SLORACH
ord in Kasama by Northern Presb of United Church of Zambia 22 Aug 1971; Service with Board of World Mission in Zambia 1970–82; admitted by

General Assembly 1983 and ind to Kirk of Lammermuir with Langton and Polwarth 5 Jul 1983.

1962 WILLIAM EWING SMITH
ord by Presb of Hamilton 7 Jan 1962; service with Overseas Council in Ajmer, Rajasthan, India 1962–72; app by Diocese of Delhi, Church of N India, to St James', Delhi Jan 1973; ind to Livingston Old 30 Mar 1978.

1973 JOHN STEIN
(FES X, 425), ord by South Kiambu Presb, Presb Church E Africa 9 Dec 1973, service in Kikuyu, Kenya; ind to Dundee Old St Paul's and St David's and Wishart Memorial 16 Mar 1976.

1979 ALEXANDER EWING STRACHAN
(FES X, 265), dem from Kilmadock on app by Overseas Council to Trinidad Greyfriars and St Ann's 22 Jul 1979; ind to Caputh and Clunie 29 Mar 1984.

1971 HOWARD GEORGE TAYLOR
ord by Church of Central Africa Presb and ind to Zomba, Malawi 13 May 1971; ind to Innellan with Inverchaolain and Toward 27 Oct 1981.

1937 ROBERT ANDERSON TROTTER
(FES IX, 427, 751), dem from Perth St Columba's on app to Indian Ecclesiastical Establishment, Lahore 29 Jun 1937; res 1948; died 15 May 1999; w Mary died 9 Apr 1989.

1981 DONALD KENNETH WALKER
ord by Presb of Inverness during assistantship at Nairn Old 14 Nov 1979; ind to St Margaret's United Church of Zambia, Kitwe 27 Sep 1981; trans to Trinity United Church of Zambia, Kalulushi, Jun 1986; Co-ordinator for Evangelism, United Church of Zambia; ind to Banchory-Ternan West 12 Jan 1995.

1973 IAN WALKER
ord by United Church of Zambia in Kafue 1 Aug 1973; app to Chingola and Chililabombwe, Copperbelt Presb, Zambia Feb 1976; ind to Garvald and Morham 15 Aug 1979.

1984 ROBERT McINTYRE WALKER
dem from Lochranza and Pirnmill with Shiskine 31 Jul 1983 on app to Samuel Bill Theological College, Abak, Nigeria; ind to Gardenstown 25 Apr 1986.

1967 JOHN CHRISTOPHER WIGGLESWORTH
app by Overseas Council 1 Oct 1967; ord by United Church of N India, Rahuri 8 Apr 1968; Presbyter, Church of N India, Ahmednagar 1 Dec 1970; introd to St Andrew's and St Columba's, Bombay 2 Jun 1972; app Lecturer, University of Aberdeen 1 Aug 1979.

1961 JAMES LINDSAY WILKIE
(FES X, 427), ord by Presb of Aberdeen 5 Jul 1959; app by Overseas Council for service in Zambia

Jan 1961; res to take up app as Africa Secretary, Divison of International Affairs, British Council of Churches, London Sep 1976.

1946 JOHN WILKINSON
(FES IX, 754), app to Church of Scotland Kenya Mission 16 Jul 1946 and served at Mission Hospitals at Tumutumu, Kikuyu and Chogoria 1946–75; Clerk to Overseas Presb of Kenya 1947–50, 1952–55; University of Edinburgh 1960–61 (BD); NHS Consultant in Public Health Medicine 1975–88; Clinical Teacher, Edinburgh University Faculty of Medicine 1979–84; ret 2 Nov 1988; FRCPE (1972); MFCM (1979); Addl children: Ewan Alastair John b 17 Jan 1956 m Maureen Beacham; d Agnes Patricia m Derek North; Publ: *Health and Healing: Studies in New Testament Principles and Practice* (Handsel Press, 1980); *Healing and the Church* (Handsel Press, 1984); *Christian Ethics in Health Care* (Handsel Press, 1988); *Making Men Whole: The Theology of Medical Missions* (Christian Medical Fellowship, 1990); *The Coogate Doctors: The History of the Edinburgh Medical Missionary Society* (EMMS, 1991); *The Story of Chogoria* (Handsel Press, 1994); *The Bible and Healing: A Medical and Theological Commentary* (Handsel Press, 1998); various articles and chapters on medicine, theology, ethics and history.

1980 JOHN MILLER WILSON
(FES X, 318, 427), dem from Dunnichen, Letham and Kirkden 6 Feb 1980 on app by Board of World Mission and Unity to serve with the Presb Church of Ghana, Ridge Church, Accra; ind to Bolton and Saltoun with Humbie with Yester 21 Feb 1985.

1993 PETER JOHNSTON WOOD
B 19 Mar 1965 at Stonehaven, s of Eric Robertson W. and Mary Watt; educ Mackie Academy, Stonehaven 1977–83; University of Aberdeen 1987 (MA); University of Edinburgh 1991 (BD), 1997 (MTh); lic by Presb of Kincardine and Deeside 4 Aug 1991; asstshp Edinburgh St John's Oxgangs 1991–92; m 6 Jul 1991 Emma Wild b 1 Sep 1969 d of Roger W. and Diana McLaren; Children: Rvari Lewis b 19 Feb 1999; ord by Presb of Kincardine and Deeside 5 Dec 1993; app by Church Missionary Society as Lecturer in Theological College, ISThA, Bunia, Congo Dec 1993.

1975 ERIC JOHN WRIGHT
ord by Presb of Glasgow and app by Overseas Council for service in Addis Ababa 1975; Bangladesh 1977–79; Lecturer in New Testament, All Nations Christian College, Ware, Herts 1979–82; introd as Assoc at Glasgow St George's Tron 1 Oct 1982.

OTHER MINISTERS

In alphabetical order

1969 ERIC DOUGLAS AITKEN
(FES X, 415), app Religious Broadcasting Asst/ Senior Radio Producer, BBC Scotland 17 Mar 1969; res on app as Asst (part-time), Edinburgh Mayfield Sep 1987; app Director (part-time), Churches Garden, Glasgow Garden Festival Oct 1987; res from Mayfield on app as Media Manager, Head of Training and Press PR Director, Buckhaven Parish Church Agency Apr 1990; ind to Clackmannan 3 Oct 1991.

1992 IAN WILLIAM ALEXANDER
B 28 Nov 1964 at Dumfries, s of William A. and Evelyn Jean Irvine; educ Douglas Ewart High, Newton Stewart 1977–83; Glasgow College (now Caledonian University) 1983–86 (BA); University of Edinburgh 1986–89 (BD); Union Theological Seminary, New York 1991–92 (STM); lic by Presb of Wigtown and Stranraer 26 Jul 1989; asstshp Edinburgh Palmerston Place 1989–91; ord by Presb of Edinburgh and app Asst at Palmerston Place 3 Jun 1990; app Education and Communication Officer, Presb United Nations Office, New York City 1 Sep 1992; app Secretary for Europe, Middle East and N Africa, Board of World Mission 1 Sep 1995; Publ: Editor of *Jane Haining* (Dept of World Mission, 1998).

1954 ALBERT DAVIDSON ALEXANDER
(FES IX, 143, 778), res as Lecturer in Hebrew and Biblical Criticism, University of Aberdeen 1953; became teacher of Classics and RE; ret 1980; died 17 Sep 1995.

1999 ROBERT SCOTT TAYLOR ALLAN
B 6 Sep 1963 at Paisley, s of Henry A. and Jane Templeman Riley; educ Castlehead High and Paisley Grammar 1975–81; University of Strathclyde 1981–85 (LLB, DLP); University of Glasgow 1987–90 (BD); Trainee Solicitor 1985–87; lic by Presb of Paisley 30 Aug 1990; asstshp Glasgow Penilee St Andrew 1987–88; Paisley High 1988–89; Glasgow Hillington Park 1989–90; Paisley Sherwood 1990–91; m 10 Jul 1987 Jane Lois Atkinson b 29 Apr 1967 d of Robert Charles Atkinson and Eileen Morton Blackett; Children: Ben Harris b 28 Apr 1990; Michael Thomas b 15 Sep 1991; Fraser John and Murray Charles b 18 May 1993; ord and ind to Larbert West 21 Jun 1991; dem on app as Education and Development Officer, Board of Ministry 31 Jan 1999.

1945 GEORGE McINNES ALLISON
(FES IX, 199, 275, 798; X, 453), app Admin Secretary, Dept of Education 17 Oct 1945; ret 31 May 1972; died 20 Mar 1987.

1990 COLIN MATHIESON ALSTON
B 16 Jul 1950 at Moffat, s of David A. and Jemima Georgina Cassells-Ballantyne; educ Moffat Academy and Lockerbie Academy 1961–68; University of Glasgow 1971–74 (BMus), 1971–74 (BD); University of Technology, Sydney 1998–99 (BNursing RN); lic by Presb of Annandale, Jul 1974; asstshp Glasgow Greenbank 1974–75; m 22 Feb 1979 Carol-Anne Petherick b 18 Dec 1954 d of James Hepburn P. and Doris Falconer; Children: James Colin b 14 Jun 1980; Jessica Helena b 15 Jan 1983; ord by Presb Church in Canada and ind to North Tyron Presb Church 30 Jul 1975; ind to Dulnain Bridge with Grantown-on-Spey 15 Dec 1980; app to Greyfriars St Ann's, Port of Spain, Trinidad 14 Dec 1987; app to Hunter Baillie Memorial Church, Annandale and The Welsh Church, Sydney, Australia 6 Sep 1990.

1994 DAVID JOHN BOYD ANDERSON
(FES X, 37), dem from Edinburgh Gorgie on app as General Secretary of Evangelical Alliance Scotland 30 Sep 1994; Addl children: Jonathan b 11 Jun 1977; Sarah b 7 Jul 1979; Malcolm b 17 Aug 1983.

1994 ROBERT ALEXANDER ANDERSON
res as Chaplain to University of Edinburgh 31 Jul 1994 and app Development Officer, Carberry Tower 1 Sep 1994; ind to Blackburn 29 Apr 1998.

1988 ROBERT SCOTT ANDERSON
B 11 Nov 1957 at Glasgow, s of William Auld A. and Jeannie Ballantyne Speirs; educ Hutchesons' Grammar, Glasgow 1967–76; University of Glasgow 1977–80 (MA), 1980–85 (BD); Open University 1996–98 (Prof Cert Management); Glen Dairy 1975–76; Student Christian Movement 1981–83; lic by Presb of Glasgow; asstshp Glasgow St John's Renfield 1985–86; m 9 Jul 1980 Jennifer Jane Paterson b 22 Jun 1960 d of John Hay P. and Ishbel Marion Mitchell; Children: Fiona Rachel; Catriona Ruth; Roderick John; app by Board of World Mission as Field Officer 1 May 1986; ord by Presb of Stirling 15 Dec 1988; Director of Scottish Churches World Exchange.

1975 THOMAS BALFOUR
(FES IX, 226, 474; X, 7, 130, 299), dem from Edinburgh Craiglockhart on app as Asst Secretary and Deputy, Church and Ministry Dept 31 Dec 1975; ret 31 Dec 1985; w Elizabeth died 6 Jul 1991; m (2) 19 Dec 1992 Muriel Logan Campbell b 16 Feb 1934, died 28 Mar 1997, d of Archibald William C. and Isabella Simpson Logan; s Derek m Yvonne Nedelea; s Jeffrey m Nancy Thain.

1997 FRANCIS DENTON BARDGETT
B 20 Jan 1948 at Newcastle-on-Tyne, s of Stanley B. and Bertha Denton; educ Fettes College, Edinburgh 1961–66; University of Cambridge 1967–71 (MA, CEd) University of Edinburgh 1980–83 (BD) (Cunningham Fellowship 1983), 1984–87 (PhD); Teaching 1971–79; Funeral Director, John Bardgett and Sons 1979–80; lic by Presb of Edinburgh 3 Jul 1983; asstshp Avoch with Fortrose and Rosemarkie 1983–84; m 28 Aug 1976 Alison Margaret Barclay d of John and Margaret B.; ord and ind to Strathy and Halladale 11 Aug 1987; introd as Community minister, Orkney 1 Sep 1993; dem to take up app as Secretary-Depute, Dept of National Mission 20 Oct 1997; Publ: *Scotland Reformed: the Reformation in Angus and the Mearns* (John Donald, 1989); *North Coast Parish: a post-clearance parish and its churches* (Thurso, 1990).

1991 WARREN ROSS BEATTIE
B 12 Dec 1960 at Dingwall, s of William Ross B. and Violet Williamson Mackenzie; educ Fortrose Academy 1972–78; University of Edinburgh 1978–81 (BSc), 1986–89 (BD), 1998 (MSc in Non-Western Christianity); Polytechnic of North London 1984–85 (DipLib); Short-term Missionary (Belgium) 1981–83; Librarianship 1984, 1985–86; lic by Presb of Edinburgh 2 Jul 1989; asstshp Edinburgh St Catherine's Argyle 1989–91; m 28 Mar 1987 Stroma Lauder b 20 Dec 1963 d of George Adam Godfrey L. and Shona Jessie Kelly Thomson; ord by Presb of Edinburgh during assistantship at St Catherine's Argyle 2 Dec 1990; app by OMF International for service in S Korea and Singapore.

1993 PAUL HARRY BEAUTYMAN
B 6 Jun 1967 at Falkirk, s of Harry B. and Anna Rowan; educ Graeme High, Falkirk 1972–85; University of Glasgow 1985–89 (MA); University of Aberdeen 1989–92 (BD); lic by Presb of Falkirk 26 Jun 1992; asstshp Ayr Castlehill 1992–93; ord by Presb of Perth and app Mission Co-ordinator 26 Jun 1993.

1978 JOHN LAMBERTON BELL
B 20 Nov 1949 at Kilmarnock, s of David Robertson B. and Marion Fulton Lamberton; educ Kilmarnock Academy 1962–68; University of Glasgow 1975 (MA), 1978 (BD); Social Work (voluntary) 1971–72; Student President 1974–75; Lay ministry 1975–77; lic by Presb of Kilmarnock 29 Jun 1978; ord by Presb of Glasgow and app as Presb Youth Advisor,

Oct 1978; app Youth Co-ordinator, Iona Community 1983; app Worship Resource Worker, Iona Community 1988; app Fellow of Royal School of Church Music (FRSCM) 1999; Publ: Editor *A Trysting Place* (Begijnhot, Amsterdam, 1979); *And the Crowd is Still Hungry* (Glasgow University, 1979); editor of *Songs of God's People* (St Andrew Press, 1988); *Wrestle, Fight and Pray* (St Andrew Press, 1993); editor of *Common Ground* (1998); Wild Goose Publs: *Poverty, Chastity and Obedience* (1984); *Songs of the Incarnation* (1984); *Heaven Shall Not Wait* (1987); *Enemy of Apathy* (1988); *Love from Below* (1989); *Many and Great* (1990); *Sent by the Lord* (1991); *Innkeepers and Lightsleepers* (1992); *Psalms of Patience, Protest and Praise* (1993); *Come all you People* (1994); *He Was in the World* (1995); *God Never Sleeps* (1995); *The Courage to Say No* (1996); editor of *A Wee Worship Book* (1997); editor of *Cloth for the Cradle* (1997); *Love and Anger* (1997); *When Grief is Raw* (1997); *The Last Journey* (1997); *Psalms of David and Songs of Mary* (1998).

1959 NEIL CAMERON BERNARD
(FES IX, 729; X, 416, 453), app Africa and Jamaica Field Secretary of FMC 20 Oct 1959; ret 1976; died 15 Jan 1991.

1973 JOHN MAXWELL BIRRELL
Project Co-ordinator, Calton Youth Ministry, Edinburgh 1973–76; Deputy Leader, Simpson House, Edinburgh (Board of Social Responsibility) 1976–77; Warden, Stroove House (Board of Education) 1977–80; ind to Carluke St Andrew's 26 Nov 1980.

1974 PETER THOMAS BISSET
(FES IX, 211; X, 28, 121, 173), dem from Bathgate High on app as Warden of St Ninian's, Crieff 8 Jun 1974; ret 1992; died 8 Jan 1994.

1981 RONALD STANTON BLAKEY
(FES X, 67, 85, 187), dem from Jedburgh Old with Edgerston with Ancrum on app as Asst Secretary, Dept of Education 1 Apr 1981; app Depute Secretary 1 Nov 1985; app Secretary, Assembly Council 1 Aug 1988; app by Board of World Mission as Interim Secretary for Management of Church's Institutions in Israel 13 Sep 1999; Publ: *Jethart's Kirk* (private, 1975); *The Man in the Manse* (Handsel Press, 1978).

1998 GRAHAM KEITH BLOUNT
B 7 Apr 1951 at Glasgow, s of George Keith B. and Caroline Victoria Brown; educ Hutchesons' Grammar, Glasgow 1960–68; University of Glasgow 1968–72 (LLB); University of St Andrews 1972–75 (BD); University of Edinburgh 1990–95 (PhD); lic by Presb of Glasgow 26 Jun 1975; asstshp East Kilbride Claremont 1975–76; m 12 Sep 1974 Audrey Sheila Gillon b 14 Oct 1953 d of Charles Colin Campbell G. and Audrey Fairway; Children: Laura Carol b 13 Nov 1981; Lindsay May b 24 May 1983; ord and ind to Glasgow Linthouse

St Kenneth's 28 Sep 1976; trans to Bridge of Allan Chalmers and also app Chaplain (part-time) to University of Stirling 12 Oct 1983; trans to Falkirk Old and St Modan's (joint ministry) 22 Jun 1990; dem 20 Sep 1998 on app as Scottish Churches' Parliamentary Officer.

1997   SCOTT BLYTHE
ord by Presb of Lorn and Mull and app Programme Worker, MacLeod Centre, Iona 5 Mar 1997; introd as Assoc (part-time) at Garthdee and Chaplain (part-time) to Robert Gordon University 15 Apr 1999.

1980   KENNETH MACKENZIE BOYD
(FES X, 441), app Research Director, Institute of Medical Ethics (part-time) 1 Jun 1980; app Edinburgh International Chaplain (part-time) 1 Jun 1981; app Senior Lecturer in Medical Ethics, Edinburgh University Medical School 1 Feb 1996; app College Cleric of the Royal College of Physicians of Edinburgh 1996; Fellowship of Royal College of Physicians 1997; non-stipendiary minister at St John's Episcopal Church, Edinburgh; Publ: *The Ethics of Resource Allocation in Health Care* (Edinburgh Univ Press, 1979); *Scottish Church Attitudes to Sex, Marriage and the Family 1850–1914* (John Donald, 1980); co-author of *Lives in the Balance: The Ethics of Using Animals in Biomedical Research* (OUP, 1991); co-editor of *The New Dictionary of Medical Ethics* (BMJ Publs, 1997).

1983   JAMES McILROY BROWN
B 13 Jun 1956 at Kirkcaldy, s of George B. and Margaret Ann Bayne McArthur; educ Kirkcaldy High 1968–74; University of Edinburgh 1974–78 (MA), 1978–81 (BD); lic by Presb of Kirkcaldy 29 Jun 1981; asstshp Edinburgh South Leith 1981– 83; m 26 Sep 1986 Heike Antje Lengenfeld b 8 Mar 1955 d of Franz L. and Ilse Oschlies; ord by Presb of Edinburgh during assistantship at South Leith 27 Jun 1982; app to Evangelische Kirchengemeinde Bochum, Pauluskirche 1 Jun 1983; app joint-pastor (responsible for English congregation) 24 Dec 1993; sole pastor from 1 Feb 1998.

1975   ISABEL COULTER BUCHAN
B 16 Mar 1949 at Glasgow, d of David Coulter Black and Catherine Black; educ Penilee Secondary, Glasgow 1961–67; University of Strathclyde 1967–70 (BSc); University of Glasgow 1970–74 (BD); Dundee College of Education 1983–84 (PGCE); lic by Presb of Paisley 27 Jun 1974; asstshp Paisley Abbey 1974–75, 1975–76; m 1 May 1976 Alexander Buchan b 1 Apr 1935 s of Alexander B. and Mary Crawford; Children: David b 17 Jun 1977; Catherine b 28 Aug 1979; ord by Presb of Paisley during assistantship at Paisley Abbey 1 May 1975; voluntary Asst in husband's charges from 1975; Chaplain to Mater and Princess Alexandra Hospitals, Brisbane, Australia 1979; app

teacher (RE), Bishopbriggs 1984, Sanday 1990; Publ: Various articles.

1987   JOHN CAMPBELL
(FES X, 122), dem from Glasgow Sherbrooke St Gilbert's to take up app as Adviser in Mission and Evangelism, Dept of National Mission 1 Jan 1987; ind to Caldwell, Uplawmoor 29 Sep 1999.

1995   JOHN PEARSON CHALMERS
B 5 Jun 1952 at Bothwell, s of Isaac MacMillan C. and Mary Ann Pearson; educ Marr College, Troon 1964–70; University of Strathclyde 1970–72; University of Glasgow 1973–78 (BD, CPS); lic by Presb of Ayr 29 Jun 1978; asstshp Glasgow Netherlee 1978–79; m 10 Apr 1976 Elizabeth Barbara Boning b 8 Aug 1955 d of Charles and Barbara B; Children: Jennifer Ruth b 13 Nov 1982; David Stuart b 11 Oct 1984; John James b 20 Dec 1987; ord and ind to Renton Trinity 14 Jun 1979; Clerk to Presb of Dumbarton 1982–86; trans to Edinburgh Palmerston Place 1 Oct 1986; app Depute Secretary, Board of Ministry 1 Oct 1995.

1991   WILLIAM JAMES CHRISTMAN
(FES X, 20, 165), dem from Ayr St Columba 28 Feb 1991 on app as Chaplain to HM Prison Shotts; res 1993.

1996   DAVID McNAIR CLARK
B 26 Feb 1948 at Glasgow, s of David Hare C. and Mary McLeod; educ Hutchesons' Grammar, Glasgow 1960–66; University of Glasgow 1966– 70 (MA), 1985–88 (BD); Jordanhill College, Glasgow 1970–71 (DEd); Teaching 1975–85; lic by Presb of Jedburgh, Jul 1988; asstshp Bearsden North 1988–89; m 29 Mar 1972 Maureen Fowlis b 22 Apr 1950 d of John F. and Angelika Eggert; ord and ind to Airdrie Flowerhill 31 Aug 1989; dem 7 Oct 1996 on app as General Director of Scripture Union Scotland.

1992   DAVID GEORGE COULTER
ord by Presb of St Andrews and app by RAChD 2 Apr 1989; app Chaplain to Loretto School, Musselburgh 20 Mar 1992; app by RAChD 21 Mar 1994.

1977   JOHN LAWLESS COWIE
(FES IX, 455; X, 20, 269, 278), dem from Richmond Craigmillar with Newcraighall 30 Jun 1977 on app by Christian Fellowship of Healing, Edinburgh; ret 3 Jul 1988; s Roderick m Ellen Douglas; s Malcolm m Carole Hoggan; s Christopher m Shona McGregor; d Rosalind m Joseph Croy; Addl publ: *People Praying* (St Andrew Press, 1972); *Growing Knowing Jesus* (St Andrew Press, 1978); *Across the Spectrum* (Handsel Press, 1993); *Ideas and Prayers for Healing Services* (Wild Goose Publs, 1995); *The Healing Works of Jesus* (Wild Goose Publs, 1999).

1991   MAXWELL DAVIDSON CRAIG
(FES X, 38, 183 (2)), dem from Aberdeen St Columba's Bridge of Don on app as General

Secretary, Action of Churches Together in Scotland 1 Jan 1991; d Sarah m Michael Wright; Publ: 'Stella: *The Story of Stella J Reekie* (Southpark, 1984); *For God's Sake . . . Unity* (Wild Goose Publs, 1998).

1985 DAVID PATRICK LOW CUMMING
(FES X, 102, 354 (2), 366), dem from Elgin St Giles' on app as Secretary Depute, Dept of Ministry and Mission 1 Sep 1985; res and ind to Kilmodan and Colintraive 31 Oct 1991.

1976 GORDON CHRISTOPHER MACLEOD CURRIE
B 18 Jun 1940 at Grantown on Spey, s of William C. and Christina Munro Weir; educ Dornoch Academy and Altyre/Gordonstoun 1952–59; University of St Andrews 1959–63 (MA); University of Edinburgh 1964–67 (BD); Moray House College, Edinburgh 1969–70 (PGCE); Teaching 1970-present; lic by Presb of St Andrews 3 May 1967; asstshp Linwood 1967–69; m (1) 9 Mar 1968 Marjory Forbes Montgomery b 11 Dec 1942 d of George M. and Margaret Forbes; Children: Andrew Christopher Forbes b 14 Apr 1971; Lorna Margaret Christine b 14 Jan 1973; m (2) 2 Apr 1986 Helen Weir Hamilton b 15 Feb 1943 d of William H. and Jessie McClure; ord by Presb of Falkirk during assistantship at Linlithgow St Michael's 3 Dec 1976; continued as Hon Asst until 1981.

1967 COLIN TRAQUAIR DAY
(FES IX, 540; X, 316, 453), res from app as Home Board Evangelist to take up app as Warden of Carberry Tower 1 Mar 1967; ret 3 Feb 1984.

1990 ROGER ALFRED FRANCIS DEAN
dem from Dennyloanhead with Haggs on app as Chaplain to Royal Caledonian Schools, Bushey, Herts 1 Sep 1990; ind to Mochrum 25 Jan 1995.

1972 ANDREW BEVERIDGE DOIG
(FES IX, 732; X, 48, 418), dem from Dalkeith St John's and King's Park 31 Aug 1972 on app as Secretary of Scottish National Bible Society; ret 1980; Moderator of General Assembly 1981–82; died 21 Dec 1997.

1972 IAN CUNNINGHAM DOUGALL
(FES X, 418), res from service with FMC in Kenya and app Chaplain to George Heriot's, Edinburgh 31 Aug 1972; res 1987 and app Headmaster of Mwambiti High School, Voi, Kenya 1988.

1999 ANDREW ALEXANDER DOWNIE
B 30 Dec 1955 at Edinburgh, s of Alexander D. and Elizabeth McDonald Bremner; educ Boroughmuir High, Edinburgh 1968–74; University of Edinburgh 1974–78 (BSc), 1984–85 (DipEd), 1989–90 (DipMin); Nazarene Theological College 1978–83 (ThB); University of London 1980–83 (BD); Moray House College, Edinburgh 1984–85 (PGCE); Lecturer in Biblical Studies 1983–84; Warden and Club Leader, Craigentinny Christian

Centre 1984–99; Teaching (RE) 1985–89; lic by Presb of Edinburgh 17 Oct 1990; asstshp Edinburgh South Leith 1990–91, St Catherine's Argyle 1991; m 30 Jul 1982 Norma Ferguson Wallace Wilson b 21 Aug 1949 d of Edward Butcher W. and Minnie Ferguson Wallace; Assoc at Holyrood Abbey 1992–94; ord by Presb of Edinburgh 11 May 1994 and continued as Assoc at Holyrood Abbey; app Chaplain (part-time) to Saughton Prison 19 May 1997; app Chaplain (full-time) to Kilmarnock Prison 22 Feb 1999.

1977 IAN BRUCE DOYLE
(FES IX, 335; X, 159, 200), dem from Glasgow Eastwood on app as Depute-Secretary, Dept of National Mission 1 Mar 1977; app Secretary 1 Sep 1977; ret 30 Sep 1991; Pastoral Asst, Edinburgh Palmerston Place from 1 Oct 1991; Addl publ: Contributor to *Local Church Evangelism* (St Andrew Press, 1987).

1957 DENIS MACDONALD DUNCAN
(FES IX, 18, 310; X, 182), dem from Glasgow Trinity-Duke Street 31 Dec 1957 on app as Editor of 'British Weekly'; Assoc Director, Westminster Pastoral Foundation, London 1971–79; Chairman of World Assoc for Pastoral Care and Counselling 1977–79; Director Highgate Counselling Centre 1973–86; Chairman of St Barnabas Ecumenical Centre for Christian Counselling and Healing 1980–92; Director of Churches' Council for Health and Healing 1982–87; Managing Director of Arthur James Publishing 1983–95; Publ: *Here is my Hand* (Hodder Headline, 1981); *Creative Silence* (Arthur James, 1983); *A Day at a Time* (Arthur James, 1984); *Love, the Word that Heals* (Arthur James, 1985); *Health and Healing, a Ministry to Wholeness* (St Andrew Press, 1991); *Be Still and Know* (Arthur James, 1995); *Solitude, Stillness, Serenity* (Arthur James, 1997); *The Road Taken* (Ecclesia Services, 1997).

1965 HAROLD CUMMING MOLLISON EGGO
(FES IX, 228; X, 54, 132, 453), dem from Dunbar to take up app as Asst Secretary and Deputy, Church and Ministry Dept 31 Dec 1965; app Secretary and Deputy 1976; ret 1977; died 19 Feb 1991.

1974 GEORGE LAMB ELLIOT
(FES X, 372, 453), dem from Inverness Ness Bank to take up app as Secretary of Stewardship and Finance Committee 1 Feb 1974; ret 4 Aug 1989; s John m Mary Quinn; s Douglas m Jill Dallas.

1989 DAVID WILLIAM ELLIS
res as Assoc at Glasgow St George's Tron on app as National Director of Overseas Missionary Fellowship 31 Aug 1989; app Minister at Large, OMF International 1 Jul 1998.

1974 ALAN DAVID FALCONER
B 12 Dec 1945 at Edinburgh, s of Alexander F. and Jean Braidwood Littlejohn; educ George

Heriot's, Edinburgh 1953–64; University of Aberdeen 1967 (MA), 1970 (BD); University of Geneva 1971 (CES); Philip's Theological Seminary, Enid, USA 1995 (DLitt); lic by Presb of Aberdeen 12 Apr 1970; asstshp Aberdeen St Machar's Cathedral 1972–74; m 6 Aug 1968 Marjorie Ellen Walters b 17 Mar 1946 d of Sydney Norton W. and Agnes Paterson Wood; Children: David Andrew b 30 Apr 1971; Rosalind Clare b 16 Jun 1973; Andrew Graham b 9 Jan 1975; ord by Presb of Aberdeen during assistantship at St Machar's Cathedral, Dec 1972; app Lecturer, Irish School of Ecumenics, Dublin 1 Oct 1974; app Senior Lecturer and Dean 1982; app Director 1 Sep 1990; app Director, Faith and Order Commission, WCC 1 Feb 1995; Publ: Editor of *Understanding Human Rights* (Irish School of Ecumenics, 1980); *A Man Alone* (Columba Press, 1987); editor of *Reconciling Memories* (Columba Press, 1988, 1998).

1982 RONALD FERGUSON
(FES X, 158), res as Community minister in Easterhouse 1979; Exchange minister with United Church of Canada 1979–80; app Deputy Warden, Iona Abbey 1 Sep 1980; Leader of Iona Community 12 Mar 1982–84 Aug 1989; Biographer (full-time) of George MacLeod Aug-Dec 1989; ind to St Magnus Cathedral, Orkney 12 Dec 1990.

1976 SINCLAIR BUCHANAN FERGUSON
(FES X, 407), dem from Unst 4 Apr 1976 on app as Editor, Banner of Truth Trust; app Professor of Systematic Theology, Westminster Theological Seminary, Philadelphia, USA 1 Jul 1982; University of Aberdeen 1974–79 (PhD).

1995 JAMES THOMSON FIELDS
B 12 Dec 1959 at Glasgow, s of Thomas Findlay F. and Christine Thomson; educ Mill Hill School, London 1973–78; University of Edinburgh 1978–82 (MA), 1982–85 (BD); Union Theological Seminary, New York 1985–86 (STM); University of Strathclyde 1992–94 (DipCouns); lic by Presb of Dumbarton 28 Jun 1985; asstshp Netherlee 1987–88; ord by Presb of Greenock and introd as Assoc at the Old West Kirk 28 Jun 1988; app Manager of Counselling Services, Yorkhill NHS Trust, Glasgow 1 Dec 1995; app Chaplain to Lodging House Mission, Glasgow 12 Feb 1998; app Chaplain to Mill Hill School, London 1 Sep 1998.

1969 DUNCAN FINLAYSON
(FES IX, 320, 799; X, 50, 308, 435), dem from Monifieth St Rule's on app as Principal of St Colm's College, Edinburgh 6 Oct 1969; res and ind to Morvern 15 Sep 1978.

1989 IAN RIDDOCK FISHER
(FES X, 104, 147), dem from Glasgow Fernhill and Cathkin 7 Aug 1989 on app as Secretary, Board of Stewardship and Finance; died 14 Sep 1992.

1972 DAVID ROSS FLOCKHART
(FES X, 329, 435, 441, 453), res as Senior Lecturer, Moray House College, Edinburgh to take up app as Director of Scottish Council for Voluntary Organisations 1972; ret 31 Oct 1991; OBE 1992; DUniv (1998).

1979 JOHN WILLIAM ARTHUR FORBES
(FES X, 352), dem from Auchterless on app to Scottish Churches Action for World Development Jun 1979; app to Charity Project Trust 1 Jan 1980; ind to Edzell Lethnot with Glenesk 17 Nov 1982.

1980 JAMES FORSYTH
(FES X, 187, 378), dem from Avoch with Fortrose and Rosemarkie to take up app as Director of Resource Centre for World Development, Glenrothes 10 Sep 1980; introd to Contin-Strathconon (term) 1 Jun 1983.

1969 IAN MASSON FRASER
(FES IX, 469; X, 278), Executive Secretary (Education and Renewal), WCC, Geneva 1969–75; Dean and Head of Dept of Mission, Selly Oak Colleges, Bimingham 1973–82; transferred to URC 1973 (until 1982); ret 15 Dec 1982; Voluntary assgn for British Missionary Societies and Boards (basic Christian communities) 1982–87; Voluntary Research Consultant to Scottish Churches Council and ACTS from 1982; d (Margaret) Anne m Sidney Eugene (Gene) Kirkley; s Keith m Hazel Street; s Ian m Kathy Morrison; Addl publ: *Live with Style* (1969); *Leisure-Tourism: Threat and Promise* (WCC, 1970); *The Fire Runs* (SCM, 1975); *Re-inventing Theology as the People's Work* (WCC, 1980); *Duty and Delight* (article later publ as *New Hymn Writing*, Canterbury Press, 1985); co-author of *Wind and Fire* (private, 1986); *Living a Countersign* (Wild Goose Publs, 1990); *Sharing Holy Communion* (Wild Goose Publs, 1994); *Strange Fire* (Wild Goose Publs, 1994); *The Try-it-out-Hymnbook* (private, 1995); *Celebrating Saints* (Wild Goose Publs, 1997); *Salted with Fire* (St Andrew Press, 1999).

1953 JOHN McCLYMONT FREW
(FES IX, 266), dem from Dennistoun 3 Oct 1953; entered teaching profession 1954; ret 31 Jul 1982; s Michael m Sylvia Biggin; d Anne m Steve Morris.

1987 MICHAEL WILLIAM FREW
dem from Alloa West 15 Jan 1987 on app as Regional Organiser for Evangelism 1 Feb 1987; ind to Carluke St John's 3 Oct 1991.

1998 ROBERT STUART McCOLL FULTON
B 31 Aug 1960 at Coleraine, s of Robert F. and Jessie Rae Young; educ Coleraine Academical Institution; University of Sheffield 1979–82 (BA); King Alfred's College, Winchester 1984–85 (PGCE); University of Glasgow 1987–90 (BD); Columbia Theological Seminary, Georgia 1989–90; Addiction Counselling 1982–84; Teaching 1985–87; lic by Presb of Ayr 6 Jul 1990; asstshp

Auld Kirk of Ayr 1990–91; m 19 May 1990 Sarah (Sally) Verner Foster b 25 Apr 1964 d of William F. and Gambrelle Glen; Children: Jessie Alexandra b 6 Jul 1991; Sarah Grace b 22 Mar 1994; ord and ind to Haggs 28 Jun 1991; dem 14 Jun 1998 on app as Special Adviser on Chaplaincy to HM Prison Services.

1995   DAVID DOUGLAS GALBRAITH
(FES X, 21), app Admin Secretary, Panel on Worship, Panel on Doctrine, Committee on Artistic Matters 1 Mar 1995; Lecturer (part-time), Diploma in Church Music, University of St Andrews 1993–; Precentor, General Assembly 1996–; app Assoc of Royal School of Church Music (ARSCM) 1999; Australian College of Theology 1999 (ThD); divorced 6 Dec 1993, m (2) 29 Feb 1996 Daphne Audsley b 8 Aug 1959 d of George A. and Joan Price; d Joanna m Peter Petrie; Addl publ: Co-author of *New Ways to Worship* (St Andrew Press, 1980); editor of *Worship in the Wide Red Land* (Uniting Church Press, Melbourne 1985); contributor to *With Strings and Pipe* (ed Gordon Graham, Univ of St Andrews, 1994); contibutor to *Urban Theology: a Reader* (ed Michael Northcott, Cassell, 1998); ThD thesis: 'The Delight of Melody with Doctrines: Ecclesiological Criteria for the Evaluation of Music for Christian Worship' (2000); founding co-editor of *Trinity Occasional Papers* and *One Voice* (journals).

1980   KATHRYN JOHNSTON GALLOWAY
B 6 Aug 1952 at Dumfries, d of John Fleming Orr and Janet Johnston; educ Boroughmuir High, Edinburgh 1964–70; University of Glasgow 1970–76 (BD, DPS); lic by Presb of Edinburgh, Jun 1976; asstshp Edinburgh Muirhouse 1976–79; Children: David John b 31 Mar 1979; Duncan Callum b 18 Aug 1981; Helen Catriona b 16 Nov 1983; ord by Presb of Edinburgh during assistantship at Muirhouse 12 Jun 1977; app Co-ordinator of Edinburgh Peace and Justice Centre 1 Sep 1980; app Joint-Warden, Iona Abbey 1 Mar 1983; Editor of *Coracle* (Iona Community) from 1989; Freelance Practical Theologian and Liturgist from 1990; Project Worker for Iona Community and Scottish Churches Action for World Development 1993–94; Worship and Counselling Co-ordinator, Orbiston Neighbourhood Centre 1995–96; Facilitator of Open Doors Project, Hillhead Baptist Church, Glasgow from 1996; Publ: *Imagining the Gospels* (SPCK, 1987, 1994); editor of *A Woman's Claim of Right in Scotland* (Polygon, 1991); *A Woman's Place: Women and Work* (St Andrew Press, 1993); *Love Burning Deep* (SPCK, 1993); *Struggles to Love* (SPCK, 1994, 1998); *Getting Personal* (SPCK, 1995); *Pushing the Boat Out* (Wild Goose Publs, 1995); editor of *The Pattern of Our Days* (Wild Goose Publs, 1996); *Talking to the Bones* (SPCK, 1996); *Dreaming of Eden* (Wild Goose Publs, 1997); *Starting Where We Are* (Wild Goose Publs, 1998); *A Story to Live By* (SPCK, 1999); numerous articles, pamphlets, papers.

1978   IAN FRANCIS GALLOWAY
app National Youth Adviser, Dept of Education Aug 1978; app Joint-Warden, Iona Abbey 1 Mar 1983; ind to Glasgow Lansdowne 8 Dec 1988.

1993   ARTHUR RAYMOND CHARLES GASTON
(FES X, 264, 267), res from app at Geneva and app Staffing Secretary, Board of World Mission 1 Nov 1993; ind to Leuchars St Athernase and Guardbridge 29 Oct 1998.

1997   RICHARD GIBBONS
B 6 May 1960 at Hamilton, s of Richard G. and Philomena Thornbury; educ Our Lady's High, Motherwell 1972–76; University of Glasgow 1992–96 (BD); Electrician 1976–81; Staff member, Glasgow Bible College 1987–90; lic by Presb of Hamilton 28 Aug 1996; asstshp East Kilbride Claremont 1996–97; m 28 Mar 1981 Ruth Langley b 13 Nov 1959 d of John L. and Margaret Thomson; Children: Michael; ord by Presb of Hamilton and app Regional Adviser in Mission and Evangelism for the Highlands 19 Jun 1997.

1972   FRANCIS SYMINGTON GIBSON
(FES X, 147, 237, 454), dem from Glasgow Fernhill and Cathkin to take up app as Asst Director of Board of Social Responsibility 1 Jul 1972; ind to Kilarrow with Kilmeny 8 Feb 1990.

1983   DAVID JOHN GRAHAM
ord by Presb of Dumbarton during assistantship at Milngavie St Paul's 15 Sep 1982; app to Glasgow Bible College Aug 1983; ind to Dirleton with North Berwick Abbey 10 Dec 1998.

1980   ALEXANDER DAVID MOORE GRAHAM
(FES X, 149), dem from Glasgow Anderston Kelvingrove 31 Jan 1980 on app as Warden of Iona Abbey; introd to Aberdeen Rutherford (term) 8 Mar 1983.

1997   ANDREW TRELAWNEY GREAVES
B 14 Jul 1951 at Edinburgh, s of Edwin Trelawney G. and Cynthia Dorothy Rackham; educ St Edward's School, Oxford 1964–68; Aston University 1973 (DIA); University of St Andrews 1980–84 (BD, DipPT); Management Trainee 1970–74; Oil Industry 1975–80; lic by Presb of Angus, 1984; asstshp Musselburgh St Andrew's 1984–85; m 3 Sep 1977 Victoria Jane Brightman b 30 May 1953 d of E C V B. and Francis Dickson; Children: Philippa b 12 Feb 1980; Rachel b 7 Aug 1982; Tom b 6 Jun 1984; ord by Presb of Edinburgh and app Chaplain to Loretto School 28 Apr 1985; Asst Director, Project Trust and minister on Coll 1987–90; ind to Glamis with Inverarity and Kinnettles 28 Sep 1990; became minister of united charge 6 Sep 1996; dem 31 Aug 1997 on app as Chaplain to Gordonstoun School.

1978   ARTHUR DAVID COURTENAY GREER
(FES X, 163 (2), 419), dem from Glasgow Kelvingrove on app by Dept of Education 1 Sep 1978; introd to Dundee Whitfield 1 Oct 1981.

1986　JAMES CARRUTHERS GORRIE GREIG
(FES X, 82), dem from Paisley St Matthew's on app as Translator, WCC, Geneva 14 May 1986; ret 22 Feb 1992; d Elspeth m Stewart Munro; s Andrew m Margaret McAllister; Addl publ: Translations of *The Charismatic Leader and His Followers* by Martin Hengel (T&T Clark, 1981) and *Law in Paul's Thought* by Hans Huebner (T&T Clark, 1984); Introd and Notes for *Witch Wood* by John Buchan (OUP, 1993) and Introds for *Supernatural Tales, The Power House* and *The Thirty-Nine Steps* by John Buchan (B & W Publs, 1997, 1999); freelance translations for WCC, CEC, LWF, WARC since 1992.

1980　DAVID GENTLES HAMILTON
(FES X, 107), dem from Bearsden South on app as Curriculum Officer, Board of Parish Education 1 Nov 1980; app Asst Director of Board; ind to Braes of Rannoch with Foss and Rannoch 31 Mar 1998.

1965　JOHN MILLEN HAMILTON
(FUF 401; FES IX, 234, 247, 541, 800; X, 454), app General Secretary of FMC May 1960; app General Secretary of Overseas Council 1965; ret 31 May 1972; died 4 May 1982.

1979　ANNE JESSIE McINROY HARPER
app Education Field Officer, Dept of Education 1 Aug 1979; ord by Presb of Paisley 28 Nov 1979; ind to Glasgow Linthouse St Kenneth's 6 Jun 1984.

1981　DAVID ARTHUR HARRIES
B 31 Dec 1925 at Cwmfelinfach, S Wales, s of David H. and Ivy Blythe; educ Caterham School and Preston Grammar 1935–41; Lancashire Independent College (Congregational); University of Manchester 1946–50 (CBK, CTh); RAF 1942–46; lic by Presb of Dunoon; m 17 Jan 1946 Eva Triantafyllou b 1 Jan 1926 d of George T. and Maria Fortouna; Children: Diane m Michael Brown; Karen; ord and ind to Ainsdale Congregational Church 5 Jul 1950; trans to Park Congregational Church, Llanelli 1 Jan 1954; app Chaplain to Royal Navy 8 Nov 1955; admitted by General Assembly and ind to Kilmodan and Colintraive 16 Mar 1977; dem 30 Jun 1981 on app as Principal Chaplain to British Sailors' Society; ret 31 Dec 1990; Publ: Co-author of *Service Book* (International Sailors' Society, 1990).

1971　WILLIAM JOHN HARVEY
(FES X, 165, 454), dem from Glasgow Laurieston-Renwick 30 Sep 1971 on app as Warden of Iona Abbey; ind to Stirling St Mark's 21 Dec 1976; trans to Govan Old 3 Sep 1981; dem to take up app as Leader of Iona Community Aug 1988; app to Craighead Institute Aug 1995; Publ: *Bridging the Gap* (St Andrew Press, 1987).

1973　HOWARD JAMES HASLETT
B 4 Oct 1944 at Belfast, s of William H. and Marion Larmour Dowling; educ Royal Belfast Academical

Institution 1955–62; University of Dublin 1962–66 (BA); University of Edinburgh 1966–68, 1969–70 (BD); Moray House College, Edinburgh 1970–71 (CEd); Teaching 1968–69; lic by Presb of Edinburgh, Jul 1971; asstshp Edinburgh St Giles' Cathedral 1971–73; m 28 Oct 1971 Agnes Alexandra Adams b 21 Apr 1945 d of William A. and Shennagh Long; Children: William Patrick b 6 Oct 1972; John Mark Fraser b 21 Sep 1977; Emma Jane b 11 Nov 1978; ord by Presb of Edinburgh during assistantship at St Giles' 26 Mar 1972; Chaplain to Edinburgh Academy 1 Sep 1973–30 Jun 1999.

1974　WILLIAM HENNEY
(FES X, 124, 313, 454), dem from Johnstone St Paul's to take up app as Asst Secretary, Dept of Education 31 Oct 1974; ind to St Andrews Hope Park 14 Dec 1978.

1999　ADAM JOHNSTON JARRON HOOD
B 27 Sep 1960 at Musselburgh, s of James Johnston H. and Alison Marshall Jarron; educ Preston Lodge High, Prestonpans 1971–77 and Stevenson College, Edinburgh 1979–80; University of Aberdeen 1980–84 (MA), 1984–87 (BD); Clerical Work 1978–79; lic by Presb of Lothian, Jul 1987; asstshp Hamilton Old 1987–89; m 5 Nov 1988 Katrina Cameron b 24 Jul 1964 d of William C. and Jane Gibson; Children: Nathan Cameron James b 3 May 1994; Abigail Alice Jane b 29 Dec 1996; ord and ind to Barrhaed Bourock 29 Jun 1989; dem to take up place at University of Oxford 1 Oct 1994; app Deputy Director, Research Centre, Queen's College, Birmingham 1 Sep 1999; Publ: *Faith as Believing and Acting* (Whitefield Institute, Oxford, 1997).

1967　WILLIAM HOWIE
B 29 Feb 1940 at Aberdeen, s of Robert Rae H. and Mary Allison; educ Aberdeen Academy 1957–60; University of Aberdeen 1956–7 (MA), 1960–63 (BD), 1970–72 (CASS); Union Theological Seminary, New York 1963–64 (STM); lic by Presb of Aberdeen 28 Apr 1963; asstshp Aberdeen Northfield 1964–67; m 19 Jul 1963 Elizabeth Ann Gill b 1 Feb 1943 d of Alexander G. and Barbara Cruden; Children: Elizabeth Jane b 23 Jul 1972; Ruth Jennifer b 30 Nov 1976; ord by Presb of Aberdeen during assistantship at Northfield 1 Nov 1964; app Development Officer, Voluntary Service Aberdeen 18 Apr 1967; app Asst Director 1 Jul 1972 and Director 1 Apr 1974.

1978　ERIC VALLANCE HUDSON
(FES X, 346), dem from Kintore 12 Mar 1978 on app as Religious Programmes Officer for Scottish Television; ind to Bearsden Westerton Fairlie Memorial 11 Jan 1990.

1986　WILLIAM FORSYTH HUNTER
ord by Presb of Perth and app Summer Mission Organiser/Youth Officer at St Ninian's, Crieff 20 Jun 1986; ind to Aberdeen Middlefield 7 Aug 1991.

1955   JOHN HENRY JARDINE
B 21 May 1925 at Glasgow, s of Henry J. and Catherine Graham; educ Bellahouston Academy, Glasgow 1937–42; University of Glasgow 1942–43, 1947–50 (MA); 1950–53; Jordanhill College, Glasgow 1958–59 (Teaching Diploma); HM Forces (Army) 1943–47; lic by Presb of Glasgow 15 Apr 1953; asstshp Govan Old 1953–55; m 26 Jan 1957 Beryl Spencer b 1 Jun 1926 d of Reginald S. and Gertrude Bellamy; Children: Mark b 9 May 1958 m Judith Reid; Paul b 25 Mar 1960 m Elizabeth Murphy; Alice b 28 May 1963 m Christopher Hoon; Ruth b 21 Sep 1964 m John Philp; ord by Presb of Glasgow during assistantship at Govan Old Oct 1953; app Youth Secretary, Iona Community 1 Sep 1955; member of Gorbals Group Ministry 22 Dec 1957 and teacher at Adelphi Secondary School, Gorbals from 1959; app Housemaster at Kingsridge Secondary School, Drumchapel Aug 1966; app Principal Teacher (English) Waverley Secondary School, Drumchapel Apr 1970; app Headteacher, Glenwood Secondary School, Castlemilk 1 Oct 1973; ret 15 Aug 1988.

1988   GORDON FRASER CAMPBELL JENKINS
(FES X, 273), dem from Dunfermline North to take up app as Deputy General Secretary, Board of Education 5 Sep 1988; app Asst Secretary, Board of Ministry 1 Jan 1991; res 31 May 1997.

1963   EMMANUEL JOHNSON
ord in India 1960; app Missionary to Ethnic Groups in Glasgow 1963; ret 1990; died 16 Jun 1993.

1998   CHRISTOPHER NEIL KELLOCK
B 26 Sep 1971 at Edinburgh, s of David John K. and Jennifer Mary Laskey; educ North Berwick High 1983–89; University of Edinburgh 1989–93 (MA), 1993–96 (BD); lic by Presb of Lothian 4 Jul 1996; asstshp Bo'ness St Andrew's 1996–98; m 4 Sep 1994 Monica Ruth Keltie b 28 Aug 1972 d of David K. and Elizabeth Hamilton; Children: Scott David b 7 Aug 1999; ord by Presb of Falkirk 3 Feb 1998; app as National Evangelist by Scripture Union, Scotland 1 Feb 1998.

1975   ISOBEL JEAN MOLLINS KELLY
ord by Presb of Edinburgh during assistantship at Pilrig Dalmeny Street 22 Sep 1974; app Asst Baird Research Fellow, Board of Education 1 Sep 1975; ind to Edinburgh Drylaw 25 Oct 1978.

1993   SHEILAGH MARGARET KESTING
B 10 Jun 1953 at Stornoway, d of Douglas Norman K. and Joan Robertson Blair; educ Nicolson Institute, Stornoway 1965–71; University of Edinburgh 1971–74 (BA), 1974–77 (BD); lic by Presb of Lewis 12 Jul 1977; asstshp Glasgow St John's Renfield 1977–79; ord by Presb of Hamilton and introd to Overtown 12 Jan 1980; ind to same charge 25 Nov 1982; trans to Musselburgh St Andrew's High 25 Jun 1986; dem to take up app as Secretary for Ecumenical Relations 1 Oct 1993.

1975   THOMAS WILLIAM KILTIE
(FES X, 148, 186, 454), dem from Airdrie West on app as Home Organisation Secretary of Overseas Council 28 Jan 1975; ret 1988; died 10 Jan 1993.

1941   ALEXANDER KING
(FUF 533; FES IX, 193, 760, 800; X, 454), app Secretary of Colonial and Continental Committee May 1941; became joint General Secretary of Overseas Council May 1964; ret 30 Sep 1966; died 25 Jan 1990.

1966   JOHN JOHNSTON LAIDLAW
B 4 Sep 1939 at Penpont, s of Francis Angus James L. and Janet Jackson Johnston; educ George Watson's, Edinburgh 1947–57; University of Edinburgh 1957–60 (MA), 1960–63; Dundee College of Education 1965–66 (HDRE); lic by Presb of Edinburgh 4 Jun 1963; asstshp Glenrothes St Columba's 1963–65; m 4 Oct 1964 Agnes Annie Leslie b 14 Jan 1928 d of John Erskine L. and Catherine Eliza Mackay; ord by Presb of Kirkcaldy 16 Oct 1964 and app Asst at Glenrothes St Columba's; Teacher of Religious Education 1966–70; Lecturer in RE, Craigie College of Education 1971–73; Adviser in RE, Dundee Corporation 1973–75; Adviser in RE, Tayside Region 1975–96; ret 31 Mar 1996.

1999   STEWART JACKSON LAMONT
(FES X, 456), app to Religious Broadcasting Dept, BBC Scotland 1 Feb 1972; ord to this post by Presb of Edinburgh 3 Sep 1972; Minister (part-time) at Abernyte 1980–82; Freelance Writer and Broadcaster from 1982; ind to Glasgow Kinning Park 2 Dec 1991; dem 31 May 1999 on app as Executive Secretary, Church and Society Commission, Conference of European Churches, Brussels; m 1 Aug 1991 Larisa Gaidakova b 23 Jul 1957 d of Victor G. and Tatiana Pushkariova; Publ: *The Third Angle* (Hutchinson, 1978); *Is Anybody There?* (Mainstream, 1980); *Religion INC* (Harrap, 1985); *Scotland 2000* (BBC Scotland, 1987); *In Good Faith* (St Andrew Press, 1989); *Church and State: Uneasy Alliances* (The Bodley Head, 1989); *The Swordbearer: John Knox* (Hodder & Stoughton, 1991); editor of *St Andrew's Rock* (Bellew, 1992); *The Life of St Andrew* (Hodder & Stoughton, 1997).

1982   JAMES BARBOUR LAWSON
(FES X, 446), ret from RAChD on app as Officer-in-Charge, Simpson House, Edinburgh Sep 1982; ind to Prestonkirk with Stenton with Whittingehame 24 Sep 1986.

1984   KENNETH CHARLES LAWSON
(FES X, 36, 130), dem from Cumbernauld St Mungo's 9 Mar 1984 on app as Adviser in Adult Education, Board of Parish Education; app Director of Ecumenical Spirituality Programme, Scottish Churches Open College 1995; ret 24 Dec 1999; Publ: Co-author of *Caring for God's People* (St Andrew Press, 1989).

1951   JOHN STEWART LOCHRIE
(FES IX, 796; X, 450), app Chaplain to Deaf People, Glasgow 15 Apr 1951; died 20 Jan 1982.

1983   THOMAS GRAEME LONGMUIR
B 26 Jul 1949 at Greenock, s of Thomas Eadie L. and Rhona Dinning McCubbin; educ The Friends' School, Lancaster 1965–69; University of Lancaster 1969–72 (BEd); University of Oxford 1972–76 (CTh, BA, MA); asstshp Summertown, Oxford 1972–76; Bicester 1972–76; ord by URC and app as Asst, Christ Church, Morecambe 10 Jun 1976; ind as Collegiate minister, Christ Church, Morecambe 10 Jun 1980; app Chaplain to Strathallan School, Perth 1 Sep 1983; Publ: Editor of *The Art of Sea Trout Fishing* (Unwin Hyman, 1989); editor of *The Record* (Journal of The Church Service Society) 1985–99; editorial board of *Songs of God's People* (OUP) and of *Common Order* (St Andrew Press); contributor to *The Expository Times* (T&T Clark).

1975   GEORGE LOCKHART LUGTON
(FES X, 213, 224, 454), app Asst Secretary and Deputy, Church and Ministry Dept 16 Jan 1975; became Secretary and Deputy 1 Aug 1977; app Joint Secretary, Ministry and Mission Dept 1984; ind to Guernsey St Andrew's in the Grange 3 Sep 1987.

1973   JOHN ROBERTSON LYALL
(FES X, 210, 454), dem from Kirkmuirhill on app as Field Officer for Dept of Education 20 Aug 1973; ind to Alvie and Insh 27 Oct 1978 and app Warden of Badenoch Christian Centre.

1972   DAVID HENRY SCOTT LYON
(FES IX, 738; X, 421, 454), app General Secretary Depute of Overseas Council 1972; app General Secretary 1975; ret 1986; Addl publ: *In Pursuit of a Vision* (St Andrew Press, 1998).

1950   ALEXANDER MACARTHUR
(FES IX, 226), ind to Penilee St Andrew's 18 Mar 1947; res charge and status 12 Feb 1950 to stand as parliamentary candidate; teaching from 1950; re-instated by General Assembly 1984; Jordanhill College, Glasgow 1950 (Teaching Cert), 1952 (HDipREd, Dip Public Admin), 1954 (DipEd), 1975 (DipAEd); Paisley Tech College 1972 (CBiol, MIBiol).

1996   FINLAY ANGUS JOHN MACDONALD
(FES X, 266), dem from Glasgow Jordanhill on app as Assoc Principal Clerk to General Assembly 1 May 1996; app Principal Clerk 1 Oct 1996; University of St Andrews 1983 (PhD); Publ: Co-author of *Children at the Table* (Church of Scotland, 1982); PhD thesis: 'Law and Doctrine in the Church of Scotland with particular reference to Confessions of Faith' (1983); sermons in *The Expository Times* (T&T Clark); articles in *Scottish Journal of Theology* (T&T Clark).

1990   JAMES WYLIE MACDONALD
B 20 Jun 1947 at Airdrie, s of Lewis M. and Joan Malone; educ Airdrie High 1960–64; University of Glasgow 1970–75 (BD); Iron and Steel Industry 1964–69; Telecommunications 1969–70; lic by Presb of Hamilton 6 Nov 1975; asstshp Armadale 1975–76; Mary Margaret Taylor b 15 Dec 1947 d of John T. and Margaret Seith; Children: Heather b 17 May 1972; Lindsay b 17 Oct 1976; Grant b 20 Mar 1979; ord and ind to Glasgow Barlanark Greyfriars 2 Jun 1976; trans to Lerwick and Bressay 6 Jul 1981; dem on app as Principal Chaplain to British and International Sailors' Society Aug 1990.

1977   DONALD NORMAN MACDONALD
(FES X, 168), dem from Glasgow Partick Newton Place to take up app with BBC 12 Apr 1977; ind to Glasgow St Columba 4 Nov 1981.

1999   WILLIAM JOHN MACDONALD
B 20 Aug 1937 at Uig, Isle of Lewis, s of Donald and Murdina M; educ Lionel Junior Secondary, Ness and Lewis Castle College, Stornoway 1949–55; Bible Training Institute, Glasgow 1961–62; University of Glasgow 1970–75 (BD, CPS); National Service 1958–60; Lay Missionary 1962–63; lic by Presb of Glasgow 26 Jun 1975; asstshp Paisley Glenburn 1963–68; m 20 Sep 1962 Jessie Ann MacLeod b 16 Mar 1940 d of Duncan and Annie M; Children: Mairi b 17 Feb 1966; Anne b 16 Jul 1970; ord and ind to Newbattle 22 Jul 1976; trans to Gairloch and Dundonnell 10 Aug 1984; dem 31 Jul 1999 on app by Dept of National Mission.

1973   DONALD FARQUHAR MACLEOD MACDONALD
(FES IX, 328; X, 1, 194), dem from Glasford 30 Sep 1972 to take up app as Principal Clerk of General Assembly and Secretary of General Admin Committee 23 May 1973; ret May 1985; died 26 Apr 1995.

1986   PETER JAMES MACDONALD
ord by Presb of Edinburgh and app National Young Adult Adviser 25 May 1986; ind to Kirkcaldy Torbain 1 Sep 1990.

1995   DONALD MACIVER
B 5 Jun 1946 at Stornoway, s of Angus M. and Christina Murray; educ Lewis Castle College, Stornoway; Napier College, Edinburgh 1963–65 (ONC); Heriot-Watt University 1965–69 (BSc); Nazarene Theological College, Manchester 1978–82 (BTh); University of London 1978–82 (BD); Apprenticeship, Ferranti Ltd, Edinburgh 1963–65; Mechanical Engineering 1969–72; lic by Presb of Edinburgh 30 Jun 1996; asstshp Edinburgh Greenside 1995–96; m 7 Aug 1981 Hazel Ellen Williamson b 23 Jul 1952 d of George W. and Margaret Maybury; Children: Kirsty Margaret b 12 Oct 1983; Lorna Mary b 28 Aug 1985; Iain Angus George b 20 May 1989; ord by Church of the

Nazarene 15 Mar 1985; admitted by General Assembly 1995; loc ten at Edinburgh Pilrig and Dalmeny Street 1996.

1973 IAN MURDO MACKENZIE
(FES X, 350), dem from Peterhead Old to take up app as Head of Religious Programmes, BBC Scotland 29 Oct 1973; ret 1989.

1984 AILSA GAIL MACLEAN
B 14 Sep 1954 at Glasgow, d of Ian Hugh McIntyre and Annie MacLeod Carson Girvin; educ Westbourne School for Girls, Glasgow 1966–72; University of Glasgow 1972–76 (BD); University of Edinburgh 1976–78 (DipChE); lic by Presb of Dumbarton, Jun 1978; asstshp Edinburgh Fairmilehead 1978–81; m 20 Aug 1988 Kenneth John Maclean b 18 Jun 1948 s of John M. and Maciver; ord by Presb of Edinburgh during assistantship at Fairmilehead 8 May 1979; loc ten Currie Kirk 1 Oct 1981; introd as Community minister at Cumbernauld Condorrat 28 May 1982; app Asst Warden at Carberry Tower 1 Aug 1984; app National Youth Adviser 1 Jun 1986; app Chaplain to George Heriot's School, Edinburgh 23 Aug 1988.

1998 MARJORY ANNE MACLEAN
B 11 Jun 1962 at Forfar, d of Maurice Renton M. and Alexa Freda Wallace Ross; educ Forfar Academy 1974–80; University of Edinburgh 1980–84 (LLB), 1984–85 (DipLP), 1987–90 (BD); lic by Presb of Edinburgh 1 Jul 1990; asstshp Edinburgh Fairmilehead 1990–91; ord by Presb of Edinburgh 5 May 1991 and app Asst at Fairmilehead; ind to Stromness 26 Mar 1992; dem 6 Nov 1998 on app as Depute Clerk of General Assembly; Publ: *Taking the Wings of the Dawn* (Stromness Church, 1994).

1987 ALASDAIR JOHN MACLENNAN
dem from Clyne 31 Jan 1987 to take up app with Dept of National Mission as Organiser for Evangelism, Highlands and Islands; res Feb 1993 and ind to Resolis and Urquhart 7 Jan 1994.

1938 GEORGE FIELDEN MACLEOD
(FES VIII, 19; IX, 270; X, 160), dem from Govan Old 31 May 1938 to become Leader of Iona Community; app life peer 1967 as Lord MacLeod of Fuinary; w Lorna died 1984; Templeton Prize 1989; Freedom of the City of Glasgow May 1991; died 27 Jun 1991; Addl publ: *The Whole Earth Shall Cry Glory* (Wild Goose Publs, 1985).

1984 FERGUS MACPHERSON
(FES IX, 741; X, 135, 422), dem from Kilbirnie Auld Kirk 19 Mar 1984 on app as World Mission Secretary to British Council of Churches, London; ret 3 Oct 1988; d Catherine m Richard Dyer; s James m Vera Stronge; d Myra m Govan Poznanovic; d Alison m John Harban; d Elspeth m Douglas Currie; s Fergus m Avril Hooks; Addl publ: *Kwacha Ngwee* (OUP, 1977); *Anatomy of a Conquest: The British Occupation of Zambia 1884–*

1924 (Longman, 1981); *North of the Zambezi—A Modern Missionary Memoir* (Handsel Press, 1998).

1993 ALLAN S MACPHERSON
dem from Cairnie-Glass with Huntly 31 Aug 1993 on app as Chaplain to Merchiston Castle School, Edinburgh.

1990 STUART DOUGALL MACQUARRIE
B 15 Oct 1952 at Glasgow, s of Archibald M. and Jessie Luke Dougall; educ Cranhill Secondary, Glasgow 1964–69; University of Glasgow 1978–79; University of Edinburgh 1979–83; Commercial Employment 1969–78; lic by Presb of Edinburgh; asstshp Govan Old 1983–84; m 17 Nov 1989 Gillian Balfour Gerry d of William John G; Children: Kirsten Gillian Lilias; ord and ind to Glasgow Toryglen 14 Jun 1984; dem 28 Aug 1990 on app by Carers National Assoc; Greater Easterhouse Council of Voluntary Organisations 1993–94; YMcA Glasgow 1994–96; loc ten Glasgow Dennistoun Blackfriars from Jan 1996; app by YMcA Glasgow May 1999.

1966 WILLIAM ROBERTSON YULE MARSHALL
(FES IX, 192; X, 109, 455), dem from Hurlford Reid Memorial on app by Overseas Council as Area Secretary (Europe, Israel and Americas) 30 Jun 1966; died 8 Jan 1981.

1992 IAIN GUNN MATHESON
B 4 Mar 1956 at Plean, s of Dugald Black M. and Maisie McPherson; educ Allan Glen's, Glasgow 1969–77; University of Glasgow 1973–77 (BMus), 1981–84 (BD); Teaching (music) 1978–81; lic by Presb of Glasgow 25 Jun 1984; asstshp Glasgow King's Park 1984–85; m 5 Feb 1994 Alison McDonald b 28 Jan 1963; ord and ind to Hamilton Trinity 28 May 1985; dem 28 Feb 1991 on app by Board of World Mission to Prague; returned Dec 1992; teaching (music) from 1996; Publ: *The End of Time* in *Text as Pretext: Essays in Honour of Robert Davidson* (Sheffield Univ Press, 1992); reprint in *The Messiaen Companion* (Faber and Faber, 1995).

1988 FIONA McDOUGALL MATHIESON
ord by Presb of Edinburgh during assistantship at Greenbank 19 Jun 1988; app Church of Scotland Youth Adviser 1 Sep 1988; app Chaplain to University of Glasgow 1 Apr 1995.

1998 ANGUS RANKIN MATHIESON
B 7 Feb 1961 at Glasgow, s of James Rankin M. and Agnes Patrick Boyd; educ Kilsyth Academy 1973–79; University of Glasgow 1979–82 (MA); University of Edinburgh 1984–87 (BD); lic by Presb of Edinburgh 5 Jul 1987; asstshp Edinburgh South Leith 1987–89; m 4 Sep 1987 Elizabeth Ann Spence b 31 Oct 1962 d of Francis S. and Jean Fowler; separated 26 Dec 1996; m (2) 1 Jul 1999 Fiona McDougall Buchan b 28 Dec 1962 d of James McLaws B. and Marion McDougall; ord by Presb of Edinburgh during assistantship at South

Leith 10 Jul 1988; introd as Community minister at Ayr St Quivox 16 Aug 1989; dem to take up app as Education and Development Officer, Board of Ministry 1 Apr 1998.

1979 STEWART GRAHAM MATTHEW
(FES X, 113), dem from Kilmarnock St Ninian's Bellfield 10 Aug 1979 on app as Adult Adviser, Dept of Education; died 13 Sep 1991.

1990 IAN DOUGLAS MAXWELL
res as Assoc at Paisley St Ninian's Ferguslie on app as Conference Manager, Carberry Tower Jun 1990; res and ind to Edinburgh Kirk o' Field Jul 1996.

1997 ROBIN JAMES McALPINE
B 10 Oct 1959 at Glasgow, s of James M. and Elizabeth Beatty Mitchell; educ Douglas Academy, Milngavie 1964–76; University of Glasgow 1976–87 (BDS, BD); Dentist 1982–85; lic by Presb of Dumbarton 5 Jul 1987; asstshp Glasgow Temple Anniesland 1987–88; m 28 Oct 1982 Anne Louise Elizabeth Beck b 27 Jun 1962 d of James B. and Elizabeth Scott Goldie; Children: Fiona Elizabeth b 8 Jul 1985; Stuart Robert b 22 Feb 1987; ord and ind to Duntocher 9 Jun 1988; dem 11 Aug 1997 on app by Board of National Mission as East of Scotland Adviser in Mission and Evangelism 18 Sep 1997.

1998 ROSS JAMES McDONALD
B 6 Aug 1966 at Falkirk, s of Coll M. and Christina McIntyre Philp; educ Grangemouth High 1971–84; University of Strathclyde 1984–87 (BA); University of Glasgow 1992–95 (BD); Princeton Theological Seminary, New Jersey 1995–96 (ThM); Retail Management 1987–92; lic by Presb of Glasgow 3 Jul 1995; asstshp Crisis Ministry of Princeton and Trenton 1996–97; Edinburgh South Leith 1997–98; ord by Presb of Glasgow and introd as Chaplain/Development Officer at Lodging House Mission 30 Oct 1998.

1988 ALEXANDER McDONALD
(FES X, 29, 129), dem from Paisley St Mark's Oldhall 11 Oct 1988 on app as General Secretary, Board of Ministry; Moderator of General Assembly 1997–98; DUniv (Open University) 1999; d Karen m Kenneth Clark.

1994 ANDREW THOMSON BLAKE McGOWAN
B 30 Jan 1954 at Glasgow, s of Alexander Baird M. and Maria Morrice Blake; educ Uddingston Grammar 1966–72; University of Aberdeen 1972–77 (BD), 1990 (PhD); Union Theological Seminary, New York 1977–78 (STM); lic by Presb of Hamilton 29 Jun 1978; asstshp Edinburgh St Cuthbert's 1978–80; m 25 Jun 1976 Jun Sinclair Watson b 12 Jun 1955 d of William Crawford W. and Jane Sinclair Riddick; Children: Scott Blake b 26 Jun 1979; David Riddick b 17 Oct 1981; Christopher Watson b 31 Mar 1986; ord by Presb of Edinburgh during assistantship at St Cuthbert's 13 May 1979;

ind to Mallaig and The Small Isles 29 Feb 1980; trans to Aberdeen Causewayend 20 Jun 1986; trans to Glasgow Trinity Possil and Henry Drummond 15 Sep 1988; dem to take up app as Director of Highland Theological Institute 1 Aug 1994; app Principal of Highland Theological College (University of the Highlands and Islands) May 1999; Publ: *Federal Theology as a Theology of Grace* (*Scottish Bulletin of Evangelical Theology* 2, 1984); *Presbytery-wide Mission* in *Local Church Evangelism* (St Andrew Press, 1987); *Thomas Boston* in *New Dictionary of Theology* (IVP, 1988); *Pray Today* (Church of Scotland, 1989–90); contributor to *Encyclopedia of the Reformed Faith* (St Andrew Press, 1992); contributor to *Dictionary of Scottish Church History and Theology* (T&T Clark, 1993); *A Biblical Approach to Education* (Care, 1993); *The New Birth* (Christian Focus, 1996); *The Federal Theology of Thomas Boston* (Paternoster Press, 1997); *The Disciples: New Lion Handbook of the Bible* (Lion, 1999); contributor to *New Dictionary of National Biography* (OUP, forthcoming).

1979 ROBIN DUNLOP McHAFFIE
ord by Presb of Glasgow during app at Trinity College Calton Mission, May 1979; ind to Glasgow Kinning Park 1 Jun 1981.

1972 DAVID McHUTCHISON
(FES IX, 739, 796; X, 450), res as Chaplain to Ruchill and Knightswood Hospitals, Glasgow to enter teaching profession 30 Sep 1972; died 6 Sep 1999.

1987 JOHNSTON REID McKAY
(FES X, 151), dem from Paisley Abbey on app as Senior Producer, BBC Religious Broadcasting 1 Jul 1987; app Editor of Religious Programmes; app to Baird Trust 1999; m (2) Evelyn Elizabeth Helen Cromar d of Thomas C; Children: Carolyn Lesley; Publ: Co-editor of *Essays in Honour of William Barclay* (Collins, 1976); *Barclay among the Scholars* in R D Kernohan (ed) *William Barclay: The Plain Uncommon Man* (Hodder & Stoughton, 1980); *Through Wood and Nails* (Gardner, 1982); *Praying for Peace* (Fount, 1991); *Reformed but Still Reformable?* in S J Lamont (ed) *St Andrew's Rock* (Bellew, 1992); contributor to P Balla (ed) *Teacher, Scholar, Friend: A Festschrift in Honour of John O'Neill* (Budapest, 1996); *This Small Pool* (Trinity St Mungo, 1997); *Daily Service 13 Mar 1997* in Lavinia Byrne (ed) *The Daily Service Prayer Book* (Hodder & Stoughton, 1998); *Is the Kirk Still Relevant?* in R D Kernohan (ed) *The Realm of Reform*; sermons in *The Expository Times* (T&T Clark); various articles in newspapers and in *Life &Work*.

1989 PETER WILLIAM MILLAR
(FES X, 157), res from service with Overseas Council in S India and became Director, Columban House, Newtonmore 1 Jul 1989; app Warden, Iona

Abbey, Iona 15 Jul 1995; Catholic Theological Union, Chicago 1994–99 (PhD); Addl children: Sulekha Mary Somerville b 25 Apr 1979; Publ: *The Dalmarnock Report* (1975); *Famous Prayers* (CLS, Madras, India, 1983); *Set Us Free* (CLS, 1985); *Letters from Madras* (CLS, 1985); *Prayers from a Columban House* (private, 1989); *Notes for a Pilgrim* (private, 1990); *A Pilgrim Guide to Iona* (Canterbury Press, 1997); *An Iona Prayer Book* (Canterbury Press, 1998), *Waymarks* (Canterbury Press, 1999).

1992 ARCHIBALD MILLER MILLOY
B 10 Jan 1946 at Kilmarnock, s of Archibald Robertson M. and Mary Stuart Carmichael Young; educ Kilmarnock Academy 1959–64; Jordanhill College, Glasgow 1964–67 (DPE); University of Glasgow 1975–78 (LTh); Fife College 1989–90 (DTrMan); Teaching (PE) 1967–73; Principal Teacher 1973–75; lic by Presb of Lanark 29 Jun 1978; asstshp Bellshill West 1978–79; m 8 Aug 1969 Sarah Dunbar Baird b 3 Mar 1946 d of Robert Livingstone B. and Margaret Dunbar; Children: Miriam Miller b 31 Aug 1975; Martin Baird b 17 Apr 1978; ord and ind to Kirkcaldy Pathhead 16 May 1979; dem on app as Regional Adviser in Mission and Evangelism, Dept of National Mission 1 Aug 1992; res on app as Regional Secretary, United Bible Societies, Europe Middle East Region 1 Aug 1997.

1972 ARCHIBALD MILLS
(FES IX, 344; X, 65, 206, 331, 455), dem from Aberdeen St Nicholas North and East 1 Sep 1972 on app as Director of Counselling and Training, Committee on Moral Welfare; app Director of Group Relations, Dept of Social Responsibility 1 Mar 1976; ret 31 Mar 1980; Children: Colin Findlay b 13 Nov 1955 m Christine Smith; Archibald Ronald b 6 Oct 1957; Kenneth Steel b 20 Jun 1959; Helen Elizabeth Marion b 11 May 1962 m Keith Bowron.

1982 ERIC GORDON MILTON
(FES X, 151, 351), dem from Jersey St Columba's 14 Apr 1982 on app as Chaplain to Queen Victoria School, Dunblane; ind to Blairdaff with Chapel of Garioch 13 Apr 1984.

1991 IAN ANDREW MOIR
(FES X, 423), res as Superintendent of Pholela Institute, Bulwer, Natal, S Africa on app as Asst Secretary of Overseas Council 18 Feb 1974; ind to Edinburgh Old Kirk 25 Aug 1983; dem 1 Nov 1991 on app by Dept of National Mission as Urban Priority Areas Adviser; s Andrew m Christine Stewart; s Neil m Julie Dyson; s Peter m Fiona Bennett.

1997 WILLIAM GRAHAM MONTEITH
(FES X, 59), dem from Flotta and Fara with Hoy and Walls 30 Sep 1994; University of Edinburgh 1994–97 (PhD); app by Scottish Student Christian Movement, Edinburgh 1997; m (2) 20 Mar 1999 Edna Jean Little b 7 Nov 1960 d of Edward L. and

Jean Blair; Children from previous marriage: Peter Graham b 24 Jun 1982; Publ: *Disability, Faith and Acceptance* (St Andrew Press, 1987).

1978 ROBERT AITKEN MONTGOMERY
(FES X, 358, 361), dem from Fordyce on app as Chaplain to Quarrier's Homes 28 Mar 1978; ind to Mount Zion, Quarrier's Village 29 May 1986; ret 25 Jul 1992; University of Glasgow (MA) 1995; s Daniel m Fiona McArthur.

1995 CATRIONA MARY MORRISON
B 29 Dec 1966 at Edinburgh, d of Peter Keith M. and Mary Brown Osler; educ Queen Anne High, Dunfermline 1978–84; University of Edinburgh 1984–88 (MA), 1989–92 (BD); lic by Presb of Edinburgh 5 Jul 1992; asstshp Prestonkirk with Stenton with Whittingehame 1992–94; m 4 Aug 1995 Marc Andreas Prowe b 26 Dec 1966 s of Harald Hans Arthur P. and Gitta Appel; Children: Ruari Emil Prowe b 3 Jul 1997; Andreas Iain Prowe b 27 May 1999; ord by Presb of Edinburgh 1 Aug 1995; app by Pauluskirche, Neustadt/Wstr, Germany 3 Sep 1995.

1986 MARY BROWN MORRISON
dem from Dunfermline Townhill on app as Adviser in Mission and Evangelism, Dept of National Mission 1 Nov 1986; ind to Carmichael Covington and Pettinain 19 Feb 1992.

1977 ALASDAIR (ALEXANDER) JAMES MORTON
(FES X, 83, 423), dem from Dumfries Greyfriars on app as General Secretary, Dept of Education 1 Oct 1977; res and ind to Maxton with Newtown 26 Sep 1991.

1974 ANDREW REYBURN MORTON
(FES X, 143, 442), res as Warden of Wolfson Hall and Senior Warden, Halls of Residence, University of Glasgow to take up app as Secretary of Community Affairs, British Council of Churches 1 Sep 1974; res to take up app as Secretary of Ecumenical and European Relations, Church of Scotland 1 Jan 1982; ret 31 Oct 1993; app Assoc Director, Centre for Theology and Public Issues, Univ of Edinburgh 1 Jan 1994; Publ: Editor of miscellaneous *Occasional Papers* of the Centre for Theology and Public Issues (CPTI, 1994 -); editor of *Beyond Fear: Vision, Hope and Generosity* (St Andrew Press, 1998).

1994 ALEXANDER WILLIAM MUNRO
B 7 Aug 1949 at Forres, s of William M. and Elsie Enid Craine; educ Forres Academy 1961–66; University of Aberdeen 1971–77 (MA, BD); lic by Presb of Aberdeen 29 Jun 1977; asstshp Aberdeen Stockethill 1977–78; m 26 Jan 1974 Cath McMillan b 7 Jun 1951 d of Hugh M. and Murray Harper Cooper; Children: Scott Alexander b 9 Jun 1974; Paul Graham b 5 May 1978; ord by Presb of Aberdeen and app by RAF Chaplains' Branch 16 Apr 1978; ret from RAF 11 Jun 1994; Chaplain

and Head of Religious Studies, The Licensed Victuallers' School, Ascot 1994–1999; app Head Teacher, Clevedon House School, Ilkley 1 Sep 1999.

1990 JOHN PRINGLE LORIMER MUNRO
dem from Arbroath Knox's with St Vigean's on app as Asst Secretary, Board of World Mission 1 Feb 1990; ind to Kinross 8 Jul 1998.

1999 JOHN ALASTAIR HILTON MURDOCH
B 18 Oct 1952 at Johnstone, s of Robert Evelyn M. and Mary Greig Adam; educ Kelvinside Academy, Glasgow and King Edward VI Camp Hill School for Boys, Birmingham 1965–72; University of Durham 1972–75 (BA); University of Edinburgh 1975–77 (BD); University of St Andrews 1977–78 (DPS); lic by Presb of Greenock, Nov 1978; asstshp Edinburgh Palmerston Place 1978–79; m 23 Jul 1977 Diana Campbell Leakey b 5 Jul 1955 d of John L. and Katherine Morrison; Children: Hope b 28 Apr 1981 and Catriona b 28 Apr 1981; Thomas b 10 Aug 1983; Alexandra b 11 Dec 1985; Guy b 12 Jul 1988; Rosamund b 21 Oct 1990; ord by Presb of Edinburgh and app by RAChD 17 Jun 1979; app Chaplain to Strathallan School 1 Sep 1982; app by RAChD 1 Sep 1983; app Chaplain to Fettes College 1 Sep 1986; introd to Gibraltar St Andrew's 26 Aug 1990; app Chaplain to Christ's Hospital, Sussex 16 Oct 1992; app Chaplain to Aiglon College, Switzerland 1 Sep 1994; ind to Glamis, Inverarity and Kinettles 31 Mar 1998; dem 31 Aug 1999 and app Chaplain to St Leonards School, St Andrews 1 Sep 1999.

1971 WILLIAM GEORGE MURISON
(FES IX, 744; X, 423, 455), res from service with Overseas Council in India 1 Jun 1971 and app by Overseas Council as Asia and Australasia Area Secretary; ret 30 Nov 1990; s William m Michelle Collin.

1986 PETER NEILSON
(FES X, 167), dem from Glasgow Mount Florida on app as National Organiser for Evangelism 1 Jun 1986; app National Adviser in Mission and Evangelism and Director of Training at St Ninian's Centre, Crieff 1 Jul 1992; introd as Assoc at Edinburgh St Cuthbert's 6 Aug 1997.

1988 ALISON MARY NEWELL
B 30 Jan 1956 at Edinburgh, d of Harry William MacPhail Cant and Margaret Elizabeth Louden; educ Kirkwall Grammar 1961–74; University of Edinburgh 1976–80 (BD); Craiglockhart College of Education; lic by Presb of Hamilton (Presb Church in Canada), Oct 1986; m 27 Sep 1978 John Philip Newell b 4 May 1953 s of William N. and Pearl Ferguson; Children: Rowan b 20 Sep 1981; Brendan b 25 Oct 1983; Kirsten b 16 Oct 1987; Cameron b 16 May 1995; ord by Presb of Hamilton, Presb Church in Canada and introd as Assoc at St Cuthbert's, Hamilton, Ontario (part-time) Oct 1986; also app Chaplain (part-time) to McMaster

University; app Joint-Warden of Iona Abbey 1 May 1988; app Chaplain to Saughton Prison, Edinburgh 1 Jan 1993; app Asst Adviser, Social Responsibility, Anglican Diocese of Portsmouth 1 Apr 1997.

1988 JOHN PHILIP NEWELL
B 4 May 1953 at Chatham, Canada, s of William James N. and Pearl Ferguson; educ Northlea Public School, Toronto, Ontario, Canada and Aldershot High, Burlington, Ontario, Canada 1958–72; McMaster University, Canada 1972–75 (BA); University of Edinburgh 1975–78 (BD), 1978–81 (PhD); lic by Presb of Edinburgh 5 Jul 1981; m 27 Sep 1978 Alison Mary Cant b 30 Jan 1956 d of Harry William C. and Margaret Louden; Children: Rowan b 20 Sep 1981; Brendan b 25 Oct 1983; Kirsten b 16 Oct 1987; Cameron b 16 May 1995; ord by Presb of Hamilton, Presb Church in Canada and app Chaplain to McMaster University 24 Sep 1982; app Joint-Warden of Iona Abbey 1 May 1988; app Asst at St Giles', Edinburgh 1 May 1992; app Warden of Spirituality, Anglican Diocese of Portsmouth 1 Sep 1995; Publ: *Each Day and Each Night* (Wild Goose Publs, 1994); *An Earthful of Glory* (SPCK, 1996); *Listening for the Heartbeat of God: A Celtic Spirituality* (SPCK, 1997); *One Foot in Eden* (SPCK, 1998); *Promptings from Paradise* (SPCK, 1998); *The Book of Creation* (Canterbury Press, 1999).

1991 DOUGLAS ALEXANDER OAG NICOL
B 5 Apr 1948 at Dunfermline, s of James George N. and Margaret Millar Oag; educ Kirkcaldy High 1960–66; University of Edinburgh 1966–69 (MA); University of Glasgow 1969–72 (BD); lic by Presb of Kirkcaldy 19 Apr 1972; asstshp St Ninian's Centre, Crieff 1972–76; m 30 Sep 1978 Anne Wilson Gillespie b 25 Feb 1953 d of Adam Moffatt G. and Mary Brash Wilson; Children: Fiona May b 27 Mar 1980; Stuart James b 22 Oct 1982; Calum Douglas b 30 Jan 1991; ord by Presb of Auchterarder during assistantship at St Ninian's Centre, Crieff 3 Oct 1974; ind to Dumfries Lochside 28 Oct 1976; became minister of linked charge with Terregles 27 Sep 1981; trans to Kilmacolm St Columba 13 Jul 1982; dem to take up app as General Secretary, Board of National Mission 1 Sep 1991.

1997 CATHERINE WEIR OWEN
B 16 Jun 1947 at Glasgow, d of Malcolm Taylor and Elizabeth Jamieson; educ Knightswood Secondary, Glasgow 1959–65; Jordanhill College, Glasgow 1965–68; University of St Andrews 1980–83 (MTh); Teaching 1968–80; lic by Presb of Glasgow 27 Jun 1983; asstshp Helensburgh West Kirk 1983–85; m 29 Aug 1987 Bryan Philip Owen b 22 Oct 1947 s of Percival O. and Winnifred Holmes; Children: Catriona b 21 May 1988; Stuart b 2 May 1991; ord by Presb of Dumbarton during assistantship at Helensburgh West 6 May 1984; ind to Wishaw Chalmers 25 Aug 1985; dem 1987;

app Chaplain to Stirling Royal (part-time) Jun 1994; app Chaplain to Tolworth Hospital (part-time) 31 Mar 1997 and to Epsom Hospital (part-time) 31 Aug 1997.

1968 ANDREW HARRY PARKER
B 6 Feb 1942 at Calcutta, India, s of Thomas P. and Barbara Gordon Harper; educ Marlborough College 1948–61; University of St Andrews 1961–64 (BSc); University of Edinburgh 1964–67 (BD); Teaching 1961–62; lic by Presb of St Andrews 3 May 1967; asstshp Dunfermline Abbey 1966–68; m 27 Oct 1977 Patricia Toublan b 18 Apr 1952 d of Henri T. and Giselle Legendre; Children: Verene b 17 Oct 1982; Rachel b 8 Aug 1984; Lydia b 9 Jun 1987; Douglas b 1 Oct 1988; ord by Presb of Dunfermline during assistantship at Dunfermline Abbey 16 Jul 1967; app by French Protestant Industrial Mission 1 Sep 1968; minister without charge since 1973; Publ: *Painfully Clear: The Parables of Jesus* (St Andrew Press, 1996).

1981 DAVID HOWARD PHILPOT
B 11 Nov 1929 at Beckenham, s of Ernest Bawden P. and Olive Miriam Ramsey; educ George Watson's, Edinburgh 1941–48; University of Edinburgh 1948–51 (MA), 1951–55 (BD); lic by Presb of Edinburgh 15 Apr 1954; asstshp Musselburgh Inveresk 1954–55; m 14 Jul 1955 Frances Buchan Wood b 3 Dec 1927 d of Andrew W. and Esther Wheeler Fowler; Children: Anne Catherine b 6 Jun 1956 m Lukas Wanjie; ord by Presb of Edinburgh Jan 1956 and app by FMC for service in Kenya; app Scholarships Secretary, WCC, Geneva 1 May 1981; ret 30 Nov 1994.

1968 VICTOR CHARLES POGUE
(FES IX, 705; X, 271, 402, 455), dem from Carnock 30 Sep 1968 on app by Dept of Education as Baird Research Fellow; ret Jan 1981; m (2) 31 Mar 1975 Margaret Helen Littlewood b 8 Aug 1916 d of George Percy L. and Margaret Fairbrother; Addl publ: *Encountering God* (1964), *Christians Now* (1977), *Who Measures the Ruler?* (1977), *Questions Jesus Asked?* (1977), *The Nicene Creed* (1981)—all publ by Dept of Education.

1949 JOHN STANLEY PRITCHARD
(FES IX, 195, 252; X, 149), dem from Williamwood 1 May 1949 on app as Asst Religious Affairs Broadcaster, BBC; app Producer of Religious Television and Appeals Organiser; ret 1970; died 11 Dec 1993.

1962 SAMUEL PAUL RE'EMI
(FES X, 424), ord by Presb of Edinburgh 1962 and app to Church of Scotland Literature Mission, Tiberias, Israel; ret 30 Sep 1977; died 26 Sep 1993; Addl publ: Hebrew trans of *God's Freedom Fighters* by D Watson (Jonah Press, 1976).

1993 PARAIC REAMONN
dem from Cockburnspath with Innerwick with Oldhamstocks 31 Aug 1993 on app as

Communications Secretary, World Alliance of Reformed Churches, Geneva.

1977 ALAN ANDERSON STUART REID
(FES X, 206, 220), res as Head of RE Dept, Matthew Arnold School, Cumnor, Oxford on app as Chaplain to Strathallan School, Forgandenny, Perthshire Aug 1977; res on app as Chaplain to University of Aberdeen, Jan 1981.

1994 ADRIAN JAMES TAIT RENNIE
dem from Glasgow Calton New with St Andrew's on app as Warden, MacLeod Centre, Iona Aug 1994; ind to Edinburgh Drylaw 15 Mar 1996.

1981 WALTER RIGGANS
B 24 Dec 1953 at Kirkcaldy, s of Walter R. and Mary Barnes; educ Dunfermline High 1958–70; University of Edinburgh 1971–76 (BD); Presb School of Christian Education, Richmond, USA 1976–77 (MA); University of Birmingham 1988–92 (PhD); lic by Presb of Dunfermline 5 Jul 1977; asstshp Glasgow Garthamlock 1977–78; m 27 May 1980, separated 18 Jul 1999; Children: Robyn Rebecca b 26 Feb 1981; Gil'ad b 21 Apr 1984; Jonathan Adam b 5 Aug 1986; Tamar b 22 Aug 1989; ord by Presb of Glasgow during assistantship at Garthamlock 15 Dec 1977; app to Church of Scotland Centre, Tiberias, Israel 1 Jan 1978; app Minister with the Israel Trust of the Anglican Church 1 Jan 1981; app Tutor in Biblical and Jewish Studies, All Nations Christian College, Ware, Herts 1 Aug 1986; app General Director, Church's Ministry among Jewish People 1 Sep 1994; Publ: *Commentary on Numbers* (St Andrew Press, 1983); *God's Covenant with the Jews* (Monarch, 1992); *Jesus Ben Joseph* (Olive Press/Monarch, 1993); *Yeshua Ben David* (Olive Press/Monarch, 1995); *Commentary on Hebrews* (Focus Publs, 1998); *Ten Drops of Wine. Jewish Spirituality for Christians* (Monarch, 2000).

1998 NIGEL JAMES ROBB
B 28 Jul 1953 at Glasgow, s of James R. and Grace Blake; educ Ardrossan Academy 1969–71; University of Glasgow 1971–75 (MA), 1975–78 (BD); Princeton Theological Seminary, New Jersey 1978–79 (ThM), 1987–89 (MTh); lic by Presb of Ardrossan 27 Jun 1978; asstshp Glasgow Cardonald 1979–80; app Assoc Chaplain to University of Edinburgh 1 Nov 1979; ord by Presb of Edinburgh 29 Apr 1981; app Lecturer in Pastoral Theology,Theological Hall, Perth, Australia 1 Jan 1983; app Lecturer in Practical Theology and Christian Ethics, University of St Andrews 1 Sep 1990; app Director of Educational Services, Dept of Ministry 1 Jan 1998; Publ: *Preaching—a manual for lay preachers* (Drummond Trust, 1992); *Let All God's People Say 'Amen'* (Univ of St Andrews, 1993), *Sermons at St Salvator's* (Univ of St Andrews, 1994); *A Time To Die and a Time To Live* (Blake, 1996); *The Preaching Triangle* (Board of Ministry, 1999).

1987 ALAN OGILVIE ROBERTSON
(FES IX, 431; X, 255, 442), res as Senior Warden, Hillhead Halls, University of Aberdeen on app as Chaplain and Head of Religious Studies at Merchiston Castle School, Edinburgh 1 Sep 1987; ret 30 Aug 1994; died 23 Oct 1999; Children: Robin Forbes Ogilvie m Clare Reihill; Timothy Alan Ogilvie; Nicola Audrey Ogilvie m Malcolm Mottram.

1992 ALEXANDER McKINNON ROGER
res from term app at Maxwell Mearns Castle 2 Nov 1992 on app as National Chaplain to Scottish Prison Service; res from app 30 Jun 1996.

1988 ROBIN ALASDAIR ROSS
B 16 Apr 1949 at Edinburgh, s of John Hugh Gunn R. and Margaret Flora Isobel Sawer; educ Edinburgh Academy 1956–67; University of Aberdeen 1967–74 (MA); University of Edinburgh 1974–75 (BD); lic by Presb of Auchterarder 29 Jun 1975; asstshp Kirkwall St Magnus Cathedral and East Church, 1975–77; m 12 Sep 1975 Isobel Ann Aikman Smith b 26 Apr 1951 d of James Aikman S. and Katherine Ann Millar; Children: Colin Magnus b 22 Nov 1977; Peter Alasdair b 28 Jun 1979; Robin Aikman b 9 Apr 1982; ord and ind to Denny Old 20 Apr 1977; dem 10 Oct 1982 and app to Tiberias, Israel 2 Feb 1983; app Middle East Secretary, Board of World Mission and Unity 8 Aug 1988; res 30 Jun 1994 to take up app as teacher of English.

1998 KENNETH RANKIN ROSS
B 31 May 1958 at Glasgow, s of Norman Rankin R. and Dorothy Kellas Hay; educ Kelvinside Academy, Glasgow 1963–76; University of Edinburgh 1976–79 (BA), 1979–82 (BD), 1983–87 (PhD); lic by Presb of Edinburgh, Jun 1982; m 29 Aug 1980 Hester Ferguson Carmichael b 10 Jul 1957 d of Alexander Calder C. and Mina Neill Mackay; Children: Barnabas Alexander Rankin b 20 Aug 1983; Gregory James Carmichael b 18 Mar 1985; Elliot Hay McKerrell b 19 Mar 1987; ord and ind to Unst 18 Sep 1982; dem to take up app as Lecturer in Theology, University of Malawi 1 Aug 1988; app Professor of Theology 10 Dec 1987; also app Parish minister, Nkanda 4 Jun 1989; dem charge and res University Chair 14 Oct 1998; app General Secretary, Board of World Mission 30 Nov 1998; Publ: *Church and Creed in Scotland* (Rutherford House, 1988); *Presbyterian Theology and Participatory Democracy* (St Andrew Press, 1993); *Gospel Ferment in Malawi* (Mambo Press, 1995); *Here Comes Your King* (CLAIM, 1998).

1988 DONALD HENDRY SCOTT
B 16 Jun 1957 at Glasgow, s of Hendry Sinclair S. and Janet McEwan Young; educ Hutchesons' Grammar, Glasgow 1969–75; University of Strathclyde 1975–78 (BA); University of Edinburgh 1979–82 (BD); Youth and Community Work 1978–79; Bus Driver 1980–83; lic by Presb of Edinburgh; asstshp Edinburgh Old Kirk 1982–83; m 21 Jun 1980 Roslyn Jane Ayre b 31 Oct 1957 d of Norman

MacKenzie A. and Audrey Anderson; Children: Keith Martin b 3 Feb 1982; Gavin Sinclair b 28 Jul 1983; Calum MacKenzie b 13 Dec 1990; ord and ind to Kilmallie 28 Jun 1983; loc ten Delting with Lunnasting and Nesting 11 Jun 1987; Presb Church in Canada, Ontario 1988–91; app Warden of MacLeod Centre, Iona 11 Apr 1991; app Director of Wiston Lodge, YMcA 1 Jul 1994; app Director of British Red Cross Society, Lanarkshire Branch 1 Aug 1997.

1993 DAVID CHARLES SEARLE
(FES X, 41, 336), dem from Hamilton Road Presb Church, Bangor, N Ireland on app as Warden of Rutherford House, Edinburgh 17 Jun 1993; d Anthea m Marc Bircham; Publ: *Be Strong in the Lord* (Christian Focus, 1995); *Truth and Love* (Paternoster, 1996); editor of *Rutherford Journal of Church and Ministry* (Rutherford House).

1995 NORMAN JAMES SHANKS
B 15 Jul 1942 at Edinburgh, s of James S. and Marjory Kirkwood Hind; educ High School of Stirling 1954–60; University of St Andrews 1960–64 (MA); University of Edinburgh 1979–82 (BD); Civil Service 1964–79; lic by Presb of Edinburgh Jul 1982; asstshp Edinburgh Murrayfield 1982–83; m 29 Jul 1968 Ruth Osborne Douglas b 10 Apr 1942 d of Hugh Osborne D. and Isabel Crammond Rutherford; Children: Marjory Jane b 25 Apr 1969; Andrew Douglas b 7 Feb 1971; David Rutherford b 15 Mar 1973; ord by Presb of Edinburgh 14 Oct 1983; app Assoc Chaplain to University of Edinburgh 26 Jun 1983; app Chaplain 1 Sep 1985; app Lecturer in Practical Theology, University of Glasgow 1 Dec 1988; app Leader of Iona Community 5 Aug 1995; Publ: *Iona—God's Energy* (Hodder & Stoughton, 1999); numerous articles on issues of church and society, urban mission, contemporary sprirituality.

1958 GEOFFREY MACKINTOSH SHAW
B 9 Apr 1927 at Edinburgh, s of John James McIntosh S. and Mina Draper; educ Edinburgh Academy 1933–44; University of Edinburgh 1944–45, 1948–50 (MA), 1950–53 (BD); Union Theological Seminary, New York; ord 1958; member of the Gorbals Group, Glasgow from 1957; elected Councillor 1970; app Leader of Administration, City of Glasgow 1973; app Convener of Strathclyde Regional Council 1974; m 12 Dec 1975 Sarah Mason; died 28 Apr 1978.

1972 HENRY ARTHUR SHEPHERD
(FES X, 329, 456), dem from Aberdeen Ruthrieston West to take up app as Asst Secretary General, Dept of Education 1 Mar 1972; ind to Balerno 18 Dec 1980; Publ: *Prolongation of Life* (St Andrew Press, 1968); *Drugs* (St Andrew Press, 1969).

1984 JOHN RICHARD SILCOX
B 27 Sep 1947 at Irvine, s of Sidney William S. and Elizabeth Blythe Gemmell; educ Dalry High 1952–67; University of Glasgow 1970–74 (BD),

1974–75 (CPS); Monsanto Textiles 1964–67; Shop Manager 1969–70; lic by Presb of Ardrossan 11 Jun 1975; asstshp Largs St Columba's 1975–76; m 2 Aug 1969 Lynda Hall Kane b 11 Dec 1948 d of George Wilson K. and Mary Dodds; Children: Christopher Raymond b 22 Mar 1972; Jonathan Wilson b 17 Aug 1974; ord and ind to Blantyre Old 16 Sep 1976; dem on app as Chaplain and Head of Dept of Religious, Moral and Philisophical Studies, Queen Victoria School, Dunblane 1 Sep 1984; Chaplain (TA) 1979–94; app Contingent Commander, Combined Cadet Force 1993; TD 1994.

1988 COLIN ANDREW MACALISTER SINCLAIR
dem from Newton-on-Ayr to take up app as General Director, Scripture Union Scotland 1 Aug 1988; ind to Edinburgh Palmerston Place 28 Aug 1996.

1999 DAVID IAN SINCLAIR
B 23 Jan 1955 at Bridge of Allan, s of John Forbes S. and Grace Margaret Cockburn; educ Stirling High 1967–73; University of Aberdeen 1973–75; University of Bristol 1976–78 (BSc); University College, Cardiff 1978–80 (DSW, CQSW); University of Edinburgh 1984–87 (BD), 1988–90 [full-time] 1991–93 [part-time] (PhD); President, Student Christian Movement 1975–76; Social Work 1980–84; lic by Presb of Stirling 1 Jul 1987; asstshp Dunblane Cathedral 1987–88; m 29 Jul 1978 Elizabeth Mary Jones b 9 Aug 1955 d of John Samuel J. and Eleanor Ann Owen; Children: Gwen Mairi b 25 Jan 1982; Euan Dafydd b 14 Jun 1984; ord and ind to St Andrews Martyrs' 1 Nov 1990; became minister of linked charge with Boarhills with Dunino 23 Jun 1993 and of linked charge with Boarhills and Dunino 1 May 1994; dem 21 Mar 1999 on app as Secretary of Committee on Church and Nation; Publ: *Dependency and the Journey of Redemption* (Centre for Theology and Public Issues, 1988); *Price, Value and Worth* (Centre for Theology and Public Issues, 1991); *Universalism* (*Theology in Scotland*, University of St Andrews, 1996).

1965 GEORGE RICHMOND NAISMITH RENDALL KNIGHT SMITH
(FES IX, 609; X, 113, 350), res as Theological Secretary, World Alliance of Reformed Churches, Geneva on app as Lecturer, Hope Trust, Edinburgh 1984; ret 2 Mar 1992; Publ: Theological articles and reviews in various journals.

1984 RALPH COLLEY PHILIP SMITH
(FES X, 283), dem as Assoc, Bearsden New Kilpatrick on app as Producer A-V Unit, Dept of Communication 1 Aug 1984; app Director 1985; ret 31 Mar 1991; app Chaplain (part-time) to Western General Hospital, Edinburgh Aug 1991; s Ralph m Lucy Inglis; Publ: *Video in the Service of the Congregation* (Handsel Press, 1991); *Surplus Baggage: The Apostles' Creed* (Wild Goose Publs, 1996).

1986 JOHN STEIN
(FES X, 425), dem from Dundee Steeple on app as Joint-Warden of Carberry Tower 1 May 1986; Addl children: Elinor Mary b 24 Feb 1976; d Dorothy m Francis Ogilvy; d Katherine m David Philp; Addl publ: *In Christ All Things Hold Together* (Collins, Eerdmans, 1984).

1986 MARGARET ELIZABETH STEIN
B 13 Nov 1943 at Turriff, d of James Munro and Margaret Elizabeth Kellie; educ Turriff Academy 1948–61; Edinburgh College of Art 1961–65 (DA); University of Edinburgh 1965–68 (BD); Moray House College, Edinburgh 1968–69 (DipRE); lic by Presb of Edinburgh, Jun 1969; asstshp Perth North 1970–71; m 20 Sep 1969 John Stein b 8 Nov 1941 s of Alan S. and Dorothea Christian Cadell; Children: Dorothy Margaret b 25 Dec 1971 m Francis Ogilvy; Katherine Elizabeth b 12 Feb 1973 m David Philp; Elinor Mary b 24 Feb 1976; ord by Presb of Dundee and assgnd to Dundee The Steeple 1 Jun 1984; app Joint-Warden of Carberry Tower 1 May 1986.

1993 JOHN STEVENSON
(FES X, 154, 268), dem from Kirriemuir Old on app as General Secretary, Dept of Education 1 Jan 1993; s Allan m Lindsay Cowan; s Douglas m Angela Watt.

1985 MARGARET LAIRD STEWART
B 26 Apr 1943 at Edinburgh, d of Alexander Pratt Elder and Mary Cowan Laird; educ Dunfermline High 1953–60; University of St Andrews 1960–67 (BSc, MBChB); University of Edinburgh 1974–77 (BD); lic by Presb of West Lothian 20 Aug 1978; asstshp Polbeth Harwood 1983–84; Edinburgh Blackhall St Columba's 1984–85; m 21 Sep 1968 Frank Ian Stewart b 16 Feb 1942 s of John Graham S. and Isobel MacArthur; Children: Eleanor Mary b 20 Aug 1970; Janet Elizabeth b 30 Jun 1972; Dorothy Rachel b 21 Sep 1978; ord by Presb of Edinburgh to post of Deputy Leader of Iona Community 24 Apr 1985; post held until 1988; Medical Doctor 1967 to present; various assistant-ships and locums; Publ: Contributor to *Dreaming of Eden* (Wild Goose Publs, 1997).

1969 IAIN KAY STIVEN
(FES X, 426), app Head of RE Dept and Chaplain, Boroughmuir High School, Edinburgh 17 Aug 1969; loc ten Wick Old 1984–86; ind to Strachur and Strathlachlan 16 Aug 1988.

1974 CHARLES GORDON STRACHAN
(FES X, 157), res as Sub-Warden, St Ninian's Training Centre, Crieff on app as Artistic Director, Netherbow Arts Centre, Edinburgh 1 Jun 1974; res from app 1980; Director of and Chaplain to Church of Scotland Centre at Tiberias, Israel 1987–89.

1997 ADRIAN PETER JOHN VARWELL
B 27 Jan 1946 at London, s of Dennis William Peter V. and Barbara Joan Trask; educ Bexley Grammar

and Eltham College 1957–64; University of Durham 1964–67 (BA); University of Aberdeen 1977 (PhD); University of Edinburgh 1979–82 (BD); Research Fellow 1969–73, 1978–79; Local Government Officer 1973–78; lic by Presb of Ross 2 Jul 1982; asstshp Dunblane Cathedral 1982–83; m 3 Jan 1970 Margaret Mary Roberts b 8 Mar 1946 d of Percy Edward R. and Constance Muriel Bargh; Children: Stephen b 1 Mar 1975; Simon b 25 Jul 1978; ord and ind to Benbecula 24 Aug 1983; dem to take up app as Director of St Ninian's Centre, Crieff 1 Oct 1997.

1957 HORACE WALKER
(FES IX, 117, 562, 801; X, 456), app Secretary of Home Board 1 Nov 1957; ret 1977; died 5 Dec 1994.

1980 DONALD STEWART WALLACE
(FES IX, 793; X, 448), app Hon Chaplain to the Queen 24 Sep 1977; ret from RAF Chaplains' Branch and app Chaplain to Royal Caledonian Schools 5 Sep 1980; ret 5 Sep 1990; Hon Chaplain and Director, Royal Scottish Corporation; Hon Chaplain and Vice-president, Royal Caledonian Schools Trust; Hon Chaplain to RAF Assoc; d Fiona m Tyson.

1985 JAMES LESLIE WEATHERHEAD
(FES X, 231, 323), dem from Montrose Old on app as Principal Clerk to General Assembly 1 Jul 1985; ret 30 Sep 1996; Moderator of General Assembly 1993–94; Chaplain to the Queen in Scotland from 1991; DD (Edinburgh) 1993; CBE 1997; s Andrew m Billinda Lawrie; Publ: *The Constitution and Laws of the Church of Scotland* (Board of Practice and Procedure, 1997).

1979 MARY KATHRYN WEIR
(FES X, 440), res as Asst Lecturer and Assoc Chaplain, University of St Andrews and ind to Gethsemane United, London, Ontario, Canada Oct 1979; University of St Andrews 1975–83 (PhD); Asst Professor of Pastoral Theology, Vancouver School of Theology 1983–88; Chaplain to Northwestern University, Evanston, IL, USA 1988–89; First Church United, Thunder Bay, Ontario 1989–92; Assoc at Canadian Memorial United Church, Vancouver 1992–94; Owner of 'Books on Bowen', Bowen Island, BC 1994–98; introd as Community minister for ministry among Deaf People and as minister of Albany Deaf Church of Edinburgh 31 Mar 1998.

1990 CHRISTOPHER PETER WHITE
(FES X, 23), dem from Edinburgh St David's Broomhouse on app as Principal of Glasgow Bible Training Institute (now Bible College) 1 Jul 1990; res from app 31 Aug 1996; three-month sabbatical to write book; introd as Assoc at Glasgow St George's Tron 12 Jan 1997; ind to Glasgow Sandyford Henderson Memorial 12 Jun 1997.

1990 IAIN ALEXANDER WHYTE
(FES X, 427), dem from Coatbridge Blairhill Dundyvan to take up app as National Secretary of Christian Aid Scotland 1 Apr 1990; app Chaplain to University of Edinburgh 1 Oct 1994.

1987 JOHN CHRISTOPHER WIGGLESWORTH
B 8 Apr 1937 at Leeds, s of Maurice Handel W. and Muriel Isabel Cowling; educ Grangefield Grammar, Stockton-on-Tees 1948–55; University of Durham 1955–58 (BSc), 1958–61 (PhD); University of Edinburgh 1964–67 (BD); Teaching 1961–64; lic by Presb of Edinburgh 19 Apr 1967; m 28 Jul 1962 Ann Rosemary Livesey b 21 Mar 1939 d of Clifford L. and Mary Clough; Children: Judith Mary b 31 Aug 1963; Karen Elizabeth b 16 Feb 1966; Sara Ann b 25 May 1967 m Kok; John Mark b 21 Oct 1968; app by Overseas Council 1 Oct 1967; ord by United Church of N India, Rahuri 8 Apr 1968; Presbyter, Church of N India, Ahmednagar 1 Dec 1970; introd to St Andrew's and St Columba's, Bombay 2 Jun 1972; app Lecturer, University of Aberdeen 1 Aug 1979; app General Secretary, Board of World Mission and Unity 1 Jan 1987; res 30 Apr 1998; Principal of St Andrew's College, Selly Oak, Birmingham until 31 Aug 1999; MBE 1977; Kerr Lectures, Trinity College, Glasgow 1990; Chavasse Lectures, Wycliffe Hall, Oxford 1994; Publ: *Which Way to Utopia?* (TRACI Journal, 1976); *Freedom of Conscience and Human Rights* (TRACI, 1977); *Salvation in Hinduism and Christianty* (TRACI, 1978); *Evangelical Views of the Poor and Social Ethics Today—The Tyndale Ethics Lecture 1981* (Tyndale Bulletin 35, 1984).

1976 JAMES LINDSAY WILKIE
(FES X, 427), res from service with Overseas Council in Zambia on app as Africa Secretary, Divison of International Affairs, British Council of Churches, London Sep 1976; app Divisional Secretary of Conference for World Mission and Deputy General Secretary, BCC, London Apr 1979; res to take up app as Executive Secretary, Board of World Mission Apr 1984; ret 3 Apr 1998.

1963 GEORGE DAVIDSON WILKIE
(FES IX, 237; X, 138, 456), dem from Port Glasgow St Martin's on app as Industrial Adviser to Home Board 1 Feb 1963; ind to Kirkcaldy Viewforth 2 May 1980.

1977 JAMES ROSS WILKIE
(FES X, 113, 355), res as Headmaster of Tynepark List-D School, Haddington on app as Director of Glenthorne Youth Treatment Centre, DHSS 1 May 1977; ind to Penpont Keir and Tynron 1 Jun 1988.

1997 JENNIFER MARY WILLIAMS
B 31 Jan 1956 at Dundee, d of Peter W. and Mary Netta Doig; educ Dundee High 1966–74; University of Edinburgh 1974–77 (BSc), 1978–79 (CQSW), Taize Community 1980–82; Social Work 1982–84; Lay Ministry, Currie Kirk 1984–87; Social Work

1987–89; University of Edinburgh 1989–92 (BD); lic by Presb of St Andrews, Jul 1993; asstshp Edinburgh St Giles' Cathedral 1996–97; ord by Presb of Edinburgh during assistantship at St Giles' 1 Sep 1996; app Chaplain to Christian Fellowship of Healing 1 Nov 1997.

1979   JOHN MACFARLANE WILSON
(FES X, 56), res as Principal teacher (RE), Blair-gowrie High on app as Adviser in Religious Education for Highland Region 1979; ret 30 Aug 1995; d Ruth m Alastair Forrester; d Elizabeth m Samuel Cumming; s David m Carol Anne Hilson.

1997   FIONA MARY McNICOL WINN
B 23 Jan 1961 at Haddington, d of David Mackie Fordyce and Jessie Knox Walker; educ Inverness High 1966–79; University of St Andrews 1979–83 (MA); Princess Alexandra School of Nursing, London Hospital 1983–87 (RGN); University of Edinburgh 1990–93 (BD); Nursing and Asst Chaplain 1987–90; lic by Presb of Edinburgh 4 Jul 1993; asstshp Edinburgh South Leith 1993–94; m 6 Jul 1991 Raymond Winn b 2 Apr 1960 s of Ronald W. and Ann Broyd; Children: Andrew John Fordyce b 12 Jun 1995; ord by Presb of Edinburgh during assistantship at South Leith 5 Jun 1994; loc ten South Leith 1 Nov 1994; app by Edinburgh North Leith as Co-ordinator of Adult Christian Education 1 Sep 1997; res from app 1999 and emigrated to Australia.

1989   IAIN ALASTAIR MACKAY WRIGHT
B 15 Sep 1957 at Edinburgh, s of William Mackay W. and Jean Henderson; educ George Watson's, Edinburgh 1962–74; University of Edinburgh 1974–77 (BA), 1979–82 (BD); Evangelische Theologische Faculteit 1994-present (PhD); lic by Presb of Edinburgh 4 Jul 1982; asstshp London St Columba's 1982–84; m 6 Sep 1986 Caroline Louise Read b 6 Mar 1964 d of Martin R. and Rosemary Buchanan; Children: Race Edward b 24 Feb 1988; Jonathan Gordon b 30 Aug 1990; Alastair Timothy b 9 Oct 1992; Rebecca Lucy b 17 Aug 1996; ord by Presb of England during assistantship at St Columba's 17 Apr 1983; ind to Falkland with Freuchie 22 Nov 1984; dem 6 May 1989 on app as Director for Care, Scotland; app Director for Care, Europe 15 Apr 1992; ind to Second Presb Church, Yazoo City, MS, USA 1 Jan 1995; ind to Covenant Orthodox Presb Church, Orland Park, IL, USA 21 May 1999.

1991   EVELYN MEIKLE YOUNG
dem from Larbert West on app as Asst/Deputy Secretary, Dept of Education 1 Feb 1991; ind to Kilmun with Strone and Ardentinny 1 Apr 1997.

1983   ADAMINA YOUNGER
ord and ind to Clydebank Radnor Park 13 Sep 1978; dem on app as Young Adult Adviser, Board of Education 15 Mar 1983; Owner of Roslea Café, Glasgow 10 Jun 1986.

MODERATORS OF THE GENERAL ASSEMBLY

1976 THOMAS FORSYTH TORRANCE, MBE, MA, BD, DLitt, DTh, DD, DSc, Professor of Christian Dogmatics, University of Edinburgh

1977 JOHN RODGER GRAY, VRD, MA, BD, ThM, DD, Dunblane Cathedral

1978 PETER PHILIP BRODIE, MA, BD, LLB, DD, Alloa St Mungo's

1979 ROBIN ALEXANDER STEWART BARBOUR, KCVO, MC, MA, BD, STM, DD, Professor of New Testament Studies, University of Aberdeen

1980 WILLIAM BRYCE JOHNSTON, MA, BD, DD, DLitt, Edinburgh Colinton

1981 ANDREW BEVERIDGE DOIG, MA, BD, STM, DD, National Bible Society

1982 JOHN McINTYRE, CVO, DLitt, DD, DUniv, Professor of Divinity, University of Edinburgh

1983 JAMES FRASER McLUSKEY, MC, MA, BD, DD, London St Columba's, Pont Street

1984 JOHN MUNN KIRK PATERSON, MA, ACII, BD, DD, Milngavie St Paul's

1985 DAVID MACINTYRE BELL ARMOUR SMITH, JP, MA, BD, DUniv, Logie

1986 ROBERT CRAIG, CBE, MA, BD, STM, PhD, DD, LLD, DLitt, Jerusalem St Andrew's

1987 DUNCAN SHAW, JP, PhD, ThD, Dr *hc* Edinburgh Craigentinny St Christopher's

1988 JAMES AITKEN WHYTE, MA, LLD, DD, DUniv, Professor of Practical Theology and Christian Ethics, University of St Andrews

1989 WILLIAM JAMES GILMOUR McDONALD, MA, BD, DD, Edinburgh Mayfield

1990 ROBERT DAVIDSON, MA, BD, DD, FRSE, Professor of Old Testament Language and Literature, University of Glasgow

1991 WILLIAM BOYD ROBERTSON MACMILLAN, MA, BD, LLD, DD, Dundee St Mary's

1992 HUGH RUTHERFORD WYLIE, MA, FCIBS, DD, Hamilton Old

1993 JAMES LESLIE WEATHERHEAD, CBE, MA, LLB, DD, Principal Clerk of Assembly

1994 JAMES ALEXANDER SIMPSON, BSc, BD, STM, DD, Dornoch Cathedral

1995 JAMES HARKNESS, CB, OBE, QHC, MA, LB, Depute Chaplain General to HM Forces

1996 JOHN HEDLEY McINDOE, MA, BD, STM, London St Columba's, Pont Street

1997 ALEXANDER McDONALD, BA, CMIWSC, DUniv, General Secretary, Board of Ministry

1998 ALAN MAIN, TD, MA, BD, STM, PhD, Professor of Practical Theology, University of Aberdeen

1999 JOHN BALLANTYNE CAIRNS, LTh, LLB, Dumbarton Riverside

OFFICIALS OF THE GENERAL ASSEMBLY

PRINCIPAL CLERK

DONALD FARQUHAR MACLEOD MACDONALD, CBE, MA, LLB	1972–1985
JAMES LESLIE WEATHERHEAD, CBE, MA, LLB, DD	1985–1996
ALEXANDER GORDON McGILLIVRAY, MA, BD, STM	*pro tem* 1993–1994
FINLAY ANGUS JOHN MACDONALD, MA, BD, PhD	1996–

DEPUTE CLERK

ALEXANDER GORDON McGILLIVRAY, MA, BD, STM	1971–1993
FINLAY ANGUS JOHN MACDONALD, MA, BD, PhD	1993–1996
MARJORY ANNE MACLEAN, LLB, BD	1996–

PROCURATOR

CHARLES KEMP DAVIDSON, QC	1972–1984
GEORGE WILLIAM PENROSE, QC	1984–1991
ROBERT ALASTAIR DUNLOP, QC	1991–

SOLICITOR AND LAW AGENT

ROBERT ARCHIBALD PATERSON, MA, LLB	1971–1995
JANETTE SYLVIA WILSON, LLB, NP	1995–

PRECENTOR

JAMES DARLING ROSS, MA	1961–1977
WILLIAM HENNEY, MA, DD	1979–1995
DAVID DOUGLAS GALBRAITH, MA, BD, BMus, MPhil, ARSCM, ThD	1996–

CORRECTIONS

Corrections applying to FES X can be found within the text of this present volume.

We have been advised of the following corrections to previous volumes (FES I–IX):

1. JAMES ESDAILE, educated at University of Edinburgh, not St Andrew's as in FES IV, 232;

2. DAVID INGLIS, born at Brechin, not Dairsie as in FES V, 402;

3. ARCHIBALD GIBSON (FES VIII, 13): Jean Pringle was not the mother of Archibald Gibson, but rather of Alexander Gibson (FES I, 166; II, 31; IV, 343). Archibald Gibson was not 'of the Gibsons of Drurie', rather the aforementioned Alexander Gibson was of this family.

INDEX OF CHARGES

Abdie and Dunbog	251	Abernethy	345
Abercorn	1	Abernethy and Dron	267
Aberdalgie and Dupplin	267	Abernyte	279
Aberdeen		Aberuthven	267
Beechgrove	299	Aboyne-Dinnet	311
Bridge of Don Oldmachar	299	Acharacle	354
Cove	299	Addiewell	24
Craigiebuckler	299	Airdrie	
Denburn	300	Broomknoll	170
Ferryhill	300	Clarkston	170
Garthdee	301	Flowerhill	170
Gilcomston South	301	High	170
Greyfriars John Knox	301	Jackson	171
High Hilton	302	New Monkland	171
Holburn Central	302	New Wellwynd	171
Holburn West	302	St Columba's	171
Kirk of St Nicholas	303	Airlie Kingoldrum and Ruthven	289
Langstane Kirk	303	Airth	215
Mannofield	303	Alexandria	189
Mastrick	303	Alloa	
Middlefield	304	North	225
Nigg	304	St Mungo's	225
North of St Andrew	304	West	225
Northfield	304	Alloway	85
Queen's Cross	305	Almondbank Tibbermore	267
Rosemount	305	Alness	358
Rubislaw	305	Altnaharra and Farr	364
Ruthrieston South	306	Alva	226
Ruthrieston West	306	Alves and Burghead	338
St Clement's	306	Alvie and Insh	345
St Columba's Bridge of Don	306	Alyth	260
St George's-Tillydrone	306	Amsterdam	395
St John's	307	Amulree and Strathbraan	260
St Machar's Cathedral	307	Ancrum	56
St Mark's	307	Annan	
St Mary's	307	Old	63
St Nicholas South of Kincorth	308	St Andrew's Greenknowe Erskine	63
St Ninian's	308	Annbank	85
St Stephen's	308	Anstruther	251
Stockethill	308	Anwoth and Girthon	69
Summerhill	308	Appin	209
Torry St Fittick's	309	Applecross Lochcarron and Torridon	372
Woodside	309	Applegarth and Sibbaldbie	63
Aberdour	328	Arbirlot	289
Aberdour St Fillan's	237	Arbroath	
Aberfeldy	260	Inverbrothock	290
Aberfoyle	225	Knox's	290
Aberlady	30	Old and Abbey	290
Aberlemno	289	St Andrew's	290
Aberlour	338	St Vigean's	290
Aberluthnott	311	West Kirk	290

INDEX OF MINISTERS